Contents

Part 2: The Star System

Part 3: Technologies

Part 4: World Cinemas

Part 5: Genre

Part 6: Authorship and Cinema

Part 7: Developments in Theory

Introduction

PAM COOK

Each new edition of *The Cinema Book* has registered the impact of seismic shifts on film studies in the intervening years. In her introduction to the 1999 volume, Mieke Bernink identified the cracks that had appeared since the early 1980s in the prevailing narrative of film history, which took a linear route from the 'great moments' of early cinema to the establishment of the classic Hollywood system. New and exciting research into early cinema and the post-classical period, and into non-Hollywood production contexts had revised not only the accepted history but the analytical and expository models on which it was based. Hollywood began to be situated within broader cultural and technological developments and its ascendancy challenged. This in turn necessitated the revision of the discipline's core areas – genre, authorship and narrative – with their roots in 1970s film theory. While classic Hollywood, genre and authorship retained a central place in the 1999 edition, narrative study was displaced and a new section devoted to theoretical frameworks discussed key issues in film theory and placed them in historical context. The emphasis on theory that had underpinned the structure of the first edition became a topic for debate in its own right as the influence of areas such as audience and reception studies, cultural studies, psychoanalysis, feminist film theory, race, queer cinema and post-structuralism was assessed.

The changes evident in the second edition indicated a transition from 1970s theory to historiography that has gathered momentum since, and has dramatically transformed the field. As a result, this third edition represents the most radical and extensive makeover yet in structure, content and approach. Advice solicited from readers was invaluable in the restructuring process, which bears witness to the modification of the hierarchies that informed previous editions and the blossoming of new research and teaching areas that have re-energised screen studies and will continue to do so. One of the third edition's most significant changes is in its treatment of Hollywood, which is now discusssed in relation to international developments from the early cinema period to the present, in recognition of the impact of globalisation on world film production, distribution and exhibition. Because of this shift in emphasis, cinematic practices considered as 'alternative' or 'oppositional' to the Hollywood model have been re-located at its edges, and are viewed as operating in tension with it. Rather than shoring up the dominance of Hollywood by perceiving it as homogeneous, central and all-powerful, the updated 'Hollywood and beyond' section stresses the dynamic interaction between film industries and the uneven development of cinema history. While the multinational conglomerates that are still referred to as 'Hollywood' retain economic power, their aesthetic and ideological hegemony can no longer be perceived as secure. The context of globalisation, diversification and the proliferation of production, distribution and exhibition sites in the wake of new technologies demands a more nuanced analysis that takes on board cultural dialogue and exchange.

One of the challenges to the centrality of Hollywood that has emerged over the past decade is the burgeoning interest in world cinema. For many years, discussion of national cinemas was confined to a handful of art-cinema movements that were far from representative of the film cultures from which they emerged, but enabled their producers to gain international visibility and kudos on film festival and arthouse circuits. Although niche marketing still limits the distribution and theatrical exhibition of non-English language films (and, indeed, of many films perceived as marginal), the increased availability of world cinema on television, video, DVD and the Internet has facilitated research in this area, which in turn has drawn attention to neglected popular cinemas that form a vital part of national film cultures. The new 'World cinemas' section reflects an increased shift of emphasis towards non-Hollywood production contexts, recognising their cultural distinctiveness as well as their transnational character in the light of global forces. It is organised alphabetically in order to avoid imposing a hierarchy of value on diverse and disparate industrial contexts that display common features as well as differences. The notion of world cinema implies a rethinking of national borders and acknowledgment of cultural hybridity, both of which are important in contesting parochial notions of national identity and the focus on the American market that constrain some approaches to national cinema.

Another innovation is a separate section devoted to star study, evidence of the continuing significance of stars in cinema history and in the industry. 'The star system' offers historical analysis of Hollywood stardom from its emergence to its transformation across key periods, such as the arrival of synchronised sound, the post-World War II reorganisation of the studio system and the increase in independent production from the 1960s to the present. A new entry on screen acting introduces an area that demands further attention, discussing performance styles from early cinema to the digital era. As stars themselves have become more powerful in the industry and the world, so their multifarious contributions to the image-making process, spanning the increasingly complex media networks that constitute 'cinema' today, have come to the fore. Audience and fan studies have revealed the creative negotiations that take place between viewers and star images, shedding new light on the contested subject of identity and identification.

One of the strengths of *The Cinema Book* is its in-depth analysis of core topics such as history, technology, genre, authorship and film theory that remain central despite the mutations affecting screen studies. The challenge facing the third edition was to retain the integrity of earlier material, which in most cases stands up extremely well, while providing shorter update essays that comment authoritatively on recent developments and identify relevant sources for readers to follow up. The earlier material and the update essays can be read together to give a longer view of each topic's history, or the update essays may be used alone as introductory pieces. The case studies adjacent to the main text and the bibliographies listed at the back of the book are intended to provide more detailed information about the areas covered in each section, and the system of cross-references directs readers to other essays in the book that cover the topic in question (see Notes on using the book, p. x).

In addition to the update essays, most of the core sections have been extensively revised. 'Hollywood and beyond' has been expanded to include material on the early and post-classical periods, contemporary women directors, new distribution, exhibition and reception contexts, African-American cinema, animation and documentary. 'Genre', which benefited from large-scale revision in the 1999 edition, has gained new entries on costume drama and exploitation cinema and has been reorganised alphabetically to avoid privileging certain genres. 'Authorship and cinema' has been given a much-needed overhaul and now exists in a slimmer version that acknowledges the historical importance of debates around auteurism and engages with the recent revival of interest in the topic. And the re-titled 'Developments in theory' is enhanced by fresh accounts of stimulating research in feminism and film, queer cinema, transnational studies, neoformalism and postmodernism. All sections have acquired additional case studies whose coverage of recent films and film-makers will particularly appeal to students.

Twenty or so years after the first edition appeared, there are now many excellent film studies textbooks available at every educational level. Students, researchers and tutors today have a plethora of resources at their command, from print media and audio-visual aids to the Internet. None of these can be considered comprehensive or complete in themselves; rather, it is a question of 'sampling' various kinds of media texts. *The Cinema Book* is one guide among many; but it does possess certain distinctive features. One is its multi-vocal approach, in which different voices argue from their own perspective. While this runs the risk of producing contradictory accounts, contradiction can be seen as the lifeblood of a discipline that thrives on debate and, indeed, was born from it. Another is its charting of debates and documenting the intellectual history of film studies as a unique field that engages productively with others. And a third is its longstanding commitment to the notion that cinema is kept alive through the circulation of ideas as well as through systems of finance, production, distribution and exhibition – a concept that is even more relevant in the current context of global electronic communications systems and renewed emphasis on transnational cultural exchange.

The third edition has been shaped by such technological and cultural forces, and subsequent volumes will undoubtedly reveal their impact even more clearly. One marker of change can be seen in the extended range of leading international contributors, continuing the trend noted in the 1999 edition. These pages are enriched by a lively diversity of approach from renowned scholars around the globe, who responded with generosity and professionalism to tight deadlines and word limits, and delivered writing of outstanding quality. My warmest thanks go to them, and to those who went before, whose work on the first and second editions made this one possible. I am also grateful to those anonymous readers who responded to the initial questionnaire with useful comments and suggestions. I am deeply indebted to the team at BFI Publishing (Rebecca Barden, Tom Cabot, Sophia Contento and Sarah Watt) for practical help, moral support and creative input during the gestation and production periods of this complex project. And I owe a great deal to friends and family (especially Sam Cook and Greg Ward) who tolerated my obsession over many months.

May 2007

Notes on using the book

Main sections, sub-sections and cross-references

The book consists of seven main sections that represent core topics (Hollywood and beyond; Technologies; Genre; Authorship and cinema) or key issues (The star system; World cinemas; Developments in theory). Each main section stands alone, or can be read in conjunction with relevant material in other sections, via a cross-referencing system.

The main sections contain sub-sections, some of which are longer, in-depth pieces from previous editions, and some of which are new, shorter update essays. The older material and the update pieces are intended to be read together to give a 'long view' of the development of each topic where appropriate, but each can also stand alone. Many essays have a dual function: to outline the history of an area of cinema, and to introduce critical writing on that area. At the end of each essay there is a short Selected Reading list that suggests further reading.

Case studies and bibliographies

Most essays are supported by adjacent case studies that explore a topic area in more detail, or provide new analyses of recent films and film-makers. The case studies also provide basic production information for the films discussed.

The bibliographies at the end of the book represent a valuable resource for readers. They are organised section by section, and provide the fullest information available for the references and selected reading lists in the main text.

Contributors' signatures

The names of authors of essays and case studies are displayed on the Contents list and in the main text. Every attempt has been made to assign the correct authors' signatures to the material from previous editions, but any mistakes or omissions will be put right in future editions.

Contributors

The Editor

Pam Cook is Professor Emerita in Film at the University of Southampton. She edited the first edition of *The Cinema Book* (1985) and was co-editor of the second edition (1999) with Mieke Bernink.

The Contributors

Richard Abel is Robert Altman Collegiate Professor of Film Studies at the University of Michigan. His recent publications include *The Encyclopedia of Early Cinema* (2005) and *Americanizing the Movies and 'Movie-Mad' Audiences, 1910–1914* (2006). Currently he is working on *Trash Twins Making Good: Newspapers and the Movies, 1911–1915*.

Michael Allen is Lecturer in Film and Electronic Media at Birkbeck College, University of London. His publications include *Family Secrets: the Feature Films of D.W. Griffith* (1999) and *Contemporary US Cinema* (2003). He edited *Reading 'CSI': Crime TV Under the Microscope* (2007) and is currently completing *Live from the Moon: Film, Television and the Space Race*.

Tino Balio is Emeritus Professor of Film at the University of Wisconsin-Madison. The 2001 recipient of the inaugural Academy Film Scholar Grant from the Academy of Motion Picture Arts and Sciences, he is currently writing a history of the foreign film market in the US from 1946 to1973.

Guy Barefoot is Lecturer in Film Studies at the University of Leicester. His publications include *Gaslight Melodrama: From Victorian London to 1940s Hollywood* (2001).

Daniel Barratt is Postdoctoral Research Fellow at the Center for Visual Cognition, University of Copenhagen. He has a PhD in cognitive film theory from the University of Kent (2005) and co-edited a special issue of the journal *Film Studies: An International Review* on the subject of film, cognition, and emotion (2006).

Tim Bergfelder is Professor of Film at the University of Southampton. His books as author, co-author and editor include *Film Architecture and the Transnational Imagination* (2007); *International Adventures: European Co-Productions in the 1960s* (2005); *The Titanic in Myth and Memory* (2004); and *The German Cinema Book* (2002).

Chris Berry is Professor of Film and Television Studies at Goldsmiths College. His publications include: (as co-author) *Cinema and the National: China on Screen* (2006); and *Postsocialist Cinema in Post-Mao China: The Cultural Revolution after the Cultural Revolution* (2004).

David Berry is a film critic and historian based at the National Screen and Sound Archive of Wales. He is the author of *Wales and Cinema: The First Hundred Years* (1994) and co-editor of *David Lloyd George: The Movie Mystery* (1998). He was film critic for the *South Wales Echo* from 1978 to 1994.

Edward Buscombe was formerly Head of Publishing at the British Film Institute and is now Visiting Professor at the University of Sunderland. His recent publications include *Cinema Today* (2005) and *Injuns! Native Americans in the Movies* (2006). He has written three volumes in the BFI Classics series.

Alison Butler teaches film studies in the Department of Film, Theatre and Television at the University of Reading. Her published research is concerned with women's cinema, experimental film and theories and practices of cinematic time. She is a member of the Editorial Advisory Board of the journal *Screen*.

Erica Carter is Professor of German Studies at the University of Warwick. She has researched and written widely on German cultural history and film. Her publications include *Dietrich's Ghosts: The Sublime and the Beautiful in Third Reich Film* (2004), and the co-edited *German Cinema Book* (2002).

Steven Cohan is Professor of English at Syracuse University. His books include *Screening the Male* (1993), *The Road Movie Book* (1997), *Masked Men: Masculinity and the Movies in the Fifties* (1997), *Hollywood Musicals: The Film Reader* (2001), and *Incongruous Entertainment: Camp, Cultural Value, and the MGM Musical* (2005).

Pam Cook is Professor Emerita in Film at the University of Southampton. She is the author of *Fashioning the Nation: Costume and Identity in British Cinema* (1996), *I Know Where I'm Going!* (2002) and *Screening the Past: Memory and Nostalgia in Cinema* (2005). She is currently working on a monograph about Baz Luhrmann.

Barbara Creed is Professor of Cinema Studies at the University of Melbourne. Her books include *The Monstrous-Feminine: Film, Feminism, Psychoanalysis* (1993), *Media Matrix: Sexing the New Reality* (2003) and *Phallic Panic: Film, Horror and the Primal Uncanny* (2005). She is currently writing a book entitled *The Darwinian Screen: the Evolution of Film Theory*.

Niamh Doheny is Assistant Director, Research and Development in the Huston School of Film and Digital Media at the National University of Ireland, Galway. She is currently completing a monograph on Oscar Micheaux's film form.

James Donald is Professor of Film Studies and Dean of the Faculty of Arts and Social Sciences at the University of New South Wales, Sydney, Australia. His publications include *Sentimental Education*; *Fantasy and the Cinema*; and *Close Up, 1927–1933: Cinema and Modernism*. He was editor of the journals *Screen Education* and *New Formations*. His current research examines the impact of Josephine Baker and Paul Robeson on European modernism.

Rachel Dwyer is Professor of Indian Cultures and Cinema and Head of the Department of South Asia at SOAS, University of London. Her recent books include *100 Bollywood Films* (2005) and *Filming the Gods: Religion and Hindi Cinema* (2006).

Richard Dyer is Professor of Film Studies at King's College, London. His recent books include *The Culture of Queers* (2002) and *Pastiche* (2006). He is currently writing a book on the film music of Nino Rota, as well as a study of the use of song in cinema.

Elizabeth Ezra teaches at Stirling University. She is the author of *The Colonial Unconscious* (2000), *Georges Méliès: The Birth of the Auteur* (2000), and *Jean-Pierre Jeunet* (2007). She is editor of *European Cinema* (2004), and co-editor of *Transnational Cinema: The Film Reader* (2006) and *France in Focus: Film and National Identity* (2000).

Leslie Felperin is a film critic and journalist whose work appears in *Variety*, *Sight and Sound*, the *Independent*, and several other publications.

Kathe Geist is an art and film historian who has written extensively on Japanese cinema. She lives and writes in Brookline and Charlemont, Massachusetts.

Christine Gledhill is part-time Professor of Cinema Studies at the University of Sunderland. She has written extensively on feminist film criticism, melodrama and British cinema, including *Reframing British Cinema, 1918-1928: Between Restraint and Passion* (2003). She is currently editing *Genre and Gender: Crosscurrents in Postwar Cinemas* and is co-organising a British Women's Film History Project.

Michael Grant has written widely on horror cinema, with particular reference to the films of David Cronenberg. Until his retirement two years ago, he was Senior Lecturer in Film Studies at the University of Kent. He is one of the founding editors of *Film Studies: An International Review*, published by Manchester University Press.

Barry Keith Grant is Professor of Film Studies and Popular Culture at Brock University, Ontario, Canada. He is author or editor of more than a dozen books, most recently *Five Films by Frederick Wiseman* (2006) and *Film Genre: From Iconography To Ideology* (2007). He served as editor-in-chief of the 4-volume *Schirmer Encyclopedia of Film* (2007).

Leighton Grist is Senior Lecturer in Media and Film Studies at the University of Winchester. He has published on classical and post-classical Hollywood, as well as on film and psychoanalytic theory. He is author of *The Films of Martin Scorsese, 1963–77: Authorship and Context* (2000).

John Hill is Professor of Media at Royal Holloway, University of London. He is co-author of *Cinema and Ireland* (1987); and author of *Sex, Class and Realism: British Cinema 1956–63* (1986); *British Cinema in the 1980s: Issues and Themes* (1999); and *Cinema and Northern Ireland: Film, Culture and Politics* (2006).

Claire Hines is Senior Lecturer in Film and Television Studies at Southampton Solent University. She is co-editor of *Hard to Swallow: Reading Pornography on Screen* (forthcoming). She has published articles on James Bond, gender representation and queerness in contemporary film and TV.

Chris Holmlund chairs Cinema Studies at the University of Tennessee. Her books include *Contemporary American Independent Film* (2005); *Impossible Bodies* (2002); and *Between the Sheets, In the Streets: Queer, Lesbian, Gay Documentary* (1997). Current projects are *American Cinema of the 1990s* and *Stars in Action*.

Dina Iordanova is Professor of Film Studies at the University of St Andrews and Director of the Centre for Film Studies. She is author and editor of books focusing on the transnational dimension of cinema; many of her publications explore the cinematic traditions of the Balkans and Eastern Europe. Her current work is on film festivals.

Sheila Johnston is a freelance journalist based in London and France. She contributes interviews and features on film and the arts to the *Independent*, the *Daily Telegraph*, the *London Evening Standard*, *The Times*, *Sight and Sound* and the *New York Daily News* among others.

Richard T. Kelly is the author of *Alan Clarke* (1998), *The Name of this Book Is Dogme 95* (2000), *Sean Penn: His Life and Times* (2004), and the novel *Crusaders* (2008); he is editor of *Ten Bad Dates With De Niro* (2007).

Geoff King is Professor of Film and TV Studies at Brunel University and author of *Indiewood, USA: Where Hollywood Meets Independent Cinema* (2008), *American Independent Cinema* (2005), *New Hollywood Cinema: An Introduction* (2002), *Film Comedy* (2002) and *Spectacular Narratives: Hollywood in the Age of the Blockbuster* (2000).

Nöel King teaches in the Department of Media at Macquarie University, Sydney, Australia. He co-edited *The Last American Picture Show: New Hollywood 1967–1976* (2004). He has published articles in *Screen*, *Undercut*, *Critical Quarterly*, *Textual Practice*, *Framework*, *Cinema Journal*, *Continuum*, *Southern Review*, *Island*, *Metro*, *Senses of Cinema*, *jacket* and *otrocampo*. He is on the editorial board of *Cinema Journal* and the advisory editorial board of *Framework*.

Barbara Klinger is Professor in the Department of Communication and Culture at Indiana University. Her recent publications include *Beyond the Multiplex: Cinema, New Technologies, and the Home* (2006) and the forthcoming 'What do female fans want? Blockbusters, *The Return of the King*, and US audiences', in Martin Barker et al. (eds) *Tolkien's World Audiences*.

Julia Knight is Reader in Moving Image at the University of Sunderland and co-editor of *Convergence: The International Journal of Research into New Media Technologies*. Her current research is looking at independent/artists' film and video distribution in the UK.

Frank Krutnik teaches film at the University of Sussex. His books include (as co-author) *Popular Film and Television Comedy* (1990); *In a Lonely Street: Film Noir, Genre, Masculinity* (1991); *Inventing Jerry Lewis* (2000); he edited *Hollywood Comedians: The Film Reader* (2003) and co-edited *"Unamerican" Hollywood: Politics and Film in the Blacklist Era* (2008).

Annette Kuhn writes and teaches on films, cinema history, visual culture, and cultural memory. She is co-editor of *Screen*; Visiting Professor at Queen Mary, University of London; Docent in Cinema Studies at Stockholm University; and a Fellow of the British Academy. Her books include *An Everyday Magic: Cinema and Cultural Memory* (2002); *Family Secrets: Acts of Memory and Imagination* (2002), and (as co-editor) *Locating Memory: Photographic Acts* (2006). Her book on Lynne Ramsay's *Ratcatcher* is forthcoming.

Tommy L. Lott is Professor in the Philosophy department at San José State University. He is the author of *The Invention of Race: Black Culture and the Politics of Representation* (1999) and co-editor of *The Companion to African-American Philosophy* (2003).

Lucy Mazdon is Reader in Film Studies at the University of Southampton. Her publications in the field of film and television studies include *Encore Hollywood: Remaking French Cinema* (2000), *France on Film: Reflections on Popular French Cinema* (2001), and she co-edited *The Contemporary Television Series* (2004).

Brian McFarlane is Honorary Associate Professor at Monash University, Melbourne, Australia and Visiting Professor in Film Studies at the University of Hull. He has published widely on Australian and British film, and on adaptation. His books include: *Novel to Film: An Introduction to the Theory of Adaptation* (1996); as co-editor: *The Oxford Companion to Australian Film* (1999); and *The Encyclopedia of British Film* (3rd ed. 2007).

Andy Medhurst works in the Department of Media and Film at the University of Sussex. He is the author of *A National Joke: Popular Comedy and English Cultural Identities* (2007) and is currently writing a book about *Coronation Street*.

Toby Miller works at the University of California, Riverside. He is the author and editor of over 20 books and also edits the journals *Social Identities* and *Television & New Media*. His latest book is *Cultural Citizenship* (2007). He has also published *The Avengers* (1997), *Global Hollywood* (2001), *Television Studies* (2002), and *Global Hollywood 2* (2005).

James Naremore is Emeritus Chancellor's Professor of Communication and Culture and English at Indiana University. His books include *The Magic World Of Orson Welles* (revised edition 1988), *Acting in the Cinema* (1988), *More Than Night: Film Noir In Its Contexts* (revised edition 2008), and *On Kubrick* (2007).

Angela Ndalianis is Associate Professor in Screen Studies in the School of Culture and Communication at Melbourne University, Australia. Her research focuses on entertainment media history and transmedia connections between film, games, comic books and other media. Her publications include *Neo-Baroque Aesthetics and Contemporary Entertainment* (2004).

Steve Neale is Chair of Film Studies in the Department of English at Exeter University. He is the author of *Genre and Hollywood* (2001), co-author of *Popular Film and Television Comedy* (1990) and editor of *Genre and Contemporary Hollywood* (2003).

Richard Neupert is Wheatley Professor in Film Studies at the University of Georgia. His books include *The End: Narration and Closure in the Cinema* (1995) and *A History of the French New Wave Cinema* (2007).

Bill Nichols is Professor of Cinema and Director of the Graduate Program in Cinema Studies at San Francisco State University. His most recent book is *Introduction to Documentary* (2001), which will soon appear in a second edition.

Geoffrey Nowell-Smith is Senior Research Fellow in the Department of History at Queen Mary, University of London, where he is researching the history of the British Film Institute. His recent publications include *Luchino Visconti* (revised edition 2002) and *Making Waves: New Cinemas of the 1960s* (2007).

Julian Petley is Professor of Film and Television in the School of Arts at Brunel University. He is the principal editor of the *Journal of British Cinema and Television* and co-editor of *British Horror Cinema* (2002). His most recent book is *Censoring the Word* (2007).

Duncan Petrie is Professor of Film at the University of Auckland, New Zealand. He is author of *The British Cinematographer* (1996), *Screening Scotland* (2000) and *Contemporary Scottish Fictions* (2004). He has just completed *Shot in New Zealand: The Art and Craft of the Kiwi Cinematographer* and a co-edited collection, *The Cinema of Small Nations*.

Alastair Phillips is Associate Professor in the Department of Film and Television Studies at the University of Warwick. He is author of *City of Darkness, City of Light: Emigré Filmmakers in Paris 1929-1939* (2004) and co-editor of *Japanese Cinema: Texts and Contexts* (2007) and *Journeys of Desire: European Actors in Hollywood* (2006).

Ashish Rajadhyaksha is Senior Fellow at the Centre for the Study of Culture and Society in Bangalore, India. He has published widely on cinema and contemporary art. He is currently co-ordinating the CSCS media archive and working on a collection of essays titled *Who's Looking?*

Jane Root was co-founder of the independent company Wall to Wall Television before moving to the BBC in 1997. She was Controller of BBC2 from 1999 to 2004, when she became Executive Vice President and General Manager of the Discovery Channel in the US.

Thomas Schatz is Professor of Film and Media Studies at the University of Texas. He has written four books about American film, including *Hollywood Genres*, *The Genius of the System* and *Boom and Bust: American Cinema In the 1940s*, and he recently edited a four-volume collection on Hollywood.

Anneke Smelik is Professor of Visual Culture, holding the Katrien van Munster chair at the Radboud University of Nijmegen, Netherlands. She recently co-edited *Bits of Life: Feminist Studies of Media, Biocultures, and Technoscience* (2007). Her research interests include digital art and culture, the performance of authenticity in fashion, and multimedia literacy.

Jackie Stacey is Professor of Media and Cultural Studies at the University of Manchester. She is author of *Star Gazing: Female Spectators and Hollywood Cinema* (1994), a co-editor of *Screen* and (with Sarah Street) of *Queer Screen: A Screen Reader* (2007). She is currently completing a book for Duke University Press entitled *The Cinematic Life of the Gene*.

Robert Stam is University Professor at New York University. His publications include *Reflexivity in Film and Literature*; *Brazilian Cinema*; *Film Theory: An Introduction*; *Literature through Cinema*; *Tropical Multiculturalism*; *François Trufffaut and Friends: Modernity, Sexuality and the Art of Adaptation*; and, with Ella Shohat, *Unthinking Eurocentrism: Multiculturalism and the Media*.

Sarah Street is Professor of Film, University of Bristol. Her publications include *British National Cinema* (1997), *British Cinema in Documents* (2000), *Transatlantic Crossings: British Feature Films in the USA* (2002), *Black Narcissus* (2004) and she is co-author of *Film Architecture and the Transnational Imagination: Set Design in 1930s European Cinema* (2007).

Julian Stringer is Associate Professor of Film Studies at the University of Nottingham and co-ordinating editor of *Scope: An Online Journal of Film Studies*. He co-edited *New Korean Cinema* (2005) and *Japanese Cinema: Texts and Contexts* (2007). He is currently writing a monograph on Wong Kar-wai's *In the Mood for Love*.

Gaylyn Studlar is Rudolf Arnheim Collegiate Professor of Film Studies at the University of Michigan, Ann Arbor. She is co-editor of four anthologies, and author of *This Mad Masquerade: Stardom and Masculinity in the Jazz Age*, *In the Realm of Pleasure: Von Sternberg, Dietrich, and the Masochistic Aesthetic*, and numerous articles on gender, sexuality and Hollywood film, most recently in *Dietrich Icon* (2007).

Yvonne Tasker is Professor of Film and Television Studies at the University of East Anglia. She is author of *Working Girls: Gender and Sexuality in Popular Cinema* (1998) and co-editor of *Interrogating Postfeminism: Gender and the Politics of Popular Culture* (2007).

Stephen Teo is Research Fellow at the Asia Research Institute, National University of Singapore, and senior research associate of the RMIT University, Melbourne, Australia. He is the author of *Hong Kong Cinema: The Extra Dimensions* (1997), *Wong Kar-wai* (2005), *King Hu's 'A Touch of Zen'* (2007), and *Director in Action: Johnnie To and the Hong Kong Action Film* (2007).

John Thompson is the author of '"Vanishing" worlds: film adaptation and the mystery of the original', in Cartmell et al. (eds), *Pulping Fictions* (1996), and 'A film of thought', in Berry and Horrocks (eds), *David Lloyd George: The Movie Mystery* (1998).

Núria Triana-Toribio is Senior Lecturer in Modern Spanish at the University of Manchester. She is author of *Spanish National Cinema* (2003) and co-author of *The Cinema of Alex de la Iglesia* (2007). She is co-editor of the series *Spanish and Latin American Filmmakers*.

Ginette Vincendeau is Professor in Film Studies and Director of the Film Studies Programme, King's College London. She has written widely on French cinema, including *The Companion to French Cinema* (1996), *Stars and Stardom in French Cinema* (2000), *Jean-Pierre Melville, An American in Paris* (2003), and *La Haine* (2005).

Paul Wells is Director of Animation in the Animation Academy at Loughborough University. His books include *Understanding Animation* (1998), *Animation and America* (2002) and *Animation: Genre and Authorship* (2002). He has made a Channel 4 documentary, *Cartoons Kick Ass* and three BBC television programmes on British animation.

Linda Ruth Williams is Professor at Southampton University, where she teaches film. She has written numerous articles on contemporary film, feminism, censorship and sexuality. She is author of four books, including *The Erotic Thriller in Contemporary Cinema* (2005), co-editor of *Contemporary American Cinema* (2006), and writes regularly for *Sight and Sound*.

Pamela Robertson Wojcik is Associate Professor in the Department of Film, TV and Theatre at the University of Notre Dame. She is author of *Guilty Pleasures: Feminist Camp from Mae West to Madonna* (1996), co-editor of *Soundtrack Available: Essays on Film and Popular Music* (2002) and editor of *Movie Acting: The Film Reader* (2004).

PART 1

Hollywood Cinema and Beyond

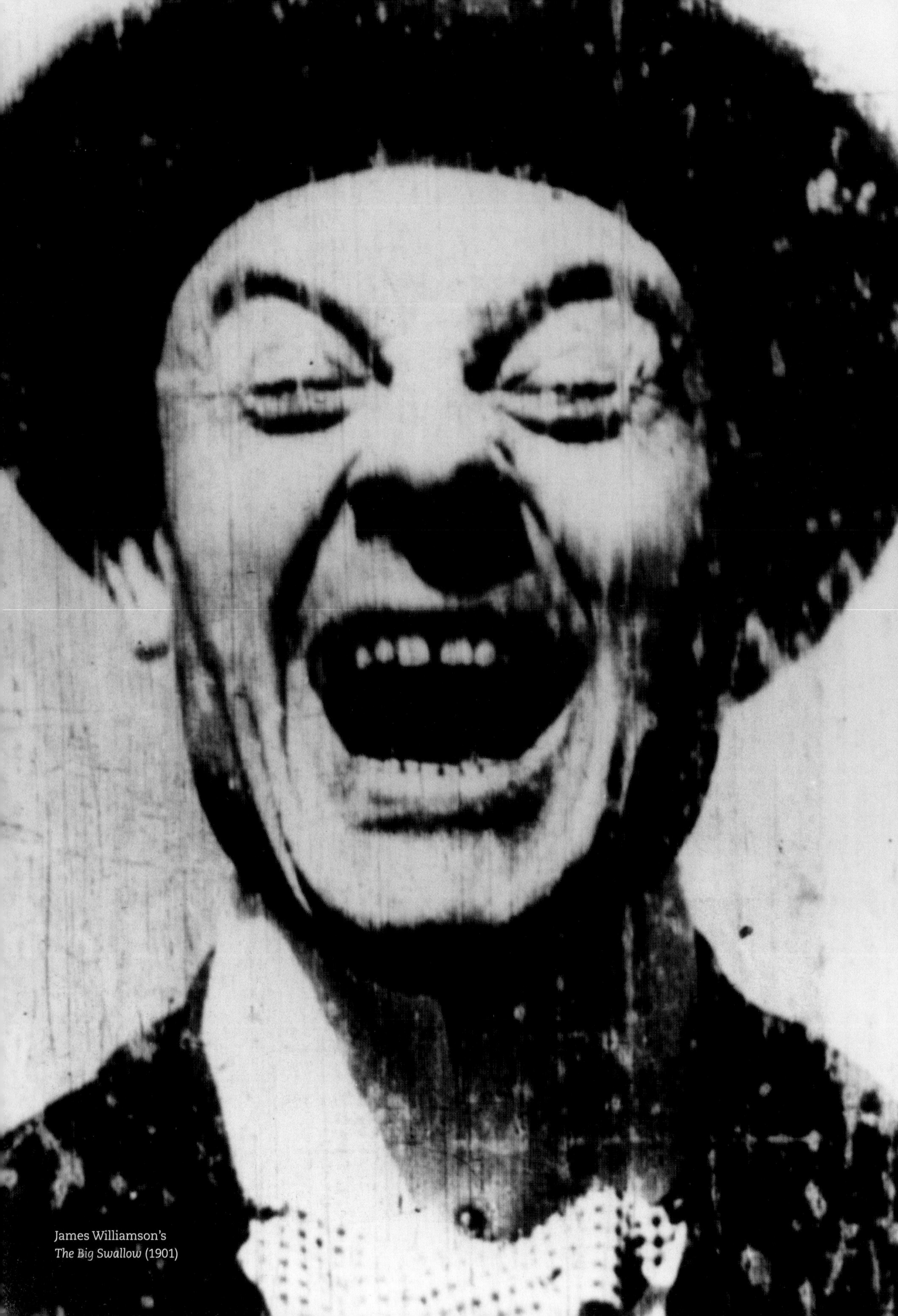

James Williamson's
The Big Swallow (1901)

EARLY AND PRE-SOUND CINEMA

RICHARD ABEL

Until recently, the history of cinema has been written according to a set of long-held assumptions about cinema's first 20 or 30 years. From Terry Ramsaye (1926) and Lewis Jacobs (1939) to Jean Mitry (1968) and Noël Burch (1986), historians conceived this period in terms of infancy or immaturity; it was a 'primitive' cinema. Built into this evolutionary account was the assumption that the best, most efficient model of narrative continuity was to be found in American cinema (whose 'father' was D. W. Griffith), in what Burch called, somewhat disparagingly, the Institutional Mode of Representation or what David Bordwell, Janet Staiger and Kristin Thompson (1985) proclaimed as the 'classical Hollywood cinema'. Early cinema was merely the workshop in which classical conventions of editing, framing and narrative were gradually crafted, to become the building blocks underpinning the edifice of classical Hollywood cinema.

Our assumptions about early cinema, however, have changed radically since the early 1980s. The impetus came from the 1978 Congress of the International Federation of Film Archives (FIAF), which brought together archivists and academics to view and discuss hundreds of fiction films (from 1900 to 1906), many of them newly rediscovered and printed. This event was a revelation that spurred scores of researchers, in a collaborative endeavour soon called the Brighton Project, to begin rethinking and rewriting the history of early cinema. This effort was supported by film archive restorations, often showcased at the annual Pordenone Silent Film Festival in Italy (launched in 1982) by Domitor (an international society instituted in 1987 devoted to the study of early cinema), and by numerous conferences and workshops, some prompted by the centennial celebrations of cinema. All this work has led historians to reconceive early cinema in several ways. One has been to re-examine the first 20 or more years of cinema's emergence worldwide, not only as an object of study for its own sake, but as a problem: how to explain what Burch (1986) aptly described as its distinctive 'otherness' in

Cinema of attractions: *The Great Train Robbery*

relation to what came later. Another has been to complicate the development of a narrative cinema, investigating the contribution of films produced outside the US, questioning the historical inevitability and dominance of the classical Hollywood model and granting equal value to alternatives or local modifications to what Hansen (2000) has redefined as a model of 'vernacular modernism'. A third has gone beyond the Brighton Project to reconceptualise early cinema from the perspective of exhibition, with its changes over time and differences across social spaces, rather than that of production and textual representation. Here, cinema is defined as a cultural practice whose meaning depends in large part on its material conditions of reception.

A cinema of attractions

One line of research has continued, after Brighton, to redraw the historical map of the cinema's first decade. A concise sign of that is the term 'cinema of attractions', first coined by Tom Gunning (and André Gaudreault) (1986). The term assumes a principle of discontinuity at work in cinema history (early cinema's 'distinctive otherness'), which Gunning extrapolates with reference to those elements that do not directly contribute to the evolution of narrative cinema. Early cinema involved an 'aesthetic of attractions' in which visual curiosity was aroused and satisfied by novelty, surprise, even shock. More specifically, it tended to show or display – as an 'attraction' – either the technical possibilities of the new medium (the moving camera in American Mutoscope & Biograph [AM&B]'s *Brooklyn Bridge*, 1899) or the spectacle of human figures (Veriscope's *The Corbett–Fitzsimmons Fight*, 1897), natural landscapes (AM&B's *Panoramic View of Niagara Falls in Winter*, 1897), and elaborately constructed decors (Georges Méliès's *Cinderella/Cendrillon*, 1899). Moreover, early films generally comprised a single, autonomous tableau or a series of tableaux/scenes, frontally framed and often static, as in photographs or on the theatre stage. The objective was to present a complete action unfolding in a homogeneous space, whether in the single-take scene of robbing and killing in Edison's *The Great Train Robbery* (1903) or in a Méliès trick film such as *One-man Band/L'Homme-orchestre* (1900), where multiple exposures and invisible editing produce a host of magical disappearances, reappearances and other transformations. In addition, the tableau's single, unified viewpoint assumed a camera relatively distant from what was being filmed, which turned human subjects into performers of physical action rather than characters. Even closer shots (James Williamson's *The Big Swallow*, 1901) served as comic and/or trick attractions. Finally, these films were sold as semi-complete products that could be finished in exhibition in different ways. All kinds of practices – variable projection speeds, re-edited or reordered shots, colours applied to the film stock, accompanying music and sound effects, lecturers offering explanations – promoted wide textual variance.

Early cinema emerged within a network of mass cultural practices throughout Europe and North America. Many of these provided familiar subjects for early films: newspaper and magazine cartoons for Lumière's *L'Arroseur arrosé* (1895), magazine photographs for Méliès's *The Dreyfus Affair/L'Affaire Dreyfus* (1899), wax museum exhibits for Pathé's *Story of a Crime/Histoire d'un crime* (1901), *féerie* plays for Méliès's *Astronomer's Dream/La Lune à un mètre* (1898), even an amusement park ride for Méliès's *A Trip to the Moon/Le Voyage dans la lune* (1902), popular stage melodramas for Edison's *Uncle Tom's Cabin* (1903), and penny press stories for Pathé's *Indians and Cowboys/Indiens et cow-boys* (1904). This material formed the basis for a dozen 'genres', and Pathé in particular took advantage of their marketability in a broad spectrum of exhibition venues. In a Boston Keith vaudeville house, one reel of film shared a programme with a dozen or more live acts (not only as 'chasers'). Each week the film performance offered something different: a short playlet, a comic or magic act, a history lesson, a current event or *fait divers*, an inexpensive tour of distant lands and peoples. On his lecture circuits, Lyman Howe – the most important American lecturer-exhibitor – shaped dozens of disparate films into a clear narrative line that allowed all three of his touring companies in 1904 to arrange a different order of scenes from the Russo-Japanese War. At the same time, on one British fairground after another, the touring Bioscope shows, having replaced the popular nineteenth-century 'ghost show', disseminated the latest news, *fait divers*, fads, comic turns and scientific wonders of that year's season. During this period, Charles Musser (1991a) concludes, it was exhibitors and not producers who exercised editorial control over films and their mode of representation.

The emergence of a narrative cinema

A second line of research continues to focus on the emergence of narrative cinema but extends Burch's critique of the historical inevitability of its dominant form. Yet historians differ over how best to conceptualise this emergence. Whereas Barry Salt (1992) still accepts a teleological model of cinema history, privileging the development of a classical Hollywood cinema, Burch himself (1986) has advanced a binary model of film practice, positing a break between an industrialised Institutional Mode of Representation and an earlier, primitive mode, which he valorises because he sees it taken up later in avant-garde films. Others, such as Thompson (1985), Gunning (1993), Richard Abel (1994) and Charlie Keil (2001), have posited a tripartite model, with a transitional period more or less distinct from, yet sharing elements with, both the cinema of attractions and the later narrative cinema. A good example from that period is Pathé's *A Policeman's Tour of the World/Le Tour du monde d'un policier* (1906), which combines a story of thievery and pursuit in Paris with several travelogue scenes (those on the Suez Canal include point-of-view-shot attractions), a secondary story of attacking 'Redskins' in the Far West, an *actualité* (a political campaign in New York) and a stencil-coloured apotheosis ending in which thief and pursuer join hands as financial partners before a huge globe and a massed group of colonial subjects.

There is general agreement, however, on the early stages of this transformation. Initially, this involved a change in spatial coherence as the autonomous tableau gave way to a synthetic space constructed out of interrelated, discrete shots. Correlated with this was a change in temporality, with greater attention given to issues of succession, simultaneity and internally generated causality. Both of these produced a new form of contiguity and sequentiality clearly evident in British chase films, from William Haggar's *A Desperate Poaching Affray* (1903) to Cecil M. Hepworth's *Rescued by Rover* (1905). As narrativisation was extended to every level of film discourse, the attractions that once served an aesthetics of display – for instance, pans, close shots, point-of-view shots – were subordinated to narrative development in films as diverse as Pathé's *The Life of a Convict/Au bagne* (1905) and Vitagraph's *The 100 to 1 Shot* (1906). Soon this system of narrative continuity included alternations between adjacent spaces (sometimes with reverse-angle cutting) and crosscut parallel lines of action, visible in Pathé films from *The Dog Smugglers/Les Chiens contrebandiers* (1906) to *A Narrow Escape or The Physician of the Castle/Le Médecin du château*

(1908). The latter film, reworked in Griffith's *The Lonely Villa* (1909), crosscuts not only between three separate locations but between close shots of the endangered wife and her rescuer-to-be husband, joined by another technological instrument, the telephone. By 1908 or 1909, in many French and American films most elements of mise en scène, framing and editing were being 're-motivated', subordinated to a causal narrative chain dependent on such devices as repetition, delay, surprise, suspense and, above all, closure.

One consequence of these changes was to wrest from the exhibitor control over the process of making meaning.

Early example of continuity editing: *Rescued by Rover*

A different kind of film narrator was constructed that positioned an audience differently, engaging the spectator (increasingly individualised) in 'stitching' together a synthetic spatial-temporal whole and a sequential process of narrative knowledge. No longer would a film's intelligibility as a story need to rely on prior knowledge and familiarity – as in Edison's *Uncle Tom's Cabin* – or on a lecturer. Consonant with this change was the increasing use of intertitles, which Pathé had pioneered in 1903. Intelligibility began to derive from what Gunning (1990), in his analysis of Griffith's early Biograph films, calls an 'internalised lecturer', from the way a film such as *The Country Doctor* (1909) told its story, selecting and organising narratively important elements from a mass of contingent details within a hierarchy of knowledge or perspective. By the time of Griffith's *The Lonedale Operator* (1911), that selection could create a concise sense of character as well as a narrative revelation in such details as the close shot of the heroine's anxious face (at the telegraph) and the close-up of a wrench she has used like a revolver to keep the villains at bay. The use to which the internalised lecturer was put varied. Whereas Griffith films usually assumed a strongly moral voice in their narration, some of Pathé's, such as *The Man with White Gloves/L'Homme aux gants blancs* (1908) and *The Mill/Le Moulin maudit* (1909), claimed the ironic voice of Grand Guignol. In the latter film, a miller kills his wife's lover, ties the body to a revolving windmill arm and binds the wife so she is forced to watch the spectacle; as he drowns himself in a nearby pool, the surface of the water grows smooth, reflecting the upside-down image of the distant windmill.

The transition from a cinema of attractions to a narrative cinema, however, did not occur at the same time, and in the same way, in every country. Rather than assume a degree of uneven development, privileging the classical Hollywood cinema, historians now are exploring the possibility of distinct, parallel developments. The American cinema, with its emphasis on individuated characters, came to depend on close shots of faces, especially those of female stars such as Mary Pickford in Biograph's *The New York Hat* (1912), and a continuity system of eyeline matches and shot/reverse-shots, as in Essanay's *The Loafer* (1911) or Vitagraph's *The Greater Love* (1912). European cinemas, by contrast, as Thompson (1985), Brewster (1990a), Abel (1994) and Tsivian (1995) argue, advanced a different mode of representation characterised by 'deep staging'. Here, the emphasis was on the precise movement of one or more characters within a set or natural landscape of considerable depth – in such films as Victor Sjöström's *Ingeborg Holm* (1913), Léonce Perret's *In the Clutches of the Paris Apaches/L'Enfant de Paris* (1913) or Yevgeni Bauer's *Twilight of a Woman's Soul/Sumerki zhenskoi dushi* (1913). As Tsivian (1995) suggests, geometrical patterns of actor positioning and movement (from a fixed viewpoint) might then define an alternative model of cinematic 'essence' or specificity in the 1910s. By the same token, Abel (1994) claims, French cinema developed an alternative model of continuity editing, perhaps most evident in Perret's films for Gaumont. Instead of eyeline matches and shot/reverse-shots, this system was marked by relatively consistent 90-degree and 180-degree changes in camera position.

However crucial ideas such as this may have become for understanding and analysing early cinema, many questions remain open to debate. Did the music and sound effects that accompanied film projections change in kind and function in the transition from a cinema of attractions to a narrative cinema? Was the gradual standardisation of sound accompaniment similar or different in the American and European cinemas? Similarly, did the processes used to colour positive

Deep staging in *Ingeborg Holm*

film prints (tinting, toning, hand-painting, stencil-colouring), all of which Pathé initially exploited more than any other company, change in kind and function in the transition to a narrative cinema? If most films were released in tinted prints by the 1910s, did that tinting function differently in the American and European cinemas, and if so, how? Finally, in the shift from one standard release format (the single-reel film) to another (the feature-length film) by the mid-1910s, did significant differences develop between the American and European cinemas? If, as Gunning (1993) argues, neither cinema of attractions nor narrative cinema can be considered a monolithic category, then silent cinema may be marked by a perpetually shifting negotiation between 'the desire to display' and 'the desire to tell a story', with the parameters of that negotiation changing from one historically specific moment or social space to another.

Exhibition and reception

Several other lines of research have reconceived early cinema by focusing on exhibition and reception. From this perspective, the cultural arena within which cinema circulated could have national, regional and even local variations, and this extended well beyond the period of a cinema of attractions. In France and the UK, films were shown in two principal venues: fairground shows and urban music halls (both drew a mass audience from the lower and middle classes). Each presented relatively long programmes – two or more hours of short films, lantern slides and live acts – although fairground shows in both countries soon featured films exclusively. The permanent urban cinemas that began to open throughout France in 1907 generally adopted this long programme format, and the larger, more prestigious cinemas soon competed directly with music halls and even theatres. In Paris, by early 1909 the Omnia-Pathé presented two daily programmes of a dozen or more Pathé films, with orchestral accompaniment and song interludes. In the UK, the fairground shows (also chiefly supplied by Pathé) developed into Great Shows with elaborate façades custom-built around massive organs. Only in 1909 did purpose-built urban cinemas begin to appear in numbers, and these adopted, as the French did earlier, the two-tiered ticketing format of the music halls: full programmes for the middle classes in the more expensive galleries and boxes; continuous shows (allowing short visits) for the lower classes on the ground floor. For the French and British, going to the cinema seems to have been class-specific (for the middle classes, it was a special occasion); it also remained tied to a long cultural history of seasonal fairs.

The conditions of exhibition and reception were quite different in the US. At first, films were shown primarily in vaudeville houses and, to a lesser extent, on lecture circuits and fairgrounds, usually as one act among many on a lengthy programme. That began to change by 1904 with the development of cheap family vaudeville venues (some in summer amusement parks) in which films featured as one of up to six acts on a programme lasting no more than an hour. By 1906, with the rapid expansion of cheap nickelodeons, programmes – several films, again usually supplied by Pathé, and illustrated songs, often totalling no more than 20 to 30 minutes – ran continuously from noon, or even earlier, to late at night. The nickelodeons served different functions depending on their location. Those in shopping districts offered a mixed class of shoppers, office workers and others (many of them women and children) comfortable places to spend time, especially the waiting time between one activity and another now so common in modern life. For single white-collar workers, nickelodeons became a significant 'woman's space' in the world of public, commercial amusements. Those in working-class (often immigrant) residential areas, according to moral reformers and the trade press, even turned into neighbourhood social centres where people could congregate. Even when larger cinemas began to appear in 1908, with programmes lasting 45 or 50 minutes, films still ran continuously so spectators could drop in and walk out whenever they wanted. For Americans, then, going

Travelling and purpose-built cinemas: (top) the New Theatre, Boston, and (above) the Omnia-Pathé, Paris, 1912

to the cinema could become part of one's everyday life (as a worker or consumer), a new source of autonomy and pleasure (for women), or a means of either renewing one's bonds with a community (for immigrants) or else rejecting them for a larger sense of social identity.

Researching exhibition conditions focuses critical attention on certain questions. The basic one is: who actually went to the cinema, according to what social categories, when, where and how often, and for what reasons? Whatever materials one might investigate – government documents, company records, ads and articles in newspapers and magazines, moral reform movement surveys, oral interviews or memoirs, even the films themselves (as they construct possible reading positions) – research on this question has to explain the historical conditions for the specific interrelations of actual spectators and films. Given the emergence of a global capitalist economy, centred in Europe and North America, geared to growing levels of consumption and the production of consumers to support such an economy, what was the role of the nickelodeons, fairground shows and first permanent cinemas? To what degree did they occupy a relatively autonomous public sphere distinct from the more comprehensive, less class-specific public sphere of the later picture palaces, as Hansen (1991) suggests, and did they offer some kind of resistance, as Burch (1990) argues, to the emergence of modern consumer society? In the US, the huge numbers of immigrants, women and children (none full citizens) going to the show weekly or even daily give such questions a particular twist. Within the context of a heightened nationalism, and heated debates over assimilation and the construction of an American identity, how did the cinema serve to train such people to take up that identity and become proper social subjects within an American culture? What was the role in that training, for instance, of the Wild West films, which became incredibly popular with urban audiences by 1909? In that westerns so quickly became the quintessential American subject, and distinctly different from Pathé's foreign film product, perhaps they not only formed the basis for what *Moving Picture World* would call 'an American school of moving picture drama', but also represented the most visible sign of an Americanisation process in early American cinema.

World War I and its aftermath

During World War I, the American film industry underwent a series of transformations that quickly led to worldwide dominance. Companies involved in different sectors of the industry merged, leading to the establishment of large, vertically integrated corporations: for example, Paramount/Famous Players-Lasky, Universal, Fox, Goldwyn, First National. Capital investment rose and production increased, especially in feature-length films, as film-making was organised along factory lines for greater efficiency. The war drastically curtailed European production and distribution, particularly in France; consequently, the American film industry found itself with a unique opportunity for foreign expansion. With exclusive control of a huge internal exhibition market (by 1920, there were some 18,000 cinemas compared to fewer than 4,000 in Germany, 3,000 in the UK and 2,500 in France), the industry could afford to seek even greater profits abroad. The major corporations adopted new distribution strategies to deal directly with more and more foreign markets, opening subsidiary offices far beyond Europe, much as Pathé had done ten years before. By the end of the war, American films dominated the distribution and exhibition markets nearly everywhere. Confronting this new Goliath of cultural imperialism put other film industries in a quandary.

Lured to Hollywood: the young Greta Garbo

On one hand, in most countries, a national cinema had to develop in negotiation with, accommodation with and/or resistance to Hollywood. On the other hand, throughout the 1920s crucial industry personnel, especially in Europe, were lured away to work in the American film industry. Germany, for instance, lost film-makers Ernst Lubitsch and F. W. Murnau as well as actors Pola Negri (who was Polish), Emil Jannings and Conrad Veidt. The Swedish film industry was damaged almost irreparably by the emigration of two major film-makers, Mauritz Stiller and Victor Sjöström, along with actors Greta Garbo and Lars Hanson. The French film industry was spared, with the exception of film-maker Jacques Feyder who left for a short stint in Hollywood in 1928 – and returned soon after French sound films became dominant in 1929–30 (see French cinema in the 1930s, p. 200).

In France itself, the response to American dominance was multifaceted. Though recovered from the war, the film industry was no longer concentrated, as in the US, but dispersed among a multitude of large, medium and small-scale enterprises. Only Pathé, Gaumont and Aubert remained involved in all sectors, but Pathé largely distributed films (Pathé-Consortium) or manufactured film stock and apparatus (Pathé-Cinéma), and in 1925, Gaumont was sold to MGM. New companies such as Albatros (with Russian émigré capital and personnel) emerged as leading French producers, and Cinéromans played a crucial role in ensuring that French films would retain a presence on French screens. Cinéromans's strategy was to institute an annual production schedule of at least four serials, standardised at eight episodes, for sequential release during the year by Pathé-Consortium. Most were costume adventures about French war heroes or outlaws from the period between 1750 and 1850: *Mandrin* (1924) or *Fanfan-la-tulipe* (1925). If the Cinéromans serials

Restoring French identity: Abel Gance's historical spectacular *Napoléon*

formed one basis for a national cinema, another was the large-scale historical spectacle films that, in resurrecting past moments of French glory (and tragedy), contributed to a collective postwar need for restoring French national identity. These ranged from *The Three Musketeers/Les Trois mousquetaires* (1921) to *The Miracle of the Wolves/Le Miracle des loups* (1924) and Abel Gance's *Napoléon* (1927) – the latter two had special premieres at the Paris Opéra. In the latter half of the decade, historical spectacle films became an important component of Film Europe, a European co-production strategy that chiefly linked the French and German industries (often with Russian émigré financing). Although films such as Carl Dreyer's *The Passion of Joan of Arc/La Passion de Jeanne d'Arc* (1927) continued to mine French history, the more successful were partly set in imperial Russia: *Michel Strogoff* (1926), *The Chess Player/Le Joueur d'échecs* (1927) and *Casanova* (1927). French realist films, a third basis for a national cinema, were often produced by small independent companies. Some were set in major cities – *Crainquebille* (1922), *The Faithful Heart/Coeur fidèle* (1923) – but most explored picturesque rural landscapes and provincial cultures – *The Earth/La Terre* (1921) and *The Hearth/L'Atre* (1920), central and southern agricultural regions; *La Belle Nivernaise* (1923), rivers and canals; *The Faces of Children/Visages d'enfants* (1925), the French Alps. Arguably, these too addressed a postwar demand for national restoration, deflecting attention from the harrowing reality of the war-devastated regions of northeastern France.

Equally significant, however, were the unique French efforts that established an alternate cinema network partly independent of the commercial industry in the 1920s. An initial stage began with Louis Delluc's editorship of *Le Film* in 1917 and ended with the deaths of Ricciotto Canudo and Delluc respectively in 1923 and 1924. Those years saw the founding of independent film journals such as Delluc's *Cinéa*, regular newspaper review columns such as that of Emile Vuillermoz in *Le Temps* and early ciné-clubs such as Canudo's Club des amis du septième art and Léon Moussinac's Club français du cinéma. From the prolific writings of Delluc, Canudo, Moussinac, Vuillermoz, Germaine Dulac and others emerged the theory and praxis of an alternative cinema that promoted a film art that could be either international or national. For the next few years, a loose network of ciné-clubs (Moussinac's Ciné-Club de France, Charles Léger's Le Tribune libre), specialised cinemas (Jean Tedesco's Vieux-Colombier, Armand Tallier's Studio des Ursalines) and film journals (Tedesco's *Cinéa-Ciné-pour-tous*) presented a relatively united front in actively promoting an alternative cinema. Popular exhibitions at the Musée Galliera (1924) and Exposition des arts décoratifs (1925), lectures at the Vieux-Colombier and regular public screenings hosted by the ciné-clubs all encouraged independent film production, built up a permanent audience and began to articulate a history of film art. In the decade's final years, a proliferation of organisations and intensification of activity had two major consequences. With the founding of Les Amis de Spartacus in 1927, the co-operative system supporting an alternative cinema verged on becoming a mass political/socio-economic movement until suppressed by the Paris police. At the same time, the exhibition network created by the ciné-clubs and specialised cinemas, which now included Jean Mauclaire's Studio 28, expanded to encompass film production and distribution, as in Pierre Braunberger's Studio-Film, formed to distribute 'all the films of artistic quality (experimental films, documentary films, films called "Avant-Garde")'. Despite its contradictions

The Great Train Robbery (USA 1903 *p.c* – Edison Manufacturing Co.; *d* – Edwin S. Porter)

This film is based on an 1896 stage play as well as accounts of actual train robberies in the Far West. Over the course of its 13 shots, an outlaw gang disables a telegraph operator, robs the passengers on a train, escapes a posse on horseback, only to be killed in a climactic gunfight. The film already departs from the usual practice of the 'cinema of attractions' in that it includes one virtual match on action and rudimentary crosscutting. Yet the robbery itself is narrated in a single two-minute static shot that may have required an exhibitor's commentary to clarify the action. Exhibitors also could place the 'emblematic close-up' at either the beginning or the end to maximise its 'shock value', which came partly from 'duping' a notorious poster for Gold Dust cleaning powder. This film enjoyed a huge success in vaudeville houses in the US throughout 1904, and later was sometimes used on the opening programmes of new nickelodeons.

RICHARD ABEL

A Policeman's Tour of the World/Le Tour du monde d'un policier (France 1906 *p.c* – Pathé; *d* – Charles-Lucien Lepine)

A Policeman's Tour of the World combines half a dozen different kinds of film, as if condensing a single programme of diverse subjects into one. Its 27 shots mix the 'attractions' of actualités, trick films and travelogues with the episodic narrative of a Paris policeman pursuing a banker-embezzler across the globe. More specifically, it includes a sequence of point-of-view shots (the thief tours the Suez Canal), a tableau (set in an opium den) in which multiple exposures create contrasting dreams for the two men, a Far West sequence (shot on location) in which the policeman rescues the thief from Native American Indians, and a close-up insert of a letter absolving the thief of guilt. This 'imperialist' adventure ends in an apotheosis tableau, with the two men (now financial partners) posing before the spectacle of a large stage-set globe surrounded by representatives of the world's peoples, over which they exert a benevolent control.

RICHARD ABEL

A Narrow Escape or the Physician of the Castle/ Le Médecin du château (France 1908 *p.c* – Pathé; *d* – Albert Capellani)

This film is based on André de Lorde's one-act Grand Guignol play, *Au téléphone* (1902), in which apaches (a criminal gang) falsely send a doctor away on a distant house call so they can break into his home and threaten his family. Unlike the stage play, or Pathé's earlier *Terrible angoisse* (1906), this film invents a 'happy ending'. Composed of 29 shots, *A Narrow Escape* is remarkable as an early example of sustained alternation or parallel editing (a frequent feature of Pathé films between 1906 and 1908). It quickly establishes adjacent spaces inside and outside the doctor's home, then alternates two lines of action (the break-in and threat versus the doctor's journey and arrival at a 'castle'), and culminates in two cut-in medium close-ups of the doctor and his wife, in matching profile (a good example of an attraction 'motivated' for narrative purposes), linked tenuously by telephone at the climactic moment of greatest vulnerability.

RICHARD ABEL

Parallel editing in *A Narrow Escape*

The Lonedale Operator (USA 1911 *p.c* – Biograph; *d* – D. W. Griffith)

Based on a script by Mack Sennett, this is a 'classic' example of Griffith's early suspense thrillers. The telegraph operator at a remote railway station falls ill, and his daughter (Blanche Sweet) has to defend the station against thieves as her fiancé races to the rescue in his locomotive. Composed of 97 shots, the film uses a multiple system of parallel editing that intercuts the locomotive engineer and his embattled sweetheart at the same time as it shows her glimpsing the thieves outside, barricading herself

Editing for suspense: *The Lonedale Operator*

in the telegraph office, and then outmanoeuvring them when they finally break in. Several cut-in medium shots accentuate the woman's anxiety as she realises her signals for help may have gone unheard, and one cut-in close-up reveals that the 'gun' she had used to hold off the thieves is actually a wrench: blue tinting in the earlier shots had kept it 'unreadable' to spectators as well.

RICHARD ABEL

The Greater Love (USA 1912 *p.c* – Vitagraph Co.; *d* – Rollin S. Sturgeon)

This western is notable as an early example of 'classical' continuity editing, especially in its repeated shot/reverse-shots (in medium and long shot): first, to link a cowboy and his lover, then to break up his duel with a rival, and finally, to intercut the two gunfighters on horseback. Its tinting and toning are also suggestive: although changes in colour sometimes distinguish day from night and exterior from interior, they primarily function to mark off one segment of the narrative from another, concisely signalling shifts in the story's development, but also serving as cues for a pianist to change the musical accompaniment.

RICHARD ABEL

In the Clutches of the Paris Apaches/L'Enfant de Paris (France 1913 *p.c* – Gaumont; *d* – Léonce Perret)

A topical feature-length melodrama in which a little girl falls into the hands of an apache gang, but is rescued by a young shoemaker who reunites her with her father. This film includes a range of mise en scène and framing strategies characteristic of European cinema just before World War I: 'deep staging' in both studio decors and natural landscapes (a good example would be the high-angle long shot from behind the father, in uniform, speaking from an apartment balcony to a cheering crowd below), moments of selective arc lighting, silhouetted figures in doors and windows, and 'pictorial' toning effects. It also displays Perret's own 'style' of continuity editing that often relied, not on shot/reverse-shot, but on 90-degree and 180-degree shifts in camera position. Finally, it is notable for sustaining narrative action across several 'breaks' between one film reel and another, taking advantage of the cinemas that could run multiple-reel films continuously (the Gaumont-Palace, for instance, began using two alternating projectors in late 1911).

RICHARD ABEL

and failures, the French alternative cinema movement not only produced valuable work on a par with that done in the Soviet Union; its legacy was also evident in the 1930s British documentary movement, the film theory and criticism of André Bazin and Jean Mitry, the American avant-garde that developed after World War II and the 1950s French film activity that eventually became known as the Nouvelle Vague (see also French cinema, p. 202).

The Chinese and Japanese cinemas present parallel, yet slightly different trajectories of development in relation to the American cinema. The Chinese film industry was located chiefly in Shanghai, the most westernised of the country's cities, where the media giant Commercial Press and the Mingxing film studio led the way in producing and promoting Chinese films. At first, according to Zhang Zhen (2005), film-makers were influenced equally by the traditional Chinese theatre and the modern, transplanted 'civilised play' (spoken drama using the vernacular); these dual influences produced sensational stories using a cinema of attractions aesthetic, as in *Victims of Opium* (1916) or the farcical *Laborer's Love* (1922). American and European influences soon led to family-problem dramas such as *A String of Pearls/Yi Chuan Zhen Zhu* (1926) that accepted yet modified the vernacular modernism of the American cinema. The most popular genre in the late 1920s, however, was the martial arts–magic spirit film that used trick cinematography, camera movement and editing to create marvellous pyrotechnic spectacles of action, as in *Burning of the Red Lotus Temple* (1928). Although the 'flying knight-errants' of most films were male, martial heroines, as in *The Red Heroine* (1929), were increasingly crucial to the genre's popularity. Perhaps the most accomplished of pre-sound films (the transition to sound was lengthy, from 1930 to 1936) were the melodramas that explicitly took up the figure of the 'new woman' and her paradoxical position in modern Chinese society. Ruan Lingyu became an emblematic star in many of these, from *Love and Duty/Lian Ai Yu Yi Wu* (1931) to *New Woman* (1935), then tragically committed suicide at age 25. Especially intriguing is the degree of reflexivity in such films as *An Amorous History of the Silver Screen* (1931) and *Three Modern Women* (1933), whose stories, set within the context of the film industry, blur the difference between actor and character. Finally, the appearance of Soviet films and Japanese radical film writing, in conjunction with the Japanese invasion of Manchuria in 1931, spurred the development of a patriotic left-wing movement whose influence can be traced in *Wild Rose/Ye Mei Gui* (1932), *Spring Silkworms/Chun Can* (1933) and *Daybreak/Tian Ming* (1933), the latter starring the athletic Li Li-li (see also Chinese cinema, p. 192).

The Japanese film industry was located in Tokyo where, during the 1910s, according to Aaron Gerow (in Abel, 2005), the dominant Nikkatsu trust produced *kyuha* or 'old school' dramas (often based on Kabuki plays, performed by male actors) that relied heavily on popular *benshi* or lecturers, and *shimpa* or 'new school' films with modern settings, sometimes influenced by French comedies. Towards the end of World War I, as American films finally reached Japan, a Pure Film Movement emerged seeking to reform and modernise Japanese cinema, especially through scriptwriting practices. The movement led to the founding of two new film studios, Shochiku and Taikatsu, which, especially after a 1923 earthquake levelled much of Tokyo, succeeded in introducing female actors, replacing *kyuha* with modernised *jidaigeki* or period films and adopting many classical Hollywood conventions, yet failed to banish *benshi*. As in China, martial arts films were especially popular in the late 1920s, but these samurai or *ronin* films tended to eschew trick cinematography and special effects and stage beautifully choreographed fight scenes deploying virtuoso camera movements, as in *Castle of Wind and Clouds/Fuun joshi* (1928). The genre was even exploited in 'tendency films' (late-1920s films with a leftist tendency) such as *Slashing Swords* (1929) in which, to avoid censorship, a stereotypical evil lord rather than class conflict causes a peasant revolt. Also as in China, the most consistently accomplished of pre-sound films (again, the transition to sound was lengthy, from 1930 to 1936) were *shimpa* melodramas whose stories revolved around one or more tragic female protagonists, a genre that had languished throughout the 1920s. Shochiku was especially invested in early films such as *Eternal Heart/Fue no shirotama* (1929), which focuses on the sacrifice of one sister for the other's happiness. At Nikkatsu, Mikio Naruse directed a series of poignant women's weepies, among them *The Unrelated/Nasanu naka* (1932) and *Farewell to You/Kimi to wakarete* (1933), in which a mother sacrifices herself for an unfeeling daughter and an ungrateful son. Yasujiro Ozu and Kenji Mizoguchi both produced early psychological masterpieces in the genre: the former with *Woman of Tokyo/Tokyo no onna* (1933), where a sister pays for her younger brother's education only to have him commit suicide when he discovers she works at a disreputable bar; the latter with *White Threads of the Waterfall/Taki no shiraito* (1933), where a music-hall artiste finances her young lover's law studies and then is mistakenly condemned to death by the very law he embodies. Finally, atmospheric crime thrillers such as Minoru Murata's *Foghorn/Muteki* (1934) uncannily anticipate the late-1930s French films of Marcel Carné (see also Japanese cinema, p. 238).

The study of silent cinema has become a 'burning passion', to cite Paolo Cherchi Usai's apt metaphor. For some, he writes, it means 'going back to the origins of a truly inflammable, even explosive relationship between image and mind' (2000, p. xix), whether that of the historian or interested spectator. But it also can mean seeing a parallel between early or pre-classical cinema and our own allegedly post-classical cinema, condensing around modes of film consumption and spectatorship. Both historical moments, Hansen (1993) argues, mark a major transition in the development of the public sphere, and the potential for a critical, utopian alternative. Our own postmodern media culture, then, may well involve a similar opening up of possibilities and interventionist options.

Selected Reading

Richard Abel, *French Cinema: The First Wave, 1915–1929*, Princeton, Princeton University Press, 1984.

Richard Abel (ed.), *Encyclopedia of Early Cinema*, Oxford and New York, Routledge, 2005.

Tom Gunning, '"The cinema of attraction": early cinema, its spectator and the avant-garde', *Wide Angle* 8 (3/4): 63–70, 1986. Reprinted in Elsaesser and Barker (eds), *Early Cinema: Space, Frame, Narrative*, London, BFI Publishing, 1990.

Kristin Thompson, *Exporting Entertainment: America in the World Film Market, 1907–1934*, London, BFI Publishing, 1985.

THE RISE OF THE AMERICAN FILM INDUSTRY

ANNETTE KUHN AND RICHARD ABEL

In 1891 Thomas Edison took out patents on two new processes, the Kinetograph and the Kinetoscope. In spite of such precautions, however, Edison underestimated the economic potential of these inventions and failed either to secure foreign rights or effectively to exploit the domestic market. In 1893, a Kinetoscope Company was set up independent of Edison to retail 'Kinetographic' material and coin-operated Kinetoscope machines, both of which Edison agreed to manufacture for a price. In the same year, Edison opened what was perhaps the first purpose-built production studio, at a cost of some $700, a sum that was soon recovered by charging $200 for every Kinetoscope sold.

The first films to flicker inside the Kinetoscopes featured such exotica as boxers, ballerinas and bears, ran only a fragment of a single reel (about 50 feet, less than a minute on average) and were watched by individual customers. In 1894, the first Kinetoscope parlour opened in New York's Broadway, and a new company – the Kinetoscope Exhibition Company (KEC) – was set up to exploit an exclusive contract with Edison to exhibit his films. Realising that greater profits could be made if more than one customer could watch a film at any one time, the KEC introduced a projection process, the Panoptikon. Other companies employing similar processes also began to appear in the mid-1890s. Among the earliest of these were Mutoscope in America and the Lumière brothers in France. In 1896 Lumière's Cinématographe and Mutoscope's American Biograph were both exhibited in New York, and the machines – rather than the material that passed through them – were clearly the main attraction. Indeed, Edison and his competitors made most of their money in these early years not from their films, which were sold outright, but from the cinematographic equipment for which they held the patents. The films themselves functioned in fact as little more than inducements to customers considering either the purchase of Kinetoscopes or the hire of an exhibition service that could provide a projecting apparatus and operator on a regular basis.

Exhibition services such as Biograph, Vitagraph, Kinodrome and even Edison's Kinetograph (each with its own different apparatus) enabled vaudeville theatres to use a single reel of motion pictures as top-of-the-bill novelties or as popular 'chasers' at the beginning and end of an advertised programme. As exhibition outlets began to multiply, first through the expansion of 'cheap' or family vaudeville and then through the conversion of storefront spaces (including penny arcades) into nickelodeons, the demand grew for more and more new films. Initially, the French magician Georges Méliès, working out of a studio in Paris, proved a crucial supplier, especially with titles such as *A Trip to the Moon/Le Voyage dans la lune* (1902) and *Fairyland/Le Royaume des fées* (1903).

It was another French company, Pathé-Frères, however, that most exploited this expanding market. By 1905, Pathé was moving into film production on a mass scale (across the full spectrum of genres) and was setting up a worldwide network of sales agencies for its films. It operated three studios (two with double stages) on the outskirts of Paris and employed more than a thousand workers in a cluster of laboratories (for developing, perforating, printing, splicing and colouring film stock). By the

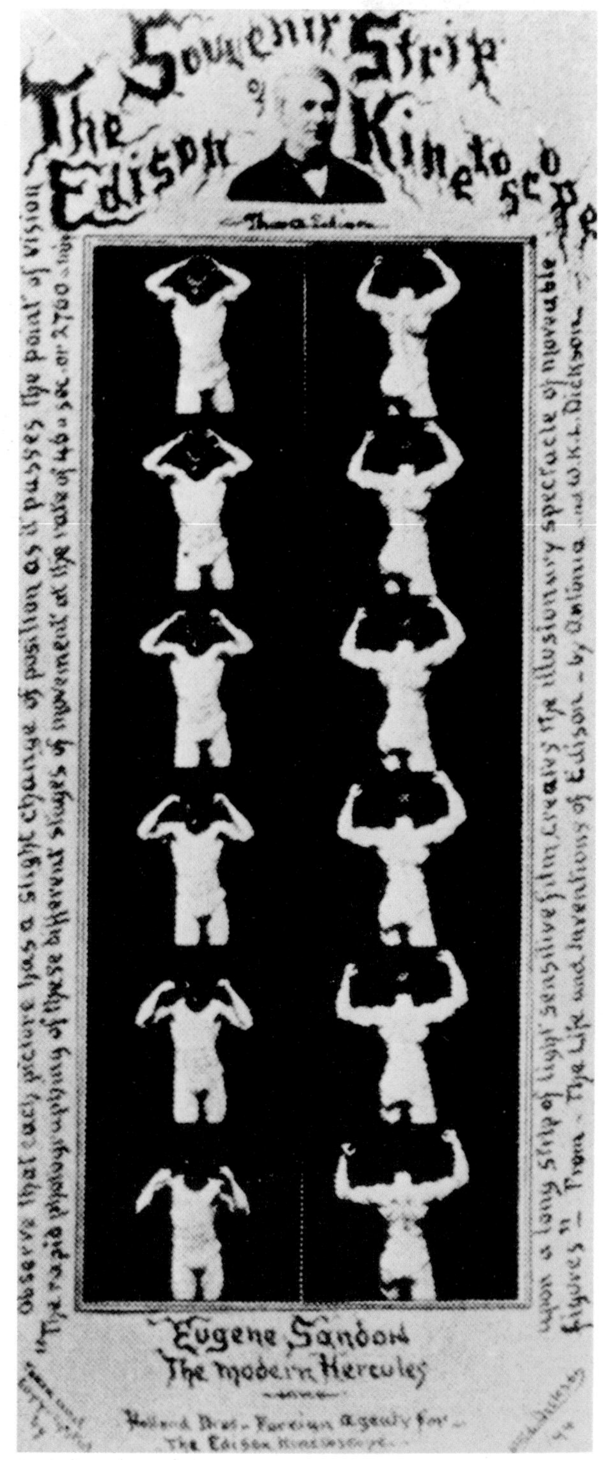

Single-reel exotica

Made for an expanding market: Méliès's *Le Voyage dans la lune*

fall of 1906, Pathé was releasing six new film titles per week, printing 100,000 feet of positive film stock per day and had advance orders for a minimum of 75 copies of each title shipped to the US. Within another year or so, the company's weekly list of titles had nearly doubled; its daily production of positive film footage had reached 230,000 feet; and it was selling on average 200 prints of each new title on the American market. This production and distribution capacity (which easily matched that of the combined American companies) arguably made the nickelodeon 'revolution' possible, and Pathé's 'red rooster' films consistently amounted to between one-third and one-half of all films circulating on the American market from 1905 to 1908 (see also Early and pre-sound cinema, p. 3).

Pathé's prominence as a film supplier opened a gap between production and exhibition, and the need for some sort of liaison was exploited by 'film exchanges' that bought, or later leased, films and then sold, or later rented, them to exhibitors. Sales and rentals were set not in accordance with studio expenditure or cinema returns, of course, but simply in proportion to purchase price, cinema size and/or film footage. By 1905, the standard length of a film was between 250 and 400 feet (4–6 minutes), although longer films of between 800 and 1,000 feet (13–16 minutes) were becoming increasingly common. At first, Pathé was able to sell its titles at a single low rate, undercutting Edison's effort to impose different prices for different 'categories' of films. As exhibition expanded, selling and rental arrangements became complicated, and by 1907 there were more than 125 film exchanges, each with its own idiosyncratic pricing practices, serving the seven or eight thousand nickelodeons in operation. In order to gain some control over these chaotic conditions (and increase their profits), some distributors such as Fred Aiken in Chicago consolidated rental exchange businesses on a large scale; certain exhibitors such as Carl Laemmle in Chicago and William Fox in New York invested heavily in rental businesses; and still others began to build up chains of cinemas (by 1910, for example, Marcus Loew's Theatrical Enterprises was reaching well beyond its base in New York). These distributors and exhibitors would soon form the nucleus of the independent sector.

The most blatant attempt to control the expanding cinema industry, however, came from Edison, who had long sought to create a monopoly through the exercise of his company's patent rights. In late 1907, a new court decision favouring Edison led to the formation of the Film Service Association that linked most of the country's rental exchanges with a majority of film manufacturers (excepting Biograph), all of whom agreed to pay licence fees to Edison. One objective of this agreement was to channel the industry's profits to the manufacturers; perhaps more important, however, it set limits on Pathé's operations. Ever wary of Edison's patent rights in the US, and unable to make the huge investment needed to establish its own viable rental exchange (it had just opened a factory for printing positive film stock in New Jersey), Pathé reluctantly agreed to Edison's terms. As the trade press became caught up in a national hysteria over 'Americanisation' and increasingly described Pathé films as 'foreign' to American tastes, the French company realised that its days of dominating the American market were numbered. By late 1908, it accepted the transformation of the Film Service Association into the Motion Picture Patents Company (MPPC, also known as the 'Trust'), which now linked Biograph and George Kleine (the distributor for Gaumont and Eclipse) with Pathé, Vitagraph, Lubin, Essanay, Selig, Kalem and Méliès as Edison licensees. As a consequence, Pathé began to shift film production to subsidiaries (not only in France but also Italy, Russia and the US), redirect film distribution to central and eastern Europe, and concentrate its investment in manufacturing cameras, projectors and negative film stock.

In 1910 the Trust had extended its technological monopoly into the field of distribution with the formation of the General Film Company, an MPPC subsidiary: ironically, this example of vertical integration was similar to the model Pathé had already established, by 1908, in France and several adjacent countries (see The classic studio system, p. 19). The General Film Company proceeded to buy up film exchanges at such a rate that by the following year only one of the former exchanges remained independent. With this single exception, General Film became the sole film distributor in the US. By this time, profits in the film industry were already enormous: in 1910, American cinemas were attracting 26 million people a week. However, this very success effectively discouraged most MPPC members from experimenting with new modes of production, distribution or exhibition, which contributed to the MPPC's ultimate downfall.

Perhaps the most prolific, and certainly the most profitable, of the American production companies in the MPPC at this period was Vitagraph. Organised in 1897 with capital of $1,000, by 1912, Vitagraph had accumulated a gross income of $6 million. At that time, the company had a staff of 400 actors, actresses, executives and technicians, and was producing about 300 films a year. Vitagraph's success probably was due to its early developments of systematic production methods, its decision to set up an aggressive sales office in Europe (with a printing factory in Paris) and its recognition that the Trust's technological monopoly was hardly sufficient guarantee of long-term economic survival. Consequently, the company began to invest in longer films and familiar faces, pioneering the production of films of two reels or more in length (30 minutes) and assembling an impressive array of popular contract performers, among them the 'Vitagraph Girl', Florence Turner, Maurice Costello and John Bunny. Unlike multiple-reel European titles then being screened as complete films (in France, Italy and Denmark), Vitagraph's *Uncle Tom's Cabin* (1910), *A Tale of Two Cities* (1911) and *Vanity Fair* (1911) were released one reel at a time through the General Film Company.

The MPPC's attempt to gain a monopoly over film production and distribution was undercut by the formation of independent companies such as Laemmle's Independent Moving Picture Company (IMP), the New York Motion Picture Company (Thomas Ince), Aitken's Mutual Film Company and the Fox Film Corporation. It also was challenged by the construction of or the renovation of existing theatres into large cinemas that could offer longer programmes (hence longer films). Moreover, in 1912 the MPPC was brought to court on antitrust charges, and by 1915 the General Film Company had been dissolved. Two years later, the Trust itself was finally outlawed by the Supreme Court. The abolition of the MPPC was not, however, a case of independent companies defeating a monopoly, nor was it merely a matter of Congress and the court system enforcing 'free enterprise'. Rather, one kind of vertical integration within the industry simply replaced another. More than anything, the Trust failed to exploit the cinematic potential of longer films (whose initial advances came in Europe) and star performers. Thus, while General Film remained committed to releasing films in 1,000-foot reels, the independents were beginning to take advantage of additional selling points or 'production values', including roadshow releases of 'foreign imports', as Adolph Zukor did with *Queen Elizabeth/Les Amours de la Reine Elisabeth* (1912), starring Sarah Bernhardt. In this context, box-office attractions assumed paramount importance.

Box-office attractions

In 1910 Carl Laemmle lured the famous 'Biograph Girl' to his Independent Moving Picture Company and took the hitherto unprecedented step of revealing her real name, Florence Lawrence, to her fans (see Stars before sound, p. 119). In 1914 William Fox, who had entered film production two years before with the formation of a studio subsidiary, Box Office Attractions, went one better by tempting director Frank Powell away from Biograph. Powell fabricated a new star persona for his first Fox film: the star was Theda Bara and the film was *A Fool There Was* (1915). Fox needed box-office attractions in order to outmanoeuvre the MPPC, and the combination of a mysteriously exotic star and a melodramatic plot provided exactly the publicity Fox had required. Indeed, Fox himself was largely responsible for that publicity: the very name Theda Bara was a suggestive anagram of 'Arab Death', and rumours were leaked to the press of Bara's 'parents' being a French artist and his Arabian mistress, and of her childhood spent under the shadow of the Sphinx, while stories were circulated of the star's smoking in public and burning incense in private and even of conducting interviews with reporters in her boudoir.

By this time, more and more licensee producers were going independent in order to exploit the flexibility of 'feature-length' films, and more and more licensee exhibitors were building or converting special film theatres. One of the directors at Biograph, for example, whose 1911 two-reeler *Enoch Arden* was released by the studio in two parts, and whose four-reel film of the following year, *Judith of Bethulia*, Biograph refused to release at all, left the Trust to work for an independent production company, Reliance-Majestic. There he began work on an ambitious adaptation of Thomas Dixon's bestseller, *The Clansman*. That director was D. W. Griffith, and the film was *The Birth of a Nation* (1915).

The original budget for *The Birth of a Nation* was $40,000, but Griffith was allowed to expand the project to 12 reels and an estimated total cost of $110,000. To protect his investment in the film, Harry Aitken – President of Majestic's parent company – formed the Epoch Producing Corporation and decided to exploit the film's extravagant length and budget by releasing it as an

Theda Bara: Fox's box-office attraction

unprecedented cinematic event. Prints were hand-tinted, and orchestral accompaniment commissioned and composed to synchronise with the on-screen action. Wherever the film was exhibited, white-robed horsemen were employed to gallop up and down the nearest streets and publicise every screening. Seat prices in New York, where the film was premiered, were increased from the usual 10–25 cents to an astounding $2. Following its premiere, *The Birth of a Nation* was 'roadshowed' across the major American cities in the larger first-run theatres. Finally, the film was released to independent distributors, and broke box-office records wherever it played. Louis B. Mayer, for instance, who operated a string of theatres in New England, made more than $50,000 from the film and with this bought Aitken's old Culver City Studio, which was later used by MGM (see MGM, p. 23). Estimates of the film's total earnings are notoriously unreliable, varying from five to 50 million dollars, but it seems certain that by 1916 a million tickets had been sold in New York alone. The film was first approved and then condemned by the National Board of Censorship; this, while barely affecting the number of screenings permitted, certainly increased the considerable publicity generated around the film. Griffith invested the bulk of *The Birth of a Nation*'s profits in his next project, *Intolerance* (1916), and, of a budget estimated at $1.9 million, Griffith advanced almost a million himself. The film was considerably less successful than its predecessor, however, and it virtually bankrupted Griffith. To finance the film, Griffith had formed the Wark Producing Corporation and the investors behind this endeavour included a number of Wall Street financiers. In seeking artistic independence from the Trust studios, Griffith instead walked into the hands of the economic empires of Morgan and Rockefeller, whose domination of the industry would be cemented ten years later with the coming of sound.

As roadshow releases and regional releases began to compete for domestic distribution and exhibitor earnings, the economic necessity of a national network of distribution became increasingly apparent. In 1914 the first such network, Paramount Pictures Corporation, was set up: it released 104 films a year to its members' circuits. To supply this amount of product, Adolph Zukor and Jesse Lasky merged their production units to form Famous Players-Lasky and, to ensure that the films they produced and distributed were all actually exhibited, introduced the policy of 'block booking' whereby exhibitors wishing to screen a particular film would be forced to book, unseen, an entire package that included this film. Famous Players-Lasky assembled a roster of 'stars' including Mary Pickford, Douglas Fairbanks, Gloria Swanson, Fatty Arbuckle, William S. Hart, Norma and Constance Talmadge as well as 'name' directors such as Cecil B. DeMille, Griffith and Mack Sennett. With the collapse of competition from the European film industry during World War I, Paramount escalated its annual output to 220 films for almost 5,000 cinemas. To counter Paramount's increasing stranglehold over exhibition, 27 of America's largest first-run cinemas combined in 1917 to form their own 'independent' distribution network, the First National Exhibitors Circuit (FNEC). During the following year, the FNEC lured Charlie Chaplin away from Mutual and Mary Pickford away from Paramount with offers of million-dollar contracts, and themselves entered into film production.

Chaplin's early film career highlights a period of 'struggle for control' in American cinema, a struggle in which stars became

A budding star: Mary Pickford in Biograph's *The New York Hat*

The struggle for artistic control: Charlie Chaplin in *The Pawnbroker*

important economic assets. At Keystone, Chaplin was artistically and economically restricted, and he subsequently moved to Essanay and a salary of $1,250 a week, where he produced 15 films, most of them two-reelers. In 1915, the year in which the General Film Company was dissolved, Essanay expanded Chaplin's two-reel *Burlesque on Carmen* to four reels. The collapse of the Trust itself immediately elevated the economic value of the stars as box-office attractions, and Chaplin left Essanay for Mutual and a weekly salary of $10,000. At Mutual, Chaplin perfected the persona of the tramp that he had developed at Essanay, and made a further 12 films, including *The Vagabond* (1916), *The Pawnshop* (1916) and *Easy Street* (1917), before leaving for First National with an eight-film million-dollar contract. Like Essanay before it, Mutual soon collapsed without Chaplin, who was at this time probably the biggest box-office draw in the US.

The origins of the studio system

By 1921 First National was linked to some 3,500 film theatres in the United States, and in 1922 added a production studio to its already extensive distribution and exhibition holdings. Recognising the threat to Paramount's profits, Zukor began by buying up cinemas himself, and by the end of 1926 had acquired a controlling interest in more than 1,000 theatres. As Paramount expanded from production through distribution to exhibition, First National responded by increasing its investment in production and distribution; the industry was becoming characterised by vertical integration (see The classic studio system, p. 19), dominated by Carl Laemmle's Universal, William Fox's Fox Film Corporation, Zukor's Paramount, the exhibitors First National and, in 1924, a fifth group, Metro-Goldwyn-Mayer – which combined Marcus Loew's cinema chain, Metro's film exchanges and the production units of Goldwyn and Mayer. As inter-company competition became increasingly fierce, film publicity and production values became crucially important in attracting both independent exhibitors and audiences to studio-specific productions. Thus while most of the packages of films distributed by these companies were of similar budgets and scales, each studio also produced occasional 'specials', often for roadshow release, and boasting huge investments, large crews and costs and impressive sets and settings. These included *The Covered Wagon* (Paramount/Famous Players-Lasky, 1923), *The Lost World* (First National, 1925), *Foolish Wives* (Universal, 1922) and *Sunrise A Song of Two Humans* (Fox, 1927).

All four of these films exploited special effects and/or elaborate sets and settings and were released as exceptional cinematic events. *The Lost World*, for example, was one of the first full-length features to use animated models, *The Covered Wagon* was the first epic western, *Foolish Wives* was a 14-reel blockbuster, while *Sunrise* employed the largest single set since *Intolerance*, covering an area a mile long and half a mile across. *The Covered Wagon* cost $350,000 and netted $1.5 million. *Foolish Wives* cost $1,400,000 and almost broke Universal. *Sunrise* cost even more. The emphasis of these specials was on literary sources – *The Covered Wagon*, for instance, was adapted from a popular novel by Emerson Hough, *The Lost World* based on a Conan Doyle story, *Sunrise* on Hermann Sudermann. These were all films based on stories already familiar to the general public that, in addition, featured the studios' biggest stars and highest-paid directors.

Meanwhile, companies with less capital found it increasingly difficult to compete with the vertically integrated majors. United Artists, for instance, which had been founded in 1919 by four of the industry's best-paid employees – Pickford, Fairbanks, Chaplin and Griffith – was only a distributor, lacking either studios or cinemas of its own and rising to major status only in the 1950s in the wake of antitrust judgments. Universal, with limited capital and only a small number of cinemas, was also frustrated in its efforts to expand. Similarly, Warner Bros., a minor but prosperous production company, found itself with neither distribution nor exhibition outlets, and so decided in 1925 to acquire the ailing Vitagraph with its national network of film exchanges.

The coming of sound and the studio system in the 1930s

In 1926 Warner Bros., in combination with Western Electric, a subsidiary of the American Telephone and Telegraph Co. (AT&T), founded the Vitaphone Corporation to make sound films and market sound equipment, and in October 1927 Warners released *The Jazz Singer*. Capitalising on the success of the 'first talkie', Warners acquired and equipped for sound the First National exhibition circuit. AT&T's corporate rival RCA swiftly responded by setting up its own sound subsidiary, RKO. By 1930, then, the film industry was an oligopoly in which five vertically integrated companies – that is, five companies with holdings in production, distribution and exhibition – dominated the American market: Warner Bros., Loews-MGM, Fox, Paramount and RKO. Three smaller companies or 'minors' – United Artists, Universal and Columbia – lacking exhibition outlets of their own, had to rely on the independent cinemas.

Of the 23,000 theatres operating in 1930, the majors controlled only 3,000 but these accounted for almost three-quarters of the annual box-office takings in the US. The majors produced only 50 per cent of the total output of the industry, but this figure represented 80 per cent of the A-films exhibited in the first-run theatres. And while the 'flagship' cinemas of each chain boasted blockbusters such as *King Kong* (1933), the second-run cinemas thrived on less ambitious genre pictures such as those produced by Warners and Universal. The coming of sound postponed for a while the effects of the Depression on the film industry, but eventually a combination of reduced receipts and increasing overheads hit the industry hard. In 1931 Warner Bros. lost $8 million, Fox $3 million and RKO $5.5 million. In 1933 Paramount went into bankruptcy with a $21 million deficit, while RKO and Universal were forced into receivership. Even MGM, the only major company not to go into debt, saw its profits plunge from $10 million in 1930 to $1.3 million three years later. Audience attendance, which had been estimated in 1929 at more than 80 million a week, fell to less than 60 million in 1932. The common stock value of the majors fell from a high of $960 million in 1930 to $140 million in 1934. To meet the crisis, President Roosevelt's New Deal administration passed a National Industrial Recovery Act (NIRA), encouraging 'fair competition' in the film industry as in other industries. A Code of Fair Competition for the Motion Picture Industry was ratified as law in 1933, and antitrust cases against the oligopoly were suspended in return for the signing of minimum-wage and maximum-hour agreements and the right to collective bargaining for employees. One of the consequences of the Depression for exhibition practices was the emergence of the 'double bill', developed as an 'added attraction' during the Depression, and allowed by the Code as fair competition. In 1935 the Supreme Court revoked the NIRA but by then the industry was too firmly reorganised to be adversely affected.

Censorship

As early as 1895 an innocuous short, *Dolorita in the Passion Dance*, was removed from an Atlantic City Kinetoscope to appease local authorities. Two years later another film, *Orange Blossoms*, was closed by court order in New York as 'offensive to public decency'. As the number of nickelodeons multiplied, a variety of pressure groups, including churches, reform groups, police and press, began attempting to exert influence on the new medium of cinema. These pressures were institutionalised in the formation of state censorship boards with the objective of outflanking possible extra-industrial 'interference' in the content of films. The Motion Picture Patents Company (MPPC) combined in 1909 with a self-appointed social research organisation to form the first National Board of Censorship (NBC).

The NBC, subsequently renamed the National Board of Review, employed rather erratic censorship principles in relation to the films it reviewed. *The Birth of a Nation*, for instance, was initially approved by the Board, only to have that approval revoked when the film met with criticism from liberal newspapers and anti-racist organisations. The MPPC, which was responsible for the production of almost two-thirds of the films made in the US, agreed to submit all its films to the Board for pre-release inspection, but the independent States' Rights system entitled individual states to impose their own censorship. In 1915 the production company of *The Birth of a Nation* took the Ohio State censor to the Supreme Court for alleged infringement of constitutionally guaranteed free speech. However, the Supreme Court dismissed the case, on the grounds that motion pictures were a 'business pure and simple' and thus not entitled to First Amendment protection.

With the collapse of the Trust and the emergence of the vertically integrated companies in the early 1920s, the need for a new national industry-appointed censorship board became increasingly pressing. In 1921 the National Association of the Motion Picture Industry (NAMPI), a consortium of representatives of the major companies, adopted a 13-point code to serve as a yardstick for the production and exhibition of films. NAMPI's code proscribed certain kinds of subject matter – illicit love, nakedness, undue violence, vulgarity and so on – but lacked the means effectively to enforce its proscriptions. A series of scandals during the next two or three years – involving Mary Pickford in an apparently fraudulent divorce testimony, Fatty Arbuckle in a rape and murder trial, and director William Desmond Taylor in a murder case – provided the excuse the industry needed: in 1922 Will Hays, President Harding's Postmaster General, was invited by the majors to head the Motion Pictures Producers and Distributors of America (MPPDA).

Since state censorship boards were becoming increasingly influential, Hays launched a fierce campaign under a 'free speech' banner aimed at defeating demands for film censorship legislation. At the same time, to offset press criticism and opposition from educational and religious organisations, the majors began to increase the output of films for 'women and children', and film-makers such as Erich von Stroheim found themselves at the mercy of censors both in the studio and at the Hays office. Stroheim complained bitterly about interference on *Foolish Wives*: 'My ears have rung with their united cry: "It is not fit for children!" Children! Children! God, I did not make that picture for children.' After several unsatisfactory years in which the MPPDA published lists of 'Don'ts' and 'Be Carefuls', Hays, together with Martin Quigley (publisher of the trade paper *Motion Picture Herald*), introduced a revised Production Code, which was adopted by the industry in 1930 and under whose terms every film made by members of the MPPDA would be censored by a Studio Relations Committee both in script and pre-release film form.

While the majors tended, at least at first, to accommodate the Code, independent productions occasionally went beyond its provisions. One such production was Howard Hughes's *Scarface* (1932), directed by Howard Hawks, which was alleged to contain scenes of hitherto unprecedented violence. On its submission to the Hays office, dozens of cuts were demanded and, knowing that without Hays's approval most theatres would refuse to screen the film, Hughes compromised and agreed to several of them. Hays then granted the film a licence, but several local censorship boards still refused to allow *Scarface* to be

Mae West in *It Ain't No Sin*, censored to *Belle of the Nineties*

Condemned by the Legion of Decency: *Baby Doll*

shown. Hughes sued these censors and as a result of the publicity that the case (which Hughes in fact won) received, the film was a huge box-office success. These events were instrumental in ensuring that the Hays office rather than the local or national legislatures became the arbiter of American film content: it was to remain so for more than two decades.

For some time the studios tended to conform to the stipulations of the Production Code, but falling attendances at film theatres during 1932 and 1933 led to the deployment of more 'daring' material, and the very adverse publicity such films received increased their box-office earnings. Mae West was a frequent target of moral crusades, and indeed after *She Done Him Wrong* (1933) West became a symbol of everything the Code condemned. Meanwhile, however, Paramount grossed $2 million during the first three months of the film's release. The Catholic Church mobilised its forces, threatened the majors with mass picketing of Paramount's theatres and formed the Legion of Decency. In 1934, under pressure from the Legion, the MPPDA abolished the Studio Relations Committee and replaced it with the more powerful Production Code Administration (PCA). By the end of the year, the impact of the Production Code on the American cinema had become apparent. The PCA followed production from the script stage through to the final editing. 'The new regulatory structure made a changed woman of Mae West ... the title of her latest film *It Ain't No Sin* was transformed to *Belle of the Nineties* and her scintillating repartee and sexual independence were toned down considerably' (Stanley, 1978, p. 196).

In 1935, partly in order to placate the PCA, a number of studios began a cycle of 'prestige' literary adaptations, which included Warner Bros.'s *A Midsummer Night's Dream* (1935), Fox's *The Informer* (1935) and Goldwyn's *Stella Dallas* (1937). According to *Fortune*:

> It is generally conceded by leaders in the industry that productions like *A Midsummer Night's Dream* ... would have been unthinkable even ten years ago, and that Hays's national publicity grapevine, reaching several millions of the 'best people' who attend movies infrequently has been the chief factor in making them possible ('The Hays Office', in Balio, 1976, p. 311).

But while prestigious Oscar-winning films such as *A Midsummer Night's Dream* and *The Informer* were being made, the studios were also engaged in producing film series and genres that could accommodate the Code and be 'fit for children'. Partly as a result of such pressure, Warner Bros. revised their gangster films to explicitly condemn gangsterism: in 1935 emphasis moved from the gangsters themselves to the G-men (FBI agents) who gallantly battled against them. Once the Code's provisions had entered cinematic currency, in fact, they informed both the style and the content of the genres themselves (see also The gangster film, p. 279).

For more than two decades the PCA was responsible for reviewing some 95 per cent of the films exhibited in the US. Indeed, as long as the industry remained vertically integrated, the power of the PCA remained virtually unchallenged. Finally, however, in 1952 the Supreme Court extended the protection of the First Amendment to the film industry. The case in point centred on Roberto Rossellini's *The Miracle/Il miracolo* (1948), which had been deemed 'blasphemous' by the Legion of Decency. While Howard Hughes continued to offend the censors with his exploitation of Jane Russell in 3-D for RKO, United Artists released a string of independent productions with 'controversial' and hitherto unpermitted subject matter. The link between the Catholic Church and the movie industry had remained intact as long as profits were high, but antitrust legislation, the rise of television and the growth of the art cinema and drive-in circuits fuelled Hollywood's hostility towards restraints, which were no longer economically viable.

The film that best illustrated – and indeed also influenced – these changes is Elia Kazan's *Baby Doll* (1956). The film received PCA approval, despite its portrayal of an unconsummated marriage between a child-wife and a middle-aged, sexually frustrated man. The Legion of Decency promptly condemned the film's 'carnal suggestiveness' as morally repellent both in theme and treatment, and Catholic cinemagoers were instructed to forego the film and picket the theatres in which it was shown (see Elia Kazan, p. 427).

Such action may have reduced the film's potential audience, but it also prompted an outcry from other religious bodies and civil liberties groups against the Church's encroachment on individual freedoms. Late in 1956 the Production Code was revised, and in the following year the Legion of Decency expanded its film classification system. Finally in 1968 a National Motion Picture Rating System was introduced, and the PCA was replaced by the Code and Rating Administration, which operates a system based on labelling films as suitable for specific audiences.

Selected Reading

Robert C. Allen, 'William Fox presents *Sunrise*', *Quarterly Review of Film Studies* 2 (3): 327–38, August 1977. Reprinted in Schatz (ed.), *Hollywood: Critical Concepts in Media and Cultural Studies*, London and New York, Routledge, 2003.

Tino Balio (ed.), *The American Film Industry*, Madison, University of Wisconsin Press, 1976.

Geoffrey Nowell-Smith (ed.), 'Silent cinema 1895–1930', in *The Oxford History of World Cinema*, Oxford, Oxford University Press, 1996.

Robert Stanley, *The Celluloid Empire: A History of the American Movie Industry*, New York, Hastings House, 1978.

THE CLASSIC STUDIO SYSTEM

ANNETTE KUHN AND THOMAS SCHATZ

The high point, economically and stylistically, of Hollywood cinema is usually seen as occurring in the years in which the 'studio system' flourished, when the film industry prospered as an oligopoly: when, in other words, the production of films was dominated almost entirely by a small number of vertically integrated companies – companies with controlling interests in the distribution and exhibition as well as in the production of films. The full consolidation of the system can be dated from around 1930, but its roots lie in the 'assembly line' methods of film-making introduced by producers such as Thomas Ince and Mack Sennett as early as 1913–15, in the first attempts at vertical integration by Paramount, First National and others in 1915, and in the opening that year in Hollywood of Universal City, the first full-blown motion-picture 'factory' for the mass production and mass marketing of the new product. When the stock market crash of October 1929 coupled with the new financial demands on the studios of the coming of sound drove a number of production companies to the wall, the way was open for a few 'majors' – companies that for various reasons managed to weather the economic vicissitudes of the time – to establish their joint control of the industry. The end of their dominance is often dated (by Gomery, 1986, and others) very precisely to 3 May 1948, when an antitrust suit filed in 1938 against the majors and the large unaffiliated theatre chains who colluded with them was finally decided, outlawing vertical integration, block booking and blind bidding. But this event, like the crash of 1929, marks only one key point in a long-term process. The majors' oligopoly was increasingly threatened before 1948 by the rapid growth in the 1940s of 'independent' production largely driven by war-related income-tax laws that encouraged top talent (such as stars and producer-directors) to go freelance.

The studios fought the 1948 decision in the courts for nearly two years, with Paramount being the first to comply by divesting its theatre chain at midnight on 31 December 1949, and MGM the last, maintaining control of its theatres until 1957. The widening of the market with the rise of television in the 1950s was an additional challenge to the integrated studio system, but the 'red scare' – the vetting of creative and technical personnel by the House Un-American Activities Committee (HUAC) – though often linked to the decline of the studios, actually hit TV production harder than film.

Of the eight companies that dominated the Hollywood film industry in the 1930s and 1940s, the 'Big Five' – Warner Bros., RKO, 20th Century Fox, Paramount and MGM – were completely vertically integrated: they owned distribution companies and chains of film theatres as well as the means to produce films. The 'Little Three' – Universal, Columbia and United Artists – were not vertically integrated, but are usually included among the majors because their films had access to the first-run theatres owned by the Big Five. During the period of mature oligopoly, the eight majors jointly owned only about a sixth of all theatres in the US, but these included most (around 80 per cent) of the first-run theatres, which generated between 50 per cent and 75 per cent of the industry's revenues – and the control of first-run exhibition gave the studios effective control over the flow of product through the entire market.

The study of the economic organisation of the film industry may be justified on a variety of grounds, ranging from an interest in its various modes of production, to a concern with the relationships between particular forms of organisation of film production, distribution and exhibition, and the films that were, on the face of it at least, the reasons for the industry's existence. If films are to be approached this way, however, some thought has to be given to the nature of the relationship between film texts and their immediate contexts. As Mae Huettig argues, there is a connection between the form taken by a film and the mechanics of the business, even if the connection is somewhat obscure ('The motion picture industry today', in Balio, 1976). How is this expressed in the Hollywood studio system as a particular form of economic organisation of film production?

How far, that is to say, did the economic organisation and the production relations (the ways in which the work involved in making films was organised) characteristic of studios determine the character of their products, the films themselves? On the side of economic organisation, the nature and provenance of capital investment in the film industry between 1930 and 1948, and also vertical integration, can be seen to have important consequences. The enormous investment required to equip studios and film theatres for sound, in combination with the effects of the general recession in the US economy in the late 1920s and early 1930s, led the industry to seek outside financial backing, usually from eastern banking groups. During the early 1930s, all the major companies in fact underwent extensive financial reorganisation, which eventually led to the domination of some of the studios by these outside sources of finance. One of the consequences of this was to reinforce the majors' dependence on vertical integration, for their assets – the collateral against which they obtained financial backing – were chiefly in the form of real estate: by the mid-1940s, about two-thirds of the majors' total capital was invested in film theatres. It has in fact been suggested that in this context the production of films by the majors was no more than a means towards the primary objective of maintaining the property value of film theatres.

Simple sets and low-key lighting in *The Public Enemy*

In this situation, the balance of power in determining the nature of the product lay largely on the side of the 'front office' – the industry's businessmen – rather than its creative personnel. The demand was for films that would secure financial return from exhibition. A 'good picture' in these terms was one that had access to first-run theatres, and hence combined production values with a certain degree of predictability. The emphasis was clearly not on the side of experimentation in film form and content.

The relations of film production characteristic of the studio system may also be examined in the light of the industry's overall economic organisation. As part of the reorganisation that took place in the major companies in the early 1930s, the studios began to organise production increasingly on an 'assembly line' basis. The main features of this form of organisation of production are highly developed divisions of labour and hierarchies of authority and control, and detailed breakdown of tasks: the industrial model for this form of organisation is, of course, the mass production of commodities pioneered by Henry Ford's car plants. Since the studio system was geared increasingly to the production of a constant flow of films to supply film theatres, there was an impetus towards organising film production along mass-production lines. This resulted in a high degree of demarcation of skills, and a breakdown of the overall production process into small parts dealt with by different groups of workers. This development is evident also in the increased tendency for workers to be employed directly by the studios and kept on studio payrolls: a characteristic not only of technicians, but also of creative personnel, as the 'contract system' for actors indicates. All this was undoubtedly instrumental in the unionisation of the film industry that took place around the mid-1930s, a trend that probably served to consolidate the effects on the industry of the division of labour and the breakdown of tasks.

The overall trend of these developments in the economic organisation and production relations of the Hollywood film industry was clearly in the direction of standardisation of the product, film. And indeed, during the period of the studio system's ascendancy, at least two forms of product standardisation may be observed. First of all, the 1930s and 1940s are commonly regarded as the golden years of the classic Hollywood film text, that is, marked by a highly specific type of narrative structure combined with a circumscribed range of cinematic expressions of narrative (see Classic Hollywood narrative, p. 45). Second, during this period, film genres – such as the gangster film, the western and the musical – were developed and refined into what is now regarded as their classic form: genre films, which are of course a means of securing standardisation, may be regarded as guarantors of a reliable return on investment .

Contrasting with this convergence towards a 'standard product' in the industry as a whole, however, was a divergence produced by the conscious need for each studio to develop an identifiable 'house style' that would differentiate its films from those of rivals, and a similar tension between standardisation and differentiation within each studio: each film had to be different, to some extent at least, to attract the paying public. These factors combined to produce the classic star-genre cycles periodically adapted to new talent that typify studio production, with in-house technical and creative personnel often forming fixed production units to maintain continuity, keep the cycle 'turning'. And the tensions were expressed in various struggles between creative personnel – directors in particular – and the front office, the business side of the industry, as well as in conflicts and disputes over the content, editing and marketing of individual films. If 'the production of films, essentially fluid and experimental as a process, is harnessed to a form of organisation which can rarely afford to be speculative . . .' (Huettig, in Balio, 1976, p. 238), we find an industry articulated by the evolving tensions and conflicts that dominated both the Hollywood studio system in its maturity as an oligopoly and the products of that system.

Selected Reading

John Belton, *American Cinema/American Culture*, New York, McGraw-Hill, 1994. Revised edition 2004.

Douglas Gomery, *The Hollywood Studio System: A History*, London, BFI Publishing, 2005.

Thomas Schatz, *The Genius of the System: Hollywood Film-Making in the Studio Era*, London, Faber, 1998.

Paramount Pictures

THOMAS SCHATZ

The history of Paramount Pictures coincided with and in many ways defined Hollywood's classical era. Created in 1916, Paramount established the prototype of the vertically integrated motion-picture company, rapidly expanding under Adolph Zukor during the 1920s into an industry colossus. Paramount foundered in the early Depression era but then rebounded in the late 1930s under Barney Balaban, and far outpaced the other majors in the 1940s – only to be cut down at its peak in 1948 by the Supreme Court's epochal Paramount Decree.

Despite its autocratic corporate management under Zukor and then Balaban, Paramount's film-making operations lacked the kind of executive leadership provided by Louis B. Mayer at MGM, Jack Warner at Warner Bros., or Darryl Zanuck at 20th Century Fox. In fact Paramount's uneven and inconsistent production management rendered it more of a 'director's studio' than any of the other majors – or rather a producer-director's studio, given its penchant for film-making 'hyphenates'. The key figure here was Cecil B. DeMille, whose epic spectacles, from the silent version of *The Ten Commandments* in 1923 to its widescreen remake in 1956, were Paramount's signature products.

Paramount also formulated successful cycles for a remarkable range of stars, including a number of European imports as well as recruits from other American entertainment fields such as radio, vaudeville and musical recording. This wide-ranging star stable indicated two important aspects of Paramount's market strategy and house style: first, the international quality and appeal of many of its films, especially in the 1920s and 1930s; and second, its continual efforts to expand and diversify its media-related interests. Paramount was in fact the first studio to establish not only a national but also a global distribution system. It also was heavily involved in a range of 'ancillary' media interests, particularly radio and television.

Thus Paramount was among the more complex and paradoxical of Hollywood's major studios during the classical era. On the one hand, it was the most aggressive of the majors in its efforts to dominate (if not completely control) the industry. Zukor was widely considered the most ruthless chief executive in the motion-picture business, and Balaban's mentality proved to be equally market-driven. But on the other hand, Paramount's top talent enjoyed far more authority over the actual film-making process than their peers at the other major studios. Indeed, film-makers such as DeMille, Josef von Sternberg, Ernst Lubitsch, Preston Sturges and Billy Wilder were the chief architects of Paramount's 'house style'.

Paramount and the studio system

From its formation in a production-distribution merger in 1916 to the final consolidation of its exhibition interests a decade later, Paramount provided a veritable blueprint for vertical integration. In the process, it created a motion-picture behemoth that other companies had no choice but to challenge and to emulate if they were to survive.

The initial merger involved three principal entities. Two were production companies: Adolph Zukor's Famous Players Film Company, a New York-based production firm created in 1912 that successfully developed feature-length films and a star-driven market strategy; and the Jesse L. Lasky Feature Play Co., co-founded by Lasky, Samuel Goldfish (later Goldwyn) and Cecil B. DeMille in 1913, which scored with its first picture, *The Squaw Man* (1914), and quickly emerged as a Hollywood-based producer of top features. The third was Paramount Pictures, a nationwide distribution company created by W. W. Hodkinson in 1914 to handle the release of Famous Players' and Lasky's films.

With the demise of the Patents Trust and the explosive growth of the motion-picture industry in the mid-teens, Zukor engineered the merger of Famous Players and Lasky (as well as a number of smaller producers) in 1916, which then merged with Paramount to create the first fully integrated production-distribution company with a nationwide marketing and sales system. Fierce in-fighting for control saw Zukor force Hodkinson and Goldfish out and then assume the presidency, with Lasky and DeMille overseeing the film-making operations of Famous Players-Lasky – Lasky as vice-president in charge of production, and DeMille as 'director general' while continuing to produce and direct his own films.

With the Famous Players facility in New York and scattered production operations in and around LA, Famous Players-Lasky was scarcely a centralised 'studio'. It was, rather, a far-flung film-making enterprise that turned out a staggering number of features – over 100 a year in the late teens and early 1920s – in Zukor's aggressive effort to corner the motion-picture market. This effort was facilitated by a block-booking policy, which involved the packaging of second-rate product along with top features. Zukor ensured the appeal of those top features by signing leading stars such as Mary Pickford, Douglas Fairbanks, Fatty Arbuckle and William S. Hart to lucrative contracts.

In direct response to Paramount's rapid expansion, a number of first-run exhibitors joined forces in 1917 to create First National Exhibitors Circuit, a nationwide distribution company that promptly moved into production, signing a number of top stars such as Charlie Chaplin and Mary Pickford to unprecedented contracts. These stars saw their salaries soar – Pickford's 1912 Famous Players salary of $500 per week, for example, hit $10,000 after the merger and then reached $350,000 per picture for First National. Despite these escalating salaries, the stars were still dependent on, in turn, Paramount and First National. Thus another crucial response to vertical integration was the 1919 formation of United Artists by Pickford, Chaplin, Fairbanks and D. W. Griffith – a veritable declaration of independence from the burgeoning studio system (see also Stars before sound, p. 119).

Zukor, meanwhile, responded to First National's challenge by moving more aggressively into exhibition in 1919–20. His build-up of Paramount's theatre chain culminated in the 1925 merger with the Chicago-based Balaban and Katz chain, giving Paramount 1,200 theatres. Zukor also expanded international operations, setting up a worldwide distribution system and investing in production and exhibition overseas, particularly in Europe. Paramount owned considerable stock in the Ufa studios in Germany, for instance, and was involved in a range of distribution and co-production deals, and in the recruitment of top German stars, directors and other film-making talent as well.

Prototype for Paramount's spectaculars: DeMille's *The Ten Commandments*

While Paramount was a model of vertical integration by 1925, its production operations remained dispersed and somewhat ill-coordinated. After the Balaban and Katz merger, however, Zukor and Lasky began to develop a more coherent production operation, based primarily in Hollywood. In 1926 Paramount moved into a larger and better-equipped Hollywood studio that became its film-making headquarters, with B. P. Schulberg installed as head of West Coast production (under Lasky). This set-up proved very successful, and after sound conversion in 1928–9, Paramount began to function as a more centralised 'Hollywood studio'.

Paramount rode the 'talkie boom' of 1929–30 to new heights, with its 1930 profits hitting a record high of $18.4 million (versus $10.3 million for Fox, $9.9 million for MGM, $7.1 million for Warner Bros. and $3.4 million for RKO). But the Depression devastated Paramount in late 1931, due largely to the company's massive theatre holdings with their debilitating mortgage payments. Paramount lost $21 million in 1932 (another industry record), and declared bankruptcy a year later. Zukor was stripped of his power but stayed on as board chairman, while Lasky, Schulberg, Selznick and other top executives left or were fired. Theatre czar Sam Katz was named chief executive, thanks largely to his close ties with Chicago and New York financiers who guided the company out of bankruptcy. A succession of studio heads from 1932 to 1936 included Lubitsch, remarkably enough, but there was no real stability in either the home office or the studio until Barney Balaban (Katz's former partner) was appointed president in 1936. Balaban installed another 'theatre man', Y. Frank Freeman, as studio head in 1938, initiating an executive partnership that would continue for two decades.

Authorship and house style

Early on, given its far-flung production operations and rapid expansion, Paramount evinced little stylistic consistency or coherence, although there were harbingers of later trends. DeMille's bedroom farces and 'modern' comedies, particularly those starring Gloria Swanson (*Male and Female*, 1919; *The Affairs of Anatol*, 1921), anticipated the sophisticated comedies of later years. And the films of Italian-born Rudolph Valentino (*The Sheik*, 1921; *Blood and Sand*, 1922) and imported German/Polish star Pola Negri (*The Cheat*, 1923; *Forbidden Paradise*, 1924) anticipated the more exotic 'continental' films of the sound era. In 1923, Paramount also produced two historical epics, *The Covered Wagon* and DeMille's *The Ten Commandments*, which were prototypes of its trademark spectacles of the next three decades.

The mid-1920s consolidation of management and production cost Paramount several top stars and film-makers, who bridled at the prospect of greater constraints over their careers.

Specialising in comedy: Leo McCarey's *Duck Soup*

In 1925–6, Valentino, Swanson and William S. Hart bolted for United Artists, while co-founder DeMille left to set up his own production unit at MGM. Lasky and Schulberg signed a number of new stars, including Clara Bow, Harold Lloyd, Emile Jannings, Gary Cooper, Claudette Colbert, Frederic March and Maurice Chevalier. They recruited several new directors as well – notably Ernst Lubitsch, Josef von Sternberg and Rouben Mamoulian, all of whom had film-making experience in Europe and were signed in 1927.

Ironically enough, in the light of DeMille's departure, these film-makers enjoyed considerable autonomy under the new regime, attaining producer-director status under the 'unit production' system developed by Schulberg and his executive assistant David Selznick. Moreover, Paramount's house style coalesced under this system and this group of film-makers. As Joel Finler has aptly noted, 'It was under the Schulberg–Lasky regime that Paramount first developed the unique style associated with the studio during its peak creative years, . . . [which] must be credited, primarily, to their many outstanding directors' (Finler, 1988, p. 162).

Paramount's production units were geared to specific star-genre cycles – von Sternberg's quasi-expressionistic Dietrich vehicles (*Morocco*, 1930; *Shanghai Express*, 1932; *Blonde Venus*, 1932), for instance, and Lubitsch's stylised musical operettas with Jeanette MacDonald (*The Love Parade*, 1929; *Monte Carlo*, 1930; *One Hour with You*, 1932). The units generally included key individuals besides the director and star; screenwriter Jules Furthman and cameraman Lee Garmes on the Dietrich films, for example. The production design on all of the Sternberg and Lubitsch films from 1927 to 1932 was done by Hans Dreier, who came to Paramount from Ufa in 1923 and would serve as supervising art director for some three decades. Indeed, Dreier, along with film-makers like von Sternberg, Lubitsch and Mamoulian (*Applause*, 1929; *City Streets*, 1931; and *Dr. Jekyll and Mr. Hyde*, 1931), fashioned a distinctly 'European' style in films designed with both the continental and American markets in mind.

This European dimension to Paramount's emergent house style was countered in two significant areas. One was the studio's remarkable comedy output, featuring established vaudeville and radio stars such as W. C. Fields, the Marx Brothers, Bing Crosby, George Burns and Gracie Allen, Jack Oakie and the inimitable Mae West. Several staff directors specialised in film comedy, most notably Leo McCarey (*Duck Soup*, 1933; *Belle of the Nineties*, 1935; *Ruggles of Red Gap*, 1935). A second factor involved the 1932 return of Cecil B. DeMille, who thereafter concentrated on his signature spectacles, alternating between epic Americana and biblical sagas, hitting his stride in the mid-1930s with *The Crusades* (1935) and *The Plainsman* (1936).

By the late 1930s, significantly, DeMille's films began to focus exclusively on American subjects while Paramount's European emphasis steadily waned. This signalled an important shift in studio style, and was related to the impending war in Europe, which wiped out the continental market in the late 1930s, and also a severe cost-cutting campaign under Balaban. Balaban curtailed Paramount's more exotic and costly fare (apart from the DeMille epics), working the domestic market with an output of contemporary drama, light comedy and women's pictures. This meant wholesale changes in the roster of stars and film-makers in the late 1930s and 1940s. Among the new stars to emerge were Ray Milland, Bob Hope, Fred MacMurray, Dorothy Lamour, Paulette Goddard, Alan Ladd, Veronica Lake, William Holden and Barbara Stanwyck. Paramount's leading film-makers of the era included producer-director Mitchell Leisen (*Easy Living*, 1937; *Midnight*, 1939; *Arise, My Love*, 1940, among others), and two staff writers who graduated to hyphenate writer-director status in the 1940s: Preston Sturges (*The Lady Eve*, 1941; *Sullivan's Travels*, 1941; *Hail the Conquering Hero*, 1944; *The Miracle of Morgan's Creek*, 1943, among others), and Billy Wilder (*Double Indemnity*, 1944; *The Lost Weekend*, 1945; *Sunset Blvd.*, 1950, among others).

While Sturges's irreverent black humour and Wilder's noir thrillers displayed the darker side of Paramount's style in the 1940s, the studio lightened things up in other areas, especially in its Bob Hope and Bing Crosby vehicles. The two completely dominated the 1940s box office, teaming with Dorothy Lamour in a cycle of hit 'road pictures' (for example, *Road to Singapore*, 1940; *Road to Zanzibar*, 1941), and enjoying enormous success as solo stars as well – Hope in a cycle of cowardly hero comedies, and Crosby in light musicals. The latter included *Going My Way* (1944), a curious blend of sentimental comedy, piety and song (with Crosby and Barry Fitzgerald as priests in a struggling New York parish), produced and directed by Leo McCarey. The film clearly struck a chord with wartime Americans, sweeping the Oscars (including Best Picture, Best Actor and Best Director) and returning over $6 million in domestic rentals.

The war boom, the Paramount Decree and the television era

Under Balaban, Paramount also increased its efforts to diversify, particularly with regard to the emerging video and television technologies. As mentioned earlier, Paramount had long pursued various broadcast-related interests – dating back to its 1928 investment in the newly formed CBS radio network. The trend continued under Balaban, with many of its biggest stars moving freely between movies and radio in the late 1930s and 1940s. Even DeMille was involved, hosting (and directing) the 'Lux Radio Theater' from 1936 to 1945. Far more significant was Paramount's heavy investment in television in the 1930s and 1940s, notably a partnership with DuMont, a video technology pioneer, and its purchase of television stations in Chicago and Los Angeles. The DuMont relationship involved not only home transmission and television sets but also theatre television; Balaban, in other words, hoped to equip Paramount's theatres with video projection systems.

World War II stalled these television-related efforts, although with the surging 'war economy', Balaban was scarcely concerned. During the war, Paramount returned to the kind of industry domination it had enjoyed two decades earlier, thanks largely to its massive theatre chain and a war-induced market boom. While Paramount's theatres had been a drag on its finances during the Depression, now they were a source of huge profits. At the war boom's peak in 1946, Paramount earned record profits of nearly $40 million, roughly twice those of its major competitors.

The war boom ended all too quickly in 1947–8, however, due to various social and economic factors – suburban migration, the baby boom, the rise of commercial television, and so on. Equally devastating was the Supreme Court's 1948 Paramount Decree, an antitrust ruling that forced Paramount (the first studio named in the suit) and the other majors to divest their all-important theatre chains and to severely curtail the sales policies that had enabled them to control the industry for decades. Moreover, the antitrust ruling enabled the FCC (Federal Communications Commission) to bar the Hollywood studios from active involvement in the television industry – a blow that was especially serious to Paramount.

Paramount handled dis-integration by splitting into separate production-distribution and exhibition firms: Paramount Pictures and United Paramount Theaters (UPT). Both entities continued to pursue television – UPT by investing in the ABC television network, and Paramount Pictures by syndicating its classic films and producing television series. Paramount's movie-related fortunes turned primarily on DeMille's epics. *Samson and Delilah* (1949) earned $9 million in domestic rentals and sparked the biblical blockbuster trend of the 1950s. DeMille followed it with his last two films and the biggest hits in Paramount's history: *The Greatest Show on Earth* (1952), which returned $12.8 million, and *The Ten Commandments* (1956), which earned an astounding $34.2 million.

The studio began to fade badly in the early 1960s, however, due to the continuing erosion of the moviegoing audience and a succession of costly flops. That led to Balaban's retirement and the 1966 sale of Paramount to Gulf & Western – the first of many studio buyouts by huge conglomerates, and a crucial step in the transition from the Old Hollywood to the New. Paramount would survive and indeed would flourish in the New Hollywood of the 1980s and 1990s (see New Hollywood, p. 60). And its resurgence, interestingly enough, has been due not only to its merger with another industry behemoth, Viacom, but also to its continued reliance on film-making hyphenates, epic-scale blockbusters, crossover stars, global marketing and media diversification – all features of studio success in the classical era.

Selected Reading

Leslie Halliwell, *Mountain of Dreams: The Golden Years of Paramount Pictures*, New York, Farrar, Straus and Giroux, 1982.

Thomas Schatz, *The Genius of the System: Hollywood Film-Making in the Studio Era*, London, Faber, 1998.

Metro-Goldwyn-Mayer

THOMAS SCHATZ

A relative latecomer to the ranks of Hollywood's integrated major studios, MGM rose rapidly to industry leadership during the late 1920s and then went on to dominate the industry throughout the 1930s and into the 1940s. With superb resources, top film-making talent and 'all the stars in the heavens', MGM specialised in A-class star vehicles for the first-run movie market. But despite its wealth of film-making talent, production at MGM was controlled by its studio executives and producers. Its films tended to project a sanguine (if not saccharine) world-view – well indicated by its penchant for historical romances, lavish musicals and family fare. Still, MGM's films appealed to critics and the Academy as well as moviegoers, as the studio managed to factory-produce what Hollywood defined as 'quality' for some three decades.

Film historians scarcely endorse that view, however, as MGM accounts for remarkably few canonised film classics or anointed auteurs – with the exception of its stunning cycle of postwar musicals (notably *An American in Paris*, 1951; *Singin' in the Rain*, 1952). But even here, aptly enough, the driving creative force was star-choreographer Gene Kelly, and the ultimate auteur was producer Arthur Freed. Thus MGM, perhaps the most accomplished of classical Hollywood studios, represents a significant challenge to an auteur-based theory of film history or criticism (see Part 6: Authorship and cinema).

The emergence of MGM

Metro-Goldwyn-Mayer was created via merger in 1924 by Loew's Inc., following the lead of other motion-picture powers in its quest for vertical integration. Created by Marcus Loew some two decades earlier, Loew's chief asset was its first-class theatre chain, centred in the New York area, which it augmented in 1920 with the purchase of Metro Pictures, a nationwide film distribution company with a modest production facility in Los Angeles. With this solid basis in exhibition and distribution, Loew's completed its expansion in 1924 with two acquisitions: Goldwyn Pictures, an integrated company whose chief strength was its massive production facility in Culver City; and Louis B. Mayer Productions, a small company geared to first-run pictures whose chief asset was the management team of Mayer and his young production chief, Irving Thalberg (then aged 25).

Metro-Goldwyn was run from New York by Nicholas Schenck, the chief executive of Loew's Inc., while the Culver City studio and all production operations were closely controlled by Mayer and Thalberg, who, along with studio attorney Robert Rubin, were known as the 'Mayer Group'. The importance of the Mayer Group was underscored by the merger agreement giving them 20 per cent of Loew's production-related profits (an exceptional arrangement in Hollywood at the time), and also by the addition of 'Mayer' to the official studio title in 1925.

Metro-Goldwyn-Mayer made an immediate impression via two huge 1925 hits, *Ben-Hur* and *The Big Parade*. But the real keys to its rapid industry rise were, first, its astute studio management team and efficient production operations; second, its well-stocked 'star stable' and savvy manipulation of the star system; and third, the effective co-ordination of production and marketing operations, keyed to a steady output of A-class star vehicles designed for the 'major metropolitan' market (and Loew's theatre holdings). While the merger gave MGM top stars such as Lon Chaney, Lillian Gish and Marion Davies, Mayer and Thalberg quickly cultivated a stable of home-grown stars including John Gilbert, Norma Shearer, Joan Crawford and Greta Garbo. MGM also signed New York stage stars Marie Dressler and John and Lionel Barrymore, enhancing the prestige value of its pictures while also appealing to Loew's predominant New York-based clientele.

Early on, Mayer and Thalberg developed a dual strategy of lavish spectacles and more modest star vehicles, with the latter frequently centred on romantic co-starring teams. After the unknown John Gilbert burst to stardom in the downbeat World War I epic, *The Big Parade*, for instance, MGM quickly developed him as a romantic lead and enjoyed tremendous success teaming him with Swedish import Greta Garbo in *Flesh and the Devil* (1926), *Love* (1927) and *A Woman of Affairs* (1928). MGM's move to sound was punctuated by a huge 1929 musical hit, *The Broadway Melody* ('All Talking! All Singing! All Dancing!') and also by *Anna Christie* ('Garbo Talks!') in 1930. Complementing these upbeat hits were more sombre 'prestige dramas' such as King Vidor's *The Crowd* (1928), Victor Sjöström's *The Wind* (1928, starring Lillian Gish) and *Min and Bill* (1930), the waterfront fable that launched Marie Dressler and Wallace Beery to top stardom.

By decade's end MGM was vying successfully with established industry giants Fox and Paramount, and the newly emerged 'major' Warner Bros. In 1929–30, at the height of the 'talkie boom' and before the Depression hit Hollywood, Metro's combined profits were $25.8 million, versus $33.9 million for Paramount, $19.8 million for Fox and $21.6 million for Warners. Interestingly enough, however, MGM did not parlay this success into expanded theatre holdings, as did its major competitors. (Paramount and Fox built their chains to over 1,000 theatres in the late 1920s, and Warners to 600, while Loew's remained at about 150.) Loew's decision to maintain a limited chain of first- and second-run houses proved fortuitous for two reasons: first, the cost of sound conversion was much lower; second and more importantly, Loew's was not saddled with the enormous mortgage commitments that devastated its chief competitors in the early 1930s.

MGM in the 1930s

MGM's Depression-era success and domination of the movie industry was simply staggering, fuelled not only by the consistent quality of its films but also by the economic travails of its rivals. Three of the Big Five (Paramount, Fox and RKO) suffered financial collapse in the early 1930s, while Warner Bros. had to siphon off one-quarter of its assets to stay afloat. Loew's/MGM, meanwhile, turned a profit every year of the 1930s and saw its assets actually increase. From 1931 to 1940, the combined net profits of Hollywood's Big Eight studios totalled $128.2 million; MGM's profits alone were $93.2 million, nearly three-quarters of the industry total.

Equally impressive was the consistent quality of its films and the industry recognition they routinely garnered. During the 1930s, MGM accounted for over 30 per cent of the Academy nominees for Best Picture (27 out of 87 pictures, including four winners), and over 30 per cent of both the Best Actor and Best Actress nominees as well (with six male and five female Oscar winners). During the first ten years of the *Motion Picture Herald*'s Exhibitors Poll of top ten box-office stars (1932–41), an astounding 47 per cent were under contract to MGM – with MGM's Clark Gable the only Hollywood star to be named in all ten years.

The consummate example of MGM's house style in the early Depression era was *Grand Hotel*, an all-star drama of star-crossed lovers (including Garbo, John Barrymore, Joan Crawford, Lionel Barrymore and Wallace Beery), which won the Oscar for Best Picture in 1932. Produced at a cost of $700,000, over twice the industry average, the film returned $2.3 million in North America alone. It emphasised glamour, grace and beauty in its polished settings and in its civilised characters – all of whom are doomed or desperate, but suffer life's misfortunes with style. Indeed, the film in many ways is about the triumph of style, expressed not only by its characters but by cinematographer William Daniels, editor Blanche Sewell, recording engineer Douglas Shearer, art director Cedric Gibbons and costume designer Adrian. Each was singled out in the opening credits of *Grand Hotel* (along with director Edmund Goulding and playwright William Drake), and they were, in fact, the key artisans of MGM's house style.

The chief architect of that style was Irving Thalberg. In the 1920s and early 1930s, MGM exemplified the 'central producer system' that dominated Hollywood at the time. While Louis Mayer handled studio operations and contract negotiations, Thalberg and his half-dozen 'supervisors' (among them Harry Rapf, Hunt Stromberg and Bernie Hyman) oversaw actual film-making. Thalberg refused to be mentioned in MGM's film credits, but his importance to the studio was well known. 'For the past five years,' wrote *Fortune* in a 1932 article, 'MGM has made the best and most successful motion pictures in the United States.' That success was directly attributed to Thalberg: 'He is what Hollywood means by MGM, . . . he is now called a genius more often than anyone else in Hollywood.' MGM's success was due to 'Mr. Thalberg's heavy but sagacious spending', noted *Fortune*, which ensured 'the glamour of MGM personalities' and the 'general finish and glossiness which characterizes MGM pictures' (Balio, 1985, pp. 312, 318).

Ambitious, innovative and costly: *The Wizard of Oz*

There were other key components to Thalberg's management and market strategy as well. He was vitally concerned about 'story values', as evidenced not only by his active role in story and script conferences, which was legendary, but also his penchant for assigning up to a dozen staff writers to a film. Thalberg was also a major proponent of using preview screenings to decide whether a picture required rewrites, retakes and re-editing. This rarely involved the original writer(s) or director, and thus evinced an ethos of 'teamwork' at MGM. Significantly, Metro's writers and directors rarely complained about the practice, as they were very well paid (by industry standards) and were deftly handled by Thalberg.

Another key factor was Thalberg's penchant for 'romance' in the form of love stories or male-oriented adventure – or preferably both, as in co-starring ventures such as *Red Dust* (1932) and *China Seas* (1935) with Gable and Jean Harlow. A more nebulous but equally important factor was Thalberg's impeccable and oft-noted 'taste', which was evident not only in his inclination for the occasional highbrow prestige picture, but also in his ability to render frankly erotic stories and situations (as in the Gable–Harlow films) palatable to Hollywood's Production Code Administration and to mainstream audiences.

While many of these qualities remained essential to MGM's house style into the 1940s, Thalberg's control of production actually ended in the mid-1930s. His ill health and an internal power struggle at Loew's/MGM (spurred by the growing resentment of Thalberg's authority and increased profit share by both Mayer and Schenck) led to a shake-up in studio management. In 1932–3, Metro began shifting to a 'unit-producer' system, with a few top executive producers – principally Thalberg, David Selznick and Hunt Stromberg – supervising high-end features, while Harry Rapf and several others produced the studio's second-rank films. (Up to 50 per cent of the other majors' pictures during the 1930s were recognisably B-movies; however, Mayer prohibited the use of the term 'B-movie' on the MGM lot, and few if any of its pictures would have qualified.)

Under the new management set-up, both Thalberg and Selznick concentrated on high-cost prestige pictures, mainly costume dramas (see Costume drama, p. 291). Many of these were very successful both commercially and critically – Thalberg's *Mutiny on the Bounty* (1935), *Romeo and Juliet* and *Camille* (both 1936), for instance, and Selznick's *David Copperfield* (1935), *Anna Karénina* and *A Tale of Two Cities* (both 1935). Stromberg, meanwhile, proved especially adept at creating successful star-genre cycles – as in the succession of Jeanette MacDonald–Nelson Eddy operettas (for instance, *Naughty Marietta*, 1935, and *Rose-Marie*, 1936), and in the 'Thin Man' films with William Powell and Myrna Loy. MGM's success continued under this new regime, but the studio was severely shaken in 1936 by two events. One was Selznick's departure to create his own company, Selznick International Pictures, which would join forces with MGM in 1939 for the most successful film in Hollywood's history, *Gone with the Wind*. The other was Thalberg's sudden, untimely death (at age 37), which marked the end of an era for MGM.

The Mayer regime: star-genre cycles and steady decline

After Selznick's departure and Thalberg's death, Mayer took charge of film-making operations, establishing a management-by-committee system that oversaw production for the next decade. While still very much a producer's studio, MGM's management ranks steadily swelled with executives who had little or no film-making experience. A few production executives like Dore Schary and Joe Mankiewicz did come up through the writers' ranks, and its top active producer, Mervyn LeRoy, had been a producer-director at Warner Bros. LeRoy's first project for MGM was *The Wizard of Oz* (1939), an ambitious, innovative and costly film that was scarcely typical of the studio's, or of LeRoy's, subsequent films. MGM took a decidedly conservative turn under Mayer, its films becoming ever more predictable and formulaic.

One indication of this conservative turn was MGM's reliance on upbeat film series with strong 'entertainment values' – best exemplified by the Hardy Family films, which the studio cranked out like clockwork, and which made Mickey Rooney (as Andy Hardy) the top box-office star in America from 1938 to 1940. Spurred by the series' huge success, Mayer developed other child stars as well, notably Margaret O'Brien (*Journey for Margaret*, 1942) and Elizabeth Taylor (*Lassie Come Home*, 1943). Mayer also favoured more wholesome depictions of love, marriage and motherhood, as seen in the rapid wartime rise of Greer Garson and her usual co-star, Walter Pidgeon (*Mrs. Miniver*, 1942; *Madame Curie*, 1943; *Mrs. Parkington*, 1944).

Garson and Pidgeon were among several co-starring teams that embodied Mayer's idealised vision of on-screen coupling – a far cry, indeed, from the hard-drinking, wise-cracking Nick and Nora Charles of *The Thin Man* a decade earlier. As Rooney outgrew his Andy Hardy role, he teamed with Judy Garland in a successful cycle of painfully wholesome post-adolescent show-musicals (including *Babes in Arms*, 1939; *Strike Up the Band*, 1940; *Babes on Broadway*, 1941). A more interesting couple, Katharine Hepburn and Spencer Tracy, emerged in *Woman of the Year* (1942), although not until their fourth outing in *Adam's Rib* (1949) did they recapture the spark of that first teaming.

While these and other MGM films did exceptional business, the studio's glory days clearly were waning in the 1940s. Indeed, due to the general fall-off in terms of product quality, along with the booming movie marketplace during the war, which favoured the studios with larger theatre chains (a reversal of market conditions in the 1930s), the once-invincible MGM was quickly surpassed by its chief competitors. In 1946, at the peak of the 'war boom', MGM's profits totalled $18 million, less than a half of Paramount's ($39 million), and well behind both Fox ($22 million) and Warners ($19.4 million). Its critical cachet was fading as well; Oscar nominations were increasingly rare, and the MGM style was looking downright anachronistic in the postwar era of film noir and social-problem dramas.

One bright spot was Metro's postwar musicals output, which included fully one-quarter of its release schedule and roughly a half of Hollywood's overall musical output during the postwar decade. Several MGM producers specialised in musicals, but the individual most responsible for its 'musical golden age' was Arthur Freed. Freed's breakthrough came in 1944 with *Meet Me in St. Louis*, a Technicolor musical starring Garland and directed by Vincente Minnelli. The success of that film enabled Freed to assemble his own production unit, which emphasised dance as well as music and relied on the talents of choreographers such as Gene Kelly and Stanley Donen. Kelly and Donen co-directed *On the Town* in 1949, confirming the currency and vitality of the Freed unit's 'dance musicals', and paving the way for such classics as *An American in Paris*, *Singin' in the Rain* (Donen–Kelly, 1952), *The Band Wagon* (Minnelli, 1953), *It's Always Fair Weather* (Donen–Kelly, 1955) and *Gigi* (Minnelli, 1957).

While the Freed unit musicals marked a sustained peak in terms of quality film-making, they were symptomatic of Metro's lavish (and thus costly) production operations. This meant narrower profit margins as changing social and economic conditions, along with the emergence of television, eroded Hollywood's audience base. Dore Schary was installed as MGM production chief in 1948 with the express goal of reducing costs, which proved impossible given the studio's entrenched production operations. In fact, MGM held out longer than any of the majors after the 1948 Paramount Decree (demanding theatre divorcement), trying in vain through legal appeals and other means to sustain the studio system in terms of both factory-based production and vertical integration.

By the mid-1950s MGM grudgingly recognised the realities of the changing media marketplace. The studio steadily shifted its film-making operations towards 'telefilm' (that is, television series) production, sold off its vault of old films to television syndicators and, in a particularly telling move, made arrangements with CBS in 1956 for a colour broadcast of *The Wizard of Oz* on prime-time television. As much as any single event in the 1950s, that signalled the end of MGM's – and Hollywood's – classical era, and the beginning of a very different period in film history.

Selected Reading

Joel W. Finler, *The Hollywood Story*, London, Wallflower Press, 2003.

Douglas Gomery, *The Hollywood Studio System: A History*, London, BFI Publishing, 2005.

Warner Bros.

ANNETTE KUHN

Warner Bros. is probably best known as the studio that introduced sound to cinema. Warners, which started in the 1920s as a small family-owned film production company, in 1925 signed an agreement with Western Electric to develop a sound system. The famous talking picture *The Jazz Singer* was released in 1927, and in 1928 the company further consolidated its position by acquiring the First National film theatre circuit, a large studio in Burbank and several prominent stars. In the same year, Warners made a net profit of more than $17 million, a record high for the film industry at that time. The momentum of this success carried the company through the following year, but by 1931 the effects of the Depression began to make themselves felt: between 1931 and 1934, the company's losses were of the order of $13 million. Warners' response to the crisis set it apart from the other major studios, and was an important factor in its economic recovery during the later 1930s.

The rationalisations made at Warner Bros. during the early 1930s involved the adoption of 'assembly line' film production methods, rigid adherence to production schedules and low budgets. During his time as head of production at Warners (between 1931 and 1933), Darryl F. Zanuck assumed much of the immediate responsibility for implementing the new regime. Throughout the 1930s, the studio was able to maintain a regular annual output of about 60 films, and unlike most of the majors managed to survive the Depression without losing managerial and financial control to Wall Street.

Warners and studio style

As Edward Buscombe has pointed out, 'studio style' is a term that occasionally crops up in film criticism, but in a loose way.

While, for example, MGM went in for large-budget costume drama and, later, musicals, and Paramount had a taste for raciness and decadence (Buscombe, 1974, p. 52), the products of Warner Bros. are commonly held as embodying studio style in a particularly marked way, combining certain genres (the gangster movies, the backstage musical and, later, romantic adventure films) with a characteristic visual style (low-key lighting, simple sets), and a kind of populism in key with the studio's rather downmarket image.

But how is the identification of a particular style or set of styles within a studio to be explained? What, in other words, is the relationship between the 'house' and the 'style'? On the one hand, the fact that Warner Bros. films are so often remembered exactly as Warner Bros. films rather than, say, as films by their individual directors may be explained in terms of the tendency inherent in the studio's institutional structure to subordinate individuals to the organisation. But the ways in which production was organised may well, in turn, be considered in relation to the economic restrictions impinging on the studio:

> Sets at Warners were customarily bare and workmanlike . . . The scale of a film could be judged by its budget, and in 1932 the average production cost per feature at Warners was estimated at $200,000, lowest of the majors except for Columbia ($175,000): MGM, by comparison, averaged $450,000 (Campbell, 1971, p. 2).

These economic conditions, it may further be suggested, had certain aesthetic or stylistic consequences. They can certainly explain the relative simplicity of the settings of many Warner Bros. films – of the action melodramas and gangster films in particular and the low-key lighting that did much to conceal the cheapness of the sets, as well as the repetitions from film to film of financially successful formulae. (*The Public Enemy*, 1931, for example, was made in only 16 days at a cost of $151,000.) It has also been argued that something less easily observable than economic restrictions may also have been instrumental in its populism during the 1930s – its use of working-class characters in films, and also the concern with social problems of the day. The notion of studio style, then, may incorporate an ideological as well as an economic component.

Warners and genre

The genre for which Warner Bros. is perhaps most famous is the gangster film (see The gangster film, p. 279). In 1931, Darryl F. Zanuck announced a series of films whose subject matter would be drawn from newspaper stories. This is the inspiration behind both *Little Caesar* (1930) and *The Public Enemy*, and the commercial success of these films determined studio policy throughout the rest of the decade. Gangster films, it was clear, made money.

From the box-office success of the 'exposé' films emerged a style of 'critical social realism'. Campbell (1971) argues that the success of these films is attributable to the fact that Depression disillusion made Warners' predominantly working-class audiences receptive to attacks on the established power structure of American society. But it seems equally likely that audiences were attracted by the action and violence in these films. Indeed, after the institution of the Production Code Administration (see Censorship, p. 17), some of Warners' more violent films were subjected to criticism from within the industry, and pressure was put on the studio to concentrate more on the enforcement of the law and less on the deeds of criminals. Warner Bros.' response was to produce a cycle of films in which the central characters are federal agents rather than gangsters: these included *'G' Men* (1935) and *Racket Busters* (1938).

The social conscience of Warner Bros.

Within its economic and ideological conditions of operation, Warner Bros.' studio policy has often been equated with a particular politics – that of President Roosevelt's Democratic New Deal. Indeed, one Warners advertisement of 1933 made this association quite explicit: 'Watch this industry turn over a New Leaf ... In the New Year ... With our New President ... And this New Deal ... New Leaders ... New Styles ... New Stars ...' (quoted in Campbell, 1971, p. 34).

It has sometimes been suggested that the studio's embrace of a relatively radical political stance is directly related to its financial and managerial independence from outside bodies. While Warners had been forced to borrow from the banks in order to expand into exhibition and invest in sound, by 1933 the three surviving Warner brothers still owned 70 per cent of the preferred stock in their company. Consequently during the 1930s Warner Bros., along with Columbia and Universal, was not subject to direct interference from Wall Street (Buscombe, 1974, p. 53).

Within the framework of the overall capitalist economy and the specific industrial enterprise of cinema, Warner Bros. as a studio was relatively independent of the Rockefeller/Morgan banking empires and was able in the short term to produce whatever films both it and its audiences wanted. Buscombe concludes that this economic independence is not unconnected with the fact that Warner Bros. made a number of pictures that were notably to the left of other Hollywood products (Buscombe, 1974, p. 53). Certainly a considerable number of early 1930s Warner Bros. productions were explicit about their endorsement of Roosevelt and the New Deal; indeed, several of the studio's films in that period even borrowed the National Recovery Administration's Eagle insignia for their credits and employed it in the choreography of its musicals (as in *Footlight Parade*, 1933). Buscombe points out, for instance:

> The famous 'Forgotten Man' sequence of *Gold Diggers of 1933* (1933) derives from Roosevelt's use of the phrase in one of his speeches . . . Pictures like *I Am a Fugitive from a Chain Gang*, *Black Legion*, *Heroes for Sale*, *Black Fury*, *A Modern Hero*, *20,000 Years in Sing Sing*, *They Won't Forget*, and *Confessions of a Nazi Spy* to mention only the best known, all testify to the vaguely and uncertainly radical yearnings which the studio shared with the New Deal (Buscombe, 1974, p. 54).

Warners' social conscience may also be seen at work in the studio's productions of World War II; indeed, Buscombe has argued that Warner Bros. was the first Hollywood studio to throw its whole weight behind government policy on the war. In place of Warners' earlier social criticism (which had to be dropped for the duration to maintain morale) came a crudely patriotic affirmation of the American way of life and an attack on pacifism, isolationism and, of course, Nazism (for example, *Sergeant York*, 1941).

Warners and authorship

In 1944, Warner Bros. released *To Have and Have Not*, a film that may be read as a typical example of a Warners wartime film with its implicit anti-isolation argument. But at the same time, it was directed by one of the studio's contract directors, Howard Hawks, who subsequently came to be regarded as an important auteur in his own right (see Part 6: Authorship and cinema). Interestingly enough, in the light of the tendency for the concept of studio style to dominate discussions of Warner Bros. films, Robin Wood has attempted to sort out the various contributing strands of the film, which he describes as

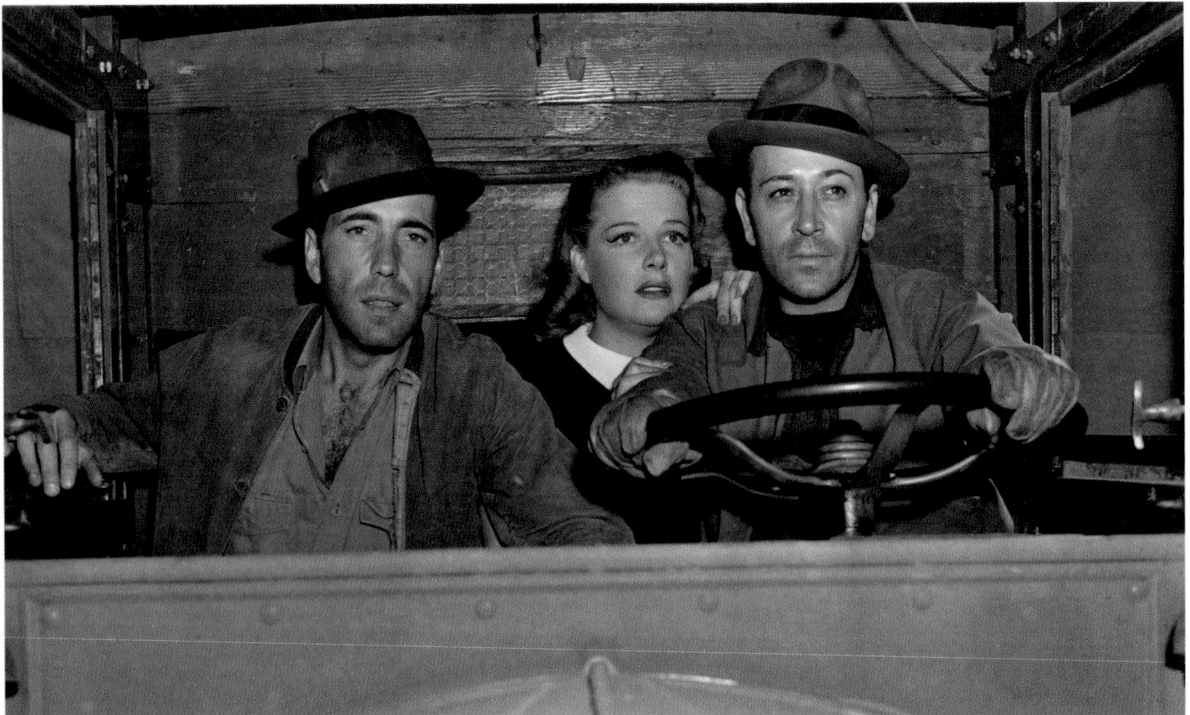

Social comment from Warner Bros.: *They Drive by Night*

> a Hollywood genre movie (species: 'adventures in exotic location') clearly conceived (by the studio at least) as a starring vehicle for Bogart, adapted from a novel by Hemingway, scripted by William Faulkner and Jules Furthman, and specifically indebted to at least two previous movies (*Morocco* and *Casablanca*) and perhaps a third (*Across the Pacific*) . . . (Wood, 1973)

While Wood isolates the studio as itself a 'contributor', he is wary of crediting it with more than a minor role. Thus while acknowledging, for example, that the lighting in *To Have and Have Not* is easily identifiable as Warners' style, Wood adds that the overall style is also 'the perfect visual expression of the essential Hawksian view'. At the same time, however, he argues that the film is marked not only by its studio provenance but also by its kinship with a certain genre: film noir. If this is the case, then *To Have and Have Not* encapsulates some of the tensions between authorship and studio style.

Similar problems arise when the work of another of Warners' contract directors, Raoul Walsh, is looked at in terms of authorship. Given the way in which production was organised at Warner Bros., once Walsh became a contract director he was obliged to work with contract crews and casts within the studio hierarchy, on projects that could capitalise both on recent financially successful formulae and also on the inclination and aptitudes of the rest of the contract staff. Discussing *The Roaring Twenties* (1939) and *They Drive by Night* (1940), Buscombe suggests:

> These films are typical of the studio for which they were made; to such an extent that one must call into question the simple notion of Walsh as an auteur who directed the style and content of his pictures. Firstly, in working for Warner Bros., Walsh was obliged to use the stars which the studio had under contract. So, *The Roaring Twenties* had Bogart and Cagney, *They Drive by Night* Bogart and George Raft . . . One can't say exactly that Walsh was forced to make gangster pictures because he had to use these stars, for they weren't the only ones available on the Warner lot. But stars and genre were, particularly at Warners, mutually reinforcing. Because the studio had Bogart, Cagney and the rest under contract they made a lot of gangster pictures; and because they made a lot of gangster pictures they had stars like this under contract. (Buscombe, 1974, p. 59)

Apart from the determining effects on Walsh's work of stars and genres, however, the character of the films' production units may also be of some importance. Thus the 'social content' of *The Roaring Twenties* and *They Drive by Night* might have something to do with the sociology of the studio's personnel:

> Mark Hellinger, who produced *The Roaring Twenties*, was a Broadway reporter in the 20s and 30s, covering New York crime stories. Jerry Wald, who helped write *The Roaring Twenties* and *They Drive by Night*, came from Brooklyn and worked with Walter Winchell on *The Graphic* in New York. Robert Rossen, who co-wrote *The Roaring Twenties*, came from the East Side in New York, where his early experiences turned him to the left politically. (Buscombe, 1974, p. 60)

Selected Reading

Edward Buscombe, 'Walsh and Warner Bros.', in Hardy (ed.), *Raoul Walsh*, Edinburgh Film Festival, 1974.

Nick Roddick, *A New Deal in Entertainment: Warner Brothers in the 1930s*, London, BFI Publishing, 1983.

The Public Enemy (USA 1931 *p.c* – Warner Bros.; *d* – William A. Wellman)

The title sequence brings together a number of gangster stereotypes, recalling for Warners' audiences the range of images of the city criminals the cinema had accumulated. Warners were not simply exploiting a genre for its sensational (in this case violent) potential but were also committed to situating that crime socially. Thus it could be argued that the prologue to the film, 'To honestly depict . . . rather than glorify', is not only a gesture to the demands for moral self-censorship by the Hays Code, it is also a statement of Warners' 'social conscience' ideology. This is exemplified in the way the film looks to socio-economic factors as the source of crime, and views the gangsters' rise to success as a result of the introduction of Prohibition. The studio's social realist aesthetic is evident in the montage of Prohibition activities, and the one-minute-long shot consisting of tracks, pans overlaid with continuous sound of the city streets, until the camera cuts to two boys coming out of the saloon. The latter also represents a virtuoso display of early sound technology.

ANNETTE KUHN

I Am a Fugitive from a Chain Gang (USA 1932 *p.c* – Warner Bros.; *d* – Mervyn LeRoy)

This is a hard-hitting film about a returned soldier (Paul Muni) who is wrongfully imprisoned for a hold-up. Warners' social realist aesthetic is visible in its observation of Depression America and its effect on the people; in one image, we see a pawnshop full of war medals; and as the hero is sentenced, the shout goes up: 'They're the ones who should be in jail', which could be seen as a clarion call for Warners' New Deal sympathies. The documentary influence is apparent in the montage (reminiscent of *March of Time* newsreels) of maps and trains, and, later, of the prisoners' picks and calendar pages. In the jail the horn sounds the same as that of the factory at the beginning of the film; an 'expressive' use of sound was characteristic of Warners' early sound films. However, it could also be argued that the focus is individualistic, in that the root causes of social injustice are shown to be the result of accidental circumstances rather than political or economic factors.

ANNETTE KUHN

Racket Busters (USA 1938 *p.c* – Warner Bros.; *d* – Lloyd Bacon)

Warner Bros.' response, partly, to pressure from the Hays Code was the revamping of the gangster genre in the mid-1930s. The central character was no longer the social outcast, the gangster, but the G-Man, the federal agent. The G-Men films retained many of the features of the earlier gangster-centred vehicles, but the iconography of the genre changed from an emphasis on the tools of the gangsters' trade to the procedure of police detection.

In *Racket Busters*, as in *'G' Men* (1935), the focus is on the police rather than the racketeers, and the credits claim that the film is 'based upon official records'. Also as in *'G' Men* and *Each Dawn I Die* (1939), authenticity is created by the use of newspaper headlines, a documentary touch reinforced by the occasional documentary-style sequence. A characteristic Warners scene is the confrontation between the mobsters and the private enterprise truck drivers. It could be argued that the early populist sentiments of Warners were being gradually transformed into a moral crusade against crime, and that consequently the commitment of the studio to situate crimes in a social context moved from centre-stage.

ANNETTE KUHN

The Roaring Twenties (USA 1939 *p.c* – Warner Bros.; *d* – Raoul Walsh)

The Roaring Twenties, like other Warners gangster films, makes an implicit connection between social deprivation and crime, with James Cagney's taxi-driver hero Eddie returning from the war to find his job gone and attempting to set up his own business as a taxi operator. This is, argues Buscombe, an example of the small-scale entrepreneurial capitalism that remains the ideal of most Warners films of the period (Buscombe, 1974, p. 56). The film combines a documentary, sociological approach to the depiction of the gangsters and their lifestyle with familiar genre iconography: for example, the

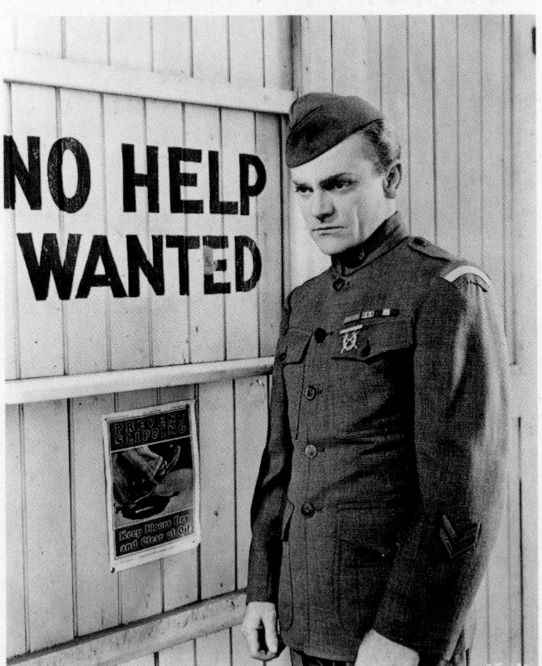

Out of a job: *The Roaring Twenties*

tommy-gun as an invention of World War I; the set-piece montage of gang warfare; the conflict between Eddie, the gangster-by-default for whom gangsterdom is the only available means of business, and the psychotic George (Humphrey Bogart) over the function of violence in their operations; the heroine (Priscilla Lane), whose classy femininity is the object of the gangster hero's sexual desire and social aspirations and who, as a consequence, is unobtainable, unlike the faithful gangster's moll (Gladys George); the role of the lawyer, who for social reasons or personal weakness gets involved with the mob but ultimately crosses the gang leader by virtue of his superior knowledge of how the system works; and the gangster's lifelong faithful friend who goes down with him in his fall.

ANNETTE KUHN

They Drive by Night (USA 1940 *p.c* – Warner Bros.; *d* – Raoul Walsh)

This represents an example of Warner Bros.' crime/thriller melodramas with elements of social comment. Warners' relative financial independence from East Coast financiers perhaps made it easier for the studio to make films that, within the capitalist film industry and by the standards of other Hollywood products, were fairly radical in terms of subject matter. The film's socio-political concerns are embodied in the Fabrini brothers, who are shown to be victims of capitalist exploitation from various directions. The independent truckers operating within this economic context co-operate to protect each other from the exploiters. Ultimately, the dominant ideology is re-established and any radicalism recuperated, in that Joe Fabrini's problems are solved on an individual basis by his takeover of the trucking business. The film noir style is evident throughout, particularly in the femme fatale stereotype, played here by Ida Lupino (see also Film noir, p. 305).

ANNETTE KUHN

Columbia Pictures

ANNETTE KUHN

Columbia's populism

Columbia, one of the 'Little Three' majors, began in 1920 as a Poverty Row company, CBC, named after the initials of its three founders, Harry Cohn, Joe Brandt and Jack Cohn. In 1924, the company was renamed Columbia Pictures, and by the end of the decade had acquired a production studio of its own and was already operating a national distribution network. In 1932, Joe Brandt was bought out by the Cohn brothers and his place on the voting trust taken by Attilio Giannini, an unorthodox banker who was also a supporter of President Roosevelt's New Deal, anathema to the Wall Street establishment. Harry Cohn replaced Brandt as president of the company – becoming the only movie mogul to be simultaneously president, production head and principal shareholder of a studio. In his role as production head, Cohn instituted the hitherto unknown practice of shooting film scenes out of sequence to ensure maximum economy, and in general, the company operated under rigid cost controls.

Throughout the 1930s, Columbia, like United Artists and Universal, supplied the cinemas owned by the 'Big Five' (MGM, Fox, Warner Bros., RKO and Paramount) with low-budget supporting features for double bills, with running times of only 70 minutes or so, few – if any – stars, and little or no prestigious production values. Around 70 per cent of Columbia's annual output of 50 to 60 pictures were in fact in this B-category. Columbia's continued solvency during the early 1930s, when so many other studios went bankrupt, is partly to be explained by the fact that the company was not itself encumbered by empty film theatres, while at the same time it enjoyed access to cinemas owned by the larger majors.

Columbia, like Warner Bros., is often regarded as an exponent of New Deal-type populism, evidenced in particular in the films of the studio's sole auteur, Frank Capra. Columbia's populism is perhaps explicable partly in terms of the company's history – its Poverty Row origins and its backing by the maverick banker Giannini – and by the fact that exactly half of the Hollywood Ten were actually employed at Columbia during the 1930s (Buscombe, 1975, p. 78; the Hollywood Ten was a group of radical directors and screenwriters who were imprisoned in the early 1950s for alleged communist subversion of the industry). Although it is clearly impossible to determine whether or not there was any deliberate policy of favouritism at Columbia towards the New Deal or left causes, it is perhaps significant that screenwriter Garson Kanin and actress Judy Holliday, both of whom worked at Columbia in the 1940s, were listed as 'subversives' in 'Red Channels', a compilation of 'radical names' by supporters in the film industry of the House Un-American Activities Committee. Indeed, *Born Yesterday* (1951), based on a play by Kanin and starring Holliday, was extensively picketed on its release by the association of Catholic War Veterans (Cogley, in Balio, 1976). Although it seems unlikely that there was a concerted communist effort at the studio, its economic structure and encouragement of 'freelancers' might well have facilitated the employment of radicals where the more careful vetting of employees by studios with large numbers of long-term contracts might not.

Capra and populism

Although the bulk of Columbia's productions during the 1930s were low-budget B-features, the studio occasionally invested in more expensive films. One such was the comedy *It Happened One Night* (1934), directed by Frank Capra. This film was enormously successful, won Columbia its first Oscars and led the company to supplement its B-feature productions with more prestigious films. After *It Happened One Night*, Capra signed a six-film contract with Columbia at $100,000 per film plus 25 per cent of profits, and was given increasingly larger production budgets. In 1936, Capra directed *Mr. Deeds Goes to Town*, which examined the unacceptable face of capitalism (in the form of anti-New Dealers) and portrayed its hero as a charitable tycoon, lending out his wealth to dispossessed farmers to give them a fresh start.

The success of Capra's films has been such that the director and the company are often equated, which has tended in fact to reduce studies of the studio to studies of Capra as an auteur. It may be argued, however, that Capra's films and the populism that characterises them might be related not simply to his personal 'vision' or to the director being 'in touch' with America, but also to the economic and ideological structures of Columbia itself.

Columbia's auteur Frank Capra at work with the cast of *You Can't Take It With You*

Stars at Columbia

> Though Columbia had contract players of its own (for example Jack Holt, Ralph Bellamy or, in westerns, Buck Jones and Charles Starrett), they could not compare in box-office appeal with the stars of bigger studios. Columbia could not afford the budgets which bigger stars would have entailed. On the other hand it could never break into the big-time without them. Harry Cohn's solution to this vicious circle was to invite successful directors from other studios to make occasional pictures for Columbia, pictures which would have stars borrowed from other studios. Careful planning permitted short production schedules and kept costs down to what Columbia could afford . . . Thus a number of big-name directors came to work at Columbia during the later 1930s, often tempted by the offer of being allowed to produce their own films. (Buscombe, 1975, p. 80)

One of Columbia's 'more expensive productions', with 'bigger stars' and a 'big-name producer-director' was Howard Hawks's *His Girl Friday* (1939) starring Cary Grant and Rosalind Russell, with Ralph Bellamy in a supporting role. Grant, like Gable in *It Happened One Night* and Cooper in *Mr. Deeds Goes to Town*, was a star from outside the studio. It was in fact a not uncommon practice in the industry to rent the stars of one studio to another. The lending studio generally received about 75 per cent more than the star's salary to compensate for its temporary loss. The borrowing studio enjoyed the advantage of the star's services without incurring the cost of a long-term contract. Perhaps something of the appeal of those Columbia films that combined its own contract players with outside stars was exactly the pleasure of seeing familiar faces in unfamiliar settings: Cary Grant, for instance, without the costume and decor with which he was associated at Paramount. Columbia's practice of bringing in outside stars (and also directors and writers) for large-budget productions would, of course, tend to militate against any deliberate or unitary political stance (for instance, on the New Deal) within the studio or its productions.

While most of Columbia's contract performers were character actors such as Ralph Bellamy, the studio occasionally succeeded in signing up a little-known actor or actress before he or she became too expensive, 'grooming' him or her for stardom itself. By the end of the 1930s, the policy of bringing in outside stars and directors and paying them percentages was proving an important part of Columbia's economic strategy, and certain stars (such as Cary Grant) returned to Columbia again and again. However, one thing the studio lacked in comparison with the other majors was a star it could claim to have created and developed for itself. By 1937, Columbia had only one female star under contract, Jean Arthur: but Arthur's resistance to publicity and her allegedly 'unglamorous' image encouraged Columbia to invest in another. Rita Hayworth, a little-known Fox employee, provided Columbia with its opportunity, and she was signed for a seven-year contract. She was at first restricted to Columbia's B-features, cast in a succession of cheap musi-

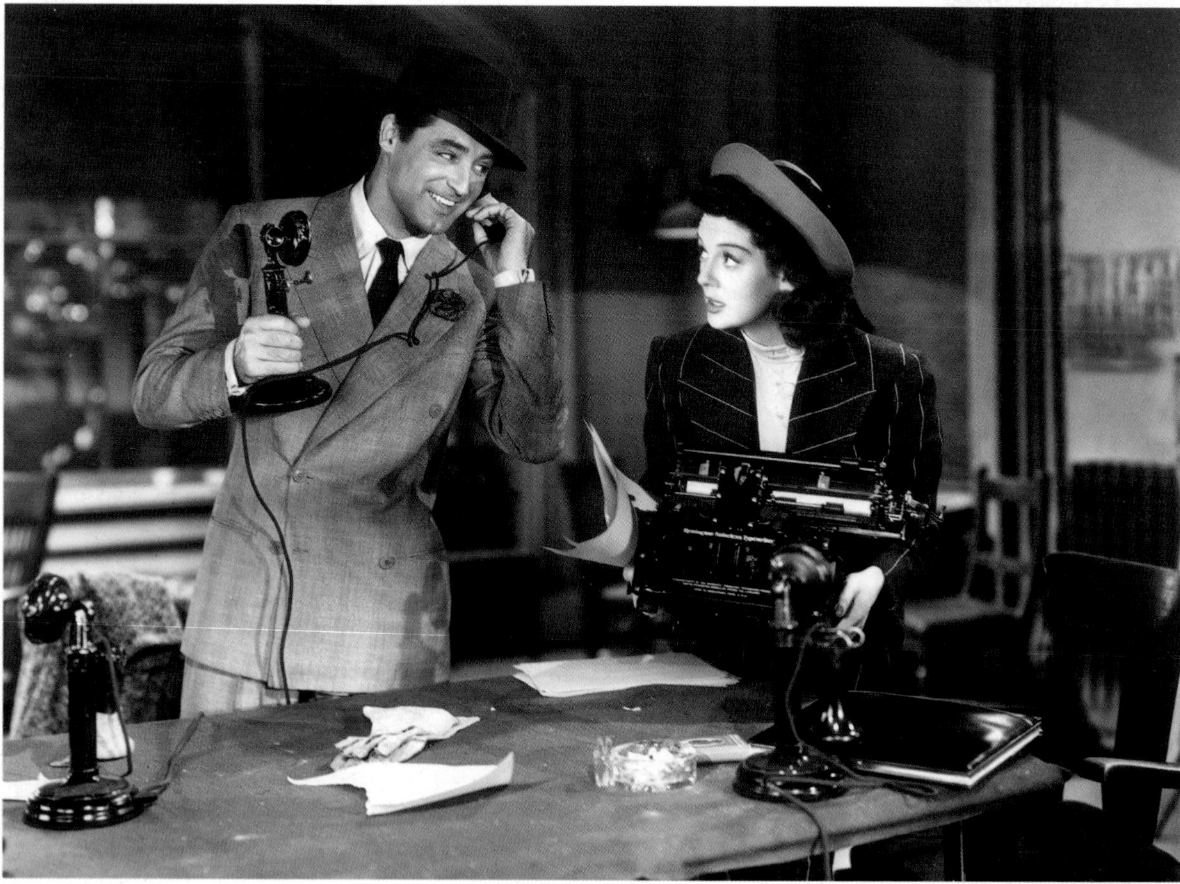

Borrowed stars: Cary Grant, 'rented' by Columbia, and Rosalind Russell in *His Girl Friday*

cals and melodramas, but after 1941 played a number of singing and dancing roles opposite Fred Astaire, Gene Kelly and other borrowed stars. By the mid-1940s, Hayworth was established, in Cohn's words, as 'the fourth most valuable property in the business' (quoted in Kobal, 1977, p. 198).

With the release of *Gilda* in 1946, Rita Hayworth became a household name: the film was a massive success at the box office, making $3 million for Columbia on its initial release. It may be argued that the combination of the Hayworth femme fatale and musical personas, and the mix of genres – the bleakness of film noir with the decor and choreography of the musical – permitted widespread publicity for the film – from pin-ups in magazines to recordings of Hayworth's (albeit dubbed-over) songs on the radio.

Columbia and the decline of the studio system

The industry-wide recession that followed the antitrust legislation in 1946 was due not only to the dismantling of the vertically integrated structures of the 'Big Five', however, but also to the rise of television, the effects of the anti-communist scare within the film industry and probably changing social trends in general. Columbia, not having been fully vertically integrated during the period of oligopoly, was in a relatively good position to survive the recession, since after divorcement they found the theatres more open to their product than before. But survival also depended on the studio's ability to differentiate its product from its rivals – who were no longer only the other studios, but television as well.

One of several strategies Columbia embarked upon in the face of fierce competition from television in the early 1950s was the adaptation of established successes, either from the best-sellers lists or from Broadway hits. *Born Yesterday* is an example of the latter policy, and Columbia paid a million dollars for the rights to Garson Kanin's play, as well as contracting Judy Holliday, its original star, to repeat her role as Billie Dawn. By this time, while the majors were being forced to reduce their assets, selling off theatres and making contract players, technicians and other employees redundant, Columbia had assembled a stable (albeit modest) of contract actors that could be economically drawn upon (as William Holden and Broderick Crawford were for *Born Yesterday*, relatively inexpensively to offset other expenditures such as, in this case, on the screenplay). *Born Yesterday* turned out to be the top box-office draw of the year for Columbia and earned the studio an estimated $4 million as well as winning Judy Holliday an Academy Award.

Columbia and television

While expensive adaptations of Broadway successes and best-sellers are obvious examples of the studio's attempts to sell its products, Columbia was also the first of the eight majors to enter television production. Unable to afford excursions into widescreen, or Cinerama, Columbia chose around 1950 to invest some of its still very limited resources in the formation of a television subsidiary, Screen Gems (the first of the majors to follow Columbia's lead, Warners Bros., did not act until 1955). Thus Columbia, more than any of its competitors, was able to produce films that both related to, and also to some extent differed from, contemporary trends in television drama. For instance, when *The Big Heat* (1953) was released, a police series, *Dragnet*,

'The fourth most valuable property in the business': Rita Hayworth in *Gilda*

was at the top of the American television ratings: Columbia was quick to exploit the trend. The violence and eccentricity of the characters in *The Big Heat*, however, illustrate how Columbia combined its exploitation of trends in television with a differentiated content. This proved a particularly important strategy for Columbia in the wake of the relaxation of censorship in the film industry after 1951.

By the mid-1950s, with television becoming increasingly popular and cinema attendance dropping, the need to differentiate cinema product from the filmed television episodes that Hollywood was itself beginning to produce had become increasingly urgent. Two 1955 Columbia releases reveal how the studio attempted to weather the crisis. Both films were made in Technicolor and CinemaScope – technologies obviously unavailable to small-screen, black-and-white television transmitters – and boasted the kind of production values that television could not hope to afford. In 1955, the first western television series made by one of the Hollywood majors – Warner Bros.' *Cheyenne* – appeared on the American networks. Screen Gems was not slow to follow suit, while Columbia's film division produced *The Man from Laramie*, one of their relatively rare A-feature westerns. The film's use not only of colour, widescreen and location cinematography, but also its violence, differentiated it successfully from its small-screen competitors.

Selected Reading

Edward Buscombe, 'Notes on Columbia Pictures Corporation, 1926–41', *Screen* 16 (3), autumn 1975. Reprinted in Staiger (ed.), *The Studio System*, New Brunswick, NJ, Rutgers University Press, 1995.

John Cogley, 'The mass hearings', in Balio (ed.), *The American Film Industry*, Madison, University of Wisconsin Press, 1976. Revised edition 1985.

Mr. Deeds Goes to Town (USA 1936 *p.c* – Columbia Pictures; *d* – Frank Capra)

Gary Cooper stars as Mr Deeds, a simple man from the backwoods who goes to New York after inheriting a fortune. The end of the film illustrates the way in which the narrative is resolved in favour of populism, validating Deeds as a hero whose qualities of innate goodness and common sense mark him out from 'the enemy': the patronising intellectuals who are isolated from the common people. Buscombe (1975) has suggested that this populism was characteristic of Columbia's output at the time. However, the ending seems to parody itself, raising the question of whether the apparent project of the film to validate populist ideology can be taken seriously.

ANNETTE KUHN

The Big Heat (USA 1953 *p.c* – Columbia Pictures; *d* – Fritz Lang)

This film deals with the violence and sadism of a gang of racketeers, and their effect on a detective, Dave Bannion (Glenn Ford), who pursues the gang in a relentless quest to avenge his wife's death. The police series was a popular form on television in the early 1950s, and this was probably an attempt to capitalise on that success while providing something more sensational than TV could offer; hence the excessive brutality, especially in the notorious scene in which the gangster Vince (Lee Marvin) viciously attacks Debby (Gloria Grahame). It has been argued (Flinn, 1974) that *The Big Heat* owes more to studio style than to either film noir genre conventions or the authorship of Fritz Lang.

ANNETTE KUHN

The Man from Laramie (USA 1955 *p.c* – Columbia Pictures; *d* – Anthony Mann)

This revenge western stars James Stewart as Will Lockhart, who sets out to avenge his brother's murder. During the 1950s, cinema capitalised on its potential for spectacle as it began to lose its audiences to the new medium of television. Westerns such as this offered the possibility of panoramic views in widescreen and colour, location shooting rather than studio sets and sensationally violent content, none of which TV could match.

ANNETTE KUHN

The Lineup (USA 1958 *p.c* – Panmar Productions/ Columbia Pictures; *d* – Don Siegel)

A Columbia film with origins more specifically in the small screen, *The Lineup* was a spin-off from a television series. Don Siegel, who had directed the pilot episode of the television version, was hired to direct the film, which was made in black and white with a cast of relative unknowns. In this case the difference between the source material (the TV series) and the spin-off was that the former had focused on the police while the latter concentrated on the gangsters: television at the time would certainly have prohibited such a focus. Siegel's film exploits this relative licence accorded the cinema by including scenes of considerable violence.

ANNETTE KUHN

Anatomy of a Murder (USA 1959 *p.c* – Carlyle Productions/Columbia Pictures; *d* – Otto Preminger)

Anatomy of a Murder also exploited restrictions placed on the content of television programmes, dealing in this instance with the subject of rape with a degree of frankness. James Stewart played Paul Biegler, a small-town lawyer defending a soldier (Ben Gazzara) charged with the murder of a man who has raped and beaten his wife (Lee Remick). Preminger had already made a number of films independently (released through United Artists) and successfully outmanoeuvred the declining censorship powers of the Production Code Administration, even releasing some of them without the PCA seal of approval (see Censorship, p. 17). The director's record in this respect may well have attracted Columbia to this film, since it was the only studio never to register with the PCA. Preminger, moreover, had a reputation for bringing films in under budget.

ANNETTE KUHN

20th Century Fox

ANNETTE KUHN

The Fox Film Corporation

The Fox Film Corporation, which was founded in 1914, took its first steps towards 'major' status in 1925 when William Fox, the owner of the company, embarked on an ambitious programme of expansion, investing in a sound process and acquiring chains of film theatres. In 1927 Fox controlled, very briefly, the production studios of Fox and MGM, Loew's and Fox's theatre chains, one-third of First National and other assorted holdings. This ambitious industrial programme was paralleled by attempts to enhance the prestige of Fox productions and the company made a number of 'specials', often adapted from Broadway hits and bestsellers. Two such blockbusters, *7th Heaven* (1927) and *What Price Glory* (1926), both of them big-budget adaptations of plays, had been successful at the box office, and Fox needed further major successes of this kind in order to offset excessive outlays incurred from production budgets and acquisitions of real estate.

This is the context within which F. W. Murnau's *Sunrise A Song of Two Humans* (1927) was produced. Indeed it has been argued that *Sunrise* should be seen as

> an integral part of one of the most carefully orchestrated and ambitious bids for power and prestige in the history of the American cinema, and in large measure *Sunrise*'s historical significance is to be found in its relation to other Fox films that were equally part of William Fox's truly grandiose scheme to control the movie industry. (Allen, 1977, p. 237)

The film cost more than $1.5 million to make and included one of the largest sets ever constructed in the history of the cinema, a section of a city, complete with elevated trains and streetcars, constructed over an area a mile long and half a mile wide on the Fox studio lot (Lipkin, 1977).

By the end of the 1920s, however, William Fox had dangerously overstretched the company with big-budget productions of this kind, as well as by his ambitions for expanding. In 1930, he was ousted from the board and in the following year the Fox Film Corporation made a loss of more than $5 million. In 1933, a combination of reduced receipts and increasing overheads forced Fox to place its theatres into receivership: in 1934, the company with two studios and a comprehensive national distribution network valued at $36 million had an annual earning power of only $1.8 million. Meanwhile Darryl F. Zanuck, former production head at Warner Bros., had set up a small independent unit without studio space of its own, 20th Century Pictures. In 1935, the Fox Film Corporation announced a merger with 20th Century: henceforth, with Zanuck as head of production, the company would be known as 20th Century Fox.

Black characters geared towards Southern taste: *The Littlest Rebel*

20th Century Fox and its stars

When Zanuck took over production at 20th Century Fox, the studio possessed two highly valuable assets, Will Rogers and the seven-year-old Shirley Temple. Charles Eckert has suggested that Temple was an asset to the Fox studios in that they held a monopoly on her star image, and were able to use that monopoly to control the distributors' choice of films. According to Eckert, the enormous commercial success of Shirley Temple's films – including, for example, *The Littlest Rebel* (1935) – has to do, in part, with their expression of a New Deal 'ideology of charity' (Eckert, 1974).

Even more successful than Temple, however, in 20th Century Fox's first year at least, was Will Rogers. Darryl F. Zanuck himself regarded the Rogers vehicle *Thanks a Million* (1935) as the film that made 20th Century Fox. By 1936, moreover, Zanuck was already expanding 20th Century Fox's small stable of stars with performers such as Tyrone Power and Sonja Henie. But Zanuck's modest stable of talent could not compete with the likes of MGM or Warners and so he made the screenplays his stars. The studio's success during this period, then, is perhaps not attributable solely to its players.

Politics and the studio

20th Century Fox's increasing commercial success during the latter half of the 1930s is commonly attributed on one hand to the appeal of certain stars contracted to the studio and on the other to the fact that its films expressed a characteristic and attractive political philosophy, which Charles Eckert characterises as 'opportunist':

> When one takes into account Fox's financial difficulties in 1934, its resurgence with Shirley Temple and its merger with Twentieth Century under the guidance of Rockefeller banking interests, one feels that the least that should be anticipated is a lackeying to the same interests that dominated Hoover and Roosevelt. (Eckert, 1974, p. 18)

In other words, the 'line' taken up in 20th Century Fox's productions of the later 1930s was basically pro-Republican. It has been suggested, for example, that the 1939 Fox production *Young Mr. Lincoln* constituted a Republican offensive against the New Deal (see *Cahiers du cinéma*'s 'John Ford', p. 462).

Fox's political 'opportunism' may not, however, be quite as straightforward as this argument suggests. How, for example, is *The Grapes of Wrath* (1940) to be explained? The production of *The Grapes of Wrath* was made possible when in May 1939 Zanuck acquired the rights to John Steinbeck's novel for an unprecedented $70,000 – the third largest amount ever paid for such rights in film history up to that time. In the 1938–9 financial year, 20th Century Fox was the third most successful studio in Hollywood (after MGM and Warners) and two of their releases from this period reached the top ten box-office grossers list. This success prompted a decision by Fox executives to produce more A-pictures – including *The Grapes of Wrath* (see John Ford, p. 464).

Prestige and critical acclaim: Henry Fonda in John Ford's *The Grapes of Wrath*

Rebecca Pulliam argues that the film represents, in fact, not a Republican but a Roosevelt/Democratic/New Deal perspective and explains this with reference to Zanuck's experiences in the early 1930s at Warner Bros. As at Warners, Zanuck's primary interest and influence was on the screenplay:

> The screenplay for *The Grapes of Wrath* was contractually bound to preserve the theme of Steinbeck's book. Zanuck stated his impression of the book's theme as '. . . a stirring indictment of conditions which I think are a disgrace and ought to be remedied'. Left-wing groups feared that he had bought the book to shelve it and see that it was never filmed. The large California growers were strongly against its production and threatened Zanuck with legal suits. The studio believed that the film might never be released in California. (Pulliam, 1971, p. 3)

Zanuck hired a private investigating firm to authenticate the novel's assertions and, having satisfied himself, refused to be thwarted by the Hays Office: 'If they . . . interfere with this picture I'm going to take full-page ads in the papers and print our correspondence'. *The Grapes of Wrath* took seven weeks and cost $800,000. At its preview the first three rows of seats were reserved for executives of the Chase National Bank, the financial backer of 20th Century Fox – and also, ironically, one of the institutions that controlled the land companies responsible for forcing the dispossessed farmers portrayed in *The Grapes of Wrath* from their land. Although the film did well commercially, it was not a massive box-office success. But it was perhaps more important to 20th Century Fox that the company won from it the prestige and acclaim that had eluded it during the 1930s: *The Grapes of Wrath* won two Oscars. The film may therefore be regarded as marking the company's move from the economic security associated with earlier pro-Republican vehicles to the aesthetic prestige associated with its productions of the 1940s.

20th Century Fox and the decline of the studio system

In the immediate postwar years 20th Century Fox embarked on a series of 'serious', 'realistic' crime films employing semi-documentary devices and often including newsreel footage of the kind Fox had made famous with their *March of Time* newsreels (see also Warner Bros., p. 26). *The House on 92nd Street* (1945), for instance, includes just such a sequence: the film was produced by Louis De Rochemont who had, in fact, launched and supervised the *March of Time* series. In 1948, 20th Century Fox followed the De Rochemont documentary-style thrillers with *Cry of the City*, which combined the latter's grittiness with the characteristics of the contemporary film noir. More important, perhaps, than either style or subject matter in these bleak urban thrillers was Fox's decisive move to location shooting, which prepared the studio for the westerns, musicals and spectaculars that were to follow the antitrust decision, and the advent of competition from the small screen and 'live' studio drama.

In the wake of the 1948 antitrust decision, declining audiences and increasing competition from television, Fox's first response was to reduce production budgets. In 1947, the average cost of a full-length Fox feature was about $2,400,000; by 1952 films were regularly being produced at less than half that amount, since location shooting actually proved cheaper than studio shooting. Both *Broken Arrow* (1950) and *The Gunfighter* (1950) illustrate such economies. They serve at the same time to illustrate the ways in which the end of vertical integration in the film industry affected not only the studios but also stars and genres, in that both films concern the activities of ageing western stereotypes – the 'veteran scout' and the 'retired gunfighter' (see The western, p. 374).

In 1952, Fox finally signed the Consent Decree agreeing to divorce its exhibition chain from its production/distribution apparatus in accordance with antitrust laws. The company could no longer guarantee the screening of its films simply by controlling first-run theatres. Moreover, by the early 1950s the celebrated 'social realism' of Fox's crime genre was hard to distinguish from innumerable television crime series such as *Dragnet* (1951–9). The company's response was to employ bigger, brighter stars – such as Marlon Brando (*Viva Zapata!*, 1952), Marilyn Monroe (*River of No Return*, 1954; *The Seven Year Itch*, 1955), Jane Russell (*The Revolt of Mamie Stover*, 1956), Monroe and Russell together (*Gentlemen Prefer Blondes*, 1953) – and specifically cinematic technologies such as colour and CinemaScope (*Carmen Jones*, 1954), Technicolor and CinemaScope (*River of No Return*). *The Seven Year Itch*, in fact, employs an explicit send-up of television in the 'dumb blonde' character of Marilyn Monroe, who makes her living by modelling for an advertising company in toothpaste commercials.

Selected Reading

Robert C. Allen, 'William Fox presents *Sunrise*', *Quarterly Review of Film Studies* 2 (3): 327–38, August 1977. Reprinted in Staiger (ed.), *The Studio System*, New Brunswick, NJ, Rutgers University Press, 1995.

Rebecca Pulliam, '*The Grapes of Wrath*', *The Velvet Light Trap* 2: 3–7, August 1971.

Tony Thomas and Aubrey Solomon, *The Films of 20th Century Fox: A Pictorial History*, Secaucus, NJ, Citadel Press, 1989.

Sunrise A Song of Two Humans (USA 1927 *p.c* – Fox Film Corporation; *d* – F. W. Murnau)

Fox recruited highly regarded German director F. W. Murnau for this prestige production, which is noted for its ambitious special effects and for bringing a European sensibility to a Hollywood film. For the scene between the Man (George O'Brien) and the Wife (Janet Gaynor) on the boat trip to the city, Fox went to the trouble of shooting on location as well as constructing a real village at the edge of a lake. The famous trolley-ride sequence demonstrates the virtuosity of the rear-projection and the use of deep-focus and long takes to ensure continuity and authenticity. The demands of realism make an interesting contrast with the use of 'Expressionist' techniques characteristic of Murnau's style. Several of the other creative personnel were European: screenwriter Carl Mayer, cinematographer Charles Rosher, and art director Rochus Gliese among them.

ANNETTE KUHN

The Littlest Rebel (USA 1935 *p.c* – 20th Century Fox; *d* – David Butler)

It has been argued that the Southern box office was of paramount importance to Hollywood in the 1930s, and that the depiction of black characters had to be geared towards Southern 'taste' to ensure a film's success. Films such as *The Littlest Rebel* romanticise the South of the Civil War. They play up paternalistic notions of chivalry and gracious living, into which blacks are accommodated as loyal family retainers or Uncle Tom figures, or by offering comic relief. Antebellum myths and values can be seen in the portrayal of the white family as a kind of aristocracy, and the incorporation of black plantation life in terms of white entertainment. Shirley Temple's star persona (one of the studio's hottest properties at the time) meshes with this appeal to an audience of white liberals, and, indeed, detracts from the presentation of the racial issues of the Civil War by supporting nostalgic myths of the South.

ANNETTE KUHN

Cry of the City (USA 1948 *p.c* – 20th Century Fox; *d* – Robert Siodmak)

Cry of the City concerns Martin Rome (Richard Conte), a gangster on the run who is pursued by a determined policeman (Victor Mature). It combines documentary style with the characteristics of film noir – a technique that was adopted by the studio in the 1940s when it began to produce bleak, urban thrillers and to move to cheaper location shooting.

ANNETTE KUHN

Broken Arrow (USA 1950 *p.c* – 20th Century Fox; *d* – Delmer Daves)

James Stewart played Tom Jeffords, a US army scout who attempts to bring about peace between the Apaches and the military. As well as the stylistic and aesthetic changes brought about by Fox's move to economise during the 1950s, *Broken Arrow* indicates a shift in the conventions of the western genre towards a sympathetic understanding of the Native American Indian as operating within the codes of his own culture. This can be seen in the character of Cochise (Jeff Chandler) who befriends Jeffords (see also The western, p. 374).

ANNETTE KUHN

RKO Radio Pictures

ANNETTE KUHN

RKO, a creation of the Rockefeller-backed Radio Corporation of America (RCA), was formed at the beginning of the era of sound in cinema. RCA had patented its own sound-on-film system – Photophone – in conjunction with its radio subsidiary NBC. In response to Warner Bros.' experiments with sound, RCA acquired its own theatre circuit, Keith-Albee-Orpheum, and a film production company, FBO. Together these groups formed the new company RKO Radio Pictures. Predictably, the studio's earliest productions were dominated by dialogue-heavy comedies and musicals.

Although the company enjoyed modest financial success in its first few years of operation, the directors were not completely satisfied, and so in order to increase production capacity and distribution outlets, Pathé, with its 60-acre studio, was purchased, and in 1931 David O. Selznick immediately instituted 'unit production', a system whereby independent producers were contracted to make a specific number of films for RKO entirely free from studio supervision, with costs shared by the studio and the producer, and distribution guaranteed by RKO. Despite a series of administrative reorganisations and policy changes within the company in subsequent years, RKO's most famous pictures – including *King Kong* (1933) and *Citizen Kane* (1941) – were nearly all produced in this way.

Selznick was also partially responsible for the construction of the Radio City Music Hall, the world's largest motion-picture house. It was felt that exhibition at Radio City would secure solid New York openings for RKO films. But this strategy proved extremely expensive, and by the end of 1932 Selznick had gone and RKO had made a net loss in that year of more than $10 million. Selznick's replacement was Merian C. Cooper, who had been acting as Selznick's adviser on evaluating future projects. One of the first films they had agreed upon had been *King Kong*. After much opposition from the studio's New York office, the film was made (at a cost of more than $650,000) and finally opened at Radio City and the Roxy. In four days it had grossed $89,931. It was the perfect film for RKO's Radio City Music Hall – for which it made a great deal of money and publicity. In 1930 RKO had announced its own inauguration as 'The Radio Titan' with full-page advertisements in the trade press, and *King Kong*, too, was launched with a massive wave of publicity.

The year of *King Kong*'s release also saw the first teaming of Fred Astaire and Ginger Rogers in the film *Flying Down to Rio* (1933). Almost immediately Astaire and Rogers became RKO's biggest stars of the decade. It is significant that as musical stars they were eminently exploitable on radio. In *The Gay Divorcee* (1934) and *Top Hat* (1935) the two stars epitomise the sophisticated musical comedy tradition that RKO had made its own, combining indolent playboy and/or heiress plots with spectacular big white sets in art-deco styles especially appropriate for the ornate decor of Radio City Music Hall and RKO's first-run theatres (see also The musical, p. 333).

After 1937, when George Schaefer became production head

Radio City Music Hall: the world's largest motion-picture house

Massive box-office hit: *King Kong*

at RKO, some of Selznick's ideas – including unit production – were revived. Schaefer claimed that he intended to concentrate the studio's energy on the production of a few big features in the hope that they would prove to be big moneymakers as well. Thus prestige productions, often produced and directed by independents, were encouraged (for example, *Bringing Up Baby*, 1938, directed by Howard Hawks) and RKO continued its musical comedy traditions with films such as *Dance, Girl, Dance* (1940), also by an outside director, Dorothy Arzner (see Part 6: Authorship and cinema).

But the most famous production at RKO under Schaefer's supervision was undoubtedly *Citizen Kane*. There can, perhaps, be no better test case of the importance of industrial determinants than *Citizen Kane*. Pauline Kael has devoted a book to the film, most of which is concerned with deciding between Orson Welles, the director, and Herman J. Mankiewicz, its screenwriter, as the film's auteurs (see Part 6: Authorship and cinema). Kael's starting point, however, is her insistence that *Citizen Kane* was not an ordinary assignment, and she goes on to argue:

> It is one of the few films ever made inside a major studio in the United States in freedom – not merely in freedom from interference but in freedom from the routine methods of experienced directors. George J. Schaefer, who, with the help of Nelson Rockefeller, had become president of RKO late in 1938, when it was struggling to avert bankruptcy, needed a miracle to save the company, and after the national uproar over Orson Welles's *The War of the Worlds* broadcast, Rockefeller apparently thought that Welles – the wonder boy – might come up with one, and urged Schaefer to get him. (Kael, 1971, pp. 1–2)

Shooting on the film officially began in July 1940 and was completed in October: a 12-week shooting schedule and a budget of $700,000 were at this period extraordinarily low for RKO prestige productions. Before *Citizen Kane* opened, Schaefer was summoned to New York by Nicholas Schenck, the president of the board of Loew's Inc., the MGM parent company that controlled the distribution of MGM pictures, and offered $842,000 if he would destroy the negative and all the prints. The reason for the offer was the well-founded suspicion that Welles and Mankiewicz had modelled the characters of Kane and Susan Alexander on the publisher William Randolph Hearst and the actress Marion Davies. Kael quotes from the trade press of the time: 'The industry could ill afford to be made the object of counter-attack by the Hearst newspapers' (Kael, 1971, pp. 3–4). When Schaefer refused Mayer's offer, the Hearst press launched a tirade of front-page denunciations of RKO and its employees, while banning all publicity of RKO pictures. RKO's usual theatrical showcase – the Radio City Music Hall – retracted its offer to screen *Citizen Kane*, and other first-run cinemas proved equally reluctant. Eventually, Warner Bros. opened the film – Schaefer was by this time threatening to sue the majors on a charge of conspiracy – but it was too late and the film was rapidly withdrawn from circulation to be reissued only in the late 1950s on the art-house circuit.

Although Kael's analysis is of the authorial contributions

of Welles and Mankiewicz, she does emphasise how different the whole feeling of *Kane* would be if it had been made at MGM instead of at RKO, and discusses the collaborative work that went into the film:

> Most big-studio movies were made in such a restrictive way that the crews were hostile and bored and the atmosphere was oppressive. The worst aspect of the factory system was that almost everyone worked beneath his capacity. Working on *Kane*, in an atmosphere of freedom, the designers and technicians came forth with ideas they'd been bottling up for years; they were all in on the creative process . . . *Citizen Kane* is not a great work that suddenly burst out of a young prodigy's head. It is a superb example of collaboration. (Kael, 1971, p. 62)

By 1942, with heavy losses, prestige again began to be seen as a less urgent priority than profits, and Charles Koerner was appointed under the slogan 'showmanship instead of genius'. Double features and low budgets became the new rule. After Koerner's death in 1946, Dore Schary was appointed his successor. Schary in his turn attempted to revive certain practices of the Selznick period, and once more RKO went upmarket, co-producing a number of films with independent production companies such as Goldwyn (*The Best Years of Our Lives*, 1946), Liberty Films (*It's a Wonderful Life*, 1947), International Pictures (*The Stranger*, 1946) and John Ford's Argosy Pictures (*Fort Apache*, 1948; *She Wore a Yellow Ribbon*, 1949; and *Wagon Master*, 1950).

In 1948, Howard Hughes acquired a controlling interest in RKO for just under $9 million, and within a matter of weeks Schary, together with 150 other RKO employees, had been sacked. In 1949, RKO signed a Consent Decree agreeing to divorce its exhibition arm from its production-distribution apparatus, in accordance with the Supreme Court's antitrust decision. In 1955, the company was sold to General Teleradio, a television production company; the RKO Hollywood studios had been acquired by Desilu in 1953.

RKO and studio style

Unlike MGM with its lavish family melodramas and musicals, Warner Bros. with its gangster films, or Universal with its horror films, RKO is rarely associated with any specific style or genre: indeed, it is often suggested that RKO is an example of a studio without a style:

> One problem was that no movie mogul had ever attached himself to RKO's banner – as did Louis B. Mayer at MGM, Harry Cohn at Columbia, and Darryl F. Zanuck at 20th Century–Fox . . . RKO's ownership was for the most part anonymous – just like the movies it put out. Today a large audience remember the famous RKO productions, but few associate them with RKO. Its roster of stars are still household names – Katharine Hepburn, Ingrid Bergman, Fred Astaire, Robert Mitchum and Cary Grant – but in time there would be other studios with which they would become more closely identified. Even the famous films, *Citizen Kane*, the Fred Astaire musicals, *The Informer*, Val Lewton horror shows, *King Kong* and *Gunga Din* – give RKO no recognisable image: the range of styles was so large, so miscellaneous, and RKO's interest in sustaining any single style or genre (with the exception of the Astaire musicals) so short-lived, that the movies blur rather than blend together. (Merritt, 1973, pp. 7–8)

One of the reasons for RKO's lack of any identifiable 'brand image' may be not so much the fact that the company lacked its own 'moguls' as the very number of such men who attached themselves to the studio, reversing its production policies and stylistic commitments so often that no overall house style ever had the opportunity to become established.

RKO and genre: the film noir cycle

Although the number and diversity of the executive regimes at RKO obviously inhibited the development of an easily recognisable studio style, the studio nevertheless did sustain one genre over a period of several years during the middle and late 1940s: the 'low-key' film noir (see Film noir, p. 305). Ron Haver associates the development of this genre at RKO with the work there of writers Daniel Mainwaring, John Paxton and Charles Schnee, and directors Nicholas Ray, Jacques Tourneur and Edward Dmytryk (Haver, 1977).

At the same time, by 1944 Charles Koerner's emphasis on low-budget, atmospheric thrillers had almost entirely replaced George Schaefer's prestige pictures and musical comedies. RKO made $5 million net in 1944, and the film noir became a formula product for the studio until the end of the decade. These films featured players such as Robert Mitchum and Robert Ryan, Jane Greer and Audrey Totter – all of them popular but none of them quite ranking with the stars of RKO's rival studios. In 1947, however, RKO's brief period of postwar profitability was punctured by losses of $1,800,000, but the studio's commitment to low-budget, low-key film-making continued.

As long as the popularity of the genre continued, losses could be attributed, at least in part, not to overspending but to declining audiences. The year 1946 was, after all, the peak box-office year in the history of the American film industry; at the end of the war it had to face competition from television and alternative leisure activities.

RKO's B-pictures

As well as the 'prestige' films produced under its various regimes, RKO also usually had a production programme of B-pictures – low-budget movies designed as second features on double bills. If the B-production units were economically restricted, they did have a degree of aesthetic and ideological independence from the front office that prestige pictures were often denied. A case in point are the films made under the aegis of Val Lewton, *Cat People* (1943) in particular. By 1942 it had become obvious that the Schaefer 'prestige' policy was not paying dividends at the box office. In 1940 the studio had lost almost half a million dollars and by 1942 had sunk to $2 million in debt. The Atlas Corporation's Floyd B. Odlum bought shares from RCA and Rockefeller until he had acquired a controlling interest in RKO. Schaefer was fired and the more businesslike Ned Depinet replaced him as head of RKO. In 1942, Depinet's vice-president in charge of production, Charles Koerner, set up a number of B-units at the studio, and Val Lewton was assigned to head one of them. Lewton's contract stipulated that he was to produce only horror films, that budgets were not to exceed $150,000, that shooting schedules were not to exceed three weeks and that running times were to average about 70 minutes. Within these limits, however, Lewton had relative freedom: he was able to select and contract a stable core of creative personnel, functioning as an independent production unit in much the same way as the units producing prestige pictures in the Selznick era. Editors (and later directors) Mark Robson and Robert Wise, scriptwriter DeWitt Bodeen, secretary Jessie Ponitz, cinematographer Nicholas Musuraca, art directors Albert D'Agostino and Walter Keller, and director Jacques Tourneur all worked together for several years in this way.

Budgetary restraint coupled with generic convention encouraged Lewton's unit to economise on labour and lighting costs by employing low-key effects. Furthermore, studio-wide set budgets, imposed by the War Production Board, limited expenditure on sets to $10,000 per picture, which meant that where possible existing sets were re-dressed rather than new sets built. The unit's first production, *Cat People*, was completed in three weeks at a cost of $134,000, and on its initial release grossed more than $3 million, saving RKO from a second bankruptcy in a year of several big box-office disasters, which included *The Magnificent Ambersons*.

Selected Reading

Richard B. Jewell with Vernon Harbin, *RKO Story*, New York, Random House, 1985.

Betty Lasky, *RKO: The Biggest Little Major of Them All*, New York, Roundtable Publishing, 1989.

James L. Neibaur, *The RKO Features*, Jefferson, NC, McFarland & Co, 2004.

King Kong (USA 1933 *p.c* – RKO Radio Pictures; *d* – Ernest B. Schoedsack/Merian C. Cooper)

This classic monster movie, at the time considered remarkable for its trick photography, was remade by Peter Jackson using state-of-the-art digital effects in 2005. The climactic moment when King Kong wreaks havoc in New York, capturing Ann Darrow (Fay Wray) and climbing the Empire State Building, provides a good example of the ambitious special effects on which RKO was banking to make the film a success. The film updated the Beauty and the Beast story, setting it against the greed of the American capitalists who exploit the mighty ape.

ANNETTE KUHN

Dance, Girl, Dance (USA 1940 *p.c* – RKO Radio Pictures; *d* – Dorothy Arzner)

RKO's investment in the women's picture: *Dance, Girl, Dance*

Arzner's accomplished film is an example of RKO's investment in the women's picture, featuring strong female protagonists, directed mainly at a female audience, and offering a critical perspective on male values from a female point of view. Generally a despised or underrated genre, at least critically, the women's pictures of the 1930s and 1940s were nevertheless box-office successes, featuring popular stars (here Lucille Ball and Maureen O'Hara), and were obviously thought of as 'bankable' by the studios.

ANNETTE KUHN

The Magnificent Ambersons (USA 1942 *p.c* – RKO Radio Pictures; *d* – Orson Welles)

Russell Merritt has usefully described the industrial atmosphere of this film's production and is cautious about privileging Welles's role as genius-victim as so many film histories have done. Instead, he situates it at a moment midway between the ousted 'prestige policy' and unit production system of Schaefer, and the economics and 'showmanship' of Koerner (Merritt, 1973, p. 18).

The Magnificent Ambersons was 'slashed from two hours to eighty-eight minutes so that it would fit on a double bill' (Haver, 1977, p. 30) and Koerner replaced the absent Welles and the ousted Mercury Theatre units with 'second unit crews . . . and then released it on a split bill with a Lupe Velez Mexican Spitfire comedy' (Merritt, 1973, p. 20). However, *The Magnificent Ambersons* was never, even under Schaefer, autonomous of economic and industrial determinants. It was based on Booth Tarkington's Pulitzer prize-winning novel, starred Tim Holt, a familiar RKO western performer, and was a melodrama about the decline of the aristocracy, reminiscent of the previous year's production of *The Little Foxes*.

ANNETTE KUHN

Cat People (USA 1943 *p.c* – RKO Radio Pictures; *d* – Jacques Tourneur)

'The wreck of *The Magnificent Ambersons* may have been taken as one monument to the Koerner regime; but from its ashes rose another: the famous cycle of Val Lewton's *Cat People*, sometimes actually filmed on the abandoned *Ambersons* sets' (Merritt, 1973, p. 18). The *Ambersons* staircase was to become a central icon in *Cat People* – re-dressed sets were much cheaper than purpose-built ones. And the fact of having to re-dress and disguise such sets encouraged an attention to detail often absent from more expensive productions. The 'bus' sequence is a useful illustration of an extremely (cost) effective and expressionist approach to concealing economies. The use of low-key lighting, low-angle camerawork, heightened sound effects and so on – animation, shadows in the swimming pool scene, silence in the walking scene – indicate the aesthetic potential in such economic imperatives. And the minute detail with which the Lewton unit was able to invest the films bears witness to the continuity and relative cohesiveness of the low-budget unit production system.

ANNETTE KUHN

Universal

ANNETTE KUHN

Universal was a relatively minor studio, one of the 'Little Three' companies (the others being Columbia and United Artists) that initially lacked their own theatres and depended for exhibition outlets on the cinema circuits of the 'Big Five' (Warner Bros., RKO, Fox, Paramount and MGM), the vertically integrated majors. The company established itself in the 1920s under the ownership of Carl Laemmle and adapted its studio to sound production relatively early: by 1930, all of its releases were 'talkies'. However, by this time the recession that affected the entire film industry had forced Universal to re-examine its approach to film production. Laemmle decided to make fewer pictures, but 'of the highest excellence that the resources of Universal City could achieve' (quoted in Pendo, 1975, p. 155).

In 1930, Carl Laemmle Jr, who had been put in charge of the studio by his father, began a series of horror films, which became Universal's speciality in the early 1930s, with the production of *Dracula* and *Frankenstein*, both 1931. In the first few years of the decade, however, the effects of the Depression made themselves felt particularly keenly at Universal, the studio's output decreased substantially, and during an industry-wide strike the studio actually closed down for several months. In 1931, film budgets were cut, production schedules shortened and static 'dialogue' shooting emphasised at the expense of 'Expressionist' visual styles. In 1933, despite Laemmle Sr's ambitions, the company entered a two-year period of receivership. The studio was re-established, after some administrative reorganisation, at the end of the decade.

However, by the mid-1940s, Universal was once again in economic difficulties. The studio's financial welfare rested somewhat precariously on Deanna Durbin and on Abbott and Costello; their pictures, while still profitable, were not doing as well as in the past (Eyles, 1978). Universal's response to this situation was to attempt to attract major stars to the studio by giving them a percentage of the profits from their films, and simultaneously to increase budgets, thereby attracting a number of independent producers. The company also merged its distribution activities with the independent production company International. This reorganisation was finalised in November 1946, when it was announced that all B-film units would be shut down immediately, whether in production or not. From then on, all Universal films were to be prestige pictures and absolutely no cheap films would be produced. What would happen, however, to B-films – rather than units – already in production? While Universal was in no position, economically, simply to abandon B-films in production, low-budget films were redundant because, with the banning of block booking, they would henceforth have to be sold individually. *The Killers* (1946) and *Brute Force* (1947), therefore, are examples of B-projects given 'prestige' treatment on very slim budgets in order to attract buyers.

Expressionist visual style in Universal's horror output: *Dracula*

Universal, studio style and genre

Universal's output of the early 1930s is identifiable primarily with a single genre, horror (see The horror film, p. 347), though they did make Lewis Milestone's anti-war epic *All Quiet on the Western Front* (1930). A consideration of Universal films of the period thus calls for an examination of the intersection of genre and studio style within a set of industrial determinants. A variety of explanations have been put forward for Universal's specialisation in the horror genre. Stephen Pendo, for example, argues:

> Depression audiences wanted the escapist entertainment which horror provided . . . Universal's contribution was to assemble the best and most imaginative technicians – cameramen, directors, make-up artists, set designers and special effects men available. Many of them had graduated with horror from the classic German silent film school. (Pendo, 1975, p. 161)

Thus, it is implied, Universal's output would be predisposed, because of the contributions of some of the studio's personnel, to the Expressionism characteristic of the visual style of horror movies. In Universal's case, too, the existence of certain types of stars in the studio's stable – Boris Karloff and Bela Lugosi in particular – would serve to reinforce the existing tendency to concentrate on this genre. Lugosi, for example, had played horror roles on the stage and had also appeared in silent horror films for Universal. Moreover, once horror films were identified as Universal's genre, stars of this type would tend to be employed at the studio. Furthermore, as a minor studio that had to establish a certain kind of 'product identification' in order to sell its films to the exhibition circuits controlled by the majors, Universal particularly needed to develop a generic area of its own.

The dominance of horror films in Universal's output of the early 1930s has also been explained in terms of the transition from silent to sound cinema – that the visual style of such films enabled the move to sound to take place as economically as possible. As far as individual films are concerned, *Dracula* illustrates this argument quite well. Production on the film was begun in 1930 as part of Universal's intended move into pictures 'of the highest excellence'. The desire to make such pictures involved attempting to recapture the visual qualities of silent cinema, which were considered in some quarters to be under threat from sound cinema with its temporary immobilisation of the movie camera. In *Dracula* there is consequently a great deal of mobile framing and minimal use of sound. The film's relative 'silence' served to increase the chilling atmosphere. There is an emphasis too on 'night' and 'outdoor' sequences with tracking shots concentrating on actors and props rather than on sets.

In *Frankenstein* the camera is considerably less mobile than in *Dracula*, and there is far more dialogue. However, *Frankenstein* compensated for lack of camera movement with use of low-angle shots and Expressionist sets. At the same time, this film was intended to be the first of a series, and is consequently less of a prestigious production than *Dracula*:

> With an eye towards sequels, the finish was reshot so that Baron Frankenstein escaped a fiery death – a fortunate change . . . *Frankenstein* was an outstanding success. This convinced Universal even more that horror pictures should henceforth be an integral part of its production schedule. (Pendo, 1975, p. 157)

Universal in the 1950s and 1960s

After the 1948 antitrust decision (see The classic studio system, p. 19) that put an end to the industry's monopolistic practices of block booking and blind selling, Universal could no longer be guaranteed exhibition of its films, and so returned to its earlier practice of providing an easily identifiable studio style and subject matter. After the late 1940s Universal's output was dominated by several genres: thrillers such as *Brute Force*, *The Killers* and *Touch of Evil* (1958); melodramas such as *Letter from an Unknown Woman* (1948), *All That Heaven Allows* (1956) and *Written on the Wind* (1957); and westerns such as *Winchester '73* (1950), *Bend of the River* (1951) and *The Far Country* (1955). The combination of such specialisation with reduced receipts and competition from television had a dramatic effect on the quantity of Universal's annual output. In 1950, for instance, Universal only released two major productions, *Winchester '73* and *Harvey*, both of which featured James Stewart: the studio was able to present stars such as Stewart because it offered them a percentage of the profits from its films. Such stars were central to Universal's success at this time.

One of the independent directors who worked at Universal during this period was Orson Welles, whose *Touch of Evil* was released in 1958. The film was shot in 1957 after Welles had been away from Hollywood for nearly ten years. According to Joseph McBride:

> Charlton Heston agreed to appear in a Universal police melodrama, thinking that Welles had been signed to direct it, when actually he had only been signed as an actor. The studio, undaunted by Welles's pariah status in Hollywood, then asked him to direct . . . he accepted with alacrity, and received no salary as writer or director. He never read the source novel, Whit Masterson's *Badge of Evil*, but found the studio's scenario 'ridiculous' and demanded the right to write his own . . . Nonplussed by the result, the studio called it *Touch of Evil* . . . and slipped it into release without a trade showing. (McBride, 1972, p. 131)

There are, however, conflicting accounts of how Welles came to direct *Touch of Evil*:

> *Newsweek* reported that Welles had been offered the film as a sop for a character role he had played previously at Universal. Charlton Heston has said he suggested Welles as director after reading the film's uncompromising script . . . but producer Albert Zugsmith . . . tells still another story. According to Zugsmith, Welles had come to Universal in the late 50s in need of money to pay tax debts . . . and Welles offered to direct the 'worst' script the producer had to offer – the Paul Monash adaptation of Whit Masterson's novel, *Badge of Evil*. (Naremore, 1978, p. 177)

Possibly the most interesting factor about the film in relation to its studio provenance, however, is the degree to which it has been seen to depart from the Universal norm of the period. Perhaps because Welles's films tend to offer themselves up immediately to an auteurist analysis, the marks of the studio are either ignored, or seem particularly difficult to determine in relation to *Touch of Evil*. It may, however, be significant that in 1958 Universal recorded $2 million worth of losses, and that since the mid-1950s, space in the Universal studio lot had been regularly rented out to television production companies.

Big stars attracted by a percentage of the profits: Orson Welles in *Touch of Evil*

Furthermore, while *Touch of Evil* was being made, 'trade papers were filled with rumours of sweeping changes within the Universal hierarchy, including reports that the film division would fold altogether in order to save their second arm, Decca records' (Naremore, 1978, p. 176).

Perhaps it was industrial indecision that permitted the 'ridiculous' (Welles's word) project of *Touch of Evil*. But the presence in the film of Marlene Dietrich, Dennis Weaver, Zsa Zsa Gabor, Joseph Cotten, Akim Tamiroff, Mercedes McCambridge, Janet Leigh, Charlton Heston and Welles himself may also suggest that *Touch of Evil* is a final example of Universal's ability to attract big stars by offering them a percentage of the profits from its films. Henceforth, almost all Universal features were to be made with an eye towards future television scheduling. By 1959, when Universal sold its studio lot to MCA, its westerns and melodramas were being undercut by competition from television. The studio's new owners divided film production into expensive blockbusters (such as *Spartacus*, 1960) on the one hand and small (often made-for-television) movies such as *The Killers* (1964) on the other. During the 1960s and 1970s, Universal's film productions became fewer as output was dominated by television production.

Selected Reading

Tino Balio, *The American Film Industry*, Madison, University of Wisconsin Press, 1976. Revised edition 1985.

Connie Bruck, *When Hollywood Had a King*, New York, Random House, 2004.

Dennis McDougal, *The Last Mogul: Lou Wasserman, MCA and the Hidden History of Hollywood*, New York, Da Capo Press, 2001.

Robert Sklar, *Movie-Made America: A Cultural History of American Movies*, New York, Vintage, 1994.

Classic Hollywood narrative

ANNETTE KUHN

In spite of the fact that the history of cinema may be approached in a variety of ways, most accounts have been dominated by a concern with cinematographic technology or by an emphasis on individual auteurs. This focus on matters strictly external to the films themselves tends to deflect attention from specific questions concerning the nature and implications of variations and developments in the 'language' of cinema. However, there are historical difficulties in the way of a proper study of film language. In particular, many early films have been lost, while those remaining in existence are rarely easily accessible for viewing. Nevertheless, work in this field is increasingly being undertaken. One of the most interesting aspects of this research is its concern to trace the process through which, by the 1930s and 1940s, a highly specific mode of cinematic representation had become dominant. In the 1930s, the cultural ascendancy of narrative cinema was complete, and a particular set of cinematic codes through which film narratives were constructed and articulated was already quite firmly in place. Noël Burch (1981) has called this set of codes the Institutional Mode of Representation (IMR). The IMR could be said to consist basically of conventions of mise en scène, framing and in particular of editing, by means of which coherent narrative space and time are set up and fictional characters individuated in ways that both engage, and are imperceptible to, the spectator.

Crucial in this process is the organisation of shots in a film according to the rules of continuity editing. Perhaps the foremost effect of continuity editing is to efface the moment of transition between shots, with the result that spectators are caught up in the film to such an extent that disbelief is suspended, and they are swept along with the story, unaware of the artifice of the means of representation. It is commonly accepted that this 'zero point of cinematic style' enjoyed its apotheosis in the Hollywood cinema of the 1930s and 1940s, the era of the 'classic' narrative system (see Bordwell and Thompson, 2004).

But all-powerful though the IMR may seem even today, its dominance is in no way historically necessary. Like all representations, the IMR exists within a particular social and historical context, and in other circumstances modes of cinematic representation might well have developed differently. The dominance of the IMR may therefore be regarded as contingent – the outcome of struggles within the cinematic institution between different modes of representation. That there is indeed nothing inevitable or final about this dominance may be demonstrated simply by pointing to the existence of many other forms of cinema. For example, narrative films made in the early years of the medium, before the IMR was fully established, look very different from narrative films of the 'classic' era. Moreover, throughout the entire history of cinema alternative approaches to cinematic representation have coexisted alongside the so-called Institutional Mode. Avant-garde and experimental cinema, 'art' cinema, various counter-cinemas and the nexus of modes of filmic address and reception in early cinema dubbed by Tom Gunning the 'cinema of attractions' all relativise the dominance of the IMR (Elsaesser and Barker, 1986; Gunning, 1990; see also Early and pre-sound cinema, p. 3).

The classic narrative system

By the early to middle 1930s, the modes of representation now held to be characteristic of 'classic' narrative cinema were more or less consolidated and had already attained a large degree of dominance, certainly in Hollywood, but also in varying degrees in film industries elsewhere. By this time, of course, sound cinema was also established. The era of classic cinema may be regarded as a period in which the cinematic image remained largely subservient to the requirements of a specific type of narrative structure. This structure is that of the classic, sometimes also called the 'realist', narrative which calls forth certain modes of narration that are then put into effect by a limited set of cinematic codes.

The classic narrative structure

In the classic narrative, events in the story are organised around a basic structure of enigma and resolution. At the beginning of the story, an event may take place that disrupts a pre-existing equilibrium in the fictional world. It is then the task of the narrative to resolve that disruption and set up a new equilibrium (see Barthes, 1993). The classic narrative may thus be regarded as a process whereby problems are solved so that order may be restored to the world of the fiction. But the process of the narrative – everything that takes place between the initial disruption and the final resolution – is also subject to a certain ordering. Events in the story are typically organised in a relationship of cause and effect, so that there is a logic whereby each event of the narrative is linked with the next. The classic narrative proceeds step by step in a more or less linear fashion, towards an apparently inevitable resolution. The 'realist' aspects of the classic narrative are overlaid on this basic enigma-resolution structure, and typically operate on two levels: first, through the verisimilitude of the fictional world set up by the narrative and second, through the inscription of human agency within the process of the narrative.

The world of the classic narrative is governed by verisimilitude, then, rather than by documentary-style realism. The narration ensures that a fictional world, understandable and believable to the recipient of the story, is set up. Verisimilitude may be a feature of the representation of either, or preferably both, the spatial location of events in the narrative and the temporal order in which they occur. Temporal and spatial coherence are in fact preconditions of the cause–effect logic of events in the classic narrative (see Burch, 1981). In classic narrative, moreover, events are propelled forward through the agency of fictional individuals or characters. Although this is true also of other types of narrative, the specificity of the classic narrative lies in the nature of the human agency it inscribes, and also in the function of such agency within the narrative as a whole. The central agents of classic narrative are typically represented as fully rounded individuals with certain traits of personality, motivations, desires and so on. The chain of events constituting the story is then governed by the motivations and actions of these characters. An important defining feature of the classic narrative is its constitution of a central character as a 'hero', through whose actions narrative resolution is finally brought about.

These actions are rendered credible largely in terms of the kind of person the hero is represented to be.

Finally, classic narrative may be defined by the high degree of closure that typically marks its resolution. The ideal classic narrative is a story with a beginning, a middle and an end (in that order), in which every one of the questions raised in the course of the story is answered by the time the narration is complete (see Barthes, 1975).

Classic codes of narrative cinema

Narratives may be communicated through various modes of expression; that is, stories can be told through a variety of media. The classic narrative is perhaps most often considered in its literary form, as a certain type of novel. However, stories may also be transmitted by word of mouth, in live theatre, on the radio and in comic strips. Film is simply one narrative medium among many but the distinguishing features of film are its mode of production and consumption, and the specifically cinematic codes by which film narratives are constructed. Cinematic codes constitute a distinct set of expressive resources that can be drawn on for, among other things, telling stories (see The early work of Christian Metz: applying Saussure, p. 511).

The classic narrative system would appear to make certain basic demands of these resources. First, it demands that cinematic codes function to propel the narrative from its beginning through to its resolution, keeping the story moving along. Second, it is important that in the narration of fictional events the causal link between each event is clear. Third, the narration called for would encompass the construction of a location, a credible fictional world, for the events of the story. Finally, it should be capable of constructing the individuated characters pivotal to the classic narrative, and of establishing and sustaining their agency in the narrative process.

Perhaps the foremost of the specifically cinematic codes is that of editing. Although editing is simply the juxtaposition of individual shots, this juxtaposition can take place according to a variety of principles. Editing in classic cinema works in conjunction with the basic demands of the classic narrative structure in highly circumscribed ways. First, the individual shots are ordered according to the temporal sequence of events making up the story. In this way, editing functions both to move the story along and also, through the precise juxtapositions of shots, to constitute the causal logic of narrative events (see *Stagecoach* case study). The specificity of classic editing lies in its capability to set up a coherent and credible fictional space, and often also to orchestrate quite complex relationships of narrative space and time.

The principles of classical editing have been codified in a set of editing techniques whose objective is to maintain an appearance of 'continuity' of space and time in the finished film; all budding film-makers have to master the rules of continuity editing. Continuity editing establishes spatial and temporal relationships between shots in such a way as to permit the spectator to 'read' a film without any conscious effort, precisely because the editing is 'invisible'. Despite the fact that every new shot constitutes a potential spatial disruption, and each gap of years, months, days and even minutes between narrated events a potential temporal disjuncture, an appearance of continuity in narrative space and time can be set up (see *Mildred Pierce* case study). The function of continuity editing is to 'bridge' spatial and temporal ellipses in cinematic narration, through the operation of such conventions as match on action, consistency of screen direction and the 30-degree rule (see Burch, 1981). Coherence of fictional space is ensured by adherence to the 180-degree rule, whereby 'the line' is never crossed in the editing of shots taken from different set-ups in a single location. Since the 180-degree rule, in particular, depends on the hypothesis that screen direction signified direction in three-dimensional space, the credibility of the fiction is maintained through a form of editing that signifies verisimilitude (see Bordwell and Thompson, 2004).

In the classic narrative system, editing is governed by the requirements of verisimilitude, hence the characteristic pattern in any one film sequence of establishing shot, closer shots that direct the gaze of the spectator to elements of the action to be read as significant, followed by further long shots to re-establish spatial relations (see *His Girl Friday* case study). Since the classic narrative sets up fictional characters as primary agents of the story, it is not surprising that characters' bodies, or parts of their bodies, notably faces, figure so frequently in close shots. Close shots of this kind function also in relation to characterisation: personality traits are represented through costume, gesture, facial expression and speech (see *Klute* case study). At the same time, relationships between fictional protagonists are typically narrated through certain configurations of close shots, particularly those where an exchange of looks between characters is implied (see *Marnie* case study). Here, editing is organised on the principle of the eyeline match, according to the direction of characters' gaze. The eyeline match also governs point of view in the shot/reverse-shot figure, which in fact reached the peak of its exploitation during the 1940s, at the height of the classic era of cinema. This method of organising the looks of protagonists, through a combination of mise en scène and editing, is a crucial defining characteristic of classic narrative cinema (see Browne, 1975/76).

The conventions of classic editing constitute a particular mode of address to the spectator. In accepting a certain kind of verisimilitude in the spatial and temporal organisation of the film narrative the spectator becomes witness to a complete world, a world that seems even to exceed the bounds of the film frame. In looking at the faces of characters in close-up, and in identifying with characters in the text through taking on their implied point of view, the spectator identifies with the fictional world and its inhabitants, and so is drawn into the narration itself. Consequently, a resolution of the narrative in which all the ends are tied up is in certain ways pleasurable for the spectator.

Although classic narrative cinema moves towards the regulation of cinematic codes according to the requirements of a particular narrative structure, it is arguable that this objective can never be completely attained (see Guzzetti, 1975). Narrative and image in film are never entirely reducible to one another, if only because the demands of the classic narrative could in fact be met by a range of conventions of cinematic narration, of which the classic system is but one. Conventions, by their nature, are subject to change. Even if the classic narrative retains its dominance as a structure, its basic requirements could conceivably be met by cinematic codes different from those of classic cinema. And indeed, since the 1950s it appears that a rather wider range of cinematic codes has entered circulation in forms of cinema that still on the whole rely on a classic approach to narrative structure. This trend is exemplified by modes of narration characteristic of films in widescreen formats (see *River of No Return* case study) and by the development of New Hollywood cinema (see *Klute* case study).

Selected Reading

David Bordwell and Kristin Thompson, *Film Art: An Introduction*, New York, McGraw Hill, 2004. Revised edition.

Leo Braudy and Marshall Cohen (eds), *Film Theory and Criticism: Introductory Readings*, New York and Oxford, Oxford University Press, 2004.

Noël Burch, *Theory of Film Practice*, Princeton, NJ, Princeton University Press, 1981.

His Girl Friday (USA 1939 *p.c* – Columbia; *d* – Howard Hawks)

In the opening sequence of the film the heroine Hildy Johnson (Rosalind Russell) and her fiancé Bruce (Ralph Bellamy) arrive at the newspaper office where Hildy formerly worked. Hildy's ex-husband Walter Burns (Cary Grant), the editor, tries to persuade her to return to her old job. Shots 1 and 2 of the film function in the classic manner as establishing shots: a tracking shot moves through a busy and crowded newspaper office. A virtually invisible lap dissolve introduces shot 2, in which the space of the office is further delineated, here in a closer shot but again with mobile framing. Hildy and Bruce are introduced into this same shot as they leave the lift adjacent to the office entrance. Shot 3 is a medium two-shot of Bruce and Hildy, shots 4, 5 and 6 a shot/reverse-shot figure. The next five shots follow Hildy back through the office, re-establishing the space already introduced in shot 1, and show her entering Walter's room with a perfect match on action that moves her from one side of the door to another. This sequence demonstrates very clearly how the classic narrative system functions through cinematic codes to set up characterisation and organise a coherent narrative space.

ANNETTE KUHN

Shot 1

Shot 2

Shot 3

Shot 4

Shot 5

Shot 6

Stagecoach (USA 1939 *p.c* – Walter Wanger Productions/United Artists; *d* – John Ford)

A stagecoach voyages to Lordsburg with a mixed group of passengers. The final part of the journey includes a chase sequence in which the coach is attacked by American Indians. Since at this point in the narrative the character traits of the protagonists are already well established, the narration is free to focus more or less exclusively on action and suspense. Suspense is generated by the familiar device of crosscutting, which in this case initially functions to establish narrative space. In the first segment of the actual chase, shots of the stagecoach and the Native American Indians alternate, and it is only later that both groups are seen within one shot. Spectator identification with the stagecoach passengers is sustained through two devices. The stage is placed first in the alternating sequence of shots in such a way that it is clearly the object of pursuit. Second, such point-of-view shots as are to be found in this sequence originate predominantly from the coach or its passengers rather than from the Native American Indians. The main burden of narration falls here on the editing, which functions almost entirely to keep the story and the action moving along. Moreover, the specific form of editing – crosscutting – generates suspense and excitement, while sustaining the spectator's identification with the passengers of the stagecoach.

ANNETTE KUHN

Mildred Pierce (USA 1945 *p.c* – Warner Bros./ First National; *d* – Michael Curtiz)

Mildred Pierce is the story of a woman's rise to success and her betrayal by her daughter and husband. Mildred (Joan Crawford), at the beginning of her second flashback, talks about the success of her restaurant business. The flashback is marked as such by conventionalised framing and editing quite prevalent in films of the 1940s, and is a mark of narratives involving complex temporal relations. A close-up of Mildred dissolves very slowly into a long shot of one of her restaurants, and Mildred's direct speech then becomes voice-over for the image as her face fades from the screen. The temporal ellipsis referred to in the voice-over ('In three years I built up five restaurants') is marked by a series of discontinuous shots punctuated by brief dissolves. In the classic narrative system the dissolve is a conventional signifier of passage of brief but indefinite time. The voice-over, which is sustained throughout the montage sequence, functions simultaneously to mark the sequence as subjective, told from Mildred's point of view, that is, and to bridge the substantial spatial and temporal ellipses dividing individual shots.

The film's opening sequence, in which the events leading up to the shooting of Mildred's husband Monte (Zachary Scott) are shown, deliberately omits a reverse-shot, which leads the spectator to believe that Mildred is the murderer. Although this could appear to be an aberration in the classic continuity system, in narrative terms it has been seen as a 'snare' that the film will eventually resolve (see Cook, 2005).

ANNETTE KUHN

River of No Return (USA 1954 *p.c* – 20th Century Fox; *d* – Otto Preminger)

This film is in CinemaScope, a widescreen format that pulled the traditional screen ratio of 1 : 1.33 out to 1 : 2.35. The Scope image is thus relatively wide in relation to its height. In *River of No Return*, as in other Scope films, a transformation in the shape of the screen image seems to have motivated a rather different approach to composition, editing and narration from that of the classic narrative system. In particular, long takes – often involving mobile framing – predominate, and in dialogue sequences two- and three-shots are much more common than shot/reverse-shots (see Widescreen, p. 154).

These variations on the classic narrative system have been hailed as conferring a greater 'realism' (in the Bazinian sense) upon the cinematic image (see Barr, 1974). So, for example, in the scene in which Calder (Robert Mitchum) is seen conversing with the storekeeper, several different sets of actions are dealt with in one single long take. Calder moves over to the window, picks up a rifle for Mark (Tommy Rettig) and exchanges some words with the boy. He then looks out of the window, moves forward and is joined from off screen by the storekeeper; both men look out onto the street. Here the space of the store is established not by the classic method of giving an establishing shot and subsequent shots that break down the space, but through 'composition in width' and mobile framing. The scene as a whole may serve as a demonstration of the potential that exists within the Institutional Mode of Representation for variation in the cinematic articulation of narratives that remain basically classical in structure.

ANNETTE KUHN

Marnie (USA 1964 *p.c* – Geoffrey Stanley Inc./ Universal; *d* – Alfred Hitchcock)

Tippi Hedren as Marnie plays a kleptomanic and sexually frigid woman who marries a rich man, Mark (Sean Connery), who attempts to 'cure' her. The scene in which Mark enters Marnie's room as she wakes up after a nightmare is constructed as a series of nine or ten alternating shot/reverse-shots. Since Marnie is not fully awake, however, and so does not see Mark, the shots of Mark are not strictly from her point of view, but those of Marnie are quite evidently from Mark's: as he moves closer to the bed, for example, the framing of the shots of Marnie contract from long shot to medium shot. In the next segment Marnie evades Mark's questions about her dream. Marnie's rival Lil (Diane Baker) passes by the bedroom door, looks into the next room and sees the book Mark has been reading: *The Sexual Aberrations of the Criminal Female*.

The extraordinarily high incidence of point-of-view shots in this scene is quite typical for a Hitchcock film. This is, of course, partly because the narratives of many of his films are actually organised around 'voyeuristic' situations. *Marnie* is no exception, and Mark's function as investigator of the enigma presented by Marnie is repeatedly condensed in the image by his gaze at her. Marnie is presented as a puzzle whose solution demands a close scrutiny, as she says to Mark: 'Stare – that's what you do' (see Mulvey, 1975; 1989).

Also in this scene optical point of view dominates the narration of a phase of an investigation. Classically, point of view functions to engage the spectator through identification with the look of a character. Here, however, identification is not simply with the character whose point of view dominates the sequence (Mark) but also, and perhaps more importantly, with the investigation that he is conducting. The solution to the enigma presented by Marnie is a necessary condition of narrative closure. An interesting variation on the point-of-view structure used here is offered by Hitchcock's *Rear Window* (1954), in which the point of view of James Stewart's incapacitated character Jeffries is shown to be flawed (see Modleski, 1988).

ANNETTE KUHN

Klute (USA 1971 *p.c* – Warner Bros.; *d* – Alan J. Pakula)

Klute is often regarded as an example of New Hollywood cinema, a variant of the classic narrative system in which a certain openness or ambiguity is admitted into the cinematic narration (see Neale, 1976). *Klute* does in fact combine quite traditional elements of classic narrative cinema with a degree of openness that would certainly have been inadmissible in the classic era. The story takes off from the conventions of the classic 1940s film noir, in that it deals both with a mystery and the process of investigation that leads to the mystery's solution. The archetypal detective-hero is Klute (Donald Sutherland), who falls in love with prostitute Bree Daniel (Jane Fonda), who herself becomes the object of the detective's enquiry.

In the first part of the film Bree is represented both as a puzzle to be solved and as an object of the gaze. Klute's face is seen in close-up, silent, bearing a penetrating look, while Bree on the other hand is twice represented as object of the gaze of an unknown, and implicitly threatening, intruder. Later, the ambiguity of the narrative is foregrounded in a scene involving Bree and her therapist, in which Bree expresses some cynicism about her relationship with Klute. This is followed by an idyllic and romantic sequence with Bree and Klute together. Because Bree's cynical voice-over continues into this second sequence, a degree of contradiction between sound and image becomes evident.

ANNETTE KUHN

GLOBAL HOLLYWOOD

Postwar globalisation

TINO BALIO

Hollywood has operated on a global basis since the 1920s, when it first became a major industry in the US. Foreign revenues regularly generated about one-third of Hollywood's total income until World War II cut off most European and Far Eastern markets, but afterwards, Hollywood set about recapturing lost territories by releasing the tremendous backlog of pictures it had produced during the war. The protective barriers established by foreign governments during the 1920s and 1930s had broken down and foreign film industries had been disrupted by the war. Hollywood, it seemed, was in an excellent position once again to dominate the international trade in motion pictures. To ensure this outcome, the major Hollywood companies formed a cartel – the Motion Picture Export Association – in 1946 to pool distribution in 13 countries closed to American films during the hostilities. Hollywood needed overseas markets more than ever. Beginning in 1947, the motion-picture business went into a ten-year slump caused by the move to the suburbs and the rise of broadcast television, among other factors. During this period, movie attendance declined by half, 4,000 theatres closed their doors and Hollywood's venerable studio system went by the board as companies disposed of their back lots, film libraries and other assets and pared producers, directors and stars from their payrolls.

In response to Hollywood's global expansion after the war, the UK, Italy, France and West Germany – Hollywood's largest foreign markets – pressed hard to protect their impoverished economies and to nurture their national film industries. Nonetheless, American film companies continued to dominate the screen overseas just as they did at home. To rekindle interest in the movies, Hollywood adopted the formula 'Make them Big; Show them Big; and Sell them Big'. Making them big meant investing in pre-tested and pre-sold properties, such as best-selling novels, Broadway hits and even successful television dramas. Showing them big meant presenting pictures in a spectacular fashion using widescreen and wide-film processes such

'Make them big': William Wyler's *Ben-Hur*

Global reach: Julie Andrews in *The Sound of Music*

as CinemaScope, Todd-AO and Panavision. Selling them big meant custom-made exploitation and promotion campaigns to ensure long theatrical runs. Blockbusters such as Cecil B. DeMille's *The Ten Commandments* (Paramount, 1956), William Wyler's *Ben-Hur* (MGM, 1959), Robert Stevenson's *Mary Poppins* (Disney, 1964) and Robert Wise's *The Sound of Music* (Fox, 1965) became worldwide hits; by the 1960s, the foreign market had accounted for about half of Hollywood's total earnings.

Globalisation meant more than just distribution; it also meant investing in production overseas – a practice known as runaway production – and marketing foreign films in the US. Runaway production entailed shooting on location overseas to give pictures an exotic flavour and to complement the new widescreen processes. It also allowed American companies to take advantage of lower labour costs, particularly in Spain and Italy. Oddly enough, the strongest incentive for shifting production overseas came from the Europeans themselves. After World War II, international trade was chaotic. To stem the dollar outflow caused by the unfettered distribution of American films, foreign governments instituted currency restrictions. Frozen funds, for example, allowed American films free entry into a country on the condition that only a portion of the earnings could be taken out. The UK was the first nation to adopt the measure and in 1948 stipulated that American film companies as a group could withdraw only $17 million a year. The remainder of the earnings was to be frozen, that is, blocked. France, Italy and Germany followed suit, with the result that American film companies began to unblock their foreign earnings by making films overseas, particularly in the principal European production centres of Rome and London, which were soon known as 'Hollywood on the Tiber' and 'Hollywood on the Thames' respectively.

Currency restrictions relaxed eventually, but countries devised other protective measures to support domestic film industries. These too had the side effect of stimulating runaway production. Take the case of the UK. In 1948, Parliament revised the quota laws to allow for the free import of foreign films. Left standing were the provisions that required British exhibitors to devote a certain amount of screen time to British films and British distributors, including American subsidiaries, to handle British product. To stimulate British film production, Parliament instituted a subsidy scheme known as the Eady Levy in 1950. Named after its author, Sir Wilfred Eady, the legislation levied a tax on theatre admissions and rebated the proceeds to producers of quota pictures. The amount rebated to an individual picture depended on the amount it collected in film rentals and the amount of tax revenue the government collected during the film's release. Any producer who made a film in the UK could qualify for this rebate, provided the film was made by a British company, including a foreign subsidiary of an American company. The amount of this assistance was of no small consequence. The Eady Levy was designed to put a premium on commercial success and when a film succeeded at the box office, it received a big reward. In essence, the plan made the rich richer. On average, the Eady Levy remitted to a quota picture an additional 35 per cent of its distribution gross in the UK.

American film companies naturally took immediate advantage of European subsidies. Rather than purchasing completed films to meet quota requirements, American companies financed annual programmes of Italian-made and British-made productions expressly tailored for the American market. Take the case of Italy. American runaway production to Italy started in the 1950s with the goal of unlocking blocked lira accounts. Rome had many things going for it. The city was within easy reach of the most disparate and colourful backdrops and had a mild climate that allowed a long season of location shooting – just like Hollywood. Rome also had an abundance of extras and horses trained for the biblical epics that came into vogue. The showplaces of Italian cinema were Rome's Cinecittà, Italy's state-owned studio built by Mussolini in 1939, and Dinocittà, a huge $11 million facility containing four immense sound stages that Dino De Laurentiis built outside Rome on a 750-acre site. Among the important American-backed productions that resulted were Mervyn LeRoy's *Quo Vadis* (MGM, 1951), William Wyler's *Roman Holiday* (Paramount, 1953), Jean Negulesco's *Three Coins in the Fountain* (20th Century Fox, 1954), Joseph L. Mankiewicz's *The Barefoot Contessa* (United Artists, 1954) and William Wyler's *Ben-Hur*.

A similar story could be told about the UK, where American subsidiaries of Hollywood companies produced over a hundred pictures during the 1950s. Many of these films produced in British studios 'were sometimes indistinguishable in look and tone from the product turned out by the home studios in California', according to Alexander Walker (1974, p. 69). The biggest box-office hit was David Lean's war epic, *The Bridge on the River Kwai* (1957). Released by Columbia Pictures, *Kwai* grossed $14 million and was shown on national television to great acclaim. By the 1960s, the American companies were taking as much as 80 per cent of the Eady Levy every year, a statistic prompting *Variety* to observe that the ever-growing 'American investment in British production has made it almost impossible to define a "British" film' (see Canby, 1962, p. 18).

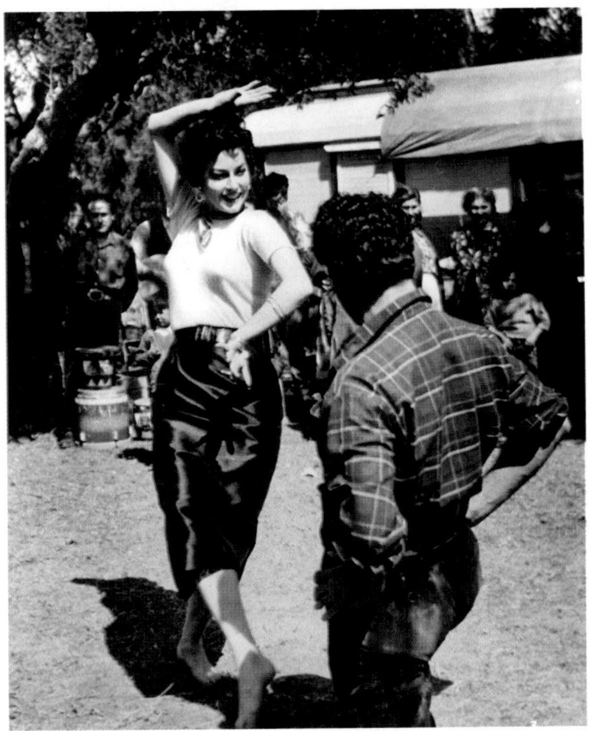

Runaway production: Ava Gardner in *The Barefoot Contessa*

Film aid laws were originally intended for development, the assumption being that state aid would eventually diminish. However, declining admissions resulting from the spread of television and more leisure time options kept European national cinemas dependent on aid for sustenance. Thus, national subsidy systems had to be supplemented by the benefits of co-production. After the founding of the Common Market in 1957, co-production became a regular part of film production in Europe. As Thomas Guback described it, co-production 'brings together financial, artistic, and technical contributions from two or more countries under criteria established by formal bilateral governmental agreements' (Guback, 1969, p. 181). The economic benefit of the scheme eased the financial strain for producers in different countries by enabling them to collect film aid twice and, if a venture were tripartite, three times. The effect of all this led to a developing European cinema, with the inevitable US participation.

Nowhere was this more marked than in Italy (see also Italian cinema, p. 231). As the Italian market opened up, Hollywood signed co-production pacts with top-ranked producers starting with Carlo Ponti, Dino De Laurentiis and Goffredo Lombardo, among others. The ventures were typically co- or tripartite productions between Italy, France and West Germany and were released dubbed into English for the US mainstream market. Often as not they teamed up American actors with Italian stars such as Sophia Loren, Gina Lollobrigida, Vittorio Gassman, Marcello Mastroianni and Silvana Mangano. What kinds of films did Hollywood produce? Every conceivable kind – romantic comedies, continental dramas, biblical epics, spaghetti westerns and melodramas. Goffredo Lombardo produced Luchino Visconti's *The Leopard/Il gattopardo* (1963) for 20th Century Fox and Jules Dassin's *Where the Hot Wind Blows!/La legge* (1959) for MGM; Carlo Ponti produced Vittorio De Sica's *The Condemned of Altona/I sequestrati di Altona* (1962) for 20th Century Fox; and Dino De Laurentiis produced Pietro Francisci's *Attila/Attila, Flagello di Dio* (1958) for Embassy Pictures and John Huston's *The Bible/La bibbia* (1966) for 20th Century Fox.

As already noted, Hollywood's international operations also meant marketing foreign films in the US. American film companies traditionally had an aversion to foreign films. The reason was primarily economic. A famous *Variety* article with the headline 'Stix Still Nix British Pix' said:

> Pix from abroad . . . are still a very long way from achieving parity of interest with the home-grown product. Imports made box-office inroads only in such areas as New York, Los Angeles, San Francisco and Boston, which had cosmopolitan populations. The mid-west and south continue to be as much citadels of isolationism in their picture tastes as in their politics. (*Variety*, 1947, p. 1)

The article appeared in 1947, but the market for foreign fare in the US changed dramatically during the 1950s as waves of films from Italy, Sweden, Japan, France and other countries fed a burgeoning art-film market (see also Art cinema, p. 83). The art-film market was devoted to the acquisition, distribution and exhibition of foreign-language and English-language films produced abroad and was originally controlled by dozens of small independent distributors operating out of New York. By the 1960s, however, the market had been taken over by Hollywood.

The film that marked the beginning of the takeover was *And God Created Woman/Et Dieu . . . créa la femme* (1956), starring Brigitte Bardot, which was distributed in the US by Kingsley-International, a former independent distributor that had become aligned with Columbia Pictures. Directed by Roger Vadim, who formulated the Bardot image, *And God Created Woman* grossed over $4 million in the US to become the biggest foreign (that is, non-English) moneymaker there up to that time. Observing these results, United Artists followed Columbia's lead in 1958 by acquiring Lopert Films, another prominent indie art-film distributor; within a decade, all the majors had gone into art-film distribution and had formed alliances with talented European film-makers by financing their pictures. French Nouvelle Vague directors were the first to attract Hollywood's attention when François Truffaut's *The Four Hundred Blows/Les Quatre cents coups* (1959), Alain Resnais's *Hiroshima mon amour* (1959) and Marcel Camus's *Black Orpheus/Orfeu negro* (1958) swept up top honours at the Cannes Film Festival in 1959. These pictures hit the American market in 1960 and grossed close to $2 million; afterwards, bidding on the films of these directors and other newcomers such as Louis Malle, Claude Chabrol, Philippe de Broca and Jean-Luc Godard became hectic as distributors, exhibitors and the critics welcomed the revolution.

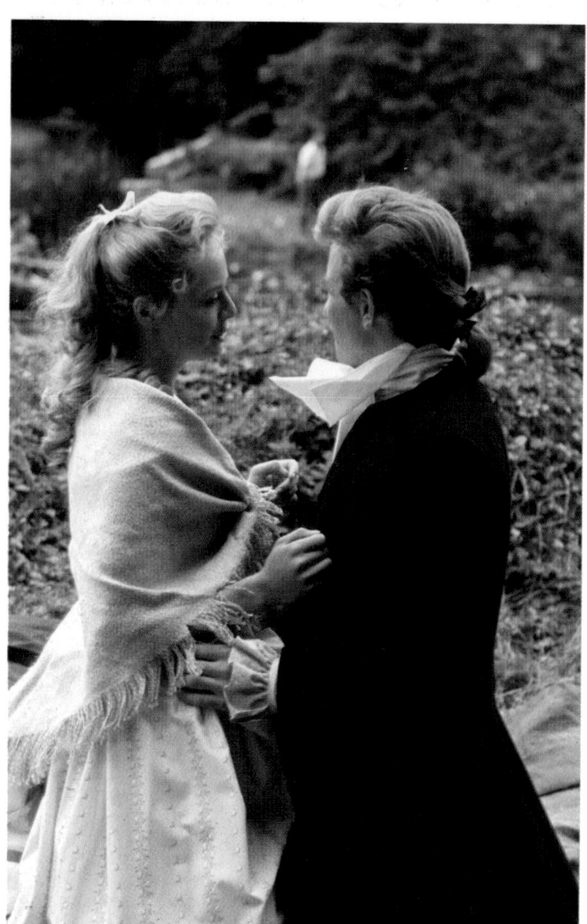

Financed by United Artists: *Tom Jones*

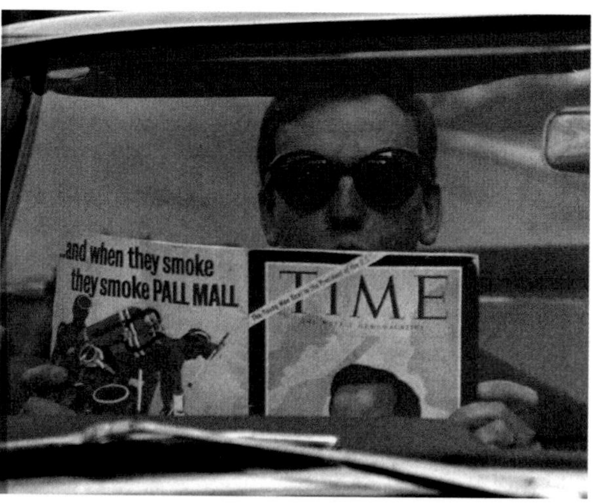

US-backed French film: *Un Homme et une femme*

United Artists was the biggest US backer of French films during this period and hooked up first with Philippe de Broca, who was known as the Mack Sennett of French films. With UA financing, de Broca made *That Man from Rio/L'Homme de Rio* (1964) and *Up to His Ears/Les Tribulations d'un chinois en Chine* (1965), two comedies starring Jean-Paul Belmondo, and *King of Hearts/Le Roi de coeur* (1966), a whimsical anti-war fantasy starring Alan Bates. United Artists' most successful commercial venture was Louis Malle's *Viva Maria!* (1966), a fun-filled comedy starring Brigitte Bardot and Jeanne Moreau that grossed over $4 million worldwide. But UA was probably best known for backing a series of small-budget pictures by Truffaut – *The Bride Wore Black/La Mariée était en noir* (1967) and *Mississippi Mermaid/La Sirène du Mississippi* (1970), homages to Alfred Hitchcock that were based on suspense novels; and the personal films *Stolen Kisses/Baisers volés* (1968) and *The Wild Child/L'Enfant sauvage* (1969). The biggest box-office hit from France in the 1960s with US backing was Claude Lelouch's *A Man and a Woman/Un Homme et une femme* (1966), starring Jean-Louis Trintignant and Anouk Aimée. Distributed by Allied Artists in the US, *Un Homme et une femme* grossed over $7 million worldwide and won the Grand Prix at Cannes and Oscars for Best Foreign Language Film and Best Screenplay in Hollywood.

After excitement with the Nouvelle Vague diminished, American producers ransacked British pop culture. So enamoured did the Americans become with the charisma of 'Swinging London' that the majors financed as many as 60 out of the 70-odd films produced in the UK each year during the latter part of the 1960s. The event that precipitated the flow of American film capital in the UK was Tony Richardson's *Tom Jones* (1963), an adaptation of Henry Fielding's ribald eighteenth-century novel starring Albert Finney. Financed by United Artists, *Tom Jones* broke box-office records wherever it played and went on to win four Academy Awards – for Best Picture, Director, Adapted Screenplay and Musical Score. A foreign film had captured the Best Picture award once before, but no foreign film had come close to *Tom Jones*'s gross: $16 million in the US and $4 million worldwide. The significance of *Tom Jones*, however, extended well beyond the box office.

United Artists financed two other noteworthy ventures that capitalised on the British pop culture scene: the James Bond films and the Beatles movie *A Hard Day's Night* (1964). The James Bond films were quintessential examples of products tailored for the international market. Financed by a major American studio, partly with British film subsidies, the films were produced by two American expatriates, Albert R. Broccoli and Harry

Tailored for international markets: Sean Connery in *Goldfinger*

Saltzman, and were based on the popular series of British espionage novels of Ian Fleming that played off cold war tensions. Shot in exotic locales, the films featured casts of mixed nationalities that were headed by a star of universal appeal – Sean Connery. Equally important, the pictures contained a lot of sex and action. The series began with *Dr. No* in 1962 and was followed by *From Russia with Love* (1963) a year later. With *Goldfinger* (1964), the third Bond picture, the series really took off. Produced on a budget of around $3 million, *Goldfinger* grossed a phenomenal $46 million worldwide the first time around. Starting with *Thunderball* (1965), the fourth entry, UA released a James Bond picture every 18 months. By 1974, the series had grossed over $350 million in rentals. Cubby Broccoli estimated that over 700 million people worldwide had seen at least one Bond picture – 'That's one in five people on earth', he remarked (Balio, 1987, p. 270).

A Hard Day's Night captured the Beatles at the height of their first enormous wave of popularity. Directed by Richard Lester, *A Hard Day's Night* premiered in London in July 1964 to smash business. Anticipating the same results for the US release the following month, UA released the soundtrack record before the picture opened and held special screenings for DJs, newspaper people, merchandisers and exhibitors. Then for the general release, UA saturated the market with 1,000 prints. This strategy generated an incredible gross of $5.8 million within six weeks and $10 million in a year, a huge success for its time. The box-office results of UA's ventures convinced other American companies to invest in Swinging London. Among the films they financed were: John Schlesinger's *Darling* (Embassy, 1965), Lewis Gilbert's *Alfie* (Paramount, 1965), Silvio Narizzano's *Georgy Girl* (Columbia, 1966), Michelangelo Antonioni's *Blowup* (MGM, 1966), Joseph Losey's *Modesty Blaise* (Fox, 1966), Karel Reisz's *Isadora* (Universal, 1968) and Donald Cammell and Nicolas Roeg's *Performance* (Warner, 1970), to name a few.

Interest in British pop culture had waned by 1968, caused in part by a Hollywood renaissance that the media called the New American Cinema (see New Hollywood, p. 60). Launched in 1967 by three hits – Norman Jewison's *In the Heat of the Night*, Mike Nichols's *The Graduate* and Arthur Penn's *Bonnie and Clyde* – the trend exhibited an unusual freedom from formula, convention and censorship that rivalled anything from Europe. The films were aimed at the counter-culture and enjoyed a new freedom of expression resulting from liberal rulings on censorship from the US Supreme Court and from the scrapping of the outmoded Production Code by the film industry in 1966. The renaissance ushered in a period of unprecedented frankness in American films that made most foreign films pale by comparison. As a result, the art-film market collapsed. Only one foreign-language film made really big money by Hollywood standards in this period: Bernardo Bertolucci's *Last Tango in Paris/Ultimo tango a Parigi* (1972). A French/Italian co-production produced by Alberto Grimaldi for United Artists, *Last Tango* had all the ingredients of a commercial art film – an American star (Marlon Brando), an esteemed European director and an erotic story. As a result of a deft publicity campaign by UA, the picture grossed $40 million in the US and $60 million in overseas markets. But *Last Tango* was a quirk and did nothing to rekindle Hollywood's interest in foreign films. Beginning in the 1970s, the majors withdrew from European production centres and once again produced their films mostly on their home turf. The new objective was to make films that appealed to a conventional youth audience and were exploitable in the so-called leisure-time market.

Pop-culture success: Monica Vitti in *Modesty Blaise*

Hollywood's attitude towards its foreign markets changed radically during the 1980s, the result of such factors as the economic growth of western Europe and the Pacific rim, the emancipation of state-controlled broadcasting, the spread of cable and satellite services, and the pent-up demand for entertainment of all types. Theatrical rentals had traditionally constituted the only source of foreign revenues for American film companies, but by 1989 they accounted for little more than a quarter. The major sources of revenue from overseas had become home video, theatrical exhibition and television, in that order. To capitalise on these conditions, Hollywood entered the age of 'globalisation'. During the 1990s, the majors upgraded international operations by expanding 'horizontally' to establish outlets in emerging markets worldwide, by expanding 'vertically' to seek an international base of motion-picture financing, and by 'partnering' with foreign investors to secure new sources of financing. Horizontal expansion led to a series of mergers and restructurings whose goal was to strengthen the means of distribution in all segments of the market. Vertical expansion led to alliances with a new breed of independent producer, such as Carolco, Castle Rock, Morgan Creek and Imagine Entertainment to enlarge their rosters (see also The major independents, p. 54). And partnering led to joint ventures with Japanese electronics manufacturers, the pre-selling of distribution rights to foreign distributors to reduce the financial exposure of big-budget pictures, and co-production deals to take advantage of film subsidies in overseas markets. Achieving these goals led to a merger movement in Hollywood that has yet to run its course.

Selected Reading

Tino Balio, *United Artists: The Company That Changed the Film Industry*, Madison, University of Wisconsin Press, 1987.

Thomas Guback, *The International Film Industry: Western Europe and America since 1945*, Bloomington, Indiana University Press, 1969.

Peter Lev, *The Fifties: Transforming the Screen, 1950–1959: History of the American Cinema Vol. 7*, Berkeley, University of California Press, 2006.

Toby Miller, Nitin Govil, John McMurria and Richard Maxwell, *Global Hollywood*, London, BFI Publishing, 2001.

The major independents

GEOFF KING

Hollywood's reach has extended in recent decades to include close relationships with various aspects of the independent sector. The Hollywood of the second half of the 20th century was one in which definitions such as 'studio' and 'independent' often became blurred, most significantly as a result of the increasingly widespread adoption of a contracted-out independent production process by the studios themselves. The majority of films that remained recognisably 'Hollywood' productions in all other respects (form and content) were produced by separate production companies, the chief roles of the studios becoming those of finance and distribution, limited to relatively small numbers of in-house productions. More distinctly different and more thoroughly independent-seeming modes of film-making continued to exist separately from the studios, ranging from the primarily avant-garde New American Cinema of the early 1960s to the youth-oriented exploitation pictures of outfits such as American International Pictures (see also Exploitation cinema, p. 298). Even here, overlaps sometimes occurred, as in the borrowings from art and exploitation cinema that fed into the radicalisation of some studio production/distribution in the 'Hollywood Renaissance' period from the mid-to-late 1960s to the mid-to-late 1970s. A long history exists of interchanges between the independent and studio realms (see Tzioumakis, 2006), but a new phase was marked in the 1990s by the emergence of what became known as the 'major independent' (Wyatt, 1998). In its principal incarnations, the major independent represents a conjunction of studio practice with aspects of a form of independent cinema (often dubbed 'indie' cinema to distinguish it from wider or more literal uses of the term) that came to prominence in the late 1980s and early 1990s.

The two companies most associated with the label 'major independent' were centrally involved in the consolidation and institutionalisation of the indie cinema that gained a high public profile in the 1990s. Miramax Films and New Line Cinema each started from very modest beginnings, booking films and/or rock concerts for college campus audiences in the 1960s. Along with other small distributors such as Samuel Goldwyn and Island/Alive and the growth of the film festival circuit, particularly the establishment of the status of the Sundance Film Festival by the end of the 1980s, they played a key role in the process through which a nascent growth in independent feature production was translated into a sustained phenomenon. By the early 1990s, each had become a substantial operation and was taken to another level after being bought by one of the major studios.

The term 'major independent' can also be interpreted more widely, to include other entities that have featured prominently in the territory that exists between the mainstream business of the studios and smaller-scale independent operations. It can encompass companies such as Orion Pictures, often described as a mini-major, formed by a group of senior executives who broke away from the struggling studio United Artists in 1978, as well as the specialist divisions created by all the major studios (alongside post-takeover Miramax and New Line) in the wake of the success of the indie sector in the 1990s. It can also include the few larger independent distributors that have remained free from any ties to the studios or their corporate owners, notably Artisan Entertainment and Lion's Gate Entertainment, the operations of which were consolidated through a merger in 2003.

The kind of cinema produced across this range of major independents varies quite considerably. It includes many features that fit into the notion of independent cinema that has been most prominently associated with the term in the past two decades – with institutions such as the Sundance Festival and the names of canonic indie film-makers including Jim Jarmusch, Steven Soderbergh, John Sayles or the Coen brothers. That is, independent or indie cinema as distinct from the prod-

Profitable 'exploitation' franchise: *Teenage Mutant Ninja Turtles*

MIRAMAX UNDER DISNEY

Ownership by Disney from 1993 gave Miramax access to increased financial resources and other assets that underlined its ability to dominate and significantly reshape the independent marketplace. It also led to a number of tensions between two very different kinds of organisations that culminated in the exit of the founders of Miramax, Harvey and Bob Weinstein, in 2005. Disney provided strong ancillary outlets to Miramax films through its clout in the negotiation of television and home video deals. This enabled Miramax to expand its strategy of paying over the odds for distribution rights and buying up large numbers of films, making it hard for other independents – studio affiliated or otherwise – to compete (Biskind, 2004). A select few of its acquisitions would then be chosen for the full Miramax treatment in terms of expensive marketing campaigns, wide releases and Academy Award campaigns, success in the latter being an important part of the establishment of the brand.

Other distributors felt obliged to follow suit if they were to remain competitive, which meant more spending on promotions and acquisitions and the use of riskier and more aggressive tactics to secure rights to attractive properties. Independents and studio affiliates were also forced to invest earlier, in the production end of the business, to secure access to product. This involved greater risks and a tendency, as Biskind suggests, towards more conservative and/or star-led properties. Miramax itself expanded further into production towards the end of the 1990s, reaching a balance of about 50/50 between production and acquisitions. It became increasingly reliant on the kind of crossover into the larger multiplex market that had been viewed earlier as a bonus, its centre of gravity shifting towards the 'prestige' end of the business, with successes such as *The English Patient* (1996) and *Shakespeare in Love* (1998), to a greater extent than the more controversial products with which it had originally made its name.

At the same time, the company's exploitation/genre division, Dimension Films, came to account for an increasing share of its box-office returns, as much as 75 per cent by 2000 (Biskind, 2004, p. 430). The penchant of the Weinsteins for marketing-via-controversy had created a number of conflicts with a studio parent whose name was a byword for inoffensive family fare. Sources of significant friction included pressure from the Catholic Church in connection with the release of *Priest* (1994), *Dogma* (1999) and *The Magdalene Sisters* (2002). The Weinstein brothers were forced personally to buy back *Dogma* from Miramax, after the intervention of Disney head Michael Eisner. Much the same was the case with Michael Moore's incendiary political documentary *Fahrenheit 9/11* (2004), eventually distributed by Lion's Gate and a new company, Fellowship Adventure Group, which was created for the purpose, after the Weinsteins repaid the original Miramax investment of some $6 million. The row over the latter was widely seen as a catalyst for the eventual departure of the Weinsteins from the company they created, to establish a new venture, The Weinstein Company, in 2005. More significant, however, might have been their ambitions to move further from the original relatively low-cost/high-profit formula that had most appealed to the studio, following Martin Scorsese's $97 million *Gangs of New York* (2002) and his $116 million *The Aviator* (2004). The post-Weinstein Miramax was destined to be a smaller and less autonomous part of the Disney empire.

GEOFF KING

ucts of the Hollywood mainstream at the levels of alternative form or content, including more 'artistic' and personally expressive tendencies or the adoption of less conventional socio-political positions (see King, 2005). Major independents have also been involved in the distribution of more commercial, mainstream-oriented features, however, as has been the case throughout the longer history of American independent cinema. The success of New Line was founded on two highly profitable 'exploitation' franchises, the *Nightmare on Elm Street* and *Teenage Mutant Ninja Turtles* series. Most of the films for which Orion is known are broadly mainstream features, including major franchise-launching titles such as the first Rambo film, *First Blood* (1982), and *The Terminator* (1984). Artisan and Lion's Gate have also profited from reliable genre/exploitation products, in addition to the distribution of some more challenging titles.

Miramax, in particular, gained its reputation through the distribution of films with a distinctly indie dimension, although its growth to a position of dominance was founded on a strategy designed to achieve a crossover to audiences larger than those usually attracted by indie fare. Key breakthrough successes included *sex, lies and videotape* (1989), *The Crying Game* (1992) and *Pulp Fiction* (1994), each of which raised the bar on previous expectations of the domestic box-office limits for indie features (from $24.7 million to $62.5 million and $107 million respectively). In each case, Miramax expanded its release strategy well beyond the confines of the exclusive art-house market to more than 500 screens for *sex, lies and videotape* and 1,100 in the case of *Pulp Fiction*. Miramax embarked on the exploitation-cinema practice of deliberately courting controversy through emphasis on the sexual dimension of some products and challenges to ratings decisions on others. Films with 'art' or 'prestige' credentials were mixed with more widely marketable material, the two dimensions sometimes combined in the same products. The company expanded during the 1980s and into the 1990s, although not without regular periods of financial difficulty. Its stability was cemented by the returns of *The Crying Game*, which established it as an attractive target for the studio takeover that came with the sale of the company to the Walt Disney Company for $60–80 million in 1993.

New Line went much the same way, initially being taken over by Ted Turner's Turner Broadcasting Corporation, in the same year as the Disney/Miramax deal, and subsequently joining Turner in merging with the Time-Warner conglomerate, home of the Warner Bros. studio, in 1996. The term 'major independent' takes on a new resonance in this context, suggesting

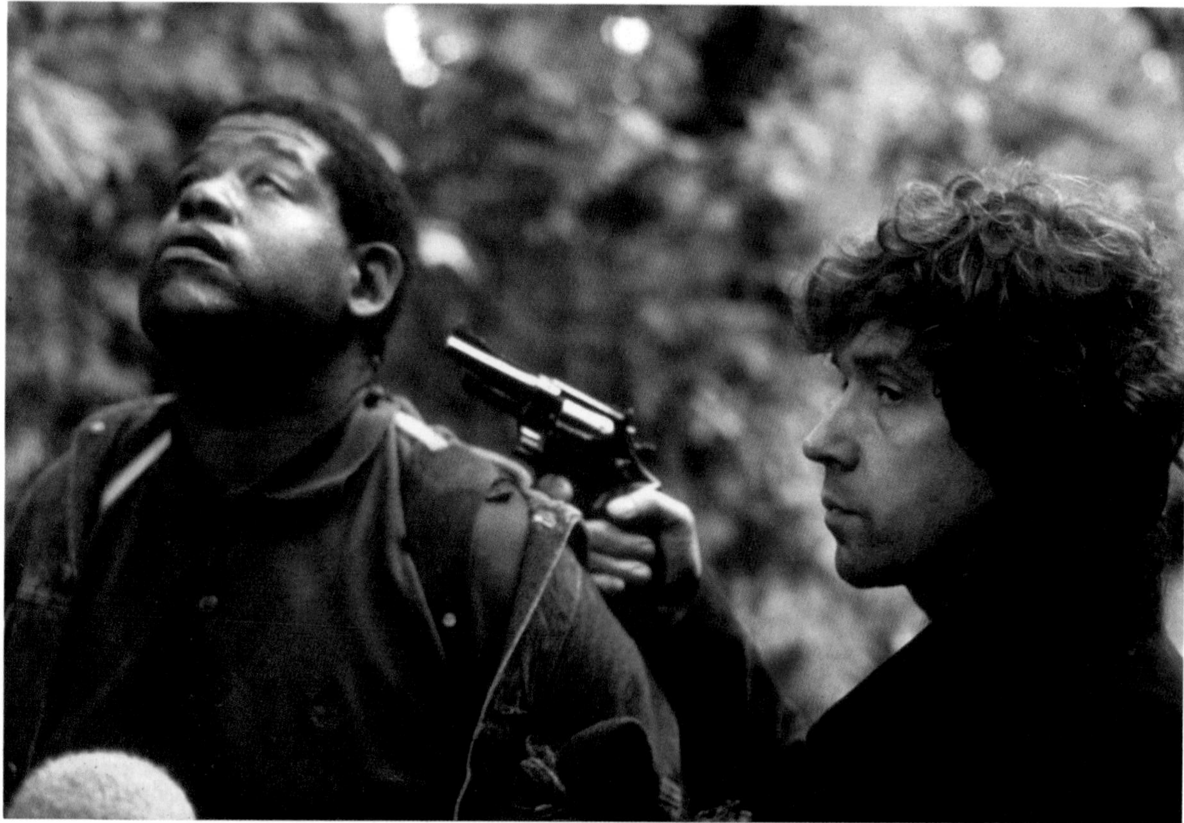

Courting controversy with Miramax: Neil Jordan's *The Crying Game*

formerly independent entities owned by the major studios rather than just independent companies that have reached a substantial scale of operations. New Line's route to this status was somewhat different from that of Miramax, although each has combined involvement in more 'arty' indie cinema with reliance on the stable profits brought by productions closer to the exploitation tradition. New Line's initial move into theatrical distribution focused on overseas art cinema and other niche products, including midnight screenings of John Waters's *Pink Flamingos* (1972). Access to additional finance led to a limited move into production from 1978 (Wyatt, 1998, pp. 76–7). The profits of the *Nightmare on Elm Street* and *Teenage Mutant Ninja Turtles* franchises enabled New Line to create its own video division and a subsidiary, Fine Line Features, that became its outlet at the more specialised art-house end of the market. Miramax, by contrast, created a separate division, Dimension Films, to handle exploitation/genre films, particularly the *Scream* and *Scary Movie* series, learning from the franchise profits achieved by New Line, without adversely affecting the higher prestige associations built around the Miramax brand.

For both Miramax and New Line, a significant degree of autonomy was maintained under studio ownership, including control of distribution and marketing strategies for their own films. The aim of the studios was to benefit from the particular specialist experience accumulated in the independent sector, avoiding a mistake made by an earlier generation of studio 'classics' divisions (created by United Artists, 20th Century Fox and Universal in early 1980s), in which less mainstream films had been handled in the same manner as the main output of the studios, generally not to good effect. In the case of New Line, much of what followed was little different from the kinds of films that would be expected from the central distribution arm of one of the majors. Fine Line continued to distribute more specialised features but was very much the sideline to a company that centred around mainstream properties such as the *Austin Powers* series (1997; 1999; 2002), major franchises such as the *Lord of the Rings* trilogy (2001; 2002; 2003) and returns to its exploitation-style roots such as the much-hyped *Snakes on a Plane* (2006).

Fine Line eventually disappeared in 2005 when New Line created a new joint venture, Picturehouse, with HBO Films, the production arm of the cable television channel, part of the Time-Warner empire. Miramax continued to work both the exploitation-oriented and prestige ends of the marketplace, with examples ranging from Quentin Tarantino's two *Kill Bill* films (2003; 2004) to *Shakespeare in Love* (1998) and high-budget features such as Martin Scorsese's *Gangs of New York* (2002). Both before and after its purchase by Disney, Miramax irrevocably altered the nature of the American independent film business, its dominance and success forcing others to follow in a number of changes, including wider release patterns and more spending on promotions, that further reduced some key distinctions between independent and studio practices (see Miramax case study).

The fate of Orion Pictures demonstrated the difficulties involved in operating at any large scale without the studio or larger conglomerate backing enjoyed by Miramax and New Line (see Tzioumakis, 2006, pp. 225–40). Orion began as a production company with a deal for distribution through Warner Bros. before moving to the status of a fully fledged producer-distributor from 1982. The company's strategy, as Tzioumakis suggests, was to focus on the low- to mid-budget range, deliberately avoiding head-on competition with the major studios at the blockbuster level around which their fortunes primarily revolved.

Working Title's radical roots: Ken Loach's *Hidden Agenda*

Orion enjoyed several years of healthy returns, notable successes including *Platoon* (1986), *Dances with Wolves* (1990) and *The Silence of the Lambs* (1991). The latter two achieved blockbuster-scale takings, but by the early 1990s the company was deeply in debt as a result of several disappointing years. It had sought to diversify, creating its own classics division in 1983 and a home video operation in 1987. Without corporate backing, however, it was unable to gain access to sufficient financial resources either to maximise the returns on its most successful films (in a number of cases, overseas rights had been sold in advance to fund production) or to ride out difficult times. Accumulated debts eventually reached $1 billion, forcing the company into bankruptcy in 1991.

If independents such as Miramax and New Line gained stability and access to new financial and other resources through takeover by studios, the studios also saw gains to be made through involvement in the indie or specialist market, most notably the high levels of profit achieved by lower-budget independent features that achieved crossover success with the mass audience. Low budgets could also result in healthy profit margins for films that performed less spectacularly, while a foot in the independent camp had the added advantage of being good for the corporate image and providing potential access to upcoming new talent. The 1990s and early 2000s saw the creation of independent or specialist-oriented divisions by all the major studios, either through the takeover of existing entities or the creation of their own operations from scratch, or a combination of the two. Sony Pictures Classics was created in 1992, inheriting the senior executive team from Orion Classics. 20th Century Fox established Fox Searchlight in 1994. Paramount Classics was launched in 1998, reduced to the status of a label within a newly formed Paramount Vantage specialist division in 2006. Universal established relationships with a number of independent labels during the late 1990s and early 2000s, eventually settling on its own Focus Features label in 2002 after taking over the noted New York independent producer Good Machine and combining it with its own affiliates.

Universal also absorbed the British major independent Working Title, producer of box-office successes such as *Four Weddings and a Funeral* (1994) and *Bean* (1997), as part of its acquisition of PolyGram from the Dutch corporation Philips in 1998. The end of Working Title's real independent status is dated some years earlier by Mike Wayne (2006), to the 49 per cent stake in the company taken by PolyGram Film Entertainment

Absorbed by Universal: Renée Zellweger in *Bridget Jones's Diary*

LION'S GATE ENTERTAINMENT

By the mid-2000s, having swallowed up Artisan Entertainment, Lion's Gate was the last of the major independents to remain free of any ownership links to the studios. Its feature release strategy had much in common with the model established by the pre-studio New Line, anchored in a line of horror and other exploitation products with potential for extension into sequel franchises of the kind likely to be solid sources of revenue on DVD, examples including *Saw* (2004; sequels 2005; 2006) and *Hostel* (2005; sequel 2007). This was combined with other releases including more prestige-garnering indie/specialist offerings such as *Girl with a Pearl Earring* (2003) and the Best-Film-Oscar-winning *Crash* (2004). Underlying the activities of Lion's Gate's motion picture division, however, was a more diversified operation that sought to create some of the securities achieved by the Hollywood majors. Founded in Canada in 1997, Lion's Gate was the product of Frank Giustra, a former investment broker, who aimed to create a smaller-scale north-of-the-border answer to Hollywood. It was born through the agglomeration of a number of existing entities, very much as it was to continue to develop up to and including the purchase of Artisan. The main initial components were Cinepix Film Properties, Canada's second-largest domestic film distributor, North Shore Studios, the country's largest studio facility, and Mandalay Television, owned by the former studio executive Peter Gruber. Its status as a company with major independent ambition was confirmed in 2000 with its $50 million takeover of Los Angeles-based producer/distributor Trimark Pictures. One of the main attractions was Trimark's library of 650 film titles, a useful source of video/DVD revenue.

Resources of this kind were also at the heart of Lion's Gate's subsequent purchase of Artisan, for $160 million plus the assumption of debt. Artisan had a more substantial library, some 6,700 features, built through a process of strategic acquisitions of back-catalogues from companies such as Republic Pictures, Vestron and Carolco, including attractive titles ranging from *Terminator 2 Judgment Day* (1991) and *Basic Instinct* (1992) to *Reservoir Dogs* (1991) and *It's a Wonderful Life* (1947). This was a valuable asset, a reliable source of revenue and collateral against which production or distribution finance could be gained: precisely the kind of resource that helps to give stability to the operations of the major studios. Artisan provided Lion's Gate with its Family Home Division, another potentially lucrative property that included rights to children's DVD franchises such as Barbie, Hot Wheels, Clifford the Big Red Dog and the Care Bears. Lion's Gate's takeover activities also gave it an important stake in the development of new forms of distribution to the home market via the Internet. Its acquisition of Trimark made it majority owner of CinemaNow, one of the pioneers of online video-on-demand, to which the major studios signed up in 2006 for new services such as permanent legal downloading and the burning of films to DVD.

GEOFF KING

in 1988, leading to a complete buy-out in 1992. Such shifts of status had a significant impact on Working Title, Wayne suggests, creating a reliance on success in the American market that shifted its output towards an emphasis on less radical material: from films of the 1980s such as *My Beautiful Laundrette* (1985) and *Hidden Agenda* (1990) towards a sequence started by *Four Weddings* and continued by *Notting Hill* (1999), *Bridget Jones's Diary* (2001) and *Love Actually* (2003). It has maintained some commitment to lower-budget and/or more challenging productions, however, its post-Universal production slate including examples such as *Thirteen* (2003) and *United 93* (2006) alongside commercial/mainstream features ranging from *Shaun of the Dead* (2004) to *The Interpreter* (2005). The complete set of studio-owned 'independent' arms was completed in 2003 with the creation of Warner Independent Pictures by Warner Bros. and the launch of Dreamworks SKG's subsidiary Go Fish. The territory occupied by these operations, along with Miramax, became known as 'Indiewood', often used as a disparaging label by those for whom studio involvement was a betrayal of the true spirit of independence, but characteristic of a hybrid brand of cinema in which markers of indie-style distinction are often combined with relatively more marketable dimensions than might be found at the radical/alternative end of the commercially distributed independent spectrum (see *Lost in Translation* case study).

The largest remaining players outside the orbit of the studios were Artisan Entertainment and Lion's Gate Entertainment. Each qualified as a major independent or mini-major studio through the scale of its involvement in film production and distribution along with other interests such as television and video/DVD. Artisan made its name through its high-profile release of *The Blair Witch Project* (1999) and established a reputation as a suitable home for unconventional indie features such as Darren Aronofsky's *Pi* (1998) and *Requiem for a Dream* (2000). Lion's Gate achieved its initial mark in similar territory, early releases including *Affliction* (1997), *Buffalo '66* (1998) and *American Psycho* (2000). Each grew through a careful strategy of diversification, an important aspect of which was the purchase of back catalogues to provide the kind of stability achieved by the studios (see Lion's Gate case study). The eventual outcome was the takeover of Artisan by Lion's Gate in 2003, creating a single entity the scale of which meant that it was more likely to survive in a marketplace still dominated by the majors.

Selected Reading

Geoff King, *American Independent Cinema*, London, I. B. Tauris, 2005.

Geoff King, *Indiewood, USA: Where Hollywood Meets Independent Cinema*, London, I. B. Tauris, 2008.

Yannis Tzioumakis, *American Independent Cinema: An Introduction*, Edinburgh, Edinburgh University Press, 2006.

Justin Wyatt, 'The formation of the "major independent": Miramax, New Line and the New Hollywood', in Neale and Smith (eds), *Contemporary Hollywood Cinema*, London and New York, Routledge, 1998.

INDIEWOOD FEATURES

Lost in Translation (USA/Japan 2003 *p.c* – Lost in Translation Inc./American Zoetrope/Elemental Films/Focus Features/Tohokushinsha Film Corporation; *d* – Sofia Coppola)

The term 'Indiewood' began to be coined in the late 1990s to describe the territory in which the line between the indie and studio sectors was becoming blurred, especially much of the output of Miramax and the other studio indie/specialist divisions. If the form of indie cinema that came to prominence through commercial distribution in the 1980s and 1990s often mixed distinctive or alternative qualities with more conventional/mainstream features, Indiewood has been taken to signify a hybrid that tends to lean more towards the latter than the former (King, 2008). It suggests the exclusion of the more challenging or radical end of the indie spectrum, examples such as the films of Todd Solondz (*Happiness*, 1998, or *Palindromes*, 2004), in favour of commercially safer films with greater potential for crossover from niche to somewhat larger audiences. Much of the responsibility for the creation of this phenomenon can be attributed to the specific strategies adopted by Miramax, particularly its award-garnering prestige productions, but Indiewood qualities can also be identified in a range of features produced by its rivals. A notable example is *Lost in Translation*, written and directed by Sofia Coppola and released by Universal's Focus Features, which earned positive reviews and numerous awards, including the Best Original Screenplay Oscar and Independent Spirit Awards (the indie equivalent of the Academy Awards) for Best Film, Director, Screenplay and Male Lead.

Lost in Translation positions itself clearly in the 'quality', specialist arena at the level of its overall tone, mood and the absence of any strong narrative drive. The story of two individuals, Charlotte (Scarlett Johansson) and Bob Harris (Bill Murray), who find solace in each other's company during enforced periods of residence in a luxury Tokyo hotel, the film is primarily a mood piece, a wry and quite touching observation of fleeting moments of human connection amid the various alienating aspects of each character's life: he an actor being overpaid to endorse a Japanese whisky, she the philosophy-graduate wife of a photographer with whom she seems to have little in common. The film faintly begins to sketch the possibility of romance between the two, but pulls back from anything like a consummation, leaving the pair heading their separate ways although only after an inaudible (thus ambiguous) final exchange that leaves a partially open-ended impression.

At the same time, *Lost in Translation* also displays more conventional dynamics. The impression of two lost souls finding one another is a familiar trope, even if not fully developed. Much of the humour offered by the film is reliant on somewhat stereotypical meetings of East and West, and the star presence of Bill Murray is central to the selling of the film. *Lost in Translation* is also keen to include its own diegetic markers of distinction, to underline the position it seeks to take up in the wider cultural field, primarily through the negative reference point provided by a minor character, a Hollywood actress presented as a crass and superficial figure who represents the cinematic pole opposite to that with which Coppola's film wishes to be associated.

GEOFF KING

Tokyo drift: Bill Murray and Scarlett Johansson in Sofia Coppola's *Lost in Translation*

New Hollywood

NÖEL KING

The notion of a 'New Hollywood' is a critical construction emerging from different accounts that describe changes in Hollywood film-making from the 1960s onwards (see Madsen, 1975; Jacobs, 1980; Pye and Myles, 1979; Schatz, 1983; *Wide-Angle*, 1983; Lewis, 1995; Colker and Virrel, 1978). Since 'New Hollywood' does not remain the same object across its different critical descriptions, we need to be aware from the outset that although these discourses target an agreed period of Hollywood film history they make different claims for what is significant about that period, producing competing accounts of 'the new' in relation to Hollywood.

Some argue that the forms of post-1970s American film-making differ little from the practices that sustained classic Hollywood cinema. David Bordwell and Janet Staiger, for example, identify in post-1960 Hollywood 'the persistence of a mode of film practice' – by which they mean the classic Hollywood style (Bordwell and Staiger, 1985). Douglas Gomery claims that 'in terms of economic structure and power, little changed in the American film industry during the seventies' (Gomery, 1983, p. 52), and in his survey of American cinema from 1930 to 1980, Robert B. Ray also argues that the traditional forms of classic Hollywood cinema persisted in New Hollywood (Ray, 1985, p. 68). Jim Hillier comments: 'In spite of all the changes that have taken place, Hollywood in the late 1980s and early 1990s does not look that different from the Hollywood of the previous forty years' (Hillier, 1992, p. 18). A similar view is expressed even within accounts that perceive a profound change (see Jacobs, 1980; Paul, 1977).

The highpoint of classic Hollywood cinema is usually thought of as occurring from 1930 to 1945, when filmgoing was a habitual national pastime and 'the movies attracted 83 cents of every US dollar spent on recreation' (Ray, 1985, p. 26). No one disputes that Hollywood went through substantial institutional changes after the 1948 Paramount Decree (see p. 19). Once the studios surrendered their theatres, the vertical integration that had characterised the mature studio system came to an end. The impact of television, the decrease in the number of theatrical films produced, the arrival of the 'package' and the 'deal' to replace the studio-era 'assembly-line' production, and changing leisure interests all led to a context in which the studios became financing and distribution entities, film production became more independent, and certain stars, directors and agents assumed a great deal of power. Pauline Kael characterised this shift of power succinctly:

> To put it simply: a good script is a script to which Robert Redford will commit himself. A bad script is a script which Redford has turned down. A script that 'needs work' is a script about which Redford has yet to make up his mind. (Kael, 1984, p. 16)

Kael wrote this in 1980 after spending a year on leave from her *New Yorker* film column working for Warren Beatty in Hollywood. There she found that the real power in the new, conglomerate Hollywood rested with the advertising and marketing people 'who not only determine which movies get financed but which movies they are going to sell' (Godard and Kael, 1982, pp. 174–5).

Three distinct moments are referred to by different critical discourses as constituting the moment of New Hollywood cinema and, although these moments overlap, they are not identical. A further degree of uncertainty derives from the tendency for critical discussion to slide between assessing recent Hollywood film as a textual artefact that is either 'better' or 'worse' than those produced under the studio regime, and/or characterising the textual form of recent Hollywood as expressive of changed production circumstances that lead to a different textual artefact.

Old and New Hollywood

For some critics New Hollywood refers to a brief window of opportunity that existed from the late 1960s to the early 1970s, when an adventurous new cinema emerged, linking the traditions of classic Hollywood genre film-making with the stylistic innovations of European art cinema (see Art cinema, p. 83). It was a period of productive uncertainty during which Hollywood opened up to new ideas because no one was sure which direction to take. In 1970, so this story goes, sclerotic studios were on the brink of economic ruin after having made a string of costly flops (usually musicals attempting to cash in on the success of 1965's *The Sound of Music*) that showed how out of touch they were with a college-educated, cineliterate 'youth audience' that had been politicised during the 1960s. This audience made hits of a cluster of so-called 'youth' or 'alternative' films of the late 1960s and early 1970s, all involving 'anti-heroes'. Films such as *The Graduate*, *Bonnie and Clyde* (both 1967), *Easy Rider*, *Butch Cassidy and the Sundance Kid*, *MASH* and *Midnight Cowboy* (all 1969) seemed to define a new period in American film-making, alliteratively described by Andrew Sarris as a cinema of 'alienation, anomie, anarchy and absurdism' (Sarris, 1978, p. 37). Directors such as Robert Altman, Mike Nichols and Arthur Penn came to the fore and actors such as Dustin Hoffman, Robert Redford and Jack Nicholson attained stardom.

This moment of 'the new' is followed by the arrival of the 'movie brats', a film-school-educated and/or film-critical generation who began making commercial American cinema with an élan that, for some, recalled the emergence of the Nouvelle Vague (see French cinema, p. 202). During the 1960s Martin Scorsese graduated from NYU film school (as Jim Jarmusch, Susan Seidelman and Spike Lee would later), Brian De Palma attended Columbia and Sarah Lawrence, while on the West Coast Francis Ford Coppola, John Milius, Paul Schrader and George Lucas graduated from UCLA and USC. They read the American film criticism of Pauline Kael, Andrew Sarris and Manny Farber, absorbing the influence of *Cahiers du Cinéma* and admiring the cinema of Federico Fellini, Michelangelo Antonioni, Ingmar Bergman, Bernardo Bertolucci and Jean-Luc Godard. Accordingly, some accounts (for example, Bernardoni,

New Hollywood icon: Robert De Niro in *Taxi Driver*

Cinema of 'alienation, anomie, anarchy and absurdism': Dennis Hopper's *Easy Rider*

1991) see this as the moment of explicit inscription within American film-making of the critical practice of auteurism, resulting in a self-consciously auteurist cinema.

Noël Carroll dubbed it a 'cinema of allusion', generated by references to other cinematic practices, particularly classic Hollywood cinema and European art cinema (Carroll, 1982). Carroll's view of New Hollywood's cinema of citation had been anticipated by Stuart Byron's (1979) claim that John Ford's *The Searchers* (1956) was the Ur-text of this New Hollywood, with references to be found in Scorsese's *Taxi Driver* (1976), Lucas's *Star Wars* (1977) and Schrader's *Hardcore* (1978). Similarly, the films that brought Peter Bogdanovich to prominence, *The Last Picture Show* (1971), *What's Up, Doc?* (1972) and *Paper Moon* (1973), were perceived as tributes to Howard Hawks and John Ford (the subject of his 1971 documentary, *Directed by John Ford*), and to classic Hollywood genres such as madcap/screwball comedy. This practice of cinematic citation continued into the 1980s with Schrader's remake of Jacques Tourneur's 1943 horror classic *Cat People* and *American Gigolo*'s 1980 homage to Robert Bresson's *Pickpocket* (1959). Schrader cites Bertolucci's *Il conformista* (1970) as 'a film I've stolen from repeatedly' and adds that the Nicolas Roeg/Douglas Cammell cult film *Performance* (1970) 'is a good one to check up on if you ever need something to steal' (Schrader in Jackson, 1990, pp. 210–11). Scorsese's *Raging Bull* (1980) alluded to, among others, Elia Kazan's *On the Waterfront* (1954), while in 1992 Scorsese remade J. Lee Thompson's *Cape Fear* (1961).

Functioning alongside the movie brats' cinema and often overlapping with it was Roger Corman's exploitation cinema. Corman's influence on New Hollywood cannot be overestimated (see also Exploitation cinema, p. 298; Authorship and cinema, p. 416). From his time with AIP through to his setting up New World Pictures, Corman provided opportunities for directors such as Scorsese, Coppola, Bogdanovich, Monte Hellman, James Cameron, John Sayles, Joe Dante, Jonathan Demme, Jonathan Kaplan, John Milius, Dennis Hopper, Ron Howard, Amy Jones and Stephanie Rothman; and for actors such as Nicholson, Robert De Niro, Bruce Dern and John Carradine. Carroll credits Corman with having established the 'two-tiered' film: 'Increasingly Corman's cinema came to be built with the notion of two audiences in mind – special grace notes for insiders, appoggiatura for the cognoscenti, and a soaring, action-charged melody for the rest' (Carroll, 1982, p. 74). A link with 'Old Hollywood' is apparent in the fact that, as Carroll (1982) and Hillier (1992) note, some of Corman's protégés likened themselves to the Hollywood professionals of the studio era.

Bordwell and Staiger (1985) observe that the New Hollywood directors were neither more youthful nor more technologically competent than their classical predecessors (pp. 372–3). Their account of the grafting of art cinema conventions onto classical traditions is also sceptical that it produced a genuinely new aesthetic: 'In keeping with the definition of a non-Hollywood Hollywood, American films are imitating the look of European art films; classical film style and codified genres swallow up art-film borrowings, taming the (already limited) disruptiveness of the art cinema' (Bordwell and Staiger, 1985, p. 375). They are equally unconvinced by claims for a new narrative adventurousness, claiming that 'most American commercial cinema has continued the classical tradition' and observing that 'the New Hollywood can explore ambiguous narrational possibilities but those explorations remain within classical boundaries' (p. 377).

This view can be set alongside Thomas Elsaesser's assertion, made a decade earlier, that the emergence of a 'new liberal cinema' marked a shift away from the classic Hollywood fictional world in which the heroes were 'psychologically or morally motivated: they had a case to investigate, a name to

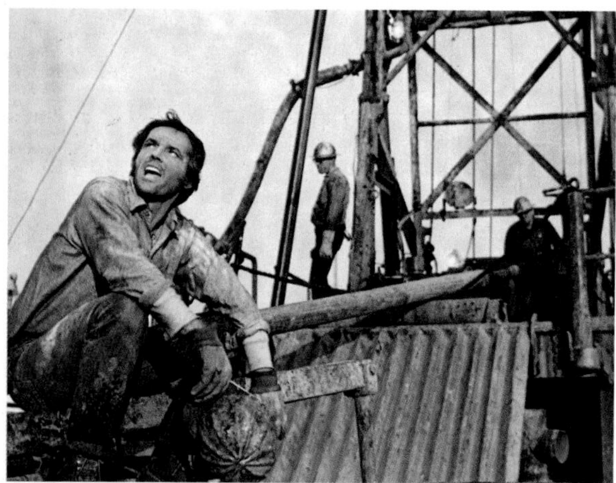

Art cinema practices in a Hollywood film: *Five Easy Pieces*

clear, a woman (or man) to love, a goal to reach', towards cinematic fictions in which notions of goal-orientation can only figure as nostalgic (Elsaesser, 1975, p. 14). According to Elsaesser, American cinema of the 1970s saw the model of the classic Hollywood film altered, as an 'affirmative-consequential model' was replaced by a more open-ended, looser-structured narrative. But Elsaesser was also careful to say that the New Hollywood cinema achieved its innovations by 'shifting and modifying traditional genres and themes, while never quite shedding their support' (p. 18).

One of the films offered by Elsaesser as evidence of a new kind of American cinema was Bob Rafelson's *Five Easy Pieces* (1970), produced by the independent BBS group, who had enjoyed great success the year before with Dennis Hopper's *Easy Rider*. David Thomson describes the way BBS productions (Bert Schneider, Bob Rafelson, Steve Blauner) 'did a deal with Columbia for a series of low-budget features that would draw on new talent' (Thomson, 1993, p. 43). This resulted in *Five Easy Pieces*, *The Last Picture Show*, *Drive, He Said* (1970), *A Safe Place* (1971) and *The King of Marvin Gardens* (1972), the first two of which were hits. For Elsaesser, such films displayed 'a kind of malaise already frequently alluded to in relation to the European cinema – the fading confidence in being able to tell a story' (Elsaesser, 1975, p. 13).

In fact, the story told by *Five Easy Pieces* invokes an enduring American myth of travelling on the open road, as well as drawing on aspects of European art cinema via the Jack Nicholson character-function. This textual device links the familiar Hollywood archetype of the hero/anti-hero as self-willed social outcast (from Huck Finn onwards) with elements of the existential protagonists of, say, an Antonioni film. Throughout *Five Easy Pieces*, Nicholson's character-function is able to cross two classes and two cultures: it functions as 'Bobby' in the world of trailers, oil rigs, bowling alleys, and as 'Robert' in the world of classical music and island homes in Puget Sound. The way Nicholson's character is presented indicates the recruitment to traditional Hollywood film practices of a specific feature of art cinema: the strategy of implying that a character will always retain an unknowable otherness, linked to art cinema's deliberate cultivation of ambiguity. As one critic said of Antonioni's films, they are 'baffling in a highly intelligible way' (Lockhart, 1985, p. 77); or, as David Bordwell described a central protocol of art cinema, it is 'read for maximum ambiguity'.

For Noël Carroll, the allusionistic interplay of New Hollywood film-makers becomes 'a major expressive device . . . to make comments on the fictional worlds of their films' (Carroll, 1982, p. 52). By 'allusion' Carroll refers to

> a mixed lot of practices including quotations, the memorialisation of past genres, homages, and the recreation of 'classic' scenes, shots, plot motifs, lines of dialogue, themes, gestures, and so forth from film history, especially as that history was crystallized and codifed in the sixties and early seventies. (Carroll, 1982, p. 52)

Stephen Neale's description of *Raiders of the Lost Ark* (1981) as a film that 'uses an idea (the signs) of classic Hollywood in order to promote, integrate and display modern effects, techniques and production values' (Neale, 1982, p. 37) nuances Carroll's view. (If we add television to the intertextual memorialisation process, Carroll's description would apply to the 1990s cinematic recovery of television memory in films such as *The Fugitive* (1993), *The Flintstones* (1994), *The Addams Family* (1991), *Maverick* (1994), *The Brady Bunch Movie* (1995), *The Beverly Hillbillies* (1993), *Mission Impossible* (1996), *The Avengers* (1998) and *The Saint* (1997). While 1950s television programmes were often spin-offs from theatrical films, in the 1980s and 1990s theatrical films plundered the television archives.) Carroll also claims that this allusive cinematic compositional practice assumed a particular reading competence on the part of its cinéliterate audience, encompassing classical genre conventions and the more recondite aspects of art cinema.

Roman Polanski's *Chinatown* (1974) has become one of the most famous and enduring examples of New Hollywood cinema (see Film noir, p. 305). It melds the Hollywood genre film with the art film, chiefly by reworking some of the hard-boiled conventions of film noirs such as *The Maltese Falcon* (1941) and *The Big Sleep* (1946). Robert Towne's screenplay helped to forge his

Plundering the television archives: *The Avengers*

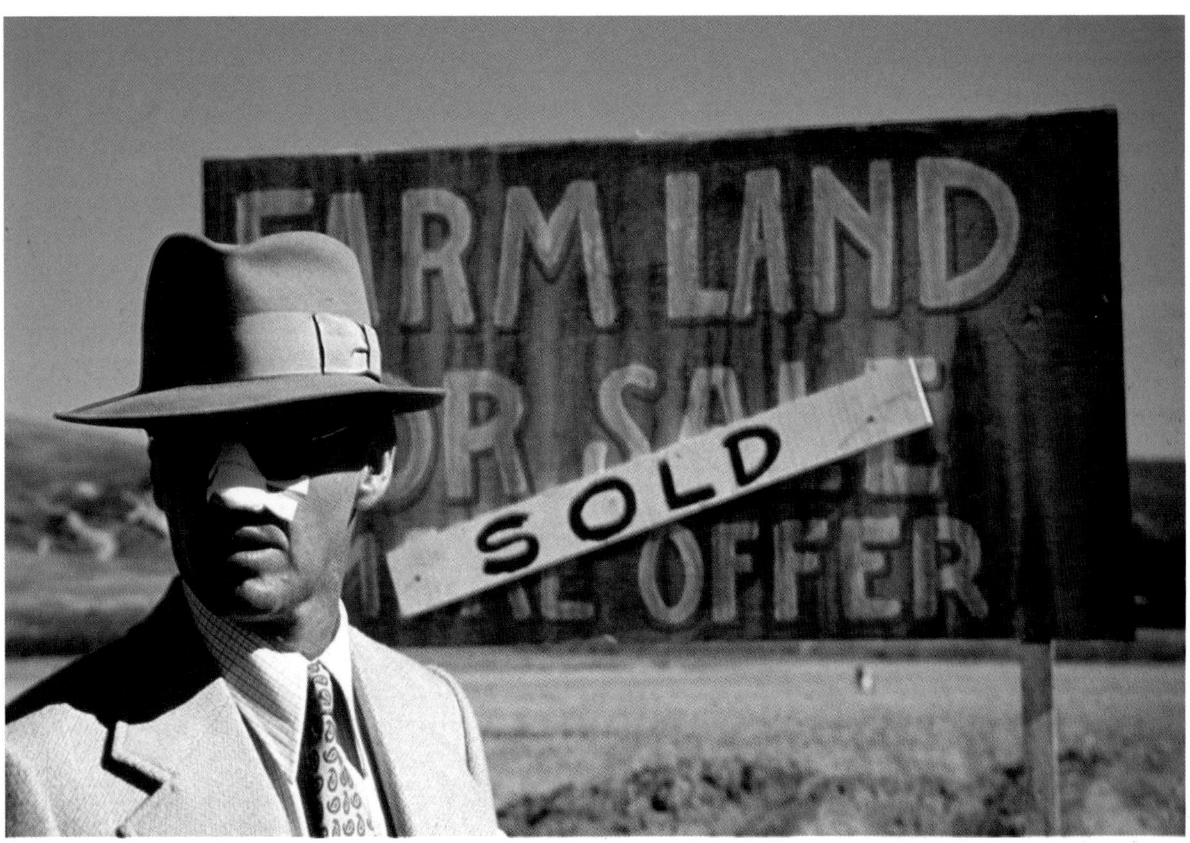

Challenging Old Hollywood genre conventions: Jack Nicholson in *Chinatown*

reputation as one of the pre-eminent New Hollywood screenwriters. It challenged one of the central conventions of the genre, in which the detective figure retells and reorganises what has happened at the end (for example, as Humphrey Bogart's Sam Spade does for Mary Astor's Brigid at the end of *The Maltese Falcon*). This convention confirms the detective's role as the one whose investigative expertise enables him to see things clearly, as they are. *Chinatown* plays with this trope when J. J. Gittes (Jack Nicholson) visits Evelyn Mulwray's (Faye Dunaway) house for the first time. As he waits at the door, an enigmatic (because unsourced) squeaking sound is heard on the soundtrack. Gittes looks in the direction of the car parked in the driveway and soon a servant comes into view, cleaning the car with a shammy. Sight and sound fall into place as we follow Gittes's look. But as the film progresses, Gittes is increasingly unable to perform his traditional detective function. He consistently misperceives people's relationships until eventually he is defeated by the fact of incest, as Evelyn spells it out for him: 'She's my daughter and my sister! Understand? Or is it too tough for you?'

After the brief period of studio uncertainty that allowed experimentation in the early 1970s, and the emergence of the 'movie brats', the next distinctive moment of New Hollywood is one on which all critics agree: the release of Steven Spielberg's *Jaws* in 1975. As Thomas Schatz puts it:

> If any single film marked the arrival of the New Hollywood, it was *Jaws*, the Spielberg-directed thriller that recalibrated the profit potential of the Hollywood hit, and redefined its status as a marketable commodity and cultural phenomenon as well. (Schatz, 1993, p. 17)

Although the post-1975 period and its financial successes are central to notions of New Hollywood cinema, in some ways it represented a relaunching of an early-to-mid-1950s Hollywood strategy that had stalled by 1970: namely, the production of a calculated blockbuster as a departure from classic Hollywood's reliance on routine A-class features to generate revenue. In his 1988 study of the studio system, Schatz had remarked on an inglorious distinguishing feature of New Hollywood: its concentration on the blockbuster. In the classic Hollywood studio system, 'ultimately both blockbuster and B-movie were ancillary to first-run feature production, which had always been the studios' strong suit – and which the New Hollywood has proved utterly incapable of turning out with any quality or consistency' (Schatz, 1988, p. 492). The post-*Jaws* world, however, was one in which blockbuster films were conceived as 'multi-purpose entertainment machines that breed music videos and soundtrack albums, TV series and videocassettes, video games and theme park rides, novelizations and comic books' (Schatz, 1993, pp. 9–10).

The media hype surrounding the theatrical release of such blockbusters as *Batman* (1989), *Dick Tracy* (1990), *Terminator 2 Judgment Day* (1991), *Hook* (1991) or *Jurassic Park* (1993) 'creates a cultural commodity that might be regenerated in any number of media forms' (Schatz, 1993, p. 29). Schatz completes his account of the New Hollywood by suggesting that it produces three different classes of movie:

> The calculated blockbuster designed with the multimedia marketplace and franchise status in mind, the mainstream A-class star vehicle with sleeper-hit potential, and the low-cost independent feature targeted for a specific market

> and with little chance of anything more than 'cult film' status. (Schatz, 1993, p. 35)

Nevertheless, his account repeatedly emphasises the imposing commodity presence of the contemporary blockbuster.

'Event' cinema and high concept

The clarity of this third moment of change is conveyed by the fact that the post-1975 blockbusters have proved the most profitable films of all time. 'Hollywood's ten top-grossing films have all been released since 1975. And even if one adjusts the figures to compensate for the dollar's reduced purchasing power – seven of the all-time blockbusters were still made between 1975 and 1985' (Hoberman, 1985, p. 58). Timothy Corrigan meditates on this changed situation by looking back on the conglomerate takeovers of the majors in the 1960s and 1970s, the later pressures from video and cable television and the way the status of the blockbuster has come to figure in the corporate thinking of New Hollywood:

> Far more than traditional epic successes or the occasional predecessor in film history, these contemporary blockbuster movies became the central imperative in an industry that sought the promise of massive profit from large financial investments; the acceptable return on these investments (anywhere from $20 million to $70 million) required, most significantly, that these films would attract not just a large market, but all the markets. (Corrigan, 1991, p. 12; see also The major independents, p. 54)

Several critics felt this form of cinema was achieved at the expense of a more meditative, adult cinema that had been present in the first two moments of the New Hollywood. Pauline Kael argued that conglomerate control of the studios meant there was less chance for unusual projects to get financed; Andrew Sarris mused that 'the battle was lost when Hollywood realized in 1970 that there was still a huge middle-American audience for *Airport*' (Sarris, 1978, p. 37); and, in a much-quoted phrase, James Monaco said: 'Increasingly we are all going to see the same ten movies' (Monaco, 1979, p. 393). As David Denby bleakly put it: 'When the studios eliminate their down-side risk, most of the time they make the same dumb movie because they are eager to pull everyone in on opening day. They want the smash hit. They're not interested in modest profit' (Denby, 1986, p. 34). The phrase that came to characterise this commercial emphasis in Hollywood's economic-aesthetic strategy was 'film event'. Hoberman explains: 'At the time of the release of *Earthquake*, Jennings Lang, its executive producer, wrote an article for *American Cinematographer* in which he proclaimed that a movie had to be an "event" in order to succeed in today's market' (Hoberman, 1985, p. 59).

Thomas Elsaesser termed classic Hollywood cinema a predominantly narrative and psychological cinema characterised by an inviolable transparency of storyline. It was a 'remarkably homogenous practice ... governed by a certain fundamental dramatic logic ... its prima facie concern is with telling a story, to analyse in fictional terms certain human situations and experiences. Its structural constraints are dramatic conflict and narrative progression' (Elsaesser, 1971, p. 6). To convey the aesthetic *realpolitik* that underlay such a form of cinema, Elsaesser relayed the anecdote of Louis B. Mayer, chief of MGM, who declared that he judged a film by whether or not his bottom ached by the time the lights came up. Mayer 'thereby indicated that a good movie, one that he was putting his money on, should activate certain psychological processes – of identification, of emotive participation or imaginative projection' (Elsaesser, 1971, p. 6).

In more recent times a different litmus test of movie entertainment is applied: that of 'high concept'. *Jaws*'s 'presold property and media-blitz saturation release pattern heralded the rise of marketing men and "high concept"' (Hoberman, 1985, p. 36). Justin Wyatt has since claimed 'high concept' as 'one central development – and perhaps the central development within post-classical cinema, a style of film-making modeled by economic and institutional forces' (Wyatt, 1994, p. 8). 'High concept' refers to a mode of film-making predicated on two things: the successful pitching of a film at the pre-production stage and the successful saturation television advertising of it after it has been made. Economics and aesthetics are linked via a notion of 'front-loading' an audience by way of pre-sold marketability ('the look, the hook and the book' as Wyatt puts it) that is deemed attractive both to television and cinema advertising. Hence the regularity with which 'high-concept' projects involve a hyped bestselling novel (a John Grisham thriller, for example), a star and a star director, and a genre strongly identified with either or both. Wyatt's example of one of the earliest 'high-concept' films is *Saturday Night Fever* (1977) with John Travolta, a project that linked television and cinema (via Travolta's television stardom), the music industry and popular cultural dance (via the Bee Gees soundtrack and nightclub disco). In contrast to this film, Bob Fosse's musical *All That Jazz* (1979) did not march to the high-concept tune, seeming to belong more to an earlier period when the art film snuggled inside the classic genre film.

It now seems clear that when *Jaws* opened at 464 cinemas and went on to become the biggest-grossing film of all time (until George Lucas's *Star Wars* topped it in 1977), the era of high concept and summer hits arrived. J. Hoberman described *Star Wars* as

> not just the highest-grossing film before *E.T.*, but arguably the quintessential Hollywood product. Drawing on the western and the war film, borrowing motifs from fantasies as varied as *The Wizard of Oz* and *Triumph of the Will*, George Lucas pioneered the genre pastiche ... *Star Wars* was the first and greatest cult blockbuster. (Hoberman, 1985, pp. 41–2; see also Science fiction and horror, p. 344)

Textual pillaging aside, *Star Wars* cost $11 million and within three years had grossed over $500 million. Lucas has said that he felt the strongest analogy was with Disney films and no Disney film had grossed as much as his film needed to in order to see profit. However, Lucas felt that the sales of products associated with his film could see the generation of sufficient profit. From *Star Wars* on we encounter the process of merchandising the contemporary Hollywood blockbuster into so many franchisable 'pieces'.

But there are other ways in which the exceptional commercial success of *Star Wars*, *E. T. The Extra-terrestrial* (1982) and *Raiders of the Lost Ark* indicates a change from the first two moments of New Hollywood. If we set aside questions concerning saturation release and merchandising opportunities, the first two moments saw an auteurist cinema explore and extend genres such as the western (*The Wild Bunch*, 1969), the gangster film (*The Godfather*, 1972; *The Godfather Part II*, 1974) and the detective-noir film (*Chinatown*; *Night Moves*, 1975; *The Long Goodbye*, 1973). For some critics, this laudable moment of thoughtful meta-filmic exploration was cast aside by the ascendancy of the late-1970s and 1980s films of Lucas and Spielberg, which marked a less philosophical, more calculatedly naïve relation to classical genres. In this lapsarian narrative, Lucas's

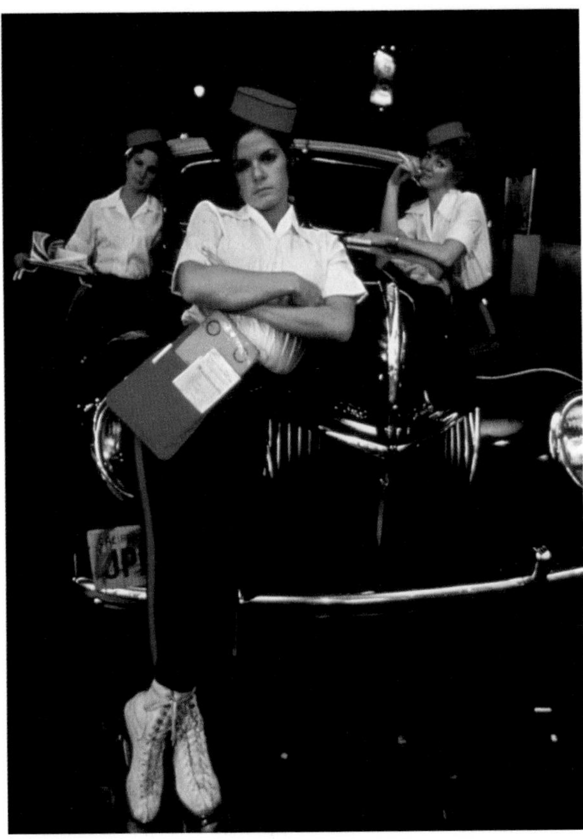

Retro-nostalgia and middle-American populism: *American Graffiti*

American Graffiti (1973) would seem a transitional text. It was adventurous in so far as it took the then unusual narrative step of basing its 45 or so scenes around as many pop songs, achieving, through the labours of Walter Murch, an innovative sonic depth of field. But the film's great commercial success (it was made for less than $1 million and recouped $55 million) foreshadowed the mix of retro-nostalgia and middle-American populism that would be found in many of Lucas's and Spielberg's blockbuster films of the late 1970s and the 1980s. For Hoberman, the success of these films meant that 'as the seventies wore on, it became apparent that the overarching impulse was less an attempt to revise genres than to revive them' (Hoberman, 1985, p. 38). Or, as Carroll wrote: 'After the experimentation of the early seventies, genres have once again become Hollywood's bread and butter' (Carroll, 1982, p. 56).

New production and reception contexts

In trying to determine how far the Hollywood cinematic institution set in place during the studio years has been transformed and to what extent the forms of classic Hollywood cinema have been modified or superseded, we now need to set those views that say 'the more things change, the more they remain the same' alongside clear evidence of change. Even if we accept that the textual form of the films we currently watch has strong similarities with the textual form of classic Hollywood cinema, it is also clear that our current modes of consuming these films are quite different from the situation that obtained into the 1960s. Earlier experiences of filmgoing involving a double bill at a neighbourhood cinema and/or a visit to a lavish art-deco 'cinema palace' have been replaced by a newer world of malls and multiplexes (see Rosenbaum, 1980; Paul, 1994). One is now used to speaking of 'screens' rather than cinemas and if it used to be the case that 'the show started on the sidewalk', the show now starts with a barrage of television advertisements preparing cinema viewers for a multi-screen release of a 'blockbuster'. *The Lion King* (1994), for example, opened on 2,552 screens. We live in a film-viewing world transformed by the delivery and reception of films such as *Jaws* and *Star Wars*. The grand social spaces of the 'picture palaces' were part of a cinematic institution less interested in gigantic hits than in a series of modestly profitable A-films, nice little earners, whereas by the 1990s we were likely to enter a diminished social space (as exhibition locales, cinemas have became smaller) in order to watch a film that is aspiring to be a smash hit. The shopping mall has become a familiar site for Hollywood fictions as well as the social site of their consumption: see, for example, *Bill & Ted's Excellent Adventure* (1988) and *Scenes from a Mall* (1991). Another instance of change can be seen in the extent to which films such as *Jurassic Park* offer themselves as kinaesthetic spectacles, linking three-act classic Hollywood screenplay structure to the sensations of a theme-park ride. From this perspective the classic Hollywood tradition is relaunched in a changed media environment, with the audience conceived as a mall shopper, freeway driver or video-game player, placed at the centre of a mobile, kinetic world. And although many contemporary critics insist that movies must now be understood as 'always and simultaneously text and commodity, intertext and product line' (Meehan, 1991, p. 62), debate persists about whether this constitutes a difference in kind or degree from earlier film-making arrangements.

John Belton (1994) points out that a process that began in the mid-1970s with the arrival of the VCR and the proliferation of cable television had a major effect on the cinema of the 1980s and 1990s (see also New distribution, exhibition and reception contexts, p. 75). The home video rental market expanded rapidly in the mid-1980s and by 1992 had reached a point where $11 billion were generated from this area as opposed to $5 billion from theatrical release. Belton also claims that the viewing habits of television watching in the home (talking back to the screen, having conversations with fellow viewers) have come to infiltrate public film viewing with a 'back to the future' effect of making today's cinemagoers resemble the earliest film viewers, who experienced film screenings as part of a mixed vaudeville entertainment programme. Tom Gunning (1986) writes that: 'Recent spectacle cinema has re-affirmed its roots in stimulus and carnival rides, in what might be called the Spielberg–Lucas–Coppola cinema of effects'.

If contemporary film viewing resembles the practices associated with early cinema, then it is not surprising that debate concerns just how decisive a change is to be found in contemporary Hollywood cinema. Hollywood has always repeated, remade and recycled earlier textual forms, either from its own history, from European and other cinemas, or from media such as television. Hollywood's recycling of European films includes *Down and Out in Beverly Hills* (1986), a remake of *Boudu Saved from Drowning/Boudu sauvé des eaux* (1932); *Sommersby* (1993), a version of *The Return of Martin Guerre/Le Retour de Martin Guerre* (1982); and *Point of No Return* (1993), a remake of *Nikita* (1990). The notion of remake or repetition now includes the 'director's cut' (for example, Ridley Scott's cut of *Blade Runner*, 1982) and sometimes (as with Sam Peckinpah's *Pat Garrett & Billy the Kid*, 1973, and *The Wild Bunch*) the 'dead director's cut'. Hollywood also plays a memorialising function when it re-releases films on their anniversary. Thus *Midnight Cowboy* and *Easy Rider* were delivered to new audiences, generating a public memory of cinema history. Releases of films on laser disc and DVD with trailers and production information, and the delivery of extra materials via websites, also demonstrate the overlap between an archiving

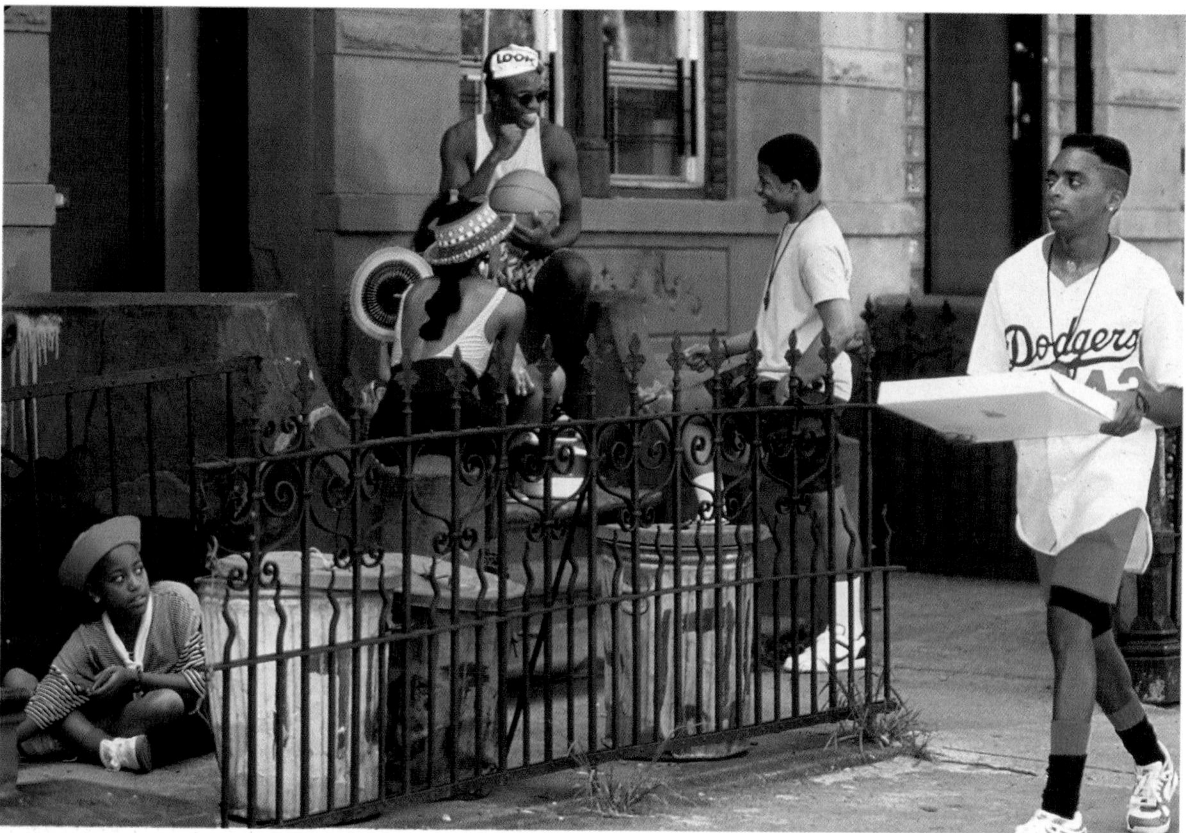

Independence and niche marketing: Spike Lee's *Do the Right Thing*

role, nostalgia and the pursuit and feeding of new markets (see also New distribution, exhibition and reception contexts, p. 75).

Some critics are nostalgic for an earlier period of New Hollywood. David Thomson, for example, remembers 1970s American cinema as 'the decade when movies mattered' (Thomson, 1993, pp. 43–7), seeing that moment as ushering in 'a terrifying spiral . . . whereby fewer films were made, more of them cost more, and a fraction were profitable' (Thomson, 1981, p. 27). Thomson laments the passing of that brief instance of productive innovation as the youth brigade took control and a counter-cultural cinema flourished. This cultural moment was lost as mainstream genre film-making was re-established by those young turks who supposedly were moving away from traditional forms of cinema towards more 'personal' films. It was this context that prompted David Denby to ask, 'Can the movies be saved?' in a familiar attack on conglomerate control:

> The movie business, perhaps American culture, has never recovered from that electric media weekend in June 1975 when *Jaws* opened all over the country and Hollywood realized a movie could gross nearly 48 million dollars in three days. Ever since, the only real prestige has come from having a runaway hit. (Denby, 1986, p. 30)

The gloom evinced by Denby and others would only have increased in the 1990s. For a film to 'open' then (that is, have the necessary enormously profitable first three days), all the same uncertainties that supposedly destabilise film production prevailed in a context that saw the cost of making and releasing the average Hollywood film spiral towards $50 million, with stars (Tom Cruise, Mel Gibson, Sylvester Stallone and Arnold Schwarzenegger) paid $20 million for a single film and 'star' directors paid $10 million (see also Contemporary stardom, p. 131). This escalation of production costs (Shapiro and King, 1996) made it essential to have the 'high-concept' elements in place to ensure that a film would 'open'.

Niche markets

In the late 1990s, some commentators saw the commercial success of low-budget independent films such as *Pulp Fiction* (1994; see case study) and *Four Weddings and a Funeral* (1994) as indicative of a new era of the major independent (Thompson, 1995; see also The major independents, p. 54). However, 'independence' increasingly functions as a niche-marketing aspect of the production-distribution policies of the majors rather than as a separate endeavour. The fortunes of African-American cinema are a case in point (see Oscar Micheaux and African-American cinema, p. 77; Blaxploitation, p. 301). Although a black film-making presence has existed since the 1910s, controversy surrounds the extent of African-American involvement and the representations of black Americans in Hollywood films. Just before the 1996 Academy Awards, Reverend Jesse Jackson protested against the paucity of black nominees and accused Hollywood of 'cultural distortion'. Denzel Washington, a major black star since the 1990s, has said that he had no one of colour to look to as he learned his craft because no black dramatic actors were stars. This situation has been partly redressed with the success of actors such as Washington himself, Whoopi Goldberg (see Contemporary stardom, p. 131), Morgan Freeman, Louis Gossett Jr, Laurence Fishburne and Samuel L. Jackson, as well as younger actors such as Angela Bassett, Cuba Gooding Jr and Halle Berry.

Spike Lee heads the list of black directors who came to prominence in the 1980s and 1990s. Lee's *She's Gotta Have It*

(1986) cost $175,000 and made $8 million, while in 1989 *Do the Right Thing* cost $6.5 million and made $28 million. Lee's success paved the way for the brief flowering of New Black Cinema in the 1990s, when the Hudlin brothers' hip-hop movie *House Party* (1990) and Mario Van Peebles's *New Jack City* (1991) each grossed more than $50 million. Many of these film-makers acknowledge the role of black film-makers of the 1960s and 1970s in making their achievements possible. Spike Lee has cited the influence of Sidney Poitier, and cast Ossie Davis, director of *Cotton Comes to Harlem* (1970), in *Do the Right Thing* and *Jungle Fever* (1991), while Melvin Van Peebles, director of *Sweet Sweetback's Baad Asssss Song* (1971), has a cameo in his son's *New Jack City*. In 1988, Keenen Ivory Wayans's *I'm Gonna Git You Sucka* pastiched the 1970s cycle of blaxploitation films such as *Shaft* (1971), *Slaughter* (1972) and *Superfly* (1972), enabling some of the original actors (Jim Brown, Isaac Hayes) to reprise their earlier performances. But Hollywood's involvement in black film-making is part of its drive towards niche marketing: it remains interested only so long as the films provide successful economic returns. When Warners refused to give Spike Lee the extra $5 million he needed to complete *Malcolm X* (1992), he eventually raised the money from fellow black celebrities Bill Cosby and Oprah Winfrey. The position of black women film-makers is even more tenuous. Julie Dash's award-winning *Daughters of the Dust* (1991) found an audience and made money but only with the help of a dedicated group of people who contacted black churches, social organisations, television and radio stations and newspapers (Belton, 1994, p. 340).

The increasing critical and consumer attention paid to independent cinema confirms the unstable nature of patterns of cinemagoing and taste. As Schatz wrote of *Jaws*:

> Hype and promotion aside, *Jaws*' success ultimately centred on the appeal of the film itself: one enduring verity in the movie business is that, whatever the marketing efforts, only positive audience response and favorable word-of-mouth can propel a film to genuine hit status. (Schatz, 1983, p. 18)

Although it is the unpredictable nature of viewer uptake that has seen 'independent cinema' take on its current importance, there are, as ever, institutional interests working in tandem with such vagaries. Steven Soderbergh's *sex, lies and videotape* (1989) won at Cannes, as did Tarantino's *Pulp Fiction*, which led Lucy Kaylin to celebrate the buoyancy of the sector: 'What *sex, lies* had hinted at, *Pulp Fiction* confirmed – that small budget, auteurist films directed and produced without big-studio interference have the potential to be not only good business, but publicity-generating, star-making, motion-picture events' (Kaylin, 1995, p. 180). The coming to prominence in the 1980s and 1990s of film-makers such as Wayne Wang (*Chan Is Missing*, 1981; *Dim Sum (A Little Bit of Heart)*, 1985; *Smoke*, 1995), Jim Jarmusch (*Stranger than Paradise*, 1984; *Night on Earth*, 1992; *Dead Man*, 1995), Allison Anders (*Gas Food Lodging*, 1992), Carl Franklin (*One False Move*, 1992; *Devil in a Blue Dress*, 1995), the Coen brothers (*Blood Simple*, 1983; *Fargo*, 1996), Hal Hartley (*Trust*, 1990; *Simple Men*, 1992) and Gregg Araki (*The Living End*, 1992; see also Queer theory and New Queer Cinema, p. 505) demonstrated the economic and aesthetic strength of the independents (see Contemporary women directors, p. 68). But in the current situation of unstable markets and their impact on the decisions made by New Hollywood's major players, nothing is guaranteed (see Postwar globalisation, p. 49).

A hard-won success: Julie Dash's *Daughters of the Dust*

Low-budget legend: Melvin Van Peebles's *Sweet Sweetback's Baad Asssss Song*

Selected Reading

John Belton, *American Cinema/American Culture*, New York, McGraw-Hill, 1994. Reprinted 2004.

David Bordwell and Janet Staiger, 'Since 1960: the persistence of a mode of film practice', in Bordwell, Staiger and Thompson, *The Classical Hollywood Cinema: Film Style and Mode of Production to 1960*, London and New York, Routledge and Kegan Paul, 1985.

Thomas Schatz, 'The New Hollywood', in Collins, Radner and Preacher Collins (eds), *Film Theory Goes to the Movies*, New York, Routledge, 1993.

Justin Wyatt, *High Concept: Movies and Marketing in Hollywood*, Austin, University of Texas Press, 1994.

Pulp Fiction (USA 1994 *p.c* – Miramax/Band Apart/Jersey Films; *d* – Quentin Tarantino)

Playing with clichés: *Pulp Fiction*

Although initially Tarantino may have seemed to be the new David Lynch, delivering a cool, stylised *petit guignol* of slapstick and slaughter, his closest links are with the 'film-school generation' and 'movie brats' of the 1970s with whom he shares a love of European cinema combined with mainstream American film.

Tarantino's name for his production company, Band Apart, is taken from the 1964 Godard film, *Bande à part*. Apparently Tarantino showed the dance sequence from Godard's film to John Travolta and Uma Thurman as an example of how he wanted the 'twist' sequence to work in his movie. And the upbeat ending of *Pulp Fiction*, in which a character killed earlier in the film jives out of a diner, shows that Tarantino has taken on board Godard's reply to Georges Franju's exasperated insistence that a film should have a beginning, a middle and an end: 'Yes, but not necessarily in that order'.

Commentary on Tarantino's work centres on the issue of graphic violence. Critical discussion of *Reservoir Dogs* (1992) focused on the fact that a character bleeds on screen for almost the entire film, and on the scene in which one of the gangsters tortures a cop. Tarantino's play with violence is in the cinematic 'blood tragedy/revenge' tradition of Sam Peckinpah's *Bring Me the Head of Alfredo Garcia* (1974), Francis Ford Coppola's *Godfather* trilogy and Tony Scott's *Revenge* (1989). His films mix 'realistic' violence with self-conscious homage, drawing attention to their relationship to earlier cinema, literature and television. When Bruce Willis chooses an appropriate weapon to intervene in the anal rape sequence in *Pulp Fiction* (baseball bat, chainsaw or samurai sword), he is choosing between movie-hero options from *Walking Tall* (1973), *The Texas Chain Saw Massacre* (1974) and *The Yakuza* (1974).

Tarantino describes this process of playing with movie clichés (such as the boxer who throws the fight, or the gangster employee who takes out the boss's girl but must not seduce her) as 'having these old chestnuts and going to the moon with them'. Believing that viewers today are so sophisticated that they can predict which way a film is heading within the first five minutes, he uses this knowledge to play with audience expectations.

In the mid-1990s the Tarantino 'effect' was all-pervasive. *Pulp Fiction* cost $6 million and made over $100 million in the US alone. Debate centred on whether Tarantino was the ultimate postmodern pastiche rip-off artist or represented something genuinely new. After *Kill Bill Vol. 1* (2003) and *Vol. 2* (2004), the jury is still out.

NÖEL KING

Contemporary women directors

YVONNE TASKER

Since the mid-1980s, female directors have operated within Hollywood in significant numbers, yet they remain a minority. The current situation is thus somewhat contradictory in that women directors are visible within, yet marginal to, the institutions of Hollywood cinema. That there is no parity between male and female directors testifies to the consistently male-dominated character of the US film industry (Martha Lauzen's 2005 research suggests that the proportion of features directed by women has rarely exceeded ten per cent and the year-on-year statistics are as likely to move down as up). Contemporary women film-makers' accounts of industry discrimination and sexism are not far removed from the experiences of earlier generations of women who have spoken of repeated setbacks and limiting perceptions of their capabilities.

Directing is a prestige role both in the film industry and outside it; this prestige is evident within film journalism, industry-generated ancillary materials (from press packs to DVD features) and academic film studies (where citing the name of the director alongside a film title remains common practice). Given the status of the role, it is not surprising that women have struggled against long-standing exclusion from this aspect of the industry, in contrast to less high-profile (though significant) areas of film-making such as editing, screenwriting, costuming, set design and production. Neither is it a surprise that the relatively low numbers of features directed by women should be a cause for concern. Thus a burst of newspaper features linked to Sofia Coppola's Best Director nomination for *Lost in Translation* at the 2004 Academy Awards (she won the award for screenwriting) speculated on the economic, cultural and institutional factors responsible for the disproportionate numbers of male directors currently working in Hollywood.

A desire to see women active in all aspects of the film industry, including high-status roles such as director or director of photography, has to do with basic issues of equity. Yet debates around women film-makers are also frequently underpinned by an assumption, or perhaps a hope, that the greater participation of women in key roles might have a significant impact on the kinds of films made in Hollywood. Such debates inevitably overlap with broader questions of gender and representation, a concern with Hollywood's reliance on, and perpetuation of, media stereotypes, from reassuring child-women to bitter career women and eroticised action heroines.

There are at least two dimensions to consider with respect to women directors who work in and around Hollywood. First, there is the involvement of women as directors of mainstream generic films, whether aimed primarily at a female market (*Bridget Jones's Diary*, 2001, directed by Sharon Maguire) or family audiences more generally (Betty Thomas directing the lucrative Eddie Murphy vehicle *Doctor Dolittle*, 1998). The possibility of a female director taking charge of a commercially significant endeavour is itself indicative of change: at least certain women are regarded as a 'safe' option in directorial terms. Women have secured such coveted positions through a number of routes, negotiating an industry in which networking is crucial. The second dimension we can identify in relation to women directors is not so much a question of their objective position within the industry but their relation to an authorial conception of the film-maker as an individual with 'vision'. Within discourses of film authorship, the metaphor of vision is typically understood in terms of creativity and artistry. Significantly, the image of the director as a visionary frequently involves an element of opposition to Hollywood's commercial logic, associating the film-maker with risk and experimentation rather than safety and reliability. These two dimensions are in tension, in that the desire to see women directors incorporated more effectively within the industry is at odds with a desire to see them reject or redefine Hollywood, whether from an explicitly feminist perspective or a more generalised creative impulse of innovation against the reproduction of formula.

JANE CAMPION

Campion achieved international visibility with the commercial and critical success of *The Piano* (1993), becoming perhaps the best-known female director of the decade. Her work as a film-maker both exemplifies and exceeds categories of national, art or feminist cinema. A New Zealander identified firmly with Australian cinema, she has long been a figure on the international stage, working in a variety of national settings. Her made-for-television adaptation of Janet Frame's novels, released theatrically as *An Angel at My Table* (1990), engaged powerfully with female creativity in the context of social containment. Features such as *The Portrait of a Lady* (1996), *Holy Smoke* (1999) and *In the Cut* (2003) use high-profile actors and incorporate the conventions of a number of genres (from heritage cinema to erotic thriller), but are hardly straightforwardly mainstream films. Similarly, while Campion's films are undoubtedly informed by feminism, dealing with questions of female desire and creativity in complex fashion, her work emphasises an almost perverse figuration of female strength, one framed by dysfunctional family groups or structures. The provocative, unruly figure of Dawn/Sweetie in Campion's debut feature *Sweetie* exemplifies this contradictory sense of a powerful female presence contained or constrained.

The extent to which this characteristic kicking against constraint is eroticised is evident in *The Piano*. Although the central protagonist, Ada, is mute within the diegesis, her subjectivity dominates the film. Ada's silence in terms of speech is counterpointed with her playing, the piano becoming a structuring metaphor for expression. The prominence accorded to Michael Nyman's score emphasises the centrality of Ada's musical voice within the film. Her resistance to the male-defined world in which she operates (most evident in her refusal to speak) situates Ada as a troublesome female, yet she is far from a straightforward cipher for feminist rebellion. One of the film's most evocative images – that of Ada, her daughter and the piano landed on a beach – tellingly pictures both characters and instrument as out of place.

The Piano's successful staging of female desire and feminine suffering in a male-dominated society indicated the possibilities of a feminist-informed art cinema characterised by visual pleasure and high production values, and capable of attracting substantial audiences. The presence of Hollywood actors (Holly Hunter and Harvey Keitel), period detail and location shooting combined with the ambiguity associated with art cinema seemed both distinctive and emblematic of a marketable art (or, in the US, independent) cinema that draws on Hollywood while serving as a counter to it. On one hand the film's relatively superficial treatment of indigenous women points to *The Piano*'s continuities with Hollywood hierarchies. However, *The Piano* employs both a relatively straightforward narrative with connections to the Gothic, and a more ambivalent and ambiguous tale associated with art cinema. Far less well received, *In the Cut* reworks film noir through themes of erotic discovery as self-discovery prevalent within women's fiction and erotic thrillers. Frannie's (Meg Ryan) inadvertent involvement in a dark world of sex and crime seemed to challenge critical definitions of Campion as feminist film-maker. *In the Cut* is an uncomfortable film in many ways; perceived by many as yielding to genre (even cliché), the film can be read as a provocative engagement with film noir's exploitation of female sexuality. From a contemporary perspective, it is Campion's ability to synthesise a range of film-making traditions that makes her films so distinctive.

YVONNE TASKER

Provocative: Meg Ryan and Mark Ruffalo in *In the Cut*

MIRA NAIR

Born in India and educated in the US, Nair is a celebrated transnational film-maker whose work is characterised by diversity. From award-winning documentaries and film essays, such as the controversial *India Cabaret* (1986), to genre cinema, Nair has demonstrated a commitment to the representation of disenfranchised, marginal figures. Her work is also centrally concerned with gender: consider the different ways in which *India Cabaret* and, ten years later, the contentious feature *Kama Sutra: A Tale of Love* (1996) question the presentation of Indian women, emphasising double standards in the former, foregrounding eroticism in the latter.

Nair attracted international attention with her debut feature *Salaam Bombay!* (1988), a fiction film that exploits the potential of vérité to convey the precarious life of its young male protagonist, who travels to the city in search of employment. Following the success of *Salaam Bombay!*, Nair worked with the conventions of genre cinema in distinctive fashion, making films in Hollywood and India. Her first US feature, *Mississippi Masala* (1991), was an interracial romance set in the American South. The film focuses on the developing relationship between Mina (Sarita Choudhury) and Demetrius (Denzel Washington), and the opposition the couple face from their respective families in terms that mobilise judgments of class, culture and race. This romantic narrative is framed by the issues posed in the film's opening sequence, set in 1972, in which the young Mina and her family are ejected from Uganda. Here Nair characteristically explores themes of diasporic identities through the frame of romance. Indeed, *Mississippi Masala*, the subsequent US feature *The Perez Family* (1995) and *Monsoon Wedding* (2001), a comedy produced in India, all stage themes of migration and cultural dislocation explored in Nair's 1982 documentary *So Far From India* within the different context of genre. Thus Nair's career to date is more than a straightforward move from documentary to feature films or vérité to genre cinema. Her work consistently demonstrates an awareness of the politics of film-making, whether that means a refusal to cast the subjects of her documentaries as passive, or using popular genres such as romance to explore power hierarchies. Nair's support for the training of film-makers in East Africa via the Maisha Film Lab demonstrates a further dimension to this political commitment: as the project's website pragmatically observes, 'If we don't tell our stories, no one else will' (see www.maishafilmlab.com).

YVONNE TASKER

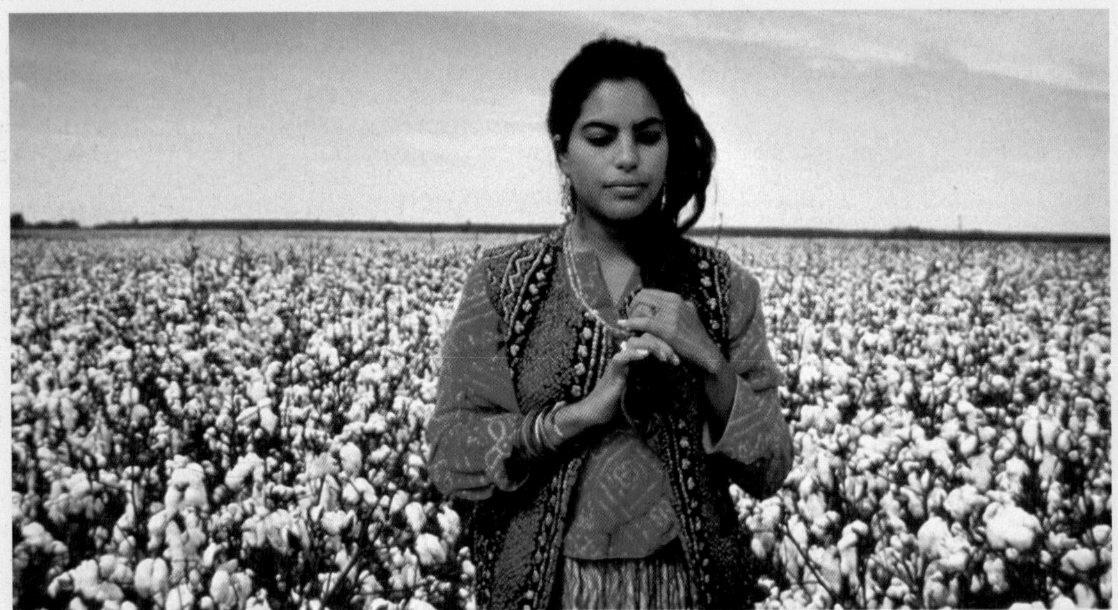

Exploring diasporic experiences through romance: *Mississippi Masala*

Coupling the often apolitical, abstracted conception of the director's vision to gender is both fruitful and problematic for feminism. The fact that women directors working in Hollywood are often associated with lower-status, female-centred genres such as romantic comedy has proved to be an additional obstacle in their assimilation to such a model of authorial vision. Nonetheless, some contemporary women directors, such as Jane Campion and Allison Anders, are evidently committed to a feminist-informed cinema that generates complex female characters. Developing films concerned with diverse female lives, exploring themes of agency, generation and desire, both women have been discussed in terms of their ability to evidence female (and for some critics, feminist) authorship. Both Campion and Anders can be reconciled to a model of female authorship and, indeed, a film-making practice shaped in many ways by feminism. Yet a conception of specifically female vision can be unhelpfully reductive, leaving little space for an account of a number of successful women directors such as Nancy Meyers or, rather differently, Sofia Coppola. Neither of these film-makers produces work that can straightforwardly be termed feminist. Nonetheless, Meyers's work as a scriptwriter, and subsequently as director of romantic comedies, undoubtedly responds to contemporary gender politics in creative fashion, while Coppola's features certainly pose issues of gender and agency.

Feminist perspectives on female authorship

In an influential study of feminism and female authorship, Judith Mayne writes that, while feminist scholarship has extensively analysed popular cinema in a process of reading against the grain, '[s]urprisingly little comparable attention has been paid . . . to the function and position of the woman director' (1990, p. 98). Here and in her study of Dorothy Arzner (1995), one of the very few female directors to work regularly in the studio era, Mayne interrogates the ways in which a woman film-maker working within dominant cinema might be seen to trouble Hollywood's gender hierarchies. Earlier feminist scholars, notably Claire Johnston (1974; 1975), have considered Arzner to be something of a limit case: a female director working in a male-dominated genre cinema who arguably produces a space for female agency, albeit of a particular kind (see also Authorship and cinema, p. 468). Since women directors were virtually absent from the studio era, feminist perspectives on classical Hollywood typically focused on textual strategies, reading films for their misogyny and for moments of resistance. Just as significantly, the energy informing the expansion of feminist film scholarship during the 1970s was also apparent in the feminist film-making that flourished within the avant-garde, and to some extent the international art cinema. Film-makers such as Laura Mulvey and Peter Wollen, Sally Potter, and Yvonne Rainer embodied a model of feminist authorship very different from the perspectives associated with a popularised concept of the male auteur producing art in the context of Hollywood's genre/star-centred studio system.

While it is the case that more published work has been devoted to experimental women film-makers, feminist scholars have demonstrated growing interest in the work of women film-makers operating in and around Hollywood, taking on some of the questions that Mayne poses as to the possibility of female authorship within a commercial context. Christina Lane (2000), for instance, analyses in detail five women directors (Martha Coolidge, Kathryn Bigelow, Lizzie Borden, Darnell Martin and Tamra Davis) who she characterises as moving from what can broadly be termed independent production to careers within Hollywood or commercial cinema. In titling her book *Feminist Hollywood*, Lane points to a very different reading of commercial film culture, emphasising the relationship and blurring of boundaries between counter-cinema and mainstream cinema consequent in part on the career trajectories of the individual film-makers who move between these spaces. Scholars such as Lane approach these questions of female and feminist authorship in a subtly transformed context that sees feminist themes played out in a diverse range of narrative and genre films.

Writing in the mid-1990s, Laurie Ouellette identifies Jane Campion as representative of 'a growing number of female directors who are negotiating feminism, along with other political and social issues, within the conventions and structures of popular narrative film-making' (1995, p. 29). The film-makers Ouellette highlights, such as Allison Anders and Nancy Savoca, can also be contextualised in relation to well-regarded directors such as Mira Nair, Marlene Gorris and Sally Potter who were active in 1990s international art cinema. These film-makers all work in different ways with feminist film-making, deploying and reinflecting the genres and codes of narrative rather than avant-garde or other experimental modes of cinema. Potter's transition from her early work in the avant-garde is indicative: from *Thriller*, her 1979 landmark reworking of *La Bohème*, to an art cinema that, while still challenging, is more accessible – for example, *Orlando* (1992), and more recently *Yes* (2004), an evocative elaboration of East/West power hierarchies (see also Feminist film theory, p. 491).

Industry and genre: women directors in Hollywood

While relatively few women directed features during the 1970s, the 1980s saw a significant expansion in the numbers of women film-makers working in and at the margins of Hollywood cinema. The decade featured a number of notable successes (critical and/or commercial) and directing debuts from women who would become important figures for those who followed them. Such diverse film-makers as Amy Heckerling, Penelope Spheeris, Susan Seidelman, Kathryn Bigelow and Penny Marshall achieved new levels of visibility in the 1980s. New York University and American Film Institute (AFI) graduate Amy Heckerling found commercial and critical success with her 1982 feature debut, *Fast Times at Ridgemont High*, an innovative teen movie combining comedy and drama. Heckerling subsequently wrote and directed the 1989 comedy *Look Who's Talking* (and the 1990 sequel, *Look Who's Talking Too*), apparently in response to her own experience of motherhood, securing a further comic success with *Clueless* (1995), a satirical teen movie that loosely adapted Jane Austen. Penny Marshall's 1980s successes with comedy (for example, the 1988 hit *Big*) paved the way for more dramatic successes in *Awakenings* (1990) and the comically inflected, female-focused drama *A League of Their Own* (1992), which uses the lives of female baseball players during World War II to elaborate themes of female aspiration, achievement and containment. Marshall's most recent film as director, *Riding in Cars with Boys* (2001), again combines comedy and drama to address the constraints shaping women's lives past and present.

Heckerling and Marshall's associations with genres such as comedy are indicative of the position of women directors more generally. Those who have scored significant commercial successes (within the top ten performing films) since the mid-1980s have typically done so in genres such as comedy or romance. Nora Ephron's *Sleepless in Seattle* (1993) is a self-reflexive romantic comedy, building on Ephron's success with the genre as a writer (the 1989 hit *When Harry Met Sally ...*, for instance) and underlining the renewed commercial potential of the genre. Ephron continued to work in romantic comedy with *You've Got Mail* (1998) and, more recently, the archly self-conscious *Bewitched* (2005). Nancy Meyers too has achieved considerable commercial success with the romantic comedies *What Women Want* (2000) and *Something's Gotta Give* (2003), films that combine strong female characters with a narrative focus on male melodramas of mid-life crisis and ageing.

In an era of escalating costs, women directors have not generally been associated with big-budget productions or with the genres (fantasy, action and adventure) that require expansive budgets for effects. But despite the preponderance of romantic and comic formats, there are women directors who have worked in more spectacular or action-oriented genres, such as Kathryn Bigelow, who has attracted considerable scholarly attention, and Mimi Leder (with *The Peacemaker* in 1997 and *Deep Impact* the following year). As Rachel Williams (2004) demonstrates, the atypicality of a female director in the genre was effectively used

ROSE TROCHE

Troche established herself as a key figure in New Queer Cinema with the low-budget lesbian romance *Go Fish* (1994), co-written with Guinevere Turner. Exemplifying the freshness of a reinvigorated independent cinema, the film employed black-and-white cinematography, an ensemble cast and a playful style. With its romance plot, direct address and location shooting, *Go Fish* seemed both innovative and familiar. The film's innovation lies in the way it plays with cultural tropes such as the makeover, investing them with significance for lesbian audiences. Max's (Guinevere Turner) courtship of Ely (V. S. Brodie) overturns the coming-out format deployed by some lesbian romances, while pivoting on the attraction between different personalities. This relationship develops within the context of a lesbian community who comment on events at length, whether with concern or humour, mirroring the film's successful address to lesbian audiences.

Independent cinema reinvigorated: *Go Fish*

New Queer Cinema was defined by a refusal of essentialist identity categories, and Troche's subsequent features, *Bedrooms and Hallways* (1998) and *The Safety of Objects* (2001), worked against expectations created by the cult success of *Go Fish* as a lesbian film (see also Queer theory and New Queer Cinema, p. 505). An exploration of sexuality and relationships centred on men, *Bedrooms and Hallways* reworked genres such as romance and romantic comedy for lesbian and gay audiences. This British comedy had European funding, and Troche has claimed that she cannot get US funding for her projects. Yet *The Safety of Objects* seemed to confirm her location within independent American cinema, echoing themes of the family as dystopian site of secrecy.

More recently Troche has worked as director and writer on Showtime's successful television series *The L Word* (2004–), a lesbian series with evident crossover markets. Troche's work on *The L Word* underlines the extent to which television functions as an important site for contemporary women film-makers.

YVONNE TASKER

as a marketing hook for *Deep Impact*, contrasting Leder's emotion-centred apocalypse to the season's rival movie *Armageddon* (1998). While Leder achieved a top ten box-office ranking for her spectacular apocalypse scenario, her subsequent feature work has focused on more emotionally led material (*Pay It Forward*, 2000), more familiar territory for female directors.

If Leder's experience suggests the possibility of movement between genres popularly regarded as male and female, critical interest in Bigelow is in some ways a function of her assumed gender transgression. Feminist critics, including Cook (2005) and Lane (2000), have framed Bigelow's 1990s features such as *Blue Steel* (1990), *Point Break* (1991) and *Strange Days* (1995) as innovative genre hybrids allowing for complex and rewarding explorations of gender and race. *Blue Steel*, for instance, exploits the gender/sexual tension of a female rookie cop, situating her as victim and avenger in response to the obsessive attentions of a serial killer. Here it is precisely the facility to redefine genre that is held to generate an authorial position for the woman director. While Bigelow's films are fascinating and evocative instances of genre hybridity, it is worth noting the desire for a disruption of the Hollywood genre system that underpins much scholarly interest in her work.

Critical expectations that women film-makers will bring something significantly different to the US film industry need to be tempered by acknowledgment of the still precarious position of those women who secure the opportunity to direct. How precarious this position is can be underlined by a consideration of patchy career patterns, particularly those of women directors who have established themselves via more challenging or unconventional material. Mary Harron was fêted for *I Shot Andy Warhol* (1996) but did not direct another feature until *American Psycho* (2000), following up in 2005 with a long-nurtured project, *The Notorious Bettie Page*. *Monster* (2003) director Patty Jenkins, a graduate of the AFI's workshop programme, has since worked in television. Following her success with the crossover hit *Girlfight* (2000), Karyn Kusama's next directorial credit was a high-profile but poorly received science-fiction fantasy, *Aeon Flux* (2005). Produced by the well-established figure Gale Ann Hurd and starring Charlize Theron fresh from her Oscar-winning success as Aileen Wuornos in *Monster*, *Aeon Flux* features the eroticised action heroine popular since the late 1990s, very different in kind from the portrayal of Diana Gusman's (Michelle Rodriguez) provocative entry into the world of boxing in *Girlfight*. The disappointing performance of *Aeon Flux* commercially is likely to hinder Kusama's subsequent career, just as the poor box-office performance of *Strange Days* seems to have impacted on Bigelow's.

Various critics have commented on the difficulty of following up a success, commercial or critical, a problem that is particularly acute for women film-makers. The more general issue at stake here has to do with the credibility of the woman director in an industry suspicious of women's capabilities. Many cite industry perceptions that women make films that do not make money as accounting for their scarcity as directors, although Lauzen notes that: 'The notion that films made by women don't earn as much just doesn't hold up' (quoted in Goldberg, 2002). Working against such assumptions, those women directors who have been active during and since the 1980s have followed a number of routes into that coveted role. Film school or other schemes (such as those supported by the AFI) have provided training and support, enabling the production of short films and the opportunity to develop projects. Both Kathryn Bigelow and Jane Campion came to film-making from a fine arts/film school background; Campion's *Peel* (1982), made while she was a film student in Australia, was subsequently awarded Best Short Film at Cannes. Both women's debut features – Bigelow's *The Loveless* (1981), co-directed with Monty Montgomery, and Campion's *Sweetie* (1989) – indicate their location in the context of art-house or counter-cinema rather than mainstream film-making. Renowned experimental film-maker Julie Dash (*Daughters of the Dust*, 1991) studied at the AFI and at UCLA during a time of intense creative and political energy in the generation of an independent black cinema in the US.

In terms of women film-makers raising funds for a project or getting attached to an existing feature, personal connections have undoubtedly been significant. While some insist that women should do more to argue their own case, seize the opportunities that do exist, many women working in the industry describe the informal networks that have proved so vital to securing finance and support as male-dominated (see Goldberg, 2002). In this context, it is noteworthy that so many women have secured an entry to directing through building on success in other areas of film production, such as performance (Jodie Foster, Kasi Lemmons, Penny Marshall, Barbra Streisand) and screenwriting (Nora Ephron, Nancy Meyers). Others have built on directing experience gained in television (Mimi Leder, Betty Thomas, Mary Harron). Indeed, television has provided a vital source of employment for many women directors including Allison Anders, Kathryn Bigelow and Rose Troche.

The greater numbers of women directing in television is telling. On one hand, there is greater permeability between the media, with television driven by a search for content. Such permeability is heightened by the ways in which companies such as HBO and Showtime have become associated with innovative film-making, with well-known women film-makers such as Mira Nair directing features for cable (for example, her 2002 *Hysterical Blindness*). Lane (2004) cites Nair, who characterises HBO as 'the independent filmmaker studio' capable of respecting a filmmaker's vision, while Anders's *Things Behind the Sun* (2001) was screened on Showtime, effectively securing an audience. On the other hand, as Lane notes, the phenomenon is doubled-edged, since: 'Even premiere cable networks are sometimes portrayed within the industry as a "female other" in relation to the "masculine" sphere of theatrical indie film' (2004, p. 200).

Independent cinema

Since the early 1990s, the viability of US independent production has provided an important space within which women film-makers have been able to develop relatively low-budget,

Resisting Hollywood hierarchies: Leslie Harris's *Just Another Girl on the I. R. T.*

distinctive films centred on women. What Kathleen Rowe Karlyn describes as independent cinema's 'self-conscious, irreverent and funky countervoice to mainstream filmmaking' (1998, p. 169) has allowed women directors opportunities to counter Hollywood's male-focused imagination. Karlyn cites Allison Anders's *Gas Food Lodging* (1992) as 'recombining and hybridizing mainstream genres' (p. 184), finding new uses for Hollywood conventions around motherhood, female sexuality and coming-of-age narratives.

Similar processes of generic appropriation and inversion can be seen at work in other mid-1990s examples, such as *Just Another Girl on the I. R. T.* (Leslie Harris, 1992) and *I Shot Andy Warhol*. *Just Another Girl* makes the most of the mobile camera, focusing on Chantel (Ariyan Johnson), an African-American teen struggling to deal with an unplanned pregnancy. Placing a young black woman firmly at the centre of the film goes against the hierarchies of Hollywood cinema. While Harris raised the money for the shoot from various sources, including grants and individuals, Miramax financed post-production and, as Lane (2004) notes, worked to get Harris into a variety of local and national media outlets while promoting the film. *I Shot Andy Warhol*, produced by Christine Vachon and Tom Kalin, both important figures in the New Queer Cinema of the early 1990s (see Queer theory and New Queer Cinema, p. 505), offers a portrait of 1960s radical feminist Valerie Solanas. It tackles a figure who personifies much of what the culture fears about feminism: political antipathy towards men, lesbianism, prostitution, female violence, madness and social disruption. Both a period piece and an attempt at feminist social history, the film did not automatically represent an entrance to directing more commercial projects for Harron.

Neither *Just Another Girl* nor *I Shot Andy Warhol* is easy to assimilate within the context of mid-1990s Hollywood. More recent films such as *Girlfight*, *Real Women Have Curves* (Patricia Cardoso, 2002) and *Monster* suggest the range of possibilities that independent production offers to women film-makers in terms of the production of a female-centred and feminist-informed cinema. Kusama's *Girlfight* juxtaposes a teen rites-of-passage drama, family melodrama and a romance plot with the generic context of the sports movie. Negotiating stereotypes of tough Latinas and 'masculine' female athletes, *Girlfight* capitalised on contemporary media interest in women's boxing without reproducing the typically exploitative terms of that interest. *Real Women Have Curves* also employs a rites-of-passage narrative, mapping Ana's (America Ferrera) transition from high school to adult life via a stint in her sister's clothing factory. The film offers an engagement with the parameters and strictures of societal standards of beauty and body size/shape as well as a critique of the exploitative economics of fashion. Casting Charlize Theron as the star of *Monster* enabled significant distribution and media attention for Jenkins's debut film, a dramatisation of the life of convicted killer Aileen Wuornos. In very different ways these films combine and make use of a range of established genres (*Monster* features tropes of Gothic horror and rape-revenge within its complex character study). Both films were innovative, and each had evident potential for marketing beyond the festival circuit. As such, they speak to the impact of commercial connections between mainstream and independent production. Indeed, as Christina Lane notes, the increasing dominance of a 'mini-major' model of independent production has impacted on women film-makers in particular, as well as working more generally to squeeze out 'avant-garde film and, to some extent, documentary' (2004, p. 195), both forms central to traditions of feminist film-making (see The major independents, p. 54). The marketability of male auteurs and the crossover potential of films with violent content frequently conflict with the projects independent women film-makers are keen to develop. Lane writes: 'From development to reception, the male-oriented gangster or thriller genres, and the quirky "loser" film, have helped to condition major independent studios' idea about what makes money and what makes film sense' (2004, p. 204).

Through the 1990s and 2000s, women directors have remained a small but constant presence working within and at the margins of Hollywood film production. It is changes in the industry as much as changes in social attitudes that have supported this development, with the impact of film school training, of directing opportunities in television and, crucially, a burgeoning independent production sector with ever-closer links to the commercial institutions of Hollywood. These factors are doubled-edged, however: though film schools have opened up to women, this does not translate into directing features; television is both a crucial source of employment and a less prestigious arena to which women film-makers are effectively relegated; and the increasing connection between independent and mainstream production ('indiewood') has resulted in an increasing emphasis on films with the potential for commercial crossover. As Lane suggests, the incompatibility of many independent films directed by women with this emphasis has tended to squeeze out women directors, particularly women of colour and those committed to more experimental material (2004, pp. 204–6).

While there is a danger of speculative or essentialist logic in linking women directors to female interest and to female or feminist authorship, it is the case that many of the women mentioned above have developed and directed films centred on female protagonists, effectively mobilising, in one way or another, themes of gender trouble. More generally, the production of a feminist-informed cinema in the context of a post-feminist culture poses new challenges to the conception of female authorship and the analysis of women film-makers. In a media culture that assumes the success or completion (and consequent redundancy) of feminism, posing questions about female authorship (or even simply drawing attention to the inequality that persists within the industry) means asserting the continuing relevance of gender politics.

Selected Reading

Christina Lane, *Feminist Hollywood: From 'Born in Flames' to 'Point Break'*, Detroit, MI, Wayne State University Press, 2000.

Christina Lane, 'Just another girl outside the neo-indie', in Holmlund and Wyatt (eds), *Contemporary American Independent Film: From the Margins to the Mainstream*, New York, Routledge, 2004.

Judith Mayne, *The Woman at the Keyhole: Feminism and Women's Cinema*, Bloomington, Indiana University Press, 1990.

Laurie Ouellette, 'Reel women: feminism and narrative pleasure in new women's cinema', *The Independent Film and Video Monthly*, April 1995, pp. 28–34.

New distribution, exhibition and reception contexts

BARBARA KLINGER

When film historians discuss film distribution, exhibition and reception, they often do so with an implicit understanding of industry practices and the film experience itself as defined by the public motion-picture theatre. With its sizeable, brilliantly lit screen, darkness and (ideally) hushed atmosphere, the theatre appears to be the quintessential venue for movie events and for defining the milieu in which audiences consume films. This comprehension continues to be important to grasping a substantial portion of cinema's circulation.

However, accounts of Hollywood cinema's theatrical life tell only a part of the story. Although commercial films have appeared outside of dedicated movie theatres since the medium's late-nineteenth-century origins, the enormity of cinema's extra-theatrical existence appears particularly clear in more recent years. In the last three decades in the US, new distribution windows have not only proliferated, but in some cases, such as VHS and DVD, have generated substantially more revenue than the box office. Along with these two formats, cable TV, satellite TV, the Internet and other venues have offered consumers movies in record numbers, transforming the American motion-picture business and moviegoing itself and making the home into a lucrative and significant locus for the film experience. Today the digital home theatre is a mainstay of movie consumption and the centre of technological innovations, from multi-channel surround-sound systems to widescreen HDTVs and high-definition DVD players, meant to rival the quality of the theatre's presentation of films without reproducing the inconveniences associated with excursions to the multiplex.

Among digital media, DVD and the Internet provide two vivid and different views of the impact of new distribution and exhibition outlets on contemporary cinema. DVD rose quickly in the ranks of home entertainment devices to become an essential source of income for movie studios and a routine feature of household movie consumption. By contrast, the Internet emerged more slowly as a possible venue for legitimate commercial film presentation, its usefulness as a window for Hollywood's wares complicated by technological, legal and economic issues.

Introduced in the US in 1997, DVD is considered the most successful home entertainment device in the nation's history in terms of its rapid penetration of the home market – faster than television, VCRs and CDs. Six years after its introduction, DVD players were in more than half of US households, with penetration rates in Europe and other overseas markets lower, but on the rise. By mid-2006, less than 20 per cent of American homes were without at least one DVD player (Pogue, 2006). Meanwhile, DVD rentals and sales were proving immensely profitable for Hollywood. By 2001, films began to generate more revenue from their DVD release than from their theatrical premieres (including such films as *The Fast and the Furious* and *Training Day*). In 2004, North American box-office tallies amounted to $10.2 billion; home video rental and purchase amounted to $25.95 billion – more than double the theatrical take – with $16 billion coming from DVD sales alone (Sporich, 2005).

VHS and earlier ancillary media paved the way for DVD, establishing foundations of distribution in brick-and-mortar outlets and mail-order companies, and making movies part of the home's entertainment landscape. But DVD's ascendancy owes additionally to its economic, technological and aesthetic advantages over VHS. DVD costs far less to manufacture than VHS; due to its quality and comparative lack of degeneration in playback, it is also more strongly identified with the sell-through market. Both of these considerations mean larger profits for studios and distributors. Further, given its audio-visual quality, DVD is well suited to the digital environments that increasingly define home entertainment. From its inception, DVD was exceptionally versatile: its equipment could play CDs, allowing it to both capitalise on the CD's success and provide a device that could perform double entertainment duty; meanwhile, it became a fixture in computers, laptops and gaming systems. Through such affiliations, DVD has been advantageously positioned to become an indispensable part of a high-tech universe of home and personal technologies.

As it has assumed a prominent role in home entertainment, DVD has elicited reconsideration of assumptions about cinema as a purely theatrical medium and of the public theatre's centrality to the business and experience of cinema. Other previous forms of home film distribution, such as network and cable television and VHS, have been immensely significant to studio economics and cinema's social circulation. However, perhaps because DVD provides an example of a particularly successful embodiment of the highly touted 'digital revolution', it has managed to challenge more visibly the notion of theatrical primacy – the motion-picture theatre's status as the principal means of introducing a film to the public. Some media executives already discuss theatrical exhibition now as nothing more than a preview for successive DVD releases, merchandising and other spin-off activities. While the issue of primacy is still subject to debate, no one would deny DVD's centrality to the media businesses, nor the fact that it has spawned a 'DVD nation' of home viewers.

DVD raises questions about another aspect of theatrical primacy as well: it undermines the intimate relationship presumed to exist between theatrical prints and authenticity. The DVD market generates multiple versions that transform films as they

Generating revenue from DVD release: *The Fast and the Furious*

originally appeared in theatres. Director's cuts, extended editions, audio commentary and other features are frequently sold to consumers as representing the director's original intentions, intentions that were unable to be realised on the silver screen for various reasons (for example, constraints on length, content and technological capabilities). These special editions are thus poised to displace the theatrical version from its usual associations with authenticity or, at least, to trouble easy assumptions about these associations. For instance, how are we to judge which version has greater authenticity: the theatrical screening of *The Lord of the Rings The Fellowship of the Ring* (2001) or the Platinum Series Special Extended Edition DVD that offers the viewer almost 30 more minutes of Tolkien/Jackson's world? As it calls attention to issues of authenticity and authorship, the multiple-version phenomenon also provokes consideration of how marketing strategies manipulate these terms as selling points.

In contrast to the media industry's and consumers' rapid adoption of DVD and its assumption of a privileged place in film exhibition, the Internet's assimilation into the home as a venue for feature films has proceeded more fitfully. On the one hand, studios have eagerly exploited the Web as a fresh display window for their goods. Ads for upcoming releases and news stories about films and celebrities abound. Websites devoted to films have also proliferated. The successful launch of *The Blair Witch Project* (1999) site, blairwitch.com – a site credited with making the low-budget independent horror film a box-office smash – helped to create a vision of the Internet as a potent promotional force. Meanwhile, fan sites (such as *Star Wars*' theforce.net) and information sites (such as IMDB.com) dedicated to films and film stars have sprung up, expanding Hollywood's horizons of advertising while providing a context for fan communities and film cultures to emerge and flourish.

On the other hand, the film industry has been reluctant to embrace the Web as a viable means of feature-film distribution and exhibition. In the early 1990s, technical problems plagued the delivery process, making the Internet an unattractive destination for films. Because feature films constitute large files, attempts to play or download them seemed interminable and could result in system crashes. The images that finally did appear were small, poor in quality and moved jerkily. In the later 1990s and early 2000s, a number of improvements, including streaming video players such as Windows Media Player and broadband technologies such as cable and DSL (Digital Subscriber Line) modems, converted the Internet into a friendlier place for watching movies. By accommodating video files' extensive data, these developments made streaming and downloading movies faster and easier, while delivering better visuals and sound. Viewers equipped with such advances could now expect reasonable quality in their Internet film experience.

Hollywood's investment in the Web, however, was not simply stymied by technological issues. The music business crisis about Napster and illegal file-sharing caused studio executives to regard the Web as a dangerous place; susceptible to pirates and hackers, it seems too risky a venue for theatrical premieres or ancillary releases of features. Indeed, the Motion Picture Association of America (MPAA) considers Internet piracy – 'the downloading or distribution of unauthorised copies of intellectual property such as movies, television, music, games and software programs via the Internet' – as a major threat to the livelihood of the studios and the corporations that own them. Film industry analysts contend that, on unregulated file-sharing sites, such as KaZaA and Morpheus, hundreds of thousands of films are swapped daily. In 2005, the MPAA estimated that its member studios (Paramount Pictures Corporation, Sony Pictures Entertainment Inc., Warner Bros. Entertainment Inc., 20th Century Fox Film Corporation, Universal City Studio LLLP and The Walt Disney Company) 'lost $2.3 billion worldwide to Internet piracy alone' (see www.mpaa.org/piracy).

Of course, Internet piracy constitutes only one form of illegal distribution. Along with other types, such as the camcording of movies in theatres and the unauthorised manufacture and sale of optical discs (that is, DVD, CD, VCD), piracy costs major US studios an estimated $6 billion annually in lost revenue (www.mpaa.org/piracy). Like the Internet, other means of illegally duplicating, distributing and selling motion pictures threaten studio profits, as they often make titles available to audiences before or during the first run in theatres. Although piracy is a problem in the US, the MPAA's deepest anxiety is aroused by international markets, where revenues for studio blockbusters often exceed those of the domestic box office. For instance, while *Titanic* (1997) took in $600 million in the US, it grossed an extraordinary $1.2 billion abroad, making it the first film to reach the $1 billion mark in global theatrical distribution (see Casenet.com/movie and Guinessworldrecords.com, 14 January 2005). Not surprisingly, the film was a hot commodity in less legitimate circles. In China alone, where pirated films constitute 90 per cent of the market, illegal distributors sold an estimated 20–25 million copies of the film (Ming, 2001).

Due to a lack of regulation and/or the ineffective enforcement of copyright laws, international black markets often operate with impunity, making legal action difficult. Spurred on by this problem, the MPAA directs an anti-piracy programme that assists law-enforcement efforts and lobbies Congress to strengthen copyright protections and international trade agreements bearing on piracy. The MPAA has also developed more sophisticated encryption processes for DVD and other venues and has hired companies such as MediaForce to locate Internet copyright violators (www.mpaa.org). Meanwhile, studios have tried to offset piracy's gains through simultaneous worldwide release of some blockbusters, in theory removing a prime incentive for purchasing pirated copies of films, which frequently appear before or shortly after theatrical release.

The film industry's reservations about the Web as a new system of distribution, resulting from uncertainty about how to control and capitalise on its powers of dissemination for feature films, have also generated a different set of tactics. Studios have entered into arrangements with Internet companies wishing to rent and sell their films. One such company, Netflix, has experimented successfully with a mail-order business meant to compete with established brick-and-mortar outlets such as Blockbuster Video. In an attempt to enter more directly into the Internet film business, in 2002 Sony, Universal, Paramount, MGM and Warner Bros. created Movielink, an on-demand Internet service that offers individual titles (encrypted to prevent file-sharing) for downloading. In a similar effort, in 2006, Universal Pictures and Warner Bros. introduced a 'download-to-own' service that serves several European markets, including the UK and Germany (Pfanner, 2006). Attempting to exploit the Internet's resources, such ventures as Movielink and download-to-own services also aim to thwart pirates by making films available inexpensively in an online environment. Given the number of films available illegally online, the studios have an uphill battle on their hands, making the future of this new venue into a hotly contested, high-stakes terrain.

Like DVD, the Internet plays an interesting role in destabilising notions of theatrical primacy. Pirated films appearing online or in kiosks compete aggressively with the theatrical box office. They often represent a de facto form of first-run distribution, while homes and other non-theatrical locales furnish the requisite exhibition screens. At the same time, akin to legitimate releases of films to the international market, piracy, whether via optical disc or the Internet, offers a wonderland of different versions of films; these knock-offs range widely in quality and may be edited, subtitled in a variety of languages and given other touches to make them suitable for destination markets. Legal or illegal, films prepared for worldwide release suggest that the multiple-version phenomenon is a defining condition of cinema's circulation in global markets.

The Internet, although not yet in place as a fully realised legitimate mode of film distribution and exhibition, shares with DVD and other forms of ancillary distribution and exhibition another challenge to theatrical primacy: public theatres no longer dominate the movie experience. In fact, in the US and many other nations, the home is equally or more closely associated with movie consumption. Whether the environment is characterised by a TV monitor and VCR, an expensive home theatre system, a high-speed Internet connection and a computer monitor, or by a laptop screen, watching movies in off-theatre sites is a major constitutive part of contemporary film culture. In this respect, recent developments suggest that the conditions, taste cultures and fandoms that characterise the home as a vital moviegoing space are worth considerable study. Such developments should also inspire exploration of the economic and experiential relationships that exist between home and theatrical modes of exhibition – not separate, but richly and intimately interrelated spheres.

Finally, although their impact is dramatic, it would be a mistake to see today's new media as responsible for utterly transforming film distribution, exhibition and reception. As the film industry continues to 'go digital' and newer technologies continue to broaden the medium's existence in homes, commercial cinema's massive non-theatrical exhibition history, stretching back to its formative years on celluloid formats through its broadcast, cablecast and VHS years to the present, awaits further research. This step is necessary to grasp how studio films have been circulated, interpreted and experienced worldwide in the home's intimate confines and in other locales that, for more than a century, have screened film entertainment for the masses.

Selected Reading

Barbara Klinger, *Beyond the Multiplex: Cinema, New Technologies, and the Home*, Berkeley, University of California Press, 2006.

Toby Miller, Nitin Govil, John McMurria and Richard Maxwell, *Global Hollywood*, London, BFI Publishing, 2001.

Kerry Segrave, *Movies at Home: How Hollywood Came to Television*, Jefferson, NC, McFarland, 1999.

Janet Wasko, *Hollywood in the Information Age: Beyond the Silver Screen*, Austin, University of Texas Press, 1994.

African–American cinema: Oscar Micheaux

NIAMH DOHENY

The success of the Harlem Renaissance in the early 20th century indicated that African-Americans were keen to represent themselves in the arts. However, there were limited options open to them in cinema. Despite the occasional interventionist film, such as *Uncle Tom's Cabin* (1927), *Imitation of Life* (1934) and the short race films made by the Christie Film Company, Hollywood offered little to African-Americans (or indeed to any non-white people). Phyllis Klotman's (1993) essay on the short-lived career of Wallace Thurman in 1930s Hollywood highlights the studios' reluctance to produce any work that dealt with African-Americans in a rounded, humanised manner. Thomas

African-American film pioneer Oscar Micheaux

Cripps's (1978) study of the writer Spencer Williams presents a similar picture of African-American impotence against studio resistance to change. Actors fared no better. Hattie McDaniel and Louise Beavers were forced to 'plump up' in order to maximise the contrast between them and their white female co-stars and were invariably cast as the domestic help (Bogle, 1997). Stepin Fetchit earned a living in the early 1930s playing a series of roles that fed off the coon stereotype. Even Paul Robeson, one of the most successful African-American actors of his day, with leading roles in Hollywood features such as *The Emperor Jones* (1933), complained in the early 1940s about the racial caricatures in Hollywood productions.

In the wake of *The Birth of a Nation* (1915), the black press renewed its calls for an independent African-American cinema. Throughout the 1910s and early 1920s, numerous newspaper columns expounded on the need for African-American film-makers to challenge the Hollywood representations of black Americans and to nurture race pride. Homesteader and novelist Oscar Micheaux made his first movie in 1919, launching a career that spanned 40 years and yielded nearly 50 feature-length films, making him the most prolific and enduring African-American film-maker in the first half of the 20th century. His films played a significant part in the development of the race movie from the start.

Working with a maximum budget of $15,000 per film, Micheaux served as writer, director, producer, distributor and promoter on his productions. In terms of distribution, the pinnacle of his career occurred in the early 1920s when he had distribution agencies in Chicago, New York, Texas, London and Paris. Although research has suggested that *Within Our Gates* (1919) and *The Brute* (1920) were exhibited in Europe, his films were not marketed to white audiences in the US, despite Micheaux's wishes (Sampson, 1995). One of the difficulties faced by early African-American film-makers was the lack of infrastructure: with no central film exchange to facilitate distribution,

Within Our Gates (USA 1919 *p.c* – Micheaux Book and Film Company; *d* – Oscar Micheaux)

Within Our Gates was Micheaux's second film and is the earliest extant production. The narrative follows Sylvia Landry (Evelyn Preer) in her quest to find financial backing in Chicago for a Southern school for African-American children. In the process, she meets and falls in love with Dr Vivian (Charles D. Lucas). An extended flashback sequence shows the lynching of her parents by a frenzied white mob in the South and her own lucky escape when a would-be white rapist, Armand Gridlestone (Grant Gorman), recognises her as his daughter from an earlier 'legitimate marriage' to an African-American woman.

Reversing *The Birth of a Nation*: *Within Our Gates*

Within Our Gates enjoyed good box-office returns on its release, despite difficulties with the censor over its lynching/rape episode (Gaines, 1993; Sampson, 1995; Peterson, 1992), a scene that marked Micheaux's unequivocal rebuttal of *The Birth of a Nation*'s racialised characterisation. Unlike Griffith's noble Klansmen, Micheaux's white lynch mob comprised men, women and children who were motivated by bloodlust rather than justice. Sylvia's rape by her white father refuted Gus's lust for Flora in *The Birth of a Nation* and in the process recast the stereotype of the black buck, driven by his insatiable obsessions with white flesh. In *Within Our Gates*, sexual transgression was the remit of the white characters alone. The historical account of interracial relations was rewritten from the viewpoint of the violated African-American in Gridlestone's attempted rape of Sylvia, rehabilitating African-American female virtue in the wake of Griffith's portrayal of the lascivious Lydia.

Another misrepresentation corrected was that of the coon stereotype. Efrem (E. G. Tatum) and Old Ned inhabit the coon role to ingratiate themselves with white society – Efrem informs on the Landrys and Old Ned degrades himself for money – but both are punished as a result. Efrem is lynched by the whites he entertained and Ned is filled with self-loathing. More importantly, with these characters Micheaux displays that the coon is simply a disguise assumed by opportunist African-Americans. Thus, he simultaneously reappropriates the caricature and exorcises it.

Besides refuting earlier misrepresentations of the African-American, *Within Our Gates* represented Micheaux's most overt effort to address the political discrimination of the black community. In several scenes, the narrative highlights the discrepancy between government spending on white and black children's education. His films were never again so openly critical of the white establishment, possibly due to the adverse reaction he received from the censors.

NIAMH DOHENY

Veiled Aristocrats (USA 1932 *p.c* – Micheaux Film Corporation; *d* – Oscar Micheaux)

This movie focuses on the light-skinned Rena Walden (Lucille Lewis), who is compelled by her brother to join him in passing for white, despite her

Problems of 'passing': *Veiled Aristocrats*

reluctance to leave her 'coal black' fiancé and her mother. Although the white community is unaware of their true identity, the African-American servants are cognisant of the fact and pity Rena in her misery. Unable to bear the charade, Rena eventually leaves her brother's comfortable house and returns home. Contemporary culture plays an aesthetic and political role in this film, as Micheaux often employs it to cultivate race pride among African-Americans.

Micheaux based the script on Charles Chesnutt's novel *The House behind the Cedars* (1900), adapting it freely to suit his own purpose. While Chesnutt's Rena emphasised the advantages of passing, Micheaux's Rena displays the misery that isolation from African-American society could bring. In this way, a character's initial rejection of the race and the black community is transformed into the film-maker's celebration of both.

The film devotes ten of its 53 minutes running time to the performance of jazz and tap numbers, and music plays an important role in the movie's race-building efforts. 'River Stay 'Way from My Door', the 1931 hit by the white writers Mort Dixon and Harry Woods, is a case in point. As it is performed by an African-American maid who assumes a broad Southern accent for the song, the piano accompaniment plays the main line from Stephen Foster's 'Swanee River' in between verses, providing an ironic commentary on the latter's misty-eyed sentiment. In 'River Stay 'Way', the river threatens to sweep away her meagre belongings and ruin her cabin. In her rejection of the river, there is also a rejection of the romanticising impulse of white minstrel songs that would cover up the hardship and suffering on which the graceful plantation life that they lamented was founded.

Less political is the inclusion of Fats Waller's hit from the previous year, 'Draggin' My Heart Around' (written by the African-American Alex Hill), performed by Mabel Garrett in an extended musical sequence that halts the plot for over six minutes. The inclusion of such musical numbers had several benefits. Apart from showcasing Micheaux's use of sound, they attracted audiences that did not have the opportunity to attend a live performance in a Harlem nightclub. *Veiled Aristocrats*' engagement with contemporary culture functions not only to display the talents of a hitherto marginalised group of performers, but also to provide its audience with the opportunity to bask in the cultural achievements of their fellow African-Americans.

NIAMH DOHENY

it was the responsibility of each film company to devise strategies that would keep costs to a minimum but maximise distribution. Most companies folded after the release of only one production, although the companies providing newsreel footage fared slightly better. One of Micheaux's rivals, the Lincoln Motion Picture Company, set up a 'wild cat' system whereby advance men brought the films from town to town to show the exhibitors, who in turn booked them for later dates. Generally the average daily rental was $25 or, in the case of theatres that could not afford this rate, a 60/40 split of the box office, favouring the film company. However, the success of this approach was dependent on the weather and not always profitable (Sampson, 1995). Lincoln's film *A Man's Duty* (1920) was the first race movie to run for two days in Oakland and Atlanta, yet it only recouped $100 gross per day (Cripps, 1977). In the early 1920s, the company folded.

For Micheaux, working in isolation away from Hollywood and other race-film producers, it was no different. His first feature, *The Homesteader* (1919), was financed by his fellow farmers, black and white, who bought stock in his production outfit, the Micheaux Book and Film Company. Aided by support from the black press, the movie was a box-office success. Distribution in the early years was arranged in a similar manner to that employed by the Lincoln Motion Picture Company, except that it was usually Micheaux who travelled among the theatres, inveigling them to hire his movie and promising that the next would be even greater. On the strength of these claims, he reputedly got exhibitors to invest in his next feature. Micheaux built up a star system, promoting his stars (many of whom were members of the prestigious Lafayette Players of New York) and organising elaborate premieres for his films, complete with limousines and spotlights. Nevertheless, Micheaux filed for bankruptcy in February 1928, though his production company was incorporated with white financing shortly afterwards and became the Micheaux Film Corporation.

Micheaux's films focused on the struggle of African-Americans to improve their circumstances, material and other, in the face of countless obstacles of an inter- and intra-racial nature. Drawing inspiration from African-American novels (some of which he penned), newspaper items and current events (such as Marcus Garvey's trial and the Rhinelander case), they emphasised the diversity of African-American identity and ambition within the black community. Initially, his films comprised a direct rebuttal to D. W. Griffith's *The Birth of a Nation*. *Within Our Gates* graphically recreated the lynching of an innocent African-American family – eschewing the convenient cut-away that Griffith employed in the scene of Gus's lynching – and reversed the earlier film's black lust for white flesh, while *Symbol of the Unconquered* (1920) challenged *The Birth of a Nation*'s glorification of the Ku Klux Klan. Nonetheless, thereafter Micheaux's work switched its focus to intra-racial conflict and achievements. Recurring themes of his films included passing (for white) and miscegenation, addressing the burning issue in the African-American newspapers of the day: how to delineate a 'Negro' identity.

By 1920, an estimated half-million African-Americans were attempting to pass for white in the US (Bowser and Spence, 2000). Reaction to these passers within African-American circles varied, as did Micheaux's treatment of the subject. For example, *Symbol of the Unconquered*, *The House behind the Cedars* (1923) and its remake, *Veiled Aristocrats* (1932), and *God's Step Children* (1938) featured characters that passed for white with varying success. In each film, passing is treated quite differently: *Symbol of the Unconquered* offers a disparaging characterisation of the passer who persecutes African-Americans and is eventually killed by the Ku Klux Klan; *Veiled Aristocrats* displays the misery and isolation of the passer, as well as the fear of discovery; *God's Step Children* offers little insight into the experiences of the passers, though it highlights their misery and they eventually commit suicide. Jane Gaines (2001) argues that passing in Micheaux's films 'undermines white attempts to create racially pure cultural spaces' (p. 158). Perhaps more importantly, like his treatment of miscegenation, it re-educated viewers about assumptions of African-American identity and self-worth.

Although the possibility of miscegenation (a theme banned by the Hays Code) was raised in many of Micheaux's movies, it only actually occurs in *Within Our Gates*. In films such as *The Homesteader*, *A Son of Satan* (1924) and *The Exile* (1931), the African-American character refuses to marry his/her love until, in a morale-boosting reversal of white-on-black exclusion, it is revealed that the white person is actually of mixed race. Thus the topics of passing and miscegenation combined to present a positive image of African-American identity that embraced a variety of people, and provided more complex characterisations of African-Americans than those in contemporary Hollywood movies. At the same time, Micheaux did not hesitate to represent the less salubrious elements of contemporary African-American life: corrupt ministers, shady gangsters and their molls vied for screen time with the sober, diligent heroes and respectable heroines.

Perhaps for this reason, his films have been criticised by some scholars, such as Joseph Young (1989) and Ronald Green and Horace Neal (1988), for capitulating to negative racial caricatures such as the coon. More recently, however, historians have seen in his work an attempt to critique and exorcise those stereotypes (Green, 2000; Bowser and Spence, 2000), reinforced by Micheaux's efforts to use his films to construct a positive racial identity for the beleaguered African-American populace. In his 1913 novel *The Conquest*, Micheaux insisted that his aim was to persuade his audience that 'a colored man can be anything'. For certain critics, this aspiration expressed an elitist preference for the middle class at the expense of the working class (Green, 2000; Gaines, 2001; Bowser, in Yearwood, 1982, p. 58). However, while Micheaux celebrates some characters' struggles to 'better themselves', he also celebrates those such as housekeepers, maids and washerwomen (for example, in *Swing!*, 1938). As Charlene Regester (2001) has noted, Micheaux's vision of elevation was more consistent with exposing social ills than vaunting economic success. Ironically, Micheaux was chastised by his contemporaries for dwelling excessively on the working class and not representing the African-American at his or her most successful (Thomas, 1925).

Others have criticised Micheaux for displaying what a contemporary review of *A Daughter of the Congo* (1930) described as 'intra-racial color fetishism' (Lewis, 1930). The debate over whether his films subscribe to criteria of white beauty (see also Gerima, in Yearwood, 1982, pp. 57–8) has been based on the prevalence of light-skinned African-American actors in lead roles. Joseph Young (1989) suggested that this indicated Micheaux's hatred of African-Americans, a view contested by Creekmur (2001) and Green (2000). Criticism has also been levelled at Micheaux's style – Cripps (1969), for example, claimed it represented a primitive attempt to slavishly reproduce Hollywood conventions that failed due to Micheaux's technical incompetence.

As more films have become available, this view has changed: Arthur Jaffa (2001) and Ronald Green (2000) have made a case for Micheaux's deliberate subversion of classical form. It could be argued that Micheaux borrowed from melodramatic form to create the 'new Negro melodrama'. While this retained certain traditional features of nineteenth-century melodrama – such as mistaken identity; talking at cross-purposes; nick-of-time rescue; and virtuous suffering – it also developed new features that functioned within a specifically African-American context. Thus Hollywood's thin characterisation of African-Americans was challenged, racial uplift was integrated and stories relevant to African-Americans were put centre-stage rather than relegated to the comic margins (Doheny, 2004).

From 1931, most Micheaux films incorporated song and dance numbers, usually performed as nightclub spots, where jazz, tap and African-American comedy acts were given free rein for the benefit of the diegetic and actual black audiences (for example, *The Girl from Chicago*, 1932; *Veiled Aristocrats*; *Swing!*; and *Lying Lips*, 1939). The performance of jazz and tap dance, both looked on as originating from African-American culture, highlighted the African-American community's specific contribution to American culture and outlined a separate identity for African-Americans. Crucially, as professional African-Americans were often shown to frequent these nightclubs and applaud the African-American performers, Micheaux made it clear that the acquisition of qualifications and a profession did not compromise their distinct 'Negro' identity, thus refuting contemporary fears that self-improvement led automatically to intra-racial social segregation.

In addition, his films offered a range of life choices to African-American audiences: his heroes and heroines were, among other things, FBI agents, policemen, teachers, singers, secretaries, housekeepers and farmers as well as gamblers, hoodlums and prostitutes. This contrasted sharply with contemporary Hollywood features, in which African-American actors were only seen as servants or jesters, or were blacked up to provide atmospheric mise en scène in plantation films (Bogle, 1997; Cripps, 1977). There was no mythification, marking or omission of the African-American in Micheaux's films: characters enjoyed social and geographic mobility and were not simply used as foils to a more glamorous white cast.

However, Micheaux's popularity did not endure. Although it has generally been accepted that the black press withdrew its support of Micheaux in the mid-1920s (Regester, 2001; Musser, 2001), the evidence suggests that this did not occur until the early 1930s and was due to several factors, not least of which was his failure to incorporate sound until 1931, four years after *The Jazz Singer* was released. Additionally, faced with the emergence of black-cast films such as *Hallelujah!* (1929) and *Hearts in Dixie* (1929), some African-American critics grew confident that Hollywood's treatment of race was increasingly sympathetic to the African-American community and rejected Micheaux's productions as amateurish and dull (Doheny, 2004). He could not match the sophisticated mise en scène and post-production facilities that were available at the Hollywood studios.

His last film, *The Betrayal* (1948), represented a return to film-making after an eight-year hiatus, but unfortunately it received uniformly bad reviews and Micheaux was bankrupted once more, and died in obscurity in 1951. He was largely forgotten until the 1970s, when the Black Filmmakers Hall of Fame began to present pioneering black film-makers with the Oscar Micheaux Award. Subsequently, his name was added to Hollywood Boulevard's stars, and the Directors Guild of America awarded him a posthumous lifetime achievement award. As more of his films have become available through specialist outlets on the Internet, interest in Micheaux's work has grown considerably and critics have come to recognise his valuable contribution to American and African-American cinema.

Selected Reading

Pearl Bowser and Louise Spence, *Writing Himself into History: Oscar Micheaux, His Silent Films, and His Audience*, New Brunswick, NJ, Rutgers University Press, 2000.

Pearl Bowser, Jane Gaines and Charles Musser (eds), *Oscar Micheaux and His Circle: African American Filmmaking and the Race Cinema of the Silent Era*, Bloomington, Indiana University Press, 2001.

Manthia Diawara (ed.), *Black American Cinema*, New York and London, Routledge, 1993.

Ronald Green, *Straight Lick: The Cinema of Oscar Micheaux*, Bloomington, Indiana University Press, 2000.

Documentary

BILL NICHOLS

Historically, definitions of documentary film prove to be varied and contentious. That documentaries address aspects of the real world, that they feature non-actors and confront social issues is commonly accepted, but this meant something different during the period of silent Soviet cinema from its meaning in 1960s America. The heart and soul of any definition arises within a specific social and historical context and it varies with time and place. This does not mean that 'anything goes', that understandings can be changed at will. It means that no single, timeless definition can capture what documentary film has been or might yet be.

Four key moments can be identified that mark significant shifts in how documentary was defined and understood. The first occurred in the 1920s when the term first came into use. The persuasive use of film took hold most vividly in the Soviet Union as the government sought ways to reach a far-flung audience of largely illiterate workers and peasants after the 1917 revolution. Dziga Vertov was the most vocal and controversial champion of documentary, although he, like Robert Flaherty, whose *Nanook of the North* (1922) is often cited as the first true documentary, did not use that word. For Vertov, films that captured life as it was, that reassembled fragments of the world into a new, transformative whole, that revealed the processes and practices that joined people into a collective citizenry were the essence of cinema itself. His works *Kino-Eye/Kinoglaz* (1924) and *Man With a Movie Camera/Chelovek s kinoapparatom* (1928) defined for him the art of cinema in a way that fiction film could never do.

His example proved tremendously influential. It demonstrated to John Grierson, who went on to head the British documentary movement of the 1930s, for example, that an alternative to Hollywood was possible. Grierson disdained film as entertainment; he advocated work that would address the pressing issues of the day. He was funded by the British government and made films to promote the interests of the state. The films were discreetly persuasive, not strident, demonstrating how the postal service did its job in Harry Watt's *Night Mail* (1936), for example. With their eloquent voice-over commentaries and carefully composed, sometimes staged, images, these works established a compelling model for documentary film-making. Grierson's model continues to provide a widely used template for many documentaries made for television and a general audience.

The second key moment occurred in the wake of World War II and culminated at the start of the 1960s. Lighter, more manageable cameras and techniques to record synchronous sound in almost any situation made new modes of documentary film-making possible. The film-maker could now observe what took place before him or her, capturing the real-time ebb and flow of actions and, most importantly, speech. This made possible the observational films of D. A. Pennebaker (*Dont Look Back*, 1967), Drew Associates (*Primary*, 1960) and Frederick Wiseman (*High School*, 1968). Such works eschewed interviewing subjects to hear what they have to say in favour of watching what they actually do, and they minimised or eliminated voice-over commentary. Viewers were invited to draw their own conclusions from what they saw.

These changes in technology allowed the film-maker to become an active participant in what took place in front of the camera. Instead of withdrawing to observe, he or she could prod or provoke subjects. Interviews and direct exchanges between film-maker and subject came to characterise this mode of participatory or interactive documentary. Jean Rouch in France was a pioneer of what he termed cinéma vérité with works such as *Chronicle of a Summer/Chronique d'un été*, 1961). Rouch filmed himself and Edgar Morin, his collaborator, interacting extensively with their subjects, six different individuals living in Paris in the summer of 1960. Both these approaches stress the present moment, as people present themselves in front of the camera, with the observational mode favouring an unobtrusive film-maker and the interactive mode favouring a participatory film-maker.

The third key moment occurred around 1980 and marks the recognition that the interactions between film-maker and subject could be organised into a narrative, often of past events.

Reconstructed: Errol Morris's groundbreaking *The Thin Blue Line*

Capturing the Friedmans (USA 2003 *p.c* – Hit the Ground Running/HBO Documentary Films/Magnolia Pictures; *d* – Andrew Jarecki)

Playing on ambiguity: *Capturing the Friedmans*

Capturing the Friedmans, along with the controversies it sparked, provides a good indication of the state of documentary today. Structured somewhat like *The Thin Blue Line* (1988) as an investigation into a crime, *Capturing the Friedmans* explores the very forms of ambiguity that the judicial system serves to resolve. Did he or didn't he? Innocent or guilty? In this case the question revolves around whether Arnold Friedman and his son Jesse committed a wide variety of brutal paedophilic acts against high-school boys who took computer-programming classes in their home. The film explores how the criminal charges and their resolution leave a swathe of factual ambiguity and emotional turmoil for everyone involved.

Capturing the Friedmans resists proving guilt or innocence in favour of examining how evidence of criminal wrongdoing is gathered, or perhaps invented, how accusations may snowball in response to police pressure and group hysteria, how suspicion, secrecy and jealousy tear a family apart, and how one family's home movies become a Pandora's box of repressed longings, romantic fantasy, intense rage and damning behaviour. Director Jarecki mixes his own interviews with family members, police officials, lawyers and others, the Friedmans' home movies made when their boys were children, and more contemporary home videos and diaries shot by two of the sons to examine how each person involved in the case constructed his or her own narrative of what happened and how it should be interpreted. The viewer is left to sort out the discrepancies between these claims as well as to experience the emotional residue of the contending allegiances, conflicting accounts and distorted perceptions that revolve around a traumatic event.

Jarecki clearly had the family's consent to make his film and yet they are exposed to renewed and not always favourable scrutiny years after the original events. Do they function as an example of the complexity of traumatic events or does the film do justice to their individual perspectives and unique situations? In its DVD release (HBO Video, 2004), it also demonstrates how ancillary material can provide a significant supplement to the stand-alone film: additional material makes clear that Arnold did have paedophilic experiences but saw them in an idealised, romantic light that contrasts vividly with the police accounts of satanic rituals and violent deeds. The additional material also includes a record of the lively discussion that followed a screening at which the presiding judge, some jurors, police officials and family members were all present. Unlike some of the more partisan documentaries that engage with political positions and social issues directly, *Capturing the Friedmans* demonstrates that documentary can not only champion a given perspective convincingly but can also explore the mysteries and ambiguities of human experience in as compelling a manner as any fiction.

BILL NICHOLS

The interview and the careful selection of archive footage were primary tools in the process of narrativisation. Emile de Antonio had pioneered this approach in his counter-history of the Vietnam War, *In the Year of the Pig* (1968), and it was then adapted by Connie Field to tell the story of women workers during World War II in *The Life and Times of Rosie the Riveter* (1980), and by Claude Lanzmann to construct a history of the Holocaust in *Shoah* (1985). Lanzmann refused, however, to include any archive footage. Instead, he built his nine-hour film entirely from interviews. This allowed him to demonstrate how the past persists in the present through the tones, gestures and expressions of interviewees. They not only recount information about the past; their bodies stand as testimony to how their experience of the Holocaust continues to shape who they are and what they say.

The fourth key moment took place in the 1990s with the rise of the theatrical documentary. These films rely more heavily than their predecessors on dramatic structure, staged or reconstructed events, and emotionally charged involvement with fascinating personalities. Errol Morris's *The Thin Blue Line* (1988) helped to pave the way for films such as *Hoop Dreams* (1994), *The Fog of War Eleven Lessons from the Life of Robert S. McNamara* (2003), *Super Size Me* (2004), *Grizzly Man* (2005) and *Fahrenheit 9/11* (2004). The willingness to revert to the fictional film-making techniques that Dziga Vertov railed against and that John Grierson regarded with disdain also marks a dramatic renaissance of the documentary form. Whether this renaissance and its reliance on fictional techniques has sacrificed documentary's claim to a privileged relationship to historical reality – an important but still unresolved issue that goes back to the 1920s – has fostered considerable debate about the authenticity and credibility of many of these newer works.

Theatrical documentaries attach considerable importance to emotional affect. They acknowledge their subjective approach and the clash of perspectives that constitutes the arena of public debate. They retain the persuasive qualities that first distinguished documentary but do so with unashamed borrowings from the repertoire of the fiction film-maker, such as individuals who possess star quality, point-of-view shots to build character identification, flashbacks, suspenseful dramatic structure, subjective interpretations of past events or states of mind, re-enactments that may depart from historical record, and powerful musical scores.

The representation of past events through re-enactments and archival footage has proved to be a particularly charged issue. Re-enactments rupture the link between the documentary image and historical record. The image still captures what happens in front of the camera with striking fidelity, but what happens in front of the camera only happens in order to be recorded. It lacks the autonomy of historical events that are recorded and then shaped into a particular argument or perspective. To what extent is staging acceptable? Can interviews be fully scripted? Can past events be recreated and different versions of an event presented to convey different conceptions of what happened? Should the subjective experience of an event be stressed, as it might be in a fiction? Can authentic archive footage from one time and place be used to stand in for similar but missing archive footage from another time and place? These questions raise ethical issues that elude categorical rules. Every documentary seeks to win the viewer's trust, which it then violates at its own peril.

The rise of a theatrical market for documentary films has been a notable development since the 1990s. More than a dozen documentaries earned over $1 million in the United States in 2005 through theatrical release. DVD and video sales have allowed many more documentaries to reach audiences efficiently, and foreign sales and distribution, mainly to television and cable outlets but also to ancillary DVD and video markets, have given documentary film-making strong financial legs to stand on. In addition, the possibility of shooting films in low-budget formats, editing them on computer software and then transferring them to commercial formats lends the home movie new and expanded meaning. Jonathan Caouette's touching and disturbing autobiography *Tarnation* (2004), for example, is reputed to have been made for less than a thousand dollars, although it has gone on to play at festivals, in theatres and on television and cable outlets in numerous countries. The critical and financial success of bigger-budget productions such as *March of the Penguins/La Marche de l'empereur* (2005), *Born into Brothels* (2004), *To Be and to Have/Être et avoir* (2002) and *An Inconvenient Truth* (2006) are evidence that the renaissance in documentary film continues to flourish.

Selected Reading

Erik Barnouw, *Documentary: A History of the Non-Fiction Film*, Oxford, Oxford University Press, 1993.

Bill Nichols, *Introduction to Documentary*, Indianapolis, Indiana University Press, 2001.

Michael Renov, *The Subject in Documentary*, Minneapolis, University of Minnesota Press, 2004.

Alan Rosenthal (ed.), *New Challenges for Documentary*, Berkeley, University of California Press, 1988.

Art cinema

ANGELA NDALIANIS

The meaning of the term 'art cinema' is difficult to pin down. Its boundaries are continually shifting, and any working definition needs to be as flexible as the diverse examples that come under its umbrella. Films separated by country of origin as well as time, such as *Seven Samurai/Shichinin no samurai* (Japan, 1954); *Breathless/À bout de souffle* (France, 1960); *Rome Open City/Roma città aperta* (Italy, 1945); *The Cabinet of Dr Caligari/Das Cabinet des Dr. Caligari* (Germany, 1919); *Beauty and the Beast/La Belle et la bête* (France, 1946); and *Ashes of Time/Dongxie Xidu* (Hong Kong, 1994), have all been labelled art films. When considering the properties of art cinema, it is crucial to take into account that it has different meanings for different audiences at specific periods (Wilinsky, 2001, p. 14).

Despite this national and temporal diversity, art films share a common trait: in form and practice, they are often defined against mainstream, commercial film industries, particularly Hollywood and its standardised system of production, distribution and exhibition. Although contemporary Hollywood operates within a radically different economic system from the classical period (and few 'Hollywood' studios today are based in Hollywood or owned outright by American companies), it has continued to maintain domination over global markets. Steve Neale has located art cinema historically as a specifically European strategy aimed at countering 'American domination' (Neale, 2002, p. 103), while others such as David Bordwell (1985) do not perceive art cinema as a strictly European phenomenon. Films such as *Rashomon* (1950), *Tokyo Story/Tokyo monogatari* (1953) and *World of Apu/Apur Sansar* (1958) are also viewed as examples of the art cinema market that burgeoned in the 1950s. Focusing on formal properties, Bordwell argues that art films such as *Rashomon*, *The Eclipse/L'eclisse* (1962) and *Cleo from Five to Seven/Cléo de 5 à 7* (1961) reveal specific patterns of plot and style that can be characterised as art cinema narration. Whereas classical Hollywood relied on storytelling practices that favoured linearity, with a cause-and-effect logic, character development and style that supported narrative progression and closure, art cinema adopts a looser narrative form that breaks up linearity and causality through the use of techniques such as ellipsis (which creates narrative gaps); 'dead time' (action that has little or no effect on narrative progression); episodic sequences paralleled by drifting, aimless protagonists; and an open-ended structure. Influenced by modernist practices, art cinema directors prioritise style and cinematic image over narrative exposition, and are frequently associated with notions of 'artistic vision'.

From cinema's beginnings, film styles emerged that provided alternative practices to those of the Hollywood studio system. The German Expressionist, Surrealist and Impressionist film 'movements' were intentionally presented as cinematic equivalents to older, 'high art' media such as painting and sculpture, while prior to World War I, the company Film d'Art focused on the production of stage classics for middle-class audiences in France (Neale, 2002, p. 105). However, the key transition period for international art cinema was the 1940s, when the Italian neo-realist films that were filmed against the backdrop of World War II and its aftermath emerged (see Italian Neo-realism, p. 233). Restricted filming conditions (including the closure of

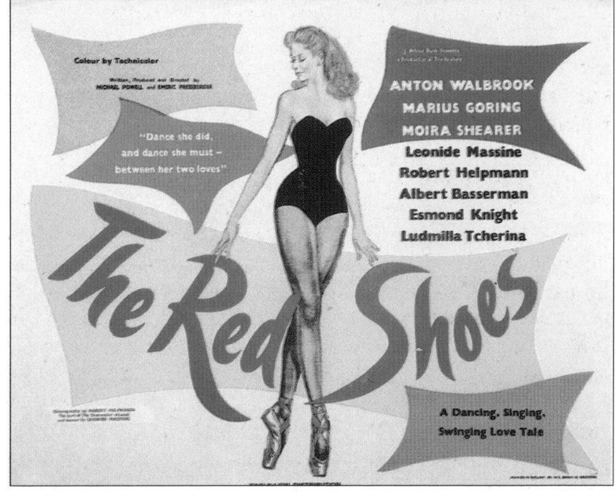

Cultural prestige in international markets: Powell and Pressburger's *The Red Shoes*

Cinecittà studios and the limited availability of film stock) provided a context that nurtured the production of a distinctive film style dominated by a 'realist' aesthetic that relied on location shooting, documentary-style hand-held camerawork, non-professional actors, grainy film stock and the loosening of cause-and-effect narrative in favour of episodic form. It was the international success of *Rome Open City* in particular that signalled a shift in exhibition practices around the world. Following its success, films such as *Bicycle Thieves/Ladri di biciclette* (1948), *The Red Shoes* (1948), *Rashomon*, *Wild Strawberries/Smultronstället* (1957) and *The Sweet Life/La dolce vita* (1960) paved the way for a niche market for international art cinema that grew in strength through the 1950s and 1960s. As Neale observes, 'art' became a strategy that local cinemas applied to make a 'critical and economic mark' on an international scale (Neale, 2002, p. 104).

Paralleling the post-war success of the art film, André Bazin (co-founder of the French film journal *Cahiers du Cinéma* in 1951) initiated a wave of film criticism that further institutionalised the phenomenon of international art cinema. Bazin's writing inspired other *Cahiers* critics – who included François Truffaut, Jean-Luc Godard, Eric Rohmer, Claude Chabrol and Jacques Rivette – to develop the *politique des auteurs* (initially coined by Truffaut), later adapted by American film scholar Andrew Sarris as the auteur theory (Sarris, 1962/63). Celebrating the work of directors such as Orson Welles, Roberto Rossellini, Alfred Hitchcock, Jean Renoir, Kenji Mizoguchi and Carl Dreyer, the *Cahiers* critics asserted that a true auteur was a film-maker who used their unique style to transcend the oppressive industrial practices imposed by mainstream film studios (see For a new French cinema: the *politique des auteurs*, p. 390). Many in the *Cahiers* group became film-makers themselves; as the Nouvelle Vague (French New Wave – a title devised by critics), they created a new auteur-driven art cinema (Marie, 2003, pp. 40–8).

Drawing on Italian Neo-realism and the modernist strategies of contemporary film-makers Chris Marker, Alain Resnais and Margeurite Duras (who adapted the literary experiments of the *nouveau roman* to the film medium), the Nouvelle Vague broke new ground in establishing an art cinema that offered modes of narration in opposition to the classical cinemas of Hollywood and France (see Vincendeau, 2004; Temple and Witt, 2004). Jean-Luc Godard, for example, experimented with editing, cinematography, sound and narrative to expose the constructed nature of film reality. *Breathless*, *The Outsiders/Bande à part* (1964), *Pierrot le fou* (1965) and *Weekend* (1967) all used extended long takes and tracking shots that drew attention to themselves, jump-cuts, direct address to camera and discontinuities between sound and image that ruptured the conventions of continuity editing. As Bordwell (1985) explains, a typical trait of art cinema is the tension between the almost obsessive drive for conveying filmic worlds objectively and that of marking the same filmic space with the stylistic stamp of the auteur – a stamp that draws attention to film as representation.

One of the myths about art cinema is that while Hollywood is primarily concerned with profit and 'empty' entertainment, art films are free from commercial constraints and encourage creativity and intellectual engagement with deeper meaning. Entangled with and perpetuating this myth is a complex social discourse about taste, quality and artistry. In reality, art cinema

Archetypal art cinema: Monica Vitti in Antonioni's *L'avventura*

The Adventure/L'avventura (Italy/France 1960 *p.c* – Cino del Duca/PCE/Société Cinématographique Lyre; *d* – Michelangelo Antonioni)

L'avventura is the film with which Michelangelo Antonioni came to international prominence in 1960, although he had made his first feature, *Chronicle of a Love/Cronaca di un amore*, ten years previously. *L'avventura* divided critics at the 1960 Cannes Film Festival, but now stands as one of the undoubted archetypes of art cinema.

The plot is simple: Claudia (Monica Vitti), her friend Anna (Lea Massari) and Anna's lover Sandro (Gabriele Ferzetti) go on a cruise in the Mediterranean. Anna mysteriously disappears, and Claudia and Sandro go in search of her, becoming lovers in the process. And that is it really. However, Antonioni's originality lies precisely in his de-emphasis of the dramatic potential of film plot with its linear problem/resolution structure and its personal conflicts between fully 'psychologised' characters. Thus Anna's disappearance, the subsequent inquest, the mystery of her whereabouts – in short, the 'essential' elements of the story as a more conventional director would have conceived it – are more or less ignored, or rather, they become only as important as Claudia and Sandro feel they are, since the way in which the story is told deliberately limits the spectator's knowledge to what the characters know.

When *L'avventura* was first released, there was much talk of it being an 'existentialist' film in that it revolved around characters who seemed alienated and out of place in their environments. And, indeed, in a statement distributed at the time of the film's Cannes premiere, Antonioni stated that people today live in a world without the moral tools necessary to match their technological skills: they are incapable of authentic relationships with each other or with their environment because they carry within them a fossilised value system quite out of step with modern times. As a result, they often attempt to find in sex or love an answer to their moral dilemma, but this too proves to be a blind alley offering neither solutions nor possibilities for self-fulfilment, let alone a substitute for outmoded values. The result is a kind of existential ennui, and it is this state that *L'avventura* so perfectly captures.

However, Antonioni's genius lies not in his use of this particular theme (which was something of a commonplace in the culture of the post-war years) but in rendering it in such distinctive visual images. The visualisation of subjective states by representational means becomes, with Antonioni, a wholly distinctive stylistic approach. To this end the director exercises an absolute control over his compositions; every aspect of an individual shot is artistically organised for the fullest effect, just as if the director were a painter or a photographer: a shot or sequence by Antonioni is marked as surely as though his signature were affixed to the celluloid.

JULIAN PETLEY

Last Year at Marienbad/L'Année dernière à Marienbad (France/Italy 1961 *p.c* – Terrafilm/S.N.F.C./ Précitel/ Como Films/Argos-Films/Films Tamara/Cinétel/ Silver Films/Cineriz; *d* – Alain Resnais)

The very fact that it is almost impossible to describe the story of *L'Année dernière à Marienbad* marks it out as a quintessential work of art cinema. Set in a vast baroque hotel, it revolves around a man, X (Giorgio Albertazzi), who attempts to entice a woman, A (Delphine Seyrig), away from a man, M (Sacha Pitoëff), by persuading her that they had met there the previous year. Whether they actually did meet or not remains a mystery.

The nature of the 'reality' of the events we see on screen is thus at the very heart of the film. As the film's writer Alain Robbe-Grillet has said:

> The whole film is the story of a persuading: it deals with a reality which the hero creates out of his own vision, out of his own words. And if his persistence, his secret conviction, finally prevail, they do so among a labyrinth of false trains, variants, failures and repetitions. (Robbe-Grillet, 1962, p. 9)

Or to put it a slightly different way, this is a film that is all plot and no story – it is impossible for the viewer to disentangle a causal, consistent, chronological story from the plot details that are presented.

L'Année dernière à Marienbad is full of ambiguities and contradictions: spatial, temporal and causal. The statue to which A and X frequently return seems constantly to shift location, A's room becomes progressively more cluttered with furniture, day and night appear to alternate within the same scene, an action may carry from one time and space to a different time and space, the narrator's voice-over account of events is often in conflict with the images shown. The entire structure of *Marienbad* is a play with logic, space and time that does not offer us a single, complete story as a prize for winning this 'game'. Or as Robbe-Grillet himself has said:

Spatial ambiguities: *L'Année dernière à Marienbad*

It will be said that the spectator risks getting lost if he is not occasionally given the 'explanations' that permit him to locate each scene in its chronological place and at its level of objective reality. But we have decided to trust the spectator, to allow him . . . to come to terms with pure subjectivities. Two attitudes are then possible: either the spectator will try to reconstitute some 'Cartesian' scheme – the most linear, the most rational he can devise – and this spectator will certainly find the film difficult, if not incomprehensible; or else the spectator will let himself be carried along by the extraordinary images in front of him, by the actors' voices, by the soundtrack, by the music, by the rhythm of the cutting, by the passion of the characters . . . and to this spectator, the film will seem the 'easiest' he has ever seen. (Robbe-Grillet, 1962, pp. 12–13)

JULIAN PETLEY

is a niche within an international market whose major selling point is its status as 'art', 'quality' and 'culture' – underwritten by the figure of the director as auteur who functions as a 'brand name', a means of labelling and selling a film (Neale, 2002, pp. 118–19; see also Authorship in cinema, p. 387). The complexity of the processes at work in the creation of art cinema becomes clear when institutional and exhibition contexts are examined. Between the 1920s and 1940s, for example, the Hollywood studios Warner Bros., MGM, 20th Century Fox, Universal, RKO, United Artists and Columbia were all actively involved in the distribution of foreign 'art' films (Wilinsky, 2001, p. 75). Furthermore, many of the films of canonic art cinema directors Federico Fellini, Roberto Rossellini, Vittorio de Sica, Luchino Visconti and Bernardo Bertolucci were produced at Cinecittà in Rome (also known as 'Hollywood on the Tiber'), the same studio that produced the spaghetti westerns of Sergio Leone and the horror films of Dario Argento. Likewise, Akira Kurosawa's *Seven Samurai* and Inoshiro Honda's *Godzilla/Gojiro*, both released in 1954, came from the same studio: Toho Co. In addition to Kurosawa, other renowned art cinema directors Yasujiro Ozu and Kenji Mizoguchi were associated with the mainstream commercial Japanese studios Shochiku and the Nikkatsu Corporation. In other words, films that to international (in particular, western) audiences may appear as marginal, foreign art cinema are often perceived as mainstream by domestic audiences in their own countries.

The exhibition spaces in which art films are screened are as integral to an understanding of art cinema as the formal properties and industrial conditions that inform their production. From the 1920s, art films were being shown at so-called 'little cinemas' in urban areas throughout the US (Wilinsky, 2001; Guzman, 2005). For example, *The Cabinet of Dr Caligari* only found an audience in the mainstream theatres after it had proved successful in the 'little cinema' exhibition space (Budd, 1986). In the 1940s, the 'little cinemas' were replaced by art-film theatres, 'small theaters in urban areas or university towns that screened "offbeat" films such as independent Hollywood, foreign languages and documentary films'; these emerging art-house spaces 'featured art galleries in the lobbies, served coffee, and offered specialized and "intelligent" films to a discriminating audience that paid high admission prices for such distinctions' (Wilinksy, 2001, p. 1).

During the 1940s and 1950s, intellectual interest in film strengthened as art-house theatres sprang up to meet the demands of a public keen to experience alternatives to mainstream Hollywood cinema. These theatres not only helped to institutionalise 'the concept of the European art film' and promoted 'the artistic concerns of the film culture' but were also integral in fostering emerging tastes and hierarchies that catered to a cultural and intellectual elite (Guzman, 2005, pp. 261–2; Wilinsky, 2001, p. 47). In addition to the exclusivity fostered by the art-house spaces, the ethos of 'quality', intellectual stimulation and 'high art' was generated by other social factors. Film institutes, university film societies, film libraries and film festivals were established throughout continental Europe, the UK, Australia, the USA and Japan.

The 1950s ushered in the first comprehensive and serious study of film as an art form at tertiary institutions. Those who attended such courses emerged as a new film-literate group of cinemagoers; taking the lead from more experimental American directors (such as John Cassavetes, Robert Altman, Arthur Penn and Stanley Kubrick), in the 1960s the directors of the so-called Film School Generation or American New Wave (for example, Martin Scorsese, Paul Schrader, David Lynch, George Lucas and William Friedkin) targeted film-literate audiences by incorporating art cinema strategies into their work while working within or at the edges of the Hollywood system. The outcome was a radical metamorphosis of the genre model that Hollywood had relied on since its inception (see Ray, 1985). Genres were deconstructed, parodied and hybridised and, true to the art cinema tradition, audiences were invited to actively participate in a game that reflexively engaged in the process of 'making meaning'.

In the 1950s and 1960s, the cinemas of other countries too began to blur the distinctions between the art and mainstream film. In the 1960s, Japanese *nuberu bagu* (new wave) directors Susumu Hani, Masahiro Shinoda, Nagisa Oshima and Seijun Suzuki deliberately transferred the aims of the Nouvelle Vague auteurs to a Japanese context (see Japanese cinema, p. 238). In the late 1970s and 1980s, a new wave of Hong Kong film-makers (Tsui Hark, Ann Hui, Yim Ho, Patrick Tam and Allen Fong, who, like the film school generation of American directors, had studied film) took up auteurist polemics, 'transcending' the conventions of genre and narrative and deconstructing and challenging the commercial system (see Hong Kong cinema, p. 224). However, once they crossed national borders and entered an international exhibition space, these Hong Kong and Japanese films often abandoned their mainstream identity and became associated with the specialised art-house circuit.

The postmodern era has further obscured traditional dichotomies between commercialism and artistry, mainstream cinema and art cinema. The self-reflexive mixing of formal strategies and codes is entwined in and supported by wider institutional practices that have encouraged various synergies and cross-cultural collaborations. Lev (1993) points to the 1960s and 1970s 'Euro-American art film' co-productions, which attempted a 'synthesis of the American entertainment film (large budget, good production values, internationally known stars) and the European art film (auteur director, artistic subject and/or style)'. The aim of films such as Michelangelo Antonioni's *Blowup* (1966), Bertolucci's *Last Tango in Paris/L'ul-*

Not clear-cut: Robert Altman's *Gosford Park*

timo tango a Parigi (1972), Wim Wenders's *Paris, Texas* (1984) and Werner Herzog's *Nosferatu the Vampyre/Nosferatu Phantom der Nacht* (1979) was to reach larger audiences than was normally the case for the art film (Lev, 1993, p. xii). Since then, art cinema has increasingly adopted mainstream conventions, and the mainstream has embraced those of art cinema. To complicate matters further, the post-1970s have witnessed the growth of independent US film distributors/producers such as Miramax, Warner Independent Pictures, Focus Features and Picturehouse (see The major independents, p. 54). These independents often support more experimental works aligned with the art-house exhibition circuit: for example, Larry Clark's *kids* (1995), Prachya Pinkaew's *Ong-Bak: Muay Thai Warrior* (2003) and Robert Altman's *Gosford Park* (2001). Yet many of these companies are subsidiaries of major film corporations: Miramax is a subsidiary of The Walt Disney Company, Focus Features of Universal Studios, Picturehouse of New Line Cinema and HBO Films. A clear-cut definition of art cinema has always been elusive, increasingly so in recent years. As the boundaries that separate mainstream and art cinema practices become ever more porous, the question 'Is there such a thing as art cinema?' comes to the fore.

Selected Reading

David Bordwell, 'Art-cinema narration', in *Narration in the Fiction Film*, Madison, University of Wisconsin Press, 1985.

Peter Lev, *The Euro-American Cinema*, Austin, University of Texas Press, 1993.

Steve Neale, 'Art cinema as institution', in Fowler (ed.), *The European Cinema Reader*, London and New York, Routledge, 2002.

Barbara Wilinsky, *Sure Seaters: The Emergence of Art House Cinema*, Minneapolis and London, University of Minnesota Press, 2001.

Animation

PAUL WELLS

Histories of animation have been dominated by the prominence of the American animated cartoon, but in recent years research and scholarship have reclaimed parallel and alternative histories of animation from across the world, which are characterised by both an imitative response to the dominant classical animation aesthetic defined by the Disney Studio in its Golden Era from 1928 to 1941, and recourse to indigenous models drawn from a range of art forms, in order to define a more distinctive style and national identity.

The form itself, evolving out of the proto-cinema of moving-image novelties such as the zoetrope (1834), the praxinoscope (1877) and the early 'trick' films of Georges Méliès and J. Stuart Blackton, was defined in the first instance by three approaches: the 'lightning sketch' film, featuring speeded-up versions of illustrators executing drawings; 3-D stop-motion animation; and primitive 'cartoons', the first largely acknowledged to be Emile Cohl's *Fantasmagorie* (1908). Arguably, though, the first animated film proper was *Matches: An Appeal* (1899), made by Briton Arthur Melbourne Cooper as a Boer War commercial, and though he later made a number of 3-D stop-motion 'toys come to life' films, it was the American context in which the confluence of comic strip, vaudeville and early effects movies led to the emergence of the animated cartoon as a quasi-industrial form. Winsor McCay's *Gertie the Dinosaur* (1914) was the first clear instance of 'personality' animation, while Otto Messmer's *Felix the Cat* films in the 1920s used the freedom of the graphic form both to ape the gags of silent film greats such as Charlie Chaplin and Buster Keaton, and to create visual jokes unique to animated film. Felix was animation's first real star.

It was the emergence of Walt Disney that led to the development of animation as an industry and a distinctive art form. His investment in research and development throughout the 1920s and 1930s in the Silly Symphonies, and the instant stardom of Mickey Mouse, led to the first full-length, sound synchronised, Technicolor, animated feature *Snow White and the Seven Dwarfs* (1937), which featured 3-D perspectives created by the multi-plane camera. Disney rationalised the cartoon, rejecting imagistic anarchy and surrealism and preferring more fully developed character animation and dramatic situation over melodramatic riffs and visual gags for their own sake. This was a consequence of investment in the animation process itself – a greater commitment to anatomically correct drawing, the stimulus of inspirational art, a recognition of the appeal of the adventure narrative in comic books, persuasive character acting and extensive storyboarding – which enabled the creation of a kind of 'realism' relevant to feature-length storytelling and the Hollywood economy.

Snow White and the Seven Dwarfs led to the acceptance of animation as a bona fide film form as well as a graphic art; a main attraction rather than a programme-filler. *Pinocchio* (1940), *Fantasia* (1940) and *Bambi* (1942) refined the form further, though Sergei Eisenstein, a great admirer and theorist of Disney's work (see Leyda, 1988, pp. 98–9), felt that *Bambi* was so much in the vein of 'hyper-realism' as to betray the intrinsically 'plasmatic' conditions of animation itself – a vocabulary used more readily by Disney's chief rivals the Fleischer studios in their Betty Boop cartoons, and in the wild urbanity of the Warner Bros.

A distinctive language: Lotte Reiniger's *The Adventures of Prince Achmed*

Ryan (Canada 2004 *p.c* – Copper Heart Entertainment/National Film Board of Canada; *d* – Chris Landreth)

In an era in which Pixar Animation studios have redefined the dominant aesthetic of feature animation, replacing Disney's classical styling with computer-generated (CG) hyper-realism, individual artists have sought to use computer-generated imagery in a more distinctive and progressive fashion. In his Oscar-winning short film *Ryan*, Chris Landreth simultaneously redefines CG aesthetics, documentary and studies of art and artists by creating a narrative about renowned Canadian animator Ryan Larkin who, having made two hugely influential films for the National Film Board of Canada, *Walking/En marchant* (1969) and *Street Musique* (1972), slipped into a life of drug and alcohol addiction, and survived by panhandling on Toronto's city streets.

Landreth found Larkin and asked him to participate in his film. Larkin, his ex-lover Felicity Fanjoy and producer Derek Lamb were interviewed by Landreth, which, along with Landreth's commentary, provides the soundtrack for the narrative. Landreth, working in a style he terms 'psychological realism', then uses CG animation to create skeletal or abstract figures in a state of physical decay and decline, who exhibit the scars, absent spaces and affects of their psychological torment as part of their external characteristics. Landreth oscillates between configuration and abstraction in visualising the deep-rooted anxieties of artists and their deep-seated fear of failure.

Landreth foregrounds the profound difficulty of the artist – both in his own experience and in Larkin's – by showing the intrinsic relationship between the artist's own experiences and their expression as art. Landreth's film is as much about his own doubts, and the way he is dealing with his own feelings about the illness and loss of his mother, as it is about the tragedy of Larkin's own decline. Indeed, it is largely because Landreth is reminded of his mother, Barbara, in the figure of Larkin that he is prompted to make the film – a perspective that leads him to challenge Larkin about his alcoholism, which prompts a violent response in Larkin and a tirade about the vicissitudes of the marketplace in determining the success or otherwise of creative practitioners.

Landreth's skill lies in the use of 'subjective' documentary; that is, while dwelling on the subjectivity of Larkin's own version of his history and predicament, he subjectivises the visual elements of the narrative, using computer technology to embrace one of animation's most distinctive aspects, the capacity to penetrate and depict interior states of consciousness, memory, fantasy and feeling. Landreth's working principle (interview with the author, February 2006) was based on writer Anaïs Nin's observation that 'we don't see things as they are. We see things as we are', which enabled him to view Larkin partly as a projection of himself, a troubled animator and artist, and partly as a vehicle through which to show how animated film itself is a profoundly self-figurative, self-reflexive form, always aware of its own codes, conventions and models of authorship. Already a classic of the form, *Ryan* speaks to animation history, past, present and future.

PAUL WELLS

Dreams and Desires: Family Ties (UK 2006 *p.c* – Beryl Productions International/S4C; *d* – Joanna Quinn)

In this third instalment of her trilogy featuring the Welsh housewife Beryl, Joanna Quinn continues her interrogation of the distinctive language of animation. Here she deliberately engages with the trials, tribulations and limits of both film theory and live-action cinematography in a hilarious narrative in which Beryl, fuelled by the various influences of Dziga Vertov, Sergei Eisenstein and Leni Riefenstahl, videos her friend Mandy's wedding.

In *Girls' Night Out* (1987), Quinn neatly reversed the assumptions of patriarchal cinema by using a male stripper as the subject of Beryl's 'female gaze', simultaneously parodying the macho bravura of masculine sensibilities and the phallic imperatives of cinematic conventions. Quinn's extraordinary draughtsmanship, fluid imagery and dynamic use of satirical caricature – all of which place her in a tradition that stretches back to William Hogarth, James Gilray and George Cruickshank – readily captured the energy of the characters and made a pointed statement about femininity, female identity and feminist idealism played out through 'the everyday'.

Reversing patriarchal assumptions: *Girls' Night Out*

The second instalment, *Body Beautiful* (1991), sees Beryl pestered by sexist factory lothario Vince and teased and criticised by her female workmates about her weight. Recalling a lifetime of feeling guilty and being persecuted about her size, Beryl responds by taking up a fitness regime at the local gym and training with a rugby team in order to enter the factory Body Beautiful contest. Competing against Vince and other lithe contestants, Beryl performs a routine rejecting everyone's criticism and the inherent sexism and pressure to conform that she experiences. Quinn cleverly uses the freedom of animation to configure Beryl's body as a musical instrument and as a newly muscled form that nevertheless speaks to the dimensions of a middle-aged woman proud of her own body and sense of being. The factory's Japanese owners vote Beryl the winner of the contest, and her victory represents more than a personal triumph, operating as a critique of male assumptions about women, and the social and cultural infrastructures that repress them.

Dreams and Desires: Family Ties engages more specifically with one of the underlying themes of the three films, Beryl's romantic and spiritual desire. Always viewed through her body, and society's dismissal of the middle-aged, Beryl harbours erotic feelings and a deep-seated need to be defined through achievement. She becomes obsessive about using her home video camera, and invests in reading about film to improve her skills. In her desire to achieve distinctive vérité, persuasive tracking shots (tying the camera to the broken leg of a man in a wheelchair) and *kino pravda* (attaching the camera to a rampant dog), Beryl manages to wreck Mandy's wedding and reception. Quinn's tour-de-force graphic renditions of amateur video making, with its unintentional views of feet, ceilings and corridors, and her extraordinary drawing skills in capturing Beryl's drunken dreams and well-intentioned blunders, confirm her as one of the most talented animators of all time.

PAUL WELLS

innovators Tex Avery, Chuck Jones, Bob Clampett, Friz Freleng and Frank Tashlin, whose work spoke directly to knowing adult audiences through more iconic and ironic characters such as Bugs Bunny and Daffy Duck.

The sense that animation was best defined by an alternative approach, however, led to the formation of UPA (United Productions of America), who embraced modern art, created affecting reduced-animation cartoons such as John Hubley's *Rooty Toot Toot* (1951) using fewer cels and movement cycles and championed more individual outlooks. Such a renaissance-style studio had antecedents in John Halas and Joy Batchelor and W. M. Larkins in the UK, whose chief influence was the work of George Pal and the Bauhaus, and was echoed in the studios of eastern Europe, most notably in Zagreb, which used 'limited animation' to create often highly politicised films critiquing oppressive authoritarian regimes. Animation in Europe was often experimental, and the work of Walter Ruttmann, Victor Bergdahl, Oskar Fischinger and later Len Lye and Norman McLaren during the 1920s and 1930s defined the form through non-linear, non-objective, abstract works and established high-quality auteur animation.

Arguably, animation remains the most auteurist of moving-image media, and artists as diverse as Ladislaw Starewicz, Lotte Reiniger, Jirí Trnka, Jan Svankmajer, Yuri Norstein, Paul Grimault, Paul Driessen and Osamu Tezuka, to name but a few, have used the highly specific language of animation, such as metamorphosis; the use of symbol and metaphor; the maximum degree of suggestion in the minimum of iconic imagery; the ability to manipulate time, timing and space; and the special capacity to depict interior states of memory, dream, fantasy, feeling and consciousness, to create artworks of distinction and distinctiveness. This independent tradition survives in the singular voices of figures such as Bill Plympton, Paul Fierlinger, Vera Neubauer, Igor Kovalyov, the Quay Brothers and Johnny Hardstaff.

In the contemporary era, Pixar Animation has defined a dominant computer-generated aesthetic in feature animation, essentially replacing Disney's classical model; Aardman Animations, through Nick Park and Peter Lord, fly the flag for 3-D stop-motion animation; and anime from Japan in the extraordinary works of Hayao Miyazaki and Mamoru Oshii has pushed at the boundaries of narrative form (see Japanese cinema, p. 241), so that animation remains progressive and developmental even as it enters the mainstream. Television has also provided a context for creator-driven work, and has enabled talents such as Gennady Tartakovsky to create groundbreaking, design-led animation such as *Samurai Jack* (2001–4). International festivals and ASIFA, the organisation promoting animators and animation globally, continue to foreground new work and champion animation history and culture. The form is represented by as many techniques and approaches as there are creative practitioners, and continues to draw upon all arts disciplines in the making of features, shorts, commercials, web-toons, installations, public displays and e-imagery.

Selected Reading

Michael Barrier, *Hollywood Cartoons: American Animation in the Golden Age*, New York and Oxford, Oxford University Press, 1999.

Esther Leslie, *Hollywood Flatlands: Animation, Critical Theory and the Avant-Garde*, London and New York, Verso, 2002.

Jayne Pilling (ed.), *A Reader in Animation Studies*, London, John Libbey, 1997.

Paul Wells, *Understanding Animation*, London and New York, Routledge, 1998.

Avant-garde and counter-cinema

ALISON BUTLER

The term 'avant-garde' was introduced into French socialist theory from military terminology in the 19th century. By the end of the first decade of the 20th century, it had been widely adopted to designate art and literature that challenged institutionalised cultural forms. The first avant-garde cinema emerged in Europe in the period 1914–30 from the ferment of modern art. To a generation of artists and writers registering the impact of modernity on every aspect of life from war to entertainment, film appealed as the medium most capable of rendering the striking new attributes of the machine age: shock and speed. Futurist artists, including Giacomo Balla and Umberto Boccioni, used techniques derived from photography and film to create dynamic effects in painting, and the 1916 manifesto *The Futurist Cinema* argued the case for a new kind of cinema:

> At first look the cinema, born only a few years ago, may seem to be Futurist already, lacking a past and free from traditions. Actually, by appearing in the guise of *theatre without words*, it has inherited all the most traditional sweepings of the literary theatre . . . The cinema is an autonomous art. The cinema must therefore never copy the stage. The cinema, being essentially visual, must above all fulfil the evolution of painting, detach itself from reality, from photography, from the graceful and solemn. It must become anti-graceful, deforming, impressionistic, synthetic, dynamic, free-working. (Cited in Hein, 1979, p. 19)

The desire to prise film from the grip of bourgeois and popular theatrical traditions came to typify much of the work of the European avant-garde. Coming mostly from backgrounds in the fine and plastic arts, which were revolutionised in the first two decades of the century by Futurism, Cubism and Dada, the earliest avant-garde film-makers sought to redefine film as a visual art (Hein, 1979; Lawder, 1975; Kuenzli, 1987). By the 1920s, three distinct variants on this project had emerged: the development of a specifically cinematic aesthetic, associated with French Impressionism (Delluc and Epstein's *photogénie* and Dulac's *cinégraphie intégrale*); the use of film to extend the scope of painting, in pursuit of, in the words of one critic, 'kinetic solutions to pictorial problems' (Barbara Rose, cited in Wollen, 1982, p. 97), seen in the works of Laszlo Moholy-Nagy, Man Ray and Marcel Duchamp; and the search for equivalences between the arts or for ways of combining them, particularly film and music, as in the work of German abstract animators Viking Eggeling's *Diagonal-Symphonie/Symphonie diagonale* (1924) and Hans Richter's *Rhythmus 21/Film ist Rhythmus* (1921), which developed from their joint experiments with 'rhythm in painting', and Walter Ruttmann's and Oskar Fischinger's 'optical music' (Russett and Starr, 1988).

Soviet avant-garde film, which evolved under the influence of Russian Futurism and Cubism in a revolutionary context, has either been discussed by some historians of experimental cinema as a related or parallel current to the French and German work (Curtis, 1971) or excluded because of its strong narrative element (Lawder, 1975). Phillip Drummond (1979) has commented that such discussions involve simplifications and exclusions and are the result of a monolithic opposition between mainstream and avant-garde that leads to a polemical drawing of the lines. A more nuanced view of the internal dynamics and tensions of the 1920s avant-garde has been possible since Peter Wollen remapped the terrain in his 1975 essay 'The two avant-gardes' (Wollen, 1982).

Wollen argues that the historical avant-garde actually comprised two quite separate tendencies: on one hand, a group of film-makers closely associated with painting and committed to formal experiment, who were part of a trend, at its most radical, towards 'an art of pure signifiers detached from meaning as much as from reference' (Wollen, 1982,

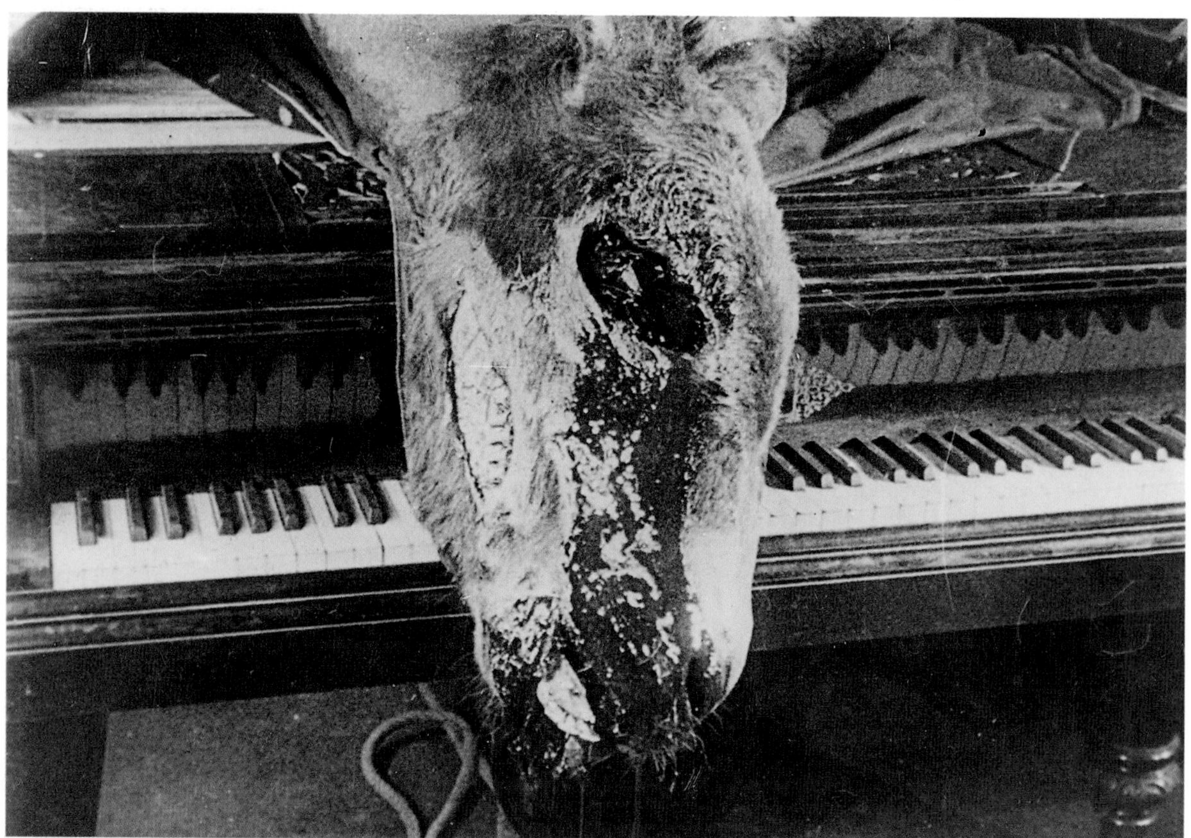

Releasing the power of the unconscious through bizarre imagery: Buñuel and Dalí's *Un chien andalou*

p. 95); on the other hand, a much smaller group around Eisenstein and Vertov whose concern with film form arose from an interest in cinema as a site for the mediation of social and political concerns. As Wollen puts it, 'What we find with the Soviet film-makers is a recognition that a new type of content, a new realm of signifieds, demands formal innovation, on the level of the signifier, for its expression' (Wollen, 1982, p. 98). By mapping the differences between the Soviet cinema of montage and western European practices contemporaneous with it onto the relationship between political and aesthetic modernism, Wollen's model suggests a more dynamic, heterogeneous history for the avant-garde.

Surrealism

Surrealism is not mentioned in Wollen's essay, but nevertheless deserves to be discussed in the context of avant-garde film-making. Despite its closeness to Dadaism, surrealism cannot be assimilated to a painterly, formalist European avant-garde. The surrealists consolidated the Dadaists' contempt for bourgeois art by repudiating all avant-gardes and denouncing purist aesthetics. They positioned themselves as a counter-avant-garde, attacking Impressionist cinema, carrying on a campaign of abuse against Cocteau and praising popular films such as Louis Feuillade's serials, Erich von Stroheim's melodramas and American crazy comedies. Playing on the codes of narrative cinema, in films such as *Star of the Sea/L'Étoile de mer* (1928), *An Andalusian Dog/Un chien andalou* (1928) and *L'Âge d'or* (1930), the surrealists created a film world in which the chance collisions of Dada were bound by obsessional desire. Instead of the illogical, non-narrative and abstract strategies characteristic of Dada films, surrealist film-makers used conventional cinematography, optical realism and narrative to invite identification, in order to make the misappropriation and rupture of these techniques all the more shocking.

Their use of narrative systems also enabled them to address social and ideological issues discursively, as in Buñuel's passionately anti-clerical documentary *Land Without Bread/Las hurdes* (1933), where the grotesque incongruities of the film's surrealist aesthetic testify to the terrible existence of the impoverished mountain people. Summing up the importance of surrealism for the history of avant-garde film, Ian Christie has written:

> The impact of surrealism has been pervasive and, in many respects, progressive. The Surrealists effectively re-defined the scope of avant-garde activity, giving it a political and a psychoanalytic dimension. Yet the immediate effect of the Surrealist counter avant-garde was a repression of modernist work in favour of neo-romantic, primitivist and eclectic activity. In the cinema, they sought to tap the 'unconscious' of popular cinema; but from *Un chien andalou* onwards, surrealism began to construct its own model of avant-garde cinema, based upon procedures of subversion, rupture and the dysfunction of dominant narrative cinema . . . In the final analysis, surrealism destroyed one conception of avant-garde activity and irrevocably altered the terms on which any future avant-garde would emerge. (Christie, 1979, p. 44)

The first flowering of avant-garde film ended with the political reconfiguration of Europe in the 1930s. In the Soviet Union, the emergence of socialist realism eclipsed the experimentalism of the 1920s. Abstract and experimental art was banned in Germany by the Nazis and fell from favour in France under the influence of the Popular Front, which favoured the direct approach of realist forms.

The post-war avant-garde

The post-war resurgence of avant-garde cinema began in the US, fostered there by cultural and industrial conditions. The arrival of scores of refugee artists fleeing the totalitarian regimes of Europe in the 1930s and 1940s brought modernism to North America, where it flourished in all the visual and performing arts. After the war, an increasing availability of 16mm equipment made film production and exhibition more accessible to those outside the industry, thus encouraging the spread of film societies, film education and amateur film-making. This also created the context in which an underground film culture could develop around organisations such as Amos Vogel's avant-garde film society Cinema 16 and the New York Film-Makers' Cooperative.

Personal film

Between the early 1940s and the mid-1960s, the North American film avant-garde took shape in 'a great burst of personal film-making' (Curtis, 1971, p. 49) that gave it its distinctive character. Across a diverse range of styles, encompassing the film poetry of Maya Deren, Kenneth Anger and Stan Brakhage, the film diaries of Jonas Mekas and self-portraits of Carolee Schneemann, and the 'trash' underground movies of Ron Rice, Jack Smith and the Kuchar brothers, the films of this period share a concern with the personal as subject matter and with the development of cinematic forms equivalent to first-person discourse. Even the abstract cinema of West Coast avant-garde film-makers such as Jordan Belson and James Whitney developed under the influence of a personal metaphysics.

The terms for discussion of these films and film-makers were set by P. Adams Sitney's *Visionary Film* (1979), which posits a Romantic tradition primarily concerned with the representation of states of mind. According to Sitney: 'The preoccupations of the American avant-garde film-makers coincide with those of our post-Romantic poets and Abstract Expressionist painters. Behind them lies a potent tradition of Romantic poetics' (Sitney, 1979, p. ix). At the core of this tradition, Sitney perceives a common concern with the phenomenology of mind: 'The great unacknowledged aspiration of the American avant-garde film has been the cinematic reproduction of the human mind' (p. 370). It should be noted that this assertion has been much criticised, not least for its vagueness with regard to the notion of 'mind' and its failure to address the role of language (Penley and Bergstrom, 1978).

Structural film

In the second half of the 1960s, an alternative to personal film emerged: structural film, defined by Sitney as 'a cinema of structure in which the shape of the whole film is predetermined and simplified' (Sitney, 1979, p. 369). Like minimalist painting or serial music, structural film foregrounds the materials and processes of film itself by substituting very explicit organising structures for the self-effacing structures of tradition (in the case of film, illusionist narrative systems). Through anti-illusionism and reflexivity, structural film attempts to approach the condition of 'pure film'. Such self-referentiality has been connected by more than one critic to the variant of modernism described by Clement Greenberg: 'It quickly emerged that the unique and proper area of competence of each art coincided with all that was unique to the nature of its medium . . . Realistic, illusionist art had dissembled the medium, using art to conceal art. Modernism used art to call attention to art' (cited in James, 1989, pp. 239–40).

Many of the structural films are systematic investigations of a restricted number of filmic codes or aspects of film's material substrate: Michael Snow's *Wavelength* (1967) explores the potentialities of the fixed frame and the zoom; George Landow's *Film in Which There Appear Sprocket Holes, Edge Lettering, Dirt Particles, Etc* (1966) investigates the relationship between the cinematic image and the filmstrip; Nam June Paik's *Zen for Film* (1964) makes projection its subject matter. The movement's British offshoot, 'structural/materialism', travelled a '*via negativa* of unprecedented severity' (James, 1989, p. 278) to a position of anti-representationalism that was much more rigorous than that of its American counterpart. Peter Gidal (an American in London) argued that representational content should be eliminated as far as possible: 'The Structural/Materialist film must minimise the content in its overpowering, imagistically seductive sense, in an attempt to get through the miasmic area of "experience" and proceed with film as film' (Gidal, 1978, p. 2). Gidal's *Room Film 1973* (1973) has been described as 'almost relentless in its denial of tangible images' (Dusinberre, 1978, p. 109).

Where most critics see a clear break between personal film and structural film, Sitney argues that structural film renewed and intensified the visionary tradition out of which personal film developed: 'The structural film approaches the condition of meditation and evokes states of consciousness without mediation; that is, with the sole mediation of the camera' (Sitney, 1979, p. 370). According to Sitney, structural film's interrogation of the ontology of film acts as a springboard for an exploration of the nature of perception, thought and feeling. Other critics, including Annette Michelson (1974) and Peter Wollen (1982), articulate an opposing view of structural film, according to which its ontological investigation is an end in itself, the only meanings produced being concerned with the medium. As Wollen puts it: 'The frontier reached by this avant-garde has been an ever-narrowing preoccupation with pure film, with film "about" film, a dissolution of signification into objecthood or tautology' (Wollen, 1982, p. 97).

To some extent, national contexts illuminate the variations in avant-garde practice. In British structural film-making, for instance, ontological enquiry was undertaken in a Marxist frame of reference rather than a phenomenological one: reflexive, anti-illusionist strategies were employed with the aim of breaking with ideology and demonstrating the materiality of filmic practice. There were also structural film-makers in Germany and Austria who were directly involved with movements such as Fluxus and Actionism, which, far from notions of ontological purity, emphasised aleatory methods of composition and mixed media.

Avant-garde versus modernism

Underlying the differences in avant-garde practice and interpretation that had emerged by the 1970s were profound differences in the assimilation of the legacy of the 1920s and the notion of avant-garde itself. Peter Wollen argues that modernism became divorced from the avant-garde when it was transplanted to the US and institutionalised in the New York art world, while the avant-garde, which centred on Paris, gained a new agenda from the events of May 1968 that led it away from modernist aesthetics (Wollen, 1981). Paul Willemen makes a similar point more trenchantly, arguing that modernism and the avant-garde 'are, in fact, two simultaneous but antagonistic tendencies' (Willemen, 1994, p. 145). Modernism, according to Wollen, is characterised by reflexivity, semiotic reduction, foregrounding of the signifier and suppression or suspension of the signified, whereas the avant-garde rejects purism and ontological speculation in favour of semiotic expansion and a heterogeneity of signifiers and signifieds. These two opposing tendencies are rooted in those of the historical avant-garde. One tendency reflects a preoccupation with the specificity of the signifier, holding the signified in suspense or striving to eliminate it. The other has tried to develop new types of relation between signifier and signified through the montage of heterogeneous elements (Wollen, 1981, p. 10).

Wollen sees structural film as a continuation of the first tendency, the modernist avant-garde of the 1920s, and the post-1968 work of, say, Godard and Straub-Huillet as a continuation of the second tendency, the avant-garde of Eisenstein and 1920s Soviet cinema. The potential of the first tendency, Wollen argues, is limited by the exhaustion of modernism, which by the late 20th century had been transposed into conceptualism and minimalism and played out in ever-decreasing circles of ontological purity. Although Wollen emphasises that these are only tendencies, pointing out, for example, that the American avant-garde is far more heterogeneous than most of its critics have acknowledged, he nevertheless sees far more potential in the tradition of montage than in the tradition of ontological purity.

Godard and counter-cinema

Unlike the American personal and structural film-makers, Jean-Luc Godard came into avant-garde film from a background in commercial art cinema. Between 1968 and 1971, Godard broke with the industry in order to work with Jean-Pierre Gorin and others in the Dziga-Vertov Group, a small co-operative set up to make political films. Writing on Godard in the early 1970s, Wollen introduced the term 'counter-cinema' as a precise description of Godard's negation of the values of mainstream cinema (in place of the term 'avant-garde', which implies being in advance of mainstream cinema in an indeterminate way).

Counter-cinema starts from the assertion that the illusionist conventions of mainstream cinema function to obscure the real conditions of its production. Ideology, by this analysis, is ingrained in mainstream film at the level of form and it is the task of radical cinema to break with that form as well as with its political contents. Central to the counter-cinema project is the attempt to involve an audience in political struggle by inviting active engagement rather than passive spectatorship. Counter-cinema therefore systematically challenges illusionism with strategies that subvert each of its major codes – disrupting linear causal relations, denying narrative closure, fracturing spatial and temporal verisimilitude, undermining identification and putting pleasure into question. In 'Godard and counter-cinema: *Le Vent d'est*', Wollen (1982) tabulates the seven deadly sins of 'Hollywood-Mosfilm' (in Godard's phrase) against the seven cardinal virtues of counter-cinema:

> Narrative transitivity/Narrative intransitivity
> Identification/Estrangement
> Transparency/Foregrounding
> Single diegesis/Multiple diegesis
> Closure/Aperture
> Pleasure/Unpleasure
> Fiction/Reality

Although a complex web of political and theoretical thought (Marx, Mao, Saussure, Lacan, Althusser) provides the intellectual background to Godard's counter-cinema strategies, the strategies themselves are more directly developed from the ideas of Brecht and Eisenstein.

From Brecht, Godard takes the idea of distanciation, embodied in devices that break the spectator's involvement and empathy and draw attention to the wider social context of the play or film. In *Wind from the East/Le Vent d'est* (1969), for example, Godard estranges the viewer by introducing 'real people' into the fiction, by using the same voice for different characters and different voices for the same character, by directly addressing the camera and insulting the audience. The crucial difference between these strategies and the superficially similar reflexive ploys of Greenbergian modernism is that Godard tries to draw our attention not to the film and its specific ontology but to the socio-economic context in which the film is made and seen.

Eisenstein's notion of montage was developed by Godard into 'a concept of conflict, not between the content of images, but between different codes and between signifier and signified' (Wollen, 1982, p. 99). Godard disrupts the traditional organisation of mainstream cinema by splitting up and recombining cinematic codes, which are distributed across the multiple channels that characterise film as a medium, and which illusionist conventions aim to unify: sound and image, time and space, character and actor. With the removal of the traditional hierarchy of filmic codes, the text becomes polyphonic: discourses are juxtaposed, recontextualised and put into conflict and dialogue with each other. Thus in *Pravda* (1970), images are accompanied by a commentary, spoken by 'Vladimir Lenin' and 'Rosa Luxemburg', which alters their meanings. Interviews with Czech workers, students and peasants go untranslated (the commentary advises: 'If you don't know Czech you'd better learn it fast'). And images from a munitions factory are intercut with images of film production. The spectator's activity in reading the film consists of assembling the various sounds and images meaningfully and evaluating the relationships between the film's many discourses.

As much as counter-cinema is a political cinema, then, it is equally a problematisation of the relationships between cinema and politics. As Wollen puts it:

> The cinema cannot show the truth, or reveal it, because the truth is not out there in the real world, waiting to be photographed. What the cinema can do is produce meanings and meanings can only be plotted, not in relation to some abstract yardstick or criterion of truth, but in relation to other meanings. (Wollen, 1982, p. 91)

However, if counter-cinema's strengths derive from this kind of analysing, then so do its weaknesses. Wollen expresses quite strong reservations about some aspects of Godardian counter-cinema. Godard's refusal of pleasure is grounded in the notion that entertainment cinema is a drug that mollifies the masses into giving up their long-term (millenarian) dreams in favour of ephemeral (false, illusory, deceptive) fantasies. Wollen finds this logic questionable as well as puritanical. He argues that in placing the reality principle before the pleasure principle, Godard overlooks the adaptive nature of the former and the transformative potential of the latter: 'Desire, and its representation in fantasy, far from being necessary enemies of revolutionary politics – and its cinematic auxiliary – are necessary conditions' (Wollen, 1982, p. 88). In addition, Godard's suspicion of fiction, which the post-1968 films equate with deception, ideology and mystification, results in a 'flattening out', as Wollen sees it, of the more complex philosophical questioning of appearance and reality, truth and lies that plays a part in his earlier films. Finally, Wollen points out that counter-cinema, by definition, cannot have an absolute existence in its own right, but can only exist as a negation of mainstream film, having been conceived as its antagonist. *Le Vent d'est* is therefore not revolutionary cinema, but a starting point for work on revolutionary cinema. Ultimately, Wollen and many others were disappointed by the outcome of Godard's 'adventures in the wilderness'. From the mid-1970s onwards, Godard gradually reverted to the forms and concerns of art cinema, leaving the pursuit of counter-cinema to others. As the revolutionary fervour of the late 1960s faded and the new politics of cultural and sexual identity emerged, a new constituency for counter-cinema took shape around feminism.

Feminist counter-cinema

Feminist counter-cinema theory emerged in the 1970s in tandem with the critique of Hollywood developed by Claire Johnston and Laura Mulvey (see Feminist film theory, p. 491). Johnston and Mulvey argued for the creation of a feminist counter-cinema on the grounds that patriarchal ideology is thoroughly embedded in film technique and cinematic convention:

> If we accept that cinema involves the production of signs, the idea of non-intervention is pure mystification. The sign is always a product. What the camera in fact grasps is the 'natural' world of the dominant ideology. Women's cinema cannot afford such idealism; the 'truth' of our oppression cannot be 'captured' on celluloid with the 'innocence' of the camera: it has to be constructed/manufactured. New meanings have to be created by disrupting the fabric of male bourgeois cinema within the text of the film. (Johnston, 1974, p. 29)

Both Johnston and Mulvey argued that since the narrative conventions, iconographic traditions and identificatory structures of mainstream film were shaped by their development in a patriarchal society, a change in content alone would merely reproduce the bias in the system. Both also rejected the idea of an essential and timeless feminine aesthetic that simply awaited discovery or clarification ('a developed tradition winding through the overt history of cinema like an unseen thread', Mulvey, 1979, p. 7). Instead, they imagined a feminist aesthetic evolved through contestation of existing forms. However, where Mulvey argued for an avant-garde women's cinema ('feminist film practice has . . . almost an objective alliance with the radical avant-garde', 1979, p. 4), Johnston, writing under the influence of *Cahiers du Cinéma*, argued for a women's cinema that would reconcile politics with entertainment. Thus Mulvey: 'Women, whose image has continually been stolen . . . cannot view the decline of traditional film form with anything more than sentimental regret' (Mulvey, 1975, p. 18), and Johnston: 'In order to counter our objectification in the cinema our collective fantasies must be released: women's cinema must embody the working through of desire: such an objective demands the use of the entertainment film' (Johnston, 1974, p. 31).

Mulvey's radical position was in tune with its times and quickly achieved wide currency on the feminist film scene. In the year that Mulvey's 'Visual pleasure and narrative cinema' was published, Chantal Akerman completed the film *Jeanne Dielman 23, Quai du commerce, 1080 Bruxelles* (1975), which was received by many feminist critics as the exemplar of Mulvey's 'passionate detachment'. Using a minimalist form comprising long takes, static camerawork and no analytic editing or reverse-shot, Akerman presented the daily existence of a widowed Belgian housewife whose routine chores include prostituting herself to support herself and her son. The three-and-a-half-hour film observed the tiny lapses in control building up to Jeanne's loss of self-control with a client, whom she murders. Most of the film's action consists of domestic labour, and it is the way that this is filmed that has led feminist critics to see it as a 'discourse of women's looks, through a woman's viewpoint' (Bergstrom, 1977, p. 118).

Mulvey's suspicion of narrative ('Sadism demands a story ...', 1975, p. 14) was also widely shared. Sally Potter's short film *Thriller* (1979), informed by 'Visual pleasure and narrative cinema' and other feminist texts, interrogated and restructured traditional narrative. The film is a reworking of the opera *La Bohème* as a film noir-style investigation by the heroine into the causes of her own death. It begins where the opera ends, with Mimi's death, and retells its story in the retrospective manner of a criminal investigation. Potter's *The Gold Diggers* (1983) is constructed as a 'semiotic shuffle' with the history of the cinema (Cook, 1984, p. 15), in which two women, Celeste and Ruby, seek answers to the riddle of their own existence as figures in a cinematic landscape. In both films, traditional narrative is displaced by reflexive critique and intertextual reference. At the same time, Potter is clearly not an anti-narrative film-maker in the sense that Brakhage and Snow are. Her films enter into dialogue with existing narratives in order to generate new narrative possibilities centring on female subjectivity.

Return to narrative

Potter's early work is situated on the brink of the return to narrative that took place in alternative cinema from the late 1970s. A key figure in this development was Yvonne Rainer. Her films, often described as ironic melodramas, work 'with and against narrative', as Teresa de Lauretis puts it (1987, p. 108), using quotation, contradiction, commentary, interruption and multiple diegeses. Rainer's approach to narrative is pragmatic: 'For me the story is an empty frame on which to hang images and thoughts which need support. I feel no obligation to flesh out this armature with credible details of time and place' (Rainer, in *Camera Obscura* Collective, 1976, p. 89). Since she began making films in 1972, her work has increasingly moved towards narrative:

> From description of individual feminine experience floating free of social context and narrative hierarchy, to descriptions of individual feminine experience placed in radical juxtaposition against historical events, to explicitly feminist speculations about feminine experience, I have just formulated an evolution which in becoming more explicitly feminist seems to demand a more solid anchoring in narrative conventions. (Rainer, 1985, p. 8)

Rainer is one of many feminist film-makers who have discovered in narrative an indispensable 'strategy of coherence' (de Lauretis, 1987) for mapping differences and making meaning. This conditional rehabilitation of narrative has been accompanied by a growing concern with fantasy and subjectivity. Bette Gordon's *Variety* (1983), Valie Export's *The Practice of Love/Die Praxis der Liebe* (1984) and Sheila McLaughlin's *She Must Be Seeing Things* (1987) all use fantasy, framed by investigative narratives, to explore the formal problems of desire and the look in women's – heterosexual and lesbian – representation. With these films, women's counter-cinema rejoins Johnston's 1974 position, although with the benefit of a period of radical negation behind it.

Inevitably this evolution has rendered some feminist films less noticeably avant-garde, as their formal problematics are embedded within a narrative infrastructure. Teresa de Lauretis argues that formalist definitions of alternative film have been renderend obsolete with the dissolution of the rigid divide between avant-garde and mass culture. Instead, she suggests that women's cinema is 'guerrilla film', which she defines in the following terms:

> In sum, what I would call alternative films in women's cinema are those which engage the current problems, the real issues, the things actually at stake in feminist communities on a local scale, and which, although informed by a global perspective, do not assume or aim at a

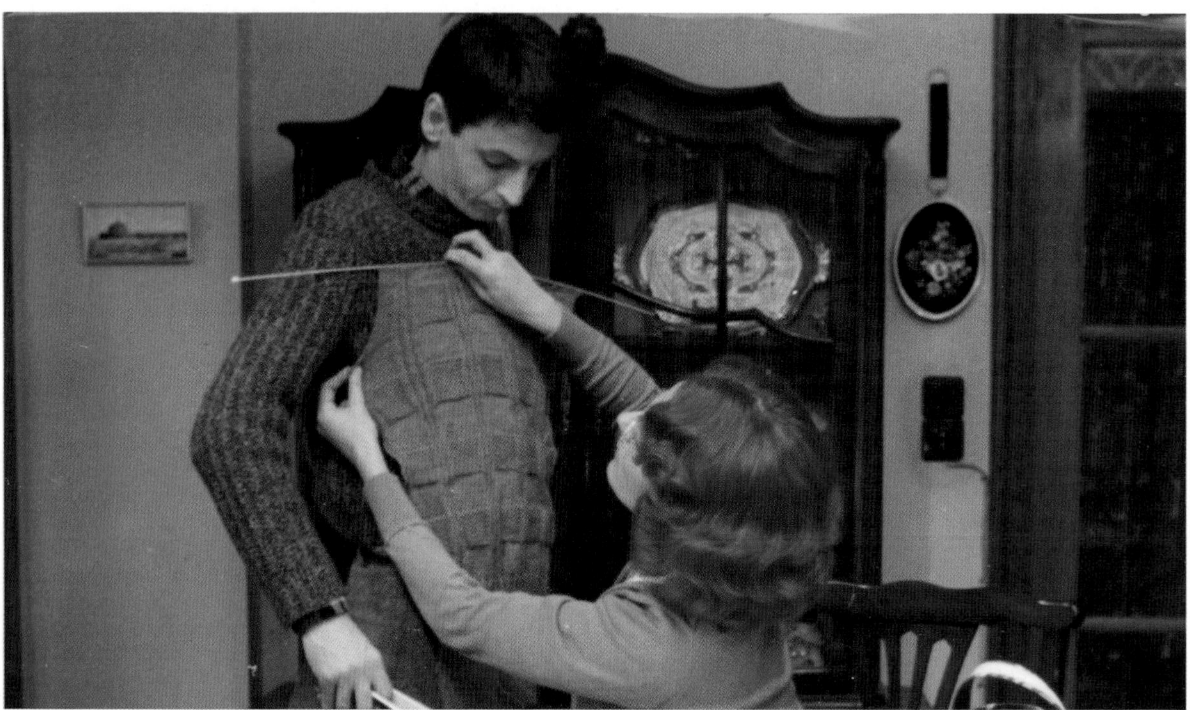

Passionate detachment: Chantal Akerman's exemplary *Jeanne Dielman 23, Quai du Commerce, 1080 Bruxelles*

Semiotic shuffle: Sally Potter's *The Gold Diggers*

> universal, multinational audience, but address a particular one in its specific history of struggles and emergence. (de Lauretis, 1990, p. 17)

This description borrows from the theory and practice of Third Cinema (see Third world and postcolonial cinema, p. 97), and might also be applied to New Queer Cinema (see Queer theory and New Queer Cinema, p. 505). Between them, these engaged cinemas have redefined the scope and nature of alternative film. Thus the work of radical film-makers such as Trinh T. Minh-ha, Isaac Julien, John Greyson and Tracey Moffatt cuts accross traditional categories such as mainstream, art cinema and avant-garde in its effort to address historically specific audiences and engage with precisely located issues. At the same time, changing media technologies have created new fields for formal innovation, ranging from video art and music video to virtual reality and the Internet. After the purism of the 1960s and the formalism of the 1970s, the combinatory, eclectic conception of avant-garde is again in the ascendancy under the influence of new politics and new media. To the extent that the current avant-garde has a common project, it is concerned with crossing boundaries between art forms, between traditions and between cultural and social identities.

Selected Reading

David E. James, *Allegories of Cinema: American Film in the Sixties*, Princeton, NJ, Princeton University Press, 1989.

Teresa de Lauretis, *Technologies of Gender: Essays on Theory, Film, and Fiction*, Bloomington, Indiana University Press, 1987.

A. L. Rees, *A History of Experimental Film and Video*, London, BFI Publishing, 1999.

Peter Wollen, *Readings and Writings: Semiotic Counterstrategies*, London, Verso, 1982.

An Andalusian Dog/Un chien andalou (France 1928 *p.c* – Luis Buñuel; *d* – Luis Buñuel)

From its startling opening sequence, in which a man appears to slice through a woman's eyeball with a cut-throat razor, to the grotesque corpses of its closing scene, *Un chien andalou* is a deliberate assault on the bourgeois artistic and social conventions of its time. Buñuel described it as 'a desperate and passionate appeal to murder'. The surrealists were interested in releasing the power of the unconscious through procedures that followed the logic of dreams. Salvador Dalí and Buñuel used bizarre imagery and incongruous juxtapositions to recreate their own dreams, almost as in surrealist automatic writing. Although some of their images, such as the rotting donkeys on pianos and the severed hand, were staged before the camera, the most visceral sequences are those where editing is used to imitate the metonymic patterns of unconscious thought, such as the sequence of puns that cuts between a moth, a mouth, a smile that is wiped off a man's face, an outraged woman frantically applying lipstick, a beard of pubic hair and an armpit. In place of linear narrative and Hollywood continuity, the film uses graphic continuity, playing on similar shapes and patterns in contiguous shots (for example, in the series of images showing a hand full of ants, a hairy armpit and a sea urchin). At the same time, its skilful parody of Hollywood style is no doubt part of its enduring success.

The similarity of the film's signifying practices to the workings of the unconscious as described by Freud has invited much interpretation (see Drummond, 1977; Sandro, 1987; Williams, 1981). Buñuel famously insisted that nothing in the film has any symbolic value, although this is clearly not the case. He may have been warning against readings of the film that would assimilate it to Impressionism or Symbolism, thereby lessening the force of its deliberate offensiveness. The subversive aesthetic of surrealism has been claimed as a precursor for American underground film-makers such as Maya Deren and Kenneth Anger (Renan, 1968), but its direct appeal to the unconscious has also been appropriated by the advertising industry.

ALISON BUTLER

Wind from the East/Le Vent d'est (France/Italy/Germany 1969 *p.c* – Anouchka Films/Polifilm/CCC Filmkunst; *d* – Jean-Luc Godard and Jean-Pierre Gorin)

Le Vent d'est was inspired by an idea of the student leader Daniel Cohn-Bendit to make a left-wing western about a miners' strike. The Dziga-Vertov Group argued that it would be impossible to make a western that was genuinely left-wing because the genre would reproduce the relations and ideology of mainstream cinema. In the event, Cohn-Bendit fell out with the film-makers and does not appear in the film. Although elements of western imagery appear, the film is above all an essay on revolutionary film-making.

In the film's dense articulation of sound and image, written and spoken language tend to dominate. An intertitle that states 'Ce n'est pas une image juste, c'est juste une image' ('This is not a just

A cinema of aesthetic adventure: *Le Vent d'est*

image, it's just an image') indicates the mistrust of the photographic form. A sequence in which members of the film company discuss the possible inclusion of still images of Stalin is offered as a demonstration of the way images can be mobilised by one side or the other in class struggle. Another sequence demystifies mainstream cinema by introducing 'a typical character in bourgeois cinema', who addresses the audience in an insulting way. The place of cinema in revolution is debated in a scene in which the Brazilian film-maker Glauber Rocha stands at a dusty crossroads and is approached by a pregnant woman with a movie camera who asks him the way to political cinema. Rocha points one way and then another, saying: 'That way is the cinema of aesthetic adventure and philosophical enquiry, while this way is the Third World cinema – a dangerous cinema, divine and marvellous, where the questions are practical ones like production, distribution, training 300 film-makers to make 600 films a year for Brazil alone, to supply one of the world's biggest markets.' The woman sets off down the path to Third World cinema, but is harassed by a red plastic ball that inexplicably gets in her way; she returns to the crossroads and takes the other path. The sequence dramatises the dilemma of the Dziga-Vertov Group as radical film-makers in the west, although whether the film solves it is another question. Glauber Rocha intensely disliked *Le Vent d'est*. Many spectators find it difficult and unpleasurable to watch, including Andrew Britton, who wrote: '*Vent d'est* is, quite simply, one of the most repressive films ever made' (Britton, 1976, p. 9).

ALISON BUTLER

Privilege (USA 1990 *p.c* – Zeitgeist Films; *d* – Yvonne Rainer)

In *Privilege*, Rainer uses a fragmentary narrative form to juxtapose different ways of thinking about privilege and the lack of it. Women are interviewed for a documentary about menopause, putatively authored by 'Yvonne Washington', Rainer's African-American alter ego. One of the interviewees, a white woman named Jenny, tells the story of an occurrence in her youth, which is narrated in flashback. Jenny's neighbour, Brenda, a white lesbian, presses charges against Carlos, a Puerto Rican man, whom she finds naked in her room. Jenny perjures herself, saying she actually saw Carlos in Brenda's apartment. Jenny subsequently has an affair with the assistant district attorney. Rainer offers this anecdote as a model of privilege, demonstrating its distribution according to the culturally coded categories of race, gender and class.

The film addresses the question of privilege not only through its content but through its forms. Rainer claims that: 'Every character in the film can be seen as either having or not having privilege, depending on race, sex, class, age. If they didn't have it, I gave it to them' (MacDonald, 1992, p. 352). She accomplishes this by privileging certain characters' points of view at key junctures in the narrative. Digna, a Puerto Rican woman, moves invisibly, omnisciently through the film, commenting ironically on the action; Carlos speaks a text by Frantz Fanon, which in turn refracts on a text by Eldridge Cleaver spoken by an African-American 'double' who replaces Carlos in some of the shots in Brenda's apartment; Jenny appears as her middle-aged self in her flashback, exchanging the privilege of youth for the privilege of hindsight. Anti-illusionist devices including reverse-shots of the film crew, direct address to camera and several appearances by Rainer in minor 'roles' serve as reminders of the privilege of the film-maker.

The film's prismatic structure of points of view, which are often irreconcilable with each other, represents Rainer's attempt to go beyond 'the limitations of feminist film theory' in order to address issues of race, age and sexuality (MacDonald, 1992, p. 346). Its coherence is not at the level of narrative or character identification but in the questions confronting the viewers about their own relationships with privilege. The dialogical form of *Privilege* opens it to a variety of readings, depending on the critic's view of the film's exposition of contradictions and assumptions in white liberal thinking. E. Ann Kaplan's sympathetic reading takes these problems as the subject matter of the film, offered as questions for the audience's consideration (Kaplan, 1997, pp. 273–80). Michelle Wallace argues that inequality is structured into the film's discursive strategies: 'The positions from which women of colour speak . . . are inferior to positions from which white women, white men, and men of colour speak' (Wallace, 1991, p. 8). Patricia Mellencamp argues that the film is trapped in its own logic: 'Caught up in the tenets of heterosexual romance (perhaps unconsciously so), *Privilege* enacts what it attempts to critique' (Mellencamp, 1995, p. 184).

ALISON BUTLER

Third World and postcolonial cinema

ROBERT STAM

Culturally rich, formally innovative and politically provocative, Third World and postcolonial cinema forms a vital current within world cinema. Taken in a broad sense, 'Third World cinema', far from being a marginal appendage to First World cinema – Hollywood's 'poor relative' – actually produces most of the world's feature films. If one excludes films made for television, India is the leading producer of fiction films in the world, producing up to 1,000 feature films a year. Asian countries, taken together, produce over half of the yearly world production. Nor is this a recent development. In the 1920s, India was already producing more films than the UK. Countries such as the Philippines were producing over 50 films a year by the 1930s, Hong Kong over 200 by the 1950s. But although the cinematic traditions of many countries later recognised as belonging to the Third World go back to the first decades of this century – Brazil's cinematic *bela epoca* occurred between 1908 and 1911 – it was in the 1960s that Third World cinema as a self-aware movement emerged on the First World film scene by winning prizes and garnering critical praise.

Third Cinema: questions of terminology

The term 'Third World' refers to the colonised, neo-colonised or decolonised nations and 'minorities' whose structural disadvantages have been shaped by the colonial process and the unequal division of international labour. The term itself challenges the colonising vocabulary that posited these nations as 'backward' and 'underdeveloped'. As a political coalition, the 'Third World' broadly coalesced around the enthusiasm generated by anti-colonial struggles in Vietnam and Algeria, and specifically emerged from the 1955 Bandung conference of 'non-aligned' African and Asian nations. Coined by French demographer Alfred Sauvy in the 1950s by analogy to the revolutionary 'third estate' of France – that is, the commoners in contrast with first estate (the nobility) and the second (the clergy) – the term posited three worlds: the capitalist first world of Europe, the US, Australia and Japan; the 'second world' of the socialist bloc (China's place in the schema was the object of much debate); and the third world proper.

The fundamental definition of the 'Third World' has little to do with crude economic ('the poor'), developmental categories (the 'non-industrialised'), racial ('the non-white'), cultural ('the backward') or geographical ('the east', 'the south') categories. These are all imprecise, because the third world is neither necessarily poor in resources (Mexico, Venezuela and Iraq are rich in oil), nor simply non-white (Argentina and Ireland are predominantly white), nor is it non-industrialised (Brazil, Argentina, India all have heavy industries), nor culturally 'backward'. Instead 'Third World' signifies an international experience of protracted structural domination.

In relation to cinema, the term 'Third World' refers to the collectively vast cinematic productions of Asia, Africa and Latin America, and the minoritarian cinema in the first world. Some, such as Roy Armes (1987), define Third World cinema broadly as the ensemble of films produced by Third World countries (including films produced before the very idea of 'Third World' was current). Others, such as Paul Willemen, prefer to speak of 'Third Cinema', which they see as an ideological project, that is as a body of films adhering to a certain political and aesthetic programme, whether or not they are produced by Third World peoples themselves (see Pines and Willemen, 1989). Originally emerging from the Cuban revolution, from Perónism and Perón's 'third way' in Argentina, and from such film movements as Cinema Novo in Brazil, the term 'Third Cinema' was launched as a rallying cry in the late 1960s by Fernando Solanas and Octavio Getino. They defined Third Cinema as 'the cinema that recognizes in [the anti-imperialist struggle in the Third World and its equivalents within the imperialist countries] . . . the most gigantic cultural, scientific, and artistic manifestation of our time . . . in a word, the decolonization of culture' (Solanas and Getino, 1983). As long as they are taken not as 'essential' pre-constituted entities, but rather as collective projects to be forged, both 'Third World cinema' and 'Third Cinema' retain important tactical and polemical uses for a politically inflected cultural practice.

In purely classificatory terms, one can posit overlapping circles of denotation. First, a core circle of 'Third Worldist' films produced by and for Third World people (no matter where those people happen to be) and adhering to the principles of Third Cinema. Second, a wider circle of the cinematic productions of Third World peoples (retroactively defined as such), whether or not the films adhere to the principles of Third Cinema and irrespective of the period of their making. Third, another circle consisting of films made by First or Second World people in support of Third World peoples and adhering to the principles of Third Cinema. And fourth, a final circle, somewhat anomalous in status, at once 'inside' and 'outside', comprising post-1970s diasporic hybrid films, for example those of Mona Hatoum, Isaac Julien, Gurinder Chadha or Hanif Kureishi, which both build on and interrogate the conventions of Third Cinema, and are therefore often referred to as 'post-Third Worldist' or 'postcolonial' (see Postcolonial cinema, p. 101). By far the largest category would be the second, the cinematic productions of countries designated as 'Third World'. This category would include the major traditional film industries of countries such as India, Egypt, Mexico, Brazil, Argentina and China, as well as the more recent post-independence or post-revolution industries of countries such as Cuba, Algeria, Senegal, Indonesia and scores of others.

The origins of Third World cinema

The Third World's cinematic counter-telling basically began with the post-war collapse of the European empires and the emergence of independent Third World nation-states (although there were, of course, implicitly anti-colonial films prior to this period of collapse). In the late 1960s and early 1970s, in the wake of the Vietnamese victory over the French, the Cuban revolution and Algerian independence, Third-Worldist film ideology was crystallised in a wave of militant manifesto essays – Glauber Rocha's 'Aesthetic of hunger' (1965), Fernando Solanas and Octavio Getino's 'Towards a third cinema' (1969) and Julio Garcia Espinosa's 'For an imperfect cinema' (1969) – and in declarations and manifestoes from Third World film festivals calling for a tricontinental revolution in politics and an aesthetic and narrative revolution in film form. Rocha called for a 'hungry' cinema of 'sad, ugly films', Solanas–Getino for militant guerrilla documentaries, and Espinosa for an 'imperfect' cinema energised by the 'low' forms of popular culture.

Although on one level the 1960s 'new cinemas' within the Third World came in the wake of the European 'new' movements – Italian Neo-realism, the Nouvelle Vague – their politics were far to the left of their European counterparts (see Italian Neo-realism, p. 233; The Nouvelle Vague, p. 202). The manifestoes of the 1960s and 1970s valorised an alternative, independent, anti-imperialist cinema more concerned with provocation and militancy than with auteurist expression or consumer satisfaction. The manifestoes contrasted the new cinema not only with Hollywood but also with their own countries' commercial traditions, now viewed as 'bourgeois', 'alienated' and 'colonised'. Just as the Nouvelle Vague film-makers raged against *le cinéma de papa*, so Brazil's Cinema Novo directors rejected the entertainment-oriented *chanchadas* and the European-style costume epics of film studios such as Vera Cruz, much as young Egyptian film-makers rejected the 'Hollywood on the Nile' tradition. And the 'new cinema' directors from India, for example Satyajit Ray, rejected both Hollywood and the commercial tradition of the Bombay musical, preferring the model of the European art film (see Hindi cinema, p. 217).

In retrospect, the Third World 'new waves' seem to have been overly binaristic in their rejection of antecedent commercial film traditions. The tendency in subsequent years has been to emphasise indigenous precursors and films (see, for example, Kamal Selim's *Determination/Al Azima*, 1939, in Egypt, and Dhirendra Ganguly's *England Returned/Bilat Ferat*, 1921, in India), and at times to recuperate, if only through parody, consecrated popular traditions. (Buñuel's critical recuperations of popular genres such as the melodrama and the *comedia ranchera* in his Mexican films of the 1950s, for example, opened a path later followed by directors such as Arnaldo Jabor and Raúl Ruiz.) After the first, 'euphoric', period of Third World cinema then, the early manifestoes were critiqued, positions were modified and updated, and cinematic praxis evolved in a whole range of directions.

Rewriting the past

According to Frantz Fanon, colonialism is 'not satisfied merely with holding a people in its grip . . . By a kind of perverted logic, it turns to the past of the people, and distorts, disfigures and destroys it' (1964, p. 210). In the face of Eurocentric historicising, Third World and minoritarian film-makers have rewritten their own histories, taken control over their own images, spoken in their own voices. It is not that their films substitute a pristine 'truth' for European 'lies', but that they propose counter-truths and counter-narratives informed by an anti-colonialist perspective, reclaiming and reaccentuating the events of the past in a vast project of remapping and renaming.

This rewriting has operated within a double timeframe: the reinscription of the past inevitably also rewrites the present. While revisionist historical films such as Luis Alberto Lamata's *Jericho/Jericó* (1991) and Carlos Diegues's *Quilombo* (1984) challenged Eurocentric accounts of the early years of European conquest and slavery respectively, other films have rewritten more recent events. Med Hondo's *An African Queen/Sarraounia* (1986), for example, tells of an African woman at the end of the 19th century who outwitted the French and saved her people from colonialism. Filipino film-maker Eddie Romero's *This Was How We Lived in Our Time, How Do You Live Now?/Ganito Kami Noon, Paano Kayo Ngayon?* (1976) treats the nationalist coming to consciousness of a Filipino just before the war against Spain in the 1890s. And Jorge Sanjines's *Courage of the People/El coraje del pueblo* (1971) dramatically restages a 1967 massacre of Bolivian tin miners, using miners as actors.

A number of films were made during the anti-colonial struggles themselves, from NLF films in Algeria (in the late 1950s), through Fidelista films during the anti-Battista campaign in the same period, to FRELIMO films in Mozambique and the work of the Radio Venceremos Film and Video Collective and the El Salvador Film Institute in El Salvador in the 1970s. But many more films were made with the luxury of historical hindsight, after the consolidation of independence. In the wake of the revolution of 1948, the Chinese film industry celebrated the victory against the Kuomintang in films such as Zhang Jungxiang's *Red Banner on Green Rock/Cui Gang Hong Qi* (1951) and Leonid Varlamov's *Victory of the Chinese People/Pobedakitayskogo naroda* (1950). Ousmane Sembène's *Emitaï* (1972), meanwhile, reached back into the relatively recent past of Senegalese resistance to French colonialism during World War II, and specifically the refusal of Diola women to supply French soldiers with rice. The same director's *Camp Thiaroye/Camp de Thiaroye* (1988) treats a similar rebellion of Senegalese soldiers who refuse to accept unequal pay in the French army, a refusal for which they are unceremoniously massacred. Mohamed Lakhdar Hamina's *Wind from the Aures/Assifat al-aouraz* (1965) tells a fictional story about Algerian popular struggle against the French. His *Chronicle of the Years of Embers/Ahdat sanawouach al-djamr* (1975) offers an epic account of the century of struggle that culminated in the Algerian revolution. Omar Khleifi's *The Dawn/Al-fajr* (1966) and *The Fellaheen/Fellagas* (1971) deal with the Tunisian liberation struggle, Sarah Maldoror's *Sambizanga* (1972) with the liberation struggle in Mozambique, and Ahmed Rachedi's compilation film *Dawn of the Damned/L'Aube des damnés* (1965) with anti-colonial struggles throughout Africa.

Many of the Third World films concerned with rewriting the past conduct a struggle on two fronts, at once political and aesthetic, synthesising revisionist historiography with formal innovation. Humberto Solás's *Lucia* (1969) rejects the conventional single fiction in favour of a complex tripartite structure. Each part is set in a different historical period (colonial 1895; bourgeois revolutionary 1933; the post-revolutionary 1960), each revolves around a woman named Lucia (creole aristocrat; middle-class urban; rural worker class), each is filmed in a distinct genre style (Visconti-style tragic melodrama; Bertolucci-style new wave political and existential drama; Brechtian farce) and each has its own visual features (dark; hazy; brightly lit). The result is to suggest that historical interpretation is inseparable from stylistic mediation. Med Hondo's *Soleil Ô* (1970), which mixes documentary and fiction, dream and dance in a poetic exorcism of colonialism, has a similar effect. The same director's *West Indies/Les Nègres marrons de la liberté* (1979) sets a cinematic opera on a slave ship, calling attention to both oppression and resistance during five centuries of colonial domination and revolt. A large number of films mingle documentary and fiction, in a politicised variation on a stylistic trademark of the Nouvelle Vague. Manuel Octavio Gómez's *First Charge of the Machete/La primera carga al machete* (1968), for example, reconstructs an 1868 battle against the Spanish in Cuba in the manner of a contemporary documentary, using high-contrast film, hand-held camera, direct-to-camera interviews, ambient light and so forth.

Allegorical interpretations

Fredric Jameson has argued that all Third World 'texts' are 'necessarily allegorical'. Even those texts invested with an apparently private or libidinal dynamic 'project a political dimension in the form of national allegory: the story of the private individual destiny is always an allegory of the embattled situation of the public third-world culture and society' (Jameson, 1986, p. 69; for an excellent critique see Aijaz Ahmad, 1986).

Although it is difficult to endorse Jameson's somewhat hasty totalisation of all Third World texts as allegorical – because it is impossible to posit any single artistic strategy as uniquely appropriate to the cultural productions of an entity as heterogeneous as the Third World, and allegory is in any case relevant to cultural productions elsewhere, including those of the First World – the concept of allegory is nonetheless a useful one. If understood in a broad sense, as any kind of oblique or synecdochic utterance soliciting hermeneutic completion or deciphering, 'allegory' is a productive category for dealing with many Third World films.

In the 1930s and 1940s in India, the female star Fearless Nadia rescued oppressed peoples from foreign tyrants in ways that were read at the time as anti-British allegories (see Ghandy and Thomas, 1991). In the more recent history of Third World Cinema, we find at least two major strands of allegory. First, there are the teleological Marxist-inflected nationalist allegories of the early period, where history is revealed as the progressive unfolding of an immanent historical design. Glauber Rocha's *Black God, White Devil/Deus e o diabo na terra do sol* (1964), for example, allegorises the people's coming to political consciousness through a stylised tale about a cowherd who moves from religious millenarianism through outlaw banditry and finally to revolution. Second, we have the modernist self-deconstructing allegories of the later period, where the focus shifts from the 'figural' signification of the onward march of history to the fragmentary nature of the discourse itself. Here, allegory is deployed as a privileged instance of language-consciousness in the context of the felt loss of larger historical purpose. Rogerio Sganzerla's *The Red Light Bandit/O bandido da luz vermelha* (1968), for instance, posits a homology, as Ismail Xavier points out, between a red-light district in a Third World country as a realm of 'garbage' and the film itself as a collection of film and mass-media refuse, and thus refuses the redemptive narrative of an earlier period (Xavier, 1997, pp. 124–63). A third variant, neither teleological nor modernist, might be found in those films where allegory serves as a form of protective camouflage against censorious regimes – where, for instance, the film uses the past to speak of the present, as in Joaquim Pedro de Andrade's *Conspirators/Os inconfidentes* (1972), or subversively adapts a classic, as in Nelson Pereira dos Santos's adaptation of Machado de Assis's story, *The Psychiatrist/O alienista* (1970).

The decline of the Third Worldist paradigm

During the 1980s and 1990s, Third Worldist euphoria slowly ebbed away in the light of the collapse of communism, the frustration of the hoped-for 'tricontinental revolution' (with Ho Chi Minh, Frantz Fanon and Che Guevara as talismanic figures), the realisation that the 'wretched of the earth' are not unanimously revolutionary (nor necessarily allies to one another), the appearance of an array of Third World despots, and the recognition that international geopolitics and the global economic system have obliged even socialist regimes to make a sort of peace with transnational capitalism.

The same period also witnessed a terminological crisis in relation to the term 'Third World' itself, which was increasingly seen as an inconvenient relic of a more militant period. Writing from a Marxist perspective, Aijaz Ahmad argues that Third World theory is an 'open-ended ideological interpellation' that papers over class oppression in all three worlds, while limiting socialism to the now non-existent 'second world' (see Ahmad, 1986; Burton, 1985). As Geoffrey Reeves puts it, the Third World concept homogenises 'markedly different national histories, experiences of European colonialism and extent of incorporation into capitalist production and exchange relations, levels and diversity of industrialization and economic development . . . and ethnic, racial, linguistic, religious, and class differences' (Reeves, 1993, p. 10).

The decline of 'Third Worldist euphoria' brought with it a rethinking of political, cultural and aesthetic possibilities. As the rhetoric of revolution began to be greeted with a certain scepticism, cultural and political critique began to develop in alternative ways. Such developments were 'post-Third Worldist' in that, while assuming the fundamental legitimacy of the anti-colonialist movement, they attempted to explore the social

An aesthetic of hunger?: Pereira dos Santos's *Vidas secas*

and ideological fissures within the Third World nations (see Shohat and Stam, 1994).

As a result both of external pressures and internal self-questioning, the cinema was itself subject to transformation. The anti-colonial thrust of earlier films gradually gave way to more diversified themes and aesthetic models, as film-makers partially discarded the didactic model predominant in the 1960s in favour of a postmodern 'politics of pleasure', incorporating music, humour and sexuality. (This diversification is evident in the trajectories of individual film-makers – see the difference between Nelson Pereira dos Santos's *Barren Lives/Vidas secas*, from 1963, and his *On the Highway of Life/Na estrada da vida* of 1981, or Fernando Solanas's *The Hour of the Furnaces/La hora de los hornos* of 1969 and his *Tango Gardel's Exile/Tango el exilio de Gardel* of 1985.)

Another development in this transformation was to do with an increased awareness of feminism. Largely produced by men, Third Worldist films were not generally concerned with a feminist critique of nationalist discourse. They often favoured the generic (and gendered) space of heroic confrontations, whether set in the streets, the casbah, the mountains or the jungle. The minimal feminine presence corresponded, more or less, to the place assigned women both in the anti-colonialist revolutions and within Third Worldist discourse. Women occasionally carried the bombs, as in *The Battle of Algiers/La battaglia di Algeri* (1966), but only in the name of the nation. More often, women were made to carry the 'burden' of national allegory (the woman dancing with the flag in *The Battle of Algiers*, the prostitute whose image is underscored by the national anthem in *The Hour of the Furnaces*) or scapegoated as personifications of imperialism (the allegorical 'whore of Babylon' figure in Rocha's films). Gender contradictions were subordinated to anti-colonial struggle: women were expected to 'wait their turn'. The minoritarian or post-Third Worldist films of the 1980s and 1990s, by contrast, while not so much rejecting the nation as interrogating its repressions and limits, suggest that a purely nationalist discourse is gravely limited. Such discourse cannot apprehend the layered, dissonant identities of diasporic or postcolonial subjectivity and focuses too much on the public sphere. So, films such as Mona Hatoum's short, *Measures of Distance* (1988), Tracey Moffatt's *Nice Coloured Girls* (1987) and Gurinder Chadha's *Bhaji on the Beach* (1993) use the camera less as revolutionary weapon than as monitor of the gendered and sexualised realms of the personal and the domestic, seen as integral but repressed aspects of collective history (see also Feminism and film since the 1990s, p. 487; Authorship and cinema, p. 437).

Displaying a growing scepticism with regard to meta-narratives of liberation, these post-Third Worldist films do not, however, necessarily abandon the notion that emancipation is worth fighting for. But rather than flee from contradiction, they install doubt and crisis at the very core of the films. Rather than enunciating a grand anti-colonial meta-narrative, they favour heteroglossic proliferations of difference within polygeneric narratives, seen not as embodiments of a single truth but rather as energising political and aesthetic forms of communitarian self-construction.

A number of post-Third Worldist diasporic film and video works explicitly link issues of postcolonial identity to issues of aesthetics. The Sankofa production *The Passion of Remembrance* (1986) thematises post-Third Worldist discourses and the fractured identities (in this case, black British identity) by staging a 'polylogue' between the slightly puritanical 1960s black radical voice of nationalist militancy, and the 'new,' more playful voices of gays and lesbian women, all within a profoundly anti-

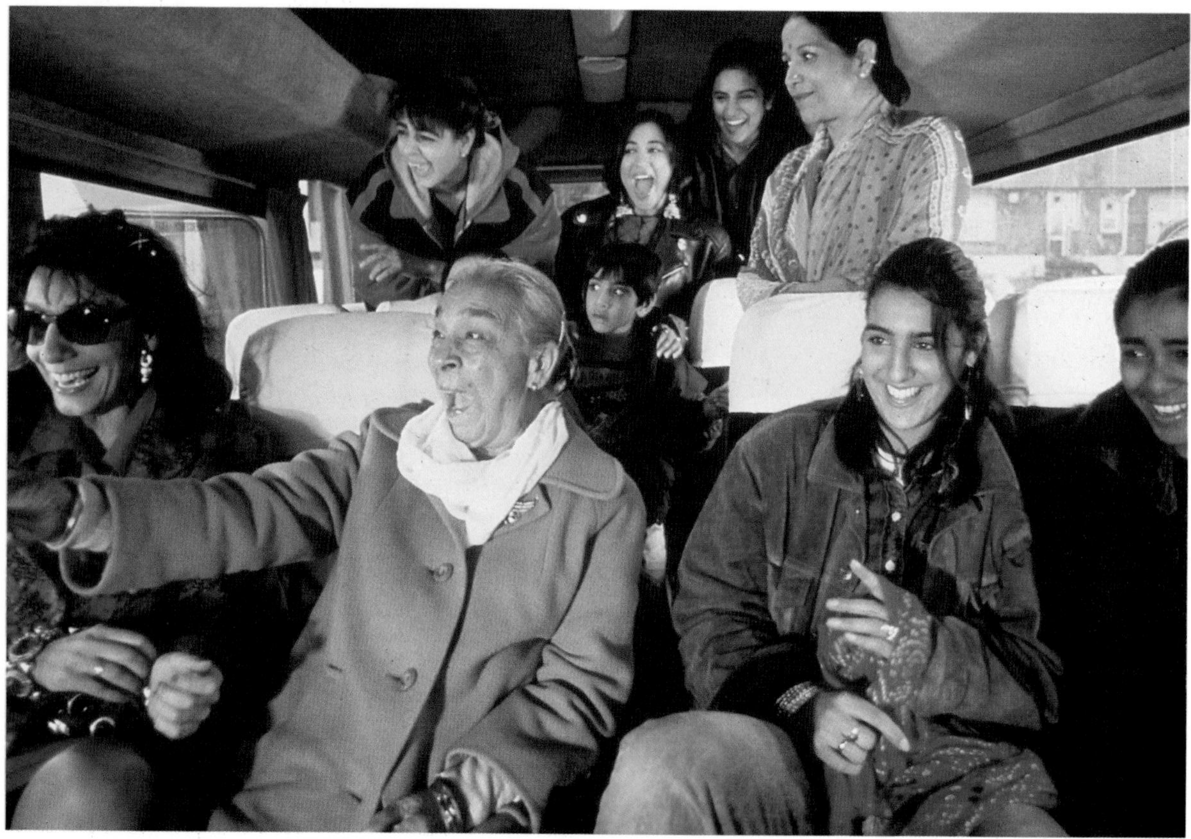

Monitoring personal and domestic lives: Gurinder Chadha's *Bhaji on the Beach*

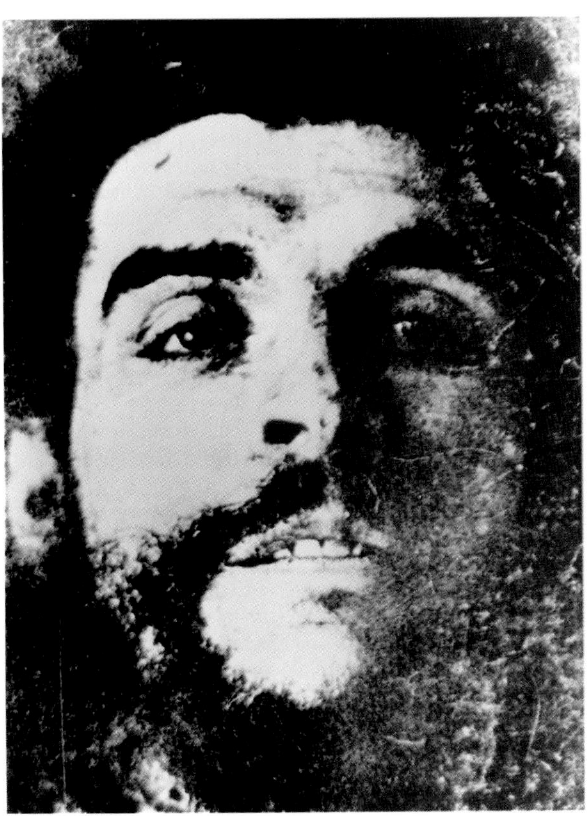

Fusing political radicalism with artistic innovation: *Hour of the Furnaces*

illusionist aesthetic. And works such as Assia Djebbar's *The Nouba of the Women of Mount Chenoua/La Nouba des femmes du Mont Chenoua* (1979), Elia Suleiman's *Homage by Assassination* (1992) and Tracey Moffatt's *Night Cries – A Rural Tragedy* (1990) break away from earlier macro-narratives of national liberation, reimagining the nation as a heteroglossic multiplicity. While remaining anti-colonialist, these experimental films call attention to the diversity of experiences within and across nations. Colonialism had simultaneously aggregated communities fissured by glaring cultural differences and separated communities marked by equally glaring commonalities, and these films suggest that many Third World nation-states were highly artificial and contradictory entities. The films produced by Third World 'postcolonials' residing in the First World (the forced or voluntary exile of Third World film-makers has led to a kind of diasporic Third World cinema within the First World) in particular raise questions about dislocated identities in a world increasingly marked by the mobility of goods, ideas and peoples that follows on from the 'multinationalisation' of the global economy.

Fourth World and indigenous media

The concept of the 'Third World' also obscures the presence of a 'Fourth World' existing within all of the other worlds, the world of those peoples variously called 'indigenous', 'tribal' or 'first nations', the descendants of the original inhabitants of territories subsequently subject to alien conquest or settlement. (As many as 3,000 native nations, representing some 250 million people, according to some estimates, function within the 200 states that assert sovereignty over them.)

First World people first became 'sensitised' to the situation of Fourth World peoples when the diverse campaigns mobilised around the global ecological crisis in the 1980s and 1990s insisted that indigenous peoples have often been the best custodians of natural resources. Film-makers translated this awareness, for better or worse, in such ecologically minded films as John Boorman's *The Emerald Forest* (1985), Ruy Guerra's *Quarup* (1989), Hector Babenco's *At Play in the Fields of the Lord* (1991) and even Menahem Golan's *The Forbidden Dance* (1990), directed by Greydon Clark.

The role of Fourth World people in First World documentaries (for example, *When the Mountains Tremble* (1983), an account of Rigoberta Menchu and the indigenous peoples of Guatemala) and in Third World films is not, of course, just a recent phenomenon. In the 1950s and 1960s, for example, the Cuzco School, in Peru, made mixed-mode documentary fictions such as *Kukuli* (1961) and *Jarawu* (1966) in the Quechua language. In Bolivia, Jorge Sanjines made feature films in Quechua such as *Blood of the Condor/Yawar mallku* (1969), which speaks of popular indigenous revolts against US-supported policies of sterilisation, and in Aymara, *Ukamau* (1966), with the collaboration of the indigenous people themselves.

Fourth World peoples more usually appear in 'ethnographic films', which of late have attempted to divest themselves of vestigial colonialist attitudes. While in the old ethnographic films, self-confident 'scientific' voice-overs purported to deliver the 'truth' about subject peoples unable to answer back (while sometimes prodding the 'natives' to perform practices long abandoned), the new ethnographic films strive for 'shared film-making', 'participatory film-making', 'dialogical anthropology', 'reflexive distance' and 'interactive film-making' (see, for example, McDougall, 1995). This new humility on the part of film-makers is evidenced in a number of documentary and experimental films that discard the implicit elitism of the pedagogical or ethnographic model in favour of a model that emphasises instead the relative, the plural and the contingent. Film-makers have experienced a salutary self-doubt about their capacity to speak 'for' the other. In Sergio Bianchi's *Should I Kill Them?/Mato eles?* (1983), a venerable Indian asks the director exactly how much money he made on the film. It is the kind of inconvenient question that would normally make its way to the editing-room trashcan. But Bianchi leaves the question in and thus voluntarily exposes his work to some of the risks of a real dialogue, and to the potential challenge offered by interlocutors. It is no longer a matter of how one party represents the other, but rather how one collaborates with the other. The goal, rarely achieved as yet, becomes to guarantee the effective participation of the 'other' in all phases of production.

Postcolonial cinema

The issue of media appropriations of the Fourth World throws into sharp focus some of the theoretical ambiguities of a term that became important in the late 1980s: 'postcoloniality'. While Fourth World peoples often invest a great deal in a discourse of territorial claims, symbiotic links to nature and active resistance to colonial incursions, postcolonial thought stresses deterritorialisation, the artificial, the constructed nature of nationalism and national borders, and the obsolescence of anti-colonialist discourse. The wide adoption, since the late 1980s, of the term 'postcolonial' to designate work thematising issues emerging from colonial relations and their aftermath clearly coincided with the eclipse of the older Third World paradigm.

Since the 'post' in 'postcolonial' suggests, on one level, a stage 'after' the demise of colonialism, it is imbued with an ambiguous spatio-temporality. 'Postcolonial' tends to be associated with 'Third World' countries that gained independence after World War II, yet it also refers to the 'Third World' diasporic presence within 'First World' conurbations. The term 'postcolonial', as Ella Shohat suggests, blurs the assignment of perspectives (Shohat, 1992). So: given that the colonial experience is shared, albeit asymmetrically, by (ex)coloniser and (ex)colonised, does the 'post' indicate the perspective of the ex-colonised (Algerian, for example), the ex-coloniser (in this case, French), the ex-colonial settler (*pied noir*) or the displaced hybrid in the metropole (Algerian in Paris)? Since most of the world is now living 'after' colonialism, the 'post' might seem to have the effect of neutralising significant differences between, say, France and Algeria, the UK and Iraq, or the US and Brazil. Furthermore, by implying that colonialism is over, the term 'postcolonial' risks obscuring the debilitating and enduring residues of colonialism.

Postcolonial theory is one of many theories to become prominent in the 1980s and 1990s that is concerned with complex, multi-layered identities and subjectivities. Terms having to do with various forms of cultural mixing, for example religious mixing (syncretism), botanical mixing (hybridity), linguistic (creolisation) and human-genetic mixing (*mestizaje*), have proliferated as a result of this concern. The emphasis on various forms of 'mixedness' in postcolonial writing calls attention to the multiple identities, already present under colonialism, but further complicated by the geographical displacements characteristic of the post-independence era. Presupposing a theoretical framework that is influenced by anti-essentialist post-structuralism and refuses to police identity along purist either/or lines – thus reacting both against the colonialist phobias and the fetish of racial purity – 'hybridity theory' also situates itself in opposition to the overly rigid lines of identity drawn by Third Worldist discourse. In the historical moment of the post-independence displacements that generated dually or even multiply hyphenated identities (Franco-Algerian, Indo-Canadian, Palestinian-Lebanese-British, Indo-Ugandan-American, Egyptian-Lebanese-Brazilian), it is clear that such lines can no longer be drawn with any confidence.

Post-independence identities, as the product of a conflictual merging, feature a more stressful hyphen, as it were, than those multiple identities deriving from a simple move from one country to another. Diasporic identities, moreover, cannot be seen as homogeneous. Displacements are often piled onto other displacements. A number of films – among them Stephen Frears's *Sammy and Rosie Get Laid* (1987), Gurinder Chadha's *Bhaji on the Beach* and Isaac Julien's *Young Soul Rebels* (1991) – bear witness to the tense hybridity of former colonials growing up in what was once the 'motherland'. In the multicultural neighbourhood of *Sammy and Rosie Get Laid*, the inhabitants have 'lines out', as it were, to the formerly colonised parts of the globe. Other films focus on diaspora communities living in countries that, if not a former imperial master, at least form part of a powerful First World. This is the case, for example, with the Indian diaspora in Canada, in Srinivas Krishna's *Masala* (1992), or the US (in Mira Nair's *Mississippi Masala*, 1991), or the Iranian diaspora in New York in Parviz Sayyad's *The Mission/Ferestadeh* (1983). Indeed, one might speak of a genre of postcolonial hybrid films. This would also include such films as John Akomfrah's *Testament* (1988, about a Ghanaian in England), Tevfik Baser's *Farewell to False Paradise/Abschied vom falschen Paradies* (1989, Turks in Germany), Barry Alexander Brown's *Lonely in America* (1991, Indians in the US), Jocelyn Saab's *The Razor's Edge* (1985, Lebanese in Paris), Ghasem Ebrahimian's *The Suitors* (1988, Iranians in the US), Mehdi Charef's *Tea in the Harem/Le Thé au harem d'Archimède* (1985, Algerians in France) and Stanley Kwan's *Full Moon in New York* (1989, Chinese in the US).

Postcolonial theory deals very effectively with the cultural contradictions and syncretisms generated by the global circulation of peoples and cultural goods in a mediated and interconnected world. What is at stake is a kind of commodified or mass-mediated syncretism. One finds proleptic expression of this kind of syncretism in the Indian film *Mr 420/Shree 420* (1955), directed by Raj Kapoor, in which the Chaplinesque tramp figure (Kapoor) sings '*Mera joota hai Japani* . . . My shoes are Japanese/My trousers are English/My red cap is Russian/But my heart is Indian'. (The song is cited in *Mississippi Masala*.) Here the protagonist insists that his syncretism is merely sartorial, since while his clothes are foreign, his heart is still Indian.

The culinary metaphors typical of multicultural discourse often imply a fondness for this kind of melange. Significantly, Indian film-makers speak of blending the *masalas* – literally, Hindi for 'spices', but metaphorically, an expression for 'creating something new out of old ingredients' – as a key to their recipe for making films (see Thomas, 1985). Indeed, as we have seen, the word *masala* forms part of the titles of two Indian diasporic films, *Masala* and *Mississippi Masala*. In the former film, the god Krishna, portrayed as a gross hedonist, appears to a nostalgic Indian grandmother thanks to an interactive VCR. While mocking the official multiculturalism of Canada, the filmic style serves up a kind of *masala*, where the language of the Hindu 'mythological' mingles with the language of MTV and the mass media.

The fact that racist tropes have been reversed and purist notions of identity rethought in postcolonial writing and cinema should not obscure the vexing question of the agency involved in 'postcolonial hybridity'. A celebration of syncretism and hybridity per se, if it is not articulated with questions of hegemony, risks sanctifying the fait accompli of colonial violence. As a descriptive catch-all term, 'hybridity' fails to discriminate between the diverse modalities of hybridity, such as obligatory assimilation, political co-optation, cultural mimicry and so forth. Syncretism, in other words, is power-laden and asymmetrical. (Africans in the New World were virtually forced to syncretise as a way of concealing and thus retaining their own religious practices behind a Euro-Christian façade.) Nevertheless, however problematic the notion of hybridity or syncretism may be, as an aesthetic strategy it has been very important.

Alternative aesthetic strategies

Post-Third Worldist, minoritarian and postcolonial cinemas have explored a wide spectrum of alternative aesthetics. This spectrum includes films (and videos) that bypass the formal conventions of dramatic realism in favour of such modes and strategies as the carnivalesque (Arthur Omar's *Triste Trópico*, 1974), the anthropophagous (Nelson Pereira dos Santos's *How Tasty Was My Little Frenchman/Como era gostoso o meu Frances*, 1971), the magical realist (Ruy Guerra's *Erendira*, 1982), the reflexive modernist (Youssef Chahine's *Alexandria . . . Why?/Iskandariya . . . Leeh?*, 1979) and the resistant postmodernist (Isaac Julien's *Young Soul Rebels*). These alternative aesthetics are often rooted in non-realist, often non-western or para-western cultural traditions featuring other historical rhythms, other narrative structures, other views of the body, sexuality, spirituality and the collective life. Ideologically post-Third Worldist, they interrogate nationalist discourse through the grids of class, gender, diasporic and sexual identities. Many incorporate para-modern traditions into clearly modernising or postmodernising aesthetics, and thus problematise facile dichotomies such as traditional and modern, realist and modernist, modernist and postmodernist.

One often encounters the view that Third World art or cultural practices are untouched by avant-gardist modernism or mass-mediated postmodernism. This view is often subliminally imbricated with the description of the Third World as 'underdeveloped', or 'developing', as if it lived in another time zone apart from the global system of the capitalist world. Like the sociology of 'modernisation' and the economics of 'development', the aesthetics of modernism (and of postmodernism) often covertly assumes a telos towards which Third World cultural practices are presumed to be evolving. The Third World, in this view, is condemned to a perpetual game of catch-up in which it can only repeat in a contorted way the history of the 'advanced' world. (A more adequate formulation would, perhaps, see time as scrambled and palimpsestic in all the worlds, with the pre-modern, the modern, the postmodern and the para-modern coexisting globally, although the 'dominant' might vary from region to region.)

The Third World, however, has known many modernist and para-modernist movements. Quite apart from the confluence of Brechtian modernism and Marxist modernisation in the 'new cinemas' of Cuba (Tomás Gutiérrez Alea), Brazil (Ruy Guerra), Senegal (Ousmane Sembène) and India (Mrinal Sen) in the 1960s and 1970s, there have been many modernist and avant-garde films in the Third World, going all the way back to films such as Rex Lustig and Adalberto Kemeny's *São Paulo: A Metropolitan Symphony/São Paulo, Sinfonia da Metrópole* (1929) and Mário Peixoto's *Limite* (1931), both from Brazil, and forward through the Senegalese director Djibril Diop Mambéty's narratively digressive *The Hyena's Voyage/Touki-Bouki* (1973) and, from Mauritania, Med Hondo's stylised *Soleil Ô* and *West Indies* to the underground movements of Argentina and Brazil, through Kidlat Tahimik's ironic anti-colonialist experiments in the Philippines.

One cannot assume, then, that 'avant-garde' always means white and European, or that Third World art is always realist or pre-modern (see Avant-garde and counter-cinema, p. 89). On the contrary, vast regions of the world, and long periods of artistic history, have shown little allegiance to or even interest in realism. Much African art, for example, has cultivated what Robert Farris Thompson calls 'mid-point mimesis', that is, a style that avoids both illusionistic realism and hyper-abstraction (Thompson, 1973). And in India, a 2,000-year tradition of theatre circles back to the classical Sanskrit drama, which tells the myths of Hindu culture through an aesthetic based less on coherent character and linear plot than on the subtle modulations of mood and feeling (*rasa*).

Syncretism

Syncretism becomes particularly appropriate to Indian cinema with reference to cinema language. The popular Hindi films of the 1950s, for example, as Ravi Vasudevan points out, mingled plots drawn from Hindu mythology and from Hollywood, with aesthetic styles ranging from a relatively realist mode to anti-illusionistic tableau effects rooted in folk painting. Many of these films were condemned by critics for what, in retrospect, appears to be their aesthetic strength – their mixing of cultural and cinematic mode. Syncretism and hybridity have also been crucial thematic and aesthetic resources in Caribbean and Latin American cinema. The region is, in any case, rich in neologisms that evoke ideas of mixture: *mestizaje, diversalité, créolité, Antillanité, raza cosmica*.

Mexican film-makers such as Emilio Fernández ('El Indio'), working with Gabriel Figueroa, carried on the tradition of the Mexican painters (Diego Riveira, David Alfaro Siqueiros, Jose Clemente Orozco) by forging a syncretistic mélange of Hollywood aesthetics with Mexican muralism. Paul Leduc picks up the same tradition at a later point, first in his *Frida/Frida: naturalesa viva* (1984), where he creates a cinematic analogue to the style of Frida Kahlo's paintings, and later in his *Baroque/Barroco* (1989), a free adaptation of Alejo Carpentier's novel *Concierto Barroco* (1974), where the themes of *mestizaje*, artistic syncretism and colonialism all come into play. Like the novel, the film has us make the same journey as Columbus and the conquistadores, but in reverse, with Mexico as the starting point. The novel's two central characters, the Mexican *mestizo* Amo and the Afro-Caribbean Filomenio, personify the racially synthetic character of Latin American culture. With scenes set in Mexico, Cuba, Spain and Italy, the film offers us a tour of the syncretic cultures of the Americas (during which we encounter indigenous fertility rituals, Afro-carnivals, Christian Holy Week processions) along with a compendium of musical styles: mariachi, Andalusian songs, salsa, bolero, flamenco, Yoruba ceremonial music, Catholic liturgical chants, in a baroque concert of musical tensions and affinities. Thus *Barroco* roots its images and sounds in a culture at once indigenous, African, Moorish-Spanish, Sephardi-Jewish and European-Christian.

Mexico is not the only South American country producing such syncretic films. In Brazil, Nelson Pereira dos Santos's *The Amulet of Ogum/O amuleto de Ogum* (1975) celebrates *umbanda*, the Brazilian religion that combines Afro-Brazilian elements – the *orixas*, a central belief in spirit possession – with Catholicism, Kabala and the spiritism of Alain Kardec. *The Amulet of Ogum* simply assumes *umbandista* values without explaining or justifying them to the uninitiated. The audience is presumed to recognise the ceremony that 'closes' the protagonist's body, and to recognise his protection by Ogum – the warrior god of metal and the symbol, in Brazil, of the struggle for justice. At the same time, the film does not idealise *umbanda*: one priest in the film works for popular liberation; the other is a greedy charlatan.

Ava & Gabriel, A Love Story/Ava & Gabriel, un historia di amor (1989), by the Caribbean (Curaçao) film-maker Felix de Rooy, meanwhile, finds artistic equivalents for the theme of hybridity in evidence elsewhere. The story revolves around a black painter in Dutch-dominated Curaçao in 1948 who wants to paint a black Madonna. Syncretism in *Ava & Gabriel* is to be found both in its painterliness and its use of language: the film is spoken in a number of languages – Dutch, English, French and Papiamento, the last itself a mixture of Dutch, Spanish and African languages. Raúl Ruiz, finally, although he does not explicitly thematise syncretism or *mestizaje*, can be seen as a syncretic diasporic artist, in that he takes all of the world's myths and forms and fictions as his province in a dazzling *combinatoire* with multicultural overtones but without a multicultural agenda. In films such as *The Three Crowns of the Sailor/Les Trois couronnes du matelot* (1983), Ruiz practises an 'aesthetic of digression', multiplying stories but always returning to a central theme or situation. Far from an austere 'aesthetic of hunger', Ruiz practises a gluttonous absorption and proliferation of styles. Within Ruiz's narratological syncretism, the entire world becomes a story or image bank on which to draw.

Archaic sources and para-modern aesthetics

As already noted, (post-) Third World artists have often drawn on the most traditional elements of their cultures, elements less 'pre-modern' than 'para-modern'. In the arts, the distinction archaic/modernist is often non-pertinent, in that both share a refusal of the conventions of mimetic realism. It is thus less a question of juxtaposing the archaic and the modern than deploying the putatively archaic (carnival, Afro-diasporic religion, magic) in order, paradoxically, to modernise, in a dissonant temporality that combines an imaginary past *communitas* with an equally imaginary future utopia. In their attempts to forge a liberatory language, alternative film traditions draw on para-modern phenomena such as popular religion and ritual magic. Here again we encounter syncretism and hybridity. In African films such as Souleymane Cissé's *The Light/Yeelen* (1987) and Saddik Balewa's *Kasarmu Ce – This Land Is Ours* (1990), magical spirits become an aesthetic resource, a means for breaking away, often in comical ways, from the linear, cause-and-effect conventions of dominant cinema.

The values of African religious culture have come to inform a good deal of Afro-diasporic cinema: for example, Brazilian films such as Glauber Rocha's *The Brute/Barravento* (1962), Ibere Cavalcanti's *The Force of Xango/A Força de Xango* (1977), Cuban films such as *Patakin!* (Manuel Octavio Gómez, 1982) and *The Amulet of Ogum*, and African-American films such as Julie Dash's *Daughters of the Dust* (1991), all of which inscribe African (usually Yoruba) religious symbolism and practice. Indeed, the preference for Yoruba religious symbolism is itself significant, since the performing arts – music, dance, costume, narrative, poetry – are absolutely integral to the religion itself, unlike other religions where the performing arts are subordinated to theology and sacred texts.

Another element of 'archaic' culture is orality: oral stories themselves and oral methods of storytelling. Many films present 'bottom-up' history conveyed through popular memory, legitimising oral history by 'inscribing' it on the screen. History, these films suggest, can also take the oral form of stories, myths and songs passed on from generation to generation. The fecundating power of oral tradition is especially apparent in African and Afro-diasporic cinema. *Yeelen*, for example, stages one of the oral epics, a kind of quest or initiation story, of the Bambara people. In Africa, the reinscription of the oral has often served a practical purpose: Sembène, for example, turned from novelist to film-maker in order to reach non-literate audiences. He wanted to become the 'mouth and ears' of society, the one who 'reflects and synthesizes the problems, the struggles, and the hopes of his people' (quoted in Pfaff, 1984, p. 29).

Here the cinema inherits the social function (but not the conservative ideology) of the *griot*, the oral archivist of the tribe, the praise singer who tells of births, deaths, victories and defeats. (The communal expression of the *griot* paradigm might be contrasted with the more individualist *caméra stylo* of the Nouvelle Vague, rooted in the romantic notion of the heroically individual auteur.) Although *griots* per se are increasingly marginal to contemporary African life (indeed, Momar Thiam's *The Troubadour/Sadaga*, 1982, charts the arc of their decline), their style of oral narration, deployed as a formal resource, informs a number of African and Afro-diasporic films (see Bachy, 1989). In Ababacar Samb-Makharam's *Dignity/Jom* (1981), for example, a *griot*-narrator narrates the themes of the film, often direct to camera. Writing about the use of narrative in Gaston Kaboré's *The Gift of God/Wênd Kûuni* (1982), Manthia Diawara (1989) delineates some of the mediations that intervene between the oral traditions themselves and their filmic re-elaboration. More important than the more superficial traces of oral literature in film (presence of the *griot*, heroes and heroines borrowed from the oral tradition), he argues, are the deep structural transformations the cinema effects in the narrative points of view. Rather than merely being 'faithful' to the oral tradition, in other words, films can transform that tradition. *Wênd Kûuni*, for example, 'incorporates an oral rendering of the tale which it also subverts'. If the *griot*'s narrative implies a restoration of the traditional order, the film points to the hope of a new order. The film thus practises the 'subversive deployment of orality', deterritorialising the story and transforming its meaning.

But oral-inflected narratives are hardly limited to African films, nor are *griots* the only agents of oral storytelling. Felix de Rooy's *Almacita di desolato* (1986) weaves legends from Curaçao, Aruba and Bonaire to narrate a symbolic battle between creative and destructive forces in a turn-of-the-century Afro-community in Curaçao. In both Hailé Gerima's *Ashes and Embers* (1982) and Julie Dash's *Daughters of the Dust*, the voiced tales of elderly women relate repressed histories of resistance passed down across the generations (see Taylor, 1986). The question of orality, then, illustrates in a striking way the folly of imposing a linear narrative of cultural 'progress' in the manner of 'development' theory, which sees people in traditional societies as mired in an inert pre-literate past, incapable of change and agency. In the arts, the aesthetic reinvoicing of tradition can shore up collective agency in the present – favouring collective engagement over consumerist entertainment, and participation over passivity (see Gabriel, 1989).

Selected Reading

Manuel Alvarado, John King and Ana Lopez (eds), *Meditating Two Worlds*, London, BFI Publishing, 1993.

Jim Pines and Paul Willemen (eds), *Questions of Third Cinema*, London, BFI Publishing, 1989.

Ella Shohat and Robert Stam, *Unthinking Eurocentrism: Multiculturalism and the Media*, New York and London, Routledge, 1994.

Ella Shohat and Robert Stam (eds), *Multiculturalism, Postcoloniality, and Transnational Media*, New Brunswick, NJ, Rutgers University Press, 2003.

Barren Lives/Vidas secas (Brazil 1963 *p.c* – Produções Cinematograficas L. C. Barreto; *d* – Nelson Pereira dos Santos)

Apart from low budgets, import duties on materials and 'under the line' production costs many times higher than in the west, Third World film-makers also confront limited, less affluent markets than those of the First World. Furthermore, they must compete with glossy, high-budget foreign films.

'Hunger' characterises not only the subject and aesthetic of *Vidas secas*, but also its production methods. The total production cost of the film was $25,000, while John Ford's *The Grapes of Wrath* (1940), made 23 years earlier on a similar theme, cost 30 times as much. Based, like *The Grapes of Wrath*, on a naturalist novel, the film tells the story of migrants driven by drought from the Brazilian northeast. The trajectory of one peasant family comes to encapsulate the destiny of thousands of oppressed migrants. *Vidas secas* cinematises the novel's third-person 'indirect free style' into a more or less direct, but still third-person, presentation of a character's thoughts and feelings. The material is articulated through the points of view of the characters, within a hierarchy of power that passes from Fabiano (Atila Iorio) to his wife Vitoria (Maria Ribeiro) down to the two boys and even the dog Baleia. We are given a kind of democratic distribution of subjectivity, deploying diverse cinematic registers: point-of-view editing; subjectivised camera movement; exposure (a blanched, overexposed shot of the sun blinds that dizzies both character and spectator); camera angle (the camera inclines with the movement of the boy's head); and focus (Baleia's vision goes out of focus as Fabiano stalks him, as if the dog were bewildered by his master's behaviour). The cinematography of *Vidas secas* is dry and harsh, like the landscape. The film's director of photography, Luiz Carlos Barreto, unable to afford the expensive 20,000-watt lights conventionally used for filling in shadowy areas in high-contrast daylight locations, turned necessity into cinematic virtue, for example by sacrificing full exposure in favour of silhouetted human figures against sun-drenched backdrops, light flaring into the camera lens, or backlit vultures perched on skeletal trees.

The mimetic incorporation of the lived tempo of peasant life forms part of the film's meaning: the spectator's experience will be symbolically dry like that of the characters. Rather than sensationalise its subject matter, only the most quotidian of events are portrayed in a world where very little 'happens'.

ROBERT STAM

The Hour of the Furnaces/La hora de los hornos (Argentina 1968 *p.c* – Solanas Productions/Groupe Cine-Liberación; *d* – Fernando Solanas)

Avant-garde militant documentaries such as *La hora de los hornos* fuse political radicalism with artistic innovation. The film orchestrates a multiplicity of styles and strategies, along with revolutionary homages to tricontinental culture heroes (Che Guevara, Frantz Fanon, Ho Chi Minh and, more problematically, Juan Perón). It raises a number of important critical issues: the convergence in the film of the 'two avant-gardes' (the political and the aesthetic); the relation between the film's open process of production and the text itself; the various strategies deployed to turn passive film consumers into active accomplices; the authors' failure to analyse the contradictions of Perónist populism; and the problematic mixture of anti-authoritarian language and demagogic manipulation. A cinematic *summa*, with strategies ranging from straightforward didacticism to operatic stylisation, the film borrows freely from avant-garde and mainstream, fiction and documentary, cinéma vérité and advertising. It inherits and extends the work of Sergei Eisenstein, Dziga Vertov, Joris Ivens, Glauber Rocha, Fernando Birri, Alain Resnais, Luis Buñuel and Jean-Luc Godard. Much of *La hora*'s persuasive power derives from its ability to give abstract concepts clear accessible form. The sociological abstraction 'oligarchy', for example, is concretised by shots of the '50 families' that monopolise much of Argentina's wealth. 'Class society' becomes the image ('quoted' from Birri's film *Throw Us a Dime/Tire die*, 1960) of desperate child beggars running alongside trains in hope of a few pennies tossed by blasé middle-class passengers. Thus *La hora* engraves its ideas on the spectator's mind.

Parody and satire also form part of the strategic arsenal of the film. Satiric vignettes pinpoint the retrograde nostalgia of the Argentine ruling class. One example is the annual cattle show in Buenos Aires, which interweaves shots of the crowned heads of the prize bulls with the faces of the aristocracy. An iconoclastic sequence titled 'Models' invokes Fanon's exhortation in *The Wretched of the Earth* to 'pay no tribute to Europe by creating states, institutions and societies in its mould'. As the commentary derides Europe's 'racist humanism', the image track parades the most highly prized artefacts of European high culture: the Parthenon, *Déjeuner sur l'herbe*, Roman frescoes, portraits of Byron and Voltaire. In an attack on the ideological hierarchies of the spectator, hallowed artworks are lap-dissolved into meaningless metonymy. The most cherished monuments of western culture are equated with the commercialised fetishes of consumer society. Classical portraiture, abstract painting and Crest toothpaste are levelled as merely diverse brands of imperial export.

ROBERT STAM

Impotence/Xala (Senegal 1974 *p.c* – Filmi Domireew/Société Nationale de Cinématographie; *d* – Ousmane Sembène)

Xala gives satiric voice to Fanon's insights concerning 'the pitfalls of national consciousness', especially the process by which the African elite comes to occupy positions formerly occupied by the colonisers. The film revolves around a fable of impotence, in which the protagonist's *xala*, a divinely sanctioned curse of impotence, comes to symbolise the neo-colonial servitude of the black elite in countries such as Senegal. (The novel and film of *Xala* were key references in Jameson's landmark essay on Third World allegory, 1986.) The protagonist, El Hadji (Thierno Leye), is a polygamous Senegalese businessman who becomes afflicted with *xala* on the occasion of taking his third wife. In search of a cure, he visits various medicine men who fail to cure him. At the same time, he suffers reverses in business, is accused of embezzlement and ejected from the Chamber of Commerce. In the end, he discovers that the *xala* resulted from a curse sent by a Dakar beggar whose land El Hadji had expropriated. He finally recovers by submitting to the beggar's demands that he strip and be spat upon; the film ends with a freeze-frame of his spittle-covered body.

In the world of *Xala*, the patriarchal structures of colonialism have given way to indigenous African class and gender oppression, precluding the utopia of liberation promised by nationalist discourse. Impotence thus betokens post-independence patriarchy as failed revolution. Here, the traditional ritual of marriage provides a structuring device for a political story. News of the protagonist's wedding-night impotence quickly spreads through the community, provoking the most diverse speculations about its origins. As Pfaff (1982) points out, each of the protagonist's wives plays an allegorical role, representing the Senegalese people at different stages and in different relations to colonisation and to tradition: the dignified, patient traditional wife

Adja (Seune Samb), the trendy westernised Oumi (Younousse Seye) and the object of sexual consumerism N'gone (Dieynaba Niang). Mulvey (1991) sees *Xala* as a reflection on the various discourses on the fetish as 'something in which someone invests a meaning and a value beyond its actual meaning or value'. Fetishism is itself allegorical, she points out, in that it calls 'attention to a nodal point of vulnerability, whether within the psychic structure of an individual or the cultural structure of a social group'. As a symptom, the fetish requires, like allegory, an act of decipherment. The Sembène film articulates the psycho-sexual with the socio-economic, turning the protagonist's impotence into a symptom of something else: the neo-colonial dependency of the black African elite.

ROBERT STAM

One Way or Another/De cierta manera (Cuba 1977 *p.c* – Instituto Cubano del Artes e Industria Cinematográfi; *d* – Sara Gómez)

One Way or Another deals with the question of machismo, and in this sense resembles other Cuban films such as Humberto Solás's *Lucia* (1969), Pastor Vega's *Portrait of Teresa/Retrato de Teresa* (1979) and Tomás Gutiérrez Alea's *Up to a Certain Point/Hasta cierto punto* (1983). Although *One Way or Another* focuses on the problem of social marginality, the question of machismo comes in through the story of the evolving relationship between Mario (Mario Balmaseda), a worker from a poor district, and Yolanda (Yolanda Cuellar), a middle-class teacher drafted to teach in the poor neighbourhood. The film deploys the metaphor of slum clearance and construction as it operates a certain 'deconstruction' both of conventional gender roles and of conventional generic formulae. Gomez weaves fictional and non-fictional segments, professional and non-professional performers, in a multi-levelled reflection on the relations between the sexes, between classes, between generations and among workers.

ROBERT STAM

Alexandria ... Why?/Iskandariya ... Leeh? (Egypt 1978 *p.c* – Misr International Films/O.N.C.I.C.; *d* – Youssef Chahine)

This semi-autobiographical film about an aspiring film-maker haunted by Hollywood dreams offers an Egyptian perspective on colonising film culture. Chahine's protagonist begins as a Victoria College student who adores Shakespeare's plays and Hollywood movies. The film is set in the 1940s, a critical period for the protagonist, and for Egypt, when Allied troops were stationed in the country and Axis forces threatened to invade Alexandria. *Alexandria . . . Why?* weaves diverse materials (newsreels, clips from Hollywood films, staged reconstructions, Chahine's own youthful amateur films) into an ironic collage. The opening credit sequence mingles black-and-white 1940s travelogue footage of Alexandria beaches with newsreel footage of Europe at war, implementing a 'peripheral' Egyptian perspective on Europe. In the following sequence, we watch a series of newsreels and Hollywood musicals along with the spectators in Alexandria. An anthology of musical clips featuring stars such as Eleanor Powell and songs such as 'I'll Build a Stairway to Paradise' are inserted into a reception context redolent of First World/Third World power relations as well as of the worldwide hegemonisation of the American Dream. The 'Three Cheers for the Red, White and Blue' number, for example, at once charming and intimidating in its climactic image of cannons firing at the camera (here the Egyptian spectator), celebrates American power and renders explicit the nationalist subtext of First World 'entertainment'.

Alexandria . . . Why? interweaves documentary and staged theatrical fiction in innovative ways. Impossibly fluid movement matches, for example, take us from newsreel material to staged footage to theatrical play. World War II actuality footage is manipulated to incorporate the film's characters, and whether these materials are diegetic or non-diegetic is deliberately blurred. The final sequence mocks the power that replaced European colonial power in Egypt after World War II: the US, deriding the chimera of Americanisation that enthrals the protagonist, and allegorically middle-class Egyptians generally. On arriving in the musical's national homeland, the protagonist is greeted by the Statue of Liberty transformed into a laughing, toothless prostitute.

ROBERT STAM

Nice Coloured Girls (Australia 1987 *p.c* – Tracey Moffatt; *d* – Tracey Moffatt)

While Third World and First World minoritarian women have experienced different histories and sexual regimes, they have also shared a common status as colonial exotics. Escaping these paradigms, *Nice Coloured Girls* interweaves tales about contemporary urban Australian Aboriginal women and their 'captains' (sugar daddies) with stories of Aboriginal women and white men over 200 years before. In sharp contrast to the colonial construction of the Aboriginal female body seen as a metaphorical extension of an exoticised land, *Nice Coloured Girls* places dynamic, irreverent, resourceful Aboriginal women at the centre of the narrative, offering a multi-temporal perspective on their 'nasty' actions – mild forms of prostitution and conning white Australian men into spending money. By shuttling between present-day Australia and past texts, voices and images, the film contextualises their behaviour in relation to the asymmetrical exchanges typical of colonial encounters. While from the vantage point of Eurocentric decorum the Aboriginal women are amoral schemers, the historical context of settler colonialism and its sexualised relations to both land and women

Self-reflexive and ironic: *Nice Coloured Girls*

switches the ethical and emotional valence. Whereas images of the past are set inside a ship, or in daylight on the shore, images from the present are set in the night-time city, pointing to the historical 'neonisation', as it were, of Aboriginal space. The film can thus be seen as a 'revenge' narrative in which Aboriginal women trick Euro-Australian men into fantasising a 'fair' exchange of sex and goods, then take their money and run.

The title of *Nice Coloured Girls* is itself ironic; it subverts the 'positive' image of 'nice' coloured girls as the objects of colonial exoticisation, valorising instead the 'negative' image of 'nastiness'. By reflexively foregrounding the artifice of its production through stylised sets, excessive performance style and ironic subtitles, the film undermines any expectation of sociologically 'authentic' or ethnically 'positive' representations. The constant changes of discursive register – vérité-style hand-held camera, voice-over ethnographic texts, subtitled oral narratives – undermine any univocal mode of historical narration. Rather than reverse the dichotomy of sexualised Third World women and virginal European women by proposing an equally virginal image of Aboriginal women, the film rejects the binaristic mode altogether by showing 'nastiness' as an understandable response to a specific economic and historical conjuncture, and finding the kernel of contemporary power relations in the colonial past.

ROBERT STAM

Sankofa (USA/Germany/Ghana/Burkina Faso 1993
p.c – Ngod GwardProductions/DiProCi/Norddeutscher Rundfunk/Westdeutscher Rundfunk/Channel Four/ Ghana National Commission on Culture;
d – Hailé Gerima)

Sankofa synthesises the modern and the traditional through an Afro-magical *egungun* aesthetic, that is, an aesthetic that invokes the spirits of the ancestors as embodiments of a deep sense of personal and collective history. Named after an Akan word for 'recuperating what's lost', the film begins with a drummed invocation exhorting the ancestral spirits to 'rise up, step out, and tell your story'. An urgent whispered voice-over says: 'Spirit of the dead, rise up and possess your bird of passage, come out, you stolen Africans, spirits of the dead, you raped, castrated, lobotomised.' This device of a collective call by a presiding spirit, turned into a structural refrain, authorises a trans-generational approach that mingles the present (a bewigged black fashion model posing against the backdrop of the Mina slave fort) and the past (the fort's former historical atrocities). In a kind of psychic and historical time machine, the fashion model becomes possessed by Shola, a nineteenth-century house slave, and is made to experience the cruelties of slavery, the rapes and the brandings, and to acknowledge her own kinship with her enslaved ancestors.

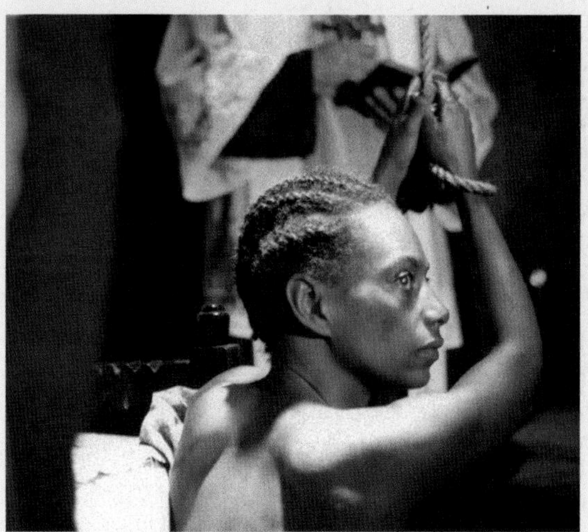

Possessed by the past: *Sankofa*

Gerima repeatedly pans over friezes of black faces, evoking an ocular chorus, bypassing an individualising point-of-view structure to evoke a community of the gaze. The narrative forms a multi-focal, communitarian *Bildungsroman*: the fashion model confronts the sources of her own alienation; the 'headman' who beats slaves becomes a double agent working for liberation. The cultural facets of African life (communal child care, herbal remedies, the primordial role of music and stories) are constantly stressed. Orality exists both as a diegetic presence – characters literally tell stories/histories of Africa, of the middle passage – and as a meta-cinematic device structuring the entire film as a collective narration where disembodied voices exhort, prophesy, exorcise, criticise, all in a 'polyrhythmic' style in which avant-garde-inflected moments of aesthetic contemplation alternate with dramatic moments of decisive action.

ROBERT STAM

PART 2

The Star System

THE HOLLYWOOD STAR MACHINE

JAMES DONALD

Although film studies only began to address the theoretical questions raised by stars in the 1970s, the fascination of film stars for both intellectual and popular audiences goes back a long way. A report on *The Film in National Life* by the Commission on Educational and Cultural Films in 1932 observed:

> A fellow of an Oxford college no longer feels an embarrassed explanation to be necessary when he is recognised leaving a cinema. A growing number of cultivated and unaffected people enjoy going to the pictures, and frequent not merely the performances of intellectual film societies, but also the local picture house, to see, for instance, Marlene Dietrich. (p. 10)

Apart from the pleasures of looking at a Dietrich, stars have also provided a useful point of reference for intellectuals' speculations around popular culture. Thus Simone de Beauvoir (1960) has used Brigitte Bardot as a scalpel with which to dissect the anxieties of French bourgeois masculinity in the 1950s, and Norman Mailer (1973) has worked over the image of Marilyn Monroe to bolster his mythologising of the American dream.

The broad range of more popular writing about stars can seem overwhelming – from histories by journalists such as Alexander Walker, to gossip, hack hagiographies and salacious muckraking. Until the mid-1970s, though, there seemed to be little inclination by film theorists to engage with the topic (see Dyer, 1979; 1998), a sign, perhaps, of the gulf between theory and popular experience, but more significantly of the difficult problems posed for the academic study of film, at whatever level, by the phenomenon of stardom. The circulation, reception and cultural currency of stars cannot be explained convincingly by exclusively textual, sociological or economic forms of analysis. More expansive conceptions of the various 'machineries' of cinema seem a step in the right direction. But in the end, as figures that (like 'Robinson Crusoe', 'Mata Hari' or 'Margaret Thatcher') condense a number of ideological themes, stars have a currency that runs beyond the institution of cinema. They require an analysis capable of explaining the resilience of these images that we pay to have haunt our minds (see Nowell-Smith, 1977, p. 12) – an account that must attend to both industrial and psychic processes.

Work has developed in two main areas. One is the diverse body of film analysis inspired by, and contributing to, feminist and gay politics. To begin with, much of this work was concerned with the appropriation of certain stars (Katharine Hepburn, Bette Davis) as figures for positive identification, as in Molly Haskell's *From Reverence to Rape* (1974); alternatively, it offered a critical diagnosis of 'stereotypes of women' or, as in Joan Mellen's *Big Bad Wolves* (1978), of male Hollywood stars as images of American patriarchy. Richard Dyer's (1979; 1998) attempt to give a firmer theoretical grounding to such concerns provoked a lively debate in which his effort to combine sociological and semiological approaches was challenged by critics drawing on a psychoanalytically oriented feminist theory (see Cook, 1979/80; 2005; Gledhill, 1982).

The other approach has followed the renaissance of more theoretically informed historical writing on the cinema. This has emphasised, on one hand, the material determinants of film production and distribution (the political economy of Hollywood, court actions and patents wars, real-estate deals and zoning agreements) and, on the other hand, the constitution of the codes of classic narrative film (see deCordova, 1982; 2001; Staiger, 1983; 1991). Such work allows stars to be analysed as marketing devices for selling films and simultaneously as organising presences in cinematic fictions (see also Spectatorship and audience research, p. 538).

The Hollywood system

'Mass culture', according to Roland Barthes, 'is a machine for showing desire. Here is what must interest you, it says, as if it guessed that men are incapable of finding what to desire by themselves' (Barthes, quoted in Mazzocco, 1982). What is

Early movie star Florence Lawrence, aka The Biograph Girl

involved, Barthes suggests, is some investment by us, the punters, which requires not conscious choice but a repertoire of unconscious processes. The object in which we make that investment is always provided for us – some would say imposed on us – by the 'machine' of culture. This machine involves not just the bricks and mortar of Hollywood studios and chains of cinemas, but also certain cultural orientations and competences (shared languages, for example, and shared conceptions of time, personality and aesthetic value) and the psychic processes whereby we enter culture and negotiate shifting, insecure positions within it.

The implications of this argument are that, in investigating the phenomenon of stardom, we are not just dealing with a person or an image with particular characteristics (talent, beauty, glamour, charisma) but with a complex set of cultural processes. The interesting question is not so much 'What is a star?' as 'How do stars function – within the cinema industry, within film narratives, at the level of individual fantasy and desire?' In considering their production, circulation and reception, for example, John Ellis has suggested a preliminary definition of a star as 'a performer in a particular medium whose figure enters into subsidiary forms of circulation and then feeds back into future performances' (Ellis, 1982, p. 1). This indicates that, from the film industry's perspective, the purpose of disseminating star images so widely is to draw audiences back into the cinema (see also Ellis, 2000). Anne Friedberg takes a similar approach, but indicates some of the complexities implied by terms such as 'performer', 'figure' and 'circulation'. 'The film star is . . . a particular commoditised human, routed through a system of signs with exchange value' (Friedberg, 1982, p. 47). The concepts of commodities, signs and exchange value suggest a model in which a homology might be established between the circulation of the star image in a circuit of exchange value that produces profit (production, distribution, exhibition) and its circulation in a circuit of semiotic use value (performance, publicity and spectatorship) that produces pleasure (see Geraghty, 2000). Just as a commodity is defined as having both exchange value (it can be bought and sold) and use value, so the two circuits of stardom are separable only analytically. For the profit to be realised, there must be at least a promise of pleasure. Enjoyment of the star has to be paid for.

This model, based on a conventional account of the elements of the cinema industry, can be fleshed out in a number of ways. It provides a useful peg on which to hang more detailed historical studies. It can be used to organise the empirical research produced within conflicting perspectives; and it can provide a reasonably accessible focus for some of the theoretical debates. Here are some possible lines of development.

Production/performance

What does a star contribute to the production of a Hollywood movie? Talent, glamour and charisma – 'that little bit extra' – might provide the terms for one answer, but they probably indicate what has to be explained rather than explain it. Richard Dyer has suggested a model that seems to offer a more useful starting point by indicating the sort of labour done by the star (Dyer, 1979, p. 18). To begin with, there is a person who constitutes the raw material to be transformed into an image or product – hence talent schools, dialogue coaches, beauticians, dazzling blond hair, nose jobs and, in Clark Gable's case, a new set of teeth. This product is both a form of capital, owned either by the studio or the individual, and also a form of raw material that, through further labour, is incorporated into another product, the film, which is sold in a market for a profit.

Star charisma: Marilyn Monroe in *Some Like It Hot*

What distinguishes stars from other performers is that, apart from their input of labour (their acting), their 'image' gives them an additional value. This is important in two ways. On one hand, it can be used to attract financial backing for a film, and on the other it provides a signal for exhibitors and audiences that this will be a particular type of film. The two aspects are closely related. Investors will only back a film that seems likely to make a profit. Hence Hollywood's task within the cinema industry has been to provide high-quality product that is both predictable enough and, at the same time, novel enough to attract and satisfy audiences. This economic function of stars was certainly recognised by 1927. In that year, the Wall Street stockbrokers Halsey, Stuart and Co. made it clear that stars, despite their high salaries, were an integral part of the studios' investment strategy:

> In the 'star' your producer gets not only a 'production' value in the making of his picture, but a 'trademark' value, and an 'insurance' value, which are very real and very potent in guaranteeing the sale of the product to cash customers at a profit. ('The motion picture industry as a basis for bond financing', Balio, 1976, p. 179)

In the earliest years of Hollywood, producers saw things differently. When films were hired out by the foot and nickelodeon audiences still paid for the novel experience of seeing pictures that moved, players remained anonymous. Most histories suggest that stars were introduced as a marketing device by independent producers trying to challenge the monopolistic stranglehold of the Patents Trust, formed by the equipment manufacturers. Janet Staiger (1991) has cast some doubt on this account, suggesting closer links to developments within the theatre (see also deCordova, 2001). But whatever the details, it is clear that stardom, along with narrative and the classic Hollywood style, became institutionalised during the second decade of the century. It would be interesting to explore the affinities in this period between the organisation of these narratives around the position of the spectator and the psychology of novelistic character, the development of the continuity style, and the role and presentation of the star on screen (see The classic narrative system, p. 45).

Stars can also provide a useful way into an understanding of Hollywood's shifting political economy. Interesting topics from this point of view might include the crisis provoked in the 1920s by the economic power of stars such as Mary Pickford, Douglas Fairbanks and Charlie Chaplin, especially when they formed United Artists (see Balio, 1976; 1985); the unionisation of Hollywood players, from freelance stars to extras, in the Screen

Actors Guild set up in 1933 during Hollywood's economic blizzard (see Ross, 1941); the contracts and work patterns imposed on their stables of stars by the oligopolistic Big Five studios from the mid-1920s until the early 1940s; the collapse of that system under pressure from antitrust suits, independent studios and newly aggressive Hollywood agents; and the bargaining power of stars in the subsequent era of packages, deals and independent production companies (see Pirie, 1981; Maltby, 1982).

What such accounts of stars as labour cannot reveal is their specific contribution to a film in terms of performance – the particular way they 'represent' a character. One approach to this question considers the clusters of connotations already associated with a star and how these create resonances for the audience watching not just Lorelei Lee but also Marilyn Monroe, not just Wyatt Earp but also Henry Fonda. Richard Dyer discusses the relationship between character and star image, pointing out that star image or persona may either 'fit' the fictional character or work to produce a disjuncture that may have ideological significance (Dyer, 1979, p. 148). Thus the star image carries powerful cultural connotations that both exceed the fictional codes of character and identification and work to bind us into the fictional world of the film. John O. Thompson (1978; 1991) has suggested that one way of understanding how these cultural connotations work in relation to specific film performances is to borrow the commutation test from linguistics, where it is used to see whether or not the substitution of one unit of sound for another produces a change in meaning. Thompson considers the difference that might result from substituting a particular facial detail and also asks what would happen if one star were to be replaced with another. What would happen if Lorelei Lee in *Gentlemen Prefer Blondes* (1953) were played not by Marilyn Monroe but by, say, Jayne Mansfield or Gloria Grahame, or Wyatt Earp in *My Darling Clementine* (1946) were played not by Henry Fonda but by John Wayne or Gary Cooper? This would enable us to separate out connotations specific to the star from those specific to the fictional character, and helps to explain the elusive and relatively unanalysed notion of 'star presence' or 'charisma'. However, there remains an argument about whether the star figure can be seen as mediating pre-existing social meanings, as a sociological approach would have it, or whether it works, together with other cinematic codes, to produce apparently coherent meaning from unstable and contradictory material (see Cook, 1979/80). It has been argued that the erotic play of the 'look' around the female star figure in classic Hollywood cinema is an integral part of the narrative drive towards closure and the reinstatement of equilibrium (Mulvey, 1975; 1989). This argument uses psychoanalytic concepts to address the question of the fantasy relationship between spectators and film and the role of the star in that relationship (see also Cook, 1982; 2005; Friedberg, 1982). Whether the emphasis is sociological, semiotic or psychoanalytic, though, the appeal of the star cannot be understood solely in the context of production and performance.

Distribution/publicity

Although less glamorous than Hollywood production and less familiar than cinema exhibition, distribution has always been at the heart of the organisation and profitability of the film industry. This is where the star's 'trademark' value and 'insurance' value come in: they embody the distributor's promise to the exhibitor of both the audience guaranteed by the familiar presence of the star and also the novelty appeal of a new vehicle.

But more important than this trade promotion, from our point of view, is the use of stars in advertising films to the public. As we have seen, John Ellis (1982; 2000) sees stars primarily as a marketing device, as an 'invitation to cinema'. This appeal is manufactured not solely by the industry's promotional and advertising machinery, but also more diffusely through fan magazines, through feature articles, news items and reviews in the press, and so forth. All these play upon the central paradoxes of stardom: that stars are both ordinary and glamorous, both like us and unlike us, both a person and a commodity, both real and mythical, both public and intimate. These dualities seem to work in two ways. They draw us into the cinema, where we can be in the presence of a more complete (moving, talking) image of the star, an idealised image. At the same time, that performance is never somehow enough and helps to fuel again our insatiable curiosity about what the star is 'really' like – hence the cycle of fandom, gossip and scandal. This view of stardom is also fostered by Hollywood's own representations of the phenomenon, most notably, perhaps, in *A Star Is Born* (1954) (see Dyer, 1982; 1991).

Exhibition/spectatorship

Consumption of a star's performance in a film has two aspects: you pay your money and you watch your film. This spectatorship is by no means a passive activity: what it involves is the most complex and hotly disputed question in the whole study of stars. Nor is it the end point of the circulation of a star, although the production–distribution–consumption model may suggest that it is. Indeed, there would be a good case for starting not with the return on capital invested in film production, but with the unquantifiable returns on our emotional investments in these pleasurable images. The pleasure derived from those moments of erotic contemplation of the spectacular figure of the star constantly threatens to spill over, to exceed the bounds of narrative that work to regulate our desires (see Mulvey, 1975; 1989). Indeed, for some spectators this excess may well overturn the delicate balance between static image and narrative flow on which classic Hollywood cinema rests. The 'management', or containment, of excess, successful or not, represents one of the ways in which Hollywood cinema attempts to hold spectators in place as consumers of its product, drawing them in with the promise of fulfilment of forbidden desires played out in the safety and secrecy of a darkened chamber. And it is widely supposed that these fantasies are awakened in ways that tend to sustain existing social definitions and relations of power.

How does this work when you or I sit watching a movie in the cinema? Here there is considerably less unanimity. There are different conceptions of the relationship between narrative and spectator. Do the structure of the narrative and presentation of bodies (especially women's bodies) on the screen implicitly address a 'masculine' spectator? If so, where does that leave the women in the audience? What is involved in identifying with a star? Can star images be read in 'subversive' ways by oppressed groups, and thus appropriated in their construction of social identities? Or is the star image simply one more cue guiding the cognitive activity of the spectator (see Clarke, Merck and Simmonds, 1982; Stacey, 1993). These are just some of the questions; the debates continue (see Stars and fans, p. 542).

Studying stars

One reason for including work on stars in courses of film study has been that, as an integral part of the machinery of Hollywood, they provide an accessible way into an analysis of its

Could this be John Wayne or Gary Cooper?: Henry Fonda as Wyatt Earp and Cathy Downs as Clementine in Ford's *My Darling Clementine*

political economy, the organisation of the narratives it produces, and the relationship between the two. A more problematic, often troubling aspect of studying stars is our own fascination with them, which can prove disturbing of apparently objective academic analysis. We do not fully understand these pleasures. We may think them too embarrassingly banal for academic study. Equally, we may be reluctant to put them under the microscope for fear they may dissolve or reveal a darker side we had only dimly and uneasily perceived. Not surprisingly, these hesitations can provoke resistance to what are, in any case, undeniably difficult theoretical questions. So what may appear at first glance an attractively straightforward topic turns out to be anything but. Here we are studying the disregarded processes of popular culture and our own place within them with no pat academic routines to provide a compensating sense of balance. That is what can make a study of stars so compelling. That cultivated and unaffected Oxford don back in the 1930s would no doubt have been able to chat lucidly about the merits of the film being shown at the intellectual film society. He may also have been able to give some account of Hollywood as a significant fact of modern economic life. He would probably have found it more difficult to give a persuasive analysis of his fascination with Dietrich.

Selected Reading

Richard deCordova, *Picture Personalities: The Emergence of the Star System in America*, Urbana, University of Illinois Press, 2001.

Richard Dyer, *Stars*, London, BFI Publishing, 1979. Revised edition 1998.

Christine Gledhill (ed.), *Stardom: Industry of Desire*, London and New York, Routledge, 1991.

Jackie Stacey, *Star Gazing: Hollywood Cinema and Female Spectatorship*, London and New York, Routledge, 1993.

ACTING IN CINEMA

JAMES NAREMORE

Even a moment's observation should make it obvious that the art of acting is extremely important to most films, and yet the critical literature on the subject is relatively sparse. In one sense, of course, movie actors are merely agents of narrative who are assisted by machinery; Lev Kuleshov famously attempted to prove that their performances can be constructed in the editing room, and Alfred Hitchcock once described them as experts in the art of 'doing nothing extremely well'. Nevertheless, the vast majority of films depend on a form of communication whereby meanings are acted out. The experience of watching them involves not only a pleasure in storytelling but also a delight in bodies, expressive movements and familiar performing skills. Perhaps we also derive pleasure from the fact that films enable us to recognise and adapt to the fundamentally acted quality of everyday life: they place us safely outside dramatic events, a position from which we can observe people lying, concealing emotions or staging performances for one another.

'Performance', it might be noted, is a much broader category than acting: we are all performers, and anyone who appears in a film, even an unwitting passerby on the street who is caught by the camera, becomes a sort of cinematic performer. Films also sometimes make use of acrobats, dancers and concert musicians who act in only a qualified sense. A person becomes a theatrical or cinematic actor of the sort discussed here when

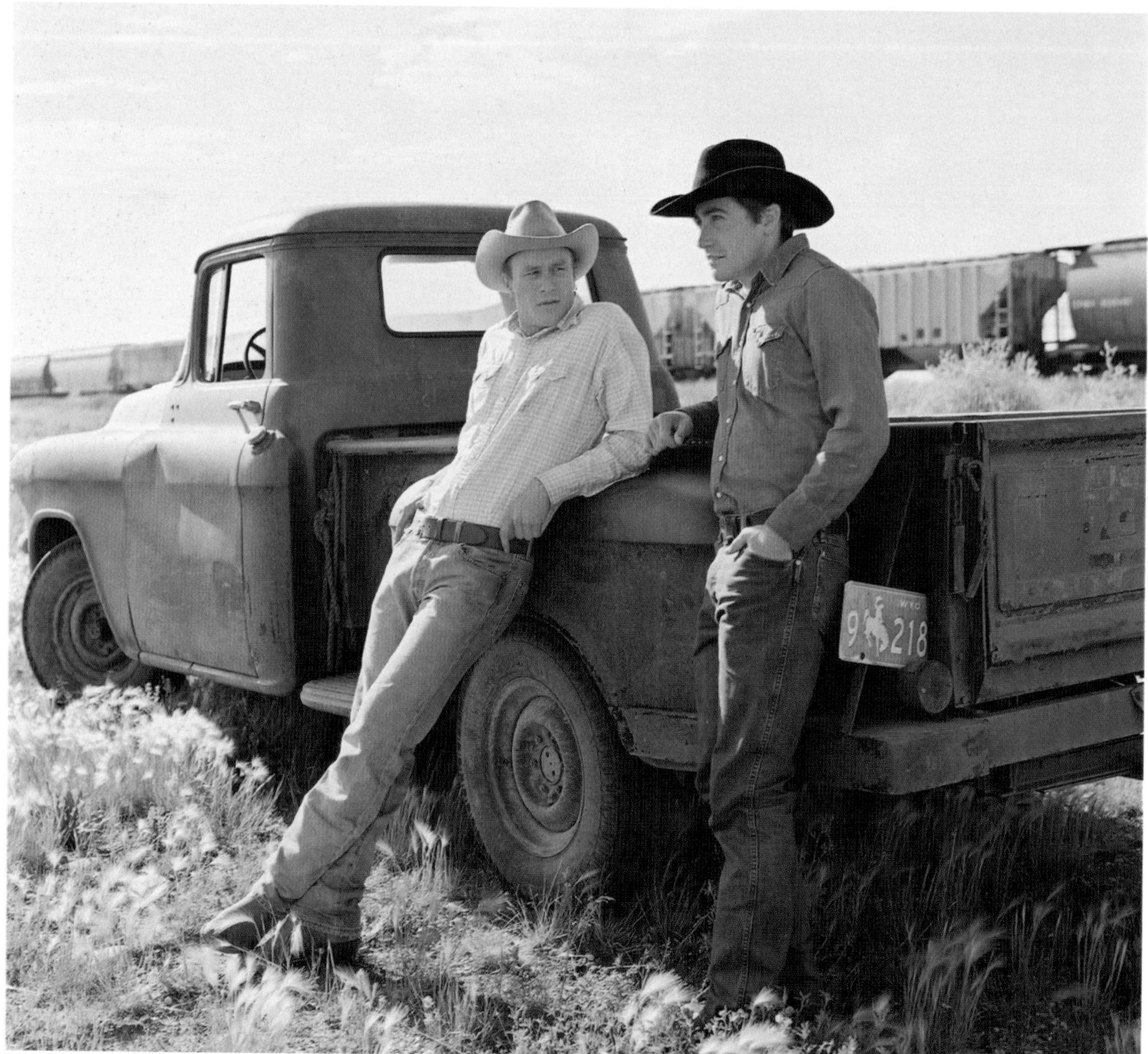

Tightly controlled performance: Heath Ledger in *Brokeback Mountain*

she or he functions as a developed character in a dramatic narrative. As with any other art form, there are no hard and fast rules for what constitutes the best film acting of this type. Certain players of the classic Hollywood era – I would name Peter Lorre, Agnes Moorehead and Mickey Rooney – create such vivid characters that they make every film they are in, no matter how good or bad, slightly better; but the dogs who played Rin Tin Tin, Asta and Lassie were also fine actors in the context of their particular films, and non-professionals have given impressive performances in fiction pictures.

All good movie actors understand the characters they play, effortlessly move to the marks that have been placed for them on the floor of the set, and have the ability to use props and costumes in expressive ways. Only occasionally do they abandon their normal mannerisms and impersonate recognisable historical figures: Helen Mirren's portrayal of Queen Elizabeth II in *The Queen* (2006) is a fine example of movie impersonation because it suggests Elizabeth without slavishly imitating her. Awards are often given for this or any other kind of performance that makes the work of the actor clearly visible – as when the actor gains or loses weight, speaks in an accent or simulates drunkenness or deformity. Acting is also made visible by dual roles or by performances within the performance. In *Mulholland Dr.* (2001), Naomi Watts plays two different personalities, one of whom is a perky young aspirant to Hollywood fame who auditions for a role in a movie at Paramount. When she prepares for the audition, she interprets her lines literally and speaks in a big, angry voice; when she arrives at the studio, however, she whispers the same lines in a steamy voice and gives them an erotic implication. We view the first performance-within-performance as 'bad' acting and the second as 'good' acting, but both are important to the film and Watts performs them equally well.

Film stars are actors (sometimes very good ones), but also iconic, extra-cinematic characters; their names circulate through all the media, their mannerisms become as familiar as the people we know intimately, and the screenplays of their films are often written to conform to the personality-images they have established. Their appearances on screen always create a double impression: it is John Wayne getting on a horse in *The Searchers* (1956), not simply Ethan Edwards (Wayne, incidentally, is 'played' by a man whose real name was Marion Morrison). Because of this effect, the star can show off acting skill by occasionally changing the sort of character she or he plays. Many of the best actor-stars – Marilyn Monroe, for example – create a single character type that they play brilliantly and definitively over and over, sometimes becoming prisoners of their creation. At an opposite extreme is a figure such as Johnny Depp, a 'postmodern' performer who has managed to become a chameleon and a star at the same time. There would seem to be no recipe for what makes a star, beyond a certain level of charisma. In most cases, the performer needs the requisite glamour and sex appeal to play leading roles in heterosexual romances and action-adventure pictures, but there are many exceptions: Shirley Temple, Marie Dressler, Will Rogers and Bob Hope were all leading players and major box-office attractions in their day.

It has often been argued that the most cinema-specific form of acting is much less ostentatious and gestural than acting on the stage – more like Naomi Watts's studio audition in *Mulholland Dr.* V. I. Pudovkin, who wrote an early treatise on the subject (Pudovkin, 1949), contended that films were ideal vehicles for what the celebrated theatrical director Konstantin Stanislavsky had described as 'gestureless moments' – scenes involving 'extreme paucity of gesture, often literal immobility', as in the cinematic close-up, when 'the body of the actor is simply not seen' (Pudovkin, 1949, pp. 334–5). Many film stars seem to be merely thinking for the camera, and performers often achieve an emotional 'subtext' through minimal gestures. Yet the exhibitionistic Fred Astaire is as important a screen actor as the supposedly introspective Marlon Brando, and Astaire's work is entirely dependent on graceful, highly stylised movements of his body – not only in dance scenes, but also when he merely lights a cigarette, sits in a chair or crosses from point A to B.

Realistic films favour restraint, as one can see in Heath Ledger's performance in *Brokeback Mountain* (2005), in which the character's tumultuous emotions are as tightly controlled as a closed fist; but comedies, musicals and costume pictures often encourage a 'stagy' style, as in the case of Steve Martin's wild abandon in *The Jerk* (1979). In fact, most movies contain a heterogeneous mix of performing styles and skills. Hollywood in the studio period usually required that supporting players, ethnic minorities and women act in more vividly expressive fashion than white male leads, and the range of expressive behaviour can be quite broad even in Method-influenced pictures: Marlon Brando is recessive in *On the Waterfront* (1954), but Lee J. Cobb chews the scenery. Notice also that certain directors impose differing styles on ensembles. By most accounts, Fritz Lang was a sadistic personality who moved actors like puppets, and Robert Altman was a sweetheart who gave them a great deal of freedom – at any rate, there is a clear difference between the geometric rigidity of the blocking in a Lang film and the roaming, freewheeling movements in an Altman film. Orson Welles wanted his players to execute actions quickly and overlap dialogue in carefully planned fashion; Stanley Kubrick, who resembles Welles in some respects, favoured an unusually

Comedic wild abandon: Steve Martin in *The Jerk*

slow, measured pace and actors who displayed over-the-top mugging (George C. Scott in *Dr. Strangelove*, 1963) or deadpan minimalism (Keir Dullea in *2001: A Space Odyssey*, 1968).

These qualifications and variations aside, the history of both stage and film acting since the late nineteenth century can be said to involve a movement from a semiotic to a psychological conception of performance, or from what Roberta Pearson (1992) terms a 'histrionic code' to a 'verisimilar code' – a phenomenon determined by changes in dramatic literature and the culture as a whole. The shift appears to have begun in the theatre of the 1850s, with the rise of the 'well-made' drawing-room drama, but it became most apparent in the period between 1880 and 1920, in the work of Stanislavsky and his followers. For at least 2,000 years previously, acting was closely related to dance and oratorical rhetoric (the very word 'actor' in English originally suggested the 'actions' of oratory), and the major form of actor training was instruction in elocution and pantomime, in which the actor learned a 'proper' diction and a vocabulary of bodily and facial 'expressions' to convey emotions.

One of the most important representatives of this pantomime school in the nineteenth century was François Delsarte, a Parisian elocutionist who made one of the earliest attempts to codify expressive gestures, and who exerted an indirect influence on the whole of silent cinema. The Delsarte system was adapted to American theatre by Steele MacKaye, the immediate predecessor of David Belasco, and it resulted in numerous 'cook-book' manuals of acting, such as Edmund Shaftesbury's *Lessons in the Art of Acting* (1889) and Charles Aubert's *The Art of Pantomime* (translated into English in 1921). It often reinforced social stereotypes or genteel mannerisms, but it was well suited to silent cinema and at its best produced remarkable performances: Lillian Gish's eloquently expressive close-ups, Charles Chaplin's balletic comedy, Lon Chaney's grotesque movement in horror films, and so forth. Its last flowering was in German Expressionism, which arrived at an approximately Delsarte-like technique via a different, modernist aesthetic; examples include *The Cabinet of Dr. Caligari/Das Cabinet des Dr Caligari* (1919), in which Conrad Veidt moves with the languorous rhythms of a trained dancer, and *Metropolis* (1927), in which the entire cast gestures in the boldest, most elemental fashion (see also German cinema, p. 207).

Relatively few actors in talking films worked along such lines (Greta Garbo and Marlene Deitrich are qualified examples), but the pantomimic or histrionic style was sometimes adopted for ironic or thematic purposes, as in Gloria Swanson's flamboyant behaviour in *Sunset Blvd.* (1950) or in Robert Mitchum's frightening performance in *The Night of the Hunter* (1955), which is a particularly clever fusion of old-fashioned melodrama and Germanic expressionism. These, however, are distinct exceptions to the rule. Where film in general is concerned, a certain tendency towards verisimilar or naturalistic acting – a movement from 'presentational' to 'representational' performance – was at work from the origins of the classic narrative cinema. Like Stanislavsky, D. W. Griffith was interested in making blocking less artificial and acting more intimate and emotionally charged, and at each stage of cinema's technical history these general aims were increasingly facilitated. The earliest, so-called 'primitive' films were devoted to straightforward action sequences, paying little or no attention to psychological motivation; the camera was usually situated at least 12 feet from the players, who moved parallel to the camera, stood in three-quarter profile when they addressed one another, and gesticulated broadly. After 1909, the camera began to move closer. The subsequent development of continuity editing, and especially of shot/reverse-shots, enabled directors to reduce the amount of visibly rhetorical blocking and track the psychological nuances on the actors' faces in a pattern of action and reaction. When sound was introduced, an elocutionary style of speech was favoured, but the invention of sensitive directional microphones eventually transformed the 'grain' of the voice and the subtler levels of timbre into important expressive instruments. A wide range of rural or working-class accents became acceptable, and multi-track sound editing, looping and sound mixing were used to record ordinary, low-key behaviour in ways that would have dazzled Stanislavsky.

Films continued to use wide shots, and directors such as Howard Hawks and John Ford were especially good at bringing the actors' bodies into play. (In a Hawks film, as has often been observed, characterisations usually arise from the way characters walk, sit or perform small actions such as tossing a coin or striking a match.) By the end of the twentieth century, however, the conjunction of digital editing systems with television-style shooting techniques, in which scenes are photographed with multiple cameras and long lenses, led to what David Bordwell (2005) calls 'intensified' continuity editing, especially in large-budget Hollywood features. 'Continuity cutting', Bordwell observes, 'has been rescaled and amped up, and the drama has been squeezed down to faces – particularly eyes and mouths' (p. 27). Big-budget movie directors usually strive for close-up 'coverage' of each line of dialogue and facial reaction, using multiple cameras and small wireless microphones attached to the bodies of the actors. As a result, close-ups dominate, space is flattened, backgrounds are blurred and the average shot length is shortened (most images are held on the screen for somewhere between two and eight seconds). In this environment, movie stars such as Tom Cruise are valued for the intensity they bring to the smallest twitch of an eyebrow.

The apotheosis of what might be called the inner-directed, Stanislavskian approach to acting, which can be a useful training for the kind of movies that centre on microscopic facial expression, was the American 'Method', particularly as taught by Lee Strasberg at the Actors Studio in New York in the late 1940s and 1950s. Much was written in the popular press in those years about the 'mumbling' and 'shambling' of Studio-trained actors, but such behaviour was more advertised than practised. Brando's clever performances as an inarticulate, sexy proletarian in *On the Waterfront*, *A Streetcar Named Desire* (1951) and *The Wild One* (1953) created the popular conception of the Method, but his greater importance was as a rebel celebrity who indicated a seismic shift in US popular culture – a new personality, related not only to the emerging postwar bohemia and the fashion for existential angst, but also to the rise of rock 'n' roll and figures such as Elvis Presley. Where Brando's acting style is concerned, Richard Dyer is correct to say that 'the formal differences between the Method and, say, the repertory/Broadway style are less clear than the known differences between how the performances were arrived at' (Dyer, 1979, p. 154). Shelley Winters, for example, was much more closely connected to Strasberg and the Actors Studio than Brando ever was, and yet Winters is seldom described as a Method actor.

Method training undoubtedly contributed to 'lifelike' performances and enabled actors to fine-tune their delicate psychological instruments. It inspired a large number of extremely talented players over the next two generations (see virtually the entire cast of *The Godfather*, 1972, and *The Godfather Part II*, 1974, in which Strasberg makes an effective appearance), but it also fostered a neglect of the physical training associated with the older pantomime tradition. In Strasberg's hands, it was narrowed down to a quasi-Freudian or therapeutic preoccupation with 'emotional memory', and most of its jargon had a familiar ring: 'private moment', 'freedom', 'naturalness', 'organic' – the keywords of romantic individualism.

Epitomising 'Method' acting: Marlon Brando in *The Wild One*

There was, however, another approach to acting, developed by the twentieth-century avant-garde and by such popular institutions as the music hall, the circus and vaudeville, which represented a counter-approach to Stanislavsky. In the period of the Russian revolution, for instance, Vsevolod Meyerhold tried to create gymnastic actors who represented a proletarian ideal, and in the same period the Soviet and Italian futurists advocated styles of performance drawn from the variety theatre, the early 'cinema of attractions' and the American comedy films of Mack Sennett. The Stanislavskian actor and the Meyerholdian actor worked from different physical assumptions (Stanislavsky stressed relaxation and Meyerhold stressed dynamic, machine-like action), and in practice they could look as different from one another as Brando and Buster Keaton. In subsequent years, Sergei Eisenstein and Bertolt Brecht, who were both influenced by futurist theatre, became interested in the stylised acting of ancient Asia. Brecht was an especially important theorist of an anti-naturalistic, anti-bourgeois form of performance in which ideology was never concealed by realistic illusion.

Although Brecht recognised that some degree of realism was essential to a committed drama and to popular taste, he emphasised that actors should produce signs (the most important of these he termed the 'gestus'), and he wanted his players to feel an emotional estrangement from their roles – an 'alienation effect' that made their performances presentational and didactic. Perhaps the best-known exponent of Brechtian acting in cinema is Jean-Luc Godard, especially in films such as *Two or Three Things I Know about Her/2 ou 3 choses que je sais d'elle* (1966), in which Marina Vlady and the other actors step in and out of their roles and frequently address the camera directly. A different but equally radical style can be seen in some of the films of Robert Bresson, who often worked with amateur players, and who advocated a form of 'automatism' in which the actor was instructed to think less about emotion than about gesture. (Alfred Hitchcock, who worked with Hollywood stars, resembled Bresson in the sense that he was impatient with Method-trained performers and was chiefly interested in actors who could produce elemental looks and gestures suitable for carefully edited sequences.)

Nearly all comic actors in film, especially the 'crazy' comics such as the Marx Brothers or Jerry Lewis, employ an entirely different style from specialists in Stanislavskian drama. By its very nature, comedy tends to be physically exaggerated, presentational, aimed at the head rather than the heart, and deconstructive of realistic conventions. Realistic acting strives for absolute expressive coherence between one shot and the next, or for a type of performance-within-performance in which the character's 'act' for other characters is plausible and convincing: see, for example, the poker-faced calm of Walter Neff (Fred MacMurray) in *Double Indemnity* (1944) when a man who might identify him as a killer is brought to his office for questioning. By contrast, broadly comic films often depend on exaggerated forms of expressive incoherence, as when Peter Sellers, in the role of Dr Strangelove, has to keep beating one of his arms down to keep it from springing up into a Nazi salute.

Since the late 1960s, there has been something of a return to movement-based, physical training of actors – a tendency prompted by such diverse figures from theatre as Rudolf Laban, Jacques Lecoq, Joan Littlewood and Julie Taymor. By the same token, several developments in digital technology – in particular CGI (computer-generated imagery), green-screen techniques and motion-capture devices – have contributed to an increased interest in pantomime. Some writers have reacted to these developments by suggesting that the new technology is a threat to the very profession of acting. In support of their argument, they point out that crowd scenes larger than Cecil B. DeMille could achieve are now composed of nothing but computerised figures, and that in *Gladiator* (2000) the face of the dead Oliver Reed as Proximo has been pasted onto the moving body of a

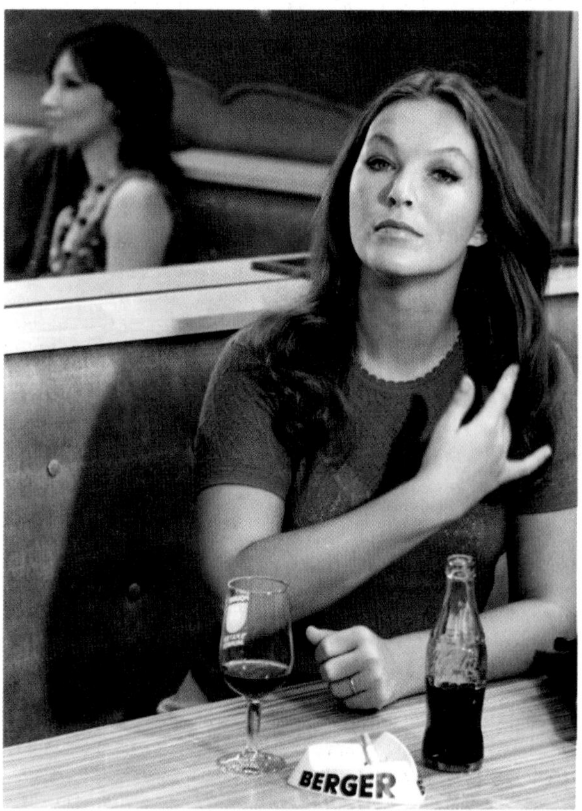

Brechtian direct address: Marina Vlady in *2 ou 3 choses que je sais d'elle*

Actors transformed into cartoon characters: *Sin City*

stand-in. Industrial society has entered an increasingly 'robotic' stage of development and digital animators the world over have spoken of their desire to achieve the 'holy grail' of 'synthespians' who seamlessly interact with human players.

Whether or not CGI is qualitatively new and will lead to such a future, it certainly increases the amount of animation in movies. We should recall, however, that animators have often worked in collaboration with actors: in 1938, for example, the Walt Disney animators copied the photographed movement of dancer Marge Champion in order to create the 'lifelike' figure of Snow White. CGI belongs squarely within this tradition, and even though it is often used to show morphing androids and missing body parts, it probably will not involve the elimination of human players. Most digital effects are recognisable, and from the time of *The Golem/Der Golem* (1920) and *Metropolis* to the time of *Blade Runner* (1982) and *Bicentennial Man* (1999), robots and simulacra have been acted by professional thespians. CGI has not so much replaced actors as required them to behave like animated figures or machines.

An obvious case in point is the *Terminator* series, in which Arnold Schwarzenegger's visibly manufactured physique and stiff acting fits perfectly with computer-generated effects. An even better example is the Steven Spielberg/Stanley Kubrick production of *A.I. Artificial Intelligence* (2001). Spielberg, who inherited the project after Kubrick's death, knew that computer animation has yet to prove that it can create believable human figures in speaking roles. (One of the most elaborate attempts to do so is *Final Fantasy The Spirits Within*, 2001, a sci-fi adventure based on video games, which uses the voices of several well-known players, but looks animated.) As a result, the robot is played by Haley Joel Osment, whose performance is especially interesting for the way it starts with a slightly digitalised, pantomimic style, very similar to what the Russian futurists called 'bio-mechanics', and then shifts, at the moment when the robot's circuits are imprinted with oedipal desire, into an analogue, Stanislavskian style that supposedly reveals his inner life or soul. (Even in the final stage of his development, he never blinks his eyes.)

A similar reversion to uncanny forms of pantomime can be seen in Peter Jackson's *The Lord of the Rings The Two Towers* (2002), for which Andy Serkis invented both a voice and a set of body movements to structure the computer animation for his character Gollum. (New Line Cinema aggressively but unsuccessfully campaigned to have Serkis nominated for an Academy Award.) Ultimately, Gollum was created from a mixture of sculpture, puppetry and digital effects, with Serkis donning a motion-capture suit and interacting with the other players on the set. Serkis also provided the 'psychological' expressions that signify his character's split personality. To elaborate these expressions further, the animators consulted Gary Faigin's *The Artist's Complete Guide to Facial Expression* (1990) and Paul Ekman's *Darwin and Facial Expression* (2006), two modern books that attempt to codify the semiotics of the face in much the same fashion as François Delsarte attempted to codify actors' gestures for the nineteenth-century stage. In other words, the digital era, coupled with the rise of fantasy and comic-strip films of various kinds, seems to involve a qualified return to a style that predates Stanislavsky. In some cases, it causes human actors to behave like clockwork instruments, but it also expands the range of performance styles. Comic-book spectaculars, for instance, can give players an opportunity to show off their skills in dual roles or to behave expressionistically. (In *RoboCop*, 1987, Peter Weller cleverly imitates Nikolai Cherkasov in Eisenstein's *Ivan the Terrible/Ivan Grozni*, 1945.)

Richard Linklater's *Waking Life* (2001) uses mini digital cameras to record a series of actors speaking improvised monologues or dialogues, which it then transforms through digital rotoscope techniques into colourful, animated imagery; this film contains a monologue about André Bazin, and everywhere it demonstrates how advanced technology can reveal the sign-making activity behind realist acting. Eric Rohmer's *The Lady and the Duke/L'Anglaise et le duc* (2001) is a costume drama set during the French revolution, and, like most of Rohmer's work, it involves actors seated in rooms holding long, realistic conversations; but it also uses digital video and computerised imaging to create a visibly artificial, painterly mise en scène around the actors. Robert Rodriguez and Frank Miller's *Sin City* (2005) is even more radical in its transformation of actors into cartoon-like characters who inhabit a world of boldly graphic designs. Where more avant-garde experiments are concerned, Michael Snow's **Corpus Callosum* (2002) serves as a compendium of things that can be done with computer technology to bend, reshape and manipulate human bodies. If these four examples are an indication, acting is crucial to the digital age. It would, of course, be possible to make digital films without actors, but that was true of motion-picture photography. In any case, at the historical moment when analogue human players seem about to be replaced by digital images, the players are with us as much as ever.

Selected Reading

Richard Dyer, *Stars*, London, BFI Publishing, 1979. Revised edition 1998.

James Naremore, *Acting in the Cinema*, Berkeley, University of CaliforniaPress, 1988.

V. I. Pudovkin, *Film Technique and Film Acting*, New York, Bonanza Books, 1949; trans. Ivor Montague.

Pamela Robertson Wojcik (ed.), *Movie Acting: The Film Reader*, London and New York, Routledge, 2004.

STARS BEFORE SOUND

GAYLYN STUDLAR

In Edison's earliest 'Black Maria' films, well-known performers from legitimate theatre, vaudeville, the circus and Wild West shows were captured for the camera on fleeting snippets of celluloid. However, none of these early performers could be called film stars or even be considered film actors. Nevertheless, actors quickly became the centre of film production, especially in the US between 1902 and 1908, as the story-centred fiction film gained ground with audiences and within a burgeoning industry.

US film-makers in particular treated the presence of professional actors in their films as an economical (and unavoidable) source of talent rather than as the opportunity to differentiate or market their product: film companies did not reveal to the public the identity of actors, who were often drawn from the lowly ranks of stock company theatricals. By contrast, the 'Films d'Art' made in France and released in the US from 1908 presented famous stars of the European stage such as Sarah Bernhardt in multi-reel films.

DOUGLAS FAIRBANKS

In the 1910s, many reformers sought to counter what they perceived to be a widespread over-feminisation of masculinity in Anglo-American culture. They found models for healthy, optimistic manhood in US President Theodore Roosevelt and in Douglas Fairbanks, Hollywood superstar. Like Roosevelt, Fairbanks was regarded as an ideal representative of Anglo-Saxon Americanism even though the actor's father, Charles Ulman, was Jewish. Fairbanks never acknowledged his complex ethnic heritage.

In 1915, despite warnings that too much emphasis on actors could lead to escalating performer costs, Triangle aggressively promoted Fairbanks as their dynamic new sensation in full-length feature films such as *The Lamb* (1916), *Double Trouble* (1915), *His Picture in the Papers* (1916), *Reggie Mixes In* (1916) and *American Aristocracy* (1916). Fairbanks's films viewed contemporary cultural anxieties surrounding masculinity through a comic lens that focused on the actor's boyish high spirits and self-confident joy. Reflecting the growing power of stars, in 1917 Fairbanks moved to the Artcraft division of Paramount, where he made films from his own scenarios and with his own production company. In 1919, he participated in the formation of United Artists, which placed control of production and distribution directly in the hands of film artists. In 1920, the star risked public outrage by divorcing his wife to wed film star Mary Pickford. The public quickly forgave them, and on their European honeymoon, fans mobbed the couple.

In the 1920s, simultaneous with Rudolph Valentino's success as a swarthy alternative to 'white' American masculinity, Fairbanks's heroes became noticeably darker, and the star was among the first to be identified with the 'suntan' as a fashion statement. Fairbanks turned away from contemporary, satirical comedies to make ambitious, large-scale costume-spectacles that continued to highlight his athletic prowess but also high-end production values and special effects. After the wildly successful costume drama *The Mark of Zorro* (1920), Fairbanks starred in *The Three Musketeers* (1921), from the Alexander Dumas novel, *Robin Hood* (1923), *The Thief of Badgad* (1924), *Don Q Son of Zorro* (1925), a two-strip colour swashbuckler *The Black Pirate* (1926), *The Gaucho* (1928) and his last silent film, *The Iron Mask* (1929).

Douglas Fairbanks in *The Taming of the Shrew*

Ultimately the gap between the actor-producer's age and his relentless staging of a juvenile off-screen presence drew criticism. After a handful of unsuccessful talkies, including *The Taming of the Shrew* (1929), the first sound version of a Shakespeare play and his only film with Pickford, Fairbanks retired from the screen. He and Pickford divorced in 1936. In 1939, after almost a decade of globetrotting, Fairbanks died of a heart attack aged 56.

GAYLYN STUDLAR

JOAN CRAWFORD

In April 1925, a studio-sponsored fan magazine contest asked readers to rename an aspiring actress named Lucille Le Sueur. The contest described the Metro-Goldwyn-Mayer Studios contract player as an 18-year-old former debutante who needed a more memorable and pronounceable name. With the announcement of the winning entry, Le Sueur – actually a 21-year-old former chorine who had run away from grinding poverty – became Joan Crawford. Such moments suggest the 'hide-and-seek' game of revelation and containment that constructed film stars as commodities in the 1920s.

After Crawford's well-received appearance as a flapper in *Sally, Irene and Mary* (1925), the Western Association of Motion Picture Advertisers (Wampas) named the actress a Baby Wampas Star of 1926. She then appeared with major stars such as Lon Chaney in *The Unknown* (1927) and John Gilbert in *Twelve Miles Out* (1927), but these roles did not create a coherent screen persona for her. At the same time, Crawford's reputed off-screen penchant for nightclubbing earned her sexually dubious nicknames in the press such as the 'Hey-Hey Girl' and the 'Whoopee Girl'.

Crawford's professional persistence, as well as her alleged acquiescence to the sexually exploitative 'casting couch' in a male-dominated industry, won her better roles, culminating in her breakthrough to stardom as Diana in *Our Dancing Daughters* (1928). This film and its sequels, *Our Modern Maidens* (1929) and *Our Blushing Brides* (sound, 1930), successfully mediated her off-screen association with 'jazz baby' values by insisting that the heroine was fun-loving but virginal.

By contrast, Crawford's off-screen persona was constantly teetering on the knife-edge of sexual scandal. In 1926, Chicago socialite Mrs Edna Cudahy thwarted the actress's very public romance with Mrs Cudahy's teenage son. Mrs Cudahy dismissively declared Crawford to be nothing more than a grasping nobody from nowhere. By 1928, fan magazine and newspaper interviews admitted to Crawford's lower-class origins and romantic misadventures. In June 1929, Crawford married the prince of Hollywood 'royalty', Douglas Fairbanks Jr. The press portrayed the union as the fitting conclusion to a 'Cinderella story'. Revelations of childhood deprivation and neglect shattered the gloss of middle-class normality that had been central to Hollywood star discourse in the 1910s, but they helped Crawford win a large measure of sympathy from female movie fans. These fans remained loyal in the 1930s, as the actress took on talkie roles that mirrored elements of her own rags-to-riches life and resonated with audiences mired in the economic anxieties of the Great Depression.

GAYLYN STUDLAR

Breakthrough to stardom: 'Whoopee girl' Joan Crawford in *Our Dancing Daughters*

With the need to make a great many films for nickelodeons, US studios developed stock companies of actors. This presented American moviegoers with the opportunity to recognise and appreciate actors, but studios, perhaps in order to avoid paying higher salaries, resisted naming their players until late 1909. At that time, the Edison Company hired and began a publicity campaign around Mlle Pilar-Morin, a French pantomime-actor who had toured American vaudeville. By early 1910, other actors who appeared in films began to be named and referred to as 'picture personalities' within motion-picture industry sources (deCordova, 1990, p. 54).

In what is often regarded as one of the watershed moments in the development of the star system, Imp studio provoked a round of newspaper publicity when, in March of 1910, the *St Louis Post-Dispatch* reported that Florence Lawrence, an Imp actress, had been run over by a streetcar. In response, Imp ran advertising featuring Miss Lawrence's name and picture, and the name of her new film *The Broken Oath* (1910), while declaring the news item to be a 'lie' promulgated by the studio's unnamed 'enemies' (deCordova, 1990, p. 58). The entire episode, including the original report of the streetcar accident, was a publicity stunt orchestrated by Carl Laemmle, Imp's founder, who wanted to draw attention to his luring Lawrence away from American Biograph. By late 1910, all major American film companies, with the exception of American Biograph, were publicising the names of their leading players in film credits as well as through a host of written publicity and visual marketing materials.

Studios exploited actors to differentiate their product, and the exploitation of actors as personalities as well as professional players took off as the industry increased storytelling capability by standardising multi-reel films in the mid-1910s. The establishment of Famous Players Film Company in 1912 signalled a shift to making films built around recognisable actors. In seeking to capitalise on the screen appearance of well-known actors from the theatre, Adolph Zukor adapted the Film d'Art model. Other companies discovered the value of exploiting the audience's interest in actors who did not have established theatrical fame but who were well known to moviegoing audiences through repeated appearances in films.

By 1914, screen actors' private lives proved to be as interesting to the public as their screen appearances. Through a rapidly developing and high level of organisation, a discursive system flourished across print media and film promotion in which discussions of actors' lives off screen as well as their roles were central. This discourse of stardom allowed the American film industry to give the star's image the widest possible circulation even as Hollywood attempted to carefully control the terms of that circulation.

By the late 1910s, the notion of the 'star' emerged from a system that shifted from an emphasis on the picture personality to a construction of the identity of the film actor whose personality was distinct from his/her on-screen roles. Rather than reveal how the star actually lived, this discourse offered tantalising glimpses of the actor's life that sought to reveal 'the truth' of the star by investigating what he or she thought about a host of topical issues. Interviews and articles exploited controversies of the time, especially those related to questions of sexuality and to the pleasures of modern consumer culture, but the star identity was figured typically as both conventional and glamorously different, committed neither to reactionary traditionalism nor to the dissipating dangers of modernity.

The star system flourished because it proved so useful in sustaining the consumption of Hollywood film product. However, in the early 1920s, this carefully orchestrated mode of constructing star identity by holding out the secret of, but simultaneously containing, the star's private life began to reveal weaknesses. In 1920, superstar Douglas Fairbanks divorced his wife to wed 'America's Sweetheart', Mary Pickford. The couple's unconventional off-screen behaviour formed an uneasy contrast with their squeaky-clean screen images, but their popularity survived this crisis. The public treatment of their marital woes heralded a change in star discourse as the moral transgressions of stars made headlines again and again in the 1920s, in the drug-related death of leading man Wallace Reid, the murder trial of comedian Fatty Arbuckle and the unsolved shooting of director William Desmond Taylor.

Seeking to contain Hollywood stars' scandalous transgression of middle-class moral norms led the Hays Office of the Motion Picture Producer and Distributors Association (MPPDA) to ask studios to insert morals clauses in actor contracts. The star scandals of the 1920s also encouraged the studios to both protect their stars from value-damaging publicity and maintain a distance between the actor's off-screen identity and his/her screen persona. This distance, a distinct change from the picture-personality model, could prevent particularly troublesome contradictions being created between the star and his/her on-screen persona.

By the end of the 1920s, the industry had created a well-honed system that worked across myriad venues to negotiate how actors were presented on and off screen as stars. As a result, stars achieved institutional supremacy within Hollywood as the primary tool for building audience loyalty and selling films.

Selected Reading

Richard deCordova, *Picture Personalities: The Emergence of the Star System in America*, Urbana and Chicago, University of Illinois Press, 1990.

Paul McDonald, *The Star System: Hollywood's Production of Popular Identities*, London, Wallflower Press, 2000.

Gaylyn Studlar, *This Mad Masquerade: Stardom and Masculinity in the Jazz Age*, New York, Columbia University Press, 1996.

STARS AFTER SOUND

ERICA CARTER

The period from 1926/27 to the early 1930s that established sound film as Hollywood's industrial norm not only set the majors grappling technologically with competing recording processes, or financially with the costs and benefits of building sound stages, hiring specialist personnel and wiring movie houses across the US and beyond for sound. The innovations of the early sound period also had significant implications for stars as film-industrial commodities, as performers and as audience favourites and box-office draw.

Film histories comparing early European and US sound have shown, first, how tenacious was the Hollywood impulse to harness the new technology to the human voice on screen. While European directors (Fritz Lang in *M*, 1931; René Clair in *Le Million*, 1931) explored sound, music and silence as formal components in film as modernist assemblage, Hollywood strove, as Janet Staiger has observed, after a classical harmony of sound and image achieved above all by a privileging of the voice in dialogue: of sound as speech, not sound as form (Staiger, 1985, p. 302). Not that consensus prevailed over the proper qualities of the Hollywood voice. In sound film's early 'quality' phase, it was the voice of the legitimate stage that found favour, as film stars were called upon to emulate the theatre actor's clear diction, articulacy, controlled pitch and agreeable tone. Early sound cinema's 'enunciative style' is exemplified for Donald Crafton in such performances (both 1929) as Norma Shearer's portrayal of the eponymous society heroine in *The Last of Mrs Cheyney*, or Ruth Chatterton's Oscar-winning fallen woman in *Madame X* (Crafton, 1997, p. 451).

Resistance to sound: Charlie Chaplin in *City Lights*

The recourse by such reputed figures as Emil Jannings to the dialogue-led performance mode of their stage roles was greeted by US critics as a welcome shift towards a theatrical style in which speech 'to a great extent govern[ed] . . . actions', and actors eschewed the 'unnaturalness' of their earlier silent films (*New York Times*, 6 December 1930; see also Riis, 2004). Yet there was no smooth transition to some putatively universal performance mode for the new sound film. The cinematic voice unleashed into film's representational repertoire a cacophony of competing dialects, accents, national and subcultural idioms, each in turn subdivided by distinctions of pitch, volume, diction, tempo, rhythm, colour and tone. Silent cinema had been celebrated by some for a supposed demotic universalism that located the actor's body as the vehicle for a 'shared universal language' (Balázs, 1924). Visible social distinctions had certainly been accentuated by narrative and mise en scène conventions that established hierarchies of 'race', class, nation or gender. Hence, for instance, the association with Jewish stereotype of German Expressionism's figures of uncanny otherness (the Golem's star of David, Nosferatu's hooked nose); or the restricted character typology assigned to black actors in Hollywood film. But what James Naremore terms silent film's pantomimic acting style (see Acting in cinema, p. 114) had the capacity to obscure distinctions in everyday bodily habitus pertaining to class in particular, but also ethnicity, nation, region, locality and so forth. Charles Chaplin's initial rebuttal of sound film, exemplified in the release of his *City Lights* (1931) as a silent feature fully four years after the coming of sound, derived in this context perhaps from his recognition of the capacity of the heterogeneous cinematic voice to dilute film's universal appeal, and undermine therefore the lovable everyman figure he embodied in his silent films. Certainly, some historians view the vocal diversity of sound film as producing a more nuanced social and geographical shading of narrative cinema's role typology, pitching, say, the quick-fire New York-ese of Mae West or James Cagney against Gary Cooper's 'western laconicism' (Maltby and Craven, 1995, p. 166) or Greta Garbo's low and sultry Swedish drawl. Hollywood's apparent trajectory towards a new cultural pluralism might be seen as exemplified, too, in the majors' short-lived enthusiasm for multilanguage versions, and in the big breaks these produced for those such as Claudette Colbert (in Paramount's English/French/German/Italian/Spanish/Swedish-language versions of *The Lady Lies*, 1929), or Bela Lugosi in his signature role in the dual-language (English and Spanish/Mexican) *Dracula* (1931).

But star historiography arguably requires a less linear method to chart the uneven and often traumatic processes that triggered, shaped or broke star careers in the transition to sound. Understandings of stars as standardised commodities within international image markets can help explain, for instance, how such figures as Marlene Dietrich or Greta Garbo could rise to international stardom by fulfilling a market role as European box-office magnets for Paramount and MGM. Studies of censorship codes and audience reception within national cinemas,

MARLENE DIETRICH

The Scarlet Empress (1934), Marlene Dietrich's penultimate film with Josef von Sternberg, confirms her as a suggestive case for a study of stars in the first sound film decade. It features Dietrich as the German Princess Sophia, who is transported to Russia to marry the halfwit Grand Duke Peter, but later deposes her husband in a *coup d'état* and rises to power as the sexually voracious and politically indomitable Catherine the Great. A marriage sequence early in the film marks a transition for Catherine in narrative terms; but it also highlights Dietrich's transitional status as a star whose collaborations with Sternberg extended for longer than for many of her contemporaries the stylistic progression from a silent cinema privileging the image and the look, to the narrative and performance dictates of classical sound.

Catherine's marriage to the idiot Grand Duke spans a full five-and-a-half minutes in which narrative cedes place to lavish ceremonial spectacle, and dialogue to a swelling choral and orchestral music track. The intertitles that bookend the sequence insert the marriage into the exotic history of the 'then so powerful' Slavic east, whose 'most sinister Empress' will be embodied by Dietrich in subsequent scenes. But Sternberg's intertitling reveals him also as a director still partially immersed – and this throughout his collaborative period with Dietrich (1929–35) – in the aesthetic sensibility of the silent film. Sternberg's pictorialism was traced by contemporary reviewers to antecedents in the Weimar silents; certainly, there are echoes of what Siegfried Kracauer (1995) termed Weimar film's 'mass ornament' in the imperial wedding, with its cluster of bejewelled, berobed and incense-swinging courtiers and priests; or its mise en scène that obscures vision and fractures perspective, with layers of curtains, veils, obtrusive artefacts (crosses, chandeliers) and flickering candle flames.

Expressionist chiaroscuro amplifies the wedding's ambivalence, its balance between the two poles of imperial magnificence and Catherine's sexual humiliation through marriage to Peter the imbecile. The sequence's concluding alternating close-ups between Catherine and her would-be lover Alexei (John Lodge) evince silent film's capacity to capture emotional nuance through an exchange of looks, while the accumulated close-ups of Dietrich at the scene's conclusion confirm her as a figure

Marlene Dietrich's European exotic allure enchants Cary Grant in *Blonde Venus*

whose aura emanates less from a persona projected through narrative and character, than from her mute but visually glorious image as star.

Contemporary reviews confirmed this view of *The Scarlet Empress* as a film that celebrated the seductions of the silent image. *Variety* (18 September 1934), for example, called it a film that 'reverts to silent film methods' in its quest for the 'pomp and flash values' of visual spectacle. The same reviewer saw Dietrich as constrained within a painterly aesthetic that never allows her 'to become really alive and vital'. Yet it may be precisely this suspension of Dietrich in an interim moment between image and narrative (or, as Donald Crafton, 1997, would have it, between the silent body and the talking mind) that locates her as a quintessential icon of the studio era in the first decade of sound. Certainly, the remarkable proliferation of studies of Dietrich, and the methodological pluralism of analyses that range from popular biographies, through feminist film theory to more recent studies of film performance and national versus transnational film, suggest that her case may crystallise important features of stardom in the period 1927–39.

Biographical studies, for instance, tell of an actress who straddled the silent/sound divide when she moved on from a career in Berlin cabaret and late Weimar film (the latter as a late addition to the German studios' stable of debutante femme fatales) to star in Sternberg's *The Blue Angel* (1930). Arriving in Hollywood in 1930, Dietrich was groomed for international stardom by Paramount executives who sought a magnet for European audiences to match Garbo at Paramount's rival, MGM. Her status in this context as emblematic star of the studio era is confirmed by the intense engagement with Dietrich in feminist studies of classical Hollywood film. Laura Mulvey (1989) used Dietrich's Sternberg films as paradigmatic cases in support of her argument that the cinematic image of woman in film induces 'fetishistic mechanisms' to circumvent an oedipal castration threat; hence, for Mulvey, Dietrich's presentation by Sternberg as 'a perfect product' that is the 'direct imprint' of a fetishistic male look.

Other critics have drawn on Dietrich's 1930s films to counter Mulvey's oedipal thesis with, for instance, accounts of a female look structured around masochistic identification (Studlar, 1988); or with a deconstructionism that sees in Dietrich's Sternbergian image a foregrounding of abstract form or surface, and applauds this as self-referentially 'confounding' that 'hierarchization of depth and surface' that grounds classical realism's truth claim (Doane, 1991, p. 56). James Naremore has recourse to Sternberg's 1930s films as the source of an 'ostentive' acting style in which Dietrich 'acts stardom' in a camp or mannerist performance mode (Naremore, 1988, pp. 131–2). A wealth of further studies draws on Dietrich's early work to explore, for instance, her gay and lesbian subcultural appeal; her place in exile film studies as an anti-fascist political icon hotly contested on both the German and US side; or the feminist allure of a screen image 'as openly sexual and lascivious as she is motherly' (Koch, 1993, p. 13).

But there remain avenues to explore: Dietrich's vocal performance, for instance, and the place of her modernist *Sprechstimme* (between singing and speaking) in a history of film voice; or by extension, her voice's intertextual relation to everyday soundscapes via radio and the record industry, and the new perspectives on star discourse that are opened by such explorations of cinematic voice and sound. The last word has yet to be spoken on Dietrich as iconic mid-twentieth-century star.

ERICA CARTER

meanwhile, amplify our understanding of Dietrich, Garbo and other European femme fatales of the classical period by exploring their symbolic function in European cinemas as home-grown erotic and/or national icons. The particular success of Garbo and Dietrich rested on the streamlining of their images simultaneously to European and US cultural convention, the latter not least through the Production Code, which moulded star images after 1930 to US moral, legal and aesthetic norms. In Dietrich's case, this produced an emphasis on her maternal and familial qualities in such films as *Blonde Venus* (1932); in Garbo's, on the moral ambiguity of her persona as an eroticised woman who nonetheless projects an image as desexualised, romantically transfigured 'woman in love' (Viviani, 2006, p. 96; see also Jacobs, 1991; Carter, 2004).

Nor was it only censorship that drew lines between the permissible and the impermissible in the talkies stars' off-screen personae and screen roles. Star careers were also made by the genre cycles of the early sound period: Maurice Chevalier, for instance, was catapulted to international prominence when his *Innocents of Paris* and *The Love Parade* (both 1929) helped trigger the early talkies' musical wave. The James Cagney of *The Public Enemy* (1931) figures similarly in genre histories as the supreme embodiment of the early 1930s gangster type (McDonald, 2000, pp. 62ff). Pola Negri and Louise Brooks fared poorly by comparison, their 'failed' transition to sound attributable in part to the anachronistic quality within classical Hollywood's emergent narrative, genre and character conventions of Negri's star image as melodrama heroine in the histrionic mode, or Brooks's – at least since her Lulu role in G. W. Pabst's *Pandora's Box/Die Büchse der Pandora* (1929) – as disarming melange of Kansas-born flapper and European vamp.

One especially rich seam mined by star studies of the early sound period is the burgeoning historiography of 'classical Hollywood'. Bordwell, Staiger and Thompson's monumental study (1985) or Jane Gaines's critical overview (1992) have helped spawn histories that locate early sound stars within a narrative of Hollywood's drive for institutional, industrial and stylistic standardisation from 1930 on. In Janet Staiger's account, for instance, the Hollywood studios' managerial shift to producer-led unit production, triggered by Columbia, Fox and Paramount in 1931, had deleterious effects for stars, intensifying already extant trends towards a commodification of star images as serially manufactured products within increasingly streamlined processes of industrial production and hierarchical control. Staiger's emphasis on stars' status as dependent labour force, and on star image and persona as standardised (typecast, stereotyped) commodities within an advanced capitalist mass-consumer industry, is reproduced in later studies such as Danae Clark's, which locates the 'sound crisis' of 1927 as one stage in a long-term process of industrial regulation that trapped actors 'between the forces of production and consumption, between bodily labour and commodified image' (Clark, 2004, p. 15). Cynthia Baron's (1999) more empirically nuanced acting history tells a cognate story of classical Hollywood's drive to regulate star performance through actor training programmes designed to standardise Hollywood modes of vocal performance, and of actorly representation of character and star.

Like all teleologies, however, this story breaks down in the face of historical contingency and cultural difference. National cinema studies, for instance, have relativised Hollywood histories of an advancing standardisation of the actor's voice, its 'moulding' (McDonald, 2000, p. 43) to narrative and genre conventions and studio codes. Charles O'Brien's study (2005) of French cinema's conversion to sound foregrounds, for example, the renewed disjuncture that sound produced between Hollywood and European star images and performance styles. French cinema's commitment until the mid-1940s to direct sound sustained an emphasis on the actor's voice as an unmediated trace of a charismatic presence – what French critics termed *phonogénie* – as opposed to the manufactured assemblage produced by Hollywood dubbing and multi-track techniques. The resurgence in film studies of performance as a scholarly object has led similarly to a rethinking of industry histories' macronarratives of studio control, illuminating instead stars' active agency. Martin Shingler, for example, describes Bette Davis as 'an actress in motion, presenting fury through her shoulders, neck, torso . . . her eyes and mouth' (Shingler, 1999, p. 49).

Similar attention to star images' ambivalence is evident in cultural studies accounts that investigate subcultural re-scriptings of star narratives and images: gay audiences' appropriations of Marlene Dietrich, for instance, or minority discourses around Paul Robeson that registered the 'black meanings' in his image and, in so doing, made these 'widely available for black people' (Dyer, 2004, p. 201; Weiss, 1993). The cultural-historical turn in film studies has further helped embed star studies historically in, say, the US transition from Depression to New Deal (an early example was Eckert on Shirley Temple, 1991); or in the convulsive US–European history of transnational migration and exile in the face of European fascism and war (Phillips and Vincendeau, 2006). In sum, studies beyond accounts of classical Hollywood open up perspectives on stars as social subjects within a historical dialectic whose ambivalences are, in the end, only partially captured by teleological narratives of the regulation, standardisation and mass commodification of stars in the transition to sound.

Selected Reading

Donald Crafton, *The Talkies: American Cinema's Transition to Sound, 1926–1931*, Berkeley, University of California Press, 1997.

Lucy Fischer and Marcia Landy (eds), *Stars: The Film Reader*, London and New York, Routledge, 2004.

Alan Lovell and Peter Krämer (eds), *Screen Acting*, London and New York, Routledge, 1999.

Janet Staiger, 'The Hollywood mode of production, 1930–60', in Bordwell, Staiger and Thompson, *The Classical Hollywood Cinema: Film Style and Mode of Production to 1960*, London and New York, Routledge, 1985.

Bette Davis presenting fury in Joseph L. Mankiewicz's *All About Eve*

STARS IN POSTWAR CINEMA

STEVEN COHAN

The 1948 Paramount consent decree (see p. 19) had significant consequences for stardom as an institution based in the motion-picture industry. Without the economic incentive to produce 40 or more films a year, studios reduced their production output; in turn, they gradually ceased their former practice of signing actors to renewable seven-year exclusive contracts with the intent of training the standouts for stardom. Without a large roster of stars on contract, the studios no longer needed to retain the machinery for the continuing development of properties for those stars and for regulating publicity about them, both of which were a means of reiterating, amplifying, but also scripting their personae. Today, one could be forgiven for thinking of stars simply as extra-filmic personalities – that is, as celebrities whose private lives justify their fame and shape how the public perceives them – forgetting that stars are manufactured commodities, too.

The transformation of Hollywood stardom into the phenomenon of public celebrity is more visible in retrospect than it was at the time. For instance, during the 1950s MGM dropped Clark Gable and Lana Turner, once indelibly linked with this studio's logo. However, MGM continued to develop new performers in their place, grooming the teenaged Debbie Reynolds and Elizabeth Taylor into adult stardom, trying out Italian starlet Pier Angeli, and signing former Columbia Pictures actor Glenn Ford. MGM also shared Grace Kelly with Paramount and borrowed young stars such as Paul Newman from other studios. Some of the era's biggest stars avoided long-term contracts and instead freelanced, the terms by which Marlon Brando headlined at MGM and Frank Sinatra returned to his former studio. In the meantime, leaving MGM did not mean the end of their careers for Gable and Turner. Trading on the iconic stature created for him by MGM, until his death in 1960 Gable continued to make action films and romantic comedies for production companies affiliated with other studios, while Turner, her career resuscitated by a scandalous murder that fed into her film roles, rebounded with a series of glossy melodramas, most of which were produced at Universal.

MGM's example summarises the state of postwar stardom, which seemed like business as usual while predicting changes that were to become more pronounced in the decades to follow. The number of stars introduced in the 1950s testifies to the continuing commercial value of star-driven vehicles: Marilyn Monroe and Gregory Peck at 20th Century Fox; Audrey Hepburn and Jerry Lewis at Paramount; Doris Day, James Dean and Natalie Wood at Warners; Kim Novak and Jack Lemmon at Columbia; and Rock Hudson at Universal. This period, moreover, is probably the last time when female and male stars sustained parity as perceived box-office draws, one major benefit of the studio system's investment in stardom as the key selling point of motion pictures.

On the other hand, a gender gap was evident when it came to older stars. Leading men from the 1930s and 1940s had little difficulty retaining their stature, often co-starring with women 30 years younger. John Wayne, James Stewart and Cary Grant achieved their greatest popularity in the 1950s, with the patriarchal connotations of their maturity adding a by-now indelible iconic significance to their screen personae. Women of that same generation, however, suffered from the industry's ageism. While some moved gracefully into television, others, such as Bette Davis and Joan Crawford, held on, but only by parodying their former personae in a cycle of horror films in which they played grotesque monsters or victims.

At the same time, several developments began loosening the studios' regulation of stardom. Once off contract, stars such as Burt Lancaster and Kirk Douglas formed their own production companies, which not only gave them more control over projects from start to finish but also enabled them to play against the typecasting of earlier roles. During the 1960s, too, a crop of talented new stars emerged – Steve McQueen, Sidney Poitier, Jane Fonda, Barbra Streisand, Robert Redford and Dustin Hoffman – who, like Brando, were notable for their lack of conformity with the more standardised look of Hollywood stardom as well as for their independence from the studio system and its protocols.

Along with the increasing presence of foreign films in the US after the end of World War II, the reopening of European markets for the studios further modified film stardom, making it more global and less identified primarily with Hollywood. To protect their own film industries, many countries enforced national quotas and restricted access to local profits for US product, which led to what was called 'runaway production' in locales outside of North America, to co-productions with

A new kind of star: Sidney Poitier: *In the Heat of the Night*

British or European film companies, and to the casting of expensive films with more of an eye towards their appeal beyond the US (see also Postwar globalisation, p. 49). An international cast was routine in the hugely successful epics that the studios treated as their prestige productions. Richard Burton, Peter O'Toole and Omar Sharif rose to prominence in such films. In the early 1960s, Sophia Loren returned to the Italian film industry after a series of lacklustre roles in Hollywood, won an Academy Award (the first granted to a performance not in English) for a film that broke with her sexy starlet image, and thereafter her popularity was not restricted to English-language films (see also Italian cinema, p. 232). Loren's frequent Italian co-star, Marcello Mastroianni, achieved international stardom without ever starring in a Hollywood film. Italy was also beneficial for Clint Eastwood, who became a star in the 1960s by way of three spaghetti westerns.

Additionally, with the lessening of studio control over a star's private life, scandalous revelations in the press became commonplace, anticipating the paparazzi now taken for granted as a byproduct of fame. Both Elizabeth Taylor's million-dollar salary and her reputation as the most beautiful woman in the world were in no small way due to continuing reports of her tumultuous off-screen life, which made for better melodrama than anything Hollywood could write and kept her in the public eye around the world even when she had no film playing in theatres. Scandalous gossip had comparable impact as material for novelists such as Jacqueline Susann, who fictionalised the biographies of Judy Garland and Marilyn Monroe. Much like James Dean's fatal car accident, Monroe's suicide, still clouded by sexual scandal and political intrigue, essentially froze her stardom in time as an icon of this era, leading to the subsequent cult appreciation of her image as distinct from her films.

Yet another source of reinvesting stars with iconic meaning came from the showings of older films on television and in revival houses. Whether viewed nostalgically (the cult audience of college students for Humphrey Bogart) or as camp (the cult audience of gay men for Joan Crawford and Bette Davis), such new currency for stars exceeded or revised what they had represented in the past. A comparable effect occurred because of the increasing politicisation of stars who became involved in the civil rights, women's liberation and anti-war movements, which gave their personae an immediacy in the public eye that exceeded their film roles. By the close of the 1960s, stardom was clearly being transformed into a phenomenon of popular culture no longer under the firm hand of the film industry.

Selected Reading

Richard Dyer with Paul McDonald, *Stars*, London, BFI Publishing, 1998. Revised edition.

Joshua Gamson, *Claims to Fame: Celebrity in Contemporary America*, Berkeley, University of California Press, 1994.

Christine Gledhill (ed.), *Stardom: Industry of Desire*, London and New York, Routledge, 1991.

DORIS DAY

Doris Day was considered the most popular star in the early 1960s, yet is mainly remembered now for playing the perpetual virgin. This impression underestimates the significance of her appeal, particularly to women. Before signing with Warner Bros. in the late 1940s, Day was a band singer known for her warm, husky voice, and she continued to record albums throughout the 1950s. Warners developed a wholesome but tomboyish persona for her in musicals, many of which capitalised on postwar nostalgia for small-town Americana. After the expiration of her contract, Day freelanced and expanded her range beyond musicals, although her films almost always featured her singing at least one or two songs regardless of the genre. Day's screen persona then appeared to change course with *Pillow Talk* in 1959. This first teaming with Rock Hudson glamorised her screen image while displaying her talent for sophisticated comedy, but it also inspired the virginal character with which she later became identified (see also Comedy, p. 270).

Oscar Levant, an early co-star, quipped that he knew Day before she became a virgin, but her many fans could well have made the same claim. Of her 37 films, only a handful portrayed her as the object of a lascivious bachelor's pursuit. If anything, Day more often than not played a mother, often widowed. The typical Day character, too, did not immediately conform to stereotypes of femininity, which is why the star could so easily cross-dress in *Calamity Jane* (1953) without damaging her image. On screen, Doris Day could fix a car, play baseball, head a union grievance committee, run a small business on her own or happily live alone as a single professional in the big city. This type of characterisation prepared the way for plots requiring her to stand up to a male authority, encouraging audience identification with her integrity and self-reliance.

Equally important, because Day sang in most of her films, her screen presence was inseparable from her voice. In *The Man Who Knew Too Much* (1955), Day's singing defines the intimacy of the mother–child bond apart from the father's dominance, and it leads to disclosure of the kidnapped boy's whereabouts. *Pillow Talk* uses Day's voice just as explicitly: from her singing about female desire during the opening credits, to the plot premise that the two stars have to share a telephone line, to the witty use of split-screen scenes and paralleled voice-overs, to her performing another song as an interior monologue expressing her own desire to consummate her romance with Hudson. That Day's voice gives expression to a strong sense of female subjectivity puts her character on equal footing with Hudson's throughout *Pillow Talk*, which makes it difficult simply to reduce her character to the perpetual virgin holding out for a marriage proposal

The independence grounding Day's persona worked with her voice to establish her characters as active, desiring women and to put pressure on the conservative closure of her films. Nonetheless, Day's star image was not without contradictions related to her success within the studio system, as Bingham (2006) points out. Her popularity owed much to her

On equal footing: Doris Day and Rock Hudson in the battle-of-the-sexes comedy *Pillow Talk*

lively roles in the 1950s but her highest standing at the box office occurred after *Pillow Talk*, when her films became more formulaic. While a simplification of Day's persona made it more reassuring and hence more bankable during a period of increasing social unrest, by the end of the decade it also made her films seem instantly outdated, resulting in that reduction of her star image to an unhappy reminder of a pre-feminist era's sexual hypocrisy.

STEVEN COHAN

PAUL NEWMAN

As a young star in the 1950s, Paul Newman was already associated with two key features that remain attached to his famous name: his deep blue eyes and his home-made salad dressing. These two contrasting associations – one condensing his erotic value as a male movie star, the other indicating his private life – outline his star image. Off screen, Newman has long been known for his lasting marriage to frequent co-star, Joanne Woodward, and their New England family life, for the Actors Studio training that has drawn him back to the Broadway stage on several occasions, and for his philanthropy and advocacy of liberal causes. Yet in his most notable films, Newman plays quite the opposite: the gorgeous, ambitious, yet morally dubious young man on the make, ready to take advantage of anyone, male or female, who crosses his path. Audiences have always responded to Newman's charismatic presence, a mark of the skill with which his acting combines with the camera's attention to his body, starting with the close-ups focusing on those famous blue eyes. However, Newman's legendary appeal owes as much to his star image, which contributes to that sense of his irresistible presence on screen.

One of many actors signed by the studios in the 1950s to emulate the rebellious, neurotic youths personified by Montgomery Clift and Marlon Brando to electric effect, Newman did not come into his own until he stepped into roles originally planned for

James Dean. This type of rebel bad boy was presented as an alternative expression of masculinity, one interpreted at the time as both a symptom of a crisis directly related to postwar culture and a critique of middle-class norms. As Klinger (1994) and Cohan (1997) both document, in the era's fan magazines, an important venue for constructing the aura of transparency central to stardom, the actors cast in the rebel mould were set off against its opposite: the uncomplicated, wholesome new star exemplified by Rock Hudson and his copycats. Although his look and performance style made Newman the logical successor to Dean after the latter's death in 1955, in fact Newman's screen persona combines the two categories. This hybridity enables Newman's characters to project dangerous intimations of amorality and open declarations of sexuality while remaining rakishly charming and desirable as a romantic lover, as in his first co-starring vehicle with Woodward, *The Long, Hot Summer* (1958).

Even when, as in *Hud* (1962), the Newman persona goes against the role, it still interacts with the film. As directed by Martin Ritt and written by Irving Ravetch and Harriet Frank Jr (the three also did *Long, Hot Summer*), *Hud* carefully lays out the title character's moral irresponsibility, predatory sexuality and cynical contempt for authority. By rights, Hud is an anti-hero who should not garner any audience sympathy whatsoever, and the film ends with him remaining alienated and unredeemed. Yet Newman's charisma makes Hud at once repulsive and attractive, a compelling figure to watch regardless of his actions. This ambivalence results from the actor's performance, his sexy appearance and his extra-filmic star image, all alluded to in Paramount's publicity for the film, which exclaimed, 'Paul Newman Is Hud'. Through this overlapping of character and star, *Hud* anticipated how the Newman persona established in the 1950s could then so easily readjust to the counter-culture attitudes of the 1960s when he played less ambivalent anti-heroes in *Cool Hand Luke* (1967) and *Butch Cassidy and the Sundance Kid* (1969).

STEVEN COHAN

Alienating yet attractive: Paul Newman as the amoral anti-hero Hud

JANE FONDA

Jane Fonda has probably reinvented herself successfully more times than any other star in Hollywood's history. Fonda's star image thus appears to cohere very loosely as an assemblage of varying identities, each one contradicting the others – Henry Fonda's daughter, sexy starlet, emancipated feminist, controversial political activist, serious actress, socially conscious film-maker, fitness advocate, consort of a broadcasting tycoon. On one hand, these identities divide Fonda's long career into self-contained phases. On the other, each identity, always widely prominent in press coverage of Fonda, never entirely cancels out the others. Fonda the Vietnam war protestor, hostilely dubbed 'Hanoi Jane' by the war's supporters, still determines how her entire stardom is seen from that single perspective, just as the poster art depicting a barely clothed Fonda as *Barbarella* (1968) still refracts a very different meaning for her stardom from yet another perspective.

However viewed, Fonda's star image greatly depends on the cultural contexts through which she has been interpreted, as Perkins (1991) demonstrates. The meanings cohering around Fonda as a star changed dramatically over time not only because her private life changed course but also because the discourses mediating her image shifted. When taken together, the many discursive frameworks equate Fonda's stardom with her celebrity status in popular culture, yet they also function to authenticate her transparency as a public figure. Regardless of whether her sincerity was believed or mistrusted at any phase of her career, and she has always elicited both responses, the effect has been the same – Fonda the movie star and Fonda the real person represent one and the same. Crucial to this effect is the way that

From innocent to activist: Jane Fonda in (top) *Barbarella* and (above) *Tout va bien*

certain elements are repeated from phase to phase throughout her career, both in her film roles and the press coverage, to structure her persona: a narrative of Fonda's innocence and education, and the tracing of this movement's significance on her body to show its effects. Each discursive reframing of Fonda specifies these elements differently, but their repetition awards an underlying unity to the persona, which is why her image could shift so radically without splintering.

The Fonda persona is most evident in the socially relevant films she co-produced after her Hollywood career revived in the late 1970s. In that era's parlance, these films stage a consciousness-raising experience for her naïve characters, referring to a Jane Fonda now publicly redirecting her anti-war activism towards liberal causes. The cartoonish *Barbarella* seems to feature a very different Fonda, but the persona is the same. *Barbarella* was one of several films she made in Europe in the 1960s with first husband Roger Vadim, who attempted to remodel her into an Americanised Brigitte Bardot. All wide-eyed innocence about the new world she encounters as a futurist space traveller, Barbarella learns how to achieve an orgasm the natural way, and her sexuality ultimately overpowers the film's villain. The poster art and slogan, 'See Barbarella Do Her Thing', were of a piece with its counter-culture ethos of drugs and sexual revolution, with the way that Fonda's on-screen nudity broke with the decorum still governing female stars in the US, and with the magazine articles recounting her own avowed emancipation as a feminist. This framework affixed Fonda's persona to the era's concern with sexual liberation, which in the 1960s was a highly divisive social issue, and it established the continuity between her films with Vadim and the risqué comedies and racy melodramas that she made for Hollywood during the same period.

STEVEN COHAN

CONTEMPORARY STARDOM

CHRIS HOLMLUND

Contemporary star-making entails increasingly complex processes. Casting and other production decisions, individual performances, marketing, media coverage, domestic and foreign box office, DVD/video and ancillary product sales, broadcast/cable/satellite television appearances, general audience and fan discussion all have an impact on the creation of star identities. Now packaged and protected by agents and entertainment lawyers, today's film stars are, as described by Barry King, 'stakeholders in an enterprise that manages their career' (King, 2003, p. 49). Salaries have skyrocketed since the 1970s, and stars wield more power than studios. Magnets for audiences, stars can be seen over and over again on television and/or computer screens. Fans voice their likes and dislikes via blogs, e-mail and websites. In popular parlance, stardom extends beyond cinema to include politicians, sports figures, singers and television personalities, among others.

In the 1970s, rising print, advertising and negative costs, the increasing interdependence of film and television, and changes in ownership of the majors combined to strengthen the hands of stars and their agents. Agencies began to offer studios talent packages, bundling together stars, directors, writers and properties. Agent fees rose, and the practice of negotiating a percentage of box-office gross started. Concerned about risk, and knowing that major stars were crucial to securing foreign markets (then half the ultimate gross; today much more), studios acquiesced, even though this sometimes meant that top-grossing hits saw no net profit. Some stars, free for the first time to steer their own careers, feared overexposure and chose to appear infrequently. David Cook (2000) identifies Barbra Streisand as a prime example: in this decade she performed in only nine films. Holmlund (2005) notes that among female stars, Barbra Streisand, Pam Grier and Ellen Burstyn were the most bankable female performers. Clint Eastwood headed the list of bankable male stars, appearing in *Variety*'s yearly top ten moneymaker charts nine times; in Cook's summary of industry statistics, Paul Newman, Robert Redford, John Wayne, Steve McQueen, Al Pacino and Burt Reynolds appeared four or more times (Cook, 2000).

During the 1980s, star salaries again spiralled upwards as agencies continued to press for higher pay by packaging talent. By the end of the decade, Eddie Murphy, Sylvester Stallone, Dustin Hoffman and Paul Newman commanded over $15 million per picture. The studios tried to fight back, signing some big stars to multi-picture contracts, without much luck. Stallone, Murphy, Robin Williams, Tom Hanks, Harrison Ford, Tom Cruise, Arnold Schwarzenegger (see case study) and Mel Gibson all emerged as superstars, appearing in movies that grossed $100 million or more. Streisand remained the most powerful female star. Yet as Stephen Prince (2002) observes, Streisand, Meryl Streep, Sigourney Weaver, Kathleen Turner and Debra Winger all earned significantly less than male stars, and men got most of the prize roles too. Independent studios, Carolco foremost among them, built themselves around star franchises, with 'hard body' action stars such as Stallone and Schwarzenegger front and centre. Cannon International competed on a lesser level, offering straight-to-video titles featuring, for example, Jean-Claude Van Damme. Home video revolutionised viewing patterns and provided the industry with new markets for both niche and big-budget, 'high-concept' films. Enlisting stars as a way to quickly illustrate plot premises and provide marketing hooks, high-concept films would seem to corral star performances. Nevertheless, according to Justin Wyatt (1994), sometimes a star's uniqueness functioned as 'excess', uncoupled from either plot or character development, as with Jack Nicholson's quirky turn as the Joker in *Batman* (1989).

The 1990s brought major shifts in media access, with profound implications for stardom. DVD rentals began to replace video; almost everyone was familiar with words such as 'e-mail', the 'Internet', and the 'World Wide Web'; and more and more people owned computers (though there was a marked divide by region and income). Many of today's stars made their first $100 million-plus film during the decade, among them Sean Connery, Bruce Willis, Matt Damon, Nicolas Cage, Julia Roberts and Leonardo DiCaprio. At the box office, Tom Cruise and Tom Hanks were the most reliable performers, but Will Smith was and remains popular with both black and white audiences; in the 1990s, he also topped the music charts.

So where does stardom stand in the 2000s? Superstars now earn over $20 million, plus a percentage for appearing in big-budget pictures. They can survive a string of failures and enjoy relatively long careers, although only Sylvester (Sly) Stallone has been a superstar for over 20 years (De Vany, 2004). People around the world refer to their favourite stars by their first names, implying intimate knowledge of the likes of Sly, Arnold, Whoopi and Clint. New synergies offer expanding options for marketing, exhibition and reception. Superstars move between studio and independent film-making, looking for more diverse roles than studio pictures alone typically offer. Some jump-start flagging careers by acting 'indie': witness John Travolta's return with *Pulp Fiction* (1994). Since 2000, with every current major studio setting up an 'independent' arm, such alternation has become easier (see also The major independents, p. 54).

Other stars are primarily known for their work in independent films. Harvey Keitel's name is enough to guarantee an independent film's production, and according to Diane Negra (2005), Parker Posey stamps a film with indie authenticity. Although most movies with high returns are made on small budgets and do not have stars (*The Blair Witch Project*, 1999, is a spectacular case in point), blockbusters do showcase stars, in part because they help to ensure longer runs. Meanwhile, the fact that directors generally have longer careers than most stars helps to explain why many contemporary stars try their hands at directing. Examples include both super- and indie stars: besides George Clooney (see case study), there is the grand old master Clint Eastwood, Tom Hanks, Nicolas Cage, Mel Gibson, Sean Penn, Jodie Foster, Ron Howard, Denzel Washington, Kevin Costner, Robert Duvall, Tommy Lee Jones, Ethan Hawke and John Turturro. Others combine acting and producing: Clooney again, Reese Witherspoon, Charlize Theron, Sandra Bullock and Don Cheadle. Yet very few stars actually make more than five films that gross over $100 million in North American markets. As of 2004, De Vany (2004) maintains, Jim Carrey topped this list; Tom Cruise, Harrison Ford, Mel Gibson, Eddie Murphy, Arnold Schwarzenegger, Robin Williams and Julia Roberts were also key players.

The differences between contemporary and classical stardom have influenced the direction of theoretical approaches. One line of enquiry has examined the economic conditions that underpin stardom today: for example, Wyatt (1994), Prince (2002), Cook (2000) and De Vany (2004). Others have approached stardom in terms of genre (Britton, 1991), audiences or fans. And there has been substantial interest in lesbian/gay/queer fans (De Angelis, 2001).

A growing body of work has concentrated on performance. King (1991) compares film and theatrical performances, arguing that Hollywood's reliance on naturalist conventions often renders a star's physical attributes more important than his or her acting range. For King, this means that 'personification' is more common than 'impersonation'. According to this argument, film stars convey authenticity differently from theatre stars. In a later article, King expands on this insight, looking at how increasing numbers of specialist departments, media outlets and viewing options change authenticity. He concludes that the stable star persona of old is gone: today's stars must parade 'wardrobe[s] of identities' (King, 2003, p. 49). To break through the 'clutter' that now characterises the world media market, contemporary stars find themselves prompted to deliver ever more sensational performances on and off screen, though this can be risky. Tom Cruise's hysterical declaration of love for girlfriend Katie Holmes on *The Oprah Winfrey Show* in 2005, when he jumped around the set, hopped on a couch and fell to one knee, attracted huge amounts of negative publicity.

Most critics agree with Dyer (1979; 1998) that like classical stardom, contemporary stardom operates on two levels, with as much commentary devoted to the star performer's off-screen life as to their on-screen appearances. Paul McDonald (1998) and Christine Geraghty (2000) conclude that the term star is now overused. In an effort to distinguish film stardom, Geraghty proposes three categories for analysis: first, the star-as-celebrity, where fame rests on biography and lifestyle, and box-office failures are not significant (for example, Richard Gere in the 1990s); second, the star-as-professional, where fame rests on work and a stable star image is paramount (for example, Whoopi Goldberg; see case study); and third, the star-as-performer, where fame rests on particular physical or acting skills (for example, Jackie Chan or Nicole Kidman). Underpinning all current lines of enquiry is the conviction that historical and cultural co-ordinates condition and impact on stardom. Thus, questions must be asked about 'what defines and delimits a "context", and what forms of context are to be judged as of most relevance . . . to the study of stardom. Such questions do not make historical studies of stars impossible, only provisional' (McDonald, 1998, p. 179).

Among topics that merit more focused attention are the labour agreements governing how film stars work around the world; the influence that stars' actual or perceived ethnicity, race, nationality and age may – or may not – have on casting and fan followings; the ways in which transnational production and regional or global reception impact on specific stars and contemporary stardom in general; and the effects that digital production, distribution and exhibition have on perceptions of authenticity.

Selected Reading

Christine Geraghty, 'Re-examining stardom: questions of texts, bodies and performance', in Gledhill and Williams (eds), *Reinventing Film Studies*, London, Arnold, 2000.

Barry King, 'Articulating stardom', in Gledhill (ed.), *Stardom: Industry of Desire*, London and New York, Routledge, 1991.

Barry King, 'Embodying an elastic self: the parametrics of contemporary stardom', in Austin and Barker (eds), *Contemporary Hollywood Stardom*, London, Arnold, 2003.

Paul McDonald, 'Supplementary chapter: reconceptualising stardom', in Dyer with McDonald, *Stars*, London, BFI Publishing, 1998.

ARNOLD SCHWARZENEGGER

'I'll be back!'; 'Hasta la vista, baby!' People across the globe imitate Arnold Schwarzenegger's heavily accented, deadpan delivery in the colossally popular *The Terminator* (1984) and *Terminator 2 Judgment Day* (1991). The relentless robot he played in the first film catapulted him to global stardom, in part thanks to the new medium of video: made for $6.5 million, the film grossed more than $80 million worldwide. Accordingly, spectacular violence escalated in action movies. *The Terminator*'s kill count of 27 makes Schwarzenegger's villain look pacific when compared with the nearly 50 people his character disposed of three years later in *Predator* (1987), or the 100-plus he destroyed in *Commando* (1985). Director James Cameron and Schwarzenegger's second collaboration, *Terminator 2*, grossing $500 million worldwide, consolidated his reputation as the supreme early 1990s 'hard body', especially since he had become a sensitive father figure.

Born to working-class parents in Austria in 1947, Arnold (as he is known to billions) is one of the most successful stars ever, with a net worth estimated at between $800 and $900 million ('ABC7 – Gov. Schwarzenegger's tax returns released'). His ticket was bodybuilding. By age 20, he was 6 feet 2 inches and 250 pounds, with a 57-inch chest, 33-inch waist, 22-inch biceps and 28-inch thighs (Bial, 1998), and by 1980 he had won 12 Mr Olympia and Mr Universe competitions. Fascinated by power from childhood, Arnold dreamed of going to the US and making it big (Andrews, 2003; Leamer, 2005). He arrived in 1968; his breakthrough came with the title role in *Conan the Barbarian* (1981). Throughout the 1980s and early 1990s, he enjoyed a string of hits with top action directors such as Walter Hill (*Red Heat*, 1988), John McTiernan (*Predator*; *Last Action Hero*, 1993), Paul Verhoeven (*Total Recall*, 1990) and James Cameron (*True Lies*, 1994). His action machos were infamous for their bloodthirstiness and one-liners. In *Total Recall*, for example, he kills his traitorous wife (Sharon Stone) while quipping, 'Consider that a divorce!'; in *Predator*, he jokes 'Stick around!' as he impales an enemy guerrilla on a tree. In the late 1980s, he branched out into comedy, scoring mega-hits with *Twins* (1988) and *Kindergarten Cop* (1990); his third attempt, *Junior* (1994), was less successful. By the late 1990s, most of his films were flops; only *Terminator 3 Rise of the Machines* (2003), for which he received $30 million, was highly profitable.

Lacking psychological depth: Arnold Schwarzenegger in *Total Recall*

An awkward actor, Arnold cuts a less romantic figure than competitors Steven Seagal, Jean-Claude Van Damme or Sylvester Stallone, although he proudly displays his naked and/or leather-clad body. 'I have a love interest in every one of my films,' he has said, 'a gun!' (Bial, 1998, p. 45). Best at characters who are unchangingly good or evil, without psychological depth, Schwarzenegger has tirelessly exercised control over his image, marketing himself as a brand on television talk shows. In public, he incessantly reinvents a persona that conflates 'the civic sphere and celebrity worship' (Indiana, 2005, p. 9). Like Sly, therefore, Arnold is a superb example not only of a star as global celebrity, but also of a '"star-as-professional" associated with quite precise variations . . . [of] displays of masculine prowess' (Geraghty, 2000, p. 189).

Schwarzenegger found the solution to his waning popularity as a film star in politics. A lifelong Republican, an American citizen since 1983 and part of the 'Kennedy clan' through his marriage to Maria Shriver, in 2003 Schwarzenegger announced his candidacy for governor of California on *Tonight with Jay Leno*. To intense media coverage, he promised to rid the state of Democratic 'girlie men'. Lacking experience, and despite exposés of sexual misconduct (Connolly, 2001; Indiana, 2005), he won. When his special propositions failed in 2005, the 'Governator' reinvented himself, moving towards the middle to win easy re-election in 2006 with a lesbian Democrat as his Chief of Staff. 'I'll be back!'

CHRIS HOLMLUND

WHOOPI GOLDBERG

Often known solely by her first name, Whoopi has appeared in over 60 films, many of them family friendly. She is the first black woman to have anchored two television talk shows, two television series and a popular TV game show, *Hollywood Squares* (1998–2004). Add to her credits stage performances, children's books, a bestseller for adults, numerous TV guest appearances and the Mark Twain prize for comedy. And who can forget her as four-time host of the Academy Awards, culminating in 1999 with a star turn as Queen Elizabeth I in white face?

A self-described 'mutt' (part Seminole Indian, Russian Jew, black, white and Chinese), Whoopi refuses the label 'African-American'. She insists she is just as American as anyone else (Goldberg, 1997). She is mindful, too, of how the label 'black actor' limits casting opportunities: 'I don't want

Whoopi Goldberg as the wistful and mostly silent Celie in *The Color Purple*

them to say, "Oh, she's a Black actor, we can't use her". I want them to say, "Oh here's a great role. Call Meryl Streep. Call Diane Keaton. Call Whoopi Goldberg"'(quoted in Noel, 1985, p. 34).

Born Caryn Johnson in 1955, Whoopi and her brother were raised by their mother in a Manhattan housing project. At age eight, Whoopi joined a children's theatre troupe; at 14, she dropped out of school to work a series of odd jobs. Addicted to heroin in the early 1970s, she kicked the habit and married her drug counsellor. In 1974, the two had a daughter, then divorced. Now calling herself Whoopi, Caryn moved west and began performing in local theatres while working and living on welfare (DeLaria, 1995; Noel, 1985; Martindale, 2000). In 1984, her one-woman comedy, 'The Spook Show', became a Broadway hit. Steven Spielberg's 1985 screen adaptation of *The Color Purple* brought national and international renown. Whoopi's performance as the illiterate, abused and mostly silent Celie was impressive in its 'wistfulness and steely doggedness' (Stuart, 1989, p. 71), earning her a Golden Globe and an Oscar nomination for Best Actress. A string of lesser films, among them *Jumpin' Jack Flash* (1986), *Burglar* and *Fatal Beauty* (both 1987) followed; all were written for white actors. *Ghost* (1990) grossed $500 million worldwide and netted Whoopi another Golden Globe and an Oscar for Best Supporting Actress (only the second given to a black woman in Academy Award history). Also immensely successful, *Sister Act* (1992; $232 million worldwide) paired Whoopi with a white lover (Harvey Keitel). As has been typical of her on-screen romances with white actors (among them Sam Elliott, Jonathan Pryce, Ted Danson, Mary Louise Parker, Gerard Depardieu and Ray Liotta), Keitel and Whoopi's sexual relationship was largely invisible. Is this why 1993 saw Whoopi as the highest-paid female star, when she earned more than $7 million for *Sister Act 2: Back in the Habit*? Other notable 1990s films, such as *The Long Walk Home* (1990), *The Player* (1992), *Boys on the Side* 1995) and *Ghosts of Mississippi* (1996), take different routes into history.

Now ageing, black and female – a triple whammy in Hollywood – today Whoopi appears primarily in supporting or cameo roles; she also voices animated films, remains a television stalwart and hosts a radio show. An outspoken liberal, she works tirelessly for human rights and other causes. Although her fashion gaffes and involvements with white men have frequently made her tabloid fodder, her richly calibrated performances deserve attention: she is expert at 'play[ing] with and against racial stereotypes, gender clichés, and sexual expectations' (Holmlund, 2002, p. 140).

CHRIS HOLMLUND

GEORGE CLOONEY

Voted 'sexiest star in television' and (twice) 'sexiest man alive', 'Gorgeous George' Clooney's effortless charisma and relaxed charm are celebrated by the popular press. They speculate endlessly about who he might marry, though Clooney clearly prefers dating and hanging out with the boys. He is often portrayed as heir to Cary Grant and Clark Gable because of his dark good looks, bedroom eyes, strong jaw and ability to wear tailored suits.

Born 1961 in Kentucky, Clooney's love of television and film stems from his father, Nick, a broadcast journalist. His aunt, singer Rosemary Clooney, also supported young George's aspirations (Cohen, 2006; Hudson, 2003). In the 1980s and early 1990s, he netted supporting roles on television shows such as *Roseanne* (1988–97) and *The Facts of Life* (1979–88). His 1994 performance as dapper bachelor Dr Doug Ross in the ensemble medical drama *ER* (1994–) launched him to stardom. Over 29 million people tuned in to see Dr Doug's final regular season appearance.

Clooney's first film break came with Robert Rodriguez's vampire/action spoof *From Dusk till Dawn* (1995). Spy-caper movies, romantic comedies and action pictures followed, most featuring him as charming ne'er-do-well. Steven Soderbergh's stylishly sizzling *Out of Sight* (1998) paired him with Jennifer Lopez. The Coen brothers' *O Brother, Where Art Thou?* (2000) lambasted his 'gorgeousness' to great effect (and won him a Golden Globe). He also won acclaim for his work in David O. Russell's anti-Gulf war film *Three Kings* (1999). 2006 brought major awards for Clooney's unshowy but gripping supporting performance as a disgraced CIA agent in *Syriana* (2005). Most financially successful have been his collaborations with super- and lesser stars in Soderbergh's *Ocean's* series (2001; 2004; 2007).

Clooney moves between independent and mainstream productions, aiming to help independent projects he believes in and to bring independent ideas into commercial film. He has become a successful director, making his first film, *Confessions of a Dangerous Mind* (2002), because he loved Charlie Kaufman's screenplay. *Good Night, and Good Luck* (2005) showcases television newscaster Edward R. Murrow (David Strathairn) and producer Fred Friendly (Clooney) speaking out against the McCarthy communist witch-hunts. The film was nominated for numerous awards and earned Clooney Academy Award nominations for Best Director and Best Original Screenplay. Clooney worked as executive producer with Steven Soderbergh for Section Eight (*A Scanner Darkly*, 2006; *Far from Heaven*, 2002), and is producer-director on the forthcoming *Leatherheads* (2007). An outspoken liberal, he admits 'I've slept with too many women, I've done too many drugs, and I've been to too many parties (see 'George Clooney biography')' to run for office, but he is dedicated to inspiring voters to ask tough questions and viewers to demand good films.

CHRIS HOLMLUND

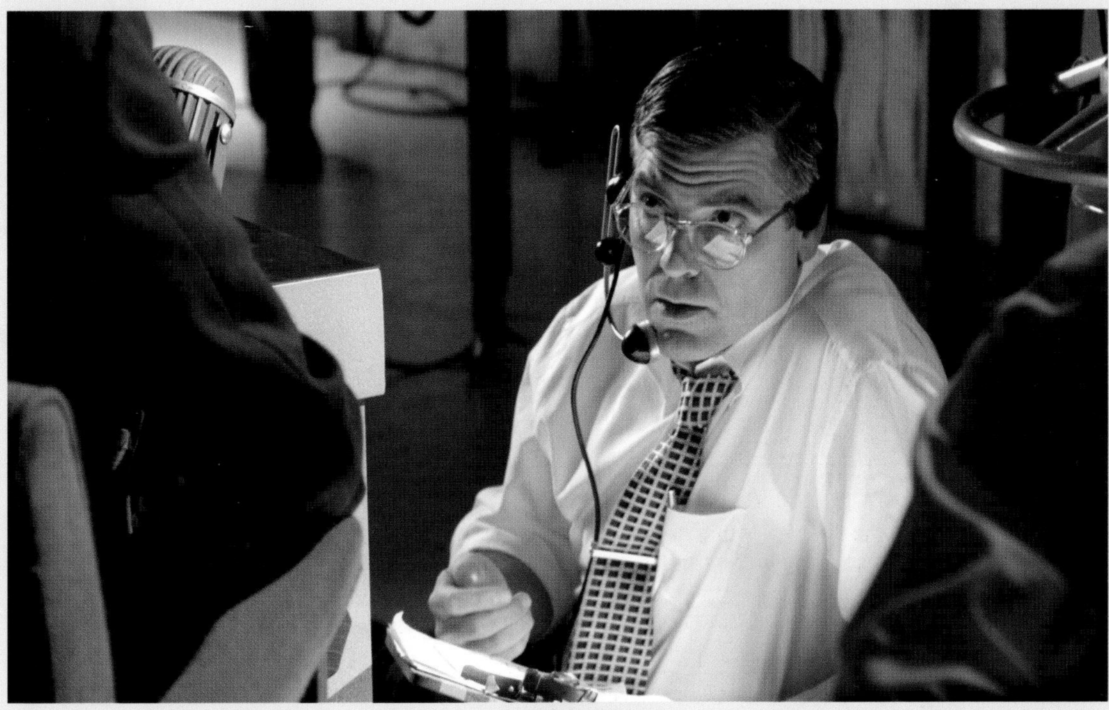

Sexiest man alive and outspoken liberal George Clooney in *Good Night, and Good Luck*

PART 3

Technologies

Keir Dullea in *2001: A Space Odyssey*

INTRODUCTION

MICHAEL ALLEN

> The motion picture did not originate as art, but as a machine. They were invented. That is, the machinery that makes pictures, and that makes them motion pictures, was invented. Thus the term motion pictures means the device as well as the art. (A. R. Fulton, 1985)

Cinema is one of the most technological of art forms. The result of an extraordinary confluence of disciplines in both science (chemistry, physics, engineering, optics) and the humanities (writing, painting, photography, drama), it began by explicitly foregrounding the apparatus. '[I]n the first moments of the history of cinema, it [was] the technology which [provided] the immediate interest: what [was] promoted or sold [was] the experience of the machine' (Heath and de Lauretis, 1980, p. 1). The machine was, effectively, inserted between the film and the viewer. Floor-standing Kinetoscopes or Mutoscopes that were hand-operated by patrons, or projectors that were visible to the crowd during film shows, testify to that technological foundation of cinema. The subject of technology and film, therefore, is central to any consideration of the cinema as a cultural and historical phenomenon.

Traditional film histories ascribe most technological innovations in the cinema to a combination of individual genius and aesthetic predestination. Peter Wollen (1980) summarises this view as seeing the history of film technology in terms of 'legendary moments' (Lumière's projector; the arrival of sound; the adoption of colour; the acceptance of widescreen). This teleological model positions technological advances as solutions to recognised aesthetic problems.

Brian Winston argues otherwise. For him, 'a technology moves from inchoate scientific knowledge (which itself is conditioned by society) to wide diffusion in society via a number of transactions' (Winston, 1996, p. 4). Therefore, within the social sphere, at a particular historical time, a certain scientific competence will exist, which creates the base potential for technological development. A transformation termed 'ideation' – the idea of the device – produces technological performances that are called prototypes. These prototypes can languish indefinitely, until external social forces produce the right circumstances to transform the prototype into invention – society must want or need the device. Winston terms this external social influence 'supervening social necessity'. When a new technology appears, it can promise substantial disruption to existing practices. That this potential is largely curbed, so that the technology can operate effectively in a prescribed area of usage, is termed by Winston the 'suppression of radical potential'. As he argues, '[n]ew technologies are constrained and diffused only insofar as their potential for radical disruption is contained or suppressed'. Winston's theory makes society, rather than 'genius inventors', the driving force for technological development.

The development of any new film technology is, therefore, grounded in its socio-economic context. Central to this argument is that any innovation and development in film technology is market-led or, at least, is in a symbiotic relationship with the market. The audience must want what the technology can provide before it succeeds and becomes naturalised. This was the case with colour and widescreen, both of which could have been adopted by the industry in the late 1920s, but had to wait until the 1950s to have the correct social and economic conditions (including, prominently, the threat from black-and-white television) present for their acceptance. In this context, it is wrong to see technologies as self-animated. 'New technologies do not simply emerge, but by virtue of their development, the market promotes their use (sometimes to the point of insistence), creating needs which the new technologies serve to commercial advantage' (Wollen, 1980). The same situation is being repeated with the emergence of multimedia and virtual reality:

> Without agreement on what these systems are expected to do, there can be no mass market. This implies making an unsuspecting public familiar with a new device and persuading it not only of its merit, but of its ease of operation. In this respect, the introduction of multimedia products into the home is a 'technology driven' push, rather than a 'culturally led' pull. (Rickett, 1993, pp. 80–1)

Part of this push occurs as a means of industrial self-regeneration. Commercial and industrial stasis, in anything other than the extreme short term, is perceived to be an undesirable state. Technological development should also, therefore, be seen as an important player in the game of product differentiation. Film companies invest in, and develop, new technologies partly in order to steal a march on their rivals and thereby improve (or maintain) their position of power within the industry. In this way, a differentiation–appropriation cycle is constructed, whereby companies differentiate themselves from one another by developing unique products, the features of which then become absorbed within the industry as standard practice. Such was the case with Warner Bros. championing sound technologies in the late 1920s, and Fox doing likewise for CinemaScope in the early 1950s. Integral to this trajectory is the opposition of short-term novelty to long-term industrial acceptance.

> Each new technological development – the advent of sound, colour, widescreen, and so on – can be seen, through a materialist scenario, to restore briefly the cinema's initial identity as a novelty, foregrounding the new technology in ways which disrupt the medium's carefully constructed, seamless surface of invisibility. (Belton, 1992, p. 14)

This disruption continues, attracting audiences by its difference and 'newness', until its frequency and longevity normalise it within the industry and the culture. At this point, usually, a new novelty is required to rejuvenate the arena.

In addition to being offered 'externally' to audiences as novelties, new technologies are also introduced 'internally' within the industry in order to improve production efficiency. This can take two tracks: improving existing practices – effectively, doing what is already being done, but faster and better – and allow-

Star Wars used cameras that were initially developed for pilot training

ing new techniques to be developed. The latter are surprisingly few. '[T]he majority of technical developments in the film industry have been aimed at facilitating extant production practices rather than at changing the "look" or sound of commercial films' (Eidsvik, 1988/9). After the first few years of film, when most of the basic techniques had been developed, any new technology tended to improve existing techniques, rather than produce a radically new film-making tool. The latest examples of this are the newly emergent digital technologies.

Each instance of technological innovation presents the industry with a number of options, variations upon the theme that the innovation generally represents. The choice of one option over another propels the trajectory promised by the innovation along a slightly different track. That is to say, significant new technologies tend to develop and/or appear during times of flux and uncertainty. Sometimes only one of these possibilities is adopted, sometimes several. An example of this would be the appearance of sound in the late 1920s, which prompted a significant debate regarding the type of sound that should be created to accompany the image track, before one option was determined upon (see Sound, p. 142). 'The road not taken is just as much a part of the cinema event as cinema itself' (Altman, 1992, p. 12).

One effect of this emphasis on specific areas of film technology is that it explicitly differentiates film from other media, such as stills photography, radio or television. Certainly, this has been a common perspective on the history of film technology, with many commentators noting the differentiation–appropriation cycle as an important trajectory for the industry as a whole. Other writers, for example Altman (1985), argue otherwise, suggesting that different media have often been linked together in such ways that their identities partly blur. The adoption of any new technological development has inevitable consequences in a number of other areas within the industry. Peter Wollen (1980) describes, for example, the knock-on effect caused by the coming of sound, which necessitated changes in lighting methods (from noisy carbon to silent tungsten lamps), film stock (orthochromatic was 'blind' to the red-biased tungsten lights, whereas panchromatic stock was not) and make-up (which had to be reformulated to look acceptable on panchromatic stock). No new technology either develops or becomes naturalised within the industry in isolation. It is always caught in a complex series of interrelations with other technologies. This issue of media identity takes on renewed importance when the new, computer-based, multimedia technologies are considered, in which several different media are combined in one site.

While it might be argued that Hollywood internally generates the technological innovations it needs, the reality is that it either usually employs or, more often, simply takes advantage of developments produced externally to itself, by 'outsiders'. 'Almost all the major technical innovations have been introduced by outsiders with the support of economic interests wishing to break into the industry . . .' (Wollen, 1980, p. 19). This is certainly the case with the development of sound technology (by electronics, record and radio companies) and digital special effects (by computer specialists for advertising and industrial presentation).

Foremost among these alternative arenas has been that of warfare. Film has always been vital to the military for propaganda purposes. In World War II, some German platoons had their own film units, responsible for gathering and immediately processing information. The difficulties of filming in dangerous or physically uncomfortable locations have forced many developments in equipment design. From improvements in lighting stemming from research into the design of searchlights, through the development of lighter cameras for reconnaissance purposes, better lenses to allow filming from greater (safer) distances, to the simulation of complex war-game scenarios in virtual reality, the results of military research have always had a major input into technological development in the cinema. Many leading figures in the development of film technology began in the audio-visual sector of the military. For example, optics professor Henri Chrétien's work during World War I on the development of naval artillery telemetry helped to lay the foundations for what would become CinemaScope; André Coutant's work in developing a small film mechanism to control the telemetry of French guided missiles eventually led to the silent-running, hand-held Éclair camera; and the computer-controlled Dykstraflex camera used on the film *Star Wars* (1977) was initially developed for a pilot training system. The ever-increasing speed and complexity of modern warfare has prompted equivalent developments in film technologies simply in order to maintain the possibility of recording and representation.

> For the United States, it was becoming an urgent matter to have new information-gathering methods at its disposal. And so it was that Eastman-Kodak came up with its Mylar-based film and Dr Edwin Land of Hycon Corporation with the high-resolution camera – both of which laid the basis for regular aerial reconnaissance over the Soviet Union. (Virilio, 1989, p. 81)

More abstractly, military technology has produced a shift from the visible and physical (face-to-face fighting in the trenches of World War I) to the invisible and virtual (combatants represented by blips on radar screens, virtual reality (VR) simulations, 'smart' missiles directed onto targets via miniature television screens mounted on the missile itself). 'Eyesight and direct vision have gradually given way to optical or opto-electronic processes, to the most sophisticated forms of "telescopic sight"' (Virilio, 1989, p. 69). This making the real unreal, invisible and virtual has had, and will have, a dramatic impact upon the development of media technologies both in the 1990s and into the first decades of the next century.

Developments in film technology have often been employed in the creation of illusion and magic. In the earliest years of cinema, for example, Georges Méliès used special cameras adapted to allow rewinding, to produce the multiple-exposure image effects that make his films so strikingly fantastic. As often, however, the production of fantastic images has been in the service of the realist aesthetic, producing a filmic world that, although logically impossible, looks completely believable. Within these terms, the aesthetic of realism dominates the history of film technology. All major technological innovations contribute towards increasing the sense of experiencing 'real life' when watching, and listening to, a film in the cinema. Each technical development is seen as helping to close the gap between the represented 'real world' and its cinematic representation. Deep-focus photography, for example, in the way it presents all elements within the same frame, is seen to be an 'unmanipulated mode of cinematic representation'. Similarly, CinemaScope, it has been argued, increases the spectator's freedom to choose what to look at and when to look at it (Barr, 1974). We can find this argument repeated for each of the other major technological innovations: colour (more like 'real life' than black and white); stereo sound (we listen to the real world in stereo); and virtual reality (the represented world can actually be experientially entered and actively engaged with, via headsets and sensitised bodysuits). In the area of the modern special-effects film, James Cameron, director of *The Terminator* (1984), discussing the special effects used to produce the alien water creature in his film *The Abyss* (1989), has commented:

The magical effect of advanced technology in *The Abyss*

> [The audience] understood intuitively what was magical about the scene. They were seeing something which was impossible, and yet looked completely photorealistic. It defied their power to explain how it was being done and returned them to a childlike state of pure entertainment. The sufficiently advanced technology had become magic to them. (Cameron, 1992, p. 7)

It may, however, be argued to the contrary that technological transitions have often involved – initially at least – the adoption of apparently non-realist aesthetic strategies, until such time as the innovation in question has entered general cinematic currency. Edward Buscombe has suggested, for example, that both sound and colour were originally associated, in the American film industry, with that least realistic of genres, the musical (Buscombe, 1978). Indeed, rather than recognising an all-embracing trend towards realism in cinema, it seems that some kind of movement between product differentiation and the eventual appropriation of such differentiation by prevailing cinematic orthodoxy has been the model for much of cinema's aesthetic development.

Selected Reading

Brian Winston, *Technologies of Seeing: Photography, Cinematography and Television*, London, BFI Publishing, 1996.

Peter Wollen, 'Cinema and technology: a historical overview', in Heath and de Lauretis (eds), *The Cinematic Apparatus*, London, Palgrave Macmillan, 1980.

SOUND

MICHAEL ALLEN AND ANNETTE KUHN

The sound era of cinema is generally dated from the release of *The Jazz Singer* in 1927 – although this was neither the first sound feature nor the first 'talking' film. Attempts to give film a voice were being made from the very beginnings of cinema: Thomas Edison's main interest in encouraging his assistant W. K. L. Dickson to develop the Kinetograph was that he hoped it would complement the Edison Phonograph. In 1895, Edison introduced his Kinetophone – an adaptation of the Kinetoscope peep-hole machine with which films were viewed using a combination film-viewer and audio-playback machine (via headphones). The device was unsuccessful, due to a combination of technical problems and public disinterest (audiences were more than satisfied with the novelty of moving pictures, even if silent), although it resurfaced briefly, and again unsuccessfully, for a second time in 1913 in a screen-projected form. Gaumont also experimented with synchronised sound films over a number of years from 1901/2, with his Chronophone. Other, unsuccessful, disc-based systems were developed by George Pomerade in 1907, E. H. Armet between 1912 and 1918, and William Bristol, from 1917.

Probably the earliest and certainly the most common method of adding sound to silent films involved the placing of actors, musicians and noise-making machines directly behind the screen. This practice was employed as late as 1915 in special roadshow presentations of D. W. Griffith's *The Birth of a Nation*. Meanwhile, the most prestigious productions – which, in the 1920s, were those shown in the lavish movie palaces – had the benefit of orchestral accompaniment, while even the smallest of cinemas, from the days of the nickelodeon until the advent of sound, employed improvising pianists. The unreliability of 'live' accompanists and developments in radio and electronic research together led to experimentation throughout the 1920s. More significant in the long term, however, was the development of photographing sound directly onto film, the first patent for such a process being issued as early as 1900 (see Early and pre-sound cinema, p. 3).

The advent of sound in cinema provides an excellent illustration of the fact that technologies are not necessarily implemented as soon as they become available. The American

All-singing, but little talking: early sound in *The Jazz Singer*

Telephone and Telegraph Company (AT&T) and the Radio Corporation of America (RCA) both conducted experiments in sound cinema from the early years of the century, but executives in the film studios were unwilling to make changes in an already profitable industry. The major film companies were all listed on the stock exchange and in 1926 the total capital invested in the industry exceeded $1.5 billion. A move to sound would involve vast expenditure in re-equipping studios and theatres and retraining casts and crews all for a commodity for which there could hardly be said to be a demand. The film industry was thus not, for the most part, keen to move from silent to sound production.

At Warner Bros., however, the situation was somewhat different. Although by 1925 Warners had built up a relatively prosperous production company, the bulk of the audiences for their films was the clientele of small independent theatre circuits and neighbourhood film theatres, and it was becoming increasingly difficult to compete with the opulent picture palaces of the vertically integrated companies. If, however, they installed sound into their studios and theatres as a direct alternative to the pit orchestras of their rivals, they might be able to compete with them. Warners impressed investment banker Waddill Catchings of Wall Street's Goodman Sachs Company with their cost accounting and strict budgetary control, and the bank agreed to finance the company through a period of carefully planned expansion. Warners then appointed Catchings to their board of directors and purchased the ailing Vitagraph Corporation with its 50 film exchanges, a worldwide distribution system and a Hollywood radio station equipped by Western Electric.

In April 1926, Warners and Western Electric co-founded the Vitaphone Corporation to make sound films and market sound equipment. In August of that year, Warners presented its first sound feature, *Don Juan*, together with a supporting programme of Vitaphone shorts, including recorded concerts and an address by Will Hays. At this point, the Fox Film Corporation decided to join the move to sound, and with the acquisition of their own sound system, began to produce sound newsreels under the Movietone banner. In October 1927, Warners followed its earlier success with the release of *The Jazz Singer*, although the film was more of a 'singing' than a 'talking' film, as the dialogue-only sections of the film were still conveyed via intertitles. By the following spring, all the majors were busily engaged in equipping studios for the transition to sound, and the Vitaphone system was rapidly revised. On both *Don Juan* and *The Jazz Singer*, the 'soundtrack' had been recorded on discs whose playing time equalled the running time of one reel of film. Because the disc-synchronisation process was rather unreliable, it was soon replaced by sound recorded directly onto film. Douglas Gomery (1985) argues that this process is an example of an economic theory of technological innovation, which posits that production processes are introduced to increase profits in three systematic phases: invention, innovation and diffusion.

By the end of 1930, Warner Bros. not only entirely controlled its former rival, First National, but had also boosted its own assets from $5 million in 1925 to $230 million. Western Electric had quickly secured contracts with all existing production companies, while AT&T's rival, RCA, responded in 1928 by creating a wholly owned integrated company of its own, RKO, to exploit its Photophone sound system. On several occasions over the next decade, RKO threatened AT&T with antitrust action because of the latter's virtual monopoly over the sound market, but by 1943 some 60 per cent of all equipment in the industry was in fact being supplied by RKO. As had been expected, sound boosted production costs to an average $375,000 per film in 1930 as against less than $80,000 a decade earlier. The conversion to sound cost the industry an estimated $500 million, and established alliances between production companies and Wall Street that were to last for many years.

The advent of sound briefly curtailed the possibilities of mobile framing only recently established in silent cinema. The new sound cameras were enclosed in soundproof booths that had to remain virtually immobile during shooting. Actors at first had to be grouped around concealed microphones. Consequently, for some time the use of close-ups was virtually abandoned as the camera was forced to keep a greater distance from the actors, and as shots became longer and cuts fewer.

Rick Altman notes that there was considerable debate in the early years of sound cinema about exactly what kind of sound should be developed to accompany the image track. This debate centred on the issue of 'sound space' – should film sound attempt to recreate the sonic landscape of real life, in which a wide number of audio elements (voices, objects, ambience) were of equal importance, or adopt some other logic whereby certain elements were privileged over others? (Altman, 1992). In the first years of sound cinema, there was an attempt to control sound quality and balance during projection, but such systems, while theoretically producing a more realistic soundscape, were practically unfeasible, and were soon replaced by processes that controlled the sound during production. At first, multiple microphones picked up the various areas of sound that were then controlled by a mixing engineer. Central to this technique was the idea that sound level should match image size (loud for close-ups, quieter for long shots). This theory was soon found to be flawed, creating a disorienting cacophony of sound. A choice was made to use only one microphone, placed closer to the camera axis, and to maintain a constant audio level, irrespective of image-framing distance. Favouring intelligibility over sonic complexity and authenticity, this process had its source in the similar sound strategies found in the dramatic theatre of the time. As such, it was dialogue-biased, and consequently narrative-biased. This process of decision-making is one instance where several options were reduced to one choice, which then became the industry standard.

Despite constant improvements in sound quality, especially at the prestige end of the market, the next decisive innovation in sound came only with the introduction, after World War II, of magnetic tape, a development aided by the Allies' capture of German technological innovations, which also included hand-held cameras and Agfacolor film stock. The great advantage of magnetic tape recording was that, unlike photographic sound that had to be chemically developed, it could be replayed immediately. The result was a greater flexibility, and greater security, in film production.

> However, every move forward has a tendency to mark a step back. Sound editors complained that, with the new-fangled magnetic sound, it was no longer possible to see the actual optical sound modulation on the track. This tended to make sound editing more difficult. (Today, with audio post-production work stations using digital sound, this facility is once again available). (Amyes, 1990, p. 3)

Later, stereophonic sound accompanied the widescreen movies of the 1950s, although only after a power struggle between Fox and Paramount. Fox initially insisted that any theatre equipping itself for CinemaScope would also have to install stereo sound equipment. However, after resistance from theatres that could not afford installation costs, and threatening progress by Paramount, who were developing an alternative widescreen system, Fox relented, and supplied their films with a variety of

The Jazz Singer (USA 1927 *p.c* – Warner Bros./Vitaphone Corporation; *d* – Alan Crosland)

The most notable aspect of the use of sound in *The Jazz Singer* is its incompleteness. Only the musical sequences and the dialogue that immediately surrounds them are carried by a recorded soundtrack. Elsewhere, dialogue-only sequences are conveyed by written intertitles, which was the standard technique of the time. This mixture of styles creates a 'text' whereby the sound sequences, which would have already been considered novel at the time, become even more so by virtue of seeming to burst forth from the silence of the film. This 'textual violence' is echoed by the actors' performances, which alternate between the overly gestural and expressive delivery of the opening and closing sequences, and the more restrained and improvisational style of the dramatic sections.

Indeed, the improvisational element of the film, partly generated by Al Jolson's status as a performer, is also a result of the demands of early sound production. The live recording of the sound onto disc at the same time as the scene was filmed meant that the performance had to continue even if the actors forgot their lines. There are moments in the dialogue between Jolson as Jakie Rabinowitz and his mother, Sara (Eugenie Besserer), when one can sense that Jolson is keeping the 'banter' from stalling. The success of these improvised exchanges precisely depends on Jolson's talent for extemporisation; the pleasure is in seeing him 'pulling it off live', reinforced by hearing him doing so as well. It is very much Jolson's performance; Besserer contributes little to these moments except acquiescent giggles.

MICHAEL ALLEN

The Public Enemy (USA 1931 *p.c* – Warner Bros.; *d* – William A. Wellman)

The opening sequence of this film is a good illustration of the way in which the studio attempted to negotiate the transition to synchronised sound recording. The tracking shot that reveals the working-class Chicago streets has a dubbed soundtrack, while the conversation between the two boys has synchronised sound, necessitating an immobile camera. Although we may experience the scene as continuous, the transition is marked by a cut that signals the difference between the two recording techniques.

ANNETTE KUHN

Jurassic Park (USA 1993 *p.c* – Amblin Entertainment/ Universal; *d* – Steven Spielberg)

Although critical and popular attention has concentrated on the visual special effects used to create the credibly moving dinosaurs in *Jurassic Park*, the soundtrack plays an equally important role, and won the film an Oscar for Best Sound in 1993. *Jurassic Park* was the first to feature Digital Theatre System (DTS) sound, in which the sound is recorded onto a digital compact disc and is then replayed on a CD-ROM machine that can read timecode.

The CD-quality sound is most apparent in the wide dynamic range found in *Jurassic Park*. The mining sequence near the beginning of the film, for example, displays a broad layering of sound, from industrial noises, metal hammers chipping away at rock, birds calling in the trees and dialogue between characters. All levels of sound – from the quietest to the loudest – are equally 'present'.

Complex, multilayered sound design: *Jurassic Park*

In the scene in which the T-Rex attacks the truck containing two children, the soundtrack begins simply with the sound of pouring rain. This sparseness helps to build suspense. The soundtrack is then broadened by the dull, resonant thud of the T-Rex's footsteps as they disturb the surface of a glass of water. The noises become increasingly layered as the fence wires begin to snap and its frame creaks under pressure from the dinosaur. When the dinosaur eventually attacks, the soundtrack reaches its fullest complexity: the roars of the T-Rex, the screams of the children, squelching mud, occasional snatches of dialogue and the continual sound of pouring rain are clearly discernible from one another, while simultaneously combining to form the dense body of sound that complements the visuals.

MICHAEL ALLEN

soundtracks. During the 1960s, Quadrophonic, Sensurround and Dolby sound were developed as a result of the acquisition of film companies by multiple-media conglomerates, who could draft technical expertise and innovations over from other sections of their media empires (most notably, the music industry).

In the early 1980s, a new sound system was developed that further redefined the experience of sound in the cinema auditorium: THX, a sound system developed by George Lucas and Tom Holman in the early 1980s, premiered as a demonstration trailer before Lucasfilm's *Return of the Jedi* in 1983. (The name is an amalgam of Lucas's 1970 film *THX 1138* and, slightly tortuously, an extrapolation of 'Tom Holman eXperiment'). THX produces a

> stable sound, extremely well defined in high frequencies, powerful in volume, with superb dynamic contrasts, and also, despite its strength and the probably large theatre space, a sound that does not seem very reverberant at all. One finds in THX theatres the realisation of the modern ideal of a great 'dry strength'. (Chion, 1994)

The result is that, even in the largest of auditoriums, the spectator has the feeling of receiving a sound meant only for them: 'The big THX theatres no longer give us a collective sound in the old style: it's inflated personal stereo sound' (Chion, 1994). A rival system, DTS (Digital Theatre Systems), premiered in 1993 with the release of *Jurassic Park*. In a curious echo of Vitaphone's sound-on-disc, the soundtrack is provided on separate CDs, synchronised to the film via timecode. In the event of a technical fault on the CD player, the system automatically switches over to a traditional analogue soundtrack running alongside the filmstrip itself.

Digital technologies of the 1980s and 1990s, imported from the music industry, have further altered the status of film sound. Chion (1994) notes that the difference both Dolby and digital sound technologies have made to modern recording techniques is that more ambient noise can be included on the soundtrack. Early sound systems were not sophisticated enough to allow the adequate and equal separation of voice, noise and music. Voice was therefore privileged, for reasons outlined earlier, and the other two components subordinated, with noise coming off worst. Modern systems allow complex layers of all three to coexist on the same soundtrack. The result is a heightened realism, in which the film's world is more fully drawn. In some sense, therefore, we are returning to the soundscape model jettisoned in the earliest years of sound.

Although virtual reality's 'heightened realism' is often described in terms that privilege the visual over the aural, in fact the role of sound in the virtual reality environment is a vital part of the toolkit for developers, being used to further distract the user's attention from the non-virtual world, and, thereby, solidify the technology's 'authority over the observer'. Digital reverb units such as the Quantec Room Simulator and the Roland Sound Space Processor allow engineers both to simulate the sound of prescribed spaces (types of room, qualities of texture) and to localise sound within a 360° horizontal, and a limited vertical, location. The general aim is to produce a 3-D audio to match the 3-D visuals of the virtual reality environment, to dismantle the sense of audio as a 'surface' projected from stereo speakers by creating, instead, the sensation that it is 'all around', and that it moves with the user as they change their physical position in space (see Jones, 1993).

Selected Reading

Rick Altman, *Sound Theory, Sound Practice*, New York, Routledge, 1992.

Michel Chion, *L'Audio-Vision*, Paris, Editions Nathan, 1990. In English: *Audio-vision: Sound on Screen*, New York, Columbia University Press, 1994; trans. Claudia Gorbman.

COLOUR

MICHAEL ALLEN AND ANNETTE KUHN

As with sound, colour was one of the aesthetic options available to film-makers from the earliest years of cinema and, as with sound, the technical problems involved in making colour films were sufficiently daunting to dissuade many practitioners from exploring its potentials for some time after its initial development. But unlike sound, which was adopted fairly quickly when social conditions made it an attractive option in the late 1920s, colour lay largely dormant for almost three decades before being fully accepted by the industry. This was due in large part to social and economic circumstances outside the control of the film industry itself.

The earliest films were hand-coloured, frame by frame. As films increased in length, and the number of prints soared, hand-colouring became increasingly less practicable. As a solution, Pathé Frères patented Pathecolor, a semi-automated device for stencilling prints according to simple colour correspondences, as one can see in *Ali Baba and the Forty Thieves/Ali Baba et les quarante voleurs* (1902), for example, where the colour of Ali Baba's yellow and red costume maintains a fair registration with his body as he moves across the screen. (The modern method of colourising black-and-white films via computer technology in some ways repeats both the process and the 'block-colour' effect of hand-colouring, albeit in a hi-tech way.) At the same time in America, less expensive tinting and toning processes converted black-and-white images to colour chemically. By the time of the transition to sound, this process was a long-standing tradition for the more prestigious productions. However, as soon as the sound-on-disc device was replaced by the recording of sound directly on film, the practice of tinting and toning was threatened because it became evident that the process affected the quality of the optical soundtrack (the dye used to stain the filmstrip also went over the soundtrack area, distorting the optical information). To combat the problem, Kodak immediately introduced a range of 17 Sonochrome positive stocks whose soundtrack areas were not affected by the dyeing process. In spite of this, however, it was eventually decided that post-production conversion of black-and-white images to colour was less sensible than actually filming with colour stock.

The principle of colour photography had been introduced in the 1850s and demonstrated in 1861 by the Scottish physicist James Clerk Maxwell. The cinematic process that first successfully employed those principles – Kinemacolour – which had been patented in 1906 and first began to appear in public film shows in 1909, employed a standard Bioscope projector fitted with a shutter of red and green filters rotating at 32 frames per second, and was a considerable commercial success. Nevertheless such 'additive' colour processes had several drawbacks, and were soon superseded by other two-colour methods, such as Kodachrome (introduced for stills photography in 1913, and adopted for movies in 1916), a 'subtractive' process in which colour images were formed directly on the celluloid rather than indirectly on the screen. In the mid-1920s, Technicolor developed a two-colour process, in which two filmstrips – one red- and the other green-biased – were pasted together to produce a composite print, but the limited effects and the various technical limitations, including the double thickness of the filmstrip and the high light levels required during filming to obtain a bright enough final image, hardly justified their expense. In 1932, it was replaced by Technicolor's superior 'tri-pack' three-colour format, in which a beam-splitting mechanism simultaneously exposed a blue/red 'bi-pack' and a separate green-biased negative. Technicolor was able to capitalise on the coming of sound by offering a process that had no adverse effect on the optical soundtrack. By means of combining superior print quality with patent control, Technicolor continued to dominate the American colour movie market for three decades.

At first, the two-colour process proved insufficiently attractive to the majors to induce them to experiment with it, and so Technicolor began to produce shorts of its own and also to provide MGM and Warner Bros. with Technicolor supervisors when the two companies began their own series of colour shorts and introduced short colour sequences into primarily black-and-white films. Finally, in 1929, Warner Bros. released two 'all-colour, all talking' features – *On With the Show* and *Gold Diggers of Broadway*, the first results of a 20-feature contract Jack Warner had signed with Technicolor. At the beginning of the new decade, when the industry began to feel the effects of the Depression, the majors, unable to withdraw from their commitment to sound, chose instead to reduce their interest in colour cinematography, and the musical – the genre with which colour had been most closely associated – was briefly considered to be 'box-office poison'. Undaunted, Technicolor invested a further $180,000 in their three-colour process, and instead of entering the market themselves, offered exclusive contracts to two independent production companies – Walt Disney and Pioneer Films. Disney acquired exclusive rights for colour cartoons and released a series of 'Silly Symphonies' that won critical acclaim, Academy Awards and massive box-office returns. Meanwhile Pioneer, after experimenting with three-colour shorts and sequences, released the first three-colour feature, *Becky Sharp*, in 1935. When Becky Sharp proved only a modest commercial success, Pioneer's executives joined forces with the independent producer David O. Selznick and, under the banner of Selznick International Pictures, absorbed Pioneer's eight-feature contract with Technicolor. There followed a string of three-colour successes, including *The Garden of Allah* (1936), *A Star Is Born* (1937) and *Gone With the Wind* (1939).

By the time the economic viability of Technicolor was established, World War II, the shrinking world market for films, and reduced budgets and production schedules curtailed the expansion of colour cinematography for some time. Into the 1950s, Technicolor improved their process to make the emulsions more sensitive; however, Eastman Color had replaced Technicolor as a negative source by 1953, because of the convenience of shooting a single negative in a smaller camera. From 1955, the name 'Technicolor' only referred to the laboratory process that produced three separately dyed negatives.

In 1935, Kodak offered Kodachrome as a new 'tri-pack' monopack for amateur use, but it took until 1943 for a professional version to appear, largely because the continued popular success of monochrome film made it an unattractive option for film-makers: in 1935, it was estimated that colour added approximately 30 per cent to production costs, which then averaged about $300,000; in 1949, this figure had fallen to ten per cent while the average costs of American A-features had risen to about $1 million. In 1948, *Variety* estimated that colour could add as much as 25 per cent to a feature film's financial return, but this was not sufficient to cover additional production costs. In 1940, only four per cent of American features were in colour. By 1951, this figure had risen to 51 per cent but in 1958 had fallen to 25 per cent as a result of shrinking budgets and the emergence of the black-and-white television market. By 1967, however, the television networks having turned to colour broadcasting, the percentage rose once more to 75 per cent, and in 1976, to 94 per cent.

Selected Reading

Angela Dalle Vacche and Brian Price (eds), *Color: The Film Reader*, New York and Oxford, Routledge, 2006.

Stephen Neale, *Cinema and Technology: Image, Sound, Colour*, London, BFIPublishing/Macmillan, 1985.

Gone With the Wind (USA 1939 *p.c* – Selznick International Pictures/Loew's Inc.; *d* – Victor Fleming)

Gone With the Wind was, from the earliest stages, designed to employ a heightened sense of colour that would be integral to the film's narrative drama. Director George Cukor and cinematographer Lee Garmes were both fired for their refusal to adhere to producer David O. Selznick's concept of a florid, theatrical look and feel that would give the film an epic quality.

Production designer William Cameron Menzies created colour sketches that established the stylised look for the production, and Technicolor was employed throughout to match the emotional mood of each scene. In the early O'Hara family evening prayer episode, for example, the colour palette and lighting are both suitably subdued; by contrast, when Rhett (Clark Gable) leaves Scarlett (Vivien Leigh) to make her own way home after the escape from Atlanta, the saturated reds connote their passionate anger. In both cases, colour is used to signify the emotional tone of character as well as scene.

The Technicolor camera was large and unwieldy, demanding twice as much lighting as standard cameras, cumbersome lens changes and substantial rehearsal time for complex action scenes. In spite of these constraints, the benefits of using Technicolor can be seen in the burning of Atlanta sequence, in which all seven Technicolor cameras then available in the US were simultaneously used to produce images of spectacular colour intensity and unforgettable vividness.

MICHAEL ALLEN

Spectacular colour intensity and unforgettable vividness: Clark Gable and Vivien Leigh in *Gone With the Wind*

She Wore a Yellow Ribbon (USA 1949 *p.c* – Argosy Pictures Corp/RKO; *d* – John Ford)

She Wore a Yellow Ribbon is, in many respects, a perfect film for the Technicolor process. Its subject matter – the attempts of a Union cavalry troop to maintain peace in American Indian territory – allows an art design that covers the range of primary colours, especially in the cavalry's uniforms (blue with yellow trouser stripes and epaulettes), the American flag (predominantly red) and the surrounding landscape (blue sky, ochre and red sand). More subtly, the various pastel shades of the women's dresses, and the many different muted colours of the American Indian costumes, all display Technicolor's wider, more sensitively hued palette range. The colour generally is soft, more so in the night scenes when colour definition is lost and takes on a murky brown quality.

In the scene where Sergeant Quincannon (Victor McLaglen) picks a fight with several soldiers in order to be sent to jail, the colour contrast between interior and exterior areas is emphasised by the constant movement between the two as the soldiers are thrown out of, and run back into, the bar. The basic uniforms, the more brightly coloured underclothes and the strong sunlight outside all confirm the ability of the Technicolor system to reproduce faithfully the required colour tones and hues, whether in direct or artificial light.

The Technicolor consultant for the film, Natalie Kalmus, acted as adviser for many of the most famous and significant Technicolor features: for example, *Mystery of the Wax Museum* (1933), *The Adventures of Robin Hood* (1938), *The Wizard of Oz* (1939) and *Meet Me in St. Louis* (1944).

MICHAEL ALLEN

Lust for Life (USA 1956 *p.c* – MGM; *d* – Vincente Minnelli)

Lust for Life was adapted from Irving Stone's novel about the life and art of Vincent Van Gogh. It was one of a number of biopics about artists and entertainers made in Hollywood in the 1950s, and one of a number of films shot wholly or partly on location. It was produced by MGM and directed by Vincente Minnelli. Minnelli's films often centred on characters, artists or otherwise who sought to impose or realise their view of themselves and the world around them. He had a long-standing interest in Impressionist and Post-Impressionist painting and was particularly keen to direct *Lust for Life*.

Lust for Life was viewed by MGM as a film that would appeal to educated adult audiences (it was initially released in a number of art-house cinemas in New York, Los Angeles and other college cities). It was also viewed as a natural vehicle for location shooting and for the colour and widescreen technologies that were increasingly being used to augment the cinema experience and to counter the appeal of television. There is some dispute as to the version of the colour process used on the film. In his commentary on the DVD (Warner Home Video, 2006), Drew Caspar states that a new version of a process called Anscolor was used. In his autobiography, Minnelli recalls that he insisted on using the old version because it was truer to the subdued tones of Van Gogh's earlier paintings and drawings as well as to the brighter tones of his later ones (Minnelli, 1975, p. 289). Either way, the process was identified on the credits as Metrocolor, and Minnelli used it not just to showcase Van Gogh's paintings, but to accent different phases in the artist's life: the first phase in Belgium is dominated by blacks and greys, the

Colour and widescreen used to augment the cinema experience: Minnelli's Van Gogh biopic *Lust for Life*

second in Holland by dark greens, the third in Paris by reds and blues, the fourth in Arles by greens, reds and yellows, and the fifth in Auvers by unstable combinations of all these different colours.

Minnelli also recalls that he was initially opposed to using CinemaScope because its proportions were different from those of Van Gogh's drawings and paintings (Minnelli, 1975, p. 288). However, he used these differences, and those between the still images of the paintings and drawings and the moving images on the cinema screen, to highlight the impossibilities inherent in Van Gogh's desire to capture the world around him, and to foreground the ways in which images of all kinds – wide or narrow, still or moving, reflected or recorded, painted or drawn – can be framed for the eyes of the viewer. This is apparent in the scenes in which Van Gogh is shown painting or drawing, which are nearly always framed to show a still rectangular image on Van Gogh's easel and the wider, often windblown scene he is trying to capture. In interior scenes, doorways, windows and in one striking case a round mirror are used as internal frames for figures and objects (see also Widescreen, p. 154).

STEVE NEALE

DEEP-FOCUS

MICHAEL ALLEN AND ANNETTE KUHN

Deep-focus cinematography, in which objects in several planes of depth are kept in equally sharp focus, is commonly associated with certain Hollywood films of the 1940s. Patrick Ogle dates its emergence at around 1941, and argues that its development was influenced by a matrix of cinematic and non-cinematic factors, such as the rise of photojournalism and social realist and documentary film movements during the 1930s, as well as the availability of new kinds of film stock, lighting equipment and lenses. According to this argument, cinematographers of this period were attempting to duplicate on film the perspective and foreground–background image size relationships seen in picture magazines. Since the normal focal length of a 35mm still camera is (relatively speaking) half that of the 35mm motion-picture camera, most still-camera pictures take in an angle of view twice as wide as that taken in by a movie camera filming the same event from the same distance. In order to reproduce the effects of still photographs, cinematographers had to use what, in motion-picture terms, were considered unusually wide-angle lenses (Ogle, 1977).

In the mid-1930s, improved arc lights that, because of noise and flicker problems, had been virtually abandoned in favour of incandescents better suited to panchromatic film stock and sound filming, were introduced specifically, at first, for Technicolor cinematography, which demanded high levels of lighting. In the latter half of the decade, however, faster film stocks became available, and while many cinematographers chose to underdevelop their footage in order to maintain the soft tones and low contrast levels they had been used to, a few opted for the possibilities of increased crispness and depth of field. In 1939, a new emulsion type was introduced that reproduced both sound and image more clearly and crisply than ever before, and, at the same time, new lens coatings were produced that resulted in improvements in light transmissions of more than 75 per cent under some conditions. This more efficient use of light led to better screen illumination, image contrast and sharpness of focus for both colour and black-and-white cinematography.

Although this conjunction of powerful point-source arc lights, fast film emulsions and crisp coated lenses were necessary preconditions for deep-focus cinematography, they were by no means sufficient. According to Ogle, for deep-focus to develop as it did, a number of essentially aesthetic choices and creative syntheses had to occur. The aesthetic in question is cinematic realism, which Ogle defines as 'a sense of presence' similar to that experienced by spectators in the theatre, in that the viewer is provided with 'visually acute high information imagery that he may scan according to his own desires without the interruptions of intercutting . . .' (Ogle, 1977). This argument echoes Bazin, for whom deep-focus brought the spectator into a relation with the image closer to that which they enjoy with reality. For Ogle, deep-focus cinematography as a recognised visual style first came to critical and public attention with the release of *Citizen Kane* (1941), though it had certainly been practised before (see Barr, 1974; Harpole, 1980). Although not obviously realistic in style, *Citizen Kane* manifested an unprecedented depth of field in the scene photographed, which led a contemporary reviewer to claim that it produced '. . . a picture closely approximating to what the eye sees . . . The result is realism in a new dimension: we forget we are looking at a picture, and feel the living, breathing presence of the characters' (*American Cinematographer*, May 1941, p. 222). For director of photography Gregg Toland, the aesthetic framework for the filming of *Citizen Kane* was always one of realism:

> Its keynote is realism . . . both Welles and I felt this, and felt that if it was possible, the picture should be brought to the screen in such a way that the audience would feel it was looking at reality, rather than merely at a movie. (Quoted in Turner, 1982, pp. 1221–2)

But the development of a deep-focus aesthetic should not be seen solely in terms of Hollywood. European directors, notably the French director Jean Renoir, were also instrumental in using it. Renoir's 1939 film *The Rules of the Game/La Règle du jeu*, for example, extensively employs deep-focus to establish and maintain the complex relationships between characters as they move around the house and gardens of the main location. In one particular scene, as Paul Schrader describes it:

> The long hallway scene . . . With so many people, how do you shoot that kind of situation? You have your actors blocked like crazy and you keep leading them off and going with them and coming back with someone else . . . He has a group shot and instead of cutting in for a close-up, he moves people out, moves in to a two-shot, pans with one of the characters to bring you to something else. Very similar to the stuff Welles was doing. (Schrader, quoted in Smith, 1995)

Although Ogle disagrees that the human eye sees in deep-focus, he believes the sense of realism celebrated by the reviewer consists in deep-focus cinematography's tendency towards long-duration sequences, avoidance of cut-aways and reaction shots, the employment of a relatively static camera, and the use of unobtrusive editing – once again echoing Bazin. Avoiding an argument based on technological determinism, Ogle insists that deep-focus could never have emerged without the timely creative input of Gregg Toland, William Wyler, John Ford and Orson Welles, and, indeed, without certain production conditions. He considers that *Citizen Kane*, for example, 'constituted a major coming together of technological practice with aesthetic choice in an environment highly conducive to creativity' (see *Citizen Kane* case study, p. 403).

Against Ogle's account, however, it has been argued (Williams, 1977) that neither technological practice nor aesthetic choice is independent of ideological and economic choices and practices, as Ogle's analysis suggests; moreover, realism is not simply an aesthetic but also an ideology, an 'ideology of the visible'. The importance of deep-focus cinematography for film criticism lies in its encapsulation of issues concerning economics and technology, aesthetics and ideology. An economic imperative might be detected, for instance, in the industry's need to mark a difference, a new kind of product; and part of the aesthetics of deep-focus may well have emerged from cinematographers' desire to assert their 'creative' status in the industry hierarchy.

Selected Reading

Patrick Ogle, 'Technological and aesthetic influences upon the development of deep-focus cinematography in the United States', in Ellis (ed.), *Screen Reader* 1, London, Society for Education in Film and Television, 1977, pp. 81–108.

Christopher Williams, 'The deep-focus question: some comments on Patrick Ogle's article', *Screen* 13 (1): 73–6, spring 1972. Reprinted in *Screen Reader* 1, London, Society for Education in Film and Television, 1977.

The Rules of the Game/La Règle du jeu (France 1939 *p.c* – Nouvelle Edition Française; *d* – Jean Renoir)

Renoir employs the deep-focus technique more frugally and more subtly than Welles's flamboyant usage in *Citizen Kane*. Indeed, it becomes an integral part of his formal armoury of camera framings and movements, which Renoir uses to describe the complex relationships between his set of characters. This is evident in the scene in which Schumacher (Gaston Modot), the gamekeeper, descends to the kitchen to confront his partner, Lisette (Paulette Dubost). She is entwined with poacher Marceau (Julien Carette), whom she is forced to hide in an adjoining room when Schumacher appears. Schumacher and Lisette meet in the foregound space, at the foot of the stairs, before moving to the kitchen table in the background. A reverse angle then frames them again in the foreground, while showing Marceau attempting to tiptoe away to the back of the room. Both foreground and background planes are kept in focus in both shots, thereby establishing and then confirming spatial relations, as well as creating the comic suspense of Marceau's attempted escape.

Everything in focus: Renoir's *La Règle du jeu*

In a later scene, the airman, André Jurieux (Roland Toutain), arrives at the house. We see two of the leading women reacting to his appearence as the camera circles around behind them to show André in the doorway. As the scene progresses, other characters appear from an opposite doorway, and walk forward from the background to join the main group milling around just in front of the camera. Again, all spatial planes are kept in focus to create the sense of a group of equals. As the scene ends, however, the action focuses on the hostess, Christine (Nora Grégor), as she recounts the history of her friendship with André. She is framed in foreground, André behind her in mid-distance; he is in blurred focus until she moves backwards to join him, when the camera refocuses on them both. The focusing obviously relates to the idea of memory and inclusion, which is the subject of the action.

MICHAEL ALLEN

The Best Years of Our Lives (USA 1946 *p.c* – Samuel Goldwyn Inc.; *d* – William Wyler)

Five years after his pioneering deep-focus work on *Citizen Kane*, Gregg Toland acted as cinematographer on William Wyler's *The Best Years of Our Lives*. A study of the post-war emotional and social problems of a group of returning veterans, the film won several Oscars in 1946, including Best Film, Best Director and Best Actor. Not, however, Best Cinematography.

Wyler and Toland's use of deep-focus can be seen in the celebrated scene in which Al (Fredric March) tries to dissuade Fred (Dana Andrews) from seeing his daughter. As Andrews enters the bar, clearly in focus, in deep background March, also in clear focus, sits with his back to the camera in a booth in the near foreground. Andrews walks the length of the bar to join March. Their tense conversation is covered in two-shots and shot/reverse-shot interchanges. The takes are generally quite long. When Andrews leaves March at the end of their conversation, he walks the length of the bar, again in full focus, and enters a phone booth in deep background. March then joins the disabled ex-sailor Homer (Harold Russell) and Butch (Hoagy Carmichael) at the piano as they show him a double-handed routine they have evolved. As they play, in one long continuous take, March alternately looks at them and glances backwards to watch Andrews as he makes his phone call. While the viewer's attention is theoretically able to freely roam the image, March's glances back and forth from background to foreground control the audience's gaze to some extent. Obviously, too, the deep-focus is used to keep all planes and areas of action equally clear, thereby increasing the scene's emotional tension.

MICHAEL ALLEN

Emotional tension between background and foreground in *The Best Years of Our Lives*

LIGHTING

MICHAEL ALLEN AND ANNETTE KUHN

In the 1890s, the major source of illumination for shooting film was sunlight. Sets were built and filmed on outdoor stages with muslin diffusers and various kinds of reflectors used to control the levels of brightness and shadow. The first film studio, Edison's Black Maria, built in 1893, had blackened walls and stages draped in black cloth. Its roof opened to adjust sunlight, and the whole building could be rotated to maximise daylight. Only occasionally did early films employ artificial lighting effects; all that was expected from lighting was that it facilitated the correct exposure of film-making. Thus the Cooper–Hewitt vapour lamps with which by 1905 several studios, including Biograph and Vitagraph, had equipped themselves, were initially used sparingly to supplement the diffused sunlight filtering through studio roofs. It was not until around 1910 – when the introduction of floor-standing floodlights permitted more distinct facial modelling and separation of actors from their backgrounds, as well as offering the possibility of simulating 'directed' lamp or window light with far greater precision than the diffused vapour lights that had preceded them – that the industry began to formulate an aesthetic of lighting, based both on economic and artistic considerations. Charles W. Handley (1954) has argued that the desire for product differentiation between the Motion Picture Patents Company and rival independent producers was a major factor in lighting innovations during the 1910s. Baxter (1975) argues instead that industry consolidation and the move to expressive use of lighting effects were harnessed to the naturalistic aesthetic evident in American theatre of the time.

By 1915, therefore, lighting for illumination was gradually being replaced by lighting for dramatic effect, and Klieg spotlights were becoming normal in studio practice. And by 1918, the conventions of lighting (revelation and expression) that were to dominate Hollywood production up to the present day, and which were grounded in the realist aesthetic that demanded the avoidance of all artificial or abstract effects, were more or less established.

As the Klieg lights came into general use, so too did three-dimensional rather than painted sets, and sunlight was finally eliminated altogether from studios. The 1920s saw the gradual conventionalisation of the use of stronger and weaker arc floodlights functioning as key (hard, direct light), fill (soft, diffused light filling in the shadows cast by key lighting) and backlighting. The coming of sound, however, called forth a new range of technological demands, including the replacement of humming carbon lights by silent mazda tungsten incandescent lamps, and the consequent changes to the more light- and colour-sensitive film stocks noted earlier.

During the 1930s and 1940s, several technological developments significantly improved lighting processes. By 1931,

Lighting advances at Edison's New York studio

Elaborate expressionistic lighting (above and top) in Von Stroheim's *Foolish Wives*

improved carbon arcs were introduced to provide the high-key bright light required by, first, two-colour, and then, in the late 1930s, three-colour Technicolor. Initially this caused technical problems related to the temperature of the bulbs, but by the end of the decade, the arrival of faster Technicolor film stock allowed a reduction in lighting power requirements for colour cinematography. During the 1930s, arc design improved, with the introduction of the Bardens arc (descended from French naval searchlights) and the Mole Richardson in 1935, all allowing greater control over a wide range of settings, from sharp spot to full flood. Further improvements reduced noise and lessened AC mains fluctuations to provide steadier output. War-developed lighting technology such as the Colortran, a relatively lightweight and mobile source that required fewer lighting units and involved a cruder use of fill lights, facilitated location filming. Until the late 1940s, studio lighting was either low key (for genres such as film noir) or high key (for genres such as the musical, as well as for deep-focus cinematography). But the codes of 'dramatic lighting' that had been established much earlier, and which demanded that lighting should be subordinated to aesthetic coherence, continued to dominate Hollywood production.

'The development of quartz-iodine (tungsten-halogen) lamps in the mid-1960s gave a much needed boost to designers of studio lighting equipment, providing them with a lamp of much smaller dimensions and greatly improved performance' (Earle-Knight, 1981). This, together with the advent of television causing studio redesigns to enable the same spaces to be used for both media, resulted in significant changes to lighting methods. Overhead lighting grids were installed, modified for film lighting (strengthened for the extra weight of film lighting units).

The technical development of studio lighting has, therefore, been governed throughout its history by a number of interlocking factors. Lights had to be of sufficient quality to ensure acceptable images; quiet enough not to interfere with sound recording; portable enough to cope with all types of location filming; and flexible enough to cope with changing production methods, most notably the merging of film and television studio production from the mid-1960s onwards. These technical considerations have always been in the service of film aesthetics, such as narrative and character development and ideological intent (see Dyer, 2002).

Selected Reading

Peter Baxter, 'On the history and ideology of film lighting', *Screen* 16 (3),autumn 1975.

Richard Dyer, *White: Essays on Race and Culture*, London and New York, Routledge, 2002.

T. Earle-Knight, 'Studio lighting 1930–1980', *The BKSTS Journal*, January 1981.

WIDESCREEN

MICHAEL ALLEN

During the first 20 years of cinema, the industry was engaged in a number of patent wars, one of which also determined the development of widescreen film formats. In August 1897, Thomas Edison was granted a patent for his 35mm motion-picture camera; five years earlier, his assistant W. K. L. Dickson had determined the 35mm standard for cinematic film stock by splitting the readily available Eastman 70mm stock down the middle to produce twice as much 35mm stock, with a 4:3 (1.33:1) ratio (Belton, 1992, p.18). The Lumière brothers adopted 35mm film in 1896, while British film-makers used 35mm stock supplied by the Blair Company. Having experimented before with film stock that produced both square and circular frame shapes, the 4:3 ratio was preferred by Dickson on both aesthetic and economic grounds. Aesthetically, the 4:3 ratio coped best with movement that was dominantly horizontal in nature. Economically, there was less wastage between frames.

In an attempt to circumvent Edison's patent stranglehold, rival film companies developed a variety of film formats. Biograph, for example, produced a 68mm format, while Lumière worked in 75mm. This variety continued until the film industry became a mass-production phenomenon.

> [T]he triumph of a single standard over the variety of standards, including wide-film formats was clearly a necessary stage in the evolution of a viable, technologically based industry which relies on mass production, mass distribution and mass consumption for its success. (Belton, 1992)

In the late 1920s, the adoption of optical sound caused a reconsideration of screen ratios, because the soundtrack demanded a significant portion of the available frame area. Considerable industry discussion regarding alternative ratios that might accommodate sound more efficiently took place at the end of the 1920s. Eventually, the Academy of Motion Pictures Arts and Sciences reinstated the 1.33:1 ratio, slightly enlarged to 1.37:1, to allow space for the soundtrack (but even with this amendment, the advent of sound had still reduced the frame area by 31 per cent).

Despite the standardisation of the 35mm screen format, experimentation with wider formats continued. In the late silent period, a number of 'spectacular' wide-film processes developed, including Abel Gance's three-screen Polyvision and Paramount's Magnascope. The novelty value of each system quickly wore off, however, and the technical demands – including cumbersome synchronisation of three cameras during filming, and three projectors during screening – were such that these particular systems never captured long-term industry attention. Experiments with wide-film formats were, however, initiated by other major studios. Fox developed the Grandeur 70mm format and persuaded MGM to adopt it. Warners, First National and United Artists chose 65mm, while Paramount went with 56mm. By early 1930, both RKO and Paramount had shifted to 65mm. There was considerable expectation that one of these formats would soon be chosen as the new industry standard. An industry-wide ban on experimentation was introduced by the Society of Motion Picture Engineers (SMPE) to block new formats being developed, and at the end of 1931 SMPE proposed a 50mm standard that was universally rejected. For a time, Fox's Grandeur format appeared to be the favourite, but changes in Fox's management structure, and the resulting company rationalisation, meant that the Grandeur process was abandoned on the eve of its potential success. As already noted, the industrial adoption of sound in the late 1920s was a further factor in the failure to standardise a wide-film format. Nor was there enough funding for research or theatre conversion. Also, audiences, entranced by the recent arrival of sound, did not demand the new feature. As a result, as Belton notes, 'Widescreen remained more of a novelty than a norm' (Belton, 1992, p. 51).

World War II and the subsequent post-war social and economic changes created conditions that were conducive to the adoption of widescreen cinema. People had become more physically active, favouring sports and action-based leisure pursuits that tempted them away from the cinema. Moreover, they had moved to the suburbs, further away from the centre of cities where cinemas tended to be concentrated. The advent of television also provided a substantial threat to the future of film as a communal entertainment experience. 'To compete with other leisure-time amusements, the motion-picture experience was in need of redefinition. Movies had to become more participatory; the movie theatre had to become the equivalent of an amusement park. The advent of Cinerama launched this revolution' (Belton, 1992).

Cinerama was a three-camera/three-projector process, each filmstrip providing a third of the full image projected onto a curved screen and synchronised with a soundtrack generator. Because of this technical complexity, however, it proved to have a number of inherent problems – it restricted shot variation, because certain close framings were impossible due to lens distortion, and it required very careful lighting and colour grading to ensure consistency across the three separate images that made up the composite widescreen image. Nevertheless, Cinerama was an industry sensation, attracting mass audiences to its literally overwhelming experience. It also provided another ideological mechanism – early Cinerama documentaries emphasising the grandeur, beauty and power of the American landscape were big hits.

Ultimately, however, CinemaScope provided the most industrially efficient format by combining a widescreen image, together with its stereo soundtrack, on a single filmstrip. Just as Warner Bros. had invested in sound in the late 1920s in an attempt to become an industry major, CinemaScope was developed by 20th Century Fox, which was, as Belton argues, 'caught up in the turmoil of an industry-wide financial crisis and self-definition' (Belton, 1992, p. 113). For a short period (1952–4), a format war once again raged, this time between Fox's CinemaScope and Paramount's VistaVision, which employed a horizontal shooting and projection system in an attempt to increase image quality. Eventually, almost every major studio (primarily, United Artists, MGM, Warners and Disney), who had all stood back nervously to watch the development of the competition between Fox and Paramount, joined Fox by agreeing to use CinemaScope. The one major sticking point – Fox's insistence on theatres being equipped with stereo sound to accompany the widescreen images – was solved when Fox relented and agreed to provide a variety of soundtrack formats for theatres to choose from. The adoption of CinemaScope had serious effects upon exhibition, with the highly capitalised theatre chains converting at great expense, and realising enormous profits as a result, while some of the smaller chains were forced out of business.

Another widescreen format, IMAX, began life as a series of Expo attractions – 1967 in Montreal and 1970 in Osaka. Between these dates, as Tana Wollen argues, 'a completely original film system had been developed in almost cottage industry conditions' (Wollen, 1993, p. 16). Originally, like Cinerama, IMAX consisted of several separate 70mm images, synchronised together. This was achieved by developing a 70mm frame that passed horizontally rather than vertically through the projector (like VistaVision, although VistaVision required non-standard projectors, whereas IMAX could be run on standard 70mm projection equipment). The 49mm x 70mm frame gives three times the exposed surface area of conventional 70mm. The IMAX sound system is free of the filmstrip itself, initially on 6-channel 35mm magnetic film, and then on a system of CDs (again, as with the DTS sound system, a curious return to the sound-on-disc system of early sound film). The exhibition sites have dozens of loudspeakers positioned around the theatre space, so that 'the sound can be positioned as much as the visual image and, since the image extends beyond the audience's effective field of vision, sound cues can be deployed to move the viewer's focus onto action in different spaces on the screen' (Wollen, 1993, p. 18). The other huge-image film system – OMNIMAX – shoots its images using a fish-eye lens. The films are then projected onto hemispheric screens angled above and below rather than in front of the audience. This extends the image beyond the field of human vision, effectively immersing the audience in the image.

The image size of both IMAX and OMNIMAX inevitably influences the type of subjects chosen for their films. As with early CinemaScope, documentaries concerning epic natural history are favoured. Certain framings have to be carefully considered, because the audience views the film image from a position lower than in conventional cinemas. Moreover, since screen size can be used to direct viewers' focus to different points of its surface, IMAX edits are paced at longer intervals to give the audience time to absorb both images and sounds (as with early widescreen formats and deep-focus). Narrative films are ill-suited to these huge-format systems. Close framings are impossible, which in turn disables the emotional intensities built via shot/reverse-shot strategies in narrative films. Moreover, both IMAX and OMNIMAX theatres have to be custom-built. While this may initially be a discouraging factor, considering the historical resistance of the exhibition sector to building costs involved in innovations such as sound and widescreen, the IMAX phenomenon might suit modern social practices. IMAX screens are currently being installed in American shopping malls to provide a one-hour entertainment/diversion/rest from the rigours of an all-day visit to this modern compendium consumer space. The acceptance of IMAX could therefore signal a significant change in contemporary viewing practices.

Selected Reading

John Belton, *Widescreen Cinema*, Cambridge, MA, Harvard University Press, 1992.

Tana Wollen, 'The bigger the better: from CinemaScope to Imax', in Hayward and Wollen (eds), *Future Visions: New Technologies of the Screen*, London, BFI Publishing, 1993.

River of No Return (USA 1954 *p.c* – 20th Century Fox; *d* – Otto Preminger)

Robert Mitchum and Marilyn Monroe in CinemaScope in *River of No Return*

In *River of No Return*, CinemaScope ratio is used to set up a series of character tensions and spectator positions. An example of this is the scene in which Harry (Rory Calhoun) lifts Kay (Marilyn Monroe) from the raft. Kay drops her valise, which then drifts downstream as the characters move away from the raft towards the cabin. The series of shots showing this action repeatedly frame the valise, either to one side of the wide frame, or in the distant background between two characters in the foreground. Director Otto Preminger has been widely perceived as employing a neutral style lacking any distinctive features. V. F. Perkins (1962) argues that 'The director presents the action clearly and leaves the interpretation to the spectator', whereas Bordwell (1985) sees the sequence

> emphasis[ing] the bundle in ways which manifest the classical aim of repeating narratively salient information, particularly through several channels. . . . It is common for a classical film to establish a locale in a neutral way and then return to this already-seen camera set-up when we are to notice a fresh element in the space. We thus identify the new information as significant against a background of familiarity.

Perkins's interpretation operates within a realist framework, seeing the widescreen frame as open and unmediated, thus allowing sufficient space for actions to occur naturally, with the spectator empowered with the responsibility of scanning the information and determining the most important elements. Bordwell's reading takes a formalist approach, suggesting that the space afforded by the wider ratio allows more information to be consciously presented to the spectator by the film-maker.

MICHAEL ALLEN

Rebel Without a Cause (USA 1955 *p.c* – Warner Bros.; *d* – Nicholas Ray)

Troubled teenager Jim Stark in *Rebel Without a Cause* was James Dean's second starring role. He fills the widescreen image with a brooding, tortured presence. Dean's Method-acting techniques are well documented, as is the resistance they engendered in his more traditional colleagues. This resistance fed into the film, increasing the palpable tension between the characters in many of the scenes.

An example occurs when Jim returns home after the fatal 'chicken-run', in which a teenager has died, to seek help and comfort from his parents. The widescreen ratio is used throughout the scene to complement and comment on the various stages of emotional manoeuvring performed by the characters. Initially, Dean sits at the foot of the stairs; the first shot shows him to the right of frame, behind the stair railings, with his mother in centre frame, and his father to the extreme left of frame. Already the mise en scène reflects the family relations: trapped son, strong, dominant mother, marginalised father.

A cut frontally shows us the contained figure of Dean; his isolation is emphasised by empty space on either side of him. He raises both arms to catch hold of the stair rail, filling the frame with an image of crucifixion. His mother and father move into the frame to stand on either side of him. A long take, as he pleads with them to hear his account of his confused emotions, preserves the length and intensity of his performance, while its conflicting, overlapping dialogue makes apparent the characters' emotional distance from one another. As the argument develops, the characters shift position, with the mother now halfway up the stairs, Dean at the foot, and his father sitting behind him. A canted angle pushes the mother into the top-left corner, and the father into the bottom-left corner, of the frame. In contrast, the subsequent cut to a closer shot of just Jim and his mother shows them close together in centre frame, again with space on either side, their physical closeness echoing their emotional intensity. In this way, the arrangement of actors across the width of, or crammed into the centre of, the widescreen frame provides a commentary on the emotional integrity of the scene.

MICHAEL ALLEN

James Dean fills the widescreen image with a brooding, tortured presence in *Rebel Without a Cause*

CAMERAS

MICHAEL ALLEN

One of the first recognised technical problems of cinema was how to take a sharp moving image that then could be clearly replayed by a projector. The technical and scientific problems posed motivated scientists and engineers to continually push forward the boundaries of design, resulting in a breathtaking profusion of cameras during the first decade of film. Many of these were minimal modifications of originals, made by unscrupulous operators eager to circumvent patent restrictions. The purpose of this 'plagiarised modification' was partly to present a new and improved product to expectant audiences.

The production of acceptably stable images, that is to say, images that encouraged the audience to think it was experiencing unmediated reality, positions film within a realist aesthetic. A parallel trajectory of early camera technology, however, was the desire to make the camera perform marvellous effects. For example, designing them to run in reverse allowed special effects to be achieved, including reverse motion and multiple-exposure images perfected by fantasy film-makers such as Georges Méliès.

At any point in film history, a variety of camera designs have coexisted; the preference for one over the other has been partly determined by demands in other areas of technology. For example, with the coming of sound, the Mitchell camera gradually became an industry leader because its viewfinder-lens mechanism was easier to use within the soundproofed blimps covering the noisy camera. Later, the CinemaScope camera won out over the Cinerama camera because its design allowed the widescreen image to be squeezed onto a single filmstrip, as opposed to the three separate filmstrips required by Cinerama.

At other times, social and economic factors created the circumstances in which new camera technologies were developed. In 1938, on the eve of World War II, Munich camera manufacturers Arnold and Richter delivered the first 35mm Arriflex camera. With a through-the-lens mirror-reflex viewfinder, a DC motor in its hand-grip and three lenses on a rotating turret, the Arriflex became one of the standard camera designs over the next 40 years (post-war, a 16mm version was built). Arriflex reflex cameras were used extensively by German newsreel cameramen during World War II. The war, with its need for reconnaissance photography, also initiated continued research into lightweight cameras that could be carried in inaccessible spaces. The Bell and Howell Eyemo and Palliard Bolex offered competition to the Arriflex. Of the two, the Bolex was more user-friendly, especially as, being spring-driven, it could be used in places inaccessible to electrical or battery-driven cameras.

Walter Bach's 16mm Auricon camera, which had a built-in optical sound system allowing both sound and picture to be recorded on the same stock, furnished a good quality, stable image and was extensively used in television news. The German TV station Sudwestfunk-Fernsehen adapted the Auricon by replacing the optical sound mechanism with a magnetic recorder. 'Either way the Auricon remained a single system device. It had recorded image and sound on one strip of film (comopt); now it recorded them on a combined strip of film and tape (commag)' (Winston, 1996, p. 79). The problems of editing commag meant its usefulness was largely restricted to 'sound-bite' use on TV news.

The documentary field provided another impetus to the development of 16mm sound technology, this time in the direction of separate sound and image devices. A new generation of documentary film-makers appeared who were intent upon not using what they saw as the staid, tripod-restricted techniques of established documentary-makers. Foremost among these was Richard Leacock, who had experienced frustration while shooting Robert Flaherty's *Louisiana Story* (1948) because he was unable to move the camera while shooting sound sequences. He and other film-makers adapted Bach's Auricon by recasting the body in a lighter metal to make it more portable. This, together with the use of camera-mounted lighting and/or faster stocks that could be used in lower-light conditions meant that film-makers could get unobtrusively closer to events as they occurred. 'All these factors contributed to create a grainy, hand-held, authentic-sound, go-anywhere style of film that was entirely new. Documentary had entered its direct-cinema phase' (Winston, 1996, p. 82).

In 1962, André Coutant marketed the Éclair – a silent-running, hand-held 16mm camera in which the weight of the lens was balanced by a film magazine shaped to sit on the shoulder, and a motor that was mounted below the lens and forward of the magazine. The Éclair was designed to be a double system, with a separate sound recorder running in sync with the camera; the recorder was called the Perfectone. Camera and recorder were connected by a cable, and a synchronising pulse emitted from the camera was recorded on one track of the tape, while the sound was recorded on the second. The system – called the Éclair NPR – was introduced commercially in America in 1963. The Nagra was introduced in the same year, and has since become an industry standard. By the early 1960s, several sync systems – including the Pilot-Tone – appeared, which involved separate units in which the camera emitted a pulse from a crystal transmitter to the tape recorder. 'By the mid-60s the modern 16mm synch sound outfit was in place – Nagra with crystal control and an NPR or Arri BL' (Winston, 1996, p. 86).

Selected Reading

Brian Winston, *Technologies of Seeing: Photography, Cinematography and Television*, London, BFI Publishing, 1996.

ALTERNATIVE PRODUCTION FORMATS

MICHAEL ALLEN

'From the moment 35mm was established as *the* professional production format, the dominant film industry has either consciously or unconsciously positioned alternative production media formats – 16mm, 8mm and video – as inferior, and as substandard' (Baddeley, 1981). The histories of these formats have seen all in turn assume the mantle of medium for the amateur, 'home-movie' hobbyist. The reasons are aesthetic, economic and social. Aesthetically, the film industry has partly identified its professional status by differentiating the quality of its 35mm product from the 'inferior' results achievable on 16mm. Socially and economically, manufacturers of equipment in all formats have identified and targeted a home market for their product, and have been keen to maintain a clear and separate identity for it. Artists interested in using 16mm, 8mm or video explicitly for their particular aesthetic qualities have always had to battle against this pejorative attitude.

16mm production

Although in existence from the earliest days of cinema, as one of the plethora of available film formats, 16mm was introduced in 1923, when the Eastman Kodak Company began to manufacture 16mm film on a safety acetate base. From the very start, it was intended both as a distribution format (in situations where 35mm prints were unusable) and, primarily, as a production format for the 'hobby' market of amateur home movies. During the 1930s, however, 16mm began to be seen as a serious production format. This required a series of technical improvements in other areas: the replacement of orthochromatic stock with panchromatic stock; the development of photoflood lighting and light meters to obtain satisfactory exposure; and the introduction of colour (16mm Kodachrome appeared by the late 1930s). In the late 1940s, Disney decided to use 16mm for its 'Wild Life Series' (the footage was later blown up to 35mm Technicolor for projection), a decision that was important in persuading professionals that 16mm was a viable format. In the early 1950s, printers with lens shutters allowed complex effects to be created from raw footage, rather than in-camera, and 'the way was open for the more robust and straightforward cameras such as the Arriflex, with its continuous through-the-lens viewing' (Baddeley, 1981). Also in the 1950s, more portable lighting was developed, and sound capabilities were improved with the introduction of the Leevers-Rich Synchropulse, which ran off a 12-volt car-type battery and recorded a sync pulse, generated from the camera onto one track of the magnetic tape. 16mm technology has played an important part in the development of many professional production techniques: non-flammable film; single-strip colour; portable cameras and lighting; and miniaturised sound equipment.

8mm and video production

Between 1947 and 1954, 16mm equipment lost ground, at least in terms of the 'home-movie' market, to the emergent 8mm format. In 1964–5, Kodak brought out their improved Super 8mm, with smaller sprocket holes allowing a 50 per cent larger frame size, magnetic sound strip offering sync sound, and simplified controls. Together, these features were sufficient to establish Super 8mm as the substandard gauge for amateur use. Camera equipment was marketed on its technical simplicity, marking it out as different from the more complex cameras used by the professional film industry. The public was persuaded that it was ever easier to capture life's unrepeatable moments with a minimum of fuss. Such a strategy is located within what Zimmerman has identified as the 'professionalisation of leisure' evident in the period, part of the home-consumer push of the 1950s and 1960s that engaged with new-found leisure time and the foregrounding of the nuclear family (Zimmerman, 1988). By the mid-1980s, both 16mm and 8mm had, in their turn, been superseded as the amateur 'home-movie' format by the video camcorder. Video offers several advantages over film formats for domestic use, primarily its instant replay capability, reusability and technical simplicity.

A political role for alternative formats has also emerged, operating at the margins of media production and society, unregulated and organised around underground systems of exhibition and distribution. This use of 'substandard' formats promised freedom of personal expression through ease of use and immediacy of results. Within this context it was important that the formats were kept separate from the industry standard, as markers of difference. 'Avant-garde and serious film-makers began to use the narrow gauges in earnest during the late 50s and early 60s' (Hudson, 1995, p. 53) and '[p]ortable video technology became available in the UK in the late 60s and, as in North America, was immediately taken up by users whose interests could be described as counter-cultural' (Marshall, 1985, p. 66). It became an important medium for young artists of the 1960s, especially as they began working outside the commercial gallery structure, and also entered the education arena. This double movement had a distinct effect upon both production practices and aesthetics, with an emphasis on self-reflexivity in an attempt to identify a definite video aesthetic in comparison with the other fine arts (Marshall, 1985). Into the 1970s, Super 8mm and video were taken up by both the women's and black movements, with their emphasis on works that give testimony to personal experience. Both formats were seen as ideal for this in their relative cheapness, ease of use and immediacy.

Selected Reading

Laura Hudson, 'Promiscuous 8', *Coil* 2, November 1995.

Stuart Marshall, 'Video: from art to independence: a short history of a new technology', *Screen* 26 (2): 66, March/April 1985.

DIGITAL VIDEO

MICHAEL ALLEN

Digital video emerged in the late 1980s when Sony began promoting 'electronic cinematography' using analogue high-definition television cameras. The initiative failed due to industry resistance, but in 1997–8, Sony introduced HDCAM (high-definition digital Betacam) with 1920 x 1080 pixel resolution, which it labelled 'digital cinematography'. Professional film-making now conventionally uses systems providing between two million and four million pixel resolution, although in 2002 George Lucas noted the recent development of a '10-million-pixel camera ... so [the potential has] gone from 2 million to 10 million – and that's much, much higher quality than film' (Magid, 2002, p. 41). The images produced are either recorded on digital tape (either in-camera or on a separate recorder) or stored as computer/server files. With the ubiquity of digital technologies such as the computer, Internet, cable and satellite, DVD and digital projection, the celluloid-based process of filming and film production is increasingly perceived as archaic.

The huge amounts of data produced with such systems cause problems of storage and manipulation. Major motion-picture productions use expensive, high-end computers capable of handling this kind of raw data. Low-end, independent productions have to use high compression rates to enable them to handle the images using less powerful computer editing equipment, with an inevitable loss of quality. George Lucas's *Star Wars Episode II Attack of the Clones* (2002) was the first major, high-budget movie shot on 24 frames-per-second digital video (Sony HDW-F900 camera), although the less well-known French film *Vidocq* (2001) was actually the first movie wholly shot digitally.

Digital cameras offer a number of advantages over their celluloid counterparts. On-set monitoring of what is being shot allows immediate visual feedback of the image quality as it actually exists. Previously, video-assist on film-based productions was used to check whether the acting and action on a take had been acceptable, rather than the image quality. The

Mike Figgis's *Timecode*: four continuous 95-minute takes arranged in a quadrant on screen

Sky Captain and the World of Tomorrow (USA/Italy/UK 2004 *p.c* – Brooklyn Films II/Filmauro/ Riff Raff Film/Blue Flower/Paramount Pictures/Natural NYlon Entertainment; *d* – Kerry Conran)

Believing no major studio would give an untried director the chance to make a feature film, director Kerry Conran began *Sky Captain* as a independent project in his bedroom, using a Macintosh home computer and commercially available imaging and editing software. It took four years to produce a six-minute section of the film, which was then shown to producer Jon Avnet, who backed the rest of the production with independently raised money to protect it from studio interference.

The film was notable for being shot entirely against blue screen, with only the actors being real, using a Sony HDW-F900 digital camera with Fujinon lenses to produce high-definition, 1080-pixel, digital images. The total control over the production environment allowed principal photography to take just 29 days. In order to fill in the 3-D world around the filmed actors, however, post-production involving over a hundred CGI artists took a further two years.

Sky Captain demonstrates that commercially available computers and imaging and editing software enable new film-makers to create credible productions outside the economic stranglehold exerted by the major studios. It is also evidence of the transformation of high-end professional production practices, a revolution that will continue to have far-reaching consequences.

MICHAEL ALLEN

Sky Captain and the World of Tomorrow: produced outside the economic stranglehold of the major studios

clarity of the digital image allows more accurate effects shots, with new elements added in precise registration to earlier ones. Furthermore, stunts and effects can be achieved 'on screen' without the need to cut away to hide certain problems, such as the shift from human actors to models or CGI effects.

The relative cheapness of low-end digital equipment such as mini DV camcorders, together with non-linear editing software capable of being run on personal computers, has transformed the independent film-making sector. Cost savings on film stock, processing and negative cutting can be significant for limited-budget productions. Aesthetically, digital filming allows new techniques to be employed, such as extremely long takes impossible to achieve using film cameras with limited-capacity film cassettes. Mike Figgis's *Timecode* (2000) was composed of four 95-minute continuous takes, arranged in a quadrant on screen, each a different angle on the same unfolding dramatic action. The Russian film-maker Aleksandr Sokurov achieved the same length continuous take for entirely different effect in his film *Russian Ark/Russki kovcheg* (2002), which portrayed centuries of Russian history as a continuous action.

The low cost and distribution of digitally created films is transforming some world cinemas whose national economies cannot readily support high-budget film-making. For example, the Burkina Faso film-maker Idrissa Ouédraogo, head of the Association of African Directors and Producers, has a vision of African cinemas showing cheaply made digital films on digital projectors: 'I learned to work in 35mm, but it's an impossible dream today' (Knight and Manson, 2005). African directors such as Appoline Traoré (*Sous la clarté de la lune*, 2004, filmed in HDTV in two weeks) are beginning to make this vision a reality. At another level, commercial camcorders are enabling a new generation of African film-makers to make zero-budget features on digital video and distribute them on DVD.

Selected Reading

Martin Lister et al., *New Media: A Critical Introduction*, London and New York, Routledge, 2003.

Mike Figgis, *Digital Filmmaking*, London, Faber and Faber, 2007.

EDITING

MICHAEL ALLEN

During the earliest years of cinema, films consisted of single shots and therefore required no editing. However, sequences of such films, especially those relating to the same subject – the Spanish–American or Boer wars, for example – were often edited together by projectionists to make up self-contained units that could be screened between the acts on a vaudeville programme.

Later in early cinema and then in the classic Hollywood periods, film editing was performed by roomfuls of workers (mainly female) who hand-crafted each physical edit. Editing on the earliest narrative films was a matter of joining together the separate shots (which were often shot sequentially), perhaps interspersed with explanatory titles. Later, when film syntax expanded considerably, the editing process became correspondingly complex, and a team of editors would work from detailed production notes to create the finished edit.

The introduction of the KEM Universal editing table at the very end of the 1960s offered a range of improvements in the editing process and enabled, for the first time on a general scale, editing to be performed by the film's director. It was a modular machine, allowing the basic table to be customised by a range of components to deal with all combinations of image and audio editing in all formats. By the early 1970s, a video version had been created, with three video cameras trained via mirrors onto the three monitoring screens. By rolling all three filmstrips and electronically cutting between video images, practice edits could be rehearsed without any cutting of the actual film. Video-assisted film editing became more commonplace by the early 1980s. The main problem was that of frame incompatibility – film running at 24 frames per second, and video at 25 (PAL) or 30 (NTSC). A 3:2 pull-down process was developed, with most film frames having a direct equivalent on the video, but some video frames having partial information from two adjoining film frames. This caused considerable problems in matching film with video frame-by-frame for editing purposes.

During the 1980s, five companies entered the electronic editing market – the Montage Computer Corp, Lucasfilm Droid Works with its EditDroid system, the laserdisc-based Spectra Image/Laser Edit, B&H Touchvision and Cinedco's Ediflex. Acceptance by the film industry was inconsistent at best. Three types of electronic editing developed: linear, random access and non-linear random access. Linear editing appeared in the early 1970s, with the CMX600 system, which used time-code identification of edit points. Edit decisions proceeded one at a time in linear fashion. It received limited acceptance at the time. Random access systems – the CMX6000 and Spectra Image/Laser Edit systems – utilise laserdisc or multiple copies of material. Laserdisc allows the editor to search to a specified point within a few seconds. The multiple-copy system requires several machines to seek scenes from various places on the tapes simultaneously. With both systems, the 'edited' sequences had to be recorded onto master videotape for viewing. With non-linear random access systems – the Montage and Ediflex – the rushes have to be assembled in sequence and transferred onto ¾-inch video. The script is fed into the computer to create a detailed coding and logging file. With the Ediflex, the keyboard is replaced with a light pen used on an operating screen, and the computer keeps track of how far into a scene the editor has cut and cues the next take to the same point. The precise timing of each edit point is logged and stored in the computer. When the final version has been approved, the assistant editor generates the edit decision list that will be used to perform the final video edit, or identify film frames for the film edit.

The 1990s has seen the development of the computer-based editing and image manipulation processes that have precipitated the large-budget, special-effects-laden blockbuster feature film. In order to preserve the quality of the original negative in the transfer from celluloid to digital image, the huge amounts of data needing to be handled – several gigabytes per minute for full-colour, full-frame images – require very powerful computers to run the programs. This has created a specialist market for digital and effects editing, such that dedicated third-party companies, who invest in the latest generation of machines, now handle much of the editing work on Hollywood productions. The field of editing is being blurred with that of special effects, as post-production work requires substantial reworking of the images on the raw footage itself at the same time as it is edited into the final work.

The advent of computer and digital editing technologies in the 1980s and 1990s has, therefore, threatened to change the relationship between time and the creative process in editing. The use of computers, the digitising of material, the replacing of film with laserdisc and/or videotape at some stages of the process in order to facilitate the creation of special effects have all made the editing process paradoxically both quicker and more complex. Some practitioners disagree with this prognosis:

> No film editing system can match the electronic editing system's speed in making numerous versions of an edit, comparing different edits, reviewing coverage, and making changes. This speed translates into either a lower ultimate editorial cost, or the ability to go further in editorial perfection, or a combination of the two. (Wasko, 1994)

Others take the opposite view, claiming that the systems may even be too fast, giving too little time for reflection on cuts, and too little lead-time into complex problem areas. The process, effectively, threatens to run out of control. As with any aspect of technical development, those using the technology need to adapt to its new capabilities. For better or worse, ever-increasing speed, instantaneous access and radical manipulation are now part of the editing process. Procedures need to be developed to maximise the opportunities these offer.

Selected Reading

Barry Salt, *Film Style and Technology: History and Analysis*, London, Starword, 1983. Revised edition 2003.

Les Paul Robley, 'Digital offline video editing: expanding creative horizons', *American Cinematographer* 74 (4/7), April–July 1993.

MULTIMEDIA TECHNOLOGIES

MICHAEL ALLEN

The impetus for the take-up and employment of 'new' technologies by the film industry has been fourfold: to provide tools for the creation of new and different images (special effects); to improve work efficiencies in production (for example, computer-controlled cinematography) and post-production (editing and special effects); to produce other types of entertainment product (video games, theme rides, virtual-reality experiences); and to develop new distribution channels (CD-ROM, satellite and cable). All four have been determined by the interrelationship of technical and economic criteria, the question being: is the technology capable of achieving the desired result and is it economical to make it do so?

The advent of the various new technologies has required a confluence of several discrete technologies – film and television, computer hardware and software, telephony, engineering and robotics – over a period of several decades. Initial research and development was conducted almost exclusively in non-entertainment arenas such as the military, science, business and training. Initial uses were therefore practical in emphasis – the improvement of cockpit control for pilots using multi-sensory headsets, or interactive laserdisc training drills for bank employees, for example. The late 1970s and early 1980s saw an adaptation of these 'extra-entertainment' applications for broad-based leisure use (initially in the form of video games). This delay has partly been due to technical limitations (mostly in the area of computers powerful enough to produce acceptable images), and partly to do with film-industry resistance (prohibitive costs, and a general mistrust of unfamiliar techniques using untried technology originating from outside the film world). Only when the equipment began to prove itself capable of delivering the goods did the film industry begin using it.

The first use of digital and computer-based technologies within the film industry was in the area of special effects. Solman places it in 1976, with what he terms the 'Effects Renaissance' (Solman, 1992). At that stage, special effects were still model-based, and computers were used only, for example, to control camera trajectory. A little later, in the early 1980s, the first completely computer-generated special effects appeared. These were marked by a certain primitiveness. The software lacked the necessary subtlety, the hardware was very expensive and few people knew how to use it. As with so many other areas of film aesthetics, what drove this effort was the desire to create new 'realities' that were wholly believable at the same time as wholly artificial. And, as with so many other areas of technological development in the film industry, such improvements were dependent on research conducted by companies in other disciplines; in this case the computer industry. Although the film industry did experiment with computer effects in films of the late 1970s and early 1980s (for example, *Alien* in 1979 and *Tron* in 1982), satisfactory computer-generated graphics had to wait until the late 1980s, by which time the computer industry had developed sufficiently powerful, flexible machines. Only then could the specialised applications be developed that were required to produce the desired cinematic special effects. These companies had developed their techniques in arenas separate from mainstream film-making – primarily advertising and computer/video games. Although in many ways financially cautious, advertising companies are by nature creatively adventurous. The drive towards the creation of new and arresting images is their *raison d'être*. As a result, the development of the techniques and the technologies necessary for creating believeable, high-tech, high-resolution images using computers was developed in an arena focused upon the quality of those images.

It comes as no surprise, therefore, that such overdetermination of the spectacularly artificial image became the staple of much of Hollywood's late-1980s and 1990s product. Baker calls this Impact Aesthetics: 'It is as if the quest for technological magic, exceeding the effects in previous movies, becomes the paramount concern . . . a preoccupation with the use of the new technologies for novel image effects' (Baker, 1993, p. 41). This manipulation of reality results in a new reality, an unreal reality (or hyper-reality). The resultant films become spectacles of technological possibility, experienced for their awesome effects as much as, if not more than, 'traditional' elements such as narrative and character development. In this sense, cinema seems to have succeeded in developing in the 1990s a distinctively different product that can compete favourably with the smaller, less overpoweringly impressive audio-visual product offered by television.

Interactive entertainments

In the mid-1990s, another significant development evolved that influenced more 'traditional' (two-hour, linear, narrative) film-making. Interactive movies are now being produced that offer the viewer/user the possibility of choosing from an image and sound database in order to construct a number of different routes through a film's narrative; in effect, to construct his or her own narrative. A variety of different scenarios are filmed, and all are put onto a CD-ROM disc. The user then begins the programme, and, when prompted by suspensions in the programme's flow, makes a decision about what should happen next. The programme then selects and displays the footage that depicts that choice. Recent productions included movie spin-offs, in which additional footage of actors and locations is shot at the same time as the film. Furthermore, original interactive movie productions (including the $6 million *Privateer 2: The Darkening*, featuring recognised stars, produced by video-games company Electronic Arts, and released in mid-1997) appeared. Such productions are 'published' on CD-ROM, to be viewed/played on games consoles, rather than 'screened' in cinemas, indicating a shift in cultural practice (see also New distribution, exhibition and reception contexts, p. 75). Most of them are made by consortia composed of the leaders in the film, video, communications and video-game markets, who recognise the potential (both creative and financial) for this type of product. By mid-1994, all major film studios had opened interactive divisions, exploring the potential that computer-based digital technologies offered. Once again, technologies developed by 'outsiders' (video games and computer companies) were taken up and adapted by the film industry as a means of regeneration, and to absorb the threat of competition within itself.

The possibilities offered by the new technologies brought with them conceptual and philosophical questions that are just beginning to be articulated and explored. Written material on the subject has largely been of a factual kind – descriptions of what the technology looks like and does – rather than abstract considerations of its implications. For film production itself, the new technologies promise potential efficiency gains, which in turn suggest changes in staffing levels and job descriptions. There is some fear in the industry that jobs will be cut because machines will be able to perform tasks more quickly and easily, and also that the technologies are developing at such speed and are becoming so specialised that practitioners will be unable to keep pace. Both fears are at least partly unfounded, but they demonstrate the nervousness that surrounds the subject of new technologies within the film industry.

Theoretical thinking on the form and content of the product has organised itself around several key issues: narrative, linearity, temporality, subjectivity and activity. These issues are explored in order to differentiate the intentions and effects of new technologies from earlier, more traditional forms. Biocca and Levy (1995) differentiate 'presence', which refers to natural perception of an environment, from 'telepresence', which refers to the mediated perception of an environment. Pennefather discusses the difference between 'participative' (video game or virtual reality) and 'contemplative' (traditional cinema) interactivity (Pennefather, 1994). Andrew Cameron compares the 'imperfective' (spectator inside the time being represented, as in virtual reality) to the 'perfective' (time completed and viewed from outside, as in traditional linear narrative) experience (Cameron, 1995). Weinbren modifies this, arguing that the particular narrative forms possible with the new technologies create a 'subjunctive' state – a 'what could have been otherwise' – as the narrative is pieced together during a session (Weinbren, 1995). For Cotton and Oliver, the 'window onto' of traditional pictorial media (painting, film) becomes the 'door into' of virtual reality, a means of intensifying the sense of actually being in the fictional experience, rather than watching it from 'outside' (Cotton and Oliver, 1993). Whatever the specific terminology used, the general agreement is that new technologies are capable of producing a more active, more involved 'receiver', who is empowered by the programme to make decisions determining the narrative structure, character make-up, time and space of the work.

The debate also concerns the implications of this for how future works will be conceived and structured – how this interactivity can be predicted and satisfied; whether it spells the end of traditional linear narrative; whether interactive multimedia narratives will actually prove satisfying as entertainment experiences.

> Much of cinema's power over us is our lack of power over it . . . It could be argued that the introduction of viewer impact on the representation is a destructive step for the cinema. The removal of the possibility of suspense is the removal of desire from the cinematic, and ultimately, the removal of the very fascination of the medium. To find interactive forms in which desire can be sustained will require the construction of a new cinematic grammar. (Weinbren, 1995, pp. 19–20)

To counter this, closure must be read in a more radical light, possibly by constructing a work around multiple diegetic narratives and temporalities, any of which can provide the necessary end to the fiction. Such potential makes Le Grice (1995) argue that the repetitive and non-linear form of interactive entertainments will position them within the avant-garde arena. This begs the question of what will be left to occupy the mainstream against which the avant-garde positions itself. It is possible that there will no longer be a recognisable 'mainstream', but rather a number of alternative forms of equal legitimacy.

Virtual reality

Virtual reality (VR) promises its user/player/participant (a term that indicates VR's multiple identities) the possibility of entering an artificial, computer-generated environment in which he or she can physically move around the space, interact with objects, characters and events, and influence the formation and progress of the narrative. Virtual reality is characterised by experiential intensity and empowerment of users. Whether its potential is fulfilled remains to be seen.

> Government money helped develop VR technology. Government funding agencies like the National Science Foundation supported much work at university research centres such as the University of North Carolina and the Massachusetts Institute of Technology. Other agencies like the US Air Force, the Navy, and NASA were instrumental in building early versions of many components. (Biocca and Levy, 1995)

Initial uses of VR have all been 'serious' in nature – providing individual training for medics, pilots or astronauts, as well as simulating large-scale military wargames that would have proved prohibitively complex and expensive to stage in reality. This complexity and expense meant that the technology was initially perceived to have no entertainment value. The 1990s saw moves to introduce it into the entertainment and domestic arenas, largely due to radical improvements in personal computer (PC) power and cost, and on the back of the over-hyped consumer interest in the information superhighway. Virtual reality has become the buzzword for all future possibilities offered by digital communications. Current emphasis is on equipment rather than implications, although Negroponte (1995) argues that VR actually refers to the experience, and thereby to the perceptions of an individual, rather than to the machine.

VR also offers new forms of meaning: 'Something new has been added with the arrival of VR, and the process of meaning construction and meaning reception will be subtly altered' (Biocca and Levy, 1995). In a way, in its attempt to create a virtual environment that, ideally, would be indistinguishable from 'real life', VR represents potentially the furthest movement yet along the realist axis – though such a perfect representation is still a significant way off. Notwithstanding this potential, the debate surrounding virtual reality, indeed its very name, positions it within the realist aesthetic. This realist agenda operates around several key terms. The vividness of the system is perceived to lie in its ability to produce a richly sensorial, mediated environment; its interactivity and responsiveness is found in the extent to which, and the speed with which, users of the medium can influence the form or content of the mediated environment, and thereby feel part of that environment; its sensory breadth resides in the number of sensory dimensions (vision, sound, touch) working together to create the virtual environment; and its sensory depth in the resolution, or 'quality', within each of those dimensions. The sense of a believable reality is therefore created through sensory overload, by several channels of information reinforcing each other's depiction of 'reality'. So, for example, a door will not only be seen to be slammed shut, it will also be heard to do so (in 3-D sound) and even felt to do so (via a dataglove that presses against parts of the user's hand).

At the same time as providing a surfeit of virtual information, the VR system simultaneously deprives the user of real-world sensory information, immersing users in the artificial environment via a head-mounted display that totally encloses the head, eyes and ears. Consequently, the only spatial, aural and relational cues possible come from the system itself. This sensory deprivation and substitution process is essential to the ability of VR to convince its users of the 'reality' of the virtual world. In a way, this can be seen as the latest stage of a process that has always been a part of cinema presentation, from the sound effects produced behind the screen during silent film shows, through 3-D and Sensurround to modern-

Terminator 2 Judgment Day (USA 1991 *p.c* – Carolco Pictures/Pacific Western/Lightstorm Entertainment/ Studio Canal1; *d* – James Cameron)

James Cameron's sequel to *The Terminator* (1984) is viewed as groundbreaking for its digital special effects – in particular, the sophistication and photorealistic quality of its images. In fact, a version of the effects, especially the morphing scenes, can be seen in Cameron's 1989 film *The Abyss*. *The Abyss* used untested computer-based effects technology to produce the fluid water creature that appears at the climax. *Terminator 2* expanded on this technical experimentation by staging extravagant stunts and by integrating the special effects to such an extent that they become virtually indistinguishable from the actors. An example of this is the scene in which the cyborg leaps into a helicopter cockpit and morphs from its cop persona into its metallic form. The motorcycle leap from building to helicopter required the post-production removal of the wires and supports used in the original stunt. Each frame of the scene was fed into a powerful computer, and the unwanted information was replaced with material copied from the surrounding area. Each completed image was then transferred back onto film. The level of software sophistication required for the morphing process can be seen in its ability to map the reflection of the human actor (the pilot) onto the surface of the metal cyborg.

For all the film-makers' intentions to integrate effects and 'live action' into a seamless whole, the impressiveness of the special effects is such that they stand out from the narrative. The foregrounding (the publicity hype) of the effects results in the film appealing to viewers for opposing reasons: first, as a narrative taking place in a fantastic, yet believable, world, involving credible characters; and second, as a display of virtuoso spectacular effects. The most sophisticated special-effects feature films depend on this tension.

MICHAEL ALLEN

Display of virtuoso special effects in James Cameron's *Terminator 2 Judgment Day*

day THX sound and IMAX screens. The difference is that with any of the cinematic systems, the spectator remains in the real world while experiencing the effect; disbelief is suspended, but not totally denied. With virtual reality, if the system eventually becomes sophisticated enough, the 'enabling of belief' promises to be total.

Cost has also been a determining factor in the physical location of the new technologies at the consumer end of the entertainment business. Affordable multimedia PCs, equipped with CD-ROM drives and capable of handling digital sound and vision, have been heavily promoted in the domestic market since 1994, and experienced an exponential sales growth from the mid-1990s. Consequently, interactive games, 'infotainment' and 'edutainment' products have become big business. Additionally, in the global communications community, where all information, whether textual, or visual and aural, is digital, the same machine can be used to view entertainment as well as to collect information of many kinds, conduct business or order shopping. Audio-visual material, in binary digit form, can be beamed by satellite, sent down cable and fibre-optic lines, or read from CD-ROM. At the end of the 1980s, with movie-theatre attendance reaching the lowest level in a decade, many consumers, through the use of VCRs and pay-per-view television, chose to view movies in their homes rather than go to the theatre.

> This trend created a need for a new form of out-of-home entertainment that could not be replicated in the home. The fact that virtual reality was perceived as a sexy new medium that could not be replicated in the home made it a prime technology to replace or supplement the ailing movie theatre market. (Negroponte, 1995)

The anticipated projection for the exploitation of virtual reality's entertainment value, then, sees it occupying a multiplicity of public locations, including games arcades and shopping malls, before entering the home when the technology has become sufficiently miniaturised and economical to create a domestic market. This trajectory echoes that of cinema as a whole, which, for the first three-quarters of its life was solely a public-space entertainment form, before it moved into the domestic arena via television and video (see also New distribution, exhibition and reception contexts, p. 75).

Selected Reading

Philip Hayward and Tana Wollen (eds), *Future Visions: New Technologies of the Screen*, London, BFI Publishing, 1993.

Joan Pennefather, 'From cinema to virtual reality', *Intermedia* 22 (5), October/November 1994.

Michele Pierson, *Special Effects: Still in Search of Wonder*, New York, Columbia University Press, 2002.

The Mask (USA 1994 *p.c* – Dark Horse Entertainment/New Line Cinema; *d* – Chuck Russell)

The special effects in *The Mask*, created by Industrial Light & Magic, make use of some of the tools developed the previous year for *Jurassic Park*. Additional effects were supplied by Dream Quest Images. The visual details of the Mask character were modified to suit comic actor Jim Carrey's unique physical features. Carrey's distinctive comic physicality also determined the style and extent of the computer-generated (CG) effects:

> Jim Carrey is such a character, sometimes people think we're creating effects when we're not, but when he goes to his extreme, we just push that a bit further ... In this case, we transitioned from Jim's head to our CG head. We made him look cartoonish by exaggerating the size of his eyes and expressions, but we rendered those images realistically. (Magid, 1994, p. 54)

The effects team used 3-D modelling software rather than what they regarded as 'clichéd morph technology' that operated only in 2-D. Over footage of Carrey, 3-D wire frames were built that were then filled out with surface detail to create the cartoonish version of the real-life original. So, for example, when the Mask spots a beautiful woman in a nightclub and transforms into a lustful wolf: 'A CG wire frame had to be built over Carrey's features in the computer, animated over several frames into a wolf's head, then rendered with photorealistic textures, highlights and shadows to blend seamlessly into the scene' (Magid, 1994, p. 55). Similarly, to create the massive pounding heart that almost bursts out of his chest, Carrey's real shirt was mapped onto an animated CG wire frame of the heart that had been superimposed over footage of Carrey. The success of the effects is achieved through a combination of prosthetic make-up on Carrey's face, computer-generated images and the actor's exaggerated physical comedy.

MICHAEL ALLEN

Titanic (USA 1997 *p.c* – 20th Century Fox/Paramount/Lightstorm Entertainment; *d* – James Cameron)

Titanic, which cost a massive $250 million to make and release and recouped over $1 billion in box-office receipts, scooped 11 Oscars at the 1998 Academy Awards. A central attraction of the film was its special effects, especially the highly convincing sinking of the ship during the second half. In fact, special effects were used from the beginning to create the 'reality' of the huge ship in port and on the open sea, and to populate it with over 2,000 passengers. James Cameron and his technical crew decided to shoot the ship 'for real', that is, as if it existed and could be filmed by, for example, cameras flying past in helicopters. To achieve this, Cameron's Digital Domain effects house had to 'force into existence' (as visual effects supervisor Rob Legato described it) the software programs and digital tools required to create

Special effects created the 'reality' of the Titanic at sea

computer-generated (CG) images of the *Titanic*. These tools can be seen in action in the spectacular single sweeping 'helicopter' shot that takes the spectator from characters standing on the bow of the ship up and over its four funnels and down its length, before twisting back to frame its stern as it sails off into the distance. Only the two initial actors are real; the rest is computer generated, including the many tiny passengers seen walking the various decks.

But these seemingly entirely CG images are used in combination with many scale- and full-sized models of sections of the *Titanic* (Cameron built 90 per cent of the ship full sized). Indeed, almost every special-effects shot or sequence in the film is a combination of actual model or actor(s) and CG imaging. It is Cameron's stated desire to make the first wholly computer-generated film (involving ostensibly 'human' figures, as opposed to the puppets of 1995's *Toy Story*).

MICHAEL ALLEN

PART 4

World Cinemas

NATIONAL CINEMAS IN THE GLOBAL ERA

ELIZABETH EZRA

The concept of national cinemas is not coextensive with cinema itself. In some ways, they can be said to have existed only since the late silent or early sound era. For the first two or three decades after the birth of cinema, films were not explicitly identified with a particular nation-state; and production companies were international, sending camera operators, films for exhibition and, before long, production subsidiaries around the world. Before the advent of intertitles around 1903, films even 'spoke' local languages, as exhibitors narrated the action for viewers while they watched the images flicker across the screen. But then, in the latter years of that decade, films made in US subsidiaries of French production companies and otherwise indistinguishable from American fare came to be branded as 'foreign' by US companies keen to stake out a domestic market for their own films (Abel, 1999). After World War I, when domination of world markets shifted definitively from France to the United States, cinema in other parts of the world was 'nationalised' economically through the introduction of state subsidies and protectionist measures, in large part as a reaction to the emergent hegemony of Hollywood. Finally, through linguistic means, the coming of sound in the late 1920s and early 1930s, before the perfection of dubbing technology, cemented the process of national identification.

Yet national cinema has never been an unproblematic category. The 20th century, with two World Wars, the demise of dynastic and colonial empires, and the end of the Cold War was a volatile period for the emergence and dissolution of nation-states (and thus of national cinemas). The fall of the Berlin Wall, for example, brought an end to East German cinema per se, which is now a historical and archival phenomenon, although former East German film-makers certainly retain a distinctive voice. And what are the institutional dynamics of a stateless cinema such as that of Palestine? National cinemas are continually in process, evolving with the ebb and flow of nation-states, and with the importance of the nation-state itself as both a geopolitical force and a conceptual entity.

Shifting political landscapes at the sub-national level too can affect a national cinema's status. Apartheid-era South African films have a problematic place within film history, and have been routinely excluded from accounts of African cinema. Since the end of apartheid, South African films have circulated more widely and have attracted much more international interest (although even then, not always without controversy: when *Tsotsi* won the Academy Award for Best Foreign Language Film in 2006, many in its home country considered the film, which was directed by the white South African Gavin Hood, to be so 'Hollywoodised' as to be almost unrecognisably South African). Then too, political forces can make national cinemas inaccessible altogether. For example, although the first Korean feature film was made in 1923, there are no extant pre-1945 feature films, because these were either destroyed during the Korean War or suppressed during Japanese imperial rule in the early part of the century.

In the 1960s and 1970s, cinema was embraced by many nation-states as a potential tool in the struggle to reassert national autonomy in the wake of decolonisation. The Third Cinema movement, which began in Latin America and was soon invoked by film-makers in Asia and Africa, at once supported these national struggles and asserted an international solidarity among Third World countries (see also Third World and postcolonial cinema, p. 97). In particular, Lusophone African states such as Mozambique and Angola adopted a form of 'guerrilla' film-making that attempted to merge Marxist theories with film practice, resulting in a politically committed cinema. Many African film-makers, including the Francophone directors Ousmane Sembène from Senegal and Souleymane Cissé from Mali, trained in the USSR, where they learned cinematic techniques from Soviet directors. Similarly, today, many South African film-makers and funding bodies view cinema as an important expression of post-apartheid democratic principles.

However, in the absence of clear principles of political commitment or propaganda, national identity is an elusive category when applied to cinema. Even the most apparently straightforward criteria of the director's nationality or audience preferences are not always helpful. For example, many of the most prominent art-house films closely identified with a national cinema have been made by foreign nationals, usually by émigré directors and other personnel. The Spaniards Luis Buñuel and Salvador Dalí made what would become the bedrock of 'French' surrealist films in the interwar period; both Charlie Chaplin and Alfred Hitchcock, two of the most celebrated auteurs of American cinema, came from the UK, and many other prominent film-makers working in the post-war era were Europeans who had emigrated to the United States. Many landmark African films of the 1950s and 1960s were made by Africans living abroad, because Africans were barred from making films in the colonial era. In recent times, the Mandarin-language international blockbuster *Crouching Tiger, Hidden Dragon/Wohu Canglong* (2000) was made by Taiwan-born Ang Lee, who now lives in Connecticut. The concept of national cinema is even less straightforward in the transnational era, when multinational co-productions are becoming increasingly common. If we look to audiences to give the term 'national cinema' meaning, then we face incoherence: viewers in West Africa prefer kung fu films and Bollywood musicals to homegrown fare, and European viewers watch more American films than films produced in their own countries. The fact that South Korean viewers began displaying a preference for domestic films over foreign films in the late 1990s has been heralded as a remarkable sign of the unusual robustness of the Korean film industry, rather than as something to be taken for granted (see Clarke, 2001). All in all, one could be forgiven for wondering if national cinema was merely a short-lived phenomenon, a temporary blip on the world cinematic radar. In the era of globalisation, is it still possible to speak of national cinemas at all, or have they receded, like the withering away of the state that Friedrich Engels so famously predicted some 130 years ago, if in a rather different context?

Certainly, and to a large extent, national cinema is a relational, conceptual category, constructed in response to the domination of American cinema, which is often conceived as the only truly globalised, or 'region-free' cinema (like the DVD players that have become a significant means of exhibition). However, the Hollywood/World Cinema dichotomy is challenged by the fact that virtually all cinemas today are deeply hybridised.

The widespread adoption of foreign film genres and narrative strategies complicates attempts to associate national cinemas with indigenous traditions or characteristics. For example, Nigerian films often incorporate Bollywood-inspired tales of good versus evil, but they also employ indigenous folkloric motifs and frames of reference. These same traditional elements could be said to bypass the national altogether, as the nation-state structure was imposed in Africa in the colonial era. Palestinian guerrilla films of the 1960s and 1970s were inspired generically by American westerns, but they were clearly not inspired by American politics. This hybridisation, moreover, does not merely reflect a one-way stream of influence from Hollywood, as films such as Quentin Tarantino's two-part *Kill Bill* (2003/4), with its overt references to Southeast Asian martial arts films, suggests (and the flourishing US independent film sector reminds us that 'American cinema' is by no means homogeneous). Nor does hybridisation imply a two-way relation between Hollywood and 'the rest', but rather a multi-directional exchange, with different patterns and currents predominating at various times and in various places around the globe. These exchanges are often uneven, but they are uneven in different ways at different times (see Transnational film studies, p. 508).

Films often acquire national status through their settings and storylines, such as the 'heritage' films of Britain and France, or the Bangladeshi film *The Clay Bird/Matir Moina* (Tareque and Catherine Masud, 2002), which, despite being made with French money, is strongly identified with its setting in the Bangladeshi war of independence from Pakistan. But setting is not synonymous with location shooting, especially when other locations are made to stand in for settings depicted on screen for financial reasons (lower production costs or tax breaks), or when sets or special effects are used to conjure up a place. At the same time, particular locales have often been represented on screen long before they come to be associated with the national identity of a body of films, as in the case of Scotland, which was represented in films such as the Ealing comedy *Whisky Galore!* (Alexander Mackendrick, 1949) well before the first indigenously-funded, full-length Scottish feature film was made, *That Sinking Feeling* (Bill Forsyth, 1979). Scenes of Africa had been familiar to viewers the world over since the beginning of the 20th century, but it was only in 1955 that what is considered to be the first sub-Saharan African film was made, the short feature *Afrique sur Seine* (Paulin Soumanou Vieyra), yet this film was shot, and set, in Paris (Sembène's 1965 *La Noire de ...*, considered to be the first feature-length film made in sub-Saharan Africa, was also set and filmed largely in France). As these and other films demonstrate, a film's national identity is not reducible to its setting.

Films made in many of the smaller nations rely heavily on financing from other countries, especially Europe. In former Communist countries, privatisation and the demise of state-run structures of production, distribution and exhibition led to a crisis in the film industry. Film-makers were forced to adopt various survival strategies to cope with the new market pressures, including relocating to or collaborating with other European countries (for example, after the collapse of Communism at the end of the 1980s, the Polish director Krzysztof Kieslowski moved his production base to France and financed his films with French and Swiss money). Today, smaller nations often band together, either to pool funds, as in multinational co-productions, or to pool creative resources, as is the case with the Advance Party initiative between Scotland and Denmark, which is producing three films made by different directors set

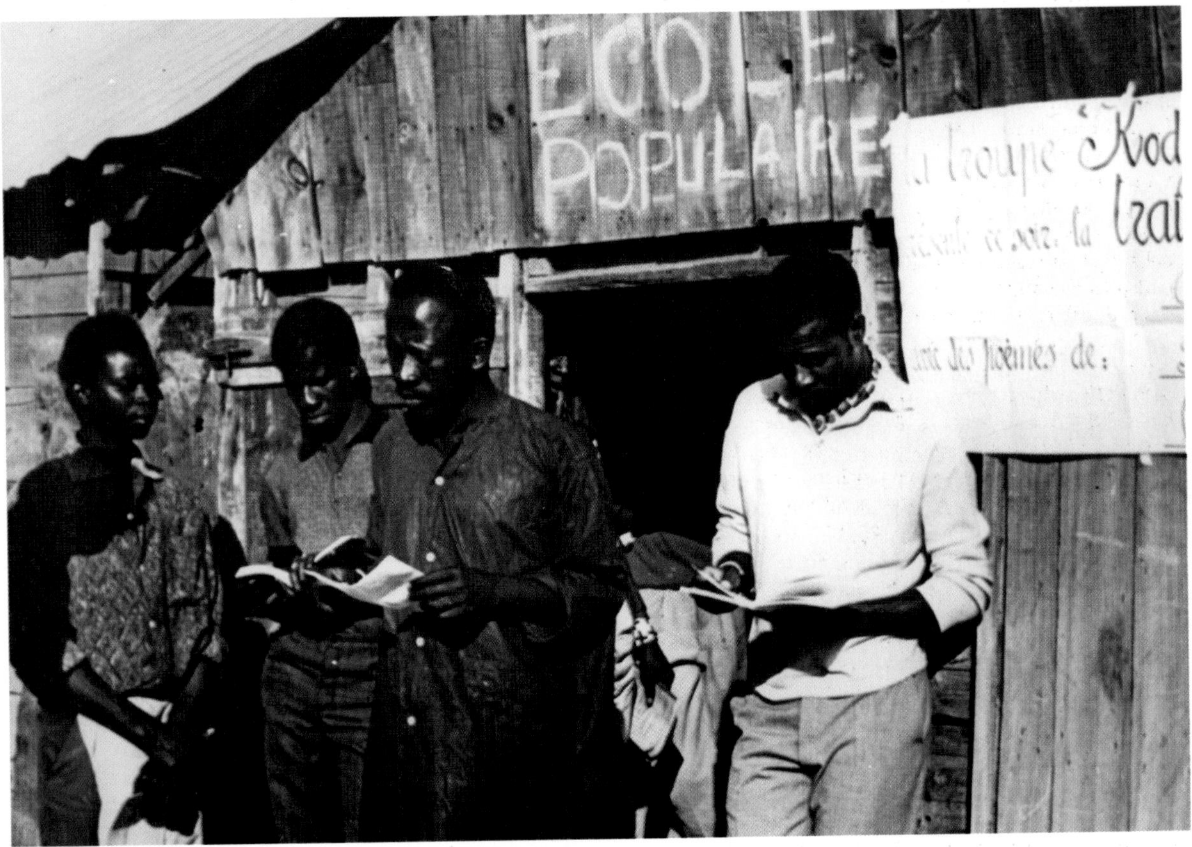

Mixed origins: Sembène's *La Noire de ...*, considered to be the first sub-Saharan African feature film, was set largely in France

Andrea Arnold's *Red Road*, the first film produced under the collaborative Advance Party initiative

in Glasgow and based on recurring characters, of which the first was *Red Road* (Andrea Arnold, 2006).

It is not only supra-national identities that problematise the concept of national cinema; these can also be complicated by sub-national affiliations. Indigenous film-makers in post-colonial or diasporic contexts (such as Aboriginal film-makers in Australia, Maori film-makers in New Zealand and Native American film-makers in the US) sometimes prefer not to be associated with their nominal nation-states, because they have oppositional political stances, and/or because they identify more strongly with their regional or tribal affiliation (or sometimes simply for the pragmatic reason that they have been more successful in obtaining financing from regional or other sub-national funding bodies). Québéquois cinema, for example, has achieved independent status within the larger body of Canadian cinema, largely because of its linguistic difference from Anglophone cinema, as well as Québec's contested national status.

Perhaps more than anything else, though, the concept of national cinema is driven by economic factors – domestically by state-funding criteria, and externally by distribution and marketing strategies. Major awards ceremonies such as the Academy Awards and the Cannes Film Festival still use national identity as a primary selection criterion, and these awards have global marketing implications. The controversy surrounding the national identity of the film *A Very Long Engagement/Un long dimanche de fiançailles* (Jean-Pierre Jeunet, 2004), which prevented it from competing in both the Academy Awards and at Cannes, hinged on the film's financing from a French subsidiary of Warner Bros. Conversely, recent Iranian cinema, though lacking in big box-office potential, has gained a high degree of cachet among international critics and on the art-house festival circuit, and in these contexts its national identity has served as a modestly effective promotional tool. National identity is also used to market films to diasporic communities around the globe. Unlike many African art films, which are often financed by European backers and circulated globally through film festivals, the indigenous Nigerian film industry (often referred to as Nollywood) produces some 600 films a year, mostly on video, many of which circulate among African communities living abroad (although widespread pirating prevents much of the profit from accruing to the Nigerian production companies). And in India, a growing number of films are aimed directly at diasporic communities. Economic factors nonetheless have undeniable cultural repercussions, and it is perhaps in the diasporic context that a national cinema retains the most affective resonance, contributing to the construction of what Benedict Anderson (1983) called 'imagined communities'.

Ultimately, very few film-makers set out to make a German film or a Taiwanese film or an American film; their films often acquire these identities retrospectively, at film festivals and in books and university courses, all of which still rely heavily on the idea of national cinema as an organising principle. Yet this principle not only has an important heuristic function, it also has significant political, economic and affective value, which indicates that, despite the problems with attempts to attribute national identities to otherwise heterogeneous bodies of films, the concept of national cinema is not in danger of disappearing any time soon.

Selected Reading

Natasa Durovicovà and Kathleen E. Newman (eds), *World Cinemas, Transnational Perspectives*, New York and Oxford, Routledge, 2007.

Mette Hjort and Scott Mackenzie (eds), *Cinema and Nation*, London and New York, Routledge, 2000.

Alan Williams (ed.), *Film and Nationalism*, New Brunswick, NJ, Rutgers University Press, 2002.

Valentina Vitali and Paul Willemen (eds), *Theorising National Cinema*, London, BFI Publishing, 2006.

AUSTRALIAN CINEMA

BRIAN McFARLANE

There is a general international perception that Australian cinema was born in the 1970s, with the successes of *Sunday Too Far Away* and *Picnic at Hanging Rock* at the Cannes Film Festival in May 1975 and 1976 respectively. Australians knew there had been a series of popular 'ocker' comedies – the *Barry McKenzie* and *Alvin Purple* films – earlier in the decade, but these were not films to win serious appraisal abroad. Or even at home, where the public liked them more than the critics did.

The history of Australian film-making is as old as that of cinema. Films of actual events were shown in Australian cities as early as 1895, but as Chris Long points out, 'From the start, Australian producers could only supplement and complement the vastly more numerous film imports' (McFarlane, Mayer and Bertrand, 1999, p. 453). The first Australian-made films were actualities (see Pike and Cooper, 1998): for example, *Passengers Alighting from the Paddle Steamer 'Brighton' at Manly* (1896), Australia's first film. But, as elsewhere, these brief actualities were stepping-stones en route to feature film-making.

The Story of the Kelly Gang, possibly one of the earliest feature films in the world

There are the usual controversies about 'firsts'. The Salvation Army Limelight Department premiered a programme (calling it a 'screening' would elide its mixed-media elements) at the Melbourne Town Hall on 13 September 1900, under the title *Soldiers of the Cross*. It comprised 15 short films, each about a minute long, depicting biblical scenes, and interspersed with over 200 slides, and a musical accompaniment of hymns and popular classics. The 'lecture', as the Army producers designated it, lasted for over two hours, but nevertheless it cannot really be thought of as a 'feature'. The title of the first Australian feature (as the term came to be understood) belongs to *The Story of the Kelly Gang* (1906), made by theatrical entrepreneurs John and Charles Tait. One of the first feature-length films shown anywhere in the world, until recently it existed only in fragments, as does most of Australia's silent film heritage. In 2007, the Australian National Film and Sound Archive released a restored version of *The Story of the Kelly Gang* on DVD that included recently recovered material.

This was a prolific period of film-making: Pike and Cooper (1998) list 106 films made between 1906 and 1913, 53 during the straitened circumstances of World War I, and 97 during the next decade. For a country with a small population, this was impressive activity. Its quality is hard to assess, and one can only echo Ina Bertrand's judgment of Australia's most famous silent film, Raymond Longford's *The Sentimental Bloke* (1919): 'This is the most important Australian production of the silent era: if there were better films produced during this period they have not survived' (McFarlane, Mayer and Bertrand, 1999, p. 442). Based on C. J. Dennis's much-loved verse-narrative, it enshrines the stereotypically demotic values supposedly held dear by the country at large. One hopes that titles by other notable film-makers of the period, such as Paulette McDonagh and Franklyn Barrett, may yet come to viewable light.

In the 1930s, Australia developed its nearest approach to a production company echoing the American studio system. The key figure here is Ken G. Hall, head of Cinesound (1932–56), who, throughout the 1930s, produced a steady stream of popular films, importing overseas stars and creating several home-grown ones, such as Shirley Ann Richards, later in Hollywood. Sound film caught the Australian industry at a low ebb, with Hollywood gaining ever firmer hold on the cinemagoing public, local film-makers facing major distribution and exhibition problems. In this climate, Hall's achievement is notable. How resonant of the decade are his films, with their stress on rural Australia (*The Squatter's Daughter*, 1933; *Tall Timbers*, 1940; those derived from Steele Rudd's 'Dad and Dave' tales of outback life: *On Our Selection*, 1932; *Grandad Rudd*, 1935; and *Dad and Dave Come to Town*, 1938), with comedies featuring stage star George Wallace (*Let George Do It*, 1938; *Gone to the Dogs*, 1939), and with melodramas such as *The Silence of Dean Maitland* (1934, previously made in 1914) and *The Broken Melody* (1938), both strongly redolent of the Victorian stage, and adventures such as *Lovers and Luggers* (1937). Arguably, Australian cinema never again produced such a genre output.

Though Hall and Cinesound dominated the 1930s output, there are other film-makers worthy of mention. F. W. Thring's Efftee Film Productions, responsible for *Diggers* (1931), the 'first commercially viable sound feature' (Pike and Cooper, 1998, p. 150), remade *The Sentimental Bloke* (1932) as a talkie, produced the social melodrama *Clara Gibbings* (1934) and starred George Wallace as *His Royal Highness* (1932) and in *A Ticket in Tatts* (1933). Paulette McDonagh's carefully wrought urban melodramas, *The Cheaters* (1930, part-sound) and the anti-war tale *Two Minutes' Silence* (1933), won considerable critical approval. And Charles Chauvel, whose chief significance lies in his wartime and post-war films, wrote and directed a series of epically inclined adventures: *In the Wake of the Bounty* (1933), starring Errol Flynn as Fletcher Christian, and mixing travelogue with drama; *Heritage* (1935), a historical chronicle highlighting conflicts in Australia's history; and *Uncivilised* (1936), charting a woman novelist's romantic adventures in the wilds of northern Australia.

World War II greatly curtailed Australian film-making: no more than ten features emerged during the years of conflict. Nevertheless, two from Chauvel warrant attention, most famously *Forty Thousand Horsemen* (1940). Explicitly intended to inspire those fighting the current war, its introductory titles and dedication highlight the soldier-bushman connection: 'These were the men from Australia and New Zealand – the Anzacs –

Charles Chauvel's melodrama *Jedda* attempted to come to terms with white liberal attitudes to the Australian Aborigines

the "mad bushmen" – the men from "Down Under"' – and more in this romantic, myth-making manner. The film enjoyed enormous success, winning particular praise for the montage that recreates the Lighthorsemen's October 1917 charge of Beersheba, which 'went a long way towards making *Forty Thousand Horsemen* the first Australian film of international stature' (Shirley and Adams, 1983, p. 163). Chauvel's other wartime film, *The Rats of Tobruk* (1944), again starring Grant Taylor and Chips Rafferty, this time joined by Peter Finch as a sensitive Englishman contrasted with more laconic local types, also paid tribute to Australians in war, but lacked the vigour of *Horsemen*.

Apart from Chauvel's films, the most notable wartime contribution to Australian cinema was that of legendary cameraman Damien Parer. He had worked with Chauvel on location-shooting for *Horsemen*, and, rebelling against the practice of re-enactment in documentary film-making, insisting on actuality shooting, he was killed while filming in action at the age of 32 – and won Australia's first Oscar for *Kokoda Front Line!* (1942). In the quarter-century following the war, documentary kept Australia's film-making skills alive. The period is not one of absolute feature-film drought, but 51 titles in the years 1945–69 hardly suggests abundance. Furthermore, nearly half, and most of the best known and most proficient, involved overseas participation. The British-backed films, especially Ealing productions such as *The Overlanders* (1946) and *The Shiralee* (1957), showed some sympathetic interest in the particularities of Australian experience, whereas the Hollywood-financed films were conventional genre pieces taking advantage of exotic locations. Films such as Lesley Selander's *The Kangaroo Kid* (1950) and Lewis Milestone's *Kangaroo* (1951) were undistinguished westerns set in a different terrain. The US/UK/Australian co-production *The Sundowners* (1960), with its star cast (Robert Mitchum, Deborah Kerr, Peter Ustinov), directed by Fred Zinnemann with feeling for time, place and rural activities, is perhaps the most attractive of these international films. Stanley Kramer's *On the Beach* and Leslie Norman's *Summer of the Seventeenth Doll* (both 1959), eclectically cast with international stars, now seem flavourless renderings of their originals.

It is not surprising that so many personnel, particularly actors, sought careers overseas: genuinely Australian films of the period were few and visiting companies tended to use Australian talents sparingly. There are, though, a few indigenous films worthy of note. Ken Hall finished his directorial career with his best film, *Smithy* (1946), a biopic celebrating aviation pioneer Charles Kingsford-Smith that was a major box-office and critical success. So was Chauvel's Queensland-set adventure, *Sons of Matthew* (1949), and the stars of both films, Ron Randell and Michael Pate respectively, went on to Hollywood careers: there was certainly not enough to detain them at home. The most notable film of the period, one that has attracted critical attention since, was Chauvel's last film, *Jedda* (1955). Both this and *Sons of Matthew* attempted to come to terms with important matters in Australian history – relationship with the land; white liberal attitudes to the Aborigines – and both articulated these with Chauvel's strong melodramatic flair. Neither, however, found much success overseas, despite title changes and substantial cuts.

Other notable productions of the postwar period were the adventure films made by Lee Robinson and Chips Rafferty, leathery icon of male Australia, and Michael Powell's *They're a Weird Mob* (1966) and *The Age of Consent* (1969), both projecting diversely attractive views of Australian life. However, Australian cinema's years of greatest significance began in the early 1970s. Throughout the 1960s, there was growing agitation for an Australian film industry, and in 1968 maverick Liberal Prime Minister John Gorton sent a fact-finding party of three on a trip to study government-funded film and television industries abroad. The ensuing legislative and institutional initiatives were a turning point, an acknowledgment that a stable industry required government support. By 1980, there had been enough sense of a film revival to warrant the appearance of several books, including one devoted wholly to the New Australian Cinema (Murray, 1980).

Two films potent enough to have sparked the revival, but that failed to do so, had overseas directors. They were Ted Kotcheff's abrasive adaptation of Kenneth Cook's *Wake in Fright* (1971) and Nicolas Roeg's *Walkabout* (1971), derived (via Edward Bond's screenplay) from James Vance Marshall's children's novel. These were very different from preceding international forays, but they were too unsettling for popular success: *Wake in Fright* offers a savage critique of the myth of mateship; and *Walkabout* is a disturbing study in intercultural relations, more poetic in treatment than mass audiences normally expect. The 'ocker' comedies noted above were hearty knockabout farces, making much of male sexual preoccupations. The *Barry McKenzie* films took satirical swipes at Britain, and were popular in an era when ties binding Australia to the 'mother country' were weakening and a new Labor government had ushered in a more sophisticated sense of nationhood.

Dominating recollections of the 1970s, though not reflecting actual numbers of films produced, were the literary adaptations, often set in the distant past – as distant as the (European-style) past can be in a comparatively new country. Joan Lindsay's 1967 novel, *Picnic at Hanging Rock*, hitherto only modestly successful, was reprinted a dozen times in the seven years after Peter Weir's 1975 film. The latter may now look swooningly self-conscious, but there is no denying the impact it made. It stood in clear opposition to the rough-and-ready comedies; it had enough sense of mystery for popular interest (even though this aspect of it is inadequately developed); it looked exquisite (schoolgirls wafting about the daunting rock surfaces); and it had the haunting notes of Gheorghe Zamfir's pan pipes on the soundtrack. It seemed like art-house fare for those who did not want to read subtitles. It ushered in a series of intelligent, sometimes too-decorous adaptations that, like *Picnic*, focused on youthful coming-of-age experiences. Bruce Beresford filmed Henry Handel Richardson's tough little 1910 novel of an author-in-the-making, *The Getting of Wisdom* (1977), changing her orientation from the literary to the musical, presumably in the interests of clearer cinematic representation; Gillian Armstrong stuck to the heroine's literary ambitions in *My Brilliant Career* (1979), a delicate rendering of Miles Franklin's feminist classic.

The literary adaptations tended to overshadow other strands of the 1970s revival. Ken Hannam's *Sunday Too Far Away* (1974), a study in social realist mode of shearers on a South Australian property, and Beresford's *'Breaker' Morant* (1979), both sober affirmations of anti-authority stances; Phillip Noyce's toughly engaging chronicle of postwar societal change, *Newsfront* (1978); the genre thrillers, Beresford's heist film, *Money Movers* (1978), and Richard Franklin's *Patrick* (1978); and, above all, George Miller's *Mad Max* (1979): these are some of the other films belonging to the period described by Dermody and Jacka (1988) as 'The Second Phase (1976–80): Seemly Respectability'. The situation was always more complex than could be accommodated by such a term. As with British 'quality' cinema, the realist and the literary tended to get the best press, but there was always more going on, including a tenacious trickle of genre films.

By the end of the decade, Australian film had acquired some sort of identity abroad, chiefly through festival attention, though *Mad Max* enjoyed enormous commercial success where it mattered – in the US, the world's largest English-speaking audience. Since then, no one (except perhaps those engaged in it) has doubted the existence of an Australian film industry. There have been good and bad years. In 2004, one film, *Somersault*, scooped the Australian Film Institute awards, not so much because this picturesque drama of youthful alienation and sexual questing was a masterwork as because the year was meagre in achievement. Fortunately, the two subsequent years found a healthier situation, with genuine competition for the awards. It is scarcely surprising that the big box-office hits have tended to be 'safe' genre pieces such as *The Man from Snowy River* (1982), a 'wallaby western', and the romantic comedy-adventure *Crocodile Dundee*

An unflinchingly graphic exercise in visceral horror: *Wolf Creek*

(1986). But even among the generically 'safe', there were endearing antipodean inflections in the 1990s and after, such as those on display in Baz Luhrmann's musicals *Strictly Ballroom* (1992) and *Moulin Rouge!* (2001), the biopic *Shine* (1996) or the gritty 'western' *The Proposition* (2005). And there was idiosyncratic acuity in the interrogation of gender stereotyping in *Muriel's Wedding* or *The Adventures of Priscilla, Queen of the Desert* (both 1994).

There has been a heartening level of ambition in recent Australian cinema (see McFarlane, 2006). It is almost as if it has outgrown a need to establish itself as a national cinema, as if it no longer needs, as in the identity-forging 1970s, to project the nation. In 2006, for instance, two venturesome films were adaptations, but not of well-loved local 'classics'. Instead, *Jindabyne* relocated a minimalist short story by Raymond Carver to the Snowy Mountains country of southern New South Wales, giving it contemporary Australian resonance. Geoffrey Wright daringly adapted *Macbeth* to Melbourne's gangland wars and, retaining Shakespeare's pentameters without deference to theatrical locutions, offered a coherent, radical reading of the play. There is nothing 'seemly' or decorous about Sarah Watts's *Look Both Ways* (2005), which confronts issues of mortality with sophistication and compassion; or *Wolf Creek* (2005), an unflinchingly graphic exercise in visceral horror. Ana Kokkinos, who made *Head On*, the rigorous 1998 drama of youthful sexual and intercultural conflict, ventured into still more daunting sexual politics in *The Book of Revelation* (2006); and Neil Armfield's *Candy* (2006), from Luke Davies's novel, is a tender and unflinching evocation of a drug-fuelled love. And perhaps most heartening was the appearance – and success – of Rolf De Heer's *Ten Canoes* (2006), the first film to be shot entirely in Aboriginal languages, and the most important contribution to the representation of Australia's indigenous inhabitants since Tracey Moffatt's films of the preceding decades – *Nice Coloured Girls* (1987), *Night Cries – A Rural Tragedy* (1990) and *BeDevil* (1993). These were films ambitious in their time, not only as the work of an indigenous film-maker but of one who went daringly beyond the bounds of realist cinema.

It was never really true that most Australian films were set comfortably in the past; or that those that were necessarily failed to engage with the indocile facts of contemporary life. Happily, the dependence of many Australian film-makers on varying degrees of government funding has not muffled imagination or outspokenness.

Selected Reading

Susan Dermody and Elizabeth Jacka, *The Screening of Australia: Anatomy of a National Cinema*, 2 vols, Sydney, Currency Press, 1987 and 1988.

Brian McFarlane, Geoff Mayer and Ina Bertrand (eds), *The Oxford Companion to Australian Film*, Melbourne, Oxford University Press, 1999.

Tom O'Regan, *Australian National Cinema*, London and New York, Routledge, 1996.

Andrew Pike and Ross Cooper, *Australian Film 1900–1977*, Melbourne, Oxford University Press, 1980. Revised edition 1998.

Newsfront (Australia 1978 *p.c* – Palm Beach Pictures/ New South Wales Film Corporation/Australian Film Commission; *d* – Phillip Noyce)

Newsfront is a key film of the 1970s revival, skilfully balancing affection for Australian mores and institutions with rigorous appraisal. Although set in the recent past (the 1950s), it is not an exercise in nostalgia, and neither Phillip Noyce's direction nor Bob Ellis's screenplay encourages indulgence. Historically valuable for the perspective it brings to bear on its recreation of shifting postwar society, it intelligently interweaves its personal story of a decent man trying to salvage his ideals with major public events. The latter – including the failed attempt to outlaw the Communist Party, the Redex motor trials, the Maitland floods and the 1956 Olympic Games – are refracted through the way they impinge on two rival newsreel companies. The film melds newsreel footage with staged action, as Len Maguire comes to terms with Australia's encroaching Americanisation (epitomised by his slick brother), with the collapse of his marriage to his uptight Catholic wife, with the death of his sidekick in the floods, and his final acceptance that television has made his work obsolete. Holding coherently together its several strands is a magisterial performance from Bill Hunter as Maguire, focus for its critique of tradition and the inroads of progress, of fidelity challenged by newer sexual freedom, of principle threatened by pigheadedness. Noyce, like compeers Peter Weir, Bruce Beresford and Fred Schepisi, went on to a Hollywood career, but it is doubtful if he has surpassed this humorous, touching evocation of a period he is too young to have known first-hand.

BRIAN McFARLANE

Jindabyne (Australia 2006 *p.c* – April Films; *d* – Ray Lawrence)

Jindabyne, like much of the prestige film-making of the 1970s revival, is an adaptation – but not of a local classic. With Terrence Malick-like parsimony, director Ray Lawrence has made only three films in over 20 years: the tediously misfiring *Bliss* (1985), the riveting urban ensemble piece *Lantana* (2001) and *Jindabyne*, his version of Raymond Carver's elliptical short story, 'So Much Water So Close to Home'. Lawrence and screenwriter Beatrix Christian have relocated this to the picturesque Snowy Mountains area, but 'picturesque' is not what they have in mind. The story leaves them with plenty of scope for development. Set in a small town, it retails the aftermath of a fishing trip on which four buddies discover a woman's dead body, but decide not to report it till they have finished their weekend's sport. The Irish Stewart (Gabriel Byrne) runs into trouble at home when his wife Claire (Laura Linney) refuses to accept his explanation and insists on seeking reconciliation with the dead Aboriginal girl's family who live on the outskirts of the town, alluding to the Australian government's difficulty in apologising for past wrongs to the indigenous inhabitants. This makes the film sound more overtly polemical than it is: its strength lies in the way it takes Carver's story as a starting-point and makes of it a film that tugs at the Australian conscience while providing engrossing personal drama. Intensely Australian, it is also utterly non-parochial.

BRIAN McFARLANE

BRITISH CINEMA

Introduction

SARAH STREET

Despite being a frontrunner in the development of early cinema, represented by pioneers such as Cecil Hepworth and the 'Brighton school' of directors, British cinema was soon hampered by American competition, which has remained at the core of its difficulties in establishing a dominant profile as a national industry resistant to the perennial vagaries of economic boom and slump. There are, however, periods, directors and genres that have made a distinctive contribution and have received international recognition. Though state support has been patchy, protectionist measures were put in place from 1927, when the government imposed quotas to free up a percentage of the market for indigenous films because it was considered important for them to reflect 'the national interest'.

During the late 1920s and 1930s, many of the technical and artistic personnel in the industry were of German origin, as well as from other parts of Europe, producing a rich stylistic and thematic corpus of films that has typified the industry throughout its history. The 1930s was a key decade when British cinema consolidated its economic infrastructure and produced popular genre films, including Alexander Korda's historical comedy *The Private Life of Henry VIII* (1933); Victor Saville's elegant musical *Evergreen* (1934), starring Jessie Matthews; Marcel Varnel's madcap comedy *Oh, Mr Porter!* (1937), featuring Will Hay; and Alfred Hitchcock's thrillers *The 39 Steps* (1935) and *The Lady Vanishes* (1938). This success provided the conditions for the further expansion of the industry in the 1940s, perceived as one of its most fruitful periods when many of British cinema's major classics were produced, including the wartime drama *In Which We Serve* (1942); the Gainsborough costume melodrama *The Man in Grey* (1943); Laurence Olivier's highly regarded Shakespeare adaptation *Henry V* (1944); David Lean's classic melodrama *Brief Encounter* (1945); and Gainsborough's *The Wicked Lady* (1945).

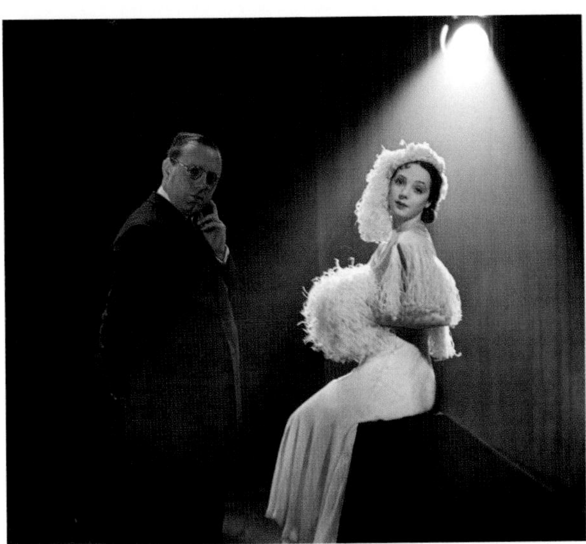

Jessie Matthews in Victor Saville's elegant musical *Evergreen*

A major classic: Laurence Olivier in *Henry V*

Partly in recognition of the importance of cinema in maintaining wartime morale, the Labour government supplemented quotas with more direct intervention, with the Eady Levy (which came into effect in 1950), a production fund created by a tax on cinema admissions, and the National Film Finance Corporation (1949), a body that provided 'end money' that supported independent producers.

The vertically integrated Rank Organisation dominated production in the 1940s and early 1950s, promoting stars as well as providing distribution outlets for independent companies such as Michael Powell and Emeric Pressburger's The Archers (see British auteurs, p. 431). Their avowedly non-realist films, including *I Know Where I'm Going!* (1945), *A Matter of Life and Death* (1946) and *Black Narcissus* (1947), made a significant contribution to raising the international profile of British cinema. The perceived tension between 'realism and tinsel' represented by these films, however, established a critical orthodoxy that favoured social realism as the expression of 'Britishness' on screen, a preference that continued until the 1970s and early 1980s, when Powell and Pressburger's films and the Gainsborough melodramas were newly appreciated, as part of the general reassessment of British cinema.

The popular films produced by Ealing Studios used comedy to reflect on contemporary social concerns while, as Charles Barr (1998) has shown, offering manifold insights into the national psyche (see Ealing Studios, p. 176). Raymond Durgnat, in his classic study *A Mirror for England* (1971), approached British cinema as an eclectic corpus of films revealing at times disturbing 'themes, undercurrents and overtones' (p. 3). Durgnat was one of the first critics to foreground genre output such as Hammer horror and Gainsborough melodrama, alongside directors such as J. Lee Thompson, Roy Baker, Basil Dearden, Frank Launder and Sidney Gilliat who were not normally included in canons of British auteurs, which typically featured names such as Carol Reed, Joseph Losey and Alfred Hitchcock.

Apart from J. Arthur Rank, another major player was John Maxwell's Associated British Picture Corporation (ABPC), responsible for successful films such as *The Dam Busters* (1955) and *Ice Cold in Alex* (1958) that explored themes of masculine identity in a postwar context. The critically applauded 'Angry Young Man'

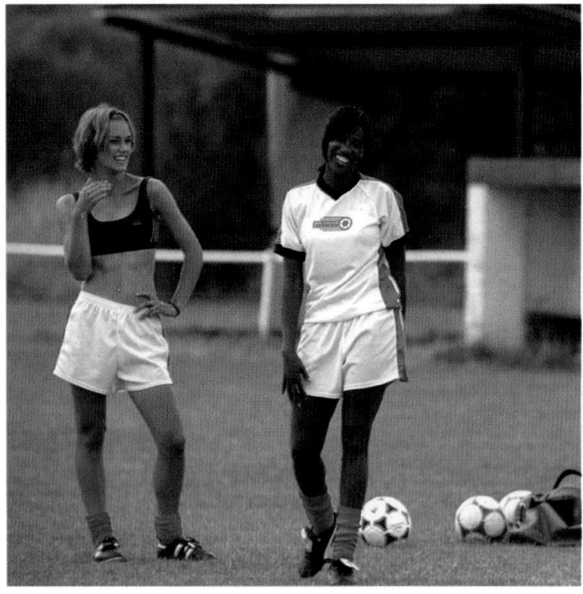

Celebrating diversity: Gurinder Chadha's *Bend It Like Beckham*

films that flourished between 1959 and 1963 (see British social realism 1959–63, p. 183) also focused on male crises and forged a further link between British cinema and social realism in critical thinking. Yet subsequent notable films such as Lindsay Anderson's surrealist fantasy *If ...* (1968), the crime film *Get Carter* (1971) and Nicolas Roeg's chilling horror/thriller *Don't Look Now* (1973) confirmed that British cinema's identity could not easily be reduced to a primary concern with social realism. And the hugely successful James Bond series, made in Britain but largely financed by American capital (see Global Hollywood, p. 52), represents a popular genre format that transcends narrow definitions of 'British' cinema in economic, industrial and aesthetic terms.

A major group of films produced from the mid-1980s, but with roots much further back in British cinema, were 'heritage' films based on classic novels by writers such as E. M. Forster and Jane Austen that were often international co-productions, and were successful in Britain and overseas. Popular period costume dramas such as Merchant Ivory's *A Room with a View* (1985) and *Howards End* (1992), Ang Lee's *Sense and Sensibility* (1995) and biopics such as *Carrington* (1994) explored questions of class and gender, and arguably influenced the aesthetics and themes of films set in more contemporary times, such as *Four Weddings and a Funeral* (1994) and *Bridget Jones's Diary* (2001). These titles contributed to a British cinema revival that included a diverse range of productions from *Bhaji on the Beach* (1993), *Small Faces* (1995), *Trainspotting* (1996), *East Is East* (1999), *Ratcatcher* (1999) and *Wonderland* (1999), to *Last Resort* (2000), *28 Days Later ...* (2002), *Bend It Like Beckham* (2002) and *Young Adam* (2003) (see also Contemporary British directors, p. 435). These films reflect on contemporary British society, each from a distinctive perspective; their diverse subject matter and transnational personnel confirm British cinema's rich eclecticism. A substantial degree of energy and dynamism has sprung from Scottish-funded (British-registered) short films and features, for example (see Scottish cinema, p. 187). But funding continues to be difficult to obtain, and access to markets dominated by American cinema remains problematic. In the mid-1980s, existing mechanisms of state support for film-making in Britain were phased out. In 2000, the UK Film Council was established to channel public funding, such as that generated by the National Lottery, into film production. British films are also typically funded as co-productions with European and US companies, highlighting the transnational nature of much British cinema.

Selected Reading

Raymond Durgnat, *A Mirror for England: British Movies from Austerity to Affluence*, London, Faber and Faber, 1971.

Andrew Higson, *English Cinema, English Heritage*, Oxford, Oxford University Press, 2003.

Amy Sargeant, *British Cinema: A Critical History*, London, BFI Publishing, 2005.

Sarah Street, *British National Cinema*, London, Routledge, 1997.

The British film industry

Ealing Studios

ANNETTE KUHN

In 1929, a company called Associated Talking Pictures was set up to exploit the advent of cinematic sound in Britain. In 1931, the company built its own sound-equipped studio in Ealing and by 1936 some 60 films had been made there, about half of them by ATP, the rest by various independents. In the financial year 1937/8, however, extravagant overproduction took its toll, forcing several studios to close down. The government responded to the crisis with a revised quota system to protect and promote British films, but American production companies were quick to exploit loopholes in the quota legislation. MGM, for instance, set up a British studio at Borehamwood making films for Anglo-American audiences with American stars and creative staff, British technicians and facilities and 'transatlantic' subjects. The first of three such MGM productions of the period was *A Yank at Oxford* (1937); on its release, MGM's Borehamwood production head, Michael Balcon, whose hopes of making high-quality Anglo-American films for the world market had been frustrated, resigned, and by the end of the year replaced Basil Dean, who had retired after running ATP since its inception. Ealing Studios Limited, which had previously been no more than a holding company for ATP's studio lot, became a production company and ATP was quietly phased out.

During the 1940s, Britain produced an annual average of 40 feature films: of these Ealing Studios provided about five. To maximise profits, Ealing and its rivals would obviously benefit from an arrangement with one of the three major cinema circuits – ABC, Odeon and Gaumont-British. By 1941, Odeon and Gaumont-British were both owned by J. Arthur Rank, who controlled 70 per cent of Britain's studio space as well as being the biggest single domestic distributor. In 1944, Rank signed an agreement with Ealing guaranteeing the screening, as top-of-the-bill attractions, of all its features as well as providing 50 per cent of the company's finances. In 1952, Rank increased its financial interest to 75 per cent, but in 1955 the relationship came to an end, and the studios at Ealing were sold to the British Broadcasting Corporation (BBC). Television had been encroaching on cinema audiences for some years and the advent of commercial television proved a major setback to Rank and Ealing. Ealing struggled on as a production company, operating from MGM's Borehamwood premises until 1959.

This sketch of the history of Ealing Studios is taken from the work of two writers on the history of Ealing, Charles Barr (1977; 1998) and John Ellis (1975). While Barr concentrates on the atmosphere of the studio and the attitudes of its personnel, Ellis examines its economic and institutional structures. Barr begins his book by analysing an example of what he sees as the studio's characteristic product. This analysis explores the analogy between the world of the film and the world of Ealing. The film in question is *Cheer Boys Cheer* (1939), which concerns the competition between a small family brewery and a large impersonal beer factory. The two firms are called Greenleaf and Ironside and, Barr argues, these names and firms stand not only for England and Germany but also for Ealing and Rank/MGM. The relation between the stories told on the screen and the experiences of the studio itself is a central theme of Barr's book.

Barr establishes that Ealing, like Greenleaf, was 'a small production centre' with 'the air of a family business, set on the village green' (Barr, 1977, p. 6). Ealing, Barr suggests, exemplifies one of the two choices for the film industry in postwar Britain, the small business; the other, collaboration with the Americans, Barr sees as epitomised by Borehamwood.

Barr is aware of the problems of a simple 'reflection' thesis in which the films act as a mirror for England, or for the studio. And he admits that 'the celebration of the little man, of the small-scale enterprise, is a traditional theme not confined to Ealing or to England; one need only refer to Frank Capra's Hollywood comedies of the thirties' (Barr, 1977, p. 6). Clearly, an equation that simply revises the traditional slogan 'film reflects society', to read 'film reflects studio' is somewhat problematic. Nevertheless, attention to industrial determinations can throw considerable light on the aesthetics of a studio's products, and not only at a level of analogy or internal reference. John Ellis, in his 1975 article on Ealing, has attempted to provide such economic and organisational data.

Ellis's emphasis is on the economics, technology and industrial organisation of Ealing. He establishes that the studio's average of five films per year were all A-features almost all with U-certificates, running some 80 or 90 minutes each and costing between £120,000 and £200,000, with the comedies averaging out at about £160,000. Each film would take about eight to ten weeks to shoot with an average of about two minutes' screen time completed every day. Ealing had its own pre-production and post-production departments at the studio, including scripting and advertising, as well as having access (between 1944 and 1955) to Rank's laboratories. The studio employed about 400 people and Ellis cites figures that support Michael Balcon's contention that at Ealing 'the most important work is done before and after a film goes on the floor' (quoted in Ellis, 1975, p. 93).

Under Balcon's leadership, studio production was stabilised with a contract staff of about 50 who constituted Ealing's 'creative elite' of directors, producers, editors, scriptwriters and cinematographers, protected by a system of internal staff promotion and a regular 'round-table' discussion of present and future projects at which all 'creative' personnel could have a say. Director Alexander Mackendrick has since commented: 'We weren't paid much but we had the advantage of being very free' (see *Positif*, 1968), but the extent of that freedom seems to

Alexander Mackendrick's acerbic comedy *The Man in the White Suit*, made at the height of Ealing's buoyant period

have depended to a considerable degree on the agreement of the staff's attitudes with those of Balcon, who had clear ideas about the boundaries within which the studio should work: 'Nothing would induce us to do anything against the public interest just for the sake of making money' (quoted in Ellis, 1975, p. 123). Ellis argues that the extremely tight production conditions had a number of effects, and describes Ealing's overall aesthetic as a combination of bland studio lighting, short takes and static camera shots, little or no reliance on 'atmospheric' music and an unusual emphasis on dialogue and performance – and thus on scripting and casting, both pre-production elements. Location sequences were kept to an economic minimum unless, of course, they cost less than sequences shot in the studio. Thus in *The Lavender Hill Mob* (1951), a scene originally scripted for Victoria Station was rewritten for Northolt Airport at 'a tenth of the price' (quoted in Ellis, 1975, p. 98).

With the signing of the 1944 Rank–Ealing agreement, the studio was able to step up its production schedule and resume its prewar policy of assembling a stable roster of contract staff while mapping out a path along which the company could profitably travel in the years to come. Charles Barr identifies the period until 1943 with the war films, and the period after 1947/8 with 'Ealing comedies', arguing that the films produced in the interval between these periods 'cover a greater range than before or since' (Barr, 1977, p. 50). Following Ellis, it might be argued that industrial conditions determined such a variety. A film such as *Dead of Night* (1945) explores the possibilities of a genre unfamiliar to Ealing and, as an anthology, allowed several apprentice talents to be tried out at less than feature length. But *Dead of Night* was an isolated experiment for Ealing. The studio consequently retreated to the cosy, familiar, rational, domestic world of the comedies. In Barr's terms, 'Ealing became typed as the safe, respectable, "U"-certificate British cinema par excellence' (Barr, 1977, p. 58). Why did Ealing fail to follow up the experiment of *Dead of Night*, which was by no means a commercial disaster? One possible explanation is Balcon's admission in an interview that

> none of us would ever suggest any subject, whatever its box-office potential, if it were socially objectionable or doubtful. We want to achieve box-office success, of course, but we consider it our primary task to make pictures worthy of that name. (Quoted in Barr, 1977, p. 58)

Yet if this is true, how did the 'horrific' *Dead of Night* ever slip through Ealing's self-censorship? Barr has argued that the supernatural nature of the film's subject sanctions its ideologically 'doubtful' content, while its episodic form functions to guarantee that those very elements remain at the level of suggestions.

If *Dead of Night* represents a closed avenue for Ealing, *The Lavender Hill Mob* and *The Man in the White Suit* (1951) are examples of the path the studio did choose to follow, that of comedy. The year 1951 was a pinnacle one for Ealing, as for the British film industry as a whole. Between 1942 and 1951, no one came in as a director from outside the studio, and a stable core of contract players and creative personnel transformed it into the cinematic equivalent of a repertory theatre company. In 1951, British censorship regulations were relaxed and the X-certificate was introduced. But in 1952, the Rank–Ealing agreement was revised, and only three years later terminated. Attendances at film theatres were diminishing considerably, film production costs were spiralling and American companies were finding it easier than ever before to exploit the British market. Moreover, in 1952 the BBC finally achieved its ambition of national television transmission, and in the following year some two million TV sets were tuned in to watch the Coronation. The cinema circuits could compete only by offering feature-length Technicolor coverage of the same event some weeks later.

In this period of low receipts and increasing competition from both television and American cinema, other film companies responded by exploiting subjects unavailable to television (for example, Hammer and the horror film), thus differentiating their products from those of the competition. Ealing, too, had either to change its production values radically or to cease production. In the end, the company took the latter course.

Selected Reading

Charles Barr, *Ealing Studios*, London, Cameron and Tayleur/Newton Abbot, David and Charles, 1977. Revised edition 1998.

John Ellis, 'Made in Ealing', *Screen* 16 (1), Spring 1975.

Gainsborough Pictures

SARAH STREET

Between 1924 and 1950, Gainsborough Pictures produced some of the most significant British films and stars. Established by producer Michael Balcon and operating from studios at Islington and Shepherd's Bush, London, Gainsborough released its films through Gaumont-British and then the Rank Organisation, which provided access to key cinemas in Britain and to overseas markets via the American companies with which Gaumont-British and Rank were linked. Known for its lower-budget, popular entertainment films across a variety of genres, Gainsborough was run by a succession of producers who had a sure sense of box-office potential and a realistic grasp of the market; these included Ted Black, Maurice Ostrer and R. J. Minney, who were responsible for promoting the distinctive, popular costume melodramas of the 1940s with which the studio is primarily identified. These were important vehicles in establishing the careers of stars including James Mason, Margaret Lockwood, Stewart Granger and Patricia Roc (see Gainsborough costume melodrama, p. 292).

While the 1940s costume melodramas have dominated assessments of Gainsborough, the company's early years were significant in advancing the careers of directors such as Graham Cutts, Alfred Hitchcock and Victor Saville, who were important figures in British silent cinema and early talkies, as well as popular stars such as Ivor Novello, Mabel Poulton and Jessie Matthews. For directors, technicians and actors, Gainsborough's position as a lower-budget studio operating within a competitive and complex film entertainment context provided a crucial training ground for experimenting with popular formulae, allowing for both technical innovation and repetition of generic styles. Working within the umbrella of vertically integrated companies that linked production with distribution and exhibition ensured that stars were well publicised. The core identities established at Gainsborough for actors such as James Mason and Stewart Granger were so strong that when they moved to Hollywood, their roles tended to replicate the personas they had acquired in the British costume melodramas, which had been exhibited across America.

In the 1920s, via its connection with Gaumont-British, Gainsborough developed links with German companies, primarily Ufa, and played a part in the 'Film Europe' movement, which consisted of intercontinental co-productions and a series of film conferences that were intended to counter Hollywood's domination of European markets. While a pan-European trade federation did not result from these initiatives, Gainsborough's

The Lodger: A Story of the London Fog
(UK 1926 *p.c* – Gainsborough Pictures;
d – Alfred Hitchcock)

Hitchcock's best-known silent film, *The Lodger* epitomises key elements of Gainsborough's identity as a British studio: the celebration of an eclectic mixture of styles, both British and European. It was based on a stage adaptation of a popular novel by Mrs Belloc Lowndes that drew loosely on the Jack the Ripper murders, which had taken place in Whitechapel in the 1880s. The film deploys a classical narrative structure while combining melodrama with techniques associated with European aesthetics. Ivor Novello, Gainsborough's major star in the silent period, plays the Lodger, a mysterious figure who rents a room in a London house and is suspected of committing a series of murders involving blonde women. This enigma propels the narrative through ten sequences fraught with ambiguities that enhance suspense, a technique for which Hitchcock later became famous. Narrative structure and mise en scène explore the film's major themes of guilt and innocence; the dangers of the city; and gender and sexuality. As well as being a thriller, *The Lodger* engages with comedy, particularly in its presentation of the working-class Bunting family and the confusion introduced by the Lodger to their everyday lives. The city, with its network of modern communications, shown spreading the news of the latest murder in montage sequences, is a problematic place where guilt and suspicion abound.

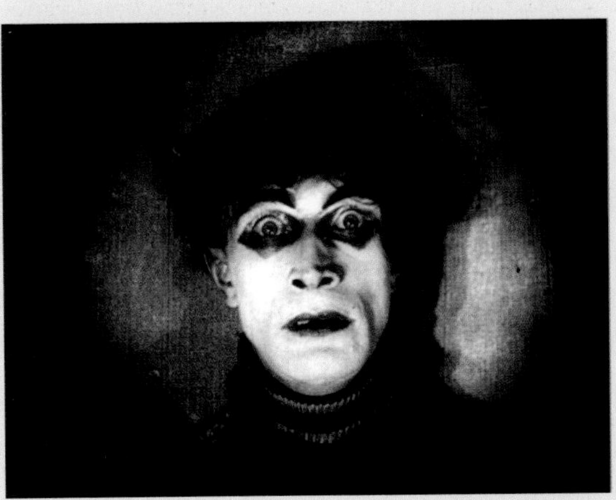

Conrad Veidt as Cesare in *Das Cabinet des Dr. Caligari*

Max Schreck as Count Orlok in *Nosferatu eine Symphonie des Grauens*

Expressionist echoes: Ivor Novello in *The Lodger*

Novello uses a non-naturalistic, gestural acting style that lends itself to ambiguity at the level of narrative and of sexuality. One shot of him looking out of a window frames his face in a manner reminiscent of the framing both of the somnambulist Cesare in Robert Wiene's *The Cabinet of Dr. Caligari* (1919) and the vampire in F. W. Murnau's *Nosferatu* (1922). This shot presents the idea of the film in tableau form: the Lodger as trapped, a victim himself, or possibly the perpetrator of horrendous crimes against women.

As in Gainsborough's later costume melodramas, which were similarly concerned with questions of gender and sexual identity, costume and props are used here in a playful, suggestive manner. An example is the use of bags that may conceal information about the murders, but at the same time emphasise the 'feminine' connotations that have been established for Novello/the Lodger. His character is pitted against the uncomplicated masculinity of the policeman Joe Betts (Malcolm Keen), in much the same way as later Gainsborough melodramas opposed characters that represented different 'versions' of gender.

SARAH STREET

involvement nevertheless marked it as a progressive and dynamic company that epitomised the transnational affiliations and identities of much British cinema during this period and later. The studio employed foreign technicians such as set designer Oscar Werndorff, and Gainsborough's comedies of the early 1930s, such as Victor Saville's *Sunshine Susie* (1931), a remake of a German musical comedy, have close affinities with contemporary German cinema.

Comedy was a staple output of the studio throughout its history. In the 1930s, notable examples starred Jack Hulbert and focused on narratives of upward social mobility. Throughout this period, Gainsborough also produced versions of the Ben Travers/Aldwych stage farces, featuring Ralph Lynn, vaudeville-inspired comedies with Will Hay, and three comedy duos known as the 'Crazy Gang' (Flanagan and Allen, Nervo and Knox, Naughton and Gold). During World War II, stars from popular radio such as Tommy Handley and Arthur Askey featured in Gainsborough's films, part of a drive to exploit proven successes in other media for the screen. In the 1940s, the studio continued to be identified with comedies, contemporary melodramas and social problem films produced by Betty Box and Sydney Box, who was the studio's last head of production, between 1946 and 1950. Thereafter, Gainsborough was fully incorporated into the Rank Organisation after a career as one of Britain's major studios that, for a quarter of a century, had produced a varied and significant contribution to popular British film culture.

Selected Reading

Sue Aspinall and Robert Murphy (eds), *BFI Dossier 18: Gainsborough Melodrama*, London, BFI, 1983.

Charles Barr, *English Hitchcock*, Moffat, Cameron & Hollis, 1999.

Pam Cook (ed.), *Gainsborough Pictures*, London and Washington, Cassell, 1997.

Sarah Street, '*The Lodger*', in Forbes and Street (eds), *European Cinema: An Introduction*, London, Palgrave Macmillan, 2000.

Hammer Productions

ANNETTE KUHN

Hammer Productions Limited was first registered as a film company in 1934, but soon after disappeared for almost a decade. In the wake of a short-lived exhibition quota imposed by protectionist postwar legislation (the Dalton Duty, 1947–8), Hammer's controlling company, Exclusive Films, was 'encouraged by the ABC cinema circuit to supply low-budget supporting features ... [and] ... this was the impetus for reforming Hammer' (Eyles, 1973, p. 22). Very rapidly it became company policy to produce films that could 'capitalise on subjects and characters that were pre-sold to the public either through radio and television or via myth and legend' (Pirie, 1973, p. 26). Adaptations of recent BBC radio programmes proved a particularly reliable and profitable source, and a cycle of low-budget B-feature quota quickies was launched, featuring such familiar radio characters as Dick Barton, PC 49 and The Man in Black.

Between 1948 and 1950, Hammer moved its production base several times from one large country house to another. The decision to use country houses rather than studios was determined by cost factors, and it proved to be one of the company's most important policy decisions, for it gave the films a distinctive style and put them in the ideal position to recreate historical/mythical subjects. In 1951, Hammer finally settled at Bray in Berkshire, in a large building that housed the company until 1968. Also in 1951, Hammer negotiated an agreement with an independent American producer, Robert Lippert, which guaranteed a 20th Century Fox release for their product in return, among other things, for Hammer's agreement to employ American stars in leading roles to ease their films into the US market. For almost four years, Hammer produced B-films starring American actors such as Zachary Scott, Paul Henreid and Cesar Romero, with the result that American studios began to see the benefits of low-budget British production of supporting features. But when the Americans withdrew from this arrangement around 1954, Hammer, like the rest of the British film industry, found itself in a critical position.

Characteristically, Hammer negotiated this crisis by changing their production policy as the structure of the industry and the expectations of the audiences changed. In the mid-1950s, there were a number of such changes for the company to exploit. At the beginning of the decade, there existed three main cinema circuits in Britain – Odeon, Gaumont-British and ABC. Rank owned both Odeon and Gaumont-British and had an agreement with Ealing. ABC, who already had a long-standing agreement with Hammer, may have decided that a degree of differentiation from Rank's Ealing comedy 'family audiences' policy was worth attempting (see Ealing Studios, pp. 176). Since the relaxation of British film censorship and the introduction of the X-certificate in 1951, Rank had only very rarely exhibited 'adults-only' films. Indeed, only one X was screened in Rank cinemas in 1956, and only 14 in the entire decade. ABC, on the other hand, showed more than 50 Xs in the 1950s, many of which came from Hammer. The mid-1950s also saw an expansion in the black-and-white television industry, with each new TV licence 'costing' approximately 100 cinema attendances a year (Limbacher, n.d., p. 15). Hammer's decision to exploit colour and X-certificate material at this point set them on the road to success. The house at Bray provided the perfect location for the period of intensive production and expansion that followed. At Bray, according to Pirie, Hammer became:

> [A] production company utterly unlike anything that the British cinema had previously known. There is a very slight echo of Ealing in the structure that emerged, but perhaps the most obvious analogy is with one of the small Hollywood studios of the 1930s and 40s like Republic or Monogram; for almost overnight Hammer became a highly efficient factory for a vast series of exploitation pictures made on tight budgets with a repertory company of actors and a small, sometimes over-exposed series of locations surrounding their tiny Buckinghamshire estate. (Pirie, 1973, p. 42)

This set-up, combined with a continuity of personnel at all levels throughout the company, enabled Hammer to produce a distinctive and professional product at low cost. Anthony Hinds, a producer and prolific screenwriter at Hammer, has summarised the studio's aesthetic/economic policy with the slogan 'Put the money on the screen' (quoted in *Little Shoppe of Horrors*, 1978, p. 40). Certainly, in the 1960s, when Hammer's budgets averaged around £120,000 per film, £15,000 or even £20,000 would be spent on sets and decor, with additional amounts spent on lighting, Technicolor and occasionally widescreens. Scripts, on the other hand, were much less expensive, deriving as they did almost entirely from radio, television, theatre, published works, myth, legend and, of course, other films.

Hammer's move into the horror cycle for which they became famous was by no means simple, though it was certainly facilitated both by the economic and industrial conditions just described, and by the social climate of Britain in the 1950s (Pirie,

Hammer's ambitious foray into horror: Peter Cushing in *The Curse of Frankenstein*

1980). The decision was helped by the peculiar attributes of the company's set-up at Bray (see Pirie, 1980, p. 13).

Paradoxically, American financial interests in the British film industry also contributed to the success of Hammer's choice of the British Gothic novel tradition as a source of inspiration. Pirie has described how:

> By the 1950s production in Hollywood had become so costly that Britain became a viable filmmaking centre for low-cost production. One of the advantages for American producers was that they could in this way spend some of the money earned from distribution in Britain which the Anglo-American Agreement of 1948 prohibited them from converting from pounds into dollars ...
> (Pirie, 1980, p. 4)

According to this agreement, American companies could only take an annual amount of £17 million out of Britain. There were, however, ways round this prohibition, co-production of films or co-ownership of facilities among them. It was, for instance, the loan capital of the National Film Finance Corporation that paid for the production of *The Curse of Frankenstein* (1957) but the film was distributed by Warner Bros. Similarly, the Eady Levy, which returned a proportion of box-office takings to the production companies of the respective best-grossing British films, was so slack in defining nationality that American subsidiaries or partnerships could easily profit from it (see also Global Hollywood, p. 50). The 'Britishness' of films set in the Victorian period and featuring a decadent aristocracy made Hammer an attractive investment for American companies and allowed the American film industry to secure an economic foothold in Britain. For a while, Hammer profited enormously from this kind of arrangement, but the bubble was to burst when the Americans eventually pulled out, leaving the British film industry in a great many difficulties (see British social realism 1959–63, p. 183). But perhaps the most influential factor was the company's ability to capitalise on the situation when their luck broke with the success of *The Quatermass Xperiment* (1955). In 1954, like Ealing ten years before, Hammer was being forced to experiment to find a new product and a new market. One 1954 production was the studio's first film in Technicolor, *Men of Sherwood Forest*. Another film, much more successful, was an experiment with a new genre – horror: *The Quatermass Xperiment* combined the then unfamiliar territory of horror with the science-fiction elements that Hammer had already explored in films such as *Spaceways* (1953). Moreover, the eccentric spelling of the word 'experiment' in the title capitalised on the film's X-certificate while also functioning as ready-made publicity. Furthermore, it was an adaptation of an already very successful BBC serial, first broadcast in July and August of 1953. 'The film opened at the London Pavilion on Friday 26 August 1955 with Hammer's fortunes at their lowest ebb and immediately began breaking box-office records both here and subsequently in America' (Pirie, 1973, p. 28).

After the unexpected success of *The Quatermass Xperiment*, Hammer commissioned another science-fiction script as well as a Quatermass sequel. Pirie points to the relationship between the themes that Hammer (and in due course many other film companies) began to approach in 1956, and the political events in the country during those crucial twelve months (Pirie, 1973, p. 31). On the very day that the greatest British anxiety movie of all, *Quatermass 2* (1957), followed *X The Unknown* (1956) into production at Bray, a headline in *The Times* read 'Giant H-Bomb Dropped'. Both films received X-certificates in Britain and were distributed as adult entertainment: once again the title *X The Unknown* simultaneously exploited and re-emphasised its certificate. In the same year, 1956, the Production Code of the Motion Picture Association of America was revised and relaxed, which widened the market for Hammer's product in the US. Nevertheless, for Hammer to survive the demise of the double bill, it was necessary for the studio to shake off their B-feature reputation and explore entirely new generic avenues in order to succeed in the American market. Hammer was thus encouraged to continue employing American actors in leading roles: Dean Jagger as the Professor in *X The Unknown*, for example, and Brian Donlevy as Quatermass.

Pirie argues that it is easy to underestimate the aesthetic and economic risk Hammer were taking in 1956 when the decision was made to elevate horror to a privileged role in their production hierarchy. 'By the time *Quatermass II* [sic] finished filming in July 1956 Hammer had more or less finalised plans for a complete change in their output ... No less than ten projects were abandoned in 1956' and in their place 'Hammer embarked on their most significant and ambitious venture so far, *The Curse of Frankenstein* which went into production at Bray on 19 November' (Pirie, 1973, p. 38), and enjoyed enormous international success. *Dracula* (1958), sponsored by Universal, soon followed:

> The final seal was set on Hammer's new status in the summer of 1958 when *Dracula* began to register its enormous success all over the world. Universal announced at this point that they would turn over to Hammer the remake rights of their entire library of horror movies. (Pirie, 1973, p. 43)

Sir James Carreras, then head of Hammer, has explained the studio's initial interest in the horror genre (rather than in sci-fi) as the result of a realisation that there had never been a *Frankenstein* or a *Dracula* in colour. Colour certainly differentiated Hammer's remakes from Universal's monochrome horror films, but this in itself was not enough. At this time, Universal's copyright expressly forbade imitation of the make-up and the neck bolts of the earlier *Frankenstein*, and for similar reasons on *Dracula* (retitled *Horror of Dracula* in the US to avoid confusion with the original) Hammer's sets were designed so as to be as unlike those in the American version as possible.

It has been estimated that between them *Dracula* and *The Curse of Frankenstein* grossed more than $4 million. That two such inexpensive films could be such a gigantic success was due in part to the interest of the American market. It also meant that sequels, spin-offs and so on were bound to follow. Eventually, having received the rights to remake Universal's entire horror library, and finally released from the copyright problems that had plagued the productions of *Dracula* and *Frankenstein*, Hammer embarked on a series of adaptations of Universal's 1930s tales of the supernatural. The proven success of previous entries in the series prompted Rank to reconsider its virtual embargo on Hammer horror films, and *The Mummy* (1959) was released in Britain not by ABC but by Rank's Odeon circuit. *The Mummy* reunited Peter Cushing and Christopher Lee for the first time since *Dracula* and proved a considerable success.

Another Rank release, *The Brides of Dracula* (1960), was Hammer's response to Christopher Lee's unwillingness to be typecast as Dracula, a role he had played in 1957 but was not to repeat until 1965. Thus, according to Pirie, Hammer were forced into the position of having to find some way of making a *Dracula* movie without Dracula. The absence of Count Dracula encouraged Hammer to compensate by adding ingredients to the formula: the brides themselves, for instance, provided an increased sexual component. However, even before 1960 Hammer were obviously aware of the need to vary the formula of the vampire myth. Once an audience has grasped the basic elements of the vampire hunters' artillery – stake, crucifix, strong daylight, communion host – the plot could all too easily subside into a succession of shopping lists. So Hammer carefully elaborated the paraphernalia and in doing so was able to persuade the audiences of the late 1950s that this time evil might just triumph (see The horror film, p. 347).

In 1968, Hammer received the Queen's Award for industry for having brought in £1.5 million from America over three successive years. However, 1968 was probably the last year in which Hammer could be certain of obtaining American distribution for its films. *The Devil Rides Out* (1968) was in fact advertised under the name of Dennis Wheatley – upon whose novel it was based – rather than that of Hammer Productions. By this time, American finance had more or less abandoned the British film industry to its fate. Having finally been forced by 1969 into vacating Bray, some of the company's confidence in the horror genre was lost with the studio. *Taste the Blood of Dracula* (1970) was advertised with the tongue-in-cheek slogan 'Drink A Pint of Blood A Day' and its deviation from formula requirements proved unpopular at the box office. Once again Hammer tried hard to differentiate their product from television: the film opens with Roy Kinnear, a familiar British TV comedian, being confronted with the horrific Technicolor Count Dracula, an opening that illustrated the complicated rituals Hammer utilised to reinvest their Count Dracula character with life at the start of each film in the series. This was the fourth Hammer *Dracula* film and, at the end of the third, the Count had fallen hundreds of yards from the battlements of his own castle to be impaled on a sharp cross. The resurrection of the Count from absolute death to life is one of the key ingredients of the series. Indeed, one film, *Dracula Prince of Darkness* (1965), took almost half its length to effect the Count's reappearance.

Following the financial failure of *Taste the Blood of Dracula*, which had compensated for the absence of Peter Cushing with other box-office attractions such as violence and sexuality, Hammer were uncertain as to the future of the horror genre. At the end of the 1960s, the company vacillated between EMI-Elstree and Rank-Pinewood, the exhibition circuits ABC and Odeon, and between straightforward horror and self-parody. With a change of management at Hammer in the early 1970s and encouragement from Warners, Hammer decided to bring the Dracula story up to date with films such as *Dracula A.D. 1972* (1972) and *The Satanic Rites of Dracula* (1973). *The Satanic Rites of Dracula* reunited Cushing and Lee, injected a number of controversial contemporary issues – such as property speculation and political corruption – and included a characteristic Hammer scene, with Van Helsing being interviewed by a television reporter. All these elements were unable to generate an audience in the UK large enough to convince American distributors that the film was worth releasing in the US. In the same year, American and British audiences were watching *The Exorcist* (1973), beside which *Dracula* was all too ordinary. Once the American horror and sci-fi cycles were under way in the mid-1970s, films such as *The Omen* (1976) and *Star Wars* (1977) were being produced in the same studios and with the same facilities that Hammer had employed. Meanwhile, Hammer returned to the source of their original success – the television spin-off. In 1972/3, for instance, Hammer released *Mutiny on the Buses*, *That's Your Funeral*, *Love Thy Neighbour* and *Nearest and Dearest*. None of these ever appeared on the American circuits. Since the late 1970s, Hammer's horror film production has virtually ceased, confining itself mainly to television series.

Selected Reading

Peter Hutchings, *Hammer and Beyond: British Horror Film*, Manchester, Manchester University Press, 1993.

David Pirie, *A Heritage of Horror: The English Gothic Cinema 1946–1972*, London, Gordon Fraser, 1973.

British social realism 1959–63

ANNETTE KUHN

In 1969, Alan Lovell described the British cinema as an almost unknown quantity, pointing to the lack of a framework for discussion as partly responsible. Lovell's complaint was echoed that same year by the influential critic Peter Wollen, who argued that 'the English cinema . . . is still utterly amorphous, unclassified, unperceived' (Wollen, 1969; 1972, p. 115; 1998), and set in motion a shift towards more thorough critical work on British cinema – work that would attempt to reconcile history and industrial conditions of production with aesthetics and would do so in interesting and productive ways. Barr's analysis of the history of the Ealing Studios can be cited as a good example (see Ealing Studios, p. 176), as can the feminist writing on the little-known 1940s Gainsborough melodramas (see Gainsborough Pictures, p. 178).

In his 1969 paper, Lovell himself provided a tentative historical analysis to explain what he perceived as the aesthetic underdevelopment of British cinema: an 'art' cinema dominated by the Griersonian ethic of documentary in the service of propaganda; an entertainment cinema hamstrung by notions of 'good taste'; and a 'New Wave' of critics-turned-film-makers (the Free Cinema movement) forced by exclusion from the feature-film industry to make documentaries. This analysis, which implies a judgment of the stultifying effects of a prevailing social realist aesthetic hostile to formal experiment, is shared by other critics. John Hill, for example, writing about the group of social realist films made around 1958–63, sees them in similar terms as emerging from the documentary prerogative in both commercial and non-commercial film-making, and 'the insulation of British culture from European modernism in the 1920s and 1930s at the very time that the "documentary spirit" was achieving its hegemony across the arts' (Hill, 1986, pp. 130–1). However, Hill points to the complex nature of the relationship between the aesthetic prejudices and procedures internalised by film-makers and film audiences alike and the final products, the films themselves. He argues that the British social realist movement related not only to an internalised aesthetic ideology but also to an external economy.

Recognising that it constituted part of a particular response to the development of postwar British capitalism, Hill is careful also to specify both the social formation and historical context in which the movement developed, and the industrial and institutional foundations upon which it was built. But he emphasises that the movement, far from simply expressing social attitudes or a response to the economic climate, actively contributed to that response 'which was likewise refracted through the particular context and struggles of the British film industry and its cinematic conventions' (Hill, 1986, p. 129). During this period, British cinema was in the process of being redefined and reorganised. Hill discusses several aspects of this transformation, including the advent of commercial television, X-certificates, the disintegration of the American majors and the impetus towards independent production, and the role of the National Film Finance Corporation. A wish to turn the tide of cinema's decline led to a certain 'openness' to new ideas that permitted 'a possibility of innovation ... subject to the demands of financial success' (Hill, 1986, p. 132). This combination of factors, then, enabled a group of socially committed directors to put into practice their aspirations, to produce a popular cinema that would reconnect with the traditional working class rather than provide escapist fantasies for its audience. The space given to those aspirations, however, lasted just as long as they proved to be commercially viable.

Alan Lovell provides another account of the short-lived success of the social realist movement. He argues that the *Sequence* film magazine critics who became independent Free Cinema film-makers in the 1950s (Lindsay Anderson and Karel Reisz, for example), together with ex-theatre directors (such as Tony Richardson), were forced into documentary because of the difficulties they faced in attempting to enter the contracting film industry. By contrast, the documentary industry was attracting increased industrial sponsorship (Lovell, 1969, p. 8). Lovell concludes that once the 'Free Cinema aesthetic' had acquired the status of a genre, it could no longer license innovation. John Hill also suggests that the social realist movement may have destroyed itself through becoming 'conventional' and hence delegitimising its claims to realism. Lovell's epitaph on the British social realists – that because of the lack of a clear analysis of the situation in British cinema at the time they became prisoners of the very situation they had criticised – is echoed in Hill's suggestion that the critique of commerce implied in social realist cinema exemplified a liberal humanist culture that was itself in crisis. The financial failure of Anderson's *This Sporting Life* (1963) signalled more or less the end of the movement and a return to 'entertainment' films, which, Hill argues, tells us something of the limits of the challenge that had been made to the industry. The control apparently given to the directors was circumscribed by a system in which the real control rested with the Rank–ABC monopoly of distribution and exhibition, which gave them the right to define what was 'entertainment' and what was not (Hill, 1986, p. 132).

However, Hill and Lovell perhaps overemphasise the influence of the documentary/Free Cinema tradition on the aesthetics and ideology of social realist cinema. Raymond Durgnat (1971) has attributed the social realist aesthetic to new developments in literature and theatre, and the impulse provided by writers such as John Osborne, Keith Waterhouse and Shelagh Delaney, novelists such as John Braine and David Storey and a new generation of actors including Albert Finney, Rita Tushingham, Rachel Roberts and Tom Courtenay (Durgnat, 1971, p. 129). According to this argument, the 'transparency' of the social realist aesthetic not only resided in cinema's alleged ability to reproduce reality unmediated but also in its apparent ability to transmit, without adversely transforming, literary texts. And most important to this aesthetic was a notion of 'quality' grounded in the established artistic status of British literature and theatre.

Whatever its origins, the brief flowering of British social

A new kind of British hero: Albert Finney as the truculent Arthur Seaton in *Saturday Night and Sunday Morning*

realism testifies to Hill's argument that as a movement it must be seen in the context of the British film industry of the time, although he tends to underestimate the influence exerted on this situation by American capital. In 1959, according to Michael Balcon, 'You couldn't run a studio in the way Ealing was run – certainly not in this country, and perhaps nowhere in the world' (Balcon, 1959, p. 133). Balcon was speaking as the newly appointed chairman of Bryanston Films, a confederation of 16 independent producers and production companies, financed by the producers themselves as well as by the distributors British Lion and by Lloyds Bank, Alliance Film Studios and Rank Laboratories, and releasing through British Lion. British Lion was modelled on the American Company, United Artists, and like United Artists lacked an exhibition circuit of its own. American financier Walter Reade's presence on the British Lion Board was part of a campaign to secure showings of British films in the United States, for without exhibition back-up they would be unlikely to make a profit in the domestic market. According to George Perry (1974) at this time: 'Up to 90 per cent of the films made in Britain derived their financing at least in some part from American sources' (p. 215). However, this financial interest was likely to be withdrawn as soon as production conditions in Hollywood improved, with disastrous effects for the British industry. When this eventually happened, British cinema in general, and the social realist movement in particular, were suddenly and radically affected.

One of the most important independent companies linked to Bryanston was Woodfall. Formed by playwright John Osborne and Tony Richardson, one of the co-founders of Free Cinema, the company was dedicated to British social realism. Bryanston Films themselves were financed by American money-men such as Walter Reade, the NFFC (National Film Finance Corporation) and theatrical impresarios such as Harry Saltzman and Oscar Lewenstein. This theatrical connection was important to Woodfall: not only were Osborne, Richardson, Saltzman and Lewenstein all identified with it, but many of the company's screenplays and performances derived from Royal Court Theatre successes. In the early 1960s, however, Reade withdrew from British Lion, Harry Saltzman left Woodfall for the James Bond series and Bryanston began producing blockbusters for the American market. In 1963, British social realism, as a coherent movement, was abruptly brought to an end.

Selected Reading

John Hill, *Sex, Class and Realism: British Cinema 1956–1963*, London, BFI Publishing, 1986.

Robert Murphy, *Sixties British Cinema*, London, BFI Publishing, 1992.

Robert Murphy (ed.), *The British Cinema Book*, London, BFI Publishing, 1997. Revised edition 2002.

Room at the Top (UK 1958 *p.c* – Remus Films; *d* – Jack Clayton)

Both Alexander Walker and Raymond Durgnat suggest a direct relationship between British society of the late 1950s and films such as *Room at the Top*. Thus, for Durgnat: 'Hints of disquiet about the time of Suez (1956) led rapidly to *Room at the Top* (1958) and *Look Back in Anger* (1959). Their success established another, and continuing mood of uneasiness …' (Durgnat, 1971, p. 13). Walker argues that working-class anti-hero Joe Lampton's envy in *Room at the Top* was the same feeling that swept the postwar Labour government to power, and was immediately recognised by movie audiences. However, Walker also points to the influence of box-office concerns and the attempt to attract international audiences, citing as evidence the casting of international star Simone Signoret and the use of the American rather than the English pronunciation of the word 'brassiere' (Walker, 1974, p. 46). In its desire to have this international appeal, Walker argues, the film plays down Joe's social origins and the class conflict in favour of the clash of generations and an emphasis on Joe's sexuality, and this is what won it its large audiences. John Hill also noted that the social realist films' attitude to class was less a positive affirmation than a displacement of it to make way for the generalised category of the 'social problem' (Hill, 1979, p. 129).

In the case of *Room at the Top*, the combination of class, youth and sex with a bestselling literary source proved enormously successful. The film took two of the 1959 Academy Awards (for Neil Paterson's screenplay and Simone Signoret's performance), made Laurence Harvey into an international star and introduced Jack Clayton to full-length feature-film-making.

ANNETTE KUHN

A Taste of Honey (UK 1961 *p.c* – Woodfall Film Productions; *d* – Tony Richardson)

Soon after Karel Reisz's *Saturday Night and Sunday Morning* (1960) opened, it was announced that Harry Saltzman was leaving Woodfall. Walker quotes Saltzman to the effect that the parting of the ways was over the filming of *A Taste of Honey*, which he felt was too provincial to appeal to an international market (Walker, 1974, p. 91).

Shelagh Delaney's play *A Taste of Honey* was acquired for adaptation at a price of £6,000, a project that Woodfall had been unable to get Bryanston to finance until the breakthrough of *Saturday Night and Sunday Morning*. Tony Richardson, having just returned from a frustrating trip to America where he had directed Delaney's play on Broadway, determined that no sets would be built for *A Taste of Honey*, and that it would be entirely shot on location. His experience of directing *Sanctuary* (1961) for 20th Century Fox in Hollywood had been less than happy. For *A Taste of Honey*, the unit was entirely based in Fulham, with the top floor of a derelict house being used as the 'rooming house' and the rest as production offices for Woodfall. An unknown actress, Rita Tushingham, played the central role; Richardson rejected an offer from American financiers to back the film if Audrey Hepburn played the part.

ANNETTE KUHN

Contemporary British cinema

SARAH STREET

From the 1980s, British cinema became particularly diverse, consisting of films orientated primarily towards domestic audiences and those intended to appeal more broadly to international markets. Trends towards co-production meant that 'British' films often included the input of US or European finance and personnel, rendering problematic any narrow definition of British films' national identity. In terms of state intervention, mechanisms established in the 1920s and 1940s (the quota system, Eady Levy and NFFC) were replaced by British Screen, a consortium that received government funding, and films benefited from tax incentives that subsequently evolved into New Labour's initiative, the UK Film Council, a private company integrating existing institutions that dispensed public funds to the film industry from 1997. National Lottery funds went into capitalising three franchises (DNA Films, Pathé and the Film Consortium) as well as to regional film investment bodies. The Council also launched a number of specific schemes to assist film-makers that catered for different types of productions ranging from the 'prestige' model to experimental films, as well as initiatives to support training, scriptwriting and digital exhibition networks. Television is another key source of funding. The BBC has invested in films since the 1970s, although on a much smaller scale than Channel Four, whose FilmFour channel was made available on digital Freeview in 2006, and screened a season of British films. Working in partnership with companies, the BBC has funded some significant films including *Sweet Sixteen* (2002), *Bullet Boy* (2004) and *A Cock and Bull Story* (2006). ITV companies have participated in film finance to a lesser extent. The expansion of cable and satellite TV has made more films available on the small screen, but movie channels are in fierce competition with sports and other popular channels.

Against this background of shifts in the nature and level of state and television support, the film industry continued to experience its historic pattern of boom and slump, although a number of companies and types of film emerged as relatively successful. At the prestige end, the international profile of 'heritage' films, from *A Room with a View* (1985) to *Elizabeth* (1998), attracted overseas investment, promoting British history, literature and locations to audiences worldwide. Spin-off genres, such as romantic comedies *Four Weddings and a Funeral* (1994), *Notting Hill* (1999) and *Love Actually* (2003), incorporated elements of heritage themes and aesthetics in contemporary scenarios. Some critics have argued that these represent a conservative bolstering of exclusive notions of 'Britishness', while others accede the films a degree of representational complexity and emphasise the pleasures they offer to audiences. The James Bond films continued to be the most popular series in cinema history, with the basic formula adapted to suit contemporary concerns. Changing attitudes towards women were reflected in the casting of

28 Days Later ... (UK 2002 *p.c* – UK Film Council/DNA Films *d* – Danny Boyle)

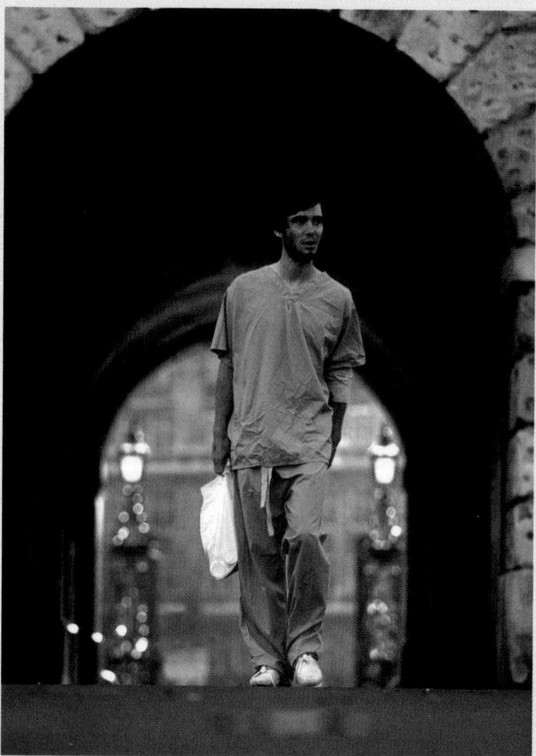

A post-apocalyptic world: Cillian Murphy in *28 Days Later ...*

Produced by the same team as *Trainspotting*, *28 Days Later ...* is a hybrid genre film (combining horror, thriller and science fiction) that explores the theme of total devastation caused by a deadly virus, known as 'the rage', that is spread after animal rights activists release an infected monkey from a research facility in Cambridge. In 28 days the virus spreads, killing all but a few survivors including Jim (Cillian Murphy), who awakes in hospital from a coma to discover that the virus has claimed thousands of lives, spreading all over the world. The unfamiliar sight of London devoid of cars and people is conveyed by digital video technology, one of the earliest uses of this format in British feature films. Jim explores the post-apocalyptic world, meeting survivors who journey with him across the country, eventually settling with others in a military encampment outside Manchester. Rather than creating solidarity, the survivors' terror of becoming infected makes them ruthless, and they turn against one another as the film develops a devastating exploration of human nature in crisis.

The film's generic hybridity and location shooting combine to produce a nightmare scenario that is rooted in realism. The scenario tapped into contemporary fears about techno-science, genetic engineering and AIDS. The stylistic energy that was evident in *Trainspotting* was repeated here and the cast (including Christopher Eccleston, who had starred in Boyle's successful thriller *Shallow Grave*, 1994, and was associated with other British 'revival' films such as *Elizabeth*) ensured that the film was a box-office success in Europe and the US, confirming the transnational appeal of much of recent British cinema.

SARAH STREET

A new kind of Bond: Daniel Craig as 007 in *Casino Royale*

Judi Dench as a feminist 'M' from *Goldeneye* (1995) onwards.

One of the most successful companies is Working Title, involved in the production of a diverse range of films representing a cross-section of contemporary British cinema, including *Four Weddings and a Funeral*, *Bean* (1997), *Billy Elliot* (2000), *Bridget Jones's Diary* (2001), *Shaun of the Dead* (2003) and *United 93* (2006). The company's access to overseas markets and co-production funding is due in large part to its link with Universal (see The major independents, p. 54). British studios are used by overseas companies and a number of blockbusters have been produced in the UK, including *Harry Potter and the Prisoner of Azkaban* (2003), which had British content but was largely American-financed. For many this situation compromises British cinema, confirming its dependency on American involvement and its inability to develop an independent infrastructure. On the other hand, co-production arrangements are a reality of contemporary film-making and these do not necessarily prevent interesting films from being made. Indeed, the critical turn in favour of transnational cinemas accentuates how in many cases co-productions and the input of non-British personnel can result in the exploration of cross-cultural themes and identities that might not otherwise be possible.

The international popularity of *Trainspotting* (1996) represented a key development in British/Scottish cinema in that it proved that a film with primarily 'indigenous' content (drug culture in Edinburgh) could be a great commercial and critical success abroad. Similarly, films with indigenous themes, including *The Full Monty* (1997), *Vera Drake* (2004) and *The Wind That Shakes the Barley* (2006), maintain an international profile for directors working within a variety of generic formats. *The Wind That Shakes the Barley*, a co-production involving Germany, Italy, Spain, the UK, France and Ireland, was about early twentieth-century English–Irish political history. It won the Palme D'Or at the Cannes Film Festival and confirmed the status of its director Ken Loach as a British auteur whose films have regularly performed well in European cinemas. Also catering to the 'art' market, Lynne Ramsay's debut feature *Ratcatcher* (1999), a formally experimental film about growing up in Glasgow in the 1970s, and *Morvern Callar* (2002) have received critical acclaim, the latter winning the Prix de la Jeunesse at the Cannes Film Festival (see also Scottish cinema, p. 187). The status of these directors is partly a result of their successful incorporation into discourses of European auteurism, which is reflected in the accolades resulting from prestigious awards at film festivals.

Selected Reading

Paul Dave, *Visions of England: Class and Culture in Contemporary Cinema*, Oxford, Berg, 2006.

Nigel Mather, *Tears of Laughter: Comedy-Drama in 1990s British Cinema*, Manchester, Manchester University Press, 2006.

Julian Petley and Duncan Petrie (eds), 'New British cinema', *Journal of Popular British Cinema* 5, 2002.

Scottish cinema

DUNCAN PETRIE

As a distinct object of study, Scottish cinema has been transformed over the last 25 years from a geographically and culturally specific sphere of representation into a small national cinema with its own distinct institutions and infrastructure, and emerging generic and thematic preoccupations. This has had major implications for the kinds of critical engagement with Scottish cinema that are possible, shifting debate from a limited but highly politicised consideration of regimes of representation to a broader and more diffuse range of institutional, cultural and textual analysis. Until the late 1980s, cinematic representations of Scotland were predominantly the creation of a metropolitan British film industry or Hollywood, while the contribution of Scots to these industries was confined to a few key individuals such as John Grierson, father of the British documentary movement; John Maxwell, the Glasgow solicitor who founded the Associated British Picture Corporation; and the director Alexander Mackendrick, responsible for such classic Ealing comedies as *Whisky Galore!* (1949), *The Man in the White Suit* (1951) and *The Ladykillers* (1955). And while Scotland has produced a number of venerable character actors, from Finlay Currie and John Laurie to Ewan Bremner and Shirley Henderson, its yield of major international stars is limited to a small group that includes Deborah Kerr, Sean Connery and more recently Ewan McGregor.

The first important critical study of Scottish cinema, the highly influential *Scotch Reels* (1982), edited by Colin McArthur, charted the pernicious influence of the discourses of tartanry, kailyard and Clydesideism on the dominant cinematic representation of Scotland and the Scots. The tartan myth ranged from a romantic idea of the noble highlander associated with the Jacobite rebellion of 1745 and the novels of Sir Walter Scott, to the more parodic and grotesque music-hall persona of Harry Lauder. It pervaded the various cinematic visions of Bonnie Prince Charlie and Rob Roy, while Vincente Minnelli's 1954 musical *Brigadoon* was described by McArthur as 'the cinematic apotheosis of this tradition' (McArthur, 1982, p. 47). Kailyard, with its inward-looking and parochial sentimentality, was found in the popular novels of J. M. Barrie, Ian Maclaren and S. R. Crocket and underpinned films such as *Whisky Galore!*, *The "Maggie"* (1954) and *Local Hero* (1983). Clydesideism, on the other hand, could embrace a more urban, working-class and industrial vision of Scotland – as demonstrated by features such as *Floodtide* (1949) and *The Brave Don't Cry* (1952) – but it eschewed any critical engagement with class conflict or industrial relations. Not only had these 'Scotch myths' ensured a chronic lack of engagement with historical and contemporary realities, but the sluggishness on the part of institutions to encourage alternative representations had contributed to Scottish film culture's failure 'to keep a historic appointment with the discourses of Marxism and modernism, the conjunction of which has dynamised analogous institutions in other cultures' (McArthur, 1982, p. 67).

Unmitigated tartanry: Gene Kelly and Cyd Charisse in *Brigadoon*

Making Scotland cool: Danny Boyle's *Trainspotting*

Stimulated by the creation of new sources of funding, including the Scottish Film Production Fund and subsequently the Scottish Screen Lottery Fund, the growth of a Scottish film industry in the 1980s and 1990s created a more diverse range of cinematic images, demanding an alternative critical response. This coincided with a renaissance in Scottish culture and the arts that engendered a greater sense of confidence in local cultural achievements, including cinema. The *Scotch Reels* polemic came under fire for ignoring films that did not fit its ideological framework, such as Michael Powell's *The Edge of the World* (1937), Powell and Pressburger's *I Know Where I'm Going!* (1945) and the celebrated trilogy of films by Bill Douglas funded by the British Film Institute in the 1970s (see case study) – an omission subsequently regretted by John Caughie (1990), one of the original contributors to *Scotch Reels*. A more fundamental revisionist critique was offered by Cairns Craig (1996), who suggested that the universality of historical process underpinning the 'Scotch myths' analysis served to deny difference and negate the need for a distinct Scottish identity, and evoked a conception of myth as a creative and progressive force.

This sense of cultural difference became more compelling with the increase in the production of Scottish films, initially with funding from London-based bodies such as Channel Four and the British Film Institute, and then with Lottery money. Key works included *Gregory's Girl* (Bill Forsyth, 1980), *Another Time, Another Place* (Michael Radford, 1983), *Venus Peter* (Ian Sellar, 1989) and *Silent Scream* (David Hayman, 1990). But the real breakthrough came in 1994 with the stylish low-budget thriller *Shallow Grave*, set in modern-day Scotland and directed by Lancashire-born Danny Boyle, which was an international critical and commercial success. The same group of film-makers went on to have an even bigger hit with *Trainspotting* (1996), a slick adaptation of Irvine Welsh's cult novel about Edinburgh junkies featuring an ensemble cast led by Ewan McGregor. By the mid-1990s, Scotland appeared the most vibrant place in British cinema, attracting established film-makers such as Ken Loach, who directed *Carla's Song* (1996), *My Name Is Joe* (1998), *Sweet Sixteen* (2002) and *Ae Fond Kiss ...* (2004), and Danish iconoclast Lars von Trier, who made *Breaking the Waves* (1996) in the Western Highlands. New local talent was also nurtured during this period, most notably Gillies Mackinnon (*Small Faces*, 1995; *Regeneration*, 1997), Lynne Ramsay (see case study), Peter Mullan (see case study), David Mackenzie (*The Last Great Wilderness*, 2002; *Young Adam*, 2003) and Richard Jobson (*16 Years of Alcohol*, 2003), who collectively have confirmed Scottish cinema's links with the contemplative and innovative tradition of European art cinema.

This burgeoning activity has also begun to invigorate and broaden the critical engagement with Scottish cinema both contemporary and historical, creating a less pessimistic analysis. While the emergence and development of 'the new Scottish cinema' has been mapped and interrogated by Duncan Petrie (2000; 2004), recent aesthetic and thematic trends have been insightfully analysed by a new generation of critics, among

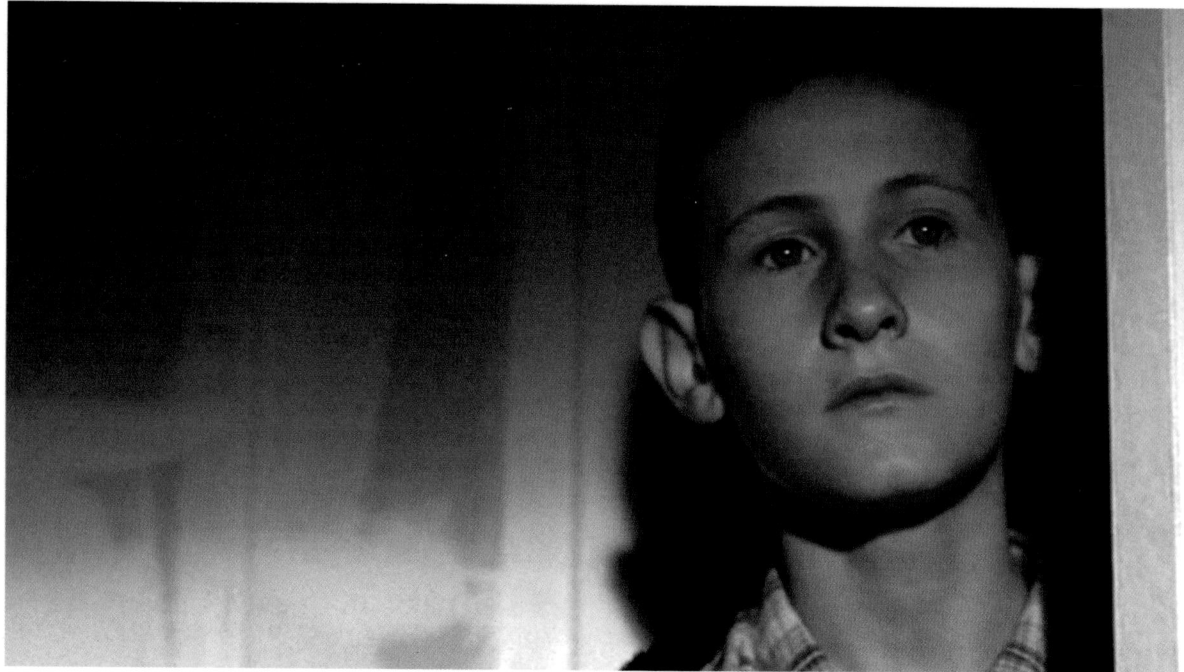

An intense meditation on childhood alienation and loneliness: Lynne Ramsay's *Ratcatcher*

BILL DOUGLAS AND BILL FORSYTH

The idea of a Scottish cinema was given an unprecedented boost by the emergence of bona fide auteurs. Bill Douglas's autobiographical trilogy – *My Childhood* (1972), *My Ain Folk* (1973) and *My Way Home* (1978) – depicted the formative years of a boy growing up in dire poverty in a Scottish mining village after World War II; the stillness and intensity of his austere black-and-white images drew comparisons with cine-poets such as Carl Dreyer, Robert Bresson and Satyajit Ray. This was augmented by his inspired casting of non-actors, notably 12-year-old Stephen Archibald, whose prematurely aged face palpably conveyed the pain and suffering of Douglas's own childhood. Douglas made only one more feature, *Comrades* (1986), before his untimely death in 1991 at the age of 57. In contrast, the films of Bill Forsyth articulate a distinctive brand of wry comedy, beginning with *That Sinking Feeling* (1979), a no-budget comedy about a group of unemployed Glasgow teenagers who plan a heist involving 93 stainless steel sinks, followed by *Gregory's Girl* (1980), the story of a schoolboy's infatuation with a girl who joins the football team; *Local Hero* (1983), about the plans of an American oil company to build a refinery in the West Highlands; and *Comfort and Joy* (1984), the story of a Glasgow disc jockey who becomes involved in a violent dispute between rival ice-cream sellers. Despite a certain whimsicality, these films abound with acute observations of masculine frailties, guaranteeing Forsyth a high profile in the British cinema of the early 1980s. Since then his star has waned, with a sequel to *Gregory's Girl*, *Gregory's Two Girls* (1999), conspicuously failing to recapture the critical or popular success of the original.

DUNCAN PETRIE

LYNNE RAMSAY AND PETER MULLAN

The end of the 1990s saw the breakthrough of two distinctive and innovative Scottish writer/directors, Lynne Ramsay and Peter Mullan, both of whom made award-winning short films under the auspices of the flagship Tartan Shorts scheme funded by Scottish Screen and the BBC before they progressed to features: with *Ratcatcher* (1999), an intense meditation on childhood dislocation, confusion and loneliness featuring a 12-year-old-boy who is consumed with guilt about his role in the accidental drowning of a friend; and *Morvern Callar* (2002), an inspired adaptation of Alan Warner's study of an enigmatic young woman whose detached fascination with the world is in direct contrast to her own existential blankness. Ramsay confirmed her talent for the impressionistic use of cinematic technique to reveal tangible surfaces and perplexing depths in the exploration of the complexities of subjectivity, emotion and experience.

Problems of Scottish masculinity: Peter Mullan's *Orphans*

While equally sophisticated, Mullan's aesthetic is more overtly expressionistic and aggressive in its emotional register. *Orphans* (1999), the story of four Glasgow siblings who in their own ways attempt to come to terms with the death of their beloved mother, is a direct meditation on the problems of Scottish masculinity that draws on a frenetic array of visual styles. It inspired Jonathan Murray (2001) to analyse it as national allegory and David Martin-Jones (2005) to see it as a compelling example of Deleuzian minor cinema. The film is also informed by Mullan's Irish Catholic heritage, which is more directly present in *The Magdalene Sisters* (2002), a scathing critique of the notorious Magdalene asylums for wayward women set in rural Ireland in the 1960s.

DUNCAN PETRIE

them Jonathan Murray (2004; 2005), who has demonstrated the positive influence of American cinema and culture on Scottish film-makers to balance the frequently acknowledged European links. Colin McArthur also returned to the fray with two studies of key pairs of films – *Whisky Galore!* and *The Maggie* (2003), and the Hollywood productions *Brigadoon* and *Braveheart* (2003) – in which he elaborated the concept of the 'Scottish discursive unconscious', a deep structure embracing tartanry, kailyard and Clydesideism that continues to exert a negative influence on the dominant representations of Scotland and the Scots.

Selected Reading

John Caughie, 'Representing Scotland: new questions for Scottish cinema', in Dick (ed.), *From Limelight to Satellite: A Scottish Film Book*, London, BFI/Scottish Film Council, 1990.

Colin McArthur (ed.), *Scotch Reels: Scotland in Cinema and Television*, London, BFI Publishing, 1982.

Colin McArthur, *Whisky Galore! and The Maggie*, London, I. B. Tauris, 2003.

Duncan Petrie, *Screening Scotland*, London, BFI Publishing, 2000.

Welsh cinema

DAVID BERRY

The notion of a Welsh screen culture might have seemed risible before 1986, when Karl Francis's *Boy Soldier/Milwr Bychan* and Stephen Bayly's *Coming up Roses/Rhosyn a Rhith* became the first two Welsh-language features (with English subtitles) to open in London West End cinemas. Both were made for S4C – the Welsh fourth channel, launched in 1982 – and embraced contemporary, distinctively Welsh issues. The films served notice of the television channel's potential for nurturing the first indigenous batch of film-directing talents for decades – even if then, as now, Wales, with its three million population, lacked an adequate industry infrastructure and the finance to create a fully fledged national cinema. (The Wales Film Council, responsible for Wales's film culture from 1993, had been succeeded by Sgrin Cymru, the Welsh Media Agency, in 1997, which was replaced in 2006 by the Film Agency for Wales, part of the Welsh Assembly's Creative Industries Department.) Later years saw the burgeoning of indigenous Welsh- and English-language film-makers such as Endaf Emlyn, Marc Evans (see case study) and Justin Kerrigan, funded largely through broadcasters.

The 1986 watershed followed seven or eight fairly fallow decades for Welsh production after the pioneers' success. The first Welsh-based film-maker of stature, William Haggar (1851–1925), made more than 30 silent shorts, mainly fiction, from 1901/2 to 1908, earning respect today for advanced editing and for the energy and brio of his few known surviving films. They include *The Life of Charles Peace* (1905), a burlesque biography of an actual murderer, and *A Desperate Poaching Affray* (1903), which influenced the American sub-genre of 'chase' films (see also Early and pre-sound cinema, p. 3). A later, extant silent feature of particular Welsh relevance is Maurice Elvey's marathon 1918 biopic, rediscovered in 1994, *The Life Story of David Lloyd George*, exploring the then British Prime Minister's political career (with ambitious crowd set-pieces and sumptu-

Virgin territory in mainstream British cinema: Endaf Emlyn's *One Full Moon*

MARC EVANS

The malaise and identity-loss of many Welsh areas after 1980s industrial upheaval found significant expression in Marc Evans's second feature, *House of America* (1997). A provocative and complex film, it presented a disastrously dysfunctional family and a community in thrall to an American opencast mining combine. The film explored the country's perceived colonisation by the English and the US, partly through an incestuous relationship between siblings living vicariously a perverted 'American dream'. Evans and screenwriter Ed Thomas suggested Wales's need for a new identity and its own mythology.

Resurrection Man (1997), a relentlessly graphic insight into Irish sectarian violence and the infamous Loyalist Shankill Butchers of Belfast, lacked adequate political context but revealed Evans's growing grasp of cinematic narrative, confirmed by his belated box-office success *My Little Eye* (2002). This adroit horror feature employed computer/digital imagery to dissect the morality of voyeuristic reality TV-style exploitation by creating a murderous, mercenary webcam entertainment. *Trauma* (2004) and the Canadian-set *Snow Cake* (2006) explored individual male grief. In *Snow Cake*, Evans made deft use of light to create a compelling sense of an independent, autistic woman (Sigourney Weaver) – the film's liberating catalyst – inhabiting her own inviolable tactile/mental space.

DAVID BERRY

ously shot Welsh childhood scenes). More enduring representations of Wales and its people emerged from 'classic' mining sound films (1937–49) directed by 'outsiders', including King Vidor's 1938 *The Citadel* (from former south Wales doctor A. J. Cronin's novel), Penrose Tennyson's *The Proud Valley* (1940) and the most iconic of 'Welsh' films – shot entirely in Hollywood – John Ford's *How Green Was My Valley* (1941). Jill Craigie's courageous *Blue Scar* (1949) raised important questions about the nationalisation of the mines. All these films had merits, but helped to create stubborn stereotypes of parochial Welsh lives revolving around pit and choir. They reflected their directors' preconceptions and were compromised as economic imperatives diluted politics or narrative. Agit-prop treatment of a Depression-crippled Wales came from non-Welsh directors, for example Ralph Bond and Ruby Grierson's *Today We Live* and Donald Alexander's *Eastern Valley* (both 1937). The next three decades produced Humphrey Jennings's lauded documentary *The Silent Village* (1943); *The Last Days of Dolwyn* (1949), an atmospheric period feature directed by actor Emlyn Williams; *David* (1951), a superbly structured documentary from Cardiff's Paul Dickson; and Jack Howells's elegiac Academy Award-winning short *Dylan Thomas* (1961).

In 1986, Karl Francis's *Boy Soldier* focused on a Valleys youth in the British army in Ireland, torn between an Irish girlfriend and her Celtic peers and a British military hierarchy contemptuous of the Welsh and their language and prepared to use him as a scapegoat. After his fiercely honest 1977 debut mining feature *Above Us the Earth*, left-wing director Francis created a powerful canon of partisan 'social realist' screen work, often set in declining pit communities and/or delving into government or media machinations (for example, *Giro City*, 1982). Francis usually worked in the English language; Stephen Bayly, however, emerged through S4C with *And Pigs Might Fly/Aderyn Papur* (1984) and *Coming Up Roses*, commenting through genre comedies on the de-industrialisation of Wales. The next decade's leading Welsh-language director was Endaf Emlyn, whose *One Full Moon/Un Nos Ola Leuad* (1991) was a riveting, mordant study of a man obsessed with religious guilt. It was set in a north Wales quarry community – almost virgin territory in British mainstream cinema. By contrast, his south Wales school-trip film *Leaving Lenin/Gadael Lenin* (1993) was humorous and questioning. Set mainly in St Petersburg, it captured a mood of bracing political change, examining personal and political loyalty and, crucially, the artist's responsibility.

Two Welsh-language films gained Academy Award nominations for Best Foreign Language Film. Paul Turner's *Hedd Wyn* (1992), celebrating a north Wales farmer-poet killed in World War I, melded fine editing, fidelity to original verses and striking battlefield scenes. Paul Morrison's story of fated love, *Solomon and Gaenor* (1999), focused on south Wales anti-Jewish racial violence circa 1911. In 2004, Amma Asante's harrowing, deeply discomforting *A Way of Life* explored present-day racism in Wales.

Successful recent features all deal with relevant modern issues. Justin Kerrigan's acclaimed 1999 'teen pic' *Human Traffic*, a disarming, buoyantly cinematic work revolving around a weekend binge, demonstrated the director's empathy with his characters and knowledge of teen vernacular. The grittier Swansea-set comedy *Twin Town* (1997), directed by Kevin Allen, offered a provocative, deliberately vulgarised view of Wales lampooning the country's cultural icons.

Paul Dickson's superbly constructed documentary *David*

Selected Reading

David Berry, *Wales and Cinema: The First 100 Years*, Cardiff, University of Wales Press, 1996.

Steve Blandford (ed.), *Wales on Screen*, Bridgend, Seren/Poetry of Wales Press, 2000.

CHINESE CINEMA

CHRIS BERRY

Cinema came to China as part of a package called 'modernity', not produced locally but delivered unsolicited from the west. As a result, it has been embroiled from its beginnings with the contentious desire to 'catch up' and become fully modern, but also to make modernity fully Chinese. The first film screenings were in 1896, when China was a declining dynastic realm that had already ceded Hong Kong to Britain and Taiwan to Japan. And they took place in Hong Kong and Shanghai, new cities that had grown up with the arrival of the west and went on to become main centres of film production. However, the first Chinese production was not until 1905, and neither in Shanghai nor in Hong Kong, but in Beijing. *Conquering Dingjun Mountain/ Ding Jun Shan* was named after the famous Chinese opera episode it recorded – making the modern Chinese. Furthermore, as a scene of martial choreography, it is the ancestor of modern martial arts films and the beginning of a long tradition of operatic cinema.

The early Chinese film industry flourished in Shanghai in the 1920s and 1930s, first in the form of supernatural martial arts popular heroism, and then in left-wing realist melodramas focused on social issues and patriotic resistance to Japan (see Early and pre-sound cinema, p. 3). These two tendencies reflect different attitudes to the modern. The former was a magical popular belief in science, the latter a rationalist belief in social and political movements whose adherents saw the supernatural as a feudal remnant. In the 1930s, the Nationalist government banned the supernatural martial arts films along with 'dialect' cinema not in the national language. This forced martial arts and Cantonese cinema to Hong Kong, stimulating the local industry and giving it its lasting character.

Shanghai was occupied during the 1937–45 War of Resistance against Japan and film-making declined. A 'second golden age' of what Leo Ou-fan Lee (1991) has called 'social realist' dramas flowered in Shanghai after the war. It included such classics as the epic of wartime corruption versus self-sacrifice symbolised by the hero's two wives, *The Spring River Flows East/Yijiang Chunshui Xiang Dong Liu* (1947). This period also produced Fei Mu's unique postwar psychological drama, *Spring in a Small Town/Xiaocheng Zhi Chun* (1948), criticised by leftists for its lack of political engagement, but often nominated as the best Chinese film ever made.

Following the establishment of the People's Republic in 1949, the film industry was nationalised. The government valued cinema for propaganda purposes. As well as tightly

Pedagogical cinema writ large: Xie Jin's highly coloured melodrama *Two Stage Sisters*

controlling the industry, it established new studios throughout the country and brought cinema to the entire population. A shift from social realism to socialist realism resulted in more thematic than stylistic changes. Where pre-revolutionary films had raised issues without offering solutions, post-revolutionary films preferred heroes from the approved worker- farmer-soldier classes and happy endings in which the Communist Party aided their success. However, there were exceptions. Possibly the most famous post-revolutionary film-maker, Xie Jin, includes films about sports heroines (*Woman Basketball Player No. 5/Nülan Wuhao*, 1957) and opera singers (*Two Stage Sisters/Wutai Jiemei*, 1964; see case study) in his repertoire.

Taiwan cinema responded to developments on the mainland with Healthy Realism in the 1960s. During the 1895–1945 Japanese occupation, little film production had occurred. During the 1950s, films in the local version of Hokkienese spoken by older inhabitants abounded, in particular local *gezaixi* opera films. But the KMT Nationalist government, which had retreated to establish its Republic of China on Taiwan in 1949 and hoped to return to the mainland, still favoured films in the Mandarin national language. In the 1960s, they also pushed Healthy Realism in Mandarin. These glossy tales resembled socialist realism, but they eulogised capitalism. Examples included the prolific Lee Xing's *Oyster Girl/Kenü* (1964), *Beautiful Duckling/Yangya Renjia* (1965) and later *He Never Gives Up/Wangyang Zhong De Yitiao Chuan* (1979), two farming films and a triumphing-against-the-odds melodrama about a disabled man, read by some as a national metaphor for the Republic of China.

Melodramas were also made in both the Cantonese- and Mandarin-language cinemas of Hong Kong in the 1950s and 1960s, along with other genre films. But swordplay and kung fu-based martial arts films made the industry world famous, with classics such as Chang Cheh's *The One-Armed Swordsman/Dubei Dao* (1967) and King Hu's *A Touch of Zen/Hsia Nu* (1969), as well as Bruce Lee films such as *Fist of Fury/Jingwumen* (1972). All three of the main Chinese cinema industries were regenerated by New Waves in the 1980s. In Hong Kong, this introduced such directors as Ann Hui, Tsui Hark, Stanley Kwan, Allen Fong and John Woo, who brought street realism to genre cinema or introduced elements of art cinema in films ranging from Woo's action classic *The Killer/Diexie Shuangxiong* (1989) to Kwan's art biopic *Center Stage/Ruan Lingyu* (1991), a tribute to 1930s silent star Ruan Lingyu. They were soon joined by Wong Kar-wai, whose Truffaut-esque romances such as *Chungking Express/Chongqing Senlin* (1994) and *In the Mood for Love/ Huayang Nianhua* (2000) made him a film festival favourite (see Hong Kong Cinema, p. 224).

The Hong Kong New Wave was energised by anxious anticipation of the 1997 integration with the mainland, announced in 1984. In mainland China, the end of the Cultural Revolution chaos in 1976 not only opened the country to the outside world but also led to disillusion with Maoism. This shaped both the Fifth and Sixth Generations (see below). In Taiwan, the waning dream of return to the mainland and the rise of film-makers who had only known life on the island produced a new cinema focused on Taiwan that rejected commercial fantasy in favour of realism. Its primary representatives are Hou Hsiao-Hsien and Edward Yang, more recently joined by Tsai Ming-Liang and others.

All three New Waves have been festival favourites, making Chinese film the leading non-western cinema today. However, with triumph overseas has come decline in box office at home and even industry collapse in Taiwan. In these difficult circumstances, the only relief has been martial arts blockbusters such as Ang Lee's *Crouching Tiger, Hidden Dragon/Wohu Canglong* (2000) and Zhang Yimou's *Hero/Yingxiong* (2002).

China's Fifth and Sixth Generations

Speaking about Chinese film-makers in generations began with the emergence of the so-called Fifth Generation in the 1980s. The demarcation of preceding generations remains disputed. But the Fifth Generation are those who graduated from the Beijing Film Academy (BFA) Directing, Cinematography and Art Directing departments in 1982. Because of the disruption of the Cultural Revolution decade (1966–76), the Fourth Generation had only graduated in 1964. The BFA did not take students every year, and the Sixth Generation graduated in 1989.

The Fifth Generation came to world attention with *Yellow Earth/Huang Tudi* (1984; see case study), directed by Chen Kaige and shot by cinematography graduate Zhang Yimou, who moved into direction with *Red Sorghum/Hong Gaoliang* (1987). The first post-graduation Fifth Generation film was *One and Eight/Yige He Bage* (1983), directed by Zhang Junzhao and also shot by Zhang Yimou. But when *Yellow Earth* screened at the 1985 Hong Kong International Film Festival, it created a sensation, because it was so different from anything anyone had seen come out of the People's Republic before.

The Fifth Generation came from divergent social backgrounds. Some were the children of the Communist cultural elite, such as the director of *Army Nurse/Nüer Lou* (1985), Hu Mei, whose father was a composer, or Tian Zhuangzhuang, who went on to make *Blue Kite/Lan Fengzheng* (1993), and whose father was a director and mother an actor who had become a studio head. Others, such as Zhang Yimou, came from humble backgrounds, in his case including political problems that had dogged his childhood. What they shared was the experience of the Cultural Revolution. They were encouraged to rebel against their parents and teachers out of loyalty to Mao. Chen Kaige has stated that the scene of betrayal by the adopted son in *Farewell My Concubine/Bawang Bieji* (1993) is based on his betrayal of his own father. When the Cultural Revolution got out of hand, this generation was sent down to the countryside, where they discovered a far less utopian reality than they had been brought up believing in.

The resulting disillusion formed in them a determination to make films different from Chinese socialist realism. However, rejecting the past also meant rejecting collectivism and embracing individualism, and they pursued different paths. Hu Mei was interested in psychology, and explored the inner voice in *Army Nurse*. Zhang Yimou and Chen Kaige pursued highly stylised film-making in their co-operation on both *Yellow Earth* and *The Big Parade/Da Yuebing* (1986). In contrast, Tian Zhuangzhuang was interested in a naturalistic realism that led him to make the documentary-like features *On the Hunting Ground/Liechang Zhasa* (1986) and *Horse Thief/Daoma Zei* (1986) about Mongol and Tibetan life respectively.

By the late 1980s, the rise of a market system was being felt. Many commentators see *Red Sorghum* as marking the end of the Fifth Generation phenomenon, and a bridge into more popular cinema. However, its theme song was adopted by the Tiananmen students in 1989. In the aftermath, life became difficult for Fifth Generation film-makers. Many compromised in the face of government pressure. Wu Ziniu, who had made such films as the exposure of the prison system *Evening Bell/Wanzhong* (1989), was soon making patriotic military films. Others stopped film-making. Hu Mei's psychological films had never made money and she disappeared only to reappear later as a highly successful director of television series.

But another small group was able to persist by attracting foreign investment. This is how Zhang Yimou made *Judou* (1990) and

Raise the Red Lantern/Da Hong Denglong Gao Gao Gua (1991), and it sustained Chen Kaige's career into the 1990s too. Ironically, Zhang was accused of pandering to foreigners by a new generation of ambitious critics in China. Gradually, pressure built on these last holdouts. Tian Zhuangzhuang was banned from film-making for several years after *Blue Kite* was screened at Cannes without permission, and *To Live/Huozhe* (1994) got Zhang Yimou into trouble. However, today, both Zhang and Chen have mellowed, with Zhang making martial arts blockbusters such as *Hero* and Chen making father–son tearjerkers such as *Together/He Ni Zai Yiqi* (2002).

The cutting-edge mantle was taken over by the Sixth Generation in the 1990s. The circumstances of their graduation were extremely inauspicious. They had to try to distinguish themselves from the Fifth Generation in the face of post-Tiananmen heights of censorship. Some gave up and went straight from the BFA into the mainstream industry. But others decided on a new route – going 'underground'. In China, 'underground' means not submitting films for censorship prior to distribution and exhibition inside China. In other words, the Chinese market is given up. This leads to low budgets and dependence on income from overseas. After making his first film, a drama about the difficulties of disabled children in China called *Mama* (1992), Zhang Yuan went underground with *Beijing Bastards/Beijing Zazhong* (1993), a film about the rock scene in Beijing. This was followed by the documentary about everyday life in Tiananmen Square called *The Square/Guangchang* (1994), co-directed with Duan Jinchuan, and a feature about gay life in Beijing called *East Palace, West Palace/Donggong Xigong* (1996).

Zhang's colleague Wang Xiaoshuai started out underground with *The Days/Dongchun De Rizi* (1993), and He Jianjun debuted with *Red Beads/Xuanlian* (1993), both of which are about depression and young artists in Beijing. These graduates from 1989 were joined later by other young underground film-makers who are also known as members of the Sixth Generation, such as Jia Zhangke, who debuted with *Pickpocket/Xiao Wu* (1997), a film about the life of a small-town pickpocket.

The Fifth Generation favoured exotic locales on the borders of the country, history and high style. In contrast, almost all the Sixth Generation films emphasised urban youth, contemporary life and naturalistic realism bordering on documentary, a mode many of them also dabble in. However, the underground mode of production was both frowned on by the government and not economically viable. Since the millennium, the Sixth Generation have come 'above ground', joining the search for investment and the domestic market. Some have found modest box-office success, but few have won critical success for their efforts so far. The eyes of critics today are on the newest film-makers, who no one has designated as a 'generation' yet.

Selected Reading

Chris Berry and Mary Farquhar, *China on Screen: Cinema and Nation*, New York, Columbia University Press, 2005.

Feii Lü, *Taiwan Dianying 1994–1999: Zhengzhi, Meixue, Jingji (Taiwan Cinema, 1994–1999: Politics, Aesthetics, Economics)*, Taipei, Yuanliu, 1998.

Stephen Teo, *Hong Kong Cinema: The Extra Dimensions*, London, BFI Publishing, 1997.

Yingjin Zhang, *Chinese National Cinema*, New York, Routledge, 2004.

Lives of contemporary Chinese urban youth explored in Jia Zhangke's film *Pickpocket*

Two Stage Sisters/Wutai Jiemei
(The People's Republic of China 1965
p.c – Shanghai Film Studio; d – Xie Jin)

Two Stage Sisters is one of the most famous and entertaining socialist realist films. Shot in a glossy Chinese Technicolor and set in the 1930s, it opens during a village opera. An escaped child bride called Chunhua hides backstage. The troupe leader's daughter, Yuehong, takes pity on her, and they give her refuge. The class status of entertainers is not as pure as that of workers, farmers or soldiers, who were the preferred protagonists of socialist realist cinema. But the opera world does provide more colourful stories. After they grow up, Yuehong and Chunhua become stars, licensing a glimpse into the glamorous lost world of pre-revolutionary Shanghai. But while Yuehong is corrupted by their manager's gifts of furs and jewels, Chunhua is introduced to left-wing culture by a Communist journalist she meets at an exhibition. This is not surprising, because Chunhua's class background as a child bride is purer than Yuehong's as the daughter of the troupe leader. Eventually, political differences cause the sisters to fall out. But after the revolution, when Chunhua has become the leader of a revolutionary song and dance troupe, they are reunited. In the final scene, the sisters float downstream on a riverboat. Chunhua puts her arm around Yuehong's shoulder and they face the camera cheek-to-cheek as Chunhua says, 'Let us remould ourselves earnestly and always perform revolutionary operas'. The lesson is made crystal clear for the viewers. Throughout the film, shot and reverse-shot sutures the audience into identification with Chunhua, as do devices such as superimpositions rendering her memories. Highly coloured melodramatic devices such as exaggerated villainy and urgent music elicit the appropriate emotions and underscore every point. This is pedagogical cinema writ large. Yet it was banned at the outset of the Cultural Revolution in 1966 because it was not pure enough, and it waited to be discovered in the late 1970s.

CHRIS BERRY

Yellow Earth/Huang Tudi
(The People's Republic of China 1984
p.c – Guangxi Film Studio; *d* – Chen Kaige)

The narrative of *Yellow Earth* could provide the frame for a conventional socialist realist drama like *Two Stage Sisters*. In the 1930s, a soldier from the Communist stronghold of Yan'an comes down to the countryside and lodges with a poor farmer's family. He is collecting folk songs that will be rewritten as revolutionary songs. He discovers terrible poverty and oppressive feudal conditions, under which his daughter Cuiqiao faces forced marriage. The soldier has to return to Yan'an, and the daughter drowns when she tries to cross the Yellow River to join him. Yet, everything about the film undermines socialist realist conventions. The symmetry and gloss of socialist realism gives way to lopsided compositions that simultaneously recall traditional Chinese painting and critical modernism. The farmers are not rosy-cheeked good souls waiting to be liberated. Wizened and obstinate, they remain faithful to feudal beliefs, and there are no oppressive landlords to blame for their condition. When the soldier finally returns to the village, only Cuiqiao's little brother runs towards him. But he cannot get close because the rest of the villagers are running in the other direction as part of a prayer ceremony for rain. As we cut back and forth between the boy and the soldier, the soldier disappears, and the disembodied voice of Cuiqiao sings a lament over the dessicated landscape. The People's Republic is founded on an absolute distinction between the old society and the new. Yet, as the soldier's journey into the shocking countryside echoes the Fifth Generation's own Cultural Revolution experiences, could the real scandal of the film be that it dares to suggest not much has changed?

CHRIS BERRY

Chen Kaige's *Yellow Earth* asks how much has changed between the old and the new China

DANISH CINEMA

Dogme 95

RICHARD T. KELLY

All revolutions in art, the playwright David Hare argues (see Kelly, 2000, p. 10), are a return to realism. Abstract painters and sculptors might beg to differ, but for cinema the claim clearly has integrity. At regular intervals in the medium's short history, particular film-makers have revolted against cinema's extravagant artifice, its wilful estrangement from life as it is lived. Instead they have proposed the camera as a tool to record and expose the world as it truly is. One problem with devising a system for such a purpose was acutely diagnosed by Roberto Rossellini: 'There doesn't exist a technique for capturing truth. Only a moral position can do it' (Gallagher, 1998, p. 267).

In their surveys of a ruined postwar nation, the Italian neo-realists stand at the head of this lineage, though they were disparate talents and made no unified claims. But a few famous realist endeavours have been based on declarations of principle: Dziga Vertov's early experiments in the 1920s *Kino-pravda* series were underscored by manifestoes. In 1956, Lindsay Anderson committed to paper the goals of 'Free Cinema'. The Nouvelle Vague had no code of practice, but one might be constructed from Jean-Luc Godard's compendious pronouncements.

Danish director Lars von Trier seemed an improbable champion of unvarnished realism, in view of the incorrigible style and pretensions of his *The Element of Crime* (1984) and *Europa* (1991), both of which received prizes for *supérieure technique* at Cannes (though Trier himself disdained such baubles). With each film, Trier issued manifestoes seemingly more attuned to the ecstasies of Futurism than the earnest sobriety of the realist vein. But by March 1995, it seemed that Trier, too, wished to get back to basics, in consort with junior colleague Thomas Vinterberg. 'We asked ourselves what we most hated about film today,' Vinterberg later told the press, 'and then we drew up a list banning it all' (quoted in Kelly, 2000, p. 5). They were joined in their project by commercials specialist Kristian Levring and ex-folk singer Soren Kragh-Jacobsen. At a conference on the centenary of cinema held at the Odeon Theatre in Paris (a site integral to the romance of May '68), Trier read this 'Dogme 95'

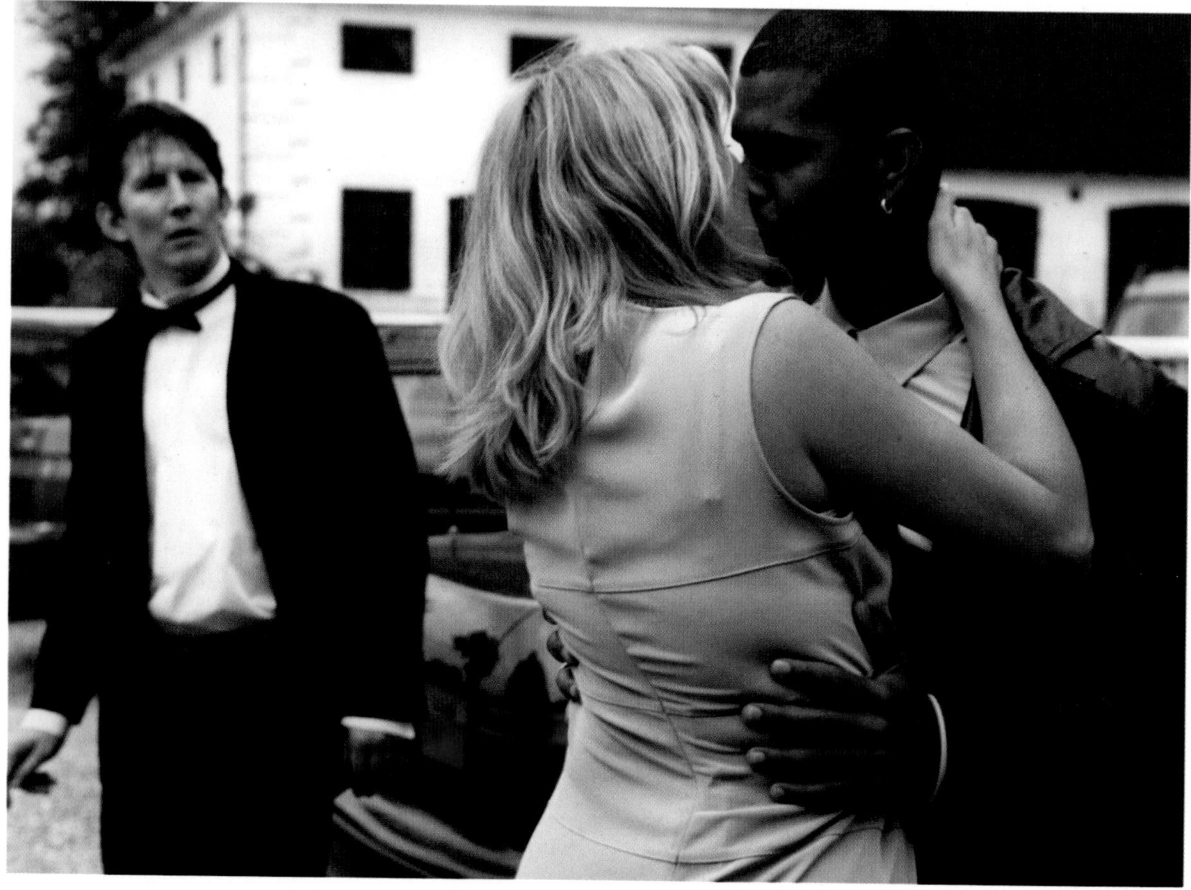

A dark mirror of Danish society: Thomas Vinterberg's disturbing *The Celebration*

manifesto aloud, then hurled into the air facsimiles printed on red paper. Quizzed by bemused journalists, he declared that he was forbidden by his 'brothers' to discuss it.

The manifesto consisted of a grandstanding prose-preamble declaring opposition to '"certain tendencies" in the cinema today' – to 'cosmetics' and 'illusion' wrought by 'trickery'. It then called for directors to pledge allegiance to a ten-point 'Vow of Chastity'. Dogme films would thus be contemporary stories, free of genre conventions and 'superficial action', shot with hand-held cameras on 35mm in natural light at authentic locations, in colour and without post-production tinkering or separation of sound and image. In a riposte to the *politique des auteurs* (see The *politique des auteurs*, p. 390), the director would not be credited.

In the absence of any actual films, critical and industry enthusiasm for Trier's plan was muted. Financing the Dogme venture was not easy, even though Trier's production outlet Zentropa were dab hands at tapping Denmark's generous public purse. Trier secured a promise from culture minister Jytte Hilden, but the Danish Film Institute, whose funding process is based on individual application and consultancy, could not blankly approve a Zentropa slate. Finally, it was the Danish national broadcaster Danmarks Radio that bankrolled the first Dogme films. With budgets tight, these would be shot on digital video and transferred to film (thus finessing the ninth rule, which decreed that 'film format must be Academy 35mm').

Trier had presented all of his earlier films at Cannes, and in May 1998 the festival gave Dogme 95 a fine baptism by selecting both Vinterberg's *The Celebration/Festen (Dogme #1)* and Trier's *The Idiots/Idioterne (Dogme #2)* for competition. Each was keenly watched and weighed up for its rough-hewn form and taboo-testing content (see case studies). *Idioterne* was deemed 'problematic' but *Festen* took a prize from Martin Scorsese's jury and became a huge hit in Denmark. Financing Dogme ceased to be a problem.

Kragh-Jacobsen's *Mifune's Last Song/Mifunes sidste sang (Dogme #3)* then emerged in 1999, a simple, romantic town-and-country comedy, full of stock figures and obligatory scenes. It won the Silver Bear at Berlin and sold to numerous overseas territories. There followed a spate of non-Danish Dogme titles, from France, Korea, Sweden, Argentina – and from the US came Harmony Korine's 1999 *Julien Donkey-Boy (Dogme #6)*. Korine, then 25, director of the unclassifiable *Gummo* (1997) and already an eminence in American avant-garde film, did not need to greatly amend his usual practice in taking the Vow of Chastity, but appeared to offer *Julien* as a gesture of creative solidarity with his Danish brethren.

By now all Dogme manoeuvres underwent scrutiny from the world's film media. The directors had begun to 'confess' to infractions of the rules on the Dogme website, and sceptics started to lambast the movement as a prank and a marketing ploy for Danish film. By late 1999, it was clear that Dogme had become an easy buzz-word for producers planning to shoot cheaply on video. Thomas Vinterberg made public his disillusion: 'Dogme is not meant to be just another low-budget *package*' (quoted in Kelly, 2000, p. 123). That October, the four brothers announced a reformation of the Dogme certification process ('from Catholicism to Protestantism', Kristian Levring joked; quoted in Kelly, 2000, p. 56), stating that they would no longer sit in judgment on submissions.

The worldwide takings for *Mifune's Last Song* proved a letdown after its Berlin sales frenzy, and by the time Levring's *The King Is Alive (Dogme #4)* took a bow at Cannes in May 2000, Dogme looked oversold, and the label a liability – regrettably, as Levring's film was a bitter, brilliant piece about a group of tourists stranded

The Celebration/Festen (Denmark 1998
p.c – Nimbus Film/Danmarks Radio TV/SVT/Nordisk Film och TV fond/Dogme 95; *d* – Thomas Vinterberg)

In 1996, Thomas Vinterberg heard a caller to a Danish talk-radio show testify to the sexual abuse inflicted upon himself and a sibling by their father, relating how he had exposed the evil through a speech at an unsuspecting family celebration. Vinterberg and his former teacher Mogens Rukov worked up this anecdote into the screenplay of *Festen*, observing the Aristotelian unities of time and place and action alongside the rituals of a certain Danish tradition: the decennial birthday dinner, with its ordeal of toasts, speeches and songs.

Autumnal patriarch Helge (Henning Moritzen) summons the extended family to his country mansion for a sixtieth birthday bash. Principal guests include reticent elder son, Christian (Ulrich Thomsen), manic son number two, Michael (Thomas Bo Larsen), and dazed daughter Helene (Paprika Steen). A second daughter has recently committed suicide. The gathering is soon seen to be rotten with fake sentiment and unspoken hatred. In the midst of the stuporous dinner, Christian rises to speak, and wincingly relates how Helge would ritually rape both him and his late sister throughout their childhoods. The cheery gathering slowly turns nasty.

With its well-heeled wardrobe and decor, one could easily imagine *Festen* shot with frosty elegance on 35mm. But digital video and the Dogme vow of chastity fling a much-needed handful of dirt at the material, giving it the feel of a disturbing and regrettable home movie. Cameraman Anthony Dod Mantle hounds the actors (even smacking into one), while the image degrades steadily as the night goes on and light sources fade. Vinterberg has happily professed debts to Henrik Ibsen, Ingmar Bergman, *The Godfather* (1972) and Shakespeare. Christian is a Hamlet figure, painfully aware he must slay the Father. (He is even visited by his sister's ghost.) And Helge certainly goads him: 'It was all you were good for' is as much as he will say of his loathsome crime.

The success of *Festen* surprised Vinterberg. He had not anticipated that audiences the world over would find bogus family get-togethers just as stifling as the Danes, who were evidently startled and gratified to gaze into such a dark mirror of their society. In 2002, the talk-show caller who had been Vinterberg's inspiration was exposed as a fantasist. In 2004, the film was adapted into a hit stage-play, its success in this form a tribute to its structural soundness and thrilling twist, though the recycling of the material for commercial exploitation felt sadly un-Dogme-like.

RICHARD T. KELLY

The Idiots/Idioterne (Denmark/France/Italy/Netherlands/Germany 1998 *p.c* – Zentropa/Danmarks Radio TV/Dogme 95/Sept Cinéma/Canal+/Liberator Productions/Argus Film Produktie/VPRO/ Zweites Deutsches Fernsehen/Nordisk Film och TV fond/Stichting Co-productiefonds Binnenlandse Omroep/SVT Kanal 1 Drama/RAI Cinemafiction/3 Emme Cinematografica; *d* – Lars von Trier)

If *Festen* shows how the Dogme rules could be midwife to a fresh take on the well-made Scandinavian chamber-piece, *Idioterne* shows how the full embrace of same could lead to willed chaos, happy accidents and humiliations. The manifesto challenges the director 'to force the truth out of my characters and settings ... at the cost of any good taste and any aesthetic considerations'. On paper this was an impossibly lofty aspiration, for Lars von Trier more than most.

A rewarding experiment: Lars von Trier's *The Idiots*

Yet Trier had invested deeply in the notion that Dogme 95 was morally bound to shake its devotees out of their bad habits, starting with Trier himself. The child of Euro-Communists, previously wary of actors and their ways, he conceived of *Idioterne* as a social experiment or workshop wherein the process was to be considered as meaningful as the product. 'We'll be as free as in the seventies', he told his company of players at the outset (see Kelly, 2000). They were and they weren't.

'The idiots' of the title are a gaggle of middle-class malcontents who decide to provoke the community about them by publicly masquerading as people with mental disabilities: 'spassing', as they call it. Under the leadership of straw-headed Stoffer (Jens Albinus), they function not unlike the Maoist cell of Godard's *La Chinoise* (1967), making guerrilla sorties from base-camp, retreating to HQ for sessions of self-criticism. Karen (Bodil Jorgensen) drifts into their number, refusing to 'spass' yet finding the group's behaviour charming, even as it starts to fracture under the weight of individual neuroses. Finally Stoffer demands that his disciples 'spass' before their own friends and families. Karen alone obliges, and so we learn that she has been missing from home since the death of her son: the idiot-experiment has done her an uncommon service.

Trier's militant adherence to his own rules inflicted savagery upon his usual style: *Idioterne* looks incredibly messy. And yet, operating a video camera himself, he clearly found a new closeness to his cast wherein he could press them to 'behave' rather than 'perform': all parties seemed to find this rewarding. Less realised was Trier's hope of founding a happy commune: as the cloistered production wore on, he grew gloomily estranged from the gang of younger actors. But the finished film expressed a fineness of feeling not observable in his work before or since. On seeing it, Godard reportedly faxed Trier a note of regard that was gratefully received.

RICHARD T. KELLY

in the Namibian desert who try to preserve their sanities by rehearsing *King Lear*. In March 2000, it was announced that henceforth a Dogme Secretariat would certify films on receipt of a director's sworn statement plus a small fee. By October 2006, more than 100 further films had been thus approved.

What, then, was the sum of Dogme's accomplishment? If a publicity stunt, it had brilliantly diverted global media attention towards some low-budget art movies from Denmark. But, with a point made, the Danes themselves moved on, leaving others to explore the Dogme rules as they wished. Like previous movements, Dogme looked strongest at its origin – distinctively Danish, it was born among graduates of the same outstanding film school, and abetted by a fine home-grown generation of actors. Clearly it reflected something of the national character, since all literate Danes know Aksel Sandermose's 1933 novel *En flyktning krysser sitt spor*, set in an imaginary town called Jante where a prohibitive ten-point code ('You shall not think you are special' and so forth) binds the citizenry.

In the wider context, it is surely fairest to view Dogme 95 as a worthy aspiration and a useful provocation than to interrogate it under hot lights. Trier, a cleverer man than most of his critics, had merely proposed something close to Bresson's maxim: 'To forge for oneself iron laws, if only in order to obey or disobey them *with difficulty*' (Bresson, 1986, p. 110). Dogme 95 was, by Trier's own admission, 'a little game', but one played in great earnest. And in doing so, the director – once a slightly irksome showboat – had made himself honourably useful to current and future debates on what exactly film is for.

Selected Reading

Stig Bjorkman (ed.), *Trier on von Trier*, London and New York, Faber and Faber, 2004.

Richard Kelly, *The Name of This Book Is Dogme 95*, London and New York, Faber and Faber, 2000.

Richard Raskin (ed.), 'Aspects of Dogma 95', *P.O.V. A Danish Journal of Film Studies* 10 (Special Issue), December 2000.

Lars von Trier, *Idioterne. Manuskript og dagbog*, Copenhagen, Gyldendal, 1998.

FRENCH CINEMA

Introduction

GINETTE VINCENDEAU

The Lumière brothers' screening at the Grand Café in Paris on 28 December 1895, which constituted the world's first public cinema screening, is a key landmark in film history. It marked the beginning of a period of rapid technological and industrial expansion in which French companies – Pathé and Gaumont in particular – dominated film trade, exporting films, machines and personnel throughout the world. The established 'grand narrative' of French cinema charts this global hegemony and its demise with World War I, when American cinema took the lead. From that point, the history of French cinema has traditionally been written (Sadoul, 1953; Armes, 1985; Williams, 1992) as a series of discrete moments dominated by great auteurs and aesthetic movements: the 1920s avant-garde, poetic realism in the 1930s (see also French cinema in the 1930s, p. 200) and the Nouvelle Vague (see the Nouvelle Vague, p. 202), by writers with either partial knowledge of, or little sympathy with, indigenous popular genres. However insightful some of these works are, they fail to account for the wealth and variety of a numerically, aesthetically and culturally important output (around 100 to 150 films a year since the early 1930s).

Since the early 1980s, scholarship on French cinema has expanded and changed dramatically under the impulse of the 'new film history', feminism, cultural studies, postcolonial studies as well as studies of nationalism. Also fundamental have been the rise of academic film studies, the greater openness of film archives and the increased availability of films on video and DVD. As a result, popular genres, stars, hitherto neglected periods, viewing practices, cinephilia, the contribution of women and film criticism itself have begun to receive due attention.

The new film history, with its insistence on a scrupulous examination of sources and film texts, on the need for the sample of films studied to be representative of the overall corpus, and on the positioning of the historian, has had an immediate impact in two areas of French film history: early cinema and the German occupation period. The work of Richard Abel (1984; 1994) has been seminal to charting French silent cinema from its pre-cinematic origins to the mature avant-garde of the 1920s, as well as placing it within an international context (see Early and pre-sound cinema, p. 3). From being ignored or dismissed as politically tainted, French cinema made during World War II has become a key object of study, but with a few exceptions (Ehrlich, 1985; Mayne, 2006), these have remained French-based (Bertin-Maghit, 2002). By contrast, the films made after the war that refer to the period (such as *The Sorrow and the Pity/Le Chagrin et la pitié*, 1969–71, or *Farewell to Our Children/Au revoir les enfants*, 1987), following Henry Rousso's groundbreaking study (1991) have proved an enduring object of fascination for international scholars (Lindeperg, 1997; Greene, 1998).

Also marked by historicity but with the added perspective of feminism, several writers have illuminatingly revisited auteur studies. Alison McMahan's volume on Alice Guy-Blaché (2002) explores the world's first woman film-maker, who directed 400 films between 1896 and 1920 in France and then America, where she owned her own studio; yet she was forgotten until her memoirs were published in 1976. Sandy Flitterman-Lewis (1996) reclaims the work of Germaine Dulac, Marie Epstein and Agnès Varda; Carrie Tarr and Brigitte Rollet (2001) examine a much wider sample of women in the explosion that followed the 1970s (see French cinema since the 1980s, p. 204).

If studies of French cinema from a feminist perspective have boosted much work in Britain (Hayward, 1993) and the US, the same cannot be said of France, still largely resistant to 'Anglo-Saxon' feminism. One exception is Noël Burch and Geneviève Sellier's (1996) re-examination of classical production from 1930 to 1960 in terms of gender relations. Their insightful analyses across an exhaustive corpus show that great auteurs and metteurs en scène alike portray gender relations in ways that chime with the historical context: the father-dominated 1930s, the 'weak masculinity' of the war years and the backlash against women in the postwar period. Burch and Sellier draw their methodology from both feminism and cultural studies, a combination – together with a wider conception of national identity – that has been most productive. Thus, studies have shifted from the director as auteur to the French star system and French stars (Vincendeau, 2000; Austin, 2003), to genre cinema (Moine, 2002), to the practice of popular film viewing in the postwar period (Montebello, 2005) or film criticism (de Baecque, 2003; Marie, 2005), to French films in relation to their Hollywood remakes (Durham, 1998; Mazdon, 2000). It is indicative in this respect that Michael Temple and Michael Witt's *The French Cinema*

Hidden from history: Alice Guy Blaché, the world's first woman film-maker

Book (2004) is organised around sections such as 'spectators' and 'business', along the more traditional 'forms', and that anthologies based around single films or groups of films now all include popular films (Hayward and Vincendeau, 2000; Hughes and Williams, 2001; Powrie, 2005).

Perhaps inevitably, this long revisionist labour also coalesces around canonical movements and directors. Thus, while directors such as Jean Renoir and Jean-Luc Godard continue to trigger reverential studies (Temple, Williams and Witt, 2004), new work brings different perspectives – for instance, gender studies of François Truffaut (Holmes and Ingram, 1997), Renoir (O'Shaughnessy, 2000) or Jean-Pierre Melville (Vincendeau, 2003), while Jean-Pierre Esquenazi's (2004) iconoclastic study drastically recasts Godard's politics in the 1960s.

Most revisited in recent years has been the Nouvelle Vague, a rereading made possible partly by its converse: a greater knowledge of the mainstream cinema that preceded it. Taking Truffaut at his word in his much-quoted vitriolic attack on the 'Tradition of Quality' (1954), critics routinely portrayed the Nouvelle Vague as a radical break from a mainstream cinema that was economically shaky or moribund (see The Nouvelle Vague, p. 202) – a view challenged by the most cursory look at production and exhibition figures; indeed, the 1950s were the heyday of popular cinema viewing in France, with a relatively stable genre and star system. Colin Crisp (1993) rightly argued that the Nouvelle Vague had more in common with what preceded it than had been maintained. Since then, Antoine de Baecque (1998) has delved into the fascinating socio-cultural context of youth at the time of the Nouvelle Vague; Michel Marie (1997) has usefully put the accent on the critical context and the key role of independent producers (challenging another cliché, that the early Nouvelle Vague films were state financed), a view expanded on by Richard Neupert (2002). A still more radical challenge comes from Geneviève Sellier (2005), who comprehensively exposes the paradox of a cinema that for all its charm and aesthetic innovation is ideologically conservative (or at least ambivalent), both in terms of politics and in its representation of femininity.

With the expansion of academic studies of French cinema in Britain and the US, the period that is proportionately receiving the greatest attention in English-language publications is that of the post-1980 era (see French cinema since the 1980s, p. 204), leaving still vast tracks unexplored, such as the popular cinema of the 1960s and 1970s. Thus, while an ever-widening spectrum of approaches now addresses French cinema in its aesthetic, cultural and ideological wealth and complexity, there is still scope for further study.

Selected Reading

Susan Hayward, *French National Cinema*, London and New York, Routledge, 1993.

Richard Neupert, *A History of the French New Wave Cinema*, Madison, University of Wisconsin Press, 2002.

Michael Temple and Michael Witt (eds), *The French Cinema Book*, London, BFI Publishing, 2004.

Ginette Vincendeau, *Stars and Stardom in French Cinema*, London and New York, Continuum, 2000.

Jean-Pierre Melville revisited: Alain Delon in *Le Samouraï*

French cinema in the 1930s

LUCY MAZDON

The powerful position occupied by the French film industry in the early years of the 20th century was to prove short-lived. The impact of World War I, along with a failure to keep up with technical developments, meant that by the end of the 1920s French film production was at an all-time low, contributing less than a quarter of the films screened in the domestic market. The gradual demise of the two major French studios, Gaumont and Pathé-Natan, culminating in their eventual collapse in 1934 and 1936 respectively, left the industry highly vulnerable to foreign competition. Moreover, French cinema was slow to adapt to sound technology, only managing to equip a handful of studios and cinemas by 1929. Technical ineptitude was matched by an aesthetic resistance on the part of some of the leading film-makers and critics of the day, who regarded sound cinema as the death knell of the experimental and the avant-garde. Jean-Pierre Jeancolas (1983) has described the early days of sound film in France as a dreadful regression, typified by clumsily produced films and the often poor-quality multilingual versions made by American studios and French producers alike.

However, by 1931 soundtrack-mixing technology had improved and in 1932 the introduction of dubbing and subtitling meant the gradual abandonment of the shooting of costly multiple versions. French film-makers, including figures such as René Clair, who had previously expressed hostility to the new technology, began to produce films that could rival their silent predecessors in terms of both commercial and critical success. Production rose from around 94 films in 1930 to 158 in 1933, gradually stabilising at between 100 and 120 films throughout the rest of the decade. Stars such as Jean Gabin, Arletty and Annabella proved highly popular with domestic audiences and many of the major box-office hits of the decade were French. Nevertheless, the industry itself did not achieve the economic or industrial stability taking root in Hollywood in the same period. It remained technically impoverished and decentralised with around 70 independent producers making one or two films a year. However, as Colin Crisp (1993; 2002) has argued, it was in spite of or perhaps even due to this industrial instability that French cinema of the 1930s flourished. French film-makers enjoyed an artistic freedom not always available to those working in the Hollywood studio system. The fragmentation of the industry resulted in great diversification in access to capital and distribution, while the absence of an over-arching censorship mechanism akin to the Hays Code was also significant. While French film-makers were subject to the authority of the *Commission de contrôle*, often strict on political and religious grounds, and occasional local censorship, they were accorded a greater degree of 'moral' liberty than their Hollywood counterparts. Interestingly, the first script of *Algiers*, John Cromwell's 1938 remake of Julien Duvivier's *Pépé le Moko* (1937), was deemed unacceptable by the Hays Office for its depiction of 'kept women', references to sex appeal, the promiscuity of Pépé and his suicide at the end of the film to escape punishment. All of this features in the original film.

Film historians have commonly described this period as a 'golden age' in French cinema. Given the nature of the industry at the time and the specific historical context of a society caught between two devastating wars and struggling under profound economic and political instability, it is perhaps surprising to see the cinema of the 1930s described in these terms. However, the period has long been held up as a high point in film history due to a very specific body of work and the input of a number of key personnel. This body of work is often described, perhaps somewhat lazily, as 'poetic realism'. Not all of the 'great' films of the 1930s are poetic realist – Renoir's *La Grande Illusion* (1937) is a case in point – and yet there is a critical tendency to use it to describe any film that deviated from the theatrical films that dominated the early years of the decade. In his seminal work on the period, Dudley Andrew (1995) argues that while poetic realism as a movement was instrumental in bringing French cinema back to critical acclaim, it only fully applies to a number of films made between 1936 and 1939 (from the birth of the Popular Front to the outbreak of World War II). Crucially, Andrew describes poetic realism as a sensibility or a mode of address that enabled 'true' poetic realist films to share with their audience a sense of immediacy and identification. Key features of the poetic realist style, exemplified in films such as Marcel Carné's *Quay of Shadows/Quai des brumes* (1938), include working-class characters often on the margins of society, evocative and yet recognisable locations, a shift from action towards milieu and atmosphere, a dark and pessimistic ending and the recurring presence of particular actors (notably Gabin, with his striking portraits of the working-class male in crisis, famously described by André Bazin as 'Oedipus in a cloth cap'). Despite these shared traits, Andrew argues that where the movement fully coheres is in its particular mode of audience address. Its bleakly fatalistic tone, its depiction of passive and powerless protagonists and its appeal to emotions over intellect assume on the part of the contemporary audience an understanding and an empathy with this dark and ambivalent worldview.

Andrew is very careful to trace the rich and complex lineage of poetic realism from the novels of Emile Zola, through other literary and artistic forms, to its links with the cinematic surrealism of the likes of Clair and Jean Vigo. This is important not only as it demonstrates the interconnections between film and other cultural forms; it also reminds us that poetic realism was not the only type of cinema produced in France in the 1930s. Indeed, Andrew points out that poetic realist films (defined according to his terms) represent only about 100 of the 1,275 films made in the decade. The subsequent canonisation of these films runs the risk of eclipsing other cinematic forms that proved much more attractive to the cinemagoing public. Musicals were hugely popular in the early years of the decade and stars such as Josephine Baker, Mistinguett and Maurice Chevalier made the transition from stage to screen. The so-called *comique troupier*, a series of comic military films with roots in vaudeville and popular theatre brought the likes of Georges Milton and Fernandel to popular acclaim. Along with the filmed theatre of writer/directors such as Sacha Guitry and Marcel Pagnol, these films made up the *cinéma du sam'di soir*, popular cinema that combined with, and eventually replaced, other forms of entertainment.

Exemplary 'poetic realism': Marcel Carné's *Le Quai des brumes*

The construction of a 'canon' of great films is telling, as it typifies a long-standing critical and academic tendency to ignore popular cinema in favour of the work of 'great directors'. In the case of French cinema, this has played a significant role in fostering a limiting notion of French film as 'art' film. Writers such as Vincendeau (1985) and Crisp (2002) have begun a deconstruction of this canon via an analysis of many of the popular genres and popular cinemagoing habits of the period. However, the notion of a 'golden age' persists and is both reflected in and engendered by the dominance of the work of the 'great' auteurs on video and DVD release.

Selected Reading

Dudley Andrew, *Mists of Regret: Culture and Sensibility in Classic French Film*, Princeton, NJ, Princeton University Press, 1995.

Jonathan Buschbaum, *Cinema Engagé: Film in the Popular Front*, Urbana, University of Illinois Press, 1988.

Colin Crisp, *Genre, Myth, and Convention in the French Cinema, 1929–1939*, Bloomington, Indiana University Press, 2002.

Ginette Vincendeau, 'Anatomy of a myth: Jean Gabin', *Nottingham French Studies* 32 (1): 19–31, 1993.

Carnival in Flanders/La Kermesse héroïque
(France 1935 *p.c* – Films Sonores Tobis;
d – Jacques Feyder)

Feyder's satire is set in Flanders in the early 17th century. The arrival of a Spanish army regiment provokes uproar and a battle of the sexes among the town's citizens, setting the feisty wife of the burgomaster (Françoise Rosay) against her weak and pompous husband (André Alerme). Clearly not a poetic realist work, the film reveals much about production of the period. The input of figures such as Alexandre Trauner, Charles Spaak, Georges Wakhevitch and Marcel Carné is striking, as it recalls the collaborative nature of film-making of the decade and the crucial input of immigrant personnel. Particularly noteworthy is the work of art director Lazare Meerson and his intricate recreation of the Flemish town of Boom. Upon release, the film was met with commercial and critical acclaim yet also provoked controversy, notably in Belgium (Feyder's country of origin), where people took to the streets protesting at its apparent allusions to Flemish collaboration with German forces in World War I. These accusations were exacerbated by German investment in the film's production and the 1936 release of a German version of the film – *The Clever Woman/Die klugen Frauen* – also directed by Feyder and starring Rosay, and which gained a Best Director award at the fascist-organised 1936 Venice Film Festival. Unlike other contemporary directors such as Renoir, Feyder here eschews contemporary themes and settings in favour of a historical costume drama. Nevertheless, his film was interpreted by many as a rather partisan response to the political exigencies of the day.

Historical satire: Françoise Rosay in *La Kermesse héroïque*

LUCY MAZDON

The Nouvelle Vague

ANNETTE KUHN

The Nouvelle Vague (French New Wave) blossomed for a brief period in the history of French cinema – between 1959 and 1963 – when certain historical, technological and economic factors combined to enable some young film-makers to influence French cinema temporarily in diverse ways. Commentators on the Nouvelle Vague have tended to focus on the film-makers, ignoring the combination of factors that permitted them to work in the way they did. Roy Armes, for example, attributed the development of a film-making new wave to the emergence of a new generation of critics-turned-film-makers. According to Armes, at the beginning of the 1950s:

> [T]he French cinema presented, on the surface at least, a rather depressing and moribund scene. No new director of the first rank had emerged ... since 1949 and the veteran directors were showing their first signs of lassitude. Experiment was rare and the newcomers of the 40s were moving towards big-budget films and international co-productions ... But beneath the surface things were stirring. Young critics under the guidance of André Bazin were laying the foundations of a new approach, particularly in *Cahiers du cinéma*. (Armes, 1970, p. 7; see French Cinema, p. 200)

James Monaco begins more cautiously with the term 'new wave' itself, admitting that, like most such critical labels, it resists easy definition. According to Monaco, the term was first used by Françoise Giroud in 1958 to refer to a 'youthful' spirit in contemporary cinema, but it swiftly became a synonym for the avant-garde in general. For Monaco himself, however, the term refers much more specifically to the work during a certain period of five film-makers – François Truffaut, Jean-Luc Godard, Claude Chabrol, Eric Rohmer and Jacques Rivette – who shared a common film intellectual background influenced on the one hand by Henri Langlois, founder of the Cinémathèque Française, and on the other by André Bazin, co-founder of the film magazine *Cahiers du cinéma*: 'Astruc sounded the call; Langlois provided the material; Bazin supplied the basic architectonics. In the pages of *Cahiers du cinéma* in the 1950s, Truffaut, Godard, Chabrol, Rohmer and Rivette argued out a new theory of film' (Monaco, 1976, p. vii).

This theory hinged on two crucial propositions: the first was that of individual authorship in cinema, the *politique des auteurs* (see The *politique des auteurs*, p. 390); the second was that of cinematic genre, of creative conventions in film language. Although simple enough, these ideas seemed perverse, and indeed they served a polemical function in the context of critical attitudes at the time. The Nouvelle Vague directors have been considered as a unitary group, therefore, largely on the grounds of their common intellectual background. The five film-makers isolated by Monaco, for example, had all written for

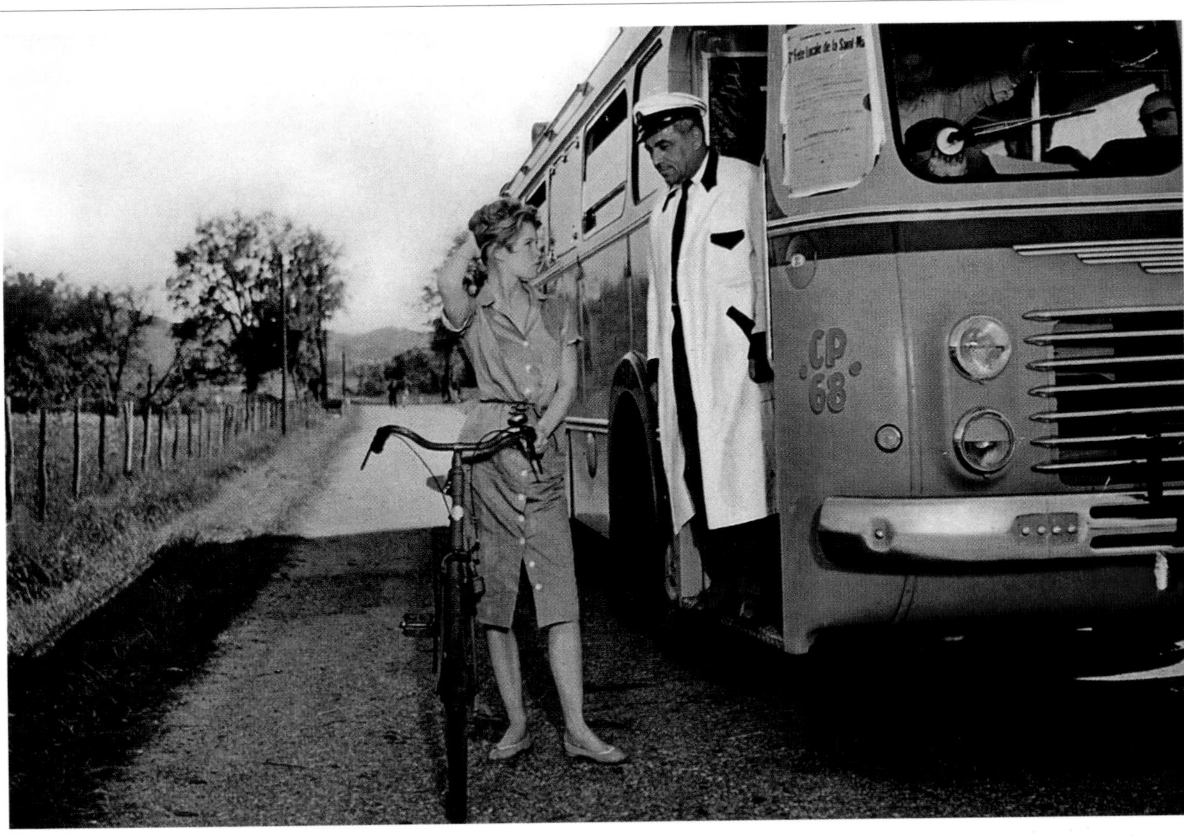

Low-budget success: Brigitte Bardot in Roger Vadim's *Et Dieu créa … la femme*

Cahiers du cinéma, and even other directors associated with the Nouvelle Vague who had not been critics had usually learned about cinema as consumers rather than as producers: of all the major film-makers of the Nouvelle Vague, only Alexandre Astruc, Roger Vadim and Louis Malle had any previous experience in the film industry.

Armes and Monaco are thus able to explain the Nouvelle Vague aesthetic in terms of film criticism, pointing to a critical response to French cinema of the 1940s – a cinema of classical virtues, literary scripts, smooth photography and elegant decor. These virtues had been repeatedly attacked by Truffaut, among others, in the pages of *Cahiers du cinéma*. By contrast, the Nouvelle Vague aesthetic was improvisational (unscripted), and its photography and editing were far less mannered than those of its predecessors. The fragmented style of many new wave films thus came in part as a response to the cohesiveness of 'quality' French cinema. Apparent improvisations in camera technique (the long take, the freeze-frame), editing (the jump-cut), dialogue, plot and performance were all deployed, because cinema was seen for the first time not as a neutral form through which something else (literature or 'reality') could be transmitted, but as a specific aesthetic system, a language in itself.

Why was this aesthetic initiative undertaken when it was? One of the Nouvelle Vague directors, François Truffaut, has described how: 'At the end of 1959 there was a kind of euphoric ease in production that would have been unthinkable a couple of years earlier' (Graham, 1968, p. 9). According to Raymond Durgnat:

> The invention of fast emulsions led to low budgets, minimum crews, location work and 'independent' finance. These new styles in aesthetics and production accompany new thematic perspectives … Commercially, the *raison d'être* of the New Wave was a renewal of tone and theme (the industry was already speaking of a '*crise des sujets*') and the cheapness of the films' budgets. (Durgnat, 1963, pp. 3–4)

During the 1950s, the film industry in France had been very closed. However, when Roger Vadim's film *And God Created Woman/Et Dieu … créa la femme* (1956) was a commercial success despite its low budget, the industry did open its doors for a while to low-budget productions, encouraging a climate of experimentation. The Nouvelle Vague constituted an attempt to make saleable films cheaply through reduced shooting schedules, the use of natural locations, day and night shooting out in the streets and the employment of small units. The Nouvelle Vague may in fact be compared with Italian Neo-realism in this respect, since both operated under similar material constraints. However, the influence of television is also apparent in French new wave cinema in a way it could not be in neo-realism. 'A certain kind of reportage and "direct" camera (shooting with a handheld camera; an acting style closer to the interview than the theatre) came into fashion …' (Siclier, 1961, p. 117).

Terry Lovell (1972) offers an outline of the characteristic qualities of Nouvelle Vague film-making, pointing to its focus on alienated, disaffected individuals who had no contact with society. She describes a number of the social conditions underlying the existence of the new wave: the advent of Gaullism, peace in Algeria, the postwar economic miracle and a crisis in the role of the French intellectual. However, she places greater emphasis on determinants relating more immediately to cinema and the film industry. According to Lovell, a significant feature of the industrial context of the Nouvelle Vague was the horizontal structure of the French film industry – in contrast with the vertical integration of the American industry (see The clas-

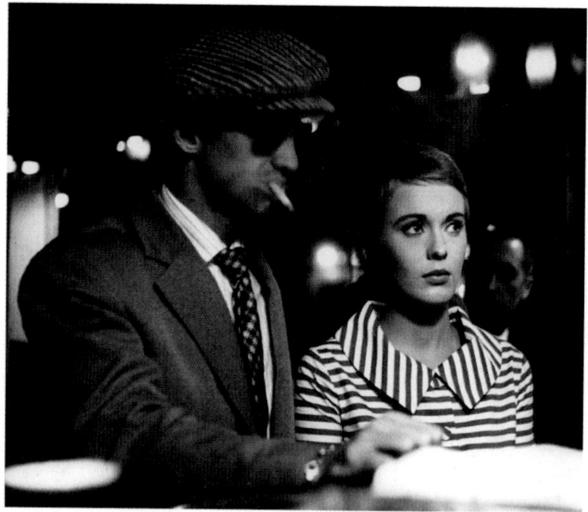

Café culture: Jean-Luc Godard's *À bout de souffle*

sic studio system, p. 19) – and the fact that state intervention in French film production is greater than in any other non-socialist country. She also points to the impact of the crisis in the French industry following World War II (Lovell, 1972, pp. 345–6). Lovell concludes that in spite of the considerable critical, theoretical and aesthetic achievements of the French new wave, at the structural level of the industry it resulted in little change, with controls being if anything tighter than they had been previously (Lovell, 1972, pp. 346–7).

Although the Nouvelle Vague is thought of as a national movement, it also had some distinctly international traits. It could be argued that its self-conscious references to Hollywood were an attempt to provide effective competition for the American films that threatened to invade French cinema screens, and at the same time make inroads into the American home market itself. Moreover, French new wave films made explicit reference to other national and international film movements: Italian Neo-realism, for example, and European art cinema, which, although primarily deployed for aesthetic reasons, could help their insertion into other European markets. A number of Nouvelle Vague films were European co-productions: Louis Malle's *Le Feu follet* (1963) was a French–Italian co-production; Alain Resnais's *The War Is Over/La Guerre est finie* (1966) was French–Swedish; Godard's *Pierrot le fou* (1965) was French–Italian, as was Jacques Rozier's *Adieu Philippine* (1962). The looseness of the plots of these films – as of other productions of this period – together with the often minimal and desultory dialogue, the fragmented scenes and shots, may perhaps have made them more easily understood by foreign audiences, who would also probably recognise the familiar Parisian and/or Mediterranean locations. It may even be argued that the geographical locations of Nouvelle Vague films correspond to a tourist's view of France in general and of Paris in particular – the café (*La Peau douce*, 1964; *À bout de souffle*, 1960; *Bande à part*, 1964; *Masculin féminin*, 1966); the airport (*Une femme mariée*, 1964; *Bande à part*); Paris streets at night (*Les Quatre cents coups*, 1959; *La Peau douce*; *À bout de souffle*; *Une femme mariée*; *Bande à part*; *Masculin féminin*); and sun-drenched summer in the countryside (*Pierrot le fou*, 1965). And the Nouvelle Vague had its own easily recognisable 'stars' – for example, Jean-Paul Belmondo in *À bout de souffle* and *Pierrot le fou*, Jeanne Moreau in *Jules et Jim* (1962), Jean-Pierre Léaud in *Les Quatre cents coups* and *Masculin féminin* – whose international familiarity might ease the films' insertion into both domestic and foreign markets.

Selected Reading

Peter Graham (ed.), *The New Wave: Critical Landmarks*, London, Secker and Warburg/BFI, 1968.

James Monaco, *The New Wave: Truffaut, Godard, Chabrol, Rohmer, Rivette*, New York, Oxford University Press, 1976. Reprinted by Harbor Electronic Publishing, 2004.

Ginette Vincendeau (ed.), *The Companion to French Cinema*, London, Cassell/BFI, 1996.

French cinema since the 1980s

GINETTE VINCENDEAU

In marked contrast to Thatcher's Britain, the arrival of François Mitterrand's Socialist government in 1981 emphatically stressed increased state help for French cinema, the policies of culture minister Jack Lang boosting support for the French 'cultural exception' that culminated in the GATT agreements of 1994. Fast-forwarding to October 2005, the revamped Cinémathèque Française reopened in Paris with four repertory cinemas, a gallery and a research library, while independent distributor Marin Karmitz inaugurated several multi-screen art cinemas (MK2), in a city already blessed with a high concentration of cinemas. Yet at the same time, French cinema continues to struggle for survival against spiralling costs of production and exhibition (aggravated by the imminent arrival of digital projection), competition from home viewing with television, DVD and the Internet, labour unrest among actors and Hollywood blockbusters.

French film production during the 1980s was buoyant, with about 120–140 theatrically distributed films every year, including a significant proportion of first films. Yet the overall decline in audiences remained a problem, and the decade saw, for the first time, American films overtake French films at the domestic box office (although the 40 per cent market share for indigenous films is still healthy compared with the rest of Europe). The period also witnessed the accelerating imbrication of film and television in terms of finance, exhibition and personnel.

The 3,000 or so films made in France since 1980 divide along the familiar lines of critically approved, 'small' auteur films, and popular movies that mostly fall foul of the French critical establishment, with various crossovers. Among these, the 1980s saw the rise of three major trends: heritage films, the *cinéma du look* and *cinéma beur*. Bertrand Tavernier's *Sunday in the Country/Un dimanche à la campagne* (1984) and especially Claude Berri's *Jean de Florette* and *Manon des sources* (1986) kick-started the heritage trend (see also Heritage cinema, p. 292), which continued with films such as *Camille Claudel* (1988) and *Cyrano de Bergerac* (1990). These spectacular evocations of the cultural patrimony continued in the 1990s. However, Patrice Chéreau's *La Reine Margot* (1994) indicated both a move by auteurs to the genre and a 'post-heritage' increase in violence and sexuality. The films are characterised by large budgets and major stars such as Gérard Depardieu, Catherine Deneuve and Isabelle Adjani.

Also with high production values, but radically different was the *cinéma du look* – exemplified by films such as *Diva* (1981), *Betty Blue/37°2 le matin* (1986), *Subway* (1985), *Nikita* (1990) and *Léon* (1994). These postmodern, youth-oriented films, borrowing from music videos and advertising, like the heritage films incurred critical wrath in France for their 'postcard aesthetics' and ignorance of the cinema (Daney, 2001), but sparked interest in Anglo-American criticism, more open to popular genres

THE NEW FRENCH EXTREMISM

Coined by James Quandt in 2004, 'New French Extremism' describes a trend in French films marked by transgressive narratives that combine violence with extreme sexuality (*Anatomy of Hell/Anatomie de l'enfer*, 2004) or pornography (*Baise-moi*, 2000), as well as shocking acts such as rape (*Fat Girl/À ma soeur!*, 2001; *Irréversible*, 2002; *Twentynine Palms*, 2003), necrophilia (*My Mother/Ma mère*, 2004), cannibalism (*Trouble Every Day*, 2001) and self-mutilation (*In My Skin/Dans ma peau*, 2002). Such extremes exist in other national cinemas too; but cultural specificity lies in the films' relationship to intellectually respectable erotic literature (from de Sade and Georges Bataille to Catherine Millet, Michel Houellebecq and Virginie Despentes), Surrealism, soft-core movies such as *Emmanuelle* (1974), explorations of sexuality by art film-makers (Bernardo Bertolucci, Louis Malle, Jean-Luc Godard) and cult exploitation figures (Jean Rollin).

Testing limits: Cathérine Breillat's *Romance*

The New French Extremism is disparate, but most films belong to auteur cinema. Catherine Breillat emerged as a figurehead with *Romance* (1999), *À ma soeur!*, *Sex Is Comedy* (2002) and *Anatomy of Hell*, and others such as Claire Denis, Philippe Gandrieux, Gaspar Noé, Bruno Dumont, Patrice Chéreau and Marina de Van are linked with it. The films are united by a desire to blur boundaries: between auteur and popular cinema, good and bad taste, high and low culture. Frequently, they import features of porn into art cinema, although thanks to their auteur status, they tend to escape censorship. While academic work explores this cinema's testing of limits (the body, the abject, sexuality in the postmodern context), mainstream media focuses on what is seen as empty provocation or a moral and political void in French society. The label helps the export of French cinema, reinforcing cultural stereotypes of Frenchness, while fitting with the global rising tide of sex and violence and appealing to younger audiences.

GINETTE VINCENDEAU

FRANÇOIS OZON

The prolific François Ozon (born 1967) occupies a distinctive place in French cinema in three ways: as a successful crossover from auteur to popular cinema, as a cinephile film-maker (paying tribute to Rainer Werner Fassbinder, George Cukor and Douglas Sirk, among others) and, last but not least, as France's first openly queer mainstream director.

A graduate of the Paris film school La Fémis, Ozon made several shorts with gay and/or extreme themes dealing with the body and the abject. *See the Sea/Regarde la mer* (1997) stirred up controversy over a scene in which a woman uses a toothbrush that has been dipped in excrement. In *Sitcom* (1998), he moved to a Buñuelian critique of the family. From that point on, Ozon's work fell within two paradigms: the comic demolition of bourgeois values (*Sitcom*; *8 femmes*, 2002; *Swimming Pool*, 2003) and understated, sombre dramas (*Under the Sand/Sous le sable*, 2001; *5x2*, 2004; *Time to Leave/Le Temps qui reste*, 2005). Stylistically, these films are, up to a point, united by pastiche and theatricality and a play on gender and sexuality, fitting notions of postmodern cinema. *Sous le sable*, *8 femmes* and *Swimming Pool* combine a fascination with beautiful ageing actresses (such as Charlotte Rampling in *Sous le sable* and *Swimming Pool*) with a ferocious undercurrent of misogyny, as they endlessly mourn the loss of their youth and sexual power. It is perhaps no accident that these have been his most popular films.

Postmodern play: François Ozon's *Le Temps qui reste*

To some extent, Ozon's popular success in France has been predicated on the erasure of his queer identity, while the latter, and his destabilisation of gender and sexuality, is central to the interest in his work outside France. But the fact that he was able to broach these topics in mainstream cinema was in itself a breakthrough.

GINETTE VINCENDEAU

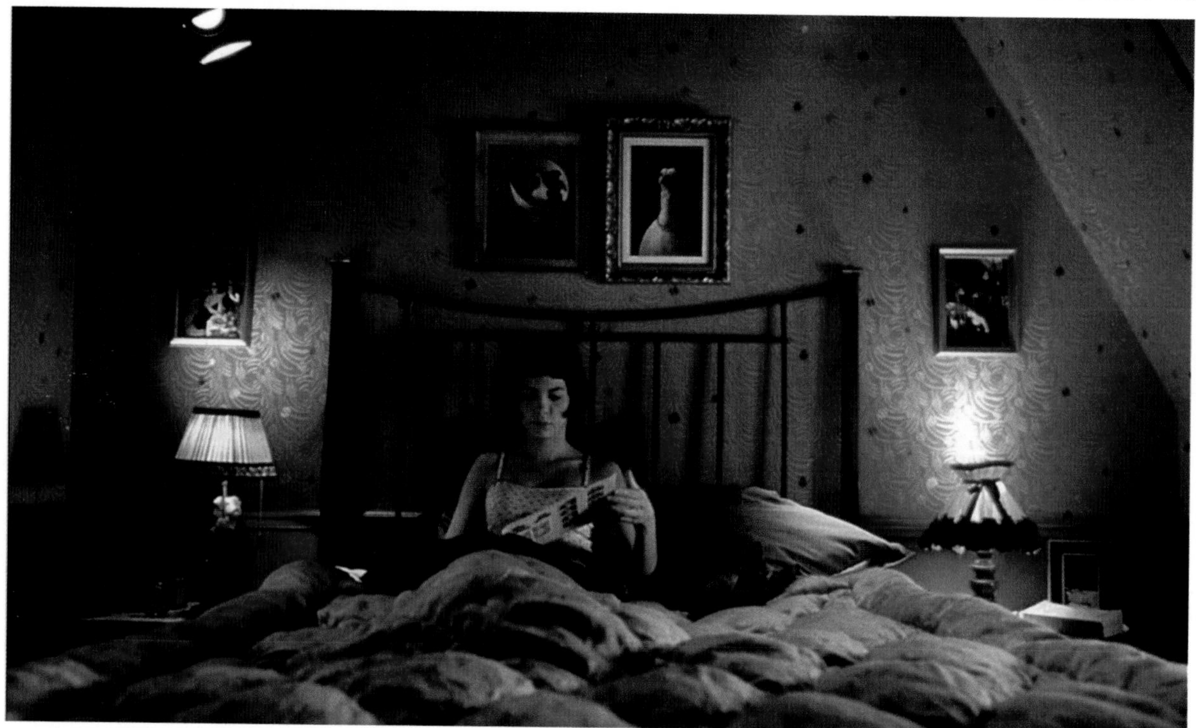

Successfully competing with Hollywood: Audrey Tatou in Jean-Pierre Jeunet's *Amélie*

and stars (Hayward, 1998; Powrie, 1997; 1999). Both heritage films and *cinéma du look* marked a return to studio aesthetics. One counter-trend was *cinéma beur*, by second-generation North African immigrants. Mehdi Charef's *Tea in the Harem/Le Thé au harem d'Archimède* (1985), among others, documented the plight of this 'minority' caught between French and Maghrebi cultures through narratives of male youth in working-class *banlieues*. While underplaying racism, the films echo the rising awareness of multi-ethnicity in the country (Bosséno, 1992; Tarr, 2005).

Paradoxically, in the 1990s as France moved to a right-wing regime, socially aware films blossomed under the heading of the *jeune cinéma français* (Prédal, 2002; Beugnet, 2000). Over 300 young French film-makers made their debut, supported by journals such as *Cahiers du cinéma*, *Positif* and *Les Inrockuptibles*, as well as prizes, state finance (one-third obtained the *avance sur recettes*) and television channels Arte and Canal+. *Jeune cinéma français* includes Xavier Beauvois, Arnaud Despleshin, Eric Zonca, Sandrine Veysset, Laetitia Masson, Laurent Cantet and Bruno Dumont, who make art films for a select audience. Others opt for more spectacular, genre-oriented cinema: Mathieu Kassovitz (who directed the international hit *Hate/La Haine* in 1995), Gaspar Noé, Jan Kounen and Christophe Gans, who make films replete with sex and violence appealing to a broader, younger audience (see New French extremism, p. 205). Generally though, and despite eschewing politics, the *jeune cinéma français* is remarkable for its combination of stylishness with an address to social issues and underclass or marginal protagonists. Shot on location in unglamorous surroundings, it offers a 'new realism' in tune with 1990s humanitarian issues such as police violence, AIDS, unemployment and immigration – on 11 February 1997, a group of 66 film-makers signed a petition calling for civil disobedience to help the *sans papiers* (illegal immigrants). In line with this socially conscious cinema is the renaissance of documentary: Agnès Varda's *The Gleaners and I/Les Glâneurs et la glâneuse* (2000); Nicolas Philibert's *To Be and to Have/ Être et avoir* (2002).

In the early 21st century, ethnic and sexual diversity has become a hallmark, with openly gay directors reaching the mainstream (see François Ozon case study), *beur* actors such as Samy Naceri, Jamel Debbouze and Roschdy Zem (all of whom starred in *Indigènes*, 2006) reaching the limelight, and a steady rise in the numbers of women film-makers, who now make up about a third of all French directors, one of the highest rates worldwide (Tarr with Rollet, 2001). On the other hand, continuity is in evidence with Nouvelle Vague film-makers (Godard, Rohmer, Rivette, Chabrol and Resnais) still active. The period has also seen the continuing popularity of indigenous comedy with *The Visitors/Les Visiteurs* (1993), *Amélie* (2001) and *The Chorus/Les Choristes* (2004), films sometimes viciously attacked as reactionary nostalgia, yet which have achieved success against Hollywood blockbusters. While the film industry sees itself in a permanent state of crisis, in 2004 film critic and historian Jean-Michel Frodon claimed French cinema as 'the first in the world' in terms of the variety of films it was able to sustain. What sounds like a chauvinistic boast nevertheless reflects the continued vitality of film production and film culture in France over the last 25 years.

Selected Reading

Elizabeth Ezra and Sue Harris (eds), *France in Focus: Film and National Identity*, Oxford, Berg, 2000.

Phil Powrie, *French Cinema in the 1980s: Nostalgia and the Crisis of Masculinity*, Oxford, Clarendon Press, 1997.

Phil Powrie (ed.), *French Cinema in the 1990s: Continuity and Difference*, Oxford, Oxford University Press, 1999.

Carrie Tarr with Brigitte Rollet, *Cinema and the Second Sex: Women's Filmmaking in France in the 1980s and 1990s*, London and New York, Continuum, 2001.

GERMAN CINEMA

Introduction

TIM BERGFELDER

Unlike other national cinemas, which developed in the context of relatively continuous and stable political systems, Germany witnessed fundamental changes to its identity during the 20th century. This has determined the periodisation of its national cinema into a succession of distinct eras and movements: the pioneering early films (1895–1918) made during the Wilhelmine monarchy; the cinema of the Weimar Republic (1918–33); the state-controlled film of the Third Reich (1933–45); an interim post-World War II occupation period (1945–9); two parallel German states in the Communist east and the capitalist west from the late 1940s to the late 1980s (with parallel and separate film industries); and finally the cinema of a reunified Germany from 1990 onwards.

Until recently, critical engagement with German film concentrated almost exclusively on three periods of its fragmented history. The first is Weimar cinema with its innovations in the fields of cinematography and set design. Weimar cinema is also known for its presumed stylistic influence on Hollywood genres such as film noir and horror, and for its acclaimed auteurs Fritz Lang (*Metropolis*, 1927), F. W. Murnau (*Nosferatu the Vampire/Nosferatu eine Symphonie des Grauens*, 1922) and G. W. Pabst (*Pandora's Box/Die Büchse der Pandora*, 1928). The second period to receive critical attention has been Nazi cinema, with its mobilisation and exploitation of film industry and technology for propaganda purposes (for example, Leni Riefenstahl's *Triumph of the Will/Triumph des Willens*, 1936, or Veit Harlan's anti-Semitic *Jew Süss/Jud Süß*, 1940). The third most commonly discussed era of German film history is the democratic reinvention of a national film culture by the generation of the West German 'New German Cinema' in the 1970s and 1980s.

Since the early 1990s, film historians have begun to fill the gaps concerning other aspects of German cinema, while standard perceptions of Weimar and Nazi cinema have been challenged or revised. Previously seen as an insignificant precursor to the more sophisticated 1920s, the films of the Wilhelmine period have been reassessed as constituting a significant achieve-

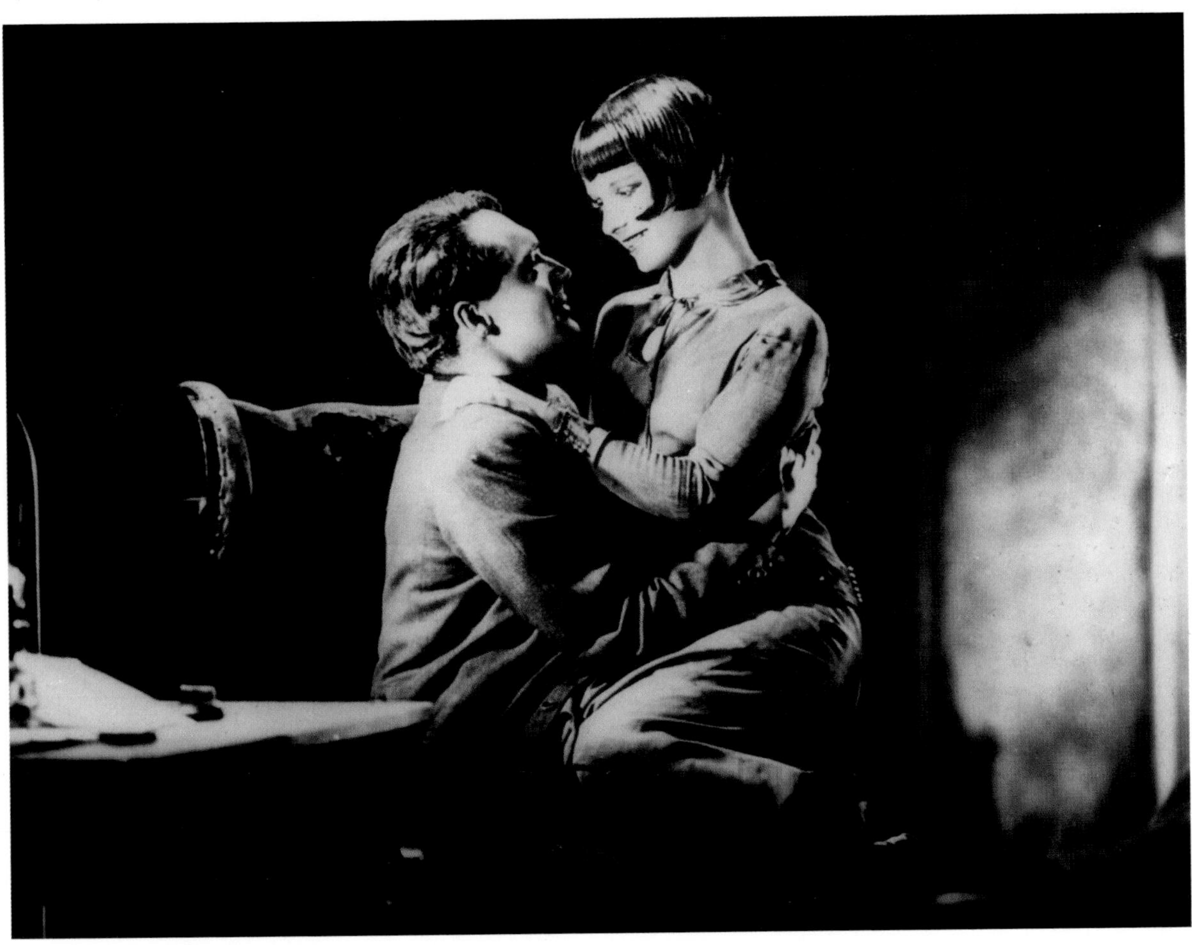

Artistic highlight of Weimar cinema: Louise Brooks in Pabst's *Die Büchse der Pandora*

ment in their own right (see Cherchi Usai and Codelli, 1990; Elsaesser and Wedel, 1996). Feminist film historian Heide Schlüpmann (1990; 1996) has argued that Wilhelmine cinema was specifically targeted at female audiences, in its focus on stars (for example, the screen diva Asta Nielsen) and genres such as social drama and melodrama. Schlüpmann has suggested that Weimar's art cinema, with its emphasis on male heroes and anxieties, marked a regression in terms of gender politics.

Meanwhile, new scholarship on Weimar cinema (Elsaesser, 2000) has expanded the canon that had been more or less fixed since the standard accounts by Siegfried Kracauer (1947) and Lotte Eisner (1969). The recurrent reduction of 1920s German film under the rubric of 'Expressionism' has been challenged, with various scholars pointing to other artistic traditions and movements, from documentary and left-wing agit-prop cinema (Murray, 1990) to animation and advertising film. Moreover, new studies have rediscovered Weimar cinema's popular traditions, exemplified by directors such as Ernst Lubitsch (Hake, 1992), genres such as melodrama (Petro, 1989), studios such as Ufa (Kreimeier, 1996) and producers such as Erich Pommer (Hardt, 1996).

Many scholars in the past decade have acknowledged that popular genres are among the most constant elements of German cinema, providing continuity across different political and historical contexts. This particularly applies to what is possibly the most typically German film genre, the *Heimatfilm* (homeland film), a specific form of rural melodrama, which, as Johannes von Moltke (2005) has documented, extends from the Wilhelmine period to its reinvention in Edgar Reitz's *Heimat* trilogy (1984–2005). New scholarship on the cinema of the Third Reich has also suggested that the dominant mode of Nazi cinema consisted of established popular formulae, which were subtly inflected by, but also sometimes had an ambivalent relationship with, party ideology (Rentschler, 1996; Schulte-Sasse, 1996; Hake, 2002a; Carter, 2004).

The output of the state-owned East German film industry, DEFA (1946–92), was largely ignored in the west during the Cold War. Since reunification, East German cinema has retrospectively emerged as a diverse corpus of films balancing political aims and artistic aspirations, and producing a range of significant film-makers (see Allan and Sandford, 1999; Byg and Moore, 2002).

Meanwhile, new research on the history of West German film from the postwar period to the advent of New German Cinema (Fehrenbach, 1995; Carter, 1997; Bergfelder, 2005; Moltke, 2005) has revised many previously held assumptions about this period, and has pointed out that the films of the 1950s and 1960s, largely comprising popular genres, achieved a remarkable level of box-office success.

Apart from popular genres, one other constant in German cinema is its international dimension. A history of German cinema encompasses the incursion of Danish and French film companies and stars into Germany in the early years of the 20th century, the influx of émigrés following World War I, pan-European production strategies of the late 1920s and early 1930s, the legacy of exiles from Hitler's Germany in the film cultures of France, Britain and Hollywood, co-productions in the post-war period, the globetrotting ventures of directors such as Werner Herzog and Wim Wenders, and the significant contributions by migrants, and children of migrants, especially since the 1990s.

Selected Reading

Tim Bergfelder, Erica Carter and Deniz Göktürk (eds), *The German Cinema Book*, London, BFI Publishing, 2002.

Weimar cinema

ANNETTE KUHN AND JULIA KNIGHT

German Expressionism

For many years, critical approaches to the films made during German cinema's Weimar period (1918–33) focused on the canon of artistically renowned productions characterised as German Expressionism (see German Cinema, p. 207). The term Expressionism (borrowed from painting and theatre and applied to a number of films made in Germany between about 1919 and 1930) refers to an extreme stylisation of mise en scène in which the formal organisation of the film is made very obvious. The stylistic features of German Expressionism are fairly specific and include chiaroscuro lighting, surrealistic settings and, frequently, a remarkable fluidity of mobile framing. The appearance of these films is often accompanied by similar acting styles and macabre or 'low-life' subject matter. The overall effect is to create a self-contained fantasy world quite separate from everyday reality, a world imbued with angst and paranoia in the face of that which cannot be rationally explained. This 'other world' often functions as a criticism of bourgeois society, though not always.

Analyses of German Expressionism have tended to focus either on German Expressionism as 'national' cinema – assuming that the films of a nation reflect its 'mentality' and do so better than other artistic media – or on German Expressionism as a label grouping together certain films by certain film-makers – emphasising the auteur rather than 'national character'. In both cases, there is a tendency to ignore the industrial context in which these films were created. Historian Siegfried Kracauer, however, writing in 1947, is an exception. Although he is ultimately interested in German Expressionism as a national cinema, he begins with a discussion of the German film industry:

> Since in those early days the conviction prevailed that foreign markets could only be conquered by artistic achievements, the German film industry was of course anxious to experiment in the field of aesthetically qualified entertainment. Art ensured export, and export meant Salvation. (Kracauer, 1947, p. 65)

Although the origins of German cinema can be traced back to the 1890s, the output of the German film industry before World War I has been perceived as relatively insignificant, with movie theatres showing mostly foreign imported films (see German Cinema, p. 207). The outbreak of war in 1914 resulted in the imposition of import restrictions, and in the absence of American, Italian, French or Danish competition, a number of German production companies were created to exploit the newly expanded domestic market. According to Kracauer (1947), the number of such companies rose from 28 in 1913 to 245 in 1919. During this period of consolidation, the German government, increasingly aware of cinema's propaganda potential for supporting an unpopular war, founded Deulig, an amalgamation of independents involved exclusively in the production of propaganda shorts, and Bufa, an agency concerned with providing frontline troops with a steady supply of films and film theatres.

By the end of the war, some industrialists were beginning to recognise the economic advantages of paying close attention to foreign audiences; accordingly in December 1917, the Universum Film Aktiengesellschaft (Ufa) was set up to facilitate further unification of the film industry. One-third of Ufa's finance came from the state, and the rest from banking interests and big business. Almost at once, Ufa became the major production company in Germany, attracting foreign film-makers and embarking on co-productions with other countries that were to give it considerable control of the postwar international market.

The end of the war, the collapse of the November uprising and massive inflation all contributed to an export boom in the German film industry that began in 1919. Of 250-odd independent production companies in Germany that year, Decla was second only to Ufa in assets and output. Its chief executive was Erich Pommer, who was convinced that foreign markets could only be conquered by artistic achievements. Perhaps the earliest artistic success among Decla's output was Robert Wiene's *The Cabinet of Dr. Caligari/Das Cabinet des Dr. Caligari* (1919) (see case study), which inaugurated a long series of entirely studio-made films. Kracauer suggests that this withdrawal into the studio was part of a general retreat into a shell, but it may also be explained in terms of rationalisation of the film industry in the immediate postwar period. *The Cabinet of Dr. Caligari* has widely been regarded as the film that first brought Expressionism to German cinema. After the war, the German film industry had concentrated on spy and detective serials, sex exploitation films and historical epics in an attempt to control the domestic and foreign markets. Though some would claim that *Caligari* was the only truly Expressionist film, it triggered a stylistic movement, derived from avant-garde painting, theatre, literature and architecture, which for a few short years became Germany's internationally respected national cinema, successfully differentiated from, and competing with, those of other countries, particularly the US.

In 1921, the year in which *The Cabinet of Dr. Caligari* was finally premiered in New York (subsequently becoming an international success), Decla was absorbed by Ufa, along with producer Erich Pommer. Two years later, Pommer became overall head of Ufa film production. One of the last Decla films to be made before Ufa took over was Fritz Lang's *Destiny/Der müde Tod* (1921). Shot in a nine-week period and involving three exotic settings – one Arabic, one Venetian and one Chinese – the film illustrated the ingredients that German companies were inserting into their films in order to appeal to the international, and particularly the American, market.

During this period, there was a considerable amount of vertical integration in the German film industry, and Ufa continued to expand throughout the early 1920s, absorbing a number of smaller production companies as well as larger enterprises such as Decla. Lang's *Dr Mabuse the Gambler/Dr. Mabuse der Spieler* (1922), for instance, was a co-production of Uco-Film and Decla, and released by Ufa. Despite its length of more than three hours, *Dr Mabuse* was successful at the box office, perhaps because it was easy to market as a thriller. Its plot, concerning a gambler who makes a fortune on the stock exchange, can be related interestingly not only to the economic conditions of contemporary Germany but also to those of the film industry itself.

Another short-lived studio, Prana-Film, supplied Ufa with its next bid for international success, F. W. Murnau's *Nosferatu the Vampire*. In 1922, Ufa's capital stock was increased to 200 million marks, and the company was able to increase its dividend from 30 per cent to 700 per cent thanks mainly to a boom in its export business (inflation notwithstanding). What *Nosferatu* lacked in 'stars' was compensated for by its Gothic subject matter and atmospheric visual style. By contrast, Arthur Robison's *Warning Shadows/Schatten* (1923) exemplified all the stylistic features of German Expressionism, but was unable to capitalise on them, apparently because the film only found a response among 'film aesthetes' and made no impression on the general public.

Ufa continued to produce, through its subsidiary Decla, large-budget and ambitious films. Lang's two-part *The Nibelungen/Die Nibelungen* (1924), for example, took a total of 31 weeks to shoot. But Ufa had overestimated the film's likely profitability. In 1924, with the settlement of German reparations under the Dawes Plan, the mark was stabilised and Germany was reintroduced to the gold standard, leading American firms to invest in the German film industry. The export boom in the film industry collapsed almost as swiftly as it had started, and the market was once again flooded with imports. By the end of the year, 40 per cent of the films being shown in Germany were American. It is not surprising, in the light of the changed situation, that *The Nibelungen* was a catastrophe at the box office. Ufa's *The Last Laugh/Der letzte Mann* (1924) met much the same fate as *The Nibelungen*, although the film's director, F. W. Murnau, was invited to Fox in Hollywood on the strength of its critical success. The fate of these two films in the context of renewed American influence signalled the end of German Expressionism. Although 'Expressionist' tendencies can be found in later German films, and its influence seen in Hollywood (particularly in horror and film noir), Expressionism as a national movement began to die out around 1924.

An industry in decline

From 1926 until 1930, income from German film exports fell to less than 50 per cent of total takings, and soon even Ufa was in difficulties. According to Julian Petley, enormously costly films aimed partly at an export art-house market clamouring for German Expressionism could not cover their production costs (Petley, 1979, p. 36). Fritz Lang's *Metropolis* provides a typical example; produced in 1927, it was the most expensive German film to date: budgeted at 1,900,000 marks, production costs eventually exceeded five million marks. At one point, the Ufa governing board had considered halting the production because of the enormous expense, but decided to complete the picture in the hope that its distribution abroad, particularly in the United States, would recoup the losses. *Metropolis* proved to be a financial failure and in April 1927, Ufa, which controlled 75 per cent of German film production, was reorganised by a new board of directors (Ott, 1979, p. 30). In producing this box-office failure, Lang had employed some 800 actors, 30,000 extras and taken 310 days and 60 nights of filming. He was never permitted such an extravagant experiment again (see Fritz Lang, p. 394).

In order to stabilise a dangerous economic situation, the major German film companies made a series of agreements, disadvantageous to themselves, with the large American companies. Ufa formed Parufamet with Paramount and MGM. The agreement was that Ufa would exhibit 20 of each of the American companies' releases in exchange for the distribution of a total of ten Ufa films by MGM and Paramount, and a loan of 17 million marks. Other German companies made similar agreements: Terra with Universal, Rex with United Artists, Phoebus, like Ufa, with MGM. Petley argues that:

> The government responded to the flood of imports with a quota law which decreed that for every foreign film released in Germany, a German film should be produced, but this resulted merely in a flood of ... cheap films often ... made solely to acquire a quota certificate .... Since the Americans wanted as many quota certificates as possible they even produced their own quota films in Germany. (Petley, 1979, p. 34)

The Parufamet deal and others like it offered the industry only temporary respite from receding receipts. These deals represented the culmination of American attempts to bring the German film industry to rely on American financial support and thus to weaken its strongest foreign competitor. In 1927, however, Alfred Hugenberg, a powerful industrialist and fer-

The Cabinet of Dr. Caligari/Das Cabinet des Dr. Caligari (Germany 1919 *p.c* – Decla Filmgesellschaft; *d* – Robert Wiene)

Made shortly after the end of World War I, *Das Cabinet des Dr. Caligari* is an indisputable classic of German cinema, an early horror film, as well as one of the first films to radically redefine the use of set design in cinema. *Caligari* combines the visual look of a contemporary avant-garde movement (Expressionism) with a story that draws on elements of the Gothic novel, the detective story and the fairytale: a mad scientist, disguised as a fairground exhibitor (Werner Krauss), descends on a small provincial German town and uses a sleepwalker (Conrad Veidt) to commit murders under his influence. Or does he?

While the film's striking sets may still dazzle audiences, they have seldom been imitated. Filmic Expressionism proved a dead end, and was quickly superseded even in German cinema by other stylistic influences. The complex narrative with its surprise ending, on the other hand, still has echoes in contemporary films. There have been endless debates regarding the framing story and flashback at the heart of the film's deception, yet *Caligari* can be interpreted in a number of ways.

Siegfried Kracauer (1947) saw the ending as a cop-out, as a triumph of authority over rebellion, and of establishment over change, while later critics (including Robinson, 1997) have read the conclusion of the film as darkly ironic. The film also suggests links to Germany's trauma during World War I – for example, the acting recalls the contorted body movements of shell-shock victims. As well as its meaning, the film's authorship has been contested. Kracauer championed the writers as the true creators of *Caligari*, while other critics have suggested the designers as the main creative force. Robert Wiene, the film's director, has more recently been rehabilitated as someone who played a crucial part in the film's gestation (Jung and Schatzberg, 1999).

TIM BERGFELDER

Striking sets: Conrad Veidt as Cesare in *Das Cabinet des Dr. Caligari*

vent nationalist, acquired Ufa, buying out all American interests in the company. Ufa's production programme was rapidly rationalised and fewer films were henceforth commissioned from independents. All but the best-funded of Ufa's rivals soon went under: as profits and production declined, only the export end of the business was expanded. Aware as the German majors were of the dangers of financial, aesthetic and technological dependence upon America, they had little alternative but to endure it.

Sound cinema, it was hoped, would cut down foreign imports because of language difficulties, while still allowing German exports to exploit the possibility of dual versions. German film companies had begun taking out patents on sound systems as early as 1924, and in 1929 an agreement was eventually signed to employ the Tobis-Klangfilm process. Some early German sound films, such as Josef von Sternberg's *The Blue Angel/Der blaue Engel* (1930), Lang's *M* (1931) and G. W. Pabst's *Comradeship/Kameradschaft* (1931), enjoyed international success. *The Blue Angel* and *M*, produced in English and German versions, made world-famous stars of Marlene Dietrich and Peter Lorre, while *Kameradschaft*, made simultaneously in German and French to suit its subject matter, was popular across Europe. By 1933, however, when Fritz Lang's *M* was finally released in America by Paramount, both Lang and Lorre were already in the US, as were Sternberg and Dietrich.

Selected Reading

Thomas Elsaesser, *Weimar Cinema and After: Germany's Historical Imaginary*, London and New York, Routledge, 2000.

Siegfried Kracauer, *From Caligari to Hitler: A Psychological History of the German Film*, Princeton, NJ, Princeton University Press, 1947. Second revised edition 2004.

New German Cinema

JULIA KNIGHT

The term New German Cinema has been used to delineate a loose grouping of films made in West Germany from the 1960s through to the early 1980s. Made by film-makers who had been born around World War II and grown up in a postwar divided Germany, these films were celebrated for their contemporary relevance and formal experimentation and were regarded as heralding the most promising development in German cinema since German Expressionism.

Initially, commentators tended to focus on the film-makers, treating them as individual creative geniuses, and examining their films almost exclusively in terms of their directors' personal visions. This critical reception was largely the result of the deliberate promotion of the new films as an *Autorenkino* (cinema of authors) by the film-makers themselves. This notion was theorised by Alexander Kluge, who believed that directors should familiarise themselves with all aspects of production, becoming *Filmautoren* with the potential to exercise a high degree of authorial control.

Due to the lobbying efforts of Kluge and others, combined with a political will to see film acquire the status of 'Kultur', the concept of an *Autorenkino* informed the film subsidy agencies that the West German government began to set up in the mid-1960s. To ensure that film-makers retained as much artistic control over their work as possible, the funding agencies encouraged them to become, for example, scriptwriters and/or producers as well as directors and to take many of the artistic, casting and editing decisions.

The dominance of auteurist film criticism in the 1960s and 1970s helped New German Cinema to attract critical acclaim as the product of gifted auteurs. Early major studies singled out a small number of (male) directors for particular attention – usually R. W. Fassbinder, Werner Herzog, Alexander Kluge, Volker Schlöndorff, Jean-Marie Straub, Hans-Jürgen Syberberg and Wim Wenders – while marginalising all other areas of work that equally formed part of the New German Cinema.

However, the key factor in the emergence of the New German Cinema was the handling of the West German film industry by the occupying powers after World War II. In order to help to both 'de-Nazify' the country and to build up the western zones as a buffer to Soviet influence in eastern Europe, the western Allies flooded West Germany with Hollywood films. As no import quotas were imposed, American companies quickly achieved a position of economic dominance in Germany by the beginning of the 1950s. To help protect this market domination, the Allies dismantled the remnants of the centralised Nazi film industry and licensed only small independent production companies in its place.

Forced to remain small-scale, the new West German film industry failed to attract substantial investment and films had to be produced relatively cheaply. Unable to compete with the expensive Hollywood spectacle, indigenous production became expressly orientated towards the home market, and during the 1950s the *Heimat* film genre with its depiction of simple country life was particularly popular. Although this popularity precipitated a brief boom for the industry in the mid-1950s, the films did not boast high production values and West German cinema soon acquired a reputation abroad for being drab, provincial and 'escapist'.

As early as the mid-1950s, representatives from the industry and film-makers had called for government intervention. Criticism reached a peak in 1961 when the organisers of the Venice Film Festival rejected all West German entries and the Federal Film Prize given annually at home went unawarded. In 1962, a group of 26 young film-makers, writers and artists – spearheaded by Kluge – published the *Oberhausen Manifesto* at the Oberhausen Short Film Festival, calling for a new cinema of artistic freedom and rejecting the German film industry.

In its criticism of the 'old' German film, the *Manifesto* also presaged Kluge's notion of an *Autorenkino*. By stressing the need for freedom from economic and other vested interests, it effectively defined the new German film as 'artistic' production in opposition to industrial modes of production. Kluge subsequently reinforced this opposition when he contrasted the new German film with the *Zutatenfilm* (recipe film): a typical industry product made up of ingredients such as stars, ideas, directors, technicians, scriptwriters and so on that could be purchased according to requirements. The comparison implied that in New German Cinema the film-makers would bring something personal to their work.

Although the government responded to this mounting criticism as early as April 1962 by announcing plans to provide public funding for feature-film production, three years passed before the first film subsidy agency – the *Kuratorium junger deutscher Film* (Board of Young German Film) – was set up. In the meantime, Kluge and co-signatory Edgar Reitz started to develop the demands of the *Oberhausen Manifesto* into a coherent education programme at the Ulm Film Institute, with the express purpose of training a new generation of *Filmautoren*. Rather than training as specialists in particular areas such as camera, scriptwriting, editing or direction – as is normally the case in the film industry – students received an all-round film-making education. Not only did a number of New German Cinema directors, including Ula Stöckl and Claudia von Alemann, study at Ulm during the 1960s, but when the Berlin Film and Television Academy opened in 1966 it followed Ulm's model.

Set up in 1965 with a brief to stimulate a renewal of German cinema, the Kuratorium funding agency provided production loans for first-time feature-film directors. Within two years, 25 films had been funded, including Alexander Kluge's *Yesterday Girl/Abschied von Gestern* (1966), which won several prizes. Other films that attracted critical acclaim were Edgar Reitz's *Mealtimes/Mahlzeiten* (1967), Peter Schamoni's *Closed Season for Foxes/Schonzeit für Füchse* (1966) and Volker Schlöndorff's *Young Törless/Der junge Törless* (1966). In contrast to the 'escapist' genre films of the 1950s, the new cinema drew on contemporary subject matter and included documentaries (for instance, Werner Herzog's *Land of Silence and Darkness/Land des Schweigens und der Dunkelheit*, 1971), formally experimental work (such as Jean-Marie Straub and Danièle Huillet's *Not Reconciled/Nicht versöhnt*, 1965) and episodic narratives (for example, Kluge's *Yesterday Girl*) alongside more conventional feature films (Fassbinder's *Katzelmacher*, 1969). Thomas Elsaesser argues that these first films bore little relation to either national or international film culture, or to any film-making traditions: 'Kluge's essays on celluloid, and even Jean-Marie Straub's or Vlado Kristl's films seemed ... inspired by what one might call "cinephobia", a revulsion against the commercial film industry and its standard product, the fictional narrative film' (Elsaesser, 1989, p. 25).

Over the next 12 years, a network of film subsidy agencies developed, providing five major sources of funding: the Kuratorium, the Film Promotion Board, Federal Film Awards, regional initiatives and television. After successive revisions, the subsidy system offered a range of types of funding – for production, exhibition, distribution, and script and project development – aimed at promoting a national cinema that was both culturally motivated and economically viable. By the late 1970s, an unprecedented half of all feature films being made were deemed to belong to the new cinema; and when Volker Schlöndorff's *The Tin Drum/Die Blechtrommel* (1979) won the Academy Award for the Best Foreign Film in 1980, one British critic commented that the New German Cinema was 'one of the most remarkable, enduring, and promising developments in the cinema of the 1970s' (Sandford, 1980, p. 6). The funding agencies also facilitated an enormous range of work that would not otherwise have been possible. In the early 1970s, the television channel WDR, for instance, produced the critically acclaimed *Arbeiterfilme* (worker films) made by a predominantly Berlin-based group of film-makers (including Christian Ziewer, Erika Runge, Ingo Kratisch, Marianne Lüdcke and Fassbinder), which focused on the lives and experiences of the contemporary German working classes. By the end of the decade, the subsidy system had also enabled a number of women film-makers (including Helke Sander, Helma Sanders-Brahms, Ulrike Ottinger and Margarethe von Trotta) to make the difficult transition from documentaries and shorts into feature-film production, which gave rise to a vibrant and critically acclaimed women's cinema.

But few of the films thus produced were box-office successes, a fact that elicited criticism at home. In 1977, for instance, Eckart Schmidt declared: 'Filmmakers like Kluge, Herzog, Geissendörfer and Fassbinder, all of whom have collected subsidies more than once, and who despite such public funding are incapable of directing a success, should in future be barred from receiving subsidies' (quoted in Elsaesser, 1989, p. 37). The increasing fragmentation of the cinema audience (due to the dominance of television, the demise of the traditional family audience and the politicisation of the student movement in the late 1960s), combined with a lack of interest from commercial exhibitors, the dominance of American distributors and the absence of a film culture in Germany (outside Berlin, Hamburg and Munich), meant that the new German film found it difficult to win a national audience.

Over the years, the film-makers themselves voiced criticism of the subsidy system. Although there was a desire to create a 'quality' national cinema, funding was often awarded with commercial priorities in mind. Consequently, the formal experimentation that characterised many of the early films gradually gave way during the 1970s to a cinema of narrative-based feature films (typified by Fassbinder's *The Marriage of Maria Braun/Die Ehe der Maria Braun*, 1979, and Wenders's *The American Friend/Der Amerikanische Freund*, 1977). Given that the cinema was completely dependent on public money, projects that addressed politically sensitive issues or were socially critical also either failed to find funding or had to adopt highly oblique approaches to their subject matter. Margarethe von Trotta's film *The German Sisters/Die Bleierne Zeit* (1981), for instance, alludes to the terrorist activity that swept across West Germany during the 1970s but does not overtly examine its causes.

By the mid-1980s, a number of critics had pronounced the demise of New German Cinema. This was partly because the directors most closely associated with it had moved abroad, and one of the cinema's most prolific directors, R. W. Fassbinder, had died in 1982. That year also saw the return to power of the CDU/CSU political union and the introduction of a more conservative approach to film policy that clearly favoured commercial projects over any form of artistic experimentation. At the same time, the cost of producing films rocketed during the 1980s, necessitating pan-European funding strategies, since national funding initiatives alone were rarely adequate.

Nevertheless, it is possible to argue that as the 1980s progressed, the aim of promoting a culturally motivated and economically viable national cinema was realised. Kluge's notion of an *Autorenkino* may have been somewhat eroded in favour of commercialism, but films such as Wolfgang Petersen's *The Boat/Das Boot* (1981), Doris Dörrie's *Men/Männer ...* (1985) and Percy Adlon's *Bagdad Café* (1987) were successful on both the art cinema and commercial circuits. Although not typical of what exemplified the New German Cinema – given their more conventional narrative structures and commercial orientation – neither were they lacking in cultural specificity.

And while some of the goals of the New German Cinema were realised in a different form, some of its more characteristic attributes persisted beyond the demise of New German Cinema as an identifiable movement. Throughout the 1980s and 1990s, a number of German film-makers, including Herbert Achternbusch (*Heal Hitler!/Heilt Hitler!*, 1986), Edgar Reitz (*Heimat II/Die zweite Heimat*, 1992), Kluge (*The Blind Director/Der Angriff der Gegenwart auf die übrige Zeit*, 1986), Elfi Mikesch (*Marocain*, 1989), Werner Schroeter (*Malina*, 1991) and Monika Treut (*My Father Is Coming*, 1991), have continued to produce innovative and challenging work of contemporary relevance. And as if in recognition of this work, the Berlin Film Festival maintained, at least until the mid-1990s, a 'New German Film' section in its International Forum of Young Film. Reitz's epic TV series, *Heimat* (1984), also demonstrated that such work could be commercially viable, when the series was sold to several major national TV networks.

As auteurist methodology began to be superseded, in the 1980s, by other critical approaches to the study of film, a number of writers (for example, Elsaesser, 1989; Kaes, 1989; Knight, 1992; Rentschler, 1984) began to reassess New German Cinema. In the process, they rescued a number of film-makers from critical oblivion – especially women directors such as Helke Sander and Helma Sanders-Brahms, who fared particularly badly in the early auteurist studies. But just as importantly, these writers explored the social, political and economic factors that helped shape the new cinema: the post-war American legacy and US cultural imperialism; the development of the film subsidy system at the cost of political and artistic censorship; modes of production, distribution and exhibition; and concern with contemporary socio-political issues such as terrorism, the Nazi past and the women's movement. These studies demonstrate that the New German Cinema, while informed by the notion of an *Autorenkino*, can only be fully understood as the product of a complex network of nationally and historically specific conditions.

Selected Reading

Thomas Elsaesser, *New German Cinema: A History*, London, BFI/Macmillan, 1989.

Yesterday Girl/Abschied von gestern
(West Germany 1966 *p.c* – Kairos-Film/Independent-Film; *d* – Alexander Kluge)

Alexander Kluge is viewed as one of the most vocal advocates of a new German cinema, and spearheaded the group of film-makers, writers and artists that drew up the *Oberhausen Manifesto* in 1962. Although he played a key role in developing the notion of an *Autorenkino*, he later criticised those film-makers who presented themselves as auteurs, and stressed the importance of the audience, arguing that 'the cinema is its spectators' (Corrigan, 1994, p. 90).

Yesterday Girl was one of the first films to be funded by the Kuratorium and, given its mix of documentary, fiction and experimental film conventions, it can be viewed as an explicit endeavour to create the new cinema called for in the *Oberhausen Manifesto*. The filmic devices employed – such as the use of intertitles to break up the narrative flow, voice-over commentary, direct address to camera and at times a non-synchronous soundtrack – have also been described as 'Brechtian'. It has been compared with Godard's work, especially *It's My Life/Vivre sa vie* (1962) and Kluge has acknowledged both Godard and Eisenstein as influences.

Yesterday Girl is based on the true story of a young Jewish woman, Anita G., who arrives in West Germany from the former GDR. According to Elsaesser (1989) the film can be read as an 'issue oriented' film about pregnancy, vagrancy, petty crime and social work, and hence represents a stark contrast to the 'escapism' of the 1950s *Heimat* films. But, in view of Anita's Jewishness and her East German background, it has also been read as being about the inseparability of past and present and the intertwining of individual and national history, a theme that frequently recurs in New German Cinema films in relation to the Nazi past. Throughout the film, Anita's presence serves as both a reminder of the Nazi persecution of the Jews and of the Communist rejection of capitalism – thus linking questions of German history and the contemporary situation of postwar divided Germany.

JULIA KNIGHT

The Marriage of Maria Braun/Die Ehe der Maria Braun
(West Germany 1979 *p.c* – Albatros-Filmproduktion /Trio-Film/WDR; *d* – Rainer Werner Fassbinder)

Fassbinder made over 20 full-length feature films and numerous television productions in just over ten years. Although he is one of the best-known New German Cinema directors, he was not part of the Oberhausen 'scene' and in fact worked initially in theatre. Whereas Elsaesser (1989) has characterised the early work of Syberberg, Herzog, Kluge and others as 'outside any recognisable tradition of film-making', much of Fassbinder's work self-consciously drew on the conventions of Hollywood genre films). Although he dealt with specifically German subject matter, his films have also been read as articulating a love-hate relationship with both Hollywood cinema in particular and American cultural imperialism generally.

Some of Fassbinder's early work, for instance, uses the gangster genre to explore the criminal underworld of Munich, such as *Love Is Colder Than Death/Liebe is kälter als der Tod* (1969) and *The American Soldier/Der amerikanische Soldat* (1970). Subsequently, he turned his attention to melodrama, influenced by the films of Douglas Sirk. In the latter stage of his career, he made what he described as German Hollywood films, such as *The Marriage of Maria Braun* and *Lili Marleen* (1981).

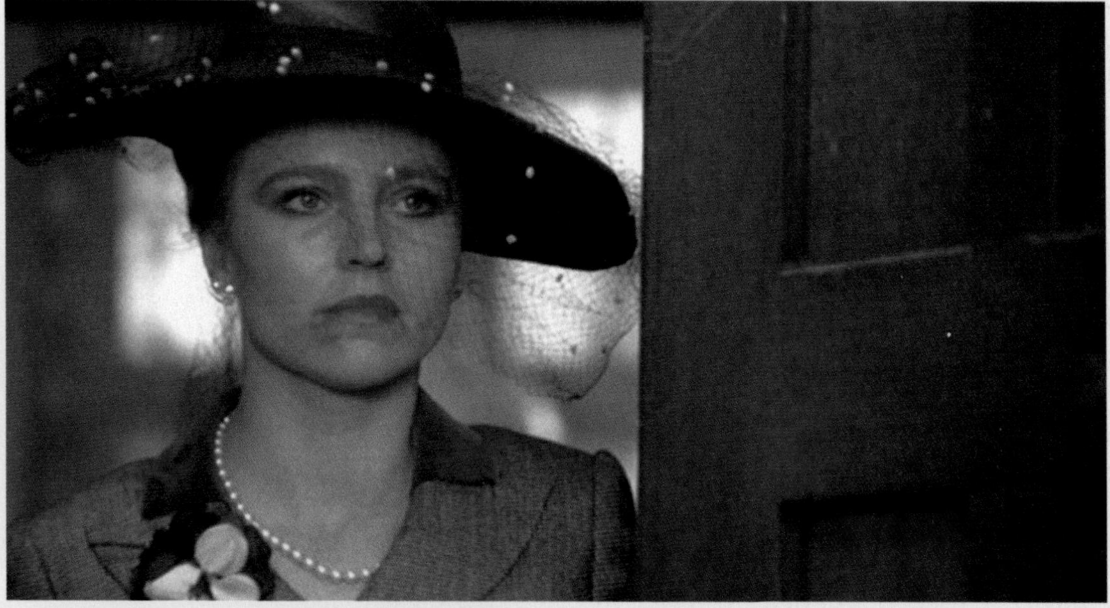

Rewriting German history: Hanna Schygulla in Fassbinder's *Die Ehe der Maria Braun*

The Marriage of Maria Braun focuses on a woman's struggle to survive in immediate postwar Germany when her husband, Hermann, goes to prison for a murder she commits. Although devoted to Hermann, Maria embarks on a long-term affair with her boss, Oswald, in order to be able to provide a home for Hermann when he is released.

According to Elsaesser (1989), the film addresses the recurring themes identified as the main preoccupations of the New German Cinema: loneliness, homelessness, isolation, fear and failure. For Elsaesser, Oswald and Maria's relationship is based on the assumption that 'sharing loneliness is the best that two people can achieve'. But since the film focuses on Maria's struggle to survive and her love for Hermann, Kaes (1989) suggests that the film also offers a 'rewriting' of German history. Not only does it highlight the purely personal experiences of the individual at the cost of exploring the political realities of the post-Nazi era, but Maria is seen as bearing no responsibility for the situation in which she finds herself.

JULIA KNIGHT

Germany, Pale Mother/Deutschland bleiche Mutter (West Germany 1980; *p.c* – Helma Sanders-Brahms/Literarisches Colloquium Berlin/WDR; *d* – Helma Sanders-Brahms)

Germany, Pale Mother caused something of a controversy on its release for its handling of the recent German past. Mixing archive newsreel footage with the conventions of art-house realism, the predominantly narrative-based film looks back to Sanders-Brahms's own childhood, her experiences of growing up in the 1950s and the lives of her parents.

However, the film was also made at the time the American TV series *Holocaust* was broadcast on German television – an event that according to contemporary observers played a key role in precipitating a 'remembering' of the Nazi past that had been systematically repressed after World War II (see Kaes, 1989, p. 30). Although partly welcomed, this process of remembering also raised unwelcome questions of who should bear responsibility for the Nazi regime. At the end of the 1970s, West Germans became preoccupied with the past and with German identity, resulting in, as Anton Kaes (1989) puts it, attempts on the part of a number of New German Cinema directors and other cultural producers 'to rewrite German history, to fit the atrocities of the Hitler period into a tolerable master narrative'.

Although Sanders-Brahms had begun developing the idea of *Germany, Pale Mother* as early as 1976, it was widely 'read' as just such an attempt. The director has stressed she wanted to make a film that dealt with those people like her parents who may not have voted for Hitler, but did not protest, resist or emigrate either. However, for many, *Germany, Pale Mother* seemed to suggest that her parents – and, by implication, others like them – bore no responsibility for the Nazi atrocities, and that rather they were simply victims of historical circumstances.

JULIA KNIGHT

Contemporary German cinema

TIM BERGFELDER

The 1980s marked a transition period in German cinema, combining a continuation of the auteur cinema of the 1970s with an increasing reorientation towards commercial modes of production, including the use of established generic formulae, serialisation of box-office hits and the creation of stars.

The fall of the Berlin wall in 1989 had a substantial impact on German cinema in a number of ways. Reunification revealed in retrospect how specifically West German the New German Cinema had been in terms of its thematic concerns. The history and legacy of the German Democratic Republic, and the continuing difficulties in overcoming 40 years of ideological division, became a recurrent post-wall narrative motif. Comedy dramas such as *Sun Alley/Sonnenallee* (1999) and *Goodbye, Lenin!* (2003) were criticised for pandering to nostalgic feelings among East Germans for their former Communist state, but also celebrated for articulating resistance against western cultural hegemony. The east–west conflict was also thematised in Margarethe von Trotta's melodrama *The Promise/Das Versprechen* (1995).

In terms of industrial infrastructure, the 1990s opened up East Germany's DEFA (formerly Ufa) studios at Babelsberg to both domestic and international productions. Becoming after reunification the most populous nation in Europe accelerated Germany's position as a crucial distribution market (Elsaesser, 1999). As a result, Hollywood investment in German production increased; in turn, German banks and production companies used tax incentives to contribute financially to international ventures (for example, *Resident Evil*, 2002). Moreover, since the 1990s Hollywood has seen a wave of German film-makers establishing themselves in the US, including directors such as Roland Emmerich (*Independence Day*, 1996) or Wolfgang Petersen (*Troy*, 2004). The internationalisation of the German film industry was, however, not all beneficial. Many of DEFA's established personnel were sidelined after the demise of the GDR. Andreas Dresen is among those East German directors who made a mark during

Nostalgia for the Communist state?: Becker's *Goodbye, Lenin!*

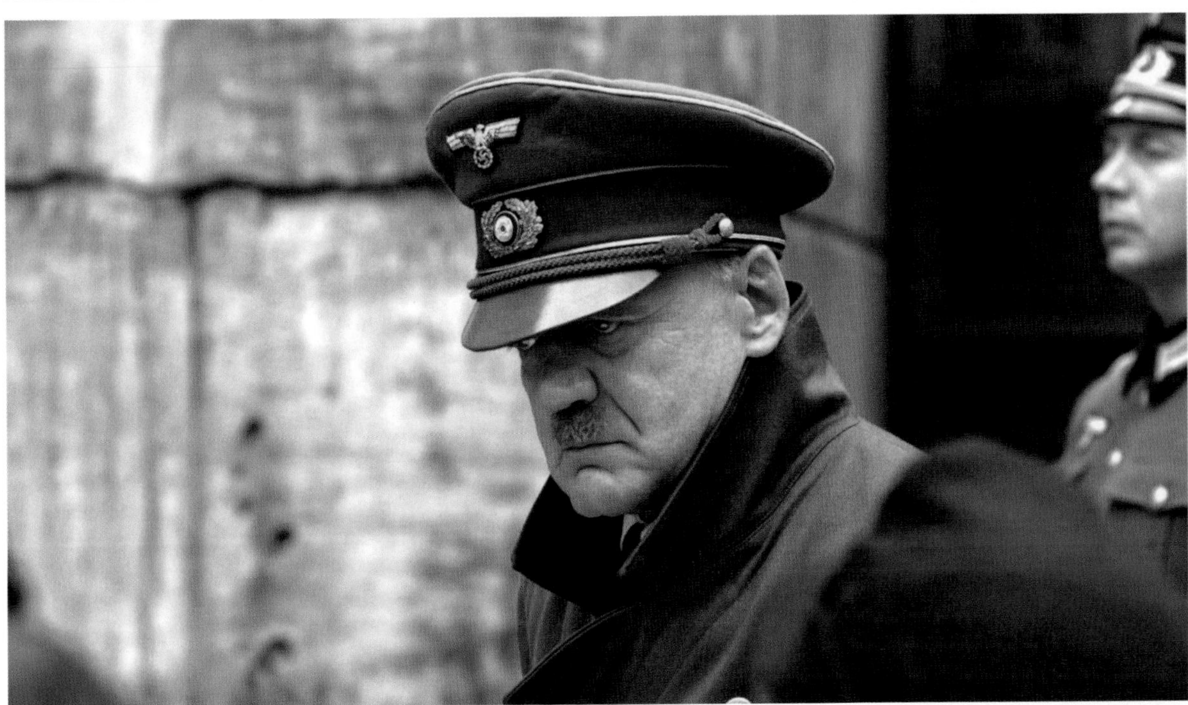

The last days of Hitler: Bruno Ganz in Oliver Hirschbiegel's *Die Untergang*

the 1990s with films that dealt with the aftermath of reunification, such as *Quiet Country/Stilles Land* (1992).

In terms of popular generic patterns, Wolfgang Petersen's *The Boat* and Doris Dörrie's *Men* can in hindsight be seen as prototypes for two dominant popular strategies during the 1990s and beyond: glossy spectacles set during the Nazi period, and romantic comedies. Joseph Vilsmaier emerged as one of the main proponents of a 'Nazi heritage' film, encompassing the battle epic *Stalingrad* (1993) and biopics such as *Comedian Harmonists* (1997) and *Marlene* (2000). Similar historical territory was covered by Max Färberböck's *Aimée & Jaguar/Aimée und Jaguar* (1998), a story of lesbian love between a Jewish woman and a German in wartime Berlin; Caroline Link's Oscar-winning *Nowhere in Africa/Nirgendwo in Afrika* (2001), about a Jewish family's wartime emigration to Kenya; and Oliver Hirschbiegel's study of Hitler's last days in *Downfall/Der Untergang* (2004).

Sönke Wortmann, meanwhile, released a series of lifestyle comedies such as *The Most Desired Man/Der bewegte Mann* (1994), and *The Miracle of Berne/Das Wunder von Bern* (2003), a feel-good story about West Germany's World Cup success in 1954. Other directors who contributed to the comedy boom in the 1990s were Detlev Buck (*No More Mr Nice Guy/Wir können auch anders*, 1993) and Katja von Garnier (*Making Up/Abgeschminkt*, 1992). Although many of these films, aptly termed a 'cinema of consensus' (Rentschler, 2000), proved domestic box-office hits, often outperforming Hollywood competition, few had a major international impact. This applies especially to the lowbrow end of the spectrum, which covers genre spoofs such as *Manitou's Shoe/Der Schuh des Manitu* (2001) and animation comedies such as *Little Arsehole/Kleines Arschloch* (1997). Much more marketable abroad have been the occasional German forays into horror films (Stefan Ruzowitzky's *Anatomy/Anatomie*, 1999) and action thrillers (Hirschbiegel's *Das Experiment*, 2001).

Despite its emphasis on popular genres, post-reunification cinema has continued to produce distinctive new auteurs. Tom Tykwer (*Wintersleepers/Winterschläfer*, 1997; *Run Lola Run/Lola rennt*, 1998; *The Princess and the Warrior/Der Krieger und die Kaiserin*, 2000; *Perfume: The Story of a Murderer*, 2006) became internationally renowned for his cineliterate, postmodern melodramas. Together with fellow directors Wolfgang Becker (*Life's All You Make It/Das Leben ist eine Baustelle*, 1997; *Goodbye, Lenin!*) and Dani Levy (*Silent Night/Stille Nacht*, 1996; *Meschugge*, 1998; *Go for Zucker/Alles auf Zucker!*, 2005), Tykwer has been one of the founding members of the production company X-Filme, which in the new millennium emerged as a creative powerhouse in German cinema. Although stylistically and thematically different in many ways, the films by Tykwer, Becker and Levy articulate the desires and anxieties of a twenty-something generation.

In contrast to Tykwer's visual fireworks is the austere style of Romuald Karmakar, which adds to the claustrophobic and oppressive atmosphere of his portrait of a Weimar serial killer in *Deathmaker/Der Totmacher*, 1995). An equally cold and stark look at the human psyche, accompanied by misanthropic sarcasm, characterises the films of Oskar Roehler, such as the powerful study of a suicidal novelist (based on the director's own mother) in *No Place to Go/Die Unberührbare*, 2000), and his adaptation of Michel Houllebecq's *Atomised/Elementarteilchen*, 2006).

Thematically, the most significant issue since the 1990s has been the cultural dialogue and conflict generated by processes of migration, and related questions of national identity. Directors from migrant backgrounds, including Thomas Arslan (*Dealer*, 1999; *One Fine Day/Der schöne Tag*, 2001), Kutlug Ataman (*Lola + Bilidikid*, 1998) and Ayse Polat (*En Garde*, 2004), have confidently mapped out a new hybrid German cinema that transcends narrow geographical or national boundaries. Exemplifying this trend are Fatih Akin's films, encompassing Scorsese-influenced portraits of ethnic gangland culture (*Short Sharp Shock/Kurz und schmerzlos*, 1998), trans-European road movies (*In July/Im Juli*, 2000) and the powerful psychodrama *Head-On/Gegen die Wand* (2004).

Selected Reading

Sabine Hake, 'Postunification cinema, 1989–2000', in *German National Cinema*, London and New York, Routledge, 2002b.

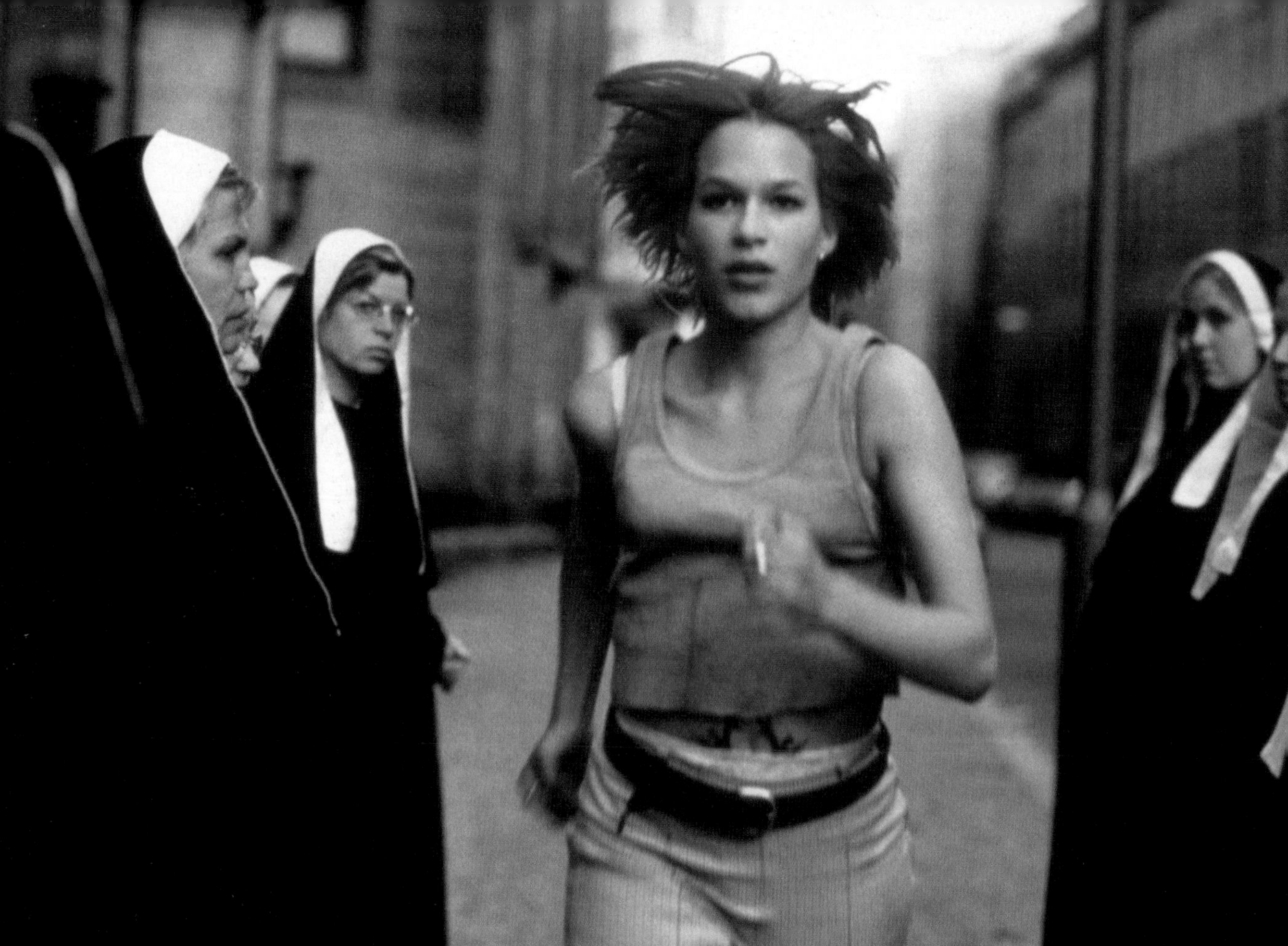

Controversial postmodern love story: Franka Potente in Tykwer's *Lola rennt*

Run Lola Run/Lola rennt (Germany 1998 *p.c* – X-Filme Creative Pool/Westdeutscher Rundfunk/Arte; *d* – Tom Tykwer)

Upon its international release, Tom Tykwer's postmodern love story, with its visually dazzling combination of live action, animation, video-games aesthetics, frenetic editing, all accompanied by a pounding trance soundtrack (composed by the director himself), made German cinema 'hip' abroad for the first time in over a decade. The film's narrative starts from the premise of a young woman, Lola (Franka Potente), who has to find a large sum of money and reach her boyfriend Manni (Moritz Bleibtreu) in a given timeframe – it is a scenario on which the boyfriend's life depends. However, the scenario is 'replayed' three times, with brief delays and coincidences leading to entirely different outcomes. Much of the film is taken up by the athletic, flame-haired Lola running through the streets of Berlin and encountering a cast of strange characters. Tykwer shows his cinephile credentials by adding a number of self-reflexive touches and popular cultural references to the minimalist narrative, including oblique visual homages to Hitchcock's *Vertigo* (1958).

Young audiences in particular embraced *Run Lola Run* as a cult film. Critical opinion, however, was divided. For some, the film provided a profound philosophical exploration of causality, memory and time, while for others Tykwer betrayed the political and social aims of the New German Cinema with an at best flashy and inconsequential melodrama, and at worst an overwrought parable that was conservative both in its moral agenda and in its gender politics. Tykwer found himself also accused of abandoning the specifically German themes the previous generation of directors had pursued. Indeed, it has been argued that Tykwer belongs to a generation of global, rather than nationally defined, film-makers, and in this he has been linked to such names as Wong Kar-wai, Lars von Trier and Baz Luhrmann. At the same time, Tykwer continues traditions that reach far back into German film history. Sabine Hake (2002b) has referred to *Run Lola Run* as a latter-day version of the 'city symphony', a cinematic genre that had its heyday in the Weimar cinema of the 1920s, while the film's complex narrative structure also has antecedents in previous German films, going back all the way to *Das Cabinet des Dr. Caligari* (see case study, p. 210).

TIM BERGFELDER

HINDI CINEMA

ASHISH RAJADHYAKSHA

India has the world's largest national film industry. It amalgamates five major 'regional' film industries based in Bombay (the Hindi and Marathi cinemas), Madras (Tamil, Telugu and Malayalam cinemas), Hyderabad (mainly Telugu), Calcutta (Bengali, Assamese and Oriya cinemas) and Bangalore (Kannada cinema). The Indian Censor Board has recorded films made in 51 languages, including Arabic, German, Persian and several Indian dialects, that is to say, languages not considered to be official by the Indian Constitution. The major industries are concentrated in eight languages. According to Censor Board figures, these were distributed in 1993 as follows: 183 Hindi, 168 Tamil, 148 Telugu, 78 Kannada, 71 Malayalam, 57 Bengali, 35 Marathi and 20 Oriya films.

The massive scale of the Indian film industry – which overtook Japan in 1971 to become the biggest in the world – its linguistic and cultural variety, geographical spread, complex aesthetic histories, combined with the relative paucity of scholarly works able to provide an understanding of this industrial-cultural sector, can mean that the subject is intimidating. For the better part of its history, the Indian film industry has survived without state support (unlike Hollywood, which benefited considerably from the US government's readiness to use strong-arm tactics, for instance, to help Hollywood achieve or maintain market domination in various regions of the globe). The Indian industry grew under colonial rule, was implicated in the independence struggle and maintained an ambivalent stance towards the government over censorship and tax legislation (the latter amounting to, on average, half the price of every ticket). The industry developed its own capital resources, at times 'unaccounted' for, that is to say, drawn from an illegal 'parallel economy', which the cinema is seen sometimes to represent. Indian cinema is thus located, economically and therefore aesthetically (although the nature of the relationship between economics and aesthetics remains to be analysed adequately), in between two realms, each with its own values: an official realm, with its economic and cultural values, and the more covert realm of the film economy, with its 'parallel' though overlapping values. In this respect, Indian cinema is simultaneously a contentious, suspect domain and arguably a key sector that, by bridging the two economies, holds the nation together while providing the main cultural force field within which the stresses and strains affecting India are manifested and contested.

Until the mid-1980s, most debates on Indian film concentrated on and deployed varieties of populist ideologies – positive or negative arguments, that is, formed around notions of mass culture versus elite culture and the cinema's seminal role in the creation of an indigenous audience in the context of pre-independence nationalisms. (After independence, cinema and the print media's populist ideologies helped form a consumption sector extending beyond the metropolitan areas.) These mass-culture debates were and are in turn framed by a larger set of arguments and positions involving, on one hand, the critique or defence of the Indian state as policy-maker, legitimator of an 'official' Indian mass culture and arbitrator of 'authenticity' and, on the other hand, an exploration of the commercial industries and the various state-sponsored art-house initiatives in the context of their claim to represent the 'reality of' Indian experiences. (These arguments, in contrast with comparable discussions in Europe and America, have only recently come to include television in their frame of reference.)

Indian cinema's relative independence from foreign investment has marked and inflected the conceptualisations of its histories. However, since relatively few film prints from its history have survived (from the 1,400 or so silent films produced, less than a dozen appear to be still extant) and other kinds of archival records are equally scarce, very little serious research has been done into the history of Indian cinema.

Instead, there has been extensive discussion of the somewhat exceptional case of a colonised nation already possessing, when independence was achieved, a well-entrenched entertainment industry. These discussions have focused largely on the regulatory role of the state in this sector of production. State-sponsored intitiatives in the film industry, as in other public sector economic areas, had to reconcile several contradictory responsibilities. The state had a monopoly over, for instance, the manufacture and distribution of raw stock and other materials as well as over the 'channelling' of the distribution of foreign films. But its role was relatively minor in attempts to diversify the culture of film through agencies such as the National Film Development Corporation, which sought to provide alternatives to mainstream cinema's market domination.

Consequently, it is quite possible to see both the history of Indian cinema and the debates surrounding and accompanying it as paralleling the history of India's private sector economy in general: determined by several initiatives seeking to foster cultural and political indigenism before independence, the industry was implicated in the promotion of a kind of 'Indianness', in bolstering the Nehruite programmes for a 'socialist form of society' as well as a mixed economy. More recently, the industry has been affected by 'economic liberalisation', a process whose impact is readily evident in the rapid changes in television caused by the entry of foreign cable networks into the country.

Some historical problems

It is possible to distinguish four main periods in Indian cinema. The first is the silent film era, dominated by the culture of *swadeshi* ('own country', a term that refers to the Indian National Congress's call to boycott all imported material and cultural goods). This phase is represented by the name of the man widely revered as the founder of the Indian film industry, Dhundiraj Govind (Dadasaheb) Phalke. As well as elsewhere in the world, this period of Indian cinema coincides with the early stages of the industrialisation of culture, a process that accelerated significantly in the latter part of the nineteenth century. In India, this generated a specific set of cultural and aesthetic problems resulting from the encounter between traditional non-perspectival representational practices and the emergent lens-based media with their inbuilt notions of perspective and space. The issues relating to this encounter are debated by Indian art and film historians (see Kapur, 1993; Rajadhyaksha, 1993) in terms of 'frontality' of pictorial composition (lack of oblique angles and problematic connections between one space and another).

These aesthetic issues parallel the more directly political and historical issue of the need to imagine a unified spatio-temporal Indian dimension suitable for independence struggles.

The second period extends from the late silent era into the 1930s, that of the studios and production houses modelled to some extent on their Hollywood counterparts. This phase ended with the onset of World War II and was marked by experimentation with styles that combined, in spite of the Hollywood organisational model, aspects of British and especially German cinemas with Indian modes of storytelling, models that characteristically do not adhere to western-style distinctions between the realms of fantasy and reality. The imperative to construct spatial coherence within multi-shot sequences and to establish an editing style seeking to convey continuity of gesture and physical movement from one shot to the next was not generally accepted or applied, as can be seen in the few surviving silent action films as well as in many 1930s works.

The third phase saw the rise of an independent industry partly funded by the tremendous, often illegal, wealth generated during the war, and consequently viewed with suspicion by the state. It is also at this stage that new, extended consumer sectors began to be addressed more directly. Aesthetically, this period is associated with the gradual consolidation of a 'classic' type of melodrama (in the literal sense of musical drama) with its own rules of narration, often derived from late-nineteenth-century popular novels that were characterised by the 'serial imbrication' of multiple storylines within one narrative stream. As well as being indebted to popular fiction, mainstream Indian cinema developed its own notions of 'character', involving exemplary figures, in whom various social pressures coalesce, surrounded by social or familial groups. Western conventions of psychological verisimilitude that transform social–historical issues into personal, internal neuroses occasionally form part of the Indian narrative canvas but do not define its notion of character, at least not at this stage (the work of Satyajit Ray represents a shift in this respect). The Indian melodrama proved to be particularly suited for exploring the tensions involved in the modernisation and secularisation of society. Melodrama interrogated the relationship between public and private, urban and rural, industrial and agricultural, capitalist and pre-capitalist modes of production and social organisation. It also dramatised in the context of patriarchy transforming issues concerning the control of women's sexuality as an older type of patriarchy mutates into a more modern one, and so on into a recognisably modern form.

The fourth period is marked by the fruition of several state initiatives sponsoring a 'new', or 'parallel', cinema movement in the 1960s and 1970s, often in regions that had not yet established local industrial infrastructure. This in turn had an impact on the development of India's state-owned television, Doordarshan, and on institutions such as the Directorate of Film Festivals, the National Film Archive of India, the Film Insitute, the National Film Development Corporation and so on. This most recent phase is marked by a greater diversity of narrative styles and aesthetic conventions in the context of the emergence of, broadly speaking, three main streams of cinema: the state-sponsored cinema that sought to develop the pioneering work of Satyajit Ray (the Indian film-maker closest to western notions of the director as auteur) in a variety of directions; the commercial cinema that refined its own melodramatic narrative orchestrations and sought to achieve greater visceral impact; and the 'middle cinema' that sought

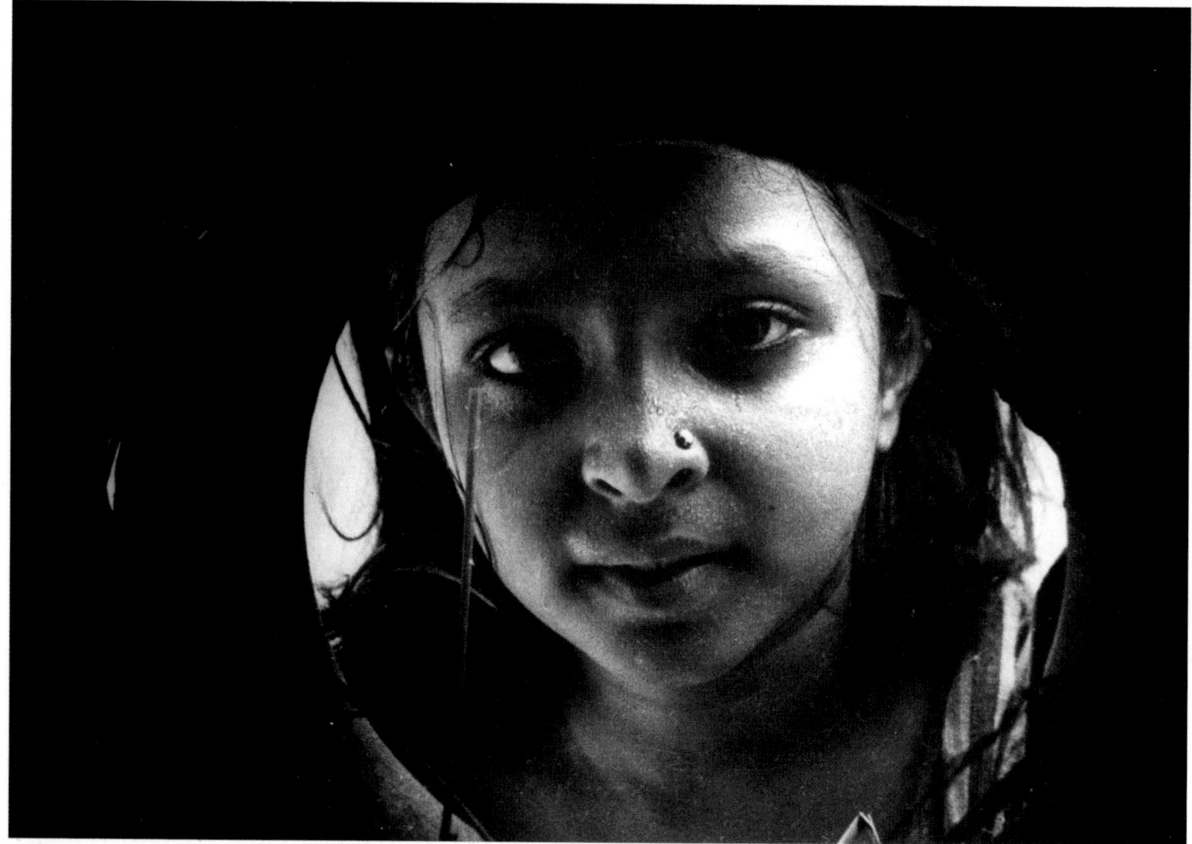

Pather Panchali, Satyajit Ray's internationally acclaimed debut feature and the first of the *Apu* trilogy

to combine elements of both of the previous tendencies (as in the work of Shyam Benegal). A fourth, numerically marginal but aesthetically tone-setting current evolved from the work of Ritwik Ghatak (1925–76) and aspires to an 'epic' mode of storytelling drawing on a variety of Indian and western representational traditions in order to elaborate a new idiom adequate to the representation of the cultural and historical complexities that are constellated in 1990s Indian society.

Some industrial issues

Phalke Films

Contrary to most accounts, Dadasaheb Phalke (1870–1944) was not India's first film director. Production in India had begun shortly after the first Lumière screenings in Bombay in 1896, mainly under the auspices of, on one hand, multinational distributors of film equipment who hired cameras and crews to make what later came to be described as documentaries and, on the other, independent film-maker-exhibitors, notably Harishchandra Bhatavdekar. In the first two decades of the 20th century, cinema grew alongside, but as a poor cousin of, the thriving Gujarati, Urdu and Hindi stage industries. However, Phalke was influential, in, first, setting up his own, domestically based, production concern (Phalke Films, founded in 1912) and, second, in aligning his enterprise with the polical economy of *swadeshi*.

Already a noted figure in the printing industry, Phalke saw his first film in 1910 (*The Life of Christ*) and was, in his own words, 'gripped by a strange spell ... Could we, the sons of India, ever be able to see Indian images on the screen?' He went on to make mythologicals using popular legends from the *Hindu Puranas* that led to his reputation as the inventor of the staple genre of India's pre-World War II cinema: the Hindu mythological (a notable early example of which was Phalke's *Kaliya Mardan*, 1919).

Phalke Films was characteristic of the small, cottage-type companies that proliferated in Indian cinema prior to the establishment of the first professional studio, Kohinoor (founded in 1918 and closed in 1932). Kohinoor was set up by D. N. Sampat, one of the most famous producers in Indian cinema whose productions (by directors such as Kanjibhai Rathod and Homi Master) were among the first successfully to address a pan-Indian audience and to boast movie stars (Raja Sandow, the Bilimoria brothers, Zubeida, Sulochana and others). Other companies followed suit: in Bombay there were the Imperial Film Company, the Ranjit, Krishna and Sharda studios, in Calcutta the Aurora Film Company and Indian Kinema, all established in the late 1920s, all attempting a variety of genres including stage adaptations, adaptations from novels and variations of American genres. Generally speaking, the most successful were those that most aptly indigenised their sources and approaches, usually within a broadly defined *swadeshi* context. For instance, Sharda's stunt and action movies starring Master Vithal adapted historical legends from India's middle ages, and there were also adventure sagas derived from Parsee Theatre's main source, Firdausi's *Shahnama*, and, of course, episodes from the *Mahabharata* and *Ramayana*. These adaptations helped to define an indigenous audience within specific distribution circuits patterned on those created by Madan Theatres, Pathé, Globe and Empire that specialised in showing American and European films, rarely overlapping with the 'native' product.

Phalke's arguments for a *swadeshi* cinema ('My films are *swadeshi* in the sense that the ownership, employees and stories are *swadeshi*') achieved virtually policy status through the work of the first major Cinematograph Committee set up in 1927. This Committee strongly endorsed the Rajput historical fantasy *At the Clang of Fetters/Janjirne Jankare* and the Rabindranath Tagore adaptation *The Sacrifice/Balidan*, both released in 1927 and hailed as Indian cinema's coming of age, proving that Indian cinema could make films that were on a par with those produced in the west. These films overcame what the Committee's report described as Indian cinema's three main limitations: an inability to tell stories, technical inadequacy and excessive length.

Prabhat Studios

Sound cinema emerged in 1931 with the release of the Parsee Theatre adaptation *The Beauty of the World/Alam Ara*, telling of the rivalry between two queens at the court of Kumarpur. Subsequently, most of the silent film studios closed down or were transformed into new companies, among the most famous of which are Prabhat, New Theatres and Bombay Talkies. This phase, between 1931 and the onset of World War II, witnessed the first of two so-called golden ages in Indian cinema (the second consisting of the famous melodramas of the 1950s). These two periods monopolise almost all critical and historical discussion on Indian film history, generating the country's first auteurs and film 'classics'.

The Prabhat studio, especially after it moved to Pune in 1933, became India's elite production house, with V. Shantaram as its star director-producer. Shantaram had emerged from the Gandharva Natak Mandali, a Marathi theatre company, and worked as actor, editor and director at Baburao Painter's Maharashtra Film Company. He then made sound versions of Baburao Painter's 20 historicals and mythologicals, later deploying a German-derived version of Expressionism for his celebrated socials (for example, *The Unexpected/Kunku Duniya Na Mane*, 1937; *Life Is for the Living/Manoos/Admi*, 1939; *The Neighbour/Shejari/Padosi*, 1941), which have been the focus for discussions of pre-1950s melodrama. Another Prabhat film, the Saint film *Sant Tukaram* by V. Damle and S. Fattelal (1936), has become the focus for seminal arguments regarding the differences between notions of 'the popular' in pre-independence India as opposed to the populist ideologies promulgated by post-independence producers (see, for instance, Shahani, 1986; Kapur, 1993; Gopal Singh, 1995).

The social dimension of genre film-making (see Rajadhyaksha and Willemen, 1994) owes much to literary adaptations produced by Prabhat and New Theatres (in Calcutta) in the 1930s, especially adaptations from the novels of Bankimchandra Chattopadhyay, Rabindranath Tagore and, later, Saratchandra Chattopadhyay in Bengal, as well as Govardhanram Tripathi (Gujarati), Hari Narayan Apte (Marathi), O. Chandu Menon (Malayalam) and others. These novels emerged from the late-nineteenth-century reform movements, which often addressed the social stresses and strains brought about by modernisation pressures as manifested in relation to changes in the status of women and the condition of the peasantry. Saratchandra especially, as perhaps twentieth-century India's most influential writer, set the terms for several stereotypes (rural India, the widow and so on) that were to recur in film melodramas that were also indebted to his convoluted narrative structures.

New Theatres and Bombay Talkies

Filming Saratchandra's stories was the method adopted by the film studio New Theatres (founded in 1931) to establish a 'respectable' cinema. (That a notion of quality should automatically imply literariness is a controversial aspect of Indian cinema in that it betrays the depth to which English ideologies penetrated 'indigenous' cultural priorities and frameworks.) The founder of New Theatres, B. N. Sircar, stated:

> [T]he first film I made was Saratchandra's *Dena Paona* (1931). The first director ... was Premankur Atorthy, the famed *littérateur*. The film was not a success. Yet I could perceive that following the path of literature would lead to the discovery of the right path ...

This approach resulted in the studio's most famous film, and one of the best-known films of pre-independence India, P. C. Barua's *Devdas* (1935), discussed extensively by Nandy (1995), for example. The eponymous character, Devdas, became a popular stereotype deployed on numerous occasions (including remakes) throughout Indian cinema: the lovesick, weak, narcissistic hero defeated by life.

New Theatres was also the studio where a host of India's best-known directors emerged: Debaki and Nitin Bose, Dhiren Ganguly and the cameraman/director Bimal Roy, the latter in his turn, after moving to Mumbai and making Hindi film, creating the conditions for the assimilation of major Bengali musicians and directors into the 'all-India' cinema.

The third major studio of the period was Bombay Talkies (founded in 1934), which had antecedents in the orientalist Indo-German and Indo-British co-productions of Himansu Rai in the 1920s (often directed by the German Franz Osten, whose career in India came to an end when he was interned as an enemy alien by the British at the start of World War II). The Bombay Talkies movies, especially Osten's work, fed a long-running debate about notions of Indianness and 'the oriental' extending into the work of Ismail Merchant and James Ivory. Initially, Osten's films were intended to break into the European market and took their aesthetic cues from Ufa in Germany (see also German Cinema, p. 208). This was also the first time that private sector capital (mainly from insurance companies) was mobilised for an industrial enterprise promising regular dividends to investors. With the hit *The Untouchable Girl/Achhut Kanya* (1936), starring Ashok Kumar and Devika Rani, the studio formulated the enduring screen image of 'village India', with its stock characters (the landowner, the peasant, the innocent hero, social evils and medieval corruption) and, most importantly, a kind of simplified Hindustani that had by then become the 'national' language. Personnel involved in Bombay Talkies went on to found the even more influential studio Filmistan, founded in 1942 but effectively launched by the Bombay Talkies hit *Fate/Kismet* (1943). The Filmistan period, which lasted for 16 years, marks the bridge between prewar and post-independence commercial Indian cinema (the so-called Masala cinema), introducing a raft of stars (Dev Anand, Dilip Kumar, Shammi Kapoor and others) and establishing the formula of the song-dance-action fantasy films that have come to be seen as typical of Indian cinema in general.

Art, industry and the state

This transition was first chronicled by independent India's first Film Enquiry Committee Report, which used strong language to comment on the shift from the prewar studio system to the postwar rise of speculators:

> Within three years of the end of the War, the leadership of the industry had changed hands from established producers to a variety of successors. Leading 'stars', exacting 'financiers' and calculating distributors and exhibitors forged ahead ... Film production ... became in substantial measure the recourse of deluded aspirants to easy riches ... (*Report of the Film Enquiry Committee*, 1951)

To a great extent this critical attitude towards the development of an utterly market-oriented mass entertainment industry bypassing the state's requirements and preferred directions of development must be seen in the context of the international and the Indian elite's acclaim for Satyajit Ray's debut film, *Song of the Road/Pather Panchali* (1955). Ray's work drew on the Bengali novel and to some extent built on New Theatres' attempt to bring literary respectability to the cinema. However, Ray pursued this project with far greater ambition and control than before. The epic story of the boy Apu's growth to adulthood in the Apu trilogy (*Song of the Road/Pather Panchali*; *The Unvanquished/Aparajito*, 1956; *The World of Apu/Apur Sansar*, 1958) clearly provided Indian cinema with its first internationally significant works of art. Joined in the late 1950s by contemporaries Mrinal Sen, later known for his Calcutta trilogy (*Interview*, 1970; *Calcutta '71*, 1972; *The Guerrilla Fighter/Padatik*, 1973), and by Ritwik Ghatak, Ray introduced a new dimension to notions of authenticity, substantially influencing what the Indian state would come to define in the 1960s and 1970s as an official aesthetic of 'good' or 'art' cinema.

On the other hand, it is also possible, and indeed necessary, to contextualise Ray's work by seeing it in relation to the tradition of the Hindi melodramas of the 1950s, the genre which has become the focus of most of the significant theoretical work on Indian cinema since the 1980s. For instance, Vasudevan's analysis of those melodramas, substantiated by the critical work of Kobita Sarkar and Chidananda Das Gupta, demonstrates how Ray inaugurated a formal opposition between melodramatic, externalised modes of representation and a more internalised, character-oriented narration coming closer to the middle-class's notion of what 'good' cinema should be like (see Vasudevan, 1993). Vasudevan discusses many of the classic melodramas of the 1950s, such as Gyan Mukherjee's *Kismet*, Mehboob's *A Matter of Style/Andaz* (1949), Raj Kapoor's *The Tramp/Awara* (1952) and Guru Dutt's *Eternal Thirst/Pyaasa* (1957), in order to analyse the narrative codes, iconic characterisations and social caste and gender identities of the characters in the films in which Ray negotiates India's transition to modernity, examining the various forms modernity can take, and assessing its limits as well as its productive capacities. The film industry's representatives tended to explain the difference between the industrial cinema and Ray's cinema in economic terms, invoking the role of state support and the attempted creation of an elite audience in contrast to the mass-entertainment approach, which tended to assume the underdevelopment of both the industry and its audiences, seeing questions of modernity either as threats to 'tradition' or as questions of the size, scale and technical infrastructure of the productions.

In the 1960s, the crucial effort to redefine the perceived splits within Indian cinema came from Chidananda Das Gupta, who introduced the phrase 'all-India film' to describe the mainstream Hindi entertainment cinema and its equivalents in other Indian languages. Das Gupta argued that this kind of cinema had taken on the role of cultural leadership, reinforcing the unifying tendencies in India's social and economic changes and providing an inferior alternative to a leadership that might have emerged had it not been for the rift between the intelligentsia, to which the leaders belonged, and 'the masses' (see Das Gupta, 1981).

Das Gupta's argument strengthened the tendency to define the mainstream Indian cinema as playing a kind of default role, making Hindi the national film language and creating, by way of the melodramas, a nationally integrative cultural domain. In the 1970s, the New Indian Cinema, sponsored by the Film Finance Corporation, intervened to redefine the terms of the debate. The New Indian Cinema itself, as a movement, is usually dated back to Mrinal Sen's satire *Bhuvan Shome* (1969) and Mani Kaul's formal experiment *Our Daily Bread/Uski Roti* (1970). The theoretical underpinning of this movement was presented by one of its most important directors, Kumar Shahani.

Kumar Shahani's films (*Mirror of Illusion/Maya Darpan*, 1972; *Wages and Profit/Tarang*, 1983; *Khayal Saga/Khayal Gatha*, 1989; *Ravine/Kasba*, 1991) and his extensive writings proclaim a radically new vanguard practice in Indian cinema underpinned by an analysis of its history. In his key essays 'Notes towards an aesthetic of cinema sound' (1985) and 'Film as a contemporary art' (1990), Shahani approaches the cinematograph in terms of its ability to deploy a sound–image dialectic, rather than in terms of an aspiration towards a technical 'realism' in camera-sound recording combinations. Shahani, detouring through Brecht, sought to recover Indian narrative traditions and art forms that would allow him to develop a new kind of 'epic' cinema. Shahani drew on Indian classical music and other performing arts to reconceptualise the very notions of narrative and sequentiality while demonstrating how these older Indian art forms in fact continued to be active within so-called lower art forms such as film and contemporary kinds of 'popular' performances. In so doing, Shahani suggests alternatives to the sterile varieties of lyrical or dramatic realisms that beset both the industrial cinema and the construction of 'Indianness' in allegedly ethnographically realist representations.

In 1975, two major box-office successes of the Hindi cinema, *Embers/Sholay*, with its many stars and an early hit song for the superstar of the 1980s, Amitabh Bachchan, and the low-budget mythological *In Praise of Mother Santoshi/Jai Santoshi Maa*, introduced a new era in which the Hindi cinema was to spearhead a major technological and cultural change via the medium of television. Earlier, in 1971, the Motion Picture Export Association of America had announced a boycott of the Indian market on account of Indian economic and cultural 'protectionism'. In 1975, as a culmination of Indira Gandhi's 'nation in danger' rhetoric shoring up protectionist economic measures, a state of national emergency was declared, the same year in which television introduced several satellite experiments preparing the way for the government's major expansion of broadcasting and media industries in the early 1980s. *Embers* and *In Praise of Mother Santoshi*, each in their own way, signalled a technological and an aesthetic readiness on the part of the Indian film industry to assimilate and propagate the upgrading of the media industry. This development had already been announced in Bachchan's earlier hit melodramas, *The Chain/Zanjeer* (1973) and *The Wall/Deewar* (1975), in which the feudal laws of kinship and the tragic vigilante hero are proposed as substitutes for the ineffectual laws and role of the Indian state. Veena Das's (1980) reading of *In Praise of Mother Santoshi* tries to account for the unexpected impact achieved by a film that presents an entirely invented legend of kinship relations, bypassing the established pantheon, and launches a mother goddess who became a popular icon, especially among working-class women.

The relevance of the work of film-makers and critics such as Shahani is that they attempt to understand the basic dynamics that structure Indian film culture as a changing force field rather than trying to fetishise some of its component factions or trends. This approach became startlingly relevant in the late 1990s when cinema had to face the massive, largely unforeseen, invasion of cable and satellite television. This latest development has received, as yet, little theoretical attention in India (or elsewhere, for that matter), even though it threatens not only cinema, but the very edifice of what has structured both the pre- and post-independence debates on Indian cinema: the Indian state as a disciplinary and regulatory authority.

Selected Reading

Chidananda Das Gupta, 'The cultural basis of Indian cinema' (1968), in *Talking about Films*, New Delhi, Orient Longman, 1981.

Tejaswini Niranjana *et al.* (eds), *Interrogating Modernity: Culture and Colonialism in India*, Calcutta, Seagull Books, 1993.

Ashish Rajadhyaksha and Paul Willemen, *Encyclopaedia of Indian Cinema*, London and Delhi, BFI/Oxford University Press, 1994. Second edition 1999.

Kumar Shahani, 'Film as a contemporary art', *Social Scientist* 18 (3), March 1990.

Bollywood

RACHEL DWYER

In recognition of its importance over the last 25 years, 'Bollywood' has now entered the *Oxford English Dictionary*. Yet this term – Bombay/Hollywood – is widely disliked and its meaning is disputed. I use it to refer to mainstream Hindi cinema, distinct from art house or cinemas in other languages.

During the 1980s, the popularity of mainstream cinema in India declined with the rise of state television that, along with 'parallel' or 'middle', often state-sponsored films, was consumed by an emerging middle class. The mainstream cinema frequently seemed a parody of itself, often referring back to the superstar of Hindi film, Amitabh Bachchan (see *Embers* case study), as a new generation of fighting heroes emerged. This cinema, despite the success of occasional big-budget films such as those of Subhash Ghai, was often poor quality and male-oriented, increasing its distance from the cinema of the middle classes. Piracy was rampant, and the VHS market grew, as did the market for music cassettes, which were easily copied and distributed. However, the late 1980s saw a growth in the youth audience as 1988's *From the Apocalypse and Back/Qayamat Se Qayamat Tak*, directed by Mansoor Khan, showcased musical romance, with a new style of music and a new generation of stars who were to dominate the next decade.

The liberalisation of the economy from state control in 1991 led to the greatest and most rapid change in India. It seemed as though Hindu nationalism (*Hindutva*) was to become the dominant ideology as Hindu/Muslim riots flared up, notably in 1992–3 in cosmopolitan Bombay, which was renamed Mumbai in 1996. However, this nationalism was paralleled by a burgeoning transnationalism in cinema, closely linked to the overseas markets of NRIs (non-resident Indians), also called the South Asian diaspora, or BritAsians in UK.

Although new television channels available on cable and satellite after 1992 looked set to seal the decline of the mainstream film, they actually fuelled its growth through showing films and film-related programmes. This and the growth of new media, notably the Internet, encouraged discourse on cinema through the creation of fan communities, circulation of reviews and press materials. The 1990s saw the return of the family audience, though transformed by the emergence of the youth audience.

Film music became 'cool' among the younger audience and a club scene grew, as innovative forms were created by the south Indian musical genius A. R. Rahman, and the global popularity of Nusrat Fateh Ali Khan's *sufi* devotional music led to an initial trickle of Pakistani pop that was coupled with the 'pizza effect' of *bhangra*, a folk form from the Punjab that was transformed in the UK and re-exported to India. Films were financed by advance sales of cassettes and CDs, reaching a peak in the late 1990s before crashing with the onslaught of downloadable

Kaliya Mardan (India 1919 *p.c* – Hindustan Cinema Films; *d* – Dadasaheb Phalke)

Dadasaheb Phalke is regarded by many as the founder of the Indian film industry. *Kaliya Mardan* is the one film of Phalke's to survive that approximates something close to its original length (which was 6,000 feet). The story tells the Pauranic tale of the child Krishna, showing his antics as he steals butter with his young friends, causing mayhem in the village while also demonstrating his godly powers. In the important final scene, young Krishna defeats the demon snake Kaliya in a fierce underwater battle, rising triumphantly to the surface as everyone mourns his assumed death. One of the most remarkable sequences is the opening in which Phalke introduces his daughter Mandakini, who plays Krishna, through a series of close-ups showing her preparing for the role in the tradition of Indian folk theatre.

Kaliya Mardan demonstrates many of the stylistic traits that the director was famous for. A crucial convention, practised in Indian cinema ever since, is the use of frontal address, with Krishna/the hero as an icon that is 'recognised' by the audience (who, represented by the villagers, is included within the frame at times) and defines several conventions of mise en scène and even a particular notion of screen realism. Phalke indicates this realism with scenes shot on location and by images showing rustic life in Maharashtra.

ASHISH RAJADHYAKSHA

Song of the Road/Pather Panchali (India 1955 *p.c* – Government of West Bengal; *d* – Satyajit Ray)

Song of the Road marked Satyajit Ray's debut and was the internationally acclaimed first film of his Apu trilogy. Set in the early years of twentieth-century Bengal, the story is told mainly through the eyes of the child protagonist, Apu. The film chronicles the entry of modernity into the rural landscape. At the end of the film, Apu's family leave their broken hut and move to Benares. The subsequent films in the trilogy show Apu growing up in Benares and Calcutta, getting married and facing the death of his young wife.

The making of the film, the technological innovations of shooting on location and assimilating the style of the Italian neo-realists (notably De Sica), including their naturalistic acting style, are issues that have been widely discussed (see Das Gupta, 1980; Robinson, 1989, which also includes an extensive bibliography). The trilogy's realism in its portrayal of rural India clearly meant a lot to the newly independent Indian intelligentsia, and can itself be placed within what is now understood as a specifically Nehruite project of modernisation.

ASHISH RAJADHYAKSHA

Guru Dutt's melodrama *Pyaasa* explores themes of exile and nationhood

Eternal Thirst/Pyaasa (India 1957 *p.c* – Guru Dutt Films; *d* – Guru Dutt)

Guru Dutt's famous melodrama about the travails of a young poet in India, played by the director himself, was the first of three films on the theme of exile and nationhood that established Dutt as one of the great exponents of melodrama in film.

Eternal Thirst tells the story of Vijay, an Urdu poet in Calcutta, and his love affair with a prostitute, Gulab. Vijay descends into squalor; rejected by his publisher, denied his rights by the husband of his former lover Meena, eventually he is believed dead. In the most astonishing sequence in the film, Vijay 'travels' through a sick, hungry and depraved India, ending up at a place where his former tormentors – who have become rich with the 'posthumous' publishing of his work – have organised a public meeting to commemorate his death. He denounces them and the hypocrisy of the state, and is overrun in the ensuing stampede. Eventually, he and Gulab leave in order to invent their own utopia elsewhere.

The film is regarded as the pinnacle of the tradition of Indian melodrama, notably in its use of music (by S. B. Burman), its elevation of the hero into an iconic presence, and its upgrading of the literary tradition and the 'socials' of 1930s film into a valid, properly cinematic idiom. Although the story claims to be original, comparisons can be made to Saratchandra Chatterjee's well-known novel *Srikanta*. Dutt's masterly camerawork, especially in the long crane shots and in the use of light and shadow, contributes to the tragic feel of the story.

ASHISH RAJADHYAKSHA

Embers/Sholay (India 1975 *p.c* – Sippy Films; *d* – Ramesh Sippy)

This big-budget hit introduced a new era of Hindi commercial cinema in the 1970s. The story is concerned with the rivalry between an ex-policeman, Thakur Baldev Singh, and a bandit, Gabbar Singh. Its style references the spaghetti western, as well as adapting scenes from the films of such directors as John Ford, Burt Kennedy, Charlie Chaplin and Sam Peckinpah. This creates an effect that Paul Willemen describes as resembling 'a skilfully designed shopping mall with the viewer being propelled past successive window displays, each exhibiting an eye-catching presentation of some aspect of the popular cinema's history'. The film broke new ground in India in its marketing strategies, with the LP of the soundtrack, and notably Gabbar's dialogues, almost outselling the music. It also introduced the new 1980s style of lumpen heroism associated with the film's writers, Salim Khan and Javed Akhtar, who claim to have authored the screen persona of Amitabh Bachchan.

ASHISH RAJADHYAKSHA

The Brave Heart Takes the Bride/Dilwale Dulhaniya Le Jayenge (India 1995 *p.c* – Yash Raj Films; *d* – Aditya Chopra)

One of the highest-grossing and longest-running Hindi films of all time, *DDLJ* draws on the style of romance created by the director's father, Yash Chopra, for the Hindi cinema, a 'glamorous realism' formed by its use of language, music and images. *DDLJ* establishes features that become key to the Hindi film of the 1990s – the use of overseas locations, the centrality of friendship to romance – while it reshapes in conservative terms the traditional problem at the heart of the Hindi film romance, namely the incorporation of the romantic couple into wider family structures. The film also showcases the superstars Shah Rukh Khan and Kajol as one of the great screen couples.

RACHEL DWYER

music files, and cinema audiences in the 2000s were affected by the high quality of cheap, often pirated, DVDs. However, from the mid-2000s, the multiplex cinema, an integral part of the new consumerist culture, has reshaped the audience through smaller theatres and more expensive tickets.

In the early 1990s, the higher production values of the south Indian cinema based in Madras (Chennai) had a great impact on Hindi film. Yet despite the popularity of certain key directors, such as Mani Ratnam, who made the last film of his nationalist 'trilogy' in Hindi, the Bombay cinema developed its own forms with the big-budget 'glamorous realism' of Yash Raj Films, headed by the veteran Yash Chopra, a lifetime member of BAFTA. Chopra's son Aditya made box-office history with his London–Punjab romance *The Brave Heart Takes the Bride/Dilwale Dulhaniya Le Jayenge*, released in 1995 and still running in Mumbai (see case study). In 2006, the group built the first major integrated studio, whose facilities are on a par with European equivalents.

Indian cinema stepped further onto the world stage in 2001, when a three-and-a-half-hour film about a cricket match between Indian villagers and the colonial rulers in the nineteenth century, *Lagaan: Once Upon a Time in India/Lagaan*, directed by Ashutosh Gowarikar, was nominated for an Academy Award.

The multiplex and the DVD have led many to predict the end of the all-India film. More interestingly, smaller, differentiated markets that show strong genre preferences (such as the gangster film and offbeat, politically engaged films) are emerging as a challenge to the dominant 'social genre' or the 'masala film'. Even big production houses such as Yash Raj Films and Mukta Arts are including smaller-budget films. However, comedy has reappeared with great success, notably in the antics of Munnabhai (Sanjay Dutt), a petty criminal with a big heart and the common touch (*Munnabhai M.B.B.S.*, 2003, and *Lage raho Munnabhai*, 2006, directed by Rajkumar Hirani). Yet, despite such successes, Indian films are poorly marketed to non-Indian audiences and very few are seen beyond South Asian communities overseas. There are too many remakes of Hollywood movies, which are often heralded as genius even though they lack character, drama and dialogue, the very features that make the Munnabhai films so popular. Songs and dance, stars, mise en scène and emotional relations between romantic couples and families are still given priority, though few directors can present these with the skill and style that has become the hallmark of Yash Raj productions.

Selected Reading

Anupama Chopra, *Dilwale Dulhaniya Le Jayenge*, London, BFI Publishing, 2003.

Rachel Dwyer, *Yash Chopra*, London, BFI Publishing, 2002.

Rachel Dwyer, *100 Bollywood Films*, London, BFI Publishing, 2005.

Ashish Rajadhyaksha and Paul Willemen, *An Encyclopaedia of Indian Cinema*, London, BFI Publishing, 1999. Second edition.

HONG KONG CINEMA

STEPHEN TEO

Hong Kong produced its first feature film in 1913, but it only became a major centre of film production in the 1930s when sound came in and production companies devoted themselves to making Cantonese feature films. The first Cantonese talkie, *White Gold Dragon/Bai Jinlong*, was produced in Shanghai in 1933; its success in Cantonese-speaking Hong Kong prompted its production company to move base to the colony, which then became a centre for the production of Cantonese films distributed in southern China and Southeast Asian countries where large Cantonese-speaking Chinese communities had settled. The Hong Kong film industry benefited from the migratory influx of Shanghai film-makers from 1933 onwards, but particularly in 1937 when Shanghai was partially occupied by Japan following the outbreak of the Sino-Japanese War. Hong Kong film production continued until the start of the Pacific War in 1941. With the exception of several wartime propaganda pictures produced by Japan, no local films were made over the duration of the war.

The Hong Kong film industry made a strong recovery after the war. With the commencement of the civil war on the mainland, Shanghai film-makers relocated en masse to Hong Kong. The migrant film-makers laid the foundation of Hong Kong's Mandarin cinema – in effect, a de facto Chinese national cinema located in the British colony when China itself was embroiled by civil war and later, after the Communist victory, cut itself off from the rest of the world. The Cantonese cinema had also revived after the war, and it became the engine of growth in the film industry throughout the 1950s. Cantonese Opera films became a popular genre that fed into the production of over 200 features annually from around 1955 onwards. Mandarin pictures posed strong competition from this period. The mogul Run Run Shaw set up the Shaw Brothers Studio in 1957 in a bid to compete with its rival, the Cathay Organisation. Both Shaws and Cathay dominated the Mandarin sector of the film industry.

The Cantonese cinema experienced an unprecedented era of growth in the early 1960s, only to decline from 1965 onwards as the Mandarin cinema, led by the Shaw Brothers Studio, spearheaded a popular movement of so-called 'new school' sword-fighting martial arts pictures that swept away the competition from the more technically backward Cantonese industry. By the end of the decade, Cantonese cinema was in terminal

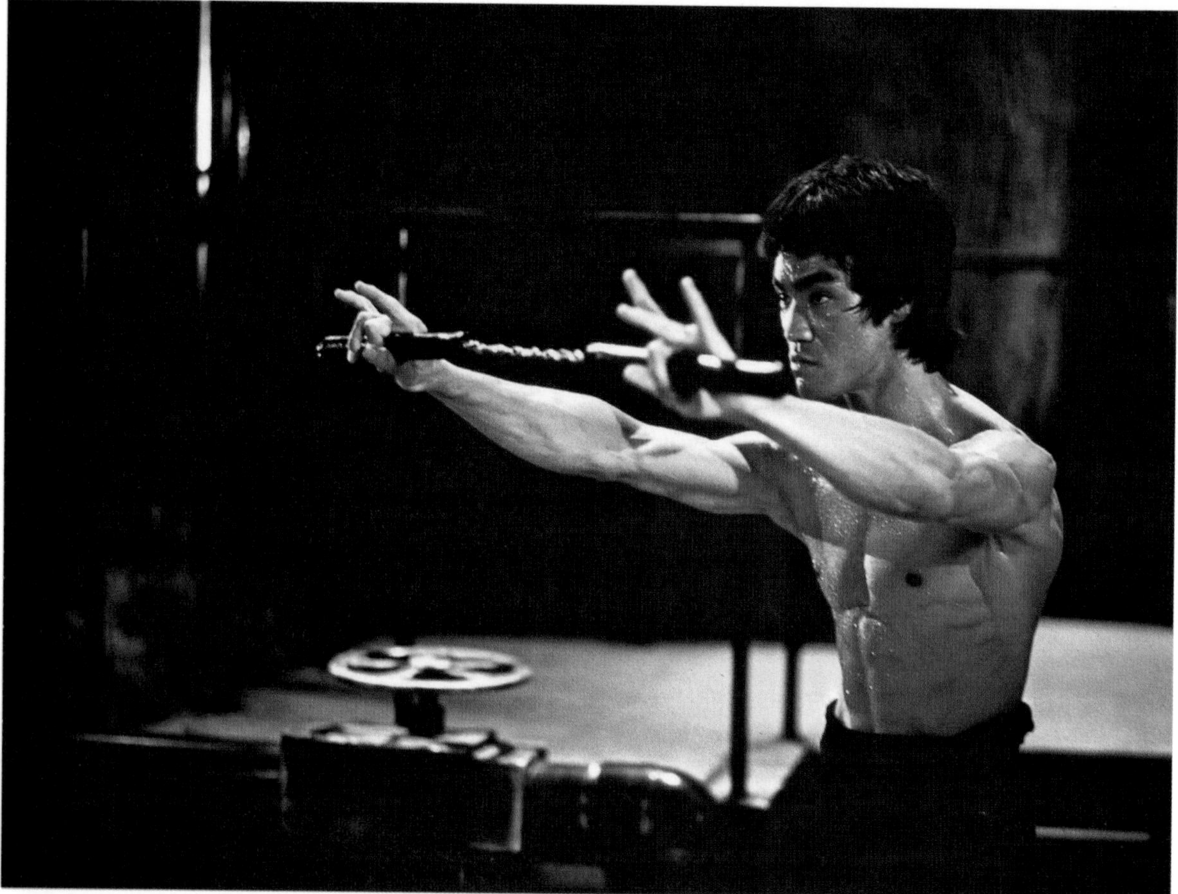

Enter the Dragon: Bruce Lee's kung fu films helped propel Hong Kong cinema into international markets

decline. The 'new school' martial arts pictures of the Mandarin cinema, exemplified by King Hu's *Come Drink With Me/Da Zui Xia* (1965) and Zhang Che's *The One-Armed Swordsman/Du Bei Dao* (1968), buttressed the pre-eminence of Mandarin films in the period 1965–71 throughout Southeast Asia and in Chinatown cinemas around the world, but it was the kung fu pictures of Bruce Lee – *The Big Boss/Tang Shan Daxiong* (1971), *Fist of Fury/Jingwu Men* (1972) and *Enter the Dragon/Longzheng Hudou* (1973) – that finally propelled Hong Kong cinema into the global market. The martial arts genre as a whole achieved international recognition when King Hu's *A Touch of Zen/Xia Nü* (1969) was awarded the Grand Prix at the Cannes Film Festival of 1975.

By the mid-1970s, Cantonese films were making a comeback with the popular comedy hits of Michael Hui (*The Private Eyes/Banjin Baliang*, 1977; *The Contract/Maishen Qi*, 1978), and Cantonese became practically the lingua franca of Hong Kong cinema when the New Wave erupted in 1979, signalling that the postwar 'baby-boom' generation had taken over the reins of the industry as the old guard of Mandarin directors died off or retired. Most of the New Wave directors had gone to film schools in the west and on returning to Hong Kong were employed in television making drama serials shot on film. The New Wave TV works had distinctive styles and touches of social commentary, expressing a clearer identification of Hong Kong citizenship that stands separately from China or Taiwan. When the New Wave directors alighted in the film industry, their films, such as Ann Hui's *The Secret/Feng Jie* (1979), Tsui Hark's *The Butterfly Murders/Die Bian* (1979) and Alex Cheung's *Cops and Robbers/Dianzhi Bingbing* (1979), combined a certain bleak allegory of Hong Kong society with the genre conventions of the crime thriller and the martial arts picture. The works of Ann Hui and Tsui Hark gradually became more commercial, with the latter making a greater impression through an idiosyncratic series of fast-paced action-adventure films laced with baroque aesthetics (such as *Peking Opera Blues/Dao Ma Dan*, 1986; *Once upon a Time in China/Huang Feihong*, 1991; and *The Blade/Dao*, 1996).

At the end of the 1980s, younger directors such as Wong Kar-wai, Stanley Kwan and Clara Law (see Transnational film studies, p. 508) entered the ranks of the New Wave, forming a 'Second Wave'. These directors tended to convey a view of Hong Kong cinema as a postmodern art form, utilising fragmentary narratives and eclectic allusions to popular culture from both east and west. In their hands, Hong Kong cinema became more recognisable as an art cinema internationally, though in fact Hong Kong films remained largely populist and strictly entertainment-oriented, over the years winning a certain reputation in the west as a cult cinema. The postmodern 'art films' of directors such as Wong Kar-wai (*Chungking Express/Chongqing Senlin*, 1994; *Happy Together/Chunguang Zhaxie*, 1997; *In the Mood for Love/Huayang Nianhua*, 2000; 2046, 2004) and Stanley Kwan (*Rouge/Yanzhi Kou*, 1987; *Actress/Ruan Lingyu*, 1991) have nevertheless managed to present a more sophisticated side of Hong Kong cinema, one that is commensurate with the best standards of film-making around the world, and offer an alternative method and vision to Hollywood's blockbuster mode.

Among the genres that have sustained the view of Hong Kong as a cult cinema are the gangster genre, the martial arts kung fu action genre and the comedy genre. The gangster pictures of John Woo, such as *A Better Tomorrow/Yingxiong Bense* (1986), *The Killer/Diexie Shuangxiong* (1989) and *Hardboiled/Lashou Shentan* (1992), centred on the world of male-bonding cops and gangsters, revolving around the theme of loyalty and betrayal. Woo's stylish direction earned him a niche in Hollywood, where he had migrated in 1992, though his subsequent Hollywood work is often compared unfavourably with his Hong Kong films. Another major Hong Kong figure who transferred to Hollywood was the kung fu star-cum-director Jackie Chan. Here again, Chan's Hollywood efforts *Rush Hour* (1998), *Rush Hour 2* (2001) and *Shanghai Knights* (2003) suffer in comparison with his Hong Kong productions such as *Project A/A Jihua* (1983), *Police Story/Jingcha Gushi* (1985), *Project A (Part II)/A Jihua Xuji* (1987) and *Who Am I?/Woshe Shei* (1998). Chan's Hong Kong films remain fresh and vibrant, not least because he managed effortlessly to customise a kung fu cinema in the form of spectacular stunts and acrobatics that he performed and choreographed with comic timing and precision (though not without a certain cost to his body in the form of physical injuries).

Chan was among a group of kung fu stars, including Sammo Hung, Jet Li and Michelle Yeoh, who made the move to Hollywood in the early 1990s, perhaps prompted by the political uncertainty of the 1997 handover of Hong Kong to China. The post-97 Hong Kong film industry has, however, been affected more by economic and social crises than political ones. An economic slump facilitated by the Asian financial crisis of 1997 (before the handover) has stubbornly persisted into the new millennium, with the result that Hong Kong produced only 50 films in 2005, the lowest ever recorded since the 1950s. In 2003, the outbreak of the SARS virus brought commercial cinemas to a standstill over the Easter holiday break (a traditional time for the release of new movies). The mishandling of the health crisis by the government, as well as its inadequate management of the economic depression and its political blunders in attempting to ram through legislation to limit Hong Kong's traditional freedoms (resulting in a massive street demonstration by the public), have all inspired film-makers to take an increasingly bleak view of Hong Kong's present and future. The crime trilogy *Infernal Affairs/Wujian Dao* (2002–4), directed by Andrew Lau and Alan Mak, depicted Hong Kong in very dark symbolic tones, interlarding a sense of dread and fatal melancholy with an absorbing drama of mutual conspiracies by the police and the triads to destroy each other's top operatives through the use of moles and double agents.

Johnnie To's *PTU*, released during the height of the SARS crisis in 2003, features cops ambling along a night beat in Kowloon (the title refers to the police tactical unit that dispatches cops to patrol the streets of Hong Kong). The cops seem weary and there is division among the ranks when the sergeant decides to help a detective search for his missing gun. The fear and misgivings of the protagonists and the dangers they face mirror the bleak vision of Hong Kong as a virtual ghost town. To is the most distinctive director of the post-97 Hong Kong cinema in that he has managed to carve out a veritable niche for himself as a cutting-edge producer-director (with his own production company, Milkyway Image) forever attempting to jump-start a depressed industry with both mainstream and offbeat productions. His reputation has grown over the period of the industry's post-1997 decline, based on a series of critically praised, stylish action pieces, including *Running Out of Time/An Zhan* (2000), *The Mission/Qiang Hu* (1999), *PTU*, *Breaking News/Da Shijian* (2004) and *Throw Down/Roudao Longhu Bang* (2004). He has effectively taken over the mantle vacated by such action directors as John Woo and Tsui Hark, who both migrated to Hollywood (though Tsui subsequently returned to Hong Kong, and has attempted several comeback efforts, including *Time and Tide/Shunliu Niliu*, 2002, and *Seven Swords/Qi Jian*, 2005, with mixed results). To's latest films, *Election/Hei Shehui* (2005) and *Election 2/Hei Shehui Yihe Weigui* (2006), portray the violent underworld of triad societies torn apart by the process of having to elect an overlord every two years. The films are an undisguised allegory of Hong Kong politics.

To's violent noir thrillers are representative of Hong Kong cinema as an industry that produces popular fare and social commentary at the same time, but some might see Hong Kong cinema as a pure entertainment industry, represented by the likes of Stephen Chow, a comedian with kung fu aspirations who showed his mettle in many so-called 'nonsense' comedies in the 1990s before making an international name for himself in *Shaolin Soccer/Shaolin Zuqiu* (2001) and *Kung Fu Hustle/Gongfu* (2004). Chow's films, like To's, seek to rejuvenate Hong Kong cinema by lifting it out of the doldrums of depression to the heights of fantasy, revealing the rich variety and complexity of Hong Kong films – from violent allegory to pure fantasy. In between, throw in the abstract but emotionally profound visions of a film-maker such as Wong Kar-wai. Wong's *2046* – the title refers to the year when the 50-year time limit for no change for Hong Kong following China's takeover ends – points to a future that is still uncertain. In fact, the future of Hong Kong cinema is increasingly tied in with the potential that China's vast market offers. How film-makers will realise that potential remains to be seen.

Selected Reading

David Bordwell, *Planet Hong Kong: Popular Cinema and the Art of Entertainment*, Cambridge, MA, Harvard University Press, 2000.

Poshek Fu and David Desser (eds), *The Cinema of Hong Kong: History, Arts, Identity*, Cambridge and New York, Cambridge University Press, 2002.

Stephen Teo, *Hong Kong Cinema: The Extra Dimensions*, London, BFI Publishing, 1997.

Esther C. M. Yau (ed.), *At Full Speed: Hong Kong Cinema in a Borderless World*, Minneapolis, University of Minnesota Press, 2001.

A Touch of Zen/Xia Nü (Hong Kong/Taiwan 1969 *p.c* – Lianbang [Union Film Company]; *d* – King Hu)

This was the seminal martial arts film that did more than any of the kung fu films of the early 1970s to introduce to the west the magical flying and fighting figure of the female knight-errant: a subsequent key attraction of Ang Lee's *Crouching Tiger, Hidden Dragon/Wohu Canglong* (2000). The film's success at the 1975 Cannes Film Festival and its wide circulation in art-house cinemas in the west made it the prototype of the martial arts art film that can 'cross over' from the local to the global. It was also a prototype of pan-Chinese production, with the employment of talent from Hong Kong, Taiwan and China: director King Hu was from Beijing while the crew and cast were from Taiwan and Hong Kong (the film was mainly shot in Taiwan by the Union studio). Hu was one of the directors responsible for reinventing the *wuxia* (martial chivalry) genre in the so-called 'new school' cinematic movement of the mid-1960s. He did this first by reintroducing the lady knight-errant as a prime action figure in *Come Drink with Me/Da Zui Xia* (1965), and second by underscoring action with the stylistics of traditional Beijing Opera. Both elements are present in *A Touch of Zen*, where the female knight protagonist, on a mission of vengeance, wrestles with the epiphanic consciousness of Zen and attempts to transcend both her nature and physicality. The action sequences, notably the famous duel in a bamboo forest, are spectacular cinematic models of their kind, combining montage technique with Beijing Opera-inspired choreography and aerobatics.

STEPHEN TEO

Chungking Express/Chongqing Senlin (Hong Kong 1994 *p.c* – Jet Tone; *d* – Wong Kar-wai)

Wong Kar-wai is the Hong Kong auteur who may have brought the Hong Kong New Wave full circle, inasmuch as *Chungking Express* looks and plays like a Jean-Luc Godard movie, evoking the freshness and technical adventurousness of the Nouvelle Vague. When Hong Kong's own New Wave broke in 1979, its aesthetics were marked by a kind of social realism closely tied to the search for local identity: many of the first works of the New Wave were crime thrillers and social dramas about dejected or rejected youth, such as Ann Hui's *The Secret/Feng Jie* (1979), Yim Ho's *The Happenings/Ye Che* (1980) or Tsui Hark's *Dangerous Encounters – First Kind/Diyi Leixing Weixian* (1980). Wong's film affirms that the style of new wave aesthetics is more or less free and improvised, and while it conjures up generic expectations it also transcends them: the film is a loose concoction of two stories, one an urban crime thriller of sorts and the other a romantic comedy featuring a policeman as the centre of a young woman's fantasy. Wong's aesthetics seem to confirm their origins in the French and other European cinemas. The film impresses as a postmodern fusion of east and west but it also betrays a curiously old-fashioned, if not outmoded, romanticism. Indeed, Wong's films such as *In the Mood for Love* (2000) and *2046* (2004) are unabashedly nostalgic ruminations about time. *Chungking Express* attempts to push forward time – it is a postmodernist romance cross-bred with MTV and Nouvelle Vague editing style, on-location realism and narrative dissonance. The accent on style conveys a feeling of edgy excitement and a sense of high-octane elation reminiscent of the days when Godard and Truffaut released their first films.

STEPHEN TEO

Kung Fu Hustle/Gongfu (Hong Kong/People's Republic of China 2004 *p.c* – Columbia Pictures Asia/China Film Co-production Corp/Huai Bros & Taihe Film Investment Co/China Film Group Corp/Film Victoria/ Star Overseas/Beijing Film Studio; *d* – Stephen Chow)

Stephen Chow's *Kung Fu Hustle* is a far more multifaceted film than is suggested by its surface appearance as a pure fantasy of kung fu martial arts. The film is a farcical comedy, which is Chow's stock-in-trade (he became a superstar in the 1990s in a series of zany farces extolling the virtues of the little man, usually hailing from the countryside in China, who always had it in him to become a big man in a city such as Hong Kong). The references in the film range from the more obvious tributes to Bruce Lee and Jackie Chan's kung fu screen

Without guns: a new aesthetic of violence in Johnnie To's *Election*

personifications (Chow's character is hybrid of the more serious side of Lee and the buffoonish quality of Chan), to the less obvious tributes to Warner Bros. cartoons (there is an allusion to *Road Runner*) and Shaw Brothers social comedies, in particular the 1973 hit *The House of 72 Tenants/Qishi'er Jia Fangke* (the film that reintroduced Cantonese into Hong Kong cinema after the dialect had disappeared for several years). *Kung Fu Hustle* borrows from the latter film its structure of a tenement setting with various tenants and an overbearing landlady.

Chow's film accentuates pure fantasy through a blend of kung fu display and CGI effects, as if suggesting that cinema is wholly illusion and magic – notwithstanding the claim made by kung fu superstars who are also genuine martial artists (Bruce Lee, Jackie Chan, Jet Li, Sammo Hung and so forth) that their kung fu is 'real' (a claim boosted by the fact that these stars often perform their own stunts). But ultimately the dialectic of fantasy and reality is immaterial to *Kung Fu Hustle*, because Chow proves that he is genuinely funny and that he could be the real King of Comedy of the new millennium.

STEPHEN TEO

Election/Hei Shehui; Election 2/Hei Shehui Yihe Weigui (Hong Kong 2005; 2006 *p.c* – Milkyway Image/One Hundred Years of Film Co/Celluloid Dreams; *d* – Johnnie To)

If John Woo's cop-and-gangster thrillers are operas-cum-ballets featuring slow-motion dances of death performed by gun-toting protagonists, this highly stylised action form is now transmuted in *Election* and *Election 2* by Johnnie To (Woo's true successor in the contemporary Hong Kong action cinema). To fashions a new aesthetics of violence where guns play no role whatsoever, though he is no stranger to directing stylised violence with guns as the prominent weapons – for example, in *A Hero Never Dies/Zhenxin Yingxiong* (1999) or *The Mission/Qianghu* (1999). The absence of guns in these two blistering allegorical works makes the violence highly abstract and strangely Gothic (*Election 2* is more representative in this respect). Despite this abstraction, the violence is powerfully palpable, and To seems obsessed with finding new ways to depict violence without the use of guns (in fact, he is innovative in his depictions of violence even with guns, as in *The Mission*).

The films do not lack symbols (if we consider that guns symbolise patriarchal authority and violence). The notion of election in the Hong Kong underworld of triad societies is symbolic of corrupt patriarchy in action, and To plays this notion for all its allegorical worth in terms of Hong Kong's relationship to China in the post-97 era, hinting ironically at China's stalled promise of letting Hong Kong citizens elect their head of government. *Election* and *Election 2* are rare examples of political critique produced by a commercial film-maker in Hong Kong cinema.

STEPHEN TEO

IRISH CINEMA

JOHN HILL

Although cinemagoing has proved a consistently popular leisure activity in Ireland, there was for many years little by way of a native film industry. There are several reasons for this. Ireland is a small country that has lacked the size of population to sustain indigenous film-making on an economically sustainable basis. Moreover, until the 1980s there was little official enthusiasm on either side of the border for encouraging film production in Ireland other than as a means to promote public information and tourism. Indeed, while the partition of Ireland (and the granting of independence from Britain to 26 of Ireland's 32 counties) in 1920 may have led to regimes that were politically hostile to each other, nonetheless the two governments shared a religiously conservative and culturally insular outlook. One of the first acts of the newly established government in the south was the passing of the Censorship of Films Act in 1923, which led, over the next 40 years, to the banning of around 3,000 films and cuts to a further 8,000. The operation of a system of state censorship was one of the few features of southern Irish society admired by the Unionist government in Northern Ireland, whose supporters vigorously opposed the showing of films that they regarded as either politically unsympathetic or morally offensive.

Due to Irish politicians and clerics' lack of enthusiasm for film, the main cinematic images of Ireland were for many years the product of cinemas elsewhere, particularly those in Britain and the US. The first fiction films to be shot in Ireland were in fact the work of the Irish-Canadian director Sidney Olcott whose American company Kalem visited Ireland between 1910 and 1912. Made prior to Irish independence, films such as *The Lad from Old Ireland* (1910) and *Rory O'More* (1911) were aimed primarily at an urban Irish-American audience predisposed to sympathise with the films' nationalist sentiments. Although these films may highlight the harsh conditions of life in Ireland under British rule, they also rely upon nostalgia for the 'old country' through their emphasis on the beauties of the Irish landscape. The association with rural simplicity was set to become one of the most common cinematic images of Ireland and achieved its most memorable expression in John Ford's Irish-American fantasy *The Quiet Man* (1952), in which a disillusioned American, played by John Wayne, is restored to psychic health on his return to the traditional Irish community of his birth.

However, given its troubled political history, the identification of the country with violent conflict was also destined to become a staple ingredient of films about Ireland. While two locally produced films – George Dewhurst's *Irish Destiny* (1925)

Healed by the Irish community: John Wayne in Ford's *The Quiet Man*

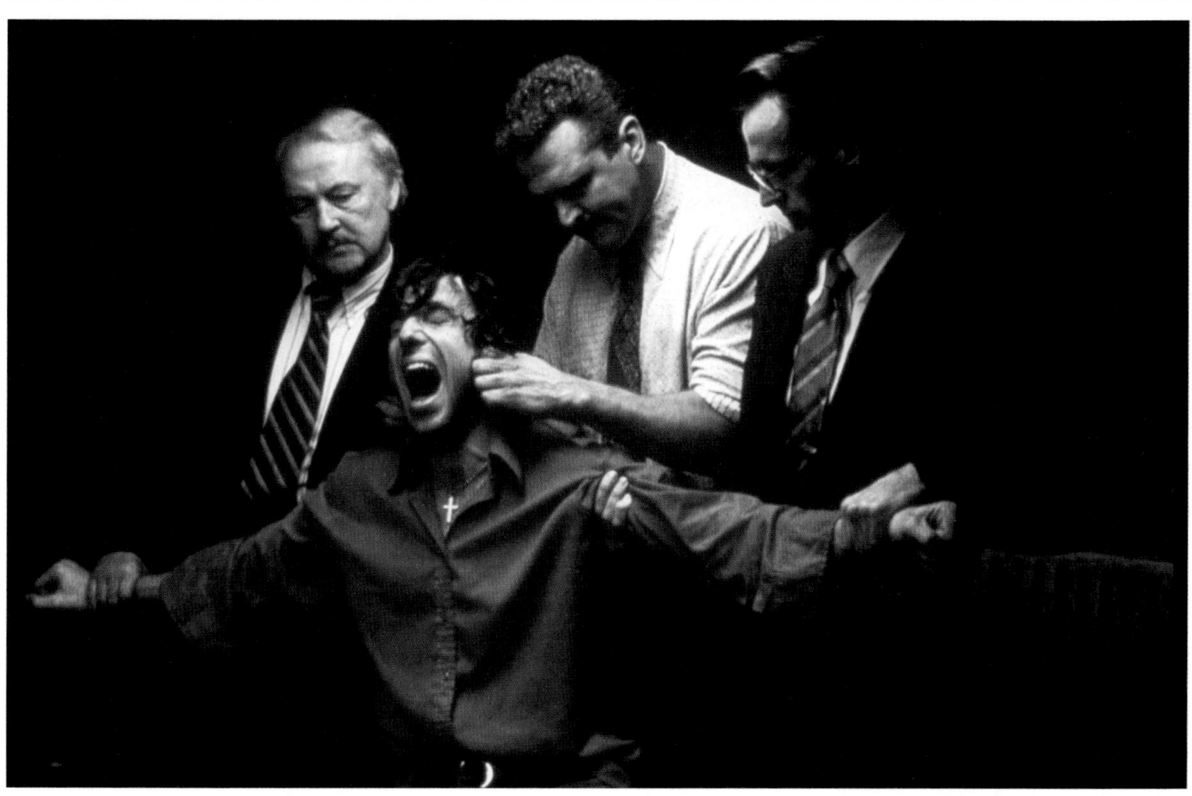

Daniel Day-Lewis in Jim Sheridan's *In the Name of the Father*, a stirring account of the wrongful imprisonment of the Guildford Four

and Tom Cooper's semi-amateur *The Dawn* (1936) – recalled the War of Independence, it was British and American films – such as John Ford's *The Informer* (1935) and *The Plough and the Stars* (1936), and Brian Desmond Hurst's *Ourselves Alone* (1936) – that achieved the greatest international visibility (despite encountering some censorship problems in both Britain and Northern Ireland). Carol Reed's gloomy film noir *Odd Man Out* (1947) emerged as the first film to deal with the conflict in the north since partition. Tracing the final hours of a dying IRA man, the film's combination of tragic narration and expressionist stylistics also established an enduring paradigm for the representation of the Northern Irish 'troubles'.

The increasing availability of public funding for film production within Ireland during the 1970s and 1980s, particularly in the south where the Arts Council Film Script Award was established in 1978 and the Irish Film Board was founded in 1981, provided opportunities for a new generation of Irish film-makers to explore Irish culture from within. However, whereas the short-lived Film Company of Ireland (1916–22) had provided support to the nationalist movement prior to Irish independence, the first 'new wave' of Irish film-making emerged at a time when many of the traditional tenets of cultural nationalism were coming under strain. In the south, Bob Quinn's groundbreaking Irish-language production, *Lament for Art O'Leary/Caoineadh Airt Uí Laoire* (1975) employed Brechtian devices to foreground the discursive construction of Irish history; the same director's *Poitín* (1977) subjected the myths of the rural west to harsh scrutiny; Joe Comerford's *Down the Corner* (1977) sought to give expression to previously unacknowledged urban working-class realities; while Cathal Black's *Our Boys* (1981) fused drama and documentary to expose the corrosive effects of a Catholic education. In the north, Pat Murphy's film *Maeve* (1981), set in Belfast, and Margo Harkin's *Hush-A-Bye Baby* (1989), set in Derry, investigated contemporary Irish republicanism from the perspective of feminism. In the wake of the Oscar-winning successes of Jim Sheridan's *My Left Foot* (1989) and Neil Jordan's *The Crying Game* (1992), Irish film-making began to move away from earlier models of art cinema and political modernism in the direction of bigger-budget, more commercially oriented forms. Sheridan secured the backing of Universal Studios for his stirring (if historically questionable) account of the wrongful imprisonment of the 'Guildford Four', *In the Name of the Father* (1993), while Warner Bros. funded Jordan's historical epic *Michael Collins* (1996). Despite the inevitable concessions to Hollywood conventions, the film's revisiting of the Irish Civil War succeeded in provoking an impassioned debate in Ireland about the historical foundations of the state (much as Ken Loach's *The Wind That Shakes the Barley* was to do ten years later). Jordan's next film, *The Butcher Boy* (1997), was smaller in scale but even more challenging. Dealing with the descent of a young boy into madness, the film audaciously mixes objective and subjective viewpoints in an unsettling exploration of the impact of modernising and internationalising forces upon Irish society in the 1960s.

Alongside the high-profile achievements of Jordan and Sheridan, there was also a steady flow of more modestly budgeted films from both north and south. The announcement of the paramilitary ceasefires in Northern Ireland in 1994 (combined with new sources of public funding through the Lottery) led to an upsurge in films taking stock of the 'troubles' and exploring the prospects for peace. However, as various films from David Caffrey's *Divorcing Jack* (1998) to Terry Loane's *Mickybo & Me* (2004) have revealed, the conflicts that have fuelled the 'troubles' have proved resistant to conversion into popular entertainment. The attempt to reimagine Northern Ireland following the onset of the peace process has been matched by a concern to give expression to the new Ireland born of unprecedented economic growth in the south. In contrast to the traditional cinematic images of rural backwardness or violent conflict, 'Celtic Tiger' films such

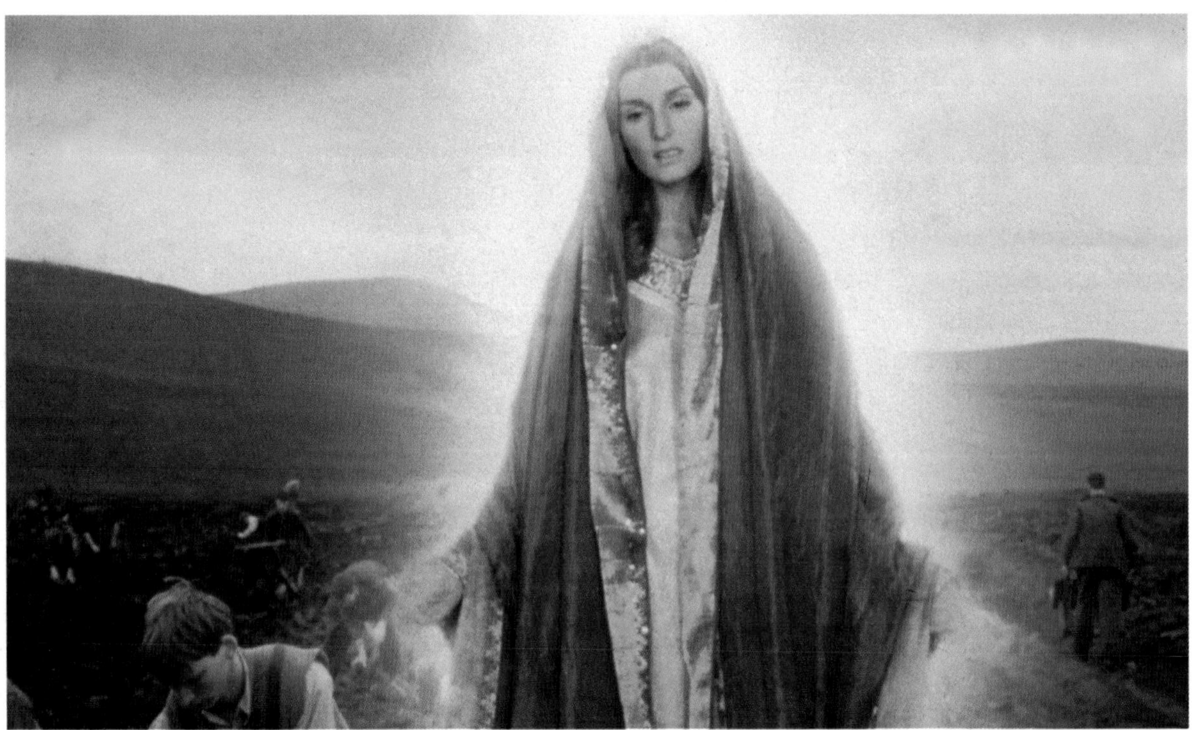

Audacious and challenging: Neil Jordan's *The Butcher Boy*

as Gerard Stembridge's *About Adam* (2000), Kieron J. Walsh's *When Brendan Met Trudy* (2000) and Elizabeth Gill's *Goldfish Memory* (2003) have associated contemporary Ireland with modern images of urban cosmopolitanism and sexual sophistication. While such images are no less mythical than those they have replaced, the political recognition of the value of supporting locally based film-making on both sides of the border has ensured that Irish cinema will continue to offer fresh perspectives on both Ireland's past and present.

Selected Reading

Ruth Barton, *Irish National Cinema*, New York and London, Routledge, 2004.

John Hill, *Cinema and Northern Ireland: Film, Culture and Politics*, London, BFI Publishing, 2006.

Martin McLoone, *Irish Film: The Emergence of a Contemporary Cinema*, London, BFI Publishing, 2000.

Kevin Rockett, Luke Gibbons and John Hill, *Cinema and Ireland*, New York and London, Routledge, 1988.

Intermission (Ireland/UK 2003 *p.c* – Company of Wolves/Bord Scannán na hÉireann/UK Film Council; *d* – John Crowley)

A surprise hit at the Irish box office, *Intermission* was a low-budget feature funded by Bord Scannán na hÉireann/Irish Film Board and the UK Film Council. While the film's success may be attributed in part to the involvement of the actor Colin Farrell, returning to Ireland following success in Hollywood, its combination of fast-moving narrative, strong acting, absurdist humour and feel for contemporary Dublin clearly struck a chord with local audiences. In doing so, the film also indicates how many contemporary Irish films establish their distinctiveness through the reworking of international forms. At the end, Farrell is heard to belt out in a thick Dublin accent a raucous version of the rabble-rousing anthem 'I Fought the Law'. Originally made famous by the American group the Bobby Fuller Four, it is the Clash's punk version that has perhaps become the best known. Farrell's interpretation of the song suggests how the film itself invests a variety of American and European cinematic influences – including the elaborate, multi-character plots of Robert Altman and Paul Thomas Anderson, the heist film, the slacker film and the black comedy of *Trainspotting* (1996) – with a local accent. In contrast to the more celebratory tone of the 'Celtic Tiger' film, *Intermission* also brings a degree of punk-like irreverence to its view of contemporary Dublin, deflating the rogue cop's pretensions to 'Celtic soul' and wreaking its revenge on the most economically privileged (the bank and store managers). While the sudden outbursts of violence (including the unexpected 'in your face' opening) have led to complaints of misogyny, this is matched by quiet moments of sensitivity (as when a distressed daughter is comforted by her mother) that make the film not only entertaining but also thought-provoking.

JOHN HILL

ITALIAN CINEMA

RICHARD DYER

Italian cinema is internationally famous for its silent epics (that influenced D. W. Griffith), postwar neo-realism (seen by many as a decisive turning point in film form) and such canonical directors as Michelangelo Antonioni, Federico Fellini, Pier Paolo Pasolini and Luchino Visconti. All these also have standing in Italy itself, not least because of their international recognition; but Italian cinema is also melodrama and comedy.

Almost everything in Italian cinema – except perhaps (and importantly) comedy – can be related back to *melodramma*. The word is ambiguous, referring both to melodrama as understood in the rest of the world and to opera, and from them both stem spectacle and stardom, adventure and thriller genres, as well as actual opera films and melodramas, and even realism.

Melodramma means literally music plus drama, with music on an equal footing with drama, expressing intense emotion experienced by the characters and usually exteriorised by them. Such exteriorisation is achieved in opera and some versions of melodrama by singing, by instrumental music expressing the characters' feelings and by gestures and postures. If there is a difference between them, it is one of scale: opera in Italy by the end of the nineteenth century meant massive, opulent spectacle and stories from mythology and history, whereas melodrama was small scale and domestic. Both were a source for the plots, performers and mise en scène of early Italian cinema as well as providing templates for most subsequent cinema. I shall trace this legacy through spectacle and melodrama, stopping briefly on the way for realism and turning finally to comedy.

Film versions of operas, with sung live or, before long, recorded accompaniment, were made from the 1900s, but most striking was the development of spectacle: immense sets, their scale emphasised by camera position and movement, the mise en scène ornate but in line with contemporary trends in design (and thus modern in feel even while evoking ancient worlds). Production of spectacle in quantity lasted from around 1908 (with *The Last Days of Pompeii/Gli ultimi giorni di Pompeii*) until the end of World War I, but it continued fitfully to be a feature of Italian film production; it was used occasionally to great fanfare in the Fascist era (for example, *Scipio the African/Scipione l'africano*, 1937) and continued to be made alongside postwar neo-realism, culminating in the energetic sado-masochism of early Christian martyrdom in *Fabiola* (1949).

Thereafter spectacle took the form of the peplum (the term refers to the short kilt worn by the heroes), adventure films set in the ancient world with heroes played by (usually) American bodybuilders. This too had its origins in the silent era, in the invention of the character Maciste for *Cabiria* (1914; see case study), which led to an early cycle of films that were vehicles for Maciste, Hercules and the rest, rediscovered in the 1950s with *Hercules/Le fatiche di Ercole* (1958), starring Steve Reeves. Peplum films did not have the scale and solidity of the mise en scène of *Cabiria* or *Fabiola*, but a comic-book aesthetic, with worlds sketched in with a few vivid details, easy spatial transitions, set-pieces of action and muscle-display and a ready mixing up of Greek, Roman, biblical, barbarian and other mythologies. They subordinated narrative coherence and plausibility to energetic spectacle and action, a principle that subsequently transmuted into, *inter alia*, the spaghetti western (beginning with *Fistful of Dollars/Per un pugno di dollari*, 1964) and the *giallo* (literally 'yellow', from the colour used for the covers of paperback crime fiction), hybrid detective horror films notable for set pieces of beautified violence and supernatural overtones.

The silent spectacle tradition also saw the emergence of the first stars, called in Italian *divi* and *dive*, gods and goddesses, a term suggesting their hyper-intense, incandescent style, caught in declamatory gestures evoking classical art. As in other cinemas, such elevated images would give way to the just-like-you-and-me image of later stardom, perhaps helped on its way by stars' roles in melodrama. The narrative substance of the spectacles was itself often melodramatic and much early Italian melodrama concerned rich people in fabulous clothes in grand mansions with impressive terraces. More importantly, silent melodrama, through the *dive*, concentrated emotional intensity in posture and gesture and this tradition, in which the body bears the brunt of emotional turmoil, continued into the sound period. In *The Blind Woman of Sorrento/La cieca di Sorrento* (1934), for instance, the two climactic moments consist of a mid-shot of the star (Dria Paola) repeating a single word ever more loudly as her eyes widen and her breathing intensifies. Italian melodrama also often has Christian resonance. In *Nobody's Child/I figli di nessuno* (1951), one of Raffaele Matarazzo's extremely popular melodramas, a boy who believes himself an orphan unknowingly encounters his mother, now a nun, on a dusty road; he cups his hand at a spring to give her water and as she walks away, the light catches her so that to him she seems a Madonna, the apotheosis of motherhood.

Both opera and melodrama had their realist dimensions, opera in the form of *verismo*, drawing on contemporary natu-

Muscular mythology: Steve Reeves as Hercules in *Le fatiche di Ercole*

SOPHIA LOREN

Sophia Loren came to prominence in the postwar years in the wave of enthusiasm for new kinds of Italian beauty that was, in its way, part of the neo-realist project. In 1950, at the age of 26, she won the Miss Italia contest; these competitions prized a beauty that was seen, against the Fascist ideals of beauty, as intrinsically Italian, an earthy voluptuousness carried in dark looks, ample bosoms and regional accents. Loren was Neapolitan, at home in her body, with challenging eyes and full mouth, neither as pretty and bourgeois as Gina Lollobrigida nor as sultry as Silvana Mangano (two other Miss Italia winners), and more apparently good humoured than either. She worked first in the mass- circulation photo-romances of the period, ensuring that she had a female fan following.

Comic skill: Sophia Loren and Marcello Mastroianni in *Ieri, oggi, domani*

The natural progression was to melodramas, and these indeed followed, including playing (blacked up) the eponymous *Aida* in 1953 (though her voice was dubbed). However, she really came into her own in comedy, where her skill and looks were allied to a tremendous sense of enjoyment. The episode 'Pizze a credito' ('Pizzas on Credit') in *Gold of Naples/L'oro di Napoli* (1954) is characteristic: her character leaves her emerald ring in her lover's room but tells her husband she must have lost it in the dough for the pizzas they make and sell, leading to a frantic search of all the customers who have just bought pizzas; her performance is exquisite, not least in its combination of humour and sexiness, as when, all the time kneading dough in a décolleté blouse, she produces a coin from her bosom to give to the priest collecting alms and then shrugs her shoulders nonchalantly at her scandalised husband. Perhaps her greatest success in comedy came in a series of films teaming her with Marcello Mastroianni, beginning with *Yesterday, Today and Tomorrow/Ieri, oggi, domani* (1963) and culminating in a late neo-realist melodrama, *A Special Day/Una giornata particolare* (1977), where she played a downtrodden housewife befriending a disgraced homosexual neighbour during a Fascist rally in Rome. Sophia Loren was indelibly Italian, which is to say, in a country so obsessively regional, specifically Neapolitan, but she was also a major international, Hollywood-style star. Undoubtedly one of the reasons for her importance in Italy is the fact that her Italianness is internationally celebrated.

RICHARD DYER

ralist authors, and melodrama dealing with the domestic lives of ordinary people, close in approach to the weekly fiction aimed at women. Neo-realism has its roots here and thus is always both realist and melodramatic. It is part of popular cinema, and canonical works such as *Rome Open City/Roma città aperta* (1945) and *Bicycle Thieves/Ladri di biciclette* (1948) are less distinct than might be assumed from the melodramas of the period (for example, Raffaello Matarazzo, and the noirish films of Alberto Lattuada, such as *Il bandito*, 1946, and *Anna*, 1951).

One byproduct of neo-realism was *commedia all'italiana* (comedy Italian-style). Comedy had been a mainstay of silent cinema since its inception, drawing on music hall and circus, producing probably the most beloved stars within Italy. The tradition had its own realism, partly in its concern with the vicissitudes of everyday life, but above all in its extreme cynicism. *Commedia all'italiana* merely added the patina of neo-realism to this, often producing comedies so coruscating in their view of humanity as to defy non-Italian ideas of what is considered funny. *Seduced and Abandoned/Sedotta e abbandonata* (1964), for instance, turns on the hilarious idea that a boy might get a girl pregnant and then refuse to marry her on the grounds that she is not a virgin, while the genial *Persons Unknown/I soliti ignoti* (1958) contains a scene in which a swaggeringly incompetent thief is run over by a bus.

This rich tradition of spectacle, stardom, melodrama and comedy is the foundation of the work of Italy's celebrated *autori* (auteurs) of the 1950s and 1960s. Visconti's work grows out of melodrama, critiquing it in *Senso* (1954) and creating operatic grandeur from working-class life in *La terra trema* (1948) and *Rocco and His Brothers/Rocco e i suoi fratelli* (1960). Fellini, rooted in circus and music hall, increasingly moved towards spectacle and artifice, at its most stunning and melancholy in *Fellini Satyricon* (1969). Pasolini too turned to spectacle in the second part of his career (*The Decameron/Il Decamerone*, 1970; *The Canterbury Tales/I racconti di Canterbury*, 1972; *Arabian Nights/Il fiore delle mille e una notte*, 1974) and worked with the greatest comic star of all, Totò, while Fellini made his last film with comic Roberto Benigni (*The Voice of the Moon/La voce della luna*, 1990). Even Roberto Rossellini and Michelangelo Antonioni worked unquestioningly in melodrama, while borrowing their aesthetic from modernism. Italian cinema has consistently sought to establish itself internationally and to borrow Hollywood models, yet has seldom at any level been untouched by the distinctive legacy of either cynical comedy or insistent *melodramma*.

Selected Reading

Geoffrey Nowell-Smith with James Hay and Gianni Volpe, *The BFI Companion to Italian Cinema*, London, Cassell/BFI Publishing, 1996.

Pierre Sorlin, *Italian National Cinema 1896–1996*, London, Routledge, 1996.

Christopher Wagstaff, 'Cinema', in David Forgacs and Robert Lumley (eds), *Italian Cultural Studies: An Introduction*, Oxford, Oxford University Press, 1996.

Mary P. Wood, *Italian Cinema*, Oxford, Berg, 2005.

Italian Neo-realism

GEOFFREY NOWELL-SMITH

A national cinema, in the full sense of the term, is not just the national production registered in a particular country but a cinema that in some way signifies itself to its audiences as the cinema through which that country speaks. By this token, the Italian neo-realism of the late 1940s and early 1950s was a quintessentially national cinema. Neo-realist films represented only a small proportion of box-office takings on the home market and their claim to signify on behalf of the nation was bitterly contested within Italy – not least by the Italian government itself. But the critical reputation acquired by neo-realism, in Italy and abroad, and the unequivocal way in which the films developed a national and popular subject matter meant that for many years 'Italian cinema' was synonymous with the neo-realist production of film-makers such as Rossellini, De Sica and Visconti, while other forms of film-making in Italy, however commercially successful, were relegated to a secondary role.

Italian neo-realism was the product of World War II and the defeat of Italian and German Fascism. Ideologically, it arose from the need, widely felt throughout Italy and most clearly articulated among intellectuals of the left, to break with the cultural heritage of Fascism and in particular with rhetorical artistic schemata that seemed to bear no relation to life as it was lived. Industrially, the conditions for the emergence of the neo-realist cinema were provided by the economic breakdown that followed the Allied invasion and the collapse of the Mussolini regime in 1943–5.

The Italian cinema had a long if not always distinguished history. Like many European national industries, it had a flourishing period just before World War I, before the Americans established their stranglehold on the world market. Of particular significance were the giant historical spectaculars (for example, *Cabiria*, 1914; see case study) that reputedly impressed both Griffith and Eisenstein and that for many years functioned as a model, for some, of what the Italian cinema should once again become and, for others, of what it should avoid. The coming of Fascism in 1922 at first affected Italian cinema very little. But throughout the 1920s, the industry was in economic and cultural decline, which the coming of sound at the end of the decade only aggravated. Having at first adopted more or less laissez-faire policies, the government took steps from about 1926 onwards to remedy the decline. The purpose of the intervention was not to create a distinctively 'Fascist' cinema, but simply an 'Italian' one, which would be economically and culturally self-sufficient. Though a number of patriotic and pro-Fascist features were produced, overt propaganda was confined mainly to the newsreels. After a brief period of experimenting with the 'art film', encouragement was given principally to the development of efficient studio production and out of this there emerged a steady stream of comedies and dramas that were designed to compete successfully, at least on the home market, with their Hollywood equivalents. To ensure that this would be possible, various protectionist measures were introduced, in the form first of quotas and then of import restrictions; these culminated in 1938 in a situation where the films from the 'major' Hollywood studios could not be seen in Italy at all, whereas those from the 'minors' could. In December 1941, with America's entry into the war, the importation of Hollywood films ceased entirely.

Although Fascism had a firm grip on economic and political life, its ability to secure popular consent was much less certain. Whereas in the 1920s, when the Fascists were struggling to consolidate their power, they did enjoy the active support of sections of the population, after 1930, when that power had been consolidated, Fascist rule became something of an empty shell, receiving little more than a formal and grudging obeisance on the part of the population at large. Political opposition, crushed in 1926, began to revive in clandestine conditions from the mid-1930s onwards. Intellectually, opposition and the seeds of a national renewal began to develop within the ranks of the Fascist organisations themselves. When war came, this opposition was to transfer itself to the ranks of the Resistance. For the cinema, key centres of the oppositional culture out of which the neo-realist aesthetic was to develop were to be found in the government-sponsored film school, the Centro Sperimentale (founded 1935), and in the Cine-GUF or Fascist university film societies.

In July 1943, Allied troops invaded Sicily. Mussolini was deposed by an internal coup, rescued by a German commando unit and restored to nominal power as head of a puppet republic based in the northern resort town of Salò. One of the more bizarre acts of this puppet regime was an unsuccessful attempt to transfer the headquarters of the Italian film industry from Rome, where the grandiose film studios of Cinecittà had been opened in 1937, to the relative safety of Venice. When the Allies entered Rome in June 1944, they found the studios deserted but intact, and turned them into a refugee camp.

The final defeat of the German forces in Italy in April 1945 left the country liberated but also under Allied military occupation pending an official transition to civilian government. The Italian film industry was saddled with a control commission dominated by American trade representatives (in military uniform), whose main objective was the reopening of the Italian market to American films. Within the Italian industry a sharp divide emerged between the exhibitors, who made common cause with the Americans in their eagerness to fill the cinemas with the Hollywood films of which the public had been deprived during the war, and the producers (supported in this by the British on the commission), who wanted import restrictions at least for the time it would take to reconstruct the indigenous industry.

It was during this immediate postwar period, before the dismantled Italian film industry had been restructured in monopolistic form, that the neo-realist cinema was able to establish itself and to achieve a modest box-office success. This was also a period of political and social ferment, in which a radical cultural project such as that of neo-realism could enjoy a lot of political goodwill among the groupings that had emerged from the Resistance and in which a public could be found for an art that sought to reflect immediate reality in simple terms. Neo-realism survived so long as these conditions lasted; when they began to change, what survived was no longer neo-realism.

Aesthetically, the 'realism' of the neo-realist movement consisted principally of a commitment to the representation of human reality. This commitment could not and did not translate itself into any precise technical or stylistic prescriptions. Insofar as there were prescriptions for a specifically realist practice, these tended to be dictated by (or rationalisations of) material conditions and were often contradictory and confused. Thus a preference for visual authenticity (coupled with the non-availability of studio space) led to a lot of scenes being shot on location, both indoors and outdoors, and also to the use of non-professional actors. But a necessary corollary of this was that sound almost always had to be dubbed or post-synchronised (which was standard Italian practice for imported films anyway), and the dubbing was generally done, not by the people whose faces appeared on the screen, but by professionals. Visual style and that of the soundtrack were thus regularly at odds with one another, with the former aspiring to a strong form of realism and the latter merely mimicking ordinary dramatic illusionism.

If this contradiction were to be avoided – as, for example, in Visconti's *La terra trema*, where the Sicilian fisherfolk speak their own lines in their native dialect – others would be generated. Thus in *La terra trema*, the use of a dialect that most audiences would find incomprehensible breaks the dramatic illusion and imposes the need for a commentary; for commercial release on the home market, the distributors in fact reverted to dubbing the film back into standard Italian. It is also noticeable that there is no consistency of camera and editing techniques in films of the neo-realist movement. The long-held deep-focus shot singled out by André Bazin as a distinguishing feature of neo-realism (as well as of the style of Wyler and Welles) is not in fact very common. The incidence of cut-aways and other elements of the editor's stock-in-trade is quite high, even in the films of Rossellini that Bazin found stylistically so exemplary. For *Germany Year Zero/Germania, anno zero* (1948), Rossellini shot the dramatic action of the film in the studio in Italy, set against back-projected material filmed on location in Berlin.

Neo-realism in fact comprised a number of tendencies, which differed in their conception of realism as well as politically and in other ways. For a while these differences were masked, but with the break-up of the united anti-Fascist 'front' and a political realignment imposed by the Cold War, the aesthetic differences also came to the fore. The disintegration of the movement in the early 1950s also coincided with the successful re-establishment of a commercial industry, supported by a centre-right Christian Democrat government, able to produce popular films in competition with the Americans. Although the political left continued for some years to promote the idea of a national cinema based on neo-realist ideals, the idea that this cinema was a homogeneous entity and that it was, or could be, the true and only 'national cinema' became increasingly hard to sustain. By the end of the 1950s, neo-realism had effectively disappeared, giving way to a mixture of 'art' and 'genre' films, some of which (for example, 'underworld' pictures) contained a certain neo-realist heritage.

The core of original neo-realism – most typically represented by the work in tandem of director Vittorio De Sica and scriptwriter Cesare Zavattini (see *Bicycle Thieves*, and *Umberto D.*, 1952) – was a strongly humanist and reformist impulse. In Zavattini's conception, the honest portrayal of ordinary life would be sufficient to create a bond between audience and film such that the protagonist would display his or her inherent humanity and the audience would grasp the nature of the circumstances that had to change if that humanity was to display itself more fully. The preferred narrative mode was realist in the sense that fictional events were portrayed as if they were real and without the sort of dramatisation that would draw attention to their fictional character. Except in the immediate postwar period, when ordinary life was experienced in quite dramatic terms, the ordinariness and lack of drama of neo-realist films of this type gave them on the whole little appeal at the box office.

Flanking the humanists, on their left as it were, stood the Marxist tendency – represented, for example, by Luchino Visconti and Giuseppe De Santis. For the Marxists, a descriptive portrayal of ordinary life was not sufficient to convey a proper understanding of the circumstances to be struggled against. Increasingly, the realism favoured by these film-makers came to be either contaminated by melodrama (rather splendidly in the case of De Santis's *Bitter Rice/Riso amaro*, 1949) or reinterpreted in the light of Marxist aesthetic theory to become a 'critical realism' that was avowedly non-naturalistic. The high point of this tendency comes with Visconti's *Senso*, which is a costume picture that offers a highly dramatised figuration of personal and class conflict in a nineteenth-century Risorgimento setting. The political-aesthetic justification for such a radical change from the style of *La terra trema* was to be found in the debate about realism going on in Marxist circles in Italy, where the *Prison Notebooks* of Antonio Gramsci had recently been published and the ideas of Georg Lukács were also beginning to circulate. An equally important consideration, however, was the change in the structure of the industry and in audience expectations. As well as being 'realist' in the Lukácsian sense of producing a narration that captures historical truth, *Senso* (starring Farley Granger and Alida Valli) was designed as a high-class entertainment film with export as well as home-market potential.

While the majority of the neo-realists remained aligned with the political left, where they were to be joined by a second wave of Italian film-makers such as Francesco Rosi and Pier Paolo Pasolini, there also existed tendencies that were either non-aligned or specifically aligned with Christian Democracy. The anti-Fascist front, which had comprised all the democratic parties during and after the Resistance, broke up in 1947/48, leaving the Christian Democrats (the Catholic party) at the head of a centre-right government, with the Socialists and Communists in opposition on the left and monarchist and non-Fascist parties on the right. Of the major neo-realist film-makers, Roberto Rossellini was the only one to throw in his lot squarely with the Christian Democrats, but other Catholic film-makers such as Federico Fellini sheltered within the same politico-cultural space and there also developed a generically Catholic form of sub-neo-realism that produced dramas of guilt and redemption. Although melodramatic in conception, these films borrowed many of the trappings of neo-realism, particularly in the choice of humdrum settings and an emphasis (Catholic, however, rather than left-reformist) on the nobility of poverty.

The case of Rossellini deserves treatment on its own. During the early part of the war, Rossellini had made feature films about the war and service life that were government-backed though not excessively Fascistic in ideology. After the fall of Mussolini in 1943, he joined the anti-German Resistance and made the first Resistance feature, *Rome, Open City/Roma città aperta*, in 1945. *Rome, Open City* tells the story of a priest and a Communist partisan that ends with the partisan being tortured to death while the priest is forced to look on, and the priest then being shot. While the film celebrates Catholic-Communist unity in resistance to the Germans, its focus is spiritual rather than political and it is the priest rather than the partisan who is the real hero.

Rome Open City was followed by two other films about war and its aftermath, *Paisà* (1946) and *Germany Year Zero*, which belong within the neo-realist mainstream, even though their existential Catholic tone is untypical of the movement as a whole. But with the series of films that he embarked on with Ingrid Bergman beginning with *Stromboli/Stromboli, terra di Dio* (1950), and even more with his film about St Francis (*Flowers of St Francis/Francesco, giullare di dio*, 1950), Rossellini distanced himself emphatically from the rest of neo-realism. Not only is the spirituality even more prominent, but the address of the films is towards European and American audiences, rather than towards Italy itself. As a commercial ploy this was not successful – none of the films was a great box-office success and *Stromboli* was mangled by RKO for American release. But the choice of direction is significant, since it mirrors the political priorities of the Christian Democrat government, which was committed both to the Atlantic alliance and to western European integration; it was also a deliberate repudiation of the 'national-popular' cultural strategy promoted by the Communists and supported by the rest of the left.

This political break with the rest of the neo-realist movement, however, did not mean that Rossellini should no longer be considered as a neo-realist in the aesthetic sense. Indeed, the case has been made, most notably by André Bazin, that Rossellini was the truest neo-realist of all. For Bazin, neo-realism was an

Melodrama combined with mythical themes:
Vittorio De Sica's *Ladri di biciclette*

Cabiria (Italy 1914 *p.c* – Itala Film; *d* – Giovanni Pastrone)

Cabiria exemplifies the fusion of epic and spectacle in Italian silent cinema. It is epic in its large-scale rendering of world historical events (the eruption of Mount Etna, Hannibal's challenge to Rome, Scipio's defeat of Carthage, Archimedes's invention of fire weapons) and of individual characters caught up in and made great by them (the heroes alert the Romans of Hannibal's advance, and their rescue of the child Cabiria from sacrifice to the God Moloch is emblematic of Roman chivalry and Carthaginian savagery). The presentation of the two heroes, patrician Fulvio (Umberto Mozzato) and brawny Maciste (Bartolomeo Pagano), deploys statuesque postures and ennobling framing, opening with shots of them singled out as men of destiny on a rocky promontory by the sea. Yet it was the slave Maciste who was to become the popular hero figure in a series of subsequent films (although in the process shedding his black identity).

Cabiria is spectacular in its sensuously overwhelming visual quality: the massive sets have a solidity staggering in comparison with both stage sets and later special effects and computer-generated (CGI) constructions of the ancient world. The scale is emphasised by canted angles that dwarf the humans, pans that indicate expanse and forward tracking shots that draw the viewer in; design pits the clean lines, open spaces and white and martial clothes of Rome against the orientalist decadent languor of Carthage, where the screen is crowded with ornate furnishing, sumptuous fabrics and furs; the spectacle of suffering is dwelt on in the whipping of Cabiria's nurse Croessa (Gina Marangoni), Maciste chained to a millstone and above all the God Moloch, a vast statue with a giant mouth into whose flames children are tossed. In short, *Cabiria*, in a blend characteristic of Italian cinema, welds together in equal measure antique ideals, stylish design, sensuous pleasures and sensual energies.

RICHARD DYER

Paisà (Italy 1946 *p.c* – Organisation Films International/Foreign Film Productions (USA); *d* – Roberto Rossellini)

Paisà, made by Rossellini in 1946 following the international acclaim of *Rome, Open City*, was among the first films to be labelled neo-realist. For Bazin (writing in 1948), it was one of the most significant events in the history of the cinema since 1940 – the other was *Citizen Kane* (1941). Both films, he believed, marked a 'decisive progress towards realism', though by very different routes. *Citizen Kane* employed deep-focus and long takes in order to preserve continuity, but paradoxically had to sacrifice verisimilitude in other ways, since the technical requirements of this shooting method virtually precluded the use of location shooting, natural light and non-professional actors. *Paisà*, by contrast, incorporated all these features: unscripted dialogue, predominantly exterior settings and 'actors' recruited on the spot, as well as an unusual dramatic form. Instead of one self-contained narrative, the film consisted of six loosely linked episodes, each set in a different part of Italy (moving from south to north with the Allied invasion)

The fortunes of war: Roberto Rossellini's *Paisà*

but sharing the common theme of the confrontation of people from different cultures thrown together by the fortunes of war. In many respects, then, *Paisà* seems to respond to the demands of the neo-realists (and of Bazin) for an unemphatic, contemplative style and a relaxed, open-ended narrative structure. However, sequences such as the retrieval of the partisan's corpse and the parachute drop in the sixth and last episode depend heavily on suspense, reinforced in the former case by incidental music and extensive crosscutting between the groups of combatants. Though the events are, as Bazin points out, elliptically presented, they fall into a coherent pattern that hardly seems 'multiple and ambiguous'. Far from being undramatic or desultory, the episode is orchestrated around a series of small climaxes that build up to a clearly signalled conclusion.

SHEILA JOHNSTON

Umberto D. (Italy 1952 *p.c* – Rizzoli Editore/Produzioni De Sica/Giuseppe Amato; *d* – Vittorio De Sica)

Umberto D reunited the team of Vittorio De Sica (director) and Cesare Zavattini (scriptwriter) who had previously worked together on *Shoeshine/Sciuscià* (1946) and the highly successful *Bicycle Thieves/Ladri di biciclette* (1948). According to Zavattini, who was perhaps the most celebrated propagandist and theorist of the neo-realist movement, the neo-realist approach to the cinema should renounce the relentless forward drive of the conventional narrative film in favour of a more leisurely pace that would savour every moment, however seemingly insignificant, for its own sake. Zavattini is often quoted as having wanted to make a film of a man to whom nothing happened. Yet his 'Thesis on neo-realism' (Overbey, 1978, p. 69) indicates that he was aware of the risk of boredom involved in rejecting a strong narrative based on drama and suspense.

Umberto D. clearly exploits the full melodramatic potential of a helpless old man and his dog. For example, the joyful (and extremely coincidental) reunion of Umberto and Flike his dog is underlined by incidental music, the chorus of barking that rises to a crescendo and a track in to Flike as he emerges from the van. The old man's acting performance at this point is also worth considering, bearing in mind the neo-realists' belief that using non-professionals would increase authenticity. The use of editing in the sequence in which the desperate Umberto encourages the dog to beg for money suggests an affectionate understanding between man and dog.

The powerful impetus of these sequences, deriving from the mythical theme of the quest (see also *Bicycle Thieves*) casts doubt on Zavattini's declared aim to defy narrative conventions. The events in the film eventually lead to the man's despair and attempted suicide, so his life could not be said to be entirely devoid of incident. It could be argued that these films' aura of inevitability blocks the neo-realist thrust towards penetrating social criticism, giving rise to a diffuse sentimentality and melodramatic fatalism.

SHEILA JOHNSTON

advance on conventional literary realism in that it was less constructed; thanks to the camera, film artists could represent immediate reality, filtering it through their consciousness, without having to impose an artificial purposive form on it. Bazin found this immediacy – an immediacy of things in themselves and an immediacy of the intervening consciousness – in Rossellini's films, far more than, for example, in the films of Visconti, which he judged realistic only in the conventional literary and theatrical sense. In a celebrated passage defending Rossellini's *Journey to Italy/Viaggio in Italia* (1954) from its Lukácsian critics in Italy, Bazin compared the construction of conventional realist art forms to that of a house made of bricks or cut stone, contrasting this to the more improvisational use of stones to provide a footpath across a stream (Bazin, 1962, p. 157).

Although the metaphor (as he himself admitted) was a bit stretched, Bazin hit on a quality that other critics too have felt to be present in many of Rossellini's films from *Paisà* onwards, and especially in *Europa '51* (1952) and *Journey to Italy*. The films give evidence of an ad hoc construction in which bits of the external world that happen to be there, together with reactions solicited from the actors/characters from the events of the filming/scenario, are fused together in an apparently unpremeditated way. It is not only the director but the spectator too who is being asked to 'make sense' by hopping over the stepping-stones. Although Rossellini's films have their own forms of contrivance, including a strong dramatic push towards a moment of spiritual illumination, and sometimes bend reality towards their purposes, it is also often the case that the film is bent to submit to elements of reality that stand outside, or in the way of, the film-maker's intentions and plans. Politically fairly conservative, Rossellini was in this respect artistically extremely radical, and has since come to be recognised as such.

Once it had so visibly split, aesthetically and politically, there was no way that neo-realism was going to be reconstituted. The Italian cinema that followed the neo-realist phase of the late 1940s and early 1950s was very different in character. Neo-realist directors continued to make films, but with very few exceptions these films were not neo-realist. The revived commercial cinema that grew up alongside neo-realism was extremely eclectic. It had room for the occasional prestige production from Visconti or Fellini, but its staple was genre films. These genres included comedies and dramas of a type that had flourished under Fascism in the 1930s and had been temporarily eclipsed in the immediate postwar years. They also included fantasy and costume pictures, generally low-budget, which engaged the talents of such masters of the genre as Riccardo Freda, Mario Bava and Vittorio Cottafavi. Along with the dramas of Raffaello Matarazzo and others, these became the Italian popular cinema, which lasted until the cinema ceased to be the major popular art. By comparison, neo-realism must be rated a popular cinema that might have been.

Selected Reading

Morando Morandini, 'Italy from fascism to neo-realism', in Nowell-Smith (ed.), *The Oxford History of World Cinema*, Oxford, Oxford University Press, 1996.

Geoffrey Nowell-Smith with James Hay and Gianni Volpi, *The BFICompanion to Italian Cinema*, London, Cassell/BFI Publishing, 1996.

Christopher Wagstaff and Christopher Duggan, *Italy and the Cold War: Politics, Culture and Society*, Oxford, Berg, 1995.

JAPANESE CINEMA

Introduction

KATHE GEIST

A Japanese woodblock print from the early 1800s shows a baby reaching for a revolving lantern on which silhouetted foxes chase each other. Spinning the lantern would have enhanced their chase. When Lumière films and projectors reached East Asia in 1897, this region of paper lanterns and shadow puppetry was well prepared to understand the possibilities of projected light. (The Chinese would name cinema 'dian-ying', electric shadows.)

Over the years, Japanese cinema has attracted the attention of many film scholars. Since the late 1980s, that attention has been focused on the question of representation. To the extent that representation in Japanese cinema differs from that in the west, some scholars see in it similarities to modernist art cinema as we know it in the west, while others see in its particular aesthetics native characteristics with a long history in the art and culture of East Asia (see Anderson and Hoekzema, 1977; Bordwell, 1988; Ehrlich and Desser, 1994; Thompson, 1977).

Among its East Asian counterparts, the Japanese film industry has enjoyed a particularly strong and uninterrupted development since 1899. Because of Japan's political domination before 1945 and its subsequent economic hegemony in the region, Japanese cinema has had a substantial influence on East Asian cinema as a whole, although each region has developed a distinctive body of work.

Disinterest in illusionism

Early Japanese film audiences were so fascinated with the film projector and its crew that one early exhibitor set up his projector on the right side of the stage and the screen on the left (see Anderson and Richie, 1982, p. 26). This arrangement allowed the audience to watch the projector as well as the film and indicates that early Japanese audiences had less interest in the illusion of reality offered by the newly invented moving pictures than in understanding how the illusion was created. In the west such an interest is considered modernist, because modernism, which came about as a critical response to the classicism that characterised western art after the Renaissance, seeks to expose the illusion of reality that classical art takes such pains to create.

Japanese painters, interested in surface decoration, played with the tensions between the surface and an illusion of depth centuries before it became a concern for modern artists in the west. Native theatrical traditions in Asia have always been highly stylised, giving little illusion of reality. In *bunraku* puppet theatre, for example, the puppet operators, though dressed in black and therefore inconspicuous, share the stage with the puppets.

Japanese of the Meiji period (1868–1912) were familiar with western art and theatre, but this did not lead them to seize the illusionist possibilities of cinema, as the example of the early Japanese exhibitor indicates. They saw no reason for a film to appear self-contained. Thus, all through the silent era, narrators, called *benshi*, stood alongside the screen and narrated the story (see also Early and pre-sound cinema, p. 3). The early Japanese silents were intentionally vague so that the *benshi* could make up the stories as they went along (see Komatsu, 1992).

As Japanese studios developed, they were organised around directors rather than producers and, copying traditional art practices, adopted a master/apprentice system in which assistant directors were assigned to learn their craft from established directors. Thus auteurism, a hallmark of the art film, was no hard-won privilege in Japan, as it frequently was in the west, but an accepted condition of film production.

Mizoguchi and Ozu

Among the first westerners to write seriously about Japanese cinema were the early *Cahiers du cinéma* critics into whose auteur theory the Japanese fitted perfectly. They particularly admired the films of Kenji Mizoguchi. They praised his lyricism and adept mise en scène, and were quick to link his work to other Japanese arts and artists such as *kabuki* theatre and woodblock artist Hokusai. Because of his preference for long takes and a moving camera, he was also compared by the *Cahiers* critics to Jean Renoir, Orson Welles and William Wyler. Noël Burch, however, disputes this similarity, noting that Mizoguchi's long takes differ from those of western directors in not being centred and rarely closing in on the actors, thus maintaining a 'non-anthropocentric' approach. Burch has suggested that Mizoguchi's long takes have the character of scroll paintings or *emakimono*, in which there is no fixed perspective (Burch, 1979).

Yasujiro Ozu, known for his contributions to the popular Japanese genre the 'home drama', also takes a 'non-anthropocentric' approach in his films. According to David Bordwell (1988) and Kristin Thompson (1977), Ozu privileges space over narration in ways that include consistently using a 360° shooting space instead of the 180° space of classical cinema, foregrounding objects that are not correspondingly important in the narrative, and cutting away to shots and shot sequences that, while related to the narrative, are not motivated by it. According to Bordwell, Ozu's consistent foregrounding of space in preference to narrative sets him apart from other Japanese directors and places him in the ranks of 'parametric' film-makers such as Robert Bresson and Carl Dreyer. Bordwell and Thompson thus see Ozu as essentially a modernist, arguing that since he was a devotee of American films, he must have been aware of the extent to which he was 'transgressing' classical film practices. Other writers, including Burch, see Ozu's film practice as rooted in traditional Japanese aesthetics and perceptions of space.

Classical *découpage* – the way in which Hollywood films are edited to put a story across – had, to a great extent, become the norm in Japan by the 1930s, and certainly Ozu knew he was flouting classical film practice. However, even as a young man, he was enthralled with the aesthetic term *mu*. *Mu* refers to the empty space in traditional painting and carries deeper Taoist and Buddhist philosophical connotations of 'void' or infinity. The transition spaces in Ozu's films, sometimes called 'empty shots', can equally be seen as expressions of *mu* rather than modernist thrusts against a classical norm.

Likewise, Ozu frequently plays with the tension between surface and depth. Often this takes the form of placing an object or face close to the camera in a space that then plunges into depth. The long alleyways typical of old Japanese cities proved

Surface and depth in Ozu's *The End of Summer*

ideal for showing off extreme depth. In *The End of Summer/Kohaya-gawa-ke no aki* (1961), Ozu graphically matches three shots, the first two shallow, the last showing a long alley. At first all three shots look the same, until one recognises the need to read much greater depth into the last one (see Geist, 1994).

Although most of Ozu's contemporaries were not as radical as he and operated within the ground rules of classical cinema, they too included 'empty shots' in their films (though not as frequently or as systematically as Ozu) and also had a tendency to call attention to surface and emphasise the decorative through flashy transitions, unusual camera angles, mirror shots and so on, consistent with the decorative tendencies in Japanese art.

Another striking feature of many East Asian films is the tendency to refer to seasons. Although at times little more than a cultural overlay, more often a deeper philosophical tendency can be seen to be at work. The notion of transience, for example – which is linked to the idea of seasons as measurements of the life cycle – is derived from Buddhism and fundamental to Japanese eschatology. Ozu's films abound in symbols of transience, passage and passing time such as clocks, smoke, trains, bridges and so on. And many of his later films, bearing seasonal references in their titles, involve marriage and death – pivotal points in the life cycle. Even Akira Kurosawa, famous for the western humanism in even his period and samurai films, makes integral use of cyclical, seasonal references. For example, *Seven Samurai/Shichinin no samurai* (1954), where a revolving mill wheel is a recurring motif, builds its story around the harvesting and planting of rice and includes a famous love scene that takes place among the spring blossoms.

Rediscovering traditional culture

Although much of what seems modern in Japanese cinema, that is, contrary to the rules of classical film-making, is rooted in traditional arts and philosophies, some of it may, as Bordwell (1995) argues, have come as a deliberate attempt on the part of the Japanese to recuperate and reaffirm their traditional culture in the 1930s and 1940s (and even more so in the 1950s after Japan's defeat in World War II). In Bordwell's view, the Japanising tendencies noticeable in films from the 1930s, for example, were conscious efforts by film-makers to reverse a trend towards westernisation that had all but overwhelmed traditional culture in the 1910s and 1920s.

A self-conscious movement such as the Japanese New Wave of the 1960s fits western patterns of modernism less equivocally, since it was intended as a revision of dominant cinema practice, not merely in the west but at home as well. However, Japanese New Wave films such as Nagisa Oshima's *Cruel Story of Youth/Seishun zankoku monogatari* (1960) or Yoshishige Yoshida's *Eros Plus Massacre/Erosu purasu Gyakusatsu* (1969) are allied to Japanese modernism, which developed its own identity in the course of the 20th century, as well as to the specific political and cultural tensions of 1960s Japan (see Desser, 1988).

In the 1980s and 1990s, Japanese film-makers looked back nostalgically at their own cinematic traditions, particularly the so-called Golden Age of the 1950s, for example Kohei Oguri's *Muddy River/Doro no kawa* (1981), shot in black and white, or Kon Ichikawa's *The Makioka Sisters/Sasameyuki* (1983). Masayuki Suo's *Shall We Dance?/Shall we dansu?* (1996), an international hit (remade by Miramax in 2004), reinvented Ozu's gently comic home drama for the age of globalisation, mediating, as Japanese cinema always has, between Japanese and western forms and traditions.

Selected Reading

David Bordwell, *Ozu and the Poetics of Cinema*, Princeton, NJ, Princeton University Press, 1988.

Noël Burch, *To the Distant Observer: Form and Meaning in the Japanese Cinema*, Berkeley, University of California Press, 1979.

Linda Ehrlich and David Desser (eds), *Cinematic Landscapes: Observations on the Visual Arts and Cinema of China and Japan*, Austin, University of Texas Press, 1994.

Arthur Nolletti and David Desser (eds), *Reframing Japanese Cinema: Authorship, Genre, History*, Bloomington, Indiana University Press, 1992.

Contemporary Japanese cinema

ALASTAIR PHILLIPS AND JULIAN STRINGER

From the success of Akira Kurosawa's *Rashomon* (1950) at European film festivals in the early 1950s, the reception of Japanese cinema outside Japan has largely been determined by the vagaries of international festival and distribution networks. For example, it was in this way that new independent film-makers such as Yoshimitsu Morita, Mitsuo Yanagimachi and Juzo Itami came to global attention during the 1980s, and the trend continued throughout the 1990s and into the 21st century, where it has increasingly been possible to view Japanese cinema in a fuller range of international and transnational contexts. Films such as Hirokazu Kore-eda 's *Phantom Light/Maborosi* (1995) and, especially, Takeshi Kitano's *Fireworks/Hana-bi* (1997) demonstrate the popularity of a certain kind of psychologically acute, formally self-aware Japanese film-making that has been well received by art-house audiences around the world. Along with the phenomenal mass appeal of horror and *anime*, this cinema continues to play a significant formative role in international perceptions of Japanese cinematic identity.

Popular domestic genres continue to flourish despite contraction in the number of films produced and competition from television and other emerging forms of mass entertainment. Popular franchises such as the long-running comic salaryman series *Free and Easy/Tsuribaka nisshi* (1988–), based on the popular *manga* and starring Toshiyuki Nishida, refract the pressures and social conflicts in contemporary Japanese society in a way that would be impossible through more direct means. In 2005, the industry notched up an enviable 41.3 per cent of domestic market share, making it one of the most successful of any developed country outside the United States. With major remaining studios Toei, Toho and Shochiku looking for successors to the phenomenally popular Tora-san and Godzilla films that dominated the vital holiday schedules of the summer and New Year periods during the 1960s and 1970s, television has proved increasingly influential. Hiroshi Fujimoto's *anime* series *Doraemon*, based on a bestselling *manga* series and television show, has proved particularly successful and the aesthetic as well as economic interrelationship between contemporary television and film is further illustrated by the hugely profitable *Bayside Shakedown/Odoru daisosasen* (1998) and its recent sequel (2003).

The 1990s also witnessed the emergence of new film-making voices sustained by the efforts of production outfits such as YES and J Movie Wars who specifically invested in independent features by women directors such as Naomi Kawase and the gay director Ryosuke Hashiguchi. Films such as *Suzaku/Moe no suzaku* (1997) and *Like Grains of Sand/Nagisa no shindobaddo* (1995) encouraged a more critical and aesthetically reflexive examination of the subjective textures of contemporary Japanese urban life. Such developments coincided with the advent of more consumer-led patterns of film distribution via satellite, cable and DVD that replaced the older circuit of cinema block bookings controlled by the now ageing major conglomerates. The success of directors such as Makoto Shinozaki and Nobuhiro Suwa owes as much to the increasingly fragmented nature of exhibition and reception within Japan as it does to their support on the global festival circuit.

Perhaps the most significant transformation in Japanese cinema has been the effect of a proliferation of pan-Asian cultural perspectives. Partly because of domestic and regional economic circumstances, and partly because of the faster and more interactive flow between countries and consumers created by new technologies, Japanese film has become more susceptible to the two-way exchange of indigenous and foreign forms of production and representation. This process is exemplified by the heightened visibility of Korean-Japanese film-makers such as Yoichi Sai as well as Japanese film companies' increasing involvement in co-productions across Asia. The intensification of the interrelationship between Japanese and other East Asian popular cultural forms has developed to the extent that a film such as Shunji Iwai's *Swallowtail Butterfly/Suwarouteiru* (1998), in which the characters speak a hybrid language derived from Japanese, Chinese and English, seems especially to belong to its time.

Selected Reading

Tom Mes and Jasper Sharp, *The Midnight Eye Guide to New Japanese Film*, Berkeley, CA, Stone Bridge Press, 2004.

Alastair Phillips and Julian Stringer (eds), *Japanese Cinema: Texts and Contexts*, Oxford and New York, Routledge, 2007.

Mark Schilling, *Contemporary Japanese Film*, New York and Tokyo, Weatherhill, 1999.

Isolde Standish, *A New History of Japanese Cinema: A Century of Narrative Film*, London and New York, Continuum, 2005.

Contemporary Japanese horror

Japan can boast a long tradition of horror film production, encompassing both the high (*Ugetsu/Ugetsu Monogatari*, 1953; *Kwaidan*, 1964) and low ends (*Lake of Illusions/Maboroshi no mizuumi*, 1982; *Evil Dead Trap/Shiryo no wana*, 1988) of the genre spectrum. However, Japanese horror's global prominence became assured with the release in the 1990s and beyond of a string of internationally successful tales of terror. Although marketing labels such as 'Asian extreme cinema' erase differences between individual titles, the list of such films is by now quite long and it encompasses the work of film-makers from several generations. The group includes veteran directors such as Kenji Fukasaku, emergent and celebrated voices of Japan's 'New New Wave' such as Kiyoshi Kurosawa and Hideo Nakata, and mavericks such as Takashi Miike and Shinya Tsukamoto. This success, in turn, has

Deadly nightmares: Kiyoshi Kurosawa's disturbing horror *Kairo*

led to the re-evaluation at recent international film festivals of previously neglected Japanese horror auteurs such as Nobuo Nakagawa (*The Mansion of the Ghost Cat/Borei kaibyoyashiki*, 1958; *The Lady Vampire/Onna kyuketsuki*, 1959).

The work of Japanese horror directors is marked by its diversity. It encompasses explorations of gender trouble in the form of avenging females (*Sweet Home/Suito homu*, 1989; *The Ring/Ringu*, 1998; *Audition/Ōdishon*, 2000); men on the rampage (*Tetsuo: The Iron Man/Tetsuo*, 1988); serial killer narratives (*Cure/Kyua*, 1998); and social dramas of apocalyptic breakdown (*Battle Royale/Batoru rowaiaru*, 2000; *Pulse/Kairo*, 2001). Such films also draw upon Japanese ghost film and Hollywood splatter-movie traditions, and enjoy close links with the production of domestic television dramas, the rise to prominence of horror novelists such as Koji Suzuki and the ubiquitous influence of Japan's high-tech games culture. The resulting mix projects an all-pervasive feeling of technological paranoia evident everywhere from the telephone and television horror of *Ring* to the murderous chip inserted into the skulls of contestants in *Battle Royale*.

Despite the range of themes and styles to be found in such films, however, Japanese horror circulates globally under the very specific unifying brand identity of 'J-horror'. Why is this, given that there is no such thing, for example, as 'I-horror' to describe the Italian horror films of Dario Argento? Clearly, the label joins together two separate terms in such a way as to suggest that there is both something particular to horror produced in Japan while also simultaneously keeping the two words apart to imply that horror is an international genre to which Japan has now contributed. In addition, the tag 'J-horror' is also reminiscent of other labels, such as 'J-Pop' (Japanese pop music) and 'K-drama' (Korean television dramas) that have originated in East Asia to name the specific regional identity of various forms of contemporary popular culture. Indeed, the growing importance of trans-Asian cultural flows in the early 21st century is demonstrated by the increased production of portmanteau horror films by Japanese and other Asian filmmakers. *Three ... Extremes/Saam gang yi* (2004), for example, collects together three short chillers by directors from Hong Kong, Japan and South Korea.

In recent years, numerous Japanese horror films have been remade in Hollywood in ways that either retain (*The Grudge*, 2004; Japanese original 2003; *Dark Water*, 2005; Japanese original 2002) or else erase (*The Ring*, 2004; *Pulse*, 2006) traces of the antecedent texts' 'Japanese-ness'. Debates over whether or not particular US remakes of Japanese horror movies are superior or inferior to the 'originals' contribute to wider discussions concerning the transnationalisation of Japanese popular culture, the centrality of horror to modern world cinema and the importance of remakes and recycling to the production and consumption of contemporary media culture. Intriguingly, all of these issues are also alluded to in the circular imagery of many Japanese horror film titles themselves, such as *The Ring*, *Spiral/Rasen* (1998), *The Whirlwind/Uzumaki* (2000) and *Pulse* – whose Japanese title, *Kairo*, translates as 'circuit'.

Selected Reading

Chris Desjardins, *Outlaw Masters of Japanese Film*, London, I. B. Tauris, 2005.

Jay McRoy (ed.), *Japanese Horror Cinema*, Edinburgh, Edinburgh University Press, 2005.

Thomas Mes, *Agitator: The Cinema of Takashi Miike*, London, FAB Press, 2003.

Thomas Weisser and Yuko Mihara Weisser, *Japanese Cinema Encyclopedia: Horror, Fantasy, Science Fiction*, Miami, Vital Books, 1998.

Anime

Anime (animated film and television programmes) forms a vital part of Japanese popular culture. It is also a global media phenomenon subject to largely unexamined processes of international circulation, translation and indigenisation. Together with *manga* (Japanese comic books) – with which it enjoys close and continuing relations – *anime* constitutes a major component of the daily lives of many Japanese as well as ever-increasing numbers of overseas consumers.

Contemporary *anime* continues a tradition of domestic film animation that is long-standing and multifarious, and which itself grew out of such enduring forms of Japanese culture as the woodblock print, the domestic shadow play and *utsushi-e* (early lantern slides). However, like much ostensibly non-representational art, Japanese 'cartoons' are frequently assigned low cultural status. Symptomatically, the 'typical' *anime* fan is therefore imagined as a gendered and socially inept *otaku* ('fanboy') who consumes too much too often and exhibits all the unprepossessing traits of a borderline obsessive. There is, however, plenty of evidence to suggest that it is not just young males who appreciate *anime*'s dynamic visual compositions, imaginative portrayals of fantastic worlds, and storylines and characters of depth and emotional complexity. It is noticeable, for instance, that much of the significant academic research on *anime* to date has been conducted by women.

Indeed, any serious understanding of *anime* cannot fail to take into account its demographic appeal across barriers of gender, class and age, as well as its cross-media existence and its broad cultural influence. The numbers involved are staggering. It has been reported that around 250 animation programmes per week are aired on television in Japan, and that in addition an average of 1,700 (short or feature-length) animated films are produced on an annual basis. Japanese animated films may circulate in movie theatres, on video and DVD, and as Internet downloads, but they also cross-fertilise with related media such as *manga* publishing and games consoles so as to spawn technological development and aesthetic innovation. *Anime* film-making skills are now in demand around the world and have been at the forefront of moves towards digital film-making. One result of this is that, at the turn of the 21st century, the lines between animated and live-action film-making are becoming increasingly blurred.

The film and television titles that attract most attention among *anime* fans and commentators not only display imagination and technical prowess, but also engage with themes of social identity (*Serial Experiments: Lain*, 1998 – TV); romance, sexuality and gender confusion (*Ah! My Goddess!/Aa! Megamisama!*, 1993; *Ranma½*, 1989 – TV); and such sensitive political issues as the post-World War II US occupation (*Grave of the Fireflies/Hotaru no haka*, 1988). *Anime* also provides in graphical art form a version of many of the live-action genres for which Japanese cinema is most famous, including the samurai film (*Ninja Scroll/Jûbei ninpûchô*, 1993); horror (*Blood: The Last Vampire*, 2000); the thriller (*Perfect Blue*, 1998); high-tech noir (*Akira*, 1988); and sci-fi (*Cowboy Bebop/Kaubôi bibappu*, 1998 – TV). In recent years, international auteurs have emerged to help give *anime* a global face as well as greater respectability. Hayao Miyazaki has produced a string of titles at Studio Ghibli that engage with Disney's legacy by reinventing Japanese tradition through an eco-friendly lens (for example, *Nausicäa of the Valley of the Winds/Kaze no tani no Naushika*, 1984; *My Neighbor Totoro/Tonari no Totoro*, 1988; *Princess Mononoke/Mononoke-hime*, 1997; *Spirited Away/Sen to Chihiro no Kamikakushi*, 2001). Mamoru Oshii followed up *Ghost in the Shell/Kôkaku kidôtai* (1995) – a key influence on the US blockbuster *The Matrix* (1999) – with script work on *Jin-Roh: The Wolf Brigade/Jin-rô* (1998), and then directing credits on *Avalon* (2001), shot in Poland, and *Ghost in the Shell II: Innocence/Inosensu: Kôkaku kidôtai* (2004). In offering mass-cultural family-oriented fare as well as subcultural sensibilities, the divergent careers of Miyazaki and Oshii present two sides of *anime*'s diverse attractions. Their films – as well as those of their many peers and predecessors – may or may not be viewed compulsively by nerdy *otaku*. However, they give pleasure to large numbers of viewers across the world, and they demonstrate that *anime* more than deserves its place in the pages of world cinema history.

Selected Reading

Philip Brophy, *100 Anime*, London, BFI Publishing, 2005.

Steven T. Brown (ed.), *Cinema Anime*, London, Palgrave Macmillan, 2006.

Jonathan Clements and Helen McCarthy, *The Anime Encyclopedia: A Guide to Japanese Animation Since 1917*, Berkeley, CA, Stone Bridge Press, 2006. Second edition.

Susan Napier, *Anime from Akira to Howl's Moving Castle: Experiencing Contemporary Japanese Animation*, Basingstoke, Palgrave, 2006.

Late Spring/Banshun (Japan 1949 p.c – Shochiku Co; d – Yasujiro Ozu)

Late Spring, the earliest of Ozu's 'marriage films', concerns a widower's ultimately successful attempts to marry off his daughter. Ozu's use of unusual spatial devices, as described by Bordwell (1988) and Thompson (1977), can be seen throughout. For example, in one scene the father is asked by a friend in which direction the sea lies. The friend points behind himself, and the father replies, 'no', it is in the opposite direction, and points behind himself. The friend asks the direction of the shrine and points to his left. The father again says 'no', and points to his right. However, because Ozu crosses the 180° line as he cuts from the friend to the father, both men point in the same screen direction, adding to the confusion. Two more requests for directions have the same result. The sequence has no narrative significance and instead serves as a commentary on Ozu's use of a 360° shooting space and his puckish delight in confounding an audience with it.

The film contains more references to traditional Japanese art than any other Ozu film – and many of the 'empty shots' are concerned with this. Certain empty shots also make reference to passing time; and several others help elucidate the odd relationship between the daughter and her father's assistant, who is engaged to someone else. The famous 'vase sequence', in which cut-aways to a vase link shots of the daughter smiling peacefully to images of her tearful face, has been the subject of much debate. Some critics see in the shot an emptiness allied to *mu* (void) that bridges the daughter's change of mood and suggests transcendence, while others see only Ozu's formal rigour and his penchant for foregrounding objects with little narrative significance.

KATHE GEIST

Sisters of the Gion/Gion no shimai (Japan 1936 p.c – Dai-Ichi Eiga; d – Kenji Mizoguchi)

Sisters of the Gion follows the attempts of two sisters, both geisha, to survive in a male-dominated world. Whereas one sister is traditional, the other is modern and tries to use men in a practical, cold-blooded way. Mizoguchi demonstrates the hopelessness of the geisha world, and the film's theme – the plight of women – is a typical concern of the director's work.

Stylistically, the film incorporates Mizoguchi's long takes, moving camera and 'non-anthropomorphic' space. In many of his long takes, a fairly distant camera is maintained – at times a travelling camera dodges behind objects and partitions to maintain its distance. A scene in which the traditional sister finds she cannot pay a delivery boy transpires in long shot with nothing in the foreground except an empty table, a sign that her penniless patron is taking no responsibility for the lunch being delivered for his sake. A crucial subsequent scene in which the modern sister undertakes to get rid of the patron also takes place entirely in long shot. Characters are usually decentred. A travelling shot in which the two sisters visit a temple generally keeps them in the right third of the frame and leaves the left two-thirds empty. Much of the film is shot with high angles reminiscent of twelfth-century scroll painting. Bordwell has suggested that high angles such as these were an attempt to revive 'Japanese-ness' in the 1930s.

KATHE GEIST

Love Letter (Japan 1995 p.c – Fuji Television Network/Robot Communication; d – Shunji Iwai)

The domestic success of Shunji Iwai's remarkable debut feature provides evidence of a wider and more subtle conception of contemporary Japanese cinema beyond the export-driven vogue for horror and *anime*. *Love Letter* is also significant for the way that its highly choreographed portrayal of female subjectivity relates to the stylised, melancholic representation of place and memory. Central to this are the finely tuned performances given by former J-Pop idol and model Miho Nakayama, who as one of Japan's most popular young performers plays both Hiroko Watanabe and Itsuki Fujii, two young women who have both known the same young man who also bears the name Itsuki Fujii.

Hiroko is the grieving fiancée of Itsuki, who has died in a mountaineering accident. On finding his former address in Hokkaido, she decides to write him a letter. She mysteriously receives a reply from Itsuki, but unbeknown to her the letter is actually from her lover's former classmate who coincidentally shares the same name and has received the note by chance. A series of curious exchanges ensues and then, with the assistance of her suitor, played by Etsushi Toyokawa (another contemporary star actor in Japan), Hiroko sets off to see the world of her fiancée's youth for herself.

The plot sounds preposterous and it certainly runs the risk of becoming fey and sentimental, but

Women's space and time: Shunji Iwai's unsettling *Love Letter*

the director's clever direction and editing constantly challenge expectations. Iwai is a veteran of Japanese music videos and popular television drama, and his mise en scène combines stately outdoor widescreen compositions with highly mobile framings in the domestic and school scenes. Also crucial to the film's ambience is the plaintive orchestral and electronic score by Remedios and the way in which Japan's wintry regional landscapes speak visually for the ambiguous presence of the past in the present.

As part of an important strand within contemporary Japanese cinema that also includes the work of Makoto Shinozaki, Hirokazu Kore-eda and Naomi Kawase, Iwai is interested in representing the modern spaces of Japan in an unfussy but highly cinematic fashion. *Love Letter* is significant for its attention to women's space and time and for Iwai's ability to harness an awareness of the fashions of Japanese popular culture to a vision of something altogether more unsettling.

ALASTAIR PHILLIPS AND JULIAN STRINGER

Pulse/Kairo (Japan 2001 p.c – Daiei/Nippon Television Network/Hakuhodo/IMAGICA; d – Kiyoshi Kurosawa)

Countless theories seek to explain what horror films are all about and how they work, yet the most fundamental of the genre's key themes has been relatively under-appreciated. Horror's great preoccupation is with the fact and meaning of death. The genre provokes fear in spectators through offering a sense of what it would be like to face the termination of existence. It is sometimes claimed that awareness of death is particularly evident in Japan because of a social belief in the omnipresence of the spirit of the dead among the lives of the living. This idea has seldom been more thoroughly explored than in Kurosawa's haunting fable *Pulse*.

Similar to the earlier *The Ring*, *Pulse* presents modern technology as the portal through which a deadly supernatural presence infiltrates the material world. A group of Tokyo office workers become concerned when a colleague fails to return a computer disc. While visiting his apartment to investigate, Michi (Kumiko Aso) witnesses strange and disturbing scenes of terror, and before long other members of the group are also being confronted with manifestations of agency above the forces of nature. It transpires that the underworld has reached its finite capacity and that the dead are now spilling over into the next available space by using a seemingly innocent website as the medium for their visitations. The living and the dead begin to coexist in a strange limbo state that drives many insane. As the virus drains life from everything around it, Tokyo is turned into a post-apocalyptic landscape from which survivors can only seek to flee.

Pulse provides numerous examples of Kurosawa's impressive command of horror conventions. Sets of a rooftop garden and a student apartment are vividly presented and the sound design, which uses contrast and definition as well as off-screen sound, is complex and nuanced. Individual scenes of ghosts materialising out of empty rooms and an aeroplane crashing overhead while Tokyo burns linger in the memory. Rack-focusing between foreground and background is handled most effectively in the astonishing scene where a woman climbs on top of a silo and then jumps off with a thud all in one shot. In the end, the two remaining survivors escape the madness by boarding a ferry bound from the city. As the ship sails on, further horrors doubtless loom large on the horizon. The final port of call is death.

ALASTAIR PHILLIPS AND JULIAN STRINGER

SOVIET CINEMA

ANNETTE KUHN

Until 1907, the only film companies operating in Russia were foreign, and the domestic market was dominated by the likes of the Lumière brothers and Pathé (see Early and pre-sound cinema, p. 3). In 1907, however, the first Russian production company, Drankov, was set up in competition with foreign films and film companies, which nevertheless continued to flourish in Russia until the outbreak of World War I and the consequent collapse of the import boom. By 1917, there were more than 20 Russian film companies exploiting a steadily expanding home market, whose output consisted mainly of literary and dramatic adaptations, and costume spectaculars. This situation was suddenly and radically changed by the October 1917 Revolution. Veteran directors, actors and technicians emigrated as a period of violent transition totally disrupted normal conditions of production. The new Bolshevik government saw film as a vital tool in the revolutionary struggle, and immediately set about reconstructing the film industry to this end. On 9 November 1917, a centralised film subsection of the State Department of Education, Narkompros, was set up. This centralisation was resisted at first by the private sector, which boycotted the state-sanctioned films, and even went so far as to destroy precious raw film stock. Lack of supplies of equipment and new film stock made production very difficult for the emerging revolutionary cinema, but nevertheless, by the summer of 1918 the first agit-trains (mobile propaganda centres) left for the eastern front, specially equipped to disseminate political propaganda through films, plays and other media to the farthest corners of Russia.

The transition from entrepreneurial to state control of film production, distribution and exhibition proved a slow and difficult process, with postwar famine and continuing political and military conflict postponing the revival of the industry until the early to mid-1920s. By 1920, Soviet film production had dwindled to a trickle, but in 1921, when Lenin's New Economic Policy encouraged a cautious short-term return to limited private investment, releases rose from 11 in 1921 to 157 in 1924. The resumption of imports in the early 1920s following the restabilisation of the economy allowed profits to be ploughed back into domestic production, and, as film equipment and stock resurfaced, the several Soviet studios by then in existence began to expand to pre-Revolution proportions. In 1922, Goskino, the State Cinema Trust, was established as a central authority with a virtual monopoly over domestic film production, distribution and exhibition in Russia, although certain companies retained a degree of independence, and film industries in the more distant republics were allowed some autonomy from Moscow and Leningrad. Studios were set up in the various

Disseminating propaganda to the farthest corners of Russia: the agit-trains

regions, such as VUFKU in the Ukraine, while others, Mezhrabpom-Russ for example, expanded in mergers with private industry. In 1923, a special propaganda production unit, Proletkino, was formed specifically for the production of political films in line with party ideology. Until 1924, films remained conventional in style, apparently untouched by the explosion of avant-garde experiment transforming the other arts in post-revolutionary Russia. Then in 1925, when the industry was allowed an increased aesthetic independence in the wake of a Politburo decision endorsing state non-intervention in matters of form and style in the arts, the new Soviet cinema entered its most exciting and formally adventurous period.

By the mid-1920s, all the production units including Goskino (renamed Sovkino in 1925), Proletkino, Kultkino, Sevzapkino and Mezhrabpom-Russ, had begun to assemble their own personnel – directors, cinematographers, editors and so on, as well as performers. Vsevolod Pudovkin worked at Mezhrabpom, Sergei Eisenstein at Sovkino, Alexander Dovzhenko at VUFKU, for example. During this period, cinema came into productive collision with the energetic theoretical and artistic activity taking place in the other arts. The work of poet Vladimir Mayakovsky and theatre director Vsevolod Meyerhold, for example, profoundly influenced the early work of Eisenstein, whose avant-garde film experiments were accompanied by an impressive body of theoretical writings that are still influential today. In the wake of the 1925 Politburo decision, Eisenstein was commissioned by the Central Committee to produce a film commemorating the 1905 Revolution. This film, *Battleship Potemkin/Bronenosets Potemkin* (1925), was premiered at Moscow's Bolshoi Theatre, an indication of its prestige. But despite a relatively positive critical response, the film's domestic release was relegated to Russia's second-run cinemas and its foreign sales delayed until pressure from influential writers, journalists and party officials induced Sovkino to send it to Berlin. Subsequently, it was a huge international success, reflecting small credit on the conservative policies of the Soviet film industry at that time. *Battleship Potemkin*'s success heralded a series of ambitious and expensive productions. In 1926, Mezhrabpom-Russ released Pudovkin's *Mother/Mat*, another prestigious film that, like *Battleship Potemkin*, exceeded average budget allowances. By 1927, all the major production units were engaged in equally extravagant and prestigious projects in order to celebrate the tenth anniversary of the 1917 Revolution.

The Jubilee films

The impulse to produce the best, as well as the first, of the tenth-anniversary films resulted in a race involving Esfir Shub and Eisenstein at Sovkino and Pudovkin at Mezhrabpom-Russ. Pudovkin won with the release of *The End of St Petersburg/Konyets Sankt-Peterburga* in 1927. Almost simultaneously, however, Sovkino completed two films recreating Russia's pre-revolutionary history entirely from archive footage – *The Great Road/Velikiy put* and *The Fall of the Romanov Dynasty/Padenie dinastii Romanovykh*. Both were compiled by Shub, who had been trained as an editor at Sovkino. Production schedules and budgets were adjusted across the board for these Jubilee celebrations. At Sovkino, for example, Eisenstein and his collaborators were ordered away from production on *The General Line/Staroie i novoe* (1929) to produce *October/Oktiabr*.

The last of the Jubilee films, *October* was not in fact released until 1928. The delayed release was due in part to the film's reliance on recent Soviet history, which by the late 1920s was the subject of intense ideological scrutiny and rewriting in the wake of Trotsky's expulsion from the party. In the event, *October* was extensively re-edited, and references to the role of Stalin's political opponents in the Revolution eliminated. The film was finally released in March 1928 to a hostile reception from the party leadership, who objected to its experimental style as 'formalist'. Simultaneously, the first All-Union Party Congress on Film Questions concluded that in future all fictional films should be accessible to the mass audience. The Congress ruled that film-makers should cease to employ formalist devices and seek instead to emphasise socialist content along strict party lines. This resolution has been seen as marking the beginnings of official sanction for a certain artistic method, that of socialist realism, which was to dominate Soviet cinema until after Stalin's death.

Away from the centre: Vertov's *Man With a Movie Camera*

Emergence of socialist realism

In the words of the 1928 Congress resolution: 'The basic criterion for evaluating the art qualities of a film is the requirement that it be presented in a form which can be understood by the millions' (quoted in Katz, 1980, p. 1076). On completing *October*, Eisenstein returned to the unfinished *The General Line* and decided to simplify his experimentations to a level more easily understood by a general audience, choosing objects like a bull, a tractor and a cream separator to symbolise the transition from primitive farming to mechanised modern agriculture, though he did not abandon his montage experiments. *The General Line* was symptomatic also of the transition to centralised control of film production: indeed, its title was changed to *The Old and the New* because the original title was criticised for implying that the film had received official sanction, which, for all its extensive re-editing on Stalin's orders, it never actually achieved. Alexander Dovzhenko's *Earth/Zemlya* (1930) was similarly symptomatic: its controversial poetic lyricism was condemned as 'counter-revolutionary' and 'defeatist', though it managed to escape outright prohibition.

Other projects managed to sidestep, if not altogether escape, the aesthetic consequences of the directives of the 1928 Congress by producing or selling films at some geographical distance from the metropolitan centres of power in the Soviet Union. The Vertov Unit's experimental *Man With a Movie Camera/Chelovek s kinoapparatom* (1928) was produced at VUFKU in the Ukraine, for instance. Vertov had been sacked by Sovkino in early 1927 and ordered to leave Moscow, in some measure no doubt because his work was regarded as overly formalist. With his editor wife, Elisaveta Svilova, and cameraman brother, Mikhail Kaufman

The milk separator: symbol of modernity in Eisenstein's *The Old and the New*

(Kino-Eye's Council of Three), Vertov made his way to the Ukraine. Between 1926 and 1928, VUFKU was engaged in an embargo on all Sovkino films, and employed the exiled Vertov on condition that his first project would be to complete the film *The Eleventh Year/Odinnadtsati* (1928), which was to have been Vertov's contribution to Sovkino's celebration of the tenth anniversary of the October Revolution. Once this film was finished, Vertov embarked on *Man With a Movie Camera*, whose formal extravagance marks it off from others in the 1920s 'City' cycle of films, exemplified by Kaufman's *Moscow/Moskwa* (1927), Walter Ruttmann's *Berlin Symphony of a City/Berlin die Sinfonie der Grossstadt* (1927), Alberto Cavalcanti's *The Book of Hours/Rien que les heures* (1926) and Jean Vigo's *A propos de Nice* (1930). Vertov continued his imaginative experiments after the advent of sound, but then gradually faded away after Stalin's consolidation of power.

Stalin's decrees under his first Five Year Plan led to increased production of documentaries in support of the Plan's industrial objectives, and in 1930 Sovkino was dissolved and replaced by Soyuzkino, an organisation directly supervised by the Politburo's Economic (rather than as previously, the Education) Department. Soyuzkino, under Stalin's appointee Boris Shumyatsky, was to function in close correspondence with Proletkino. It also officially adopted the resolution of the 1928 Congress in determining its aesthetic policy. After a brief transition period in which some interesting sound experiments emerged (for example Vertov's *Enthusiasm*, 1931), the coming of sound in 1930, combined with government-imposed restrictions on form and content, encouraged an increasing realism of dialogue and character. Musicals and literary adaptations dominated the film industry's output, though there was also a spate of historical biopics celebrating the achievements of Lenin and Stalin. Eisenstein's first sound film, *Alexander Nevsky/Aleksandr Nevski* (1938), was made during this period, after a campaign by Shumyatsky to discredit and humiliate the director, which involved hostile government interference in the production of *Bezhin Meadow/Bezhin lug* (1937), and finally abandonment of the project. Only after a painful confession in which he was forced to renounce *Bezhin Meadow* was Eisenstein assigned the patriotic *Alexander Nevsky*, an important project intended to strengthen Russian national identity in the face of the growing threat from Nazi Germany. In 1938, Shumyatsky was sacked, though there was no change in policy as a result.

The administrative reshuffling in the film industry that followed, combined with the outbreak of World War II, led to a reduction in film output and a revival of the documentary. During the war, film industry personnel were evacuated from Moscow to remote parts of the USSR, and feature-film production gave way to morale-boosting political propaganda in the form of documentary material gathered from the fronts. *Alexander Nevsky*, which had been made as implicit anti-Fascist propaganda, was withdrawn in 1939 in the wake of the German–Soviet Pact. In 1940, Eisenstein, having emerged from disgrace for his formalism in 1938, was appointed artistic head of Mosfilm, the revamped Soyuzkino, and in 1945 won the Stalin Prize for Part I of *Ivan the Terrible/Ivan Grozni*. The following year, Eisenstein began work on a sequel, but Part II met with none of the support that had greeted Part I, and its release was postponed for a decade. During the Cold War period, Stalinist repression reached its highest level, repudiating the faintest hint of formalism as deviation from socialist realism, and several films were banned outright. It was only in 1956, three years after Stalin's death, that the effects of Khrushchev's denunciation of some aspects of Stalinism allowed a gradual withdrawal from the aesthetic orthodoxies of the Cold War years and a return to a more 'poetic' cinema. Chukhrai's *Ballad of a Soldier/Ballada o soldate* (1959) is an illustration of this liberalisation. However, Nikita Khrushchev's enforced retirement in 1964 and the reintroduction of state controls in the film industry under the auspices of the Cinematography Commission of the USSR Council of Ministers resulted in another retreat to prestige literary adaptation and 'safe' historical reconstructions, until the late 1960s, when an international co-production programme resulted in a broadening of scope (for example, the Japan/USSR co-production, Akira Kurosawa's *Dersu Uzala*, 1975).

Selected Reading

Jay Leyda, *Kino: A History of the Russian and Soviet Film*, London, George Allen and Unwin, 1973. Revised edition 1983.

Richard Taylor (ed.), *The Eisenstein Reader*, London, BFI Publishing, 1998.

Richard Taylor and Ian Christie (eds), *The Film Factory: Russian and Soviet Cinema in Documents 1896–1939*, New York and London, Routledge, 1988. Revised edition 1994.

Richard Taylor and Ian Christie (eds), *Inside the Film Factory: New Approaches to Russian and Soviet Cinema*, New York and London, Routledge, 1994.

The Battleship Potemkin/Bronenosets Potemkin
(USSR 1925 *p.c* – Sovkino; *d* – Sergei M. Eisenstein)

After the success of *Strike/Stachka* (1925), Eisenstein was commissioned by the appointed Jubilee committee to direct a film to celebrate the abortive 1905 Revolution, which became *Battleship Potemkin*. Eisenstein took the Potemkin mutiny as the central metaphor for the Revolution.

Eisenstein worked closely with cameraman Tissé on the film and the famous 'Odessa steps sequence' required radical new filming techniques to put the director's ideas into practice (see Leyda, 1973, p. 195). The editing was planned in advance and the film was photographed accordingly. The principle behind the cutting was the editing together of disparate images to produce new ideas, which would emerge from the collision itself rather than the individual images. This idea has much in common with theories of counter-cinema (see Avant-garde and counter-cinema, p. 89) and with the linguistic theories that influenced much structuralist work on cinema (see Structuralism and its aftermaths, p. 510).

The 'Odessa steps sequence' is an example of Eisenstein's agitational cinema, using montage to build a tension that finally provokes a violent emotional response. It is also interesting as an attempt to make history itself the motivating force of the action, rather than individual men and women. If the Revolution speaks through the combination of images, however, the staging of events still clearly rests with Eisenstein. Later he would be heavily criticised for this manipulative approach to his material.

ANNETTE KUHN

The Fall of the Romanov Dynasty/Padenie dinastii Romanovykh (USSR 1927 *p.c* – Sovkino and the Museum of the Revolution; *d* – Esfir Shub)

This film is an example of Shub's pioneering work in the development of reconstructed documentary. She put enormous energy into researching and collecting her material, often a difficult task given the poor condition and fragmentary nature of the newsreel clips. By editing the pieces together according to a system of juxtaposition of connecting images, she was able to achieve effects of irony, absurdity and pathos that few of the pieces had intrinsically. Through this editing technique she gave Russia's history and its progress towards socialist reconstruction great emotional power.

Although her work was held up as an example of pure 'factography' (clearly, by its very nature it could never aspire to the visual stylistic flourishes of Eisenstein, Vertov and others), there is a level of playful irony in the films that could be seen as characteristic of Shub's approach.

PAM COOK

The Great Way/Velikii put (USSR 1927 *p.c* – Sovkino and The Museum of the Revolution; *d* – Esfir Shub)

This was Shub's October anniversary film, for which she meticulously combed through all the newsreels made in the ten years between 1917 and 1927. She found that in themselves those newsreels did not provide a record of how the country had been transformed into a new socialist state; she had to reconstruct that process herself by re-editing the original newsreel material. In the debates about the relative ideological merits of the 'played' and the 'unplayed' film, Eisenstein's *October/Oktiabr* (1928) was unfavourably compared with Shub's documentary montage reconstruction. It was thought that Eisenstein let his worldwide reputation as a great director interfere with his relationship to his material, while Shub's films resolutely refused to deviate from the task of representing historical truth. Yet it can be argued that Shub's techniques are just as emotionally manipulative as Eisenstein's, involving a high degree of personal intervention on her part. The played/unplayed debate raised acutely the question of the place of individual contributions to historical materialist analysis and to the process of history itself.

PAM COOK

Earth/Zemlya (USSR 1930 *p.c* – Ukrainfilm; *d* – Alexander Dovzhenko)

The end sequence of *Earth*, with the villagers and family mourning the young village chairman Vasili, offers a demonstration of 'poetic' modes of organising relations of space and time in narrative film. Thus it includes several instances of 'creative geography': for example, at one point the father of the dead boy is transported between shots from his son's deathbed to a hilltop, while the spatial transition is bridged by a match on action. Here the verisimilitude of fictional space is opened to question by a foregrounding of the cinematic language used to articulate spatial relations. But at the same time, the device is an economical way of effecting a spatial transition required by the narrative.

Later, there is a sequence of three identical shots showing the father sitting at a table grieving. Each of these fairly lengthy shots is punctuated by a slow fade out and in. Whereas in creative geography, spatial coherence is broken, here it is the conventional articulation of narrative time that is infringed.

ANNETTE KUHN

Controversial poetic lyricism in *Earth*

SPANISH CINEMA

NÚRIA TRIANA-TORIBIO

Introduction

It took Spanish cinema about two decades after 1896 to grow out of its beginnings as a fairground attraction and its position of cultural marginality to become a fairly viable industry attracting the attention of investors and audiences. By the 1920s, main cities (Barcelona first and Madrid subsequently) developed a more or less sustained production, with a Golden Age in the early 1930s in terms of audience numbers, popularity of the star system and stability of the industry. This period coincided with Spain's short-lived democracy of the Second Republic (1931–6) and offered apprenticeships for film-makers (such as Luis Buñuel), production companies (CIFESA) and national stars whose importance came to fruition in subsequent years. Film magazines (*Nuestro Cinema*, *Popular Film*) discussed the medium and debated wider cultural-political issues. In 1936, a military coup and a civil war (1936–9) destroyed democracy, forcing many film professionals into exile, and dealt a deathly blow to modernity by ushering in a period of regression to ultra-Catholic and anti-democratic policies. Cultural life was decimated, but the status of cinema as a popular medium hardly suffered. Censorship and shortages shaped the genres used, as well as the settings and the talent available, but under adverse conditions, iconic films were made both by those compliant with the regime (for example, Juan de Orduña's *Love Crazy/Locura de amor*, 1948) and by those who soon contested its values (L. G. Berlanga and Juan A. Bardem's *Bienvenido, Mr Marshall!/Welcome Mr Marshall*, 1952).

The 1960s became a period of economic strength for the dictatorship after it cut deals with European and US governments. Spain had to become attractive to foreigners by showing more than its 'natural beauty', and cinema was chosen as a useful accessory to signal 'modernity', albeit a cosmetic one. J. M. García Escudero, a civil servant of the regime with a deep knowledge of and interest in cinema, was put in charge of a strategy that would ensure that a section of the national production could be of interest beyond Spain. The 1960s was the decade in which film festivals throughout Europe were either created or revamped and also a time when showcasing production in them became a measure of a national cinema's success. The strategies put in place produced crops of new film-makers who saw Spanish cinema through the next two, three and in some cases four decades (producers such as Elías Querejeta or directors such as Mario Camus, Basilio Martín Patino or Carlos Saura). In close proximity to this 'New Spanish cinema', the popular genres perpetuated a conformist agenda and tamed foreign influences for its wide internal audience. Film-makers

Almodóvar's critically acclaimed films stimulate interest in Spanish cinema: Carmen Maura and Penélope Cruz in *Volver*

such as Pedro Masó, Pedro Lazaga (in the roles of producer/scriptwriter and director) and stars such as Marisol (Pepa Flores), Sara Montiel and Alfredo Landa became associated with a cinema that was popular but was uncritical of the regime, retrograde in its desire for continuity and fearful of the modernisation that Europe could bring, which maintained the links with traditional genres and stars.

The mid-1970s brought the death of the dictator and the tortuous but allegedly bloodless return of democracy. Cinema, particularly popular cinema, needed reinvention and politically engaged art cinema became witness and 'actor' of Spain's democratic transition. Saura's iconic *Cousin Angélica/La prima Angélica* (1974) and *Raise Ravens/Cría cuervos* (1975) performed this double function. When the Partido Socialista Obrero Español (Spanish Socialist Party) was elected in 1982, the makeover began in earnest. Film-maker Pilar Miró's ambitious contribution as head of cinema was to fashion measures to make Spanish production worthy of the label 'European Cinema' and to eradicate genre cinema associated with the past. Approved films tackled the traumatic political and cultural heritage (Saura's *Carmen*, 1983; Jaime Chávarri's *Bicycles Are for the Summer/Las bicicletas son para el verano*, 1984; Camus's *The Holy Innocents/Los santos inocentes*, 1984) and promoted the repressed identities of Basques and Catalans (Antoni Ribas's *Victory/Victoria*, 1984, and Imanol Uribe's *The Death of Mikel/La muerte de Mikel*, 1983). Spanish film-makers won international acclaim for democratic Spain: in 1984, Cannes bestowed its main awards on Camus, Francisco Rabal and Alfredo Landa for *The Holy Innocents*. The latter's emergence from the retrograde roles of Francoist popular cinema into democratic ones was a metaphor for the change pursued by Miró.

However, Spanish audiences rejected most of these didactic new films created by the well-intentioned legislation and flocked to see escapist 1970s Hollywood blockbusters. A new generation of film-makers, for whom the Miró model of cinema was unappealing but who were helped by its funding, took a different approach to cinema: they did not dismiss entertainment in favour of sober tales about the past. Iván Zulueta, Fernando Trueba, Fernando Colomo and Pedro Almodóvar, among others, bore witness to the cultural atmosphere of early democracy Madrid. The *movida* was a cultural movement that erupted with the end of censorship, shook the cultural world of the capital and rippled throughout Spain. A surge of creativity and strength coexisted with a backlash against the politicisation of cultural life of the late dictatorship; the *movida* was suffused with hedonism and the experience of foreign cultural movements after decades of censorship. Almodóvar, Carmen Maura and Zulueta are among those involved in film-making within this movement, whose effects are still felt.

Almodóvar adopted a collage of popular genres and stars from past Spanish cinema, with Hollywood melodrama as an aesthetic and thematic guide, and put women centre-frame in a male-centred filmic tradition. The groundbreaking *Women on the Verge of a Nervous Breakdown/Mujeres al borde de un ataque de nervios* (1988) used these ingredients to great international acclaim. Almodóvar's strategies, controversial for the establishment within Spain, indicated a modernity that attracted national and international attention and signalled to new generations possibilities for film-making (such as the use of genre

Torrente, the Stupid Arm of the Law/Torrente, el brazo tonto de la ley; Mission in Marbella/Torrente 2: Misión en Marbella; Torrente 3: The Protector/Torrente 3: El protector
(Spain 1998; 2002; 2005 *p.c* – Iberamericano Films/Rocabruno Producciones/CARTEL; Lolafilms/Amiguetes Entertainment; Amiguetes Entertainment; *d* – Santiago Segura)

Santiago Segura is the protagonist, scriptwriter, director and co-producer of three of the biggest box-office successes in Spanish film's history. Each comedy focuses on the adventures of a corrupt Madrid policeman, José L. Torrente. As Meritxell Esquirol and Josep Lluís Fecé claim, the *Torrente* series is a unique phenomenon in the context of Spain's cultural industry. It was the first Spanish blockbuster conceived and launched alongside unprecedented merchandise and multimedia publicity campaigns (Esquirol and Lluís Facé, 2001, p. 34). Many commentators see in the series a depiction of a politically incorrect and retrograde universe of excess, a return to the 'values' of Francoism and a backlash against the Europeanisation of democratic Spain. What can be said about the *Torrente* series' popularity is that it demonstrates the enduring appeal of Francoist genre cinema, one of the main components recycled in the series, in spite of all the efforts to eradicate it.

NÚRIA TRIANA-TORIBIO

Work in Progress/En construcción (Spain/France 2001 *p.c* – Ovideo TV/Arte/Canal+/Institut National de l'Audiovisuel/Televisión de Catalunya/Wanda Vision/Nirvana Films; *d* – José Luis Guerin)

Before 1975, it was almost impossible for film-makers to make documentaries in Spain. The only sanctioned company was NODO (the regime-controlled Noticiarios y Documentales). This is one of the reasons why this mode of film-making has been embraced by contemporary generations. Another reason is the prestige of the *engagé* cinema within Spanish tradition: *cine social* (social cinema) is one of the most acclaimed trends by critics. *En construcción* is an account of the work in a building site in the centre of Barcelona. Digging the earth to insert the foundations, the construction team finds remains of uncertain origin and we witness the ponderings of the bystanders about Spain's violent past. The film zooms into the lives of characters soon to be made homeless by a process of gentrification of the once working-class *barrio*. It also follows the daily routines and thoughts of a North African worker.

Critics and audiences have welcomed documentaries. In 2005/6 women documentary film-makers gained success; Mercedes Álvarez with *The Sky Turns/El cielo gira* (2004), which focuses on the emptying countryside, and the team Marta Arribas and Ana Pérez with *Memory Train/El tren de la memoria* (2005) on the generation of Spanish emigration to Germany in the 1960s.

NÚRIA TRIANA-TORIBIO

Recent documentary success: Marta Arribas and Ana Pérez remember the 1960s Spanish emigration to Germany in *El tren de la memoria*

cinema) different from the approved model. Almodóvar – with his brother Agustín Almodóvar – created the production company El Deseo that guarantees his independence, permits his thematic and stylistic evolution as a film-maker and kickstarted other careers (for instance, Álex de la Iglesia's with *Mutant Action/Acción mutante* (1993).

Contemporary Spanish cinema

In the mid-1990s, the PSOE's rule started to flounder and Spanish cinema, dependent on subsidies, was affected greatly. The financing system of the 1980s was all but abandoned. The right-wing Partido Popular's policies ostensibly encouraged cinema to pay for itself and from 1996 the state proposed to liberalise cultural sectors, the audiovisual among them. In this industrial climate, film-makers who had secured a relatively strong position in the industry in the 1980s – Almodóvar, Bigas Luna, Colomo or José Luis Cuerda – continued their production (indeed, Catalan auteur Bigas Luna's work gained international recognition) and, in some cases, ushered in new talent: Cuerda was responsible for financing Alejandro Amenábar's *Thesis/Tesis* (1996) and Colomo facilitated Icíar Bollaín's *Hello, Are You Alone?/Hola, estás sola?* (1996). Barry Jordan and Rikki Morgan-Tamosunas (1998) argue that the late 1980s and early 1990s witnessed 'a burgeoning in the number of women filmmakers achieving releases and, in some cases, significant critical and popular success' (p. 121). However, almost a decade later, it is the case that most of these women found it difficult to make more than one film; Bollaín remains one of the few women with a solid film-making career.

Some younger film-makers, such as Julio Medem and Juanma Bajo Ulloa, secured a foothold through the financing of the Basque autonomous government, but only Medem managed to continue working. He commands backing from influential mainstream critics in Spain's press and relies on the art-house international appeal of films such as *Sex and Lucía/Lucía y el sexo* (2001). Almodóvar's work continues to garner critical respect and inspire interest in Spanish cinema worldwide. Among his successes are *All about My Mother/Todo sobre mi madre* (1999), which won the Academy Award for Best Foreign Film in 2000, and *Volver* (2006), whose entire female cast was recognised at Cannes in 2006 with the Best Female Actor Award.

According to the European Audiovisual Observatory (EAO) (2006, pp. 4 and 27) and in keeping with a worldwide trend, attendance at cinemas is falling nationally, although less rapidly than in other western countries. However, Spanish cinema's market share in 2005 increased to a healthy 16.7 per cent, although not quite reaching the 2001 benchmark of 17.8 per cent. The number of productions has increased steadily since the late 1990s. This increase has been helped enormously by the number of co-productions with partners such as France, the UK, Argentina and Chile. Some of these are international successes: Lucrecia Martel's *The Holy Girl/La niña santa* (2004), co-produced by El Deseo in Spain and Lita Stantic in Argentina, among others.

Spanish cinema has consolidated a transnational presence with stars such as Penélope Cruz, Antonio Banderas and Javier Bardem. Transnational European stars such as Carmen Maura, Sergi López or Victoria Abril continue to succeed and the traffic of talent within Spanish-speaking countries gathers momentum. Spanish cinema's next challenge within a globalised industry is not simply to maintain its position but also to open up to the voices and experiences of future generations of non-European/non-white Spanish men and women film-makers.

Selected Reading

Peter W. Evans (ed.), *Spanish Cinema: The Auteurist Tradition*, Oxford, Oxford University Press, 1999.

Alberto Mira, *The Cinema of Spain and Portugal*, London, Wallflower Press, 2005.

Paul Julian Smith, *Desire Unlimited: The Cinema of Pedro Almodóvar*, London and New York, Verso, 2000. Second edition.

Núria Triana-Toribio, *Spanish National Cinema*, London and New York, Routledge, 2003.

PART 5

Genre

HISTORY OF GENRE CRITICISM

Introduction

CHRISTINE GLEDHILL

While literary genre criticism has a long history, it was introduced into anglophone film criticism comparatively recently, in the mid-1960s and early 1970s (Buscombe, 1970; Pye, 1975). In cinema itself, generic forms were one of the earliest means used by the industry to organise the production and marketing of films, and by reviewers and the popular audience to guide their viewing. In this respect, genres – like stars a decade later – emerged from the studio system's dual need for standardisation and product differentiation. The genres, each with its recognisable repertoire of conventions running across visual imagery, plot, character, setting, modes of narrative development, music and stars, enabled the industry to predict audience expectation. Differences between genres meant different audiences could be identified and catered to. All this made it easier to standardise and stabilise production (see The classic studio system, p. 19).

These industrial associations account for the late entry of generic categories into film criticism, which, in its attempt to divest itself of its literary or sociological heritage, sought to demonstrate the presence of individual artists (auteurs) despite rather than in relation to industrial conditions (see The auteur theory, p. 410). Genre conventions in Hollywood cinema had, of course, been remarked upon by film criticism before genre itself became a theoretical issue. But here the term 'convention' was used pejoratively, referring to the second-hand meanings and stereotypes associated with mass production that militated both against the personal expression of the artist and the authentic portrayal of reality. When auteur criticism took on the cause of Hollywood cinema, it was committed to reproducing the author as 'artist' in what was largely genre product. In Colin McArthur's view (1972), this meant sifting the 'irrelevancies brought to particular works' by studio personnel and genre conventions in order to lay bare the core of thematic and stylistic motifs peculiar to the film-maker.

The relationship of genre and auteur criticism will be pursued later. Important to note here is that cinematic genre criticism grew out of the growing dissatisfaction with auteur analysis of Hollywood product that, Tom Ryall (1978) argues, 'tended to treat popular art as if it were "high culture"'. Seminal to this work of reassessment were essays written in different contexts in the 1950s by André Bazin on the western ('The western, or the American film par excellence', and 'The evolution

John Ford's *The Searchers*: for Bazin, the western was 'the American film par excellence'

of the western', both 1971), focusing on two genres that were central to early genre criticism's concern with popular art (see The western, p. 374; The gangster film, p. 279).

In the 1960s, Laurence Alloway wrote an influential piece in *Movie* (1963) and mounted and wrote an introductory booklet to an important season at the Museum of Modern Art in New York, *Violent America: The Movies 1946–64* (1971). His approach was rigorously uncompromising in its insistence on formulae and ephemera as the basis of the popular Hollywood cinema claimed as the product of great 'artists' by the auteurists. In the early 1970s, several articles on genre appeared in the British journal *Screen*, and three books were produced concentrating on the two genres central to the debate – *Horizons West* (Kitses, 1969), *Underworld USA* (McArthur, 1972) and *The Six-Gun Mystique* (Cawelti, 1971) – and here for a while the theoretical debates around genre stopped. As auteur theory was challenged by the emphasis of cine-semiotics on the text itself as the site of production of meaning and author and spectator positions, so the specificities of genre were lost in the general concern with narrative and processes of signification.

Meanwhile, in the 1970s interest shifted from the western and gangster genres that had dominated the 1960s, to exploration of film noir. This was a generic category used by film criticism rather than the industry. It demarcated a body of films that could be explored in the new terms introduced into Anglo-Saxon criticism from the French journal *Cahiers du Cinéma*. Under the influence of a revival of interest in Marxist aesthetics, *Cahiers du Cinéma* detached itself from its championship of Hollywood auteurs; it suggested a system of categorisation that would discriminate between those films whose formal organisation reinforced their manifest ideological themes, and those that through a process of fracture and disjuncture exposed ideological contradictions. Under this rubric a whole range of Hollywood films, which auteurism had virtually been unable to place, could be appropriated for critical validation. In the late 1970s, in response to the assimilation of psychoanalysis and feminism by film theory, melodramas were seen to provide excellent material for the investigation of these interests. As in the case of film noir, a neglected, if not despised, area of Hollywood production was brought into critical view (and feminist film theory has since taken up the even lower-rated women's picture as an adjunct to work on melodrama), but little in these investigations took the issues of genre theory itself much further. Exceptional in this respect was a study by Will Wright (1975), which attempted a structuralist analysis of the western (see p. 378). In the preliminaries to his analysis of the western itself, Wright attempted to adapt Lévi-Strauss's concept of myth to an explanation of how genre conventions represent problems and shifts in social meanings – in how a society communicates with itself. However, the book's concentration on an individual genre begs the question of how genre itself operates in cinema and what questions are posed by a genre approach to cinema.

In the late 1970s, two studies attempted in different ways to revitalise work on the question of genre. Tom Ryall's *Teachers' Study Guide* (1978) on the gangster film set out to analyse the work and debates of the 1960s and 1970s, clarifying the main issues, and to relocate these in relation to structuralist and post-structuralist questions about ideology and signification. In so doing, he attempted to indicate how genre criticism could be useful to the student of film. Stephen Neale's monograph, *Genre* (1980), rather than historicising such debates (a task taken on by Paul Willemen in his short introduction), attempted to recast them, conceptualising genre in terms of linguistic and psychoanalytic theory. Before looking more closely at these ideas, however, it is necessary to ask precisely what are the questions posed by a genre approach to cinema.

What is genre criticism?

Tom Ryall (1978) distinguished genre criticism from the two approaches dominant at the time of its development: auteurism, and an earlier tradition that saw films as providing social documents. He saw as a central concern of genre criticism the relationship between the art product, its source and its audience. Both auteur and 'social document' approaches use a linear model of this relationship, privileging artist or social reality as the originating source of the art product, which, representing their expression, is then consumed by its audience. In contrast, Ryall suggested, the model offered by genre criticism is triangular, with art product, artist and audience as three equally constituting moments in the production of the text – a view that posits a dynamic and mutually determining relationship between them. The basis of this equality lies in the way the conventions of genre operate. They provide a framework of structuring rules, in the shape of patterns/forms/styles/structures, which act as a form of 'supervision' over the work of production of film-makers and the work of reading by an audience. As a critical enterprise, genre analysis, which looks for repetitions and variations between films rather than originality or individuality, was developed as a more appropriate tool for understanding popular cinema than authorship theories. Following the structuralist intervention and revival of Marxist aesthetics, genre analysis enabled film criticism to take account of conditions of production and consumption of films and their relationship to ideology. Thus Ryall placed his original triangle – film/artist/audience – in two concentric circles, the first representing the studio, or particular production institution – the film's immediate industrial context – and the second representing the social formation – here American society, western capitalism – of which the film industry and cinematic signification are a part. Whereas the triangular model displaces the notion of a single originating source, the concentric circles displace an earlier Marxist linear model used to account for historical and social determination – in which the base is seen as unproblematically reflected in the superstructure. In this reconceptualisation, art and society are not opposed to each other as two abstract and discrete entities; rather art is understood as one of the social practices in which society exists. Ryall's model, then, attempted to grasp the range of determinants – historical, economic, social, cinematic, aesthetic, ideological – involved in the production of meaning in the cinema, without foreclosing on the question of which element dominates in any given instance.

Ryall's conceptual models enable us to establish the general ground of genre criticism. When we move from this overall project to the particularities of how it works, however, we confront many of the problems that have dogged genre criticism in the cinema. While the existence of the major genres is in some ways a self-evident fact, the business of definition and demarcation is less clear-cut. Description gets tangled up with evaluation, both of which snag on the problem of historical change – new films often deny accepted definitions and appear to the genre critic to mark a decline from 'classic' examples. The problem of evaluation reappears in the need for genre criticism to sort out its relation to auteurism and the relative weight it gives to the play of conventions compared to the work of the author in the production of particular genre films. The understanding of genre formulae and conventions as a form of cultural tradition poses the problem of how to conceptualise the relation between cultural and other social practices and the ideological roles of the different genres; and this involves consideration of the studio system as part of this relationship. Finally, given that film theory went on to focus on the production of meaning across all texts, and through all cinematic strategies, we have to ask what pertinence genre criticism can have to this project.

Genres: problems of definition

Work on individual genres sooner or later comes up against the problem of where one genre stops and another begins. Much early genre criticism concentrated on producing accounts of defining characteristics for particular genres. To do this the critic must start out with at least a provisional notion of what constitutes the genre. Andrew Tudor points succinctly to the problem in this:

> To take a genre such as the 'Western', analyse it, and list its principal characteristics, is to beg the question that we must first isolate the body of films which are 'Westerns'. But they can only be isolated on the basis of the 'principal characteristics' which can only be discovered from the films themselves after they have been isolated. (Tudor, 1974, p. 135)

The danger here is that the 'provisional notion' crystallises around certain films or a certain period of genre production as a prescriptive 'essence'. Earlier developments then become an 'evolution' towards a 'classic' moment and later deviations constitute decline or decadence. This is very clearly indicated in the work of the two founding critics of genre study of film, André Bazin and Robert Warshow: both wrote seminal pieces about the western, but both picked on different films from different periods as classic examples of the essence of the genre (see The western, p. 374). At issue here is the place of differentiation within the type in genre analysis. Looking to historically discarded literary genres such as Elizabethan revenge tragedy or Restoration comedy as models, Robert Warshow saw repetition rather than differentiation as providing the aesthetic force of a genre:

> For a type to be successful means that its conventions have imposed themselves upon the general consciousness and become the accepted vehicles of a particular set of attitudes and a particular aesthetic effect. One goes to any individual example of the type with very definite expectations, and originality is to be welcomed only in the degree that it intensifies the expected experience without fundamentally altering it. (Warshow, 1970, pp. 129–30)

Laurence Alloway (1971), on the other hand, writing in the context of late-1960s developments in genre theory, resists the temptation to establish 'classic' timeless dimensions in popular forms. He insists on the transitional and ephemeral character of any particular period of genre production. Rather than attempting definitive accounts of particular genres or genre films, he writes about 'cycles, runs or sets', so drawing attention to the shifts and differences that constitute 'internal successive modifications of forms'. Colin McArthur's study of the gangster film (1972) extends this view of differentiation within particular forms to the problems of demarcating one form from another. He argues that one must talk about the gangster/thriller, because the limits of each form are fluid, constituting a spectrum with an infinite number of gradations. He describes the 40-year development of this sprawling genre as 'a constantly growing amoeba, assimilating stages of its own development' (McArthur, 1972, p. 8). Antony Easthope (1979/80) has suggested the usefulness of Tzvetan Todorov's argument that a specific genre should be understood as an abstract, theoretical and provisional structure, incarnated in specific examples, but itself transformed by each new production so 'any instance of a genre will be necessarily different' (Easthope, 1979/80, p. 40). Stephen Neale similarly argues against attempts to define genres as discrete, strictly differentiated and fixed systems in which the critic searches across the range of cinematic codes for relationships of repetition representing rigid rules of inclusion and exclusion. Neale's position, discussed more fully below, emphasises the role of 'difference' in generic production (see also Vernet, 1978).

However, even with a flexible model, empirical assumptions will enter any discussion of specific genres. If these are to be rigorously founded, the critic must decide which of the cinematic codes are pertinent to the definition of a particular genre. In his survey of the early development of British genre criticism, Tom Ryall (1978) identified three broad sets of terms used to net the constituents of individual genres: socio-historical actuality, thematic/ideological constructions deriving from history, and iconography or visual imagery.

Iconography

The notion of iconography was perhaps particularly influential in the work of the 1960s and early 1970s on genre, because it offered a parallel course to the one already laid out by the auteur validation of Hollywood films. If to literary minds their plots were corny and the dialogue banal, this was because the literary critic had no language to cope with cinema as a visual medium. Auteurism developed the notion of mise en scène to fill this gap; genre critics turned to iconography. Edward Buscombe (1970), for instance, argued forcibly that it was in terms of iconography – rather than, for example, narrative structure or rhythm – that the dynamic of particular genres should be specified: 'Since we are dealing with a visual medium we ought surely to look for our defining criteria at what we actually see on the screen ...' (Buscombe, 1970, p. 36). Whereas mise en scène provided the means of materialising the author's personal vision, the notion of iconography gave life to the conventions of generic production, investing them with historical and cultural 'resonances' that, put to work in new combinations and contexts, could produce new articulations of meaning. By iconography, Buscombe meant recurrent images, including the physical attributes and dress of the actors, the settings, the tools of the trade (horses, cars, guns, etc.). Colin McArthur (1972) makes a similar categorisation for the gangster/thriller, attributing to these icons a degree of formal organisation – a 'continuity over several decades of patterns of visual imagery' (McArthur, 1972, p. 24). Although iconography was undeniably 'visual', McArthur in a later unpublished BFI seminar paper, 'Iconography and iconology' (1973), located it in the 'profilmic arrangements of sign-events'. In other words, it was not produced by specifically filmic codes but was taken up and transformed by cinema from cultural codes already in circulation.

Crucial to the functioning of such iconic conventions is the cumulative knowledge and expectation of the audience:

> In *Little Caesar* (1930) a police lieutenant and two of his men visit a nightclub run by gangsters. All three wear large hats and heavy coats, are grim and sardonic and stand in triangular formation, the lieutenant at the front, his two men flanking him in the rear. The audience knows immediately what to expect of them by their physical attributes, their dress and deportment. It knows, too, by the disposition of the figures, which is dominant, which is subordinate. (McArthur, 1972, p. 23)

This knowledge provides the ground on which the 'popular' in the commercial cinema attains its dynamic, the means

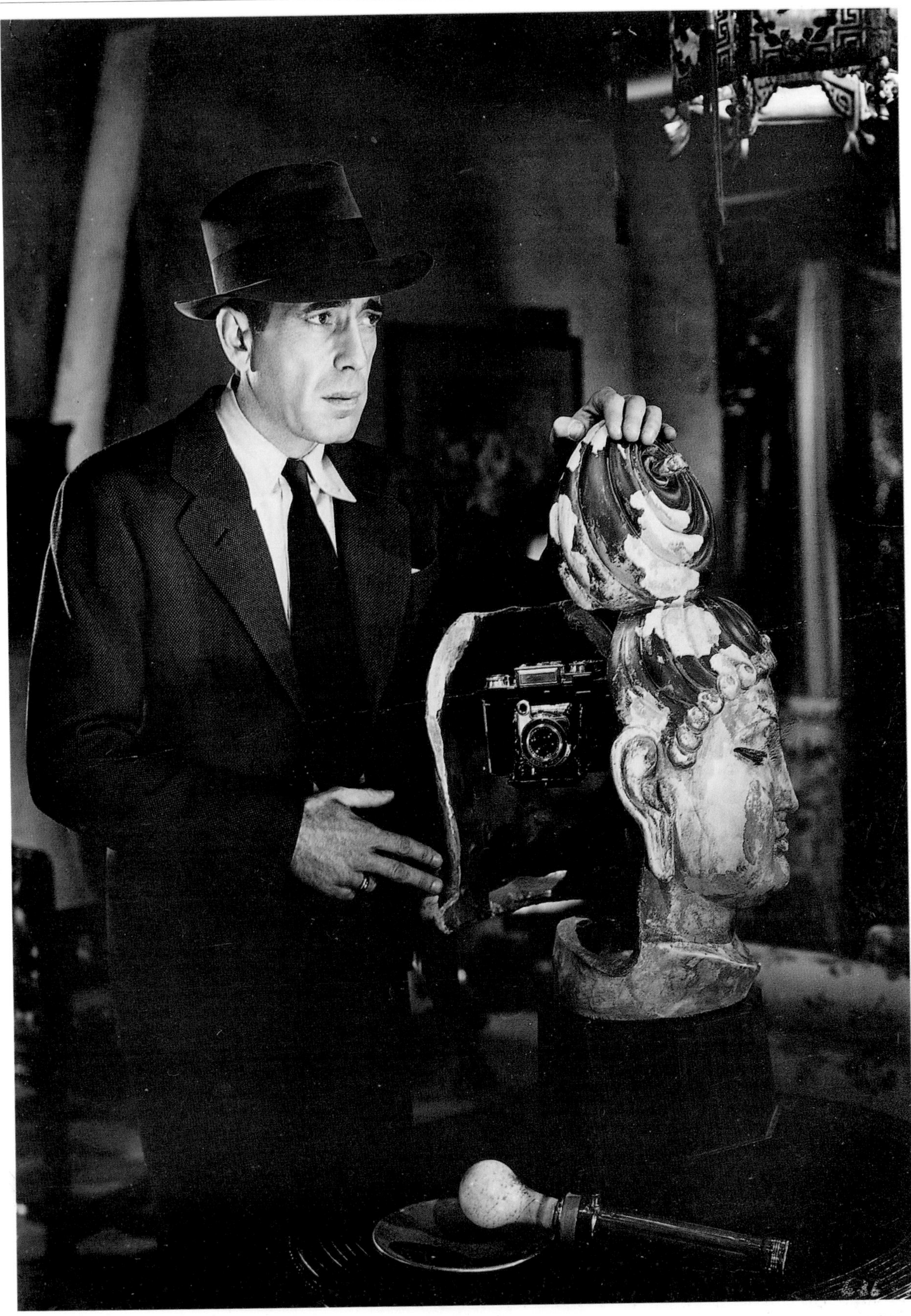

Gangster/crime film iconography: Humphrey Bogart in *The Big Sleep*

by which significance, art, is produced sometimes without the artist; for accretions of the cinematic past in generic convention generate a set of expectations in audiences and these provide, as Bourget (1977) has suggested, opportunities for their disruption, postponement or displacement; disturbances not necessarily attributable to individual film-makers.

Buscombe has given a celebrated example of iconography at work in his account of the opening of *Guns in the Afternoon* (1962):

> Knowing the period and location, we expect at the beginning to find a familiar Western town. In fact, the first few minutes of the film brilliantly disturb expectations. As the camera moves around the town, we discover a policeman in uniform, a car, a camel, and Randolph Scott dressed up as Buffalo Bill. Each of these images performs a function. The figure of the policeman conveys that the law has become institutionalised; the rough and ready frontier days are over. The car suggests, as in *The Wild Bunch*, that the West is no longer isolated from modern technology and its implications. Significantly, the camel is racing against a horse; such a grotesque juxtaposition is painful. A horse in a Western is not just an animal but a symbol of dignity, grace and power. These qualities are mocked by it competing with a camel; and to add insult to injury, the camel wins. (Buscombe, 1970, p. 44)

Of course, it could be argued that while the genre allows for the introduction of the car into a western under pressure from the industry to mine relatively unworked aspects of its relation to the historical west – in this case the closing of the frontier – only the baroque sensibilities of a Sam Peckinpah could have dreamed up the camel. However, it is the accumulated tradition of the western that allows a camel to produce so forceful a shock and sense of estrangement.

It can be seen from these examples that while iconography is manifested in visual terms, it contains considerably more than simple visual imagery – dress connotes character, the three gangsters formation will initiate certain movements in plot, and so on. Moreover, in particular visual motifs, iconography focuses a wide range of social, cultural and political themes that are part of the currency of the society for which it works. The art criticism of Erwin Panofsky was often cited by critics looking for a visual rather than literary heritage to illuminate cinematic conventions. Colin McArthur (1973) argues that the iconography of the western or ganster films carries cultural meanings that are 'read' by contemporary western audiences in much the same way that an ordinary Frenchman of the thirteenth century could 'read' Chartres Cathedral and that a seventeenth-century Venetian could 'read' Francesco Maffei's painting of Judith of Bethulia. This aspect of iconography provided the source of some debate with auteur critics, and the ground on which the genre critics attempted to argue a more subtle relation between socio-historical actuality and particular genres.

Iconography dominated genre study as long as the western and gangster genres remained the focus of empirical interest – perhaps because of its capacity to mediate between historical traditions and particular cinematic forms. However, despite its basis in visual imagery, iconography fails to take account of the finer detail of visual style – camera movement, lighting, editing, for example. Nor does it deal with patterns of narrative structure. And while it enabled the critic to infer action and character attributes in a film's play of meaning, the shift of interest into new generic areas – film noir, or melodrama for instance – found the 'iconographical programmes' that seemed appropriate to the western or gangster film restricting, so that the notion of genre was often displaced in favour of visual style or dramatic modality (see Place, and Harvey, in Kaplan, 1978). A further problem was the tendency of the focus on iconography to produce taxonomies that, while they provided the underlying structure of individual genres and were an extremely useful empirical tool for collating the range of cultural knowledge such genres assumed, could offer little illumination of any particular example beyond its membership of a particular genre (see Ryall, 1978, pp. 13 and 24–6). Thus genre criticism would often turn back to authorship to account for individual films, and both Jim Kitses and Colin McArthur provide authorship case studies, though qualified ones, to follow on their seminal accounts of the western and gangster/thriller genres respectively (see Genre and authorship, p. 258).

The problems of an iconographical approach to genre were displaced by the British appropriation of semiotics and structuralism in the 1970s, which seemed to offer a totalising account of the production of meaning in the cinema. However, semiotics and structuralism tend to work at an abstract, formal level, and while they may explain how iconography functions, the iconographical programmes worked out by the earlier genre critics provided an empirical base for locating particular genres and a means of tracing the historical and cultural traditions that give them their social dimension. Later writing on melodrama, for instance – a genre with very fluid boundaries, many subgeneric offshoots and a complex relation to other forms and traditions – has, arguably, suffered from the absence of such empirical groundwork in its frequent lack of precision.

History and ideology

The foregoing discussion of iconography has already broached the question of the relation of cinematic genres to historical traditions and cultural conventions. This dimension was important to the evaluation of Hollywood genre films in terms of popular rather than high art. In the case of the western and gangster film, these connections could be traced to historical actuality itself:

> The western and the gangster film have a special relationship with American society. Both deal with critical phases of American history. It could be said that they represent America talking to itself about, in the case of the western, its agrarian past, and in the case of the gangster film/thriller its urban technological present. (McArthur, 1972, p. 18)

While it is evident that, for these genres at least, history provides basic subject matter and many aspects of form, the question that confronts genre study is how the relation of history to fiction is to be understood. McArthur's notion of a society 'talking to itself' suggests less a search for historical reconstruction or, in the case of the gangster film, reflection, than what Tom Ryall calls the 'social perception of historical actuality'. This shifts the focus from historical 'fact' to ideology; here, as Tom Ryall (1978) suggests, the historical raw material of a genre is perceived in terms of a network of thematic constructions – for instance, Jim Kitses's (1969) analysis of the history of the west in American consciousness as a conflict between the themes of garden versus wilderness (see The western, p. 377).

At issue here is the relation of socio-historical reality and cultural and aesthetic convention. On one hand, as Colin McArthur (1972) points out, our ideas about the American west or Prohibition are as likely to be gleaned from the cinema as from history books. On the other, Robert Warshow has argued that once historical reality is taken up in an aesthetic process, aesthetic determinations take over: genre films refer not to historical reality but to other genre films and they evolve according to the rules of generic production:

> Moreover, the relationship between the conventions which go to make up such a type and the real experience of its audience or the real facts of whatever situation it pretends to describe is only of secondary importance and does not determine its aesthetic force. It is only in an ultimate sense that the type appeals to its audience's experience of reality; much more immediately, it appeals to previous experience of the type itself: it creates its own field of reference. (Warshow, 1970, pp. 129–30)

Neither of these positions confronts the problem of determining what meanings are being circulated. However, together they raise interesting questions about the interplay between ideologies and aesthetic conventions in the construction of 'social perceptions of history'. Judith Hess (1977) starts from the position that generic convention, as a product of formulaic repetition for a capitalist-financed studio system, can only produce meanings in support of the status quo. Genre films drew audiences and were financially successful 'because they temporarily relieved the fears aroused by a recognition of social and political conflicts' (Hess, 1977, p. 54). They did this by encouraging 'simplistic solutions – the adherence to a well-defined, unchanging code, the advocacy of methods of problem solving based on tradition' (Hess, 1977, p. 55). Clearly, behind such a view of the working of convention in the cinema is the assumption that films address the problems of the real world directly, and provide solutions on a realisable level. Genre films are indictable because they construct reality according to outworn, reactionary conventions. An opposite view, in relation to the gangster film, is put by Robert Warshow, who argues that the popularity of this genre rests not in its official solution to a social problem – 'crime does not pay' – but its ability to provide at an imaginative level a quite different response to American society:

> [T]he importance of the gangster film, and the nature and intensity of its emotional and aesthetic impact, cannot be measured in terms of the place of the gangster himself or the importance of the problem of crime in American life ... What matters is that the experience of the gangster as an experience of art is universal to Americans.
>
> ... [T]he gangster speaks for us, expressing that part of the American psyche which rejects the qualities and demands of modern life, which rejects 'Americanism' itself ... the gangster is the 'no' to that great American 'yes' which is stamped so big over our official culture and yet has so little to do with the way we really feel about our lives. (Warshow, 1970, pp. 130, 136)

For Warshow, generic convention is distinct from the social reality on which it feeds, thus allowing the possibility of ideological criticism. The aesthetic compulsion of generic repetition then suggests, as it were, a neuralgic point – 'there is something more here than meets the eye'.

The emergence in the late 1960s of a concern with the workings of ideology in cinematic forms found a progressive potential for genre in the requirement for differentiation at the commercial as well as aesthetic level – the difference being precisely what draws the audience back into the cinema for the pleasure of repetition, and what makes 'the same' perceptible (see The classic studio system, p. 19). Jean-Loup Bourget (1977) argued that 'wherever an art form is highly conventional, the opportunity for subtle irony or distanciation presents itself all the more readily' (Bourget, 1977, p. 62).

The concept of radical reading – suggesting that generic conventions allow meanings to be constructed against a film's ideological grain – introduces a further problem in the task of relating genres to socio-historical reality: the question of whether the meanings we construct for a genre are those understood by the audience who went to see the films when they first appeared, or those which belong to a contemporary perception of both socio-historical and cinematic actuality. This means respecting the historical conditions of production and consumption (see Ryall, 1978, pp. 11–12) and drawing on the understanding given us by semiotics of the potentially multiple meanings of any signification and our dependency on particular cultural contexts for specific readings.

Genre and industry

So far discussion has focused on how authorial concerns and socio-historical reality have been seen as caught up in the interplay between aesthetic structures and their audiences – arguably producing something far removed from either social actuality or a director's intentions. It remains to consider the place of this activity in the film industry and the wider institution of cinema. While history has often been posed as a source of a genre's subject matter, and social or psychic reasons credited with maintaining an audience's interest in a particular genre, the economic organisation of the film industry along the lines of commodity production is cited as the reason for the existence of genres themselves. As the market for entertainment is notoriously difficult to predict and control, profit is dependent on the successful identification and capture of particular audiences. Generic production grew out of the attempt to repeat and build on initial successes. The studio system developed to facilitate such production: 'Each genre had its regular scriptwriters, sometimes on a yearly contract, its directors, its craftsmen, its studios' (Metz, 1974, p. 122). Tom Ryall describes how 'the standardisation of product obliged by the economic necessities of large scale industrial production led to particular studios concentrating on particular genres' (Ryall, 1978, p. 4). And Edward Buscombe argued that at Warner Bros., 'stars and genre were ... mutually reinforcing' (Buscombe, 1974, p. 59) – the presence of Cagney and Bogart on contract there favoured production of gangster films and vice versa (see Warner Bros., p. 26). Moreover, if a studio spent a lot of money acquiring a star or another sort of 'generic asset' – such as an elaborate western townscape or nightclub set – the cost could be spread over extended periods of production and returns maximised against capital outlay.

It was not only production that was organised along generic lines. Distribution and exhibition sought to market films and attract audiences by mobilising a set of expectations through advertising and promotional gimmicks, while film journalism and critical reviewing perpetuated generic divisions by working within generic expectations and assumptions.

In this context, it has been argued that any study of Hollywood or the studio system must be a study of genre. The problem, however, is not to identify the economic rationale for genres, but to know what such knowledge tells us about this particular aspect of cultural production. Tom Ryall argues that it indicates one set of constraints in the production context of film-making that must be taken into account but not accorded sole determination over the end products. This context, particularly in an entertainment industry, is not and cannot function monolithically. Not only is product differentiation an economic necessity, but:

> The production personnel of a film will include a number of people whose practices fall under the general rubric of 'the creative', e.g. directors, scriptwriters, actors, actresses, designers and so on. A corpus of individuals whose ideology of film will inevitably differ from that of those whose primary allegiance is to a Wall Street finance house. Any description of the Hollywood system will have to take account of the many different, often contradictory, tendencies which jostle with each other during the production of a film. (Ryall, 1978, p. 32)

Stephen Neale (1980) tried to extend the purchase of industrial consideration on genre by utilising the concept of cinematic institution or machine developed by Christian Metz and Stephen Heath among others, and taking a cue from Ryall's references to generic marketing and reviewing practices. From this perspective, the industry is seen not so much as an economic or manufacturing system, but rather as a social institution constituted in a number of discursive practices that include both production and consumption. Genres are not simply the outcome of a certain kind of studio organisation but involve the consolidation in the spectator of a set of viewing orientations, expectations and positions. Behind this lies an attempt to provide a more dialectical model of the relation between industry, text and audience and to conceptualise it as a process rather than a series of reflections between a number of discrete, fixed and static positions. This reconceptualisation of the film industry as cinematic institution prepared the ground for Neale's interest in locating genre within a general, psychoanalytic theory of narrative.

Genre and authorship

Having outlined the different ways in which genre criticism was established, it remains to consider how its relation to authorship was conceived after its initial challenge to this tradition. Only Laurence Alloway appeared to accept the total displacement of the author by generic convention, arguing that collective authorship and diffusion of responsibility are the actual working conditions of Hollywood and that authorship is therefore much less appropriate than genre theory in analysis of the American cinema:

> The rhetoric of art discussion tends to require ... personal authorship and a high level of permanence, criteria not easily satisfied in the popular cinema ... reflex homage to personal originality too often makes us dismiss as aesthetically formulaic a negligible film that may be an interesting, valid, even original development within the convention. (Alloway, 1971, p. 60)

At the other extreme is the view that while indubitably genre conventions exist, their productivity is dependent on the animating power of an author:

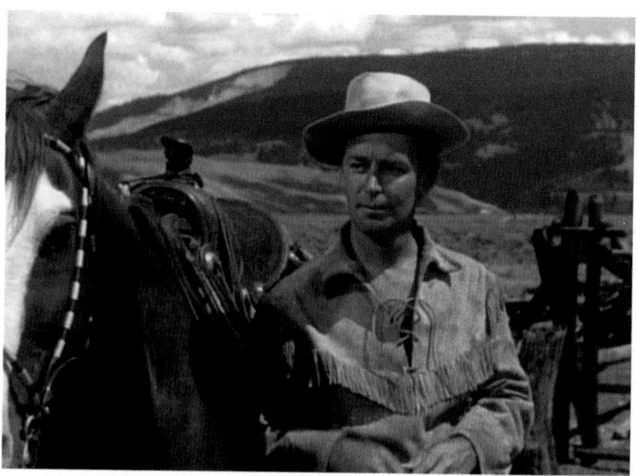

America's agrarian past in *Shane* ...

> If genre exists as a distinct quantity it is in erms of a repertoire of stock situations, selected from the events of the American frontier, that are themselves unspecific, ambiguous and intrinsically without meaning ... neither a structure of archetypal patterns and myths nor of history is sufficiently precise to constitute a genre, nor do recurrent locations, clothes and props do more than signal a temporal and geographical context for a film. (Collins, 1970, pp. 74–5)

Thus history and myth are mediated through the obsessions of the author to animate the conventions of the western with a power attributed by Buscombe and others to the genre itself.

Most genre criticism, however, avoids the extremes of either of these positions, positing a relation between genre conventions and authorial concerns that in different ways could be beneficial to the latter. In one view, there can be a coincidence between genre and author that enables the director to use its conventions as a kind of shorthand, enabling him or her to go straight to the heart of his/her concerns and express them at a formal level through the interplay of genre convention and motif – a common view, for instance, of the relation between John Ford and the western (see John Ford, p. 461). In another view, the author works in tension with the conventions, attempting to inflect them, so as to express his or her own vision in the differences set up between the expected playing out of the convention and the new twists he or she develops – a vision expressed in counterpoint (see McArthur, 1972, p. 17; The auteur theory, p. 410). A third view posits genre as a beneficial constraint that provides a formal ordering and control over the drive to personal expression, preventing its dissolution in an excess of individualism and incomprehensibility, but at the same time capable of containing a certain non-naturalistic dimension – the theatricality or Expressionism of a baroque sensibility. Colin McArthur argues such a position in relation to Jules Dassin, whose work within the apparent greater freedom of European cinema he sees as inferior to his earlier Hollywood productions.

Finally, it remains to note that authorship was often the only recourse for genre critics who wanted to move from discussing the constituents and functioning of the genre itself to discussing their operation in particular films. If genre films could not be evaluated against some presupposed definitive model, then their particularity had to be netted by overlaying another grid, and authorship was the obvious one to hand.

... and its urban technological present in *Machine Gun Kelly*

Both the major book studies of genres that culminated the first phase of genre study, *Horizons West* and *Underworld USA*, devoted their second halves to looking at individual genre films categorised by author. Thus the question of the place of the author did not disappear. Moreover, the difference in *Underworld USA* between the chapters on John Huston and Nicholas Ray suggest that genre and author codes do have different weight in different cases and that these distinctions may parallel those between auteur and metteur en scène (see The *politique des auteurs*, p. 390).

Genre: redirections in the 1980s

Both Tom Ryall (1978) and Stephen Neale (1980) imply in their respective assessments of the first 'wave' of genre criticism the need to place genre within a more 'totalising' theory of cinema. Tom Ryall draws on the concepts of 'cultural production' and 'reading' as a means of shifting genre criticism from the circular and taxonomic tendencies of its earlier phase. The notion of cultural production places film-making as one more practice in a 'network of social practices which constitute a social formation' (Ryall, 1978, p. 24). It therefore stands in dynamic relationship to these practices, overlapping with them, mediating them, participating in a shared body of cultural knowledge or group of discourses, while at the same time operating within its own history and productivity. From this perspective, film-making is in the business of producing or reproducing and circulating varieties of pleasure and cultural meaning. Access to cultural meaning is through the activity of reading, understood as the mobilisation of a particular set of conventions and audience expectations. Genre study for Ryall, then, becomes the 'elaboration of perceived meaning where the individual film is tied to its generic roots on the basis of the reading process' (Ryall, 1978, p. 26). The point is not to allocate particular films to their respective genres, but to investigate the implications of our being able to do this at all. Such an examination of how and why the perceived meanings of a film are produced in particular contexts is not tied to the specific text, but can pull back to look at the social motivations and expectations that governed its production, marketing and consumption.

For Stephen Neale, Ryall's approach, although giving valuable insight into the way genre can be reconceptualised, is not totalising enough. Film-makers and audience, history, industry and society still retain a degree of discreteness and autonomy, confronting each other as a series of dichotomies rather than in a dialectic process. For Neale, any aspect of film must be understood in terms of the social process of cinema as a whole. Working within a psychoanalytic framework, this must in turn be understood in terms of the role of signification in producing and regulating subjectivity. Here subjectivity is understood not as a discrete and fixed identity. Three basic propositions are important in this respect. First, that the subject is driven by the desire to repeat a past pleasure that can never be attained, because something can only be perceived as the same through a gap of difference. Second, that identity is always conferred from the position of another – a 'you' is essential to the meaning of 'I'. (All signification repeats this basic pattern, constructing interpersonal subject positions that speaker and addressee must fill in order for signification to take place.) Third, that in consequence of one and two, an autonomous and stable identity can never be attained; rather subjectivity is a process, in which individuals move in and out of positions constructed for them in the various discourses that constitute society.

By virtue of these propositions, genres have to be seen as specific modes of the narrative system, which function to exploit and contain the diversity of mainstream cinema. As components of the cinematic machine, they represent 'systems of orientations, expectations and conventions that circulate between industry, text and subject' (Neale, 1980, p. 19). Above all, genres work on the terrain of repetition and difference that it is the work of narrative to regulate. Neale is at pains here to stress repetition and difference as a relation rather than as distinct elements. There can be no difference except insofar as it emerges from repetition and, vice versa, it is only the element of difference that allows repetition to become visible.

Genres, then, are not discrete systems, consisting of a fixed number of listable items and separated out from the rest of cinema, but 'constitute specific variations of the interplay of codes, discursive structures and drives involved in the whole of mainstream cinema' (Neale, 1980, p. 48). In order to locate the 'specific variation' of a particular genre, we have to know how narrative organises the codes and discourses that are its material. Narrative is 'a process of transformation of the balance of elements that constitute its pretext; the interruption of an initial equilibrium and tracing of the dispersal and refiguration of its elements' (Neale, 1980, p. 20). Generic specification starts therefore with a consideration of the way in which equilibrium and disruption are articulated. Difference between genres occurs in the particular discourses invoked, the particularity of emphasis on and combinations of elements that are shared with other genres – for instance, the relative placing and relations between the discourses of law and heterosexual love are what differentiate the melodrama from the film noir, not the exclusivity of one kind of discourse to one genre. Such different emphases and relations between different discourses produce different positionings of the subject. Genre specification can therefore be traced in the different functionings of subjectivity each produces, and in their different modes of addressing the spectator.

Neale's intervention into genre criticism represents an attempt to reorientate the task of genre specification in order to achieve a greater flexibility in demarcation – for instance, the emphasis on the relation of repetition and difference allows for the textual productivity of overlaps and contradictions – and a greater sense of how genre may draw on other forms of cinematic signification. As it stands, his account operates at a highly abstract level, the specification of discourses appearing no easier than the categorisation of icons, and often relying on an already established iconographic base as clues to their presence.

Genre theory since the 1980s

STEVE NEALE

While studies, theories and histories of individual genres have appeared in great numbers since the early 1980s, studies, theories and histories of genre as such have been few and far between. Within film, media and cultural studies, general theorising, in particular, has tended to focus on issues of narrative, representation, race and ethnicity, sexual difference, identity and spectatorship, and to explore the merits and limits of postmodernism, post-structuralism, semiotics, psychoanalysis, cognitive psychology and formalism. Nevertheless, some general theories – and some general questions – have been both advanced and debated.

In two books published in the early 1980s, *Hollywood Genres: Formulas, Filmmaking, and the Studio System* (1981), and *Old Hollywood/New Hollywood: Ritual, Art, and Industry* (1983), Thomas Schatz put forward a number of general ideas about the cultural function and significance of Hollywood's genres, about the nature of Hollywood's genre system and, in the second book in particular, about the changes wrought to both by the demise of the studio system and the rise of what he and others have called 'the New Hollywood' (see p. 60). Starting from the premise that Hollywood's genres have their basis in the economic impulse to repeat or to build upon commercially successful formulae, that this basis was further underpinned on one hand by the routines and practices of studio production and on the other by the reciprocal links between producer and consumer, artist, industry and audience that he sees as integral to the way genres and the industry as a whole tend to work, Schatz argued that these formulae are not only socially and culturally meaningful, but that they perform what he calls a 'ritual' function for the audience and hence for American society as a whole. Borrowing the term, and the idea, from Henry Nash Smith's book *The Virgin Land* (1950), and acknowledging the limits and qualifications necessitated by some of the commercial and technological aspects of the cinema, Schatz nevertheless sees genres and genre film-making, as Smith sees pulp fiction and pulp writing, 'as a form of collective cultural expression' (Schatz, 1981, p. 13), and hence as a vehicle for the exploration of ideas, ideals, cultural values and ideological dilemmas central to American society. Each genre possesses its own 'generic community' and tends to deal with its own set of dramatic and ideological conflicts and problems. Thus:

> What emerges as a social problem (or dramatic conflict) in one genre is not necessarily a problem in another. Law and order is a problem in the gangster and detective genres, but not in the musical. Conversely, courtship and marriage are problems in the musical but not in the gangster and detective genres. (Schatz, 1981, p. 25)

In this way, genres possess their own individual identity and significance, but also belong to a larger generic and cultural system. This system is in turn divisible into genres of two basic kinds or types: genres of 'determinate space' on one hand, and genres of 'indeterminate space' on the other:

> In a genre of determinate space (western, gangster, detective, et al.), we have a symbolic arena of action. It represents a cultural realm in which fundamental values are in a state of sustained conflict. In these genres, then, the contest itself and its necessary arena are 'determinate' – a specific social conflict is violently enacted within a familar locale according to a prescribed system of rules and behavioral codes. (Schatz, 1981, p. 27)

In addition, and in part because conflict in the genres of determinate space centres on the nature and control of the space, the setting itself, its props, its inhabitants and their dress, tend to figure significantly in a developed and highly coded visual iconography. (Hence the extent to which the concept of generic iconography was developed in relation to genres of this kind.) By contrast:

> [G]enres of indeterminate space generally involve a doubled ... hero in the guise of a romantic couple who inhabit a 'civilized' setting, as in the musical, screwball comedy, and social melodrama. The physical and ideological 'contest' which determines the arena of action in the western, gangster, and detective genres is not an issue here. Instead, genres of indeterminate space incorporate a civilized, ideologically stable milieu, which depends less upon a heavily coded place than on a highly conventionalized value system. Here conflicts derive not from a struggle for control of the environment, but rather from the struggle of the principal characters to bring their own views in line either with one another's or, more often, in line with that of the larger community.
>
> Unlike genres of determinate space, these genres rely on a progression from romantic antagonism to eventual embrace. The kiss or embrace signals the integration of the couple into the larger cultural community. In addition, these genres use inconographic conventions to establish a social setting – the proscenium or theater stage with its familiar performers in some musicals, for example, or the repressive small-town community and the family home in the melodrama. But because the generic conflicts arise from attitudinal (generally male–female) oppositions rather than from a physical conflict, the coding in these films tends to be less visual and more ideological and abstract. (Schatz, 1981, pp. 27–9)

In *Old Hollywood/New Hollywood*, Schatz puts forward similar ideas. However, he also argues that since the decline of the studio system, the genre system and its ritual function have broken down. A 'radical', 'experimental' or 'modernist' group of film-makers made genre films that self-consciously 'examined the very nature of the genres themselves and their ongoing cultural appeal (Schatz, 1983, p. 27):

> Gangster films like *Bonnie and Clyde* and *Mean Streets*, detective films like *The Long Goodbye* and *The Conversation*, musicals like *New York, New York* and *All That Jazz*, westerns like *Ulzana's Raid* and *McCabe and Mrs Miller*, war films like *The Deer Hunter* and *Apocalypse Now*, romantic comedies like *Annie Hall* and *Smile* – these and other films were designed for widespread distribution and are genre films, but they finally do more to challenge and reflect upon their generic heritage than to mindlessly sustain it. (Schatz, 1983, pp. 27–8)

Generic blockbusters such as *Love Story* (1970), *The Poseidon Adventure* (1972), *The Sting* (1973), *Jaws* (1975) and *Star Wars* (1977) did attract 'the closest thing to a "mass audience" in the New Hollywood', 'but often this was due as much if not more to the hype of the marketing campaigns than the quality of the films themselves' (Schatz, 1983, p. 20). In short, 'without the steady production and audience feedback of the old integrated system, the ongoing discourse – the process of cultural exchange – between audience and industry has ended' (Schatz, 1983, p. 26). Ended too, therefore, is genre's ritual function.

Schatz's work is mentioned in passing by Rick Altman in his book on *The American Film Musical* (1987). Altman notes that while Schatz and other champions of the ritual approach to genre like John Cawelti (1971; 1976), Leo Braudy (1976), Frank McConnell (1975), Michael Wood (1975) and Will Wright (1975) were all fundamentally 'attributing ultimate authorship to the audience, with the studios simply serving, for a price, the national will', 'a parallel ideological approach was demonstrating how audiences are manipulated by the business and political interests of Hollywood' (Altman, 1987, p. 94). Citing *Cahiers du Cinéma*, *Jump Cut* and *Screen* as vehicles of the latter (a trend to which Neale, 1980, also clearly belongs), Altman is at pains to stress the irreconcilable differences between the two approaches:

> Whereas the ritual approach sees Hollywood as responding to societal pressure and thus expressing audience desires, the ideological approach claims that Hollywood takes advantage of spectator energy and psychic investment in order to lure the audience into Hollywood's own positions. The two are irreducibly opposed. (Altman, 1987, p. 94)

Altman is here content to note that these two approaches 'continue to represent the most interesting and well defended of recent approaches to Hollywood genre film' (Altman, 1987, p. 94). He himself goes on to argue that the ritual and ideological functions or dimensions of genre are, in fact, negotiable, variable, unpredictable, a position that is echoed by Neale who argues that the ritual approach tends to ignore 'the role of institutional determinations and decisions, bypassing the industry and the sphere of production in an equation between market availability, consumer choice, consumer preference, and broader social and cultural beliefs' (Neale, 1990, p. 64), and that the ideological approach is open to charges of 'reductivism, economism, and cultural pessimism' (Neale, 1990, p. 65). He instead proposes 'context-specific analysis' (Neale, 1990, p. 65).

Altman's discussion of the ritual and ideological approaches to genre occurs during a broader discussion of genre and genre theory. During the course of this broader discussion, he offers both a model – or conceptual grid – for the analysis of individual genres, and a framework – or procedure – for the analysis of genre as such. First, following Fredric Jameson (1975), he argues that one can distinguish between 'semantic' and 'syntactic' approaches to genre and genres:

> While there is anything but general agreement on the exact frontier separating semantic from syntactic views, we can as a whole distinguish between generic definitions which depend on a list of common traits, attitudes, characters, shots, locations, sets, and the like – thus stressing the semantic elements which make up the genre – and definitions which play up instead certain constitutive relationships between undesignated placeholders – relationships which might be called the genre's fundamental syntax. The semantic approach thus stresses the genre's building blocks, while the syntactic view privileges the structures into which they are arranged. (Altman, 1987, p. 95)

He then goes on to argue that these two approaches are complementary, not mutually exclusive, to propose that every genre possesses semantic traits and syntactic characteristics, and to argue in addition that

> When genres are redefined in terms of their semantic and syntactic dimensions, new life is breathed into the notion of genre history. Instead of simply enumerating the minor variations developed by various studios or directors within a general, fundamentally stable generic framework, genre history based on a semantic/syntactic hypothesis would take as its object three interrelated concerns: 1) the introduction and disappearance of basic semantic elements (e.g., the musical's deployment of a succession of styles – from operetta and chansonnier crooning and opera to swing and folk to rock and nostalgia); 2) the development and abandoning of specific syntactic solutions (e.g., the move from the early sound period identification of music with sadness, usually in three-person plots assuring a sad, solitary odd-man-out, to the post-1933 emphasis on music as celebration of a joyous union of opposites, in the culture as well as the couple); 3) the ever-changing relationship between the semantic and syntactic aspects of the genre (e.g., the way in which diegetic music, the musical's semantic element par excellence, is transformed from a flashy but unintegrated element of spectacle into a signifier of success and a device for reversal of the traditional image-over-sound hierarchy). (Altman, 1987, pp. 97–8)

Like Schatz's distinction between genres of determinate and indeterminate space, Altman's distinction between generic semantics and generic syntax remains unexplored and untested by others. It is attractive in its economy, and in the methodological purchase it appears to offer genre theorists and genre historians. However, as Altman himself points out, questions – particularly questions of definition and clarification – remain. To what extent, for instance, can a musical style (like operetta, folk or swing) be considered a semantic element, a building block, to use Altman's term, of the musical considered as a genre? To be sure, different musical styles convey different meanings. They therefore perform a semantic function. But surely the building blocks of the musical are not musical styles, but, simply, songs and passages of music? (And not all of them are diegetic: passages of dance in numerous musicals are accompanied not by diegetic but by non-diegetic music; what matters, both in songs and in passages of dance, is that, as Altman himself points out, the hierarchy of image over sound is reversed, and the body and its activities on the one hand and the means and devices of cinematic enunciation on the other are organised around, and subordinated to, sound, music and the soundtrack.) Moreover, insofar as the style of music used in a musical acquires a generically specific semantic dimension, surely that dimension is syntactically governed? These particular questions relate to the two more general questions Altman raises himself: 'Just where ... do we locate the border between the

Redefinition of the musical, with no place for *Bambi*

semantic and the syntactic? And how are these two categories related?' (Altman, 1987, p. 99). These questions, and others, remain unexplored.

Altman's propositions about the semantic and syntactic dimensions of genre arise in the context of a more general concern with the aims and procedures of genre analysis. The aims include the identification and explanation of the attributes of a genre, an explanatory account of the genre's history, and an account of 'the way in which the genre is moulded by, functions within, and in turn informs the society of which it is a part' (Altman, 1987, pp. 14–15). Central to these aims is the establishment of a generic corpus, a group of films that can clearly be considered as musicals or westerns, horror films, gangster films and so on. Within this context, Altman considers the role of industrial and journalistic discourse and its terms. It is a role he considers crucial in establishing the possible presence or existence of genres, but of limited value in nearly all other respects. Even here,

> The fact that a genre has been posited, defined, and delimited by Hollywood is taken only as prime facie evidence that generic levels of meaning are operative within or across a group of texts roughly designated by the Hollywood term and its usage. The industrial/journalistic term thus founds a hypothesis about the presence of meaningful activity, but does not necessarily contribute a definition or delimitation of the genre in question. (Altman, 1987, p. 13)

For Altman, the location of an industrial term, and of the group of films to which that term has been applied, is merely the first step in a multi-stage process. Having established a preliminary corpus in this way, the role of 'the genre critic' is to subject the corpus to analysis and to locate a method for defining and describing the structures, functions and systems specific to as many of the films within it as is possible. The next step is to redefine the corpus in the light of the critic's analysis:

> Texts which correspond to a particular understanding of the genre, that is which provide ample material for a given method of analysis, will be retained within the generic corpus. Those which are not illuminated by the method ... will simply be excluded from the final corpus. In terms of the musical, this would mean admitting that there are some films which include a significant amount of diegetic music, and yet which we will refuse to identify as musicals in the strong sense which the final corpus implies. (Altman, 1987, p. 14)

Having thus established a final corpus, the critic is then in a position to produce a history of the genre, and an account of its social significance.

Altman's own analysis of the musical, and his own redefinition of its corpus, is itself impressively comprehensive and inclusive in scope. However, despite the many merits of his analytical definition, he finds himself excluding from a redefined corpus films such as *Dumbo* (1941) and *Bambi* (1942), and able only to include films such as *The Wizard of Oz* (1939), Fox's Shirley Temple films and Universal's Deanna Durbin vehicles by means of a particularly tortured and circuitous argument. And it is with this stage of Altman's procedure, and the limited role it assigns industrial and journalistic discourse, that Stephen Neale (1990) takes issue. Neale disagrees with the proposition that the aim of generic analysis is the redefinition or rearrangement of a corpus of films:

> Such an aim is in the end no different, in effect if not in intention, from ... the worst, pigeon-holing inheritances of neo-classical literary theory. We can easily end up identifying the purpose of generic analysis with the rather fruitless attempt to decide which films fit, and therefore properly belong to, which genres. We can also end up constructing or perpetuating canons of films, privileging some and emoting or excluding others. (Neale, 1990, p. 31)

In addition, an aim such as this is in danger of curtailing the very cultural and historical analysis upon which Altman rightly insists as an additional theoretical aim. The danger lies not only in the devaluation of industrial/journalistic discourses, but in the separation of genre analysis from a number of the features that define its public circulation. These features include the fact that genres always exist in excess of a corpus of films; the fact that genres comprise expectations and audience knowledge as well as films; and the fact that these expectations and the knowledge they entail are public in status (Neale, 1990, p. 31).

Neale continues, quoting Todorov (1976, p. 102), and moving on to place industrial and journalistic discourse, and the discourses of promotion and publicity that surround the films themselves, at the heart of genre study. Borrowing Gregory Lukow and Steve Ricci's term 'inter-textual relay' to refer to these discourses (Lukow and Ricci, 1984, p. 29), he writes:

> As Todorov has argued (while himself tending to equate genres solely with works): One can always find a property common to two texts, and therefore put them together in one class. But is there any point in calling the result of such a union a 'genre'? I think it would be in accord with the current usage of the word and at the same time provide a convenient and operant notion if we agreed to call 'genres' only those classes of texts that have been perceived as such in the course of history. The accounts of this perception are found most often in the discourse on genres (the metadiscursive discourse) and, in a sporadic fashion, in the texts themselves.
>
> As far as the cinema is concerned (Todorov here is writing about literature – and High Literature at that), this metadiscursive discourse is to be found in its inter-textual relay. Clearly, generic expectations and knowledges do not emanate solely from the industry and its ancillary institutions; and clearly, individual spectators may have their own expectations, classifications, labels and terms. But these individualized, idiosyncratic classifications play little part, if any, in the public formation and circulation of genres and generic images. In the public sphere, the institutional discourses are of central importance. Testimony to the existence of genres, and evidence of their properties, is to be found primarily there. (Neale, 1990, pp. 51–2)

Neale goes on to argue that industrial and journalistic labels and terms constitute key evidence of and for the history and the historicity of genres: 'they ... offer virtually the only available evidence for an historical study of the array of genres in circulation, or of the ways in which individual films have been generically perceived at any point in time' (Neale, 1990, p. 52). This is important, because 'both the array and the perceptions have changed', and Neale goes on to give two examples. He points out on the one hand that 'the western', as an established term of generic description, only came into existence in or around 1910. It is therefore unlikely that the term was applied to *The Great Train Robbery* (1903), which has often been classified since as an important early western. He in addition quotes Charles Musser (1984), who argues that *The Great Train Robbery* is best understood, and was understood at the time, not as a western, but as a crime film that drew also on the paradigms and conventions of melodrama, 'the chase film' and the 'railway genre'. On the other hand, Neale points out that the terminology used in the catalogues of film companies in the early part of the century indicates considerable differences between the generic regimes characteristic of early cinema and the more familiar regimes of the studio and post-studio era. He quotes both from the Kleine *Complete Illustrated Catalog of Moving Picture Machines, Stereoptikons, Slides, Films* (1905, p. 5) and from the *Biograph Bulletins*, 1896–1908 (1971, pp. 59–73).

Thus, instead of the westerns, horror films and war films of later years, the Kleine Optical Company's catalogue for 1905 lists films in the following groupings:

1. Story
   a. historical
   b. dramatic
   c. narrative
2. Comic
3. Mysterious
4. Scenic
5. Personalities

Meanwhile, Biograph's 'Advance Partial List' of films for sale in 1902 lists its 'subjects' under the following titles and headings: Comedy Views, Sports and Pastime Views, Military Views, Railroad Views, Scenic Views, Views of Notable Personages, Miscellaneous Views, Trick Pictures, Marine Views, Children's Pictures, Fire and Patrol Views, Pan-American Exposition Views, Vaudeville Views and Parade Pictures (p. 55).

This kind of work is pursued in Neale's article 'Melo talk: on the meaning and use of the term "Melodrama" in the American trade press' (1993) (see Melodrama, p. 316), and also in *Genre and Hollywood* (1999). The latter, in addition, takes up a number of questions raised by Alan Williams (1984) in a review of Schatz (1981) and Neale (1980), and attempts to set forth a number of new ideas and new definitions. Williams's questions are fundamental:

> Perhaps the biggest problem with genre theory or genre criticism is the term genre. Borrowed, as a critical tool, from literary studies ... the applicability of 'genre' as a concept in film studies raises some fairly tough questions. Sample genres are held to be Westerns, Science Fiction Films, more recently Disaster Films, and so on. What do these loose groupings of works – that seem to

> come and go, for the most part, in ten- and twenty-year cycles – have to do with familiar literary genres such as tragedy, comedy, romance, or (to mix up the pot a bit) the epistolary novel or the prose poem. (Williams, 1984, p. 121)

He continues:

> For the phrase 'genre films', referring to a general category, we can frequently, though not always, substitute 'film narrative.' Perhaps that is the real genre. Certainly there is much more difference between *Prelude: Dog Star Man* and *Star Wars* than there is between the latter and *Body Heat*. It's mainly a question of terminology, of course, but I wonder if we ought to consider the principal genres ... as being narrative film, experimental/avant-garde film, and documentary. Surely these are the categories in film studies that have among themselves the sorts of significant differences that one can find between, say, epic and lyric poetry. (Williams, 1984, p. 121)

Responding to this, Neale first points out that the genres and genre categories characteristic of literature are by no means always as systematically coherent or long-lived as Williams appears to suggest. Comedy, romance and tragedy are all long-lived as terms, but the criteria that define them and the types of work the terms encompass have in each case shifted radically over time (see Beer, 1970, on romance; Koelb, 1975, on tragedy). In addition, the western and science fiction are literary genres as well as being genres in the cinema. Even the disaster film has its analogue in a series of novels written in the late 1960s and early 1970s (for example, novels such as *Airport* by Arthur Hailey and *The Poseidon Adventure* by Paul Gallico).

This leads to a second point: western novels, science-fiction novels (even disaster novels) are frequently thought of, precisely, as genre fiction, a term that marks a division between this kind of fiction and 'literary fiction' or simply 'literature' proper. The latter is usually considered the province of 'genuine' literary art and 'authentic' authorial expression. The former, by contrast, is usually considered formulaic, artistically anonymous and therefore artistically worthless. However, as Kress and Threadgold (1988) and Threadgold (1989) have shown, there is a distinct history to these kinds of attitudes and to the ways in which genre and conceptions of genre have figured within them. An almost symmetrical inversion has occurred since the end of the eighteenth century. Prior to the advent of Romanticism, industrialisation, urbanisation, mass literacy and the regular production of fiction of all kinds for the mass market, genre, and the kind of order and decorum it implied, was valued and promoted as a mark of high culture, and as in contrast to the anarchy, the lack of order – the lack of genre – seen as characteristic of low culture (political pamphlets, ballads, chapbooks and the like).

Genre, then, has always been a value-laden term and has always been used to mark divisions between (as well as within) fields of artistic production. Ideology rather than logic has always governed or overshadowed definitions of genre. Thus in support of Williams's argument, there is no logical reason whatsoever why avant-garde films and documentaries should not be considered as genres, particularly as they both possess their own infrastructures of production, distribution, exhibition, promotion and critical discussion – their own intertextual relays and their own terms of description – in addition to their own conventions and textual features. There is no logical reason either why 'the narrative film' should not be treated as a genre. However, Neale's third point is that there is equally no reason for the categories 'narrative film' and 'western' (or 'science fiction' or 'disaster film') to be treated as mutually exclusive. Most texts, and most films, are multiply generic: *Star Wars* and *Body Heat*, to use two of Williams's examples, are simultaneously 'films', 'fiction films', 'Hollywood films' and 'narrative feature films'; the former is also 'science fiction', 'space opera' and/or 'action-adventure', and the latter a 'thriller' (and possibly also 'neo-noir').

This point stems, finally, from a discussion of definitions and debates about genre within speech-act theory, pragmatics and philosophy. Both speech-act theory and pragmatics are branches of linguistics. They are concerned with language in use, and in particular with the rules and conventions governing the production, reception and comprehension of specific kinds of linguistic utterance in specific kinds of context (see Blakemore, 1992; Davis, 1991; Enkvist, 1991; Leech, 1983; Levinson, 1983; Lyons, 1981; and Mey, 1993). Issues of genre are central to pragmatics and speech-act theory because generic expectations and conventions characterise all forms and instances of utterance, not just those conventionally thought of as aesthetic. As Mary Louise Pratt points out,

> Genre is not solely a literary matter. The concept of genres applies to all verbal behavior, in all realms of discourse. Genre conventions are in play in any speech situation, and any discourse belongs to a genre, unless it is a discourse explicitly designed to flaunt the genre system. (Pratt, 1981, p. 176)

Jacques Derrida (1992) has criticised aspects of speech–act-orientated genre theory on the grounds that texts can always exceed or evade specific expectations, labels and contexts. He would therefore contest the notion that texts 'belong' to genres. He would also deny, though, that any utterance, text or discourse could ever escape being generic. A particular utterance, text or discourse might well be able to 'flaunt' a particular 'genre system'. But it could never entirely evade what he calls 'the law of genre', for the simple reason that all utterances, whenever they are actually encountered, are always encountered in a context of one kind or another, and are therefore always confronted with expectations, with systems of comprehension, and in all probability with labels and names.

From this perspective, all films, like all linguistic utterances, 'participate' (to use Derrida's term) in genres of one kind or another – and usually in several at once. The laws of genre – and the laws of genres – are thus exclusive neither to Hollywood nor to the commercial cinema in general. They pervade the cinema, films and the viewing of films as a whole.

Selected Reading

Rick Altman, *Film/Genre*, London, BFI Publishing, 1999.

Barry Keith Grant, *Film Genre: From Iconography to Ideology*, London, Wallflower Press, 2007.

Steven Neale (ed.), *Genre and Contemporary Hollywood*, London, BFI Publishing, 2002.

Thomas Schatz, *Hollywood Genres: Formulas, Filmmaking, and the Studio System*, New York, Random House, 1981. Reprinted by McGraw-Hill, 1988.

ACTION-ADVENTURE

STEVE NEALE

The term 'action-adventure' is nowadays used mainly to describe what was perceived in the 1980s and 1990s to be a new and dominant trend in Hollywood's output, a trend exemplified by the *Alien* films (1979; 1986; 1992; 1997); the *Indiana Jones* films (1981; 1984; 1989); the *Rambo* films (1982; 1985; 1988); the *Die Hard* films (1988; 1990; 1995); and the *Terminator* films (1984; 1991; 2003), as well as by films such as *Total Recall* (1990), *Point Break* (1991), *The Last of the Mohicans* (1992) and *Braveheart* (1995).

This trend encompassed a range of films and genres – from swashbucklers to science fiction, from thrillers to westerns and war films – and was a clear instance of Hollywood's propensity for generic hybridity and overlap. The term 'action-adventure' has been used, though, to pinpoint a number of features common to these genres and films: a propensity for spectacular physical action; a narrative structure involving fights, chases and explosions; the deployment of state-of-the art special effects; and an emphasis in performance on athletic feats and stunts. The nature of this emphasis has often been accompanied by a focus on the 'hyperbolic bodies' and physical skills of the stars involved: Arnold Schwarzenegger (see also Stars, p. 132), Sylvester Stallone, Dolph Lundgren, Bruce Willis, Brigitte Nielsen, Linda Hamilton and others. It is thus not surprising that two major books published on these films – by Susan Jeffords (1994) and by Yvonne Tasker (1993) – explore the ideological implications of this emphasis on the athletic body.

In the wake of her 1989 book, Jeffords's aim is 'on the one hand to argue for the centrality of the masculine body to popular culture and national identity while, on the other, to articulate how the polarizations of the body altered during the years of the Reagan and Bush presidencies' (Jeffords, 1994, p. 13). Her argument is that:

> Whereas the Reagan years offered the image of a 'hard body' to contrast directly to the 'soft body' of the Carter years, the late 1980s and early 1990s saw a re-evaluation of that hard body, not for a return to the soft body but for a rearticulation of masculine strength and power through internal, personal, and family-oriented values. Both of these predominant models ... are overlapping components of the Reagan Revolution, comprising on the one hand a strong militaristic foreign-policy position and on the other hand a domestic regime of an economy and a set of values dependent on the centrality of fatherhood. (Jeffords, 1994, p. 13)

In arguing her case, Jeffords links a reading of the narrative structure of the films she discusses to the policy statements of Reagan, Bush and their spokespeople. However, she does not specify a mechanism through which the presidential ideolo-

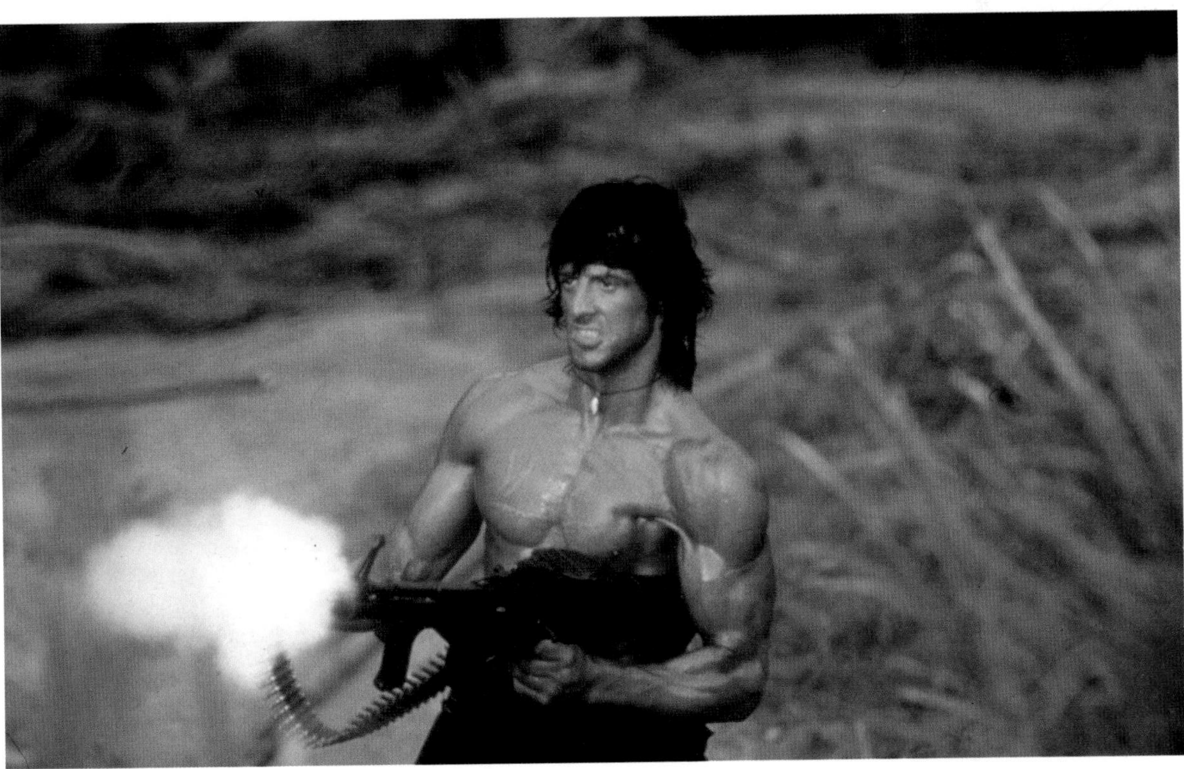

The 'hard bodies' of 1980s action heroes: Sylvester Stallone as John Rambo in *Rambo First Blood Part II*

gies she discusses find their way into the films. She is therefore forced to rely on analogy. This is a procedure – and a problem – common to many ideological analyses of genres and cycles; in this case, Jeffords's analysis dovetails with arguments made about 1980s action films by Britton (1986); Kellner and Ryan (1988); Sartelle (1996); Traube (1992); and Wood (1986). Other writers have taken a different view, both about the ideological significance and scope of 1980s action films, and about their aesthetic characteristics and values. Pfeil (1995), for instance, argues that the category of 'white, heterosexual masculinity' that often underpins these analyses is not as monolithic as is often implied, that the films are often multivalent (combining appeals to the populist left as well as the right), and that distinctions need to be made between them, particularly between those produced by Joel Silver at Warners and Fox – the first two *Die Hard* films and the first two *Lethal Weapon* films – and others such as *Batman* (1989) and *Total Recall*. For Pfeil, the former are sites in which 'fantasies of class- and gender-based resistance to the advent of a post-feminist/post-Fordist world keep turning over, queasily, deliriously, into accommodations' (p. 28), and in which, within a 'very specifically white/male/hetero American capitalist dreamscape, inter- and/or multi-national at the top and multiracial at the bottom ... all the old lines of force and division between races, classes and genders are both transgressed and redrawn' (p. 2). While 'the rhythms of excitation and satisfaction in these films' assert male violence, 'their own speeded-up processes of gratification undermine any claim to male authority' (p. 8). The repeated spectacle of 'torn but still beautifully exposed slick-muscled bodies' raises rather than answers a number of questions:

> How do we distinguish between their (re)assertion of gendered difference and their submission to the camera ... as objects of its gaze and our own? What, likewise, is the boundary line between the diehard assertion of rugged male individualism and its simultaneous feminization and spectacularization? (p. 29)

Similar points have been made by Willis (1998) and by Tasker (1993). Tasker points to the ambivalent populism of many of these action films, and to the fact that the muscular hero within them is often literally 'out of place': 'Increasingly ... the powerful white hero is a figure who operates in the margins, while in many senses continuing to represent dominance. This is an important trait in many action pictures and is central to the pleasures of the text' (Tasker, 1993, p. 98). Equally central are style, spectacle, atmosphere and tone. Tasker is particularly interested in the knowing visual excess and the tongue-in-cheek humour characteristic of these films. She is therefore particularly insistent that ideological readings based solely on an analysis of their plots may be reductive, misleading, or both. As an example, she cites *Red Sonja* (1985), a sword-and-sorcery follow-up to Schwarzenegger's *Conan* films (1981; 1984). Early in *Red Sonja*, we learn that Sonja herself (Brigitte Nielsen) has rejected the sexual advances of queen Gedren. She becomes a swordswoman, and it is in this guise that she encounters Schwarzenegger as Kalidor:

> An analysis of the ideological terms at work in a film like *Red Sonja* is not difficult – the film follows Sonja's journey to a 'normal' sexual identity, or at least the rejection of lesbian desire. After the initial 'threat' of lesbianism, Sonja becomes a masculinised swordswoman who refuses Kalidor/Schwarzenegger until he can beat her in a 'fair fight'. (Tasker, 1993, p. 30)

However, the comedy and the excess permeating the presentation of the fight and the 'texture' of the film as a whole 'call into question the very terms deployed – the "normal" sexual identity to which Sonja is led' (Tasker, 1993, p. 30).

Tasker continues, noting the extent to which exaggeration and parody are involved in the presentation of the body in these films. For her this means that the body and the terms of its gender can become the site of transgression and play, the focus of an attention that can make strange, as well as reinforce, norms of gender and sexual identity. Similar points are made by Holmlund (1993) in an article on *Lock Up* (1989) and *Tango & Cash* (1989), though while stressing the extent to which in these films heterosexual masculinity is presented as 'masquerade', she concludes by noting that: 'Masculinity may be only a fantasy, but as the success of Sylvester Stallone's films, including their invocation by right-wing politicians like Reagan and Bush, so amply demonstrates, masquerades of masculinity are eminently popular, and undeniably potent' (Holmlund, 1993, pp. 225–6). Her conclusion thus dovetails as much with Jeffords's position as it does with Tasker's.

Related issues and disagreements are raised by the 'women warrior' films discussed by Tasker, films such as *Fatal Beauty* (1987), *China O'Brien* (1991) and the *Alien* trilogy, and by what Brown (1996) and Willis (1998) see as an increasing trend towards 'hardbody heroines' and 'combative femininity' in action films in the 1990s. An additional complication here is the fact that *Fatal Beauty* centres on a black female star, Whoopi Goldberg (see Stars, p. 133), and thus constitutes an exception to what most commentators have perceived not just as an ethnic bias in action-adventure, but as a systematic project of marginalisation, demonisation and subordination towards non-whites whose immediate roots lie in the racist and imperialist policies of Reagan and Bush (see also Marchetti, 1989).

One way to contextualise, if not necessarily to resolve, these issues and debates is to locate the films within a tradition. 'Action-adventure' is not a new term. It was used by *The Film Daily* in 1927 to describe the Douglas Fairbanks film *The Gaucho* (1928). And it was used, among others, to categorise 'The New Season Product' in *The Motion Picture Herald* in 1939. Used separately, the terms 'action' and 'adventure' have an even longer history, and films in the action-adventure tradition have been a staple of Hollywood's output since the 1910s.

With its roots in nineteenth-century melodrama and in a principle strand of popular fiction, action-adventure has always encompassed an array of genres and sub-types: westerns, swashbucklers, war films, disaster films, space-operas, epics, safari films, jungle films and so on. As Sobchack points out: 'Although these groups of films may appear a disparate lot, their patterns of action and character relationships display characteristics which clearly link them together and distinguish them from other genres' (Sobchack, 1988, p. 9). 'In a sense', he continues, echoing Cawelti (1976),

> all non-comic genre films are based on the structure of the romance of medieval literature: a protagonist either has or develops great and special skills and overcomes insurmountable obstacles in extraordinary situations to successfully achieve some desired goal, usually the restitution of order to the world invoked by the narrative. The protagonists confront the human, natural, or supernatural powers that have improperly assumed control over the world and eventually defeat them. (Sobchack, 1988, p. 9)

Questioning 'normal' sexual identity: woman warrior Brigitte Nielsen in Richard Fleischer's *Red Sonja*

Set 'in the romantic past or in an inhospitable place in the present', the exotic milieux and the 'flamboyant actions of the characters' in the adventure film afford numerous opportunities for filmic spectacle (Sobchack, 1988, p. 10). Its basic narrative structure, meanwhile, gives rise to two characteristic variations. 'One focuses on the lone hero – the swashbuckler, the explorer who searches for the golden idol, the great hunter who leads the expedition, the lord of the jungle'. The other, the 'survival' form, most apparent in war films, prison films and disaster films, 'focuses on a hero interacting with a microcosmic group, the sergeant of a patrol, the leader of a squadron, the person who leads a group of castaways out of danger and back to civilization' (Sobchack, 1988, p. 12). As Marchetti points out, the plots in adventure films of all kinds are usually episodic, 'allowing for wide variations in tone, the inclusion of different locations and incidentally introduced characters, and moments of spectacle, generally involving fights, explosions, or other types of violence' (Marchetti, 1989, p. 188). It might be noted that among the variations in tone to which Marchetti refers, tongue-in-cheek humour and knowingness are as common in swashbucklers as they are in modern action-adventure films. And it might also be noted that even where locations are restricted, as they often are in prison and submarine films, space, the control of space and the ability to move freely through space or from one space to another are always important.

In his discussion of the swashbuckler, Sobchack notes that the hero is 'defined as much by his physical expressiveness as by his good deeds' (Sobchack, 1988, p. 13). He also argues that in the survival genres, 'women play a decisive role in the success or failure of the group', thus returning us to issues of gender and the body within the context of the adventure film as a whole. Displays of the male body and of the hero's physical prowess are traditional in all kinds of adventure films, especially those of the lone-hero variety. Swashbucklers themselves tend to rely more on costumes and coiffeur than muscles (though as Richards, 1977, points out, displays of the naked male torso – often in scenes of torture or violence – are regular features of such films). But the reverse is the case in the Tarzan films and in epics such as *Samson and Delilah* (1949). And just as modern performers such as Schwarzenegger and Stallone are well known for their physique, so too were Victor Mature, Burt Lancaster (who trained as an acrobat) and Johnny Weismuller (who played Tarzan at MGM and RKO, and Jungle Jim at Columbia, and who was once an Olympic swimmer).

These displays reach back to Elmo Lincoln's performances as Tarzan in the late 1910s and 1920s and Douglas Fairbanks's performances in films such as *The Three Musketeers* (1921), *Robin Hood* (1923) and *The Thief of Bagdad* (1924; see case study) (see Richards, 1977; Koszarski, 1990; and Taves, 1993). They include the performances of such muscular stars as House Peters, Richard Talmadge, Jack Tunney and Joe Bonomo in the numerous adventure serials, 'railroad melodramas' and circus films that pervaded the 1920s, as well as those of Tom Mix, Ken Maynard and others in stunt-orientated westerns such as *Riders of the Purple Sage* (1925), *The Arizona Wildcat* (1927) and *The Glorious Trail* (1928). They also include performances of various kinds in the stunt-based aviation films of the late 1920s and early 1930s, the Errol Flynn films made at Warners in the mid- to late 1930s and early 1940s, the Tyrone Power films made at Fox in the late 1940s, the postwar cycle of adventure films featuring the likes of Robert Taylor, Burt Lancaster, Alan Ladd and Cornel Wilde, postwar epics such as *Spartacus* (1960), *Ben-Hur* (1959) and *El Cid* (1961), and the numerous adventure serials, Tarzan films and jungle melodramas that appeared throughout the 1930s, 1940s and 1950s. As Tasker points out: 'The appearance of ... "muscular cinema" during the 1980s calls on a much longer tradition of representation' (Tasker, 1993, p. 1).

Selected Reading

Susan Jeffords, *Hard Bodies: Hollywood Masculinity in the Reagan Era*, New Brunswick, NJ, Rutgers University Press, 1994.

Gina Marchetti, 'Action-adventure as ideology', in Angus and Jhally (eds), *Cultural Politics in Contemporary America*, London and New York, Routledge, 1989.

Yvonne Tasker, *Spectacular Bodies: Gender, Genre and the Action Cinema*, London and New York, Routledge, 1993.

Brian Taves, *The Romance of Adventure: The Genre of Historical Adventure Movies*, Jackson, University Press of Mississippi, 1993.

The Thief of Bagdad (USA 1924 *p.c* – Douglas Fairbanks Picture Corp/United Artists; *d* – Raoul Walsh)

The Thief of Bagdad exemplifies the prestige adventure film of the 1920s in which the hero is called upon to demonstrate courage, initiative and physical endurance, ultimately triumphing over what seem to be impossible odds. An epic fairytale, it features extravagant sets and breathtaking choreography, underlining the long-established associations between action and spectacle. The film's construction of an elaborate fantasy world (Bagdad as 'dream city of the ancient East') draws on orientalist imagery, with the East serving both as visual extravaganza in its own right and as a context for the spectacle of Douglas Fairbanks's star body. As the thief Ahmed, Fairbanks is introduced in a position of repose suggestive of both exoticism and indolence; that impression is rapidly supplanted by the star's characteristic physical exuberance as Ahmed steals, struts around and scales the set. His desire for the princess (Julanne Johnston) sets Ahmed on a route to personal transformation, an adventure framed as spiritual quest. In this way, the film sets in motion an effects-laden adventure narrative. Ahmed faces physical humiliation at the hands of palace guards before traversing a series of challenging landscapes, defeating both monsters and treacherous human opponents in order to claim his prize (marriage to the princess).

Primarily a vehicle for Fairbanks, *The Thief of Bagdad* is also notable for Anna May Wong's breakthrough appearance as a Mongol slave. While her role as treacherous anti-heroine staged one of the defining stereotypes against which she struggled throughout her career, Wong's presence and performance proved compelling. Indeed, the film epitomises Hollywood's orientalist adventure tradition, underlining the centrality of discourses of race and constructions of otherness to American action/adventure cinema. As in this film, these discourses are frequently displaced geographically and/or temporally through tropes of travel or the fairytale past (see also Stars: Douglas Fairbanks, p. 119).

YVONNE TASKER

Die Hard (USA 1988 *p.c* – 20th Century Fox/Gordon Company/Silver Pictures; *d* – John McTiernan)

Hugely successful (it has generated three sequels), *Die Hard* features many of the tropes associated with the genre in the 1980s: a wisecracking hero; bi-racial male bonding; an emphasis on the suffering white male body; and spectacular, effects-laden action. The film involves highly condensed action in both temporal and spatial terms: cop hero John McClane (Bruce Willis) must race against time to save the hostages (including estranged wife Holly) held by robbers masquerading as terrorists in a high-rise building. Part luxurious office suite and part construction site, the high-rise set provides a series of visual contrasts – McClane navigates the building in unconventional style, crawling through ventilation ducts and elevator shafts – that counterpoint its core themes of populist class conflict. McClane's blue-collar, ordinary American guy is opposed to the inadequate or compromised masculinity of his opponents, whether represented by the corporate culture of the Japanese-owned company in which Holly (Bonnie Bedelia) works, the European villains who have taken possession of the building or the obstructive official forces of the police and FBI. Assisting McClane against these enemies is a buddy character, the African-American cop Al Powell (Reginald Veljohnson), who keeps in touch with him via radio, first distrusting and then defending the unknown 'fly-in-the-ointment' against his commanding officer's hostile instructions. Such bi-racial pairings were a staple of Hollywood action in the decade, typically functioning to suggest the inclusive character of the white populist hero without questioning his position of authority.

YVONNE TASKER

White populist hero: Bruce Willis as John McClane in *Die Hard*

Artful action in *Crouching Tiger, Hidden Dragon*

Crouching Tiger, Hidden Dragon/Wohu Canglong (People's Republic of China/Taiwan/USA/Hong Kong 2000 *p.c* – United China Vision/Zoom Hunt International Production Co/China Film Co-production Corp/Asia Union Film & Entertainment/Columbia Film Production Asia/Sony Pictures Classics/Good Machine/Golden Harvest; *d* – Ang Lee)

The US success of Ang Lee's *Crouching Tiger, Hidden Dragon* marked an intensification of the incorporation of action conventions into international art cinema, a trend evident in the marketing and distribution of films such as *Nikita* (1990) and *Run Lola Run/Lola rennt* (1998) (each in different ways foregrounding the figure of the female fighter or action protagonist). Ang Lee had acquired a reputation for thoughtful independent films exploring the complexities of the family, such as *The Wedding Banquet/Xi Yan* (1993) and *The Ice Storm* (1997), and his production of an epic fight film attracted considerable attention. In addition, the relative novelty of female fighting leads in Hollywood cinema (at least within the context of prestige productions) meant that *Crouching Tiger* could be effectively promoted and framed as an innovative departure, one that had the potential to invest one of US cinema's most commercially successful genres with critical kudos.

Crouching Tiger centres on the youthful figure of Jen Yu (Zhang Ziyi), whose resistance to the strictures of her gender and class is expressed through theft, fighting and cross-dressing disguise, culminating in her choice to jump from a cliff in the film's final scene. Jen's theft of the Green Destiny sword initiates the film's action and signals the transgressive status of her character; the theft represents a challenge to Li Mu Bai (Chow Yun-Fat), and Jen is opposed on the one hand to the virtuous but rule-bound Shu Lien (Michelle Yeoh) and on the other to the more straightforwardly villainous Jade Fox (Cheng Pei-Pei). Thus the film stages the conflicting demands of personal desire, duty and responsibility. This conflict is associated with an opposition between sexual freedom and repression, which makes *Crouching Tiger, Hidden Dragon* resonate with contemporary gender culture in the US. Combat represents both physical freedom and the acceptance of rules that explicitly constrain desire (the suppression of Shu Lien and Mu Bai's longing for each other).

As a westernised reworking of Chinese cinema, *Crouching Tiger* is a marker not only of artful action but also of a hybrid form. Challenged by some for its 'Hollywoodisation' of Chinese film conventions, celebrated by others for its feminism, the film exemplifies a transnational cinema that seeks to address different audiences through its reworking of the cinematic past. The subsequent US release and promotion of Zhang Yimou's *Hero/Ying Xiong* (2002) and *House of Flying Daggers/Shi Mian Mai Fu* (2004) cemented this association between Chinese cinema and art-house action films.

YVONNE TASKER

COMEDY

STEVE NEALE

In the late 1980s and 1990s, a number of books on comedy appeared – among them Gehring (1994), Horton (1991), Karnick and Jenkins (1995a), Neale and Krutnik (1990), Palmer (1987), Rowe (1995a) and Sikov (1989; 1995) – indicating a significant revival of interest on the part of film critics, theorists and historians. In various guises, comedy has always been a staple of Hollywood's output. It has also, since the days of Chaplin, been a topic of critical debate, though generally within evaluative paradigms compatible with liberal humanist values, hence within frameworks of concern that have tended to focus on issues of aesthetic integrity, self-expression, and direct or indirect social and cultural worth (for example, Agee, 1958; Mast, 1976; McCaffrey, 1968; Robinson, 1969; and, to some extent, Cavell, 1981). Aesthetics, evaluation and socio-cultural issues are by no means absent from more recent books. But the agendas within which they are working are in general rather different from those governing earlier writing and research. They include feminism, gender and sexual politics; structuralism, semiotics, post-structuralism and psychoanalysis; cultural studies, race and ethnicity; and the 1980s turn towards archival and historical research.

The diversity of topics addressed and approaches adopted in these books is in part related to the multifaceted nature of comedy itself. Encompassing a range of forms, sites and genres – from jokes to intricately plotted narratives, from slapstick to farce, from satire to parody, from shorts and cartoons to features – comedy can also entail an array of defining conventions – from the generation of laughter to the presence of happy endings to the representation of every life – and is able in addition to combine with or to parody virtually every other genre or form (Neale and Krutnik, 1990). It is therefore hardly surprising that discussions of comedy have drawn on a variety of disciplines – from philosophy to narrative theory, from anthropology to psychology and psychoanalysis – and that most comprehensive overviews tend to combine a multi-disciplinary approach with a breaking down of the subject into a number of distinct topics, aspects and themes.

Most discussions of comedy begin by acknowledging a basic distinction between what might be called its comic units – gags, jokes, funny moments and the like – and the narrative and non-narrative contexts in which they occur. This distinction is important, both because it links to issues of film history, and because it raises questions about definition and hence about the criteria governing comedy as a genre. For many commentators, gags, jokes and funny moments are fundamental to all forms of comedy, and hence to definitions of comedy either as a single genre or as a diverse but related cluster of genres and forms. An initial distinction can then be drawn between those in which they occur outside, or predominate over, narrative contexts and narrative concerns, and those in which they do not. Hence Horton's proposal that:

> Comedies are interlocking sequences of jokes and gags that place narrative in the foreground, in which case comedy leans in varying degrees toward some dimension of the non-comic (realism, romance, fantasy), or that use narrative as only a loose excuse for holding together moments of comic business (as in a Marx Brothers' film). (Horton, 1991, p. 7)

This proposal is made in response to Mast's emphasis on narrative, and in particular to his thesis that 'There are eight comic film plots' (Mast, 1976, p. 4). It echoes the proposals and critiques of Jerry Palmer, who argues that Mast's typology suffers from logical inconsistencies – it includes the 'parody of genres' and the 'sequence of gags' as plots – and avoids the issue of funniness by focusing on the 'maximum' units of comedy (such as plots) rather than 'minimum' units such as jokes and gags (Palmer, 1987, p. 28). To be fair to Mast, it is worth pointing out that he emphasises 'comic climate', the way in which what happens in a plot is signalled as comedy rather than drama (Mast, 1976), and that for some time in the west, comedy was defined as a narrative with a happy ending, a definition that avoids the issue of gags, jokes and comic climate altogether (Neale and Krutnik, 1990). Nevertheless, Palmer's, Horton's and subsequent critiques – like those of Karnick and Jenkins (1995) – clearly point to the inadequacies of Mast's typology, and of any approach to comedy that ignores its minimum units.

Palmer argues that gags, jokes and funny moments are not only fundamental to comedy, but they exhibit similar structural and logical features. These include a preparation stage and a culmination stage (often in the form of a verbal or visual punchline), an instance or moment of shock or surprise (a peripetia or reversal of fortune), and a system of logic – 'the logic of the absurd' – in which the plausible and the implausible always combine, but in unequal measure: while plausibility is always present, implausibility is always dominant, and it is this dominance that allows us to perceive the events, actions and utterances with which we are presented in comedy as comic (rather than poetic or tragic), and that thus endows them with what Palmer calls 'comic insulation'.

Palmer goes on to argue that these features mark comic plots and situations as well; thus although comic units of all kinds have their own shapes and structures, they are susceptible to a degree of narrative integration. Elsewhere, Gunning (1995) and Crafton (1995) have debated the extent to which such integration is possible, the extent to which gags, jokes and other comic units necessarily undermine or diverge from the narrative contexts in which they may be found. For Crafton, gags and jokes are inherently digressive. If narrative can be defined

> as a system for providing the spectator with sufficient knowledge to make causal links between represented events ... the gag's status as an irreconcilable difference becomes clear. Rather than providing knowledge, slapstick misdirects the viewer's attention, and obfuscates the linearity of cause–effect relations. (Crafton, 1995, p. 119)

For Gunning, some gags are susceptible to narrative integration and can themselves be perceived as possessing narrative features, especially if narrative is itself reconceived as a 'process of integration in which smaller units are absorbed into a larger overarching pattern and process of containment' (Gunning, 1995, p. 121). Neale and Krutnik (1990), meanwhile, seek to identify degrees of integration, ranging from purely digressive gags and jokes to fully integrated 'comic events'. They also draw on the work of Coursodon (1964) and of other French writers such as Lebel (1967), Mars (1964), Pasquier (1973) and Simon and Percheron (1976) in drawing up a scale of structural complexity in gags, ranging from the simple 'comic effect' (a funny expression, a pratfall, a single, self-contained piece of comic action) to the elaborate 'articulated gag', which may involve a multi-stage chain of events and effects.

A great deal of attention has been paid to gags, jokes and other comic units. (In addition to those cited above, see Carroll, 1991; Jenkins, 1986; and Sweeney, 1991.) Aside from their intrinsic interest, there are two fundamental reasons for this. The first is that they are points at which laughter is designed to occur, and can therefore act as a focus for ideas, theories and debates about laughter and humour. The second is that they are bound up with the early history of comedy in cinema, and with a number of specialist producers, directors and performers, from Mack Sennett to Jerry Lewis, from Frank Tashlin to Woody Allen, from Laurel and Hardy to Hope and Crosby, and from Charlie Chaplin and Buster Keaton to Danny Kaye, Steve Martin and Jim Carrey.

Laughter and humour have, of course, been discussed for hundreds of years. No single theory has dominated the study of these topics in the cinema. Mast occasionally draws on Bergson (1956) and Freud (1976; 1985). Eaton (1981), Neale (1981) and Neale and Krutnik (1990) draw on – and to some extent modify – Freud's ideas. Neale and Krutnik also draw on the work of Olson (1968). And Palmer draws on the work of Douglas (1968). Douglas also features in Palmer's later book (1995), an overview of theories of laughter and humour. His central argument here is that laughter and humour are multi-dimensional, hence that most theories of humour are partial. He considers these theories under four main headings: 'occasion' (theories that stress the contexts and rules that permit, encourage or solicit humour and laughter); 'function' (theories that stress the social and psychological purposes of humour and laughter); 'structure' (in which work on the shape and the logic of gags and jokes comes into play); and what he calls 'limits' – the points, psychic and social, at which humour or laughter can simply fail or disappear. In his discussion of structure, he notes that most modern theories of humour involve notions of incongruity, and this is certainly true of most theories of jokes and gags in the cinema, including his own. However, he also notes that such notions and forms may be historically and culturally 'local', specific to the west in the modern era, rather than universal (Palmer, 1995, p. 143).

Local or not, gags, jokes and slapstick humour in general have formed the basis for a tradition in film comedy that is virtually as old as film itself. (Gunning, 1995, contains a lengthy discussion of what is perhaps the first example, Lumière's *L'Arroseur arrosé*, 1895.) Derived initially from existing forms of variety entertainment, notably vaudeville and music hall, but also the circus, the comic strip, burlesque and revue, and fed by later forms such as radio, television and nightclubs, this tradition has been treated as a site within which a whole series of comic performers, including most of those listed above, have been able not only to present their skills, but also to subvert or to question narrative values and conventions – and occasionally socio-cultural ones as well.

A particularly influential account of this tradition is found in Seidman (1981). Under the heading of 'comedian comedy', Seidman proposes an array of distinct – and eccentric – characteristics, themes and devices linking performers and films within this tradition and differentiating both from those found elsewhere in Hollywood comedy and in Hollywood cinema in general. Seidman starts from the premise that nearly all the performers within this tradition began their careers, honed their skills and established their personae outside the cinema, in media and in forms of entertainment geared to live or quasi-live performance, and hence to the possibility – or the illusion – of direct interaction with an audience. He goes on to note the prevalence in their films of devices that draw on and foreground these contexts and characteristics, and that thereby conflict with, contradict or undermine the norms characteristic of most other Hollywood films and hence of most other Hollywood genres – asides and direct address to camera, allusions to the artificial nature of films and their devices, and allusions to the world of show business outside the fictional universe of any particular film.

The comedians in comedian comedy are thus privileged figures, able to step outside and to play with the rules governing most narrative films and their genres. But they are also anomalies and misfits. In the films, they often portray eccentric or deviant characters, characters given to dreaming, to disguise, to regression and to bouts of madness. To that extent, the opposition between eccentricity and social conformity found elsewhere in Hollywood comedy is here internalised as an aspect of the comedian's character, one that is inextricably linked to his or her performance skills, and one that is therefore irresolvable.

In recent years, the concept of comedian comedy has been refined, extended and modified (Krutnik, 1984; 1995). It has also been criticised as ahistorical (Jenkins, 1993; Karnick and Jenkins, 1995). The male-centredness of comedian comedy has been noted. And the extent to which masculinism and masculinity are rehearsed, explored, endorsed or undermined has been looked at in detail (Bukatman, 1991; Krutnik, 1994; 1995; Rowe, 1995a; Sanders, 1995; and Winokur, 1996). In response, several studies appeared of Mae West (Curry, 1995; Hamilton, 1996; Rowe, 1995a). In addition, given the 'low' – and popular – status of comedian comedy, and given the prevalence within it of Jewish performers and personnel, a number of studies have introduced (or reintroduced) issues of ethnicity and class (Jenkins, 1993; Musser, 1990b; 1991; and Winokur, 1996).

Meanwhile, a number of studies have appeared that either question any absolute distinction between comedian and narrative, situational or 'polite' forms of comedy, or seek to draw attention to the presence of the latter in early film and thus to question or modify the ways in which the early history of comedy in the cinema – and the careers of particular comic performers – have been written (Bowser, 1990; Gartenberg, 1988; Krämer, 1988; 1989; 1995; Koszarski, 1990; Musser, 1990a; Neale and Krutnik, 1990; Riblet, 1995). This can be seen both as a reaction to the canonic dominance of slapstick comedy and slapstick performers in accounts of early cinema, and as a sign of the revival of interest in narrative and in situational traditions and forms.

Of these, romantic comedy has received the greatest attention in recent years, at least in part because of its revival by Hollywood in the mid-1980s under the guise of what Neale and Krutnik have termed 'the new romance' (Neale and Krutnik, 1990; Krutnik, 1990; Neale, 1992). Neale and Krutnik argue that the emergence of the new romance, as exemplified by films such as *Blind Date* (1987), *Roxanne* (1987), *When Harry Met Sally ...* (1989) and *Only You* (1992), constituted the revival not just of an 'old-fashioned' genre, but also of an ideology of 'old-fashioned' heterosexual romance and hence of the rituals, signs and wishes that mark it. Its appearance followed a period in the 1970s and early 1980s during which significant challenges had been mounted to that ideology, and during which romantic comedy itself seemed either to have taken the form of Woody Allen-like 'nervous romances' (Neale and Krutnik, 1990; Krutnik, 1990), or else to have disappeared altogether (Henderson, 1978).

Recent work on new romances such as *Moonstruck* (1987) by Rowe and others suggests that the new romance may not be as ideologically homogeneous as Neale and Krutnik have proposed (Rowe, 1995a; 1995b; Evans and Deleyto, 1998). Meanwhile, many of these discussions echo debates about the 'screwball' films of the 1930s and 1940s, about films such as *The Awful Truth* (1937) and *Bringing Up Baby* (1938). The screwball cycle, which emerged in 1934 with *It Happened One Night* and *Twentieth Century*, has been seen as one of the few 'genres of equality' to have emerged during the course of the studio era (Woodward, 1991). On the other hand, it has been seen as a cycle that, in and through its aesthetic characteristics – an energetic mix of slapstick, wisecracks, intricately plotted farce and the comedy of manners combined with vividly eccentric characterisation and a disavowable undercurrent of sexual innuendo – served to revivify the institution of marriage and traditional gender relations at a time when both were being bolstered by government policy following periods of intense turbulence, challenge and change during the Jazz Age and the early years of the Depression.

In contrast to the screwball films, little has been written on the 'sex comedies' of the 1950s and 1960s – films such as *Pillow Talk* (1959) and *Lover Come Back* (1961) – aside from Neale and Krutnik (1990) and writing on Doris Day in Clarke, Merck and Simmonds (1981). There has been a revival of interest in the 'sophisticated' comedies of romance, sex, marriage and remarriage that preceded the screwball cycle in the late 1910s and the 1920s, especially those directed by Cecil B. DeMille (Higashi, 1994; Musser, 1995). However, there are as yet no histories of romantic comedy in Hollywood that encompass all these trends. Neale (1992) proposes a number of basic conventions, including 'the meet cute', 'the wrong partner', the learning process the couple nearly always have to undergo and the initial hostility it eventually dispels. And Babington and Evans (1989) discuss a number of individual romantic comedies from distinct periods and cycles.

The existence of comedies of remarriage (the term derives from Cavell, 1981) suggests an area of overlap between romantic comedy and domestic comedy. However, like other forms of narrative comedy, and in curious contrast to the attention given to domestic and familial drama, domestic comedy remains largely unexplored. The same is true of parody and satire. Works by Hutcheon (1985) and by Rose (1993) are largely concerned with literature, or with art forms other than the cinema. Both note that parody and satire involve imitation, citation and reference. And both note that they are not always comic in intention or effect. Neale and Krutnik (1990) refer briefly to satire and parody in the cinema. And Crafton (1995) discusses the role of caricature and parody in Warner Bros. cartoons.

Satire – the debunking of prevalent social norms, institutions and mores – is clearly central to any theory or discussion of comedy's socio-cultural role and significance. Comedy has often been viewed as either actually or potentially subversive, or at least an inherently positive force for social renewal and social change. This view has long been influential in literary studies of comedy, and often finds an echo in the cult of slapstick, comedian and low forms of comedy in particular. It has been revived through the writings of Bakhtin (1968), in the work of those such as Fischer (1991), Paul (1991; 1994), Rowe (1995a; 1995b) and Winokur (1996), who have used or adapted Bakhtinian ideas, especially the stress on the upturning of the social world and its rules in all forms of carnival comedy.

Others, however, have offered a different view. Neale and Krutnik (1990) argue that deviations from the norm are conventional in comedy and hence that 'subversion' is a licensed and integral aspect of comedy's social and institutional existence. And Purdie (1993) has explicitly attacked the views of Bakhtin and others, arguing that all forms of comedy involve a recognition of the norms whose transgression they entail, and hence a claim to social membership at the expense not only of those who are comedy's butts, but also of those who do not get its jokes. Either way, it is likely that, as is the case with most genres, comedy's ideological significance and impact varies from film to film, cycle to cycle, and audience to audience, and is probably best assessed at specific and local levels rather than through universal generalisations.

Selected Reading

Stanley Cavell, *Pursuits of Happiness: The Hollywood Comedy of Remarriage*, Cambridge, MA, Harvard University Press, 1981.

Peter William Evans and Celestino Deleyto (eds), *Terms of Endearment: Hollywood Romantic Comedy of the 1980s and 1990s*, Edinburgh, Edinburgh University Press, 1998.

Andrew S. Horton (ed.), *Comedy/Cinema/Theory*, Berkeley, University of California Press, 1991.

Kathleen Rowe, *The Unruly Woman: Gender and the Genres of Laughter*, Austin, University of Texas Press, 1995a.

Lover Come Back (USA 1961 *p.c* – Universal/ Seven Pictures/Nob Hill/Arwin Productions; *d* – Delbert Mann)

Lover Come Back was the second in a series of sophisticated sex comedies pairing Doris Day and Rock Hudson. It shares with its predecessor, *Pillow Talk* (1959), a mise en scène that flaunts a glossy high-consumer lifestyle (sumptuous fashions, lavish apartments, exclusive restaurants, fancy cars); and a narrative of sexual subterfuge that pits a wolfish playboy against a resistant career woman. *Lover Come Back* adds to the earlier film's concoction a satire of the values and strategies of America's industry of desire, the advertising business – Day and Hudson play account executives for rival Madison Avenue companies. Hudson's Jerry Webster is a semi-parodic take on the urban bachelor fantasy. The playboy, a recurring figure in the sex comedies of the 1950s and 1960s, is an idealised figure of male liberty that is opposed to the domesticated suburban husband. Jerry Webster not only embodies a fantasy of untrammelled, 'uncastrated' masculinity, but his approach to advertising reveals that he is also a master of seductive manipulation – he boasts that 'given a well-stacked dame in a bathing suit' he could sell aftershave lotion to beatniks. By contrast, Carol Templeton (Doris Day) attempts to establish an ethical

Playboy at work: Rock Hudson in the satire on advertising *Lover Come Back*

grounding for the business of selling. The opposed value systems of the two are outlined when they compete for the Miller Wax account: Carol's efforts are easily outstripped by Jerry's elaborate bribery – alcohol, showgirls – of the company's millionaire owner.

As a woman who resists seduction, both personally and professionally, Carol's discourse is mined to expose the sexuality she 'represses'. She is the butt of numerous sexual jokes: when she declares that the agency to win the account will be 'the one that shows Mr Miller the most attractive can', the film cuts immediately to a chorus-line of bunny-girls hired by Jerry to wiggle their backsides for Miller's entertainment. Equating the consumer object with the fetishised female body, this gag insinuates that, as a woman, Carol is wrong to assume she can find a place in the advertising industry's enterprise of seduction. The film develops the negative value of Carol's ambitions by doubling her with the showgirl Rebel Davis (Edie Adams), an alternative 'career woman' who subjects herself readily both to Jerry's seductions and to the system of commercial representation that will transform her body into an all-purpose signifier of consumerised desire.

The satire of advertising practice (Jerry creates an advertising campaign for a non-existent product – VIP; to capitalise on the success of the campaign, he decides to invent a product to fit the sales pitch) overwhelms the amorous narrative in the first half of the film. When Carol meets Jerry, she mistakenly assumes him to be the chemist hired to work on the mystery product. Seizing upon her misapprehension, Jerry continues to masquerade as 'Linus Tyler', so he can trick her into bed. The 'Tyler' that Jerry constructs is a male image tailored to the interpretation of Carol's desiring self, an image that reflects back her own qualities – dedication, honesty, sensitivity, sexual inexperience. At the same time, however, the identity masquerade throws up for examination conflicting figurations of masculinity: Webster is split into an aggressive 'masculine' persona and a more passive, 'feminised' persona. Even though, for contemporary viewers, Hudson's high-profile outing as a gay man brings into sharp relief the element of performance integral to his 1950s image as an idealised heterosexual male, the performative status of gender identity – especially male identity – is foregrounded in the comedies of the 1950s and 1960s.

The subterfuge plot provokes Carol's extended humiliation, as Jerry lays siege to her sexual defences – hence, as the film has it, to her professional identity. But as she is on the verge of surrendering herself, Carol learns of his duplicity, and exacts her revenge. The manipulation and hostility of Jerry's behaviour does not amount to a viable model for union, so the film engages in several frantic and convoluted narrative manoeuvres as a means of shifting the emphasis from the elaboration of seductive enterprise to a generically conventional marital resolution. An advertising-council hearing degenerates into an orgy as they test the VIP product generated by Webster's chemist – candy that is super-saturated with alcohol. Jerry and Carol awaken the next morning in a Maryland motel room, with a marriage licence in tow. But while VIP allows Carol's sexual defences to be circumvented, Webster experiences a quite staggering role reversal. All of a sudden, he is desperate to embrace his own 'castration' by remaining wedded, while she wants nothing to do with him. After a lengthy separation, they remarry nine months later, as Carol is wheeled into a hospital delivery room to give birth. This cynically slick observance of Production Code morality makes clear the film's lack of commitment to the concept of romantic marital union. By making the route to the union so ridiculous, *Love Come Back* signals a termination of the indulgences of the 'good life' while stripping the renunciation of any force. The emphasis on Jerry's extreme change of character also excludes any portrayal of the radical adjustment Carol must make in sacrificing her career ambitions for the vocation of motherhood. The final image of Carol, prone and powerless on the hospital trolley, constitutes an overpowering vision of the 'taming' of the independently minded career woman.

FRANK KRUTNIK

The Patsy (USA 1964 *p.c* – Paramount/Patti Enterprises; *d* – Jerry Lewis)

Jerry Lewis was the last star comedian under long-term contract to a major film company of the Hollywood studio era – he was signed to Paramount Pictures in 1948, with partner Dean Martin, and remained with the company until 1965. After the traumatic dissolution of his successful ten-year partnership with Martin in 1956, Lewis triumphantly re-established himself as a solo performer and continued as a top box-office attraction. His long-lasting success, and the protection accorded to him by Paramount, enabled him to make a series of eccentric and controversial films in the 1960s, which he starred in, directed, co-wrote and often co-produced. Together with eight comedies Lewis made with directorial mentor Frank Tashlin (from *Artist and Models* in 1955 to *The Disorderly Orderly* in 1964), these films were highly regarded by French ciné-critics – such as Jean-Luc Godard, who proclaimed Lewis a 'genius' – but castigated by American reviewers, who read Lewis's ambitions as rampant egomania. Lewis's self-directed project reached its apogee in *The Patsy*, a highly idiosyncratic, personal art film masquerading as a comedian comedy. *The Patsy*, like *The Errand Boy* (1961), addresses the processes of stardom, comedy and the entertainment business, but it also more explicitly invokes Lewis's own public image and career.

Comedian comedy: Jerry Lewis in *The Patsy*

The narrative of *The Patsy* concerns the making of an entertainment star. After the death of famous comedian Wally Brandford, his staff decide they will train 'some nobody' – the painfully inept bellboy Stanley Belt (Jerry Lewis) – to take his place. Stanley's body continually sabotages the professionalised showbiz routines he is taught, however, and fearing disaster the Brandford team abandons him as he is about to make his debut on *The Ed Sullivan Show*. Their desertion spurs Stanley to prove he is not at the mercy of the showbiz machine – he improvises a sketch, 'A Big Night in Hollywood', which propels him to stardom. The Sullivan appearance puts Stanley in a commanding position, where he can turn the tables on his erstwhile manipulators. But success has its costs: as he fires off instructions to his former puppet masters, the business-suited ex-bellboy acts with the polished self-assurance (and implicit self-regard) of callous swinger Buddy Love, the monstrous alter ego of meek chemistry professor Julius Kelp in Lewis's *The Nutty Professor* (1963). As the danger of corruptive egomania is introduced as a possible consequence of stardom, and Lewis drops the fictional mask of Stanley Belt to reveal himself as 'Jerry Lewis', Hollywood director, the film ends with Lewis commanding the film crew of *The Patsy* to break for lunch. As this final scene implies, Lewis hijacks the Hollywood comedian comedy, to transform it into a highly unconventional vehicle for a discourse of the self. Stanley's path to stardom is interlaced with knowing references to Lewis's own career: the record act he performs briefly during his stand-up debut echoes Lewis's own first showbiz speciality; the bellboy costume evokes his first self-directed film, as well as his youthful stint as a bellhop in the Catskills; and the *Ed Sullivan* performance is adapted from a sketch on one of his own solo TV shows from 1957.

The Patsy is the most acutely self-mythologising of Lewis's films: it celebrates the ascendancy of the multifaceted creative presence 'Jerry Lewis' over the familiar Lewisian misfit, Stanley Belt. This flamboyant auteurist agenda directly interferes with the way the film operates as a comedian-centred film. While American critics were outraged by the 'unfunniness' of Lewis's self-directed films, many French critics recognised that Lewis was no longer content to be 'simply funny'. From the start, his performance represented a very extreme form of 'low' physical comedy, through which he created a wild, at times discomforting spectacle of deformation built upon verbal and bodily unruliness, sexual confusion, gender-role slippage, and a fragmented or uncentred sense of self. *The Patsy* reveals Lewis's performative hyperbole taken to even greater extremes – as is illustrated by the sustained spectacle of embarrassment created from Stanley's first appearance in the film, his body erupting in painful slow motion under the withering gaze of the Brandford retinue. At such moments, Lewis extends the spectacle of pain and embarrassment rather than forcing a quick, clean wrap-up – thus exposing the discomfort that precisioned gag-making can disavow. In the films he directed, Lewis frequently toys with the familiar techniques of visual comedy by diverting the gag from its signalled trajectory, or refusing a conventionally ordered build-up. Rather than providing the expected mechanism of disruption and reordering, Lewis's gags play with the conventional forms, procedures and discursive registers of film comedy, initiating a process of deformation that denies a comfortable place to laugh from. The clearest example of such meta-nagging is *The Patsy*'s stand-up routine, where a conventional mode of comic performance is turned inside out.

FRANK KRUTNIK

Miss Congeniality (USA/Australia 2000 *p.c* – Warner Bros./Castle Rock Entertainment/Village Roadshow Pictures/NPV Entertainment/Fortis Films; *d* – Donald Petrie)

Traditionally, classic Hollywood romantic comedy focused on the apparently mismatched heterosexual couple, overcoming conflicts and obstacles in order to move towards their happy union. As a contemporary rom-com, *Miss Congeniality* follows this formula, but the predictable romance that develops between FBI agents Gracie Hart (Sandra Bullock) and Eric Matthews (Benjamin Bratt) is pushed away from the centre and towards the margins of the narrative, which instead focuses on the question of female identity and the performance of gender – contributing to the film's queer appeal. *Miss Congeniality* plays with the conventions of this popular Hollywood genre to provide its audience with an alternative union, which is the happy marriage of masculine and feminine characteristics within Gracie's personality. Thus it is Gracie herself, rather than the couple, who undergoes a significant change.

Miss Congeniality makes use of stereotypes and much of the comedy derives from gendered attitudes to hair, make-up, costume and behaviour. The film's opening scenes establish Gracie as a feminist tomboy who does not fit the accepted social definition of femininity. Consequently, she is a misfit who exhibits typically masculine characteristics: she is aggressive, violent and clumsy. However, Gracie's transformation begins when she goes undercover as a contestant in the

Gender performance: Sandra Bullock's makeover in *Miss Congeniality* adds to the film's queer appeal

Miss United States beauty pageant. The transformation initially takes place only at a physical level, as she is forced to endure a painful, *Pygmalion*-style makeover to masquerade as beauty queen Gracie Lou Freebush. It is a role that requires her to learn feminine posture and behaviour, producing a disjunction between her on and off-stage personas that is exaggerated for comic effect. In many ways, this clash is characteristic of the classic romantic comedy, which has always explored tensions of gender roles and identity between the sexes. But at the same time, *Miss Congeniality* updates this tradition, since its focus remains on Gracie and the relationship (or romance) she builds with the audience. Furthermore, during her involvement in the pageant, Gracie experiences an inner metamorphosis that truly changes her. This occurs as a result of her having to act feminine and as a result of her interaction with the other contestants. Finally, Gracie is successfully able to blend her masculine and her newfound feminine character traits to become an empowered, well-rounded and above all popular individual awarded the title of 'Miss Congeniality'. This journey into the self is often found in Hollywood's 'new romances', and represents a variation on the traditional romantic comedy evident since the 1980s (Krutnik, 2002).

Miss Congeniality raises questions about whether the modern romantic comedy reinforces gender roles or whether it challenges them. On one hand, Gracie's role-play transgresses gender binarisms, demonstrating their artificiality and that the image of femininity can be manipulated. On the other, Gracie learns to conform, negotiating her individuality within the demands of societal expectation and approval. It is worth noting, though, that the unconvincing heterosexual union between Gracie and Eric that provides the generic happy ending to this film is problematised by its sequel, *Miss Congeniality 2: Armed and Fabulous* (2005), which instead plays on the (sexual) chemistry between Gracie and her new female FBI 'partner', Sam Fuller (Regina King) (see Hines, 2008).

CLAIRE HINES

Down With Love (USA/Germany 2003 *p.c* – 20th Century Fox/Regency Enterprises/Jinks-Cohen Co/Mediastream Dritte Film; *d* – Peyton Reed)

Down With Love offers a postmodern take on romantic comedies of the 1950s and 1960s, in particular those starring Rock Hudson and Doris Day as the mismatched couple whose initial hostility to one another the narrative strives to overcome. It is also an example of the contemporary American film industry's intensified drive to exploit merchandising tie-ins via links with fashion, music and publishing. The film is set in 1960s New York, allowing it to stage an extravagant, seductive retro look and style that is both nostalgic and an update, so that it consciously presents itself as pastiche for a sophisticated audience of cinéphiles. Although the marketing targeted mainly female viewers with an interest in fashion and contemporary rom-coms, the film's ironic treatment of its subject and focus on modern sexual mores (post-feminism and 'lad' culture) indicate an intention to appeal to male consumers as well.

The film is a knowing homage, taking the already stylised features of its source texts (including costume and sets, technological gags such as split screen, performance style and narrative contortions) several stages further. Arrogant journalist and man-about-town Catcher Block (Ewan McGregor) and bestselling author Barbara Novak (Renée Zellweger) are pitted against one another professionally and romantically; their sidekicks Peter McMannus (David Hyde Pierce) and Vicki Hiller (Sarah Paulson) are their alter egos: Peter is the timid obverse of Catcher, whose sexual predator persona he unsuccessfully tries to imitate, while Vicki is the girlfriend desperate to find love, in contrast to Barbara's assertion of female sexual independence. A guest appearance by Tony Randall as the head of Barbara's publishing house nods towards his role as Rock Hudson's insecure friend in the 1960s comedies.

Much of the humour in *Down With Love* revolves around the differences and similarities between 'then' and 'now', with the retro impulse used to point up the fact that the Hudson–Day couple and the 'battle of the sexes' in which they were engaged prefigured the emerging feminist movement, while the McGregor–Zellweger conflict enacts the dilemmas of post-feminism, taken to mean a period in which women's demands for equality have largely been achieved. This produces a double irony: on one hand, Barbara's professional success and sexual independence validates the gains made by *Cosmopolitan*-style feminism; on the other, it is perceived as generating a backlash in the form of Carter's unreconstructed, manipulative masculinity. It is no accident that Ewan McGregor's character, performance and body language echo urbane bachelor figures such as Cary Grant and James Bond as well as Rock Hudson, a reminder of the continuing importance of the narcissistic male to the consumer economy.

In its mannered stylisation, *Down With Love* could be perceived as so arch as to be unfunny, and a cynical attempt to exploit style at the expense of substance. On the other hand, it might be seen as a new kind of comedic enterprise, capitalising on the pleasures offered by nostalgia and using pastiche's ironic potential to produce a playful commentary on the traditions and evolution of the rom-com genre itself.

PAM COOK

CONTEMPORARY CRIME

STEVE NEALE

Criminals, crime, victims of crime, and official and unofficial agents of law, order and justice have featured in films since the turn of the century. The earliest American crime films include *A Career in Crime* (1900), *The Bold Bank Robbery* (1904), *The Adventures of Sherlock Holmes* (1905) and *The Lonely Villa* (1909). They were followed in the early 1910s by films such as *The Monogrammed Cigarette* (1910), *One of the Honor Squad* (1912), *Suspense* (1913) and *Detective Burton's Triumph* (1914) (see Langman and Finn, 1994).

The Monogrammed Cigarette shows how the daughter of a famous detective solves her first case. *The Bold Bank Robbery*, as its title suggests, depicts the robbery of a bank by a gang of thieves. And *The Lonely Villa* shows a woman and her children besieged in their home by burglars and their eventual last-minute rescue by the woman's husband. Broadly speaking, the differences in emphasis between these three films – the first with its focus on an agent of investigation and on detection, the second with its focus on the perpetrators of crime and on criminal activity, and the third with its focus on the victims of crime and on their response – correspond to the differences in emphasis characteristic of the three principal genres of crime as a whole: the detective film/investigative thriller, the gangster film and the suspense thriller. As is often the case in the American cinema, these genres and their characteristics overlap and cross-fertilise each other in individual cycles and films. *The Big Combo* (1955), for instance, can be seen as a hybrid gangster and detective film. And *Underworld USA* (1960), a gangster film, nevertheless involves a mystery, a process of investigation and an (unofficial) agent of justice – elements normally characteristic of investigative thrillers. In addition, as Derry (1988) points out, the suspense thriller can focus on individual criminals as well as on victims, and can thus encompass films such as *The Day of the Jackal* (1973). Nevertheless, all three genres remain distinct, at least as tendencies, and by and large can be charted with respect to three major figures: the criminal, the victim and the agent of law and order; and two major aesthetic effects: suspense and surprise.

The detective film

Discussion of the detective film has been dominated by debate about film noir, and hence by debate about the hard-boiled detective and the hard-boiled tradition in general. Even scholars such as Cawelti (1976) and Schatz (1981), who neither use nor debate film noir as term, tend to focus on the hard-boiled tradition and hence on films such as *The Maltese Falcon* (1941) and *Farewell My Lovely* (1944) that are central to most versions of the noir canon. As a result, detective films made prior to the 1940s, and those that are generally considered to be neither noir nor hard-boiled, have either been ignored or mentioned in passing as inauthentic counterpoints to noir and the hard-boiled tradition. Thus very little has been written about these films beyond the occasional enumeration of titles, cycles and dates. Film noirs and the hard-boiled tradition are discussed below (see pp. 305–15). Here, attention will be paid to ideas and findings relevant to all detective films and investigative thrillers, beginning with research into their origins and the theories put forward to explain their genesis, socio-cultural role and popular appeal. Because of the preoccupation in film studies with noir and the hard-boiled tradition, many of these ideas derive from research on detective fiction rather than from research on the detective film as such.

Most commentators cite the following as key to the development of detective and investigative fiction in the late eighteenth and nineteenth centuries: the Gothic mystery; William Godwin's novel, *The Adventures of Caleb Williams*; the memoirs of Vidoq and the memoirs, fictional and real, of other detectives and policemen; Edgar Allan Poe's Dupin stories; 'city mystery' fiction (books such as Eugene Sue's *The Mysteries of Paris* and George Lippard's *The Quaker City*); Victorian sensation fiction (especially the novels of Charles Dickens, Wilkie Collins, Charles Reade and Mary Elizabeth Braddon) and its counterpart on the stage; the American dime novel; American pulp fiction; the novels of Emile Gobariau, and, of course, Sir Arthur Conan Doyle's Sherlock Holmes stories.

There are differences in emphasis among and between different commentators, depending on the extent to which stress is laid on the elements of enigma and investigation or on the figure of the detective. These differences, and the distinctions that underlie them, are important, both because the investigation of a criminal enigma need not necessarily be undertaken by professional detectives (witness many of Hitchcock's films), and because narratives centred on detectives – or the police – need

Focused on investigation: Al Pacino in *Serpico*

not necessarily focus on a process of investigation, as witness *Detective Story* (1951), *The Offence* (1973) and *The Onion Field* (1979). Moreover, even if, like *Serpico* (1973) and *Prince of the City* (1981), they do, they need neither stress nor entail a central enigma. Indeed, it is a basic tenet of Hamilton (1993), Hoppenstand (1982) and Panek (1987; 1990), who have written specifically about the American tradition of crime fiction, that American detective stories, with their roots in the dime novel and pulp literature, have always been concerned as much with action and adventure as they have been with the solving of mysteries. And as Matthew Solomon (1995) has shown, dime novels, pulp fiction and the action-adventure tradition were as much a source of early American (and European) detective films as the tradition that placed the emphasis on ratiocination.

Among the conditions of existence of modern investigative fiction and the figure of the fictional detective, commentators have cited the emergence in the nineteenth century of the professional detective, professional detective agencies and a professional police force; the secularisation of concepts of crime, sin and punishment (Cawelti, 1976; Knight, 1980); urbanisation, population growth and the reconfiguration of class (Cawelti, 1976; Hutter, 1983; Kaemmel, 1983; Porter, 1981); concomitant shifts in attitudes towards criminals and the police (the heroisation of the latter and the demonisation of the former) (Mandel, 1984; Porter, 1981); and the introduction of scientific and bureaucratic procedures for tracking down and capturing criminals as part and parcel of what some, following Foucault (1979), have seen as a wholesale shift towards a mode of social control based – literally and figuratively – on a particular model of surveillance (Cawelti, 1976; Palmer, 1978; Porter, 1981). The weight of some of these factors – together with the fact that in most detective stories the enigma is resolved, the criminals caught and punished, and order restored – have led many to see the genre as almost inevitably conservative (in particular, Kaemmel, 1983; Mandel, 1984; and Porter, 1981).

Foucault wrote that the nineteenth century witnessed a fundamental change in the dominant 'episteme' of punishment and crime, a change in which 'we have moved from the exposition of the facts or the confession to the slow process of discovery; from the execution to the investigation' (Foucault, 1979, p. 69), and of which the detective story itself is both product and sign. One way of reading this change is in terms of the development of a post-romantic cult of mystery (Alewyn, 1983). Certainly, the generation of mystery and the provision of (rational) solutions to it have played a central part in accounts of the pleasures and structures involved in investigative fiction. Caillois (1983), for example, argues that: 'At bottom, the unmasking of a criminal is less important than the reduction of the impossible to the possible, of the inexplicable to the explained, of the supernatural to the natural' (p. 3), while psychoanalytic accounts stress the relationship between enigma and mystery, the desire to know and fantasies of the primal scene (Pederson-Krag, 1983; Neale, 1980; Porter, 1981).

The aesthetics of investigative fiction have been discussed in some detail, especially by those working within a structuralist, formalist or neo-formalist framework. Drawing on remarks made by one of the characters in Michael Butor's novel *Passing Time*, Tzvetan Todorov makes the point that most whodunnits contain not one story but two: the story of the crime and the story of the crime's investigation. Using this point as a basis, he goes on to distinguish between the whodunnit proper and the thriller. The latter, he argues, 'suppresses the first and vitalizes the second. We are no longer told about a crime anterior to the moment of the narrative; the narrative coincides with the action' (Todorov, 1977, p. 47). Instead of curiosity, the effect here is one of suspense, and it is worth noting that its characteristics dovetail with the action-adventure tradition mentioned above.

The formalist concept of retardation, meanwhile, is central to Porter's account of detective fiction. Here, emphasis is placed on the means by which the revelation of the first story – the story of the crime – is forestalled by various digressive means and devices. These include peripeteia: 'A discovery or event involving deflection or rebound from progress toward resolution. Examples of this are parallel intrigues, including rival investigations or love motifs that intermittently suspend the principal investigation, and false trials and false solutions' (Porter, 1981, p. 32). They also include

> the antidetective or criminal, who may remain passive and not impede the Great Detective's search or actively intervene in a variety of ways to prevent unmasking or capture. There are also other blocking figures, such as recalcitrant or confused witnesses, false detectives like Watson or Lestrade, who take time misrepresenting the evidence, and false criminals or suspects. (Porter, 1981, p. 32)

In addition, they include the taciturnity of the detective, false clues, 'the episodes themselves, which, as in an adventure novel or odyssey, intervene in greater or lesser numbers between a given point of departure and a fixed destination' (Porter, 1981, p. 33), and passages of extended description and dialogue.

In *Narration in the Fiction Film* (1985), David Bordwell draws on a number of formalist concepts in his discussion of the detective film. He reworks the notions of *syuzhet* and *fabula* to mean on one hand, the narrative events and cues with which the viewer is actually presented, and on the other, the narrative as a whole, including those events and actions the viewer is left to infer. From this perspective, the *fabula* in the detective film is seen to consist both of the story of the crime, and also, depending on the nature of the film, of portions of the story of the investigation. The *syuzhet* is marked by the manipulation of information concerning the story of the crime, and by retardation in the story of the investigation.

For Bordwell, the crux of the detective film is knowledge, and in particular its suppression and restriction, and this accounts both for its modes, styles and tactics of narration, and for the 'emotional states' to which it often gives rise:

> The detective film justifies its gaps and retardations by controlling knowledge, self-consciousness, and communicativeness. The genre aims to create curiosity about past story events (e.g., who killed whom), suspense about upcoming events, and surprise with respect to unexpected disclosures about either story [fabula] or syuzhet. To promote all three emotional states, the narration must limit the viewer's knowledge. This can be motivated realistically by making us share the restricted knowledge possessed by the investigator; we learn what the detective learns, when she or he learns it. There can be brief marks of an unrestricted narration as well ... but these function to enhance curiosity or suspense. By restricting the range of knowledge to that possessed by the detective, the narration can present information in a fairly unselfconscious way; we pick up fabula information by following the detective's enquiry. Again, the narration can signpost information more overtly, but this is occasional and codified. (Bordwell, 1985, p. 65)

In illustrating these points, Bordwell refers to *The Big Sleep* (1946) and *Murder My Sweet/Farewell My Lovely* (1944), both of them generally regarded, as already mentioned, as hard-boiled and noir. In her discussion of *Terror by Night* (1946), Kristin Thompson (1988) draws on a similar set of precepts and concerns but applies them instead to a Sherlock Holmes film, one in a series made at Universal in the 1940s. Thompson's aim is neither to elucidate the workings of the investigative thriller nor to validate *Terror by Night* as a genre film. It is rather to validate the use of formalist ideas as a means by which to illuminate the workings of what she calls 'the ordinary film' (see Post-theory, neo-formalism and cognitivism, p. 530). Concentrating on the general issues of knowledge and retardation, she argues that the film is not a straightforward murder mystery, as might be expected, but rather a film that 'in its second half ... becomes more oriented toward suspense; we wonder not, who is the murderer, but will the detective find out who he is in time?' (Thompson, 1988, p. 62). The film contains investigative material and an initial mystery, but these elements function as delaying mechanisms, as means by which to build up those forms of suspense associated with the thriller rather than the classic Holmes whodunnit as such.

The extent to which films such as *Terror by Night* have been neglected is a symptom not only of the dominance of noir in academic writing on the detective film, but also of the dominance of neo-noir in Hollywood's output since the late 1960s. While detectives of a relatively traditional kind have appeared with regularity on television, they have, unlike investigative thrillers, been almost completely absent from the cinema. Partly as a consequence, contemporary critics, theorists and historians have rarely been prompted to examine traditional detective films in more detail.

Selected Reading

David Bordwell, *Narration in the Fiction Film*, London, Methuen, 1985.

Dennis Porter, *The Pursuit of Crime: Art and Ideology in Detective Fiction*, New Haven, CT, Yale University Press, 1981.

Tzvetan Todorov, *The Poetics of Prose*, Ithaca, NY, Cornell University Press, 1977.

The gangster film

CHRISTINE GLEDHILL

Until the emergence of genre criticism, writing on the gangster film was divided between censorship issues and journalistic accounts of the historical phases and thematic and iconographic features of the genre and its various subgenres. Until the 1970s, Warshow's 'The gangster as tragic hero' (1970) was almost the sole attempt to deal with the aesthetic and ideological significance of this enormously popular and endlessly proliferating genre, supported by a somewhat different, more generalised approach in Lawrence Alloway's *Violent America* (1971), which concentrated on the depiction of violence. It was not until the arrival of one of the founding texts of genre criticism, Colin McArthur's *Underworld USA* (1972), that in Tom Ryall's words, 'a systematic attempt to define the genre, and to indicate the achievement within it of a selection of notable auteurs' (Ryall, 1979, p. 14) emerged.

Insight into the reasons for this early neglect can be gleaned from Andrew Tudor's (1974) account of the genre where he compares it unfavourably with the western, characterising the 'urban nightmare' so often attributed to the gangster film as a 'brutal universe ... mechanistic, offering little in the way of social and emotional riches' (Tudor, 1974, p. 201). This says much about what the western contributed to establishing genre criticism as a way of talking seriously about popular culture: 'Unlike the western there is no code governing the violence, no set of rules for the regulation of this war of all against all' (Tudor, 1974, p. 201). A feminist perspective might suggest that what is at stake here is the too naked expression of a certain form of male heroics. The gangster's 'self-interested individualism is totally unfettered ... It is the cowboy's world but without his integrity and without his sense of character' (Tudor, 1974, p. 202).

Clearly, one problem that confronted early genre criticism in relation to the gangster film was its seemingly symbiotic relation to contemporary events as circulated in a sensational press rather than to an already mythologised history. As Tudor puts it:

> The construction of the genre was almost contemporaneous with the construction of the events themselves ... It was stimulated by the late 20s boom in publicity for gangster activities. The fame of Capone and the notorious St Valentine's Day massacre of 1929 created a storm of publicity. Quick to see the possibilities, the studios reacted, and on the crest of this wave came Mervyn LeRoy's *Little Caesar*. (Tudor, 1974, pp. 196–7)

Another related problem confronted by film criticism was the extreme fragmentation of the genre, whose 'classic' period lasts, according to most accounts, only three years, but which was preceded by a flourishing and highly distinctive type of gangster film in the 1910s and the 1920s – one in which emphasis was placed on the gangster's repentance, self-sacrifice and moral regeneration – and which was followed by fragmentation under what Schatz summarises as 'threats of censorship, boycott, and federal regulation' (Schatz, 1981, p. 82).

This fragmentation can be enumerated in terms of various cycles, phases and subgenres: the G-Man cycle, film noir, crime melodramas and so on. The mythic coherence that could be attributed to the western and that supported claims that it connected with long-established traditions was difficult to establish for the gangster film, with its seemingly opportunistic shifts and turns according to changes of the physiognomy of crime and law enforcement in America – Tudor cites, for instance, the lack of anything like the 'Garden-Desert thesis' for the gangster film (Tudor, 1974, p. 196). A succinct account of how changes in 'the reality of American crime' surface in generic change can be found in McArthur (1972, pp. 64–5).

For early criticism, the apparently close relation between generic change and contemporary reality encouraged notions of 'reflection'. This was made all the easier by the association of the classic gangster film with Warner Bros., widely known for its 1930s 'social issue' movies, and with the development of sound by that studio, again popularly understood as an instrument of realism. This supposed realism contributed, and still contributes, to recurring 'moral panics' about the effects of the films' violence, glorification of the criminal and misogyny on young audiences, and consequently the history of the genre has been interlaced with censorship problems. Beyond this, early work on the genre was much concerned with tracing the appearance of different cycles and subgenres in terms of social sources, subject matter and dominant conventions, much of which is taxed with problems to do with periodisation, cycle demarcation and definition and ultimate origins (see Whitehall, 1964; French, 1967/8).

The gangster film as an experience of art

In this context, Warshow's seminal 'The gangster as tragic hero' (1970) attempted to break the grip of readings of gangster films as if they reflected or were accountable to historical or sociological renderings of American contemporary reality:

> The importance of the gangster film, and the nature and intensity of its emotional and aesthetic impact, cannot be measured in terms of the place of the gangster himself or the importance of the problem of crime in American life. Those European moviegoers who think there is a gangster on every corner in New York are certainly deceived, but defenders of the 'positive' side of American culture are equally deceived if they think it relevant to point out that most Americans have never seen a gangster. What matters is that the experience of the gangster as an experience of art is universal to Americans. (Warshow, 1970, p. 130)

In Warshow's view, the data of social reality are reorganised to produce a reality of the imagination whose referential field is other gangster films rather than the 'real world'.

The gangster/thriller as iconography

Writing on the gangster film produced as part of, or since, the emergence of genre studies, has generally taken Warshow's argument as its starting point. Most notable within the first category was McArthur (1972), one chapter of which was concerned to lay out the basic unity of the genre's iconography, which he understands as 'the continuity over several decades of patterns of visual imagery, of recurrent objects and figures in dynamic relationship' (McArthur, 1972, p. 23). These stable iconographic elements can be divided into three categories (see Ryall, 1978):

1. The physical presence, attributes and dress of the actors and actresses and the characters they play;
2. The urban milieux in which the fiction is played out;
3. The technology at the characters' disposal, principally guns and cars.

These elements recur consistently, in spite of shifts between different phases or subsets of the genre. As Ryall argues, McArthur's iconographical approach enables him to produce a flexible, dynamic account of the genre, whereas Warshow's attachment to the 'rise-and-fall' narrative freezes the genre at an early point in its development (Ryall, 1978, p. 18).

The gangster film and ideology

McArthur's book constituted a groundbreaking exercise in making visible and delineating the genre. Two major problems remained: one, to offer a convincing analysis of the relationship of the genre to reality that would also account for generic change; the other, to extend the account of the aesthetic and imaginative reach of the genre beyond the limitations of the classic moment as in Warshow, or of a concentration on iconography at the expense of all the other elements in a film production, both cinematic and extra-cinematic. The debates about ideology and aesthetics that superseded generic criticism would seem to have ideal material in the gangster film, but on the whole, recent studies of the genre have not chosen this route, preferring to elaborate the genre's formal development in terms of production histories – studios, censorship, technologies – or in terms of narrative and cinematic codes. Ideological readings tend to be sensitive to textual appraisals of what Warshow describes as the obverse of the American dream, the 'urban nightmare'. In this respect, the gangster/thriller is most often poised between the western on the one hand and the horror film on the other.

Warshow (1970), having rescued the gangster from reductionist 'realist' readings, had to go on to define and defend the significance of this perverse 'creature of the imagination'. The loss of tragedy to American culture is the cornerstone of Warshow's argument. American capitalism claims to eliminate tragedy from human experience by making individual happiness the ostensible goal and rationale of all its social arrangements. This ethos in turn destroys the conditions for the production of tragic art, which depends on a social order that subordinates the fate of the individual to 'a fixed and supra-political ... moral order or fate' (Warshow, 1970, p. 127). However, if banished from 'official ideology', the 'tragic sense' does not disappear, because of fundamental contradiction between the ideals of equality and individualism, and the ambiguous nature of happiness when conceived in terms of 'success'. Happiness as success not only pitches the individual against others, inviting his or her downfall, but breeds its obverse, a 'sense of desperation and inevitable failure' (Warshow, 1970, p. 129). This, argues Warshow, is 'our intolerable dilemma: that failure is a kind of death, and success is evil and dangerous, is ultimately – impossible' (Warshow, 1970, p. 133). The gangster film enables this dilemma to be played out and resolved in a way that its message is both 'disguised' and involves the minimum of distortion: 'The gangster is the "no" to that great American "yes" which is stamped so big over our official culture and yet has so little to do with the way we really feel about our lives' (Warshow, 1970, p. 136).

The notion that the gangster film represents 'the modern sense of tragedy' is frequently assumed and will be returned to. Similarly, the link between the gangster film and capitalist ideology has been elaborated by many critics. For some, the problems posed by the contradictions of capitalism open onto wider philosophical issues to do with appearance, reality, the individual and society, self-assertion and death.

The formal history of the gangster film

Jack Shadoian (1977) has offered one of the more interesting developments of the Warshow thesis. In place of iconography, he utilises the idea of 'structure' as the form's unifying principle. His deployment of this concept in relation to other cinematic codes such as narrative, mise en scène and lighting enables him to mount an interesting history of the way the necessities of generic and formal change produce shifting possibilities of pleasure and meaning. Less successful perhaps are his occasional attempts to link these shifts back to political and social realities of the time.

Shadoian's thesis is that the basic structure of the gangster/crime film is 'ready-made for certain kinds of concerns' (Shadoian, 1977, p. 3). Along with Warshow and several other commentators since, who see the fictional gangster as 'a product of advanced urban civilisation', Shadoian argues that these concerns arise out of the contradictions of the 'American dream' in the context of industrialism and post-industrial corporate capitalism – for instance, 'between America as a land of opportunity and the vision of a classless, democratic society' (Shadoian, 1977, p. 5) – contradictions that come to a head in the gangster film in the drive to success, 'the urge for it, the fear of it, the consequences that both having it and not having it entail' (Shadoian, 1977, p. 5).

The structure that emerged with the classic gangster film carried these contradictions with it. The legal and social status of the criminal produced a figure, the gangster, outside of and opposed to society, who 'violates a system of rules that a group of people live under' (Shadoian, 1977, p. 3). The position of the

Between the classic gangster film and film noir: Humphrey Bogart and James Cagney in *The Roaring Twenties*

hero as outside but related by conflict and violence to society produces a perspective from which that society must be viewed; in this way 'meanings emerge, whether deliberately or not, about the nature of society and the kind of individual it creates' (Shadoian, 1977, p. 3). In this respect, the gangster differs from the western 'outlaw'; in the west, society – civilisation – has yet to be constructed and fought for. The gangster/crime film speaks to the 'American dream' at a different stage.

From his starting point in the formal and aesthetic working of the genre, Shadoian moves on to a flexible account of its ideology in which the personal, psychic and political intertwine. Central to his analysis is its construction of the contradictions of capitalism as the simultaneous summoning and restriction of desire. Above all, the gangster/crime film deals with desire confronted by constraint. It pits 'basic human needs in opposition to a world that denies them' (Shadoian, 1977, p. 119). 'The gangster', says Shadoian, 'is a creature who wants, and although he shares this trait with characters in other genres, the degree of his compulsion is probably unique' (Shadoian, 1977, p. 14).

In Shadoian's analysis, the gangster/crime film develops towards inward and existential examination of human existence in modern American corporate society, accompanied by the increasing formalisation of the genre, and indeed of cinema itself. He discerns, for instance, a shift from the use of the gangster outside as a means of gaining a new perspective on society to a film noir concern, expressed in an increasing use of 'symbol, metaphor and allusion', with the nature of society itself, in which the distinctions between gangster and society, and society and self become confused and a new 'flavour of guilt and atonement' replaces the 'amorality, cynicism and self-confident' behaviour of the classic gangster hero (Shadoian, 1977, p. 120).

The formal history of the genre illuminates this shift. The 'classic' gangster took off from a known public fascination with real criminals, already being processed by sensational journalism. The films quickly diverged from reality, while maintaining a realist address. They were, in Shadoian's terms, travelogues and documentaries into alien territory – the world of the gangster, whose otherness became increasingly marked by stylisation, which prepared the ground for the genre's transformation when the combined forces of censorship, the passing of the Depression, the logic of generic renewal and sophistication made the gangster's heroic rise and near tragic fall no longer a viable structure. *The Roaring Twenties* (1939) and *High Sierra* (1941) stand nostalgically poised between the world of the classic gangster offering 'resonant myths of defeat that echoed with heroic, positive reverberations' and the more pessimistic world of film noir where 'views of freedom and possibility narrow' (Shadoian, 1977, p. 59). In the 1950s, the existential confusion of film noir shifts into a new organisation of the basic structure of gangster versus society. 'If noir scrambled the terms of the opposition, the 1950s inverts them' (Shadoian, 1977, p. 211).

In the era of affluence, crime and corporate capitalism are equated, an equation that not only inverts the 'classic' gangster's position as outsider, but also the struggle celebrated by the western, in which civilisation is attained by overcoming primitivism and savagery. In the 1950s gangster film, the evils of civilisation can only be purified by a reversion to instinctive actions and emotions. In this period, the gangster has gone the farthest in achieving control, reason, logic and precision and has consequently lost contact with his real self more than others. Within the overall structure of the gangster film, then, 'When the gangster … becomes that which he used to oppose, the genre finds his substitute, one who can assume his former function' (Shadoian, 1977, p. 214). The hero who will combat society as crime in the name of the American dream is one who has to detach himself from society. If he is a policeman, since the force

A dramatic focus for everyday problems: *Angels With Dirty Faces*

is incorporated into crime, he must 'act independently of the machinery'. This process of detachment involves the hero being 'restored to his fundamental drives, his basic instincts' (Shadoian, 1977, p. 212), and occurs only through the agency of violence, the reassertion of desire once embodied in the gangster.

With the end of the 1960s and entry to the 1970s, Shadoian argues that the genre, in line with the overall development of cinematic codes, reaches a point of sophistication and self-referentiality that makes the shift towards modernism inevitable. The unfeasibility of representational storytelling forces the genre into evasive strategies such as replaying stories from the past, or creating characters and heroes 'who can scarcely be defined as human' at all (Shadoian, 1977, p. 291). A further consequence of this shift is an increase in violence and the creation of 'highly aggressive fictions that have little regard for facts' (Shadoian, 1977, p. 291). Use of colour and the dominance of auteurs further heighten violence and anti-realism. Violence in this sense has to be understood aesthetically:

> The brutalisation of the audience, which took on systematic form in the 50s, has detached itself from urgent content and become an aesthetic factor with its own logic of communication. It has become the genre's core experience, and its ultimate statement. (Shadoian, 1977, p. 8)

Studio, technology and style

The emergence of the gangster film as a distinct genre in the 1930s, and its reputed realism and contemporaneousness, has often been associated with the consolidation of Warner Bros., which produced many of the 'classic' titles. Nick Roddick explores the association of Warners in the 1930s with the 'social conscience' movie, arguing that there exists 'a certain similarity between American social history and the themes produced by Warners during the 1930s' (Roddick, 1983, p. 65) (see Warner Bros., p. 26).

The studio system was developed as a means of rationalising production in relation to the market: 'There was an identifiable audience need to be met, and the studio system was designed to meet it as economically – and therefore as profitably – as possible' (Roddick, 1983, p. 10). The major studios set out to produce clear and differentiated identities to avoid duplication of effort, specialising in 'a particular kind or style of film' (Roddick, 1983, p. 8).

The development of sound, in which Warners played a large part and which contributed to its studio identity, shifted Hollywood production generally in the direction of realism and away from fantasy and the exotic. Warners followed the route of realism and contemporaneity with a heavy emphasis on what can be loosely designated 'social problem' pictures, although Roddick points out that only just under one-third of Warners output in the 1930s dealt with contemporary American society and 'the vast majority bear little or no immediate social message' (Roddick, 1983, p. 73). Nevertheless, Warners did consciously identify themselves with the New Deal. The question is what such identification could mean ideologically or aesthetically. Warners, a more emphatically 'family' business than any of the other majors, was also 'the most tightly run, economical and streamlined of the big five during the 1930s' (Roddick, 1983, p. 22). Yet while Warners were geared to 'a mass-production system', what they were producing for consumption was, quite consciously, 'art'. The relationship of their films to the real world, Roddick argues,

> was not a direct one: it was an aesthetic one. What is more, the terms in which the films are discussed in the studio memos – structure, balance, impact, pacing, credibility – are terms which are basically concerned with the artistic, not the physical nature of the product. Even in cases where financial considerations are clearly the origin of the memo, the aim is always to get the best effect in the most economical way. The criterion remains, in the final instance, artistic. How else is 'the best effect' to be designated? (Roddick, 1983, p. 25)

With a liberal leaning towards contemporary issues, a pressure towards realism increased through a heavy investment both of capital and identity in sound, and an equal pressure towards maximising use of studio space and avoidance of costly location work, the implicit aesthetic problem for Warners was how to turn reality into drama and narrative. As Roddick points out, a tradition already existed in the fiction of Balzac, Dickens and their derivatives for the association of social realism and crime, an association made vivid in the 1930s as gangsterism, and potential social breakdown consequent upon prohibition and the Depression, hit the newspaper headlines. Crime movies, then, 'provided a potentially perfect formula for fulfilling Warners' early talkie policy of realistic and at the same time popular entertainment' (Roddick, 1983, p. 77). Not only did they give 'a dramatic focus to fairly ordinary problems or aspirations – poverty, unemployment, sexual inadequacy, alienation, ambition, greed – by making them criminal motives' (Roddick, 1983, p. 77), they also offered in the criminal 'a hero whose antisocial individualism could speak to the contradictions of capitalist ideology, be romanticised and identified with by the audiences of the small-town and neighbourhood theatres' (Roddick, 1983, p. 99) to which the gangster films were directed.

Roddick identifies two levels of production in Warners' output of contemporary pictures in the 1930s. While the more directly 'social problem' pictures ranged across genres, taking in crime thrillers, gangster films and newspaper films, and were, because of their importance to the studio's corporate image, 'allocated top writers, major stars and comparatively large budgets ... and were road-shown in the major theatres with strong promotional campaigns guaranteeing them longer than usual runs' (Roddick, 1983, p. 78), the consolidation of the 'classic' gangster film itself was a more tightly generic and economical affair. Such films

> were relatively cheap to make, since they used contemporary dress, sets (seedy restaurants, backroom offices and hotel rooms) and exteriors that rarely if ever called for anything other than

> the standing sets of the backlot. Additionally, once the formula was perfected – as early, basically, as 1931 – the scripting and pre-production process was ideally suited to Warners' streamlined studio methods. (Roddick, 1983, p. 99)

They were also extremely popular, and clearly provided an economic and an aesthetic base to the more prestigious productions. Eventually, it would seem, the aesthetic force of generic convention displaced the foregrounding of social issues in Warners' crime movies, which came to be seen rather as 'mystery melodramas' (Roddick, 1983, p. 82).

In considering the ideological significance of studio policy, Roddick is concerned to dispel either a too radical, or too recuperative view of Warners' social realism. He cites Hans Magnus Enzensberger's comment on advertising – 'that it is not the creation of a false need, but the false meeting of a real need' (Roddick, 1983, p. 8) – in order to suggest the contradictions inherent in the consolidation of studio style and genre as a means of 'manipulating' the market. The liberal ideology of the studio bosses, the commitment of studio style to a 'hard-hitting' realism, meant in Roddick's view that inevitably, 'in tackling the symptoms, Warners should tackle some of the causes' for instance of the Depression or Fascism (Roddick, 1983, p. 74). The limitations of what could be done were set both by the contradictions of liberalism's attempts to make capitalism work and by the demands of fiction. Social responsibility, economic self-interest and the demand for narrative resolution made it a sine qua non 'that a film which tackled a problem had to offer a solution, even if the real-life problem seemed likely to remain unsolved for some time to come' (Roddick, 1983, p. 66). Nevertheless, 'the contradictions of American society in the 1930s were the material on which the studio drew, if not something it necessarily set out to highlight' (Roddick, 1983, p. 66). If the studio by its very nature and situation could not produce social change, its product was a medium through which indirectly a need for change could be registered.

Thomas Schatz's chapter on the gangster film in *Hollywood Genres* (1981) follows the general line pursued by Warshow, Shadoian and Roddick, and offers some interesting elaborations on the latter's concern to trace the interplay of studio, technology, aesthetics and ideology. Sound, he argues, not only effected a decisive shift towards realism, but was the catalyst for the consolidation of the crime film as a staple of the studio's output, contributing much to its aesthetic formalisation. Warners' experimental *The Lights of New York* (1928)

> demonstrated that sound effects and dialogue greatly heightened the impact of urban crime dramas. As later films would confirm, synchronous sound affected both the visual and editing strategies of gangster movies. The new audio effects (gunshots, screams, screeching tyres, etc.) encouraged film-makers to focus upon action and urban violence, and also to develop a fast-paced narrative and editing style ... Similarly the gangster persona itself – with his propensity for asserting his individual will through violent action and self-styled profiteering – offers an ideal figure for cinematic narrative elaboration. The fact that his assertiveness flaunts social order even heightens his individuality. (Schatz, 1981, pp. 85–6)

Like other writers, Schatz argues that the aesthetics of the genre organise a range of meaning around the gangster hero of far greater imaginative power than the attempts of censorship bodies to assert against him the values of the status quo (see Censorship, p. 17). One good reason for this perhaps is that the gangster speaks, if contradictorily, for the status quo, for its buried underside as well as its affirmative goals. As Schatz comments, 'the urban lone wolf's brutality and antisocial attitudes in Hollywood films are simply components of an essentially positive cultural model – that of the personable and aggressive but somewhat misguided self-made American man' (Schatz, 1981, p. 84). It is therefore perfectly possible, when the Hays Code intervenes, to shift the role of hero from gangster to cop and maintain the same expressive style:

> Cagney as gangster in *The Public Enemy* is basically indistinguishable from that of Cagney as government agent in *G-Men* ... He may be advocating a different value system in each role, but his self-assured swagger, caustic disposition, and violent demeanour are basic to each. (Schatz, 1981, p. 84)

Clearly, part of this continuity is to do with the star, and several commentators (such as McArthur, 1972) have noted the importance of the stars of these films – Cagney, Robinson, Bogart, Muni *et al.* – to the consolidation of the genre's conventions.

Schatz sees the ideological significance of the classic gangster film as stemming from the interplay of such aesthetic factors with the conditions of production and consumption of genre, to which the studio had to submit. Once a business is mounted in the field of entertainment, promulgation of safe ideologies is complicated by the technical and aesthetic requirements of the 'product': 'Despite the film industry's avowed efforts to support the status quo ... film-makers and audiences were cooperating in refining genres that examined the more contradictory tenets of American ideology' (Schatz, 1981, p. 95). For,

> camerawork, editing, dialogue, characterisation, and even the star system work together to engage our sympathy for the criminal. So from a technical (as well as thematic) standpoint, the gangster-hero functions as an organising sensibility in these films, serving to offset the other characters' naive moralising and to control our perception of his corrupt, Kafkaesque milieu. (Schatz, 1981, p. 93)

In this respect, the death of the hero is not a sop to the various pressure groups that concerned themselves with the morality of Hollywood. It is an aesthetic and ideological necessity, which recognises both sides of the contradiction that provides the dynamic of the genre. The appeal of the gangster is his ability to grasp those goals for which the status quo says we should strive despite the minimal options it offers. 'For a brief time, at least, the gangster is on top of his own pathetically limited world' (Schatz, 1981, p. 89). The strength of this appeal qualifies the apparent endorsement of social order of the genre's ending; paradoxically, the gangster's 'very death is the consummate reaffirmation of his own identity' (Schatz, 1981, p. 90).

The necessity of this ending has the same formal force as 'the romantic embrace which resolves the musical comedy, or the gunfight which resolves the Western' in maintaining 'a narrative balance between the hero's individuality and the need for social order' (Schatz, 1981, p. 90). But it is balance that is arrived at, not the elimination of one side of the contradiction in favour of the other. (This accounts perhaps for critical unease with more recent variants of the genre, with what is often seen as the proto-Fascist police movie exemplified in the Eastwood *Dirty Harry* series, in which the cathartic end in death is denied.)

The death of the gangster: tragedy or melodrama?

For most critics, the moralistic intentions behind many of the gangster films' tacked-on endings of retribution are far outweighed by the imaginative necessity of the hero's death. It is this – the inevitability and mode of the gangster's death – that permits critics' frequent appeal to tragedy as a justification for taking the genre seriously (in much the same way as the western claims prestige as epic). As Steve Jenkins (1982, p. 44) suggests, the death of the gangster is qualitatively different from death in other genres. Death comes with an inevitability that precludes suspense, often arbitrarily and always with finality. The gangster dies at the hand of fate, isolated, and yet a public spectacle. What makes this death appear tragic is variously defined. Jenkins, noting that the gangster's death generally ends the film, offers the suggestive comment that 'the genre concentrates on the progress of an individual male character ...' (Jenkins, p. 44). As we have seen, Warshow finds the ending tragic because its rise-and-fall structure contains within it the failure of a struggle for individual self-assertion with which we identify, but which we also know society cannot allow. Schatz pursues an identification of the tragic in the gangster film by looking for the gangster's tragic flaw, which he isolates as 'his inability to channel his considerable individual energies in a viable direction' (Schatz, 1981, p. 88). However, he immediately qualifies this by suggesting society itself is partly responsible, 'in that it denies individual expression and provides minimal options to the struggling, aggressive male from an inner-city, working-class background' (Schatz, 1981, p. 89). Shadoian, in claiming that the gangster film offers a 'tradition of popular tragedy in film', cites the 'combination of hubris, social fate and moral reckoning' (Shadoian, 1977, p. 15) in the gangster's story, arguing that *Little Caesar* (1930) is to the gangster film what *Oedipus Rex* is to Greek tragedy. Crucial to his argument are the gangster's choice of his fate, and the awesomeness of his overthrow.

What is interesting here is the need to rediscover the tragic and the sense that it has to be redefined in 'modern' terms. It is also notable that the designation, tragedy, is applied almost exclusively to the 'classic' gangster films of the 1930s with their clear rise-and-fall structure. Shadoian goes so far as to suggest that the interaction of the needs provoked by the Depression with a cinema still in its 'age of innocence' was productive of a tragic catharsis in the classic gangster film denied to later phases of the genre. However, melodrama, closely related to tragedy, may provide a different understanding of the conflicts and violence that make the gangster's death seem tragic.

Robert Heilman (1968) and Peter Brooks (1976) have both discussed the relationship between tragedy and melodrama. Heilman's concern is to preserve the category of tragedy from its frequent, mystifying reduction to melodrama. Awesomeness of fate, even if chosen, does not by itself define the tragic hero. What is crucial is his internalisation of conflict, his coming to awareness of division within and of his own responsibility. Brooks seeks to historicise the distinction by suggesting that the two forms belong to different sets of historical socio-economic and cultural circumstances. Following a somewhat similar line to Warshow, Brooks argues that tragedy belongs to a social hierarchy, organised around the monarchy and church,

Melodrama and the gangster film: Bette Davies takes the stand in *Marked Woman*

which integrates individual lives to a transcendental, sacred order, embracing the forces of good and evil. Brooks, like Heilman, sees our identification with the hero's coming to self-awareness, his introspective contemplation of his internal divisions, as the source of tragedy's lesson. The downfall itself relates back to communal sacrificial rites, and is a mechanism for catharsis rather than insight.

However, with the destruction of traditional social hierarchies bringing to an end the transcendental sacred order, the problem arises of how to found a new ethical order; how to prove the existence of good and evil and find the means for their expression within a secular framework and in a way that would satisfy the ethical and psychic needs of the new bourgeois 'individual'. For Brooks, melodrama attempts to do this by finding a new moral order 'occulted' within individual lives lived in an everyday, ordinary world. Thus, melodramatic rhetoric seeks to 'infuse the banal and the ordinary with the excitement of grandiose conflict' (Brooks, 1976, p. 40). Good and evil can only be grasped as features of personal life; thus 'they are assigned to, they inhabit persons who indeed have no psychological complexity but who are strongly characterised' (Brooks, 1976, p. 16). What such rhetoric entails is a 'victory over repression', which is 'simultaneously social, psychological, historical and conventional' (Brooks, 1976, p. 41). Such victory means saying – asserting – what social and verbal constraints do not permit to be said; it means forcing language beyond its limitations as a symbolic system to yield fullness of meaning and identity to speakers and audience in moments of 'ringing identification' (Brooks, 1976, p. 42).

The gangster/crime film can be understood in terms of the ethical-psychic terms offered by Brooks. We have already noted Shadoian's 'the gangster is a creature who wants'. Schatz also suggests the primal nature of the gangster's self-assertion: 'Destiny may kill him, but the intensity of the hero's commitment to his fate indicates that power and individuality are more important than a long life' (Schatz, 1981, p. 94). The gangster/crime film provides a context in which the desire for power and acquisition can be named and asserted against all the codes that would control and repress it. Nevertheless, such desire cannot overthrow the social order. As Brooks comments:

> The ritual of melodrama involves the confrontation of clearly identified antagonists and the expulsion of one of them. It can offer no terminal reconciliation, for there is no longer a clear transcendent value to be reconciled to. There is, rather, a social order to be purged, a set of ethical imperatives to be made clear. (Brooks, 1976, pp. 16–17)

This inability to move beyond the bourgeois world is found in the gangster/crime film. For instance, Shadoian observes that 'The genre offers no alternative to the American way of life. America's political, social and economic flaws are not hidden, but the system, in principle, is never seriously argued with' (Shadoian, 1977, p. 11). The capacity of the genre to transmute the values of society and gangster allows a critique of society to emerge. However, 'Upper-middle, middle-class, or prole heroes continue in the same system after convulsing it. In the end they act on behalf of its ideal nature' (Shadoian, 1977, p. 11). In this context, the function of the tableau-like endings of gangster films noted by Steve Jenkins can be set in a wider perspective:

> At the moment of the gangster's death these female characters are placed in opposition to the representatives of the law in a recurring tableau-like representation of the significance of that death ... By placing the dead gangster between the law (man) who stands over the body, and the woman, who often kneels by it or cradles the dead man's head, the distinction is clearly made between the official 'meaning' of the death (public enemy dealt with) and its resonance for the audience's emotional investment in the character, the spectator's interest in the gangster's human qualities, which is developed through the woman's romantic interest. (Jenkins, 1982, pp. 47–8)

Clearly, from Brooks's account of the melodramatic, both sets of meanings carry weight. The distance of the genre from tragedy may be responsible for the poverty of the 'official' meaning: 'Nor is there, as in tragedy, a reconciliation to a sacred order larger than man. The expulsion of evil entails no sacrifice ... There is rather confirmation and restoration' (Brooks, 1976, p. 32). Melodrama's fundamental Manichaeism discerned by Brooks may also account for the apparent division in the hero that leads some critics to label him a tragic figure. Schatz, for instance, argues that 'the ultimate conflict of the gangster film ... involves contradictory impulses within the gangster himself' (Schatz, 1981, p. 85). But his account of this conflict hardly suggests the introspection and coming-to-self-awareness of the tragic hero: 'This internal conflict – between individual accomplishment and the common good, between man's self-serving and communal instincts, between his savagery and his rational morality – is mirrored in society ...' (Schatz, 1981, p. 85). More appropriate perhaps is Brooks's contention that if the melodramatic protagonist be conceived as

> theatre for the interplay of manichaeistic forces, the meeting place of opposites, and his self-expressions as nominations of those forces at play within himself – himself their point of clash – the role of character as a purely dramaturgic centre and vehicle becomes evident. (Brooks, 1976, p. 101)

Charles Eckert (1973/74) has offered a different evaluation of the relation of melodrama and realism in the gangster film. The search for a 'moral occult' in his view is less a need to refind categories of good and evil than to impose a displacement of the origin of social conflict in class. Drawing on Lévi-Strauss's theory that 'a dilemma (or contradiction) stands at the heart of every living myth ... The impulse to construct the myth arises from the desire to resolve the dilemma; but the impossibility of resolving it leads to a crystal-like growth of the myth through which the dilemma is repeated, or conceived in new terms, or inverted ...' (Eckert, 1973/74, p. 18), Eckert contends that the melodrama of the gangster film displaces the class conflict that is at the centre of much of its Depression/Prohibition-originated material into a series of oppositions of ethics – the good life versus the wrong; of region – the rural small town versus the city; and of lifestyle – the snobbish rich versus the true proletarian. While the 'realist' scenes of *Marked Woman* (1937) dealing with the problems of the prostitute/witnesses' 'attempt to conceptualise the dilemmas that the women face' (Eckert, 1973/74, p. 17), the crucial question, why the poor are poor, is displaced into the oppositions floated by the melodrama, which themselves achieve resolution in the figure of the gangster, in whom melodrama discovers the villain, an exploiter characterised less by his role as capitalist than by his sadism. In Eckert's terms, then, ethical conflict framed as a 'moral occult' is the mystified means of reconciliation to the status quo. What are occulted are the 'real conditions of existence' – the social relations and forces of production.

The suspense thriller

STEVE NEALE

In part, perhaps, because it has been so associated with the work of one particular director, Alfred Hitchcock, the suspense thriller as a genre has received little attention. There are books on thrillers, suspense and suspense films (Davis, 1973; Gow, 1968; and Hammond, 1974, for instance). But most of them suffer from imprecision and/or from a tendency to focus on an array of generically disparate films. An exception here is Charles Derry (1988). While marked by Hitchcock's shadow, and while marred by a tendency to concentrate almost exclusively on films made since the late 1940s, Derry's book is rigorous, systematic and otherwise wide ranging in its choice of examples.

Derry notes that suspense thrillers focus either on victims of crime or on pursued and isolated criminals. One of their distinguishing features is therefore a lack of attention to official detectives or the police, and this is the basis of Derry's definition: 'The suspense thriller', he writes, is 'a crime work which presents a generally murderous antagonism in which the protagonist becomes either an innocent victim or a nonprofessional criminal within a structure that is significantly unmediated by a traditional figure of detection' (Derry, 1988, p. 62).

Given that this is a broad – though precise – definition, one that encompasses films as diverse as *North by Northwest* (1959), *The Manchurian Candidate* (1962), *Wait Until Dark* (1967) and *The Postman Always Rings Twice* (1946), Derry goes on to identify six major sub-types. The first is 'the thriller of murderous passions', which 'is organized around the triangular grouping of husband/wife/lover. The central scene is generally the murder of one member of the triangle by one or both of the other members. The emphasis is clearly on the criminal protagonist ... [and] ... The criminal motive is generally passion or greed' (Derry, 1988, p. 72). Examples include *Double Indemnity* (1944), *Blood Simple* (1984) and *Body Heat* (1981). The second is 'the political thriller', a category that includes *Seven Days in May* (1964), *All the President's Men* (1976), *The China Syndrome* (1979) and *Blow Out* (1981). Films such as these 'are organized around a plot to assassinate a political figure or a revelation of the essential conspiratorial nature of governments and their crimes against the people. These films generally document and dramatize the acts of assassins, conspirators, or criminal governments, as well as the oppositional acts of victim-societies, countercultures, or martyrs' (Derry, 1988, p. 103).

The third type is 'the thriller of acquired identity', which is exemplified by films such as *The Running Man* (1963) and *Dead Ringer* (1964). These films 'are organized around a protagonist's acquisition of an unaccustomed identity, his or her behavior in coming to terms with the metaphysical and physical consequences of this identity, and the relationship of this acquisition to a murderous plot' (Derry, 1988, p. 175).

Fourth and fifth are 'the psychotraumatic thriller' and 'the thriller of moral confrontation'. The psychotraumatic thriller is 'organized around the psychotic effects of a trauma on a protagonist's current involvement in a love affair and a crime or intrigue. The protagonist is always a victim – generally of some past trauma and often of real villains who take advantage of his or her masochistic guilt' (Derry, 1988, p. 194). Examples include *Spellbound* (1945), *Marnie* (1964), *Hush... Hush, Sweet Charlotte* (1964) and *Body Double* (1984). The thriller of moral confrontation is exemplified by films such as *The Window* (1949), *Strangers on a Train* (1951), *Sudden Terror* (1970) and *Outrage* (1973). It is 'organized around an overt antithetical confrontation between a character representing good or innocence and a character representing evil. These films often are constructed in terms of elaborate dualities which emphasize the parallels between the victim and the criminal' (Derry, 1988, p. 217).

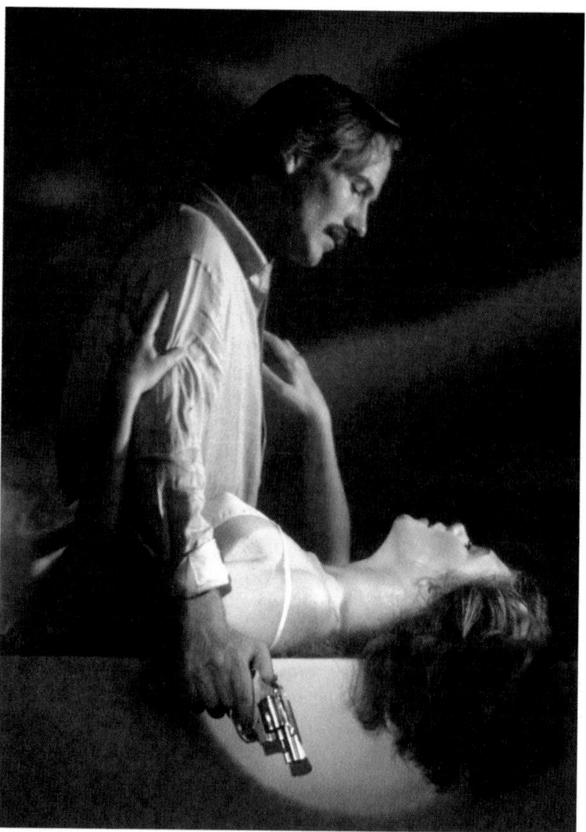

A suspense thriller of murderous passions: Lawrence Kasdan's *Body Heat*

The sixth and final sub-type is 'the innocent-on-the-run thriller', which is 'organized around an innocent victim's coincidental entry into the midst of global intrigue' and in which 'the victim often finds himself running from both the villains as well as the police' (Derry, 1988, p. 270). Examples include *The Man Who Knew Too Much* (1955), *The Parallax View* (1974), *Three Days of the Condor* (1976) and *Into the Night* (1985).

In addition to constructing these categories, Derry also addresses the issues of thrills and suspense. In discussing thrills, he draws on the work of psychoanalyst Michael Balint (1959), and in particular on Balint's distinction between 'philobats' (lovers of thrills) and 'ocnophobes' (haters of thrills). He notes that thrillers tend to plunge ocnophobic protagonists into deadly – and thrilling – situations in which familiar objects, spaces and activities are replaced by – or become – objects, spaces and activities that are unfamiliar and threatening. In discussing suspense, he distinguishes between the role of surprise and the role of curiosity. He argues that suspense is not necessarily related to the resolution of enigmas or to 'the vague question of what will happen next' (Derry, 1988, p. 31). It is dependent, instead, on 'the expectation that a specific action might take place': 'the creation of suspense demands that enough information be revealed to the spectator so that he or she can anticipate what might happen; suspense then remains operative until the spectator's expectations are foiled, fulfilled, or the narrative is frozen without any resolution at all' (Derry, 1988, pp. 31–2). In the interplay between expectation and narrative development in suspense, what becomes suspended is time:

'During those moments that suspense is operative, time seems to extend itself, and each second provides a kind of torture for a spectator who is anxious to have his or her anticipations foiled or fulfilled' (Derry, 1988, p. 32).

In insisting on the importance of specific information and knowledge, Derry's argument parallels the argument put forward by Dove (1989). For Dove, as for Derry, suspense 'is dependent to a greater degree upon what the reader has been told than upon what he wants to find out. The more the reader knows (without knowing everything), the more he wants to know' (Dove, 1989, p. 4). Dove, however, is less interested in sub-types than in broad generic variations on the structures that he sees as fundamental to all forms of suspense. These structures comprise four phases or states:

> 'Cumulation' (the phase that accommodates the development of promises, clues, questions, tensions which will determine later developments); 'postponement' (the phase in which the promise of early resolution is deferred); 'alternation' (the period of doubt, where the chances regarding the outcome are uncertain); and 'potentiality' (the crisis, in which the chances appear to be favoring a given outcome). (Dove, 1989, p. 50)

These phases mark developments and shifts in the 'relational components of the story' (Dove, 1989, p. 51), and it is here that generically specific variations tend to occur.

These components include a 'mover', 'A', an 'object', 'B', the tensions involved in the confrontations between them, 'C', and the exclusion of possible solutions or directions that would resolve the story too quickly, 'D'. In the thriller, where the basic issue is: 'What is going to happen?', the identity of 'A' and 'B' are obvious: 'no question who or what is the menace, or the victim. "C" is generated by the conflict of "A" vs "B." The "D" component is clearly defined, as are the phases or states' (Dove, 1989, p. 59). In the '"pure" or non-detectional mystery', the question is: 'What is happening? "A" (the person, problem, menace) is not identified until late; "B" (the identity menaced) emerges somewhat earlier. "C" arises from the disturbance created by loss of security … [and] "D" is the vulnerability/inadequacy of "B"' (Dove, 1989, p. 60). In the detective story, the question posed is: 'What really did happen? In this story "A" is the detective, the element that makes the story move … "B" is the problem, which would include the guilty person(s) … "D" is … the obscured past, which hold[s] the story in bounds … [And] "C" is the repeated revelation-frustration of the detective's pursuit' (Dove, 1989, p. 60). And in the 'tale of the Supernatural', the question is: 'Is anything happening? "A" and "B" are customarily ambiguous, "A" often so until the end, and "B" may not emerge until late in the story … "C" is frequently present before "A" or "B" … [And] "D" is the irrationality-uncertainty-perversity-invulnerability of "A"' (Dove, 1989, p. 61).

Dove's book concentrates on written fiction, and his terminology (alphabetical and otherwise) is occasionally eccentric and difficult to follow. However, his formulae work as well for films as they do for novels, and he allows throughout for hybrids and combinations. The extent to which his formulae extend beyond the traditional realms of crime to encompass the supernatural is (yet another) indication of the extent to which popular genres are rarely tidy and self-contained, even, perhaps especially, from a structural point of view. Further confirmation that this is the case can be found in historical surveys of crime films of the kind produced by Langman and Finn. As in Dove's – and Derry's – books, categories and sub-types tend to abound. Here, though, they are founded less on form than on content, less on structural characteristics than on cyclical features and variations. They include 'The courtroom film' (Langman and Finn, 1995a, pp. xii–xiii), 'The newspaper-crime film' (Langman and Finn, 1995a, p. xiii), 'The exposé drama' (Langman and Finn, 1995b, pp. xviii–xix) and 'The social conscience drama'. While some of the films within these categories are marked by the structural features analysed by Dove and Derry, others are not. Whether regarded as genres or as sub-types, the point is that they rarely feature in critical or theoretical discussions of the crime film.

Selected Reading

Charles Derry, *The Suspense Thriller: Films in the Shadow of Alfred Hitchcock*, Jefferson, NC, McFarland Press, 1988.

Charles Eckert, 'The anatomy of a proletarian film: Warners' *Marked Woman*', *Film Quarterly* 27 (2): 10–24, winter 1973/4. Reprinted in Nichols (ed.), *Movies and Methods Vol. II*, Berkeley, University of California Press, 1985.

Steve Jenkins, *The Death of a Gangster*, London, BFI Education, 1982.

Nick Roddick, *A New Deal in Entertainment: Warner Bros in the 1930s*, London, BFI Publishing, 1983.

Scarface (USA 1932 *p.c* – Caddo Company/United Artists; *d* – Howard Hawks)

Loosely based on the Al Capone story, *Scarface*, along with *The Public Enemy* (1931) and *Little Caesar* (1930), has contributed to the definition of the 'classic' gangster film, exhibiting a rise-and-fall structure and many of the iconographic and thematic elements later developed in the genre. The gangster hero in these films is depicted as a paradoxical figure, at once representing the worst in society and the best in his striving towards the goals of the American dream: wealth, individualism, success, power. All the iconographic elements of the genre are visible: cars, guns, hats and coats, backroom gangsters and brash frontmen. The emphasis on consumerism, particularly clothes, indicates increasing wealth and status: for example, lapel flowers, smoking jackets, handkerchiefs, the array of shirts and the interior-sprung mattress shown to Poppy (Karen Morley). Poppy herself is part of Tony Camonte's (Paul Muni) success, for in the gangster film, accession to gang leadership is often worn by taking the leader's girlfriend.

Also demonstrated is the extravagant violence of these early films, which provoked attacks from censorship bodies. Here it is exemplified in the total destruction of the restaurant (cf. *The St Valentine's Day Massacre*, 1967, where this incident is repeated), and by the introduction of the machine gun. Socio-economic explanation of the gangster is suggested in Camonte's gleeful wave at the Thomas Cook sign, 'The World is Yours'.

If the film is more violent than its two 'classic' contemporaries, however, it is also more comic – and indeed, Robin Wood (1981) identified *Scarface* as one of Hawks's comedies. For example, the antics of Angelo juggling between the telephone and a stream of hot water are used to counterpoint the destruction of the restaurant. In this context, the figure of Scarface is offered as an innocent primitive and much of the comedy in the film comes from this – for example, Camonte's reply to Poppy's suggestion that his flat is 'kind of gaudy': 'Isn't it though? Glad you like it.'

CHRISTINE GLEDHILL

The Roaring Twenties (USA 1939 *p.c* – Warner Bros.; *d* – Raoul Walsh)

This film demonstrates a number of gangster film motifs: the *March of Time* documentary style; sociological explanation of the gangsters and their lifestyle, characteristic of Warners' 1930s gangster films; the set-piece montage of gang warfare; the raid on a rival warehouse and narrow escape; the conflict between the gangster for whom crime is a matter of material survival, represented by Eddie (James Cagney), and the psychotic gangster, George (Humphrey Bogart); the heroine, whose classy femininity is the object of the gangster's sexual desire and social aspiration but who is unobtainable, in contrast to the gangster's faithful moll, Panama (Gladys George); the role of the lawyer, who for social reasons or personal weakness gets involved with the mob but ultimately crosses the gangster leader by virtue of his superior knowledge of how the system works; and the gangster's lifelong and faithful friend who goes down with him in his fall.

On the other hand, the film also signals the shift from the 'classic' gangster film and G-Men cycle towards film noir, in what Shadoian (1977) calls its 'ambiguously elegiac perspective' on the gangster motifs. In this respect, the authorship of Raoul Walsh is significant in that his other crime melodramas for Warners, *They Drive by Night* (1940) and *High Sierra* (1941), also exhibited a noir dimension. Here it is exhibited in the Expressionist architecture and lighting of the warehouse raid, the unsocially motivated cynicism and the psychotic violence of George (see Warner Bros., p. 26).

CHRISTINE GLEDHILL

Dirty Harry (USA 1971 *p.c* – Warner Bros./Malpaso; *d* – Don Siegel)

Dirty Harry is a big-budget 1970s police thriller using as its central protagonist the psychotic policeman in place of the psychotic gangster of earlier decades. It is both representative of the police movie subgenre and of the work of its director, Don Siegel, who had directed earlier psychotic gangster pictures such as *Baby Face Nelson* (1957) and *The Lineup* (1958). It also marks the collaboration between Clint Eastwood and Siegel and the inception of the Dirty Harry character, and exemplifies the interplay between genre, author and star.

William Park (1978) has described the police movie as a union of psychological melodrama and observation of social conditions. The cop hero is both isolated and a representative American Everyman, positioned between black and Hispanic minorities on the one hand and Wasps on the other. Having worked his way up through the force, he despises middle-class liberalism and its conscience-ridden advocacy of civil liberties; on the other hand, he works with a black or Hispanic partner – here, Chico Gonzales (Reni Santoni). He lives alone, has no private life and is up against a source of corruption that is unseen but penetrates even the precinct. The cop hero fights corruption on all sides motivated by an idealistic moral anger that justifies his breaking all laws, except the policeman's taboo against taking a bribe.

Siegel himself contributed to the development of this character in *Coogan's Bluff* (1968) and *Madigan* (1968), the former marking the transposition of Eastwood's 'Man With No Name' from its enormous popularity in spaghetti westerns to a contemporary American urban setting, in which the cynical policeman confronts an obstructive, short-sighted police bureaucracy. In *Dirty Harry*, Harry is up against the liberalism of the mayor, whose vote-seeking allegiance to civil rights means he cannot identify, let alone act against, evil when it confronts him. The villain, Scorpio (Andy Robinson), is isolated, sadistic and sexually perverted. This element seems removed from the journalistic strand of the movie, which deploys the hunt/chase structure to incorporate elements of social observation – for example, signs of social tension in the use of blacks and symbols of protest movements (Scorpio's peace badge buckle).

The union of melodramatic structure and signifiers of political minority opposition has produced conflicting ideological assessments of the police movie subgenre, the Dirty Harry character and this film. For instance, Harry's confrontation with the black bank robber parallels Scorpio's sadistic games later in the film. Hero and villain are both isolated loners and Harry displays both sadism and voyeuristic tendencies. The issue is how far this parallel suggests a critique of Harry's attitudes and how far it exemplifies a cynicism on the part of the film in which there is limited choice between Fascism and madness.

CHRISTINE GLEDHILL

Blue Steel (USA 1990 *p.c* – Lightning Pictures/ Precision Films/Mack-Taylor Productions; *d* – Kathryn Bigelow)

Blue Steel represents a stylish post-feminist update of the police thriller. It is a hybrid of cop movie and serial killer film, with a rape-revenge subplot and elements of family melodrama. In addition, it puts a maverick female cop and her problems with the male-dominated police hierarchy centre-stage. In 1991, Jonathan Demme's *The Silence of the Lambs*, starring Jodie Foster as an inexperienced woman

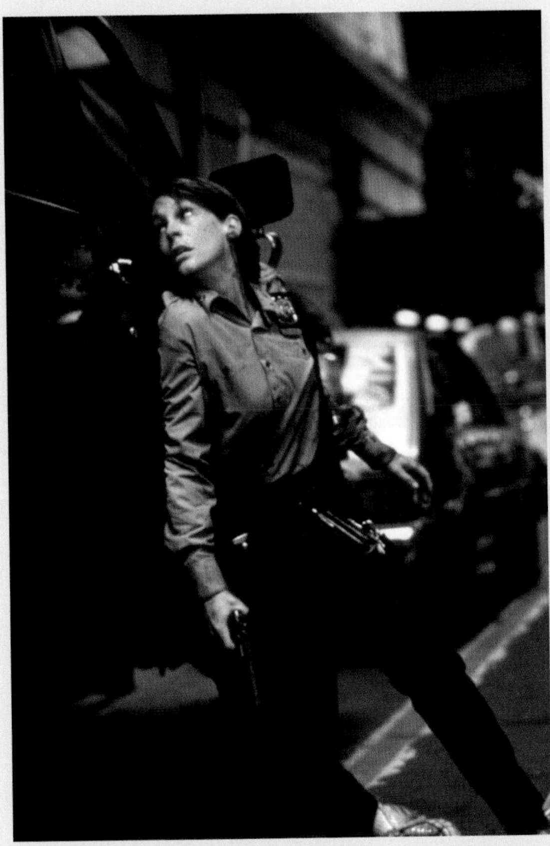
Unsuitable job for a woman: Jamie Lee Curtis in *Blue Steel*

detective hunting down a serial killer, covered similar territory. Kathryn Bigelow's film, while it does not have the high production values of *The Silence of the Lambs*, is in some ways a more radical examination of the dilemmas faced by women working in dangerous male environments.

The story features rookie cop Megan Turner (Jamie Lee Curtis) who kills an armed gunman during a robbery, but is then suspended when the gunman's weapon is not found. The gun has been picked up by a psychotic serial killer, financial trader Eugene Hunt (Ron Silver), who tracks her down. Unaware of his identity, Megan begins an affair with Eugene, but becomes increasingly uneasy as their relationship turns violent, and he attacks those close to her. In an extended denouement, after Eugene attempts to rape Megan, she pursues him through the city streets in a bloody shootout, finally killing him. Bigelow, who co-scripted the film with Eric Red (*The Hitcher*, 1986; *Near Dark*, 1987; *Cohen & Tate*, 1988), leaves Megan's motivations for becoming a cop obscure, while indicating that she is regarded (particularly by men) as a freak and (by her male colleagues) as incapable of doing the job. Megan is given a rudimentary backstory in which her father's violence towards her mother is seen as contributing to her interest in law enforcement, but in general she is presented as a maverick risk-taker who breaks many of the rules of police procedure.

At the heart of the film, and alluded to in its title, is gun fetishism, which is depicted as central to Eugene's psychosis and to Megan's attraction to him. This represents a dark twist on the doppelganger relationship between cop and criminal, and is used by Bigelow to explore gender boundaries, to question the masculine death drive (see also *Point Break*, 1991) and to highlight issues of power and control. In *Blue Steel*'s closing moments, after Megan kills the monstrous Eugene in a shootout that explicitly foregrounds the devastating physical effects of gunfire, she drops her own gun in a gesture that intimates both her loss of identity and the nihilism characteristic of the genre.

PAM COOK

Heat (USA 1995 *p.c* – Monarchy Enterprises/ Regency Entertainment/Forward Pass Productions/Warner Bros.; *d* – Michael Mann)

Crime films frequently represent the gangster or criminal as a doppelganger of the law-abiding protagonist. However, in its story of a cold-blooded killer and thief attempting one last score and the detective determined to bring him down, *Heat* emphasises the continuities between them rather than their differences. In John Huston's classic caper film *The Asphalt Jungle* (1950), the shyster lawyer remarks that 'Crime is merely a left-handed form of human endeavour' – a view that seems to be endorsed by Michael Mann's film. As much a melodrama as a crime movie, *Heat* is structured as a series of comparisons between professional thief Neil McCauley (Robert De Niro) and streetwise detective Vincent Hanna (Al Pacino), focusing on their troubled relationships and domestic lives as well as their respective avocations.

McCauley's motto is to have no attachments, 'nothing in your life that you can't walk out on in 30 seconds flat if you spot the heat around the corner', a creed he attempts to live by. Yet Hanna too lives this way, interrupting important moments in his personal life to answer police calls on his pager. Although one man acts to enforce the law while the other seeks to circumvent it, both are loners whose tough masculinity has alienated them from emotional attachments to women. While Hanna triumphs in his final confrontation with McCauley, allowing the plot to meet the demands of generic closure, both men are seen to have suffered because of their fear of emotional relationships.

Often unjustly criticised for being an empty stylist, writer/director Michael Mann displays his distinctive visual style in *Heat*, using a cool colour palette and depicting Los Angeles as an environment of alluring high-tech surfaces. Detective Hanna alludes to this in his sarcastic remark to his partner, Justine, that they live in her 'ex-husband's dead-tech postmodernist bullshit house'. In *Heat*, this postmodern ambience is crucial to the film's theme, for the bright, clean technological world it depicts contrasts starkly with the brutish, messy violence of the characters. This contrast is visualised in the image of McCauley's empty beach house, suffused in blue light, with a gun on a table in the foreground dominating the diminutive figure of McCauley in the background – the melancholy fate of men who sacrifice human connection and risk all for material gain.

BARRY KEITH GRANT

Inside Man (USA 2006 *p.c* – Universal/GH Two/ Brian Grazer Productions/Imagine Entertainment/ 40 Acres and a Mule Filmworks; *d* – Spike Lee)

Like many of Spike Lee's films, *Inside Man* mobilises genre conventions to explore the director's interest in issues of race, class and power in American society. It begins as a crisp caper film, with a band of robbers efficiently sealing off a bank and holding the employees and customers hostage; but soon *Inside Man* changes from focusing on the craft of the caper to probing the privileges of power. Just as the police are fooled by a sensationally faked video of a hostage execution, so viewers are lured by genre expectations into watching a more ambitious movie. Some contemporary reviews criticised the film for allowing the suspense of the heist plot to dissipate by revealing what is hidden inside the safe-deposit box early on, but this is less a flaw than a deliberate strategy. Indeed, it is in the spaces between its narrative conventions that the film's real concerns lie. *Inside Man* begins with the leader of the gang, Dalton Russell (Clive Owen), addressing the camera directly, saying that we should listen to his words carefully – a scene unmotivated by the plot, but a trope used by Lee since *Do the Right Thing* (1989) to signal seriousness of purpose.

As the tense standoff with police unfolds, a series of overlapping conflicts involving the police, the mayor, the chief hostage negotiator, Detective Keith Frazier (Denzel Washington), the president of the bank (Christopher Plummer) and a mysterious woman, Madeleine White (Jodi Foster), begin to play out. Plot points involving a rabbi, a Sikh bank employee and an Albanian worker and his ex-wife explore the relation of ethnicity, race and gender to social power. Dressed in white and placed in a white mise en scène, the aptly named Ms White wields power over even the mayor, gaining access to the crime scene and the robbers. Her power lies in her possession of information about those she manipulates; in similar vein, the robbers are not after money, which they leave untouched in the bank vault, but secret details of the bank president's collaboration with the Nazis during World War II.

Ultimately, the film has numerous 'inside men', including the mayor, the bank president and gang mastermind Russell, who is literally hidden inside the bank as he recites his opening monologue. The film shows that when power is at stake, everyone jockeys for an inside position, whether it involves cancelling parking tickets or promotion to detective. And despite the generically determined ending in which the black detective trumps Ms White, *Inside Man* makes it clear that the powerful elite remains white America – the Man on the inside – pulling strings behind the scenes.

BARRY KEITH GRANT

Probing the privileges of power: Denzel Washington in Spike Lee's *Inside Man*

COSTUME DRAMA

Introduction

PAM COOK

Costume dramas (films that reconstruct a historical past) have always been a staple of popular cinemas worldwide. Costume performs key functions in narrative films of all descriptions, whether documentary or fiction. Yet costume design is one of the least explored of all aspects of the film-making process, and most textual analyses prefer to minimise its contribution to the activity of making meaning. This section looks at some of the reasons for this, and at the multiple roles performed by costume in film, focusing on costume drama but extending its reach to cinema generally.

Costume dramas are distinguished by their foregrounding, or putting on display, elements of film that are traditionally associated with craft (in that they depend on artisanal skills such as sewing, or in the case of set design, carpentry, construction and painting) and teams of craftspeople. Costume and sets are considered to be part of mise en scène; thus they are often perceived as passive elements in the scene that is staged for the camera rather than as active participants in creating an overall 'look' or style. This active, creative role is attributed to the director, and to those such as cinematographers, scriptwriters, composers and occasionally editors who work with the director to bring to life his or her 'artistic vision'. Costumes and sets play a vital part in sustaining narrative unity (ensuring continuity, establishing period, indicating character, producing a coherent sense of space and so forth), but this is only one factor in their repertoire. The ways in which costume functions in cinema vary dramatically according to cultural and historical context, technological developments and the demands of genre and markets. In certain circumstances, such demands can mean that costume design becomes so prominent that it disrupts narrative unity, or sidelines narrative altogether. It can exceed its basic function by drawing attention to the presence of a particular designer, whose visual 'signature' then competes for attention with that of the director and other creative personnel; by eroticising a star's body to the extent that their sexual allure overrides narrative or genre expectations; by inducing a reverie that takes the viewer into realms outside the film; and by symbolising aspects of meaning that narrative and dialogue cannot directly express.

The dominance of auteur theory, with its emphasis on the director's control of mise en scène, ensured that the creative contribution of costume and set designers was obscured or relegated. Traditional genre analysis regarded costume as part of the iconography of the western, gangster film, musical, historical film and so on. For many years, film studies' attention to the operations of narrative and ideology in classic Hollywood took precedence over analysis of visual codes, except to see the latter as subservient to the former. Influential feminist approaches that stressed the negative aspects of the eroticised female body in classic Hollywood as a vehicle for masculine voyeuristic and fetishistic fantasies, or used theories of masquerade to point to the absence of woman, contributed to prevailing views of costume as contaminated by regressive ideology. Early star studies, with its emphasis on the positive role of star charisma in transcending narrative and ideology, implied that fetishistic aspects of costume could play a less ideologically compliant role in cinematic representation (see Dyer, 1979; 1998). But costume itself was still seen as an adjunct to the star image rather than an independent entity with its own language.

The studies of melodrama and the women's picture that emerged in response to women's perceived marginalisation by classic Hollywood began to carve out a more dynamic function for costume, sets and props. Thus costume, colour and other facets of visual design were studied for their symbolic potential in providing information about a character's state of mind, or an ironic counterpoint to narrative events, much in the same way as music was used in melodrama (see Melodrama, p. 316). Subsequent analysis of the cycle of costume melodramas produced by the British studio Gainsborough Pictures in the 1940s (see p. 292) took these debates further, projecting costume as an independent discourse that celebrated the wayward heroines' social and sexual transgressions and used costume's exotic and erotic attributes to visualise, in coded form, female sexuality.

The cross-dressing scenarios typical of costume dramas enabled masquerade to be reassessed as a way of performing, playing with and travestying traditional gender identities (see Kuhn, 1985; Garber, 1992; Butler, 2006). A major study of costume in cinema appeared (Gaines and Herzog, 1991) that presented a spectrum of conflicting and contradictory approaches, from those that saw costume as reinforcing classic cinema's oppression of women, to those that perceived it as offering female spectators the pleasures of creative play with the identities constructed by cinema. Coinciding with burgeoning interest in audience response and fan discourse, this study stressed the significance of costume reaching outside the film text to production and reception contexts, connecting to the wider culture through its sartorial language. As a result, interest in the role of costume in cinema grew, broadening the scope of earlier work to include male dress, and issues of national identity, race and ethnicity (see Cook, 1996; Bruzzi, 1997).

However, costume's elevation received a mixed reception in some quarters. While costume was a key feature in the heritage film debates of the late 1980s and 1990s (see p. 292), it was perceived negatively as contaminated by conservative values, and its spectacular dimension characterised as distracting from the progressive potential of the narrative. Dissenting voices reiterated the value of spectacle, pastiche and irony in offering viewers more subversive pleasures, in an echo of earlier divisions of opinion. Such debates have brought costume design into the limelight, but approaches to costume, and to costume drama itself, continue to be typified by ambivalence. This ambivalence could be said to stem from deep-rooted cultural attitudes that perceive costume on the one hand as carnivalesque and potentially disruptive of 'normality', and at the opposite extreme, as preserving the status quo. Depending on context, costume drama can fulfil either or both of these functions (or neither).

Although the studies outlined here opened up the topic as a fruitful area for further research, such research has been intermittent, and is generally subsumed within broader discussions. This is surprising in the light of contemporary cinema's trend towards design-led productions and the industry's intensified drive to capitalise on commodity tie-ins with fashion, for example. The growth of interest in history and memory also provides fertile ground for discussion of costume's role in the processes of historical reconstruction (see Cook, 2005). The history of costume in cinema has potential in other ways too: not least to highlight the creative agency of designers, many of whom were and are women, and enable a new map of cinema history to be drawn.

Selected Reading

Stella Bruzzi, *Undressing Cinema: Clothing and Identity in the Movies*, London and New York, Routledge, 1997.

Pam Cook, *Fashioning the Nation: Costume and Identity in British Cinema*, London, BFI Publishing, 1996.

Sybil DelGaudio, *Dressing the Part: Sternberg, Dietrich and Costume*, Madison, NJ, Fairleigh Dickinson University Press, 1993.

Sarah Street, *Costume and Cinema: Dress Codes in Popular Film*, London, Wallflower Press, 2002.

Gainsborough costume melodrama

SARAH STREET

Since the early 1980s, the study of Gainsborough melodramas has challenged dominant views of British cinema as primarily informed by stylistic and thematic forms of realism that had become associated with notions of 'quality' and critical 'value'. The popular cycle of costume melodramas produced by Gainsborough Pictures in the 1940s used historical settings, escapist narrative formulas and opulent-looking costumes and sets created on small budgets to score significant box-office successes. Nevertheless, they were widely dismissed by critics at the time and in subsequent writing. As film historians (Aspinall and Murphy, 1983; Harper, 1994; Cook, 1996) began to ask questions about the significance of these films for their contemporary culture, it became clear that this neglected subgenre had much to say, particularly about gender inequalities.

Gainsborough was associated with a variety of genres (see Gainsborough Pictures, p. 178), but the first really successful costume melodrama was *The Man in Grey* (1943), set partly in the eighteenth century, starring Margaret Lockwood, Phyllis Calvert, Stewart Granger and James Mason. This film established a formula for later box-office hits, notably *The Wicked Lady* (1945), set in Restoration England (see case study). These films, which often adapted popular novels, were set in the past and featured feisty, wilful heroines who challenged the prevailing masculine order, even if in the end they did not succeed in completely overthrowing it. Studies of contemporary audience reaction, completed by J. P. Mayer (1948), revealed that although the films were set in the past, viewers identified with the dilemmas facing the characters. In the context of World War II, when many people experienced temporary freedoms, had extra-marital relationships and travelled within and outside the country in an unprecedented way, the films tapped into contemporary concerns, which accounted for their box-office success.

A distinctive feature of Gainsborough costume dramas is that they express much of their rebellious sensibilities through sets and costume. Although the films were released in a context of war and postwar austerity, they provided an opportunity for audiences to 'enter into a world of fantasy where freedom and pleasure were coterminous' (Harper, 1994, p. 131). Elizabeth Haffenden, who designed the costumes for the cycle with Joan Bridge, exploited the arrival of 'New Look' fashions in historical designs that were anachronistic yet 'fitted' people's expectations of what was worn in the past. With its emphasis on an 'hour-glass figure' that accentuated the waist, bust and hips, the New Look was perfectly suited to emulation via the compelling heroines of the melodramas, such as Jean Kent in *Caravan* (1946). The films celebrated excessive displays of femininity that, as argued by Harper (1994) and Cook (1996), encouraged oppositional readings that relished transgressive female desire at a time when some of the freedoms enjoyed during World War II were being curtailed. The rebellious heroines were often pitted against more conventional, conformist women who usually triumphed with narrative closure; nevertheless, the feisty women were seen as more appealing for their audacity and daring.

While the Gainsborough costume dramas can be related to gender issues, they are important registers of the national psyche in other respects. Their fascination with exotic outsiders, particularly gypsies, in films such as *Madonna of the Seven Moons* (1944), *Caravan* and *Jassy* (1947) signals an eclectic affinity with 'foreign' locations and styles that was typical of much of Gainsborough's output (Cook, 1996). This allowed art directors such as John Bryan and Andrew Mazzei to indulge themselves and delight their audiences with European-inspired decorative designs that ranged from rococo to Expressionism. The critical acknowledgment of this aspect of Gainsborough, which drew on debates about cinematic melodrama (see Melodrama, p. 316), was important in establishing that mise en scène and costume can constitute independent discourses that offer excessive visual pleasures to audiences, and linger in the memory as thrilling encounters with opulence associated with sexual transgression.

The Gainsborough costume melodramas represented a high point in the celebration of 'wicked ladies' in British cinema, which according to Harper (1994) ended in 1950 with the studio's demise, when more docile female stereotypes dominated the screen. Their resuscitation had important consequences for the analysis of British cinema, since they highlighted aspects that had been neglected: a fascination with transnational identities; overt representations of gender and sexuality; the false distinction between 'realism' and 'tinsel'; and the importance of visual style.

Selected Reading

Sue Aspinall and Robert Murphy (eds), *BFI Dossier 18: Gainsborough Melodrama*, London, BFI, 1983.

Pam Cook, *Fashioning the Nation: Costume and Identity in British Cinema*, London, BFI Publishing, 1996.

Sue Harper, *Picturing the Past: The Rise and Fall of the British Costume Film*, London, BFI Publishing, 1994.

J. P. Mayer, *British Cinemas and Their Audiences*, London, Dennis Dobson, 1948.

Heritage cinema

GINETTE VINCENDEAU

While costume films have formed an unbroken strand of international films since their origins, the term 'heritage cinema' refers to (initially European) period films that emerged in the 1980s: *Chariots of Fire* (1981), *A Room with a View* (1985), *Babette's Feast/Babettes Gëstebud* (1987), *Jean de Florette* and *Manon des*

Challenging the prevailing masculine order: Margaret Lockwood in *The Wicked Lady*

sources (1986; see case study). Box-office success ensured the continuation of the trend with, among others, *Howards End* (1992), *La Reine Margot* (1994), *Cyrano de Bergerac* (1990), *Elizabeth* (1998), *Shakespeare in Love* (1998), *Le Temps retrouvé/Time Regained* (1999), and productions ranging from Mexico (*Like Water for Chocolate/Como agua para chocolate*, 1992) to the US (*The Age of Innocence*, 1993) and Australia (*The Piano*, 1993).

Heritage films do not constitute a genre. However, they share characteristics that give them unity as far as industry, audiences and critics are concerned. They are made by respected film-makers (for example, the Merchant–Ivory–Jhabvala team), with large budgets, sumptuous production values and stars. The films adapt 'popular classics' (by writers such as Jane Austen, Charles Dickens, E. M. Forster, Alexandre Dumas, Emile Zola and Marcel Pagnol) or draw on the lives of famous artists and monarchs. Importantly, some common traits distinguish them from earlier costume dramas. After the more naturalistic 1960s and 1970s, heritage cinema marked a return to classical narrative and polished mise en scène. They also shifted the focus from story to decor. Earlier costume films used the past as a background for swashbuckling adventure or romance (as in the Gainsborough costume melodramas; see p. 292) without bothering too much about accuracy. By contrast, heritage films are concerned with the minute reconstruction of the past: grand houses, landscapes, rituals, costumes and objects. They echo 'museum aesthetics' and the rise of heritage tourism (Urry, 2002). Generally, they celebrate rather than critique the past. And here lies the main reason for their controversial status.

From the start, heritage films provoked strong attacks. Cairns Craig (2001), Tana Wollen (1991) and Andrew Higson (1993) saw them as reactionary, offering a narrowly English, white and bourgeois vision of the British past – partly linked to an audience perceived as middlebrow, middle-aged and middle class. Higson (1996; 2003), the most prolific heritage cinema critic, also argued that the lavish mise en scène inhibited any subversive discourse, even in apparently trenchant narratives (see also Hill, 1999). This conservativeness was linked to the Thatcher years, fostering a nostalgic gaze at an idealised past in order to avoid present realities – although this British-centric perspective does not necessarily translate to other national cinemas, notably French (Powrie, 1997; Vincendeau, 2001a). The films' pastiche of the past was also seen as failure of imagination, and heritage cinema adduced to the postmodern obliteration of history (Jameson, 1991).

Delirious postmodern melange: the intense visual excitement of costume in Baz Luhrmann's *Moulin Rouge!*

Equally polemical counter-views emerged. First, echoing Raphael Samuel's *Theatres of Memory* (1994), heritage films were seen as a possible forum for a popular history 'from below' (Light, 1991), and the films' earlier critics were accused of elitism. Gender was another line of counter-attack. Dyer (2001), Monk (2001; 2002) and Pidduck (2001; 2004) noted that heritage films were open to women and gay writers, and to a sympathetic representation of homosexuality. They also reclaimed the films' strong woman-centred nature, against the misogyny of critics who saw their address to a 'feminine' audience as a weakness.

Along with the increased internationalisation of heritage films, arguably a 'post-heritage' phase has been reached, in which decorous, middlebrow stories are challenged or 'invigorated' by higher levels of sex, violence and politics in films such as *Elizabeth* and *La Reine Margot* (Monk, 2001; 2002; Pidduck, 2001; 2004). Nevertheless, the successful *Sense and Sensibility* (1995) and *Pride & Prejudice* (2005) show that women-orientated, lovingly crafted recreations of the classic literary heritage can also contain feminist discourses and address young, modern audiences.

Selected Reading

Andrew Higson, *English Heritage, English Cinema: Costume Drama since 1980*, Oxford and New York, Oxford University Press, 2003.

Julianne Pidduck, *Contemporary Costume Film: Space, Place and the Past*, London, BFI Publishing, 2004.

Ginette Vincendeau (ed.), *Film/Literature/Heritage: A Sight and Sound Reader*, London, BFI Publishing, 2001b.

Tana Wollen, 'Nostalgic screen fictions', in Corner and Harvey (eds), *Enterprise and Heritage: Crosscurrents of National Culture*, London and New York, Routledge, 1991.

Contemporary costume drama

PAM COOK

Although costume is important to all cinema and to every genre, it takes on particular significance in costume drama, where its spectacular and symbolic dimensions are brought to the fore, often at the expense of narrative. The classic western and gangster film secure authenticity by referring to documented historical evidence, even though they reconstruct an imaginary past (see Genre, p. 252). Costume drama, despite its dependence on extensive research and advice from consultants, and despite its setting in the historical past, to a greater or lesser extent eschews authenticity in favour of fantasy. It is driven by visual display rather than historical veracity, which means that even in its more transparent or realist modes its primary aim is to generate an aesthetic and emotional response from viewers. A central element of its appeal is nostalgia: it recreates the past as a pleasurable zone where escapist fantasies can be enjoyed. Even those films that have been perceived as motivated by 'serious' intent (such as the Merchant–Ivory–Jhabvala literary adaptations) reveal a tension between their seductive visuals and their presumed high-culture aspirations (see Higson, 1993; Heritage cinema, p. 292).

This tension is reinforced by another. Costume's function as indicator of period is not necessarily legible to audiences, who may have rudimentary knowledge of the history of dress. Designers overcome this by incorporating recognisable contemporary fashion into period design, creating a hybrid of modern and historical styles. Thus the past recreated in costume drama is deliberately anachronistic, interleaving 'today' with 'yesterday'. This conforms to Pierre Sorlin's (1983) observation that history in cinema is always an amalgam of past and present. Sorlin also claimed that such representations influence our ideas of 'proper' history. It is feasible, then, that costume drama's emphasis on the affective dimensions of historical reconstructions could enlighten viewers about the psychological and emotional investments involved in creating history. This is not to devalue proper history, but to acknowledge the role played by the imagination in its execution (see Cook, 2005).

Contemporary costume dramas cover a range of subgenres or cycles: biopics (*Finding Neverland*, 2004; *Miss Potter*, 2006; *Factory Girl*, 2006; *Becoming Jane*, 2007); epics (*Alexander*, 2004; *Troy*, 2004; *The New World*, 2005); musicals (*Moulin Rouge!*, 2001; *Dreamgirls*, 2006); swashbucklers (*Master and Commander: The Far Side of the World*, 2003; *House of Flying Daggers/Shi Mian Mai Fu*, 2004); and literary adaptations (*Memoirs of a Geisha*, 2005; *A Cock and Bull Story*, 2005; *Perfume: The Story of a Murderer*, 2006) among them. This diverse collection is united by spectacular visual design, an emphasis on personal and intimate relationships, and a creative play with source materials. Many of them are popular 'event' movies, evident in their high production values and intensive marketing campaigns, but they also cross over to art-house audiences, not just because of their high-culture connotations, but because of their sophisticated use of the conventions of period drama. The costume drama has always been a knowing and self-reflexive genre; arguably its preoccupation with image, style and form has come into its own in the post-modern era (see Pidduck, 2004).

Selected Reading

Pam Cook, *Screening the Past: Memory and Nostalgia in Cinema*, Oxford and London, Routledge, 2005.

Julianne Pidduck, *Contemporary Costume Film: Space, Place and the Past*, London, BFI Publishing, 2004.

Pierre Sorlin, *The Film in History: Re-staging the Past*, Oxford, Blackwell Publishers, 1983.

The Wicked Lady (UK 1945 *p.c* – Gainsborough Pictures; *d* – Leslie Arliss)

Set in Restoration England, *The Wicked Lady* concerns the exploits of Lady Barbara Skelton (Margaret Lockwood), a woman who steals her best friend's fiancé and then becomes bored with her marriage. To find excitement and adventure, she pretends to be a highwayman, taking to the road each night, eventually linking up with Jerry Jackson (James Mason), a notorious highwayman with whom she has a sexual relationship. She is presented as a ruthless murderer who stops at nothing to get her way; the narrative punishes her for these transgressions with her eventual death. Lockwood's performance grants her some sympathy, but above all she comes across as a fascinating and dynamic personality. Her presentation as a 'wicked' character who challenges convention is visualised by her costume, designed by Elizabeth Haffenden.

As Harper (1994) has noted, Lockwood's first appearance on screen is marked by visual opulence. Silk and fur are used to create a costume resplendent with sexual symbolism, with its vulval pleats and folds, motifs that are echoed in her 'vortex' hairstyle and other dresses. This excessive femininity is contrasted with her more masculine 'action' costuming when she is on the road with Jerry, her sexual ambiguity here providing further confirmation of her relish in challenging social norms. In this way, the film establishes a compelling 'costume discourse' that counters the more conservative narrative closure intended by the scriptwriters.

SARAH STREET

Backward glance: Emmanuelle Béart in *Manon des Sources*

Jean de Florette/Manon des sources (France/Italy/Switzerland 1986 *p.c* – Renn Productions/ Films A2/Rai Due/DD Films/ Télévision Suisse-Romande (TSR)/Antenne 2/Investimage/ Cofimage; *d* – Claude Berri)

This two-part rural melodrama marked the debut of French heritage cinema. The lavish super-productions featured major players: Gérard Depardieu, Yves Montand, Daniel Auteuil and Emmanuelle Béart, but arguably their true 'stars' are the writer Marcel Pagnol and the landscape. *Jean de Florette* and *Manon des sources* are based on Pagnol's Provençal novels, one of which (*Manon*) he had himself filmed in 1953, in the hills behind his childhood village. Modernisation meant that Claude Berri had to find more remote spots.

Rather than the middle-class milieu of the British heritage films, *Florette* and *Manon* reach back to French rural roots in the interwar period, precisely when they were vanishing. Berri casts a backward glance at settings that, in the meantime, have become prime tourist destinations, a virtual open-air museum. *Florette* and *Manon* have been seen as highly nostalgic and celebratory, yet on close inspection they offer a dystopian portrayal of the farmers as grasping, cunning and treacherous. The discrepancy between glorious mise en scène and dark narrative is particularly marked, though it did not stop *Cahiers du Cinéma* from attacking the films as 'too academic'. Nor did it prevent the films from attracting huge audiences (7.3 million and 6.6 million spectators respectively in France alone) and generating quasi-sequels, from *La Gloire de mon père* (1990) and *Le Château de ma mère* (1991), based on Pagnol's memoirs, to Stella Artois commercials. Twenty years on, *Florette* and *Manon* still participate in the Provence and Pagnol tourist industry.

GINETTE VINCENDEAU

Moulin Rouge! (USA/Australia 2001 *p.c* – 20th Century Fox/Bazmark; *d* – Baz Luhrmann)

Moulin Rouge! is an example of the convergence of costume drama with the musical, resulting in a delirious postmodern melange of sounds and images that consciously collapses boundaries of time and place. It occupies a position at the extreme edge of the costume drama spectrum, where the most stylised examples belong. There is not a single frame that does not wear its irony on its sleeve; yet it does not sacrifice affect, and subjects the viewer to a rollercoaster experience of mixed emotions.

The film was nominated for eight Academy Awards and won two: Best Art Direction and Best Costume Design, reflecting the prominence of visual design in the production, but also recognising its extraordinary inventiveness. Designer Catherine Martin's costumes and sets were based on meticulous research into late-nineteenth-century styles, sourced from archive photographs and paintings, and then mapped onto contemporary fashions to produce a modern, multi-layered version of turn-of-the-century bohemian Paris. The Moulin Rouge interiors were recreated using dramatic colour, texture and lighting to invoke an exotic, eroticised ambience that transmitted the intense visual excitement that characterised this period of cultural and technological change. At the same time, images borrowed from classic cinema (most visible in Nicole Kidman's costumes recalling Marilyn Monroe, Marlene Dietrich and Rita Hayworth) etched further layers of representation, reminding viewers that the past is only accessible through such processes of recycling. Besides its sophisticated use of visual design, *Moulin Rouge!* is notable for its relentless motion, epitomising the forward rush to modernity that has devastating effects on the lives of its protagonists.

PAM COOK

Pride & Prejudice (USA/UK/France 2005 *p.c* – Universal/Scion Films/Working Title/ Studio Canal; *d* – Joe Wright)

This cinematic version of Jane Austen's most famous novel came ten years after the 1995 BBC television mini-series and one year after the Bollywood-style spoof, *Bride & Prejudice* (2004). *Pride & Prejudice* is a perfect example of heritage mise en scène in its deployment of bucolic English landscape and great houses; indeed, architectural historians criticised its 'overkill' number of stately homes (including Chatsworth House, Haddon Hall and Stourhead Gardens). From the 'humble' Bennet home to Darcy's palace, *Pride & Prejudice* features superb interiors in self-consciously painterly compositions, their visual splendour a perfect setting for the romantic music, the attractive costumes and upper-class rituals (balls, tea parties, dinners). Yet it combines these classic heritage features with an appeal to a young audience, notably through the casting of Keira Knightley as Elizabeth Bennet and a gesture towards realistic detail – the actresses wear little visible make-up, and hairstyles are relatively dishevelled.

Unlike Patricia Rozema's *Mansfield Park* (1999), this version of *Pride & Prejudice* has no political exposé of the sources of aristocratic wealth. Instead, the film artfully points out the modern status of these great houses, as Elizabeth sees Darcy's home on the day it is 'open for visits'. In contrast to Emma Thompson's feminist adaptation of *Sense and Sensibility* (1995), *Pride & Prejudice* (which she co-scripted) recasts the seminal Austen text about the marriage-market into a 'rom-com', in line with the previous work of production company Working Title, who advertised the film as 'from the makers of *Bridget Jones's Diary*'. It seems the strategy of reaching a wide audience worked, as *Pride & Prejudice* grossed over £14 million in the UK alone.

GINETTE VINCENDEAU

Marie Antoinette (Japan/France/USA 2006 *p.c* – Columbia/Pricel/Tohokushinsha/American Zoetrope; *d* – Sofia Coppola)

Like *Moulin Rouge!*, *Marie Antoinette* set out to reinvent the period costume film. In interviews, Coppola announced her intention of making a personal film that created an intimate portrait of the young Marie Antoinette that would be very different from the conventional biopic, and would dispel many of the myths surrounding its heroine. It was an ambitious production, shot on location at Versailles, where production designer K. K. Barrett embellished the palace's imposing surroundings with pretty, ultra-feminine decor, props and fashions, creating a stylised environment that visualised Marie Antoinette's youthful perspective. Colour design privileged light, pastel shades, while Milena Canonero's Oscar-winning costumes

A fresh look at the past: Kirsten Dunst in Sofia Coppola's *Marie Antoinette*, which set out to reinvent the biopic

emphasised symbolic, affective and emotional aspects, and, like the music soundtrack, mixed period and modern styles. The results were controversial, with critical opinion split between those who condemned Coppola's 'frothy' approach to history for its lack of substance, and those who admired the film's creative reinvention of the past.

These debates crystallise the ambivalence surrounding costume drama; on one hand, the spectacular staging of history is desired; on the other, taking too many liberties runs the risk of travestying the past. Yet it is precisely this tension between dramatic spectacle and authenticity that drives contemporary costume dramas, and provides fertile ground for discussion of history and representation, and the processes of historical reconstruction. *Marie Antoinette* was also distinguished by an intensive publicity campaign covering many different media, from websites, DVD and CD production to television and fashion tie-ins with magazines such as *Vanity Fair*, *Vogue* and *Dazed and Confused*, confirming the film's and Coppola's reputation as contemporary, stylish and cool.

PAM COOK

EXPLOITATION CINEMA

LINDA RUTH WILLIAMS

Exploitation film has a long history in world cinema. Despite differences of opinion about exactly who or what is being exploited, the term 'exploitation' in its loosest form has wide cultural currency. An exploitation aesthetic, drawn as much from lurid poster and promotional campaigns as from the content of films such as *Reefer Madness* (1938), *The Tingler* (1959) or *Blood Feast* (1963), has infiltrated mainstream fashion, art and music as insistently as it has studio film-making. Exploitation cinema is usually defined as a low-budget form of film-making that 'exploits' particular sensational, shocking and taboo subjects (violence, perversion, drugs, cruelty, abnormality, sex and its perils) in genre feature film or pseudo-documentary format. Because exploitation films often excite the curiosity of the viewer or provoke active physical responses (lust, disgust, terror), these thrill-films (and their makers) have been seen as 'exploiting' the desire of audiences to indulge in guilty cultural pleasures. The origin of the term, however, derives from the bold marketing techniques early exploitation producers deployed in promoting their product, promising stimulating stories 'ripped from the pages of life'.

Indeed, exploitation can be defined by its rich history of distinct forms of exhibition, from the carnival sideshow to the grindhouse cinema to the sex shop. Sometimes exploitation distribution practices have influenced the mainstream, from 'four walling' to saturation booking, utilised first by 'exploiteers' (Schaefer, 1999, p. 2) 'to generate quick profits before negative word of mouth could set in' (Cook, 2002, p. 16) before becoming common practice in Hollywood from the 1970s onwards. The opportunity offered for delivering extreme spectacle directly into the living room by the domestic VCR has also been particularly valuable for fringe film-makers. Working at the very cheapest end of low-budget production, exploitation cinema has reacted swiftly to moral panics and social scandal, making quickie movies for popular audiences about the most sensational and anxious topics of their moment (for example, Edward D. Wood's *Glen or Glenda*, 1954, which capitalised on sex-change news stories). These films are prone to attracting a cult audience, partly because of their extreme or perverse subject matter, partly because micro-budgets and fast turnaround make for low production values, resulting in a 'so bad it's good' aesthetic. Cult audiences have delighted in viewing oppositionally, attracted rather than put off by wobbly scenery, wooden acting and poor scripts. Judgments of high artistic quality have no place in the reception of exploitation cinema. Continuing fondness for Wood's films rests entirely on his curious aesthetic and the poverty of his technique.

Exploitation cinema is also discussed in the context of cult cinema because of the fan cultures it elicits. Horror, docu-

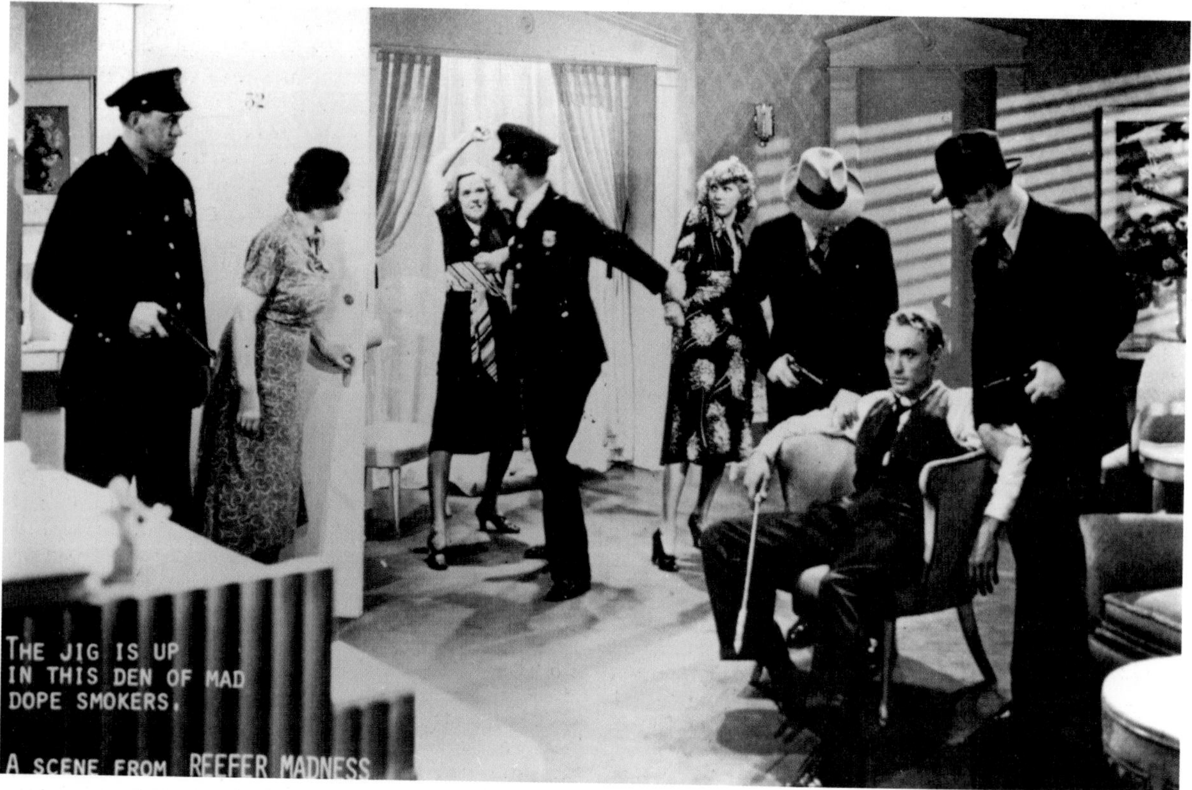

Reefer Madness aka *Tell Your Children*: the dangers of drugs exposed

horror and cannibal movies (*The Last House on the Left*, 1972; *Faces of Death*, 1978; *Cannibal Holocaust*, 1979) have generated 'paracinematic' subcultures of audience response (Sconce, 1995) linked to their extreme gross-out spectacles. That in some territories 'extreme' titles have been refused a classification or banned due to social worries about 'harm' and 'effects' (particularly in relation to children) has meant that exploitation cinema has acquired an even more intense aura of the forbidden. Exploitation has also annexed the softer face of weirdness, in the form of kitsch or camp, displayed in rock 'n' roll movies (see also Teenpics, p. 367), monster movies and sexploitation, and engendering an ironic counter-taste response to cheap film-making.

However, exploitation historian Eric Schaefer argues that there is a significant difference between B-movie producers from the classical period and exploitation film-makers proper, who are even further down the cinematic food chain. The origins of exploitation lie in the 1920s, with the term first being used in print in the early 1930s (Schaefer, 1999, pp. 3–4). Schaefer defines the form through a set of specific exhibition, distribution and stylistic practices that connect means of production (the lowest of budgets, unskilled crew and performers, short production schedules) to the 'threadbare' look of the resulting films. These early independent exploiteers also strayed from mainstream Hollywood's regulation codes, churning out films focused on subjects prohibited in both A and B production. By the 1950s, when independent production houses began to make movies tailored to drive-in and grindhouse youth audiences, and names such as Sam Arkoff and Roger Corman were put on the map, the terms of taboo had shifted, as they would again in the early 1970s following the MPAA's new classification categories, in the wake of which hardcore and harder violence found a foothold in more conventional locations. Since the 1960s, then, the history of exploitation has been on the one hand concerned with the pursuit of more extreme spectacle and on the other a story of mainstream absorption of exploitation's stock-in-trade.

Exploitation subgenres

Exploitation film history in the US can been understood as developing through the rise and fall of certain subgenres. Schaefer (1999) discusses white slave pictures in the teens and 1920s as proto-exploitation titles, while the main body of his history, from the 1930s to the late 1950s, examines a diverse group of subgenres, including drug films (for example, *Assassin of Youth*, 1937; *She Shoulda Said 'No!'*, 1949); health-related morality stories (*Damaged Goods/Marriage Forbidden*, 1937; *Mom and Dad*, 1947); nudist films (*The Unashamed*, 1938; *Garden of Eden*, 1954); 'exotic' films (*Virgins of Bali*, 1932; *Lash of the Penitentes*, 1937); and atrocity films (*Halfway to Hell*, 1954; *Mau Mau*, 1954). While purporting to educate about the perils of whichever vice or fringe phenomenon they examine, such titles simultaneously deliver a vicarious pleasure in salacious excess. This has remained a trait of the form, even in the ostensibly more liberated, less guilt-fuelled post-1970s period.

But when histories such as Schaefer's are read in light of exploitation since 1960, it is also clear that this is an evolving form that has long 'exploited' its own ancestry for the most marketable ideas. The ethnographically related exotic film, featuring naked 'natives' or 'savage' practices in geographically Other locales, developed into the 'mondo' (or shockumentary) movie, while the atrocity film, focusing more on violence and death than vice and sex, is read as ancestor of both mondo and the gore film. The teenpics and creature features of the 1950s also have precedents in earlier movies, while prefiguring post-1970s disaster movies and the resurgence of sci-fi. The roots of 1960s sexploitation are in earlier burlesque forms, yet sex-flicks such as Doris Wishman's nudist films (*Nude on the Moon*, 1961; *Gentlemen Prefer Nature Girls*, 1962) or her later collaboration with Chesty Morgan, or Russ Meyer's notorious breast-fests (*Faster, Pussycat! Kill! Kill!*, 1966; *Mondo Topless*, 1966; *Vixen!*, 1968), also exploit the opportunity of a more liberated climate, and look forward to subsequent softcore genres such as women-in-prison films and the erotic thriller, as well as to hardcore itself (see Gorfinkel, 2000; Bowen, 1997; Luckett, 2003; Crane, 2000. Bowen calls Wishman 'the most prolific woman filmmaker of the sound era', p. 66).

Post-1970, a distinct new roster of exploitation genres, such as blaxploitation, splatter horror and the rape-revenge film, promised new futures for old cinematic sensations. The US was always a key import market for exploitation material from other territories, but this became more intense from the 1960s onwards, with vogues for genres such as the martial arts film (Hong Kong), the wrestling film (Mexico), the aforementioned mondo movie (Italy and Germany as well as the US), softcore 'erotic' cinema (France, UK and Hong Kong) and pornography (Scandinavia). It should also be noted that high-culture art films from Europe and Asia were sometimes distributed in the US by independent labels associated with exploitation cinema, blurring the line between high and low (see Betz, 2003, pp. 217–18).

Exploitation and the mainstream

That exploitation cinema is a ready resource for more mainstream, studio-funded products has long characterised discussion of its history. The case of Corman – perhaps the most celebrated name associated with exploitation genres – is interesting here. Corman came to prominence in the 1950s as a producer/director for low-budget independent American International Pictures (AIP), making teenpics (*Sorority Girl*, 1957), sci-fi (*It Conquered the World*, 1956) and creature-features (*Attack of the Crab Monsters*, 1957), before directing a celebrated series of Edgar Allan Poe adaptations in the early 1960s, then developing fodder more in tune with a mid-60s fascination with drugs and motorcycle culture (*The Wild Angels*, 1966; *The Trip*, 1967; *Gas-s-s-s*, 1970). As one of US cinema's most prolific film-makers, Corman has focused mostly on production since the 1970s under the auspices of his own companies, New World, Concorde and New Horizons. He is also known for his nurturing of hot new talent, poached from film school because they were enthusiastic as well as cheap (see also Authorship and cinema, p. 416). Corman protégés (Francis Ford Coppola, Martin Scorsese, Jack Nicholson *et al.*) are the best-known examples of the creative exchange between high/low film-making strata that has characterised exploitation/mainstream history. However, Corman has also always encouraged women: the 'Corman alternative film school' provided what Williams calls 'an alternative "off-Hollywood" route' for film-makers such as Stephanie Rothman, Amy Holden Jones and Katt Shea, 'which has gone some way towards compensating for the prevailing sexism of the mainstream industry' (Williams, 2006, p. 306). Corman's shift of emphasis since the 1970s has often been attributed to a sense that the post-*Jaws* blockbuster ate up the ideas of standard Corman-esque sensation fodder, but this must be read in light of Schaefer's (1999) argument that the better-funded independents of the 1950s (of which Corman was a part) had themselves already contributed

John Boorman's *Deliverance* traded on the sensational nastiness of previously fringe forms of exploitation

to the death of earlier exploitation cinema, by reworking 'classical' exploiteers' stock-in-trade in a way that would be friendlier to a drive-in youth culture.

The 'mainstreamisation' of exploitation material and distribution tactics since the late 1960s is a well-discussed aspect of US cinema. In October 1968, a new ratings system was introduced in the US, overseen by CARA (the Code and Rating Administration; after 1977 the Classification and Rating Administration), which effectively legitimised representations of exploitation-style material (sex and violence) in mainstream locations and movies. Films such as *The Exorcist* (1973), *Deliverance* (1972) and *Straw Dogs* (1971) traded on the sensational nastiness of previously fringe forms; *Jaws* (1975) was the first proto-blockbuster to deploy exploitation pre-release marketing tactics and saturation booking. Why endure the grindhouse if you could see creature-features and vigilante flicks at your local mall? Exploitation's traditional stomping-ground was under threat. But the latter-day exploiteer is nothing if not tenacious. When *Jaws* absorbed his material and audiences, he developed new ones. New genres and subgenres evolved (blaxploitation, the martial arts film), while others were strengthened by fracturing into what we might loosely call new forms of the A- and B-feature, in horror, fantasy and sexual cinema. The rise of the blockbuster must then be seen as an opportunity as much as it was a threat to small-scale independent producers. Cook states that: 'In the twelve months between June 1975 and June 1976, 300 independent films were produced, representing an investment of $100 million outside the majors. Of these, some 80 percent were R- and PG-rated action-adventure or exploitation dramas' (Cook, 2002, p. 19).

If the blockbuster, made by now studio-based film-makers who had learned their trade with Corman, annexed sci-fi, fantasy and the sequel, a new development was just around the corner that would offer more lucrative opportunities. The story of exploitation cinema post-1975 (when Sony introduced the first home-viewing video and recording system) must largely be told in the context of the radical transformation in exhibition opportunities and the distinct audiences that home viewing enabled (see also New distribution, exhibition and reception contexts, p. 75). Video (and later DVD, PC and cable) facilitated different kinds of viewing pleasure, and allowed low-budget film-makers to flourish in new ways. The 'exploitation' of this opportunity has meant that formerly fringe forms of film-making now constitute huge sections of the industry. Some exploitation genres in particular (hardcore porn, gross-out schlock horror) were tailor-made, or could be tailored to, the privacy of domesticity, or the intimacy of watching with a partner or a group of peers (exploitation, however mainstreamed, is not family fare). The 1980s and 1990s were then a 'boom or bust' time for film-makers working on a shoestring but with the potential to make a huge profit; production and distribution companies rose and fell on the crest of this home-viewing gold rush.

The pattern of international distribution of 'taboo' materials is complex and region-specific, inflected by local censorship and cultural/religious practices. Nevertheless, the move from exhibition in the limited theatrical locations traditionally associated with exploitation genres to the presence of a VCR in (nearly) every living room proved an unprecedented opportunity. Williams (2005, pp. 253–71) discusses the importance of the sofa as reception space for sexual material, and both hard and softcore pornography are now made with the privacy of home or hotel room in mind. However, the stratification of exhibition across public and private spaces (cinemas on the one hand, and cable/VCR/pay-per-view on the other) has only augmented the (involuntary, plagiarised or acknowledged) exchange of material and personnel between exploitation 'fringe' and studio 'centre'.

So the mutual feeding frenzy between major and exploitation producers continues: Carol J. Clover emphasises the interrelationship of influence between low- and high-budget horror, focusing on how themes and issues dealt with in an unrefined way at the fringes find their way to the mainstream. This relationship is articulated via a psycho-cultural model of avowed consciousness (mainstream cinema) and the disavowed-repressed (exploitation, subsumed by mainstream cinema): horror, then, trades in images of repression, and is itself the repressed of mainstream film-making (Clover, 1992a, p. 20). According to Clover, this is underpinned by a relationship of influence whereby the mainstream 'exploits' as its resource fringe cinematic tropes:

> The direction of trickle here is up, not down. ... No aficionado can see *The Silence of the Lambs* or *Mortal Thoughts* without thinking of the low-budget, often harsh and awkward but sometimes deeply energetic films that preceded them by a decade or more – films that said it all, and in flatter terms, and on a shoestring. (1992b, p. 18)

Kim Newman also makes the point that working outside of the strictures of A-feature pressures has always meant that a certain level of experimentation could prevail (Newman, 1996, p. 513). Mainstream genres thus repress the energies of 'low' exploitation films while simultaneously feeding off their ideas and images, which are recycled in a safe, sanitised form.

The history of sexual cinema charts a similar course, though the 'class' stratification here is more complex than the high/low dynamic that Clover examines (studio-funded horror/exploitation slasher). The rise of the hardcore pornography industry is the single most significant development in exploitation film-making in the post-classical period: 'At $10 billion, porn is no longer a sideshow to the mainstream like, say, the $600 million Broadway theatre industry – it is the mainstream' (Rich, 2001, p. 51). Throughout the 1960s, intrepid distributors were finding a niche in US markets for Scandinavian films containing unsimulated sexual images (*I Am Curious – Yellow/Jag är nyfiken – gul*, 1967), sometimes legitimised by a European art-film aura, at other times legitimised by the presence of a pseudo-doctor figure narrating a reassuring message, or travelogue footage giving a socially important guise or educative veneer to exploitation fodder (see Williams, 1991, pp. 96–8; Cook, 2002, pp. 271–4). Such films are understood to have paved the way for the popular cultural explosion of what came to be known as 'porno-chic': hardcore pornography, heralded by the release of *Deep Throat* in 1972, made briefly fashionable for 'ordinary' middle-class audiences. The rest is history: hardcore survived and thrived on a hugely lucrative transition to video and then DVD, and is now one of the biggest sectors of the US entertainment industry. Exploitation it remains; fringe it certainly is not.

Parallel to this is the softcore industry, first developed through 'sexploitation' film-making in the 1960s and 1970s, and then in the new subgenres of the erotic thriller and sexually inflected gore cinema. Since the 1990s, hardcore has garnered increasingly sophisticated critical attention (see, for example, Williams, 1991; 2004; Church Gibson, 2003; Lehman, 2006). However, it is softcore that is 'the Cinderella of sexual theory' (Williams, 2005, p. 270), provoking both the guiltiest audience pleasures (Andrews, 2006, p. 257) and the least critical attention of all exploitation genres (see also Schaefer, 2008; Sconce, 2007).

Clover's important study was one of the highlights of a wave of serious academic readings of trash aesthetics in general and horror in particular, and there has been a rash of histories pleading the progressive case for contemporary exploitation since 2000 (see Quarles, 1993; McDonagh, 1996; Read, 2000; Mendik and Harper, 2000; Mendik and Schneider, 2002; Jancovich *et al.*, 2003). Williams and Andrews (2006) also read their exploitation subject matter as, if not politically progressive, then at least challenging the psycho-sexual politics of Hollywood film-making. The film studies precedent for counter-reading is Pam Cook's 1976 *Screen* article, updated in 2005. But we might also see exploitation cinema as a form that has long been read against the grain by popular audiences, from early 'sex hygiene film' viewers ignoring warnings against venereal disease while relishing forbidden spectacle, to dope-fuelled hippies of 1960s counter-culture enjoying *Reefer Madness* despite its ostensible condemnation of drug use. In an era in which mainstream film-makers can make a $53 million multiplex homage to sleaze entitled *Grindhouse* (Quentin Tarantino and Robert Rodriguez's 2007 collaboration), perhaps exploitation cinema no longer needs to be brought in from the cold.

Selected Reading

Carol J. Clover, *Men, Women and Chain Saws*, Princeton, NJ, Princeton University Press, 1992a.

Mark Jancovich, Antonio Lázaro Reboll, Julian Stringer and Andy Willis (eds), *Defining Cult Movies: The Cultural Politics of Oppositional Taste*, Manchester, Manchester University Press, 2003.

Kim Newman, 'Exploitation and the mainstream', in Nowell-Smith (ed.), *The Oxford History of World Cinema*, Oxford, Oxford University Press, 1996.

Eric Schaefer, *'Bold! Daring! Shocking! True!': A History of Exploitation Films, 1919–1959*, Durham and London, Duke University Press, 1999.

Blaxploitation

TOMMY L. LOTT

In cinema studies, blaxploitation is a term often used dismissively to refer to a formulaic style of commercial film-making employed by Hollywood studios in the early 1970s to capitalise on an untapped black audience that constituted one-third of the total market. The African-American rebellion, with its heightened black consciousness, provided the social, cultural and political context for the birth of this new black cinema. The emphasis many scholars have placed on periodi economic shifts in the movie industry to explain the green-lighting of blaxploitation-style films again in the early 1980s and early 1990s overshadows the fact that a younger generation of black and white film-makers have reclaimed classic blaxploitation aesthetics. Although the industry's economic shifts have played a key role, economic factors alone cannot account for the persistence and appeal of blaxploitation in contemporary film-making (Ward, 1976; Guerrero, 1993; Reid, 1993; Rhines, 1996).

Criticism of blaxploitation cinema gravitates towards blaming Hollywood studios. While this line may apply to a group of formulaic black hero films that were crafted by white writers and directors to market to black audiences during the early 1970s (Reid, 1993), it seems inappropriate to a black independent production such as *Sweet Sweetback's Baad Asssss Song* (1971). It is also important to acknowledge that studio films such as *Shaft* (1971) and *Superfly* (1972) were made by black film-makers during the same period. The idea that white-orientated studios

Criticised for its alignment with the establishment: Richard Roundtree in Gordon Parks's blaxploitation classic *Shaft*

were prone to manufacture superficial caricatures of black life is a standard critique of blaxploitation films (Massood, 2003). Underlying this argument is the idea of an alternative black cinema devoted to a more authentic representation. Too often this demand for authenticity trades on a contested positive-negative image dichotomy (Yearwood, 1982; Taylor, 1988).

The controversy surrounding 1970s blaxploitation films emanated from several quarters within the black community. In the Black Panther party's newspaper, Huey Newton (1971) argued that *Sweetback* succeeded in portraying the development of a collective revolutionary consciousness in the black lumpenproletariat. The array of positive image advocates who were opposed to the sex and violence in the film included members of an assimilation-minded black middle class, as well as cultural nationalists. This moral debate coincided with the emergence of a black independent film movement focused on combating the studios' one-dimensional image of black people. Politically conscious and college-trained, this new generation of black film-makers responded with a battery of independent productions that aimed to provide an alternative. Black film-makers who worked with Bill Greaves on the Public Broadcasting Station's *Black Journal* (1969–71) in New York and those associated with UCLA's Third Cinema collective employed cinema as a mode of political art and cultural expression that aimed to educate more than to entertain black audiences (Taylor, 1986; Lott, 1999a). The intellectual tone of such work distanced black audiences, but some of the films have had a lasting influence on the present generation of black film-makers. Over the past three decades, structural changes in the film industry, along with advancements in digital technology, have contributed to the waning of this movement. In terms of numbers of black films produced by studios, nothing has come close to the black film cycle of the 1970s. Nonetheless, blaxploitation aesthetics continue to thrive in mainstream films such as Quentin Tarantino's *Jackie Brown* (1997) or John Singleton's *Shaft* (2000).

The polarities that once existed between independent and commercial film-making have been cross-pollinated by a younger generation of black film-makers bent on reaching a mainstream audience. HBO films such as Joe Brewster's *The Killing Zone* (2003) and Cheryl Dunye's *Stranger Inside* (2001) draw on both independent and commercial cinema. Another kind of interbreeding involves gangsta rap music and blaxploitation cinema, represented by films such as Hype Williams's *Belly* (1998), Master P's *I'm Bout It* (1997), the Hughes brothers' *Menace*

Pam Grier as Jackie Brown in Tarantino's blaxploitation homage

Samuel L. Jackson in John Singleton's remake of *Shaft*

II Society (1993) and Ernest R. Dickerson's *Never Die Alone* (2004). Prior to the 1960s, black urban folklore had been articulated through an oral rap tradition involving mainly music and poetry. Along with gangsta rappers, the new wave of blaxploitation film-makers have become the visual progenitors of the black urban folklore expressed in 'ghettocentric' rap music. The resonance of films such as *Sweetback* and *Superfly* with black audiences, then and now, is due to the fact that the street hustler and the 'bad nigger' are among the most compelling images in urban black male folklore and in black cinema. Needless to say, it is a masculine folklore filled with the tricksterism of pimps and hustlers who are more than willing to subordinate women and exploit other black people. While this aspect was tempered somewhat by the inclusion of a female version of the black hero in films such as *Coffy* (1973), *Foxy Brown* (1974) and *Cleopatra Jones* (1973), critics have argued that this image is consistent with dominant views of black women. A further transition occurred with films such as *Superfly T.N.T.* (1973), *Shaft in Africa* (1973) and *Black Mama, White Mama* (1973) as blaxploitation film-making shifted from location shooting in inner cities to international settings.

The golden age of blaxploitation cinema is often associated with the boom in black movies that occurred between 1970 and 1974 (Murray, 1973; Leab, 1975; Bogle, 2003; Guerrero, 1993; Rhines, 1996). Three of the classic films from this period, *Sweetback*, *Shaft* and *Super Fly*, have been criticised for employing a black hero formula that simply reverses the Hollywood master narrative (Leab, 1975; Bogle, 2003). Critics sometimes read *Shaft* and *Superfly* as studio attempts to co-opt *Sweetback*'s political ideology of rebellion, resulting in an analysis that reduces all three films to sex, drugs and violence (for example, Bogle, 2003). However, Gordon Parks Jr's protagonist in *Super Fly*, who successfully challenges a corrupt system of law enforcement, is a far cry from Gordon Parks Sr's black detective in *Shaft*, who validates that system. Indeed, a highlight of the *Superfly* narrative for black audiences is its latent critique of Shaft's alignment with the establishment. There is also much to learn from paying closer attention to black films produced during this period that were outside of the so-called action genre, as well as many studio productions that do not fit the black hero formula (Cripps, 1978; Massood, 2003). Greater attention to the diversity of studio films from this era, as well as to some of the black independent productions, enables a more nuanced account.

Despite the controversy surrounding *Sweetback*, it was a socially conscious black independent production made specifically for a black mass audience – and the response was overwhelmingly favourable. Undoubtedly the hyperbolic images of sex and violence added to the film's entertainment and commercial value. Unlike many later blaxploitation films, however, these were not simply gratuitous features. Van Peebles's film-making style, including his use of the anti-hero, has been likened to Jean-Luc Godard and *Sweetback* has been deemed 'essentially a European art film set in Watts' (see Massood, 2003, p. 95). Van Peebles imbued his urban folk tale about the triumph of an underdog male hustler-criminal with the black revolutionary spirit of the late 1960s to construct, as he claimed, 'a victorious film' (Van Peebles, 1971, p. 36). The financial success of *Sweetback* prompted the studios to begin turning out movies that exploited the black hero formula. According to Nelson George, in 1971 a quarter of all films in production were slated for a black audience (George, 1994, p. 52).

Black music is an essential feature of blaxploitation. In *Sweetback* and *Shaft*, the music combines with the narrative to create a black aesthetic that permeates the visual portrayal of violence, crime, drugs and urban poverty (Howell, 2005; Watkins, 1998). Since the blaxploitation era, a music-based black aesthetic has been employed in more benign films, such as *Wild Style* (1982), *Breakin'* and *Breakin' 2: Electric Boogaloo* (both 1984), *Beat Street* (1984), *Krush Groove* (1985) and *Tougher Than Leather* (1988), that were produced during the rap craze of the 1980s. Ingredients of a black aesthetic closer to 1970s blaxploitation appear in hard-edged mainstream films such as *King of New York* (1990), *The Return of Superfly* (1990) and *Original Gangstas* (1996), as well as in those by New Black Cinema black film-makers, such as *New Jack City* (1991), *Straight Out of Brooklyn* (1991), *Boyz N the Hood* (1991), *Juice* (1992) and *Menace II Society*, that were released during the 1990s black film boom (Watkins, 1998).

Attempts to define the boundaries of blaxploitation open up questions of whether all the studio-produced black films made during this era count as blaxploitation and whether all the independently produced films eschewed the blaxploitation aesthetic. As late as 1979, Jamaa Fanaka, a film student trained at UCLA but an anomaly among the Third Cinema students, released *Penitentiary*, a story about prison boxing that was such a box-office success he went on to make two sequels. His earlier films, squarely in the blaxploitation tradition, included *Welcome Home Brother Charles* (1975) and *Emma Mae* (1976). Another black independent film-maker, Fred Williamson, is well known for playing black hero characters in studio productions such as *Black Caesar* (1973), *Hell Up in Harlem* (1973), *Bucktown* (1975), *The Soul of Nigger Charley* (1973) and *The Legend of Nigger Charley* (1972). Interviewed in Isaac Julien's documentary *Baadasssss Cinema* (2002), he is highly critical of the image of black men in Hollywood films; yet his commitment to the black hero formula is displayed in many of his own independent productions.

The blaxploitation films produced by Williamson and

Fanaka during the blaxploitation era caution against assuming either that black independent film-makers were always against using a blaxploitation aesthetic, or that this was a stance black film-makers working on studio-produced films were unable to take. Melvin Van Peebles's *Watermelon Man* (1970), a comedy about a white bigot who is horrified when he awakens one day to discover that he has turned black, was an independent production for Columbia. Ossie Davis directed *Cotton Comes to Harlem* (1970), a film based on a Chester Himes novel. With strong literary credentials, this film employs a black aesthetic to tell a story about black life in Harlem; nonetheless, it was shot as a farcical comedy. Bill Gunn wrote the screenplay for *The Landlord* (1970), another humorous film set in Harlem. All three went on to direct films during the blaxploitation era.

Ed Guerrero has pointed out that, of the 91 films produced from 1970 to 1973, 'forty-seven can be considered models of the Blaxploitation formula' (Guerrero, 1993, p. 95). If, however, more than half of the studio productions did not fit the formula, this suggests a need to reassess blaxploitation era film-making. After having his first film, *Stop* (1970), shelved by Warner Bros., Bill Gunn secretly shot *Ganja and Hess* (1973) as an art film. It was hailed by critics at the 1973 Cannes Film Festival and is considered by film scholars to be one of the best black films ever made. After directing *Trouble Man* (1972), Ivan Dixon produced and directed *The Spook Who Sat by the Door* (1973), Sam Greenlee's story about black guerrilla warfare. Sidney Poitier directed a western, *Buck and the Preacher* (1971), with the aim of educating audiences about a black presence on the frontier. The Billie Holiday story was the subject of *Lady Sings the Blues* (1972), produced by Motown's Berry Gordy, who later directed *Mahogany* (1975), both of which featured Diana Ross and Billy Dee Williams. Two blaxploitation stars, Ron O'Neal and Bernie Casey, were in *Brothers* (1977), a thinly disguised account of the relationship between black activist Angela Davis and prison revolutionary George Jackson, with music by Taj Mahal. A Negro Ensemble Theatre cast that included Cicely Tyson, James Earl Jones, Glen Turman and Louis Gossett Jr appeared in *The River Niger* (1976), a story about survival in a poor black urban community. This cursory listing shows that the association of blaxploitation-era film-making with action movies is the result of critical attention that has focused on controversial films at the expense of other endeavours.

The action-orientated blaxploitation films that capitalised on *Sweetback*'s success opened the door for films that attempted to expand the black market. Following the success of *Super Fly*, Gordon Parks Jr directed a western, *Thomasine & Bushrod* (1974), and Ron O'Neal directed the *Superfly* sequel, *Superfly T.N.T.*, from a screenplay by Alex Haley, whose Pulitzer Prize-winning novel was the basis for the television mini-series *Roots* (1977). After *Shaft's Big Score!* (1972), Gordon Parks Sr directed *Leadbelly* (1976), a biopic of blues and folk singer Huddie Leadbetter, while besides *Cotton Comes to Harlem* and *Gordon's War* (1973), Ossie Davis directed *Black Girl* (1972) and *Countdown at Kusini* (1976). These independent efforts suffered at the box office due to lack of support from black audiences.

As the blaxploitation era came to an end, there were a number of commercially viable black films aside from those that fit the blaxploitation action genre. Michael Schultz directed black film classics *Cooley High* (1975) and *Car Wash* (1976) and went on to make the politically astute comedy *Which Way Is Up?* (1977), a remake of a 1972 Lina Wertmüller film. In the same year, he made *Greased Lightning*, a fictional biography of black auto racer Wendell Scott. Comedian Richard Pryor's characters in Schultz's films are treated with a dignity that is largely absent in the films Pryor made with white directors. Although the highest-grossing black film of the 1970s was the Sidney Poitier crime comedy *Let's Do It Again* (1975), not all of the commercially viable alternatives to black action films were comedies. There were dramatic productions such as *The Bingo Long Traveling All-Stars & Motor Kings* (1976), a light, but sobering, treatment of racism and the Negro Baseball League, and *Cornbread, Earl and Me* (1975), which remains one of the best dramatic treatments of police violence in the black community.

When considering the impact blaxploitation films have had on subsequent generations of film-makers, distinguishing between economics and aesthetics is paramount, for a contemporary black film can be assimilated to the blaxploitation paradigm by virtue of either. With regard to aesthetics, a film is usually categorised, and dismissed, as blaxploitation when the film-maker is charged with an over-reliance on stereotypical characters in ghetto settings and a gratuitous use of sex and violence. With regard to economics, often the comparison with blaxploitation-era films is made on the basis of the ratio of investment to profit. Ossie Davis's *Cotton Comes to Harlem* fits the blaxploitation paradigm on both criteria. It grossed $15.4 million from an initial investment of $2.2 million, and the use of visual images that resonated with black urban experience were ingredients of a black film-making style that became commonplace in later ghettocentric films (Guerrero, 1993, p. 81). With a closer alliance to the black independent tradition of Oscar Micheaux (see African-American cinema, p. 77), Spencer Williams and Ralph Cooper, Ossie Davis was well aware of the importance of using black culture in black-audience films.

In his comparison of the black film boom of the early 1990s that capitalised on the popularity of gangsta rap with the blaxploitation era, S. Craig Watkins emphasises economic criteria (low budgets, limited distribution and inexpensive marketing) to show a similar pattern of investment-to-profit ratios in both cases (Watkins, 1998, p. 189). This suggests that blaxploitation is primarily a marketing term for what he terms ghettocentric black films. In this economic sense, it can refer to disparate aesthetic strategies employed by black directors in films such as *Boyz N the Hood*, *Straight Out of Brooklyn*, *Menace II Society*, *New Jack City*, *Posse* (1993), *Deep Cover* (1992) and *Jason's Lyric* (1994). For reasons to do with aesthetics, blaxploitation should not be thought of only in terms of a marketing category – and certainly not only a black market. Contemporary versions of 1970s blaxploitation films, whether they are spoofs such as Keenen Ivory Wayans's *I'm Gonna Git You Sucka* (1988) or Malcolm D. Lee's *Undercover Brother* (2002); films that use blaxploitation-style cinematography such as Jim Jarmusch's *Ghost Dog: The Way of the Samurai* (1999) or Quentin Tarantino's *Pulp Fiction* (1994) and *Kill Bill Vol. 1* (2003); or new versions of classics such as *Shaft*, *Superfly* and *Foxy Brown* (1974), are usually aimed at a mainstream market and are expected to compete well with other blockbuster productions.

In retrospect, complaints about the quality of 1970s blaxploitation films based on their low-budget aesthetics seem misguided. Black independent masterpieces such as Julie Dash's *Illusions* (1982), Charles Burnett's *Killer of Sheep* (1977) and Hailé Gerima's *Ashes and Embers* (1982) display film-making acumen of a very high order, despite their low budgets. These black independent film-makers have demonstrated that sometimes the raw, unpolished look of a cheaply made film can be an aesthetic asset.

Selected Reading

Ed Guerrero, *Framing Blackness: The African American Image in Film*, Philadelphia, Temple University Press, 1993.

Paula J. Massood, *Black City Cinema: African American Urban Experiences in Film*, Philadelphia, Temple University Press, 2003.

S. Craig Watkins, *Representing: Hip Hop Culture and the Production of Black Cinema*, Chicago, University of Chicago Press, 1998.

FILM NOIR

JANE ROOT

> Whoever went to the movies with any regularity during 1946 was caught in the midst of Hollywood's profound post-war affection for morbid drama. From January through December deep shadows, clutching hands, exploding revolvers, sadistic villains and heroines tormented with deeply rooted diseases of the mind flashed across the screen in a panting display of psychoneuroses, unsublimated sex and murder most foul. (Quoted in Schatz, 1981, p. 111)

This article from a 1947 *Life* magazine is revealing not only for the way in which, at a time when the genre was still young, it manages to touch on many of what were later to be seen as the essential elements of film noir, but also for the high moral tone it adopts towards 'panting', 'morbid drama'. At a time when few popular American films were taken seriously, concern about the explicitness of the sexuality and, curiously in the light of later work, the 'realism' of the violence of noir, amounted to moral panic. Critics' dislike was compounded by economic snobbery: the low budgets and B-film status of many film noirs were seen as a priori proof that the films were 'trash'. Within this framework, the noir films by émigrés whose earlier work was considered 'art' were seen as particularly lamentable. As documented by Jenkins, it became an English and American critical truism to decry Fritz Lang's decline into the production of what Gavin Lambert, for instance, saw as mere 'workmanlike commerce' (Jenkins, 1981, p. 2).

The major period of noir production is usually taken to run from *The Maltese Falcon* in 1941 to *Touch of Evil* in 1958. Even after this, however, British and American critics failed to take film noir seriously. As Paul Schrader comments, 'For a long time film noir, with its emphasis on corruption and despair, was considered an aberration of the American character. The western, with its moral primitivism, and the gangster film, with its Horatio Alger values, were considered more American than the film noir'. Schrader goes on to suggest that the fundamental reason for the neglect of noir was the importance of visual style to the

The portrait comes to life: Edward G. Robinson and Joan Bennett in Fritz Lang's *The Woman in the Window*

form: 'American critics have been traditionally more interested in theme than style … it was easier for the sociological critics to discuss the themes of the western and the gangster film apart from stylistic analysis than it was to do for the film noir' (Schrader, 1972, p. 13).

In France, the situation was very different. Initially, interest focused on the links between noir films and the writing of the 'hard-boiled' novelists such as Raymond Chandler, Dashiell Hammett, Cornel Woolrich, James M. Cain and Horace McCoy, who all either wrote screenplays or source novels for noir films. The phrase film noir itself derives from the *série noire* books – mainly translations of the above-named American writers. Interestingly, it seems that this examination of writers as one of the sources for film noir became, in the UK and US, a method of ascribing respectability – see, for example, Jenkins's comments on the overvaluation of the role of the literary Hammett in histories of film noir compared with the contribution of, for example, Woolrich (Jenkins, 1982, p. 276).

Equally relevant to the French context was the rise of authorship theory via the *politique des auteurs* (see The *politique des auteurs*, p. 390). The re-evaluation of noir films by particular directors, especially Fritz Lang, John Huston, Nicholas Ray, Sam Fuller and Robert Aldrich, involved a new depth of investigation and, especially, a close examination of mise en scène. The basic aim of such studies was, however, the tracing of continuities across careers rather than the lateral investigation of work produced in particular periods and production contexts. The most interesting questions about noir do not concern the marks of directorial difference. Rather, the crucial issue, as phrased by Silver and Ward, is that of 'cohesiveness': the wide influence of noir across the work of different directors and genres. Silver and Ward take a random sample of seven film noirs and note that 'different directors and cinematographers, of great and small technical reputations, working at seven different studios, completed seven ostensibly unrelated motion pictures with one cohesive visual style' (Silver and Ward, 1981, p. 3).

Although it is generally accepted that crime and criminal acts provide the basis for the majority of noir films and the noir style (see Durgnat, 1974), the influence of noir spreads beyond the gangster/thriller genres influencing melodramas, horror films, detective movies, even (although this would not be universally agreed) westerns and musicals. Indeed, Schrader has suggested that noir can be seen as touching 'most every dramatic Hollywood film from 1941 to 53' (Schrader, 1972, p. 9).

Suicidal impulse: William Holden and Gloria Swanson in *Sunset Blvd.*

Categories and definitions

Given the potential expansiveness of the term, noir demanded both a theoretical system that could pin down what it was that made noir *noir*, and criticism that examined its generic marks and investigated the structural, thematic and visual systems integral to the whole series of films. Before work on defining the crucial elements of noir and an examination of their workings could begin, however, preliminary attempts were made to categorise those films that seemed central to noir.

The first book-length study of noir (Borde and Chaumeton, 1955) began this work by mapping out various recurrent themes within noir (violence, crime, psychological emphasis) and relating these to particular films. This in turn provided the basis for Durgnat's eccentric and amorphous (1974) article that listed nearly 300 films under headings such as 'psychopaths', 'gangsters' and 'middle-class murder'. The latter category was subdivided into lists including 'corruption of the not-so innocent male' (such as *Double Indemnity*, 1944; *The Postman Always Rings Twice*, 1946); 'woman as heroic victim' (*Rebecca*, 1940; *Gaslight*, 1944) and 'mirror images' (*Rebecca*; *The Woman in the Window*, 1944). Durgnat's article, written in 1970, was influential in mapping the territory but it pointed up the need for more rigorous and specific definition – for many, his inclusion of films such as *2001: A Space Odyssey* (1968) was mere provocation.

Paul Schrader touches on what he sees as some of the recurring visual marks of noir – the majority of the scenes lit for night, rain-drenched streets, doom-laden narration, compositional tension rather than action and a fondness for oblique lines and fractured light. Generally appreciative of Durgnat's categorisation, Schrader suggests that the family tree is structured around a halting of the upwardly mobile thrust of the 1930s. 'Frontierism has turned to paranoia and claustrophobia. The small-time gangster had made it big and sits in the mayor's chair. The private eye has quit the police force in disgust, and the young heroine, sick of going along for the ride is now taking others for a ride'. Writing more historically than Durgnat, Schrader identifies an intensification of this downward movement as the noir period continues and categorises noir temporally by subdividing it into three main periods. These are: wartime 1941–6 (characterised by 'the private eye and the lone wolf … studio sets and more talk than action', for example *The Maltese Falcon*; *Gilda*, 1946; *Mildred Pierce*, 1945); postwar realistic 1945–9 ('crime in the streets, political corruption and police routine' and 'less romantic heroes', for example *The Killers*, 1946; *Brute Force*, 1947); and finally, psychotic action and suicidal impulse 1949–53 ('the psychotic killer as active protagonist, despair and distintegration', for example *Gun Crazy*, 1950; *D.O.A.*, 1950; *Sunset Blvd.*, 1950) (Schrader, 1972, pp. 11–12).

Both Durgnat and Schrader state that they do not see film noir as a genre. Instead, Schrader suggests that it should be seen as a period or movement similar to German Expressionism or Italian Neo-realism. Critics of this use of the term claimed that unlike these movements noir did not involve an overt, or even implicit, commitment to a political/aesthetic programme and that to imply that it did misrepresented the divergent attitudes of noir film-makers and noir's precise industrial production context.

Janey Place (1974; 1978) also uses the term 'movement' and justifies her use of it in some depth. She claims that 'unlike genres, defined by objects and subjects, but like other film movements, film noir is characterised by a remarkably homogeneous visual style with which it cuts across genres' (Place, 1978, p. 39). In the 1974 article, Place and Peterson attempt to identify the elements of this 'consistent thread'. They outline the difference between the dominant 'high-key lighting style' that eliminates 'unnatural' shadows on faces and gave 'what was considered to be an impression of reality' and noir's chiaroscuro 'low-key lighting' that eschews softening filters and gauzes and 'opposes light and darkness, hiding faces, rooms, urban landscapes – and by extension, motivations and true character – in shadow and darkness'. The night scenes integral to film noir would, in the *blanc* style, have been shot 'day for night' with special filters. A central element of the noir look, however, was the high-contrast image and jet-black (rather than *blanc* grey-black) skies given by 'night for night' shooting. Place and Peterson go on to describe noir's mise en scène 'designed to unsettle, jar, and disorient the viewer in correlation with the disorientation felt by the noir heroes'. Typically, they argue, noir is distinguished by the use of 'claustrophobic framing devices' that separate characters from each other, unbalanced compositions with shutters or banisters casting oblique shadows or placing grids over faces and furniture, 'obtrusive and disturbing' close-ups juxtaposed with extreme high-angle shots that make the protagonist look like 'a rat in a trap'. Overall, the visual style of noir as described by Place and Peterson amounts to a disorientating anti-realism that exists in opposition to the harmonious *blanc* world of the realist film.

Place's insistence on the distinguishing character of the visual style of the noir is challenged in an article by James Damico (1978). Arguing against the view of noir as movement and for it as a genre, Damico claims that the visual style of noir is actually an iconography. He suggests that the common denominator of noir films is their narrative structure and proposes a model by which film noirs may be isolated, objectified and their examination facilitated:

> Either because he is fated to do so by chance, or because he has been hired for a job especially associated with her, a man whose experience of life has left him sanguine and often bitter meets a not-so-innocent woman of similar outlook to whom he is sexually and fatally attracted. Through this attraction, either because the woman induces him to it or because it is a natural result of their relationship, the man comes to cheat, attempt to murder, or actually murder a second man to whom the woman is unhappily or unwillingly attached (generally he is her husband or lover), an act which often leads to the woman's betrayal of the protagonist, but which in any event brings about the sometimes metaphoric, but usually literal destruction of the woman, the man to whom she is attached, and frequently the protagonist himself. (Damico, 1978, p. 54)

While Place's and Damico's respective uses of the terms 'movement' and 'genre' are closely argued in relation to their individual stress on either visual style or narrative structure, other writers have used them differently, or have opted instead for 'series', 'cycle' or 'subgenre'. Subsequent authors have not automatically accepted Damico's contention that his schema provides an alternative reading of noir that is in opposition to accounts stressing visual style. For example, Paul Kerr's article on the industrial context of the B-film noir unproblematically includes both Place and Damico in a general introduction to the genre's characteristics (Kerr, 1979/80, p. 49). Sylvia Harvey, meanwhile, offers a useful synthesis within a framework that accepts visual style as the most fundamental aspect of noir. The defining contour of the genre, Harvey suggests, is dissonance: 'the sense of disorientation and unease' produced by 'that which is abnormal and dissonant' (Harvey, 1978, p. 32).

The historical specificity of film noir

Underlying all these different attempts at categorisation of noir lies the issue of its historical specificity. How did it become so dominant in Hollywood for more than 20 years, touching (one might almost say consuming) almost every genre while retaining a specific visual and narrative structure? What caused it to decline? And if, as this line of questioning suggests, there was a relationship between historical period and the stylistic and thematic elements of noir, how should this relationship be characterised?

Before dealing with how various theorists have answered these questions, it is important to signal the debate about the delineation of the genre's historical period. Following Schrader, most critics have understood the major period of noir to fall between 1941 and 1958 (Schrader, 1972, p. 8), although the search for immediate precursors has been a popular academic occupation (Flinn, 1972, for example, claims that the 65-minute B-movie *Stranger on the Third Floor*, 1940, is the earliest film noir). This strictly time-bound view is, however, implicitly challenged by some listings. Durgnat's family tree lists a number of titles made outside of the 1941–58 period, including several more usually seen as precursors, such as Warner Bros.' gangster films. A more complex challenge to Schrader's time limits comes from Silver and Ward (1981), whose book includes synopses of later films that were clearly influenced by noir, often to the point of intentional homage. The genesis of films such as *Klute* (1971), *Hustle* (1975), *Body Heat* (1981) and Schrader's own *American Gigolo* (1980) was provocatively prefigured by his comment that 'as the current political mood hardens, filmgoers and film-makers will find the film noir of the late 40s increasingly attractive' (Schrader, 1972, p. 8). These later films may be better described as 'film *après* noir', as suggested by Larry Gross (Gross, 1976), but this merely recasts, rather than eliminates, questions about the relationship between noir and its specific historical configuration.

Industry and aesthetics

Borde and Chaumeton (1978) comment briefly on the influence of German Expressionism, which they see as transmitted chiefly through the agency of émigré directors such as Fritz Lang and Robert Siodmak, but then go on to say that noir is better understood as a 'synthesis' of 'the brutal and colourful gangster films' made by Warner Bros., the horror films associated with Universal and the 'detective fiction shared by Fox and MGM'. They also identify in the genre the 'inexhaustible sadism' of animation, the 'absurdity and casual cynicism' of American comedy and the influence of certain realist and/or social commentary films, notably LeRoy's *I Am a Fugitive from a Chain Gang* (1932) (Borde and Chaumeton, 1978, p. 63). Rather than helping to explain why a synthesis in the form of noir should have taken place during the 1940s and 1950s, the diversity of their sources tends to obscure the issue. They do make it clear, however, that noir grew from within the American as well as European industries.

Schrader's account stresses the historical time limits of genre, but does little to explain the industrial context for the 'halting of 30s optimism' except to speculate that the end of the Depression and World War II freed the industry from the task of 'keeping people's spirits up' (Schrader, 1972, p. 9). His combination of a listing of sources (to which others have added *Citizen Kane*, 1941) linked to a vague statement of postwar gloom can be seen as the most dominant paradigm for understanding the industrial/aesthetic context for noir.

Film *après* noir: detective Donald Sutherland hunts down Jane Fonda in Alan J. Pakula's *Klute*

Paul Kerr challenges the generality of such accounts, suggesting a re-examination of the conjuncture between 'a primarily economically determined mode of production known as "B" film-making' and what were primarily ideologically defined modes of 'difference' known as the film noir (Kerr, 1979/80, p. 65). More specifically, Kerr argues that some of the stylistic features of noir such as night-for-night shooting, disorientating lighting and camera angles, and the generation of tension through editing and short bursts of extreme violence, were direct results of economic factors such as the desire to thwart union restrictions and use stock footage. Furthermore, production took place in the context of the need to demonstrate a clear difference from the realism of A-films, with which the B-noirs were paired in double bills. Kerr's account goes on to examine the decline of noir, which he relates to various technical developments, such as Technicolor, which were the products of an ideological pressure for increased verisimilitude, and changes in the economic structure of the industry, particularly the anti-monopoly Bill of Divorcement that contributed to the end of the double bill (Kerr, 1979/80, pp. 56–65).

Genre and social context

Kerr's article is explicitly written as a counter-attack on the series of books and articles that dealt with the wider social/economic/political configurations of the noir period. Again, Borde and Chaumeton (1978) offer a fairly typical account. They suggest the influence of 'vulgarised' psychoanalysis in America and the publicity given to crime. While both of these form recurring elements in noir narratives, Borde and Chaumeton's comments lack historical specificity. A more detailed and influential account of noir's social context can be found in Colin McArthur (1972). McArthur notes that 'it is useless to try to align the wholly fictitious events of the thriller with actual events', but then goes on to speculate on the reasons for the emergence of the thriller as film noir. These 'speculations' include the aftermath of the Depression, the war and the Cold War, and the 'general mood of fear and insecurity' produced by an uncertain future. 'It seems reasonable to suggest,' he continues, 'that this uncertainty is paralleled in the general mood of malaise, the loneliness and angst and the lack of clarity about the characters' motives in the thriller'. McArthur also cites the misogyny associated with 'the heightened desirability and concomitant suspicion of women back home experienced by men at war' and the horrors of Auschwitz and Hiroshima, which he sees echoed in a shift from 1930s gangsters overtly concerned with the social origins of crime to noir thrillers such as *Dark Corner* (1946), 'a cry of loneliness and despair in a sick world' (McArthur, 1972, pp. 66–7).

These speculations are suggestive, but McArthur offers few clear indications as to how they are actually articulated in the texts. Furthermore, there is a paradox in his positing a relationship between the social/psychological formations of a particular period and angst, a term that is ahistorical. Given the point in the development of critical theory at which the study was undertaken, it is perhaps inevitable that McArthur falls back on auteurist notions to explain the connection between these events and the texts. It was, he suggests, the 'sour and pessimistic sensibilities' of directors such as Lang, Siodmak and Billy Wilder, 'forged in the uncertainty of Weimar Germany and decaying Austria-Hungary', that provide the vital link between film noir and America in the 1940s and 1950s.

The connection between 'postwar gloom' and the 'meaninglessness', 'depression' and 'angst' of noir became almost de rigueur in critical analyses. Perhaps the most extreme examples linking an apparently angst-laden period and noir via the agency of auteurs is found in the articles about noir and existentialism. Robert G. Porfirio (1976), for example, attempts to connect French existentialist philosophy to noir through 'hard-boiled' writers, especially, and dubiously (see Jenkins, 1982), Hammett and Ernest Hemingway. Writing about the Flitcraft parable, for instance, included in the novel *The Maltese Falcon* was taken from but omitted from the film, Porfirio claims it reveals that 'Spade is by nature an existentialist, with a strong conception of the randomness of existence'. Porfirio's analysis implicitly depends upon making an unproblematic leap between the historical configurations within which existentialism developed in France and the 'world' that exists within the noir texts.

Women in film noir

A very different approach to the historical context of noir can be seen in the feminist writing collected in *Women in Film Noir* (Kaplan, 1978; 1998). Making a decisive attempt to shift discussion away from angst, these writers concentrate on the structuring role of patriarchal ideology within the texts. Their interest in noir comes from an understanding of the period of its growth as one of social and economic transition following the disruption of the war years, producing problems for male power and control, and a concern to analyse the genre's treatment of women. Kaplan, for instance, notes that:

> The film noir world is one in which women are central to the intrigue of the films, and are furthermore usually not placed safely in ... familiar roles ... Defined by their sexuality, which is presented as desirable but dangerous, the women function as an obstacle to the male quest. The hero's success or not depends on the degree to which he can extricate himself from the women's manipulations. Although the man is sometimes simply destroyed because he cannot resist women's lures, often the world of the film is the attempted restoration of order through the exposure and then destruction of the sexual, manipulating woman. (Kaplan, 1978, pp. 2–3)

In contrast to the seamless, unproblematic assimilation of existentialism by the noir text assumed by Porfirio's article, these feminist analyses emphasise the text as a site of contradiction. Thus, rather than searching for symbolic truths residing statically within the text, many of the writers (such as Gledhill, Johnston and Cook) are concerned to discern structural relationships that they then rework through conceptual frameworks provided by Marxist and psychoanalytically influenced feminism. Gledhill, for instance, says that to understand the significance of film noir for women,

> It would be necessary to analyse the conjuncture of specific aesthetic, cultural and economic forces; on the one hand the ongoing production of the private eye/thriller ... on the other, the post-war drive to get women out of the workforce and return them to the domestic sphere; and finally the perennial myth of woman as threat to male control of the world and destroyer of male aspiration – forces, which in cinematic terms, interlock to form what we now think of as the aberrant style and world of film noir.
> (Gledhill, 1978, p. 19)

Gledhill's analysis of film noir is based on examination of a series of structural elements that open up contradictions around the ambiguously placed noir women. Her 'five features' of noir are: the investigative structure of the narrative that 'probes the secrets of female sexuality within patterns of submission and dominance' (p. 15); flashbacks and voice-overs that can sometimes open up a textual gap between a male narrator and the woman he is investigating, as in *Gilda*; a proliferation of points of view, with, typically, a struggle between men and women; unstable characterisation of the heroine, who is likely to be a treacherous femme fatale; and the sexualised filming of this heroine, who is also enmeshed in the contradictory visual style of noir.

This last point is expanded by Place (1978). Working from the basis provided by her earlier work with L. S. Peterson (1974), Place examines the visual motifs through which two archetypical women – the spider woman and the nurturing woman – are articulated. Writing about the spider woman, Place comments that 'the sexual woman's dangerous power is expressed visually' and details her inconography: long hair, cigarette smoke as a cue for immorality, a habitat of darkness and, perhaps most importantly, a domination of composition, camera movement and lighting that seems to pull 'the camera (and the hero's gaze with our own) irresistibly with them as they move' (Place, 1978, p. 45). Despite her apparent power, the femme fatale 'ultimately loses physical strength' and is actually or symbolically imprisoned (Place, 1978, p. 45). For Place, however, this visual and narrative containment is not what is retained from noir. Instead, it is the power of the femme fatale that we remember, 'their strong, dangerous and above all exciting sexuality' (Place, 1978, p. 37).

Place's analysis signals the importance in these analyses of the different emphases placed on the recuperative potential of noir – that is, on the extent to which the text is able to contain and mask the social contradictions structured into its narrative and visual systems. Here there is considerable divergence between theorists. Unlike Place, and Dyer (1978), who argues for Gilda/Rita Hayworth's 'resistance through charisma' to textual and ideological containment in *Gilda*, Pam Cook (1978) offers a reading of *Mildred Pierce* in which the film's textual organisation works to suppress the heroine's discourse 'in favour of that of the male', with Mildred finally designated guilty by the law and returned to a subordinate domestic role. Gledhill's (1978) examination of *Klute*, an example of what has been described as 'film *après* noir', discerns a similar final positioning for a different, but equally equivocal heroine – redefinition, yet again, as guilty. These feminist analyses made a provocative intervention into critical debates about film noir, which have generally been characterised by a masculine perspective on the part of critics and a concentration on the existential dilemmas of the noir hero.

Noir and neo-noir

STEVE NEALE

Since the early 1980s, what Larry Gross initially identified as 'film *après* noir' has – usually now under the heading of 'neo-noir' – become a major contemporary phenomenon. In addition to obvious homages and remakes such as *The Postman Always Rings Twice* (1981), *Against All Odds* (1984) and *Night and the City* (1994), nearly every crime thriller made in Hollywood is now almost automatically labelled as noir or as neo-noir by reviewers and critics in the trade press, in newspapers and listings magazines, and in specialist film journals alike. In tandem with these developments, academic writing both on noir and on neo-noir has itself become a major phenomenon. With 'noir classics' from the 1940s and 1950s now also regularly recycled on video and on television, 'film noir' has become firmly established.

Recent writing on neo-noir – a term perhaps first established in the 1992 edition of Silver and Ward (pp. 398–443) – has distinguished between trends, modes and cycles within what tends to be viewed, nevertheless, as a single phenomenon. Leighton Grist, for instance, carefully distinguishes between what he calls 'modern', 'modernist' and 'postmodern' instances of neo-noir. 'Modern' neo-noir, exemplified by films such as *Harper* (1966) and *Farewell, My Lovely* (1975), tends to introduce 'a number of signifiers of modernity', signifiers that can include 'an updated setting, the use of colour, greater sexual frankness, and the transmission of decidedly modern attitudes and mores' (Grist, 1993, p. 267). 'Modernist' neo-noirs, made more or less at the same time, include *Point Blank* (1967), *The Long Goodbye* (1973), *Chinatown* (1974) and *Taxi Driver* (1976), and are marked by a 'questioning of the conventions and discourses of film noir narrative'. 'Essentially challenging crucial ideological assumptions embedded in the genre, these films enact a process of formal and thematic demystification' (Grist, 1993, p. 267). In 'postmodern' neo-noirs, by contrast, noir's 'generic conventions may be reprised, but rarely interrogated' (Grist, 1993, p. 274). Marked by what he sees as an uncritical deployment of allusion and pastiche, 'postmodern' neo-noir is above all a feature of the 1980s and 1990s, and is exemplified by films such as *Body Heat*, *Blade Runner* (1982) and *The Hot Spot* (1990).

Recent writing on noir itself is divisible into a number of distinct and different trends. First, there are a number of articles and books that tend to summarise, reorder or recycle the tenets of earlier accounts. Among these are Crowther (1988), Walker (1992) and Palmer (1994). Palmer's book contains an innovative chapter on 'The noir woman's picture', and a concluding chapter on neo-noir. Walker's introductory summary is both succinct and thorough, usefully dividing the protagonists who enter or who are plunged into what he calls 'the noir world' between 'seeker heroes' (often detectives, policemen or investigative figures of one kind or another) and 'victim heroes'. He also suggests that 'film noir is not simply a certain type of crime movie, but also a generic field: a set of elements and features that may be found in a range of different films' (Walker, 1992, p. 8).

Maltby (1992), Neve (1992), Polan (1986) and Telotte (1989) all address themselves to the issues of noir's original historical context and significance. Polan and Telotte see noir in terms of contemporary discursive structures and preoccupations. For Polan, noir's conventions and devices, its differences and defamiliarisations, relate to various crises within America's social and symbolic order in the 1940s. For Telotte, noir was a privileged site for expressing and exploring the difficulties and problems of communication in a changed postwar world.

Maltby's and Neve's accounts are both more empirically based and more partial and specific in focus. Maltby is concerned with the contemporary significance of those films subsequently labelled as noirs for leftists and liberals working in Hollywood in the late 1940s or commentating on its output and its trends. Citing Siegfried Kracauer, John Houseman, Abraham Polonsky and others, he shows how, among other things, liberal worries about the contemporary mass media and about the future of purposeful social commitment and activity now that the war against Fascism was over found expression in a number of anxieties about contemporary crime films. John Houseman, for instance, complained about 'their absolute lack of moral energy' and 'their listless, fatalistic despair' (Maltby, 1992, p. 41). These anxieties were exacerbated by the onset of the Cold War and by the hearings at the HUAC, and Maltby himself goes on to argue that at this point the paranoid rhetoric of noir took a decidedly rightward turn.

Similar ground is covered by Neve. He, however, is concerned to demonstrate a strong left-wing and liberal current in noir throughout the 1940s and the early 1950s, citing writers, directors and producers such as Edward Dmytryk, Robert Rossen, Adrian Scott, John Berry, Joseph Losey, Albert Maltz, Dore Schary and Orson Welles, and films such as *Cornered* (1945), *The Stranger* (1946), *They Won't Believe Me* (1947), *Force of Evil* (1949), *Where Danger Lives* (1950), *The Narrow Margin* (1952) and *The Prowler* (1951).

Continuing but to some extent also reorientating earlier work on gender, women and the figure of the femme fatale, a further trend in recent writing on noir has been an attention to issues of masculinity. For Frank Krutnik (1991) and for Deborah Thomas (1992), issues of masculinity are central to film noir, which they see as dramatising and exploring 'a particular crisis in male identity' (Thomas, 1992, p. 59). Both tend therefore to read noir's female characters as functions of male dilemmas and male anxieties. For Thomas, the 'redemptive' or 'domesticating' woman is as threatening for the male protagonist as the femme fatale, while for Krutnik the femme fatale tends to 'represent conflicting elements within male identity' (Krutnik, 1991, p. 63). For Krutnik, though, the problems faced by noir's male protagonists extend beyond their relations with women. Women are only one source or index of more general 'disturbances in or threats to the regimentation of masculine identity and social/cultural authority' in the 1940s (Krutnik, 1991, p. 164). Krutnik here echoes Dyer (1978), and also Florence Jacobowitz, who argues that noir is a 'genre wherein compulsory masculinity is presented as a nightmare' (Jacobowitz, 1992, p. 153).

Elizabeth Cowie (1993) also addresses the issue of gender, but her argument is a different one – indeed, she is explicitly critical of those who stress the masculine orientation of film noir. She draws attention to the frequent role played by women as source novelists and as scriptwriters for noirs, to the absence of femmes fatales in numerous noirs, and to the extent to which noirs such as *Raw Deal* (1948) and *Secret Beyond the Door* (1948) are 'women's stories'. She goes on to argue that while the issue of sexual difference in noir is always crucial, the gender of its originators and of its protagonists, together with the gender appeal of the films themselves, is much more variable than most commentators on noir have hitherto been willing or able to acknowledge.

Cowie is in general highly sceptical about noir as a category, and about the coherence of the phenomenon the term is usually used to identify:

> The term has succeeded despite the lack of any straightforward unity in the set of films it attempts to designate. Unlike terms such as the 'western' or the 'gangster' film, which are relatively uncontroversial ... film noir has a more tenuous critical status, a devotion among aficionados that suggest a desire for the very category as such, a wish that it exist in order to 'have' a certain set of films all together. Film noir is in a certain sense a fantasy. (Cowie, 1993, p.121)

Cowie's scepticism is tempered by her thesis that noir 'names a certain inflection or tendency which emerges in certain genres in the early 1940s' (Cowie, 1993, p. 129), one in which 'American cinema finds for the first time a form in which to represent desire as something that not only renders the desiring subject helpless, but also propels him or her to destruction' (Cowie, 1993, p. 148).

Vernet (1993) points on one hand to historical contradictions and nonsequiturs in those accounts that link noir to hard-boiled fiction. Noir is argued to be a postwar or 1940s phenomenon. Yet hard-boiled fiction emerged in the 1920s and 1930s, and film versions were made in the 1930s. On the other hand, he points to political and ideological factors predisposing the discovery (or invention) of film noir by intellectuals and cineastes in postwar France. In addition, he argues that the Expressionist visual style and the chiaroscuro look reputedly specific to noir and hence to the 1940s and 1950s is in fact a long-standing tradition in American cinematography, one that not only predates the 1940s, but also the 1920s, the period in which those associated with Expressionism in Germany first began to make Expressionist films.

Neale (1999) mobilises these points and others in arguing that noir is as a critical category and as a canon of films both logically and chronologically incoherent. He points to inconsistencies in versions of the canon (some include films such as *Suspicion*, 1941, and *Secret Beyond the Door*, while others do not), and to historical anomalies in arguments proposing that a category including films such as *Stranger on the Third Floor*, *The Maltese Falcon* and *This Gun for Hire* (1942) is a postwar phenomenon. He argues that the significance attributed to noir as an index of contemporary American society is disproportionate to the number of films involved and tends to ignore the nature and diversity of Hollywood's output as a whole. He argues, in addition, that a number of the features said to be characteristic of noir – the use of chiaroscuro, for instance, and the use of flashback and voice-over, scenarios of destructive and murderous passion, an emphasis on perverse forms of character motivation and behaviour and on the depiction of extreme mental states, and a stress on suspicion, distrust and deceit in the depiction of relations between male and female protagonists – can all be found in genres and cycles – such as the Gothic woman's film and Val Lewton's horror series at RKO – that proponents of noir tend to regard as either non-canonic or marginal. And he argues, conversely, that a number of canonic noirs lack some or all of these features. All in all, he suggests, the notion of noir, and the attachment to it of film scholars, critics, theorists and historians, now functions to block rather than to facilitate historical research. Meanwhile, somewhat paradoxically, the widespread dissemination of what was once an esoteric critical term has, in tandem with the advent and ubiquity of neo-noir, ensured that 'film noir' itself now has a generic status it never had in the 1940s and 1950s.

Selected Reading

Ian Cameron (ed.), *The Movie Book of Film Noir*, London, Studio Vista, 1992.

Mary Ann Doane, *The Desire to Desire: The Woman's Film of the 1940s*, Bloomington, Indiana University Press, 1987.

E. Ann Kaplan (ed.), *Women in Film Noir*, London, BFI Publishing, 1978. Revised edition 1998.

Dana Polan, *Power and Paranoia: History, Narrative, and the American Cinema, 1940–1950*, New York, Columbia University Press, 1986.

Double Indemnity (USA 1944 *p.c* – Paramount; *d* – Billy Wilder)

Barbara Stanwyck's performance as Phyllis Dietrichson in *Double Indemnity* represents one of the most powerful and disturbing noir portraits of a femme fatale – the destructive, duplicitous woman who transgresses rules of female behaviour by luring men with the promise of possessing her sexually and then using them for her own, murderous, ends. Immensely successful despite early studio qualms about the 'appropriateness' of a thriller with such a dark heroine, the film had a substantial effect on later noirs.

One of the characteristics of noir films is their use of voice-over narration. In the scene following on from the renowned double entendre-filled first meeting between bored housewife Phyllis and insurance salesman Walter Neff (Fred MacMurray), we hear Neff's voice-over delivering a classically hard-boiled, retrospective description of events. It is not until a little later that we see that he is in fact dictating it into an office machine for the benefit of Keyes (Edward G. Robinson), Neff's father figure and in Claire Johnston's (1978) analysis 'signifier of the patriarchal order'. Discussing narration in her essay on *Klute*, Christine Gledhill comments that for the audience

> the temporal separation of the moment of telling and the event told lead to something of a dislocation between what they observe and the storyteller's account of it. This aspect is intensified in that the storyteller is often proved wrong by subsequent events and may even be lying. (Gledhill, 1978, p. 16)

Neff's voice-over suggests that he despises Phyllis and wants to be rid of her, while the audience knows that this is not the case. Later that evening, Phyllis arrives at his apartment. As Johnston points out, yet again a gap is created, this time between image and voice-over: 'The voice-over suggests an appointment which the image denies: "it would be eight and she would be there"' (Johnston, 1978, p. 105).

Barbara Stanwyck snares Fred MacMurray in *Double Indemnity*

During this meeting at his apartment, Phyllis is identified visually and through the voice-over with the darkness in the apartment and with the rain. During the whole scene, Walter is softly lit, while at certain moments the chiaroscuro low-key lighting makes her appear jewel hard. Most crucially, the interaction between Phyllis and Walter is both sexual and violent. The real moment of sexual catharsis is not the first kiss, but the embrace that follows Walter's commitment to help her to kill her husband. The importance of the intention to do violence to Mr Dietrichson is outweighed by the sadistic eroticism between the two of them.

The death of the transgressive woman – in a narrative that closely adheres to Damico's (1978) ideal noir structure – does not end the film. With Phyllis's death, the gap between retrospective narration and image can be resolved into a present. The trajectory of *Double Indemnity* follows the shattering of the friendship between Keyes and Neff and the imperilling of the smooth workings of the insurance system (and the patriarchal order it represents) by Neff's involvement with the world of women. In particular, Phyllis concretises Neff's unacknowledged desire to 'buck the system' by testing the fallibility of Keyes and, in Johnston's analysis, the law he represents. The elimination of her and her challenge to the patriarchal order means that the film can finish with a brief re-establishment of the homoerotic relationship between Keyes and Neff, signified by their affectionate ritual with Neff's last cigarette.

JANE ROOT

Kiss Me Deadly (USA 1955 *p.c* – Parklane Pictures; *d* – Robert Aldrich)

Kiss Me Deadly was made comparatively late in the noir cycle and represents its most extreme and psychotic vision. Unlike some earlier films, the noir world of *Kiss Me Deadly* is not a substratum of society into which the protagonist gradually and inexorably slips. Mike Hammer (Ralph Meeker), a seedy private detective who specialises in providing evidence in divorce cases, is already part of that world when the film begins, and the anti-realist noir style is therefore present from the very first frames in the night-for-night shooting of the road, with its white lines emphasised almost to the point of abstraction, while the half-naked body of the hysterical, running woman is disturbingly segmented by the framing. This is accompanied on the soundtrack by the noise of her frenzied breathing and followed by the credits, which scroll up, disconcertingly, in reverse.

Mike Hammer, unlike earlier noir heroes (such as Sam Spade), is an entirely unsympathetic character: morose, violent and stupid. Narrative and mise en scène mark him as a man trapped by forces beyond his control. These elements, especially when linked to the extreme violence of the film, have allowed *Kiss Me Deadly* to be seen as a prime example of 'existential' noir. At the same time, the film is useful for discussion of the sexual dissonances of noir. Hammer's encounters with women, for example, are all marked by female sexual aggression. Lily Carver (Gaby Rodgers), who makes an explicit play for Hammer, causes world destruction at the end of the film through rampant 'female' acquisitiveness coupled with a desire to look at the forbidden. Velda (Maxine Cooper), meanwhile, is given a position of power from which she criticises both Hammer and the entire trajectory of the film (in her speech about his pursuit of 'the great whatsit' halfway through). It could be argued that the occurrence of this speech criticising the male quest right at the centre of the film produces a radical disjuncture in a genre predicated upon such a quest.

JANE ROOT

Mean Streets (USA 1973 *p.c* – Taplin-Perry-Scorsese Productions/Warner Bros.; *d* – Martin Scorsese)

Mean Streets exemplifies the New Hollywood cinema of the late 1960s to mid-1970s, discussion of which has noted its debt to art cinema: narrative fragmentation, introspective protagonists, generic self-consciousness and detailed social realism. Location shooting, long takes and intimate, shaky hand-held camerawork characteristic of cinéma vérité complement the naturalistic representation of a specific subculture to afford a 'documentary' picture of New York's Little Italy that convinces, despite being shot largely in Los Angeles. However, this documentary representation is also stylistically heightened by a battery of anti-realist devices that flags the 'new wave': jump-cuts, slow motion, 'unmotivated' camera movement and often intrusive music.

In generic terms, the film's claustrophobic Expressionism bears out Scorsese's claim that *Mean Streets* 'became a very clear attempt at doing a film noir in colour' (*Pulp Fictions: The Film Noir Story*, 1995). Other noir elements include the film's mainly night-time, seedy urban setting, the representation of an oppressive, inescapable milieu, and a narrative concern with figures who exist within or on the fringes of the criminal underworld. Structurally *Mean Streets* recalls the classic gangster film. Caught between his ambitions as a scion of the local don and the demands of his Catholic conscience, between materialism and morality, Charlie's (Harvey Keitel) situation replicates a familiar thematic/ideological opposition. Moreover, *Mean Streets* exhibits numerous gangster film motifs, whether one considers iconography (suits, cars, guns), character (Giovanni as godfather, Charlie as 'family' heir, Shorty as hitman) or incident (meetings, deals, threats, a car chase, shootings).

Even so, as in much New Hollywood Cinema, genre shifts from being predominantly a means of representation to being, in part, an object of representation. Through this, the film engages in a revision of generic conventions that implicitly

Film noir in colour: Harvey Keitel leads a life of crime in Scorsese's gritty *Mean Streets*

confronts their underlying assumptions. *Mean Streets* inverts the ideological emphasis of the gangster film by representing the mob not as a criminal 'other' but as the dominant patriarchal norm, while Charlie's Catholic conscience is placed as transgressive, and the film ends with him effectively defeated by Little Italy's criminal mores.

LEIGHTON GRIST

Chinatown (USA 1974 *p.c* – Long Road Productions/ Penthouse Productions/Paramount; *d* – Roman Polanski)

Made at a time when Hollywood's staple genres were undergoing intense revision, nostalgic evocation or comic parody (see New Hollywood, p. 60), *Chinatown* has been seen as a film that alludes to – and critically reworks – the conventions, ideology and mythology of the traditional hard-boiled detective film in a number of recent critical assessments, including Cawelti (1995), Eagle (1994), Gallafent (1992) and Grist (1992).

Evocation, allusion and critical revision are apparent from the start. The credit sequence, with its black-and-white Paramount logo, its art-deco graphics and its romantic – and nostalgic – trumpet theme, clearly serves to signal past styles and conventions. But the film's first images (explicit black-and-white photos of an adulterous affair) and its opening scenes (shot in Panavision and Technicolor, at times accompanied by a minimal, fragmentary and atonal score and containing Jake Gittes's declarations that he is a businessman, that his motive is money and that divorce work is his 'metier') serve to highlight a series of differences – and dissonances – between the traditional and the modern. And they serve to foreground a process of revision rather than nostalgia.

Many of the film's revisions centre on the figure of the private eye. Not only is he unashamedly involved in divorce work (something that, as Cawelti, 1995, and others point out, traditional private-eye figures such as Philip Marlowe explicitly eschew) he is also naive (for all his surface cynicism), inept as a hard-boiled wit and generally out of his depth, especially when he adopts the role of moral crusader. As Grist points out, from the moment he is set up by the fake Mrs Mulwray (Faye Dunaway), 'he finds himself in a situation beyond his control' (Grist, 1992, p. 270). His interventions make things worse, his deductions are nearly always wrong (catastrophically so in the case of Evelyn Mulwray and her daughter) and his overestimation of his own abilities ('I won't make the same mistake twice') eventually fatal. The enigmas of the plot involve forms of sexual and political corruption and power Gittes (Jack Nicholson) is totally unable to anticipate.

The figures of Noah Cross (John Huston) and Evelyn Mulwray are central. Cross has been seen by

Eagle (1994) as a descendant of the corrupt and powerful father figures characteristic of numerous 1940s noir films. Evelyn Mulwray, meanwhile, is seen as a character that not only evokes but also undermines the figure of the noir femme fatale. While she is at times duplicitous, her duplicity is justified both by her knowledge, and by her motives; Gittes's lack of trust in her is one of the factors that lead directly to the film's tragic denouement. On both counts, commentators have seen the film as mounting a critique of patriarchal ideology.

Cross's given name – Noah – interconnects with biblical and water motifs that pervade the film. One of the major clues, Mulwray's glasses, is found in the pool in his garden, connecting the water motif with a third strand of imagery: eyes, spectacles, eye-like shapes and optical devices. It is a mark of the care with which this and other strands of imagery are thought through that the flaw in Evelyn's eye echoes the broken tail light on Hollis's car and is in turn echoed by the nature of the gunshot wound that kills her. Thus it could be said that visual appearances always prove to be deceptive and that this strand of imagery can be read as a pun on the term 'private eye'.

LEIGHTON GRIST

L. A. Confidential (USA 1997 *p.c* – Monarchy Enterprises/Regency Entertainment; *d* – Curtis Hanson)

Film noirs often depict their doomed characters as entrapped by technology and media. In 1950s noir, television frequently figured as the embodiment of technology, its surveillance ability and tightly framed images contained within the big-screen film image acting as a cogent expression of the genre's fatalistic vision. *L. A. Confidential*, however, set in early 1950s Los Angeles, invokes television less for its ominous portent than as portraying a false image of police work as efficient and reliable. The television show *Badge of Honor* for which Detective Jack Vincennes (Kevin Spacey) acts as technical adviser presents as false a picture of the police as *Hush-Hush*, the tabloid that manufactures celebrity scandals, does of Hollywood. *Badge of Honor* is a by-the-book police procedural series that recalls Jack Webb's popular television programme *Dragnet* (1951–9). But in contrast to such representations, *L. A. Confidential* shows the tarnished underside of the police badge.

A policier that depicts the Los Angeles Police Department (LAPD) as a world driven by politics and corruption, *L. A. Confidential* is concerned with the importance of image on several levels. The LAPD is preoccupied with its public image. Beginning with the unwarranted beating by police of some Latino suspects, the Department spins evidence of internal corruption so that the stories reported in the newspapers show it as cleansing the town of crime and acting heroically. The significance of positive images papering over vice is reflected in one of the film's subplots involving a high-class pimp named Patchett (David Strathairn), whose call girls are surgically altered to resemble famous movie stars.

The narrative dispels any conception of the police as selfless protectors of society. Each of the three detectives who become involved in investigating a multiple slaying in a café – Vincennes, Ed Exley (Guy Pearce) and Bud White (Russell Crowe) – has different motivations and limitations. Patchett uses his call-girl racket to blackmail wealthy citizens in order to finance the construction of a major freeway, thus implicating the bedrock of commerce in corruption in a manner reminiscent of the foundational neo-noir *Chinatown* (1974). The plot convolutions, which rival *The Big Sleep* (1946) for complexity, mirror the layers of corruption that reach as far as the chief of police and the District Attorney.

BARRY KEITH GRANT

A History of Violence (Germany/USA 2005 *p.c* – Media 1 Filmproduktion/Benderspink/New Line Cinema; *d* – David Cronenberg)

A History of Violence represents a move away from the body horror characteristic of David Cronenberg's earlier work, from *Shivers* (1975) to *The Fly* (1986). While the film is an adaptation of a graphic novel, Cronenberg made it wholly his own, as he did in his versions of the novels *Naked Lunch* (1991) and *Spider* (2002). Although there are one or two close-ups of faces turned to bloody pulp by gunfire, the horror in *A History of Violence* is more psychological than physical. Rather than a horror tale about grotesque bodily mutations externalising unreleased anger (for example, *The Brood*, 1979), this is a noirish morality tale about violence that has been internalised within the apparently normal.

Family man Tom Stall (Viggo Mortenson) lives a peaceful small-town life, but unbeknown to everyone including his loving wife, Edie (Maria Bello), he was once a brutal gangster named Joey Cusack. An unexpected turn of events causes his violence to emerge in the form of self-defence against two killers, eventually outing his past to other gangsters looking for him, and to his family. Stall is appropriately named, for no matter how hard Tom tries to suppress his violent self, it inevitably emerges like the return of the repressed. Initially, Tom refers to Joey in the third person, but ultimately he must accept his killer identity. Tom's transformation into Joey in front of his family home as he kills three gangsters with swift and decisive skill is akin to the transformation scene in many classic horror films, but without the monster make-up.

Though *A History of Violence* takes something from horror, it also borrows from the crime film and film noir. Many crime films feature narratives in which gangsters are represented as evil doubles of the good guys; in Cronenberg's film, the two are combined in the same character. And like numerous noirs, *A History of Violence* depicts a world of dark impulses and corruption lurking beneath the surface of the social order. The serial killers shown at the beginning suggest that violence is pervasive, a point further emphasised when Tom's previously docile son Jack (Ashton Holmes) explodes in a violent rage, putting the school bully in hospital. The irony of the ending, in which Tom is accepted at the dinner table by Edie and Jack when he returns home from his night of murder, echoes the critique of the family and the American dream found in gangster films and film noir.

BARRY KEITH GRANT

Trapped by the past: Maria Bello in Cronenberg's film noir update *A History of Violence*

MELODRAMA

CHRISTINE GLEDHILL

Problems of definition

The study of melodrama as a cinematic genre is a recent development. It achieved public visibility in 1977, when the Society for Education in Film and Television commissioned papers for a study weekend, some of which were subsequently published in *Screen* and *Movie* in the UK and in *The Australian Journal of Screen Theory*. Around this time and since, a spate of articles has appeared in British, French and American film journals and interest in the genre has been extended to work on television, particularly soap operas.

The British foundations of this work were laid in two very different contexts. In 1972, a small independent film journal, *Monogram*, opened a special issue on melodrama with a detailed and seminal account of the historical sources and aesthetics of the 'great Hollywood melodramas of the 50s', written by Thomas Elsaesser as part of a project of re-evaluating American cinema. Then in 1974, *Spare Rib*, a general interest magazine for the women's movement, published a review by Laura Mulvey of Fassbinder's *Fear Eats the Soul/Angst essen Seele auf* (1974) in which she used the film's acknowledged homage to Douglas Sirk's *All That Heaven Allows* (1956) to argue a case for feminist interest in the genre. Elsaesser's and Mulvey's contributions represented two very different approaches to melodrama, and dominant film theory and feminist work coexist uneasily on this terrain.

One major source of difficulty in the ensuing debate is the diversity of forms that are gathered under the heading of melodrama. Until the 1970s, the term hardly existed in relation to the cinema except pejoratively to mean a 'melodramatic' and theatrical mode that manipulated the audience's emotions and failed aesthetically to justify the response summoned up. The film industry used the category to denote dramas involving the passions – hence crime melodrama, psychological melodrama, family melodrama. Closely related are two further categories, the woman's film and romantic drama. To these, film critics have added the maternal melodrama and the argument that most American silent cinema should be considered as melodrama, with the work of D. W. Griffith constituting a virtual subset of its own. Ascription of literary and theatrical sources is equally diverse, running from Greek tragedy, through the bourgeois sentimental novel, Italian opera to Victorian stage melodrama. In the face of such confusion, arguments that melodrama constitutes a 'mode' or 'style' crossing a range of different periods and forms are persuasive. However, this does not evade the problem of generic definition, for writers on melodrama have been united in seeking to trace in it the convergence of capitalist and patriarchal structures, a project that requires historical, cultural and formal specificity. The categories set out above belong to particular phases of generic production and particular socio-historic circumstances – although with considerable overlapping and transformation of material between them.

Lack of generic specificity may arise in part from the fact that interest in melodrama first entered film criticism via the channels of mise en scène and the auteur. Criticism from this standpoint (such as *Movie*) saw in the work of Nicholas Ray, Vincente Minnelli, Max Ophuls and Otto Preminger a transformation of banal and melodramatic scripts through the power of authorial vision expressed in mise en scène. Later, film criticism that re-evaluated Hollywood in terms of ideological textual analysis looked to mise en scène for a formal play of distanciation and irony. The work of Douglas Sirk was discovered around 1971 and lined up alongside Ophuls and Minnelli, preparing the ground for the central place occupied by melodrama in debates on ideology and film aesthetics during the 1970s, and at the same time allowing more critical space to the role of generic convention (see Halliday, 1971; Willemen, 1971). These beginnings in mise en scène and ideological criticism account for the tendency of much writing on melodrama to focus on the 1950s family melodramas made by a small number of auteurs, Minnelli, Ophuls, Ray, Preminger and Sirk (see Schatz, 1981). This contrasts with the constitution of film noir as a critical category that led to the greater visibility of a corpus of non-authorial works. On the other hand, more recent work on the woman's film, which is not so predicated on preceding film critical traditions, has allowed a much wider range of titles to emerge.

Early feminist investigation of Hollywood had dismissed much of the work validated by auteurism as enshrining a male viewpoint on the world that was oppressive to women. However, Molly Haskell's (1979) influential chapter on the woman's film of the 1930s and 1940s drew attention to a whole area of submerged and despised production, featuring domestic or romantic dramas centred on female protagonists played by stars valued by the women's movement. Critical work on melodrama has tended to elide the woman's film with the family melodrama. Only feminists have drawn attention to the woman's film as a category of production aimed at women, about women, drawing on other cultural forms produced for women often by women – such as women's magazines or paperback fiction – and to raise questions about the aesthetic and cultural significance of this gender specification.

Theorising family melodrama

While on the surface appearing far removed from the western and gangster film, genres whose plots are often rooted in actual historical events, the family melodrama is nevertheless frequently defined as the dramatic mode for a historic project, namely the centrality of the bourgeois family to the ascendancy and continued dominance of that class. For example, Geoffrey Nowell-Smith argued that 'melodrama arises from the conjunction of a formal history proper (development of tragedy, realism, etc.), a set of social determinations, which have to do with the rise of the bourgeoisie, and a set of psychic determinations which take shape around the family' (Nowell-Smith, 1977, p. 113). This description places melodrama within a network of different concerns, the relationship between which is at issue according to the theoretical and political commitments of the writer.

One problem that emerges is the relation between the socio-historical conjuncture that gives rise to a particular form and its subsequent aesthetic development and history. Another set of problems is introduced in the meeting of Marxism and feminism, which offer competing notions of patriarchy, capitalism and bourgeois ideology, sex and class as key terms for the analysis of the family in melodrama. When Freudian psychoanalysis is brought to bear on melodrama, interesting tensions are pro-

Tugging at the heartstrings: Lillian Gish in D. W. Griffith's *Hearts of the World*

duced between the application of those ideas in film theory and in feminism. The feminist emphasis on the problem of the construction of femininity in patriarchal culture introduces questions of gender in relation to both the industrial and aesthetic constitution of a form: what, for instance, is the relation between specific audiences and the forms produced in their name? How is the male oedipal scenario – so often cited as the bedrock of classic narrative cinema and frequently the explicit subject matter of 1950s melodramas – to be understood in forms that offer an unusual space to female protagonists and 'feminine' problems, and are specifically addressed to a female audience?

The question of gender is also a factor in the argument as to whether melodrama is better considered as an expressive code rather than a genre and as to whether it can be considered 'progressive' or not. The taxonomies that arise out of genre analysis bring into focus iconographic motifs, themes and situations that have a material or structural force in feminist analysis of women's lives, but which in mise en scène analysis produce metaphorical significance on behalf of patriarchy. Similarly, ironic distanciation or disruption at the level of style may seem progressive in giving the spectator, both male and female, access to 'structures of feeling' normally closed off, but do little to shift the social relations between the sexes represented at the level of plot and character. Such shifts of emphasis characterise the complexities of the melodrama debate.

Melodrama as a problem of 'style and articulation'

Writing in 1972, Elsaesser's approach draws on the 1960s concern to validate Hollywood through mise en scène analysis and the post-1968 interest in irony, distanciation and ideological criticism, reworking both in the context of his own concerns with aesthetic affect. Much of Elsaesser's article is concerned to counter the conventional relegation of the form for its blatant use of 'mechanisms of emotional solicitation' (Elsaesser, 1972, p. 8). He counteracts this view from two main directions. First, he seeks to show how the aesthetics of melodrama as a popular and commercial form give access to truths about human existence denied to more culturally respectable forms such as European art cinema. Second, he seeks to demonstrate how it is possible under certain social and production conditions for the melodrama to be ideologically subversive.

In common with other critics, Elsaesser establishes melodrama as a form that belongs to the bourgeoisie. In its first manifestations – which Elsaesser cites as the eighteenth-century sentimental novel and post-Revolution romantic drama – it constituted an ideological weapon against a corrupt and feudal aristocracy. The bourgeois family's struggle to preserve the honour of the daughter from despotic and unprincipled aristocrats marked a contest over space for private conscience and individual rights. Elsaesser identifies certain features in early bourgeois melodrama as important to its later developments:

the capacity of the eighteenth-century sentimental novel and romantic drama to make individual conflicts speak for a society that, he argues, lies in the popular cultural tradition it inherited, leading from the medieval morality play to music-hall drama, the most significant aspect of which was its 'non-psychological conception of the dramatis personae' (Elsaesser, 1972, p. 2); and formal devices such as ironic parallelism, parody, counterpoint and rhythm. Another significant feature is the siting of the struggles of individualism in the family. For Elsaesser, the family is not, except in early forms of melodrama, important in itself as a political institution; rather, through the highly charged formal motifs of melodrama, it provided a means of delineating social crises in concretely personalised and emotional terms.

These constituents of the melodrama – its non-psychological conception of character and formally complex mise en scène, its containment of action within the family and consequent emphasis on private feeling and psychic levels of truth – enable Elsaesser to construct the family melodrama of the 1950s as the peak of Hollywood's achievement. According to Elsaesser's argument, by the time melodrama was taken up in the cinema it was already saturated with significance beyond the specific socio-historical conditions that gave rise to it. He therefore looks to cinematic history to illuminate how the strategies of melodrama are realised in film. He argues that in the beginning, all silent cinema was forced into a melodramatic mode – not simply because of its temporal closeness to Victorian popular forms (see Fell, 1974; Vardac, 1949), but because the requirements of expression outside verbal language fortuitously pushed the medium into modes that favoured a melodramatic worldview. While the coming of sound meant the dominance of the verbal register and a consequently different dramatic mode, the development of new technologies in the 1950s – colour, widescreen, deep focus, crane and dolly – often in the hands of German directors with backgrounds in Expressionism, made a complex visual mise en scène again possible, in which the spoken word would be submerged as only one strand in a musical counterpoint.

Coincident with the development of the technology for such a dramaturgy was the popularisation of Freudian psychoanalysis in America in the 1940s and 1950s. The family reappears as a site of dramatic action, though in a far different ideological context from its heroic stance in the emergence of melodrama as a bourgeois form. The domestic melodrama provides not the exterior spaces of the western or urban gangster film to be conquered by a hero, who, in search of oedipal identity can express himself in action, but a closed self-reflexive space in which characters are inward looking, unable to act in society (Elsaesser, 1972, p. 10).

Not only do the location and mores of the family reduce the scope for dramatic action, but the characters themselves, in line with the melodramatic tradition, are unaware of the forces that drive them. The intensity and the significance of the drama, then, are not carried in what the characters say, or in the articulation of inner struggle as in tragedy: rather it is the mise en scène of melodrama, providing an 'aesthetics of the domestic', that tells us what is at stake. The 'pressure generated by things crowding in on the characters ... by the claustrophobic atmosphere of the bourgeois home and/or small town setting' (Elsaesser, 1972, p. 13) is intensified through the demand of the 90-minute feature film for compression of what may be far more expansively expressed in its literary sources. There is, Elsaesser argues, a sense of 'hysteria bubbling all the time just below the surface' and a 'feeling that there is always more to tell than can be said' (Elsaesser, 1972, p. 7).

Elsaesser draws on Freudian concepts for the interpretation of mise en scène, arguing that the aesthetic strategies of 1950s melodrama function similarly to Freud's 'dream-work'. Sometimes this is a matter of the stock characters' lack of self-awareness producing an explicit form of displacement at the level of the plot:

> The characters' behaviour is often pathetically at variance with the real objectives they want to achieve. A sequence of substitute actions creates a kind of vicious circle in which the close nexus of cause and effect is somehow broken and – in an often overtly Freudian sense – displaced.
> (Elsaesser, 1972, p. 10)

In other cases, it functions 'by what one might call an intensified symbolisation of everyday actions, the heightening of the ordinary gesture and a use of setting and decor so as to reflect the character's fetishist fixations' (Elsaesser, 1972, p. 10).

This account provides the basis of Elsaesser's argument that in the hands of gifted directors and at the right historical moment, it can be used to critique the society it represents. Key terms here are pathos and irony. The externalisation of feelings and reactions into decor, gesture and events objectifies and distances emotions, producing pathos or irony

> through a 'liberal' mise-en-scène which balances different points of view so that the spectator is in a position of seeing and evaluating contrasting attitudes within a given framework ... resulting from ... the total configuration and therefore inaccessible to the protagonists themselves.
> (Elsaesser, 1972, p. 15)

Thus melodrama can suggest causes beyond individual responsibility, to be found on a 'social and existential level' (Elsaesser, 1972, p. 14).

The melodramatic aesthetic gains its social force in a circular movement of displacement: while capitalist society creates psychic problems that become acutely focused in family and sexual relations, so events within the family are displaced outwards into the mise en scène indicating forces that exceed specific family conditions. From this position, Elsaesser suggests that the shift in 1950s Hollywood from the linear trajectory of the active hero conquering the spaces of the west or the city, to the impotent hero trapped within a domestic interior and confined by the codes of behaviour appropriate to the family, indicates a shift in the ideological conditions obtaining under postwar advanced capitalism. The melodramatic form had come full circle from its initial championing of individual human rights via the bourgeois family's struggle against a feudal aristocracy to a later critique of the ideology of individualism in which the bourgeois family becomes the site of the 'social and emotional alienation' consequent on a corrupt individualism and the failure of the drive to self-fulfilment (Elsaesser, 1972, p. 14).

The major distinction between Elsaesser's position and the work that followed later lay in his use of Freud and Marxism. While noting the rich potential of Freudian subject matter for Hollywood melodrama and assuming rather than analysing the oedipal hero as dominating the form, it is on the formal mechanisms of a Freudian 'dream-work' that Elsaesser bases his argument for the rich and complex significance of the melodrama's mise en scène. And what he takes from Marxism is not so much a classical definition of class relations as a notion of alienation translated into existential terms. Consequently, his arguments do not analyse or distinguish between class and gender relations in Hollywood melodrama, beyond the displacement of one into the other, 'the metaphysical interpretation of class conflict as sexual exploitation and rape' that, according to Elsaesser, dominates the form throughout its history (Elsaesser, 1972, p. 3). This means that the question of how a female protagonist may affect plot structures or the trajectory of the hero's oedipal drama remains unexamined. Furthermore, the emphasis on melodrama as 'form' and 'mise en scène' neglects questions that generic specifications would have raised; for instance, the distinctions and relations between the woman's film, romantic drama, family melodrama – questions important to an understanding of the place of women in melodrama. Issues of class and gender, but particularly of gender, were to figure in the next stage in the emerging debate about melodrama.

Sex and class in melodrama

Later work on melodrama was to prise Elsaesser's groundbreaking work away from its metaphorical and existential proclivity for mise en scène analysis. What followed was either a more sociological approach to its subject matter (see Kleinhans, 1978; French, 1978), which understood the family as a political institution and site of real oppression, particularly for women; or work influenced by the development of feminist film theory that produced accounts of the social or sexual positions made available in the narrative to protagonists and spectators. Here mise en scène, rather than being metaphorically resonant, was seen as symptomatic, indicating the 'return of the repressed', or insoluble contradictions.

Central to the debates that emerge in these reassessments of melodrama is the significance of the bourgeois family as a product of patriarchy and capitalism. At issue here is how the social relations of capitalist production – class – articulate with the social relations of capitalist/patriarchal reproduction – the family. Once the bourgeoisie stops rising, it is no longer easy to see in it a direct symbolisation of class struggle – as is argued of the eighteenth-century sentimental novel or post-Revolution romantic drama, for instance. However, the family is felt to be related to class at an ideological level. On one hand, it seems to operate as a trans-class institution; on the other, it reproduces individuals as class subjects. The family, however, does not simply secure class subjects; it also produces sexed individuals. Arguably, the neuralgic point for debates around cinema melodrama is the interrelation of sex and class. In this respect, Freud and Marx compete to provide the terms of analysis of the family; according to which authority is given more emphasis, the family is viewed as the site of sexual repression (Nowell-Smith, 1977; Mulvey, 1977/78) or of displaced socio-economic contradiction (Kleinhans, 1978). From Freud is taken the oedipal drama, particularly the moment of castration and repression; from Marxism the concept of the division between productive and personal life, in which the contradictions inherent in the alienated labour of capitalist production are supposed to be compensated for within the family, where, however, they are merely displaced (see Kleinhans, 1978).

The male oedipal crisis

Geoffrey Nowell-Smith (1977) located melodrama as a bourgeois form by distinguishing its address from that of classical tragedy. Whereas tragedy does not depict the class to which it is addressed, the social relations depicted in melodrama presume authority to be distributed 'democratically' among heads of families rather than vested in kings and princes. Thus 'the address is from one bourgeois to another bourgeois and the subject matter is the life of the bourgeoisie'. While this apparent egalitarianism avoids questions about the class exercise of power, the relation between social power and gender becomes potentially more visible – less a question of the symbolisation of one by the other (see Elsaesser, 1972) than of their articulation together. The paternal function becomes crucial in establishing both the right of the family to a place in the bourgeois social hierarchy and, through the mechanism of inheritance, the property relations that underpin this position. The problem for the family is the possible failure of the father to fulfil this function suitably, together with the risky business of raising the son into a patriarchal identity in order that he may take over his property and his place within the community. One root cause of such possible failure is the confinement of sexual relations within the family – evoking the oedipal drama – and the problematic position of women there.

However, while Nowell-Smith makes the relations of power, gender and sex more visible, he still leans towards a masculine construction of melodrama. Like Elsaesser, he distinguishes melodrama from the western in the way it closes down on potential social action and turns inward for its drama. Although he does not make the home an existential space, it becomes simply the arena of the 'feminine' characterised by passivity and negativity. Feminist film theory had argued that representation of the 'feminine'as positive, rather than 'non-male', was impossible within the framework of classic Hollywood narrative. Nowell-Smith draws on such arguments to deal with the 'feminine' presence in melodrama. While acknowledging it frequently figures female protagonists, he argues that 'masculinity' still constitutes the only knowable heroic norm, so that acute contradictions are involved in the production of active female characters. The space allowed female characters, while it cannot represent femininity, facilitates an exploration of problems of male identity.

From here, Nowell-Smith goes on to give an account of melodrama as a patriarchal form, taking the oedipal drama (more literally than does Elsaesser) as its subject matter. The Hollywood melodrama of the 1950s is structured in terms of conflict between the generations, in which the son has to accept his symbolic castration by the father before he can take up his place in the patriarchal and bourgeois order, proving himself, by becoming both an individual and like his father, capable of reconstituting the family unit for the next generation (Nowell-Smith, 1977, p. 116).

Like Elsaesser, Nowell-Smith draws on Freud for an understanding of the mechanisms of melodramatic narrative and mise en scène. However, rather than concepts elaborated in *The Interpretation of Dreams*, Nowell-Smith deploys Freud's account of a childhood fantasy, the 'family romance', and his theory of conversion hysteria. The family romance provides the means of understanding the melodrama as being both about the family, foregrounding female characters, and about patriarchal identity. In the family romance, the child questions its parenthood, exploring through the question 'Whose child am I?', or 'would I like to be?', different family arrangements. Thus the structure allows differential and even taboo sexual relations to be explored, reorganised and eventually closed off in the final resolution of a reconstituted family to which melodrama is committed.

However, Nowell-Smith argues, such resolution is consequent on castration and therefore on repression; for fiction, this means an initial laying out of the problems, entry into the fantasy, which, nevertheless, cannot be articulated explicitly. This

Daydreamer: Jane Wyman longs for Rock Hudson in Douglas Sirk's *All That Heaven Allows*

leads Nowell-Smith to the notion of mise en scène as 'excess' – a 'too much' of music, colour, movement that indicates not simply a heightening of emotion but a substitution for what cannot be admitted in plot or dialogue, a process for which Freud's theory of 'conversion hysteria' provides an analogy (Nowell-Smith, 1977, p. 117). From a perspective that views classic Hollywood in terms of the 'classic realist text', such 'hysterical moments' can be seen as a breakdown in realist conventions, where elements of the mise en scène lose their motivation and coherence is lost. Such moments of breakdown cannot be done away with by a 'happy end' but represent the 'ideological failure' of melodrama as a form, and so its 'progressive' potential.

Melodrama and real life

Chuck Kleinhans offers a different perspective. A Marxist–feminist sociology of the family, rather than Freudian theories of sexuality, provides the premiss of his arguments: 'Since bourgeois domestic melodrama emerges with the ascension of capitalism, and since it deals with the family, it makes sense to look at the family under capitalism to better understand melodrama' (Kleinhans, 1978, p. 41). He characterises the social relations of capitalist production in terms of a split between 'productive' work and personal life now confined to the home – the sphere of reproduction. The alienation of the labour process within capitalist forms of production is disguised and compensated for in the notions of personal identity and happiness supposed to be found in the family, a bourgeois conception of 'people's needs' shaped by the ideology of individualism. At the same time, women and children are marginalised outside production and confined to the home, while women become responsible for providing the fulfilment that capitalist relations of production cannot – a need whose source lies outside the family and therefore cannot be achieved. 'This basic contradiction forms the raw material of melodrama' (Kleinhans, 1978, p. 42).

Kleinhans argues that, in the piling on of domestic conflict and disaster, in its concentration on 'the personal sphere, home, family, and women's problems' (Kleinhans, 1978, p. 42) and its closeness to real life, melodrama deals more directly than many other genres with themes and situations close to its audience's experiences. In so doing, its function is similar to that of the family itself, displacing social contradiction, working through the problems of keeping the family intact at the cost of repression and women's self-sacrifice. In these terms, melodrama is a profoundly conservative form. Its penchant for ambiguity, far from providing an ironic critique of bourgeois society, disperses critical focus among a number of possible readings. In *All That Heaven Allows*, for instance, the unsuitability of Cary's second marriage to her gardener is equally and indifferently a problem of class, of age, of lifestyle – thus attenuating the film's purchase on its subject matter. For Kleinhans, these films are symptomatic – indicating the strategies of bourgeois ideology for evading structural problems. They are not, however, instances of ideological breakdown or aesthetic radicalism and it is only analysis from quite a different position to that of the film that can reveal its project.

The two voices of melodrama

Laura Mulvey's (1977/78) contribution shifts the emphasis away from melodrama as a 'progressive' genre by reinserting questions about the place of women both in the subject matter of melodrama and in its conditions of production and consumption. While sharing some of Kleinhans's concerns, her feminist perspective produces a very different intervention. Kleinhans sees the family as a product of capitalist social relations residing in the split between 'productive' and 'reproductive' life: patriarchy does not enter as a term in his analysis, and, as with Elsaesser, the question of gender specificity in melodrama disappears.

For Mulvey, however, it is in patriarchy that the pertinent and irresolvable contradictions lie. For her, the notion that melodrama exposes contradictions in bourgeois ideology by its failure to accommodate the 'excess' generated by its subject matter (see Nowell-Smith, 1977) fails to understand either the degree to which family and sexual relations are constituted as contradictory or the role of melodrama in providing a 'safety valve' for them. Drawing on Helen Foley's view (about Aeschylean tragedy) that 'over-valuation of virility under patriarchy causes social and ideological problems which the drama comments on' (Mulvey, 1977/78, p. 54), Mulvey argues that 'ideological contradiction is the overt mainspring and specific content of melodrama, not a hidden, unconscious threat' (Mulvey, 1977/78, p. 53). Consequently, mise en scène can no longer be the means of privileged critical access to progressive interpretation, but rather, in 1950s Hollywood melodrama, represents the specific aesthetic mode that distinguishes it from tragedy, working overtime to carry what the limited stock figures of bourgeois melodrama cannot consciously be aware of, 'giving abstract emotion spectacular form' (Mulvey, 1977/78, p. 55). Thus Mulvey closes off the notion of a formal subversiveness being inherent in the melodramatic mode.

Instead, she looks to the production conditions of melodrama and its relation to its imputed female audience, whose material and cultural conditions of existence the form, despite the 'symbolic imbalance' of narrative structures, was forced to acknowledge: it is, after all, the patriarchal need for coexistence with women that produces the crisis melodrama seeks to alleviate. Because she insists on the real contradictions of patriarchal ideology for women, rather than their metaphorical significance for men, Mulvey begins to show how melodrama can both function for patriarchal ends, bringing about a narrative resolution of its contradictions, and at the same time perform a quite different function for women: offering the satisfaction of recognising those contradictions, usually suppressed (Mulvey, 1977/78, p. 53).

This view leads Mulvey to distinguish between those films that are 'coloured by a female protagonist's dominating point-of-view' and those that deal with male oedipal problems by examining 'tensions in the family, and between sex and generations' (Mulvey, 1977/78, p. 54), constructing the hero as Elsaesser's and Nowell-Smith's victim of patriarchal society. Sirk, she argues, worked in both traditions, his independently produced *The Tarnished Angels* (1958) and *Written on the Wind* (1957) conforming to the second pattern, his work for Ross Hunter at Universal, who specialised in women's pictures (see *All That Heaven Allows*), belonging to the first. Women's pictures, variously known in the trade as 'weepies', 'sudsers' or 'four handkerchief pictures', were tailored to the female matinée audience, generally deriving from women's magazine fiction or novelettes, and had a tangential relation, yet to be fully explored, to the family melodrama derived from the bourgeois novel. These films are characterised by an attempt to reproduce the woman's point of view as central to the narrative, and if there is subversive excess in melodrama, this is where Mulvey locates it. Whereas the patriarchal mode of melodrama is able to produce some form of readjustment of its values, some reconciliation between the sexes, the attempt to entertain the woman's point of view, to figure feminine desire, produces narrative problems of an order impossible to tie up, except in the fantasies of women's magazine fiction. In *All That Heaven Allows*, Cary, a widowed mother of two, past child-bearing age, is able to unite with her younger, employee lover only when a last-minute accident renders him bedridden and incapable. However, such a fantasy, while resolving certain of the narrative's contradictions, touches on 'recognisable, real and familiar traps, which for women brings it closer to daydream than fairy story' (Mulvey, 1977/78, p. 56).

Progressing the debate

Two major and interlinked areas of debate emerged from Mulvey's and Nowell-Smith's interventions. The first concerns the 'obscured dialectic between class politics and sexual politics, bourgeois ideology and the patriarchal order' (Pollock, 1977, p. 106); the second, the question of whether gender difference can be said to have aesthetic consequences in fictional structures.

The repressed feminine

Griselda Pollock (1977) takes up the first issue in a consideration of what precisely is repressed in the oedipal moment. She notes confusion in discussion of melodrama as to whether its representation of the family signifies an interrogation of bourgeois family relations, or the displacement of contradictions found in bourgeois social relations, or both. Behind this lies an issue about the primacy of patriarchal or of capitalist relations – of sex or class determination. Pollock wants to argue the necessity of thinking of the family, and the place of women within it, as a product of both in dialectical articulation together. In this respect, she sees both Nowell-Smith (1977) and Mulvey (1977/78) as in danger of 'reifying sexuality outside the social formation', arguing that 'the contradictions which *All That Heaven Allows* exposes are between different social positions, not just irreconcilable desires or the sexuality of women' (Pollock, 1977, p. 110). Taking issue with the view that femininity in patriarchal culture is unrepresentable because unknown and unknowable, Pollock argues that femininity can be produced only as specific social positions. In western society, the social position of mother is crucial to the perpetuation both of capitalist social relations and patriarchal dominance, demanding the subjugation of female sexuality in social and cultural life. From Pollock's perspective, the women's point-of-view movies and male oedipal dramas have one thing in common: the relocation of the woman as mother, a position that, while fathers may disappear, be rendered silent or impotent, dominates the conclusion of these films.

However, such relocation faces the problem of 'the extraordinary and disruptive role played by the woman's uncontained, withheld or frustrated sexuality in the dynamic of the narrative' – which includes 'female sexuality outside familial roles' (Pollock, 1977, p. 111) and the continued sexuality of mothers. This leads Pollock to posit the 'repressed feminine' as the key to understanding melodrama. In her terms, the 'feminine' represents a psycho-sexual position, hypothetically available to either sex, but foregone and repressed in the reproduction of sons in the patriarchal, masculine position and daughters as mothers. What is important here is that femininity is understood not simply as an empty, negative, passive space, but something positively 'lost' in the construction of the social and sexed subject positions necessary to patriarchal, bourgeois society. Although Pollock does not do so, the fantasy of the family romance could be invoked here to explain the patriarchal function of both women's film and male family melodrama. In one of its forms, it allows the child to disown the father and fantasise the mother's independent sexuality with another man. This, for the male child in particular, allows both an exploration of incestuous desire and identification with the female position; for the female child, it allows a refusal of the repression required for the confinement of female sexuality to reproduction.

Taking up Mulvey's (1977/78) 'safety valve' theory of melodrama, Pollock goes on to suggest that many of the contradictions exposed in 'progressive' analysis of melodrama are in fact ones that patriarchal and bourgeois culture can contain. And this is as true of the women's picture tradition as of the male family melodrama; the woman's point of view in *All That Heaven Allows* is not in the last analysis what is disruptive. Cary in fact is offered as a passive spectator of her own fate, quite in line with patriarchal ideology, whereas in *Home from the Hill* (1960), on the surface a male melodrama, the figure of the woman, totally robbed of point of view, holds nevertheless enormous control in the disposition of narrative events.

Pollock's intervention in the debate constitutes a useful appraisal of its theoretical assumptions. She attempts to construct terms in which the women's picture and family melodrama can be thought through together in terms of a problematic that embraces the dialectic of sex and class. However, attractive as Pollock's conception of the source of potential disruption in melodrama might be, the notion of the 'feminine position' outside of patriarchal and bourgeois social relations is highly abstract, and not much further forward in providing a sense of the articulation of sex and class that she demands.

Class and sex in the maternal melodrama

Christian Viviani (1980) is concerned with 'woman' as an already culturally coded figure capable of mobilising audience response towards new conceptions of social organisation. He attempts an analysis of the ideologies reworked in a subset of Hollywood melodrama that appears to effect a passage between its Victorian forms, epitomised in the work of Griffith, and the woman's film – a subset that Viviani dubs 'the maternal melodrama'. His analysis of this subgenre in the 1930s deals with the transformation of European, Victorian themes under pressure from New Deal ideology. In this, the role of woman as mother is pivotal, suggesting something of the way issues around female sexuality and maternity can be dramatised as a displacement or resolution of class issues (see Elsaesser, 1972). Viviani's contention is that as a fictional mode, melodrama seeks to move its audience emotionally by an appeal to everyday feelings and experiences that are then magnified in intensity through a complexity of baroque incident and coincidence. The fallen mother is a figure who can readily summon up such feelings, particularly for the male audience for whom she carries a charge of oedipal eroticism. At the same time, the sexual transgression of the mother is capable of evoking not only a moral but also a class register, for the variations in moral attitude to her speak different class ideologies.

The dramaturgical structure on which this is based, and which was adopted by Hollywood from the European Victorian stage, involved

> a woman [who] ... separated from her child, falls from her social class and founders in disgrace. The child grows up in respectability and enters established society where he stands for progress ... The mother watches the social rise of her child from afar; she cannot risk jeopardising his fortunes by contamination with her own bad repute. Chance draws them together again and the partial or total rehabilitation of the mother is accomplished, often through a cathartic trial scene. (Viviani, 1980, p. 7)

A mother's love: Barbara Stanwyck as Stella in *Stella Dallas*

This basic structure could be organised ideologically according to two different codes of judgment, one moral, the other social. For the European-influenced and smaller cycle, the woman's fall 'was traceable to her adultery, committed in a moment of frenzy and expiated in lifelong maternal suffering' (Viviani, 1980, p. 6). In Hollywood, this vein represented a female equivalent to Warshow's 'gangster as tragic hero' (see The gangster film as an experience of art, p. 280). Although still morally condemned, the heroine's descent into the 'more realistic, more tawdry or desperate ambiance of music halls and furnished rooms' marked an opposition to the permanence of the bourgeois household, a 'veritable ideal of this thematic, totally impregnated by Victorian morality' (Viviani, 1980, p. 8). Her fate of 'anonymity and silence' was the opposite of the tale favoured by Hollywood of success and rise to fame. However, though admitting its potentially critical slant on European aristocratic moral codes, Viviani argues that this cycle looked decidedly reactionary from the perspective of the New Deal:

> Heroines who are submissive, resigned, sickly, even naive ... defenceless, lacking in energy or decisiveness were hardly good examples for the movie-going public of 1932 and 1933 who needed to be mobilised to face the economic crisis. The direct lineage of Madame X was an uncomfortable reminder of an earlier state of mind which had led to the Wall Street crash. (Viviani, 1980, pp. 9–10)

As America became more isolationist and nationalistic, the moral codes of the maternal melodrama shifted gear. The foundations of such a shift had been laid in the work of Griffith, who had performed the necessary transposition from a European aristocratic urban milieu to an American, petit bourgeois and rural one, which both bore the brunt of an ideological criticism (as, for instance, in *Way Down East*, 1920), but was capable of regeneration. New Deal ideology, according to Viviani, 'is incarnated halfway between city and country' (Viviani, 1980, p. 12), and it is the figure of woman with her culturally given connection to nature, who can facilitate this incarnation, which both castigates 'the residue of an outworn morality' hung on to by the idle city rich and the rigidity of rural society in the name of the 'pantheistic philosophies of Thoreau and Whitman'. In the American maternal melodrama of the 1930s, epitomised by *Stella Dallas* (1937), the motif of maternal sacrifice is rearticulated in relation to themes closer to American society of that time: 'prejudice, education, female understanding, the "good marriage" of the children' (Viviani, 1980, p. 10). In this context, moral sin is replaced by social error and a new kind of heroine can emerge whose sacrifice is less dumb acquiescence to an inevitable and remote fate than a struggle to survive in a society whose values need correcting: 'Integrated into the world of work, she unconsciously participates in the general effort to bring America out of the crisis; she is set up as an antagonist to a hoarding, speculating society, repository of false and outworn values' (Viviani, 1980, p. 12).

Her child becomes a stake in this regeneration, not taken away from the mother as in the European cycle, but given up 'to insure him an education, a moral training that only a well-placed family can give him' (Viviani, 1980, p. 13). 'These films recount the tale of a woman's loss due to a man's lack of conscience and show her reconquering her dignity while helping her child re-enter society thanks to her sacrifices. It is a clear metaphor for an attitude America could adopt in facing its national crisis' (Viviani, 1980, p. 14).

The figure of the mother could effect such ideological work because of the powerful emotions she calls up in the viewer, producing 'an illusion destined to mobilise the public in a certain direction, an illusion that transposed the anguish of an era, an illusion ... knowingly grounded in eroticism' (Viviani, 1980, p. 16). By implication, the power of such eroticism to effect displacement or resolution of class difference lies in the flexible class definition of the woman. On the one hand, this is dependent on familial and sexual placing, transgression of which produces the woman in the position of outcast. On the other, ideologies of maternity and femininity – for example, the woman sacrifices self for child, or acts out of true love for a man – can be utilised to argue for an ideological shift in the moral balance of power between different class forces.

Feminist approaches

Laura Mulvey's essay 'Visual pleasure and narrative cinema' has been seminal in suggesting the role the figure of woman plays in patriarchal fiction. Her concern there, as she has since explained it (see Mulvey, 1981), was to examine the masculinisation of spectator position and identification in classic Hollywood cinema. However, as she herself argued (1977/78), a female protagonist at the centre of the narrative disturbs this structure. This view has led to work by feminists on the possible aesthetic consequences of gender difference. Pam Cook (1978) argued that *Mildred Pierce* (1945) represented a mixed-genre film in which the male voice of film noir combated the

A mother's guilt: Joan Crawford is economical with the truth in *Mildred Pierce*

female voice of the woman's film, with both narrative structure and mise en scène enacting the subordination of the latter to the former. Barbara Creed (1977) considered the narrative consequences of the generic necessity of the woman's melodrama (in her terms, any melodrama that supports a central heroine) to produce the figure of the woman as leading protagonist. She investigated the differences between the narrative structures developed to cope with a female protagonist and those that characterise most other genres. The problem the melodramatic structure faces is one of producing drama while conforming to social definitions of women in their domestic roles as wives and mothers (Creed, 1977, p. 28).

From a small group of women's pictures, she derives a typical narrative structure capable of supporting a central feminine protagonist 'which involves a pattern of female role transgression; the entry of an exceptional male; marked change in the heroine's point of view; suffering and sacrifice; and, finally, her acceptance of a more socially desirable role' (Creed, 1977, p. 28). She goes on to show how in the three women's pictures she studied, the discourse of the doctor is used to bring the transgressing woman's viewpoint into line with the accepted codes of feminine behaviour. For Creed, the displacement of the female protagonist's dilemma into mise en scène and into a range of other characters, far from combating an ideology of individualism, simply restates her problem in terms of other people's needs – reproducing a scenario in which the woman does not speak, but is spoken for (Creed, 1977, p. 29). Like Kleinhans, she sees melodrama as interesting for the questions that an analysis constructed elsewhere – by Marxism or feminism – can show it touching on but not able to ask. Whereas in Kleinhans's case there are questions of capitalist relations of production and class, Creed suggests that the unspoken question of women's melodramas is to do with the taboo subject of female sexuality.

Melodrama and the status quo

Most accounts of melodrama in literature and cinema, including those discussed above, agree on one thing: that in its post-revolutionary bourgeois forms, the boundaries of the field in which it operates are those of the established social order as lived in everyday domestic terms. For instance, Stephen Neale argues that whereas in most other genres the establishment of law and order is the object of the narrative, melodrama focuses on problems of living within such order, suggesting not 'a crisis of that order, but a crisis within it, an "in-house" rearrangement' (Neale, 1980, p. 22).

Jean-Loup Bourget presents the same idea in ideological rather than moral terms: 'America after questioning the myth of progress, urbanisation and socialisation, is content with a rhetorical question and at the end of the story reinstates the same belief' (Bourget, 1978, p. 32). Elsaesser concretises these generalities in an acute description of the mise en scène of the domestic, arising from an account of *Hilda Crane* (1956), which, he argues, 'brings out the characteristic attempt of the bourgeois household to make time stand still, immobilise life and fix forever domestic property relations as the model of social life and a bulwark against the more disturbing sides in human nature' (Elsaesser, 1972, p. 13). Thomas Schatz, in a survey of 1950s melodramas, notes the paradoxical narrative function of marriage and the family, which provides both dramatic conflict and resolution. Of *Young at Heart* (1955) he argues: 'We have seen the central characters as either victimised by or utterly hostile to the existing social-familial-marital system, but somehow romantic love and parenthood magically transform familial anxiety and despair into domestic bliss' (Schatz, 1981, p. 229).

The necessity for melodrama to produce dramatic action while staying in the same place gives it a characteristically circular thematic and narrative structure – many cinematic melodramas start out from a flashback so that their end literally lies in their beginning. And it gives melodrama a characteristically ambiguous modality and address, which has given rise to different interpretations. Bourget, writing about the romantic dramas of 1940s Hollywood, describes their hesitation between, on the one hand, a heavy-handed moralistic realism, operating in parable-like fashion in support of the bourgeois family, and on the other, the disbelief of whimsy, of escape offered by 'romance'. Stephen Neale, writing from a psychoanalytic perspective, describes this ambiguity of melodrama as a form of pathos to do with the narrativisation of desire, which, by its very nature, can never be fulfilled (Neale, 1980, p. 30).

While these accounts vary in the degree to which they see subversive potential within, or despite, such constraints, they are alike in concentrating on formal analysis of the genre. Only a feminist interest in the relation of the films to the lives of their audiences has suggested that the formal ambiguity within which the genre works is neither simply a meretricious ploy to soak the drama for all the pathos it is worth without confronting serious issues, nor a mass medium's attenuation of the tragic vision, but provides a structure that relates to the material conditions of women's lives.

What appears as the affect of form in one critical context is given a material reality in another. This observation is not quite the same as noting the 'real life' occurrence of events that seem exaggerated or absurd in the films. Links between the form and the lives of the presumed female audience are commonly made by industry, establishment critics and feminists. The audience for women's pictures and melodramas is most often characterised as composed of frustrated housewives, oppressed by the duties of motherhood and marriage, by sexual frustration and lost fantasies of romantic love. In this view, the women's pictures and melodramas of the 1940s and 1950s gave cultural expression to these frustrations, offering in vicarious outlets escapist fantasy, rage, or sublimation. In the words of Molly Haskell (1979), the films represent 'soft-core emotional porn for the frustrated housewife'.

What the industry and Marxist feminism have in common is an implicit view of the housewife's life and the emotions it calls forth as being narrow, circumscribed, petty, boring and frustrated. Critics, and many of the directors and writers involved in these films, regard them with contempt or mild patronage, looking for value in what can be made of the situations in terms of the 'human condition'. Hence the great interest in the notion of the form's power lying in its capacity to subvert its content. Recent work on melodrama, however, has ceased to look for textual progressiveness. This is partly due to the displacement of mise en scène by a psychoanalytically construed concept of narrative as the key to a film's ideological operation. In this view, classic narrative functions precisely to engage with 'difference' – whether social, sexual or unconscious – but always from the reassuring perspective of 'the same' to which everything is returned at the end. From quite a different approach, the notion of progressive reading has become suspect because of the formalism that constitutes meaning textually, without reference to the reading situation and practices of actual audiences. Further work on melodrama and the woman's film has been pursued predominantly by feminists, proceeding in two main directions: one a formal, narrative/discourse-orientated approach; another, frequently focusing on TV soap opera, an audience-orientated approach. The former is concerned to analyse the work performed by narrative structure and the process of enunciation when a female protagonist is posited as subject of desire and discourse rather than its object (see Lea Jacobs, 1991; Mary Ann Doane, 1983). The latter traces a homology between the ambiguous modality of melodrama, its circular structure, and the contradictions within which women's lives are constructed. The woman's film and melodrama provide fictional structures and forms of pleasure that reproduce a 'female' subject, and at the level of the text some of the material conditions in which women live (see Modleski, 1979; Brunsdon, 1981). In these terms, the duplicitous complexity with which Kleinhans charges *All That Heaven Allows* – where the displacement of problems to do with class, age, sexuality into female problems of personal relations renders them simply confusing – is not so much a question of ideological poverty in the analysis of class or age, but of the difficulty of mapping the 'question of femininity', of women's issues, across other social definitions.

Melodrama and the woman's film since the 1990s

STEVE NEALE

In 1987, many of the articles discussed above were collected together and introduced by Christine Gledhill in *Home Is Where the Heart Is: Studies in Melodrama and the Woman's Film*. Far from signalling the culmination of work in these areas, this publication coincided with and helped to promote and focus additional research, including books by Lang (1989), Byars (1991), Jacobs (1991), Basinger (1993), Klinger (1994) and a further collection of articles edited by Bratton, Cook and Gledhill (1994), based on papers delivered at a major international conference on melodrama held in London in 1992. In addition, E. Ann Kaplan discussed melodrama and the woman's film at some length in *Motherhood and Representation* (1992), and the directing and scripting of women's pictures by women were discussed by Judith Mayne (1994) and by Lizzie Francke (1994) respectively.

Each of these books and studies presented new insights and/or new research. Lang's book was the first systematic study of the 'family melodramas' directed by Griffith, Vidor and Minnelli. It included extensive discussion of *The Crowd* (1928), as well as *Stella Dallas* and *Ruby Gentry* (1942), *Madame Bovary* (1949), *Some Came Running* (1958) and *Home from the Hill*, placing these films within the context of familial, oedipal and patriarchal issues and concerns.

Byars's book was a study of gender in the films of the 1950s, and highlighted the extent to which the films themselves drew on and interacted with wider social and cultural debates and representations. Focusing on men as well as women, she extended the canon of films traditionally discussed by referring in detail to films such as *Picnic* (1955), *From Here to Eternity* (1953), *A Streetcar Named Desire* (1951), *All That Heaven Allows* and *Imitation of Life* (1959). She also addressed issues of class and race.

Klinger also focused on the 1950s, specifically on the films directed by Douglas Sirk. Eschewing traditional auteurism and conventional textual analysis, Klinger's concern was to trace the contemporary contexts within which Sirk's films, their devices, their stars and their style were understood. Her approach represents – and seeks to bring together – renewed interest in historiography and historiographical research on one hand, and interest in audience research and in the multiple readings of films produced by audiences on the other.

Kaplan situated an array of films and film cycles from different periods in cinema's history within and across changing – and unchanging – ideologies and representations of motherhood. Within this context, she considered topics such as the maternal woman's film, themes of maternal sacrifice and paradigms of motherhood such as 'Angel' and 'Witch'.

Jacobs considered in detail a particular cycle of films – the 'Fallen Woman' films of the late 1920s, the 1930s and the early 1940s – which in many ways represented and embodied a challenge to traditional ideologies of motherhood and femininity. Focusing on the issue of self-regulation and self-censorship, and using specific archival case files, Jacobs's study demonstrates on the one hand how social ideologies and the practices of the film industry interacted at a specific point in time, and on the other how that process of interaction was always also a process of negotiation, a two-way or sometimes a three- or four-way process whose results – the films themselves – were often highly complex, ambiguous and contradictory.

These characteristics were also stressed by Mayne in her study of the work of Dorothy Arzner, and in Francke's account of the work of several generations of female scriptwriters in Hollywood. They also formed the basis of Basinger's account of the woman's film. For Basinger, as for many others:

> What emerges on close examination of hundreds of women's movies is how strange and ambivalent they really are. Stereotypes are presented, then undermined then reinforced. Contradictions abound, which at first sight seem to be merely the result of carelessness, the products of commercial nonsense. But they are more than plot confusion. They exist as an integral and even necessary aspect of what drives the movies and gives them their appeal. These movies were a way of recognizing the problems of women, of addressing their desire to have things be other than the way they were offscreen. (Basinger, 1993, p. 7)

Unlike others, Basinger offers a 'working definition' of the woman's film that extends well beyond the traditional canon, the traditional label and the traditional confines of 'melodrama'. 'A woman's film', she writes, 'is a movie that places at the center of its universe a female who is trying to deal with emotional, social, and psychological problems connected to the fact that she is a woman' (Basinger, 1993, p. 20). It thus includes – or should include – 'Rosalind Russell's career comedies, musical biographies of real-life women, combat films featuring brave nurses on *Bataan*, and westerns in which women drive cattle west and men over the brink' (Basinger, 1993, p. 7).

The point that Basinger makes here is clearly both polemical and logical. It is also a point that raises questions about generic labels and terms, and about the relative weight to be accorded institutional terms – the terms used by Hollywood, and by contemporary reviewers, critics and journalists – as opposed to those used and defined by subsequent theorists and subsequent historians. Similar questions have been raised by Ben Singer (1990) and by Steve Neale (1993), who have researched the deployment and definition of 'melodrama' as a term both inside and outside Hollywood, and its relationship to female-centred narratives on the one hand, and to the woman's film on the other. Both find significant differences between the understanding and use of the term in and around the film industry and other contemporary institutions of entertainment – the theatre, and in Neale's case television and radio – and the understanding and use of the term in and around film, media and cultural sudies.

Broadly speaking, both Singer and Neale have found that 'melodrama' meant 'thriller', and hence was used principally to describe and to label crime films, adventure films, war films, westerns and horror films. Singer, who is concerned with the 1900s, the 1910s and the 1920s, quotes from a 1906 article entitled 'The Taint of Melodrama': 'Ask the next person you meet casually how he defines a melodramatic story, and he will probably tell you that it is a hodge-podge of extravagant adventures, full of blood and thunder, clashing swords and hair's breadth escapes' (Singer, 1990, p. 95). Neale, who is concerned with the sound period through to the end of the 1950s, quotes from an issue of *Life* magazine (27 August 1925, p. 26):

> Melodrama, on the screen, is identified almost entirely with fast physical action; cowboys or sheiks or cavalrymen riding madly across country, men hanging by their teeth from the ledges of skyscrapers, railroad wrecks, duels, heroines floating on cakes of ice toward waterfalls, and every known form of automobile chase.

He also quotes from numerous trade reviews, and notes that the only two films made by Hollywood with the word 'melodrama' in the title – *Manhattan Melodrama* (1934) and *Washington Melodrama* (1941) – were both thrillers or crime films.

As Singer and Neale both point out, women's pictures – and films marked generally by domestic settings, by romance and/or by pathos and sentiment – were called dramas, not melodramas, and Neale goes on to speculate that this use of the term may derive from theatrical genre, 'drama'. The only female-centred films regularly described as melodramas were, precisely, action films and thrillers of one kind or another, from the 'serial queen' adventure films that Singer discusses – *The Perils of Pauline* (1914), *The Exploits of Elaine* (1914–15), *The Hazards of Helen* (1915) and others – through such female-centred aviation films as *Tail Spin* (1939) and *Women in the Wind* (1939), to the numerous female-centred detective films and Gothic thrillers of the 1940s – *Murder among Friends* (1941), *Second Chance* (1947), *Mary Ryan, Detective* (1949) and *Gaslight* (1944), *Shadow of a Doubt* (1948), *Undercurrent* (1946) and *Secret Beyond the Door* (1948). (For further discussion of the aviation films, see Paris, 1995, pp. 114–16; for further discussion of the Gothic thriller, see Waldman, 1983; Walsh, 1984; Doane, 1987; Barefoot, 1994.)

Neither Neale nor Singer denies a relationship between the woman's film, as traditionally defined, and nineteenth-century theatrical melodrama. But they both point to the heterogeneous – the multi-generic – nature of nineteenth-century melodrama. And they both point to the possibility that the meaning of melodrama as a term may have altered as melodrama itself altered and changed. Singer argues that there was a division between cheap, popular, sensational melodrama and highbrow and middle-class theatre at the turn of the century. Despite the fact that elements of nineteenth-century melodrama fed into the latter, the former became the site of an equation between 'melodrama' and thrills, spills and action, blood, thunder, villainy and vulgarity upon which commentators, critics, audiences and reviewers in film and in the theatre increasingly drew. Neale's argument is similar, though, drawing on Rahill (1967), he places the division further back in time, arguing for a correspondence between the woman's film and what Rahill calls 'modified melodrama', a form of melodrama that emerged initially in the second half of the nineteenth century, and in which:

> The 'heart' became the target of playwrights rather than the simple nervous system, and firearms and the representation of the convulsions of nature yielded the centre of the stage to high-voltage emotionalism, examination of soul-states, and the observation of manners ... The unhappy end became common. (Rahill, 1967, p. xv)

Neale argues that it was this form of melodrama, an inheritor of *drame*, which became known simply as drama. The action-based forms fed first in the theatre and then in the cinema into action-based genres of various kinds and tended to retain the melodrama label. Some of these points were made some time ago by Michael Walker (1982), who sees nineteenth-century melodrama as a matrix both for action genres and what he calls 'melodramas of passion'.

It is clear that melodrama, the woman's film and the precise nature of the relationship between them remain key areas of debate and research. It is equally clear, as numerous commentators have pointed out (for example, Vardac, 1949; Fell, 1974) that melodrama is related to other genres, and that further research – and debate – is needed in this area as well.

Selected Reading

Jeanine Basinger, *A Woman's View: How Hollywood Spoke to Women, 1930–1960*, London, Chatto & Windus, 1993.

Christine Gledhill (ed.), *Home Is Where the Heart Is: Studies in Melodrama and the Woman's Film*, London, BFI Publishing, 1987.

Barbara Klinger, *Melodrama and Meaning: History, Culture, and the Films of Douglas Sirk*, Bloomington and Indianapolis, University of Indiana Press, 1994.

Ben Singer, 'Female power in the serial-queen melodrama: the etiology of an anomaly', *Camera Obscura* 22: 94–5, January 1990. Reprinted in Abel (ed.), *Silent Film*, New Brunswick, NJ, Rutgers University Press, 1995.

A Fool There Was (USA 1915 *p.c* – William Fox/ Box Office Attractions Company; *d* – Frank Powell)

This film plays on a typical theme of nineteenth-century stage melodrama – the disaster that besets a respectable family when its head falls prey to a fashionable vamp (a stereotype instituted in Theda Bara's role here, and which made her a star). Examples of early film melodrama style can be found in the film's use of the static camera, the lack of close-ups and the reliance on natural light sources. Viewed from the perspective of 1950s family melodramas, this can be seen as a lack of technological development; or it can be understood as the continuity, even fulfilment, of certain nineteenth-century theatrical traditions (see Vardac, 1949). Melodramatic effects, for instance, are produced by the crosscutting between pathetic scenes of the wife with her angelic daughter or in church, and the scenes of dissolution at the vamp's apartment or of despair in the husband's home, wrecked through his squandering time and money on his mistress and drink. The husband himself becomes the site of a struggle between two representations of women: the wife, who hearing of the vamp's desertion declares 'If he is as you say my place is with him', and the dark-haired sexual woman. Melodramatic expression is carried, as in the theatre, by furnishing and fittings – a chaise-longue, a card table, half-empty bottles and glasses, costume – the wife's squashed-down hat, the furs and silky gowns of the vamp, and significant gesture – the vamp's stare that drives the wife from her husband's arms. The scene utilising the staircase was to become a standard feature of a cinematic rhetoric in the expression of melodramatic confrontation (see also *Written on the Wind*, 1957). Here, the husband is tempted to return to wife and daughter until the vamp appears in her nightdress at the top of the stairs to drive them away, causing the husband to collapse, his hand reaching through the banister in a gesture of helpless appeal. The necessary reliance on natural light is turned to theatrical affect by lighting schemes exploiting the dramatic conflict of darkened rooms pierced by shafts of light as curtains and blinds are drawn or closed. And a substitute for the play of light and shade is found in the wreaths of incense that swathe the vamp in her apartment, evoking an atmosphere of decadence and mystery.

CHRISTINE GLEDHILL

Way Down East (USA 1920 *p.c* – D. W. Griffith; *d* – D. W. Griffith)

Way Down East was based on a Victorian melodrama of the same name. Griffith bought the rights in 1920, at a time when films were moving away from melodrama to become more naturalistically rooted in contemporary issues. Both play and film, as Kozloff (1985), Lennig (1981) and Kauffmann (1972) have observed, drew on certain themes and specific events in Thomas Hardy's *Tess of the D'Urbervilles*.

The melodramatic origins of the film are evident in the stereotypical characters (virginal heroine, clean-cut hero, idealised mother, stern father, shrewish busybody), as well as in instances of narrative coincidence, such as when the heroine Anna (Lillian Gish), having started a new life in another town, happens to be seen by her ex-landlady, who knows the secret about her dead illegitimate baby. The film also contains several inexplicable moments that seem to operate from what Peter Brooks (1976) calls the 'occult realm'. Foremost among these are the scenes showing David (Richard Barthelmess), who has yet to meet Anna, waking from a bad dream while she gets married to the villain, and the one in which David 'senses' Anna's arrival at his farm although it is spatially impossible for him to see her.

But *Way Down East* is not just unadorned melodrama. According to Cardullo, 'Filming the whole of Anna's story, as opposed to solely the plot of the play, gave Griffith one large advantage; he could make it appear less melodramatic, or better, he could enhance the realism of the melodrama' (Cardullo, 1987, p. 17). Melodrama, although often forming the emotional core of Griffith's films, is always accompanied by a sense of the 'photographically realistic'; we are shown – we see – concrete realities, with locations and interiors 'made real' through meticulous detail. In narrative terms, Griffith usually chooses to show us events rather than allowing them to take place off screen. For example, with the ice-flow rescue of Anna at the film's climax: 'In the play, we only hear of Anna's incredible rescue. In the film, her rescue becomes credible because we see it happen …' (Cardullo, 1987, p. 17). The rescue off stage allows Poetic Justice to claim at least a partial role; in the film, the rescue is all down to David's (and Barthelmess's) courage in actually braving the rapids. It becomes an almost strictly human act.

Significantly, whereas the play opens with Anna's arrival at the Bartlett farm, and only gradually reveals her secret, Griffith chose to tell the story chronologically. In the play, therefore, Anna's guilty secret is gradually revealed to both spectator and other characters at the same time. In the film, the spectator knows the secret as it happens, well in advance of the scene that finally reveals it to the other characters. Thus viewers are positioned with Anna throughout the film, intensifying the emotional affect of the melodramatic chain of events.

MICHAEL ALLEN

Sunrise A Song of Two Humans (USA 1927 *p.c* – Fox Film Corporation; *d* – F. W. Murnau)

The plot of this film is typical of nineteenth-century domestic melodrama, involving the temptations held out to a young farmer, living happily with his wife and child, by a city vamp, who consumes his small financial resources and finally suggests murdering his wife. The iconography of the domestic melodrama is everywhere: the oil lamps, soup bowls, peasant bread and chequered tablecloth signifying domestic virtues; conflicting representations of femininity – the wife and mother with blonde hair pulled back flat in a bun, associated with traditional peasant country life, the sexual woman in silky garb, black bobbed hair, smoking, jitterbugging and associated with the modern city; the moon and mists over the marshes as the site for the young farmer's succumbing to the murder plot. This iconography contributes to the extreme moral polarities between which the man is pulled, and which are intensified by the non-individualisation of the protagonists, designated only as the man, the wife and the woman from the city.

While much of the film's iconography, melodramatic structure and mise en scène looks back to nineteenth-century theatrical melodrama, it also looks forward in its style to the full development of cinematic melodrama. Notable in this respect is, first, the influence of German Expressionism that Murnau brings to Hollywood, particularly in the distorted perspectives of the interior sets, the stereotyping of the woman from the city, the dramatisation of typography in the

High emotions: country boy George O'Brien is seduced by city vamp Margaret Livingston in Murnau's *Sunrise*

intertitles that spell out the murder plot, the split screen, superimpositions and dissolves that link the woman and the city; second, Murnau's development of the moving camera, which led Bazin to put him on the side of the realists. Arguably, however, the moving camera (for instance, to bring the young farmer to the city woman on the marshes) and the long-take, deep-focus tracking shot that allows us to travel with the young couple on the trolley from lakeside to city are part of the externalisation of emotion into cinematic mise en scène that Elsaesser (1972) describes as the hallmark of full-blown Hollywood melodrama in the 1940s and 1950s.

Finally, the film's use of sound marks its transitional status. For while it utilises a synchronous soundtrack, it fulfils the nineteenth-century melodramatic ideal of reducing dialogue in favour of music and pictorial mise en scène, adding only a few expressive sound effects.

CHRISTINE GLEDHILL

Stella Dallas (USA 1937 *p.c* – Samuel Goldwyn Inc; *d* – King Vidor)

This is a classic and much-debated woman's film, so designated because of its central woman protagonist, its 'feminine' subject matter and its address to a female audience. These features overlap with the melodramatic mode insofar as domestic subject matter, family relations and the expression of 'feelings' are seen as both sources of the melodramatic and belonging to the feminine province. In this context, and given the cultural ghetto in which the woman's film existed until recently, the melodramatic becomes a pejorative designation, associated with tear-jerking pathos and sentimentality, provided frequently by the presentation of women as victims of their circumstances or nobly self-sacrificing. Christian Viviani (1980) has described a shift in the articulation of the maternal self-sacrifice theme in 1930s Hollywood when, under pressure from New Deal ideology, the motif of the mother's fall and degradation gave way to her energetic attempts at recovery, providing a more upbeat ending. It is this spirit that motivates *Stella Dallas*, where the motif of maternal sacrifice is called on to collaborate in the portrayal of the family as a means to upward mobility and social hope. Stella's (Barbara Stanwyck) 'failing' is not so much the utilisation of her charms to catch a rich man as a means of escaping her Depression-oppressed family, but her refusal to tone down her ambitions and lifestyle in order to match those of her upper-class husband, or to suppress her sexuality once a mother, and then later allowing her bonding with her daughter to replace conjugal relations. Stella's punishment is the crushing realisation that her lack of financial and social capital will hinder the possibility of a 'happy', upwardly mobile marriage for her daughter. She therefore proves her superior motherhood by deliberately alienating her daughter to make such a marriage possible, thereby loses for ever the relationship that motivates the sacrifice.

The debate about the film is how to understand the implications of the ending. Does it represent the punishment of the erring mother, or is it more contradictory? Arguments that this is the case point to the difference in the maternal sacrifice theme when played out in a woman's film. The scene in which Laurel (Anne Shirley) turns down the offer of a fur coat is an interesting example of this, where Laurel is entranced with the 'good taste' and economic well-being of the Morrison household to the detriment of Stella's good-hearted vulgarity. The scene is played out through women's magazine iconography – the dressing table, mirror, cold cream and hair bleach – and the activities of the 'feminine' world. However, this iconography does not simply dramatise the problem of female upward mobility; it also plays on the dependency of such mobility on the right appearance, a rightness that has little to do with the real underlying relations between mother and daughter.

This suggests a second twist to the maternal sacrifice theme offered by the woman's film. E. Ann Kaplan has argued (in Gledhill, 1987) that the mother/daughter bond characteristic of the woman's film is potentially threatening to patriarchal social and sexual relations. This, Kaplan argues, gives a special meaning to the film's ending when Stella is forced to accede to the sacrifice of the bond so that her daughter can enter heterosexual monogamy and contribute to social progress, while she herself is reduced to mere spectatorship, outside the scene of action. However, Linda Williams gives a different inflection to the ending by concentrating on its address to a female audience (in Gledhill, 1987). Williams argues that the multiple identification through which the 'feminine' is constructed in the film means that the female audience identifies with the contradictions of Stella's position itself. The only possible unifying point of identification is Stephen Dallas (John Boles), who, however, is totally lacking in empathy. The audience stand-in at this point is Helen Morrison (Barbara O'Neil), the only person to recognise Stella's sacrifice, and who purposefully includes Stella into the scene patriarchy would exclude her from by leaving the wedding parlour curtains open. We see Stella's patriarchal placement, but feel the loss of mother and daughter to each other.

CHRISTINE GLEDHILL

Gaslight/The Murder in Thornton Square (USA 1944 *p.c* – Loew's Inc/MGM; *d* – George Cukor)

The nineteenth-century theatrical roots of Hollywood melodrama are explicitly drawn upon – and transformed – in *Gaslight*. The film's stage origins, its Victorian setting and its melodramatic narrative led *Variety* to comment that the film verges 'on the type of drama that must be linked to the period on which the title was based', but also to compliment it for 'lacking the ten-twenty-thirty element that had been a factor in the stage play'. The reviewer's reference is to the 10, 20 and 30 cent admission charges levied at the beginning of the century by theatres specialising in lowbrow melodrama (see Rahill, 1967, pp. 272–83). The MGM production values clearly indicate more prestigious aspirations, but the Victorian furnishings displayed in *Gaslight* have the additional function of forming a decorous surface that conceals but at the same time accentuates the force of the film's melodramatic material. Thus the scene in which the married couple attends a musical recital lends itself to the display of production values characteristic of many period films, but also allows the melodrama to be acted out behind this ornate façade. Indeed, the decorum of the occasion partly serves to heighten the force of the disruption.

Ornate setting for repressed feelings: Ingrid Bergman and Charles Boyer in *Gaslight*

The fact that in *Gaslight* the husband (Charles Boyer) and wife (Ingrid Bergman) have a relationship tantamount to that of oppressor and oppressed has allowed it to be interpreted as a critique of patriarchy and the institution of marriage. Key issues here are the confirmation or denial of the heroine's perception, and her ability to articulate her fears. Thomas Elsaesser lists *Gaslight* as belonging to a cycle of 'Freudian feminist melodramas' – films 'playing on the ambiguity and suspense of whether the wife is merely imagining it or whether her husband really does have murderous designs on her' (Elsaesser, 1972, p. 11). Other writers have related the cycle to a 'female Gothic' tradition, given a particular inflection by the shifting demands made on women in wartime and postwar America (see Waldman, 1983).

In *Gaslight*, there is confirmation of the heroine's point of view. But if this signifies a validation of female experience, it can be argued that it also ushers in a restoration of the patriarchal order. The detective who comes to the wife's rescue and confirms what she has seen and heard provides a sympathetic male to counterbalance the figure of the tyrannical husband. The narrative closure also serves to locate the film within the codes of classic Hollywood cinema – the sensationalism of the melodrama is ultimately contained by the film's narrative resolution. The question here is to what extent can this resolution accommodate what has gone before?

GUY BAREFOOT

Written on the Wind (USA 1957 *p.c* – Universal-International; *d* – Douglas Sirk)

This film was central to the rediscovery of melodrama in the early 1970s, when a revaluation of Douglas Sirk as auteur (see also Douglas Sirk, p. 451) pointed to the ideological critique that his ironic mise en scène operated on 1950s middle-class America.

Its plot enacts a typical family melodrama in which the constriction of its range of action is reinforced by the circularity of its flashback structure and the hopeless, limited and incestuous channels for its protagonists' desires, locked as they are within the bourgeois patriarchal family. Behind Kyle Hadley's (Robert Stack) impotence lies his father's (Robert Keith) failure as patriarch, further manifested in the excessive, misdirected desire of his daughter Marylee (Dorothy Malone), expressed here in the displacement of her desire for Mitch (Rock Hudson) into her active pursuit of a lower-class petrol-pump attendant. In this respect, the plot foregrounds the interconnection of class and sexuality that Elsaesser (1972) and others contend is central to melodrama, class struggle being enacted as a problem of desire, in which female sexuality plays an ambiguous but central role (see Pollock, 1977).

The play of class and sex is carried in the iconography of the film – all the signs of conspicuous bourgeois consumption of the Hadley mansion, the oil pumps working incessantly against the skyline, the contrasting colours and costume of the conflicting couples – particularly reds associated with Marylee (sports car, flowers, negligée) and the cool green twinsets of Lucy (Lauren Bacall). Such use of decor, costume and consumer goods is typical of Hollywood family melodrama, as is the use of the space of hallway and landings where characters cross paths, eavesdrop, exchange confidences, malicious innuendo or accusations. Overlaying 1950s melodramatic plot structure and iconography is the special injection of Sirkian irony into its excessive mise en scène; his play with cliché (the nodding mechanical horse and grinning child that confront Kyle at the moment he believes himself impotent); an obsessive play with mirrors (Mitch's entrance with a drunken Kyle over his shoulder is first caught in a hallway mirror); screens and windows (Marylee looking through her window panes to the policeman and the petrol-pump attendant); and above all an Expressionist use of colour, which breaks with realist conventions for the sake of wresting ironic contrasts from objects and faces (the harsh lighting and make-up on Lucy's and Mitch's faces as they attempt to soothe Kyle at the country club, where the palm-court music is also in striking contrast to the extreme emotions expressed by Kyle).

Mismatched: Dorothy Malone lusts after Rock Hudson in *Written on the Wind*

Sirkian mise en scène can also be read in terms of the repression so often said to provide melodrama with its outbreaks of expressive excess, which in turn draws its audience into the emotional drama rather than putting them at a critical distance. The breaking out of repression at the level of plot, florid mise en scène and crosscutting typical of melodramatic style are epitomised in the climactic scene where the father falls to his death down the staircase while daughter Marylee dances wildly and erotically to blaring pop music in her bedroom. The scene also exemplifies the extension of 'musical counterpoint' so crucial to nineteenth-century theatrical melodrama into visual and aural mise en scène (see Elsaesser, 1972).

CHRISTINE GLEDHILL

In the Mood for Love/Huayang Nianhua Hong Kong/France 2000 *p.c* – Block 2 Pictures/Jet Tone/Paradis Films/Orly Films; *d* – Wong Kar-wai)

Though melodrama has largely been discussed as a western European phenomenon, as a popular form it extends beyond national boundaries. One of the richest examples occurs in Chinese culture, where melodrama is found in theatre, opera, literature and film (see Chinese cinema, p. 192). Many of the tropes perceived as specific to Hollywood melodramas and women's pictures are present in Chinese cinema, from the social realist dramas to the stylised art movies of the Fifth Generation film-makers. But although these iconographic, narrative and thematic elements resonate across national contexts, their expression is specific to their cultural and historical origins.

Hong Kong director Wong Kar-wai is known for his stylish, postmodern adaptation of Hong Kong genre movies, themselves indebted to Hollywood (see Hong Kong cinema, p. 224). *In the Mood for Love* has been seen as a tender reworking of Chinese cinema melodramas such as Fei Mu's 1948 *Springtime in a Small Town/Xiaocheng Zhi Chun*, which told the story of a married woman's unconsummated love for a young doctor, and her inability to free herself from a loveless marriage. Fei Mu's film, which was controversial in China because of its focus on inter-personal relationships rather than politics, had at its centre key melodramatic themes: the passage of time, memory and coincidence. The heroine's decision to stay with her ailing husband has been perceived as conservative and nostalgic, harking back to a period of moral and social stability. *Spring-time in a Small Town* resonates with David Lean's World War II women's picture *Brief Encounter* (1945), which told a similar story of frustrated adulterous passion and was received with ambivalence by contemporary audiences because of its nostalgia for prewar values (see David Lean, p. 432).

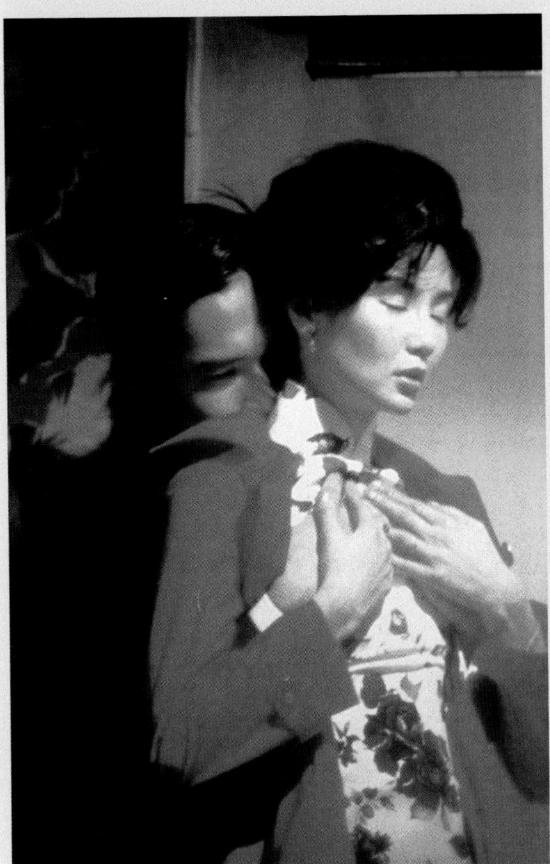

Desire deferred: Tony Leung and Maggie Cheung in *In the Mood for Love*

Several commentators have remarked on the similarities between these films, Douglas Sirk's 1950s melodramas and Wong's *In the Mood for Love*, which is set in 1960s Hong Kong and concerns a married woman, Mrs Chan/So Lai-chen (Maggie Cheung) who suspects her husband of having an affair with the wife of Chow Mo-wan (Tony Leung), living in the same crowded apartment building (see Teo, 2005). As these two share their fears, they embark on their own tentative affair, though it is not clear whether it is consummated, and the story ends with So Lai-chen returning to her husband, leaving Chow Mo-wan bereft. Wong's exquisite staging of this scenario of passion deferred is poetic in its play with ritual, repetition and lost opportunities, and it wears its debt to Hong Kong cinema and culture on its sleeve, both in its allusive visual design and in its eclectic use of music. The film's use of classic melodrama to evoke the transience of Hong Kong's culture and communities testifies to the enduring power of the genre and to its transnational nature.

PAM COOK

Far from Heaven (USA/France 2002 *p.c* – Vulcan Productions/Focus Features/Killer Films/John Wells Productions/Section Eight/USA Films/Clear Blue Sky Productions/TF1 International; *d* – Todd Haynes)

Todd Haynes's appropriation of Douglas Sirk's 1950s melodramas in *Far from Heaven* has been the subject of much debate. Its strategy of quotation and allusion has been seen by some as draining Sirk's films of their powerful emotional affect, and by others as using pastiche and irony to intensify emotion (see Dyer, 2006). Indeed, on its release, the film sparked a controversy about the value of pastiche. Its reworking of classic melodrama has also been controversial among feminists (see *Camera Obscura*, 2004).

Haynes's film can be approached from a different perspective. It borrows from several different Sirk films to create a new, multi-layered object: a reflection on the limitations of 1950s melodrama in dealing with its socio-political context, and a retrospective look at 1950s America

A sense of loss: Julianne Moore and Dennis Haysbert relive the past in Todd Haynes's Sirk tribute *Far from Heaven*

that attempts to make visible the social problems that Sirk's films could not confront or express directly. The result is a poignant play on 'then' and 'now' in which both are interleaved with one another, creating a sense of loss that echoes the tragic scenarios of Sirk's films, while allowing a fragile intimation of hope. The film may be seen as using nostalgia politically to activate a sense of lost ideals in its post-feminist, post-civil liberties audience, at the same time as recognising the achievement of some political aims. Thus it can be said to encourage historical reflection by generating the emotion of loss (see Cook, 2005).

As an essay on melodrama, *Far from Heaven* takes the famous visual excess of Sirk films such as *All That Heaven Allows* (1956) and *Written on the Wind* (1957) a stage further. Haynes uses costume, props, saturated colour and high-contrast lighting as a self-conscious homage to Sirk, but also to create a different aesthetic that might be called 'hyperbolic'. Hyperbole is a literary term that refers to a form of rhetoric; it employs exaggeration to produce a vivid impression in the reader, and it can be linked to the 'purple prose' characteristic of pulp romance fiction. In Haynes's Sirk tribute, it is represented by a knowing, symbolic use of costume and visual design that both alludes to its source texts (and the way they have been discussed in film studies), and refers to its own creative reinterpretation of those films. Like Wong's *In the Mood for Love*, *Far from Heaven* is both a love letter to past melodramas and a celebration of the genre's enduring relevance and vitality.

PAM COOK

THE MUSICAL

STEVE NEALE

The Hollywood musical is a product of the advent of sound, of the industry's commitment to an ethos and to forms of entertainment represented, among other things, by the theatrical musical, by Broadway and by Tin Pan Alley, of its stake in the music publishing, recording and radio industries (acquired during the conversion to sound in the late 1920s), and of developments in and on the musical stage in America and elsewhere during the previous 80 to 90 years. Film versions of stage musicals such as *The Merry Widow* and *The Student Prince*, and of operas such as *Carmen* and *La Bohème*, had been produced during the silent era. So, too, had filmed records of dancers and dances. As Collins (1988) points out, these and nearly all other films were usually accompanied by live music, and were often shown in contexts and venues that included musical performances of one kind or another. As he goes on to argue, it was the presence and popularity of these musical acts that helped prompt the first experiments with sound in the mid-1920s, and that helped function as a model for the preludes and shorts produced by Warners and others at this time. And as he goes on to suggest, the ensuing 'tension between live musical acts and film presentation', between 'the increasing technological sophistication of the medium ... and the sense of nostalgia for a direct relationship with the audience' has marked the musical ever since, providing the focus for such studies as those by Feuer (1993) and Altman (1987), and the motivation for his own concentration on the 'ever-shifting relationship between performance, spectacle, and audience' (Collins, 1988, p. 270). In the meantime, as Wolfe (1990) has pointed out, the established nature and shape of the musical short helped govern the use of musical sequences in *The Jazz Singer* (1927), the film usually cited as the first feature-length musical. During the course of the next three years, over 200 musical films of one kind or another were made, and despite a decline in the number of musicals produced and released in the early 1930s, the musical had re-established itself as a routine component in Hollywood's output by 1934 (Altman 1996; Balio, 1993; Barrios, 1995).

The musical has always been a mongrel genre. In varying measures and combinations, music, song and dance have been its only essential ingredients. In consequence, its history, both on stage and on screen, has been marked by numerous traditions, forms and styles. These in turn have been designated by numerous terms – 'operetta', 'revue', 'musical comedy', 'musical drama', 'the backstage musical', 'the rock musical', 'the integrated musical' and so on. As we shall see, historians, critics and theorists of the musical sometimes disagree about the meaning of some of these terms. As we shall also see, some invent their own. Nevertheless, it is possible to provide some basic definitions, to indicate areas of debate and disagreement, and in the process to highlight the extent to which the musical has always been, despite its accessible and effortless image, multifaceted, hybrid and complex (Collins, 1988, p. 269).

Revue, to begin with, is usually uncontentiously defined as a series of comic and musical performances lacking a narrative framework (lacking what in the theatre is called a 'book'), and unified, if at all, only by a consistent style, design or theme, a common set of comic targets, or a single producer, director or venue (Bordman, 1985; Kislan, 1980). Pure revue in the cinema is rare, though there was a vogue for revue in the late 1920s and early 1930s when as Balio, citing Walker (1979), points out, it 'was used by producers to showcase stars and contract players and to offer "proof positive that everyone could now talk, sing and dance at least passably well"' (Balio, 1993, p. 211). And as Delameter points out, the influence of revue is evident in the backstage musical, where the show in preparation is usually a revue of one kind or another (Delameter, 1974, p. 122).

One of the distinguishing marks of operetta, by contrast, is the presence of a book. Important too, though, is the nature of the book, the nature of the setting, and the nature and importance of the music (in 1946, *Variety* argued that 'In operetta the score is the primary consideration ... The book, dancing (if any), comedy (if any), production and acting (if any) are all secondary to the music and singing' (p. 49). To quote Rubin: 'Operetta is characterized by its European origins, its elegance and sophistication of tone, its use of melodic, waltz-time music, its picturesque and exotic settings, and its strongly integrative organization around a melodramatic, romance-oriented book' (Rubin, 1993, p. 48). In the cinema, operetta is usually exemplified by the films of Jeanette MacDonald and Nelson Eddy (*Sweethearts*, 1938; *Rose-Marie*, 1936) and others, all based on stage hits by proponents of American operetta such as Victor Herbert and Sigmund Romberg, and all produced as a series by

On with the show: Lloyd Bacon's classic backstage musical *42nd Street*

Hunt Stromberg at MGM (Balio, 1993); by a cycle of stage adaptations made in the late 1920s and early 1930s (Balio, 1993); and, as an offshoot of this cycle, by a group of four Maurice Chevalier films made at Paramount: *The Love Parade* (1929), *The Smiling Lieutenant* (1931), *One Hour With You* (1932) and *Love Me Tonight* (1932), all highly acclaimed by critics for their risqué wit, and for their inventive use of editing, space and sound (Altman, 1987; Balio, 1993; Knight, 1985; Mast, 1987).

Operettas of a fairly traditional kind continued to be made in the 1940s and 1950s, some of them as vehicles for new musical stars such as Kathryn Grayson and Howard Keel, and some of them also, like the remakes of *The Desert Song* (1952) and *Rose Marie* (1954), as contributions to a contemporary vogue for action, adventure and spectacle (always in colour, and often in CinemaScope, Todd-AO or VistaVision too). However, the fact that so many of the 1950s film were remakes is significant. For most commentators argue that by then, traditional operetta as a form capable of generating new work was moribund or dead (Bordman, 1981; Kislan, 1980). However, some, for example Bordman (1981) and Traubner (1983), argue that it had already given rise to a new form, 'musical drama' (or 'the musical play').

Musical drama is usually exemplified by a tradition of Broadway musicals that begins with *Show Boat* in 1927, and runs through *Oklahoma!* (1943), *Carousel* (1945), *South Pacific* (1949) and other works by Rodgers and Hammerstein, *Brigadoon* (1947), *My Fair Lady* (1956) and other works by Lerner and Loewe, and shows such as *West Side Story* (1957) and *Fiddler on the Roof* (1964), all of which have been made into films, and many of which were roadshow productions in the 1950s and 1960s, a period in which Hollywood increasingly turned to Broadway for pre-sold, prestige material (Collins, 1988). Along with a tendency to use what Delameter calls '"big" voices' (Delameter, 1974, p. 123), one of the hallmarks of musical drama – one of the elements it derives from operetta – is the importance of its storyline (one that could accommodate pathos, dramatic conflict and even on occasion an unhappy ending), its attention to situation and character, and the 'sharply integrative' organisation of its music, its singing and its dancing. Integration of this kind became an ideal not only among those who wrote, directed and choreographed musical dramas, but also among critics, theorists and historians. It has tended to produce a canonic crest-line, a tradition of landmark films, shows and personnel. Although as Solomon points out, 'There is no evident reason' for preferring integration (Solomon, 1988, p. 71), and although there are significant differences between Broadway's crest-line and Hollywood's, both have resulted on occasion in partial and distorted accounts of the musical's history.

The notion of integration and the idea of 'the integrated musical' appear at first sight to be straightforward. However, as Mueller (1985) has pointed out, things are not necessarily as simple as they seem. Focusing on the relationship between the musical numbers and the plot, he argues that there are at least six different possible permutations, from numbers that are 'completely irrelevant to the plot', to those 'which contribute to the spirit or theme' or 'which enrich the plot, but do not advance it', to those 'which advance the plot' (Mueller, 1985, pp. 28–9) either through their setting and narrative function – it is here that he tends to place the backstage musical – and/or through their lyrical content.

The precision Mueller seeks to bring to the concept of integration is unusual. Most uses of the term are rather vague. It can act as a synonym for almost any form of motivation, and sometimes even as a synonym for stylistic or aesthetic coherence. This is one reason why its history, both on stage and in the cinema, is also rather vague. There is no doubt that operetta and musical drama are important. But a number of the films and shows cited by Mueller and others are musical comedies. This is certainly true of the Astaire–Rogers film made at RKO in the 1930s, the principal focus of Mueller's account. It is also true of the Princess Theatre shows written by Guy Bolton, Jerome Kern and P. G. Wodehouse in the late 1910s, often cited as early examples of integration by historians of the musical on stage (among them Bordman, 1982; Kislan, 1980; Smith and Litton, 1981).

Issues of integration notwithstanding, musical comedy has always been more heterogeneous than operetta or musical drama, as befits a genre – or subgenre – whose origins lay as much in the minstrel show, vaudeville and other forms of variety entertainment as in turn-of-the-century farce (Bordman, 1982; Smith and Litton, 1981). What has remained constant has been a commitment to comedy and the comic, to popular and vernacular styles of music, song and dance, and a willingness to sacrifice coherence or integration for the sake of either or both. Most Hollywood musicals are musicals of this kind. Films such as *College Holiday* (1936) and *Road to Morocco* (1942) have always outnumbered films such as *West Side Story* (1961), *Swing Time* (1936) and *Meet Me in St. Louis* (1944).

Alongside formal and subgeneric categories such as these, the musical has often been discussed under the headings provided on one hand by the names of its producers, directors, choreographers and performers, and on the other by the names of the studios responsible for its production. Once again, though, treatment of these topics has been somewhat uneven, governed more by critical taste and ideological preoccupation than by historical precision. During the studio era, for instance, most of the major and minor companies made musicals. But research into the production policies and output of these companies has been uneven, and this is as true of the musical as it is of other genres. Thus while there is a whole book devoted to the output of the Freed unit of MGM (Fordin, 1975), there are no book-length studies of the musicals produced by Fox, by RKO, by Warner Bros., or by Paramount, let alone those produced by Columbia, Universal or Republic. Moreover, while scholars such as Mordden (1988) and Schatz (1988), respectively, document Warners' role in the revival of the musical in the early 1930s, and MGM's numerical dominance of the genre in the postwar period, they are not really able to account for either. The same is true of Collins's account of Paramount's propensity for operetta, Warners' propensity for contemporary settings and backstage conventions in the 1930s, and MGM's propensity for self-reflexivity in the 1940s and 1950s (Collins, 1988). And the same is true of Rubin's observation that Fox's musicals in the 1940s tended on the one hand to feature big hands and exotic settings and on the other to eschew 'integration, coherent narrativity, consistent characterization, or even simply logic' (Rubin, 1993, p. 159). In addition, aside from Fordin's book on Freed, there are no detailed studies of the work of unit producers such as Charles Rogers, Hunt Stromberg, Joe Pasternak or Pandro S. Berman, though it should be noted that Schatz (1988) contains references to all these figures, and a particularly interesting account of the roles played by Rogers and Pasternak in the development of a formula for Deanna Durbin's musicals at Universal in the late 1930s.

Pandro S. Berman is probably best known as unit producer on the Astaire–Rogers musicals at RKO in the 1930s. These films, and Astaire's role within them as choreographer and director of musical numbers as well as singer, dancer and star, have been subject to extensive analysis, not least as relatively early examples of integrated musicals on screen. Mueller's (1985) book-length study documents in detail the modes of integration in these and other Astaire films, Astaire's eclectic style as choreographer, the traditions of dance upon which he drew, and in particular his style as choreographer for the camera, filming and editing sequences of dance in such a way as to preserve the integrity of the body and the space within which it moved.

Along with the work of Ernst Lubitsch and Rouben Mamoulian at Paramount in the early 1930s, the Astaire–Rogers films are generally cited as important points of reference for the work of Vincente Minnelli, Gene Kelly, Stanley Donen and others at MGM in the 1940s and 1950s. Minnelli's commitment to integration is well documented in his interviews and autobiography (Minnelli, 1974; Delameter, 1981). From this point of view, Elsaesser's (1981) account of Minnelli's films is exemplary. As he points out, the central characters are engaged in a struggle to assert their identity, to articulate their vision of the world. In the musicals they succeed, and a key device in this respect is what Genne (1984) has termed 'the dance-drama', lengthy sequences of dance in which the terms of the struggle are laid bare. Dance-dramas were also used by Donen and Kelly, who were equally committed to integration. Where they differ from Minnelli is in their preferences for stories involving strong male friendships, in their deployment of a sparser, brighter and more evenly lit mise en scène, and in their use of what Genne calls 'street dances' (like 'Singin' in the Rain') in preference to the 'festive' or 'party' scenes that tend to figure in Minnelli's films.

Minnelli, Donen, Kelly and Astaire all tended to contrast their work with that of Busby Berkeley, not least on the grounds of integration, motivation and display. However, as Rubin has pointed out, Berkeley's work – both on screen and on stage – belongs to a tradition that includes the circus, nineteenth-century extravaganza, the Wild West Show and the spectacular revue, a tradition that has always eschewed integration, and one whose persistence leads him to argue that 'the history of the musical ... [is] ... not so much a relentless, unidirectional drive toward effacing the last stubborn remnants of nonintegration, but a succession of different ways of articulating the tension and interplay between integrative (chiefly narrative) and nonintegrative (chiefly spectacle) elements' (Rubin, 1993, pp. 12–13). Rubin points out that in films such as *The Gang's All Here* (1943), Berkeley sought 'to spectacularize the entire film' (Rubin, 1993, p. 161), to turn the conventional relationship between the narrative and the numbers inside out. Alain Masson (1981) makes a similar point about George Sidney's work, arguing both that Sidney systematically exploited the artifice and the disjunctive potential of the musical and that his critical reputation has tended to suffer as a result.

Berkeley's work has also been criticised for what Lucy Fischer (1981) has called its 'optical politics'. In an analysis of *Dames* (1934), Fischer points out that women literally become two-dimensional images, subordinated to a voyeuristic gaze whose instrument is the camera and whose source is resolutely male. In this context, it is worth nothing that Berkeley made a number of musicals with Esther Williams in the 1940s and 1950s, and that along with Sonja Henie and Eleanor Powell, Williams is one of a trio of female performers whose films have been analysed by Faller in terms of what he calls their 'subversive power' (Faller, 1992, p. v). In each case, Faller sees the relationship between the narrative and the numbers as the site of a potential contradiction between the powers and performance skills demonstrated in and through the numbers and the ideological work of the plot. Thus Henie's solitary skills as a skater and Williams's solitary skills as a swimmer so dominate the numbers in their films that narratives that seek to pair them up with men 'fail to contain' them (Faller, 1992, p. 205). Meanwhile, Powell's skills as a dancer result, almost uniquely, in narratives that centre as much on a successful career as on domesticity or romance.

The relationship between gender, narrative and spectacle in the musical has been explored in the case of male performers too. Cohan, for example, argues that Fred Astaire's 'male image' is grounded in 'the so-called "feminine" tropes of narcissism, exhibitionism, and masquerade' (Cohan, 1993, p. 48), while Rickard (1996) argues not only that the dance sequences in the Astaire–Rogers films serve to sexualise Astaire's masculinity, but also that this sexualisation is authorised for the audience by Rogers's gaze. More traditional analyses of star personae and musical performance skills can be found in Babington and Evans (1985), who discuss Jeanette MacDonald, Maurice Chevalier, Fred Astaire, Ginger Rogers and Gene Kelly. As well as Kelly and Astaire, Delameter (1981) discusses Alice Faye, Betty Grable, Danny Kaye, Bill Robinson and others, though principally as dancers rather than as actors, singers or stars. Reflecting the tendency to focus on dance rather than music and song in the Hollywood musical, he also discusses choreographers such as Hermes Pan, Robert Alton, Jack Cole, Michael Kidd and Bob Fosse.

This account has so far focused on the studio era. However, although the musical is often viewed as a quintessential studio form, and although the number of musicals produced has certainly declined since the 1960s, the genre has by no means disappeared entirely. Aside from the occasional 'revisionist' musical such as *Nashville* (1975) and *All That Jazz* (1979), viewed by Collins (1988, p. 277) as 'metafictional' extensions of the self-

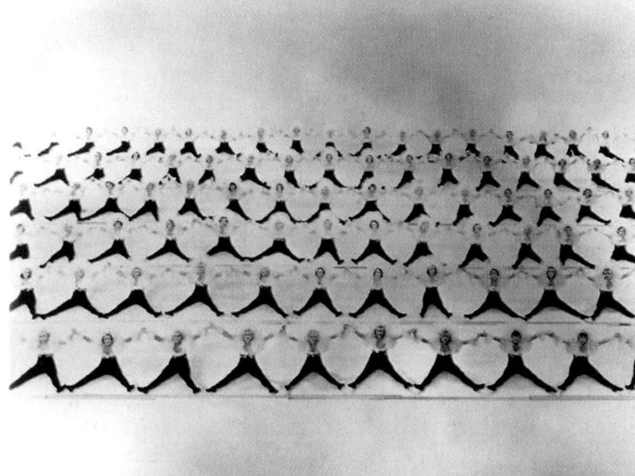

Optical politics: the female body reduced to two-dimensional spectacle in Busby Berkeley's *Dames*

The power of performance: the subversive Eleanor Powell in Norman Z. McLeod's *Lady Be Good*

reflexive Freed unit films, and aside from the even more occasional revival of something akin to the traditional musical such as *Evita* (1996), the numerically dominant form over the last 30 years has been the rock musical.

The rock musical was born in the 1950s with teenpics such as *Jailhouse Rock* (1957) and *The Girl Can't Help It* (1956). Apart from research on the synergistic connections between the film and popular music industries and their effects on musical films, debate since then has tended to focus on the extent to which it has challenged or changed the values and conventions of the traditional Hollywood musical. For Grant, the anarchic rebelliousness and raw sexuality associated with rock 'n' roll in the 1950s were potentially disruptive of the genre's commitment to romance and community. He argues, however, that by 'the stressing of rock's potential for community, and the taming of rock's energy through a deliberate moulding of its stars ... rock 'n' roll changed much more than ... the musical film' (Grant, 1986, p. 199). For Telotte (1980), by contrast, the musical has changed fundamentally since the 1950s, not because of its music, but because of a shift in the balance between its 'real' and its 'ideal' components. On one hand, musicals such as *Grease* (1978) and *The Wiz* (1978) 'tend to integrate the musical components at the expense of a realistic plot. As a result they seem to deny or denigrate the reality of the world that has given birth to the music' (Telotte, 1980, p. 3). On the other, musicals such as *Saturday Night Fever* (1977) and *The Buddy Holly Story* (1978) realistically motivate singing and dancing as diegetic action while setting them in counterpoint to a narrative world otherwise filled with difficulties, dangers and frustrations. In this way, they address the limitations – as well as the potential – of music and dance as means of escaping, transcending or changing the everyday world.

The 'escapist' status of the musical has been addressed at length by Dyer, Feuer and Altman. For Dyer (2002), musicals offer aesthetically 'utopian' solutions to real social needs and contradictions. The same is true for Feuer, who stresses the extent to which its artificial, quasi-modernist devices serve the conservative ends of showbiz by seeking to bridge the gap between producer and consumer and create in its stead an illusion of community. In this way, the Hollywood musical can be seen as a form of modern industrial mass entertainment that nevertheless 'aspires to the condition of folk art' (Feuer, 1993, p. 3). For Altman (1987), the resolution of contradictions and oppositions is not just a function of the musical, but also a method of analysis. Wishing to construct a rigorous critical definition of the musical, and a systematic history of its forms, its cultural functions and its history, Altman constructs a corpus of films on the basis of perceived structural, stylistic and ideological characteristics, all of which entail opposition and mediation. Central to the corpus is a 'dual-focus' structure in which 'the text proceeds by alternation, confrontation, and parallelism between male and female leads (or groups)' (Altman, 1987, p. 107), and in which a romance plot and a couple (or couples) provide the basis for the construction and reconciliation not just of differences of gender, but also – depending on the film – of differences of class, age, wealth, personality, outlook and so on as well. What this means, among other things, is that traditional narrative values such as causality and motivation, and the conventional opposition between the narrative and the numbers, are displaced by structures and devices of comparison and contrast whose role is to articulate the dualities with which any particular film is concerned. Among these devices are 'the audio dissolve' and the 'video dissolve'. Where the former 'superimposes sounds' (Altman, 1987, p. 63) in moving from one portion of the soundtrack to another (from conversation, for example, to music and song), the latter serves to connect 'two separate places, times, or levels of reality' (Altman, 1987, p. 74). Each device thus serves both to mark and to bridge oppositions.

Altman also constructs a new typology of musical forms. Using the relationship between the musical's romance plot and its ideological oppositions as a basis, he suggests that there are three basic musical types: 'the fairytale musical', in which 'restoring order to the couple accompanies and parallels ... restoration of order to an imaginary kingdom'; 'the show musical', in which 'creating the couple is associated with the creation of a work of art (Broadway show, Hollywood film, fashion magazine, concert, etc.)'; and 'the folk musical', in which 'integrating two disparate individuals into a single couple heralds the entire group's communion with each other' (Altman, 1987, p. 126).

Altman's book is the most sustained and detailed attempt to provide a theoretically rigorous account of the Hollywood musical. However, while it encompasses an impressive array of films and examples, and while its typology is convincing, it is not without its problems. Like Dyer (2002) and Feuer (1993), Altman tends to argue that the musical always resolves the contradictions with which it deals. This position is not uncommon among theories of genre. But it tends on the one hand to obviate the need for further research, since the answers to questions about ideology in particular are always known in advance. On the other, it tends to underestimate the extent to which musicals such as *Brigadoon* and *Maytime* (1937) blatantly signal their resolutions as unreal, and the extent to which musicals such as *West Side Story* and in particular *It's Always Fair Weather* (1955) (Babington and Evans, 1985; Wood, 1975) lay the costs of their resolutions uncomfortably bare. Meanwhile, Altman's insistence on the centrality of romance and a dual-focus structure is problematic, both because these elements characterise most romantic comedies as well as many musicals, and because some musicals lack either or both. Aside from *The Wizard of Oz* (1939), an example acknowledged by Altman himself (1987, p. 104), one might cite *Ziegfeld Follies* (1944), which as a revue lacks an overarching plot; *Hold That Co-Ed* (1938), in which the dual

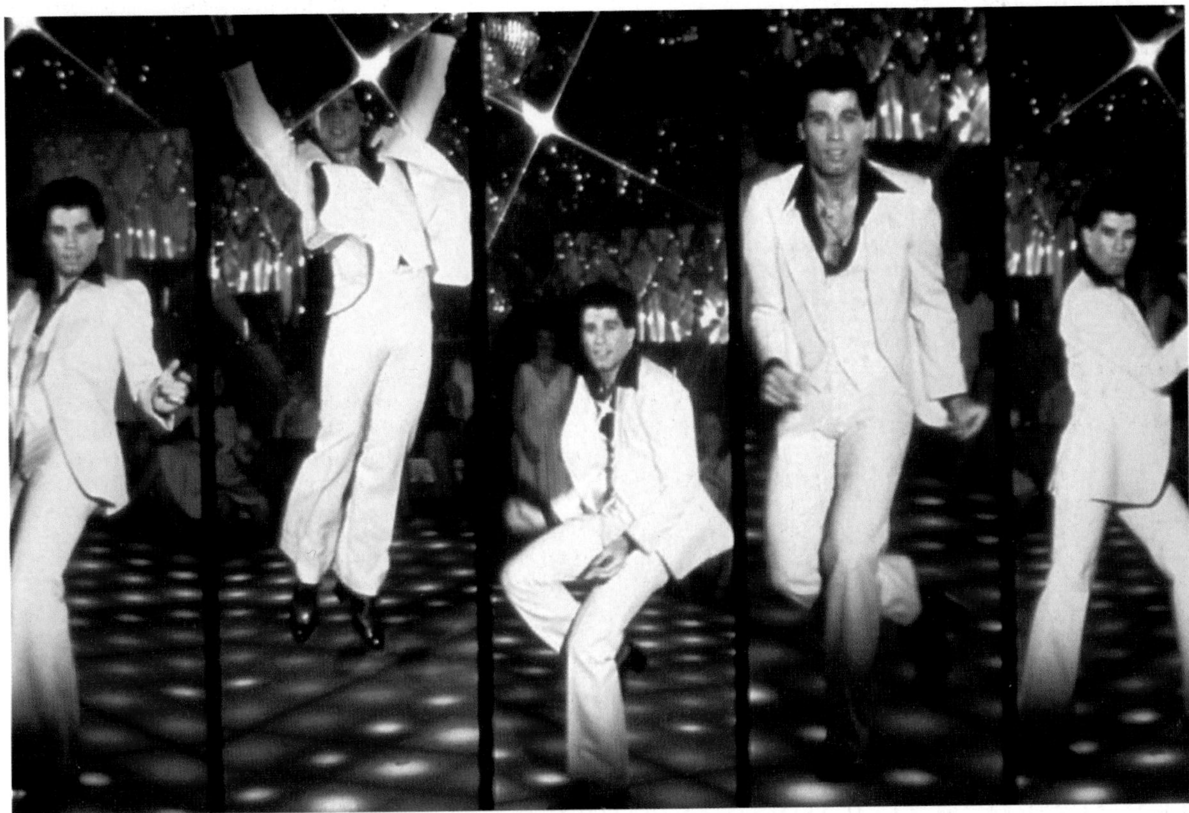

Rites of passage: John Travolta escapes through disco in *Saturday Night Fever*

cultural values of skilful, hard work and entrepreneurial flair are embodied in the alliance between a football coach and a local politician rather than in the film's perfunctory romance; *Poor Little Rich Girl* (1936), a Shirley Temple film that lacks both a romance and a dual-focus structure; *Jupiter's Darling* (1955), which is triple- rather than dual-focused; and *Meet Me in St. Louis*, which contains two romances, neither of which is dual focus in nature, and neither of which embodies the film's central opposition between domestic and familial harmony and domestic and familial discord.

Responding to an earlier version of these ideas (Altman, 1981), Babington and Evans cite *Gold Diggers of 1933* (1933) and *Easter Parade* (1948) as exceptions (1985, p. 80). While less ambitious than Altman, their own discussions of these and other musicals tend to be more attentive to the genre's multifarious nature as well as to the films' specificities. To that extent, their approach shares the virtues of those ideologically orientated analyses that are more localised and context specific, and more focused on particular issues, aspects, periods, performers and films than Altman's.

Selected Reading

Steven Cohan (ed.), *Hollywood Musicals: The Film Reader*, New York and London, Routledge, 2002.

Jane Feuer, *The Hollywood Musical*, London, Macmillan, 1982. Reprinted 1993.

John Mueller, *Astaire Dancing: The Musical Films*, New York, Wings Books, 1985.

Martin Rubin, *Showstoppers: Busby Berkeley and the Tradition of Spectacle*, New York, Columbia University Press, 1993.

Gold Diggers of 1933 (USA 1933 *p.c* – Warner Bros.; *d* – Mervyn LeRoy)

Discussion of the 1930s musical usually sets up Busby Berkeley and Fred Astaire as contrasting poles. In the teleological version of the genre's history, it is Astaire's intimacy that is acclaimed as advancing the musical towards its later integrated and 'realistic' modes, while Berkeley becomes a dead end of baroque spectacle.

For Leo Braudy, Berkeley's 'attitude towards individuals is that of a silent film director, iconographic and symmetric'; Braudy also points up the crucial distinction between Berkeley's and Astaire's roles in their films – Berkeley the 'non-participating choreographer-director', Astaire the 'dancer-choreographer himself ... a participant' (Braudy, 1976, p. 142). To put it simply, Berkeley contributed a great deal to the use of movement in cinema, but almost nothing to dance (see Delameter, 1981).

Gold Diggers of 1933 (choreographed by Berkeley) is one of the musicals Richard Dyer (1977; 2002) singles out for analysis in 'Entertainment and utopia'. He sees the relationship between numbers and narrative as particularly problematic in this film, given its explicit narrative concern with the effects of the Depression: 'The thrust of the narrative is towards seeing the show as "solution" to the ... problems of the characters; yet the non-realist presentation of the numbers makes it very hard to take this solution seriously' (Dyer, 1977, p. 8).

This is clearly the case with the 'Shadow Waltz' – one of Berkeley's more fanciful set-pieces, yet interestingly atypical in its relative lack of overt sexual symbolism. While the female body is as usual the raw material for aesthetic composition and scopic concentration, the end result is, for Berkeley, a little tame, even prim. With the exception of one shot of reflected legs, the mise en scène is not directly voyeuristic. This is perhaps not unrelated to the number's slight straining after European high cultural values (it is, after all, a waltz).

Dyer's argument is less convincing in relation to 'Remember My Forgotten Man', although this number is a prime example of his categories of intensity and – all the more powerful because inflected negatively – community. It, too, is not typical Berkeley, nor even typical of the genre, in being direct social comment, worlds away from the same film's 'Petting in the Park' or any of the Astaire love ballads. It was certainly read as aberrant by some critics in the 1930s: 'I can take most war films cheerfully on the chin, but I want none of them in musical comedies, where they certainly do not belong. For downright offensiveness and bad taste, that last reel wins the Croix de Garbage' (quoted in Roth, 1981, p. 55).

Precisely why seriousness and social awareness were thought so incompatible with a musical rendering, even so early in the genre's history, is an intriguing question. Certainly 'My Forgotten Man' shows that the attempt could be brought off; indeed the number now strikes us as one of Berkeley's most impressive, demonstrating his undeniable mastery in the orchestration of space, spectacle and editing without the usual stress on fetishistic voyeurism.

ANDY MEDHURST

Top Hat (USA 1935 *p.c* – RKO Radio Pictures; *d* – Mark Sandrich)

Like all the Astaire–Rogers films, this can profitably be considered in terms of its sexual politics, the ideology of the perfect romance. *Top Hat* offers a particularly pure example of the way in which heterosexual desire in the musical 'occupies a central as opposed to a secondary or peripheral place in the discursive ensemble ... its presence is a necessity, not a variable option' (Neale, 1980, p. 23).

The two couple-dances, 'Isn't This a Lovely Day' and 'Cheek to Cheek' could, with appropriate caution, be analysed in terms of the significactory potential of non-representational signs, for although, as Dyer says, the methodology for any such reading remains particularly undeveloped (Dyer, 1977, p. 4), a clear difference between these dances is perceptible.

Reinforcing heterosexual romance: Fred Astaire and Ginger Rogers couple-dance in *Top Hat*

'Isn't This a Lovely Day' offers a rare pleasure in mainstream cinema – the couple as equals. It is the courtship dance that has the same structural function in all Astaire–Rogers films, as the antagonistic couple forget their personal animosity in the joy of shared dancing. The dance is in one respect Astaire's pursuit of Rogers, but it never becomes an oppressive celebration of male prowess. The star personas of the couple are a contributing factor – Astaire is not the conventional macho hero, Rogers is never the demure feminine heroine. In this dance, their equality is further reinforced by Rogers's 'masculine' clothes (dress being one of the key non-representational signs). The dance becomes a mutual game, the couple's joy further multiplied by the realisation that each knows the rules of the other's game. Once again, this is a reading of non-representational signs, in this case gesture. The setting is 'rural' (in the park) as opposed to the glossy interiors that serve as the space for the later dances in each of their films, and they end by shaking hands rather than kissing. They remain equal in dance (whatever the relative skills of the performers) as long as signifiers of conventional romance are avoided.

The different complexion of the second couple-dance, 'Cheek to Cheek', indicates the importance of non-representational signs. Now the dancers are in evening dress, Rogers's dress a particularly elaborate 'feminine' creation. The setting is the nightclub, interior glamour as opposed to pastoral outdoors. The style of dancing has changed, traditional gender roles are as strongly reinforced here as they were unnecessary earlier; aspirations to the balletic have replaced the previous informality. The couple's steps are now organised around his dominance ('leading' is the appropriate dance term) where they had been identical or humorously competitive. If 'Cheek to Cheek' reinforces the terms of classical Hollywood romance, then 'Isn't This a Lovely Day' at least suggests an alternative, perhaps utopian view, of romance based on equality.

This shift from dislike to mutual discovery to conventional romance recurs not only throughout this and other Astaire–Rogers films, but throughout most musicals, comedies and romances in Hollywood production. The Astaire–Rogers relationship has assumed mythic status as an ideal of the ideology of romance, so that the responsibility of analysis lies with teasing apart the contradictions in that ideology. In their progression from side-by-side to cheek-to-cheek, these films clearly close down more egalitarian possibilities. However, the existence of the earlier dances of mutual discovery raises the question of whether subversive moments can escape eventual narrative recuperation.

ANDY MEDHURST

Meet Me in St. Louis (USA 1944 *p.c* – Loew's Inc/MGM; *d* – Vincente Minnelli)

Meet Me in St. Louis is in part the product of an interest in and celebration of rural and provincial America at the time. It was also one of the first in a cycle of films to feature a nostalgic, turn-of-the-century setting, a theme that emerged in the mid-1940s and continued into the early 1950s (other examples include *Mother Wore Tights*, 1947, and *Cheaper by the Dozen*, 1950). It is considered exemplary of the integrated musical produced by Vincente Minnelli and Gene Kelly/Stanley Donen at MGM.

The film is divided into four parts: spring, autumn, winter and summer. Each part begins with a framed sepia photograph of the Smith home in St Louis; these still images – which slowly transform into motion and colour – introduce one of the film's key thematic elements: the house. The opening musical number, 'Meet Me in St. Louis', introduces the interior of the house, the Smith family members and their housekeeper, as the song is 'passed' from one to another and from room to room. The 'travelling song', as Beth Eliot Genne (1984) terms it, derives from the opening number of Rouben Mamoulian's *Love Me Tonight* (1932), and was a standard feature of the Minnelli and Donen/Kelly musicals at MGM; of note is its synthesis of camera movement, decor, character movement, gesture and music.

Following the introduction of a secondary romance plot (between the older sister, Rose, and her beau, Warren), the film's principal romance is inaugurated (once again through song), when young Esther (Judy Garland) sees her new neighbour, John (Tom Drake) – when 'the girl next door' first encounters 'the boy next door' (characters derived, as Genne points out, from the backyard musicals in which Garland began her career). Importantly, neither romance is dual focus in nature, nor do they consistently embody the film's main thematic oppositions: John and Warren espouse the same values as Esther and Rose, and bring complication and conflict only insofar as at various points they are (mistakenly) perceived to be a threat to the Smith family, its unity and its location in their house in St Louis. However, it is the father who is the main vehicle of thematic and dramatic opposition, as it is his job move to New York that jeopardises the stability of the household.

Esther and John actually meet and fall in love during a party at the Smith house (and in particular during the virtually wordless 'gaslight' sequence, a kind of numberless number, and the 'Over the Banister' song that follows). The party is one of several 'festive sequences' in the film (and in the work of Minnelli generally). These sequences serve, among other things, to mark the relationship between the Smith family and the wider local community in St Louis, and to articulate the integration of the one within the other. The autumn section contains the Halloween sequence, a variant that serves to articulate a counter-current or underside, one in which a resident within the community is feared and attacked, and is marked as not belonging.

Central to this sequence is the youngest daughter, Tootie (Margaret O'Brien), who is a vehicle for the expression of an underside to the cosiness of familial and provincial life and values, often in and through images (verbal and visual) of hysteria, violence and death. For the most part, these expressions are marked as comic. But they take on a seriousness and desperation when in the winter section she destroys the snowmen she has built in the garden. Here, in a quintessential Minnelli sequence, the frustration of wishes and desires finds articulation in the destruction of a decor, and in the destruction, specifically, of the products of artistic and imaginative vision. Significantly, it is this act that leads to the father's change of heart (filmed amid a half-empty house, its contents packed away for the move to New York), allowing the desires of Tootie and Esther and of the other members of the family finally to prevail amid the carefully choreographed decor of the 1904 World's Fair.

STEVE NEALE

Singin' in the Rain (USA 1952 *p.c* – Loew's Inc/MGM; *d* – Gene Kelly and Stanley Donen)

Following *On the Town* (1949), *Singin' in the Rain* is the second film Gene Kelly and Stanley Donen made together at MGM (a third, *It's Always Fair Weather*, was released in 1955). It can be categorised in a number of ways: a musical comedy involving (mild) satire and parody; an integrated backstage musical; a 'show musical' (which is how it is categorised by Altman, 1987); a 'catalogue' musical (a vehicle for the numbers written by a particular composer, songwriter or songwriting team – here the team of lyricist Arthur Freed and composer Nacio Herb Brown); and also as a vehicle for Gene Kelly as singer, dancer and star, and for Kelly's (and Donen's) ideas about dance and the presentation of dance in musical film.

However, one of the film's major features is the extent to which it escapes, mixes and modifies some of these categories. Its film-industry setting means that it becomes a 'backscreen' rather than a backstage musical. As Beth Eliot Genne has argued, the style pioneered by Donen and Kelly in *On the Town* – the use of bright, evenly lit primary colours, spare sets and an accelerated pace – is here mixed with elements derived from the work of Minnelli – notably the extensive use of the boom camera in the filming of some of the numbers, the incorporation of a dance-drama and the occasional use of chiaroscuro (evident, for instance, in the title number) (Genne, 1984, p. 357). And as Peter Wollen has argued, the film is at one and the same time a show musical, a folk musical and a fairytale musical – a combination of all three of Altman's categories (Wollen, 1992, p. 55).

In addition, while most of the film's musical numbers are motivated (and hence integrated) by their showbiz context, by diegetic performance and/or by situation, character and plot, play is made with some of the devices used to motivate numbers and hence with the concept of integration. For example, 'Broadway Rhythm', itself a mix of dance-drama and conventional backstage production number, is introduced as an idea for a production number for the film being made within the film. It so obviously fulfils this function for *Singin' in the Rain* itself, and hence exceeds its motivation as a mere idea, that the line that follows its conclusion – 'Well, what do you think R. F.?' – becomes a joke.

'You Were Meant for Me' is one of a series of courtship dances that occur in Kelly's films. The courtship dance was a feature of the Astaire–Rogers films, but Kelly's dance style and persona is very different. Whereas Astaire's style combines ballroom and tap, and is known for its detachment, poise and control, Kelly's technique is a combination of ballet, modern dance and tap, and is noted for its athleticism, energy and slapstick (explored in the 'Make 'Em Laugh' number that Kelly choreographed for Donald O'Connor). In addition, whereas Astaire is associated with 'high society', Kelly is considered more 'proletarian', more virile and masculine: 'For Kelly, obsessed with the validity of male dance, the presence of the body was all-important, a male body that is acceptably exhibitionist in its athleticism' (Wollen, 1992, p. 57). Partly for this reason, Kelly's films, while concerned with heterosexual romance, are always also concerned with male friendship (see Delameter, 1981; Genne, 1984).

As Babington and Evans point out, Kelly's persona also contains an element of self-assured self-regard and fake charm. The characters he plays have consequently often to be chastened (and frequently are conmen or hams) (Babington and Evans, 1985, p. 183). In *Singin' in the Rain*, these elements are linked to Don's character prior to his encounter with Kathy. They are also linked to the themes of artifice and deception, authenticity and truth that pervade the film, and, via the differences between Don's verbal account of his early career and the visual account the film provides, to the opposition or mismatch between sound and image that provides one of their principal vehicles. Peter Wollen goes so far as to argue that 'the core issue in the film is that of the relationship between sound and image. Things can only end happily when, so to speak, a properly "married print" is produced, in which voice and image naturally joined together' (Wollen, 1992, p. 55). He goes on to say that: 'The underlying theme is that of nature as truth and unity, versus artifice as falsehood and separation' (1992, p. 55). However, things are a little more complex than this. As 'You Were Meant for Me' shows, artifice can be authentic; the real opposition is between honesty and dishonesty, truth and falsehood, whether in the realm of artifice, or in the realm of nature.

STEVE NEALE

Sweet Charity (USA 1968 *p.c* – Universal; *d* – Bob Fosse)

By the late 1960s, the moment of production of this film, the musical was in most respects stranded by shifts in industrial practice and cultural sensibility. The traditional audiences for cinema were largely captured by television, and the mainstream musical could hardly be expected to redirect itself towards the new youth market, since that market's preferred musical entertainment had little to do with Irving Berlin or Rodgers and Hammerstein. The Elvis Presley films were an attempt to combine the old cinematic practice with the new musical practice, but they functioned largely as objects for fan adoration. Hollywood was deceived by the great success of *The Sound of Music* (1965) into investing in other expensive musicals, such as *Sweet Charity*, which flopped.

Despite its commercial failure, however, *Sweet Charity* has been seized on by devotees of the musical, and, more importantly, Bob Fosse has been

Director Bob Fosse too determined to be modern with *Sweet Charity*

hailed as the new saviour-auteur of the genre. Recognised as a major choreographer on films such as *The Pajama Game* (1957), Fosse directs dance in a distinctive and immediately recognisable way (see Delameter, 1981). 'Hey, Big Spender' has taken its place in the nostalgic repertory of Hollywood musical numbers. But to obtain a perspective on *Sweet Charity* beyond the authorial and adulatory, the film must be considered in terms of its historical moment.

'Hey, Big Spender' is memorable for reasons that go beyond talent – it is the most sexually direct musical number since the heyday of Berkeley. And it can be so because of relaxed censorship laws – moreover, it needs to be so to receive the description 'adult' intended to attract a late-1960s audience. (Fosse was to capitalise on such social nuances again with *Cabaret* in 1972, Hollywood's first foray into decadent chic.) 'If They Could See Me Now', however, is of a different register. Editing trickery apart (and the film can be dated now by the self-congratulatory flashiness of the editing), this number is a throwback to vaudeville. The film is trying to have it both ways – the so-daring sleaze of 'Big Spender' and the old-fashioned barnstorming of 'If They Could See Me Now'. The use of top hat and cane in the latter clearly marks it as an attempted tribute to earlier musical styles, but the effect is muddled.

Sweet Charity was also acclaimed for introducing a central star performance reminiscent of the genre's classic period (see Kobal, 1971). Shirley MacLaine performs a creditable impersonation of a musical star, but she is indulged by Fosse (especially in 'If They Could See Me Now') to an extent undreamed of in, say, the 1940s musical. The very notion of an old-style musical star functioning in the late 1960s seems anachronistic. MacLaine's one register is the relentless projection of being lovable – difficult to bring off in any context, and floundering in misplaced energy in *Sweet Charity*, where Fosse's determination to be modern is uppermost. The jagged, mannered stylisation of a number like 'The Aloof' cannot coexist with the gushing warmth of MacLaine without resulting in a seriously ruptured text.

ANDY MEDHURST

Saturday Night Fever (USA 1977 *p.c* – Paramount/ Robert Stigwood Organisation; *d* – John Badham)

Few films are as iconic, but few are as frequently, mockingly parodied. It is often hard to disentangle *Saturday Night Fever* as an actual text from the nest of associations and assumptions that have clustered around it. Looked at dispassionately (if that were possible), it is an urban melodrama about disenchantment and escape, with its dream of escape represented by the space and sounds of the disco. That its vision of utopia is musical places the film squarely in that tradition of seeing the genre as concerned with the fantasy of release from everyday drabness and material constraints. The flashing disco floor is in this sense a small-scale Brigadoon, a magical arena that opens up at certain times to allow transportation to a better, finer world. The fact that the film centres on couples (and larger groups) dancing to music that we do not see performed on screen also aligns it to the 1930s musicals of Fred Astaire and Ginger Rogers.

In many ways, then, this is a film that holds true to key conventions of the musical's heritage, but other aspects of its representational repertoire mark it out as breaking new ground. Its Italian-American crime trappings, for example, seem to draw on a somewhat diluted Scorsese aesthetic – so that it sometimes feels like *Mean Streets* (1973) with handclaps – or a grittier episode of a 1970s TV crime drama – at which points it becomes *Kojak* (1973–8) in falsetto. Above all, it remains fixed in the public mind as the film that brought disco music to a commercial peak, so that perhaps more than any other musical, its sounds (those endlessly ridiculed Bee Gees harmonies) are just as instantly evocative as its sights (John Travolta's white suit and that pulsating dance floor). The film's unwarranted reputation as a 'guilty pleasure' resides primarily in the still-prevailing sonic snobbery that refuses to see disco music as anything other than kitsch.

ANDY MEDHURST

Strictly Ballroom (Australia 1992 *p.c* – M & A Film Corporation/Australian Film Finance Corporation; *d* – Baz Luhrmann)

Whereas *Velvet Goldmine* (1998) strives to be 'queer' (see case study), *Strictly Ballroom* is content to remain, and luxuriate in, camp. Its unrepentant devotion to a clichéd Cinderella-meets-her-prince storyline, its embrace of the slightly frayed glitz of the ballroom dancing milieu, and its sheer delight in the filming and framing of heterosexual love played out to an emotion-yanking soundtrack revealed a deep affection for the genre to which it paid conscious, but never too self-conscious, homage. In many ways, it is not so much a musical as a film about how fabulous life could be if it were like a musical. It testifies to the magic of the genre rather than merely reproducing it, yet manages to stop short of the hyper-artificiality of director Baz Luhrmann's later *Moulin Rouge!* (2001).

Moulin Rouge! has its devotees, but those who prefer *Strictly Ballroom* could explain their preference by pointing out that in the earlier film Luhrmann was able to demonstrate the interplay between ordinariness and artifice that is one of the genre's hallmarks. By showing the constricting conformity of the life that needs escaping from, the triumph of dance-floor escape is all the more palpable. The film's national identity is also noteworthy, as it helped to usher in a new breed of Australian cinema that put on the global map that country's perhaps

Sequinned excess: Tara Morice and Paul Mercurio in Baz Luhrmann's tribute to the musical *Strictly Ballroom*

surprising appetite for sequinned excess. As Fran leaves behind ugly duckling status to enter Scott's embroidered embrace in *Strictly Ballroom*, the seeds are sown not just for Luhrmann's unfolding mission to eliminate drabness but also for the drag extravaganza of *The Adventures of Priscilla, Queen of the Desert* (1994), the Abba-hymned bittersweet fairytale of *Muriel's Wedding* (1994) and the rebirth into diva-hood of Kylie Minogue.

ANDY MEDHURST

Velvet Goldmine (UK/USA 1998 *p.c* – Channel Four/Velvet Goldmine Production/Zenith Productions/Killer Films/Single Cell Pictures/ Newmarket Capital Group/Goldwyn Films International/Miramax Films; *d* – Todd Haynes)

The musical has always been a genre besotted with artifice, but *Velvet Goldmine* is notable for its determination to shift that fascination with surface and play in a more self-consciously intellectualised direction. Made at the height of the brief fashionableness of New Queer Cinema (see p. 505), its knowingly aloof tone revealed rather starkly the gulf between the film-makers bound up in that micro-movement and the tastes of audiences less stirred by the minutiae of queer aesthetics. On paper, the film should work, not least because in choosing to forge a screen musical from a non-cinematic pop genre, it at least had the wit to select glam rock, which in its early 1970s heyday often drew heavily on the pizzazz and eroticism of classic Hollywood. In doing so, however, glam added a British fascination with sexual ambiguity, and it is this dimension that *Velvet Goldmine*'s director Todd Haynes correctly identifies as a watershed in the public visibility of cultural queerness. The difficulty with the resulting film, however, is that it cannot shake off its air of clever postgraduate dissertation, and fails to transmute its conceptual aims into a wholly satisfying textual outcome. Put cruelly, it is a musical designed to theorise about rather than enjoy, replacing the joy and the verve of the genre's peaks with something theorem-like and emotionally null. A showily convoluted narrative and some unhelpfully arch performances (Ewan McGregor's lively turn being the honourable exception) further conspire to push away most viewers, leaving them thirsty for something more vulgar, more alive and more truly glamorous.

Velvet Goldmine, like *Saturday Night Fever* and *Strictly Ballroom*, centres on a youthful male rite of passage, an emphasis that both aligns the (post)modern musical with the teen film and attempts, probably without much chance of success, to masculinise this most un-masculine of genres.

ANDY MEDHURST

SCIENCE FICTION AND HORROR

Science fiction

STEVE NEALE

As has often been noted, it is sometimes difficult to distinguish between horror and science fiction. Not only that, it can at times be difficult to distinguish between horror and the crime film, and science fiction, adventure and fantasy as well. Films such as *Frankenstein* (1931), *Psycho* (1960) and *Wait Until Dark* (1967), and *Star Wars* (1977), *E.T. The Extra-terrestrial* (1982), *The Thing* (1982) and *The Hound of the Baskervilles* (1939), all in their own ways testify to the propensity for multiplicity and overlap among and between these genres in Hollywood. It is therefore hardly surprising that watertight definitions of science fiction and horror – or for that matter fantasy, adventure and crime – are hard to come by. Nor is it surprising that articles and books on science fiction and horror often discuss the same or similar films. However, if there are areas and instances of hybridity and overlap, there are also areas and instances of differentiation – few would describe *Dracula* (1931) as science fiction, just as few would describe *Silent Running* (1972) or *Logan's Run* (1976) as horror films. In consequence, horror and science fiction will be treated separately.

There are numerous definitions of science fiction. Some are normative and exclusive, designed to distinguish between 'good' and 'bad' science fiction or to promote a particular form or trend. This is especially true of those that comment on written science fiction, and of those concerned to distinguish between its 'pulp' and its 'literary' forms on one hand, and its written and filmic forms on the other. Some, like Richard Hodgens, are more descriptive and all-embracing. 'Science fiction', he writes, 'involves extrapolated or fictitious science, or fictitious use of scientific possibilities, or it may be simply fiction that takes place in the future or introduces some radical assumption about the present or the past' (Hodgens, 1959, p. 30; cited in Sobchack, 1988, pp. 17–63; see also Hardy, 1986, pp. ix–xv; Kuhn, 1990). What this means, among other things, is that in science fiction, science, fictional or otherwise, always functions as motivation for the nature of the fictional world, its inhabitants and the events that happen within it, whether or not science itself is a topic or theme.

As a term, 'science fiction' was first used in the nineteenth century, but only became fully established in the late 1920s in and around American pulp magazines such as *Amazing Stories*, and in particular *Science Wonder Stories* (James, 1994, pp. 7–11). It thus largely postdated the vogue for 'invention stories', for 'tales of science', for 'tales of the future' and for the '*voyages imaginaires*' that were associated in particular with Jules Verne, and which characterised the late nineteenth and early twentieth centuries (James, 1994, pp. 12–30). This vogue coincided both with a second industrial revolution, a new machine age and a cult of scientific invention, and with an acceleration of the processes of colonial expansion and imperial rivalry that had already fuelled a tradition of exploration stories, adventure stories and tales of territorial conquest. It also coincided with the invention of film, itself seen as a new scientific and technical marvel.

The earliest generic vehicles for this vogue were 'trick films' such as *The X-Ray Mirror* (1899) and Méliès's *voyages imaginaires*, both of which helped to establish the bond between science fiction, special-effects technology and set design that has remained a feature of the genre ever since (Barnouw, 1981; Brosnan, 1974; Frazer, 1979; Hammond, 1974; Hutchison, 1987). In 1910, the first filmed version of *Frankenstein* helped establish a link between science fiction and horror in the cinema, a link that was to be reforged in Gothic mode in the 1930s, in apocalyptic mode in the 1950s and in body-horror mode since the late 1960s. A little later, series and serials such as *The Exploits of Elaine* (1914), *The Flaming Disc* (1920) and *Terror Island* (1920) helped to cement a similar link between science fiction, action and adventure. This link was maintained in the 1930s and 1940s by low-budget serials such as *Flash Gordon* (1936), *Batman* (1943) and *Superman* (1948) and revived in the form of the upmarket blockbuster by George Lucas and others in the late 1970s. Finally, a tradition of large-scale speculations on the future of modern society – and allegories in science-fictional form about its current condition – was established in Europe by films such as *Metropolis* (1927), *La Fin du monde* (1931) and *Things to Come* (1936). It was revived in America, usually on a more modest industrial scale, during the course of the boom in science fiction in the 1950s, then again in the late 1960s and early 1970s with films such as *The Day the Earth Stood Still* (1951), *On the Beach* (1959), *Planet of the Apes* (1968) and *Soylent Green* (1973). Since then it has tended to merge into the horror and action-adventure traditions, and to become ever more dystopian in outlook. These are the principal forms of science fiction in the cinema. They thus incorporate most but not all of the categories or 'templates' into which science fiction as a whole is divided in Pringle (1997). These templates are listed as 'space operas', 'planetary romances', 'future cities', 'disasters', 'alternative histories', 'prehistorical romances', 'time travels', 'alien intrusions', 'mental powers' and 'comic infernos'.

Although there are several books that detail the history of these trends (notably Baxter, 1970; Hardy, 1986; and Brosnan, 1978), science fiction in the cinema has tended to lack a tradition of critical theory. There is a great deal of writing about individual films, periods and topics, but very little about science fiction as a genre. The major exceptions here are Sobchack's *Screening Space* (1988) (a reworking of her 1980 *The Limits of Infinity*), the section on science fiction in Schatz (1983) and J. P. Telotte (1995).

Screening Space begins with a chapter on definitions, and moves on to consider iconography, and the genre's use of language and sound. Sobchack concludes on one hand that 'Although it lacks an informative iconography, encompasses the widest possible range of time and place, and constantly fluctuates in its visual representation of objects, the SF film still has a science fiction "look" and "feel" to its visual surfaces' (Sobchack, 1988, p. 87). This 'visual connection' between SF films

> lies in the consistent and repetitious use not of *specific* images, but of *types* of images which function in the same way from film to film to create an imaginatively realized world which is always removed from the world we know or know of. The visual surface of all SF film presents us with a confrontation between a mixture of those images to which we respond as 'alien' and those we know to be familiar. (Sobchack, 1988, p. 87; original emphasis)

The past meets the future: Charlton Heston is marooned on *The Planet of the Apes*

Thus: 'The major visual impulse of all SF films is to pictorialize the unfamiliar, the nonexistent, the strange and totally alien – and to do so with a verisimilitude which is, at times, documentary in flavor and style' (Sobchack, 1988, p. 88).

This relationship between the strange and the familiar is, she argues, as pertinent to the soundtrack as it is to the image. Vocabulary and language are often highlighted as issues in science fiction. In *2001: A Space Odyssey* (1968), for example, 'we are constantly made aware of how language – and, therefore, our emotions and thought patterns – have not kept up with either our technology or our experience' (Sobchack, 1988, p. 177). And sound itself – the sound of machinery, of natural forces and 'the sound of the alien' (Sobchack, 1988, p. 218) – functions in films such as *Five* (1951) and *The Thing* (1951) both as a generic marker, and as one of the points at which the strange and familiar meet.

Focusing almost exclusively on the 1950s, Sobchack argues that: 'The milieu of science fiction is one of contested space, in which the generic oppositions are determined by certain aspects of the cultural community and by the contest itself' (Sobchack, 1988, p. 86). The contest here is the contest between 'the human community' and some kind of 'alien or monstrous force' (Sobchack, 1988, p. 86). The milieu, whose attributes are usually 'a direct extension of America's technological capabilities', may be a small town, a city or even the world as a whole (Sobchack, 1988, p. 86). However, the distinction between the human community and the alien force is by no means always straightforward. In films such as *It Came from Outer Space* (1953) and *Invasion of the Body Snatchers* (1956), the distinction is blurred: 'The members of the community so utterly assimilate the group values that they are turned into automatons' (Sobchack, 1988, p. 87). It becomes hard to tell alien and human apart. In this way, within a constellation of generic concerns that includes nature, science, technology, social and communal organisation and that which is alien or other, the idea of the human, upon which the dramatisation of these concerns centrally depends, is broached as an issue.

For Telotte (1995), the issue of humanness lies at the heart of science fiction, and it is focused in particular by the figure of the robot and by its most recent avatar, the cyborg. He traces the function and the meaning of these figures in films from *Metropolis* on, placing them within both their cyclic and cultural contexts. Thus he sees such 1930s films as *Mad Love* (1935), *Bride of Frankenstein* (1935) and *Island of Lost Souls* (1933) as depicting in the then current horror mode 'violent efforts to redefine the human body as some sort of raw material' for scientific artifice and experiment (Telotte, 1995, p. 86), and hence as expressing contemporary concerns about the subjection of the human to the powers of technology and science. He sees the serials of the 1930s and 1940s as revealing 'a growing fascination with the technological and its potential for reshaping the human' (Telotte, 1995, p. 18), while at the same time drawing a line between the two through stories that 'repeatedly celebrate a human might and human feelings, particularly a human determination to stay something other than a subject, serialized thing' (Telotte, 1995, p. 100). He sees such 1950s films as *Forbidden Planet* (1956) as marking a 'newly recognized ability to duplicate anything, including the human body' (Telotte, 1995, p. 19), and such 1970s films as *Westworld* (1974), *Futureworld* (1976) and *Demon Seed* (1977) as expressing 'growing anxieties' both about 'our place' in a world in which that capacity has been enhanced by artificial intelligence (Telotte, 1995, p. 19) and about the ensuing loss of 'all distinction between the public and the private' (Telotte, 1995, p. 146). And finally, in the 1980s and 1990s, as 'science fiction … returned to the level of popularity it enjoyed in the 1950s' (Telotte, 1995, p. 148), he sees films such as *Blade Runner* (1982), *Cherry 2000* (1986), *Total Recall* (1990), *RoboCop* (1987) and *Terminator 2 Judgment Day* (1991) repeatedly depicting the body 'as an image that is constantly being reconfigured and presented for display' (Telotte, 1995, p. 149), and repeatedly using the robotic to interrogate, to blur and often to reverse the polarities between the artificial and the human. While the trend in the 1980s was 'toward showing the human as ever more artificial', the trend in the 1990s has been 'toward rendering the artificial as ever more human' (Telotte, 1995, p. 22).

As Telotte is well aware, the boundaries of the human and the issues of difference they raise are rendered more complex by the fact that they necessarily include issues of sexuality, ethnicity and gender. Following Haraway (1985), such issues have been explored in a number of essays edited by Kuhn (1990) and by Penley *et al.* (1991). Nearly all these essays refer at least in passing to *Alien* (1979) and to *Blade Runner*, films that have become canonic touchstones not just for discussions of difference, but also for those engaged in debates about postmodernism and the nature of postmodern aesthetics and representation.

Aside from Bruno's (1990) article on *Blade Runner*, an essay that touches on time, space, memory, history, pastiche, simulacra and the definite absence of authenticity, the concluding chapter in Sobchack's 1988 book is probably the most sustained attempt to engage with these issues. Sobchack argues that since the 1960s, science fiction in the US has undergone a number of fundamental changes. These changes

> go much further than a simple transformation of the nature and manner of the genre's special effects or of its representation of visible technology. Whether 'mainstream' and big-budget or 'marginal' and low-budget, the existential attitude of the contemporary SF films is different – even if its basic material remained the same. Cinematic space travel of the 1950s had an aggressive and three-dimensional thrust – whether it was narrativized as optimistic, colonial, and phallic penetration and conquest, or as pessimistic and paranoid earthly and bodily invasion. Space in these films was semantically inscribed as 'deep' and time as accelerating and 'urgent'. In the SF films released between 1968 and 1977 … space became semantically inscribed as inescapably domestic and crowded. Time lost its urgency – statically stretching forward toward an impoverished and unwelcome future worse than a bad present. (Sobchack, 1988, pp. 225–6)

With the release of *Star Wars* and *Close Encounters of the Third Kind* (both 1977), a further transformation occurred: 'Technological wonder had become synonymous with domestic hope; space and time seemed to expand again' (Sobchack, 1988, p. 226). Finally, during the course of the 1980s, postmodern norms take hold:

> Most of today's SF films (mainstream or marginal) construct a generic field in which space is semantically described as a surface for play and dispersal, a surface across which existence and

Beyond human: Kurt Russell takes on 'the entity' in John Carpenter's *The Thing*

An impoverished and unwelcome future: Daryl Hannah and William Sanderson in Ridley Scott's *Blade Runner*

> objects kinetically displace and display their materiality. As well, the urgent or hopeless temporality of the earlier films has given way to a new and erotic leisureliness – even in 'action-packed' films. Time has decelerated, but it is not represented as static. It is filled with curious things and dynamized by a series of concatenated events rather than linearly pressured to stream forward by the teleology of the plot. (Sobchack, 1988, pp. 227–8)

Sobchack cites films such as *Liquid Sky* (1983), *Strange Invaders* (1983) and *Night of the Comet* (1984) as examples of what she means. Whether her argument applies to films such as *Aliens* (1986) and *Terminator 2* remains open to question.

Selected Reading

Donna Haraway, 'A manifesto for cyborgs: science, technology and socialist feminism in the 1980s', *Socialist Review* 80: 65–108, 1985. Reprinted in *Simians, Cyborgs and Women: The Reinvention of Nature*, London and New York, Routledge, 1991.

Annette Kuhn (ed.), *Alien Zone: Cultural Theory and Contemporary Science Fiction Cinema*, London, Verso, 1990; *Alien Zone II: The Spaces of Science Fiction Cinema*, London, Verso, 1999.

Constance Penley, Elisabeth Lyon, Lynn Spigel and Janet Bergstrom (eds), *Close Encounters: Film, Feminism and Science Fiction*, Minneapolis, University of Minnesota Press, 1991.

J. P. Telotte, *Replications: A Robotic History of the Science Fiction Film*, Urbana, University of Illinois Press, 1995.

The horror film

CHRISTINE GLEDHILL

For some time, horror films had comparatively little serious discussion, and only in the second half of the 1970s was the genre put on the agenda of film studies. From 1935 to the late 1940s, accounts of local authority bannings of H-films and of reports on their harmful social effects, especially on children, proliferated in the British trade press. The 1950s witnessed renewed panic around the spectacular international success of a native development of the genre by the Hammer studio (see Hammer Productions, p. 180) and British film journals carried articles on the psychology of the genre. Quite distinct was the French response: during the 1950s and 1960s, French journals located the genre within the category of the *fantastique* and made links with Surrealism, as well as investigating the new British contribution largely ignored at home. Then in the late 1960s, two books appeared by Carlos Clarens and Ivan Butler arguing for the horror film as art, pointing to the long literary tradition of 'the art of terror', and chronicling a history of the genre in the cinema. These groundbreaking contributions were followed in the early 1970s by a spate of books on both sides of the Atlantic devoted to the monsters and stars of the horror film, offering historical and psychological studies. Anglo-Saxon journals in the meantime devoted space to 'special effects' and returned again to the question of social/psychological significance of the 1970s boom in horror with violence, frequently against women. In the late 1970s/early 1980s, feminists mounted public protest at the perpetuation of a widespread cultural misogyny by such films.

The titles of the 1970s horror film books reveal the emergence of a cultist knowledge stored up over the decades by the closet horror film addict. Robin Wood has commented on this characteristic:

> The horror film has consistently been one of the most popular and, at the same time, the most disreputable of Hollywood genres. The popularity itself has a peculiar characteristic that sets the horror film apart from other genres: it is restricted to aficionados and complemented by total rejection, people tending to go to horror films either obsessively or not at all. They are dismissed with contempt by the majority of reviewer-critics, or simply ignored. (Wood, 1979, p. 13)

This attribute of the horror film's popularity is further illustrated by the number of specialist journals devoted to its different aspects – *Midi-Minuit Fantastique*, *Twilight*, *Cinefantastique* (US), *The Horror Élite*, *L'Écran fantastique*, *Vampyr*, *Little Shoppe of Horrors* and so forth. All this attests to the special relationship of the horror film with its aficionados that early on became the centre of critical attention and arguably inhibited theoretical elaboration of the genre. Frequently, the form is identified by industry and critics alike as aimed at the 'youth market' or 'adolescents of whatever age' (see Evans, 1973; Kapsis, 1982; Wood, 1979).

However, the relegation of the horror film was not solely a result of critical disdain for its supposed audience. Other factors arose from its mixed heritage and development in a wide range of different forms and cultures, which appear to defy coherent categorisation. Historical approaches demonstrate a heterogeneity of inputs and developments rather than the integrated evolution of generic tradition attributed to the western or gangster film – for example, Universal's Gothic horror films of the 1930s; German Expressionism; 1950s science-fiction monster movies; Hammer horror in the UK; Roger Corman's Poe cycle; the onset of the psychological thriller with *Psycho*, all cited in T. J. Ross's introduction to *Focus on the Horror Film* (1972). A tension remains between older European traditions and Hollywood, producing the problem of relating the forms that developed in the European art cinema in terms of the *fantastique* or supernatural (see Clarens, 1968) and the formation of a popular Hollywood genre. As with melodrama, the origins of the horror film looked back to European literary traditions – the Victorian Gothic novel, for instance – and a central strand of the genre has retained its mythical European location, 'Transylvania'. This heterogeneity is increased by the input of two European movements, German Expressionism (see Eisner, 1969), and Surrealism, the former often cited as indispensable to the 'horror style' of Hollywood, the latter arguably more influential on European developments in the work of, for instance, Franju or Dreyer, or 'Europeanised' directors in Hollywood such as Roman Polanski. Some critics attempt to get round this impasse by defining the horror film in terms of its aesthetic effect – its intention to horrify. Andrew Tudor argues, for instance, that the heritage from German Expressionism was important because 'the style itself is capable of infecting almost

The revenge of marine life in Jack Arnold's cult horror film *Creature from the Black Lagoon*

any subject matter with its eerie tone ... the sense of mystery, of lurkers in the shadows is the constant factor' (Tudor, 1974, p. 208). However, the mechanics of the horror movie did not provide the material for the elaboration of the existential/moral dramas central to early attempts to regain classic Hollywood for serious critical consideration. For example, both Andrew Tudor, who writes mainly about Gothic horror, and Brian Murphy, who deals with 1950s science-fiction monster movies, agree that the genre offers a 'never-never land' governed by absolutely inflexible laws:

> Men turn into werewolves only but always on nights of the full moon; vampires always dislike garlic, cast no reflection in mirrors, and can be destroyed only by having their hearts pierced with a wooden stake; and it is the nature of Frankenstein's monster that he can never be destroyed ... horror's never-never land is bearable because it is so entirely rational. (Murphy, 1972, p. 34)

The Gothic mode in particular, with its self-referentiality, refused elaboration in more social terms. Thus several commentators have argued (Ross, 1972; Tudor, 1974) that of all the genres the horror film shows least connection with American history, thereby cutting it off from a major source of legitimation. This, added to the rigid simplicity of the horror film's conventions, deprives it of the resonances that inform and deepen, for example, the western or gangster film (Tudor, 1974). As a result, and compounding the problem, the directors and stars of the horror movie have generally been unable to escape the pejorative implications of cultism and failed to win acclaim as auteurs of the cinema.

The chief route to cultural legitimation, therefore, has been through popular anthropological or Freudian/Jungian reference, which assumes 'inside us a constant, ever-present yearning for the fantastic, for the darkly mysterious, for the choked terror of the dark' (Clarens, 1968, p. 9). As the capacity of religion and its equivalents to fill this need receded with the advance of rationalism and technology in the nineteenth century, the simultaneous discovery of the unconscious and the cinema released a new source of imagery for 'rendering unto film ... the immanent fears of mankind: damnation, demonic possession, old age, death, in brief the nightside of life' (Clarens, 1968, p. 13; Butler, 1970). For Clarens, this symbolic approach to the horror movie provides clear, normative boundaries. Thus *Psycho* and its imitators are rejected because, 'in Jungian fashion, I feel more compelled to single out and explore the visionary than the psychological' (Clarens, 1968, p. 13). Similarly, he excludes much European work because it uses horror as a means rather than as an end in itself. This emphasis leads him to speculate that the horror movie declines in the late 1960s when horror ceases to be clothed in mythic forms. Other critics have turned to the notion of aesthetic affect as a source of evaluation. So, for example, distinctions are drawn between the horror produced by suggestion – the terror of the unimaginable – and the *guignol* effects of things seen. The former is often associated with the European tradition, or the New (and Europeanised) Hollywood of Polanski and others, while the latter is identified as the Hollywood Gothic or more recent 'splatter' movies: 'Sublime terror rests in the unseen – the Ultimate Horror. Things seen, fully described, explained, and laid to rest in the last reel or paragraph are mere horrors, the weakest of which are the merest revulsions over bloodshed and dismemberment . . .' (Rockett, 1982, p. 132).

Ivan Butler (1970) identifies the promise of 'too much' – the production of expectations that cannot possibly be rendered in visual terms – as a major aesthetic problem of the horror film, and dissociates his claims for the genre as art from any tendency towards 'beastliness for its own sake'. These attempts to establish both the boundaries of the genre and a basis for its evaluation have not gone unchallenged. David Pirie's book (1973), largely about the horror films produced in the 1950s and 1960s by the English production company Hammer, argues that the aesthetics of Gothic horror are based on the act of showing rather than on suggestion. And in a more recent study, Charles Derry (1977) has charted not only the emergence of three distinct subgenres in the decades following *Psycho*, but has traced their historical predecessors in the 'classic' horror movie and other genres. From this preliminary investigation of critical approaches to the horror movie, a broad distinction emerges between those seeking predominantly psycho-sociological explanation of the genre – what it represents for its audiences – and those attempting to analyse the aesthetic affects offered to the audience by the play of the genre's conventions.

Psycho-sociological explanation

The problem facing all such accounts is to explain the meaning of the monster, or of the threat that produces the horror. 'Normality' is our everyday common-sense world – in more recent interpretations, the world of the dominant ideology, sanctioned by the established authorities. As suggested above, approaches to this problem via the notion of reflection have been thwarted by the horror film's lack of historical or social context, although where the genre borders on science fiction, political readings become possible. The outcropping of mutant monsters in the horror/science-fiction films of the 1950s are frequently understood as reflecting a 'doom-centred, eschatological fear' provoked by Cold War politics and the nuclear deterrent, which yet relied on the scientist and 'co-operation with the military' for protection (see Murphy, 1972, pp. 38–9). Ernest Larsen argues in similar vein that those horror films that take up aspects of the disaster movie – for instance *Alien* and *Dawn of the Dead* (1978) – 'advance ... the notion that modern technology is so overwhelming that it tends to obliterate any possibility of its liberatory use ... science has, as the handmaiden of capitalism, created an uncontrolled monster' (Larsen, 1977, p. 30).

Such readings suggest that traditional sources of horror in the unknown or the supernatural are less potent to the post-

Doomed: zombies in George Romero's *Dawn of the Dead*

Nature turns abnormal: a crisis of confidence in rational thought worked through in Alfred Hitchcock's *The Birds*

World War II western audience than the horrors that society has already perpetuated and seems in some scenarios likely to exceed – horrors often referred to as the 'American nightmare'. Such a premise provides the basis for at least two of Charles Derry's (1977) subgeneric categories for the modern horror film, though, in his account, the forms they take derive from cinematic history. Thus he distinguishes first, 'the horror of personality', inaugurated by *Psycho*, where the horror, rather than projected in a monster and so distanced and externalised, is now seen to be 'man' himself (see case study). Such a source of horror requires not supernatural or pseudo-scientific but psychological explanation, and represents a response to the escalation of violence, mass killings and the Kennedy assassination of the early 1960s. The *Dr Jekyll and Mr Hyde* series, Hitchcock's 1940s psychological thrillers and film noir have all contributed to the generic realisation of this popular obsession. The second subgenre Derry labels 'the horror of Armageddon', which in continuity with the 1950s science-fiction mutant-monster cycle, and exemplified by *The Birds* (1963), deals with a 'normal aspect of nature that turns abnormal', resulting in 'a struggle that is obviously ultimate, mythical and soul-rending' (Derry, 1972, p. 50). Such films Derry sees as representing a 'modern, cataclysmic corner of our everyday fears' traceable to anxiety about the spread of totalitarian, automaton-like political regimes and the threat of nuclear warfare. Their narratives are articulated in three major themes, proliferation, besiegement and death, the first and the last of which serve to demarcate this cycle from another closely related one, the disaster movie. Derry's final category is 'the horror of the demonic', which reverts to the presence of evil forces as a time-honoured explanation of the horror of the world, thereby suggesting the possibility of a moral order in the wings. While Derry's cataloguing of the conventions and strategies of these subgenres and his sensitivity to cinematic and generic traditions illuminate the development of the horror movie, his appeal to eruptions of violence in society to explain its existence tends to assume a relationship between films and society in which the former directly reflect the latter rather than mediating or representing it.

The notion of the 'nightmare' opens up a different and more common approach to understanding the horror film through popular Freudianism and anthropology. Concepts of the unconscious, of repression, of the cinema as an analogy for dreaming, displace the literalism of the 'reflection' thesis. With varying degrees of sophistication, they are used to explain the monster as that which must be excluded, or repressed, so that the western drive towards technological progress and world domination can proceed. According to this view, the threat is neither external to society, nor to the cinema. Rather the horror movie represents a medium in which the underside of the 'normal' world makes its appearance in a play of fantasy and ritual. Notions of the primordial, the tribal, figure centrally in this scenario, and sexuality is a key component. Depending on the politics of the writer, this perspective leads to a view of the horror film as adaptive (Evans, 1973), symptomatic (Kennedy, 1982; Snyder, 1982) or potentially progressive (Williams, 1980/81; Wood, 1979). Walter Evans, for example, works on the commonly attributed youth of the audience for horror to advance the view that the Gothic horror film's appeal is to 'those masses in American film and TV audiences who struggle with the most universal and horrible of personal trials: the sexual traumas of adolescence'. In a later account, he argues that monster movies 'respond to a deep cultural need largely ignored in western society … the need for rituals of initiation' (Evans, 1975, pp. 124–5).

Harlan Kennedy, on the other hand, uses the terminology of the 'unconscious' and 'id' to explain the recent resurgence of werewolf movies in terms of atavistic throwbacks manifested in political behaviour. Watergate and the facts and imagery of Vietnam that are now beginning to receive popular circulation, the guilty conflation of the Vietcong abroad and the Native American Indians at home, the 'wolf-like features of Richard Nixon', all point in the American cinema of the 1980s to an obsession with the horror of the split personality.

The impulse displayed here to explain the modern horror film in terms of a specifically American crisis of conscience is characteristic of many recent accounts of the genre. Rather than political traumas, many writers focus on the American 'way of life' as symptomatic of the distortions and repressions consequent on the development of American capitalism. Consumerism is identified as a prime symptom, behind which stands middle-class life, or the family and patriarchal social relations as sources of horror – for example *Night of the Living Dead* (1968), *The Hills Have Eyes* (1977), *Communion* (1976), *Martin* (1976). Stephen Snyder (1982), for example, argues in relation to *The Shining* (1980), *The Texas Chain Saw Massacre* (1974), *Burnt Offerings* (1976) and *Halloween* (1978) that 'the notion of … (middle-class) life as tantamount to the world of horror has been mushrooming'. This location of horror in the home is symptomatic of a 'network of anxieties … often realised in terms of the troubling insatiateness which underlies the structure of American family life' (Snyder, 1982, p. 4). Rather than a 'Watergate syndrome', Snyder identifies in the American 'collective psyche' a 'leisure culture syndrome' (Snyder, 1982, p. 5), in which 'traditional masculine values of conquest coupled to a mindless consumerism' threaten to unhinge 'our sanity' (Snyder, 1982, p. 4). Tony Williams (1980/81) takes this argument further, seeing the family as a key institution for the production of individuals in the social roles required for the perpetuation of the – patriarchal – state and therefore itself an instrument of repression and supported by other apparatuses of oppression, the church, the police and so on. The source of horror, then, is not so much in the family's economic role but in the monstrous reactions that inevitably erupt against its repressiveness when fantasy attempts to obliterate what cannot be changed by political means. In the terms of Williams's argument, the horrors of Vietnam are not perpetrated by werewolf-like authorities. Vietnam simply provides the opportunity for a re-enactment of the monstrous fantasies engendered within the heart of the repressive patriarchal family.

The return of the repressed

The most sustained discussion of the horror film in such terms has been provided by Robin Wood in his introduction to a booklet, *American Nightmare*, produced to accompany a season of horror films at the Toronto Festival of Festivals (1979). Wood attempts to provide a teleological account of the post-*Psycho* American horror film as the appropriation and reworking of European traditions in popular cultural forms relating to the American way of life. Wood's analytical apparatus, drawing on Marcusean Freud, combines the notion of ideology as a form of social conditioning with a view of the unconscious as the receptacle of energies repressed by the patriarchal family. Citing Gad Horowitz's distinction between basic and surplus repression, Wood argues that 'surplus repression' in western civilisation occurs in the production of individuals conditioned to be 'monogamous, heterosexual, bourgeois, patriarchal capitalists' (Wood, 1979, p. 8). What is repressed is sexuality, in its fullest, polymorphous sense, in the interests of producing narrowly defined gender roles, and the strictly functional deployment of the individual's creative energy. The tensions consequent on such repression and the threatened return of the repressed are siphoned off 'through the projection onto the Other of what is repressed within the Self, in order that it can be discredited, disowned, and if possible, annihilated' (Wood, 1979, p. 9). Exploiting the analogy of cinema and dream, and its degraded status as escapist entertainment, the horror movie is able to escape both inner and outer censor to explore in the figure of the monster – a stand-in for 'the Other' – the nature of the sexual energies repressed and denied:

> One might say that the true subject of the horror genre is the struggle for recognition of all that our civilisation represses and oppresses: its re-emergence dramatised, as our nightmares, as an object of horror, a matter for terror, the 'happy ending' (when it exists) typically signifying the restoration of repression. (Wood, 1979, p. 10)

Significant here is not escape from the real world, but what is escaped into. The distance from the 'reality' evoked by fantasy makes radical criticism of that world possible. In fact, the centre of energy in the horror film, as most commentators point out, is the monster: 'the definition of normality in horror films is in general boringly constant'. It is rare for the monster not to be treated sympathetically, for, 'central to the effect and fascination of horror films is their fulfilment of our nightmare wish to smash the norms that oppress us' (Wood, 1979, p. 27). From this basis, Wood goes on to deal with the American form's development. While normality has always, in the horror film, been represented by the 'heterosexual, monogamous couple, the family, and the social institutions (police, church, armed forces) that support them' (Wood, 1979, p. 26), and often defined in terms of dominant American stereotypes, even when the action takes place in Europe, the monster and its associates were, in the early period of Gothic horror, conceived as foreign. Wood argues that

Mia Farrow takes on the supernatural in Polanski's *Rosemary's Baby*

this represents for the early horror film a mechanism of 'disavowal' while at the same time allowing horror to be located in a 'country of the mind'. The various phases of the horror film – such as the Val Lewton cycle of the 1940s, the extra-terrestrial invaders or mutant monsters of the 1950s – can, then, be seen as 'the process whereby horror becomes associated with its true milieu, the family ... reflected in its steady geographical progress towards America' (Wood, 1979, p. 29). In post-*Psycho* movies, the doppelganger is not a foreign phenomenon but integral to the psychic life of the American family.

Wood argues for the potential progressiveness of the horror film in the focus of its destructiveness and its ambivalence towards the 'monsters' who destroy:

> While by definition the monster is related to evil ... horror films ... are progressive precisely to the degree that they refuse to be satisfied with this simple designation – to the degree that, whether explicitly or implicitly, consciously or unconsciously, they modify, question, challenge, seek to invert it. (Wood, 1979, p. 23)

In Wood's view, this ambivalence offers the possibility of a challenge to 'the highly specific world of patriarchal capitalism' (Wood, 1979, p. 23). The pleasures such films offer their makers and audiences is the release of repressed energies and the destruction of those social norms that demand the repression in the first place. Opposed to this progressive, or 'apocalyptic', strand in the horror films is the 'reactionary wing', defined in its designation of the monster as nothing but evil. This strand confuses repressed and aberrant sexuality with sexuality itself, its ideological project being the reinstatement of repression in the name of normality, supported by a Hollywood version of Christianity. Such films serve the dominant ideology by allowing some release of repressed energies only to rename them evil and cynically justify their further repression.

Horror as affect

The approaches discussed above share a belief in the possibility of understanding the horror film in terms of historically and culturally specific meanings already in circulation in the society that has produced them. Notions derived from anthropology and psychoanalysis such as the 'collective unconscious', 'repression', the 'id', the 'interpretation of dreams' support readings of the hermetic, self-referential fantasy world of the horror film as the working through in 'irrational' imagery of material lodged in the unconscious, material not to be found in the epics of history or social contemporary reality that provide the more intellectually acceptable explanations of the western or the gangster film. The advent of 'personal politics' in the 1970s, and the socio-historical critiques of the family and sexuality, provides a theoretical, if controversial, grounding to claims for the social relevance of the horror film.

However, the horror film has also been approached in terms of what it does to the audience, rather than what it represents. The significance of the horror film is not so much in the content released through its symbolic imagery – primitive fears, repressed energies and so forth – but the way it plays on insecurities as to the basis and adequacy of rational explanation. The audience goes to horror films not only to see things to be feared, or that have been repressed, but to experience fear, to explore the outer limits of knowledge and of cinematic representation itself.

W. H. Rockett (1982) argues that the horror film has to manoeuvre delicately between the contradictory needs of the aesthetic territory it inhabits. In an epistemological and cultural universe dominated by an Aristotelian logic, the overriding compulsion of representation is to produce order by demonstration, showing an action's origins, development and ultimate consequences. The horror film attains the dimensions of terror to the extent that it can resist the Aristotelian compulsion to 'open the door, and show what is behind it'.

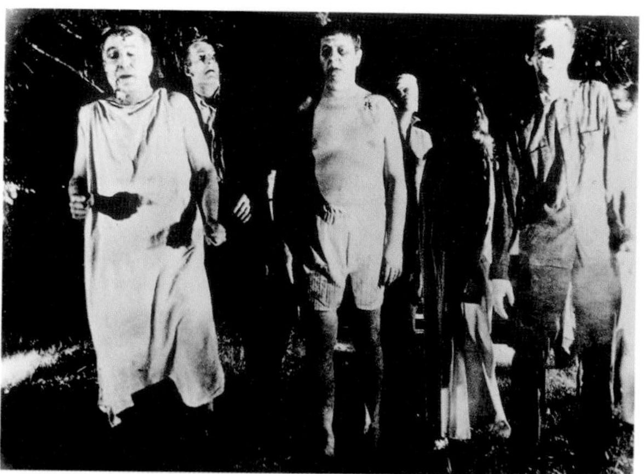

Bringing it all back home in Romero's *Night of the Living Dead*

> Terror relies on convincing the audience of the fallibility of the logic we assume governs the world. To achieve this the horror film makes the audience oscillate between terror (of uncertainty), horror and revulsion (both at things ultimately glimpsed or shown) and finally relief. It can achieve this through a play with off-screen space, or with space hidden in the frame, 'to emphasise what we do not see', or by breaking not simply the 'fixed laws of Nature' but one or more of the laws of the horror film ... which the 'fixed laws' aficionados of the genre have come to believe in with an almost religious fervour. (Rockett, 1982, p. 133)

Moreover, although the horror film may be compelled to open the door, to show the audience something of what is behind, the oscillation between the reassurance of suspended disbelief and the experience of terror is maintained by the door being closed again, to produce further uncertainty. Finally, Aristotelian closure may be denied if the monster's destruction is left in question. However, Rockett's description of this fine balance rests on a judgment of value: those horror films that go for quick sensation and show all and more fall victim to the Aristotelian logic and fail to reach the sublimity of terror. Terror depends, however, on the existence of the ground rules that are to be questioned; implicitly, it also depends on the Aristotelian gullibility or debased tastes of the audience that sustains them.

The post-structuralist approach

Stephen Neale in his monograph on genre (1980) attempts to elucidate the horror film's form and address in relation to its circulation in critical discourse – an attempt, in other words, to account for all the work described so far. A major distinction between his approach and those discussed above is the place he finds for so-called anti-realist, anti-Aristotelian or 'progressive' elements within the embrace of classic narrative cinema, where they play their part in the contradictory functioning of the dominant ideology. Neale's position derives from the link Lacanian psychoanalysis makes between the oedipal scenario consequent on the child's confrontation with sexual difference and 'castration', and the functioning of language. This link knits together three dimensions of human experience. First, desire is haunted by lack, depends on it for its existence and continuation and in the Freudian/Lacanian scenario is primarily about repossessing the plenitude and unity experienced in infancy with the mother. Second, structural linguistics state that in language there are no positive terms; meaning arises in the gap, the difference, between terms. Third, while castration inaugurates desire and compels the child to separate from the mother and enter the symbolic order, achieving individual identity in language, language itself institutes in the subject a splitting of identity: 'I' achieves its meaning only in relation to an implied 'you'. The patriarchal subject, then, is one driven to construct an illusory identity, unity, coherence on a foundation of lack, difference, separation. In this context, the unconscious is not so much a receptacle for repressed contents that in a liberated society would emerge comfortably into the light of day (see Wood, 1979; Williams, 1980/81), but a consequence of the human subject's endeavour to construct meaning out of difference, for any attempt to possess the object of desire through coherent, full representation also calls into play its opposite, its founding lack.

According to this perspective, the activity of representation is a fetishistic process that seeks to disavow lack by instituting presence elsewhere (for example, in cinema the fetishisation of the star's hair or clothing, producing a perfection that obscures the 'castration' threat of female sexuality). However, as Neale argues, the fetishistic substitute implicitly acknowledges its instituting lack, involving a play on the motif of presence/absence and a 'splitting of belief' in the subject – 'I know very well this is so, and yet ...'. From the psychoanalytic perspective, then, the pleasures and fascinations of classic narrative cinema arise out of its capacity to play on these contradictions – especially as they centre on sexual difference – while at the same time it preserves the integrity of subjective identity outside the contradictions that found it. The fetishism of cinematic representation takes place on three interrelated levels. First, following Christian Metz, Neale argues that the fascination of the cinematic image itself derives from its play of presence and absence – we know that the events and figures we watch on the screen are not really there, yet we believe we grasp them as though in some way they were more real than life. Second, the function of classic narrative structure is to command 'the viewer's adherence to a coherent and homogeneous diegesis' (Neale, 1980). In other words, the fetishism of fiction has to be supported by the production of the conditions in which the audience will accept the make-believe, will be willing to suspend disbelief, accept the fiction as a 'real world', and so support the reality-effect of classic Hollywood. Finally, further and specific 'regimes of credence' – conventions of verisimilitude – are produced by the different genres.

In this context, Neale sees the horror film as bound up with fetishism in an overdetermined way. For a start, in the body of the monster it addresses directly the question of sexual difference and castration. But also, in relation to the foregoing discussion, its fetishistic fictionality is trebled in that it deals in areas predefined as pertaining to imagination, fantasy and subjectivity. Genres such as the gangster, war film or western, focusing on questions of law/disorder, derive their regimes of credence from discourses and codes defined as 'non-fiction' – such as newspaper reporting, sociology and historical documentation. The horror film, on the other hand, dramatises questions about the definition of the 'human' and the 'natural' against the concept of the 'unnatural/supernatural'. The order it refers to is metaphysical, its narrative disequilibrium produced in the disjunction between the 'real' world and the 'supernatural'. The narrative quest of the horror film, then, is to find that discourse capable of solving this disjunction, explaining events (Neale, 1980, p. 22). Given that the discourses mobilised by the horror film are 'characterised as representing not factual reality but poetic or psychological realities', the 'kinds of legitimating documents and references employed ... will tend to be ancient texts, parapsychological treatises, myths, folklore, religion' (Neale, 1980, p. 37).

Clearly, the maintenance of verisimilitude, the 'splitting of belief' in the audience, is harder for fantasy genres such as the horror film, hence the requirement for 'rigorous conventionalisation' noted by some of its critics, and its cultural marginalisation as fodder for adolescents and children. At the same time, the cinematic work involved in making credible an avowedly fictional world produces the particular brand of fetishistic fascination – with special effects and so on – exhibited by the cinephilia of the aficionados. Accepting that the neuralgic point of narrative in the horror film is sexual difference, and that its successful suspension of disbelief produces effects – horror, anxiety, fear – 'linked to the problematic of castration' (Neale, 1980, p. 39), the horror film, Neale argues, engages the spectator directly in the play of fetishism. This is taken further in the materialisation of the monster. While the fascination with the monster brings the spectator close to the source and terror of desire and close to the truth of his condition as a patriarchal subject, the fetishistic structure of cinematic narrative ensures that the monster also acts as a displacement of this lack:

> Hence the monster may represent the lack, but precisely by doing so it in fact functions to fill the lack with its own presence, thus coming to function as a fetish simultaneously representing and disavowing the problems of sexual difference at stake. (Neale, 1980, p. 44)

This happens in two ways. First, in the narrative search for the means of controlling the 'play of the monster's appearance/disappearance', in order to contain the lack in place of which the monster appears. Second, in the emphasis the horror film puts on the 'appearance' of the monster, the special effects used both to make the monster terrifying and convincing and to highlight the key moments of its first appearance or birth, and of its destruction. From this investment in the fetishistic moment, Neale concludes, against the 'horror by suggestion' critics, that it is essential for the genre that the monster is physically materialised.

Neale elaborates further the significance of the monster in relation to sexual difference. The monster is defined as monstrous in relation to notions of masculinity and femininity. However, these categories intersect with and are complicated by definitions of the 'monstrous' versus the 'human'. On one hand, the notion of the 'human' does not recognise sexual difference, producing homogeneity in place of heterogeneity. On the other, the monster is rarely without human traits. Its heterogeneity, then, could be seen as a displaced instance of the sexual difference for which it acts as a fetish: the monster's consequently double heterogeneity 'functions to disturb the boundaries of sexual identity and difference' (Neale, 1980, p. 61). Nevertheless, Neale goes on to speculate, since the monster is frequently given male gender and woman is his victim, his desire for the woman – whether lustful or homicidal – could be understood as representing the horror that female sexuality produces for the male subject in the castration scenario.

In your dreams: Leatherface is the monstrous, uncontrollable 'id' in Tobe Hooper's *The Texas Chain Saw Massacre*

In Neale's account, then, the violence and sexual ambiguity of the monster, whether Gothic creature or deranged psychotic, the hovering of the horror film around the abnormal and taboo, far from representing a release of the repressed and a challenge to the patriarchal status quo, simply offers a fetishistic feast in acknowledgment and perpetuation of the perversity on which patriarchy is founded, the simultaneous fascination with and, disavowal of, female sexuality: 'The horror film is concerned ... not only with curiosity, knowledge and belief, but also, and crucially, with their transgressive and "forbidden" forms'. From this, he argues, arises the dominance of religious, or religio-scientific, forms of explanation within the horror film, and of critical accounts of the genre 'rooted in mysticism and other forms of irrationalism' (Neale, 1980, p. 45).

Feminism and the horror film

Several commentators on the horror film have pointed out the role of woman as victim – a role treated with increasing viciousness as the sexual violence of recent cycles increases. Stephen Neale's account of the monster from a Lacanian psychoanalytic perspective suggests that its association with sexual difference and the castration scenario makes it a representation of female sexuality itself. However, the interpretative consequences of this argument have been challenged in Linda Williams's (1983) reintroduction of the question of the woman's 'look' into psychoanalytic accounts of the mechanisms of classic narrative structure. Accepting the notion of the voyeuristic nature of cinematic pleasure in which the woman's look is denied in order to secure the safe identification of a male audience with the male hero's gaze at the objectified female, and accepting also that the horror film makes a special play with the relations of looking, knowledge and desire, Linda Williams offers a different system of interpretation, submitting the Lacanian scenario to the empirical realities of female sexuality: women are not castrated, a fact that a symbolic system found on such a notion has to negotiate somehow.

The interest of the horror film for Linda Williams is that it provides an exception to the general denial of the woman's look in the cinema, for a central moment of these films is the gaze of the heroine at the monster. On one level, the woman is punished for daring to look; instead of the mastery that is conferred on the male gaze, the act of her looking paralyses the woman and enables the monster to master the looker. However, Williams goes on to question the meaning of the woman's look, and of her relation to the monster, arguing that the power of the monster lies not in its castration, but in its sexual difference from the 'normal male': 'In this difference he is remarkably like the woman in the eyes of the traumatised male: a biological freak with impossible and threatening appetites that suggest a frightening potency precisely where the normal male would perceive a lack' (Williams, 1983, p. 87).

To ground this rereading of sexual difference, Williams interrogates the notion of woman as a 'castrated version of the man'.

Drawing on Susan Lurie's 'Pornography and the dread of woman' (1980), she argues that the mother's traumatic representation of sexual difference to the male child lies in her not being castrated: she does not possess a penis, yet is not mutilated, thus suggesting a totally other, non-phallic potency. Similarly, 'the monster is not so much lacking as he is powerful in a different way' – as, for example, is the vampire. This then leads Williams to argue that the woman's look at the monster

> is more than simply a punishment for looking, or a narcissistic fascination with the distortion of her own image in the mirror that patriarchy holds up to her; it is also a recognition of their similar status, as potent threats to a vulnerable male power. (Williams, 1983, p. 90)

This rereading of the castration scenario then enables Williams to account for several features of the classic horror film: the 'vindictive destruction of the monster'; the frequent sympathy of the female characters for the plight of the monster; their similar constitution 'as an exhibitionist object by the desiring look of the male'; the frequent weakness of the male heroes; and 'the extreme excitement and surplus danger when the monster and the woman get together' (Williams, 1993, p. 90).

This is clearly a reading against the grain of a dominant view of how female sexuality is represented, a reading made easier by the Gothic horror film's use of mythical figures. The coming of the psychological thriller in the 1960s, however, with its abandonment of mythic monsters and its self-conscious Freudianism, makes the possibilities of such subversive reading more problematic. *Peeping Tom* (1960), which along with *Psycho* inaugurated the cycle, is, according to Williams, exceptional in that it offers 'a self-conscious meditation on the relations between a sadistic voyeur/subject and the exhibitionist objects he murders', for what the woman sees at the moment of confrontation is not the monster but her own reflection literally distorted in the concave mirror he holds up to her. The film marks a break in 'the history of the woman's look in the horror film' in that it constructs a heroine who refuses to recognise herself in the mirror: 'She sees it for the distortion it is and has the power to turn away, to reject the image of woman as terrified victim and monster proffered by the male artist' (Williams, 1993, p. 93). The cost of such a breakthrough, however, is a simultaneous refusal of 'the only way patriarchal cinema has of representing woman's desire': Helen can resist because she is without sexual desire herself. *Psycho*, and the cycle it inspired, including the controversial *Dressed to Kill* (1980), display no such self-consciousness about the structures they operate. These films reduce the gap between woman and monster, so eliminating that flash of sympathetic recognition that in Gothic horror suggests the 'possibility of a power located in her very difference from the male' (Williams, 1993, p. 96).

In the modern psychological thriller/horror film, 'the monster who attacks, looks like and, in some sense, is a woman', and we are asked to believe 'that the woman is both victim and monster', for she is 'responsible for the horror that destroys her' (Williams, 1993, p. 93). For Williams, the 20 years between *Psycho* and *Dressed to Kill* saw an intensification of this shift so that 'the identification between woman and monster becomes greater, the nature of the identification is more negatively charged and women are increasingly punished for the threatening nature of their sexuality', to the point that, in the recent spate of 'women-in-danger' exploitation films and 'video nasties', the psychopathic murderer is rarely seen: the body of the female victim is the only visible horror in the film.

Body horror

MICHAEL GRANT

Subsequent approaches to the horror film may perhaps best be characterised, at least initially, with reference to a special issue of *Screen* that appeared in 1986, adorned with a graphic still from *The Evil Dead* (1982) and entitled 'Body Horror'. The articles included in the issue concentrate on the representations of bodily mutilation as these appeared in works of the period such as the zombie films of George Romero, David Cronenberg's *Shivers* (1975), *Rabid* (1977) and *The Brood* (1979), as well as *Last House on the Left* (1972) and *The Texas Chain Saw Massacre*. The films in question are characterised by one of the contributors, Philip Brophy, in the following terms:

> The gratification of the contemporary horror film is based upon tension, fear, anxiety, sadism and masochism – a disposition that is overall both tasteless and morbid. The pleasure of the text is, in fact, getting the shit scared out of you – and loving it; an exchange mediated by adrenalin. (Brophy, 1986, p. 5)

Brophy goes on to describe American horror films of the 1970s in terms of what he calls 'horrality', a mode of textual manipulation whereby the spectator's feelings and expectations are self-consciously played upon by the film he or she is viewing. These are films that at once foreground themselves as constructions and terrorise their audiences by means of this very constructedness and self-conscious artifice. For Brophy, a film of this kind '*knows* that you've seen it before; it *knows* that you know what is about to happen; and it knows that you know it knows you know' (Brophy, 1986, p. 5; original emphasis). Self-awareness and the horrific effect come together in the destruction of the body, a destruction that is shown explictly on screen. A prime example is the opening scene in *Scanners* (1981), where by the sheer power of thought a scanner blows the head of another scanner apart, a process seen in all its physical detail. In the last scene of the same film, we see the transformation of Vale's body as his brother, Revok, scans him and gains power over him: 'Veins ripple up the arm, eyes turn white and pop out, hair stands on end, blood trickles from all facial cavities, heads swell and contract' (Brophy, 1986, p. 9).

For Brophy, body horror is taken to its logical limit by John Carpenter's *The Thing*, the horror of which derives from the Thing's total disregard for, and ignorance of, the human body (see case study). This results in a violent and self-conscious melding of spectacular display and horror, exemplified in the transformation of a severed head into a spider-like entity, as legs extend themselves from it in real time, turning it upside down to become a mobile body of extraordinary monstrosity. As the crew watch it walk out of the room, one of them says: 'You've got to be fucking kidding!', a line that identifies the film's display as a horrific and comic transgression that affects those on screen as it does the audience, and at the same time draws attention to it as a special effect, a spectacular violation of the limits of what it is to represent the human body. The humour of the scene, for Brophy a crucial characteristic of the modern horror film, has much in common with that of *The Evil Dead*, being 'mostly perverse and/or tasteless' (Brophy, 1986, p. 12) and having its source in the EC comics of the 1950s. The result is a cinema of the moment, concerned neither with past nor future, existing only for immediate effect.

Brophy's article is descriptive, contenting itself with noting certain of the major features of modern horror. Barbara Creed's piece, published in the same issue, 'Horror and the monstrous-feminine: an imaginary abjection', offers by contrast a theoretical reading of the horror film based on psychoanalytic concepts deriving from the work of Julia Kristeva. Creed turns to Ridley Scott's film *Alien* in an attempt to clarify the issues this raises – issues of otherness and the monstrous-feminine. By 'monstrous-feminine', she refers to woman seen from the point of view of Freud's understanding of castration – as shocking, terrifying, horrific, as the site of abjection. The theoretical underpinnings for this project, to be found in Kristeva's *The Powers of Horror* (1982), aim to establish the abject as a new theoretical entity beyond meaning, beyond the confines of the human (as understood within patriarchal society), but which nonetheless can be given significance within a psychoanalytic (Lacanian) understanding of the formation of the subject. Creed's purpose is to show the inescapable relevance of this to an analysis of dominant culture and the subordination of women within that culture.

Kristeva pictures the abject as a place where meaning collapses, where 'I', the subject, am not. The abject is thus to be identified with what threatens life, and it must, therefore, be radically excluded from the place of the living subject. The abject, in other words, is all that the subject excludes in order to be what it is, to have the identity that it does. The abject is, for Kristeva, what in Judaism is characterised as 'abomination': sexual perversion, murder, the corpse, incest and the feminine body. In effect, the abject concerns everything that figures in the archaic relation to the mother. Given this context, it is hardly surprising that Kristeva considers the ultimate in abjection to be the corpse. The body expels from itself wastes such as faeces and urine and by so doing continues to live. The corpse represents a condition in which waste has encroached upon everything; the body has become its own waste product, and the living subject is no longer the one who expels: in an ultimate reversal, it is itself the object of expulsion. Thus, the corpse – at least within the Old Testament tradition – is wholly abject. It constitutes a basic form of pollution, a body without a soul. It is this notion that Creed applies to horror films. Bodies without souls, such as vampires and zombies, and corpse-eaters such as ghouls, comprise the basic iconography of the horror film, an iconography of abjection.

Creed takes this further when she argues that the major project of the horror film is the construction of the maternal figure as abject. She considers that, within our culture, central images of pollution are related to the mother – in particular, images of menstrual blood. These images of pollution are horrific, since images of this kind, of blood, pus, faeces, vomit and so on, signify a split between two orders: the maternal authority and the law of the father. These images of waste threaten an integral and unified subject that is constructed as such within the symbolic, the world of meaning, of social order and paternal law, and, as a result, they induce loathing and disgust. At the same time, these images hark back to an archaic period when the child's relation to its mother was such that it did not experience embarrassment and shame at the emergence of its bodily wastes. Thus, images of filth and waste give rise not only to fear and loathing but also to pleasure, a perverse pleasure deriving from the archaic mother–child relation, which was marked by untrammelled playing with the body and its wastes. The menstrual blood in *Carrie* (1976) is taken by Creed to give significant backing to this argument.

This approach allows Creed her fundamental point, that 'the central ideological project of the popular horror film' is 'purification of the abject' through what Kristeva calls 'a descent into the foundations of the symbolic construct' (Creed, 1986, p. 53). This means that the horror film brings about a confrontation with the abject such that the abject (the zombie, the vampire and so forth) is ejected and the boundaries of the symbolic, of the human world, are re-established. Horror films are a kind of modern defilement rite in which all that threatens the rule of order and meaning, all that is of the Other, is separated out and subordinated to the paternal law. This project is, for Creed, fundamentally reactionary, and she finds it in *Alien*, which represents 'the monstrous-feminine in terms of the maternal figure as perceived within a patriarchal ideology' (Creed, 1986, p. 56). The archaic mother, the monstrous-feminine, is present in the film as primordial abyss, manifest in the alien spacecraft, as well as in the images of blood and the all-devouring, toothed vagina.

The same presence is also embodied in the monstrous figure of the alien born from the rupturing of Kane's chest, and in the Nostromo's computer, Mother, whose children, born from the sleeper-pods of the spaceship at the beginning of the film, are devoured by the toothed alien during the course of the narrative. The archaic mother is not represented as such in these scenes, nor indeed does she appear at any point in the film's subsequent development. She is, however, present in the mise en scène, in the womb-like imagery of the alien craft, with its tunnels leading to the rows of hatching eggs, and in the body of the Nostromo, the mother ship. Present in the voice of the controlling computer, she is also present in the birth of the alien, who is her representative, and in its destruction of the Nostromo's crew. For Creed, the archaic mother informs all things, though she is localised in none of them.

It is the underlying strategy of *Alien* to contain this pervasive alterity, this radically ungraspable and unrepresentable Other, within a structure that makes of the alien the mother's fetish. That the alien is the mother's phallus is made perfectly clear when it arises from Kane's body. However, the alien is more than a fetish: 'It is also coded as a toothed vagina, the monstrous-feminine as the cannibalistic mother. A large part of the ideological project of *Alien* is the representation of the maternal fetish object as an "alien" or foreign shape' (Creed, 1986, p. 68).

The film finally signals the accomplishment of its phallocentric project in its presentation of Ripley's body as she undresses just before her final confrontation with the alien in the escape capsule. We have here a reassuring and pleasurable image of the 'normal' woman, the humanity of whose maternal feelings are expressed in her stroking the cat as if it were her baby. The final sequence not only disposes of the alien, but also represses 'the nightmare image of the monstrous-feminine' that has been constructed in the film 'as a sign of abjection' (Creed, 1986, p. 69). Thus, at the end of *Alien*, the abject is literally expelled from the image in a restoration of the symbolic order (see case study).

The question of the body is also addressed in psychoanalytic terms by Carol Clover (1992). Her concern is predominantly with the slasher movies of the 1970s, such as *The Texas Chain Saw Massacre* and *Halloween*), films that lead her to reconsider certain of the assumptions she sees as basic to much recent academic and theoretical writing about mainstream Hollywood. Her argument begins from Laura Mulvey's well-known contention that the cinematic gaze is structured by male or masculine perceptions, something that is made clear when the object of the gaze is a woman. For Clover, Mulvey's position amounts to saying that

> [t]he cinematic apparatus ... has two ways of looking at a woman, both organised around defending against her 'castration' and both of

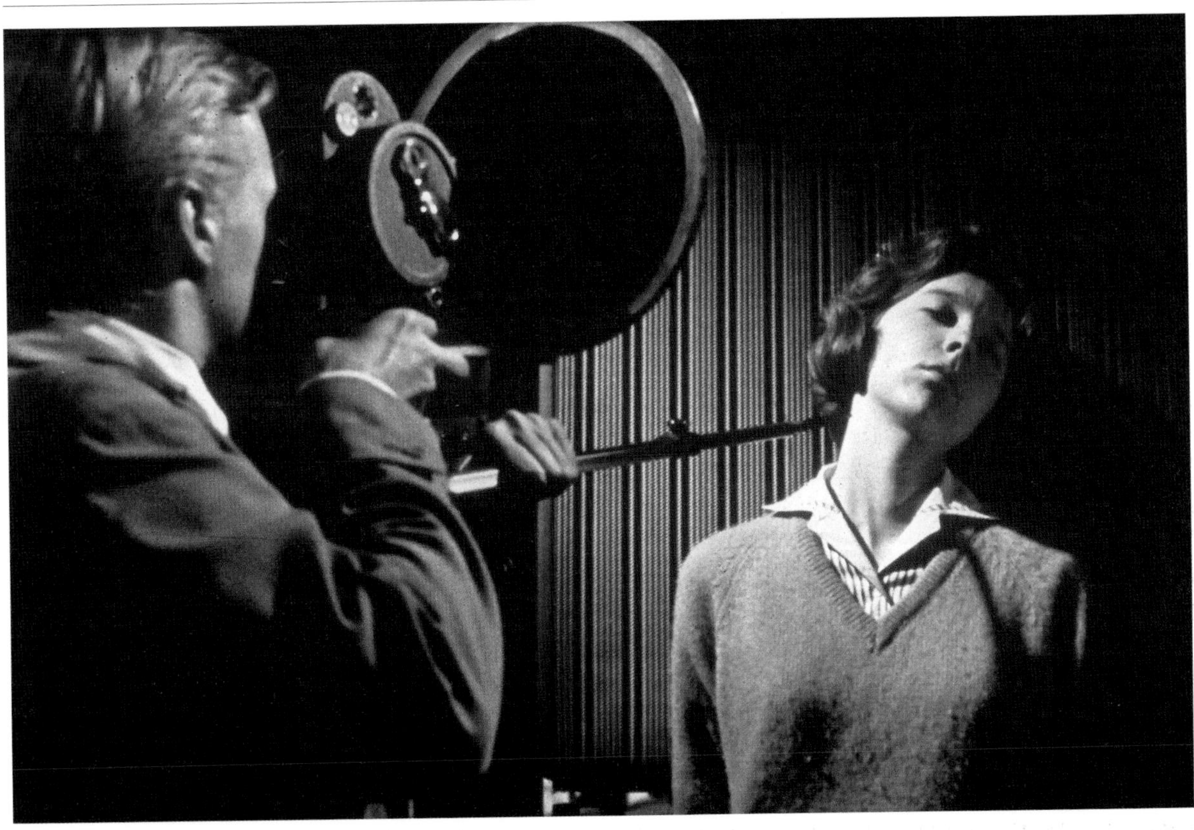

The monster's human face: Carl Boehm victimises Anna Massey in Michael Powell's *Peeping Tom*

> which, therefore, presuppose a male (or masculine) gazer: a sadistic-voyeuristic look, whereby the gazer salves his pleasure at female lack by seeing the woman punished, and a fetishistic–scopophilic look, whereby the gazer salves his unpleasure by fetishizing the female body in whole or in part. (Clover, 1992, p. 8)

However, Mulvey's account by no means exhausts the pattern of identification and subject position put into play by slasher films. Brian De Palma's *Carrie* is a case in point: though the camera positioning invites us to take up the perspective of Carrie's tormentors, the overall development of the film is such that by the end the viewpoint that prevails is Carrie's own. Our involvement with her sufferings earlier in the film is essential to our coming to sympathise with, and to understand, her revenge on her school and her final destruction of her mother. Clover's project leads her to question one of film theory's 'conventional assumptions', namely that 'the cinematic apparatus is organized around the experience of a mastering, voyeuristic gaze' (Clover, 1992, p. 9).

This means that Clover tends to concentrate on matters of point of view and identification. For the male viewer, seeking a male character to identify with, there is, in her view, little to hang on to. Of the good characters in slasher films, characters such as boyfriends or schoolmates of the girls, few are developed and even those who acquire some presence in the narrative soon die. Traditional authority figures, such as policemen, fathers and sheriffs, are usually risibly incompetent, and are themselves often killed, leaving the girl, the film's protagonist, to confront the killer on her own. As for the killer, he is usually invisible or scarcely seen during the first part of the film, as in *Halloween*, and what is revealed when finally we do get to see him is not something that is likely to evoke sympathy. He is often fat, deformed, or dressed as a woman, or more extremely, as in *The Texas Chain Saw Massacre*, wearing a mask of human skin. The killer may even be a woman. Any male viewer of *Friday the 13th* (1980) who thinks to identify with the killer is in for a rude awakening, when he discovers in the film's final sequences that the killer is not a man at all but a middle-aged mother. In any event, the killer is either himself killed or otherwise thrust out of the narrative. No male figure of any significance survives to tell the tale.

The main character of these films is the final girl, such as Laurie in *Halloween*, and hers is the main storyline. As Clover remarks, she is intelligent and watchful, being the first to recognise that something is wrong and the only one able to deduce the extent of the threat posed by the killer. Her perspective comes close to our own understanding of the situation:

> We register her horror as she stumbles on the corpses of her friends. Her momentary paralysis in the face of death duplicates those moments of the universal nightmare experience – in which she is the undisputed 'I' – on which horror frankly trades. (Clover, 1992, pp. 44–5)

She is the slasher film's hero, and by the end our attachment to her is almost complete.

This shift of perspective from the masculine to the feminine becomes, for Clover, the aesthetic base of the slasher genre, a feature she addresses in terms of what she calls 'the play of the pronoun function'. An example of this is the opening sequence of *Halloween*, in which we view the action in the 'first person' before it is revealed to us who that first person actually is. A continuous shot shows us a murder from the killer's point of view, a point of view that a reverse-shot reveals finally to be that of a six-year-old boy, Michael Myers. In *Friday the 13th*, 'we' stalk teenagers over the course of the film, and are invited to think of 'ourselves' as male, due to glimpses of 'our' booted and gloved body, items conventionally coded as masculine. By the end, however, 'we' are revealed as female. Similar uncertainties as to sexual position inform *Dressed to Kill* and *Psycho*. This unsettling of spectatorial position is embodied particularly in the final girl. In films such as *Hell Night* (1981) and *The Texas Chainsaw Massacre 2* (1986), the active investigating look is that of the final girl, making the killer the object of the look and herself the spectator. Though it is through the killer's eyes that we see the final girl at the beginning of the films, it is through her eyes that we see the killer, often around the middle of the film and increasingly towards the end. The gaze therefore becomes female. This would seem to reverse the priorities associated with classic Hollywood cinema: 'The female exercise of scopic control results not in her annihilation, in the manner of classic cinema, but in her triumph; indeed, her triumph *depends* on her assumption of the gaze' (Clover, 1992, p. 60; original emphasis).

What the slasher film offers, then, is a profound variation on the classic structure; in these films, the categories of masculine and feminine, which are traditionally correlated with male and female, are unified in one and the same character, who is anatomically female and whose point of view the spectator is encouraged to share. In the killer, we find a feminine male and in the hero a masculine female. This, however, is not the whole of the character of the final girl. While she can be described as masculine, she also registers as feminine in her fears and doubts. Even in her final struggle with the killer, she shifts between strength and weakness, attack and flight, fear and anger, error and effectiveness. Like her name – Laurie, Terry, Will, Marti, Ripley and so on – she is female and androgynous. She is 'not masculine but either/or, both, ambiguous' (Clover, 1992, p. 63).

The final girl, then, appears as a figure that, for Clover, embodies a dialectic or logic of representation underpinning the aesthetic effectiveness of the slasher film. It is this approach that informs her discussion of one of the most subtle and complex of modern films, Michael Powell's *Peeping Tom*, whose protagonist, Mark Lewis, is male. Her argument is that Powell is interested in Mark the assaultive gazer, the one who kills with his camera, inasmuch as he is the outcome of Mark, assaulted gazer assaulted, that is, by his father, whose investigation into the physiology and psychology of fear involved filming his son's childhood in unremitting and excruciating detail. It is in this context that Clover sees Mark's suicide as the act of a tragic figure. If the film opened with a scene of pure aggression, it closes on a scene of pure helplessness, a helplessness made evident by the sound of a recorded dialogue from his childhood. As Mark dies, we hear a voice we take to be his father's, saying 'Don't be a silly boy; there's nothing to be afraid of'. After the screen darkens, we hear the voice of a small boy: 'Goodnight, Daddy – hold my hand'. The film is thus structured around Mark's experience of fear and pain. His assaults on women, assaults carried out by his camera, are not simply sadistic; they are inseparable from and 'animated by his own historical pain' (Clover, 1992, p. 176). In other words, *Peeping Tom* is a film crucially concerned with male lack, a characteristic it shares with the slasher films of a later period. At the end of *Peeping Tom*, Mark's suicide is accomplished in an ecstatic act

Animal instincts: Geoff Goldblum mutates into a monstrous insect in *The Fly*

that unites him with the female subjects of his earlier killings. It is an act of castration that takes place on camera and that is effected by the camera, and it unites Mark's actual assumption of the feminine position with his recognition of it. The film's enactment of the sado-masochistic dialectic thus involves at the same time a self-conscious and self-reflexive articulation of the dialectic of film and spectator.

The psychoanalytic approach to horror cinema has been challenged by Andrew Tudor (1989). His book offers a cultural history of the horror movie, and it is from this context that Tudor's objections emerge. He finds psychoanalytic accounts to be 'inordinately reductive', insofar as they presuppose the credibility of a particular outlook to which the widest possible range of cultural phenomena are to be subordinated. The terms of the theory are also the terms in which the reading is constructed, the result being that the revealed meanings are presupposed by the method of uncovering them. There is a further, related problem: the readings produced are esoteric, and are excluded by definition from the conscious understanding of any audience. As against this, Tudor proposes to study narrative structures, his intention being to distinguish three main types of narrative, each of which he derives from the analysis of a set of paired oppositions. Thus, horror narratives routinely place a 'known' world under threat from an 'unknown' of some sort, with the narrative development involving a series of moves from order to disorder and back to order. The oppositions that he tabulates are of the following kind: in line with the basic contrast between known and unknown, he places the secular everyday against the supernatural; 'normal' sexuality against 'abnormal' sexuality; social order against social disorder; culture against nature; health against disease, and so on. On the side of the known stands 'Good', while 'Bad' is subsumed under the unknown. On the basis of how these contrasts interrelate, Tudor goes on to distinguish between three types of narrative: narratives of knowledge, invasion and metamorphosis.

The knowledge narrative, exemplified by the 1931 *Frankenstein* (see case study), is based on contrasts between life and death, and normal and abnormal physical matter. The narrative pivots on the way Frankenstein's scientific knowledge and expertise mediate between these contrasted elements. As a result either of Frankenstein's intent or of his 'meddling' with what is best left alone, this knowledge gives rise to that which threatens the order and security of the known, familiar world. This in turn leads to a period of disorder and rampage, brought about by the monster, during which time attempts are made to overcome the threat, attempts based on the very knowledge that induced the disruption in the first place. Eventually, the monster is subdued and order restored. Invasion narratives, in which the unknown simply invades the known, are all rampage: the monster appears and goes on the rampage, until the customary blend of knowledge and expertise returns it to the unknown. Examples include *Jaws* (1975), *Alien*, *The Fog* (1979) and the *Dracula* films.

The most complex and interesting narrative form is that of metamorphosis. It involves many of Tudor's basic oppositions, the most significant being the contrasts between the conscious and the unconscious self, normal and abnormal sexuality, sanity and insanity, social order and disorder, and health and disease. In modern films, the unconscious self becomes equated with abnormal sexuality, disorder, insanity and disease, engendering psychological patterns of considerable richness and subtlety. Metamorphosis narratives may also combine with the other two types, resulting in invasion narratives that become fused with stories of physical change and transmutation, as in *The Thing* (see case study), or knowledge narratives involving extreme alterations in bodily states, as in 'body horror' films such as Cronenberg's *The Fly* (1986). The metamorphoses may befall either individuals or groups, so that in Jekyll-and-Hyde stories, for example, we have knowledge precipitating a disorder embodied in the man of knowledge himself, as well as narratives including *Psycho*, where Norman's abnormal psychic state leads to a transformation of his whole being, *Peeping Tom*, *Halloween*, *The Exorcist* (1973), *A Nightmare on Elm Street* (1984) and *Videodrome* (1982). Group narratives include *The Crazies* (1973) and Romero's zombie films, beginning with *Night of the Living Dead*, as well as the earlier works of Cronenberg, such as *Rabid* and *Shivers*.

Tudor does not lay down either necessary or sufficient conditions for defining 'horror'. A common criterion for the identification of horror, bodily mutilation, is not part of his typology. Furthermore, a comedy such as *The Mask* (1994) can be located in accord with his criteria on the borderline between metamorphosis narratives of the individual and group types. The value of Tudor's analysis derives from the discrimination it encourages between what seem to be two historically distinct worlds of horror. At some point in the 1960s (perhaps the pertinent film is *Psycho*, which may be thought to enact just this shift from one world to another), a marked alteration in emphasis took place, with films prior to the period exhibiting a relative security in their values, and films after it inviting the label 'paranoid'. Earlier films presuppose a world in which disorder is ultimately subject to human intervention, while the authorities, such as the police and the army, and institutions, such as the law courts, educational bodies and hospitals, remain credible embodiments of social and cultural meaning. In films of the later, paranoid type, 'both the nature and the course of the threat are out of human control, and in extreme metamorphosis cases, disorder often emerges from *within* humans to potentially disrupt the whole ordered world' (Tudor, 1989, p. 103; original emphasis).

The nature of the two conditions may be graphically exemplified by the contrast between *The Thing from Another World*, made in 1951, and John Carpenter's 1982 reworking, *The Thing*. In the world of 'secure' horror, the contrasts that hold sway, those between life and death, normal and abnormal, human and alien, and so on, are clearly marked as contrasts between what is human and what is external to the human, and thus what threatens the human is more easily defended against. In 'paranoid' horror, the principal oppositions are internal to the human condition: conscious/unconscious, health/disease, sanity/insanity, and so on, insinuate the unknown into the known in ways not found in earlier examples of the genre. Cronenberg's *The Fly* exemplifies the mode characteristic of the later kind of film, as do the slasher films discussed by Clover (1992), and the 'body horror' cinema addressed by psychoanalytic criticism. The world presupposed by these films is different from that of earlier horror. The earlier sense of a world whose moral and social order is worth defending has disappeared, as has the sense that institutions and authorities have a legitimate claim on the loyalties and co-operation of the protagonists. The new order is one that came to definitive birth with Romero's *Night of the Living Dead*.

Jonathan Lake Crane (1994) continues and develops Tudor's historical approach. For Crane, *Night of the Living Dead* initiates a cinema of nihilism, in which 'Altruism, respect for others, and valiant acts will have the same nil effect on material circumstances as those actions that are motivated by baser desires and feelings' (Crane, 1994, p. 14). It is in this film that Crane finds the supreme expression of contemporary nihilism, which pivots on the figure of the last survivor, the black male, Ben. Despite his extraordinarily heroic efforts in repelling the zombie attack on the farmhouse, in pulling the other defenders together and working out a plan of defence, he is mistaken for a zombie, and casually shot by a redneck member of the posse. We then see grainy still images of his body being dragged away on a meathook, being thrown on an unlit pyre and then incinerated. As Crane puts it, 'Ben's strong presence vanishes instantly with his ridiculous and unnecessary death' (Crane, 1994, p. 14). This line of argument does not encourage Crane to support the position on abjection that we have seen Creed take up; he is, on the contrary, opposed to psychoanalysis, like Tudor, because of what he sees as its excessively reductionist mode of explanation. Not only this, but Kristeva and others have gone wrong in arguing that terror, in whatever form it takes, is always a question of the 'I'. This is to make the matter of response to the horror film 'a private escapade, a lonely search for solitary satisfaction, a simple matter of individual psychological economy' (Crane, 1994, p. 38). It is to cut the films off from the times and culture of the people who made and understood them, and to confine the horror cinema within the constrictions of the 'I'.

For Crane, on the other hand, new horror films do not entertain the unconscious, but instead offer 'meaningless death in response to the terrors of everyday life' (Crane, 1994, p. 39). Contemporary horror frees itself from the conventions of the past, conventions that, it would seem, include the subjectivity described by psychoanalysis, and turns its attention to terrorising the body in ways that mean nothing to any but contemporary audiences. Crane's position finds succinct expression in his account of John Carpenter's version of *The Thing*: 'When [the protagonists] perform superbly, they die. When they screw up, they die. Whatever happens, they die' (Crane, 1994, p. 137). Modern films regard efficacious knowledge as 'a quaint chimera', and 'they work, like deadly and incurable epistemological viruses, to destroy all we once took on faith' (Crane, 1994, p. 138). The value of Crane's work lies in the degree of clarity he introduces into how we think about horror films. His procedure, like Tudor's, is descriptive; in this it differs profoundly from earlier, more ambitious attempts to 'theorise' horror cinema as a whole.

Selected Reading

Philip Brophy, 'Horrality: the textuality of contemporary horror films', *Screen* 27 (1): 2–13, January/February 1986. Reprinted in Gelder (ed.), *The Horror Reader*, London and New York, Routledge, 2000.

Carol J. Clover, *Men, Women and Chain Saws*, London, BFI Publishing, 1992.

Barbara Creed, 'Horror and the monstrous-feminine – an imaginary abjection', *Screen* 27 (1): 44–70, January/February 1986. Reprinted in *The Monstrous-Feminine*, London, Routledge, 1993.

Robin Wood, 'Introduction', in Britton, Lippe, Williams and Wood (eds), *American Nightmare: Essays on the Horror Film*, Toronto, Festival of Festivals, 1979.

Frankenstein (USA 1931 *p.c* – Universal; *d* – James Whale)

The creature of Whale's *Frankenstein* is both helpless and powerful, worthless and godlike, abject and sublime, a contrast that is central to the figure's aesthetic power.

The paradoxical nature of the monster is made apparent in the creation scene, set in Henry Frankenstein's laboratory. Out of the darkness of the storm comes the creative energy of lightning, a fusion of light and fire giving life to a creature of darkness and death. As T. R. Ellis (1985) has argued, the monster's fear of fire is tied, first, to his own violent origins and, second, to the Promethean overtones of the film. The monster (Boris Karloff) seems to remember the shock of his birth and the place of fire in it. The monster's fear arises from Promethean mythology: Prometheus created man, and stole fire from heaven to ensure the survival of the being he had made. Henry Frankenstein (Colin Clive) also calls on fire to endow his creation with life, but 'the great ray' is natural not divine. The creature's extreme fear of fire derives, therefore, from his origin in the non-divine, the human. Whale uses the suffering and confusion induced by the monster's conflicted nature, and endured by him throughout the film, as an expression of the paradox inherent in his creation.

Henry is not simply a crazed version of a figure from ancient myth. Frankenstein also subverts themes and images from Christianity. If Frankenstein has created a new Adam, then, in Ellis's words: 'This "Adam" will never inhabit a garden of Eden, but a world of pain and fear' (Ellis, 1985, p. 48). At the moment when the creature's hand first moves, indicating that he is alive, there was dialogue that was censored before the release of the print as we now have it. Henry exults: 'Now I know what it is to be God'. One of the paradoxes fundamental to the Christian conception of the Incarnation is manifest in the Crucifixion, where Christ, the Creator, dies at the hands of His creation. Henry's death at the windmill is an echo and parody of this: he too dies at the hands of what he has created. The blasphemy of the idea is evident in the burning arms of the windmill outlined in a fiery cross against the blackened sky.

The film not only plays on religious connotations from the Crucifixion, it also inverts the ultimate mystery, the Resurrection. The opening scene in the graveyard presents Henry and Fritz (Dwight Frye) as 'Resurrection men', grave robbers, in a setting that makes extensive use of images of the cross, a statue of the crucified Christ and a statue of death. It is against this background of death that Whale cuts to a close-up of Henry holding on to the casket he and Fritz have raised out of the earth. In an echo of Christ at the tomb of Lazarus, he says: 'He's just resting, waiting for a new life to come'. Thus, the film begins with a pseudo-resurrection, and ends with what is, despite the tacked-on ending, final and irrevocable death, a narrative progression that itself seems a parody of the Passion of Christ. Jonathan Lake Crane (1994) has argued that the monster is an outcast whose fate calls into question the assumptions and values of the 'normal' world, the estate of the Frankensteins and the village community that serves it. However, if we place the film against the romantic background of Mary

Shelley's novel, we may think that the subversive perversity of its conception of the creative act, an act more like that of an artist than the scientist, goes further than Crane allows. In Henry Frankenstein, Whale has created a character whose will and ambition serve to undermine the very foundations of paternal heritage and identity.

MICHAEL GRANT

Psycho (USA 1960 *p.c* – Paramount/Shamley Productions; *d* – Alfred Hitchcock)

For Robin Wood, the death of Marion Crane (Janet Leigh) in *Psycho* is 'probably the most horrible incident in any fiction film' (Wood, 1965, p. 109). It is the meaninglessness of it that shocks him and, he would argue, the audience. The murder seems irrational and useless: it ruptures the identification with Marion that the film has thus far been at pains to build up, overwhelming a fictional universe characterised by neurosis with nightmare and psychosis. Marion's decision to steal Cassidy's $40,000 and her subsequent flight from Phoenix to Fairvale seem the result of neurotic compulsion, a compulsion we are induced, by music and techniques of identification, to sympathise with. Her confrontation with Norman Bates (Anthony Perkins) thus becomes 'the core of the film'. The scene establishes a continuity between the normal and the abnormal, between Marion's neurotic compulsion and the psychotic behaviour of Norman, that survives the ensuing brutal disruption. With Marion's death we have no one except Norman with whom to identify. As a result, the techniques Hitchcock earlier employed to align us with Marion are then used to make us 'become' Norman, the remainder of the film being a descent into the depths of his 'psychological hell-state', his 'chaos-world' (Wood, 1965, p. 110). This means that the film's central protagonist, in whose psyche the major characters are united, is the spectator. Lila Crane's (Vera Miles) exploration of the Bates's mansion is our exploration of Norman's psyche, and her confrontation with mother in the cellar is our confrontation with the wellsprings of Norman's being.

Central to most accounts of *Psycho* is the shower scene. As the bloody water spirals in an anti-clockwise direction down the plughole, the camera cranes down after it into the blackness. As it then tracks back from the dark pupil of Marion's dead eye, the camera takes on the anti-clockwise movement of the water. The lacuna between these two moments is the elision of death, the point at which the film represents a lack beyond representation. It is here that we may recognise the film's principle of organisation; the enactment of an intrusion or rupture, which the film both can and cannot show. It is evident in a pattern of repetitions that find expression in a number of ways, including the doubling of actions (the hotel in Phoenix echoed by the Bates's motel, Marion's narrative duplicated by Norman's, and so forth) and physical similarities between characters, such as Marion and Lila.

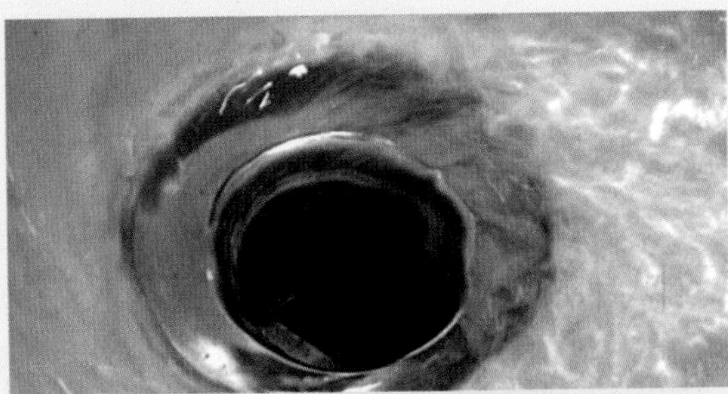

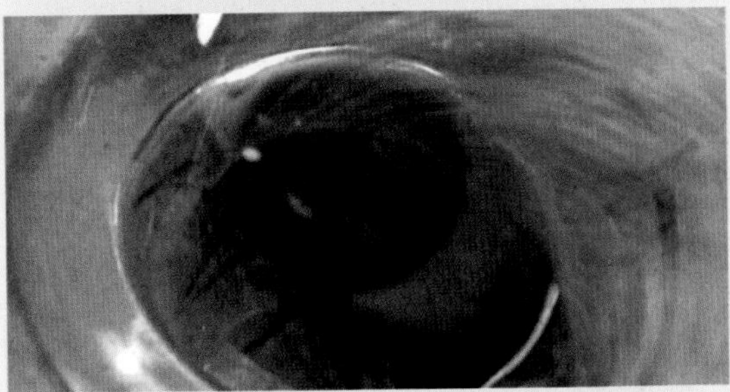

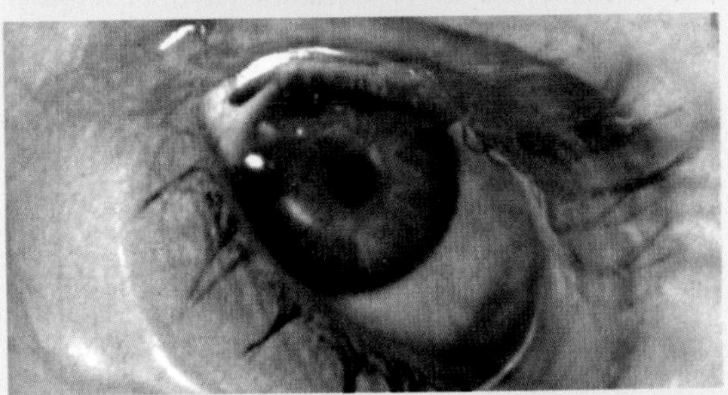

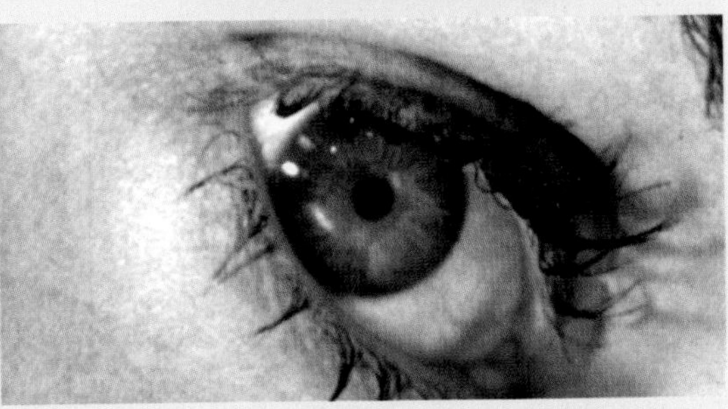

Marion Crane's death visualised in *Psycho*

Explained by their being sisters, their likeness is reflected in similarities between Sam Loomis (John Gavin) and Norman Bates, a likeness that requires more elucidation, drawing on the confrontation between two types of sexuality, one seemingly 'normal', the other rotted from within. Similarly, one might cite Lila's sudden shock as she encounters her own reflection in a mirror in Mrs Bates's bedroom. This encounter between self and self is repeated and transformed later in the scene in the cellar, when Lila confronts Mrs Bates's dead body, animated by light from the bulb swinging from the ceiling, as simultaneously the 'living' body runs shrieking towards her from the opposite end of the cellar brandishing the knife that killed her sister.

Lila is confronted by one person in two bodies. The most striking coinherence of two persons in one body is the superimposition of mother's skull onto Norman's face, as Norman is finally possessed by her. The sequence is played out with Norman looking directly at the camera, and with only the film's viewers present. It may be in part this close engagement with Norman that reminds us here of Marion, whose dead eye stared directly into the camera as she lay on the bathroom floor after her annihilation at mother's hands, the mother who is now heard saying 'They can see she wouldn't hurt a fly'. Mother's words are audible only to the film's audience, Norman's lips remaining fixed until the scene ends with his enigmatic smile. The final emergence of mother is therefore something that takes place only for us. It is an event that is grimly sardonic and humorous: in ascribing guilt to Norman, she is proclaiming her liberation from the confines of her son's inadequate psyche. She creates herself by annihilating her own creation. The superimposition, visible only to the viewer, of mother onto Norman is continued into the next and final shot of the film, the withdrawal of Marion's car from the swamp where Norman had concealed it. Here death emerges out of death: the self-conscious use of filmic devices effects the transcendence of death in the very images that celebrate its triumph of negativity. The end of the film is thus not simply ambivalent: it is poised between two different ways of understanding the significance of death, and commits itself to neither.

MICHAEL GRANT

Star Wars (USA 1977 *p.c* – Lucasfilm/20th Century Fox; *d* – George Lucas)

At the time of its initial release, *Star Wars* was the biggest box-office hit of all time. It served to reorientate late-1960s and 1970s science fiction away from

> the bittersweet questioning of tendencies within modern society [as exemplified by films like *Planet of the Apes* (1968), *Soylent Green* (1973) and *Rollerball* (1975)] to an unabashed celebration of escapism, gee-whizz heroics and innocence [as exemplified by *Close Encounters of the Third Kind* (1977), *Superman – The Movie* (1978) and *Star Trek – The Motion Picture* (1979)]. (Hardy, 1986, p. 290)

Accompanied by a major merchandising campaign, *Star Wars* is an early instance of what Justin Wyatt has called 'high-concept' film-making, in which 'the style and look of the films ... function with the marketing and merchandising opportunities structured into the projects in order to maximise profits within a conglomerized, multi-media industrial environment' (Wyatt, 1994, p. 190). In spawning two further 'episodes', *The Empire Strikes Back* (1980) and *Return of the Jedi* (1983), the film also became an instance of 'post-classic' (or post-studio period) sequel or series production. In addition, it helped to pioneer a new generation of special effects (in particular 'motion control', the computerised control of the camera movements used in filming models, especially model airships), and the use of Dolby stereo. Moreover, *Star Wars* is a relatively early and highly influential instance of the use of allusion and pastiche as dominant stylistic devices in post-1960s Hollywood films (see New Hollywood, p. 60).

There are allusions in *Star Wars* to a number of films: C-3PO is modelled on the robot Maria in *Metropolis* (1927); the bombing raids and serial dog-fights have their origins in *Twelve O'Clock High* (1949), *The Dam Busters* (1955) and *633 Squadron* (1963); the victory celebration at the end is based on sequences in Leni Riefenstahl's *Triumph of the Will/Triumph des Willens* (1936); and the return of Luke Skywalker (Mark Hamill) to his aunt and uncle's burnt-out homestead is modelled on a similar scene in John Ford's *The Searchers* (1956). However, although such allusions arguably help to cue or to reinforce some of the film's major generic points – notably science fiction, the western and the war film – they are neither foregrounded as such, nor employed to develop the narrative, its characters or themes. By contrast, the science-fiction adventure serials of the 1930s and 1940s, the genre 'memorialised' (to use Noël Carroll's term) through much of the film's pastiche, are more central in their effects, not just on the characterisation, storyline and setting, but also on its structure and style of narration (Carroll, 1982).

This is evident from a storyline that ranges across the galaxy, and which pits a small group of heroes against an ostensibly more powerful set of villains in a mission to save it from total domination, to the adoption of the procedures of serial construction. The latter are articulated through cuts back and forth between locations and actions; a narrative built on 'cliffhanging' moments; and the cuts to, from and into continuing conversations or actions as the film moves from scene to scene, often via such 'old-fashioned' devices as the horizontal or vertical wipe. The principle of serial construction is established at the start – labelled 'Episode 4' – with a set of rolling titles serving to summarise the story so far, which then plunge straight into a continuing action: the pursuit and capture of Princess Leia (Carrie Fisher) and her spaceship by Darth Vader (David Prowse) and the forces of the Empire. This sequence also highlights two of the principal formal and technological elements that update and modernise the film: its visual effects and sound. While the first shot displays the use of models (and motion control), it also shows off the possibilities of Dolby stereo and of modern multi-track recording: the roar of the spaceships, the whizz and the rattle of laserfire, the squeaking first line – 'Hear that?'.

In using and updating a minor genre, *Star Wars*

arguably illustrates the Russian formalist thesis that aesthetic innovation proceeds by means of the adoption of the principles of hitherto uncanonised art (see Erlich, 1981) The film's particular combination of naivety and sophistication, innocence and knowingness, also helped to initiate what Robert Ray (1985) and others have seen as a major tendency within post-1960s Hollywood cinema and post-1960s mass culture as a whole.

STEVE NEALE

Alien (USA/UK 1979 *p.c* – Brandywine Productions/ 20th Century Fox; *d* – Ridley Scott)

To characterise something or someone as alien is to characterise them as Other. This at least is an assumption that seems appropriate to a film such as *Alien*, as Annette Kuhn (1990) makes clear. Drawing on nineteenth-century definitions of the alien and on law from the same period concerning immigrants, Kuhn shows how new ideas concerning the treatment and regulation of immigrants entered our culture at the turn of the century, a period coinciding with the origins of cinema. She sees a connection between these ideas and the treatment of extra-terrestrials in both literary and cinematic science fiction. Aliens are seen as threatening, insofar as their numbers, visibility and 'difference' are such as to constitute the opposition: Them versus Us. There are aliens, such as the lone voyagers in *The Day the Earth Stood Still* (1951) and *E.T. The Extra-terrestrial* (1982), who come as messiahs, to save us from the effects of our technology and arrogance. Aliens of this kind are not threatening. Kuhn argues that, in all these cases, the Them/Us divide can be mapped onto other divisions, such as culture versus nature, reason versus instinct and good versus evil. These boundaries are shifting and permeable, and nowhere more so than in *Alien*.

The alien of this film, and of the rest of the *Alien* series, is one of the most threatening ever devised in the cinema, and the Them/Us divide maps unambiguously onto an opposition between the human and the non-human. However, as Kuhn points out, the non-human can be subdivided further 'into the techno-products of corporate culture (Ash, the Company's android; Mother, the spaceship's duplicitous computer system) as against the rampantly fecund, visibly Other alien, a manifestation of monstrous Nature' (Kuhn, 1990, p. 13). Nonetheless, the narrative dynamic is such that the overall movement of the film blurs these distinctions. The alien takes over the Nostromo, the crew's 'home', after penetrating Kane's (John Hurt) body and then bursting out of it. In a manner reminiscent of John Carpenter's *Halloween* (1978), Ridley Scott makes effective use of off-screen space in order to suggest not only that the alien threat is everywhere, but also that it menaces the very possibility of a human space. This sense of threat comes to a climax in the final sequence, when Ripley confronts the alien in the escape craft. After destroying the Nostromo, she places the cat in a sleeping pod, and settles back at the control console in relief. As she does so, she notices the shiny metallic shape of the alien coiled among the pipes and ducts of the craft's engine. She strips down and steps into a pressure suit, and eventually expels the creature by opening the inner world of the craft to the outer world of space: she defeats the alien by accepting the utterly alien universe of intergalactic vastness. We see the escape craft from the alien's point of view, as it is blasted into the void by the power of the engines, and we hear its cries of distress.

The marriage of the organic and inorganic in Ridley Scott's *Alien*

What is remarkable about *Alien* is the complexity of its presentation of what is alien. The alien eggs are discovered in a ship belonging to a civilisation of which we learn nothing, except that its technology seems one in which the organic and inorganic have been intimately married. We see one long-dead member of the crew, the nature of whose death we subsequently come to understand. As for the alien itself, we learn little or nothing in this film of its origin, though its sole purpose seems to be annihilation and conquest. Furthermore, there is alienness of another kind at work, that of the company, represented by Ash (Ian Holm) and Mother. It is the lack of humanity in the company's concern with power and profit that forces the crew members into contact with the alien, and brings about their eventual destruction. This theme is developed in the later films, *Aliens* (1986), *Alien³* (1992) and *Alien Resurrection* (1997), as is the complementary theme of motherhood. By the time Ripley plunges to her death in *Alien³*, giving birth to the creature that is forcing its way out of her chest, the values of the company have been wholly repudiated. Ripley herself takes on the role of alien mother, and in doing so accepts her death. Her acceptance of death is an unequivocally human act, and yet paradoxically it requires that she accept the alien within her. The categories of human and alien are thus inextricably bound up with one another, and the opposition between Them and Us is undermined. This constitutes a major critique of the values of the company and the culture of profit and exploitation it represents.

STEVE NEALE

The Thing (USA 1982 *p.c* – Universal/Turman-Foster Co; *d* – John Carpenter)

Noël Carroll has argued that monsters in horror films are both threatening and impure (Carroll, 1990, p. 43). They pose a psychological threat to individual identity (*The Exorcist*, 1973), a moral threat to the underlying order of society (*Rosemary's Baby*, 1968) or, as in the case of *The Thing*, a cosmic threat to the entire organic and human world. The idea of impurity involves the transgression of two or more fundamental cultural categories. This means that monsters are constructed out of various combinations of disparate elements. One such combination is fusion, a process involving the transgression of such categorical distinctions as inside/outside, living/dead, insect/human, machine/flesh. Examples include vampires, mummies, ghosts and zombies, creatures who are both living and dead. Elements from contradictory categories are fused or condensed together to form a single creature with a unified identity. Fission is the other basic type, in which contradictory elements are distributed over different identities. Examples include doubles, alter egos and werewolves.

However, the entity in *The Thing* evades Carroll's system. It exhibits elements of both fission and fusion, and neither of these. As a fission monster, it is spatially split across the members of Science Station 4, and also temporally divided, insofar as it imitates first a dog (which carries it from the Norwegian to the American station) and subsequently various crew members. Blood tests reveal it to be an entity composed of an infinite number of copies of itself. It also exemplifies fusion, as the dead specimen that Dr Copper (Richard Dysart) and MacReady (Kurt Russell) bring back from the Norwegian station makes clear. The conclusion Copper draws from his examination is that the chaotic mass of tissue appears to have died in the process of forming itself into a single entity out of many distorted and barely recognisable shapes. Towards the end of the film, after the Thing, in the form of Blair (A. Wilford Brimley), has killed Garry (Donald Moffat), MacReady attempts to destroy it with dynamite. The Thing displays itself in spectacular fashion, seeming to recapitulate all the beings, human and otherwise, it has ever been. Here the entity appears as a fusion that transgresses the ontological boundaries between human, animal and alien, as well as those between the living and the dead, and the temporal boundaries that separate the past from the present. However, it differs from the fusion monsters described by Carroll insofar as it does not achieve a stable homogeneous identity: when the entity manifests itself, it reveals itself as always elsewhere, as unlocatable. During the metamorphosis of the dog, or the extraordinary transformation of Norris's (Charles Hallahan) head into a spider-like creature with legs, the sheer exuberance of the exhibition suggests the excessive and ungraspable nature of what is seen. If the Thing can be said to exist at all, it is as a process of metamorphosis rather than as an entity with identifiable properties and qualities. This lack of definition not only reinforces our sense that the mode of being of the Thing is undecidable, it also shapes the narrative. When MacReady and Childs (Keith David) face each other surrounded by the dying flames of the burning camp, the question of who may or may not be the Thing is not merely left open but cannot be resolved. The lack of closure enacts the radical, primordial otherness of the monster. The narrative dynamic embodies in itself the nothingness or absence from which we are to imagine the Thing as still emerging.

Thus, what is crucial to the film is not so much the actions the station crew take in response to the Thing, but the Thing itself, or rather, the lack or absence it embodies. This means that the film's spectacular special effects are the pivot around which the spectator's interest turns. This point is made disparagingly by Steve Jenkins in a highly adverse review: 'The special effects, in true "modernist" fashion, exist in and for themselves' (Jenkins, 1982, p. 159). However, the reason for this self-reflexive mode of the effects can be justified as a consequence of the entity's existence as a kind of neither/nor: the more palpably it makes itself present, the more evidently it is absent. In this sense, Jenkins is right: to display effects in this manner is highly 'modernist'. Present in its absence, absent in its presence, the modernist text is precisely one that makes these antinomies palpable. This also describes the psychoanalytic fetish, and Carpenter's emphasis on effects can be linked with the fetishism of special effects in films contemporary with *The Thing*, such as *Alien* (1979) and *Star Wars* (1977). Steve Neale has argued that the effects in these films 'depend upon and intensify the fetishistic aspects of "fantasy" in particular and of the cinema and its signifier in general' (Neale, 1980, p. 105). If this is so, *The Thing* moves beyond the reification of its effects in order to engage its audience with the lack of representation as such. Its horror is not only that of the transgression of cultural categories but of what lies beyond categorisation, beyond the limits of the thinkable. It is to imagine the Thing as a sublime and impossible object.

MICHAEL GRANT

Dead Ringers (Canada/USA 1988 *p.c* – Mantle Clinic II/Morgan Creek/Téléfilm Canada; *d* – David Cronenberg)

Dead Ringers seems to demand interpretation. Cronenberg himself provides a key: 'In *Dead Ringers* the truth, anticipated by Beverly's parents – or whoever named him – was that he was the female part of the yin/yang whole. Elliot and Beverly are a couple, not complete in themselves. Both characters have a femaleness in them' (Rodley, 1992, p. 147).

It is certainly the case that repression and female sexuality are central to an understanding of the horror film in general and to *Dead Ringers* in particular, as Barbara Creed (1990) has demonstrated. Nonetheless, this kind of approach by no means exhausts the significance of the film. As Pam Cook has noted, one of the most striking features of *Dead Ringers* is that it avoids generic categorisation and interpretation: '[The film's] poeticism defies the rational explanation which would give the audience a spurious sense of mastery' (Cook, 1989, p. 4). At the centre of this is the complex handling of the notion of twins that is inseparable from the concept of the double. This is a theme central to psychoanalysis, and is explored by Otto Rank (1979), for whom the double is intimately related to problems associated with narcissism. Rank shows how self-love of the kind exhibited by Oscar Wilde's Dorian Gray, the love of a subject for its image or double, which excludes love of another person, has two aspects: love, and hate or fear. This ambivalence within narcissism is a form of defence against narcissism, a defence necessary to allow the subject its own identity, which is otherwise threatened by that of the other, the double, the self-image. *Dead Ringers* can be seen as an instance of this dialectic. As Beverly is drawn ever more deeply to Claire (Geneviève Bujold), participating in and abetting her use of drugs, and abandoning himself to sexual passion, so his narcissism returns him to his twin: his double. And yet, according to Rank, the relation of younger to elder brother is always fraught with rivalry. The younger brother 'is, as it were, a reflection of his fraternal self that has come to life; and on this account he is also a rival in everything that the [elder] brother sees, feels, thinks' (Rank, 1979, p. 75). The ensuing complexities are manifest in the way Elliot gradually succumbs to Beverly's drug-taking and loss of control, a reversal of dominance similar to that explored by Cronenberg in *Scanners* (1980).

It is this dialectic of reversal that allows Cronenberg to transform and go beyond much that is basic to the horror film, including the 'body horror' that had characterised some of his own earlier work, such as *Rabid* (1977), *Scanners* and *Videodrome* (1982). This further level of complication enters the film with the introduction of the theme of the Siamese twins, Chang and Eng. The force of this depends on the thematic emphasis on the split between mind and body: the Mantle twins are, in effect, one body split in half, while their minds seem joined (as Elliot puts it, he and Beverly share the same nervous system). It is in this context that Cronenberg is inclined to speak of the Mantle twins as monstrous, as creatures 'as exotic as *The Fly*' (Rodley, 1992, p. 144), a film that he describes as 'metaphysical horror' (Rodley, 1992, p. 134). Here Cronenberg invokes the 'metaphysical' poetry of the seventeenth century in which normally unharmonious elements are violently yoked together (Rodley, 1992, p. 131). The result is a combination of dissimilar elements and the discovery of unforeseen resemblances in things apparently unlike. Throughout the film, we are presented with such resemblances in things apparently unlike, and the violent revelation of dissimilarity or difference in what seems similar.

MICHAEL GRANT

The Blair Witch Project (USA 1999 *p.c* – Artisan Entertainment/Haxan Films; *d* – Daniel Myrick and Eduardo Sanchez)

Released in 1999 and quickly becoming a cult hit, *The Blair Witch Project* seemed to offer innovative synergistic possibilities for cinema and digital media at the cusp of the millennium. In addition to suggesting a new direction for marketing with the relatively young medium of the Internet, the film opened up a fresh aesthetic for the once-vibrant horror genre, which had grown stale. While horror cinema had become elaborate displays of digital effects, with graphic images of bodily violation, *The Blair Witch Project*, made on a budget of around $40,000, employed a more subtle approach that recalled the classic horror films produced by Val Lewton in the 1940s.

The film's narrative premise is explained in the opening titles: 'In October of 1994, three student film-makers disappeared in the woods near Burkittsville, Maryland, while shooting a documentary about the town's witch legend. A year later their footage was found'. *The Blair Witch Project* consists of this 'found footage', supposedly shot by the students with hand-held video cameras in grainy black and white and colour. A mockumentary about a failed documentary, *Blair Witch*'s camcorder aesthetic enhances its chilling reality effect by employing the visual conventions of observational cinema. Its vérité approach was also employed during production, as the unseen directors would leave mysterious bundles, slime backpacks and make frightening noises, generating real confusion and anxiety in the three actors. This realism was further aided by the film's novel Internet campaign, which provided a detailed backstory about the Blair Witch legend as if

Legend becomes fact in *The Blair Witch Project*

it were based in historical fact, including mock police reports, diaries, interviews and news about the disappearance of the student film-makers. So extensive and convincing was this 'documentation' that the real Burkittsville became a tourist attraction, and the film one element of a super-text involving numerous promotional and marketing tie-ins.

Stylistically, *The Blair Witch Project* relies on ambiguity and a deft use of off-screen space and sound to suggest the unknown. These techniques work to evoke elemental fears of the dark and of being lost – childhood terrors that are conjured up in the film's final images of one of the students standing with his face to the wall like a little boy being punished. Despite the narrator/camerawoman Heather's (Heather Donahue) disclaimer that 'It's very hard to get lost in America these days', the film recalls a specific tradition of American horror in its depiction of the woods as dark and deep, a place of evil to be feared, that stretches from Puritan captivity narratives to contemporary horror films such as *The Descent* (2005).

BARRY KEITH GRANT

War of the Worlds (USA 2005 *p.c* – Paramount/ Dreamworks/Amblin Entertainment/Cruise-Wagner Productions; *d* – Steven Spielberg)

H. G. Wells's 1898 novel *The War of the Worlds* was adapted as a radio play by Orson Welles and broadcast on Halloween night in 1938, causing panic among some listeners who, apprehensive about impending war in Europe, believed that invading Martians had landed in New Jersey. Like Welles's famous broadcast, and the first film adaptation in 1953, which drew on Cold War anxieties, Steven Spielberg's version taps into contemporaneous concerns, in this case post-9/11 fears about terrorism.

For the most part, the film is faithful to Wells's novel; perhaps its biggest departure is the premise that the Martian machines have been buried under the earth for eons, animated by aliens parachuted into them like terrorist 'sleeper' cells under our very noses that are suddenly awakened. The attack begins in New York City, site of the 9/11 attacks on the World Trade Center, and then spreads to the world beyond. A downed passenger jetliner that crashes onto a house in which protagonist Ray Ferry (Tom Cruise) and his children hide is a resonant image for post-9/11 consciousness; indeed, Ray's son Robbie (Justin Chatwin) asks if the attack is the work of terrorists. In Wells's novel, the Martians land in England – then a world power with a global empire – ruthlessly laying it to waste in a horrifying tale of the colonisers being colonised; likewise, in Spielberg's film, the Martians begin transforming the environment into their habitat, indifferent to and intolerant of indigenous terrestrial life. The US is saved by mere bacteria, organisms that 'God in his wisdom' has put on Earth, so that American and, by extension, western culture is represented as human and natural.

The film's ending, in which Ray improbably finds both his son and estranged wife safe in her parents' Boston home, with the entire street inexplicably unscathed by the Martians' onslaught, has been dismissed by many as Spielbergian sentimentality. This scene has its counterpart in the novel; but Spielberg did rework Wells's story as a family melodrama about an absent father. Ray's quest to deliver his children safely to their mother becomes a personal journey in which he learns to become a responsible parent. Initially self-absorbed and full of anger, Ray matures as a man and father by the end, an oedipal trajectory found in many of the director's other films.

BARRY KEITH GRANT

Tom Cruise resolves oedipal problems in Steven Spielberg's *War of the Worlds*

TEENPICS

STEVE NEALE

A period in life between childhood and adulthood has been recognised by most societies in most periods of history (Graff, 1995). However, during the course of the twentieth century in America and elsewhere in the industrialised west, this period has tended to increase, and alongside a series of social policies, practices and institutions that have increasingly treated those under 20 as both distinct and separate from adults, two key terms have emerged in America to mark it: 'adolescence' (a term first coined by psychologist G. Stanley Hall in 1904), and 'teenager' (a term first used in the popular press in the 1920s, and first fully established during the course of the World War II) (Kett, 1977). According to Maltby, a '"self-conscious subculture" of the young developed during the 1920s and 1930s as a largely urban white middle-class response to the increasing leisure opportunities afforded by changing social attitudes' (Maltby, 1989, p. 140). But as he goes on to argue, the first fully commercialised, cross-class, transnational – though for the most part equally white – forms of teenage culture emerged in America in the 1950s, as significant numbers of young people with increasing amounts of disposable income and leisure time comprised for the first time in the west both an increasing proportion of the population as a whole and an expanding sector of the market for services and goods.

In parallel fashion, Hollywood has always made films about young people (Considine, 1981). It has also made films designed or presumed to cater for what it called 'the juve trade' – juvenile spectators. (There is a distinction between the two. Films about the young are not necessarily addressed to the young; films presumed to address the young do not necessarily focus on or feature young characters. The 'bad boy' films of the late 1890s and early 1900s were presumed to appeal to nostalgic middle-class men [Krämer, 1998], while B-westerns and action serials, which featured adult characters and actors, were often presumed to appeal to young teenage boys, and animal films such as *National Velvet* (1944) and *The Yearling* (1946) were aimed at an audience of families.) However, the teenpic itself is normally held to emerge, like modern teenage culture, during the course of the 1950s.

One of the conditions underlying its emergence was a growing awareness on Hollywood's part of the importance of the teenage audience. Flying in the face of the industry's presumption that: 'Everyone who was not too young, too old, too sick, or living in the remotest backwoods' attended most movies most of the time (Quigley, 1957, p. 21), audience research conducted in the late 1940s indicated that: 'Age [was] the most important personal factor by which the movie audience is characterized' and that 'the decline of movie attendance with increasing age is very sharp' (Lazarus, 1947, pp. 162–3). Coming at a time when the industry faced unprecedented challenges and changes in the form of divorcement and divestiture, competition from television and other leisure pursuits, suburbanisation, a shift in audience demographics, a precipitous decline in ticket sales and audience attendance, these findings reinforced the growing importance of the teenage market for films and of targeting this market by drawing on aspects of teenage culture and by catering for teenage interests, tastes and concerns (Doherty, 1988).

A reflection in part of the industry's uncertainties, the teenpic was at this point heterogeneous, multi-dimensional and often contradictory in its forms, concerns and modes of address. A number of genres, traditions and production trends, some of them quite distinct, contributed to its initial development. First, there were mainstream dramas and social-problem films such as *The Wild One* (1953), *Blackboard Jungle* and *Rebel Without a Cause* (both 1955), each of them produced by mainstream studios (Columbia, MGM and Warner Bros. respectively), and each of them drawing on a tradition of films about juvenile delinquency, juvenile wildness and juvenile crime that stretched back as far as the 1920s and 1930s and that included films such as *Flaming Youth* (1923), *Dead End* (1937) and *Wild Boys of the Road* (1933). However, their immediate origins lay in two separate cycles of juvenile delinquency films made during and just after World War II that included films such as *Youth Runs Wild/Are These Our Children?* (1944) and *I Accuse My Parents* (1944) on the one hand, and *Gun Crazy* (1950), *City across the River* (1949) and *Knock on Any Door* (1949) on the other. The idea and the image of the juvenile delinquent continued to colour films of all kinds made about teenagers in the 1950s and early 1960s, from sensationalised crime dramas and social-problem films such as *Girls in Prison* (1956) and *Juvenile Jungle* (1958) to musicals such as *Jailhouse Rock* (1957) and *West Side Story* (1961), though distinctions need to be made between those films that sought, at least ostensibly, to condemn juvenile delinquency, those that sought to understand it and those that sought, either way, to use it to appeal either to a teenage or adult audience.

The cultural context within which delinquency emerged as an issue at this time has been explored by Gilbert (1986), and the industrial context within which the films emerged by Doherty (1988) and Betrock (1986). Gilbert stresses the extent to which a realignment of the relations between the media, the market, the teenage consumer, teenage tastes and teenage behaviour threatened hitherto dominant patterns of cultural authority. Doherty and Betrock emphasise the heritage and the growing influence of independent production and 'exploitation'.

Sidney Poitier and Glenn Ford deal with teenage problems in *Blackboard Jungle*

The term 'exploitation' originally referred both to the publicity techniques used to maximise a film's commercial potential and to the making of films that drew on topical, controversial or otherwise easily saleable subjects (see also Exploitation cinema, p. 298). During the studio era, both types of exploitation were common. But they were governed and controlled by the industry's organisations, notably the MPPDA (the Motion Picture Producers and Distributors of America) and its successor, the MPAA (the Motion Picture Association of America), and those films that exploited topics banned by the Production Code were refused a seal of approval and denied access to the theatres controlled by the majors (Schaefer, 1999). However, films that deliberately flouted the Code were produced by small-scale independents for independent distribution and exhibition, and many of these films – among them *The Burning Question/Reefer Madness/Tell Your Children* (1938), *High School Girl* (1934) and *The Road to Ruin* (1934) – used youthful deviance as a framework for dealing with exploitable 'adult' topics such as drugs, prostitution, unmarried motherhood and venereal disease (Muller and Farris, 1997). Following divorcement, the MPAA found it more difficult to enforce the Code. Meanwhile, the decline in audiences and in the number of films produced by the majors meant that many exhibitors were crying out for films to show, preferably films with exploitable potential, and films that would appeal to those still going to the cinema on a regular basis and to those whose tastes were not catered for by television. As a result, a number of small independent producers and production companies such as Samuel Arkoff, Allied Artists and American International Pictures (AIP), together with a handful of unit producers at mainstream studios, such as Sam Katzman at Columbia and Albert Zugsmith at Universal, began to tailor their films to the teenage market and to 'marginal' (rather than mainstream) adult audiences, to adopt the techniques and the practices of exploitation, and in the process to defy or at least test the limits of the Production Code and the bounds of 'good taste' as established by the MPAA. Many of these films were about juvenile delinquency and juvenile crime, and the resulting mix of mainstream and independent productions, practices and genres, and of adult, marginal adult and teenage components and points of appeal, is just one index of the 'ambivalence' James Hay sees as fundamental not just to the teenpic, but to teenage culture in general (Hay, 1990, p. 336).

A similar ambivalence marks other 1950s and early 1960s trends and genres, not least 'weirdies' and rock 'n' roll and pop films and musicals, and not least because a similar mix is characteristic of them all. '"Weirdie" was inexact nomenclature for an offbeat science fiction, fantasy, monster, zombie and/or shock film, usually of marginal financing, fantastic content, and ridiculous title' (Doherty, 1986, p. 146). Developing alongside cycles of 'adult' science-fiction and low-budget monster films made by the majors, produced both by the majors themselves and by independents such as AIP, weirdies in particular sought to capitalise on the popularity of horror and science fiction with teenage spectators. Hence the appearance alongside *The Incredible Shrinking Man* (1957), *I Married a Monster from Outer Space* (1958) and *The Deadly Mantis* (1957) of films with titles such as *I Was a Teenage Werewolf* (1957) and *Teenagers from Outer Space* (1959).

Films such as these drew on and fed into a wider teenage culture that included horror and fantasy comics. Other films drew on pop and rock 'n' roll. Following the use of 'Rock around the Clock' on the credits of *Blackboard Jungle*, Sam Katzman produced the first rock 'n' roll musical, *Rock around the Clock* (1956), the following year. Unlike *Blackboard Jungle*, an adult-orientated social-problem film, *Rock around the Clock* was, as Doherty points out, 'the first hugely successful film marketed to teenagers *to the pointed exclusion of their elders*' (Doherty, 1986, p. 74; original emphasis). It was arguably, therefore, the first modern teenpic, as well as the progenitor of a cycle of rock 'n' roll films that included *Shake, Rattle & Rock!* (1956) and *Rock Rock Rock!* (1956), both produced by independents, and *The Girl Can't Help It* (1956) and *Rock, Pretty Baby* (1957), both produced by the majors.

These cycles and genres were soon joined by hot-rod films such as *Dragstrip Riot* (1958) and *Hot Rod Girl* (1956), by calypso and beatnik films such as *Calypso Joe* (1957) and *The Rebel Set* (1959), and by what Doherty calls 'clean teenpics', musicals and light romances such as *April Love* (1957) and *Gidget* (1959) that recall a tradition stemming back to the Deanna Durbin, Mickey Rooney and Judy Garland films of the late 1930s and early 1940s (Considine, 1981), which parallel what some have seen as the incorporation and neutralisation of rock 'n' roll by the white musical establishment (Martin and Segrave, 1993), and which Doherty himself argues addressed teenagers and teenage concerns within an unambiguously white, middle-class adult framework of values. 'In the clean teens baroque phase, AIP's Beach Party cycle (1963–5), parents were banished altogether', he writes.

> As compensation, though, there was little in this portrait of teenage life that would disturb a worried father. Adults were usually absent, but their values were always present. Fulfilling the best hope of the older generation, the clean teenpics featured an aggressively normal, traditionally good-looking crew of fresh young faces, 'good kids' who preferred dates to drugs and crushes to crime. (Doherty, 1986, p. 195)

Doherty's views are echoed by Morris (1993). However, there are a number of unspoken and perhaps rather glib assumptions at work here, not just about the relative merits of preferring dates to drugs and crushes to crime, but also about the relationship between teenage and adult values, about the ethnic politics of early rock 'n' roll, about rebellion and deviance as hallmarks of teenage authenticity, and, indeed, about the authenticity of teenage culture itself. As Graff points out, despite 'striking legacies, images, and myths to the contrary', there are numerous 'paths' to growing up, not just one (Graff, 1995, p. xiii). And as Lewis argues, 'When we are talking about youth we are talking about a fundamentally mediated culture, one that continues to re-present itself in terms of the products it buys, the art that defines it, and the art it defines as its own' (Lewis, 1992, p. 4). It is this 'dialectic of cultural autonomy and media appropriation' that lies at the heart of the teenpic, and that helps generate the ambivalence noted by Hay (1990), and the conflicts and contradictions to which that ambivalence gives rise.

Underlying the extent to which marginalised films, marginalised filmgoing practices and marginalised venues such as drive-ins 'contributed to the formation of teen spectators and a "teen culture" in the 1950s' (Hay, 1990, p. 335), Hay points out that teen films often 'co-opted, parodied or resisted' the preferred genres and 'narrative practices of US film culture' (Hay, 1990, p. 336). However, he also points out that teen films and teen culture were never 'wholly autonomous' (Hay, 1990, p. 336). They too could be co-opted and resisted. The ensuing conflicts and contradictions often found articulation in 'rites-of-passage' narratives, in stories that placed their protagonists 'betwixt and between' (Hay, 1990, p. 336) adulthood and childhood, and that explored issues of autonomy, identity, allegiance and difference in the context of the teenage peer group on the one hand and adult society on the other, and in the ways in which – and the extent to which – hitherto dominant generic norms were inflected or reworked in the process:

> These films in some fashion involve narrative conflict both over finding one's place within a relatively autonomous society of youths and over defining, negotiating and resisting differences between youth and adulthood. In the sense that teenpics were given to modelling conflict in this manner and through generic conventions that also deterritorialized and reterritorialized the conventions of traditional Hollywood genres, they can be said to define doubly the relation of 'the minor' to a 'parent' culture. (Hay, 1990, p. 336)

The clean-teen films of the late 1950s and early 1960s are particularly exemplary of the problems and issues at stake here, especially insofar as they tend to centre on female characters, and share a number of the features and concerns of contemporary woman's films such as *Picnic* (1955) and *Peyton Place* (1957), as Hay points out. But subsequent teenpics are exemplary too, not least because, for demographic reasons, teenagers have since then comprised 'the primary battleground for commercial motion picture patronage in America' (Doherty, 1986, p. 231); because: 'Since 1960, teenpics have been an industry staple, if not the dominant production strategy for theatrical movies' (Doherty, 1986, p. 231); and because the relationship between what is marginal and what is central, what is minor and what is mainstream has shifted and changed.

There have been important variations in the nature and volume of teenpics since the early 1960s. In the late 1960s and early 1970s, 'youth movies' drew much more on an image of counter-cultural rebellion than on an image of irresponsible juvenile delinquency. And as 'the boundaries between counter (film) culture and mainstream (film) culture all but evaporated' (Doherty, 1986, p. 233), films such as *The Graduate* (1967), *Bonnie and Clyde* (1967), *Easy Rider* (1969) and *Five Easy Pieces* (1970) mounted serious critiques of the parent culture. Following a crisis wrought by overproduction in the late 1960s and early 1970s, and in the wake of a counter-culture in general decline, the industry resumed production of teenpics in regular numbers in the late 1970s and 1980s. Some, such as *Halloween* (1978), *Night of the Comet* (1984) and *A Nightmare on Elm Street* (1984), were low-budget horror, sci-fi and slasher films. Some, such as *Caddyshack* (1980) and *National Lampoon's Animal House* (1978), were 'gross-out' or 'animal' comedies. Some, such as *Sixteen Candles* (1984), *Pretty in Pink* (1986) and *The Breakfast Club* (1984), were teen-centred dramas and romances. And some, such as *Rumble Fish* (1983) and *River's Edge* (1986), were teen-centred art or social-problem films. They were joined by bratpack westerns such as *Young Guns* (1988) and *Young Guns II* (1990) and by musical biopics such as *Great Balls of Fire!* (1989) and *La Bamba* (1986). (For an overview of teenpics since the late 1970s, see Bernstein, 1997.)

Teen-friendly time travel in Robert Zemeckis's *Back to the Future*

Despite their generic diversity, these films can all be defined as teenpics because they all focus on teenage characters. However, issues of definition are complicated by the fact that since the early 1970s, Hollywood has been decisively 'juvenalised' (Doherty, 1986, p. 235): not only do most Hollywood films aim to cater for a teenage audience, but directors and producers such as George Lucas and Steven Spielberg, who as Doherty points out were 'reared on the teen-oriented fare of the 1950s' (Doherty, 1986, p. 235), have helped through films such as *Star Wars* (1977) and *Raiders of the Lost Ark* (1981) to establish a teen-friendly trend towards big-budget action, adventure and fantasy films, and through films such as *American Graffiti* (1973) and *Back to the Future* (1985) to establish a trend towards the recycling of 1950s teenage culture. Generic definition is further complicated by the fact that both Doherty and Lewis (1992) detect what Doherty describes as a 'palpable desire for parental control and authority' in post-1960s teenpics (Doherty, 1986, p. 237), and by the fact that so many teenpics are marked by what he terms 'double vision':

> As teen-oriented movies have become the industry's representative product, the throwaway, unconscious artistry of the 1950s has been supplanted by a new kind of calculated and consciously reflexive teenpic ... Thus films aimed at teenagers are not only more carefully marketed and calculating created, they also function more explicitly on two levels. *Fast Times at Ridgemont High* (1982) and *Risky Business* (1983) are teenpic-like in their target audience and content, but their consciousness is emphatically adult. (Doherty, 1986, p. 236)

These points recall and refocus some of the questions raised by Hay (1990). When reference is made in *Clueless* (1995) to a 1970s tennis player, an early 1960s historical epic and an eighteenth-century novel, who are these references aimed at? When in *Back to the Future* a rites-of-passage narrative is set in the 1950s, and focused not on the young male protagonist but on his father, and when in *Stand by Me* (1986), a rites-of-passage narrative, again set in the 1950s, is recounted by an adult male in retrospect, whose fantasy is being enacted? To whom is that fantasy addressed? What process of negotiation and exchange, of deterritorialisation and reterritorialisation is taking place? Along with developments such as the advent of black teenage films, the trend towards pre-teen films in the early 1990s and a recent decline in the proportion of teenagers in America's population, in the proportion of teenagers attending Hollywood's films and therefore in the volume of teen-orientated films, questions such as these testify to the complexity and interest of a genre that has for years been important to Hollywood, but more rarely, it seems, to genre critics, theorists and historians.

Selected Reading

Jonathan Bernstein, *Pretty in Pink: The Golden Age of Teenage Movies*, London, St Martin's Press, 1997.

Thomas Doherty, *Teenagers and Teenpics: The Juvenalization of American Movies in the 1950s*, Boston, Unwin Hyman, 1988.

Jon Lewis, *The Road to Romance and Ruin: Teen Films and Youth Culture*, New York and London, Routledge, 1992.

Rebel Without a Cause (USA 1955 *p.c* – Warner Bros.; *d* – Nicholas Ray)

Today, the name James Dean is often suffixed by the definition 'the first American teenager'. There were, of course, many cinematic teenagers before Dean, such as the delinquents of *Blackboard Jungle* (1955) and Marlon Brando and his biker gang in *The Wild One* (1953). In fact, the famous exchange in the latter between a local girl and Brando – 'What are you rebelling against?' 'What've you got?' – forms a kind of genetic code for the nameless anomie and disaffection that runs through so many of the rebel-teen dramas that followed. *Rebel* was released by Warner Bros., who, like other studios in the mid-1950s, were becoming increasingly aware of the advisability of tapping the teen market in the context of shrinking audiences.

Disaffected teen delinquents in films before *Rebel* were almost always from deprived backgrounds or just plain 'born bad'. *Rebel* broke new ground by portraying middle-class alienated teens. Against the background of the growing suburbanisation of the US in the 1950s and the consequent upward mobility, it is easy to understand why *Rebel* and Dean's performance were embraced by teenagers, most of them middle class themselves rather than the urban 'street rats' of earlier films.

Dean's status as an icon rests less on his originality than on the fact that his image collates a number of key teenage discourses: nameless angst; a frustrated longing for both peer and parental approval balanced against a certain freedom from social regulations; and, most importantly, eternal youth born out of the fact that he died young in a car accident in 1955, encapsulating the live-fast-die-young philosophy. Of the three films in which Dean appeared, Nicholas Ray's melodrama is responsible, far more than the period literary adaptation *East of Eden* (1954) or the generational saga *Giant* (1956), for founding this 'first teenager' reputation and elucidating these discourses. One of the most memorable (and oft-quoted) expressions of teen angst is found in Jim's cry 'You're tearing me apart!', provoked by his parents' squabbling over him in the police station at the start of the film. To a certain extent, like the delinquent dramas before it, *Rebel* wants to account for teen angst as experiential, stemming from dysfunctional family life rather than from human essences. What makes it so resonant is that it is an archetypal teenpic at the same time as being atypical in its complex deployment of erotic subtexts.

The film provides a cod-Freudian explanation of Jim's disaffection: his apron-wearing, henpecked father (Jim Backus) is, in the parlance of the time, 'castrated', provoking a crisis in masculinity in his son. This crisis is displaced onto the homoerotic strain that underlines Jim's friendship with Sal Mineo's Plato. The erotic charge between father and son, reinforced by the tilting camerawork and Dean's intense performance, in the scene where Jim begs his father to stand up to his mother, is echoed in the scene where Plato – having become the ad hoc son to Jim's father with Judy (Natalie Wood) as mother – upbraids Jim for leaving him to go off to make love with Judy. The reproach can be read on one level as Plato's re-enactment of the original abandonment by his absent father, but also as a lover's criticism. With hindsight, the repressed sexual tensions in the film are reinforced by our knowledge of Mineo's homosexuality and Dean's reputed bisexuality. Perhaps less remarked upon, though, is the hint of incest in Judy's anguished relations with her own father, who we learn called her a 'dirty tramp' because of her lipstick at the beginning of the film, and who subsequently rejects his daughter's attempts to sit on his lap.

But beyond these domestic tensions, *Rebel* offers another explanation (again, typical of the 1950s) for Jim Stark's alienation: existential malaise. The film is sprinkled throughout with watered-down

Natalie Wood struggles with an adolescent crisis in Nicholas Ray's *Rebel Without a Cause*

existential notions, or at least a kind of atheistic pessimism: Jim's problem stems as much from his abandonment in a lost, mechanistic and uncaring universe, devoid of meaning, as it does from faulty parenting and gender confusion. Our first sight of Jim is of him abjectly lying on the pavement playing with a mechanical monkey. This introduces a theme of animality, elaborated on later when Jim describes his home as a 'zoo' and imitates the sound of a bull.

Rebel also reprises the notion of the essential triviality of being, dwarfed by a larger cosmos and the forces of fate (that kill Buzz): 'From the infinite reaches of space, the problems of man seem trivial and naive indeed', intones the astronomer's voice in the observatory scene. The spectral sense of the inevitability of death that *Rebel* brings to the fore is yet another reason why this film and James Dean helped to 'invent' the teenager.

LESLIE FELPERIN

Grease (USA 1978 *p.c* – Paramount; *d* – Randal Kleiser)

After the release of *American Graffiti* in 1973, the 1970s and 1980s saw a number of films – including *American Hot Wax* (1977), *Porky's* (1981) and *La Bamba* (1986) – that were set in the 1950s and 1960s and addressed both a youth audience and older viewers who had grown up in those decades. US television series such as *Happy Days* (1974–84), loosely modelled on *American Graffiti*, and its spin-off *Laverne & Shirley* (1976–83) received top ratings. Although films and television series had used historical settings before, this particularly virulent preoccupation with the 1950s was interpreted by some commentators as evidence of a different order of nostalgia, one shaped by postmodernism. The film's incorporation of both 1950s iconography and allusions to films of the era can be read as 'pastiche', which Fredric Jameson (1992) has described as a significant feature of postmodernism: 'the imitation of a peculiar and unique style, the wearing of a stylistic mask, speech in a dead language … without parody's ulterior motive, without the satirical impulse'.

Contrary to Jameson's claim that pastiche is humourless, there is evidence of postmodern irony in *Grease*'s pastiche of the 1950s; however, it is hardly satirical, compared to, say, John Waters's *Hairspray* (1988). *Grease*'s story – hingeing on whether or not the lovers, clean-cut Sandy (Olivia Newton-John) and tough-guy Danny (John Travolta), will manage to find common ground – sticks fairly closely to its generic frame of reference, the clean-teenpics of the late 1950s and early 1960s.

Grease lays out an intertextual relay of allusions to reinforce its pastiche. In one song, Betty Rizzo (Stockard Channing) makes fun of Sandy by imitating her and comparing her to Sandra Dee, one of the best-known wholesome actresses of the period. Annette Funicello, a 1950s teen pin-up who appeared in Disney's *The Mickey Mouse Club* (1955–9) and later co-starred with Frankie Avalon in AIP Beach Blanket movies, is name-checked, while Frankie Avalon appears as a guardian angel in the number 'Beauty School Drop-out'. With its white studio-set backdrop and elaborate costumes, this sequence, and the 'Greased Lightning' number, imitate the fantasy-sequence numbers of films of the period (*An American in Paris*, 1951; *Funny Face*, 1956). Although the audience is invited to smile at the knowingness of these allusions, the film also encourages identification with Sandy and Danny: when Sandy sings 'Hopelessly Devoted to You', no satire is detectable, thus reinforcing *Grease*'s status as pastiche rather than parody or satire.

Jameson's analysis critiques postmodernist texts' plundering of other periods as repackaging iconography for consumers in a late-capitalist economy. *Grease* was enormously successful at the box office and certainly generated capital for its producers. In a manner increasingly common for blockbusters from the 1970s onwards, the film was promoted and exploited prodigiously through merchandising, with the soundtrack album and spin-off singles achieving vast worldwide sales. As with *Saturday Night Fever* (1977), which also starred John Travolta, the success of *Grease*'s soundtrack demonstrated that films, particularly those aimed at the youth market, could function as part of a larger 'synergistic' franchise involving numerous products, including albums, T-shirts, videos and games.

LESLIE FELPERIN

kids (USA 1995 *p.c* – Independent Pictures/Shining Excalibur Pictures/Guys Upstairs; *d* – Larry Clark)

Following a day in the lives of a group of New York street teens, Larry Clark's controversial debut feature offers a bleak and uncompromising vision of contemporary youth culture and adolescent sexuality. With *kids*, Clark expressed his desire to make 'the teenage movie that America never made', a film about adolescence that aims to 'tell it like it is' (Schrader, 1995, p. 74).

kids' extended opening scenes observe 16-year-old Telly (Leo Fitzpatrick), the film's anti-hero and self-titled 'virgin surgeon', expertly coaxing a nervous young girl into bed. Afterwards, Telly boasts of his first conquest of the day to sidekick Casper (Justin Pierce), describing his obsession with seducing virgins whom he then swiftly abandons. The remainder of the film sees Telly focus his sexual energy on deflowering 13-year-old Darcy (Yakira Peguero), while at the same time it is revealed that one of his previous victims, Jennie (Chloë Sevigny), has tested HIV-positive. As Telly was Jennie's first and only sexual partner, she vows to find him and pass on this information.

Scripted by 18-year-old Harmony Korine (see *Gummo* case study) and shot using documentary techniques, *kids*' tone and visual style capture the speech, attitudes and behaviour of its hedonistic

The alienated teens of Larry Clark's *kids* are depicted with unsettling authenticity

characters as they aimlessly roam the streets of Manhattan. In addition to skateboarding, these teens, whose lives are devoid of any parental involvement, are free to pursue a range of reckless recreational pleasures, including unprotected sex, drug and alcohol use, violence and theft. As Richard Benjamin notes, *kids* accurately portrays the major social problems affecting adolescents in the early 1990s: 'absentee parents, limited employment opportunities for urban youths, the prevalence of drugs, violence, the rise of HIV and other STDs' (Benjamin, 2004, p. 38).

In the media, *kids* has been cited as a cautionary tale about unsafe sex and the threat of AIDS, and criticised for its exploitative and voyeuristic images of teen sexuality. Much of the controversy surrounding the film results from then 53-year-old Clark's (and thus also the viewer's) ambiguous relationship with his subject matter. Questions of moral ambiguity focus on the unsettling frankness and intimacy with which Clark presents graphic scenes of teen sex. This ambiguity is further heightened by the documentary style he adopts: while appearing to contribute to the film's claim to authenticity, in practice it works to blur the line between fiction and reality. Significantly, *kids* signalled Clark's transition from still photography (see, for example, his photographic books *Tulsa*, 1971, and *Teenage Lust*, 1983) to film-making. His subsequent films *Bully* (2001) and *Ken Park* (2002) continued to explore teenage delinquency, subcultures and sexuality on screen.

CLAIRE HINES

Gummo (USA 1997 *p.c* – Independent Pictures/ New Line Productions; *d* – Harmony Korine)

Understanding Harmony Korine's *Gummo* as a teenpic requires a broader historical context. The US film industry in the 1980s and 1990s saw the flowering of the 'indie' movie. Like its parallel term 'indie music', the 'independent' or 'indie' prefix originally referred to a film's financing. Instead of being developed and produced by a major studio, the archetypal indie film was made by a production company and co-financed by an independent distributor (which could be one and the same). Miramax, co-producers of *Hardware* (1990) and *Smoke* (1995), and New Line, co-producers of *Hairspray* (1988) and *My Own Private Idaho* (1991), were two of the major independent producers/distributors of the 1980s and 1990s. However, they were bought by Disney and Turner Broadcasting respectively in 1993 and, like almost every other independent outfit, their 'independence' is now really a matter of style and marketing (see The major independents, p. 54).

The discourse of the indie film overlaps with 'cult' and 'underground' movies, all of which are marked by notions of authenticity, subversiveness and estrangement from the mainstream. Just as a jangly guitar sound is the cornerstone of the indie music sound, today independence in film is a matter of aesthetic and thematic tropes, such as grainy or unpolished cinematography, disjunctive or sparse soundtracks, obfuscatory or fragmentary editing, little-known stars and narratives that concern offbeat stories and often youthful, marginalised characters. For this youth-orientated audience, an indie film's value is measured partly by its distance from the polish, coherence and digestibility that are seen as defining mainstream cinema. The wider this distance, the richer the film is in 'subcultural capital' (in a phrase coined by Sarah Thornton, 1995, adapted from Pierre Bourdieu). In cruder terms, the more shocking to adult audiences, the better! *Gummo* emerges from this context.

The son of a documentary film-maker, Korine began his film-making career at the age of 18 by writing Larry Clark's controversial *kids* (1995; see case study), which featured an abundance of teenage sex. Journalistic and publicity discourse around that film pivoted on Korine's youth, the way that Clark met him through a mutual interest in skateboarding and the fact that Korine had 'lived the life' – all of which increased his authenticity and that of the film. In interviews, Korine stressed the improvised nature of *Gummo* and his personal familiarity with the people depicted in it. The film focuses on characters living in a Midwestern town that some time before suffered a tornado. We meet few adults, and there is a suggestion that this catastrophe has swept away moral frameworks and, in a sense, prompted the fragmentary, discontinuous style of the film. As Gavin Smith (1998) observes, 'With all authority and social restraints swept away by an act of God, Korine's kids live in a world where all transgression seems permitted and unchallenged'. Two of the protagonists, adolescents Tummler (Nick Sutton) and Solomon (Jacob Reynolds), spend their time looking for stray cats to kill, which sparked controversy in both the US and the UK. With its violence and strenuous refusal to judge its characters or their actions, the film positions itself at the other end of the spectrum from the clean-cut tradition of teenpics.

In the UK, *Gummo*'s status as a 'cool' indie film was enhanced by its being championed in style magazines such as *Dazed and Confused* and the more marginal film magazines such as *Neon*, and vilified by 'establishment' newspapers such as the *Evening Standard*. This confirmed its status as a work resolutely opposed to the recuperating strategies and generic conventions of many rites-of-passage teenpics and belonging to its own indie youth-orientated tradition.

LESLIE FELPERIN

Cruel Intentions updates *Dangerous Liaisons* for teen consumption

Cruel Intentions (USA 1999 *p.c* – Columbia Pictures/Cruel Productions LLC/Original Film/Newmarket Capital Group; *d* – Roger Kumble)

Based on Choderlos de Laclos's eighteenth-century novel *Les Liaisons dangereuses*, *Cruel Intentions* is part of a popular cycle of 1990s high-school teenpics that reworked literary classics. This group of adaptations also includes: *Clueless* (1995), based on Jane Austen's *Emma*; *10 Things I Hate about You* (1999), based on William Shakespeare's *The Taming of the Shrew*; and *She's All That* (1999), based on George Bernard Shaw's *Pygmalion*. Typically, these films use the generic conventions of the teenpic to update the setting, central characters and story of the original text for a young audience. In the case of *Cruel Intentions*, this appeal to a youth market was further aided by Sarah Michelle Gellar's casting as the villainous Kathryn Merteuil, exploiting her popularity in the cult television series *Buffy the Vampire Slayer* (1997–2003).

Set against the backdrop of a Manhattan prep school, *Cruel Intentions* transforms Laclos's French aristocrats into rich high-school kids who conform to familiar stereotypes (the socialite, the virgin, the jock, the male libertine). This provides the film adaptation with a teen context in which social standing and sexual reputation (good and bad) are both competitively judged and fiercely protected. Like the novel, the film begins with a wager: Kathryn bets her stepbrother Sebastian Valmont (Ryan Phillippe) that he will not be able to seduce the headmaster's chaste daughter Annette Hargrove (Reese Witherspoon) before the next school term begins. In order to ensure that this wager still appears shocking to a contemporary audience, the film plays on the (socially taboo) sexual tension between the stepsiblings – Kathryn offers Sebastian a visit to her bed if he wins.

Whereas Laclos's eighteenth-century polemic exposed the moral corruption of the French aristocracy, *Cruel Intentions*' focus on the manipulations of its unscrupulous adolescent characters uncovers modern standards of high-school acceptability and pressures to conform. In the film, a rich girl's unacceptable suitor is no longer poor, as in the original – he is black; and a gay footballer's fear of being outed means that he is vulnerable to blackmail. The other principal modification of Laclos's novel is the clear opposition established between love and sex, good and evil. Contrary to the ending of *Les Liaisons dangereuses*, Annette does not die, as Sebastian's willingness to save her life at the cost of his own suggests that virtue is victorious over evil. *Cruel Intentions*' moralistic ending thus makes the teenagers' penalties for using sex as a weapon exceptionally plain, for while Sebastian is finally redeemed by his love for Annette, Kathryn's unrelenting hypocrisy is exposed and her actions condemned.

CLAIRE HINES

THE WESTERN

CHRISTINE GLEDHILL

Arguably, the western represented the starting point of genre criticism in the UK, contributing to the popular culture debate evidence of the capacity of Hollywood formula films to produce works of significance and value. In the 1960s, discussions of genre mostly used the western as their chief example, and were less interested in the critical problems of the notion of genre itself than they were in demonstrating the value of western films.

Alan Lovell characterised the critical context of this debate thus:

> For Anglo-Saxon critics, the western is typical of most of the vices of the mass media. It is endlessly repetitive, utterly simple in form and expresses naive attitudes. For French critics, the western contains nearly all the things they most admire in the American cinema, its directness, its intelligence, its energy, its formal concerns. (Lovell, 1967, p. 93)

This work of reclamation reflected its British context in the struggle to deflect, sometimes by incorporating, a Leavisite literary tradition, and in its concern to argue via the western for the place of Hollywood films in education. Two main concerns can be traced: the first, the status of the western as popular art and the capacity of such forms to handle questions of value and morality; and the second, the contribution of convention to great films or the work of great directors (see Hall and Whannel, 1964).

The western and history

A key notion in the validation of the Hollywood western has been its relation to history and to national cultural motifs. As we are repeatedly told, the material of the western is drawn from a brief period in the winning and settling of the American frontier:

> Hollywood's west has typically been from about 1865 to 1890 or so ... within its brief span we can count a number of frontiers in the sudden rush of mining camps, the building of railways, the Indian wars, the cattle drives, the coming of the farmer. Together with the last days of the Civil War and the exploits of the badmen, here is the raw material of the western. (Kitses, 1969, p. 8)

How the west was won: the building of the railroads dramatised in John Ford's *The Iron Horse*

Mythologising the west: John Wayne battles faceless hordes of 'savages' in Ford's *Stagecoach*

Although a widespread anti-mass-media view of the western was that it travestied the west, only a few serious approaches to the genre attempted to found their arguments on its historical truth. The French critic Jean-Louis Rieupeyrout (1952) argued enthusiastically that the pleasures of the western derive from its reconstruction of the adventures of the frontier. He had spent much time researching the sources of individual western films and considered that proof of authenticity should change condescending attitudes to the form. However, the potential naivety of his notion of historical reflection is mitigated by his accepting as historical sources secondary elaborations in oral folklore, and newspaper journalism, so that an imaginative response to frontier tales becomes part of the fabric of history. The majority of commentators, however, have been concerned with either the contribution of history to the thematic structure and narrative functioning of the western, or with the transformations performed by successive fictionalisations of the west.

The problem of relating history and the western has been posed in different ways. One form of the question is to ask why this particular brief stretch of history is capable of sustaining such a wide range of cultural elaboration over so long a period. Two answers emerge. One, from the perspective of cultural history, argues that the conditions of existence in the west put into particularly sharp focus and provided imagery for a deep-seated ideological tension in America's view of itself and of progress – a tension axed around the conflicting ideals of unfettered individualism and community values represented in opposing views of the west as desert or garden. The second, looking for greater socio-economic precision, argues that within these narrow geographic and temporal boundaries assembled an exemplary cross-section of social types, representing a range of economic and social interests in struggle and caught in a variety of activities eminently susceptible to the kind of narrativisation that can illuminate the underlying play of historical forces.

From such approaches arises a second way of posing the history/western question, that is, the relation of fictionalised history not simply to the past it represents, but to the contemporary audiences for whom it is constructed. While some critics see the genre as crucially linked to the American problem of national identity (see Kitses, 1969; 2004) and imply the enduring viability of a set of representations produced out of a particular historical experience for succeeding generations, others argue for greater historical determinism, attempting to link different phases of western production to changes in economic and ideological conditions (Wagner, 1961; Wright, 1975), or even to particular political leaders in power (French, 1973).

For critics in the first category, a crucial factor is the precise moment in the conquering of the west that the western takes up – a moment critical in the formation of America as a nation, balanced between the past and the future, 'when options are still open' (Kitses, 1969, p. 12). Most critics agree that the fact that this moment of choice is past intensifies its possibility for ideological elaboration. Options closed off by history and a developing social order can safely be reopened, nostalgically indulged, judged and closed off again (see Pye, 1977/78; Warshow, 1970).

The implication that the western is specific to American culture and history raises the question of the genre's almost universal appeal and its production in different cultural contexts, such as the Italian westerns made between 1965 and 1975. Rieupeyrout (1952) deals with this problem by assuming a universal fascination with enacted history. Bazin (1971) sidesteps it by asserting a mythic dimension through which the western finds in frontier history sympathetic material for reworking older and more universal themes. Other critics assert the importance of the movement westward and of America itself for older European nations, the 'idea of the west' having dominated western civilisation since classical times (Kitses, 1969, pp. 8–9).

Founding fathers: Bazin and Warshow

Most influential in Anglo-Saxon criticism of the western were André Bazin's two essays, 'The western, or the American film par excellence', and 'The evolution of the western' (both 1971), and Robert Warshow's 'Movie chronicle: the westerner' (1970), all written in the 1950s. Both writers were concerned with defining the essence of the western film in order to locate its cinematic and cultural significance. They examine the development of the genre and attempt to determine its outer boundaries, so that they can distinguish acceptable transformations from violations. At the centre of their investigations stands a 'classic example' against which they evaluate earlier and later developments. Writing, however, from different perspectives and in different cultural contexts, both their choice of example and their estimation of the value of the western differ.

As a celebrated proponent of cinematic realism (see Bazin, p. 525), Bazin's account of the genre's realism is surprisingly oblique as he steers round the obvious pitfalls of a naive view of the relationship between the western and history: 'The relations between the facts of history and the western are not immediate and direct, but dialectic. Tom Mix is the opposite of Abraham Lincoln, but after his own fashion he perpetuates Lincoln's cult and memory' (Bazin, 'The western', 1971, p. 143). Between history and cinema, a process of mythologising has taken place: 'Those formal attributes by which one normally recognises the western are simply signs or symbols of its profound reality, namely the myth. The western was born of an encounter between a mythology and a means of expression ...' (Bazin, 'The western', 1971, p. 142).

For Bazin, myth is an idealisation of historical reality; the historical and sociological conditions of the west permit imaginative elaborations dealing with fundamental realities that exceed the particular moment, replaying in contemporary form metaphysical and moral dramas that recur throughout the history of cultural expression. The particular myth that Bazin elaborates is 'the great epic Manicheism which sets the forces of evil over against the knights of the true cause' (Bazin, 'The western', 1971, p. 145), at the centre of which is the woman posed as representative of the good. This myth is demanded by the actual sociological conditions of the west and the role of women in the conquering and civilising of the frontier, but it both points back to earlier cultural forms, for instance the courtly romance, and also works through problems of the ambiguous relation of law and social justice, or morality and individual conscience, endemic to civilisation itself.

For Bazin, the ideal example of this mythologising of history is *Stagecoach* (John Ford, 1939) made during a brief period (1937–40) in which the western arrived at its classic peak, that 'ideal balance between social myth, historical reconstruction, psychological truth, and the traditional theme of the western mise-en-scène' (Bazin, 'The evolution of the western', 1971, p. 149). Against this classic achievement, Bazin poses the post-war emergence of the 'superwestern', which, under pressure to deal with serious themes appropriate to the times and self-conscious of its own history, effectively treated the western as 'a form in need of a content', stepping outside the parameters of its own concerns to bring in 'aesthetic, social, moral, psychological, political or erotic interest, in short some quality extrinsic to the genre and which is supposed to enrich it' (Bazin, 'The evolution of the western', 1971, p. 151). *High Noon* (1952) and *Shane* (1952) are examples of this tendency. However, Bazin argues, the traditional western did not die, but continued to be nourished at its popular base, in the B-westerns churned out in great numbers during the 1950s, such as *The Gunfighter* (Henry King, 1950); or by older directors whose experience in western traditions was not to be deflected by new trends, for example *The Big Sky* (Howard Hawks, 1952). The 1950s also produced a group of newer directors who managed to make a class of western that, while developing a more contemporary flavour, did not break with the spirit of the true western, a class that Bazin termed 'novelistic', characterised by their lyricism and their sincere rather than patronising approach to the form, such as *Johnny Guitar* (Nicholas Ray, 1954), *Bend of the River* and *The Far Country* (Anthony Mann, 1952 and 1954).

Like Bazin, Robert Warshow, writing in 1954, sets out to define the essence of the western, and like Bazin, he sees its value in its capacity to handle moral ambiguity in traditionally epic terms. However, while Bazin writes from a Catholic/ existentialist perspective and locates the struggle between good and evil as informing history itself, Warshow is concerned with the aesthetic realisation of ideological conflicts attendant on the development of twentieth-century American capitalism. His concern, as for many writers on the western since, is the relation of the individual to society, the westerner rather than the western. Warshow defines the western hero in relation to the same problematic that, he argues, produced the gangster as tragic hero. The latter's acquisitive urge and inevitable defeat represents 'the "no" to that great American "yes" which is stamped so big over our official culture and yet has so little to do with the way we really feel about our lives' (Warshow, 1970, p. 136). However, while the gangster's desperate need to prove himself drives him from one bout of activity to another, the westerner is self-contained, knows his worth and needs only to be able to live by his code. In this respect, he represents a type of hero, of individualism, not realisable in twentieth-century society. In these terms, the historical west is important only inasmuch as it is past – 'Where the westerner lives it is always about 1870 – not the real 1870, either, or the real west ...' (Warshow, 1970, p. 141) – and insofar as the material it offers the cinema, 'the land and the horses', provides a 'moral openness'. In the western, guns are carried openly rather than secretly as in the gangster film, forcing the hero into moral self-responsibility. The other crucial aspect of this hero for Warshow is his relation to violence. Unlike the opportunism of the gangster, the westerner's violence is a statement of his being, and he waits for the quintessential moment in which to express this (Warshow, 1970, p. 140).

For Warshow, then, the central problem of the western is individual masculine identity and the violence necessary to its expression. His conception of the place of women in the western is the antithesis of Bazin's, for whom woman is the object of a metaphysical struggle between good and evil. In Warshow's account, the role of women is associated with the establishment of community and the necessary qualifications of individualism and violence brought by the civilising of the frontier. Prior to this moment, 'the west, lacking the graces of civilisation, is the place "where men are men": in western movies, men have the deeper wisdom and women are children' (Warshow, 1970, p. 138).

The western's move from primitivism to full maturity Warshow cautiously attributes to a deeper realism – more in terms of philosophical outlook and the ageing of the stars than in terms of historical truth. The western grows up when it foregoes its innocent Romanticism and recognises the tragic limitations of the frontier ethos, as for instance in Henry King's *The Gunfighter*. However, when the impulse to realism breaks totally with this ethos and the code of the westerner for the sake of a '"reinterpretation" of the west as a developed society', we arrive at a different genre, social drama for which the western setting is irrelevant except as a backdrop. *High Noon* provides an example of this kind of breakdown. Warshow also identifies an opposite tendency away from realism towards an aesthetic embalming of western conventions in response to their mythological and cinematic potential. Here Bazin's exemplum *Stagecoach*, and Ford's later *My Darling Clementine* (1946) stand accused.

The western's formal history

Both Bazin and Warshow define the essence of the western and choose their classic examples with scant reference to the historical development of the genre, basing their judgments on their own respective metaphysical and ideological concerns. Alan Lovell (1967) sought a more objective way of establishing the parameters of the genre by examining its formal history. Such an attempt, he argues, must take account of the themes and forms introduced into the western through its source materials and of how it combined, displaced or transformed these in its movement towards establishing a coherent and stable structure. Lovell defines four principal elements that contributed to the formation of the western genre:

> 1. A structure drawn from nineteenth-century popular melodramatic literature, involving a virtuous hero and wicked villain who menaces a virginal heroine;
> 2. An action story, composed of violence, chases and crimes appropriate to a place like the American west in the 19th century;
> 3. The introduction of the history of the migration westwards and the opening of the frontier signalled in such films as *The Covered Wagon* (1924) and *The Iron Horse* (1924); and
> 4. The revenge structure, which was present by the time of *Billy the Kid* in 1930. (Lovell, 1967, p. 97)

For Lovell, the history of the western over the next 20 years can be understood in terms of the working of these elements into a coherent formal structure. From this perspective, *My Darling Clementine* becomes the classic centre of the genre. In this film, the narrative is structured by the revenge theme, which is itself integrated into the historical theme of civilising the west, as the hero's quest for personal revenge is translated into the establishment of law and order for the nascent township of Tombstone, under the influence of the heroine schoolteacher from the east (see John Ford, p. 451).

Although not all these elements necessarily recur in every western since *My Darling Clementine*, the structural balance identified in that film, Lovell argues, is determining in the genre's subsequent development. Against frequent assertions that 1950s westerns broke with their primitive past to become more adult, sophisticated and individualised, Lovell argues for the continuity between pre- and postwar westerns, positing a tradition that runs from *My Darling Clementine* through *The Gunfighter* to *Guns in the Afternoon* (1962), and citing the shared characteristics of *The Left-handed Gun* (1958), often seen as one of the 'more modern' westerns, and *My Darling Clementine*. From this perspective, shifts in emphasis in the genre become interesting not in terms of breaks with a classic past but rather in terms of significant differences produced in relation to a maintained continuity. Thus *The Oxbow Incident* (1943), maligned by Warshow for its illegitimate concern with problems of social organisation in the west, becomes interesting for its recasting of familiar elements in a darker, more pessimistic tone.

From this position, Lovell goes on to argue against the assumed naivety of the prewar westerns, and against the attribution of a precocious progressivism to the so-called adult westerns of the 1950s – sympathetic treatment of the Native American Indian, for instance, may be less a contemporary concern with racial questions than an exploration of ambiguous attitudes to the coming of civilisation to the west that are contained in the structure of the genre. However, Lovell does not deny that 1950s westerns also bear the marks of the prevailing climate of ideas or of the influx of a postwar generation of new and more cinematically conscious directors. But rather than a transformation of the genre, this represents 'the imposition of a new sensibility on the old forms', and Lovell argues that 'part of the fascination of the western in the 1950s results from the confusions caused when this ... comes into contact with the traditional forms of the genre' (Lovell, 1967, p. 101). It is then arguable that some of these films are simply confused, but that others such as *Guns in the Afternoon* or *The Tall T* (1957) demonstrate the productive power of genre confronted with 'new sensibility'.

Horizons west

Jim Kitses's 1969 book (revised edition 2004) on the western and western directors represents an attempt to deepen knowledge of the genre by consciously confronting, in its influential first chapter, many of the problems of generic criticism exhibited in earlier writings on the subject, namely prescriptiveness, the task of relating the western to history and the problem of understanding it as myth. Whereas Alan Lovell tackles the problem of arbitrary prescriptiveness by describing the history of a central tradition, Kitses attempts a synchronic and structural account of the genre's basic elements. Thus he takes account of the genre's complex historical and socio-cultural inheritance in order to propose, rather than a central model, 'a loose, shifting and variegated genre with many roots and branches' (Kitses, 1969, p. 17), which can account for films made at any period. History, in his account, is not the record of the genre's development but what has made the genre so fruitful.

Kitses sees history as contributing to the western in two ways. First, it provides the national cultural tradition in which the western is rooted and to which it speaks; and second, in a narrower sense, it offers as 'raw material' that brief historical span that covers the opening of the American frontier, 1865–90.

For a definition of the particular cultural tradition underlying the western, Kitses turns to Henry Nash Smith's seminal 1950 study, *Virgin Land*. Citing a range of political and cultural output, Nash Smith identifies as central to America's national consciousness an ambiguous attitude to the west, torn between the symbols of garden and desert. Several commentators have seen this ambiguity as providing much of the thematic preoccupations of the western (see Lovell, 1967; McArthur, 1969). Under the master opposition, wilderness/civilisation, Kitses elaborates a series of antinomies that together represent a 'philosophical dialectic, an ambiguous cluster of meanings and attitudes that provide the traditional/thematic structure of the genre' (Kitses, 1969, p. 11). The shift in meanings from the top to the bottom of each set of oppositions – the wilderness starting with the individual and freedom and ending with tradition and the past, while civilisation starts with the community and restriction and ends with change and the future – demonstrates both the flexibility of the structure and the ideological tension that it embodies. While the structure animates many forms of cultural activity, the use of frontier history in the western brought it into particularly acute focus, for the period was placed 'at exactly that moment when options are still open, the dream of a primitivistic individualism, the ambivalence of at once beneficent and threatening horizons still tenable' (Kitses, 1969, p. 12). A third factor in the genre's appropriation of frontier history was that it had already been reworked in folkloric and mythic terms. Kitses attempts to differentiate the varieties of meaning attendant on the concept of myth, and to distinguish between a mythic dimension frequently attributed to twentieth-century popular culture, and the tales of gods and heroes handed down through oral traditions from classical and medieval times. While the western does not represent myth in the latter sense, it 'incorporates elements of displaced (or corrupted) myth on a scale that can render them considerably more prominent than in most art' (Kitses, 1969, p. 14). Such incorporation takes place through the western's particularly varied inheritance from the popular literary forms in which frontier history was first reworked. Following Northrop Frye's definition of archetypes, Kitses argues that different literary modes are characterised by types of hero and patterns of heroic action. Central to the western was the mode of romance 'which insisted on the idealisation of characters who wielded near-magical powers' (Kitses, 1969, p. 15), and provided 'the movement of a god-like figure into the demonic wasteland, the death and resurrection, the return to a paradisal garden' (Kitses, 1969, p. 20).

However, the incursion of morality play, melodrama, revenge tragedy into the tradition together with the input from Wild West shows and cracker-barrel humour meant that the western could develop within different modes and draw on a rich and complex profusion of mythic and archetypal elements. Finally, the cultural resources of the western are enriched cinematically by the repertoire of visual iconography most frequently commented on in generic studies (Buscombe, 1970; Collins, 1970).

Thus Kitses provides an account of the western as a four-part structure:

1. Frontier history
2. The thematic antinomies of wilderness/civilisation
3. Archetype
4. Iconography

Contrary to the argument that a non-prescriptive genre criticism must be limited to description (see Ryall, 1970), Kitses sees in the conceptual richness of the western genre a potential source of value, capable of realisation in the hands of 'the artist of vision in rapport with the genre' (Kitses, 1969, p. 20). The peak of authorial westerns, however, is dependent on the structure produced by a particular social, cultural and formal history, a structure, moreover that includes the existence of the large popular audience who supported the development of the 'mass production at the base', which in turn 'allows refinement and reinvigoration' at the peak (Kitses, 1969, p. 21). Thus: 'The western is not just the men who have worked within it ... an empty vessel breathed into by the film-maker' (Kitses, 1969, p. 26) but represents a vital structure 'saturated with conceptual significance' (Kitses, 1969, p. 21).

The western as myth

Will Wright's (1975) much debated intervention in discussions of the western (see Frayling, 1981a) sought to shift the looseness of its validation in terms of general moral or archetypal themes, cultural or psychological conflicts. He insists first that the significance of the western must be located in its appeal to contemporary popular audiences, which are subject to historical change, and second that it must be treated as an aspect of communication, subject to the rules that govern the production of symbolic meaning. He calls on the structural linguistics of Saussure and Roman Jakobson and the structural anthropology of Lévi-Strauss to support his argument that all human endeavour is an effort to communicate meaning. In Wright's view, the work of myth or mass culture is not to achieve emotional expression of problems arising elsewhere, in the psyche or cultural climate, but itself contributes to them through the forms of knowledge it produces. Thus in the cinema, the western myth 'has become part of the cultural language by which America understands itself' (Wright, 1975, p. 12). What interests Wright in structuralism is its promise of a methodology for understanding scientifically how social communication works. Where he differs from the structuralists is in his retention of a sociological concern to analyse what meanings are produced in particular societies in given historical periods. What he is attempting then is to make content analysis more rigorous (Wright, 1975, p. 10).

In approaching the western from this standpoint, Wright starts out from a number of basic premises. First, integrating Lévi-Strauss's view of primitive myth with Kenneth Burke's narrative theory, Wright contends that modern societies, despite the apparent authority of science, history and literature, still have recourse to myth as a means of producing knowledge of and order in the world. Second, he argues that westerns represent industrially produced stories made from mythic material already in social circulation that are amenable to the same, if liberalised, kind of analysis that Propp used on the Russian oral folk tale or Lévi-Strauss on the myths of tribal peoples. Third, he asserts that because analysis of the western as myth stresses the social and historical (rather than formal, authorial or industrial) production of meaning, its mythic significance can only be found in what the mass of people went to see. The 'classic' westerns are those most popular in the period in which the genre achieves clear definition and contours, not examples chosen in terms of a schema already constructed in the critic's mind, whether generic, cultural or authorial. Box-office popularity is in its turn an indicator of the 'meanings viewers demand of the myth' (Wright, 1975, p. 12). Wright therefore confines his structural analysis to those westerns that grossed $4 million dollars or more. From these films he seeks to derive the 'communicative structure of the western' (Wright, 1975, p. 12), and from shifts in the structure over the decades to reveal a pattern of change and development 'corresponding to changes in the structure of dominant institutions' (Wright, 1975, p. 14).

Wright's final premise is that the history of the American west supplies the western with appropriate material for the production of myth. This it does in two main ways. First, it furnished a dramatic concatenation of social types and actions productive of the kinds of oppositions from which, in Lévi-Straussian terms, myth is made; and second, these character types and actions were capable of carrying the meanings and shifts in meaning that could make sense of the social conflicts dominant in American society at any one time (Wright, 1975, p. 6).

The meaning of the myths circulated by the western is located in two basic structures: one of binary oppositions in which its characters are placed; and another, the organisation of these characters' functions into narrative sequences. Here Wright uses the Proppian notion of 'character function' – which he interprets as a single action or attribute referring to roles performed in the plot – as a link between Lévi-Straussian oppositions and an argument mounted by the philosopher Arthur Danto, that any narrative sequence, insofar as it describes a change in an initial state of affairs, also includes an explanation of it. In the explanatory function of narrative, combined with the representative function of the characters, Wright finds the power of the western myth to provide 'a conceptual response to the requirements of human action in a social situation' (Wright, 1975, p. 17). On this basis, Wright proceeds to categorise the plots of westerns in terms of their constituent 'character functions' and the way character functions are organised into narrative sequences and narrative sequences into plots.

Wright's final task is to provide 'an independent analysis of the social institutions of America and demonstrate the correlation between the structure of the western and the structure of those institutions' (Wright, 1975, p. 130). This is not a relation of direct causation. Wright argues, however, for institutional determination on the way individuals live their lives, a determination that may be in conflict with the cultural traditions and values of a society, because institutional requirements tend to change more rapidly. This then produces 'a conceptual dilemma ... for the people of the society' to which a myth such as the western speaks. Drawing on social analysts such as Kenneth Galbraith, Jürgen Habermas and C. B. MacPherson (a somewhat heterogeneous grouping of authorities), he argues that 'the classical western plot corresponds to the individualistic conception of society underlying a market economy', that 'the vengeance plot is a variation that begins to reflect changes in the market economy', and that 'the professional plot reveals a new conception of society corresponding to the values and attitudes inherent in a planned, corporate economy' (Wright, 1975, p. 15).

The language of reflection here indicates the weak link in Wright's conception of the social function of myth: cultural production and social institutions confront each other as discrete entities, the influence of box-office returns providing the only explanation as to why film-makers should provide audiences with the cultural models of social action necessary for their survival as institutions change. Moreover, the predominance of 'myth' in his analysis necessitates excluding many aspects of the film-making and reading process that intervene between the institutional needs of society and the finished film. This leads to a view of genre cinema as essentially conservative. For Wright assumes that, in its reliance on a structure of binary oppositions, 'myth depends on simple and recognisable meanings which reinforce rather than challenge social understandings' (Wright, 1975, p. 23). Works by individual artists, however, construct more complex, realistic and unique characters, that are not amenable to analysis by binary opposition. Thus the 'social action' proposed by any particular phase of a genre is seen as adapting to institutional demands rather than resisting them or exploring their contradictions.

Gregory Peck (above) is outside the civilised society represented by Helen Westcott (right) in Henry King's *The Gunfighter*

Gender and sexuality in the western

Disagreement may arise over the place of women in the western, but most commentators assume its address to a male problematic and a male audience. For instance, John Cawelti in *The Six-Gun Mystique* (1971) argues that the western speaks to adolescent or working-class males about 'the conflict between the adolescent's desire to be an adult and his fear and hesitation about the nature of adulthood' and 'the tension between a strong need for aggression and a sense of ambiguity and guilt about violence' that the working-class male feels in relation to the authority of corporate America (Cawelti, 1971, pp. 82 and 14).

In very different terms, Raymond Bellour (1979) has argued that the western depends upon 'a whole organised circuit of feminine representations (the young heroine, the mother, the saloon girl, the wife, etc.) without which the film cannot function' (Bellour, 1979, p. 88). For Bellour, the western is a variation of the classic Hollywood narrative text (see The classic narrative system, p. 45) that, in line with the nineteenth-century novel, centres on the symbolic figure of the woman as source of the disruption that sets off a narrative trajectory of male desire and its ultimate resolution in heterosexual couple formation.

Feminist response to the dominance in the western of a male-defined problematic has taken two forms. Jacqueline Levitin (1982) has attacked the western for the circumscribed roles it gives women. She analyses their function in catalysing the choices that face the hero, and the narrative contortions undergone by those exceptional westerns that attempt to support a female hero – for instance, *Johnny Guitar* (1954). She also suggests that the historical west offered opportunities for greater

Suzy Amis becomes a western hero in Maggie Greenwald' s *Ballad of Little Jo*

freedom and social power for women, as well as potential female hero figures, which are transformed and traduced in the process of producing patriarchal fiction. In this respect, she argues that the history of the west provides material that could be colonised by feminism. The problem in her account is the assumption that all that is required is greater historical accuracy; she seems to ignore the work of fantasy and fiction at play in the childhood memories she cites of identification with the male hero, and the problems of finding forms that will fulfil this task for women.

The question of the female audience and the western was taken up by Laura Mulvey in a consideration of how women deal with the male system of spectatorship she had analysed (1981; 1989). Mulvey draws on Freud for an argument both about how the Western relates to the male oedipal scenario and about the transsexual identification of women with male heroes described by Levitin. In both cases, what she sees at work is a fictional indulgence of the fantasy of omnipotence belonging to the pre-oedipal phase, experienced by both boys and girls, before the socially required gender positions are taken up. This phase is characterised by narcissism, allowing for object choices and identifications based on similarity rather than difference, so that boys and girls are able to take up one another's positions. This forms the basis of transsexual identification. Despite its hypothetical freedom from social categorisation, Mulvey notes that the pre-oedipal phase is nevertheless conceived in traditionally 'masculine' terms – as active, phallic. For the boy, the oedipal passage into 'manhood' requires forsaking the fantasy of omnipotence, submission to sexual difference ('masculinity') through the castration scenario, and the channelling of his desire towards the woman positioned within the couple, marriage. For the girl, passage through the oedipal phase requires not merely channelling active desire towards the correct goal, but forsaking it altogether by taking up the feminine position traditionally conceived as 'passive'. However, because of the relative weakness of the castration scenario for women, the 'active' fantasies of the non-gender-specific pre-oedipal phase are never entirely repressed.

The western serves the pre-oedipal fantasies of the gendered audience in two distinct and gender-specific ways. If, as Bellour suggests, the oedipal resolution of 'couple formation' is the implicit goal of every western, the 'not marriage' choice, Mulvey argues, is also central to its agenda. The indulgence of this male fantasy, involving a disavowal of the feminine sphere, frequently leads in the western to a splitting of the hero: 'Here two functions emerge, one celebrating integration into society through marriage, the other celebrating resistance to social demands and responsibilities, above all those of marriage and family, the sphere represented by woman' (Mulvey, 1981, p. 14).

In the first option, 'the fiction "marriage" sublimates the erotic into a final closing social ritual'. In the second, the male spectator is offered 'a nostalgic celebration of phallic, narcissistic omnipotence ... difficult to integrate exactly into the oedipal drama' (Mulvey, 1981, p. 14) – the hero rejects the woman and rides alone into the sunset. However, the dominance of the male hero, and role of woman as a signifier in a male scenario in this as in most genres, does not, Mulvey argues, mean the films do not address the female spectator. They do so through the mechanism of transsex identification in which pre-oedipal 'active' and narcissistic fantasising, never finally repressed in women, is given cultural outlet and reinforcement by the logic of narrative grammar, which

> places the reader, listener or spectator with the hero ... In this sense Hollywood genre films, structured around masculine pleasure offering an identification with the active point of view, allow a woman spectator to rediscover that lost aspect of her sexual identity, the never fully repressed bed-rock of feminine neurosis. (Mulvey, 1981, p. 13)

From this perspective, it could be argued that in the western, female pleasure may be derived from its offering to women identification with a male figure asserting desire in pre-oedipal terms, the male fantasy of self-sufficiency serving women's own ambivalence towards the 'correct' feminine position.

Mulvey's argument, and the western's exclusive bias towards the white male hero, was taken up and subjected to a trenchant critique by Tania Modleski (1999). Modleski claimed that male writers on the genre had consistently supported its focus on the white male hero, and that only a radical shift in perspective could open up new stories, and new histories of the west. For Modleski, Maggie Greenwald's feminist revisionist western *Ballad of Little Jo* (1993) offered an example of such radical rethinking (see case study).

Male spectators and the western

In his book *Genre* (1980), Stephen Neale touches briefly on the question of spectatorship and the western from the masculine perspective. Laura Mulvey had argued in 'Visual pleasure and narrative cinema' (1975; 1989) that the role of the male hero for the male spectator is that of an ideal ego, through whose gaze the spectator gains symbolic possession of the female body placed as the central spectacle in the fiction. Neale is interested in Paul Willemen's (1976) qualification of this argument, in which he points out that in the Freudian scenario the scopophilic instinct (the drive to look) is in the first instance 'auto-erotic', taking as its object the subject's own body. If the cinema can be seen as pleasuring such formative desires, then the male body can be 'a substantial source of gratification for a male viewer' (Willemen, 1976, p. 43). Mulvey had suggested that the narrative function of the hero acts in part as a deflection of such desires insofar as they threaten the social taboo against homosexuality. Neale takes this further, arguing that the spectator's gaze at the male hero is legitimated, 'rendered "innocent"', because in following his actions eroticism is deflected into the hero's pursuit of the woman, who constitutes an ideologically acceptable sexual object. What interests Neale is the way the western plays on this ambiguous production of the male hero as an object for the spectator's gaze. He argues that many of the structural antimonies of the western, described by Kitses, can be set in opposition around the way the hero's body is represented, 'opening a space for ... the male as privileged object of the look' (Neale, 1980, p. 58). Thus the opposition law/outside law can be set up in the way the body of the hero, 'through the codes of dress, comportment, movement, adornment' (Neale, 1980, p. 58), relates to those of Native American Indian, outlaw, townspeople, farmers, elaborated through similar codes; or in the dynamic oscillation between natural landscape and township, realised in the play of 'light, texture, colour' over the male figure, and in the pace and rhythm of his movements. For Neale, the drama of the western revolves around its exploration of various modes of the inscription of law on the human body. Since it is the hero who engages with the law, the father/son relationship dominates the scenario, and the western can be said to be 'about' the male half of the oedipal trauma (Neale, 1980, p. 59).

Italian westerns

The representation of sexuality and gender identity in the western received a revealing inflection in the decade of Italian production of what became known as the 'spaghetti western' (1965–75), a period associated most strongly with the names of directors Sergio Leone and Sergio Corbucci, and the American star Clint Eastwood, whose fame was made by the Dollars Trilogy. Little serious work has been done on how the popularity of this subgenre affects the demarcation of the western, although Christopher Frayling (1981b) attempted a pioneering work of archival research on this phenomenon in which he mounted an argument that Leone's films, at least, represent a critique of Hollywood's reconstruction of the west and its meanings. The films clearly mark a challenge to the dominance of Hollywood over genre production, complicating the question of the relation of genre motifs to the culture that produced them, and demonstrating the work of translation and transformation that goes on between cultures, especially in the cinema. Anglophone critics of the period were appalled at what they saw as a travesty of the traditional western and its time-honoured values. Behind the outrage at what was considered gratuitous violence and sexual sado-masochism can be sensed an unease about the production of a more rampant, less romanticised expression of masculine identity. On the whole, it is the Eastwood/Leone Dollars Trilogy through which this period of production has entered film studies, and the films are liable to be discussed as much in terms of the Eastwood image and how it speaks to a post-1960, 'post-feminist' crisis in male identity as in terms of its contribution to and development of western traditions.

Westerns in the 1980s and 1990s

EDWARD BUSCOMBE

In the 1970s and early 1980s, Hollywood appeared to have given up on the western. The genre lacked appeal to the youth market that now constituted the dominant part of the audience. Other genres such as horror and science fiction offered more immediate sensations. But the end of the 1980s saw a cautious revival, led by *Young Guns* (1988), a version of the Billy the Kid story that attempted to retool the genre for contemporary filmgoers by casting 'bratpack' actors such as Emilio Estevez, Kiefer Sutherland and Charlie Sheen.

In the 1990s, there was a concerted effort to counter criticism of the western's ideological shortcomings with a series of politically correct films. Kevin Costner's *Dances with Wolves* (1990) was a pro-Native American Indian story, though still told from a white man's point of view. Black westerns (*Posse*, 1993) and 'feminist' westerns (*Bad Girls*, 1994; *The Quick and the Dead*, 1995) attempted to contest the centrality of the white male to the narrative structure. But instead of trying to subvert the very idea of masculinity upon which the western had traditionally relied, their strategy was simply to show that blacks and women could be just as tough as men. Only *Ballad of Little Jo*, with its story of a woman who passes as a man and who falls in love with a feminised Chinese man, tried to work against the stereotypes. *Unforgiven* (1992) is not a radical work, but its story of a reluctant gunfighter (played by Clint Eastwood) dragged out of retirement to avenge a wronged woman manages some subtle digs against racism and sexism – and ageism too, considering that Eastwood was over 60 when he made the film.

The so-called 'new western history' developed by professional historians has amply demonstrated that western films have barely scratched the surface when it comes to dramatising the role of women, blacks, Native American Indians, Hispanics and other ethnic minorities in the American west (Cronon, Miles and Gitlin, 1992; Nelson Limerick, 1987; Nelson Limerick, Milner II and Rankin, 1991). History is a rich source of material for those who would offer narratives other than those dominated by the macho white male. A few films such as US 'independent' director Jim Jarmusch's *Dead Man* (1995) encroach on this territory. But Hollywood seems reluctant to take the plunge. While it no longer has confidence in the certainties of the traditional western, it lacks the ability to imagine what would take their place. It may be that only when women and minorities are better represented in the film industry will the western genre undergo some genuinely radical mutations. But that position seems a long way off.

Selected Reading

André Bazin, 'The western, or the American film par excellence' and 'The evolution of the western', in Gray (ed. and trans.), *What Is Cinema?*, Vol. 2, Berkeley, University of California Press, 1971. Revised edition 2005.

William Cronon, George Miles and Jay Gitlin (eds), *Under an Open Sky: Rethinking America's Western Past*, New York, W. W. Norton, 1992.

Jim Kitses, *Horizons West*, London, Secker and Warburg/BFI, 1969. Revised edition BFI Publishing, 2004.

Tania Modleski, 'A woman's gotta do ... what a man's gotta do? Cross-dressing in the western', in *Old Wives' Tales: Feminist Re-visions of Film and Other Fictions*, London, I. B. Tauris, 1999.

Joan Crawford as Vienna displaces male action from the centre in Nicholas Ray's baroque western *Johnny Guitar*

My Darling Clementine (USA 1946 *p.c* – 20th Century Fox; *d* – John Ford)

At the centre of this romantic western (typifying Bazin's 'classical' form and period of the genre) is the figure of Wyatt Earp (Henry Fonda). Thematically, this hero, cattleman-cum-town marshall, represents the rugged individualism of the frontier consciousness, assured in male company and as an agent of legal justice, but uneasy as a member of the burgeoning white community and especially in the company of women.

Structurally, the figure is an agent of eastern expansion into the west, pacifying Native American Indian and destroying outlaw. The positive qualities of the west are expressed in conditions of early settlement through community life, crackerbarrel wit, dance and music, all characteristic qualities of John Ford's authorship (see John Ford, p. 451).

In the same way that the west is seen in its negative and positive aspects, so too is the east. The schoolteacher, Clementine (Cathy Downs), provides positive elements such as education and stability, seen as necessary to the utopian promise of western settlement, elements that are celebrated in the scene at the dance in the shell of the new church under the sign of the Stars and Stripes. The negative elements – vice and decadence – are embodied in the figure of the consumptive Doc Holliday (Victor Mature).

As an agent in the transformation of positive eastern values into the west, and the ejection of all negative values from the west, Earp's centrality is clear. Interestingly, despite the essential nature of that agency to the narrative and ideological project of the film, the figure's unease is evident. This phenomenon can be viewed as presaging generic shifts in the role of the gunfighter, authorial developments in Ford's view of America as well as exemplifying the characteristic laconic liberalism of the star persona of Henry Fonda.

CHRISTINE GLEDHILL

Johnny Guitar (USA 1954 *p.c* – Republic; *d* – Nicholas Ray)

Johnny Guitar is an example of the 1950s baroque western that deviated in significant ways from the conventions of the earlier romantic form: for example, in its representation of a stylised landscape and decor contrasting with the ornate interior of Vienna's place (hanging chandelier, grand piano, red-suffused lighting) and the dark, windswept, barren exteriors. An impulse towards myth and melodrama is also revealed in the central conflict between the two female adversaries.

The mythic dimension can be seen in the frenzied performance of Mercedes McCambridge as Emma, whose black widow's weeds lead the mob of settlers and townspeople. Elements of melodrama emerge from the treatment of Vienna (Joan Crawford) as a central agent in the fortunes of the partly criminalised all-male group. Her isolation from both these groups can be identified in the action (the quietness as she lights the lamps and sits at the piano) and in the organisation of spatial relations during the scene of the search, where the contrast of her white dress with the predominant blacks and reds around her is notable. It is here, too, that the coded social and sexual antagonisms between the two monumental female adversaries can be located.

The film also demonstrates the significant displacements affecting the conventions of the western when the protagonists are female. The most revealing displacement is the marginalisation of male action as the dramas of gunfighters/outlaws and settlers/ranchers alike are subordinated to the central female conflict (see Nicholas Ray, p. 413).

CHRISTINE GLEDHILL

Guns in the Afternoon/Ride the High Country (USA 1962 *p.c* – MGM; *d* – Sam Peckinpah)

In the opening sequence, Joel McCrea as Stephen Judd rides into a little town in the Californian Sierras. Judd, a former sheriff, is down on his luck and needs a job. As he rides slowly up the main street, he sees crowds waving and cheering. Bemused, he acknowledges the applause, but a uniformed policeman makes it clear the cheering is not for him, shouting at him to get out of the way as a motorcar rushes past, scaring his horse. Then down the street come a horse and a camel, racing to the finishing line.

The incongruity of the camel and the anachronism of the car are a shock to the viewer expecting a traditional western. Change is everywhere – and decay too. Judd is feeling his age. 'I expected a younger man', says the banker to whom he applies for a job. 'I used to be,' Judd replies ironically. At the funfair, he discovers his old partner Gil Westrum (Randolph Scott), kitted out in a fake Buffalo Bill wig and buckskins, posing as the Oregon Kid and running a crooked shooting gallery. The old west has been reduced to a threadbare parody.

These opening scenes introduce the theme that Peckinpah was to develop in the rest of the film, and in much of his subsequent work: that of the ending of the west. The question he poses is, how can the traditional code of the western survive into an era when the certainties that underpin it have eroded? Individual morality has been replaced by corporatism, greed and cynicism; even Judd's partner betrays him, though he is redeemed in a final act of heroism.

In Peckinpah's films, the white male hero is subjected to a series of ordeals, moral and physical, that test to the full his ability to retain his integrity and sense of self. Typically, Peckinpah's heroes cannot adjust to a world that has overtaken them. There is no community that they can relate to, only, if they are lucky, a few kindred souls, doomed like them to assert their defiance in acts of heroic resistance. *The Wild Bunch* (1969), Peckinpah's masterpiece, is his most extreme demonstration of the tragedy of heroes in a world that has no use for them.

CHRISTINE GLEDHILL

Unforgiven (USA 1992 *p.c* – Warner Bros./Malpaso; *d* – Clint Eastwood)

William Munny and his companion, the Kid, have finally accomplished their mission and killed the man responsible for mutilating a young prostitute. Waiting outside town for a rendezvous with those who hired them, the two men discuss their deed. Munny, a veteran gunfighter reluctantly brought out of retirement for this job, is reflective and undemonstrative. The Kid, who up till now has been full of youthful bravado, is in shock, giving way to alternate outbursts of boasting and remorse. Deep down, as Munny senses, he is aghast at what he has done. In a scene remarkable for facing up to the act

Facing up to killing: Clint Eastwood in *Unforgiven*

of violence at the heart of the western genre, Munny articulates what it has taken him a lifetime to learn:

'It's a hell of a thing, killing a man – you take away all he's got and all he's ever gonna have.'

'Yeah, well,' says the Kid, 'I guess he had it coming to him.'

'We all have it coming, Kid,' says Munny.

Unforgiven is not a feminist film, but it takes seriously the issue of violence against women. It is not an anti-racist film, but Morgan Freeman's role as Munny's companion is one of the best a black actor has had in a western. Ultimately, William Munny behaves in a typical western hero manner – he goes out and shoots the bad man. But the film does not shy away from the consequences of what it means to kill another human being. *Unforgiven* is a film made in full knowledge of everything that has been said against the western – its racism, sexism, its obsession with violence. It negotiates in a subtle and cunning way an accommodation with the critics of the western, yet manages to preserve the fundamentals of the genre all but intact.

EDWARD BUSCOMBE

Ballad of Little Jo (USA 1993 *p.c* – Fine Line Features/PolyGram Filmed Entertainment/Joco; *d* – Maggie Greenwald)

Before making this extraordinary feminist western, Maggie Greenwald had caused a stir with her stylish adaptation of Jim Thompson's crime novel *The Kill-Off* (1989), in which she had changed Thompson's plot to suit her own ends. *Ballad of Little Jo*, also scripted by Greenwald, undertakes a similar enterprise of creative rewriting, this time of the hallowed version of the history of the west celebrated by the classics of the genre. No matter how many times the western has been revised, or how self-reflexive it becomes, it retains its focus on the white, male hero at the expense of others who made a significant contribution to the building of the west. *Ballad of Little Jo* does not simply replace the western hero with a woman, it plays on the irony at the heart of the story: if Little Jo was able to pass as a man, then how many other western 'heroes' were actually women in disguise? Such an irreverent question shakes the very foundations of the genre, which may be one reason why Greenwald's film, though admired by feminists (Modleski, 1999), has received little critical attention (but see Kitses, 1998).

Greenwald's take on the western is given added bite by the fact that it was based on documented events. The 'real' Little Jo cross-dressed as a man for many years and her masquerade was only discovered when she died. In Greenwald's hands, the story becomes one of survival and desire, as Jo (Suzy Amis) builds her own homestead in an isolated spot away from the other townspeople and falls in love with the Chinese man (David Chung) who becomes her housekeeper and lover. Their relationship remains secret, emblematic of a whole 'hidden history' of transgressive relationships that the western occasionally hints at, but can never fully accommodate, except at its margins.

Greenwald uses the themes and iconography of the genre (costume, landscape, civilisation versus wilderness, lawless violence) to full effect, creating a hostile world in which women are at best tolerated, at worst abused and marginalised. Little Jo's assumed masculine identity is not always secure: she has to eradicate all signs of effeminacy in order to be accepted in the community. Like the classic westerner, Little Jo exists outside civilised society, preferring to live a way of life that calls into question its ideals of democracy and progress. When she finally gives up any idea of returning to the east to rejoin her family and her illegitimate son, realising that she will not be accepted there either, her decision to remain living as a man resonates with that of many of the genre's reluctant heroes (such as Wyatt Earp in *My Darling Clementine*, 1946, or Ethan Edwards in *The Searchers*, 1956). Male identity allows her freedoms that she would not otherwise have, in the west or the east.

One of the film's greatest pleasures is the music by David Mansfield, who invests the haunting score with a sense of plangent yearning that makes Little Jo's lonely existence appear both poignant and heroic, and provides a fitting accompaniment to the sublime landscapes, whether lush and verdant or harsh and frozen, against which her battle for survival and existence plays out.

PAM COOK

PART 6

Authorship and Cinema

Holly Hunter and Anna Paquin in Jane Campion's *The Piano*

INTRODUCTION

PAM COOK

Debates about authorship in cinema occupied a privileged position in film studies from the 1950s – when the French journal *Cahiers du cinéma* formulated the influential *politique des auteurs* – until the early 1980s when the academic focus shifted towards audience and reception studies. Basically a polemical critical strategy aimed at 'quality' French cinema and the writing that supported it, the *politique* proposed that, in spite of the industrial and collaborative nature of film production, the director, like any other artist, was the creative source of the finished product. This proposition has been appropriated, attacked and reformulated in many different ways, and its long-lasting relevance to critical debates is some indication of the value of *Cahiers*' initial polemic.

Historical and political changes, particularly since the late 1960s, brought about a radical rethinking of the underlying assumptions of traditional auteur study of cinema, and an assault on the ideology of the artist as sole creator of the artwork. Appropriating concepts from structural linguistics, semiology and psychoanalysis, film theory in the 1970s began to question the underlying assumptions of auteur theory such as 'aesthetic coherence', 'self-expression' and 'creativity'. In spite of these onslaughts, auteur study was not destroyed, but rather transformed: from a way of accounting for the whole of cinema into a critical methodology that poses questions for film study, and for cultural practices in general. The history of this transformation is traced in this section.

The question of authorship and its application to cinema has sometimes been presented ahistorically. For example, American film critic Andrew Sarris reformulated *Cahiers' politique* as 'the auteur theory', transforming the original polemic for a new cinema of auteurs into a critical method for evaluating films (mostly Hollywood films, some European art cinema) and creating a pantheon of 'best directors' that is still effective in film criticism today. In many film courses (and many cinema programmes), the notion of the 'great director' remains important to the way cinema is learned and understood. Recognising the marks of 'greatness' in film can be a source of pleasure for some spectators, just as recognising the elements of genre can offer pleasure as well as knowledge. These pleasures are used in the marketing of films to attract audiences by offering the possibility of using their specialist knowledge of cinema.

All too often, the critical assaults on authorship have refused to take on board these pleasures, ending up in the impasse of puritanical rejection. A historical approach helps us out of that impasse, because it attempts to show how and why auteur theory emerged and was transformed, beginning the work of understanding different critical attitudes to cinema, the diverse pleasures we get from it and how they change over time.

Cinema as art or commodity?

Before the *politique des auteurs* emerged in France in the 1950s, traditional film criticism (largely sociological) assumed that the industrial nature of film production prevented a single authorial voice making itself heard (or seen) in film. For some critics, this meant that cinema could not be regarded as art: a commodity product at the service of the laws of the capitalist economy, it could do no more than reflect the ideology of the capitalist system. For others, cinema only achieved the status of art when a film or body of films could be seen as the expression of certain intentions carried out by an individual person, who was an artist by virtue of his or her struggle against the industrial system of production. Few artists achieved this empirical control; Danish film-maker Carl Dreyer is an example of a director whose career can be defined by his uncompromising insistence on control of production: his status as one of the great artists of cinema resides as much in his intransigence vis-à-vis the industry as in the aesthetic quality of the relatively small number of films he was able to make (see Nash, 1977). The 'butchering' of many of these films by 'uncomprehending' (commercially motivated) distributors is seen as further evidence of the fundamental antagonism between art, or the interests of the artist, and the interests of commodity production. The artist is portrayed as an isolated, heroic figure struggling for creative autonomy against the interference of outside bodies.

The artist as creative source

The idea that the individual artist is the source of true creativity can be traced back to historical shifts that have radically changed the position of the artist in society. Before the Renaissance, the artist was seen as a craftsman producing useful objects: God was the locus of creativity rather than man. When creativity was extended to painters and poets, the divine gift of inspiration and genius was relocated in the artist, who was directly dependent upon the patronage of the ruling class. A division emerged between the craftsman or artisan who produced for consumption, and the artist whose innate genius presented a potential challenge to the prevailing social order. However, the artist's autonomy was limited by his or her dependence on the patronage of the ruling class.

The emergence of the capitalist commodity economy changed the traditional relationship of the artist to society from direct dependence on patronage to indirect dependence on a large, anonymous group that was always expanding: the market. This shift produced a new conflict: on one hand, the artist was now able to exploit the market to sell the results of his or her labour to the highest bidder; on the other, the forces of the market were resisted by the romantic notion of 'artistic genius' struggling for autonomy in opposition to 'commercial, socially conformist art' (see Murdock, 1980).

In a capitalist economy, art is a commodity subject to the laws of the market: the division between mass-produced culture and art proper merges with the distinction between craftsman and artist to marginalise the artist from society. Since artistic activity cannot be totally rationalised according to the laws of profitability governing commodity production, it can only survive through state intervention in the form of subsidies, in which case the artist is guaranteed minority prestige status, subsidised by a society of which only a tiny part represents his or her audience. The minority status of art performs

Hitchcock's name given prominence on the hoarding advertising *The Man Who Knew Too Much*

a double function: to guarantee critical approval for those who control it (the subsidising agencies), and to provide a safe, licensed space for artistic activity, necessarily marginalised. This marginalisation effectively neutralises the potentially critical voice of the artist in society.

The practice of attributing cultural products to the name of an individual artist ensures that they are marketed in a particular way, as 'art' rather than 'mass production', and consumed by a knowledgeable, niche audience. However, the distinction is far from clear-cut: art is constantly appropriated by popular culture, and vice versa. It could be argued, then, that the status of any cultural product as art (or otherwise) depends less on its intrinsic aesthetic value, or indeed on any intrinsic property, than on the way it is taken up and exploited by the laws of the market, or by a particular interest group.

The function of authorship in cinema

The distinction between 'art' and 'commercial product' has its own history in the development of cinema, and has different functions at different moments. In the early days of Hollywood, for example, as the commercial potential of cinema was recognised, the rush to exploit that potential meant that innovation and experiment were at a premium. In the relatively open context of the early Hollywood industry, copyright laws were minimal, leading to widespread pirating. The practice of marking a film with the logo of its production company grew up as a way of protecting the rights of the company over the film, but the logo could also function as a mark of authorship, and hence as a guarantee of artistic value. The aesthetic experiments that emerged from Hollywood in this period were admired by Russian and European avant-garde film-makers. In Hollywood itself, the films were marketed as exceptional cinematic events: their status as art was part of their commodity value, and the mark of the presence of the 'artist' (Griffith's logo, Chaplin's 'Tramp' persona) performed a function in the marketing process.

There is, however, a danger in reducing the concept of authorship to the status of a simple function (see Foucault, 1979). As the history of auteur study in cinema shows, authorship can be taken up in multiple ways. It could be argued, for example, that after the arrival of synchronised sound, the notion of film as art gave way in Hollywood to the idea of popular entertainment, although a place was reserved for prestige productions that were often literary adaptations. In this case, the creative source was taken to be the writer of the original work rather than the director. As the strength of the major studios grew, producers and stars became more important in the marketing process than directors. At the time of the *politique des auteurs*, then, the idea that a Hollywood film could be attributed to the intentions of an individual director, as it was in the case of art cinema, had a polemical impetus. It attempted to break down the barrier between art cinema and commercial cinema by establishing the presence of artists in the apparently monolithic commodity production of Hollywood. Although the idea of the director as artist was prevalent in writing on art cinema at that time, it was not as significant in writing on Hollywood.

In the wake of auteur theory's polemic for popular cinema, and the anti-auteurist politics that followed the social and cultural upheavals of May 1968 in France, art cinema became unfashionable in film criticism. It also declined in economic importance, and its distribution and exhibition became restricted to small art-house and film society circuits. Yet its aesthetic impact on cinema in general increased rather than waned. New Hollywood Cinema of the 1960s, for instance (the films of Robert Altman, Arthur Penn, Francis Ford Coppola *et al.*) owed much to art cinema (see New Hollywood, p. 60). The director's name once again became important in marketing Hollywood cinema: hoardings advertised 'Samuel Fuller's *The Big Red One*' and 'John Carpenter's *Halloween*' alongside '*Don Giovanni*: a film by Joseph Losey' and '*Kagemusha*: an Akira Kurosawa film'. Paradoxically, art cinema suffered from critical neglect at a time when the division between art cinema and popular cinema was breaking down.

Authors in art cinema

Tracing the emergence of art cinema after World War II, David Bordwell (1979) gives a cogent account of the ways in which it differs from classic narrative cinema. He sees the loose narrative structure of art cinema as motivated by a desire for realism, defined as an attempt to represent 'real' problems in 'real' locations, using psychologically complex characters to validate the drive towards verisimilitude. Social, emotional and sexual problems are reflected in individual characters, and are only significant in so far as they impinge upon the sensitive individual.

This drive towards realism may seem incompatible with the idea of a creative artist as source of meaning in art cinema: the artist's signature or style is intrusive and disrupts verisimilitude. Yet, Bordwell argues, art cinema uses authorship to unify the film text, to organise it for the audience's comprehension in the absence of familiar stars and genres. Art cinema addresses its audience as one of knowledgeable cinemagoers who will recognise the characteristic stylistic touches of the author's oeuvre. The art film is intended to be read as the work of an expressive individual, and a small industry is devoted to informing viewers of particular authorial marks: career retrospectives, press reviews, television programmes and DVD 'extras' all contribute to introducing viewers to authorial codes.

In art cinema, then, the informed, educated audience looks for the marks of authorship to make sense of the film, rather than to the rambling story or the characters, who are often aimless victims rather than controlling agents. Audience identification shifts between characters and author: the audience is often given privileged information over the characters (as with the 'flash-forward' device), which strengthens identification with the author. Although apparently at odds with the realist project of art cinema, this controlling authorial discourse provides the final guarantee of 'truth' for the audience: if the realism of locations and character psychology represents the world 'as it is', the authorial discourse can be said to confirm the essential truth of the individual's experience of that world. This textual organisation differs from that of the 'classic realist text', which follows the logic of cause and effect, features goal-oriented characters and strives for resolution (see Classic Hollywood narrative, p. 45). However, the dominance of authorial discourse is by no means secure in art cinema: Bordwell sees the art film in terms of a shifting, uneasy relationship between the discourses of narrative, character and author. In this way, art cinema maintains hesitation and ambiguity rather than the resolution of problems: the essential ambiguity of life reflected in art.

If, as Bordwell claims, art cinema can be established as a distinct mode, different from classic Hollywood or the modernist avant-garde, there are nonetheless interesting areas of overlap. Some 'classic' works (for example, those of Douglas Sirk, John Ford or Fritz Lang) display stylistic affinities with art cinema, while Alfred Hitchcock's films emphasise the narrational process, authorial discourse and problems of point of view in much the same way as the art film. On the other hand, some modernist film-making has taken up and extended art-cinema strategies (Carl Dreyer, Alain Resnais or Jean-Marie Straub and Danièle Huillet, for example) and some radical filmmakers have questioned it (as in the case of Jean-Luc Godard). One useful way of approaching art cinema might be in terms of its relationship to, or difference from, other modes of film-making. For instance, while it could be argued that New Hollywood owes much to art cinema, conditions of production are different in Hollywood, so that Hollywood art films represent a complex transformation of the codes of art cinema, and the role of the director as author (see Neale, 1976).

It could be assumed that the transformation of traditional auteur analysis has made it difficult to take the idea of the auteur seriously. However, the name of the director-as-author did not cease to be important in the marketing of film, and while film theory may have abandoned straightforward auteur analysis, much of the criticism in 'quality' newspapers and film journals remains devoted to the idea of the director as artist. The influence of art cinema on New Hollywood and the growth of the popular art movie have resulted in the extension of the function of the author/artist, at one time limited to art cinema, to popular cinema, where the name of the director can be deployed to attract a larger knowledgeable audience (rather than the minority audience of art cinema proper) for commercial cinema. A study of art cinema in terms of authorship could offer insight into the viewer's pleasure in recognising the indicators of authorship in cinema in general. Art cinema could provide a means of critical entry into commercial cinema, not in terms of the confirmation of traditional auteur analysis, but in the interests of understanding the relationship between art cinema and commercial cinema in order to question the conventional division between 'art' and 'entertainment' (see also Art cinema, p. 83).

Selected Reading

David Bordwell, 'The art cinema as a mode of film practice', *Film Criticism* 4 (1): 56–64, 1979. Reprinted in Fowler (ed.), *The European Cinema Reader*, London and New York, Routledge 2002.

Michel Foucault, 'What is an author?, *Screen* 20 (1): 13–33, spring 1979. Reprinted in Rabinow (ed.), *The Foucault Reader*, New York, Pantheon Press, 1984.

Graham Murdock, 'Authorship and organisation', *Screen Education* 35: 19–34, summer 1980. Reprinted in Alvarado, Buscombe and Collins (eds), *The Screen Education Reader*, New York, Columbia University Press, 1997.

Stephen Neale, 'New Hollywood cinema', *Screen* 17 (2): 117–22, summer1976.

FOR A NEW FRENCH CINEMA: THE *POLITIQUE DES AUTEURS*

PAM COOK

The *politique* was signalled by Alexandre Astruc's 1948 article 'The birth of a new avant-garde: la caméra-stylo', calling for a new language of cinema in which the individual artist could express his or her thoughts, using the camera to write a world-view, a philosophy of life. Astruc was writing as a left-wing intellectual and film-maker in postwar France, where the social fragmentation and isolation of the left led to reconstruction and stabilisation formulated in individual rather than political or collective terms. During the war, the Americans had developed lightweight 16mm cameras, which enabled film-making in small groups as opposed to the methods of studio production in Hollywood or France. This, combined with the growth of television, made the possibility of wider access to the means of production seem real and immediate. After World War II, French intellectuals and film-makers were able to see previously unavailable Hollywood films at the Cinémathèque in Paris. Against this contradictory background, the European intellectual tradition that saw the artist as a voice of dissent in society took on a polemical force in film criticism (see Buscombe, 1973).

The film-makers and critics who subsequently wrote for *Cahiers du cinéma* were interested in questions of form and mise en scène and in theoretical analysis of the relationship of the artist and the film product to society. They rejected the untheorised political commitment of other journals of film criticism in France at the time, notably *Positif* (see Benayoun, 1962). The *politique des auteurs* emerged in opposition not only to established French film criticism, with its support for a 'quality' cinema of serious social themes, but also to the political criticism of the left that ignored the contribution of individuals to the process of film production (see Truffaut, 1954; 1976).

André Bazin

It is sometimes tempting to dismiss the *politique des auteurs* as a simple manifesto for individual personal expression, which is why it is helpful to understand the context (such as the upheaval in left-wing politics in the 1950s, the Cold War, anti-Stalinism) from which it emerged. It was partly the status of personal feelings within left-wing cultural struggle that was at stake in the early formulations of the *politique*, both in the pages of *Cahiers* and in its relationship to the film-making practice of the Nouvelle Vague. Although this polemic was often lost in the process of appropriation, it remained relevant to arguments in film theory (see Hess, 1974).

There was lively debate within *Cahiers* about the *politique*. The shift towards the film-maker/director as the source of meaning was resisted by André Bazin, who believed that the film-maker should act as a passive recorder of the real world rather than manipulator of it – a contradictory position, in the light of his admiration for Hollywood directors such as Orson Welles and Alfred Hitchcock. There were political implications in the disagreement: Bazin's notion of society as based on the interdependence of individuals and social forces was at odds with the idea of a society of conflict and opposition espoused by many of *Cahiers*' younger writers. At the same time, Bazin criticised the notion that a body of work could be ascribed to an individual auteur as though the individual was not part of society and history, subject to social and historical constraints (see Bazin, 1957/1968). Bazin argued for a sociological approach to film that would take into account the historical moment of production. However, when it came to his own analysis of the work and directors he considered important, his position often led him to a dead-end (see also Structuralism and its aftermaths, p. 525).

Bazin's criticism of the *politique* was perceptive: the evaluation of films according to the criterion of the 'great director' who transcended history and ideology was the least productive aspect of the *politique des auteurs*, together with the importance given to the critic's personal taste that went with it.

Auteur versus metteur en scène

Closely linked to this discussion about the status of the individual artist in artistic production was the distinction the auteur critics made between auteur and metteur en scène. The idea of mise en scène (the staging of the real world for the camera) was central to the interest in form and cinematic language that many *Cahiers* critics shared, but their notion of the individual artist as primary source of meaning in film led them to make a distinction between those directors who simply directed (who had mastered the language of cinema) and those who were true auteurs, in the sense that they created a coherent worldview and manifested a uniquely individual style across all their films. Again Bazin differed: a film's mise en scène should efface individual style to allow the inner meaning to shine through naturally so that the spectator could come to his or her own conclusions without being manipulated. Bazin's emphasis on the transparency of cinematic language was at odds with many *Cahiers* critics' interest in manipulating the language of cinema to express the director's personal concerns. Bazin's argument comes close to eliminating human intervention in the process of production altogether (see Wollen, 1976).

This defence of style against transparency (film as window on the world) and realism (film capturing the truth of reality) remained important to the *Cahiers* critics even through the reassessments that took place in that journal during the 1960s under the impact of structuralist theory. The structuralist attack on humanism and personal expression was to have major repercussions for the *politique* and for the centrality of the individual artist within it. Nonetheless, the basic argument that the director of a film should be considered an important source of meaning in that film remained relevant to debate in film studies, though the terms of the debates had changed.

Style and theme

Jean Renoir

French film-maker Jean Renoir's career spanned more than 40 years; he worked in many different production situations and is now considered one of the great film artists, whose films display a consistency of cinematic style and thematic concerns. He was a major influence on Nouvelle Vague film-makers such as François Truffaut, and a favourite auteur of André Bazin because of his subtle use of mise en scène. His style, based on absence of montage, deep-focus photography and fluid camera movement, exemplified the transparency of approach that Bazin argued could most effectively reveal the essence of the real world for the spectator. Equally, Renoir's humanist view of the world expressed in the way he integrated actors with objects and space coincided with Bazin's interest in the way cinema could be used to express the relationship between individuals and society as one of mutual interdependence (see Bazin, 1971).

These stylistic and thematic concerns can certainly be seen in Renoir's work. But it is also evident that history (the 1930s Popular Front in *The Crime of Monsieur Lange/Le Crime de Monsieur Lange*, 1935; the impending World War II in *La Grande Illusion*, 1937) and different production situations (his work in America) also had an impact on the films. While auteur study sometimes allows us to understand films better by detecting the director's concerns over a body of work, it should not obscure questions of history and ideology as equally important determining factors, not only on the films but on the way we read them. Today's viewers, used to different forms of realism in cinema and television, may find Renoir's mise en scène excessive, even melodramatic.

Renoir made over 35 films between 1924 and 1961. Any serious attempt to approach his work as an auteur would need to look carefully at as many of these films as possible. His work is used here to discuss one aspect of the *politique des auteurs*: the use of the name Jean Renoir as a means of classifying and evaluating films according to the assumed presence of a consistent personal vision or worldview. This auteurist approach could be questioned by a consideration of Renoir's work in the context of the 1930s Popular Front, which affected a whole generation of French film-workers, and the different production conditions he met in America (see Fofi, 1972/73; Rivette and Truffaut, 1954).

JEAN RENOIR

Boudu Saved from Drowning/Boudu sauvé des eaux (France 1932 *p.c* – Productions Michel Simon; *d* – Jean Renoir)

Renoir's consistent interest in the idea of 'natural man' is manifest here in the person of Boudu, who flouts polite conventions and is restless and disruptive within the bourgeois milieu of the man who saves him from drowning. This concern with the positive antisocial values of the anarchic outsider can be traced as a theme throughout Renoir's work, but since this film was made in the 1930s during his involvement with left-wing politics, it is equally relevant to place this concern within the context of French cinema of the time and to take into account the collaboration between Renoir and Michel Simon (Boudu). Simon co-produced the film under the banner of his own production company, while Renoir wrote and directed. The character of Boudu, the anarchic renegade in opposition to petit-

Renoir's celebration of 'natural man' (Michel Simon) in *Boudu sauvé des eaux*

bourgeois values, is in many ways a vehicle for Simon, who was often associated with such roles (for example, in Jean Vigo's *L'Atalante*, 1934).

In terms of Renoir's characteristic mise en scène, the film uses deep-focus photography and moving camera to indicate a coherent space that the camera reveals, disclosing people and objects as if by accident. Bazin saw Renoir's use of camera movement to integrate actors and space as exemplary of a style that captures reality for the spectator, with the camera acting as an 'invisible guest' at the scene to be filmed.

PAM COOK

The Crime of Monsieur Lange/Le Crime de Monsieur Lange (France 1935 *p.c* – Films Obéron; *d* – Jean Renoir)

A film made directly out of Renoir's political commitment to the Popular Front and its ideas of the unity between white-collar and labouring workers against capitalist businessmen and employers. The idea of unity in a common cause, here represented by the workers' co-operative, is central to much of Renoir's work, whether that cause be war (*La Grande Illusion*, 1937), art (*French Can-Can*, 1955) or social change as in the case of this film. Contradictions arise and are resolved by group solidarity and mutual caring, but the continued existence of the problem boss, Batala (Jules Berry), can only be resolved by extreme and violent action. Lange (René Lefèvre) must become a hero (like Arizona Jim) and kill the villain, placing himself outside the law for ever. It could be argued that a dark note of irony overshadows the 'happy ending'. Lange sacrifices himself (and Valentine) for the co-operative, and finally a group of workmen helps them to escape. The co-operative survives at the expense of individual sacrifice.

In terms of mise en scène, Renoir characteristically creates a coherent and identifiable space, centred on the courtyard where all communal discussion and action take place. Individual workers move between the courtyard and their workplaces in the block, and the fluidity of movement of the actors between on-screen and off-screen space, combined with a naturalistic use of sound, makes the interaction between individuals and group, and the sense of solidarity, especially convincing. However, the 'Arizona Jim' subplot, with its emphasis on fiction and fantasy, seems to work against the realism of Renoir's style, thus complicating the overall meaning of the film and its endorsement of Popular Front ideology.

PAM COOK

La Grande Illusion (France 1937 *p.c* – Réalisations d'Art Cinématographique; *d* – Jean Renoir)

The context of war is used to work through Renoir's concern with class and cultural differences and human affinities. The aristocrat, the bourgeois, the intellectual and the 'common man' have different attitudes and manners. War is said to make them all

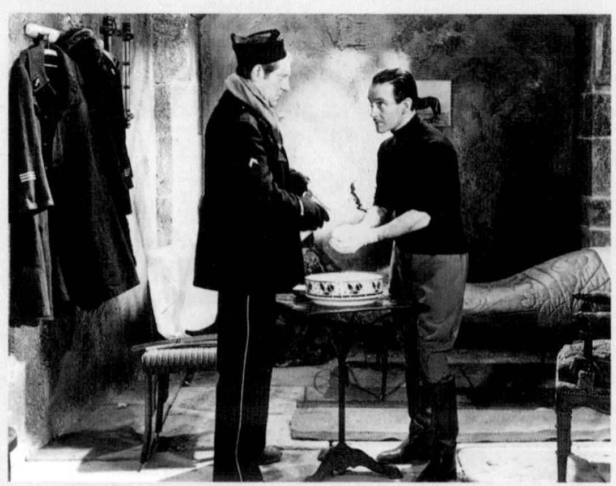

Jean Gabin and Pierre Fresnay face class differences in *La Grande Illusion*

equal, but the French aristocrat de Boêldieu (Pierre Fresnay) has more in common with von Rauffenstein (Erich von Stroheim), his German enemy, than with his fellow Frenchmen. His solidarity with them is based on patriotism and a 'gentlemanly' sense of generosity that causes him to sacrifice himself so that they may escape successfully. Renoir's sympathy for the aristocrats and their doomed way of life is evident in his treatment of their relationship: a characteristic humanism. Yet it is arguable that this can appear contradictory, undermining humanism by putting blatantly Fascist remarks in the mouth of von Rauffenstein, and raising the question of how far sympathy for individual human beings can be maintained when the primary struggle is against Fascism. The idea of 'unity in a common cause' is more complex and contradictory here than in *Le Crime de Monsieur Lange* (1935), manifested in the differences between characters and the fragmentation of space. However, Renoir's mise en scène, the use of deep-focus, long takes and sideways and panning shots can be seen as realistic, depicting a world fragmented by war into which death, loss and fear are constantly erupting. This mise en scène seems to endorse the film's central pacifist theme, emerging from the policies of the Popular Front.

PAM COOK

The Rules of the Game/La Règle du jeu (France 1939 *p.c* – Nouvelle Edition Française; *d* – Jean Renoir)

This film is another complex exploration of social differences – this time in the context of a house party where the love intrigues of high-society guests are mirrored by parallel activities among the servants – in which contradictions are raised and left unresolved. Renoir uses the theatrical conventions of farce to explore the extent to which personal relationships, and by extension social structures, are based on pretence, accident and misunderstanding. The idea of 'social cohesion' is brought into question as it becomes clear that social unity is illusory, based on an acceptance of deceit.

If the stability of the status quo is based on illusion and deceit, who has the greatest vested interest in maintaining the illusion? The upper classes, evidently; but they cannot totally control events, much as they try. A servant's sexual jealousy can cause chaos in the system. The film reflects Renoir's growing concern with the opposition art (artifice) versus life (reality), and the overlapping of the two. In terms of his relationship with the Popular Front, he has returned to his bourgeois roots in the subject matter of his film, but his treatment of the theme is lucid and detached. The hunt in which the houseguests take part is shown as a metaphor for the exploitative power of the upper classes. The apparent naturalism of the mise en scène is offset by the incident in which the Marquise (Nora Grégor) sees her husband and his mistress through binoculars, and misreads what she sees. The audience knows what is happening, the Marquise misinterprets the scene because of her subjective position. This disjuncture between objectivity and subjectivity reflects Renoir's awareness that appearances are deceptive. The question remains: does Renoir's humanism, his concern for each of his characters and their vested interests, obscure the serious social questions about class differences that the film raises?

Renoir's interest in theatrical conventions, and in acting, relevant to all his work, is particularly important in this film, where it becomes part of the thematic structure.

PAM COOK

This Land Is Mine (USA 1943 *p.c* – RKO Radio Pictures; *d* – Jean Renoir)

Renoir co-wrote (with Dudley Nichols), co-produced and directed this film, made during his period in the US under the auspices of RKO, who also provided the facilities for Orson Welles's *Citizen Kane* (1941). It is interesting to see how the context of a Hollywood studio production and actors affected the film, which looks quite different from his earlier work. The film won an Academy Award for sound recording.

The theme is typical Renoir: a community divided by war, misunderstandings and deception. The demands of Hollywood narrative can be seen in the use of a central character through whose maturing consciousness the problems are resolved, and a touch of 'American Freud' can be discerned in the relationship between Albert (Charles Laughton) and his possessive mother (Una O'Connor). The studio sets look strangely constricting in relation to the characters compared with the realistic locations used in earlier films. How then do these factors – the use of stars as central protagonists, the psychological realism of the Hollywood narrative, the conditions of studio production – combine to affect the place of this film within the Renoir oeuvre constructed by auteur study? The theme of war, collaboration and resistance is characteristic, but the director's point of view may have been affected by different conditions of production. Renoir was criticised for his attempt to make a propaganda film about the Nazi occupation that gave a less than heroic view of occupied France.

PAM COOK

The Woman on the Beach (USA 1947 *p.c* – RKO Radio Pictures; *d* – Jean Renoir)

This is another example of Renoir's American work, again for RKO. The film is almost entirely dominated by the requirements of the film noir genre as it developed in the postwar US. In contrast to earlier films, the narrative problems here are internalised in terms of individual psychology, projected against a dreamlike Expressionist set. With its theme of solitude and formalised mise en scène, the film seems most relevant to later Renoir:

> It was a story quite opposed to everything I had hitherto attempted. In all my previous films I had tried to depict the bonds uniting the individual to his background. The older I grew, the more I had proclaimed the consoling truth that the world is one; and now I was embarked on a study of persons

Charles Bickford and Joan Bennett face marital problems in *The Woman on the Beach*

whose sole idea was to close the door on the absolutely concrete phenomena which we call life. (Renoir, 1974)

How, then, was Renoir's perspective changed by the experience of working in postwar America? It is unlikely that the expressive use of montage and fragmentation of space would have gained approval from André Bazin. When seen as a transition to late Renoir, as auteur study prescribes, it seems less strange. But despite Renoir's words above claiming that his own point of view is expressed in the film, the conditions of Hollywood production, and the generic conventions of film noir, could be said to have as much claim on the final product as Renoir's authorial vision.

PAM COOK

French Can-Can (France/Italy 1955 *p.c* – Franco London Film/Jolly Film; *d* – Jean Renoir)

Made after his return to Europe, this represents an example of mature Renoir in which the relationship between art (artifice) and reality (life) is developed and explored. Although the film pays homage to the Impressionist painters and the popular theatre of turn-of-the-century France in its use of colour photography, music and spectacle, it is pessimistic about the potential of art to change anything. Danglard's (Jean Gabin) belief in the importance of the can-can as art has the quality of an obsession imposed as a repressive discipline on the girls he employs, whom he also exploits. Since he labours under such extreme financial difficulties and is always on the verge of bankruptcy and imprisonment, his involvement with the theatre seems perverse, and his final exhortation to Nini (Françoise Arnoul) that the artist must dedicate himself totally to his or her art seems to be an argument for 'art for art's sake'. This cynical view of the relationship between art and life contrasts sharply with earlier films such as *Le Crime de Monsieur Lange* (1935), and the use of a single central character (Danglard) as a focus for identification tends to obscure contradictions arising from the subject matter (such as that between the pleasurable aspects of the can-can as spectacle, and the repression/distortion/exploitation of the female body on which it depends).

PAM COOK

The Vanishing Corporal/Le Caporal épinglé (France 1962 *p.c* – Films du Cyclope; *d* – Jean Renoir)

It is interesting to compare this film with *La Grande Illusion* (1937). Thematically, it has many of the same preoccupations. But whereas in *La Grande Illusion* the struggle against Fascism is given real importance, here the urge to escape, the concern with 'freedom', is seen as a human obsession, a perversity in the face of the obvious advantages in staying in prison, and opting out of the struggle.

Human perversity is shown in one of the scenes at the end of the film: the sombre funeral procession that the French POW escapees join appears bizarre in the context of war that values life so cheaply, and in the train the over-friendliness of the drunken German to the Frenchmen makes a mockery of human relationships, and threatens their safety. The French corporal (Jean-Pierre Cassel) and his friend admire the trouble-free life of the peasant couple, yet they themselves are perversely driven to return to Paris and give up the comradeship that the war has provided, each going their separate ways. The comic emphasis and use of sentimentalised characters barely obscure the implications that human impulses exist in their own right, irrespective of social realities. The will to escape takes on the aspect of a childish game, and at the end of the film the question remains – what is there left to fight for? Considered in the context of Renoir's earlier films made with the Popular Front, the question takes on added poignancy.

PAM COOK

Fritz Lang

Fritz Lang's career is similar to Renoir's in some ways: he worked as scriptwriter and director in the German film industry in the 1920s and early 1930s, leaving to go to Hollywood in the mid-1930s, where he had a prolific career except for a brief period in the 1950s when he claims to have been blacklisted (see Bogdanovich, 1968, p. 83). His work is generally divided by critics into 'early' and 'late', German and American, and critical opinion differs as to the relative merits of each.

In the context of the *politique des auteurs*, Lang's work demonstrates how authorship can be traced across apparently totally different sets of films, such as German and American Lang, to confer the status of art on commercial cinema. Lang's American films have been described as artistically inferior to those he made in Germany. But *Cahiers du cinéma* (see no. 99, 1959) was interested primarily in Lang's American work as part of their polemic for a reassessment of American cinema in general, and they were responsible for rescuing Lang's American films from the dismissive category of routine commercial production to which they had been relegated, tracing a consistent worldview through them, and a consistent use of Expressionist mise en scène that had its roots in the German films.

There are problems with locating a director's work so firmly within a particular artistic movement such as German Expressionism. First, the use of a term borrowed from modernist painting and theatre tends to locate the film as art rather than commodity production, endorsing the notion of self-expression and obscuring the complex processes involved in producing a film (see Petley, 1978). Second, the term 'Expressionist' can be used to cover such a variety of formal practices in cinema that it becomes meaningless. However, the value of placing Lang's work historically within German Expressionism is that as an author he can be shown to be working within a specific historical and cultural context (see Johnston, 1977). Expressionism itself is generally regarded as a movement that arose directly out of social change in Europe at the turn of the century: Expressionist artists attempted to express this changing, fragmented world and the alienated place of the individual within it. In Germany, Lang used Expressionism to explore his interest in social criticism, an interest that can be directly related to a historical moment. However, the modernist momentum behind the German Expressionist movement and the artistic experiments that flourished in the postwar boom of the early 1920s in Germany cannot be directly mapped onto Lang's work in Hollywood. Rather, his American films show the way in which a director's social and artistic concerns are transformed by different production contexts (see German cinema, p. 207).

Selected Reading

André Bazin, 'La politique des auteurs', *Cahiers du cinéma* no. 70, April 1957. Translated in Graham (ed.), *The New Wave*, London, Secker and Warburg/BFI Publishing, 1968.

John Caughie (ed.), *Theories of Authorship: A Reader*, London, Routledge and Kegan Paul/BFI Publishing, 1981.

FRITZ LANG

Destiny/Der müde Tod (Germany 1921 *p.c* – Decla-Filmgesellschaft; *d* – Fritz Lang)

This was Lang's first major film as a director, and an example of his use of Expressionist motifs, such as the obsession with allegory and myth as a framework for representing individuals (in this case the innocent young lovers) destroyed by the repressive forces of a hostile world. The Expressionist mise en scène creates an enclosed imaginary world in which human figures are overpowered by the huge sets. The film is pessimistic about the fate of individuals. However, if human desire ultimately cannot prevail against destiny, here represented by Death, who controls the narrative, nevertheless in his three tales the protagonists are entirely motivated by the need to resist such a cruel and inevitable fate.

PAM COOK

Dr Mabuse the Gambler Part 1: The Great Gambler – A Picture of Our Time; Dr Mabuse the Gambler Part 2: Inferno, A Play About People of Our Time/Dr Mabuse, der Spieler 1. Teil: Der Grosse Spieler – Ein Bild unserer Zeit; Dr Mabuse, der Spieler 2. Teil: Inferno, Ein Spiel von Menschen unserer Zeit (Germany 1922 *p.c* – Uco Film/Decla-Filmgesellschaft; *d* – Fritz Lang)

Lang began his career by writing scripts for detective films and never lost his interest in this genre as a medium for expressing a critical view of society. Expressionist art is full of representations of evil, supernatural figures who attempt to control events but are ultimately controlled by them, and the master criminal and hypnotist Mabuse (Rudolf Klein-Rogge) is one of these. But the film does not entirely condemn him: the police are also subject to the movement of events, and while Mabuse and Inspector von Wenk (Bernhard Goetzke) struggle against each other, they are both at the mercy of a hostile world. The power relationship between them allows Lang to highlight the social system that produces such manipulative monsters. Characteristically, the power-crazed Dr Mabuse tries to control the destiny of others by using disguise and hypnosis to lead his enemy von Wenk to his death. *Dr Mabuse* can be seen as an early example of a theme central to all Lang's work: the danger of trusting appearances. However, Mabuse's apparently supernatural powers do not make him omnipotent: his attempt to kill von Wenk is foiled, indicating that he is as much at the mercy of events as his victims. Mabuse's fantasies of himself as superman finally bring about his destruction.

PAM COOK

The Nibelungen Part 2: Kriemhild's Revenge/Die Nibelungen 2. Teil: Kriemhilds Rache (Germany 1924 *p.c* – Decla-Filmgesellschaft/Ufa; *d* – Fritz Lang)

Die Nibelungen is based on the Teutonic saga that describes the destiny of the hero Siegfried, of which there are many versions. The form of the legend allows Lang to explore the theme of the individual pitted against fate. In Part One (*Die Nibelungen 1. Teil: Siegfried*, 1924), Siegfried marries Kriemhild before being betrayed and killed by her brother. In Part Two, the innocent Siegfried is replaced as protagonist by his revengeful widow, Kriemhild (Margarete Schön), whose obsession brings about chaos, manifested in the mise en scène by a tension between geometric composition and the fluid movement of actors within the frame. Kriemhild's unnatural rigidity and manic gaze emphasise her transformation into the manipulative monster who is ultimately defeated by her obsession. She can be seen as a forerunner of the American Lang's femme fatales: women as destructive, erotic forces created by a violent male-dominated society. The destructive power of revenge is also explored in *Fury* (1936), Lang's first film in the US.

PAM COOK

Metropolis (Germany 1927 *p.c* – Ufa; *d* – Fritz Lang)

Expressionism is usually seen as an artistic movement in theatre and painting arising out of the economic reconstruction of Germany after World War I. A so-called 'agrarian mysticism' was manifested in a revulsion against city life and the dehumanising exploitation of technology by capital. While it would be wrong to characterise this idealism as proto-Fascist, the Expressionist emphasis on the irrational and the primitive could in some cases seem like a retreat into mysticism. It is interesting here to compare Expressionism with Futurism, which saw itself as a revolutionary modernist movement committed to the enormous

Formalised, geometric mise-en-scène represents social order in *Metropolis*

potential for social change offered by technological advances. Somewhere between the humanism of Expressionism and the anti-humanism of Futurism lies *Metropolis*, which can be read as a criticism of the manipulative capitalist system that both oppresses the people and transforms them into a monstrous destructive power. The irrational resurgence of the masses is not entirely endorsed by the film: rather they are seen as victims of a manipulative system, and the demolition of the machines by the workers does not bring about the annihilation of that system itself (see Kracauer, 1947). The reintroduction of a formalised, geometric mise en scène, broken up during the scenes of revolution, testifies to the re-establishment of order. Beneath this final resolution lies a question: 'But who now holds the power?'. The abstract Expressionist mise en scène enables a critical space to open up: it represents social structures topographically, so that each of the characters is seen to inhabit an ideological position rather than appear as a coherent psychological entity. The final resolution could be seen as ironic rather than positive, offering audiences the possibility of a critical perspective.

PAM COOK

M (Germany 1931 *p.c* – Nero-Film; *d* – Fritz Lang)

This film marks an aesthetic turning point in Lang's work, which can be placed historically. The postwar boom during which Expressionism had flourished came to an end, and a new psychological realism emerged, supported by the introduction of sound, which made it possible for individual psychology to be represented through characters' speech. The fragmentation of society came to be reflected in the tormented individual psyche. 'M' (Peter Lorre), like the driven protagonists of Lang's later American films, is seen as a victim of the tension between his desires and a hostile environment.

The world is divided between two organisations: the police and the criminals, who join forces to track down the child-killer M. 'Normality' is the state of uneasy equilibrium between them, which is disturbed by the irrationality of the murderer of children, and which must be restored at all costs. When M defends himself in a long speech that has little effect on criminals or police, we are made aware of the limitations of a so-called rational society that relies on repression to maintain normality. M's challenge to society takes the form of an individualistic struggle against his fate: in Lang's

Victim of society: Peter Lorre in *M*

worldview, such a struggle can reveal the mechanisms of the system, but it can never defeat it. It is the individual who is ultimately defeated, and the rational, hierarchical organisation that survives. Yet it is arguable that this makes clear that the underside of normality is a destructive drive that allows its victim no pity and will tolerate no questioning. In arousing the spectator's compassion for M, Lang also makes it possible to criticise normal society. An alternative to the individual's self-defeating struggle can be seen in the organisation of the community into social action.

PAM COOK

Rancho Notorious (USA 1952 *p.c* – Fidelity Pictures/RKO Radio Pictures; *d* – Fritz Lang)

Lang's career in Hollywood began in 1935, following a short stay in France, where he directed *Liliom* (1934). Rumour has it that he left Germany after being asked by Goebbels to become head of the German film industry. He seems to have had less freedom in the Hollywood studio system than in Germany, and experienced some interference in his projects. His Expressionist style and interest in the psychological thriller format were well suited to the studio system, and in general he collaborated on scripts and controlled the sets for his films. Nevertheless, his interest in social criticism and formal experiment (he was influenced by Bertolt Brecht, with whom he collaborated on *Hangmen Also Die*, 1943) had to be reconciled with the demands of genre, and although the political climate of America in the 1930s and early 1940s was reasonably sympathetic to these interests, in the 1950s Lang apparently found it difficult to get projects off the ground for a short period.

Femme fatale: Marlene Dietrich in *Rancho Notorious*

Rancho Notorious can be seen as an example of the intersection of these conflicting interests. The film was a reworking of the western revenge genre in terms of Brechtian strategies (evident in the fragmented, episodic narrative and the use of songs to break into the storyline) intended to distance the audience from the spectacle. Completely recut by the studio, much of the film's self-reflexiveness became subservient to the demands of narrative and the psychology of the vengeful hero. Yet Lang's interests surface: the rancher hero (Arthur Kennedy) is a detective figure following a trail of clues to find his fiancée's killer; obsessed with revenge, he is transformed into a monster with a manic stare; Altar Keane (Marlene Dietrich) is depicted as a femme fatale, highlighting the obsessional nature of the masculine desire that creates her as fetish object; and the abstract, stylised mise en scène, especially the use of colour, recalls Lang's Expressionist beginnings. The film remains a strange, atmospheric reflection on the revenge western.

PAM COOK

The Big Heat (USA 1953 *p.c* – Columbia; *d* – Fritz Lang)

This film was primarily a genre piece: a police thriller based on a *Saturday Evening Post* serial. However, Lang's interests coincided well with the genre. Cop Dave Bannion (Glenn Ford) is fighting the racketeers who control the corrupt city administration. Obsessed with revenge following his wife's death, he becomes involved in the violent, brutal underworld with its disturbed and psychotic figures, taking on some of its malign features in the process. The unstable gangster's moll (Gloria Grahame) is one of the tragic victims of this sadistic, diseased world. As with all Lang's American films, the question remains whether his view of the individual's struggle with society is pessimistic, or whether he sees a way out in organised community action.

PAM COOK

Beyond a Reasonable Doubt (USA 1956 *p.c* – RKO Teleradio Pictures/Bert Friedlob Productions; *d* – Fritz Lang)

This was Lang's last film in America, and it is sometimes thought to be the most definitive statement of his preoccupations. The reporter hero Tom Garrett (Dana Andrews) finds himself caught between two opposing organisations: the opponents of capital punishment, and the law. He poses as a murderer in an attempt to prove the fallibility of circumstantial evidence, becoming obsessively caught up in the masquerade and his wish to beat the system. The result is a schematic, abstract work in which identification with the characters is difficult, if not impossible: instead the emphasis is on the inhumanity of a system reflected in the increasingly inhuman obsessions of the central protagonist. The abstraction of the geometric compositions, the minimal schematic narrative, all combine to produce a bleak criticism of a ruthless, hostile society that can be pushed to its limits but never overcome, except, perhaps, by organised community action. The world of the burlesque and its exploitation of women's bodies provide a significant aspect of Lang's social criticism.

PAM COOK

Auteurs and metteurs en scène

The distinction between auteur and metteur en scène introduced by *Cahiers* critics was intended to support the idea of a cinema of personal vision, displaying through a distinctive style the presence of an auteur. Like much of the polemic behind the *politique*, it drew attention to significant factors that had not been considered before, and raised questions that are still unresolved in film criticism.

The term mise en scène refers to the staging of events for the camera, but can also be used loosely to mean the formal organisation of the finished film, the 'style' in which film-makers express their personal concerns. Sometimes film-makers are said to master the mise en scène competently, but the overall meaning is not perceived as their own, in which case they qualify as metteurs en scène rather than true auteurs. In auteur study, these criteria provide one way of distinguishing between 'good' and 'routine' or 'bad' films and directors.

The distinction auteur/metteur en scène led to some unfortunate evaluations by film critics, and to some critical pantheons originating in, and supporting, subjective tastes (see The auteur theory, p. 410). It had its roots in the traditional division between 'art' and 'entertainment' that had previously prevented cinema from being taken seriously. Part of the 'scandal' created by the *politique* was caused by its application of such criteria to popular American cinema, generally thought of as mass entertainment and incompatible with the interests of art proper.

Alfred Hitchcock

For the *Cahiers* auteur critics, Alfred Hitchcock was the classic auteur: a master of cinematic mise en scène who created an unmistakable and homogeneous worldview, controlling the audience so that they were completely at the mercy of his intentions. Hitchcock's habit of making cameo appearances in his films contributed further to the myth, but more than this his worldview is intimately bound up with the mechanisms of cinematic language and the relationship of spectator to film. Many of Hitchcock's films deal with the activity of looking or spying, given a centrality that transcends the plot, so it can be argued that a narrative of human psychology emerges in which characters and cinema audience are involved in a play of exchange of looks. This drama of exchange opens up a scene of obsession, guilt, paranoia and phobia in which author, characters and audience are all implicated, but which Hitchcock as author ultimately controls (see Wollen, 1969).

It was this aspect of Hitchcock's work, interpreted as raising serious questions of morality, that intrigued and influenced many *Cahiers* critics and film-makers, especially Claude Chabrol, Eric Rohmer and François Truffaut, whose films contain many direct references to Hitchcock (see Truffaut, 1968).

Cahiers' approach was echoed by Robin Wood (1978), who argued that Hitchcock's American work not only explored moral dilemmas through its obsessional characters, but also included the audience in the drama, forcing them to acknowledge previously unrecognised moral ambiguities in themselves. Raymond Bellour (1977), writing under the influence of French structuralist and psychoanalytic theory, used Hitchcock's work to demonstrate the closed structure, in formal and ideological terms, of the classic Hollywood text.

Many of Hitchcock's films use the detective or spy genre as a pretext for exploring the predatory aspects of human behaviour, be it in a sexual or a political context. It has been argued, using psychoanalytical concepts that attempt to go beyond 'Hollywood Freud', that Hitchcock's work exemplifies a cinema in which voyeurism and scopophilia (the drive to look) are manipulated in such a way that 'the male gaze' (of author, characters and spectators) predominates, thus raising the question of the subordinate place of women in Hollywood cinema. Victim and predator may seem at some points to be interchangeable in Hitchcock's work but ultimately, the argument goes, the drama is resolved in favour of the male and at the expense of the female, confirming patriarchal ideology. Hitchcock's work is seen as drawing attention to that ideology, at the same time as representing its apotheosis (see Mulvey, 1989; see also Feminist film theory, p. 491). Hitchcock's interest in the drama of looking is not only reflected in his choice of the investigative thriller genre as a form of expression: he is considered a master of the classic point-of-view structure in which a shot of a character looking is edited together with a shot of what they are looking at. This structure has been identified as a basic element of continuity in Hollywood narrative cinema (see Classic Hollywood narrative, p. 45) and Hitchcock uses it frequently to build narrative suspense. He also breaks the rules of continuity to destabilise audience expectations and create a sense of unease.

The *Cahiers* auteur critics who championed Hitchcock saw him as the major exponent of cinema at its most pure. They liked his manipulation of the language of editing because it corresponded to their own interests as film-makers, and because the worldview expressed was that of the isolated individual trapped in a hostile world not of his or her own making, an alienation manifested in Hitchcock's use of the fragmentation of montage editing. Later theoretical work (for example, Mulvey, 1989; Modleski, 1988) attempted to reassess Hitchcock's films in terms of ideology rather than the criteria of the 'purely cinematic'. More recently, critics have drawn attention to the influence of Hitchcock's experiences in the UK on his American films (for example, Wood, 1989; Barr, 1999), while Hitchcock's contribution to building his own status as auteur has been documented (see Kapsis, 1992).

In order to establish Hitchcock as a true auteur, the critic must be able to trace the development of a consistent theme, expressed in a style that is perfectly suited to that theme, across all his films. The films that do not fit the critic's construction of Hitchcock's worldview are either ignored, or treated as minor or flawed works. These gaps and inconsistencies can provide the basis of a challenge to traditional auteur study by drawing attention to its partial approach, and to the need for a historical analysis to explain those films considered uncharacteristic.

Selected Reading

André Bazin, 'Hitchcock versus Hitchcock', in LaValley (ed.), *Focus on Hitchcock*, Englewood Cliffs, NJ, Prentice-Hall, 1972.

Robert E. Kapsis, *Hitchcock: The Making of a Reputation*, Chicago, University of Chicago Press, 1992.

Tania Modleski, *The Women Who Knew Too Much: Hitchcock and FeministTheory*, New York, Routledge, 1988.

Robin Wood, *Hitchcock's Films Revisited*, New York, Columbia UniversityPress, 1989.

ALFRED HITCHCOCK

Blackmail (UK 1929 *p.c* – British International Pictures; *d* – Alfred Hitchcock)

Hitchcock worked in the UK until 1939; his films of this period were dismissed for many years as inferior to his American work, until they became the subject of a major reassessment (see Wood, 1989; Ryall, 1996; Barr, 1999). As a young film-maker, he spent time in Germany where he encountered German aesthetics and working methods that formed one of many influences on his British work, in which he experimented with the technological possibilities of cinema. *Blackmail*, which was made in silent and sound versions, is one of the earliest British sound features, and uses disjunctures between sound and image characteristic of many of Hitchcock's films (see Weis, 1982).

The story concerns a young woman, Alice White (Annie Ondra), who kills a man who tries to rape her and is then blackmailed by an unscrupulous witness. As well as its innovative use of sound, the film features an experimental deployment of montage editing (cutting shots of the dead man's arm against shots of the heroine's legs as she walks home after the murder, building to the climax of the landlady's scream when she discovers the body) and of the zoom-in for dramatic effect. These devices both depict Alice's subjective state of mind and engage the audience's emotions, a strategy found in much of Hitchcock's work. *Blackmail* also plays with the 'act of looking', for example in the use of pictures that return the looks of the guilty protagonists: the jester looks mockingly at Frank, and the policeman looks sternly at Alice.

Alice can be seen as one of Hitchcock's earliest guilty, aberrant females (see also *Under Capricorn*, 1949; *Psycho*, 1960; *The Birds*, 1963; *Marnie*, 1964) and sound is employed expressively to stress her guilt.

Hitchcock plays with sound and image in *Blackmail*

The emphasis on the word 'knife' in the scene in which Alice is overwhelmed by fear of being found out is a particularly effective use of sound to portray her obsessional state of mind (Ryall, 1993).

PAM COOK

Foreign Correspondent (USA 1940 *p.c* – Walter Wanger Productions/United Artists; *d* – Alfred Hitchcock)

Between 1935 and 1938, Hitchcock made a cycle of British thrillers that brought him international renown. He moved to the US in 1939 and this was his second film made there (the first was the

Selznick-produced *Rebecca*, 1940). Not generally regarded as a major Hitchcock work, it nevertheless provides an example of transition between his British and American work, particularly in the use of comedy and parodied English stereotype characters, which traverse and disrupt the forward drive of the thriller narrative. Looking forward to later work, note the use of apparently innocent objects to suggest threat or problem (for example, the mass of umbrellas shot from above as the assassin escapes; the windmills that become a significant feature in the plot; the errant derby belonging to the comic Englishman that leads to a vital clue). Thus the director/auteur and the spectator share a joke initiated by the former, at the expense of, and for the pleasure of, the latter – a play with the spectator characteristic of both British and American Hitchcock. Joel McCrea's American reporter, like many of the protagonists in Hitchcock's thrillers, finds himself out of his depth on foreign territory (Europe on the brink of war).

PAM COOK

Mr. & Mrs. Smith (USA 1941 *p.c* – RKO Radio Pictures; *d* – Alfred Hitchcock)

Hitchcock's interest in the relationship between couples, which he portrays as perverse, can be found in most of his films. Often the couple is yoked together unwillingly, or under difficult circumstances, united by a sexual desire that is bound to be frustrated. This film shows the workings of male desire in its worst light: in order to reconcile himself with his wife, Ann (Carole Lombard), after she has thrown him out on discovering that their marriage is not legal, the hero David Smith (Robert Montgomery) must spy on and pursue her, and disrupt her plans to marry another man, causing everyone concerned acute embarrassment. Beneath the comedy lies the darker side of personal relationships: the sado-masochism of the male/female relationship, the overturning of social and moral codes under the impact of sexual desire, and the consequent prevalence of paranoia, which seems to be totally justified in Hitchcock's worldview.

PAM COOK

Shadow of a Doubt (USA 1943 *p.c* – Universal Pictures/Skirball Productions; *d* – Alfred Hitchcock)

One of Hitchcock's themes in which *Cahiers* critics (including Bazin) were particularly interested was the 'double' relationship between characters in which guilt was transferred from one to the other (see Bazin, 1972). One character takes on the features of another so that the question of a fixed identity attributable to one person becomes problematic: examples from Hitchcock's films would be *Strangers on a Train* (1951), *Psycho* (1960) and *Vertigo* (1958), although the theme appears frequently in some form. The concept is particularly disturbing when the relationship is between members of the same family, as in Psycho, where the identities of mother and son are fused and in conflict. It is rarely explicitly recognised, however, that this doubling of identities introduces a perverse sexual element into the narrative, and it is often this very perversity that motivates events.

In this film, the perverse doubling is between young Charlie Newton (Teresa Wright) and her adored Uncle Charlie (Joseph Cotten), who unknown to her is a murderer. Hitchcock uses two different genres to underline the splitting of the characters' identities: the thriller/film noir, to which the psychopathic killer belongs, and the small-town melodrama, locus of the 'nice' family into which he intrudes. Hitchcock was particularly fond of the thriller genre because of its potential for dramatising the splitting-of-identity theme, and he objected to the fact that Hollywood produced so many 'women's pictures', the category into which the small-town melodrama conventionally falls. Thus the trouble in the superficially normal family, trouble represented by naive Charlie and her fantasies of excitement, is given another disturbing dimension by the introduction into the scene of her 'double' and namesake, Uncle Charlie, visitor from another, much more sinister world.

PAM COOK

Under Capricorn (USA 1949 *p.c* – Transatlantic Pictures; *d* – Alfred Hitchcock)

By the late 1940s, Hitchcock's international reputation was well established. He co-produced many of his films of this period, and arguably had sufficient control in Hollywood to do as he wished (this film and *Rope* were made by the production company Hitchcock set up with Sidney Bernstein). In 1948, he experimented with long takes in *Rope*, only cutting when the film itself ran out and had to be replaced. This produced 10-minute-long takes that were unusual in Hitchcock's mise en scène, since the long take generally excludes the shot/reverse-shot point-of-view technique for which he is well known, and which forms the basis of his narrative suspense. *Under Capricorn*, a period costume melodrama set in Australia, is also a deviation from the usual Hitchcock method, employing long takes and moving camera and very little shot/reverse-shot, in a totally stylised manner. It could be argued that Hitchcock uses the moving camera in such a way as to draw attention to it as a camera, reminding the spectator that she or he is not actually present at the scene in the same way as the director. The camera movements are often gratuitous, independent of narrative or character; this device is reminiscent of the 'unchained camera' used by German film-makers in the 1920s. The scene in which Henrietta (Ingrid Bergman) comes down the staircase dressed for the ball, watched by her husband Sam (Joseph Cotten) and suitor Charles

(Michael Wilding), demonstrates an interesting use of the movement of a tracking shot into a close-up of the ruby necklace held behind Sam's back, which, the audience sees, he hurriedly hides. This shot replaces the conventional 'reaction shot' in which his feelings would be revealed by the expression on his face. It might be interesting to discuss how this substitution of shots affects the meaning of the scene, if at all, and what sort of position is created for the viewer in relation to the characters. It is characteristic of Hitchcock to emphasise small gestures in this way to create a sense of unease that cannot be easily explained.

PAM COOK

Psycho (USA 1960 *p.c* – Shamley Productions/ Paramount; *d* – Alfred Hitchcock)

After *Under Capricorn* and *Rope* were both unsuccessful, Transatlantic Pictures folded. *Psycho* was made by Hitchcock's company Shamley Productions, under which banner he produced many of his television series. It has been noted that in Hitchcock's films the viewer is often held in a state of anxiety that may or may not be resolved by the narrative (in *The Birds*, 1964, for instance, it is arguable that it is not). This 'mise en scène of anxiety' is played out on many levels, not least in the sexual relationships between characters. It has been argued (see Mulvey, 1989) that Hitchcock's films organise the play of looks between characters and cinema audience in terms of the dominance of the male (heterosexual) gaze. The relationship between male and female characters is perceived as a struggle based on dominance and subordination in which the former finally dominates the latter, thus neatly resolving the narrative in favour of patriarchal ideology. This account has been influential in discussion of the ideological implications of Hitchcock's films, especially in *Psycho*, where fear and guilt is induced in the female protagonist by the investigatory looks of male characters, and her inability to escape these looks places her in a subordinate and vulnerable position. The notorious knife attack on Marion Crane (Janet Leigh) in the shower could also be seen in terms of an attempt to link the 'look' of the camera and of the audience with the aggression of the stabbing, thus reducing the female protagonist to the status of object rather than subject: the female transgressor is not, as she thought, in command of her own destiny, the power of the 'look' is taken from her (the image of Marion's dead, unseeing eye is significant in this respect) and she is fixed as an object.

Hitchcock with Janet Leigh on the *Psycho* set

However, it can also be argued that the question of sexuality is complicated in *Psycho* by the fact that both Marion Crane and Norman Bates (Anthony Perkins) have masculine and feminine characteristics. Like many of Hitchcock's heroines (see *Blackmail*, 1929; *Marnie*, 1964; *The Birds*, 1963), Marion transgresses conventional gender roles by becoming active rather than passive, by becoming a thief in order to get what she wants. Similarly, although Norman as voyeur is male, and his 'look' at Marion could be assumed to be male, as a killer he is bisexual (part mother/part son), and this gender ambiguity (we never know which part is dominant) is unresolved at the end, even though it is 'explained' by the psychiatrist. Indeed, it could be argued that Norman's dead mother is at least partly responsible for his aggression towards women. What kind of fantasy/pleasure is evoked for the spectator when the boundaries of 'male' and 'female' are destabilised in this way (see Modleski, 1988; Williams, 2000)?

PAM COOK

The Birds (USA 1963 *p.c* – Alfred J. Hitchcock Productions/Universal; *d* – Alfred Hitchcock)

This is one of three Hitchcock films based on Daphne du Maurier's fiction (see also *Jamaica Inn*, 1939; *Rebecca*, 1940). Wilful young socialite Melanie Daniels (Tippi Hedren), like many Hitchcock heroines, takes destiny into her own hands and pursues rugged Mitch Brenner (Rod Taylor) to his home in Bodega Bay on the California coast, reversing the conventional male/female roles. In doing so, she appears to trigger an inexplicable attack by hordes of malevolent birds on the Bodega Bay community, culminating in a horrific assault on Melanie herself by the birds. The film compares with *Psycho* in that it shows an independently curious woman, an active subject, as the object of violent aggression and punishment. The theme of aggression is manifested at the level of mise en scène in the use of montage, low-angled shots and the composition of characters within the frame based on disequilibrium.

There is a characteristic Hitchcockian use of point of view in the scene in which Melanie, motivated by curiosity and dread, moves towards the stairs and the attic door behind which the birds are massing. This strategy serves a double function: to build suspense from the rhythm of shot/reverse-shot, and to emphasise Melanie's subjectivity through point of view before she is reduced to a senseless victim following the vicious bird attack in the attic. Immediately after Melanie regains consciousness, she looks straight into the camera and defends herself with flailing arms against its 'look', equating it with an act of aggression.

Hitchcock mixes genres once again, as the romantic melodrama becomes a science-fiction horror story in which the apparently untroubled surface of a community (and Mitch's family) is radically disturbed. At the end of the film, as the traumatised characters attempt their escape, it is not at all clear that the threat and whatever caused it have been overcome.

PAM COOK

Marnie (USA 1964 *p.c* – Geoffrey Stanley Inc/ Universal; *d* – Alfred Hitchcock)

Marnie (Tippi Hedren), like Marion Crane in *Psycho* (and other Hitchcock heroines), challenges the social order: not only is she a compulsive thief who steals large sums of money from her employers but she is a mistress of disguise, changing her identity at will to avoid being caught. This double problematic (female aggression and masquerade) could be seen as particularly threatening to a society in which men control the exchange of money and the place of women. Characteristically, Hitchcock develops the explicitly sexual aspect of this problem through the relationship of dominance and subordination between Marnie and one of her 'victims', Mark Rutland (Sean Connery), who sets out to reform and control her: Marnie is an object of desire and curiosity for Mark because she is apparently impervious to his sexual allure. Mark's compulsive desire to master the problem provides the central drive of the narrative, and as usual in Hitchcock's films the characters are shown to be the victims of their own desires so that the narrative resolution (in which Mark brings about Marnie's 'cure') is profoundly ambiguous. Both protagonists are in the grip of their compulsions, but Mark's go unexamined; the 'problem' is displaced onto the female character. It has been argued that Hitchcock's films dramatise the place of woman in patriarchal society as the locus of male problems and fears (Mulvey, 1989; see also Modleski, 1988).

The opening scenes provide an illustration of this argument: the camera tracks the figure of the unknown woman in such a way as to mark her as an object of obsessive curiosity – the viewer sees what she does but is denied her face. The viewer watches as she substitutes one identity for another, washing black dye from her hair. Curiosity and suspense build until the shot in which she lifts her head and looks straight into the camera. The moment is explicitly erotic and marked as transgression: the rule 'Don't look at the camera' is broken as Marnie exchanges looks with the audience. Her subjective desire is explicitly marked as a threat, tinged with excitement, that motivates both Mark and the viewer to seek its cause and cure. As so often in Hitchcock, the relationship between the protagonists and the audience is seen as perverse and sado-masochistic.

PAM COOK

Auteur and studio

Orson Welles

Orson Welles's flamboyant personality, his turbulent relationship with the film industry and his struggles for artistic control have contributed to a critical consensus that ascribes style and meaning in the films to Welles himself. The fact that Welles directed, wrote and acted in most of them has given credibility to this view, and Welles himself has supported it:

> Theatre is a collective experience, but cinema is the work of a single man, the director ... You've got to have all your helpers, all the necessary collaborators; it's a collective endeavour, but in essence a very personal outcome, much more than the theatre to my mind, because film is something dead, a band of celluloid like the blank sheet on which you write a poem. A film is what you write on the screen. (Welles, quoted in Wollen, 1977, p. 26)

In the context of 1940s Hollywood studio production, this view perpetuates the myth of the lone individual struggling against the dictates of a monolithic commercial organisation, the industry, which prioritises profit rather than art. The idea that cinema is produced in the same mode as writing (which echoes Astruc's argument for the *caméra-stylo*, see p. 390) is hardly tenable in the context of Hollywood studio production, where 'writing' (the script) is a separate area of work, often (though not always) placed lower in the hierarchy than that of the director.

Nevertheless, Welles's persistent struggle against the interference of the industry makes his films illuminating examples of cinema authorship at a time when the studio system in Hollywood was robust, and studio control over the process of production was such that the contribution of the director was often effaced altogether. However, as Welles himself was aware, that contribution was dependent on other factors than the presence of 'genius' and 'personal vision': 'If I were producer–director, if I had a financial interest in the production, it would all be different. But my services are hired and on salary alone I was at the mercy of my bosses' (Welles, quoted in Wollen, 1977, p. 26).

The legend of Orson Welles (his dazzling artistic virtuosity that could not survive in the philistine world of Hollywood, condemning him to wander from country to country, working when and where he could) has by and large determined the way in which his work has been approached by critics. Even when it has provoked bitter controversy (see Kael, 1971), that work is generally seen in terms of authorship, rather than in historical terms for its place in the development of studio technology, for instance, or as an indication of the politics of 1930s and 1940s Hollywood (see, however, Carringer, 1992; Mulvey, 1992). Welles came to the film industry from radical theatre and radio, a political and aesthetic background that may have clashed with the prevailing ideology of the studio system, but nevertheless found a place there, however unstable. His films appear markedly different from other studio products of the time in that they combined the techniques of deep-focus photography, wide-angled lenses, upward-tilting shots, lighting from below, long tracking shots and sets with ceilings in ways that went against the grain of the prevalent realist aesthetic. At the same time, they take full advantage of studio resources and technology.

These stylistic differences were glossed over by Bazin, who greatly admired the films of Orson Welles – surprisingly, since those films depend above all on the techniques of 'expressive montage' that Bazin was arguing against, and Welles's style is hardly 'self-effacing' (see Bazin, 1978). All his films have a distinctive mise en scène and a consistent worldview (see the interview in Wollen, 1977). It is difficult to see how Welles's films correspond to Bazin's ideas about the 'democratic' realism offered by the development of deep-focus photography at this point in cinema history. For this reason they can be useful in testing Bazin's argument (see André Bazin, p. 390) and to test the assumptions of auteur theory by looking at Welles's work in terms of its productive tensions with the studio system and the industry of 1940s Hollywood.

Selected Reading

André Bazin, 'William Wyler or the Jansenist of *mise-en-scène*', in Williams (ed.), *Realism and the Cinema*, London, Routledge and Kegan Paul/BFI Publishing, 1980.

Robert L. Carringer, *The Making of 'Citizen Kane'*, Berkeley, University of California Press, 1992.

Laura Mulvey, *Citizen Kane*, London, BFI Publishing, 1992.

ORSON WELLES

Citizen Kane (USA 1941 *p.c* – Mercury Productions/RKO Radio Pictures; *d* – Orson Welles)

One of the most critically highly rated films of all time, *Citizen Kane* is regarded by many as an example of the young Orson Welles's artistic genius; he produced, co-wrote (with Herman J. Mankiewicz), starred in and directed the film – an apparently classic case of cinema authorship. In spite of the fact that Welles acknowledged the importance of cinematographer Gregg Toland's contribution, and others have debated whether scriptwriter Mankiewicz is the real author of the film (see Kael, 1971), *Citizen Kane* retains its reputation as the first Wellesian masterpiece, a stylistic tour de force that continues to hold canonical status. Stylistic virtuosity is one of the film's primary pleasures, not least the knowing play with the conventions of Hollywood cinema (the biopic genre, the March of Time newsreels) that makes it notably different from studio films of the time. André Bazin (1978) hailed *Citizen Kane* as inaugurating a new period in cinema: a break with Russian 'expressive montage' and the shot/reverse-shot editing of American narrative films in the 1930s, in favour of the democratic realism of deep-focus photography. Welles and his collaborators employed a variety of cinematic techniques for symbolic rather than realistic effects: deep-focus photography, low-angled shots and the constructed ceilings made necessary by depth of field, wide-angle shots, overlapping dialogue and whip-pans in the marriage sequence. Deep-focus photography combines with shot/reverse-shot, sound and lighting to symbolise the increasing distance and alienation between Kane and his second wife, Susan Alexander (Dorothy Comingore). In some cases, special effects are used to give the impression that the camera achieves the impossible (for example, in the rooftop sequence).

Kane himself is the kind of ambiguous hero who recurs in Welles's films. Welles's populism ensures that the film is on one level critical of Kane, his will

Wellesian masterpiece: Joseph Cotten and Orson Welles in *Citizen Kane*

to power and inevitable moral decline (Wollen, 1969). Kane's story is told after his death by a succession of 'witnesses' from different perspectives and has the quality of detective fiction. However, the film's basis in melodrama gives its theme a tragic dimension: Kane is a villain almost in spite of himself, a tragic hero caught in contradictions he cannot control. Reputedly, Kane was loosely based on William Randolph Hearst, a newspaper tycoon with massive interests in the film industry. The legal action taken by Hearst failed to prove the connection, but it delayed the release of the film and made it difficult for RKO to find bookings, and Welles was never allowed such artistic freedom again (RKO Radio Pictures, p. 38).

Citizen Kane is interesting from a number of perspectives: as part of the Welles oeuvre; for its technical virtuosity, made possible by the studio technology of the time; in relation to the power politics of the Hollywood industry; and for its enduring place in critical pantheons, in spite of its box-office failure.

PAM COOK

The Magnificent Ambersons (USA 1942 *p.c* – Mercury Productions/RKO Radio Pictures; *d* – Orson Welles)

Citizen Kane was something of a critical success, but it was not commercially successful. Welles had a similar production set-up at RKO for *The Magnificent Ambersons* (his own company of actors and the technical resources of the studio at his disposal) but the studio took a much greater part in supervising the film to make sure that this time it recouped their investment (RKO Radio Pictures, p. 38).

The film's central figure is once again an egocentric male protagonist (Tim Holt) whose arrogance finally causes his downfall. The story concerns the disintegration of an aristocratic American family under pressure of social change, but the social dimension was submerged by the studio's insistence on emphasising the melodramatic elements of the film, and cutting it accordingly.

Welles's style, which consists of a combination (or rather conflict) of opposing strategies, such as moving versus static camera, close-up versus long takes, light versus dark, whispering versus shouting, gives the world created in the film a sense of turmoil and upheaval. Characteristically, it is fragmentation and contradiction that dominate rather than unity; however, this fragmentation, manifested in the behaviour of the protagonists and the dissolution of the family and its traditions, is not only characteristic of Welles's worldview: it is prevalent in Hollywood cinema of the 1940s, for example in film noir (Film noir, p. 38). Welles may have been less of an anomaly in Hollywood than is sometimes thought.

PAM COOK

Touch of Evil (USA 1958 *p.c* – Universal Pictures; *d* – Orson Welles)

It is arguable that Welles's best films were made in Hollywood, where he had the resources of the studios at his disposal, and where his turbulent relationship with the industry created the conditions in which he became established as an auteur. Although he participated in many films, particularly as an actor, his own output was relatively small and he had numerous uncompleted projects, a symptom of the mutual distrust with which director and studio regarded one another. In the context of Hollywood production values, the demands of narrative, genre, the star system and the need to produce commercially viable products, the baroque world and flamboyant style of Welles's films may seem self-indulgent, asserting the value of art and the artist against commerce. Yet this stylistic excess has been seen as testing the limits of Hollywood studio production, threatening to overturn them and therefore revealing them as limits (see Heath, 1975).

Touch of Evil was directed by Welles after an absence from the Hollywood industry lasting ten years; for much of that time he worked in Europe. The film ran into problems with Universal, who gave Welles carte blanche throughout the shooting, then prevented him from completing the cutting, and cut some of it themselves. Welles's grotesque portrayal of bloated, corrupt cop Hank Quinlan dominates the film, a drama about drugs and murder set on the US–Mexican border.

Welles's excessive style is manifested in extreme camera angles and violent fragmentation of shots, and in low-key light/dark contrasts typical of Expressionist mise en scène and of film noir. Excess is also marked in the extensive use of tracking camera that underlines the obsessional 'tracking' of Quinlan by morally upright drugs investigator Mike Vargas (Charlton Heston). The sense of a perverse, nightmarish world is emphasised by the mise en scène, and by the way Vargas is shown struggling to follow and eavesdrop on Quinlan, a struggle with which the spectator is encouraged to identify, but which, because of its marked perversity, brings the relationship between the two men into question. Although Quinlan is depicted as evil and must be exposed by Vargas, it could be argued that Welles pushes at the limits of the conventions to question the narrative resolution, implicating the spectator in questions of moral ambiguity. The use of the border as a setting, and the reversal of ethnic stereotypes (the Hispanic Vargas is the one with principles, while the American cop Quinlan is completely amoral), adds further ambiguity.

Welles's stylistic and thematic concerns were generally consistent, especially in those films he made in Hollywood. A comparison of his Hollywood films with those he made outside of the Hollywood studio system could be useful in exploring the notion that artistic freedom is only possible outside the constraints of commodity film production.

PAM COOK

The Nouvelle Vague

The Nouvelle Vague (French New Wave) covers a brief period in French cinema history from 1959 to around 1965, when certain historical, technological and economic factors combined to enable some young film-makers to influence French cinema in very diverse ways (The Nouvelle Vague, p. 202). When Roger Vadim's film *And God Created Woman/Et Dieu … créa la femme*, 1956) was a commercial success in spite of being made on a low budget, the French industry opened its doors temporarily to low-budget production. Technological developments contributed to keeping costs low and enabled film-makers to experiment with lightweight, cheaper equipment and stock. Many young film-makers started out as critics, concerned with attacking the likes of René Clément, Jean Delannoy, Henri-Georges Clouzot and others who made up the established French quality cinema.

It suddenly became possible for a group of young French film-makers to experiment with expressing their personal concerns on film, to become auteurs in their own right. They admired the technical skill and the personal vision of the great Hollywood directors: much of their work is in homage to them. At the same time, they celebrated low-budget American B-features, and they wanted to experiment with new cinematic forms in opposition to established genres and stereotypes. They borrowed widely from the rich traditions offered by the great moments of world cinema, giving them a new immediacy made possible by technological and economic developments. The Nouvelle Vague took cinema out of the studio and into the streets, celebrating its newfound possibilities.

As might be expected, this cinema of experiment and change could not continue to be commercially successful, and by 1964 the backers had seen enough box-office failures to make them more cautious. The experimental flowering died for the most part. Some film-makers were absorbed into the industry; a few survived outside it, to continue to make films that have influenced world cinema and whose directors have, like their Hollywood mentors, achieved the status of auteur in the eyes of the critical establishment (see Kinder and Houston, 1972, p. 181).

The economic and ideological context in which the French New Wave emerged is discussed elsewhere (see The Nouvelle Vague, p. 202). Between 1959 and 1965, the work of the Nouvelle Vague directors was particularly interesting in relation to the *politique des auteurs* and its defence of popular American cinema.

Jean-Luc Godard

Jean-Luc Godard has continued to be the most radically experimental and the most politically aware of the Nouvelle Vague directors, constantly raising new problems that are formal, to do with cinematic and other kinds of language; political, to do with transforming existing social structures; and intellectual, concerned with the history of ideas (see Williams, 1971/72).

As one of the *Cahiers* critics who argued polemically for the artistic value of popular cinema, Godard made films that not only reflected those concerns, but also had far-reaching implications for film-making as well as theoretical film criticism. His films constantly refer outside themselves to other films, other traditions, using this method of inter- and extra-textual reference and quotation to bring together apparently incompatible ideas and forms to contradict and conflict with each other. Arguably, it is this process of questioning and transformation that makes Godard such an important and influential modern director. During the upheavals of 1968 and after in France, Godard, like many intellectuals, became politicised and his film-making practice changed. The pre-1968 films are discussed here in the historical context of the Nouvelle Vague and its relationship to the *politique des auteurs* (see Auteurism, Godard and counter-cinema, p. 467).

JEAN-LUC GODARD

Breathless/À bout de souffle (France 1960 *p.c* – SNC/Productions Georges de Beauregard/Impéria; *d* – Jean-Luc Godard)

This was Godard's first feature, and one of the earliest Nouvelle Vague films to be financially successful. Godard scripted and directed the film, but he collaborated with Claude Chabrol and François Truffaut, and with cinematographer Raoul Coutard. In addition, editor Cécile Decugis has been credited with the jump-cuts that are so important to the film's rough-edged style. Nouvelle Vague film-makers often worked together, although each had different concerns and developed in different directions. The film can be seen as a tribute to Hollywood, particularly low-budget crime films, but the Hollywood homage is ambivalent, as the French 'hero' is destroyed by his obsession with all things American.

The plot is inspired by the American gangster movie, and petty criminal Michel (Jean-Paul Belmondo) models himself on the iconic Humphrey Bogart, mimicking his image on movie posters. The references to other films, and to other popular forms such as comics or newspapers, are employed to show that film is an intertextual medium, made up of influences from other arts. It is not simply a question of filling the film with 'in-jokes', although this is part of the pleasure in watching it, but of bringing diverse elements into conflict. For example, the documentary style of the film and its use of real locations conflict with the allusions to Hollywood stereotypes to reveal the conventional nature of both: neither can be seen as embodiments of 'truth'. However, the exuberant use of hand-held moving camera in this case appears to support the romantic celebration of individual freedom that underpins many Nouvelle Vague films, and the philosophy of the *politique des auteurs*.

This celebration is given an ironic twist as the amoral Michel's fascination with American popular culture and his independent American girlfriend (Jean Seberg) leads to his betrayal and death. He is also typical of the aimless protagonists of European art cinema (Authors in art cinema, p. 389).

The low-budget, spontaneous quality (natural lighting, natural sound and fast-moving hand-held

Sami Frey, Anna Karina and Claude Brasseur mimic the American musical in *Bande à part*

35mm camera) combined with use of real locations are played off against Hollywood studio production. At this stage in his career, Godard tried to encourage critical insight in the audience without losing the pleasurable experience that cinema offers.

PAM COOK

The Outsiders/Bande à part (France 1964 *p.c* – Anouchka Films/Orsay Films; *d* – Jean-Luc Godard)

Godard's films from this period have influenced a new generation of film-makers (Quentin Tarantino, for example, named his production company Band Apart). The title refers to a group of renegade outsiders (Anna Karina, Sami Frey and Claude Brasseur), thieves who prey on bourgeois society, but are doomed to failure. Based on a popular American thriller (*Fool's Gold* by Dolores Hitchens), the plot has been stripped down to its basic elements, resisting direct involvement or identification.

Nevertheless, the spontaneity (almost childlike innocence) of the protagonists is extremely seductive, and is celebrated on one level. The self-reflexive mixing of genre conventions has the effect of denaturalising them; for example, the romantic isolation of the characters is set against their dance, which is a knowing reference to the American musical. As with *A bout de souffle*, the mimicking of American cinema by French characters is both lighthearted and tragic. Godard invites viewers to celebrate, enjoy and criticise traditional pleasures offered by cinema.

The conventions of the thriller genre are reduced to their most schematic elements: for example, the climactic 'shootout' from which all tension is removed. The narrative conventions appear banal because of Godard's ironic treatment of them: they are revealed as conventions. The reworking of familiar forms and stereotypes to create new meanings here presages his radical work on cinematic language in later films.

PAM COOK

The Married Woman/Une femme mariée (France 1964 *p.c* – Anouchka Films/Orsay Films; *d* – Jean-Luc Godard)

Godard uses a banal plot – a melodrama of the affair between a bourgeois mother/housewife (Macha Méril) and her actor-lover (Bernard Noël) – to raise questions about cinematic language and social conditions.

The film plays with disjunctures between sound and image, visual and verbal signs, subjective monologues and documentary-style images, and positive and negative photographic images to reveal the interrelationship of different language systems, and the way they come together to make up cinema. He takes the different systems apart and recombines them to create new meanings (for example, through the use of visual/verbal puns), which is not simply an intellectual exercise, but a creative activity similar to that of modern poets.

The heroine's fragmented interior monologues are also akin to poetry, reflecting her status as woman/housewife/consumer rather than presenting her as a psychologically coherent character. The sequence of the lovers in bed, which is an explicit reference to another Nouvelle Vague film, Resnais's *Hiroshima, mon amour* (1959), uses the fade-out to fragment narrative. Godard's treatment of the central female protagonist here raises questions about the representation of women in his work overall.

PAM COOK

Pierrot le fou (France/Italy 1965 *p.c* – Rome-Paris Films/Productions Georges de Beauregard/Dino De Laurentiis Cinematografica; *d* – Jean-Luc Godard)

This is another adaptation of a popular novel (*Obsession* by Lionel White) where Godard disrupts the fiction in order to question the romantic aspirations of the protagonists. The debt to Hollywood is evident in the use of the gangster film theme of the couple on the run from a hostile society, but the film uses various formal strategies to question the notion of escape. Its protagonists are doomed, by the conflict between their inner desires and the violence and corruption of society, to destruction. Godard uses CinemaScope and colour to emphasise the seductive nature of their dream of an idyllic paradise. However, social reality constantly interrupts the idyll, and the pair are driven back into society, which finally kills them. In spite of Godard's evident ambiguity towards politics at this stage, the film anticipates the explicitly political concerns of later work.

The central theme is that of the escape of the young couple from civilisation. Godard's strategy of fragmenting the narrative by juxtaposing written texts with film image is much in evidence. Godard has often been accused of a puritanical distrust of the seductive potential of the cinematic image: here, Scope and colour emphasise the lush beauty of the fantasy island, while written texts constantly intrude to 'jog' the spectator out of the fiction in the direction of politics.

The film's basic romanticism is conservative in some respects: for example, in the representation of Marianne (Anna Karina) as instinctual and Ferdinand (Jean-Paul Belmondo) as the thinker, and in the anarchism of Ferdinand's final nihilistic gesture of self-destruction: the only alternative, it would seem, to utopianism.

PAM COOK

Masculine Feminine/Masculin féminin 15 faits précis (France/Sweden 1966 *p.c* – Anouchka Films/Argos-Films/Svensk Filmindustri/Sandrews;*d* – Jean-Luc Godard)

Masculin féminin looks forward to later Godard in which political questions are raised more explicitly. The problem presented here is the relationship between the 'personal' and the 'political'. The hesitant, tentative relationship between two young people (a man involved in Communist Party politics and a woman involved in herself and pop music) is used as the basis for an enquiry into sexual relationships and the representation of sexuality.

The narrative is divided into sections, or 'acts', indicating Godard's growing interest in Brecht's theories of epic theatre and the use of tableaux to break up narrative fiction. Note the use of the 'interview' sequence to disrupt identification with characters.

Godard can be seen to be moving towards a rigorous theoretical style in which camera movement, long takes and editing are used in an abstract manner to foreground and question the language of cinema. This strategy attempts to place the spectator in a critical position vis-à-vis the film (and its protagonists), raising the question of pleasure, a question that for Godard was a political priority (as indeed it was for Brecht).

In the context of the Nouvelle Vague, Godard's use of Jean-Pierre Léaud can be compared with the actor's different treatment in films by François Truffaut. In the 'interview' sequence, Paul (Léaud) answers that 'la tendresse' is the most important thing in his life: a reference to Truffaut, who had become associated with this expression, and to Léaud's appearance in Truffaut's films. This intertextual reference, a form of quotation, has the effect of emphasising the fact that Léaud is an actor, and a 'sign' whose meaning can change according to different contexts. The difference is significant, since Godard's project is, increasingly, to criticise notions of human spontaneity and freedom, whereas Truffaut is often concerned to celebrate them, and to mourn their loss.

PAM COOK

Critical positions in *Masculin féminin*

François Truffaut

Truffaut's critical writing for *Cahiers du cinéma* in the 1950s was passionate and flamboyant, denouncing established French cinema in favour of the technical expertise, inventiveness and 'personal vision' of certain Hollywood films (Howard Hawks, Raoul Walsh, Samuel Fuller, John Ford and above all Alfred Hitchcock) and of 1930s French cinema (Jean Renoir in particular). Truffaut's article 'A certain tendency of the French cinema' (1954) was important in marking the critical shift towards the *politique des auteurs* by the *Cahiers* critics. Yet Truffaut's importance as a polemical critic does not seem to be carried over into his films. Unlike Godard, who has constantly tested and developed his critical and theoretical ideas with an intellectual toughness that has allowed him to grow and change, Truffaut (one of the Nouvelle Vague directors who survived to found his own production company) seems to have remained locked within a conservative romantic ideology (which is indeed one strand within the auteurist position) and his work – influenced by French cinema of the 1930s, the films of Alfred Hitchcock and the American B-picture – has remained within the conventions of narrative cinema. According to Don Allen:

> The word 'revolutionary' might be applied to Truffaut in two senses only. First because he was committed to the violent destruction by spectacular critical attacks of what he judged bad; secondly, and more literally, because 'revolution' for him has implied turning the wheel back to his cinematic golden age, the 30s. The cinema which Truffaut advocates is firmly based on the best characteristics of this period, and in particular on the total authorship and consequent directional freedom of such lyrical film creators as Jean Renoir and Jean Vigo. (Allen, 1974, p. 13)

Selected Reading

Colin MacCabe, *Godard: A Portrait of the Artist at Seventy*, London, Bloomsbury, 2003.

François Truffaut, 'A certain tendency of the French cinema', *Cahiers du cinéma* 31, January 1954. Translated in Nichols (ed.), *Movies and Methods Vol. I*, Berkeley, University of California Press, 1976.

FRANÇOIS TRUFFAUT

The 400 Blows/Les Quatre cents coups (France 1959 *p.c* – Films du Carosse/SEDIF; *d* – François Truffaut)

The films Truffaut made with Jean-Pierre Léaud playing Antoine Doinel (as a boy, then growing up into an increasingly conformist young man) are reputed to be based loosely on the director's own life. Truffaut has endorsed this view, and his appearance as an actor in some of his films seems to confirm the personal nature of his work.

Elements of this autobiographical mode deserve to be explored further. Jean-Pierre Léaud/Antoine Doinel may 'stand for' François Truffaut, but other factors intrude to complicate any simple idea of self-expression. *Les Quatre cents coups*, for instance, owes much to Jean Vigo's 1933 film about young boys at a strict boarding school, *Zéro de conduite*, while the use of camera movement to capture 'real space' is reminiscent of 1930s Renoir films. In the late 1950s and early 1960s, films about young people were common; indeed several of the Nouvelle Vague film-makers worked with this topic. It could be argued that Léaud/Doinel represents much more than 'Truffaut'.

Truffaut's interest in the theme of individual freedom and spontaneity is manifested in the opposition between sequences shot on location in Paris, where the camera is moving, tracking and panning, and closed interior scenes, where the camera is predominantly static. Motion is used to represent freedom (Antoine and René are constantly running) and stasis to represent confinement, a structural polarisation that runs through the film. Arguably, the presence of structure questions the idea of absolute freedom, since it is only in opposition to confinement that freedom exists (see Kinder and Houston, 1972). This is the question that underlies the final shot of the film: a freeze-frame in which Antoine, free at last from reform school, is left totally alone in a reductio ad absurdum of romantic individualism.

PAM COOK

Jules and Jim/Jules et Jim (France 1962 *p.c* – Films du Carosse/SEDIF; *d* – François Truffaut)

Truffaut's concern with exploring the complexities of the idea of individual freedom is worked through in *Jules et Jim*, which was an adaptation of the novel by Henri-Pierre Roché. The representative of spontaneity here is a woman, and the effects of her behaviour are reflected in the triangular relationship between herself and Jules (Oskar Werner) and Jim (Henri Serre) rather than in any resistance to social institutions, as in *Les Quatre cents coups* (see Stam, 2006).

Catherine, played by Jeanne Moreau, represents the primitive forces that are both the source of creative activity (art) and the impulse behind mindless, nihilistic destruction. The social background is that of the bohemian intellectual spirit in Paris before World War I, fragmented and shattered by the war and the rise of Fascism. Jules and Jim have a peaceful and productive rapport that is transformed when Catherine enters their lives, and is never to be regained. She represents the freedom they desire, which ultimately destroys them and their relationship.

The disruptive force of Catherine's wild and instinctual impulses is manifested in her unease in her marriage to Jules, reflected in the use of a restless, wandering camera and the constant motion of the protagonists. The effects of displacing the

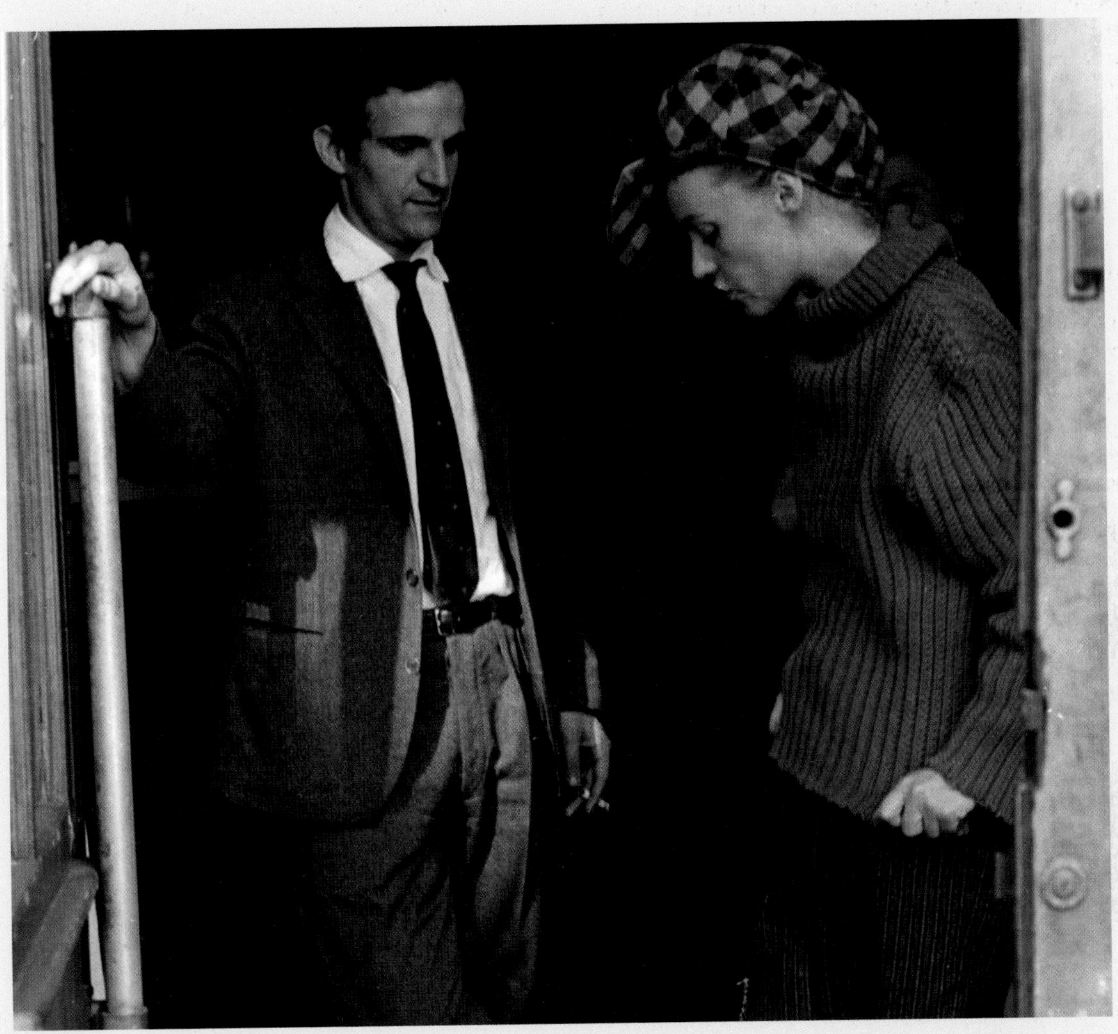

Truffaut directs Jeanne Moreau as Catherine on the set of *Jules et Jim*

contradictions inherent in the idea of individual freedom onto a female character is, it could be argued, to create her as a monster who constantly threatens the apparent stability of the male world. Jules and Jim are the victims of their own self-destructive fantasies, but the film does not explore the extent to which Catherine is also the victim of those fantasies.

PAM COOK

Silken Skin/La Peau douce (France 1964 *p.c* – Films du Carosse/SEDIF; *d* – François Truffaut)

One of Truffaut's preoccupations (shared by other Nouvelle Vague film-makers) was with the institution of marriage and the problem it presents for men, a theme also central to many Hollywood films. *La Peau douce* owes much to Hitchcock (for example, *Vertigo*, 1956) in its portrayal of a man trapped and destroyed by his desires. Like most Truffaut heroes, Pierre Lachenay (Jean Desailly) looks for freedom, which is conceived in terms of the options offered by bourgeois society, in this case an obsession with a young and beautiful mistress as a way out of a sterile marriage.

The film can be seen in terms of Truffaut's debt to American cinema, especially to the work of Hitchcock and his view of male sexuality as constantly under threat, manifested here in the use of a weak, obsessive hero destroyed by his own fantasies. It could usefully be compared with Claude Chabrol's *La Femme infidèle* (1968), in which Stéphane Audran plays an errant wife whose infidelity destroys her lover and her husband, to show contrasting treatment of the same theme, and with Agnès Varda's *Le Bonheur* (1965) – an ironic view of male fantasies from a woman's perspective (from the only woman director in the Nouvelle Vague; see p. 472).

PAM COOK

THE AUTEUR THEORY

PAM COOK

Andrew Sarris and American film criticism

Andrew Sarris wrote film criticism in the late 1950s when America was still embroiled in Cold War politics, which partly explains why he took up *Cahiers*' argument directed at the criteria of established film criticism (see Murray, 1975). Postwar American film criticism (typified perhaps by the writing of James Agee) had been primarily sociological, asserting the value of social realism. The best films, it was argued, were those 'quality' productions that dealt with serious social issues: this was how the 'art' of film was described. The 1940s and 1950s in Hollywood had produced a vast number of popular entertainment films in general dismissed by critics for their blatant commercialism, which was considered incompatible with serious art. The critical mood changed when in the 1950s, Hollywood began to sell old movies to television, making it possible for many people to re-view and reassess the earlier work of those directors considered to be at their peak in the 1950s.

In the late 1950s and early 1960s, Andrew Sarris wrote for small magazines such as *The Village Voice* and *Film Culture*, the locus of lively debate. Ironically, at the same time as he began arguing for the auteur theory and popular American cinema, that cinema and its mass audience were beginning to fragment and many of his friends were involved in actively opposing it through their film-making practice (in 1961, the New American Cinema Group published in *Film Culture* a 'revolutionary manifesto' for a new independent cinema in opposition to Hollywood). After the repressive climate of 1950s America, a cultural shift in the 1960s towards greater intellectual freedom enabled polemical writing to flourish. Sarris's critical polemic was directed against social realism in favour of formal concerns, against 'serious art' in favour of the 'art of popular cinema'. It had a double impetus: towards re-evaluating Hollywood films as worthy of critical consideration, and towards using the director as a criterion of value (rather than the stars, the screenwriter or the producer). This emphasis on the director and on formal concerns was linked to the postwar reorganisation of the Hollywood studio system and the growth of small-scale production facilities, which allowed greater individual access to technical resources: many artists in America had begun experimenting with 16mm film after the war, for instance. Some of the social conditions that gave rise to the French *politique des auteurs* also contributed to the emergence of the auteur theory in America. Although Sarris was not a film-maker, he came into contact with the Nouvelle Vague at the Cannes Film Festival in 1961 and spent a year in Paris in 1962 watching old Hollywood films at the Cinémathèque. He was the editor of the English-language version of *Cahiers du cinéma* published in London and New York, and was responsible for introducing the *politique des auteurs*, translated as the auteur theory and transformed into a system of evaluating and classifying Hollywood cinema. In *The American Cinema* (1968), Sarris was to establish a critical pantheon that graded directors according to the extent to which their personal vision transcended the hierarchical industrial system within which they worked.

Earlier, in 'Notes on the auteur theory in 1962' (1962/63), he had clarified his version of the auteur theory, which, he emphasised, was not prescriptive. It was a means of evaluating films a posteriori according to the director's technical competence, the presence of a distinct visual style and an interior meaning that arose precisely from the tension between directors and the conditions of production with which they worked. At this stage, auteurs were not limited to American cinema, but in *The American Cinema* Sarris elaborated his 'theory' (which might better be called a rationalisation) in terms of Hollywood cinema, and included some other major directors who were said to have influenced those working in Hollywood. Sarris never denied the importance of recognising both social conditions and the contributions of other workers besides the director in the production process, but he claimed that in the case of great directors, they had been lucky enough to find the proper conditions and collaborators for the full expansion of their talent. Nevertheless, he rarely, if ever, mentions collaborators and manages to summarise the career of Orson Welles without mentioning cinematographer Gregg Toland, screenwriter Herman J. Mankiewicz or production conditions. One of Sarris's most vocal opponents, Pauline Kael, devoted *The Citizen Kane Book* (1971) to the refutation of his theory that the director alone was the author of a film.

The basis of Sarris's argument in 1962 was the conviction that although it was impossible to deny the importance of history (the social conditions of production) in understanding any work of art, it was equally important not to reduce the work to its conditions of production. Recognition of the contribution of individual personal concerns was important therefore as part of the argument against sociological criticism, which saw film as a direct reflection of 'reality', without human mediation. To this extent he took issue with André Bazin (see p. 390) as well as with contemporary American film criticism.

Another important strand of his argument was the recognition of the artistic achievements of popular Hollywood cinema:

> After years of tortured revaluation, I am now prepared to stake my critical reputation, such as it is, on the proposition that Alfred Hitchcock is artistically superior to Robert Bresson by every criterion of excellence, and, further, that, film for film, director for director, the American cinema has been consistently superior to that of the rest of the world from 1915 through 1962. Consequently, I now regard the auteur theory primarily as a critical device for recording the history of the American cinema, the only cinema in the world worth exploring in depth beneath the frosting of a few great directors at the top. (Sarris, 1962/63, p. 130)

In his introduction to *The American Cinema*, Sarris developed this argument, classifying Hollywood in terms of its directors, and in terms of a hierarchy, running from 'pantheon directors' (the best) down to 'miscellaneous' (the least distinguished). Like any pantheon, Sarris's classifications are questionable, subject to personal taste and historical change. Nonetheless, it can be argued that the assumptions underlying his argument (that there are 'good' and 'bad' directors, 'good' and 'bad' films, and that these evaluations can be accounted for simply in terms of the auteur theory) are an important element in the way that films are consumed. Part of the pleasure in evaluating films is to be able to differentiate between 'good' and 'bad', and it is easy to forget that these judgments are both subjective and culturally specific. The auteur theory, in so far as it privileges one area of cinema over others, and the director over other factors in the process of production, encourages the acceptance of these assumptions as natural rather than open to question. However, Sarris's categories (and it is surprising how far they have continued to hold good in film studies) could be used to provoke questions. For example: what is the value of assessing the quality of a film, or body of films, according to the consistency of their 'worldview'? Does it matter which worldview is presented, and how?

'Pantheon directors': D. W. Griffith

Sarris argued that the history of American cinema could be written in terms of its great directors:

> Very early in his career, Griffith mastered most of the technical vocabulary of the cinema, and then proceeded to simplify his vocabulary for the sake of greater psychological penetration of the dramatic issues that concerned him ... The debt that all film-makers owe to D. W. Griffith defies calculation. Even before *The Birth of a Nation*, he had managed to synthesize the dramatic and documentary elements of the modern feature film. (Sarris, 1968, p. 51)

According to this argument, cinema history can be explained through the contribution of a few 'great men', and indeed, this is the way Griffith is usually regarded. His film career spanned the history of the industry from its beginnings to the introduction of sound, and in that time he played a major role in its development. He has been credited with inaugurating a specifically cinematic language (and style of acting), which was to become the basis of American narrative film through skilful editing together of panning shots, extreme long shots, full-screen close-ups and judicious use of split screen, dissolves, iris and other masking devices. This cinematic vocabulary was available to other film-makers working at that time, but Griffith's worldwide reputation among critics and film-makers as a pioneering artist of the cinema arose from the way in which he combined these elements to produce profoundly moving epic statements about history and its impact on the men and women who were caught up in it. He was not afraid to embark on extravagant experiments and broke away from the Biograph company in 1914 when his extravagance apparently became too much for them, and he set up his own production company, in partnership with others.

Despite the well-documented controversy surrounding the racist content of *The Birth of a Nation* (1915), Griffith's skill with editing and his experimental flair, although closely tied to narrative, were influential on film-makers all over the world. The montage tempo of *Intolerance* (1916), for instance, was admired by the cinematic avant-gardes in France and Russia for the way it managed to convey abstract ideas and feelings, taking the language of cinema much further than the one- or two-reel comedies and dramas produced within the studios (see Bordwell and Thompson, 1979, pp. 293–8). Griffith's films were also different for the way they dealt with the great epic themes of history and civilisation, investing cinema with a prestige generally denied it in relation to the other arts; at the same time, he tried to reach the widest possible audience by using popular forms such as melodrama to convey the 'humanity' of his characters. This combination of the epic and the personal, of history and melodrama, became the basis of classic Hollywood narrative cinema (see Early and pre-sound cinema, p. 3).

While there is no doubt that the exploitation of cinema's potential for spectacle and emotional involvement in Griffith's films was instrumental in establishing the artistic reputation of American cinema throughout the world, it is doubtful whether this great step forward can be put down to Griffith himself, as Sarris's argument (and others) would suggest. Griffith's work, and his auteur status were made possible by a combination of historical, technological, economic and ideological factors that formed the basis of the expansion of the Hollywood industry and its growing hegemony. Griffith's critical reputation as 'the father of American cinema' obscures the contribution of many of his collaborators, and of those other adventurous film-makers and entrepreneurs whose aesthetic experiments were equally important to the development of cinematic language (see Gunning, 1993; McMahan, 2002).

D. W. GRIFFITH

The Birth of a Nation (USA 1915 *p.c* – Epoch Producing Corp/David W. Griffith Corp; *d* – D. W. Griffith)

This film was Griffith's first major independent production; he had already directed well over 200 films by this stage. Large-scale epic production was not confined to Griffith: it was a feature of both the contemporary American and Italian cinema. The scale of the production envisaged by Griffith, his reputation for being intractable and the controversial subject matter discouraged investment from traditional sources, so that Griffith had to finance and distribute the film independently.

The Birth of a Nation is not only significant in relation to the development of Hollywood narrative cinema, but also in terms of its ideological implications, which are linked with its narrative structure. The combination of epic historical spectacle and family melodrama forms the basis here (as in other films) of a humanist ideology dedicated to individual freedom and the resolution of all contradictions of class, race and sex in terms of an ideal unity. In Part Two, where the Ku Klux Klan is depicted as saving the South from annihilation, unity is represented as the unity of whites against the emancipated blacks. This gives an ideological perspective on the value placed on family unity, and on the unity of the couple, in this film and other Griffith films. *The Birth of a Nation* was based on a racist novel, *The Clansman*, whose author Thomas Dixon Jr acted as consultant on the film, and its racist content has been the subject of much

Complex storylines and montage editing employed by Griffith in *Intolerance* were admired by film-makers across the world

controversy. Interesting comparisons have been drawn between Griffith's work and that of pioneer African-American film-maker Oscar Micheaux, which has also proved controversial (see African-American cinema, p. 77).

Griffith's development of cinematic narrative and spectacle, and his combination of historical epic and melodrama, demonstrates a particular use of narrative fiction films as powerful, moving political propaganda. When compared with Russian cinema of the time (Eisenstein and Pudovkin, for example), in spite of cross-fertilisation, ideological differences emerge. If the epic quality of *The Birth of a Nation* encourages us to forget the way it elides and suppresses contradictions because of its spectacular dimension, the Russians exploited cinematic strategies in order to produce contradiction and criticism: a very different view of the function of art, and the artist, in society.

PAM COOK

Intolerance (USA 1916 *p.c* – Wark Producing Corp/Majestic Motion Picture Co; *d* – D. W. Griffith)

Intolerance is considered to be a virtuoso work: those cinematic strategies that Griffith had been developing in earlier films came together here to form a complex and moving combination of technique and spectacle.

The narrative structure is based on the intercutting of four different stories illustrating social intolerance and its effects at different historical periods. Apart from the difficulty the spectator may have in following four separate plots, the variety of technical devices contributes to the overall effect of complexity that gives the film the quality of a historical tableau, or tapestry, in which detail is ultimately less important than the movement of history itself. How far can this effect be attributed to the intentions of Griffith? The translation of traditional material (the Modern Story is borrowed directly from popular melodrama, for instance) into a sophisticated, innovative cinematic language can be seen as a high point in Griffith's development of the multiple-plot narrative, and as a breakthrough in the silent cinema of this period. It was a time of technical innovation generally, in Hollywood and the rest of the world, and this film influenced film-makers in France and Russia. The Russians in particular admired its use of montage editing to bring together different stories and themes, and to manipulate the spectator's emotions, although it is debatable whether they would have subscribed to the theme of democracy based on individual freedom.

PAM COOK

Hearts of the World (USA 1918 *p.c* – D. W. Griffith; *d* – D. W. Griffith)

A combination of documentary and melodrama, this film's theme is the destructive effect of war on family and personal relationships. The scenes of war are spectacular, but in general the film underwrites the necessity of defending democracy and individual freedom by dwelling on the drama of personal suffering.

Some documentary footage was used, and the war provides the background to the drama, so that the film works as powerful humanist propaganda. Scenes of love, caring and happiness in the family and between the boy and girl are dwelt upon: this innocence is shattered by the war, and the girl in particular (played by Lillian Gish) is forced to come to maturity through personal suffering and unhappiness, a characteristic that became part of Gish's star persona. The suffering imposed on the family and the couple by the mobilisation order and the devastation of war is taken to almost grotesque lengths when the girl, distraught after the destruction of her village, finds the boy unconscious on the battlefield and lies down beside him.

PAM COOK

'The far side of paradise': Nicholas Ray

Sarris introduces Section II of *The American Cinema* thus: 'These are the directors who fall short of the pantheon either because of fragmentation of their personal vision or because of disruptive career problems' (Sarris, 1968, p. 83).

This second section is potentially more interesting than that of the 'Pantheon directors', because it raises the question of how far the idea of 'personal vision' can be maintained in the context of Hollywood studio production. For many auteur critics, Nicholas Ray was the supreme example of the artist whose vision transcended conditions of production; for others, he was the opposite: a Hollywood hack. The extremes of critical positions surrounding Ray's films match the extreme differences between those films, and the inconsistencies manifested by many of them. In some cases, the violence of the themes reverberates on the level of form so that they push the boundaries of the Hollywood codes of representation. Together with the myths surrounding Ray's dramatic conflicts with the Hollywood studio hierarchy, this contributes to an image of Ray as the archetypal romantic artist, in a continual state of crisis vis-à-vis the world (see also Orson Welles, p. 402). Paradoxically, the overall sense of crisis and fragmentation that characterises Ray's work, its 'unevenness', have made it possible for auteur critics to construct it as an oeuvre, seeing in its moments of perception a unified personal vision (see Perkins, 1972). Thus such radically different films as *They Live by Night* (1948), *Rebel Without a Cause* (1955) and *Johnny Guitar* (1954) can all be seen as manifestations of a theme of almost mythic dimensions: 'Moral crisis and salvation, a thirst for liberty, the clash of the individual and society, and the beauty of those ideals which men and women will pursue past all discretion to the point of their own annihilation' (Wilmington, 1973, p. 46).

Joan Crawford thirsts for liberty in *Johnny Guitar*

Sarris's call for a sense of proportion in relation to Ray's work, and his hint that it might be productive to look at the films from the point of view of Ray's relationship to the industry (Sarris, 1968, p. 107) is perceptive. The fragmentation of the director's worldview can be seen as the result of contradictory elements that highlight the difference between each film rather then their similarity, differences that can be attributed to their place in history and changing circumstances.

Ray's film career can be roughly divided into four phases: the years at RKO Studio (1948–52); an independent phase between 1954 and 1958; an 'epic' period (1961–3); and a final phase in which he rejected Hollywood completely, working in Europe and latterly in New York on underground, experimental projects. His best films are generally thought to belong to the first two phases, although there are several 'bad' films there too; by locating the films in their production context, the evaluations made according to the criteria of the auteur theory can be reassessed (see Andrew, 2004).

NICHOLAS RAY

They Live by Night (USA 1948 *p.c* – RKO Radio Pictures; *d* – Nicholas Ray)

Based on the novel *Thieves Like Us* by Edward Anderson, this was Nicholas Ray's first film for RKO, which at that time was in the 'progressive' hands of Dore Schary. Ray came from radical community theatre into postwar Hollywood; this is probably the only project he was able to film as he wished. The film, which belongs loosely in the sub-film noir category 'gangster couple on the run', is a sympathetic portrayal of the illusion of freedom cherished by the two young protagonists (Farley Granger and Cathy O'Donnell), forced to live outside the law and trying to realise their own desires from their position as outsiders. This attempt brings them into conflict with the system from which they are seeking to escape and which ultimately destroys them. The romanticism of the couple cannot be denied: their innocence and playful naivety might seem absurd, were it not for the fact that it is opposed to a hostile and threatening social system that allows no room for romantic fantasy. Meaning resides in this play of oppositions: from the point of view of the lovers, normality appears grotesque, yet their innocence is also unreal, and we know that they are doomed (see also *You Only Live Once*, 1937; *Bonnie and Clyde*, 1967; *Pierrot le fou*, 1965). Ray returned to the theme of rootless young people again (in *Knock on any Door*, 1949; *Rebel Without a Cause*, 1955), often depicting them at odds with social institutions such as the family or the legal system. The extent to which this theme in itself can be regarded as critical of American society provides an interesting area for debate: what is the role of genre, or narrative, for instance, in articulating such criticism? How far is social criticism possible within the classic Hollywood system of representation?

PAM COOK

On Dangerous Ground (USA 1952 *p.c* – RKO Radio Pictures; *d* – Nicholas Ray)

They Live by Night spent two years in the vaults of RKO before being released. Howard Hughes arrived at the studios, demanding personal approval on everything in the production process: consequently, Ray often found himself with uncongenial projects (*A Woman's Secret*, 1949; *Born to Be Bad*, 1950 – widely regarded as two of Ray's 'bad' films from this period).

The innocents: Farley Granger and Cathy O'Donnell on the run in *They Live by Night*

At the end of the 1940s, Ray was reunited with his sympathetic producer John Houseman and regained some of the control he had lost. He worked on the script of *On Dangerous Ground*, which can be seen as a development of preoccupations in *They Live by Night*, looking forward to later films.

The protagonists of this film are victims of a destructive society, which is mirrored in their own violence. Mise en scène and editing (Sarris called Ray's style 'kinetic') emphasise conflict and fragmentation, which is not seen as exclusive to city life, but has spread to the country too: the brutality of cop Jim Wilson (Robert Ryan) is seen as the effect of a social system built on repression of human desires. Characteristically, Ray depicts social repression as one of the root causes of psychological disturbance, but the psychologically disturbed hero was a common feature in Hollywood of the 1950s across many genres, as was the film's theme in which the policeman hero makes a journey from the urban landscape of the police thriller/film noir to the pastoral haven of the American countryside. In this film, the haven or sanctuary is fraught with danger, perversion and a sense of loss.

PAM COOK

The Lusty Men (USA 1952 *p.c* – Wald/Krasna Productions/RKO Radio Pictures; *d* – Nicholas Ray)

This film, Ray's last in black and white, was made at the end of his 'apprenticeship' with RKO; Mike Wilmington argues that he was surrounded by so many excellent collaborators that it is not easy to single out his contribution (Wilmington, 1973/74, p. 35).

All the RKO films might be regarded as 'work in progress': they are stylistically very different, even when a consistent theme can be detected in them. Yet all of Ray's oeuvre displays this stylistic inconsistency, manifesting a willingness to experiment and explore the limits of cinematic language. Victor Perkins (1972) constructs a coherent, unified auteur from this experimental principle. Alternatively, the Ray oeuvre could be seen as the site of multiple contributions, constantly shifting, in which the contribution of Nicholas Ray is sometimes dominant, sometimes not, according to the specific historical moment in which each film was produced, and the different contexts in which they are received.

In terms of Ray's treatment of genre, the thematic opposition between disorder (rootlessness) and normality (stability) is here transposed onto the rural setting of the rodeo film, a subgenre of the western. An opposition is drawn between 'rodeo' (male: rootlessness/isolation) and 'home' (female: stability/family), both terms seen as incompatible. Typically, the obsessions of the characters in the fiction, their inability to control their impulses, drive the narrative forward, and ultimately the problem is resolved through death.

In comparison with other Ray films, the muted (almost realistic) mise en scène gives this film a rigour and certainty of style that differs from the 'experimental' excess that is said to characterise Ray's oeuvre overall. Nonetheless, it can be argued that it occupies a pivotal place in that oeuvre, looking back to the concerns of earlier films and forward to *Johnny Guitar* (1954). The strength of Susan Hayward's portrayal of Louise Merritt is interesting in this respect. She seems to be the first of Ray's 'strong' heroines, to be developed in splendid ambiguity in *Johnny Guitar* (see Haskell, 1974), a film considered by some to be Ray's personal statement against the McCarthy witch-hunts (for example, Kreidl, 1977).

PAM COOK

Johnny Guitar (USA 1954 *p.c* – Republic Pictures Corp; *d* – Nicholas Ray)

Kreidl (1977) describes *Johnny Guitar* as a political western with a female hero, an anti-McCarthy parable made during self-imposed exile in Spain. In fact, the film was shot in Arizona; but certainly its theme of a disenchanted outsider (Sterling Hayden) who returns home to find a land ravaged by hatred, distrust and revenge that he must find the strength to resist is both characteristic of Ray's work and appropriate to Cold War America.

Kreidl argues that Ray is more clearly the sole author of *Johnny Guitar* than of *Rebel Without a Cause*, which was a collaborative effort. It seems Ray had a high degree of control over the production: the film was made away from the scrutiny of Hollywood executives, and he was associate producer. His stylistic signature can be seen in the symbolic use of colour to code the different characters and the expressive use of sets and decor.

V. F. Perkins (1972) also emphasises the importance of decor and mise en scène as an expression of Ray's recurring preoccupations. He points to the division in *Johnny Guitar* between 'upstairs', where Joan Crawford's Vienna has her private, feminine retreat, and 'downstairs', the public, masculine, violent world where she must shed her femininity to survive.

Indeed, the political themes of the film are partly worked through in terms of gender: in order to resolve the unhappy situation, Johnny must become stronger, more masculine, which in turn allows Vienna's 'true' femininity to emerge. Vienna's oscillation between masculinity and femininity has been seen by feminist critics as offering the possibility of a positive role for women in the western (Haskell, 1974), as a feminist critique of the western (Cook, 2005), and more negatively as a symptom of the way the genre activates women's predisposition to transsexual identification only to finally replace them, albeit uneasily, in the feminine position (Gender and sexuality in the western, p. 379).

PAM COOK

Rebel Without a Cause (USA 1955 *p.c* – Warner Bros.; *d* – Nicholas Ray)

The box-office success of *Johnny Guitar* led to an offer from Warner Bros. to direct a film in the new 'youth movie' genre. Kreidl (1977) traces the different conditions and contributions that affected the final product, in his view a collaborative venture representing the way in which Ray preferred to work. Nonetheless, Kreidl considers this Ray's finest work, and finds it ironic that its international success rests largely on the presence of James Dean, whose performance as young Jim Stark is exemplary of Hollywood 1950s Method acting (see Acting in cinema, p. 114).

Kreidl argues that the film breaks with the classic Hollywood narrative tradition, and points to Ray's characteristically dislocated mise en scène combined with horizontal composition to exploit the potential of CinemaScope. He sees the upside-down shot and the tilted camera used in the family confrontation scene as code breaking in the context of Hollywood emerging from the Cold War.

V. F. Perkins (1972), however, sees these strategies in classical terms as the perfect representation of Ray's ideas, projecting the world as he and his angry, alienated characters experience it. For Perkins, the 'chicken run' represents Ray's worldview in microcosm: life as a meaningless, chaotic journey towards death, unless one stops to question it, as Jim Stark does, in order to find an alternative. In addition to the place it occupies in the Ray canon, the film is now regarded as an iconic example of the teenpic (see p. 370).

PAM COOK

The True Story of Jesse James/The James Brothers (USA 1957 *p.c* – 20th Century Fox; *d* – Nicholas Ray)

Rebel Without a Cause was a commercial success, enabling Ray to work in Hollywood at a time when widescreen processes and colour (the film industry's weapons against television) were increasingly significant. Technological developments in CinemaScope and colour in the 1950s contributed to the emergence of a new kind of super-western, spectacular in style and dealing with psychological themes, of which this film is an example.

Like many of Ray's films, *The True Story of Jesse James* is regarded both as hack work and masterpiece. The genre components are strong, but Ray's concerns might be seen in the treatment of the outlaw band as both alienated from and trapped by the society it opposes. The violence within the gang is matched by the violence that society uses against the threat that the outlaws represent to capitalism (in the form of the railroad and the banks).

While Ray's sympathies can be seen to lie with the renegade outlaws, his use of mise en scène to depict the violent confrontations between them and the established social order suggests an interest in social conflict itself, an interest that can be traced throughout his work. Ray's 'mise en scène of violence' could be compared with other westerns of this period (such as those of Anthony Mann or John Ford) to discuss different treatments of these common themes of violence and social unrest.

PAM COOK

Film as disposable commodity product: Roger Corman

Sarris places Roger Corman in 'Oddities, One-Shots, and Newcomers', although he lists as many as 25 films directed by Corman between 1955 and 1967, many of which represent a consistent contribution to a genre (the Poe cycle of horror films and the gangster films). Apart from its value as a 'scandalisation' category, this section – which includes Charles Laughton, Howard Hughes and Ida Lupino – usefully demonstrates the contradictions in an auteur theory that depends on a conception of individual personal vision transcending conditions of production and material. Behind Sarris's summary dismissal of Corman's work lies the implication that he fails to produce high art from popular culture, and so falls short of being a true auteur.

There have been attempts to reclaim the status of auteur for Corman (see Will and Willemen, 1970; Dixon, 1976). Despite this, the interest of Corman's work lies in its resistance to the criteria imposed by Sarris's auteur theory, and the hierarchies of value implicit in his judgments.

Corman's cheaply made exploitation films remain firmly linked to the context of independent production at the edges of Hollywood in the 1950s and 1960s and, rather than displaying any tension or opposition, seem to revel in their own 'trashiness'. Style and meaning, and a certain knowing, camp quality, appear to emerge directly from conditions of production, as much as from the director's personal vision. The profit motive, the impetus to make 'a quick buck', is so dominant that the auteur's artistic intentions seem to recede in the face of this assertion of film as disposable product, while coherence, or lack of it, seems to reside rather in genre conventions and production values.

Auteur theory demands that popular entertainment cinema be taken seriously, on a level with art. The exploitation material with which Corman works depends on ripping off, and often parodying, more upmarket expensive productions. Since it does not take Hollywood seriously itself, and overtly displays this lack of seriousness, it is difficult to reconcile with the demands of the auteur theory to distinguish between 'good' and 'bad' films. Stock characters and situations, poor acting and bad direction are the hallmarks of exploitation films, and, it has been argued, their strength (see Cook, 2005). They cannot be considered 'classic' works, nor are they interested in being classified as such; instead, they feed on classic cinema.

Sarris stresses that authorship is discerned retrospectively by the critic, who looks closely at a film or a body of films to abstract the essence of the auteur. The role of the critic is one of contemplation and reassessment, and in this respect auteur theory attempts to break with the ideology of mass production of films for immediate consumption. Low-budget exploitation films are generally produced for immediate consumption (via alternative distribution and exhibition circuits such as drive-in cinemas, video and DVD, and the Internet) and their value is assumed to be exhausted when they cease to make money. The disposable ideology of 'trash' exploitation films seems to be incompatible with the notion of the discerning critic analysing and evaluating films according to their status as classic works. Exploitation films are often reviled by quality critics, while many receive little or no critical attention. However, the role of low-budget exploitation in nurturing new talent led to some film-makers who cut their teeth on such material in the 1960s and 1970s becoming major players in New Hollywood (Martin Scorsese, Joe Dante, Jonathan Kaplan). Critics began to look at the early exploitation output of these directors in a new light, and to reassess the cultural value of exploitation, its relationship to art cinema and its impact on mainstream production (see Exploitation cinema, p. 298; Cook, 1985; Hillier, 1986).

Selected Reading

Andrew Sarris, 'Notes on the auteur theory in 1962', *Film Culture* 27, winter 1962/63.

Andrew Sarris, *The American Cinema: Directors and Directions 1929–1968*, New York, Dutton, 1968.

ROGER CORMAN

Machine Gun Kelly (USA 1958 *p.c* – El Monte Productions/AIP; *d* – Roger Corman)

Corman had already directed and produced around 20 films, all cheaply made using 'sensational' material and saturation booking to exploit all the potential markets. With this film, the independent company American International Pictures (AIP), which would become one of the best-known exploitation producers, was cashing in on the 1950s cycle of gangster movies (often remakes of 1930s films) popular with young people on the drive-in circuits.

Machine Gun Kelly was shot in black and white using Superama, one of many widescreen processes tried out in the 1950s as the film industry geared itself up to fend off the challenge posed by television. In true exploitation style, it features less well-known actors, cheap sets and spectacular violence. David Will argues that the film resembles a comic strip but goes on to say that, like pop artist Lichtenstein, Corman redefines the 'validity of the lowest forms of commercial cinema' (Will and Willemen, 1970, p. 74). However, the conditions in which Corman worked as director and producer were very different from those of a painter, involving collaboration with a team of writers, technicians and actors, and a large degree of entrepreneurial skill. Before attributing to him the status of artist, the contributions of R. Wright Campbell (script) and Floyd Crosby (cinematography) to this film would have to be considered. One reason why Corman's work does not fit easily into Sarris's auteur theory is that the process of exploitation production militates against the attribution of authorship to a single source. In this context, the reconstruction of a body of films under the name 'Corman' privileges one element of the production process at the expense of others that may equally contribute to meaning and style.

An auteurist construction of this film as a Corman work finds his personal concerns in the treatment of its gangster protagonist. Kelly (Charles Bronson in his first leading role) is a pathological hero (see also *The St. Valentine's Day Massacre*, 1967) incapable of 'normal' relationships, created by a dysfunctional society. However, the pathological hero is also a feature of the gangster genre: the 'Corman variation' on the genre can be seen in the bleak pessimism of this film, which implies that the only possible resolution is the complete destruction of society as it exists in order to rebuild from scratch.

PAM COOK

The Haunted Palace (USA 1963 *p.c* – Alta Vista Productions/AIP; *d* – Roger Corman)

By 1960, both Corman and AIP were well established. Corman himself became a major international director whose films opened film festivals worldwide and were the subject of articles in European critical journals. The series of Gothic horror films known as the Poe cycle (*House of Usher*, 1960; *Pit and the Pendulum*, 1961; *The Premature Burial*, 1962; *Tales of Terror*, 1962; *The Raven*, 1963; *The*

Gothic tale: Vincent Price in *The Haunted Palace*

Haunted Palace, 1963; *The Masque of the Red Death*, 1964; and *The Tomb of Ligeia*, 1964) reflect this change in their more expensive production values, artistic aspirations and use of more respectable literary source material. *The Haunted Palace*, promoted by AIP as an Edgar Allan Poe vehicle to cash in on the cycle's success, was actually based on a H. P. Lovecraft story. It comes towards the end of the cycle, which finished with *The Tomb of Ligeia*.

Critical renown and respectability did not, however, affect the basically commercial nature of the films, which continued to revel in their own trash conventions. Typical elements of the Gothic horror genre include the theme of black magic, which undermines and is opposed by the community; the rational man of science who believes himself able to explain everything; the 'good' woman as victim; and the themes of psychic possession and physical deformity. The Corman variation on the conventions can be seen in the melancholy atmosphere of decadence and social decay; the opposition between civilised manners and aggressive primitive desires in one pathological individual; an obsession with death and the past; and a pervasive sense of doom and despair. In terms of style, the contributions of art director Daniel Haller and cameraman Floyd Crosby, both regular Corman collaborators, are significant. Haller is noted for his ability to make cheap sets look expensively mounted, and Floyd Crosby for his fluid camerawork. The importance of actor Vincent Price (here playing Charles Dexter Ward) to the branding of the Poe cycle cannot be overestimated.

PAM COOK

The Tomb of Ligeia (USA 1964 *p.c* – Alta Vista Productions/AIP; *d* – Roger Corman)

The basic elements of the Gothic horror genre are present here in the form of the decaying aristocratic society; the possession of a person by supernatural forces; and the inclusion of a dream sequence to indicate the preoccupation with primitive desires repressed by society.

Auteur critics have detected Corman's interests in the concern with the past; the return of the repressed; the divided pathological hero tortured by the past and death; and with female sexuality as a potential force for the destruction of society. In this film, the tortured hero, Verden Fell (Vincent Price), is destroyed in Ligeia's arms in the apocalyptic blaze that concludes the narrative.

The treatment of female sexuality in this film can be related to Corman's general interest in strong, destructive female figures, and is interesting as a precedent for many of the films he later produced for his own production/distribution company, New World Pictures (1970–83), which built up a reputation for producing films with a feminist bent in exploitation packaging (see Morris, 1974; 1975).

In the context of Corman's thematic concerns, the use of popular Freudian psychology in this film should also be noted. In one sense, it is 'camped up' as part of the commodity film package but it is also powerfully and seriously used in the scene in which Rowena/Ligeia (Elizabeth Shepherd) is hypnotised, and in her dream.

PAM COOK

The St. Valentine's Day Massacre (USA 1967 *p.c* – Los Altos Productions/20th Century Fox; *d* – Roger Corman)

This film is an example of Corman's move into big-budget production. An interesting comparison could be made with the low-budget *Machine Gun Kelly* (1958), to discuss different production values and approach, and with contemporary historical period gangster films such as Joseph Pevney's *Portrait of a Mobster* (1961), Arthur Penn's *Bonnie and Clyde* (1967) and Corman's *Bloody Mama* (1970). During the 1960s, graphic depictions of violence became more common in mainstream cinema.

The film, based on the gang wars between Al Capone (Jason Robards) and Bugs Moran (Ralph Meeker), has a semi-documentary framework: the opening legend states that 'every character and event herein is based on real characters and events' and the film's voice-over commentary gives biographical facts about each character as they appear. This device creates an epic sense of the inevitability of fate, which has often been seen as fundamental to the gangster genre. Will argues, however, that this film is different in that violent action is employed by Corman to reveal the rules and rituals of the gangster's world, rather than as a defining characteristic of that world (Will and Willemen, 1970, p. 75). Corman's own interest in, and respect for, the conventions of the genre have been seen in the use of colour and Panavision (for example, the plush red velvet of Capone's 'boardroom', suggesting his power and the extent of his aspirations; the deployment of Panavision to suggest domination of space and territory). Capone himself is a monstrous, psychopathic figure in the tradition of the genre, and of Corman heroes. The extreme violence portrayed in the flashback (shot with red filter) elevates violence to the level of ritualistic exchange between the gangs, drawing a parallel between the gangsters and American big business. Corman retired from directing in 1971 but remained active as producer and distributor. His influence on American independent cinema has been immeasurable (see p. 61).

PAM COOK

AUTEUR THEORY IN BRITAIN

PAM COOK

The British critical context: *Movie* magazine

The British authorship debate, as it emerged in the magazine *Movie* in the 1960s, was formulated rather differently because of historical factors specific to British culture. British critical tradition had its roots in an art criticism that stressed the importance of the critic's personal taste in assessment of works of art; a literary criticism that stressed the social and moral function of art, and the importance of the author's unified worldview as a criterion of value; a general cultural resistance to industrial modes of production geared to entertainment rather than art; and a Marxist social criticism that regarded mass media as essentially manipulative and dangerous, to be counteracted by the insights of a critical elite. This tradition was challenged by the 'popular culture debate' in the 1950s and 1960s, in which film criticism played an active part (see Lovell, 1975; Rohdie, 1972/73).

These conflicting strands came together in the pages of the magazines *Sequence* and *Sight and Sound*, who were inclined to dismiss Hollywood cinema as unworthy of serious critical attention and to value European art cinema as a cinema of personal vision and integrity. Some of the critics who wrote for these magazines were also film-makers unable to find work in the contracting British film industry and forced to work as independents (Lovell, 1969).

At the time the new wave was developing in France (see The Nouvelle Vague, p. 202), the British film-making tendency that came to be known as the Free Cinema movement appeared, committed to the idea of 'personal vision' that underpinned the *politique des auteurs*, but without its emphasis on popular American cinema. Many of the Free Cinema film-makers went on to work in the British industry (Lindsay Anderson and Karel Reisz among them), carrying this commitment with them (see British social realism 1959–63, p. 183).

Generally speaking, British film criticism had perceived authorship as opposed to the industrialised mass production of

Tony Richardson's *Look Back in Anger* was a key film of the 60s British new wave

Hollywood entertainment films: this argument assumed that art cinema should be taken seriously, whereas Hollywood was controlled by capital, whose interests it reproduced. In this context, the magazine *Movie* appeared in 1962 with an energetic attack on these defensive critical positions and on British cinema itself for its lack of style and imagination (see Perkins, 1972). Although they were not all in agreement, many *Movie* writers compared the mediocrity of British cinema with the technical expertise of Hollywood and put the former down to a cultural context that precluded the possibility of British directors achieving any artistic control. They pointed to the climate of critical opinion that ignored questions of form and demanded 'quality' pictures with serious social themes, and to the lack of British auteurs with their own personal style. They argued that how a film put over its theme was indistinguishable from what it attempted to say, prioritising detailed analysis of mise en scène as a critical approach, because it was in the formal organisation of film that meaning was to be found, not in any relation it might have to society. This emphasis on formal analysis was the link between *Cahiers' politique des auteurs* and *Movie*'s auteur theory, but *Movie* critics lacked the film-making context of the Nouvelle Vague that gave *Cahiers* its polemical force. They also lacked the strong national cinema, Hollywood, which lent strength to Andrew Sarris's arguments; but it was to Hollywood that the *Movie* critics turned as part of their attack on British cinema.

Movie's attack on British cinema for its lack of inventiveness, based as it was on an auteurist position that saw only that style and personal vision were absent, failed to analyse the economic, social and ideological factors underlying the British production context and, by looking towards Hollywood as a model, paradoxically supported the domination of British film production by the American industry. The concentration on the formal organisation of the film text itself at the expense of other forms of analysis led to a reinforcement of some of the least productive aspects of the auteur theory: the 'good' film as the coherent, non-contradictory expression of the director's personal vision and the task of evaluation given to the perceptive critic whose insights marked them off from the ordinary viewer. However, *Movie*'s championing of the auteur theory and popular Hollywood cinema at this point had far-reaching effects on British film criticism, initiating debates that still continue. Its contribution to film education has been considerable; many *Movie* writers were teachers engaged in debate about the status of film studies in schools and universities, concerned to establish film as a serious object of study on a level with other arts such as literature and music. Their support of Hollywood as a cinema of auteurs was important to this struggle.

Free Cinema and British realism

The critical tradition against which *Movie* directed its attack (primarily *Sequence* and *Sight and Sound* critics and the film-makers who emerged from Free Cinema) had also defined itself in opposition to current values in British cinema. Critics such as Lindsay Anderson and Karel Reisz argued in the pages of *Sequence*, and later in *Sight and Sound*, for a new cinema that would discard outmoded artifice in favour of the simplicity and freshness of personal observation of everyday reality. In 1947, Anderson criticised Rossellini's *Paisà* (1946) for its lack of personal statement and in 1955 condemned *On the Waterfront* (1954) for its flashy excesses of style, for masking its right-wing ideology with a display of technical tricks. In this article, Anderson described his view of the artist:

> The directors whom Tony Richardson would be more justified in castigating are surely those false creators with professional talent beyond the ordinary, with heavyweight pretensions, but without equivalent honesty, insight or sensibility who undertake significant subjects only to betray them. It is less a question of 'dominating' one's material than of being truthful about it. (Anderson, 1955, p. 130)

Although as socialists these writers were interested in popular cinema as a means of reaching a large audience, they positioned themselves against the artificiality and stereotypes of Hollywood, which they saw as conformist, in favour of a personal, poetic observation of reality, an affectionate look that respected its material enough to avoid distortion. In this approach, meaning pre-existed the film, and was brought to life by the director with the minimum of interference. The *Movie* critics argued against this that meaning was inseparable from form (mise en scène) and that only through close attention to the cinematic language specific to each film could meaning be deduced, constructed after the event.

As co-founders of Free Cinema, Lindsay Anderson, Karel Reisz and Tony Richardson made 'personal' documentaries on 16mm (such as *O Dreamland*, Anderson, 1953; *Momma Don't Allow*, Reisz/Richardson, 1955) during the 1950s until the industry opened up to the production of social realist feature films For a brief period, the film-makers of this British New Wave (also known rather dismissively as the 'kitchen sink' cycle) were able to resist the monopoly of large-scale production set-ups in order to maintain artistic autonomy (see Hill, 1986). The Woodfall Group, formed by John Osborne and Tony Richardson in 1958 to make a film of the successful stage play by Osborne, *Look Back in Anger*, was criticised in *Movie* for its commitment to a social realism that put lofty themes before a feeling for cinema (see Perkins, 1972).

For Alan Lovell, the Free Cinema/*Sequence* current emerged out of specific social and historical factors and disappeared for similar reasons:

> The impact was not a sustained one. Under the pressure of a situation that neither its aesthetic nor its economic and social analysis of the cinema could properly cope with, the Free Cinema/*Sequence* position was modified into one simplified diagram of the cinema, a mixture of Marxist and liberal attitudes – art is personal expression, personal expression is extremely difficult with a capitalist economic system, the artist's position is a very difficult one in our society. (Lovell, 1972, p. 158)

When the Free Cinema/*Sequence* film-makers moved into the feature-film industry in the 1960s, they took with them this combination of personal expression and sense of social responsibility. Their unwillingness to compromise may account for the small number of films they actually made and the fact that those films now seem to belong to a particular moment in British film culture. *Movie*'s attack on British social realist films of the 1960s and on British film culture in general for its lack of style and auteurs did not take account of their historical context. The very absence that *Movie* deplored has opened the way to critical approaches to British film history that reconstruct it in other terms than those that demand the presence of auteurs as a criterion of value (see British cinema: auteur and studio, p. 438).

Lindsay Anderson

Although Lindsay Anderson is acknowledged to be one of the most controversial and influential of British film directors, he directed fewer features after the late 1960s (though *O Lucky Man!*, 1973, *Britannia Hospital*, 1982, and *The Whales of August*, 1987, were generally critically well received) and moved into making films for television. Anderson's oeuvre covers his critical writings for *Sequence* and *Sight and Sound*, sponsored promotional films, work in the theatre as producer, director and actor, television commercials and films made with the Free Cinema movement, besides his feature films (see Lovell and Hillier, 1972). Conventionally, auteur theory would look for a consistent worldview across all this work and indeed it would be possible to detect a continuity of thematic and stylistic concerns (such as a committed left-wing view of British society and an interest in aesthetic issues). However, those concerns have made it difficult for Anderson to work consistently within the British film industry, which has only periodically been open to aesthetic innovation, and those feature films he has made often seem confused and contradictory rather than homogeneous. Lovell argues that in the context of an entrenched bias towards realism in British cinema, the production of non-naturalistic films within the feature-film industry constitutes a major achievement (see Lovell, 1975/76).

As a vocal member of the Free Cinema movement, Anderson argued for the freedom of the film-maker to make personal statements through his or her films, that those statements should act as a commentary on contemporary society and should reflect the commitment of the film-maker to certain basic values for which he or she should be prepared to fight. Anderson's 'basic values' might be described as a kind of militant liberal humanism that saw the weaknesses of liberalism in its lack of commitment rather than in its theoretical or political position.

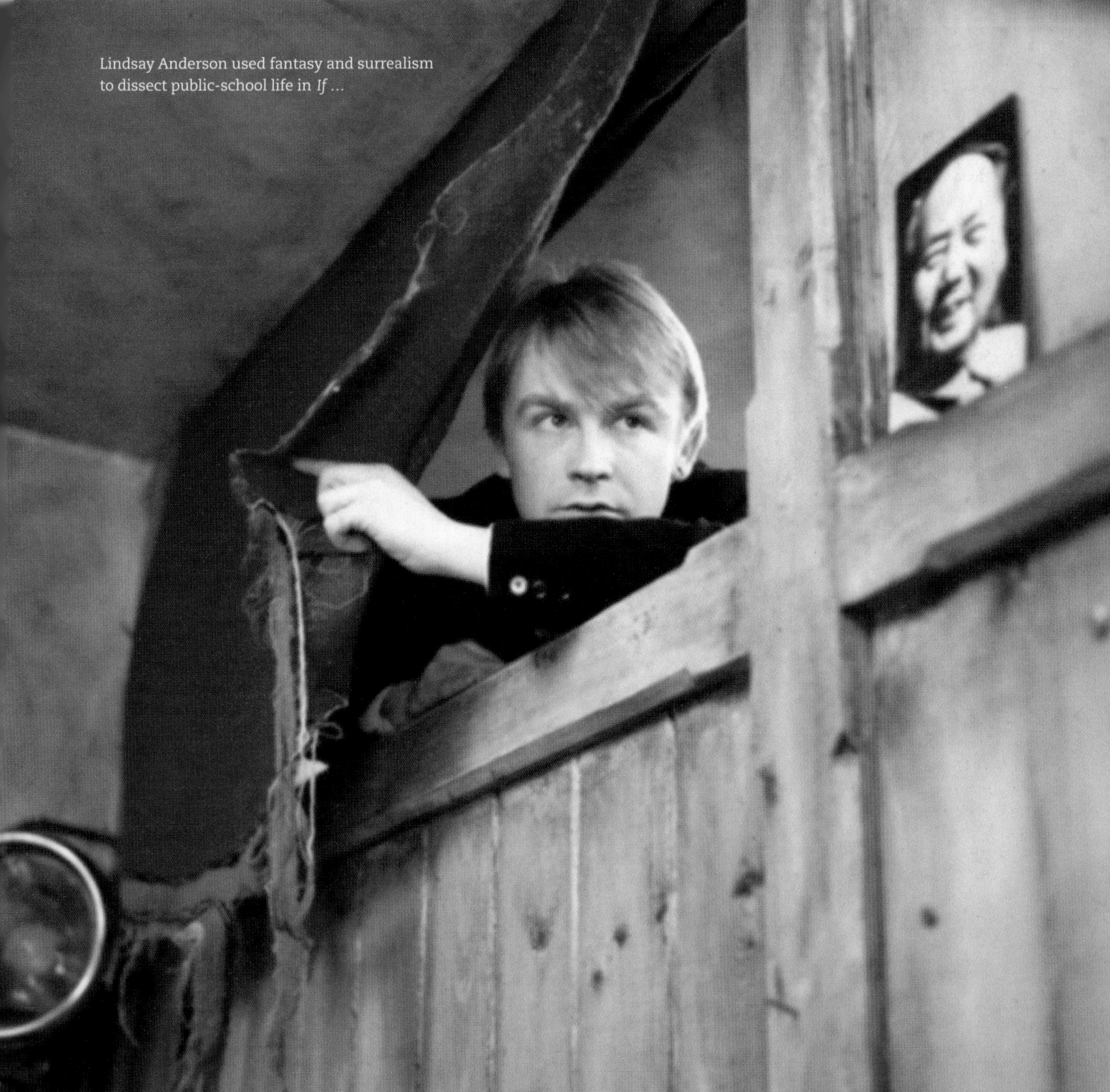

Lindsay Anderson used fantasy and surrealism to dissect public-school life in *If ...*

The aesthetics of Free Cinema were basically those of documentary reportage; however, they were never simply documentary. The use of sound–image disjunctions in Anderson's *O Dreamland* is an example of the way that the 'objective' documentary mode could be transformed into personal commentary. Although the documentary strand of Free Cinema seemed compatible with British realism, the freedom of personal expression strand was less easy to accommodate, and many of the Free Cinema directors, including Anderson, who moved into the industry found themselves at odds with it. Anderson's interest in surrealism and in broadly Brechtian ideas derived from British theatre can be seen in all his feature films and distinguished them from prevailing ideas of British social realism. Those interests are perhaps most clearly displayed in *If ...* (1968) and *O Lucky Man!*, albeit in an uneven and contradictory way. The tension between subjective and objective, interior and exterior is worked through in *This Sporting Life* (1963), which is seen as one of the final flourishes of the British New Wave (see Hill, 1986).

Karel Reisz

Karel Reisz co-directed *Momma Don't Allow* with Tony Richardson and made *We Are the Lambeth Boys* (1959), both as part of the Free Cinema project; the concerns expressed in those films can be detected in his first feature film, *Saturday Night and Sunday Morning* (1960), based on the novel by Alan Sillitoe and one of the key British New Wave films. Its sympathetic treatment of working-class life, presented through the point of view of its truculent hero, played by Albert Finney, has been viewed as problematic because of the film-maker's middle-class perspective.

In an interview for *Cinéma International* in 1967, Reisz described his style:

> The style in which you make a film reflects faithfully what you have to say; there are no two ways of saying the same thing. The way you hold the camera reveals exactly what you have chosen to reveal. In my case, it's a question of filming based much more on observation than on abstraction. This implies a tendency to use the camera in the most simple way; I want the people in front of the camera to feel very free in their movements, instead of having to change places for the camera, that is in terms of the camera. (Reisz, 1967, p. 690)

This formulation echoes Lindsay Anderson and the commitment of the Free Cinema film-makers to personal observation, social commitment and sincerity of style. In terms of theme, Reisz's later films, such as *Morgan – A Suitable Case for Treatment* (1966) and *Isadora* (1968), show a preoccupation with unconventional individuals, often artists or intellectuals, at odds with a restricted and unsympathetic society. It is difficult to see a direct connection with Free Cinema here. Although Reisz shared the basic principles of Free Cinema, it is arguable that his personal concerns moved away from those principles in a way that Anderson's, for instance, did not.

Selected Reading

John Hill, *Sex, Class and Realism: British Cinema 1956–1963*, London, BFI Publishing, 1986.

Robert Murphy (ed.), *The British Cinema Book*, London, BFI Publishing, 1997. Revised edition 2002.

Impotent: David Warner as Morgan and Vanessa Redgrave as Leonie in Reisz's *Morgan – A Suitable Case for Treatment*

LINDSAY ANDERSON

This Sporting Life (UK 1963 *p.c* – Independent Artists; *d* – Lindsay Anderson)

This Sporting Life is generally regarded as the last of the British New Wave films: it was received well by critics but performed badly at the box office. Produced by Karel Reisz and scripted by David Storey from his own novel about northern working-class life, it remains a compelling work, startlingly modern in its approach and execution. The moody, percussive score by Roberto Gerhard and the expressive black-and-white photography combine to create a sense of epic poetry, while the brooding physicality of Richard Harris as miner-turned-rugby star Frank Machin, and the brittle fragility of Rachel Roberts's Mrs Hammond have the emotional power of Greek tragedy.

The narrative structure is unusually complex for a New Wave film, based on flashbacks from Frank's perspective that sit uneasily with the more exterior, objective sequences (for example, the cut-in documentary footage of crowds at the rugby stadium, which is reminiscent of Free Cinema). There is a tension throughout between personal self-expression and objective reality, almost literally embodied by the inarticulate Machin, that adds to the atmosphere of pent-up violence and emotion. The film exemplifies the 'poetic realism' to which the New Wave film-makers aspired, giving it an added dimension. It has been compared to European art cinema, but it is equally indebted to Hollywood, particularly in Harris's performance as Machin, who strongly resembles the Marlon Brando of *On the Waterfront* (1954). The film is clearly a very personal work, and its pessimism about the social changes affecting the traditional British working-class way of life under the impact of consumerism can be traced back to the Free Cinema films. Nevertheless, it stands up as a powerful statement by Anderson about British life, cinema and culture.

PAM COOK

If ... (UK/USA 1968 *p.c* – Memorial Enterprises/ Paramount; *d* – Lindsay Anderson)

Co-produced and directed by Anderson, this film is interesting both as an explicit, if not entirely coherent, expression of his personal concerns and also as a break with realism.

The film combines fantasy and social satire in a critique of British public school life and mores and was influenced by Jean Vigo's *Zéro de conduite* (1933). Anderson admired Vigo, Humphrey Jennings and John Ford as personal film-makers whose styles, in his view, demonstrated sincerity and honesty.

The film was made in colour and black and white and, although this was partly due to economic pressures, it adds to the stylisation. The effect of this stylisation was to give viewers a critical distance, denying them the pleasure of identification. Tony Richardson's *Tom Jones* (1963) had used 'Brechtian' distancing devices to great comic effect, and had been highly successful in America. Unfortunately, *If ...* did not repeat this success. Anderson's use of surrealism here indicates his interest in repressed desires and their return in the form of destructive fantasies, and in the role of fantasy and the imagination in political action.

PAM COOK

KAREL REISZ

Saturday Night and Sunday Morning (UK 1960 *p.c* – Woodfall Productions; *d* – Karel Reisz)

Adapted from the novel by Alan Sillitoe and scripted by him, this film marked an important moment in Reisz's career. It was an unprecedented box-office success, and quickly became one of the most critically respected of the New Wave films. Reisz adhered to the principles of Free Cinema in attempting to reconstruct with maximum authenticity and minimum distortion the daily life of a young working-class man at odds with his provincial background. However, the film departed from Free Cinema in its use of the strategies of narrative fiction to 'get inside' the psychology of its central protagonist Arthur Seaton (Albert Finney).

As an example of British social realism, the film is related to the 'youth problem' genre prevalent in the 1950s and 1960s; Albert Finney's muscular portrayal of a rebel anti-hero, engaged at times with his society yet alienated from it, has often been taken to account for the success of the film (see British social realism 1959–63, p. 183). Finney was one of a group of new male stars who were significantly different from the 'stiff-upper lip' types that had largely dominated British cinema.

Reisz's concerns can be seen in the treatment of Arthur's critical view of his society, expressed in his behaviour and his voice-over. The working-class male protagonist, whose problems are represented in sexual as much as class terms, is set against a provincial industrial background that he seeks to escape because of its narrow, restrictive moral codes. Arthur's virility and amoral attitude are closely linked to his disenchantment with the conditions of his existence; although this perspective derives from the novel, it is also reminiscent of Free Cinema's middle-class portrayal of working-class life.

PAM COOK

Morgan – A Suitable Case for Treatment (UK 1966 *p.c* – Quintra Films; *d* – Karel Reisz)

This began life as a BBC TV play written by David Mercer, who also scripted the film; it is an example of the close relationship between film and other media (literature, theatre, television) in British cinema at the time. Although Reisz had moved away from his background in Free Cinema, an element of social criticism remained: Morgan's 'madness' enables him to see what is wrong with the world.

The film illustrates the kind of dramatic situation that John Osborne's *Look Back in Anger* introduced into English drama ten years earlier – the young male protagonist (played by David Warner, at the time a brilliant young theatre actor) is an eccentric left-wing artist whose rebellion against bourgeois society pushes him towards madness. Class differences hinder his relationship with his girlfriend Leonie (Vanessa Redgrave), and they can only express their attraction through fantasy. In terms of Reisz's work, there is a development away from the social realist format of *Saturday Night and Sunday Morning* (1960) towards surrealism in the depiction of Morgan's state of mind. The sexuality of the hero remains a central theme; however, his sexual competence is in question here. Morgan's impotence is in sharp contrast to the virility of Arthur, the working-class rebel hero of *Saturday Night and Sunday Morning*, though ultimately both are portrayed as victims of their society.

PAM COOK

Movie and mise en scène analysis

Although each *Movie* critic writes about film from a different perspective (see Perkins, 1972/73), they share an approach to film criticism that can be traced back to a British tradition of literary criticism, best exemplified perhaps by the journal *Scrutiny*, especially contributors such as F. R. Leavis, L. C. Knights and Denys Thompson, and the debate about the value of mass culture in which it was engaged (see Filmer, 1969). The 'popular culture debate' hinged upon an opposition between traditional high art and popular mass culture. For some critics, the former was capable of providing moral insights for the perceptive reader, while the latter, because it was mass-produced for the entertainment of a passive popular audience, could do no more than reproduce the status quo. Cinema, as part of the mass media, was placed in the category of popular culture (see Collins, 1981). During the early 1960s, left-wing critics began to question the inferior status given to the mass media, arguing that it was not a monolithic phenomenon and that it offered the possibility of reaching a mass audience in a way that high art, which was only available to a privileged minority, did not. As a result of this debate, Hollywood, seen as the mass cinema par excellence, began to be reassessed. The auteur theory, which insisted that statements from individual directors were possible even in the Hollywood system of commodity production, performed an important function in the attempt to break down resistance to mass art. At the same time, methods of film analysis were carried over from the literary criticism tradition. This tradition emphasised the organic relationship of form to content, and close analysis of the text as a means of discovering the themes and values embedded in it.

Movie's approach, based on detailed attention to form, merged with that strand of the *Cahiers' politique* that saw analysis of mise en scène as a way of discovering an author's themes or moral values. Some confusion exists about the term mise en scène in film criticism, partly because it is imported from theatre and partly because of its collapse into auteur theory, where it came to mean 'style' or 'formal conventions'. Strictly speaking, mise en scène refers to the practice of stage direction in the theatre in which things are 'put into the scene', that is, arranged on the stage. When applied to film, it refers to whatever appears in the film frame, including those aspects that overlap with the art of the theatre: setting, lighting, costume and the behaviour of the figures. By this definition, the term does not include specifically cinematographic qualities such as photographic elements, framing and length of shot, camera position, and movement, or editing. In formal analysis of film, then, mise-en-scène analysis is only one important area demanding attention. By extension from theatre to cinema, the term has come to mean the director's control over what appears in the frame, and the way the director stages the event for the camera. *Cahiers du cinéma* took this a stage further by making an evaluative distinction between auteur and metteur en scène in which the latter would be concerned simply with the craft of staging events for the camera rather than with organising the whole film according to a personal vision (see The auteur theory, p. 410).

While *Movie* critics subscribed to the auteur theory as an evaluative method, their concept of mise en scène was broader than *Cahiers*' and referred to the overall formal organisation of films, their 'style'. *Movie*'s brand of mise en scène analysis is based on a deductive method whereby detailed description of films is seen to be the basis for criticism, a method that sees film criticism as a practical activity rather than as a theoretical project. *Movie*'s attachment to this form of mise en scène analysis and auteur theory at the expense of other approaches seems to have led it into a critical impasse. By virtue of its own criteria of value (for example, criteria of classicism, such as the organic unity of a given film or body of films), it was forced to resist the impact of historical change, whether this was manifested in new film-making practices that did not embody classical unity and coherence or in new critical theories, such as Jean-Luc Godard, or Soviet cinema (see the exchange of views between the *Movie* critics in Cameron, 1972, p. 19, and in 'The return of *Movie*', *Movie* 20, spring 1975, p. 1). Indeed, it could be argued that the combination of a deductive empirical method and auteur analysis cut many *Movie* writers off from engaging with more general political and ideological questions.

One of the oldest debates in film criticism is between the advocates of the art of mise en scène (see André Bazin, p. 390

) and the advocates of the art of montage editing (for example, Sergei Eisenstein), a debate that has tended to polarise issues rather than open up discussion of the interrelationship between the two methods of construction (see Henderson, 1976). Without collapsing the different positions of the *Movie* critics into the Bazinian worldview, it is possible to trace in some of their arguments a preference for a cinema of mise en scène untroubled by obtrusive editing or camera movements and a predilection for a classic cinema that eschews blatant formal effects in favour of a style that is adequate or equivalent to content. *Movie*'s pantheon (see Cameron, 1972) is headed by the great classic Hollywood directors Alfred Hitchcock and Howard Hawks, closely followed by a range of directors whose styles, the overall composition of their films, are seen by *Movie* to be entirely compatible with their themes or values.

Movie can be credited with initiating a critical debate in the UK about the artistic value of popular cinema; it is, however, debatable whether its basic critical preconceptions were very different from those of *Sight and Sound* against which it argued; it simply applied these values to a different body of films – Hollywood rather than art cinema. After 1975, however, it attempted to come to terms with the different questions raised for British film criticism by structuralism and semiology and with the contradictions raised for its own critical position by New Hollywood.

Joseph Losey

Two articles on the films of Joseph Losey in *Movie Reader* (1972) provide different examples of *Movie*'s critical method.

Paul Mayersberg writing on *The Damned* (1961) starts with a close analysis of the opening sequence of the film, from which he proceeds to deduce Losey's symbolism (themes or values). He supports the analysis by reference to other Losey films in which he traces similar values, returning to close analysis of *The Damned* to find other themes, which in turn he relates to other Losey films, in a constant movement from the particular to the general. Mayersberg points to the importance of mise en scène as a conveyor of meaning in Losey's work:

> In his use of decor as an element in the construction of his movies Losey has no equal in the cinema. He and [Richard] Macdonald devise a setting that will characterise the person associated with it: the white simplicity of the psychiatrist's room in *The Sleeping Tiger*, the angrily contrasted surface textures of Stanford's flat in *Time Without Pity* conveying the moody violence of the man, the nudes in Bannion's flat [in *The Criminal*] which give the appearances of luxury, but are in reality no more than a grandiose extension of the pin-ups on the walls of the prison cells. (Mayersberg, 'Contamination', 1972, p. 74)

Charles Barr's article ('*King and Country*', 1972, p. 75) also uses close analysis of the film to indicate his dissatisfaction with its 'cerebral' quality, nevertheless acknowledging that its schematic formal beauty articulates with logical precision the hopelessness of its theme. Barr makes reference not only to other Losey films but also to other Hollywood films, and to Shakespeare's *King Lear*, to show how *King and Country* differs both from standard British films and from other anti-war films.

Both these approaches move from the specific (the film text) to the general (other film texts), constructing the auteur's personal values from analysis of single films and tending to ignore historical factors like conditions of production, or even the director's known interests and ideas. In the late 1960s, some British Marxist structuralist film critics took *Movie* to task for its resistance to general theoretical and political questions and for the emphasis placed on the critic's interpretation of the films rather than on more 'objective' criteria. It could be argued that Mayersberg and Barr evaluate Losey according to their own personal taste and that a more objective approach would place Losey in his historical context. However, it should be remembered that *Movie*'s attempt to validate Losey as a cinema auteur was part of their attack on British cinema for its lack of style. Losey had difficulty finding work in the UK after he was blacklisted in America, a fact that *Movie* saw as symptomatic of the stalemate situation in the British film industry at that time.

JOSEPH LOSEY

The Criminal (UK 1960 *p.c* – Merton Park Studios; *d* – Joseph Losey)

Joseph Losey's career began in American radical theatre in the 1930s. His work as a theatre director was influenced by Russian theatre and by the theory and practice of Erwin Piscator and Bertolt Brecht with the Berliner Ensemble, about which he wrote several articles. He collaborated closely with Brecht on a theatre production of *Galileo Galilei* just before directing his first feature film for RKO, *The Boy With Green Hair* (1948), and has acknowledged the Brechtian influence on his work in general.

Losey's cinema is primarily intellectual. In an interview in *Image et Son* 202 (1967), he described his wish to stimulate thought in the audience (p. 21) through the use of an abstract mise en scène that encouraged critical distance rather than emotional involvement and identification with characters (p. 25). In the context of Brecht's ideas, the 'cerebral' quality that Charles Barr objected to in *King and Country* (*Movie Reader*, 1972, p. 75) can be seen to form the basis of Losey's work. Barr's resistance to the 'alienation effect' is perceptive and perhaps symptomatic of a critical approach that distrusts any signs of formal excess that might disturb the balance of form and content.

Because of his left-wing views, Losey was blacklisted by the House Un-American Activities Committee and came to England in 1951, where he had some difficulty at first in finding work because of restrictions on the number of foreign directors allowed to work in the UK (see Roud, 1979). After completing several low-budget productions in between directing commercials for television, he had a success with *Blind Date* (1959), produced by Independent Artists and Sydney Box Associates, which led to a larger budget for *The Criminal*. The story, scripted by Alun Owen and the uncredited Jimmy Sangster, dealt with prison life and organised crime. It attracted Losey because he saw a parallel between the rigid criminal code and the organisation of big business. The film was not a success in the UK, but when it opened in Paris in

1961 French critics acclaimed it as a masterpiece and Losey as a great director. It was largely due to the support of the French critics that Losey's reputation as an international auteur was established, making it possible for him to gain a measure of artistic control over his projects.

PAM COOK

Eva/Eve (France/Italy 1962 *p.c* – Paris Film/Interopa Film; *d* – Joseph Losey)

The critical success of *The Criminal* in France established Losey's artistic reputation and caused French actress Jeanne Moreau to suggest his name as director of *Eva*. The production laboured under constant difficulties: disagreements between Losey and the producers over the script, Moreau and Losey both ill, the producers pushing Losey to complete the film. The music Losey wanted (Miles Davis and Billie Holiday) was unobtainable and the producers forced him to cut the film drastically to keep costs low, finally making further cuts without his consent (see Rissient, 1966, pp. 129–30).

In spite of these difficulties, the film is considered to be one of Losey's most important, both in its conception and its theme. Carefully structured in a prologue, three acts and an epilogue, it deals with an impossible relationship between a strong independent woman and a puritanical working-class Welshman (Stanley Baker, who had starred as Johnny Bannion in *The Criminal*) who assumes his right to dominate her and is finally destroyed by his obsession. The film contrasts two characters from different social backgrounds to point up contradictions in the notion of sexual liberation. The portrayal of Eva by Jeanne Moreau is cold and detached and her 'independence' is established simply by her ability to control her own sexuality and to humiliate Tyvian through it. The interaction of class and sexual struggle in the film is interesting in relation to British New Wave films of this period that also attempt to deal with the subject of changing social values.

PAM COOK

Joseph Losey on the set of *The Damned*

The Damned (UK/USA 1963 *p.c* – Hammer Film Productions/Swallow Productions/Columbia; *d* – Joseph Losey)

The expatriate Losey worked for Hammer at Bray Studios on this science-fiction film: an unlikely partnership that resulted in one of the most pessimistic of all Hammer's postwar science-fiction films, revolving around an insane government plot to preserve radioactive children from the outside world and an American tourist (Macdonald Carey) and woman-hating teenage gang leader (Oliver Reed) who stumble on the results.

The Damned is staple Hammer diet: sensational science fiction full of violence; but it also manifests Losey's characteristic use of mise en scène and his political concerns. Some of the director's preoccupations can be seen in the parallel drawn between the obsessional government scientist Bernard (Alexander Knox) and the mindless violence of gang leader King, and in the opposition drawn between Bernard the scientist, preoccupied with death, and Freya the artist (Viveca Lindfors), dedicated to life. The use of the innocent but deadly children to represent the contradictions between absolute purity (non-contamination) and the corruption of the system that has brought them into being is reminiscent of Losey's first feature, *The Boy with Green Hair* (1948).

PAM COOK

Accident (UK 1967 *p.c* – Royal Avenue Chelsea; *d* – Joseph Losey)

Losey collaborated with Harold Pinter on the screenplay of *The Servant* in 1963, which had taken up the themes of sexuality, class and relationships of domination and subordination in the confrontation between master and servant. Pinter's concern with using the suggestive possibilities of language to make apparently normal situations seem strange and full of hidden menace meshed well with Losey's precisely structured mise en scène to create a nightmarish world of corruption in which the characters were turned in on themselves, obsessed with their own destruction.

Accident, their second collaboration, also dealt with a closed world, and starred Dirk Bogarde as Oxford don Stephen; it is set in an academic community, ruthless and compulsively claustrophobic, in which class and sexual tensions erupt, disturbing the narrative continuity of the film. Discontinuities of time and place in the construction of the film contribute to a 'strangeness' that is intended to alienate the spectator, much as the central protagonists of all Losey's films feel themselves to be alienated, displaced in a world that imposes its rules upon them, destroying their individuality.

The studied formalism of this film, combined with the highly mannered performances from the actors, is typical of Losey's later work. The themes of the closed community with its stifling moral code, and of class and sex struggles as destructive and self-defeating, recur in his films. The mysterious Anna (Jacqueline Sassard), who is a catalyst, or agent of destruction, represents one of the dangerous, sexually emancipated women who appear throughout Losey's work (Melina Mercouri in *The Gypsy and the Gentleman*, 1957; Micheline Presle in *Blind Date*, 1959; Jeanne Moreau in *Eva*, 1962; Sarah Miles in *The Servant*, 1963; Monica Vitti in *Modesty Blaise*, 1966).

PAM COOK

Elia Kazan

Movie 19 (winter 1971/72) is devoted to a study of Kazan's career and consists of a lengthy interview and extensive bio-filmography as well as detailed critical analysis of several films.

One reason why this detailed knowledge of the man, his background and ideas should be seen to be important in this case is the assertively personal quality of Kazan's films and the extent to which they manifest the shifting concerns of someone caught up in, and acutely aware of, changing historical circumstances. There is a strong autobiographical thread in Kazan's work: he cannot be said to have a detached view of the world; like Losey, he is aware of the need to formulate a political position and engage the audience in critical activity. He differs in that he inscribes himself, as a human being rather than as an artist, across his work. This aggressive self-display has caused some English critics to distrust his films, seeing in its 'flashy excesses of style' (see Anderson, 1955), an overemphasis on the individual's role in history, or a vulgarity of expression that betrays the function of the artist: to educate with restraint, without rhetoric (Wood, 'The Kazan problem', 1971/72). It could be argued that it is precisely the unevenness and the emotional excess in Kazan's work that make it interesting, raising questions about the relationship of art and the artist to society and to politics, and of the individual to history.

Kazan's background in the left-wing radical theatre of 1930s America, where issues of style and politics, art and society were constantly debated, left a legacy of social realism, naturalism and agitprop throughout his films, providing a sometimes uneasy mixture with classic narrative cinema – an uneasiness that it might be productive to explore. Similarly, Kazan's growing interest in psychoanalysis and sexuality is often represented as a disturbing force intruding with some violence into a social order that maintains a precarious balance. This mixture of politics and sexuality in Kazan's work attracted French critics, as did the acknowledged influence of John Ford (see Tailleur, 1971; Ciment, 1974). The response of British critics has been more ambivalent. The contributors to *Movie* 19 were split between those who found his work uneven, lacking balance and restraint (Robin Wood, V. F. Perkins) and those who found this unevenness the symbolic expression of Kazan's worldview (Jim Hillier, Michael Walker).

Selected Reading

Michel Ciment, *Conversations with Losey*, London, Methuen, 1985.
Richard Schickel, *Elia Kazan: A Biography*, London, HarperCollins, 2005.

ELIA KAZAN

A Streetcar Named Desire (USA 1951 *p.c* – Charles K. Feldman Group/Warner Bros.; *d* – Elia Kazan)

Kazan collaborated with Tennessee Williams on this film; he directed two movies from Williams's plays (*A Streetcar Named Desire* and *Baby Doll*, 1956) and directed several for the stage throughout the 1950s. It was independently produced, and manifests Kazan's roots in radical theatre. The ideas about acting that emerged from the Actors' Studio, co-founded by Kazan in 1948, can be seen in Marlon Brando's performance as Stanley Kowalski, which gains value and authenticity because of its directness and immediacy in contrast to the mannered acting style of Vivien Leigh (Blanche Dubois). A tension is set up between 'honesty' (realism) and 'hypocrisy' (artifice), a conflict that recurs throughout Kazan's work. In this case, Kazan's populist politics can be identified in the value placed upon Stanley's virile working-class persona: his violence is shocking, but it seems to be justified in the face of Blanche's social pretensions. The extreme femininity of Vivien Leigh's performance has the effect of emasculating and devaluing the middle class. Questions arise about the way that ethnicity, class and sexuality interact to reinforce certain class positions and identifications for the audience, and the contribution of acting, gesture and mise en scène to this process. How does the power of Brando's performance affect the way the audience views the sadism and brutality of the Stanley Kowalski character and mitigate our sympathetic response to Blanche as his victim? Is it conceivable that the sexual and ethnic roles could be reversed?

PAM COOK

Viva Zapata! (USA 1952 *p.c* – 20th Century Fox; *d* – Elia Kazan)

In 1951–2, Kazan became directly involved in the proceedings of the House Un-American Activities Committee by giving testimony to the Committee against some of his colleagues, and critics have seen a direct relationship between these events and the films Kazan went on to make in the 1950s. Kazan himself characterised his position as antagonistic to any party line and in favour of intellectual freedom, while still retaining his left-wing sympathies, and insisted that the films he made during and after his testimony were more explicitly left wing.

Kazan worked closely with John Steinbeck on the script for this film; they were both interested in the complex figure of Emiliano Zapata, who was a leading figure in the 1910 Mexican revolution. Kazan seems to have identified with him directly, seeing a parallel between the Mexican rebel's life and his own at that time (see Ciment, 1974, p. 89).

Elia Kazan (in white shirt) directing on the set of *Viva Zapata!*

Of note is the way Kazan uses the crosscutting editing technique basic to Hollywood narrative cinema, combined with music, to create intense excitement, involving the spectator in a process of identification with the ambiguous figure of Zapata (Marlon Brando) and his peasant supporters. Comparison with *A Streetcar Named Desire* (1951) raises the question of Kazan's manipulation of audience response through editing and mise en scène.

PAM COOK

On the Waterfront (USA 1954 *p.c* – Horizon Pictures/Columbia Pictures; *d* – Elia Kazan)

Apparently, Fox had cut *Man on a Tightrope* (1953) without Kazan's permission. Kazan insisted on cutting rights on *On the Waterfront* and following its success he became an independent producer with absolute rights on all his projects.

The central theme of individual conscience and social responsibility has been seen as an attempt by Kazan to re-establish his political integrity after giving evidence to the House Un-American Activities Committee (the film was scripted by Budd Schulberg, who like Kazan had 'named names' to HUAC). Kazan himself characterised all his films of this period as emerging from a desire to question himself and the world around him. Indeed, the narrative of *On the Waterfront* revolves around the idea of the difficulty of taking a political stand, as the reluctant hero Terry Malloy (Marlon Brando) struggles with pressure from all sides to 'do the right thing'. Lindsay Anderson (1955) was one critic who saw the ending of the film as validating right-wing individualist politics, a view that perhaps failed to take the whole film into account. As with much of Kazan's work, a problem remains with the use of narrative and a central heroic figure as a focus for political issues. Terry Malloy is the charismatic character with whom the audience is intended to identify, rejecting with him the political and moral positions offered by the other characters. The extent to which Brando's performance strengthens this identification, overcoming any questions we may have about the film's political stance, is open to debate. In relation to *A Streetcar Named Desire* (1951), for instance, there are important differences between Stanley Kowalski, characterised as essentially masculine and embodying a virile immigrant strength that arguably represents the New America, and Terry Malloy, a character who exists precisely in order to question those values, but finds himself unable to discard them completely, since he must 'become a man'.

The relationship between Terry and Edie Doyle (Eva Marie Saint) represents the problem posed in gender terms: the gentleness embodied in Edie, and her 'feminine' virtues, are also to be found in Terry (he is an ambiguous character in this respect). These 'feminine' qualities of caring and tenderness are to some extent validated by the film. However, they are qualities associated with passivity, and Edie rejects them in Terry because the political struggle against the union bosses requires 'masculine' toughness. To a certain extent she also rejects her own traditionally 'feminine' role by becoming more politically active after the death of her brother. Terry is required to 'be a man' in the struggle for freedom, and the extent to which political struggle is identified with 'masculine' qualities, in this film and in Kazan's work in general, is an interesting issue. Terry's stand for democracy against corruption in the unions leaves him battered and bloodstained, raising a question mark over the value of individual heroism at the same time as celebrating it.

PAM COOK

Baby Doll (USA 1956 *p.c* – Newtown Productions; *d* – Elia Kazan)

This is Kazan's second film version of a Tennessee Williams play (*27 Wagons Full of Cotton*) and is interesting as an early example of a more explicit expression of sexuality on the screen that emerged in America during the 1950s and 1960s. In spite of pressure from the Catholic Legion of Decency, Kazan refused to make any changes and persuaded distributors Warner Bros. that the notoriety would help to sell the picture. The gigantic sign that advertised the film, showing its star Carroll Baker in a crib sucking her thumb, is now legendary (see Censorship, p. 17).

Kazan shared Williams's obsession with the crumbling way of life in the South and with the idea of the virile immigrant-outsider who acts as a force for change and renewal. Kazan wanted Marlon Brando to play this role, but he refused and newcomer Eli Wallach took the part of Silva Vaccaro. Characteristically, the political questions are represented in terms of sexual problems: Karl Malden as Archie Lee Meighan represents the old South; his inability to fulfil his side of the marriage agreement in material terms is explicitly linked with his sexual frustration and his 19-year-old wife Baby Doll's arrested development.

Baby Doll is the first of Kazan's films in which black characters from time to time act as a chorus, commenting on the whites' behaviour (see also *A Face in the Crowd*, 1957, and *Wild River*, 1960). However, Kazan claimed that he intended to portray the bigoted white Southerners sympathetically (if comically) in this film and saw it as the beginnings of a more liberal position in his work.

In terms of mise en scène, the stylised contrast between white and black is striking and was intended to represent symbolically the death of the old South in the face of new blood: the immigrants and the blacks. White is associated with femininity and weakness, black with masculinity and strength (see interview with Kazan, *Movie* 19, 1971/72, p. 9).

The opposition between blonde woman and dark man here can be compared with other Kazan films (Eva Marie Saint versus Marlon Brando in *On the Waterfront*, 1954, Lee Remick versus Montgomery Clift in *Wild River*). Kazan's complex, ambivalent version of blonde femininity is embodied in the performance of Carroll Baker as Baby Doll, who combines arrested sexual development with material acquisitiveness. At the same time, in common with other Kazan heroines, she represents a catalyst for change.

PAM COOK

A Face in the Crowd (USA 1957 *p.c* – Newtown Productions/Warner Bros.; *d* – Elia Kazan)

Kazan worked closely with writer Budd Schulberg on the screenplay, which was adapted from Schulberg's short story 'Your Arkansas Traveler'. The film relies on a mixture of realism (in the location scenes, the choice of some Nashville natives as actors and in the journalistic format) and psychological fantasy in its portrayal of common man 'Lonesome' Rhodes's meteoric rise to fame and tragic downfall. It is partly a satire on television, which was rapidly poaching popular audiences from radio and cinema.

In the context of Kazan's work, his preoccupations can be seen in the depiction of the left-wing intellectual (Walter Matthau as Rhodes's scriptwriter Mel Miller) as basically impotent; the juxtaposition of personal relationships and political beliefs (the perverse sexual attraction between Patricia Neal's Marcia Jeffreys and Andy Griffith's thuggish 'Lonesome' Rhodes); and the distinction drawn between surface appearances and underlying reality, here played out in the tension between what the public sees and what goes on behind the scenes.

PAM COOK

Wild River (USA 1960 *p.c* – 20th Century Fox; *d* – Elia Kazan)

Of all his work, this film perhaps shows most clearly Kazan's debt to John Ford, in its humanising of political questions, its nostalgia for those values inevitably threatened by progress and its lyrical approach to its subject.

Kazan had been fascinated by Roosevelt's New Deal policies, particularly in the context of the Tennessee Valley Authority, where he spent time when he was a Communist in the 1930s; he described the film as the story of his love affair with the people of Tennessee and New Deal policies (see Ciment, 1974). Colour and CinemaScope were used to full effect to capture the seductive power of the Southern landscape.

The basic thematic conflicts are between city and country, intellectual and uneducated, bureaucracy and traditional values, manifested in the relationship between the Southern Garth family and the Tennessee Valley Authority Agent (Montgomery Clift) who tries to move them off their island, becoming deeply involved with them in the process.

The central relationship between Carol Garth Baldwin (Lee Remick) and Chuck Glover (Montgomery Clift) revolves around the river; Carol represents the lure of 'the natural', the 'feminine' qualities that the intellectual bureaucrat feels he is lacking, to which he is attracted, but of which he is also afraid, because he must prove himself as a man. On the other hand, the stubbornness of matriarch Ella Garth (Jo Van Fleet) in refusing to leave her home represents the toughness and courage of the rural community. Chuck must somehow reconcile his admiration for the land and its people with the human cost of progress. The mise en scène depends on widescreen framing and long takes, which seems to support the validation of 'natural qualities' projected by the film, although Kazan has suggested that the absence of montage editing was forced on him by the aesthetics of the CinemaScope shape and that the style of the film was not intentional (Ciment, 1974, p. 122).

PAM COOK

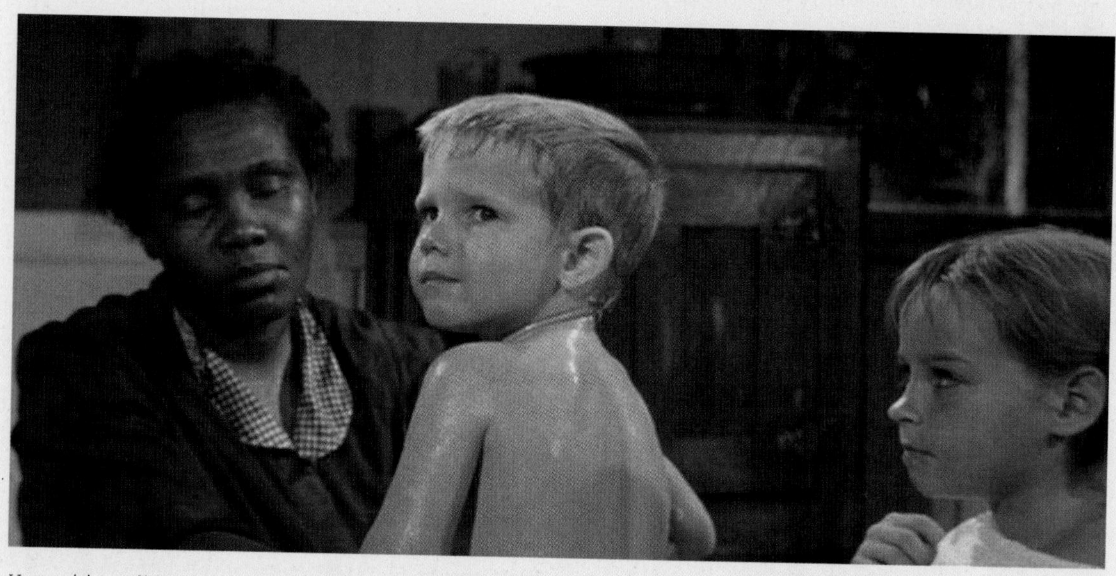

Humanising political issues: *Wild River*, Kazan's tribute to John Ford

British auteurs

British cinema has not generally been regarded as a cinema of auteurs. This may be one of the reasons it is perceived as less successful in international terms than some other smaller-scale national cinemas: in order to differentiate themselves from Hollywood, national cinemas often position themselves as art cinema, depending on the names of directors who possess a recognisable style, and the kudos of film festival awards, to appeal to niche audiences of cultured, knowledgeable viewers. The art-film strategy can be successful in allowing smaller national cinemas to compete with Hollywood in domestic and world markets (see, for example, Pedro Almodóvar and Spanish cinema; or Wong Kar-wai and Hong Kong cinema). However, international status can also result in the loss of national specificity, as art-house directors attract the interest of the major conglomerates and their work is absorbed into a 'global' (usually perceived as Hollywood) aesthetic (for example, French film-maker Jean-Pierre Jeunet's *Alien Resurrection*, 1997; or the Australian Baz Luhrmann's *Moulin Rouge!*, 2001).

British cinema's reputation as a realist cinema with its roots in documentary is somewhat at odds with the idea of a distinctive personal style on which auteur status depends. However, realism itself is an aesthetic that can take on many different manifestations (see, for example, the 'poetic realism' of Free Cinema and the British New Wave, p. 420); and it can be deployed creatively to distinguish one director's work from another's. In recent years, the art-house strategy has been significant in raising the profile of British cinema in the all-important American market and elsewhere. Film-makers such as Merchant–Ivory, Mike Leigh, Ken Loach, Michael Winterbottom and Lynne Ramsay (p. 189) have all used different varieties of realism to establish an art cinema niche for their work, which is identified as British auteur cinema across the globe.

There have, of course, always been significant British directors with international reputations. But historically, these figures have tended to be discussed in terms of their social, institutional and industrial contexts rather than as auteurs in their own right. (If they are treated as auteurs, as in the case of Alfred Hitchcock, it is generally the American work that receives most critical attention; see p. 398.) This bias towards contextual analysis could be seen as an advantage, since it avoids the individualism typical of much auteur theory. British auteurs have often emerged from a background of group work and collaborative activity with specific cultural and social roots, which could provide a challenge to traditional auteurist approaches.

Nevertheless, the art-house strategy and its reliance on auteurs have been significant in British cinema history at different times. One such moment is the 1940s, often viewed as a 'golden age' when British films were able to compete successfully with Hollywood in the domestic and American markets. This success encouraged film-makers and critics to mount a campaign for a postwar 'quality' British cinema defined in terms of humanism, realism and restraint (see Ellis, 1978). During the ensuing intense debates, a consensus was created around a canon of works that were seen to conform to quality-film standards, while anything aesthetically excessive was heavily criticised or rejected. David Lean was one of those whose work was generally approved, while the films of Michael Powell and

Wendy Hiller as Joan Webster discovers a magical Scotland in Powell and Pressburger's *I Know Where I'm Going!*

DAVID LEAN

Brief Encounter (UK 1945 *p.c* – Cineguild/ Independent Producers; *d* – David Lean)

Brief Encounter was based on the playlet 'Still Life' by Noël Coward, who co-wrote the screenplay with Lean, Ronald Neame and Anthony Havelock-Allan, and is also credited as producer. Now celebrated as one of the high points of British cinema, it was greeted with derision by some British audiences on its release in 1945 because of its outmoded view of national mores and morals. By contrast, quality critics of the time hailed the film as a masterpiece, praising its realism and holding it up as a model of what British cinema should be.

'Realism' seems a strange term to use in relation to a film that is characterised by artificiality. *Brief Encounter* is a melodrama dealing with the suppression of sexual desire by social forces (Dyer, 1993). Its heroine, Laura Jesson (Celia Johnson), is a middle-class housewife whose (unconsummated) affair with an ambitious young doctor, Alec Harvey (Trevor Howard), disrupts her safe family life and puts at risk everything she thought she held dear. The mise en scène, the sound and the lead players' performances become increasingly abstract and intense, with strong contrasts of light and dark employed to express the characters' inner torment. The emotional sequences are counterpointed by archly comic interludes featuring the stationmaster Mr Godby (Stanley Holloway) and the buffet manageress Myrtle Bagot (Joyce Carey). The broad humour of these scenes highlights the repression and stuffiness of the world of the middle-class would-be lovers, whose affair can only blossom elsewhere, in Laura's fantasies or on another continent (Alec decides to emigrate to South Africa, vainly hoping that Laura will join him).

The plot is convoluted, as Laura recalls her meetings with Alec over several weeks. This narrative complexity adds to the film's 'difficulty'; at the same time, it is an expression of Laura's unstable psychological state, as she remembers and misremembers what happened. This 'Expressionist' quality, together with Celia Johnson's subtle, luminescent performance, provides the psychological realism that critics admired. Laura Jesson seems to epitomise a British femininity caught up in social change, yet unable to grasp available opportunities. In that sense, *Brief Encounter* remains a powerful statement about British culture and society in transition at the end of World War II. It is also an example of Lean's melodramatic style and concern with identity crisis in characters caught up in forces they cannot control, evident in films from *Great Expectations* (1946) to *The Bridge on the River Kwai* (1957), *Lawrence of Arabia* (1962) and *A Passage to India* (1984).

PAM COOK

Emeric Pressburger occupied a more ambivalent and contested place in the canon. Both Lean and Powell and Pressburger emerged from the buoyant, expansive and ambitious climate of 1940s British cinema, which enabled them to achieve international reputations. However, the career trajectories of these film-makers were very different.

David Lean

Director David Lean's association with cinematographer Ronald Neame and producer Anthony Havelock-Allan on the critically acclaimed naval drama *In Which We Serve* (1942) led to the formation of their company Cineguild Productions in 1944. Cineguild was responsible for a handful of prestige productions that helped to sustain the reputation of quality British cinema until the company's demise in the late 1940s. These included the adaptations of Noël Coward's plays *This Happy Breed* (1944), *Blithe Spirit* (1945) and *Brief Encounter* (1945) and the Charles Dickens adaptations *Great Expectations* (1946) and *Oliver Twist* (1948). Between 1943 and 1949, Cineguild operated under the umbrella of the J. Arthur Rank Organisation; in order to mount a determined assault on the American market, film magnate Rank formed a loose association of independent producers (which included Powell and Pressburger's company The Archers and Frank Launder and Sidney Gilliat's Individual Pictures) to whom he extended the relatively lavish facilities of his studios and a high degree of creative autonomy in return for the production of prestige films he could sell abroad, particularly to the Americans (see Macnab, 1993). Rank's Independent Producers Ltd (IPL) experiment only survived for a few years, but it was responsible for generating some of the most ambitious and internationally respected British productions. The ethos of IPL was intended to be collaborative, though this rarely extended to co-operation between the different companies. Nevertheless, Lean's early career, before and during IPL, was characterised by collaboration, not least with Noël Coward on *In Which We Serve*, *This Happy Breed*, *Blithe Spirit* and *Brief Encounter*.

This emphasis on collaboration, together with his reputation for careful attention to detail, may be responsible for David Lean's classification as a master craftsman rather than full-blown auteur. It is also the case that there is a division between his early work, with its focus on intimate portrayal of characters in confined settings, and the later sweeping historical epics such as *The Bridge on the River Kwai* (1957), *Lawrence of Arabia* (1962) or *Doctor Zhivago* (1965). Nevertheless, a consistent set of concerns can be traced across this body of work: with the nature of Britishness; with gender and sexuality; and with the impact of historical change on people's lives. In terms of style, Lean's expressive (even Expressionist) mise en scène and use of sound and music lend powerful emotional resonance to his films from *Brief Encounter* to *A Passage to India* (1984). Auteur or metteur en scène, he is a major proponent of quality British cinema at its best.

Powell and Pressburger

After many years in the wilderness, Michael Powell and Emeric Pressburger's films have now achieved the status of masterpieces of British cinema. Popular successes at the time of their release, they were greeted with incomprehension by many critics of the day, who found it difficult to come to terms with their aesthetic excesses and were bemused by their sprawling, dreamlike narratives. Although Powell and Pressburger (and

An Englishman abroad: Peter O'Toole explores his sexual and national identity in David Lean's epic *Lawrence of Arabia*

Powell in particular) had been championed by isolated voices such as Raymond Durgnat (1965; 1971) and Kevin Gough-Yates (1971), and idolised by the French (see Lefèvre and Lacourbe, 1976, pp. 274–5), it was the publication of Ian Christie's *Powell, Pressburger and Others* (1978) that initiated a wholesale revaluation of the place of the duo in British film culture. This was the first time that the collaborative working practices of their company The Archers, formed in 1943, which brought together émigré film-makers from continental Europe and British technical and creative personnel, had been seen in the context of 1940s British cinema. It was also the first time that their body of work had been examined in depth, and its controversial nature explored. Christie's book revealed an undercurrent of xenophobia in the focus on Michael Powell as the 'author' of The Archers' films, to the exclusion of Emeric Pressburger's contribution – a tendency that persists, even though Pressburger's work has higher visibility today (see Macdonald, 1996). It is telling that though Michael Powell's centenary was widely celebrated in the UK in 2005, Pressburger's centenary in 2002 was generally overlooked.

Since *Powell, Pressburger and Others*, partly as a result of the general reassessment of British cinema, the significance of Powell and Pressburger's films has been widely recognised, and they have achieved the critical kudos that so often eluded them. Their working methods and creative ambition flourished in the context of J. Arthur Rank's IPL experiment, and their productions of this period were instrumental in raising the international profile of British cinema at the time and subsequently. Their maverick, risk-taking approach to technology and their stylised, vivid use of image and sound may have owed more to continental European aesthetics than to prevailing notions of realism in British film culture – but this very quality of difference challenges the perceived dominance of realism and restraint in British cinema, as well as the perceived national identity of that cinema. Similarly, the emphasis on collaborative production practices, encapsulated in the attribution of joint authorship to both Powell and Pressburger on The Archers' productions, goes against the grain of auteur theory, since style and meaning cannot be vested in the director or any single figure.

Selected Reading

Pam Cook, *I Know Where I'm Going!*, London, BFI Publishing, 2002.

Kevin Macdonald, *Emeric Pressburger: The Life and Death of a Screenwriter*, London, Faber and Faber, 1996.

Geoffrey Macnab, *J. Arthur Rank and the British Film Industry*, London and New York, Routledge, 1993.

Sarah Street, *Transatlantic Crossings: British Feature Films in the USA*, NewYork, Continuum, 2002.

POWELL AND PRESSBURGER

I Know Where I'm Going! (UK 1945 *p.c* – The Archers/Independent Producers; *d* – Michael Powell and Emeric Pressburger)

This film was conceived during a hiatus in The Archers' production schedule. The spectacular extravaganza *A Matter of Life and Death* (1946) had been delayed due to the temporary unavailability of Technicolor; to fill the gap, Powell and Pressburger decided to make a more modest film, a simple love story set in the Scottish Highlands and shot in black and white. *I Know Where I'm Going!* was intended to be more straightforward in conception and execution than earlier productions such as *The Life and Death of Colonel Blimp* (1943) and *A Canterbury Tale* (1944), which had been greeted with incomprehension by many critics (though Erwin Hillier's stunning cinematography for the latter received lavish praise). Nevertheless, the Scottish romance was extremely ambitious in its adventurous use of special visual effects, which involved an innovative use of rear projection employed to recreate Scotland at Rank's Denham studios. One of the most impressive set-pieces was the complicated Corryvreckan whirlpool sequence, staged using models, location footage and rear projection on one of Denham's water tanks.

Such technological and aesthetic ambition was characteristic of all The Archers productions, and played an important role in raising the international profile of British cinema during the 1940s – particularly in the US, where their films were admired. But despite the British settings of many of their films, including this one, it has been argued that their vision of Britain and Britishness owes more than a little to the continental European émigrés who contributed their skills and experience, and their memories (see Cook, 2002). In the case of *I Know Where I'm Going!*, this included cinematographer Erwin Hillier, production designer Alfred Junge and composer Allan Gray, in addition of course to Pressburger himself. Macdonald (1996) has argued that Pressburger's contribution to the films extended beyond that of scriptwriter to input into the visual dimension, in the tradition of the German film industry in which he worked for many years. Powell and Pressburger's collaborative working methods, whereby each draft of the script went through many changes after intensive discussion, also suggest that creative vision cannot be attributed to one or the other.

Pressburger had wanted to make this film for some time; it is the story of a wilful young woman (Wendy Hiller) who sets out on a journey to marry her boss, one of the wealthiest men in the UK, on a remote Scottish island, but falls in love with an impoverished young laird (Roger Livesey) and is forced to revise her priorities. In the inventive hands of The Archers, it became a reflection on materialism, evoking Scotland as an enchanted realm, a refuge from the pressures of modern existence. Like all their films for IPL, it also enabled the technical resources of Rank's studio set-up to be put on display.

PAM COOK

The Red Shoes (UK 1948 *p.c* – The Archers/Independent Producers; *d* – Michael Powell and Emeric Pressburger)

Powell and Pressburger were known for their total disregard for realism, which put them at odds with

Delirious Technicolor dreamscape: Moira Shearer follows her destiny in *The Red Shoes*

the critical consensus in wartime and postwar Britain. *The Red Shoes* is one of the most dazzling and vivid examples of this, as it eschews the distinction between art and reality. It concerns a young ballet dancer, Vicky Page (newcomer Moira Shearer), who finds herself torn between her artistic ambitions and her love for talented composer Julian Craster (Marius Goring) when she falls under the spell of her power-crazed mentor Boris Lermontov (Anton Walbrook), director of the ballet troupe for which they both work. The film is a delirious Technicolor fantasy in which Vicky's tragic story mirrors that of the Hans Christian Andersen fairytale and the ballet-within-the-film inspired by it. Thus it is far more than a film of the ballet, as Vicky's destiny is first visualised through her intense performance of *The Red Shoes*, and then inexorably unfolds at the film's climax. The ballet sequence itself is a tour de force of visual special effects in which Vicky's emotional torment is dramatised through nightmarish images and sets evoking surrealism, cubism and abstract expressionism.

Production designer Hein Heckroth and cinematographer Jack Cardiff produced a modernist, painterly look for the film through saturated colour and dramatic lighting that help to evoke the excitement, conflict and neurosis of the artistic world. Surprisingly, in the light of The Archers' European heritage, the film presents a dark and pessimistic view of creative collaboration between the British characters and the impresario Lermontov, who was based on the notorious director of the Ballets Russes, Sergei Diaghilev. This pessimism may have been connected to the escalating Cold War. *The Red Shoes* was better received in the US than in the UK (see Street, 2002) and is reputed to have influenced Gene Kelly's staging of the 17-minute ballet sequence in *An American in Paris* (1951).

PAM COOK

Contemporary British directors

Stephen Frears

Stephen Frears began his film-making career in the 1960s as assistant director on Karel Reisz's *Morgan – A Suitable Case for Treatment* (see p. 424) and then on *Charlie Bubbles* (1968) and Lindsay Anderson's *If ...* (see p. 423). He worked regularly as a television director in the late 1960s and 1970s, making his feature-film debut with *Gumshoe* (1971), starring Albert Finney as a would-be private eye. His background in television produced critical successes such as *Bloody Kids* (1980), co-scripted by Stephen Poliakoff, and *Saigon: Year of the Cat* (1983), written by David Hare. Following the quirky feature *The Hit* (1984), a low-key thriller starring Terence Stamp, Frears achieved a cinematic triumph with *My Beautiful Laundrette* (1985). Scripted by Hanif Kureishi, the film centred on an interracial love affair between Omar (Gordon Warnecke), the son of a Pakistani immigrant (Roshan Seth), and Johnny (Daniel Day-Lewis), an ex-member of the National Front. A low-budget production shot on 16mm, the film was originally intended for television rather than theatrical release. After an ecstatic critical reception, it was distributed internationally on 35mm and became a huge, controversial success (Geraghty, 2004).

My Beautiful Laundrette was followed by a biopic of Joe Orton, *Prick up Your Ears* (1987), written by Alan Bennett, and *Sammy and Rosie Get Laid* (1987), Frears's second collaboration with Hanif Kureishi. Both received a respectable critical response, and Frears then went to the US, where he directed *Dangerous Liaisons* (1988), *The Grifters* (1990), for which he received a Best Director Academy Award nomination, and *Accidental Hero* (1992). The next ten years, when he oscillated between British television and the US film industry, saw a patchy series of films including *Mary Reilly* (1996), *The Van* (1996), *The Hi-Lo Country* (1998) and the acclaimed *Dirty Pretty Things* (2002), which dealt with the experience of immigrants living in contemporary London. In 2003, Frears worked with screenwriter Peter Morgan on the television film *The Deal*, a dramatisation of the relationship between British Prime Minister Tony Blair and Chancellor Gordon Brown and the supposed deal between them about the leadership of the Labour Party. Morgan and Frears collaborated again on *The Queen* (2006), which was nominated for numerous awards in 2007, including ten BAFTAs and six Oscars. *The Queen* made skilful use of archive documentary material to produce a funny and poignant account of the political events surrounding the death of Princess Diana.

Frears is one of British cinema's most highly regarded directors, yet he has decided not to take the familiar path of permanent emigration to the US. Instead, he moves between the British and American industries – a successful strategy that

Daniel Day-Lewis and Gordon Warnecke in Stephen Frears's ground-breaking *My Beautiful Laundrette*

is adopted by many contemporary international film-makers. His career is distinguished by collaboration with writers, and he has consistently given credit to collaborators, seeing his role as a director to facilitate and enable the talents of others rather than to project his individual vision, and downplaying his status as auteur. Despite viewing television as primarily a writer's medium, Frears has achieved some of his most innovative work in that medium, which, with the increasing interaction between TV and feature-film companies, provides valuable production and exhibition opportunities for British film-makers (see Contemporary British cinema, p. 185).

Danny Boyle

Like Stephen Frears, Danny Boyle worked in theatre and television before making his feature-film debut with *Shallow Grave* (1994). A black-comedy-cum-thriller set in modern-day Scotland, this featured an accomplished early performance by Ewan McGregor as Alex, one of three flatmates who get caught up in a murder. Cheekily reminiscent of Coen brothers films such as *Blood Simple* (1983), *Shallow Grave* was an immediate success for its production team – director Boyle, producer Andrew Macdonald and writer John Hodge. It demonstrated an assured sense of visual style and genre, and contributed to the Scottish cinema boom of the 1990s (see also Scottish cinema, p. 187). But the huge success of the team's next feature, *Trainspotting* (1996), adapted from Irvine Welsh's cult novel and starring Ewan McGregor as Renton, totally eclipsed the earlier film at the time of its release and subsequently. *Trainspotting* was set in Edinburgh and dealt with the underground drug counter-culture that provided uncomfortable insight into the city's seamy underside. Rich with irony, stylish and featuring a 'cool' contemporary pop

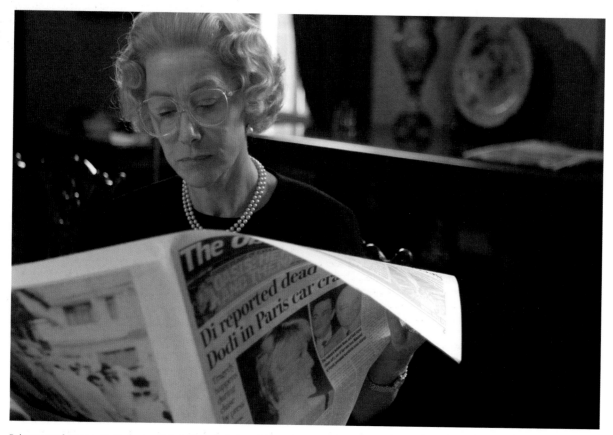

Poignant and unexpectedly funny: Helen Mirren in Frears's *The Queen*

Hot property: Danny Boyle's ambitious sci-fi thriller *Sunshine*

soundtrack, the film was supported by an aggressive and innovative marketing campaign that ensured international success (see Smith, 2002).

The success of *Trainspotting* made the team hot property, and they embarked on their first America-set venture, *A Life Less Ordinary* (1997), a quirky romantic-comedy-cum-thriller starring Ewan McGregor and Cameron Diaz that had British funding. This was followed by the more expensive production *The Beach* (2000), an adaptation of Alex Garland's book starring Leonardo DiCaprio, funded by 20th Century Fox. Both these films had limited success, and Boyle returned to the UK to direct two BBC television films, *Vacuuming Completely Nude in Paradise* and *Strumpet* (both 2001). Boyle's next feature outing was *28 Days Later …* (2002), a science-fiction film shot on digital video. Scripted by Alex Garland and produced by Andrew Macdonald's company DNA Films, it was set in a post-apocalyptic London where a few survivors struggle to stay alive (see Contemporary British cinema, p. 186). 2004's *Millions* centred on two young boys who accidentally find the proceeds of a train robbery and have a week to spend the money before they are discovered. Boyle's next project, the sci-fi thriller *Sunshine* (2007), was set 50 years in the future, when a team of astronauts is sent to reignite the failing sun in order to save the earth from extinction. Andrew Macdonald's DNA Films was involved in this production, with Fox Searchlight handling distribution.

In common with other contemporary British film-makers, Danny Boyle followed spectacular success in the UK with uneven results in the US, and a consequent return to his British roots. Despite their patchy critical and box-office performance, his films have acquired a cult reputation for their individual style and adventurous approach to film-making. His collaborative working methods are typical of British film production, as well as of independent cinema generally.

Gurinder Chadha

Gurinder Chadha is one of the few successful women directors to emerge from British cinema. Her first directorial venture was *I'm British But …* (1989), a stylish 30-minute documentary about young Asians in the UK featuring an innovative use of Bhangra and Bangla music, made for the British Film Institute's New Directors scheme with the participation of Channel Four. Her next production, the short fiction film *A Nice Arrangement* (1991), a comedy about arranged marriage featuring a performance by Meera Syal, was produced by FilmFour, the production arm of Channel Four. In the documentary *Acting Our Age* (1991), elderly Asians living in Southall recalled their experiences of living in the UK. All these concerns came together in Chadha's first feature, *Bhaji on the Beach* (1993), which followed three generations of Asian women from Birmingham on a daytrip to Blackpool. The witty script by Chadha and Meera Syal, and the non-moralistic approach, contributed to the film's critical and commercial success. *Bhaji on the Beach* consolidated Chadha's reputation as a distinctive new talent, and it won numerous awards. It was also hailed as a breakthrough to a different kind

Exploring race and ethnicity with style and verve: Aishwarya Rai in Gurinder Chadha's Bollywood-style musical *Bride & Prejudice*

of British-Asian cinema with broad appeal and crossover potential (see Malik, 1996). Chadha went on to direct a two-part television film, *Rich Deceiver* (1995), about a working-class woman who keeps her substantial win on the football pools a secret from her husband, and a number of television documentaries. Her next feature project, *What's Cooking?* (2000), was set in America, and partly funded by the Sundance Institute. A lively comedy scripted by Chadha with her husband Paul Mayeda Burges, it explored ethnic identity by contrasting the Thanksgiving celebrations of four families – African-American, Latino, Jewish and Asian. In 2002, Chadha directed the huge commercial and critical success *Bend It Like Beckham*, starring Parminder Nagra, Keira Knightley and Jonathan Rhys Meyers in a story about two young women's ambitions to become professional footballers, and the difficulties they encountered. Chadha's ability to explore issues of race and ethnicity with subtlety, style and visual verve were displayed in *Bride & Prejudice* (2004), a Bollywood-style musical version of Jane Austen's *Pride and Prejudice* that gave this most English of stories a transnational inflection by relocating it to modern-day India, America and the UK.

Chadha has established an international reputation as a director who continues to make a vibrant contribution to British-Asian cinema, to British television and to world cinema. Her films question what it means to be British, in a national and transnational context, but in typically populist style she has also taken on projects that deal with topics other than race (for example, *Rich Deceiver*). Her next project was expected to be a film version of the long-running television series *Dallas* (1978–91), backed by US independent Regency Enterprises. In common with many of her contemporaries (see also Four contemporary directors, p. 479), Chadha has benefited from the interaction between the film and television industries (see also Contemporary women directors, p. 68), the growth of the independents in the US and the proliferation of co-production finance in the global era.

Selected Reading

Christine Geraghty, *My Beautiful Laundrette*, London, I. B. Tauris, 2004.

Sarita Malik, 'Beyond "the cinema of duty"? The pleasures of hybridity: black British films of the 1980s and 1990s', in Higson (ed.), *Dissolving Views: Key Writings on British Cinema*, London and New York, Cassell, 1996.

Murray Smith, *Trainspotting*, London, BFI Publishing, 2002.

British cinema: auteur and studio

Ealing Studios

While traditional auteur study concentrates on the director as source of meaning at the expense of conditions of production, analyses of production contexts often fail to account for the director's contribution altogether. If auteur theory places the director in conflict with industrial modes of production, then paradoxically it is precisely those industrial conditions that allow auteurs to flourish. Two studies on Ealing Studios by John Ellis (1975) and Charles Barr (1999) attempted to relate conditions of production to ideological readings of the films, with important consequences for auteur analysis. John Ellis traced in detail the nexus of working relationships and methods within the apparently homogeneous group known as 'Ealing', showing how the group's reputation for working together as a team, or 'family', was based on a hierarchical division of labour between 'creative workers' and technicians, with producer Michael Balcon retaining final control. Within this framework, members of the 'creative elite' consisting of producers, directors and scriptwriters collaborated in the early stages of pre-production, but Balcon's decisions were final. Director Robert

Hamer, for instance, constantly found his projects vetoed because his concerns were significantly different from those of the studio. At production stage, too, requirements of time, space and money dictated certain shooting methods that produced a particular style of film: short takes and static shots. Some directors (Hamer again, and Alexander Mackendrick) who wanted to work differently found this very difficult. Rushes were viewed by the editor in consultation with Balcon rather than with the director, but final editing was done in collaboration with the director, a situation that could lead to conflict, as it did on *Kind Hearts and Coronets* (Ellis, 1975, p. 103).

This historical analysis of the institutional framework within which the film-makers worked revealed the contradictions underlying the prevailing view of the studio as a liberal and democratic working team; by showing how the concerns of some directors were in conflict with the studio's attempt to perpetuate an 'Ealing product', it began to differentiate between films, arguing that the product cannot be seen as homogeneous. This approach suggests that the organisational structure of Ealing militated against the emergence of auteurs, though directors such as Hamer and Mackendrick have been given that status in retrospect – and, indeed, their differences with the studio have been used to establish them as auteurs (Barr, 1999).

'Made in Ealing' described how the hierarchial organisation and system of controls in operation at Ealing Studios under Michael Balcon both supported the project of producing a particular kind of 'quality' film and effectively prevented other, different projects from being realised. Ellis showed that the personal concerns and methods of working of some directors (notably Robert Hamer, but also to a certain extent Alexander Mackendrick and Thorold Dickinson) were generally at variance with the interests of the studio. Charles Barr (1999) has argued along similar lines that there is a 'mainstream' Ealing (nonetheless important and interesting for being so) manifested mainly in the films of Basil Dearden and T. E. B. Clarke, and an 'oppositional' Ealing (the films of Robert Hamer and Alexander Mackendrick) that not only shows different concerns from the 'mainstream' but reflects critically upon it. Barr's reading of Hamer and Mackendrick placed them in their historical context, showing how they contradict and undermine the Ealing project in general while working within its different genres and stereotypes and how they indirectly reflect upon the frustrations experienced by those film-makers whose interests conflicted with those of the studio. Auteur analysis here has the advantage of differentiating between a body of films in such a way as to bring out contradictions, thus challenging dismissive critical accounts that stress the homogeneity of the films produced by Ealing. Barr combined several different forms of reading – ideological, historical and auteurist – to build up a complex and fascinating account of the work of Ealing Studios that leads to a reassessment of those films in which auteur study plays an important part. Both Ellis and Barr concentrated on the conflicts between directors and studio head Michael Balcon, seeing the 'oppositional' films as a result of that conflict. However, there are other potentially critical voices in the film-making process – that of the writer, for instance. It should be possible to read some Ealing films in terms of multiple conflicting contributions, so that the director is not always seen as the major, or only, critical voice.

Robert Hamer

Ellis described the relationship between Hamer and Ealing Studios in terms of Hamer's antipathy to certain of the studio's fundamental values, which made his career there somewhat uneasy: 'His attitude to the studio was one of profound ambivalence ... He existed at the extreme edge of, but still within, the community of ideas and assumptions which the studio held' (Ellis, 1975, p. 95).

The extent to which Hamer was part of the community of ideas and assumptions that the studio supported is open to debate. In a detailed analysis of *Kind Hearts and Coronets* (1949), Charles Barr (1999) attempted to show the ways in which the film's complex and multi-layered structure works against the form of realism prevalent in the Ealing 'mainstream' to produce meanings that undermine its common-sense humanism and, more than this, inscribe a scenario of frustrated desire that comments both on British society itself and on Ealing's depiction of it. The dispute between Hamer and Balcon over the editing of the trial sequence is usually described in terms of different interests: Balcon wanted to emphasise the class aspects of the scene, Hamer was interested in the sexual aspects. This illustrates another point of conflict between Hamer and Ealing: the studio's attitude towards sexuality is generally recognised to have been repressive, linked to ideas of 'good taste' and 'quality' as hallmarks of British cinema, and to notions of sexuality that place women safely within the family and men in the public, cultural sphere (Ellis, 1975). Hamer is known to have been interested in sexual and psychological themes and Charles Barr makes a good case for his films as forming part of an 'underground current' in British cinema: the cinema of sex and violence that surfaces in the Gainsborough productions of the 1940s (Gainsborough Pictures, p. 178) and in the films of Powell and Pressburger (p. 434), burgeoning forth in Hammer Productions (p. 442) a decade later.

ROBERT HAMER

Dead of Night (UK 1945 *p.c* – Ealing Studios; *d* – Robert Hamer [*The Haunted Mirror*])

John Ellis argues that the basic strategies of Ealing's realist cinema were closely linked to those of classic narrative cinema. Formal innovations were contained within a project that carried with it 'a certain mode of watching', encouraging the audience to recognise (or rather misrecognise) itself in the representation of full and finished characters, coherent entities living at the centre of society (Ellis, 1975, p. 107).

Ellis emphasises that this process of identification is complex and that Ealing managed to pose some real social problems in this mode. It is tempting to see Hamer's section of Ealing's portmanteau film *Dead of Night, The Haunted Mirror*, as a metaphor for the process of recognition/ misrecognition and as a criticism of it. The complacent middle-class hero Peter Cortland (Ralph Michael) finds the coherence of his own identity and then the ordered pattern of his life split and fractured by violent images from some mysterious past projected by the mirror, images that gradually take him over and transform him into a madman, violently possessed by sexual

Michael Redgrave in Ealing's portmanteau film *Dead of Night*: a rare foray by the studio into the horror genre

jealousy. The Ealing image of the 'ideal hero', represented by Ralph Michael, could be seen to be radically questioned in this film, so that the viewer's identification is hindered. The role of the heroine in restoring the status quo could be discussed in relation to Ealing's representation of women. In a sense, Joan Cortland (Googie Withers) controls the narrative: she gives Peter the mirror, and her presence seems to dispel the 'other world'. Finally, she defeats it by smashing the mirror.

The film can also be seen as a link with later developments in the British horror film, where a complacent social order is disturbed by repressed forces. After *Dead of Night*, Ealing did not open the gate to the dark 'other world' again. Instead, it accepted the terms of constraint on sexuality and violence that *The Haunted Mirror* implicitly criticises.

PAM COOK

Kind Hearts and Coronets (UK 1949 *p.c* – Ealing Studios; *d* – Robert Hamer)

An ironic satire on the British class system, co-scripted by Hamer, this film features Dennis Price as the dispossessed Louis Mazzini who plots to gain a dukedom by killing off eight members of the aristocratic D'Ascoyne family (all played by Alec Guinness) who stand in his way. Ealing's predilection for realism and restraint, particularly in the areas of sexuality and violence, is challenged by Hamer's frank portrayal of sex and murder here. In addition to the witty play with Alec Guinness's performance, the film employs voice-over in an innovatory manner. The overall effect is of a dark, sophisticated comedy that not-too-subtly lampoons British manners and mores – perhaps one reason why it has gained a critical reputation as a masterpiece of British cinema. At the same time, it puts on display the skills of the character actors with which that cinema is identified.

PAM COOK

Alexander Mackendrick

The status of auteur conferred upon Hamer and Mackendrick is justified in terms of readings of their films that reveal the tensions they display with all that Ealing represents. However, Ealing itself did not remain the same and the differences of inflection between the films of Hamer and Mackendrick are as much the result of the changing historical situation as of different personal concerns.

Mackendrick was active in Ealing from 1949 onwards; according to Barr (1999), by the early 1950s Ealing's buoyant period was more or less over, the self-effacement of the individual in the Ealing community was consolidated and sexuality was more or less excluded from the films. The established order was now to be learned from, rather than questioned. It is against this background of stifling conformity that Mackendrick co-wrote and directed *The Man in the White Suit* (1951), a biting satire of British antipathy to creativity and innovation. For Barr (1999), Mackendrick's Ealing films are cruelly satirical, especially in their treatment of the English; Colin McArthur, on the other hand, sees the director's films *Whisky Galore!* (1949) and *The Maggie* (1954) as self-lacerating (see McArthur, 1982, 2002; see also Kemp, 1991).

ALEXANDER MACKENDRICK

The Man in the White Suit (UK 1951 *p.c* – Ealing Studios; *d* – Alexander Mackendrick)

Charles Barr (1999) sees this film, about a young scientist who invents a fabric that never gets dirty and never wears out, as a critical statement about England governed by consensus and about the relationship of opposition between the old and the new, between father and son.

John Ellis (1975) provides a reading of the film that places it more centrally (less critically) with Ealing's output, drawing on a description of the studio's 'creative elite' as a group of middle-class intellectuals who conceived of 'the people' in a certain way, as petty bourgeois shopkeepers and clerks rather than factory workers. Ellis criticises *The Man in the White Suit* for concentrating on individuals 'at the point of exchange' rather than workers 'at the point of production'. However, it could be argued that it is through this emphasis on 'the point of exchange' that the film is able to criticise the social relationships that 'mainstream' Ealing takes for granted: relationships between workers and bosses, between father and daughter, between men and women, as organised by capitalism – not necessarily a conscious criticism, since Mackendrick himself

Phyllis Calvert and Jack Hawkins form a bond with Mandy Miller in Mackendrick's moving melodrama *Mandy*

saw the film in psychological terms, as a hysterical comedy demonstrating that in a psychotic world, neurotics can appear normal (see Cohn, 1968).

Charles Barr analyses a scene in which the heroine Daphne (Joan Greenwood) is asked to use her sexuality to get inventor Sidney Stratton (Alec Guinness) to change his mind, and responds by making a point of putting a price on her services, a scene that is a good example of Mackendrick's use of comedy to make a critical statement about social relationships. In Barr's view, the ruthlessness of this scene is closer to Godard or Buñuel than to mainstream Ealing (Barr, 1977, p. 142). Daphne can be seen as a significantly different type of heroine from the Ealing ideal of femininity. The character tests the limits of the stereotype, much as *The Man in the White Suit* itself can be seen to test the limits of the Ealing comedy genre.

One way of exploring these questions about Mackendrick's relationship to Ealing might be to compare those films he made for the studio with those he made after he left. It is arguable that the later films, while superficially different, show the same underlying structural and thematic concerns and the same critical intelligence: towards Hollywood and America in *Don't Make Waves* (1967) and towards the adult world in *A High Wind in Jamaica* (1965) and *Sammy Going South* (1963) (see Simpson, 1977).

PAM COOK

Mandy (UK 1952 *p.c* – Ealing Studios; *d* – Alexander Mackendrick)

As a social-problem melodrama dealing with the attempts by young mother Christine Garland (Phyllis Calvert) to obtain treatment and education for her deaf-mute daughter (Mandy Miller), this film represents a break with Mackendrick's Ealing comedies. Nonetheless, it displays equal flair and imagination. British bureaucracy is seen as malignant, embedded in a social system that distrusts innovation, and is unwilling to be flexible. Mackendrick draws a moving and sympathetic portrait of a family torn apart as Mandy's father, Harry (Terence Morgan), encouraged by his rigid mother (Marjorie Fielding), is unable to come to terms with his daughter's disability.

The liberal, progressive educationalist Dick Searle (Jack Hawkins) forms a paternalistic relationship with Mandy and her mother that promises to grow into something more as the young girl blossoms under his care and begins to learn to speak. However, in Ealing style, the film holds back from developing the bond between Christine and Searle; instead it shows Harry coming round to Searle's approach once he sees Mandy's progress. Despite the fact that it is Christine's determination that makes it possible for Mandy to connect with normal society, Harry is back in charge as the head of the family at the end. There is a characteristic irony, however, in his gesture of restraint when Christine moves to follow Mandy as she runs out to meet the other children at the end (see Cook, 2005).

In terms of style, Mackendrick uses tight framing to suggest constraint and claustrophobia, and to emphasise Mandy's sense of isolation. His use of sound is startlingly innovative, as he invites the viewer to experience the deaf-mute child's imprisonment in a world of silence. Although Mackendrick's Ealing comedies have received more critical attention, this film remains one of his most accomplished and personal works.

PAM COOK

Hammer Productions

The approaches to Ealing Studios outlined above locate the films historically within multiple, often contradictory, elements that contribute to their meanings, in contrast to traditional auteur study, which attributes meaning simply to the assumed intentions of the director. This kind of contextual analysis acknowledges the director's contribution, although it is not necessarily always the most important or the most helpful in understanding particular films. These analyses of Ealing attempted to show how auteurs such as Robert Hamer and Alexander Mackendrick emerged from specific conditions of production. The apparent similarities between Ealing and Hammer (see Hammer Productions, p. 180) and the fact that Hammer was born as Ealing died, apparently giving life to the side of British cinema that Ealing suppressed (concerned with psychology, sexuality and violence), suggest that a contextual analysis might also be useful in differentiating between the films produced by Hammer.

However, in one of the most impressive critical accounts of Hammer, David Pirie (1973) took a traditional auteur approach in which Terence Fisher emerged as the Hammer director par excellence, creating his own worldview from basic studio material. Pirie argued that Fisher's romantic vision (which he traced back to the director's pre-Hammer productions) transforms even the most banal low-budget project (such as *The Devil Rides Out*, 1967) into a work of classic distinction, making a qualitative difference between Fisher and other directors in much the same way as the *Cahiers* critics, and others, differentiated between auteurs and metteurs en scène.

By all accounts, Hammer directors seem to have had very little personal control over their films. They were employed on a freelance basis, had little to say about casting and scripts, and had to work strictly within the constraints of time, money and space imposed by low-budget commercial production. Under such conditions, the contributions of production workers other than the directors (such as the set designers, for instance) were important, especially in making cheap horror films look expensive. With this in mind, one might ask whether a traditional auteur approach is adequate to understanding Hammer's films (see Hutchings, 1993).

Terence Fisher

One of the functions of the auteur theory is to bestow the status of art on apparently trivial material by showing how a director's oeuvre displays a consistency of style, theme and structure that differentiates it qualitatively from other work in the same genre, allowing us to look at it in a new way. Auteur study can be useful in critical reassessment of areas of cinema history previously neglected or dismissed, such as British cinema, opening up areas of pleasure and aesthetic judgment that differ from those offered by genre study or study of production conditions.

The sensational, exploitation material with which Hammer studios made its name outraged critics when it first appeared. One way to begin the work of reassessment would be to examine the historical reasons for the (temporary) unacceptability of this material to 'serious' British film criticism. Another way would be to give new value to the material by viewing it, as Pirie does, in the context of the literary tradition of Romantic poetry and Gothic writing in British culture. This perspective, combined with auteur analysis, allowed Pirie to argue convincingly that Hammer produced a revolutionary kind of popular art, so that it became possible to re-view the Hammer films and give them 'quality' status in retrospect. If Fisher's films remain within the bounds of the 'quality film', however, other Hammer films do not (for example, Peter Sasdy's *Taste the Blood of Dracula*, 1969), which suggests that Pirie's approach might not be applicable to the entire Hammer output.

Pirie took the work of Terence Fisher as a test case: by establishing Fisher's status as an auteur, he demonstrated that Hammer films were worthy of the serious critical attention so often denied to them. Significantly, he saw Fisher's art as that of a nineteenth-century storyteller, comparable to that of the best Gothic novelists, tracing in his films a coherent worldview based on a strict dualism, an ambiguity towards sexual excess and the body, and a strong belief in the power of rational thought to overcome evil and corruption. It is interesting to speculate to what extent Fisher's work can be identified with the 'mainstream' Hammer product and how far his style and thematic concerns meshed with the interests of the studio. By all accounts, Fisher and Hammer were in complete harmony, which was not the case with all their directors (see *Little Shoppe of Horrors* 4, April 1978).

Selected Reading

Charles Barr, *Ealing Studios*, Moffat, Cameron & Hollis, 1999.

John Ellis, 'Made in Ealing', *Screen* 16 (1): 78–127, spring 1975.

Peter Hutchings, *Hammer and Beyond: British Horror Film*, Manchester, Manchester University Press, 1993.

David Pirie, *A Heritage of Horror: The English Gothic Cinema 1946–1972*, London, Gordon & Fraser, 1973.

TERENCE FISHER

Dracula (UK 1958 *p.c* – Hammer Film Productions; *d* – Terence Fisher)

Fisher inaugurated Hammer's horror cycle with *The Curse of Frankenstein*, which was greeted with critical outrage when it appeared in 1957, but became a huge box-office success. Hammer was quick to capitalise on this success, and *Dracula* went into production about a year later. Pirie's detailed analysis of the film relates it specifically to Bram Stoker's novel, stressing its essentially British version of the legend and describing how Fisher's allusive style apparently meshed perfectly with the studio's concern to convey visually Dracula's sensuality and its effect on women (Pirie, 1973, p. 86).

Dracula reunited Christopher Lee (Count Dracula) and Peter Cushing (Van Helsing), who had both appeared in *The Curse of Frankenstein*. These two actors, together with Fisher's restrained, minimal style, became the hallmark for Hammer horror films. Fisher reinvented the classic Dracula myth by pitting Lee's charming and sophisticated Count against Cushing's zealous and obsessive Van Helsing. Their final showdown is reminiscent of a swashbuckling action film. Although disliked by contemporary critics, *Dracula* has become known as one of Fisher's most stylish works.

PAM COOK

The Mummy (UK 1959 *p.c* – Hammer Film Productions; *d* – Terence Fisher)

Pirie attributes the mise en scène entirely to Fisher, although some of its 'pictorial sensuality' can be put down to the work of regular Hammer art director Bernard Robinson (Pirie, 1973, pp. 57–8). Part of the success of the Hammer horror cycle was due to the studio's ability to draw on a team of talented creative personnel, such as scriptwriter Jimmy Sangster, who wrote the screenplays for *The Curse of Frankenstein* (1957), *Dracula* (1958) and *The Mummy*.

The violation of an Egyptian princess's tomb is the pretext for a revenge curse on a family of British archaeologists. A primary opposition set up in the film is a political one between British imperialism and Egyptian culture, and the 'return of the repressed' theme centres here on the struggle between a 'primitive' culture and so-called civilisation. This compares with similar struggles between primitive forces and scientific reason in the *Dracula* and *Frankenstein* films directed by Fisher for Hammer. Pirie attributes this dualism to Fisher's worldview, but it is also a requirement of the genre (see The horror film, p. 347).

PAM COOK

Peter Cushing confronts Britain's colonial past in *The Mummy*

Rational man: Peter Cushing as the obsessive Van Helsing in Terence Fisher's *Dracula*

The Hound of the Baskervilles (UK/USA 1959 *p.c* – Hammer Film Productions/Universal; *d* – Terence Fisher)

Fisher's work is often admired for the precision with which he unfolds a narrative: he has been described as a master storyteller. According to Pirie, Fisher's most successful films are those in which the lines are drawn with absolute clarity. In this version of Conan Doyle's Sherlock Holmes story, Pirie sees a stark opposition between Holmes's rational Victorian milieu and the demonic cruelty of the Baskerville legend (Pirie, 1973, pp. 56–7). The opening sequence shows this spatial division, as it moves from the 'legend' to the rational context of Baker Street. In Fisher's worldview, reason overcomes evil, and Holmes (Peter Cushing) is one of the rational, obsessive heroes that recur in his films.

The opening sequence provides an interesting contrast with John Gilling's *The Plague of the Zombies* (1966) in which the doctor hero is, unlike the 'Renaissance Man' Sherlock Holmes, as susceptible to the threat represented by repressed evil as the other characters in the film. The characters in Gilling's film do not represent schematic oppositions: the scientist figure (played by André Morell, who played Dr Watson in *The Hound of the Baskervilles*) is not the rational, 'objective' character personified by Peter Cushing, who uses knowledge as a defence against 'evil'. Instead he is an agnostic, experimental scientist who admits that there are areas of thought and experience that defy the tyranny of reason. For this kind of character it is necessary to become actively involved in these areas, risking his rational objectivity.

PAM COOK

The Brides of Dracula (UK 1960 *p.c* – Hotspur Films/Hammer Film Productions; *d* – Terence Fisher)

In agreeing to direct this film for Hammer, Fisher laboured under the difficulties imposed by the absence of Christopher Lee as Count Dracula. *Dracula* (1958) had been an enormous success and in order to cash in on this, Hammer were forced to find a way to make a sequel without Count Dracula himself. Jimmy Sangster's initial script went through many changes, and in the final version Peter Cushing's Van Helsing (one of Fisher's scholar-heroes) became the main protagonist. Pirie identifies some characteristic Fisher touches, particularly in the film's finale, where Van Helsing uses his expert knowledge of vampire lore and not inconsiderable physical skills to overcome the vampire Baron Meinster, Count Dracula's disciple (Pirie, 1973, pp. 88–9).

Also of note in this film is the implied lesbian sexuality; although only an oblique reference here, it was to reappear in more explicit form in later Hammer products, which became increasingly sensational.

PAM COOK

Dracula Prince of Darkness (UK/USA 1965 *p.c* – Hammer Film Productions/Seven Arts/Warner Pathé; *d* – Terence Fisher)

This was the second of Fisher's *Dracula* films to feature Christopher Lee as the Count. Pirie places Fisher's 'artistry' in this film on a par with European art cinema, evoking a comparison with Ingmar Bergman's *Winter Light/Nattvardsgästerna* (1962), and regretting that Hammer proceeded to hand over the *Dracula* series to a succession of directors. According to Pirie, none of the subsequent films can quite compare with Fisher's (Pirie, 1973, pp. 89–93). A different and more critical treatment of the myth is offered by Peter Sasdy's *Taste the Blood of Dracula* (1969). In contrast to Fisher's schematic treatment of the Dracula legend, Sasdy's version is based on a more complex conception of the implicitly destructive relationship of Count Dracula to 'normal' society. Sasdy is concerned with psychological and social rather than metaphysical themes and he bases them on physical eroticism rather than spiritual values.

Sasdy's mise en scène is restrainedly surreal, stressing the fantasy aspect of oral eroticism and the destructive drives that underlie it. The bourgeois façade of Victorian society is seen to be cracking open at the seams under the impact of all that it represses. *Taste the Blood of Dracula* goes far beyond the bounds of taste set by Fisher's work and indicates some of the changes Hammer introduced into its products to maintain its audience.

PAM COOK

The Devil Rides Out (UK 1968 *p.c* – Hammer Film Productions/Associated British Pathé/Seven Arts; *d* – Terence Fisher)

Pirie evaluates this film as one of the high points of British cinema, and places it in a specifically English tradition of horror. According to Pirie, Dennis Wheatley's unremarkable novel is transformed by Fisher and scriptwriter Richard Matheson into a Gothic tale of good versus evil. Wheatley's novel linked Satanism to Communism; in Matheson's script, the threat was transferred to the heart of British society. Pirie refers to the scene in which Mocata, the head of the coven, visits the Eaton household in search of the young couple who have been taken from his clutches, and to the film's climax in which the four agents of good spend a night within the pentacle assailed by the forces of evil, arguing that the subtle script combined with Fisher's allusive and restrained mise en scène produce a new and powerful aesthetic masterpiece consistent with Fisher's dualistic worldview (Pirie, 1973, pp. 60–4).

PAM COOK

AUTEUR THEORY AND STRUCTURALISM

PAM COOK

French intellectual context

The 'structuralist controversy' (as it came to be known) emerged from the fierce debates raging among left-wing intellectuals in the universities of Paris during the mid-1960s. These debates caused reverberations in British intellectual life that are still felt today (see also Structuralism and its aftermaths, p. 510).

The year in which *Movie* first appeared (1962) was also the year of publication in Paris of anthropologist Claude Lévi-Strauss's *La Pensée sauvage* that included a challenge to Jean-Paul Sartre's 'developmental' view of history and was to bring forward debates with far-reaching effects in many disciplines: linguistics, literature, anthropology, history, sociology, art, music, psychoanalysis and, not least, philosophy and politics. In contrast to the existentialists, Lévi-Strauss argued that history does not reveal the present as the necessary culmination of events in the past: rather, history offers us images of past societies that are structural transformations of those we know today, neither better nor worse. In this sense, modern 'man' is not so much a superior development of his antecedents as a complex amalgam of different historical levels that can be shown to coexist in our modern minds (Leach, 1970). This view of 'man' as the result of the interaction of historical forces rather than occupying a position of superiority in relation to the past set in motion an intellectual shift that was to recast the problems posed by nineteenth-century thought and demand that they be looked at in a new way.

Structuralism, by drawing attention to the underlying sets of relationships both within and between cultural objects (or events), claimed that it was these relationships that should occupy the attention of the analyst rather than the search for some pre-existing essential meaning hidden behind the mask of language. Structuralism and the allied discipline semiology were a radical challenge to those empirical methods that took for granted as pre-given the objects of its analysis. However, as its critics were later to point out, structuralism itself fell into some of the ideological traps it was so anxious to avoid: the search for 'underlying structural relationships' often involved a reduction of those relationships to a fixed, static underlying structure, waiting to be revealed; and structures themselves were often seen as existing outside of time and place, outside of history. Nonetheless, the fundamental challenge of structuralist thought remained, and in the intellectual climate of Paris took on a social and political dimension.

Political implications of structuralism

The Marxist philosopher Louis Althusser, one of the most influential writers to advocate the importance of structuralist theory for political philosophy and criticism (though he denied that he was a 'structuralist'), made an attempt to define the historical moment or 'conjuncture' that made possible the development of this theoretical work in France (Althusser, 1969).

Althusser's ideas about ideology and representation were profoundly influential on British cultural theory, particularly the film theory of the journal *Screen*. He attempted to establish the 'relative autonomy' of ideology from the economic base of society, taking issue with the orthodox Marxist view that cultural artefacts were directly determined by economic factors on the grounds that such a view ignored the way in which the different elements of the social formation interact to affect one another at any given moment (see Spectatorship and audience research, p. 538).

Althusser's ideas formed part of a historical movement in which traditional disciplines such as philosophy, linguistics and literary criticism became increasingly politicised and in which theory was given an active role in determining political strategy and practice. Broadly speaking, the 'structuralist method' took issue with the notion that human beings could be conceived of as 'free' individuals in control of society. It argued, on the contrary, that while individuals ('man') might experience themselves as the origin and source of all meaning, action and history, and the world as an independent constituted domain of objects, in fact both individuals and objects were caught up in a system of structural relationships and it was this system that made the construction of a world of individuals and things, the construction of meaning, possible (Belsey, 1980).

The focus of attention for structuralist critics was language, but language as an activity of construction rather than as a mask for inner meaning that the critic could conjure up at will. Literary texts had certain reading practices built into them, some of which contributed to the process of reproducing capitalist relations of production, while others challenged or resisted that process. Classic realist fiction, the dominant literary form of the 19th century, addressed the reader as the central point from which the meaning of the text would emerge: the reader matched the author as the controlling source of the coherence and intelligibility of the text. Some twentieth-century modernist literary practices, on the other hand, were structured to produce contradiction rather than harmony and coherence, and these avant-garde texts challenged the central place given to author and reader in classic realism. Instead of a search for immanent meanings, intentions or causes, such texts demanded the abandonment of attempts to master and control meaning in favour of an activity of reading that can never exhaust the meaning of the text, but is rather a process of reading and writing in which texts are constantly transformed. The structuralist impulse to displace universal categories such as 'man' and 'human nature' from their 'natural' place at the centre of the world and history has political implications, since an understanding of individuals and society as formed contradictorily rather than essentially or finally fixed provides the basis for theories of radical social transformation. However, the 'de-centred self' proposed by structuralism also posed problems for political action.

Ideology and the subject

It has been argued that structuralism was concerned from the beginning with the dissolution of the notion of 'man' as a full and original presence, the source of all meaning. Stephen Heath, for instance, one of the first British critics to write about structuralism in relation to literary criticism, argued that 'structure' should be understood as a process, or network of processes, whereby individuals are put in place in society and that language played an important part in 'calling up' individuals, thereby transforming them into 'subjects' in society (Heath, 1972, pp. 35–6).

This account of 'the subject', developed from Althusser (1971), implies that while individuals may experience themselves as possessing a consciousness that enables them to freely form the ideas in which they believe, in fact this experience is an imaginary or ideological one, based on misrecognition. The ideological construction of subjects as individuals free to exchange their labour is seen to be important to capitalist relations of production, which therefore seek to perpetuate it, using language as their means. Broadly speaking, then, ideology cannot be thought of as a set of ideas or thoughts that individuals can take up and discard at will. Rather, it consists in the material practices and representations within which the subject is inscribed and is largely unconsciously acquired. Returning to questions of authorship, while traditional criticism envisages the work of art as the expression of the intentions of the individual artist containing an identity that can be directly recovered by the critic, structuralism proposes that the 'author', far from controlling the meaning of the work, is an effect of the interaction of different texts, or discourses, which have their own autonomy.

Language as convention

Many critics of structuralism thought that it tended to rely on a rather mechanistic concept of the subject as a fixed structure, totally at the mercy of language. Later, when structuralism was displaced by semiotic analysis, Julia Kristeva and writers from the theoretical journal *Tel Quel*, principally concerned with modernist practices of writing that attempt to disturb the ideological construction of the subject as unified and coherent, drew on psychoanalytic and linguistic theory to develop the concept that the subject itself is no more than the marks left by the process of intersection of different and conflicting texts. The 'I' that we use to designate our presence as individuals was seen as a convention, or code, that was the result of the interaction of a number of codes, rather than a unified expression of the individuality of the person using the code. Moreover, this emphasis on the conventional nature of language enabled the semioticians to give language a material base in society and history, independently of individual language users, who inherited a set of institutional conventions without which they would not be able to communicate. These conventions pre-dated the writer and continued to be readable in his or her absence (Culler, 1975). By evacuating the coherent, intentional subject from language in this way, semiotics hoped to bring into play new, revolutionary practices of writing that would mobilise unconscious desires as a force for social change.

The end of the author?

Structuralist and semiological criticism insisted that language functions independently of the author: does the individual author then disappear? While the theoretical interventions of structuralism may have called into question some of the fundamental premises of traditional critical approaches, the influence of these ideas has been uneven, especially in the UK and the US. Moreover, the sway of the author remains powerful as a social institution and it would be utopian to assume that structuralism or new practices of writing could have achieved its annihilation. In France, the structuralist intervention paved the way for radical changes in cultural practices, particularly in cinema after the political upheavals of May 1968, when the attribution of individual authorship to films was attacked as part of an assault on traditional methods of production, distribution and exhibition. In the UK during the 1970s, the French ideas were influential in producing new theories and practices of cinema. Sylvia Harvey has argued that the importation of these ideas into British and American criticism occurred at the expense of the theoretical and political context that engendered them in France:

> Those ideas which, in France, were the product of a momentary but radical displacement, a critical calling into question of all the levels of the social formation, have become in Britain and the United States little more than a hiccup in the superstructures, a slight grinding of gears in that social machine whose fundamental mode of operating has not changed. (Harvey, 1978, pp. 1–2)

This argument tends to underestimate the extent to which cultural practices in the UK were affected by French theory and politics (the development of independent oppositional cinema during the 1970s, for instance). The French debates are marked by a consciousness of their social, political and historical background, which adds vigour and relevance to their arguments, a process of self-reflection that at its best takes nothing for granted. Their insertion into anglophone culture transformed these arguments.

Structuralism and British film criticism

It is perhaps significant that the first indications of the intervention of structuralist ideas into British film criticism should circulate around the work of Jean-Luc Godard, a French critic and film-maker whose ideas were profoundly affected by French structuralist thought and by the political upheavals in France. It is also significant that this discussion first appeared in the pages of *New Left Review*, since it is largely through the writings of a small but influential group of left-wing intellectuals that structuralism emerged in the UK. This emergence, in contrast to the French situation, has been slow and painful, symptomatic perhaps of an intellectual tradition that is firmly entrenched in empiricism and distrusts theoretical enquiry.

The beginnings of 'English cine-structuralism'

The debate between Robin Wood and Peter Wollen about Jean-Luc Godard in *New Left Review* in 1966 offers an opportunity to see a confrontation between one kind of critical approach developed in the pages of *Movie* (see above p. 419), and a Marxist criticism influenced by structuralism that was to be developed in the journal *Screen* in the 1970s. It also offers an opportunity to see an early example of the way in which structuralist ideas 'seeped into' British film criticism, producing problems and contradictions. As Peter Wollen (pseud. Lee Russell) points out in his article, there is no simple opposition between his approach and that of Robin Wood, but there are important differences of emphasis that produce conflicting views of Godard's work and of the function of the artist in society.

A sense of tradition: Robin Wood

Wood isolates a single central theme in Godard's oeuvre around which all the other themes cohere: 'the sense of tradition'. Through detailed analysis of one scene in *Bande à part* (1964), he argues that Godard's view of contemporary society is a pessimistic one: seeing it as fragmented, lacking cultural tradition, the film-maker looks back nostalgically to a time when a rela-

Bitter self-parody?: Godard's *Les Carabiniers*

tively stable society enabled the great classic tradition (defined by Wood in terms of 'harmony') of art to appear. For Wood, Godard is a modern artist who constantly tries to resolve the problem of the lack of stable cultural tradition by fabricating his own tradition, essentially personal rather than social. Even Godard's 'most savage statement of discontinuity' in *Les Carabiniers* (1963) is seen as bitter self-parody: his position is characterised as a tragic one. In Wood's view, the relationship of form to content is perfectly equivalent; the style and structure of the films express Godard's tragic statement that the loss of tradition leads to the loss of personal identity and relationships.

It is possible to trace in Wood's approach to Godard's work a clear statement of the critic's own humanist concerns and it was this approach with which British Marxist film critics took issue. Nevertheless, the differences between Wood's and Wollen's approaches are not always clear-cut: the articles mark a historical point of transition rather than a break.

Unresolved contradictions: Peter Wollen

Lee Russell/Peter Wollen agrees that the issue of tradition is a 'key' one in studying Godard (rather than 'the essential one') but points to a difference of approach in his article that is more than a difference of opinion: it is 'a clash of worldviews'.

Wollen begins, not with an inner theme, but with French society and politics: the social and historical context for Godard's work. He traces a set of structural oppositions running through the films: action versus destiny, culture versus society, art versus tradition. These oppositions form unresolved contradictions in the films, they do not cohere to form an ideal unity. Indeed, the artist, in Wollen's view, far from being a central unifying force in society, is generally marginal to it, sometimes antagonistic, often simply indifferent. Wollen goes on to criticise Godard's romantic individualistic position and the absence of politics in the films, an absence of which the film-maker is aware and which he regrets. According to Wollen, Godard's way forward from his despairing view of society should be in the direction of politics, which is 'the principle of change in history'. A very different view of the artist and of art in society can be seen at work here. Far from transcending society with a unique and unifying personal vision, the artist is placed firmly within history: no longer the romantic 'outsider', his or her task is to contribute to social change through the critical activity of political film-making.

However, like Wood, Wollen retains a central place for Godard as auteur in this article and still subscribes to the critical method that depends on bringing forward meanings hidden behind language. Nevertheless, it is possible to see the beginnings of a shift away from the notion of the auteur as originating source of the work towards the idea of the work as a set of contradictory relationships between structural elements that interact to produce the author's worldview rather than express it. Wollen is working towards a 'worldview' that is less that of a coherent totality, the expression of a pre-given set of ideas, than a collage of different positions transformed in the process of history. Underlying Wollen's arguments is a criticism of the relativism of subjective criticism and a desire to move towards a more rigorous objective method. At the same time, Wollen is careful to point out that he is writing from a particular position, which he elaborates in the course of the article. The subjectivity of the critic is not denied, but it is beginning to be called into question.

Wollen was to revise his position on Godard in the light of his post-1968 films, developing his argument about thematic oppositions in Godard's work into a political strategy of film-making that would counter, or oppose, Hollywood cinema, and assessing his contribution as a political film-maker (see Auterism, Godard and counter-cinema, p. 467). The dualism of Wollen's structural criticism (elaborated in *Signs and Meaning in the Cinema*, 1969; 1972; 1998) came under attack with later developments in anglophone film theory, as did his attempt to make an alliance between structuralism and auteur theory (see Auteur structuralism under attack, p. 454). But the problems in Wollen's arguments do not detract from the contribution they make to shifting the ground of British film criticism away from empiricism towards a different problematic: the relationship of science and theory to artistic practice and to politics.

Auteur structuralism: Geoffrey Nowell-Smith

The 'English cine-structuralists' as they came to be called, after Eckert and Henderson (see Auteur structuralism under attack, p. 454), were not a homogeneous group. Though they shared a concern with developing materialist methods of analysis, the use of structuralism differed from critic to critic. Indeed, the Marxist framework within which each critic worked was also very different and often contradictory. One of those approaches is represented by Geoffrey Nowell-Smith, in his book on Visconti (1967), who states his intention of retrieving Visconti's work from the place assigned to it by traditional criticism:

> This does not mean exalting the later work at the expense of the earlier, but making it one's primary concern to consider the work as a whole, as the product of a single intelligence, and to seek out the connections between each film at whatever level they are to be found. In Visconti's case the connections are multifarious and can be traced in his choice of actors, his use of decors, his concern with certain historical questions and so on. The development of

> each film out of the problems posed by the last can also be easily demonstrated. But there are further links within his work which exist at a deeper level, less easily discernible and which are perhaps even more important. (Nowell-Smith, 1967, p. 9)

Nowell-Smith emphasises that he is not using auteur structuralism to support the idea that every detail of a film is the sole responsibility of its author, the director, or as a mode of evaluating films as 'good' or 'bad'; rather it is a 'principle of method' around which the critic organises his or her work. 'The purpose of criticism becomes therefore to uncover behind the superficial contrasts of subject and treatment a structural hard core of basic and often recondite motifs' (Nowell-Smith, 1967, p. 10).

However, as Nowell-Smith demonstrates, auteur structuralism is not so much an answer to the early excesses of the auteur theory as a problem in itself. In narrowing the field of enquiry to the internal formal and thematic analysis of the work, it tends to ignore the possibility of historical changes affecting the basic structure, and the importance of non-thematic elements and mise en scène. Moreover, certain directors, of whom Visconti is one, cannot be discussed simply in structuralist terms, because external factors of history and production are so important to their work. Nowell-Smith begins with a defence of auteur structuralism that is radically questioned by the critical method he then chooses to adopt: discussion of Visconti's work not only in terms of its internal relationships, but also in its social and historical context.

To characterise these early auteur-structuralist writings as theoretical failures would be to misunderstand the nature of theoretical enquiry, which proceeds from problem to problem rather than looking for 'correctness' or immediate solutions. It would also be to underestimate the value of polemic in critical debate. Most of the auteur structuralists reformulated their original positions, although the project of a materialist enquiry remained.

Selected Reading

Peter Wollen, *Signs and Meaning in the Cinema*, London, Secker and Warburg/BFI Publishing, 1969. Revised edition 1972; expanded edition 1998.

Geoffrey Nowell-Smith, *Visconti*, London, Secker and Warburg/BFI Publishing, 1967. Revised edition 1973.

Structuralism, individualism and auteur theory

Structuralism, from its beginnings, posed itself against those forms of criticism that regarded the work of art as a closed, self-sufficient system in which the intentions of the author were to be found. In *La Penseé sauvage* (1962), anthropologist Claude Lévi-Strauss attacked Sartre's existentialist concept of the ego as consciousness, fully present to itself and freely able to create its own values. According to Lévi-Strauss, the final goal of the human sciences is not to constitute 'man' but to dissolve him. In a well-known remark about the language of myth, he refuted the idea that 'man' could be conceived of as a 'language user', existing outside structures and therefore able to master and use them at will: 'We are not therefore claiming to show how men think in myths but rather how the myths think themselves out in men and without men's knowledge' (quoted in Leach, 1970, p. 51).

Lévi-Strauss introduces the Freudian concept of the unconscious to explain the way in which (as he sees it) the human mind assimilates the deep structures that are seen to underpin all social organisation and forms of communication. In his attack on the notion of the individual self, Lévi-Strauss collapses individuality into a formulation of the human mind as a kind of 'collective unconscious' that assumes the universality of the structures he identifies. Individual myths, indeed all individual 'utterances', are different versions of these universal structures: emphasis is put upon the structures rather than on the utterances. This approach tends to be ahistorical, denying the particularity of different kinds of utterance, and returns constantly to the presence of a structure hidden in the myth. It has been pointed out that, like the critical tradition it is supposed to reject, it assumes the presence of an intention, whether this intention is shifted over to the side of the myth itself, or back to the 'human mind', conscious or unconscious.

In a radical rereading of Freud, French psychoanalyst Jacques Lacan also offered a challenge to the self-sufficiency of the individual subject, redefining the unconscious not as a deep well or reservoir of repressed thoughts or feelings, but as 'structured', indeed as 'structured like a language'. Far from being a place, Lacan argues, the unconscious is in fact a network of deep structural patterns in which our conscious thinking and discourse are intimately caught up, in the same way as the act of speech is transformed by the underlying linguistic structures (see Benoist, 1970). Freudian psychoanalysis does not attempt to recover the intention hidden behind each utterance, or to seek out the underlying structures, but by paying close attention to the relationship between the conscious discourse and what is absent from it (an absence marked by jokes, slips of the tongue, and so forth), it attempts to throw light upon the structural activity that produced the discourse. According to Lacan (1977), the individual self is not, as traditional ego-psychology would have it, a unified ego, but is constantly produced and transformed by the activity of the unconscious, a 'self' divided between the unconscious id and the conscious ego, which can never be captured or reconstituted as a coherent presence that transcends language and society.

The Marxist philosopher Louis Althusser (1971) drew on Lacan's theories when he attempted to reformulate Marx's concepts of identity and alienation into a 'theory of the subject': the unconscious network of structures that simultaneously holds people in place and produces the illusion of 'free men'.

How does this sustained attack on 'individuality', 'presence' and 'intention', the attempted dissolution of 'man', relate to the principles of auteur study, which precisely depends upon the presence of an authorial (authoritative) voice as the prime source of meaning in the work? If the author/subject is constituted only in language, and language is by definition social and independent of any particular individuality, then why does the author return, as it does in some structuralist accounts of film? The early work of Christian Metz, for instance, depends upon a literal application to cinema of the linguistic distinction between *langue* and *langage*, defining cinema as a language without a *langue*, or underlying system of rules, a realm of pure performance or expression, which seems to confirm the idea of authorship in its conventional sense. In the absence of a general *langue*, there is only the singular usage, and the language user (the author) is free to express his or her intentions directly. Significantly, this notion of language as direct expression also appears in Astruc (1948), one of the earliest defences of the *politique des auteurs* (see p. 390). It is hardly surprising, then, that auteur structuralism was also caught in this dilemma: the attempt to redefine the auteur as a structure, an 'effect' rather than a punctual source of meaning in the film(s) nonetheless retained the notion of the underlying intention present in the basic structures, and therefore failed to displace conventional auteur theory (see Nowell-Smith, 1970).

Cultural politics and auteur theory

Cahiers' category 'e'

The events of May 1968 heralded radical changes in French film criticism that were to have a profound effect on British criticism too. Dissatisfied with its early auteurist work, the French journal *Cahiers du cinéma* began a series of articles on cinema, ideology and politics that drew on the development of French structuralist thought in politics, psychoanalysis and literary criticism within the framework of an explicitly Marxist approach. The project of this politicised film criticism was to develop a new theory and practice of the cinema and the fierce debates that followed (principally between *Cahiers du cinéma* and *Cinéthique*) were taken up in the UK in the pages of the journal *Screen*, which allied itself to this programme of political and theoretical struggle when it emerged in a new form in 1971.

The following years also saw the proliferation of radical film-making groups dedicated to making political cinema and to mounting an attack on the existing structures of the film industry. Technological and economic developments made small-scale film production more viable and an increasing political awareness among film-makers and film critics meant that the ideological function of Hollywood cinema came under scrutiny. Hollywood was seen as the principal agency of cultural imperialism in its domination of world cinema; for many people the task of revolutionary cultural struggle was to dismantle its hold on the popular imagination, to produce new, politically aware audiences. To this end, attention was turned towards the question of how to find new structures, new forms to express new revolutionary content: the debates of the Russian formalists, the ideas of Brecht became the models for film-makers and critics (see Harvey, 1978).

Internal criticism: Henry Fonda in John Ford's *Young Mr. Lincoln*

The refusal of dominant cinema also involved an attack on hierarchical production systems in favour of collective working methods and rejection of the idea that any individual should be enshrined as the author of a film. Auteur criticism, which focused on the director as central controlling presence, was seen as supporting the hierarchical division of labour and the individualist ideology of the dominant system. However, there was disagreement about how that system should be conceptualised. Critics were divided between those who argued for the necessity of building alternative structures 'outside' the dominant mode of production and those who argued for a theoretical concept of the dominant mode that would allow for intervention within it.

The journal *Cahiers du cinéma* did not subscribe to the notion of Hollywood as an ideological monolith and struggled to produce a theoretical conception of the commercial industrial system, and of the place of the director within it, that allowed more space for contradiction. In an influential editorial that appeared in *Cahiers du cinéma* in the autumn of 1969, the editors proposed dividing films into seven categories 'a'–'g' according to whether they allowed ideology a free passage, or whether they attempted to turn ideology back upon itself to reveal the contradictions that it was the nature of ideology to efface. The fifth category, 'e', was defined as those films that seem at first sight to belong firmly within the ideology, but which reveal on closer inspection that:

> An internal criticism is taking place which cracks the film apart at the seams. If one reads the film obliquely, looking for symptoms, if one looks beyond its apparent formal coherence, one can see that it is riddled with cracks: it is splitting under an internal tension which is simply not there in an ideologically innocuous film. This is the case in many Hollywood films, for example, which while being completely integrated in the system and the ideology end up by partially dismantling the system from within. (Comolli and Narboni, 1969, quoted in Harvey, 1978, p. 35)

Cahiers cited the films of John Ford, Carl Dreyer and Roberto Rossellini as examples of this category and their subsequent analysis of Ford's *Young Mr Lincoln* (1939) demonstrated the importance of the authorial sub-code in that film to the process of internal criticism. Thus films that appeared to be basically 'reactionary' (that is, instruments of the dominant ideology) could, on rereading, prove to be 'progressive' in so far as they produced a criticism of that ideology. *Cahiers du cinéma* followed up its definitions of classes of films with analyses of individual texts (*Young Mr. Lincoln*; *Sylvia Scarlett*, 1936; *Morocco*, 1930) to demonstrate how they each challenged dominant ideology in specific ways. *Cahiers'* approach allowed for the possibility of progressive texts to be found in Hollywood cinema and it was this position that had most effect on the theoretical work of *Screen*. Auteur criticism in the UK began to look at the films of certain Hollywood directors in terms of the way they resisted dominant ideology, laying bare its operations. Those directors whose work seemed to offer a radical criticism of the system through manipulation, conscious or unconscious, of its language were the most important; their work was evaluated according to the extent to which it could be read as breaking with the traditional pleasures offered by mainstream cinema, which attempted to seduce the audience into losing itself in a self-contained fictional world, putting its doubts and questions aside.

The 'progressive' auteur: Douglas Sirk

One of the basic premises of the critical ambivalence towards Hollywood in the early 1970s was that the project of mainstream cinema is illusionist; that is, that it attempts to create an illusion of reality on the screen in such a way that the spectator becomes totally absorbed in the spectacle and is prepared to accept the illusion as 'truth', at least for the time spent viewing the film. Any critical resistance is overcome and the ideology of mainstream cinema is accepted as 'natural'. This argument depends upon the idea that while all ideology is actually inconsistent, bourgeois ideology struggles to overcome its own inconsistencies. 'Progressive' cinema, then, can be defined as anti-illusionist, or anti-realist, in the sense that it works to produce those contradictions that bourgeois ideology attempts to efface. In order to do this, it must work on the illusionist strategies of mainstream cinema to disturb the 'illusion of reality', to remind the spectator that the illusion is ideological rather than natural, that it can therefore be questioned. Not all non-realist films can be seen as progressive, however: many Hollywood films are blatantly unrealistic, while still preserving the illusion of a coherent self-contained world that becomes imaginatively real for the period of watching. To qualify as progressive, a Hollywood film would have to be perceived as producing a criticism, at some level, of its manifest ideological project. A subtext would be discernible that works against the grain of that project, denaturalising it.

The films of Douglas Sirk provide an opportunity to examine the influence of these ideas on British film theory. Sirk was a European left-wing intellectual with a background in art history and the German theatre of the 1920s and early 1930s. He was not only familiar with the debates about art and politics in the Soviet Union and Germany during that period: he had lived through the advent of the Third Reich and the consequent campaign against left-wing artists and intellectuals that signalled the demise of one of the most thriving periods in German theatrical history, a theatre of criticism and social commitment (see Elsaesser, 1972). Sirk's theatrical productions owed much (formally at least) to the Expressionist emphasis on mise en scène, on the supremacy of gesture, light, colour and sound over the spoken word, which drew attention to the symbolic aspect of the stage-spectacle rather than its realism. At the same time, he was interested in the controversial political dramas of Bertolt Brecht and Arnolt Bronnen, which were designed to shock the conventional, primarily middle-class German theatre audience. As the Nazi authorities interfered more and more with the running of the theatre, Sirk turned to the cinema, becoming a director for Ufa, since there was still considerable freedom for directors within the German film industry at that time (1934) (see Halliday, 1971a, p. 35). His success was established with the melodrama *Final Accord/Schlussakkord* (1936), and continued with *To New Shores/Zu neuen Ufern* (1937), which shows explicitly Sirk's interest in the ideas

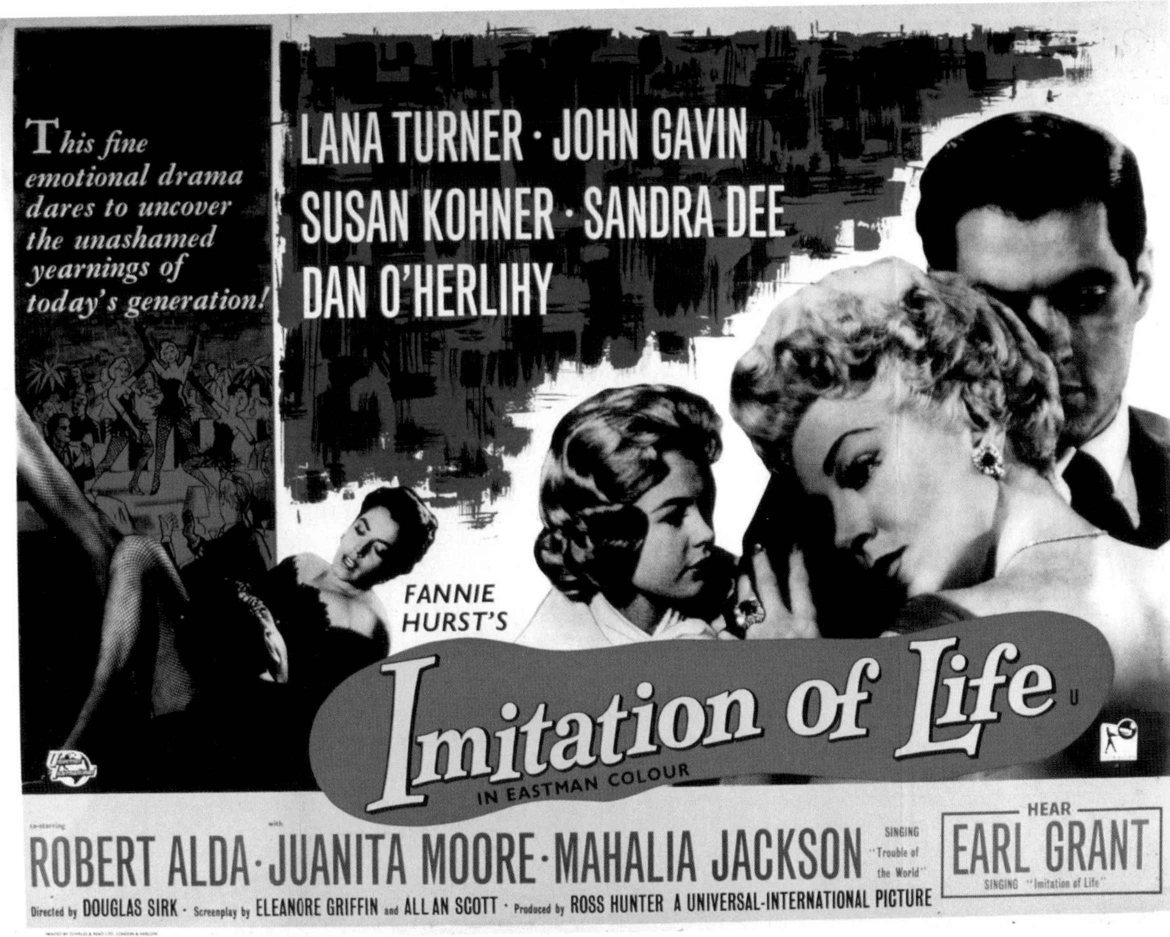

Sirk tackled social and political issues in overblown melodramas such as *Imitation of Life*

of Brecht and Kurt Weill and in film as social criticism. Thus, before he moved to America in 1937, Sirk's theatrical productions and German films reveal the extent to which he was able to transform the materials at his disposal in his own interests.

Sirk's first experience of Hollywood (between 1939 and 1949) was rather bleak (in common with that of many European émigré directors). Working as a contract scriptwriter for Columbia, he was consistently denied work as a director, in spite of successes with films made by independent producers. After a year spent in Germany in 1949, where he found the film industry more or less destroyed, he returned to America and signed up as a director with Universal. After a few years, he began to impose his own style and personal concerns on the material handed to him by producer Ross Hunter and others, in the form of sometimes 'impossible' scripts. He gradually gained more control over his projects and, with the help of collaborators (photographer Russell Metty, scriptwriter George Zuckerman, producer Albert Zugsmith), a group of melodramas emerged that have been identified as characteristically Sirkian, showing the same interest in form and politics as his German theatre and film work, albeit less explicitly (see Halliday, 1971a; Mulvey and Halliday, 1972).

The argument for Sirk as a 'progressive' auteur rests on the assumption that he was working as a director in uncongenial circumstances (Nazi Germany in the 1930s, America in the 1950s). His own political beliefs and interests as a left-wing intellectual were under attack, he was working in a hierarchical industrial situation and therefore did not have complete control over his projects, yet he managed to produce work that can be read as critical of the prevailing ideology at one level, not necessarily the most obvious one. One problem with this argument is that the films chosen by critics to illustrate it (*Schlussakkord*, *Zu neuen Ufern* and *La Habañera*, 1937, from the 1930s, the Universal melodramas from the 1950s) were all produced at a time when Sirk had considerable control over his projects (see Halliday, 1971a, p. 35; Mulvey and Halliday, 1972, p. 109). Moreover, it is well known that he had several sympathetic collaborators within Universal studios, which makes it difficult to argue that Sirk was totally responsible for the 1950s melodramas associated with his name. It has also been argued that it is the overt project of melodrama as a genre to act as a safety valve, siphoning off ideological contradictions and deliberately leaving them unresolved (see Melodrama, p. 316). From this perspective, Sirk would appear to have been less in tension with his material, producing a hidden, underlying criticism, than at one with it; any criticism of the prevailing ideology to be found in his work could therefore be seen as overt and, moreover, sanctioned by that ideology (see Klinger, 1994).

The argument for the 'progressivity' of Sirk's films raises important questions about the relationship of authorship to genre, of directors to the conditions in which they work and of how ideology is produced in films.

Selected Reading

Jon Halliday, *Sirk on Sirk*, London, Secker and Warburg/BFI Publishing, 1971a.

Barbara Klinger, *Melodrama and Meaning: History, Culture, and the Films of Douglas Sirk*, Bloomington, Indiana University Press, 1994.

Laura Mulvey, 'Notes on Sirk and melodrama', *Movie* 25, winter 1977/78. Reprinted in Gledhill (ed.), *Home Is Where the Heart Is: Studies in Melodrama and the Woman's Film*, London, BFI Publishing, 1987.

DOUGLAS SIRK

To New Shores/Zu neuen Ufern (Germany 1937 *p.c* – Ufa; *d* – Detlef Sierck [Douglas Sirk])

After the enormous success of *Schlussakkord* (1936), Sirk's first full-blown melodrama, he went on to direct this film, which he described as incorporating his interest in melodrama as a vehicle for encouraging social criticism in the audience and in characters who are uncertain about their aims in life and so find themselves going in circles – the 'tragic rondo' (see Halliday, 1971a, pp. 47–8). Jon Halliday describes the film as a tough social criticism of the British ruling class and colonialism in nineteenth-century Australia (Halliday, 1971b). The tragic, vacillating figure in this case is Sir Albert Finsbury, a weak British officer.

The trial sequence usefully demonstrates Sirk's interest in adapting Brecht–Weill for cinema. The trial of Gloria Vane (Zarah Leander) is introduced by an old woman singing a song about Paramatta (the women's prison in Australia to which Gloria is about to be consigned by a class-prejudiced court) outside the courtroom; she has a large placard with a number of pictures on it: the camera passes from her to the courtroom where Gloria is sentenced, back out to the placard, whereupon a picture of Paramatta dissolves to Paramatta itself. This explicitly Brechtian strategy has the effect of drawing attention to the formal construction of the film and, some would argue, introducing a critical distance for the audience.

This scene also shows Sirk's interest, influenced by German Expressionism, in using mise en scène to create an independent, dreamlike world on the screen entirely divorced from 'reality'. Sharp contrasts of light and dark combined with stylised acting and sets are an extension of the theatrical conventions of melodrama.

PAM COOK

Zarah Leander in the dock in *Zu neuen Ufern*

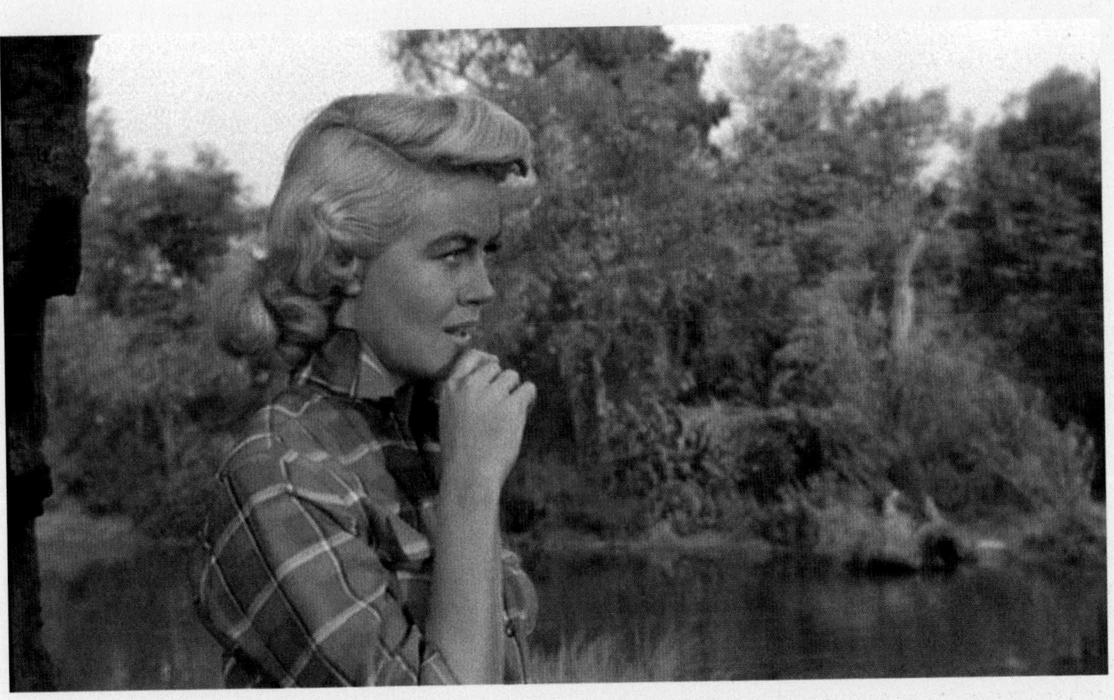

A mise en scène of emotional excess: Dorothy Malone goes back to nature in *Written on the Wind*

All That Heaven Allows (USA 1956 *p.c* – Universal International; *d* – Douglas Sirk)

One of Sirk's women's pictures (see also Melodrama, p. 320), this film has been praised both as a critique of American bourgeois values (Halliday, 1972) and as a poignant working through of the contradictions faced by women in patriarchal society (Mulvey, 1977/78).

The film presents events through the point of view of its central female protagonist Cary (Jane Wyman), using the visual codes of mise en scène to indicate her state of mind. This ironic use of mise en scène can be read either as an attempt by the director to comment on the conservative values supposedly adhered to in the melodrama's subject matter, or as part of the melodramatic convention in which stylised mise en scène is used to offer the audience privileged information over the characters (Elsaesser, 1972). Klinger (1994) has argued that Sirk's mise en scène can be seen as supporting 1950s ideologies of sexuality and consumerism.

In the family melodrama, it has been argued, dramatic conflict is engendered by working through the contradictions, particularly for women, of heterosexual monogamy and motherhood. *All That Heaven Allows* centres these problems in the point of view of its heroine and her difficulties in following through her desires, arguably producing problems for the classic Hollywood narrative that are out of the director's control. From this perspective, the film is less a 'progressive text' than a safety valve for painful ideological contradictions (see Mulvey, 1977/78).

PAM COOK

Written on the Wind (USA 1956 *p.c* – Universal International; *d* – Douglas Sirk)

Sirk's theatrical background can be seen in the organisation of the mise en scène: strong primary colours, contrasts of dark and light, exaggerated acting and gestures combine to produce a world dominated by physical and psychological violence, marked by an emotional excess that threatens to overturn the stability of the established order. This film is a tragic melodrama, concentrating on male Oedipal problems with the patriarchal order (see Mulvey, 1977/78).

Kyle Hadley (Robert Stack) is an example of one of Sirk's vacillating characters (cf. Cary in *All That Heaven Allows*, Sir Albert Finsbury in *Zu neuen Ufern*), but his hysterical response to his supposed sterility has also been identified as one of the basic motifs of tragic melodrama. The 'negative' destructive impulses of Kyle and his sister Marylee (Dorothy Malone) are played off against the 'positive' qualities of the 'good' couple, Mitch (Rock Hudson) and Lucy (Lauren Bacall), to produce a criticism of the patriarchal American family and the ideals of masculinity and femininity on which it depends. Marylee's orgiastic 'dance of death', linked to her father's fatal heart attack, explicitly draws a parallel between excessive female sexuality and the overthrow of the patriarchal order, a view of female sexuality as threat that is common in American cinema and that is arguably mobilised here in the interests of social criticism.

The symbolic use of colour in the mise en scène to refer to the values held by different characters is typical of melodramatic conventions, but could also be seen as a particular use of ironic commentary by the director in order to distance the audience from their emotional response and induce a critical awareness (that is, as a 'Brechtian' strategy that can undermine the pathos and catharsis characteristic of tragedy as a form).

PAM COOK

Auteur structuralism under attack

Signs and Meaning in the Cinema

Peter Wollen's defence of auteur structuralism in *Signs and Meaning in the Cinema* (1969; 1972; 1998) is perhaps the most cogent argument for the retention of the auteur theory in some form or other. The problem of authorship and cinema is not satisfactorily resolved by the attempts on the part of proponents of some of the more reductionist and formalist developments of structuralist method to dissolve the auteur altogether into the generalities of other structures. The theoretical problems inherent in British auteur structuralism have often been pointed out (Eckert, 1973; Henderson, 1973). Henderson's careful reading of Wollen's chapter on the auteur theory reveals the lack of theoretical foundation in auteur structuralism and the empiricism underlying many of Wollen's rhetorical strategies. It also points to the fundamental incompatibility of the two critical approaches, which produces contradictions in the arguments that must finally destroy auteur structuralism itself: that is, while auteur theory as it stands (and as it is retained by Wollen) rests on the principle that the subject is the producer of a unique or distinctive meaning, the structuralism of Lévi-Strauss and others is founded upon the interchangeability of subjects in the production of meaning. Henderson's impressive demolition of auteur structuralism is the prelude to a criticism of structuralism itself in the light of theoretical developments emerging from the French *Tel Quel* group and others, which called for a new theory of textual operation and of the place of the subject in the process of production of meaning (Henderson, 1973, p. 33). Nonetheless, as Henderson himself points out, it is only in the destruction of auteur structuralism itself that the new question can be liberated. The value of auteur structuralism resides in the problems it poses and the questions it provokes.

Wollen argues that auteur structuralism provides a critical approach that can retain the impetus of the original *politique des auteurs* (that is, to decipher the presence of authors in Hollywood film production as opposed to European art cinema) while avoiding its excesses by providing the more objective criteria of basic structures rather than subjective ones of personal taste. Structuralism allows the critic to define a core of repeated motifs in the director's oeuvre: however, it must also analyse the system of differences and oppositions that marks one film off from the others in the oeuvre, and that produces meaning in each film. It is not enough to reduce films to basic oppositional structures: the critic must also pay attention to the whole series of shifting variations within and between films. Different levels of complexity of combination mark the work of some directors as 'richer' than others. For Wollen, Ford's work is richer than Hawks's because Hawks's films can be summed up in terms of schematic sets of oppositions, whereas Ford's work manifests many different and shifting levels of variation. It is interesting that Wollen retains the categories of 'good' and 'bad' films that structuralist method could, in theory at least, have dispensed with. In the first edition of his book, Wollen discounts the importance of other contributions (such as those of the star or the studio) to the production of meaning in film: the auteur structure, for him, is the primary or dominant one. Strangely, it is at this point of greatest tension between auteur theory and Lévi-Strauss's structuralism that Wollen calls on Lévi-Strauss and equates film with myth (Wollen, 1969, p. 105). For meaning in myth is indeed collectively produced: there is no place in myth for the individual language user.

An important part of Wollen's polemic is his reformulation of auteur theory in terms of the auteur as unconscious catalyst rather than intentional presence, an argument he elaborates in the Postscript to the 1972 revised edition:

> Auteur analysis does not consist of retracing a film to its creative source. It consists of tracing a structure (not a message) within the work, which can then *post factum* be assigned to an individual, the director, on empirical grounds. It is wrong, in the name of a denial of the traditional idea of creative subjectivity, to deny any status to individuals at all. But Fuller, or Hawks or Hitchcock, the directors, are quite separate from 'Fuller' or 'Hawks' or 'Hitchcock', the structures named after them, and should not be methodologically confused. There can be no doubt that the presence of a structure in the text can often be connected with the presence of a director on the set, but the situation in cinema, where the director's primary task is often one of coordination and rationalisation, is very different from that in the other arts, where there is a much more direct relationship between artist and work. It is in this sense that it is possible to speak of a film auteur as an unconscious catalyst. (Wollen, 1972, p. 168)

While there is clearly a tension at work here between the traditional notion of structure as present in the work (noted by Henderson) and a new formulation of the auteur as a 'fiction' in the text rather than as intentional subject, this new formulation precisely looks forward to the theory of meaning production that Henderson argues for. The auteur as catalyst can be read as one element in the play of assemblage of different elements that makes up the film text(s).

The auteur as structure: Howard Hawks

A comparison of the different critical approaches to the work of Howard Hawks taken by Robin Wood (1968; 1981) and Peter Wollen (1969; 1972; 1998) demonstrates basic differences in conceptualising the auteur theory and Hawks's place within it, which illuminate the historical context for British auteur-structuralist criticism.

Both writers are concerned with the status of film as an art

At the periphery of Hawks's male group: Miriam Hopkins in *Barbary Coast*

and its relationship to the other, established arts. Both use the auteur theory to support the contention that film does indeed deserve the status of 'art' rather than (or as well as) 'entertainment' by demonstrating that Hawks's work is on a par with the great classical tradition (which in Wood's case means Shakespeare, Bach, Mozart). While Wood supports this tradition in opposition to modernism, however, Wollen is primarily concerned, especially in the Postscript to the revised edition of *Signs and Meaning in the Cinema* (1972), with a defence of modernism that attacks the roots of Wood's critical assumptions.

An intuitive artist

Wood argues that art is defined by the extent of the artist's personal involvement with his material and not by the common distinction between 'art' and 'entertainment', which is virtually meaningless when applied to the classical tradition. The classical tradition is opposed to the modern tradition in that in the former the artist develops an already existing language rather than developing a new one. Hawks belongs in the classical tradition because he is totally unselfconscious; he does not draw attention to the forms he uses, therefore his work is ultimately unanalysable: the critic responds intuitively and spontaneously to the intuitive and spontaneous work that is the film. Although Hawks worked within many of the Hollywood genres, his personal vision transforms those genres; therefore he should be classified not according to genre, but according to his way of looking at the world. For Wood, Hawks's only limitation as an artist is his refusal to think of himself as such and his commitment to film as commercial entertainment. Hawks's masterpieces were produced in those moments when he was 'suddenly completely engaged by his material', when his 'intuitive consciousness' is fully alerted.

A structure of reversal

Wollen (1969; 1972; 1998; p. 53 in 1998 edn.) uses Hawks as a test case for auteur theory. Hawks is a director who is generally judged on the basis of his adventure dramas and found wanting. It is only by looking at the whole of his work, at the crazy comedies as well as the dramas, that a core of repeated motifs emerges that give added dimension to the films and makes it possible for the critic to decipher a Hawks worldview through the play of oppositions and reversals between the dramas and the comedies. Wollen is critical of that worldview and supports his criticisms by differentiating between Hawks's work and that of Ford and Boetticher: they are all concerned with similar problems of heroism and masculinity, but the problem is articulated quite differently by each one. For Wollen, the strength of Hawks lies not in his spontaneous, intuitive artistry but in the systematic organisation of structural reversals throughout his work as a whole. Wollen does not subscribe to Hawks's values, as Wood appears to, but this does not prevent him from attempting to establish Hawks's status as an auteur on the basis of criteria that go beyond his personal taste as a critic.

Hawks versus Ford

Both writers compare Hawks with Ford, arriving at totally different conclusions. Wollen sees Ford as going beyond the question of the value of individual action to society and to American history: Ford does not simply validate American individualistic values, he begins to question the historical basis of these values. Hawks, on the other hand, finds the solution to individual isolation in the camaraderie of the self-sufficient all-male group, cut off from society, history and women, who are a threat to this male world.

For Wood, the comparison between Hawks and Ford reveals Hawks to be the more modern of the two artists, because the idea of a stable social tradition is absent from his work. While Ford looks back nostalgically to lost values, Hawks deals with the problem of modern society by rejecting it, by creating his own world of personal loyalties in which an ideal society would be one in which the individual had maximum possible freedom from social constraints. 'Within the group, one feels an absence of *civilised* sensibility, but the strong presence of the uncultivated, instinctive sensibility that must underlie any valid civilisation: intuitive-sympathetic contact, a sturdily positive, generous spirit' (Wood, 1968, p. 92).

A feminist view

One might wish to question the value of any view of society in which the 'sturdily positive, generous spirit' does not extend beyond the male group to the other half of society: women. Women exist at the periphery of Hawks's male group, at the point at which it threatens to break down. It is this representation of 'woman' as a point of tension or anxiety in male society – in effect a troublesome question that refuses to go away – which has attracted the attention of feminist film critics to Hawks's work. Hawks's films appear to epitomise the workings of patriarchal ideology in the way that they represent the 'otherness' of women as a threat that can only be resolved (uneasily) by the initiation of this 'other' into the codes of male society: in effect, by recognising and then recuperating the 'otherness', the difference of women.

Selected Reading

Jim Hillier and Peter Wollen (eds), *Howard Hawks: American Artist*, London, BFI Publishing, 1996.

Peter Wollen, *Signs and Meaning in the Cinema*, London, Secker and Warburg/BFI Publishing, 1969; 1972; 1998.

Robin Wood, *Howard Hawks*, London, Secker and Warburg/BFI, 1968. Revised edition BFI Publishing, 1981.

HOWARD HAWKS

Scarface (USA 1932 *p.c* – Caddo Productions/United Artists; *d* – Howard Hawks)

This film belongs in the so-called 'classic' cycle of the gangster film in which the gangster hero is depicted as a paradoxical and schizophrenic figure, representing the worst in society and the best, in so far as he is striving towards the goals of the American dream (wealth, individualism, success and power). In the context of Hawks's work, however, Robin Wood has identified *Scarface* as one of his comedies. Tony Camonte (Paul Muni) is presented as an innocent primitive with whom the audience should sympathise rather than pass moral judgment. Much of the comedy resides in the way that the male characters are ridiculed (as in the comic violence involving Angelo and Camonte's innocent enjoyment of his own bad taste). Wood pays close attention to Hawks's mise en scène to demonstrate how the audience is both drawn in to enjoy the gangsters' sense of complete freedom through violence, and yet distanced by the horror of it (Wood, 1968, p. 64). The combination of farce and horror makes the film truly disturbing, and it could be argued that Hawks here presents a completereversal (and possible criticism) of the values he seems to justify in the dramas.

Wollen sees this opposition between the comedies and the dramas as vital. In the comedies, the retrograde, Spartan heroism of the dramas is exposed to reveal their underlying tensions: the regression to infantilism and savagery and the sexual humiliation of the male (Wollen, 1972, p. 91). If in the dramas man is master of his world, in the comedies he is its victim. It is in this opposition that Hawks's value as an auteur is to be found, because it lends complexity to the representation of sexuality in his work as a whole.

PAM COOK

Bringing Up Baby (USA 1938 *p.c* – RKO Radio; *d* – Howard Hawks)

Wood characterises Hawks's comedy as extreme, and compares it to the Marx Brothers. He sees it as celebrating the male's resilience, his ability to retain an innate dignity in the face of humiliation (Wood, 1968, p. 68). For Wood, this film is based on the opposition between duty and nature, order and chaos, superego and id, the oppositions manifested in the struggle between the man and the woman in the progress from order to chaos and back to order

Dignity in the face of humiliation: Cary Grant squares up to Katharine Hepburn in *Bringing Up Baby*

again. The safety of David's (Cary Grant) world is shattered by Susan's (Katharine Hepburn) anarchistic behaviour and can only be precariously rebuilt, leaving the spectator with an uneasy feeling that the male–female couple relationship will never be ideal. Wood points to the representation of the woman in this film as an anarchic, destructive natural force, dominating the weak and foolish male intellectual.

Wollen agrees that the comedies are the reversal of the dramas in that the hero becomes victim and that Hawks's comedy often centres around sex and role reversal (domineering women and timid, pliable men). The association of women with nature, and therefore with danger and disruption, is common to Hawks's films in general – although *Scarface* presents an interesting variation on this theme in that these primitive forces are represented by a male hero. Hawks generally keeps the male and female worlds strictly apart: when they are combined in one character (such as Tony Camonte), they lead to self-destruction.

The comedy in this film is again farcical, sadistic and destructive. It could be argued that Hawks undermines the ideology of male heroism only at the expense of putting forward a view of women that mirrors the fears and anxieties of men. Another argument might be that the use of structural oppositions and reversals in this work allows the ideology to be presented in a schematic form, thus inviting the audience to criticise it.

PAM COOK

His Girl Friday (USA 1939 *p.c* – Columbia; *d* – Howard Hawks)

His Girl Friday is one of Hawks's mature comedies that works out the sets of oppositions outlined above in an extremely complex structural network, using all the elements described by Wood and Wollen as specific to the comedies, but reversing many of them. A structural study of Hawks's work is useful for revealing the varied and shifting combinations of basic structures that are possible. Wollen argues that the greater the complexity of combinations, the richer the work becomes.

The male world is again opposed to the female world, but this time amorality and irresponsibility lie with the former and the latter is associated with a desire for stability, home and family. Both worlds are controlled by men: the frenetic newspaper office by the unscrupulous Walter Burns (Cary Grant) and the home and marriage scene by the stolid, safe insurance salesman Bruce (Ralph Bellamy). Hildy (Rosalind Russell) is torn between the two: her 'feminine' qualities enable her to be critical of the moral chaos of the newspaper world but in the end, in an extraordinary reversal, she rejects marriage and respectability and takes her 'natural' place in that world as a 'newspaperman'.

Hildy is an example of Hollywood's 'positive heroines' and of the use of this stereotype by Hawks. She holds her own in an exclusively male world and is critical of it. However, it is arguable that the 'positive heroine' only succeeds in Hawks's male world because she behaves like a man: her 'femininity' is negated. This sexual reversal is illustrated in terms of verbal language: at first Walter dominates Hildy and Bruce by his command of words, but later the situation is reversed when Hildy tells Walter off. Her verbal diatribe is the mirror image of his; similarly, her rugby tackle, which brings down the Sheriff, is 'heroic' in a masculine sense and heralds her final capitulation to Walter Burns's demands that she rejoin the male world of the newspaper. Nevertheless, Hildy's struggle to retain her own identity and the impossibility of that struggle produce an ironic commentary on the problems of sexual difference that is characteristic of Hawks's work.

PAM COOK

Sergeant York (USA 1941 *p.c* – Warner Bros.; *d* – Howard Hawks)

Apparently atypical of Hawks's work, this film nonetheless represents a validation of the virtues of individual heroism. Alvin York (Gary Cooper) is an ordinary man forced by circumstances (America's involvement in World War I) to become a reluctant hero. While violence and heroism are against his principles, he sacrifices those principles for the sake of his country and discovers that he is, in fact, a 'natural' hero. This structure is similar to that of *His Girl Friday*, and the values attached to home life and community, while initially opposed to those attached to war, are eventually shown to be interchangeable with them. It could be argued that the reversal of oppositions in this film works to validate the ideology of individual heroism and patriotism.

PAM COOK

To Have and Have Not (USA 1944 *p.c* – Warner Bros.; *d* – Howard Hawks)

Harry Morgan (Humphrey Bogart) refuses to commit himself to help the French patriots escape until he finds himself directly and personally involved, and even then political action against Fascism is justified in personal terms, so that the film appears less an anti-Fascist statement than a validation of individual action against corrupt authoritarian forces. The first meeting between Slim (Lauren Bacall) and Harry is interesting because of the woman's self-assurance and insistence on meeting the man on equal terms. However, this is immediately undermined in the sequence in which Harry forces Slim to return the wallet she has stolen, thus asserting his mastery and control of her.

The uneasy relationship between Slim and Harry is characteristic of Hawks's work. Peter Wollen has

Male bonding: Kirk Douglas in *The Big Sky*

pointed to the ritualistic quality of Hawks's male groups: one of the ways in which women enter the group is by learning the rituals, by acting like men. Slim's 'feminine', 'caring' qualities are rejected by Harry because they threaten his self-sufficiency. The only way she can help him is by subscribing to his code, in effect, by becoming 'masculinised'.

Robin Wood (1976) takes this film as a test case for his view of the auteur theory. One of the arguments that critics of auteur study of films put forward is the collaborative nature of film production in Hollywood: the director's contribution is only one among many, and not necessarily the most important one. *To Have and Have Not* would seem to support this view: it is a genre movie (adventures in exotic locations) conceived by the studio (Warner Bros.) as a starring vehicle for Bogart, adapted from a novel by Hemingway, scripted by William Faulkner and Jules Furthman and specifically indebted to at least two other films (*Morocco*, 1930, and *Casablanca*, 1942). Starting with his conception of Hawks's worldview, Wood looks carefully and in detail at all these possible contributions in order to establish that the film is in fact 'quintessentially Hawksian'.

PAM COOK

The Big Sky (USA 1952 p.c – RKO Radio Pictures/Winchester Pictures; d – Howard Hawks)

The idea of love between men recurs in Hawks's films and has been explicitly acknowledged by him. It appears most clearly in the westerns and it could be argued that it is fundamental to this genre.

Robin Wood does not see the male relationships in Hawks's films as homosexual, since they coexist with, and often finally yield to, heterosexual love. For Wood, the love between men is an immature relationship that gives way in the progress of the hero to maturity and responsibility (that is, heterosexuality and marriage).

Wollen, however, refers to 'the undercurrent of homosexuality' in Hawks's films , which he sees as closely linked to the director's idealisation of the all-male group and rejection of women. Men are equals, whereas women are closely identified with nature and the animal world (cf. *Bringing Up Baby*, 1938, *Gentlemen Prefer Blondes*, 1953). Marriage, and the heterosexual relationship, is a threat to the integrity of the elite male group.

Narrative plays an important role in resolving the complex network of 'perverse' relationships running through the film: the relationships between the two men, between the American Indian woman and two white men (one sadistic, the other tender) and between the white men and American Indian woman are resolved ambiguously and, it could be argued, in a somewhat arbitrary fashion. It could seem that Hawks's view of these relationships is at odds with the demands of narrative resolution. Hawks's particular inflection of the 'male love' theme seems to pose it in opposition to heterosexual love, as an ideal in contrast to the problems inherent in homosexuality, thus raising sexual difference itself as a problem.

PAM COOK

Gentlemen Prefer Blondes (USA 1953 p.c – 20th Century Fox; d – Howard Hawks)

This film is one of Hawks's comedies in which sexual role-reversal is predominant. Wollen points to the scenes of male humiliation (for example, Jane Russell's number in which the Olympic athletic team are reduced to passive objects) as an example of Hawks's comic strategy of reversals.

Wood sees this film as one of Hawks's failures: while all the essential elements are there, they do not fuse into a satisfactory coherent whole. However, Richard Dyer (1979) has argued that this lack of coherence is one of the most interesting aspects of the film: the 'lack of fit' between the different elements, in particular, what Dyer sees as the miscasting of Marilyn Monroe in the part of Lorelei, works to

Excessive: Marilyn Monroe in *Gentlemen Prefer Blondes*

Angie Dickinson as the feisty Feathers is conquered by John Wayne in *Rio Bravo*

undermine the consistency of Hawks's worldview.

Of all the genres within which Hawks worked, the musical seems the most unlikely: indeed, *Gentlemen Prefer Blondes* is his only musical and is generally referred to as one of his comedies. While viewing the film as a comedy is revealing in the context of his other work, it is interesting to speculate on his use of the musical numbers here to point up moments of extreme tension between the male world and the threat to it represented by the female. The 'excessive' nature of the musical numbers has been pointed out by Robin Wood, who finds them vulgar and crude. If, as Wood argues, *Gentlemen Prefer Blondes* represents a break in Hawks's work with his usual 'classical' style, it could be seen as one of the points at which the ideology of his worldview begins to fall apart at the seams, making it particularly useful for an ideological reading.

PAM COOK

Rio Bravo (USA 1959 p.c – Armada Productions/ Warner Bros.; d – Howard Hawks)

Robin Wood argues that this film lies firmly within the tradition of the western, at the same time representing the most complete statement of Hawks's position that exists. Genre and director fuse perfectly.

Wood points to the positive qualities of the male group in *Rio Bravo*, seeing in the relationships between the men a moral vision that confirms Hawks's 'spirit of generosity' (Wood, 1968, p. 48). Peter Wollen sees it slightly differently: the self-sufficient all-male group represents an exclusive elite, imposing severe tests of ability and courage on its members (Wollen, 1972, p. 82). Wollen's shift of emphasis makes Hawks's treatment of the male group seem oppressive rather than positive, particularly in relation to women, who never really become full members of the group however hard they try to prove themselves worthy (Wollen, 1972, p. 86).

Some feminist critics (for example, Molly Haskell, 1987) have defended Hawks's 'positive heroines' as strong female figures. However, it is arguable that Feathers (Angie Dickinson) is first recognised as a problem for the male hero, Chance (John Wayne), when she takes the initiative, and is then recuperated as a threat when the hero conquers her, precisely confirming Hawks's view of the necessity for strong male heroes. In this context, the threat of male humiliation is expressed through the use of screwball comedy in the scene between Feathers and Chance at the end of the film. On the level of mise en scène, the exoticism of Feathers's room, the sharp contrasts between red and black, seem to reinforce her function as a sign of threat to the stability of Hawks's male world. It could be argued that Hawks takes John Wayne's star persona to an extreme point of stylisation, so that it almost becomes self-parody, undercutting the masculine values of stoicism and self-sufficiency normally associated with the western hero.

PAM COOK

AUTEUR STUDY AFTER STRUCTURALISM

PAM COOK

The passing of auteur structuralism

British auteur structuralism had attempted to bring together two apparently incompatible theories to resolve the problems inherent in both. On the one hand, it tried to preserve a place for the individual in artistic production, generally retaining the notion found in the *politique des auteurs* of the artist as a potentially critical voice in society. On the other, it saw the individual as enmeshed in linguistic, social and institutional structures that affected the organisation of meaning: the individual was not a free human being in control of the work, whose conscious intentions could be simply retrieved or decoded by the critic. What could be decoded was an authorial system, not to be confused with a real author, which was only one code among many others and not always dominant (see Wollen, 1972). Nevertheless, auteur structuralism, as a method of 'reading', still posited the auteur code as dominant, since it rarely attempted to account for any other codes. So, while claiming to dissolve the auteur into a generality of codes, it continued to provide a partial analysis that maintained a place for the author, still seen as the director, at the centre of their work.

The contradictions inherent in auteur structuralism created the need for new theoretical enquiry to deal with them. At the same time, the historical context in which auteur structuralism first emerged had changed. In France after 1968, a new emphasis on art as political practice brought the idea of individual authorship into question. Also in question was the structuralist 'method' itself, in so far as it was used to decode an abstract, static code or system outside history and society. What was needed, it was argued, was a more dynamic concept of the text that took account of the processes within which it was constantly transformed.

British film criticism produced diverse answers to the theoretical problems generated by auteur structuralism. Peter Wollen (1972) argued for a bringing together of modernist art practice that draws attention to the text as a system of signs, and a theory of language (semiology) that would break with the functionalist approach that saw the work as the expression of thought or intention. The work, he argued, generated meanings through an internal conflict of codes, independently of author or critic; it was a kind of 'factory where thought was at work': author and reader collaborated to produce different and conflicting meanings or interpretations, an activity that would always be 'work in progress' and could never provide a comprehensive, final or 'correct' meaning.

Ed Buscombe (1973) suggested three possible ways out of the impasse of auteurism, all of which would displace the traditional notion of the auteur: a sociology that would attempt to understand how society makes sense of cinema; a theory that would examine the effects of ideology, economics and technology on the cinema; a history that would look at the language of cinema and the effects of films on other films.

Stephen Heath (1973) argued that it was precisely this shift, or displacement, of the idea of the individual auteur at the centre of the work that was in need of theorisation. Close textual analysis, and the employment of psychoanalysis as a tool of analysis, would reveal not the presence of the author, but the play of the unconscious across a body of films and the ways in which the system of each particular film constructed a set of positions for the spectator that determined his or her relationship to the film.

These arguments seemed to signal the end, at least in theoretical film study, of auteur study as it had been known. The shift of emphasis towards the text as the place where meaning was produced, and towards analysis of ideology militated against the classification of films under the name of an author/director. Some textual analysis continued to draw on the idea of an 'authorial code' that could be detected in individual films: this code was not important in itself, however, except as part of the textual system. The question raised for film study by the death of auteur structuralism (a death, it could be argued, implicit in its formation) was an awkward one: why study 'authorship' at all?

Geoffrey Nowell-Smith (1976) argued that the process of assemblage by which a film is put together to be marketed militated against the attribution of a single meaning to one intentional source. From this perspective, authors and critics could not be seen simply as 'effects', dispersed across the textual system. It was precisely the authorial sub-code, or the fragmented marks of authorship, that enabled the critic to reconstruct a coherent auteur. There was no necessary fit between the process of commodity production and that of consumption, but neither should be seen as somehow escaping its place in the social formation.

If the author code can be seen, then, as one of the organising principles of coherence in the film that enables us to grasp meaning, to read it, the problem still remains of what methods to use to identify the marks of the author as distinct from the other elements. So, paradoxically, the post-structuralist debates about authorship and cinema, far from evacuating the problems, had the effect of drawing attention to questions of different methods of 'reading' films, and to the social function of criticism itself.

Historicising auteur study

The question raised by structuralism for film theory was 'why study authorship?', the answer to which can partly be found in the multiple problems auteur analysis raises for film criticism in general; the history of auteur criticism can be seen as the history of different methods of reading films, and of the shifting and complex relationship between spectator/critic and film. Different critical approaches to the work of an auteur can be brought together to demonstrate the historical specificity of 'authorship' as a category and the way in which different readings depend upon and produce different relationships between author, film and spectator. In the study of Hollywood cinema in particular, auteur analysis can be posed against other approaches to the text (for example, through genre, or industry) as a principle of opposition that goes against the grain of the industrial system. The difference between the critics' construction of the auteur and the real director's own assessment of his or her films helps to show that the auteur is indeed a construction, which cannot necessarily be related back to the intentions of a real person. This more complex, historical approach to authorship demonstrates the partiality of different methods of studying cinema, rather than posing one method as more adequate than others.

John Ford

John Ellis (1981) has outlined the principles of a historical approach to studying authorship. Ellis's approach is limited to a consideration of a director working within the Hollywood system over a long period whose status as an auteur in film criticism changes with history. Furthermore, the best kind of director for the purpose would be one whose own account of his work was decidedly not theoretical: interview material could then be used to point up differences between critics' and director's statements. The approach is based on the study of a wide range of critical texts and a large number of films, all of which should show as many differences as possible: the more 'unevenness' there is between texts and between films the easier it is to demonstrate that auteur study is an ideological project that attempts to unify and systematise. There are very few directors who would fulfil these requirements. John Ford is an obvious choice because of his veteran status in the Hollywood industry, his critical reputation as a monumental artist of the cinema and the ability of his films to engage the audience on many complex levels. Ford's relationship to the industry and to critical taste is complicated: his film-making career covers artistic experiments, genre films, studio product and independent productions; his critical reception has varied from Academy Awards to complete disdain. Moreover, many of his films take as their subject matter questions of imperialism, racism and sexism in American society and history: some of them (for example, *Young Mr. Lincoln*, 1939; *The Wings of Eagles*, 1956) seem to undermine their ostensible ideological message through their textual operations, raising the question of the viability of relating them back to the director's intention (or to any other intentional source).

This approach has the advantage of illuminating the notion of authorship as well as the work of the chosen auteur and, because of the emphasis on the process of reading, is able to confront questions of ideology, personal taste and politics in relation to film study. Since it is structured specifically around John Ford and his relationship to the Hollywood industry, however, and it seems as though Ford is the only director whose work could be utilised in this way, the problem remains of how to approach authorship with different directors and in other production situations. For example, the concept of authorship retained by Ellis is the one of opposition to the institutional structures of Hollywood (genre, industry): one question would be whether other institutional structures (for example, New German Cinema, art cinema, independent cinema) bring into play different principles of authorship.

As Ellis points out, the attention given to different critical texts in his approach is not just a way of establishing relative differences between them: a marked distinction emerges between those accounts that assume the relationship between the director and his films is one of continuity of self-expression (for example, Andrew Sarris, see p. 410), and those that distinguish between the man Ford and the auteur construction 'Ford' (for example, Peter Wollen, 1972). In the first case, these readings, combined with interview material, can be seen to perform a particular function in the construction of a persona that will contribute to the process of marketing the Ford commodity. The second kind of readings work against this by positing a 'Fordian system', which is the result of the critical activity of reading rather than the discovery of an expressive essence. In these terms, authorship study is posed as an operation of reading and criticism rather than the straightforward consumption of the Ford commodity.

The difficulty of systematisation, the extent to which any attempt to construct a Fordian system falls short of the complete Ford oeuvre, can be shown by examining the ways in which Ford films contradict one another, undermining the possibility of attributing a set of positive values to Ford or 'Ford'. The use of star John Wayne, for instance, in many different and often contradictory roles, works against the idea of a Fordian world-view outside of history and change (and indeed, against the idea of a Wayne persona outside of history and change).

A comparison of films from the 1930s indicates the extent of the differences and contradictions. *The Informer* (1935) and *The Grapes of Wrath* (1940) appear as 'quality' films with serious intent: they seem more worthy of critical attention/approval than genre films such as *Steamboat Round the Bend* (1935) or even *Stagecoach* (1939), partly because 'Fordian concerns' can be discerned more easily in them. Such a comparison raises quite directly questions of authorship, genre, industry and critical taste (that is, what viewers expect from a 'good' movie). One of the positive aspects of auteur study employed to decode an underlying authorial system is, it could be argued, the way in which it takes issue with critical notions of some films as more 'culturally respectable' than others. However, close analysis of film texts can point to the contradictions within them that seem to fragment or undermine any unifying discourse (for example, *The Wings of Eagles*, *Young Mr. Lincoln*).

In this way, Ellis argues, auteur study can be seen to raise a multitude of questions both for itself and for other critical methods. At the same time, it can be revealed as a partial approach that ignores questions of the industry, except as a set of constraints or limitations on expressivity, or questions of production of meaning in film texts, except as the expression of the author's intentions. Looking at authorship as an activity of reading can raise the general question of criticism and its role in relation to film, for instance, by highlighting the way in which textual operations always tend to exceed or escape attempts to delimit their meanings by critical writing.

The author as 'discursive subject'

Auteur structuralism had insisted that the author should no longer be thought of as a 'real' person existing independently of the films, the intentional source of meaning, and that a new formulation was required that located him or her as producer of meanings within the films themselves. One such formulation defined the authorial 'voice' as a code, or sub-code (see Wollen, 1972), one of many codes that made up the films and that could be objectively defined by reference to the films in question. However, there still remained the problem of the status of the auteur code; why should it be privileged over others, such as those of genre, or studio? Moreover, the emphasis on the film text as a set of objectively definable codes tended to stultify it, fixing meaning in a somewhat mechanical way. What was needed, it was argued (Heath, 1973; Nowell-Smith, 1976) was a theory of meaning production that understood the particular way in which each text worked to produce meaning: objective knowledge of the codes required to decipher meanings was not enough – a 'reading' of the text implied attention to the process of interaction of codes in producing a particular message. This notion of the text as the intersection of various codes stressed the multiplicity of codes at work in any utterance and hence the importance of recognising the effects of different texts upon one another (their 'intertextuality'). The author was not simply an objectively definable sub-code, but rather a 'discursive subject' identifiable as a 'speaker' in the text through the network of different discourses by which it is made up. This discursive subject did not reside in a single point of view or authorial position: it was produced in the interaction of discourses, and itself contributed to the production of meaning. It was the particular historical manifestation of a general set, or system of codes, of specific modes of writing (*écriture*) in circulation at any given moment in a given society. This concept of the 'discursive subject' had the advantage of constituting the subject as productive at the same time as determined by forces of history and language, thus avoiding more mechanical structuralist formulations of the 'subject structured by language'.

The idea of the author as discursive subject, produced by the film text defined as a network of discourses, offered a more flexible account of the relationship between text and reader in which the latter, while clearly now seen as equally responsible with the author (if not more so) for constructing meanings, was also caught up in history and society. Thus different readings would produce different, historically specific meanings, and the text was no longer seen as a finished, complete object: it was transformed by, and accumulated meanings in, the historical process of reading. The reader's codes intersected the codes in the text, of which the authorial code was one, to produce meaning (see Brewster, 1973).

Cahiers du cinéma's 'John Ford'

This idea of the 'text' as constituted by the interaction of different historically specific codes provides the context for the collective text by the editors of the French film journal *Cahiers du cinéma*: 'John Ford's *Young Mr. Lincoln*' (1972). After 1968, *Cahiers* reformulated its position on authorship and cinema, producing a programme of work that would approach cinema as an ideological system and a table that classified films according to the relationship each film held with the dominant ideology. The fifth category in the table referred to those films that seemed at first sight to be caught within the dominant ideology, but on closer inspection were revealed to be cracking apart under the tension of internal contradictions (see *Cahiers*' category 'e', p. 450). A 'symptomatic' reading would reveal the contradictions and demonstrate the extent to which the film dismantled the ideology from within.

Cahiers' symptomatic reading of *Young Mr. Lincoln* attempted to uncover cracks in the system of the film, disjunctures between the different codes that made up the text, specifically between the generic framework of the film (the 'early life of the great man' genre), its fictional sub-codes (the 'detective story' plot superimposed on the genre) and the Fordian authorial sub-code. According to *Cahiers*' argument, while the generic code allowed the film to present Lincoln (against historical evidence) as the great reconciler, in accordance with the ideological project of the film to promote a Republican victory in the American Presidential election of 1940, this code was contradicted by others at work in the film: the detective-story plot that made Lincoln ambiguously both the 'bringer of the truth' and the involuntary puppet of the truth, and the Fordian sub-code (working in parallel to the detective story) that identified Lincoln with his dead mother and dead ideal wife (vehicle of the truth of the community) at the same time as presenting him as implementer of the truth of the community. These two codes work against the depiction of Lincoln as the 'great reconciler', turning him into a kind of monster. In order to implement their symptomatic reading, *Cahiers* employed a code of psychoanalytic decipherment that also worked, in parallel with the detective-story code and the Fordian sub-code, against the 'early life of the hero' generic code to subvert the manifest ideological project of the film.

There are several problems inherent in this analysis: for instance, *Cahiers* did not establish the 'ideological project' of *Young Mr. Lincoln* except by reference to the intentions of Darryl F. Zanuck – head of production at 20th Century Fox – largely ignoring the role played by political and economic factors. Moreover, their use of psychoanalysis as a tool of decipherment tended to remove the film from its historical and political background: thus their reading of the generic code and its ideological motivation in this film could be seen to give it too much importance, leading to an underestimation of the importance of the Fordian system in the film. These problems point to an interesting contradiction: while attempting to displace the author (Ford) as intentional source of the film, the *Cahiers* analysis ends up by confirming the importance of the Fordian authorial system to *Young Mr. Lincoln* and by implication the continuing relevance of auteur analysis in the study of American cinema.

Selected Reading

Ben Brewster, 'Notes on the text "*Young Mr Lincoln*" by the editors of *Cahiers du cinéma*', *Screen* 14 (3): 29–43, autumn 1973.

Edward Buscombe, *Stagecoach*, London, BFI Publishing, 1996.

John Ellis, 'Teaching authorship: Ford or fraud?', in Gledhill (ed.), *Film and Media Studies in Higher Education*, London, BFI Education, 1981.

Peter Wollen, *Signs and Meanings in the Cinema*, London, Secker and Warburg/BFI Publishing, 1972. Expanded edition 1998.

JOHN FORD

The Informer (USA 1935 *p.c* – RKO Radio Pictures; *d* – John Ford)

This film, set during the 1922 Irish rebellion, was acclaimed by critics as a masterpiece when it first appeared because of its formal concerns (its 'Expressionism' and return to the imagery of silent cinema) and incorporation of serious social themes of hunger and unemployment in Ireland in the 1920s. Later it was to be condemned by the same criteria: as formally pretentious and approaching its theme with an over-serious sentimentality (see Anderson, 1981).

In terms of the Fordian system, Victor McLaglen is one of Ford's repertory of actors and the comic-grotesque quality of his performance as Gypo Nolan, his weakness set beside his basic humanity, can be found in his performances in other Ford films. The IRA is described by Sarris (1976) as 'the ultra-Fordian community': comparison of its treatment here with Fordian communities in other films (such as the families in *My Darling Clementine*, 1946, or the army in *She Wore a Yellow Ribbon*, 1949, and *Sergeant Rutledge*, 1960) might illuminate the influence of Irish Catholicism on his work. Peter Wollen (1972) sees a development in Ford's career in terms of a shift in structural oppositions: from an

Ford's divided *Stagecoach* community comes together to defeat the threat of the Native American Indian

identity between 'civilised versus savage' and 'European versus Indian' to their separation and final reversal so that in *Cheyenne Autumn* (1964) it is the Europeans who are savage, the victims who are heroes. How does *The Informer* fit into this pattern of shifting antinomies? Does Wollen's structural model apply to the whole of Ford's work, or only to the westerns?

Ford made this film for RKO – the 'studio of his conscience ... of his moral commitment to his material' (Sarris, 1976) as opposed to Fox, 'his bread and butter base' – and a comparison could be drawn with *The Grapes of Wrath* (1940, Fox) to discuss how far differences might be attributable to studio policies (see The classic studio system, p. 19). The prestige production of *The Informer* might be attributable to Ford's concern with taking on projects at this stage in his career that would further his reputation and give him more control: hence the collaboration with Dudley Nichols and the adaptation of a serious novel.

PAM COOK

Stagecoach (USA 1939 *p.c* – Walter Wanger Productions/ United Artists; *d* – John Ford)

Critical opinion has generally been united over this film, hailing it as a 'classic', in spite of the fact that it is blatantly a genre piece with no 'artistic' pretensions: in fact, the western-genre conventions completely submerge the origins of the film in a novel by Guy de Maupassant (turned into a western story by Ernest Haycox).

Wollen's structural antinomies (civilised versus savage, European versus American Indian) are worked out in terms of the opposition between the savage Apache and the beleaguered stagecoach 'community'. The community is riven with contradictions of class and sexuality between the various characters, but these contradictions are transcended by the primary opposition between American Indian savage versus American civilised values, allowing the extermination of the Native American Indian to be validated and celebrated. It has been argued that this view of American history is reversed and questioned in other Ford films (Wollen, 1972).

The landscape of Monument Valley has become a kind of stylistic signature in Ford's westerns, raising the question of how to identify the marks of authorship in relation to genre conventions. In this film, it figures as an imaginary landscape, part of a mythical 'creative geography' (see Buscombe, 1992).

Stagecoach has often been held up as an example of the classical art of narrative based on montage editing prevalent in Hollywood cinema of the 1930s (see Bazin, 1967). The film thus provides an opportunity to look closely at the organisation of shots and the relationship between image and sound that provide the basis of this narrative system. It can be argued that Ford breaks many of the classical conventions.

Although the film is clearly a genre piece, and also an example of 'classical' narrative cinema, it could be argued that it nonetheless deals with 'serious' questions (class, sexuality, race) as much as *The Informer* (1935) or *The Grapes of Wrath* (1940), in spite of the fact that critics do not generally give it the status of a 'quality' film.

PAM COOK

The Grapes of Wrath (USA 1940 *p.c* – 20th Century Fox; *d* – John Ford)

The story of a family's migration from Oklahoma to California, this was the film that established Ford's reputation as a great poet of American cinema; paradoxically, it is difficult to identify it as belonging only to Ford without ignoring the contributions of, for example, Nunnally Johnson's adaptation of Steinbeck's novel, Gregg Toland's photography, not to mention producer Darryl F. Zanuck.

In terms of the Fordian system, Ford's reputed populism could be detected in the depiction of the Joad family as a community and the role of the mother in unifying the family. Arguably, however, this populism emerges as much from Steinbeck's concerns, or from New Deal ideology, as from a 'Fordian system'. Comparison with other Ford films (such as *Young Mr Lincoln*, 1939; see p. 462) and with other Hollywood populist films (such as Frank Capra's) could illuminate this question. Sarris (1976) argues that Steinbeck's criticism of American society is undermined by New Deal homilies.

The structural opposition between wilderness (or desert) and garden identified by Wollen (1972) as the master antinomy in Ford's films is worked out here in terms of the opposition between the Oklahoma dustbowl and the luxuriant promised land of California, which proves to be less than ideal. The journey, or quest, of the Joad family has been identified as part of Ford's thematic system: the search for the promised land involves a movement between desert and garden that changes in emphasis, and therefore in meaning, from film to film.

It is arguable that the film's aesthetically beautiful images, attributable to Ford and Toland, are in conflict with the angry, critical words of Steinbeck and Johnson, a conflict produced perhaps by Ford's desire to enhance his directorial career at this time with prestige productions (Sarris, 1976).

PAM COOK

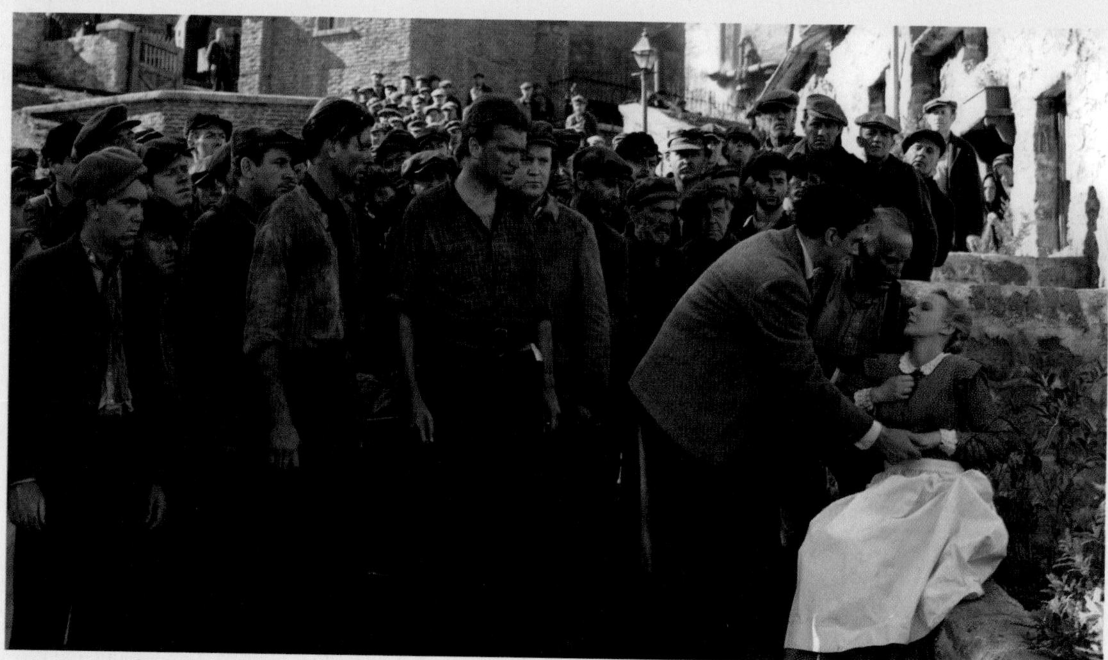

Set in the Welsh mining valleys, *How Green Was My Valley* mourns the loss of community and family values

How Green Was My Valley (USA 1941 *p.c* – 20th Century Fox; *d* – John Ford)

A lavish, prestige production that Ford took over from William Wyler in the early stages of preparation and that won five Academy Awards, including Best Director. The film draws attention to its literary origins in a novel by using the device of voice-over narration through which a central character (the boy Huw Morgan) remembers the past.

The film centres on family and community, a thematic element in many Ford films, but here providing the entire motivation for the film. The combination of nostalgia for past values and the representation of the community as the location of positive values such as loyalty, discipline and gallantry have been identified by Robin Wood (1968) as Ford's major preoccupation. Whereas the fragmentation of the family in *The Grapes of Wrath* (1940) provides the basis for a criticism of social conditions, *How Green Was My Valley* seems to look back to the Depression as a time when social conditions destroyed family unity, the project of the film being to mourn its loss.

In terms of genre, the film belongs to a certain type of family melodrama prevalent in Hollywood in the 1940s (see Higham and Greenberg, 1968). Ford's films often used melodrama to move the audience and this film is one of the all-time great weepies; yet it also combines 'serious' political questions with a genre not usually valued highly for its seriousness.

PAM COOK

My Darling Clementine (USA 1946 *p.c* – 20th Century Fox; *d* – John Ford)

After World War II, Ford's reputation fell into something of a critical decline (see Sarris, 1976). This film was his second western in 20 years and it did little to restore that reputation.

It is arguable that the traditional conventions of the genre (action sequences, gunfights) are displaced or transformed by the emphasis placed in this film on domestic activity; that is, on day-to-day activities of personal hygiene, dressing up, courting, going to church and so forth, which represent the civilising forces that take over the desert/wilderness, transforming it into a cultivated garden.

Wollen (1972) sees the progress of Wyatt Earp (Henry Fonda) from 'nature' to 'culture' as relatively unproblematic compared with other Fordian heroes (such as Ethan Edwards in *The Searchers*, 1956). The scene in the barbershop is seen by Wollen as symbolic of this progress: the barber 'civilises' the unkempt Earp, splashing him with honeysuckle scent (an artificial rather than a natural perfume), thus marking his transition from nomad to settled, civilised man, administrator of the law. However, it could also be argued that Earp's progress can only be measured against the decline of Doc Holliday (Victor Mature), which is seen in terms of the loss of an anarchic spirit that is the basis of poetry and subversive sexual energy. Moreover, Earp's bearing during his transformation remains stiff and unwieldy, even in the communal dance sequence. The transition from nature to culture is heavily marked as comic, and could be seen as more problematic than Wollen allows. Furthermore, the highly stylised mise en scène (extreme perspectives, predominance of long shots and 'Expressionist' lighting) might offer the audience a critical distance both on the genre conventions and the narrative events.

The opposition between the two women, Clementine (Cathy Downs) and Chihuahua (Linda Darnell), is also interesting in terms of the transition from nature to culture discussed by Wollen in relation to the central male character. This taming of energy is often depicted in Ford's films as necessary but regrettable, so that the films seem to question the 'progress' of history.

PAM COOK

Fort Apache (USA 1948 *p.c* – Argosy Pictures/RKO Radio Pictures; *d* – John Ford)

Sarris (1976) argues that the last two decades of Ford's career were the most vigorous in that 'he became fully his own man'. Contemporary critics, however, did not agree, and saw the later Ford as self-indulgent, relegating him to the status of an honoured has-been, now engaged in reworking tired old themes with the same stock company.

Peter Wollen's (1972) structural approach can be seen as an attempt to redress the critical balance. By looking for underlying patterns of shifting oppositions, he was able to argue that the shifting pattern became more complex as Ford's work developed. *Movie*, following *Cahiers du Cinéma*, had declared its preference for Sam Fuller over Ford; in the mid-1960s *Cahiers* re-evaluated Ford, but only in terms of 'key' auteur films.

Wollen's approach provided the possibility of looking again at the whole of Ford's work, and not necessarily in terms of 'good' and 'bad' films, rather in terms of an underlying 'Fordian system'. Although this approach attempted to come to terms with the unevenness of Ford's work, with its differences and contradictions, Wollen himself deals mainly with westerns, which seem most amenable to analysis according to structural oppositions. The question still remains of how the more 'aberrant' works fit into the schema. Ford's work seems to resist schematic systematisation, which is what makes it so useful for a critical approach to auteur study.

This film was the first in a series of cavalry westerns that demonstrated a changing attitude towards the Native American Indians in Ford's work. It could be argued that this liberalised attitude in the films was less a political shift (on the part of Ford or anyone else) than a way of dramatising the conflict of values within the cavalry community. Wollen may be right in pointing to a reversal between the oppositions savage (Native American Indian) and civilised (European) in Ford's later work, but it is not a simple reversal in which the Native American Indians take the place of the Europeans at the centre of the drama. However, the film does include a point-of-view shot from the perspective of the American Indian characters in one scene, an unusual occurrence at the time.

This film also marks the shift from Henry Fonda to John Wayne as the hero of Ford's films. The confrontation between Captain York (Wayne) and Lieutenant Colonel Thursday (Fonda) is useful for discussing the iconographic differences between the two stars as deployed in the Fordian system.

PAM COOK

The Searchers (USA 1956 *p.c* – C. V. Whitney Pictures/Warner Bros.; *d* – John Ford)

As John Ellis (1981) argued, Ford's work can be used to raise a wide range of questions about the ways in which films are produced and consumed and the critical methods employed to analyse cinema. *The Searchers* is a paradigmatic case: it has achieved the status of a key text in film studies for the possibilities it offers as the site of different, often conflicting, analytical methods that work productively with and against one another.

The film's perceived usefulness in different contexts can be partly ascribed to its problematic place in the Fordian oeuvre, which makes it necessary to look outside the film itself for an explanation of its 'lack of fit'. Critics are deeply divided in their evaluations. Anderson (1956), for example, denies that the film has any place in the humanistic worldview he defines as Ford's, while Wollen (1972) sees the film as perhaps Ford's most complex working through of the opposition wilderness/garden that forms the basis of his work. For Wollen, the complexity lies in the overlapping of these oppositions within and between characters, particularly between Ethan Edwards (John Wayne), a tragic hero torn apart by the divisions Native American Indian/European, savage/civilised, nomad/settler; his 'opposite', Scar (Henry Brandon), the Native American Indian chief with whom he shares many characteristics; his companion in the quest to find Debbie, part-Cherokee Martin Pawley (Jeffrey Hunter); and the European family of homesteaders who represent the eventual transformation of wilderness into garden. This structural complexity enables the film to complicate, perhaps undermine, any simple progress from wilderness to garden, savage to civilised, which may be seen as its manifest ideological project.

For Wollen, then, Ford's particular inflection of material basic to the mythology of the western forms a subtext or code that contradicts the genre's ideological bias, an analysis that can be used to challenge allegations that the film is racist. However, as John Caughie points out (1975/76), even if it could be proved that a critique of racism was 'intended', the narrative resolution in which Debbie is returned to the white community and the 'natural order' restored at the very least removes the sting from the critique. Caughie also argues that the wilderness/garden opposition is supported by a sexual division in which men are active participants in the struggle towards civilisation and women passively represent the values for which they are fighting. It would seem, then, that the complexity noted by Wollen is not present at every level.

PAM COOK

Sergeant Rutledge (USA 1960 *p.c* – Warner Bros.; *d* – John Ford)

Wollen (1972) identifies a transition in Ford's work that equates 'non-Americans' (Irish, Native American Indians, Polynesians, blacks) with the traditional values of the American dream that America itself has lost. It could be argued that this appropriation of other races in the service of 'American' values is imperialistic, to say the least. While the representation of the black Rutledge is often seen (see Ellis, 1981) to be a more liberalised view of the black Americans than in Ford's earlier work (for example, *Judge Priest*, 1934; *Steamboat Round the Bend*, 1935; *The Sun Shines Bright*, 1953), this 'liberalisation' seems to involve divesting Rutledge of both his blackness and sexuality, superimposing the values of courage and nobility associated with the American cavalry and so producing Rutledge as a 'noble savage' figure who transcends racism. The position of the black soldier is never raised in terms of his relation to the Native American Indians, the white man's ideology is accepted and the Apache are unquestionably regarded as the enemy, the destruction of whom will enable the black soldiers to become free Americans.

John Ellis (1981) argues that the film produces a commentary on racism by taking the myth of black super-sexuality as its central problem, displacing the myth in favour of the proposition that blacks are asexual; Rutledge becomes a human being only in so far as he forswears his sexuality. This forswearing of sexuality in a higher cause can be traced in other Ford films (*My Darling Clementine*, 1946; *She Wore a Yellow Ribbon*, 1949; *Rio Grande*, 1950). According to Ellis, the film is only able to raise the problem of race and sexuality in this way because of its tightly coded narrative structure: the trial device enables commentary to be carried out at all points of ambiguity in the story, with returns from flashbacks to the cross-examination of witnesses. Thus multiple meanings are limited and controlled, and the film articulates its position against a certain kind of racism based on the myth of black super-sexuality. Ellis's account focuses on the way in which narrative structure contributes to the construction of meaning in the film, independently of the intentions of the author.

PAM COOK

THE AUTHOR NEVER DIES

PAM COOK

By the mid- to late 1970s, cinematic authorship had undergone radical revision, from a polemical intervention that insisted on the primary role of certain directors in producing style and meaning (see The *politique des auteurs*, p. 390; Auteur theory, p. 410) to a theoretical construction that perceived the director as an idea, as a sub-code among the many codes that competed for attention in film texts. Creative power had shifted from the film-maker to the reader; the latter interacted with film texts to produce many different kinds of meanings and analyses, depending on context. Before long, as film studies moved towards a 'historical turn' in which the experiences of actual spectators were granted prominence (see Spectatorship and audience research, p. 538), the director waned in importance – and, indeed, seemed to disappear altogether, at least in theory.

The dissolution of the author in film theory coincided with a major shift in cultural politics that emerged in the wake of the upheavals following May 1968 in France, which had a profound effect on independent film-making. To many engaged in cultural practice on the ground, what was needed was not simply a deconstruction of ideology, but a fundamental reorganisation of the industrial system of production, distribution and exhibition from which a new, revolutionary cinema could emerge, not only political in content, but 'made politically' (see 'The Estates General of the French cinema, May 1968'). This refusal of industrial, hierarchical methods of working was accompanied by a rejection of individual authorship. Many newly politicised film-makers formed small independent groups dedicated to collective working methods, skills-sharing and to producing films for small and specific political audiences. Jean-Luc Godard joined with other young Maoists to form the Dziga-Vertov Group during this period; Vertov's name was used less as an authorial inspiration than for his practice, his battle to produce a cinematic language adequate to express the 'truth' of class struggle.

This emphasis on the need for a totally new practice of cinema was influential on the growth of independent film-making in the UK during the 1970s. But initially it emerged as a discussion of what forms this new cinema should adopt and was expressed, perhaps surprisingly, in quite conventional auteurist terms. Jean-Luc Godard's work was taken up by Peter Wollen as exemplary of what a materialist oppositional cinema, a 'counter-cinema', might be (see Avant-garde and counter-cinema, p. 89).

Auteurism, Godard and counter-cinema

In his Postscript to the second edition of *Signs and Meaning in the Cinema* (1972), Wollen argued that since Hollywood provided the dominant codes with which films are read, it was only in confrontation with Hollywood that anything new could be produced; according to Wollen, this kind of confrontation, interrogation and criticism could be found in the work of Jean-Luc Godard. In 'Counter-cinema: *Vent d'est*' (1982), he took this argument a stage further by elaborating on those values of 'orthodox' cinema with which Godard's 'counter-cinema' took issue, evaluating his work up to 1972 in terms of its increasing opposition to, or break with, Hollywood cinema. Wollen claimed that Godard's method of 'negation', or contrast, enabled him to produce a revolutionary materialist cinema that took account of 'Hollywood-Mosfilm' (Godard's term for 'bourgeois capitalist cinema') while working to criticise it. For Wollen, the value of this method was that it created questions and disagreements in Godard's films, setting up a different relationship between spectator and films from that of traditional cinema, which he characterised in terms of narrative coherence and identification, the generation of pleasures that aimed to satisfy or reassure the film viewer rather than to involve him or her in debate. However, Wollen criticised Godard's rather puritanical rejection of the fantasy pleasures offered by mainstream cinema, arguing that a 'revolutionary' cinema must take on board the relationship between pleasure, entertainment, fantasy, ideology and science produced in film (see Avant-garde and counter-cinema, p. 92).

Wollen's account dealt with a period in which the ideas of structuralism, semiology and psychoanalysis, combined with a cultural politics emerging from the events of May 1968, explicitly informed Godard's work. It is questionable whether the strategies identified by Wollen could be effective outside that particular context. Nevertheless, his polemic for the necessity of developing a new, oppositional film-making practice was influential on subsequent debates about independent political cinema in the UK.

Godard and history

Godard himself has insisted that the political upheavals in France represented for him not so much a break with the past as the possibility of developing the ideas he was already formulating (see MacCabe, 1980). He had already collaborated with Maoist militants on some films when in the immediate aftermath of 1968 it became possible for him as a film-maker to commit himself to engaging in totally new methods of work. Although his Maoism waned with the disintegration of French Maoism in 1972, the commitment to alternative methods of work remained. However, in Godard's case those alternative methods have not remained the same. There are evident differences between the films emerging from his collaboration with Jean-Pierre Gorin and others in the Dziga-Vertov Group in 1969–70 and after the dissolution of the group in 1972. In 1974, he set up his own production company away from Paris in the French Alps with Anne-Marie Miéville: the films and television programmes they produced show a further shift of concern towards the investigation of the relationship between the personal and the political. In the 1980s, Godard returned to using fictional forms and stars in his film projects – *Every Man for Himself/Sauve qui peut (la vie)* (1980); *Hail Mary/'Je vous salue, Marie'* (1984) and others – while at the same time pursuing his fascination with history in 'documentaries' about cinema (for example, *Histoires du cinéma*, 1993).

Godard has reinvented himself and his working methods many times, in response to historical and cultural change (see MacCabe, 2004). Nevertheless, his work shows a persistent preoccupation with theory and politics, with the technology and

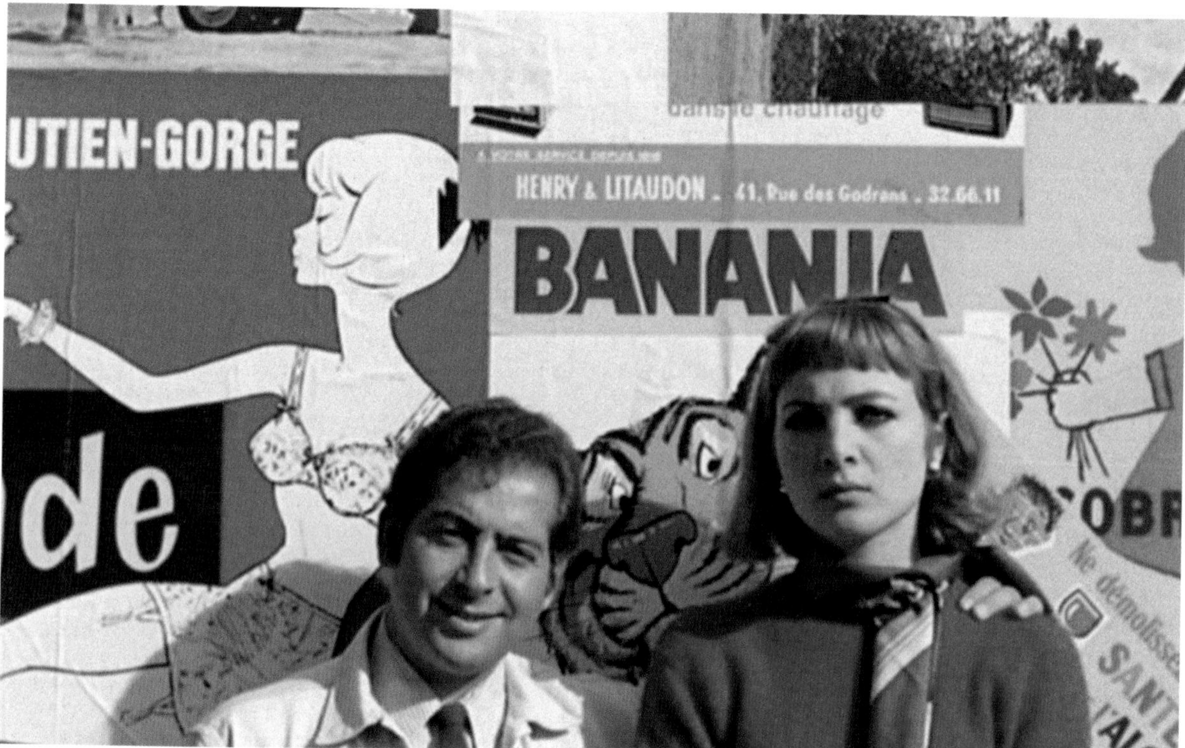

Towards a revolutionary counter-cinema: *Weekend*, Godard's scathing attack on the bourgeoisie

language of cinema and the circulation of images in society, and with formulating new audio-visual languages (although the form of those preoccupations constantly mutates, sometimes quite radically). More recently, he turned to reflecting on memory and history (*In Praise of Love/Eloge de l'amour*, 2001). One of the lessons of the political upheavals in the late 1960s that remained with Godard was the idea of cinema as 'social practice': that is, a political commitment to bringing cinema into relationship with people's everyday lives, a different relationship from the perceived escapism of 'normal' cinemagoing or television viewing. This involves changing the traditional ways in which films are produced, distributed, exhibited and consumed. Because of his constant drive to reinvent audiovisual media, Godard remains one of the most revered film-makers in cinema history (see Temple, Williams and Witt, 2003). His work is endlessly exciting because it is capable of raising a multitude of questions about all aspects of cinema and politics, and shows how the film-maker is caught up in history rather than being consciously in control of the work. This implies a different, nuanced view of the notion of agency in auteur study and makes it difficult to apply traditional critical criteria to that work, although this has been done (see Perkins, 1972; Harcourt, 1974). The aggressive 'intertextuality' of Godard's films, that is, the ways in which they break with classical unity of forms to assert their critical, dialectical relationship with other films, other texts and media, other ideas and historical situations, accounts for his continuing relevance over more than 45 years of film-making.

Selected Reading

Raymond Bellour and Mary Lea Bandy (eds), *Jean-Luc Godard: Sound + Image*, New York, Museum of Modern Art, 1992.

Colin MacCabe, *Godard: A Portrait of the Artist at Seventy*, London, Bloomsbury, 2004.

Peter Wollen, 'Counter-cinema: *Vent d'est*' and 'The two avant-gardes', in *Readings and Writings*, London, Verso, 1982.

Auteurism and women directors

Wollen's counter-cinema polemic was taken up by feminist film theorists in the early 1970s (see Avant-garde and counter-cinema, p. 93). In particular, Claire Johnston (1974) called for a new women's cinema that would confront the ideology of mainstream cinema by developing the means to challenge its depiction of reality. By countering the conventions of Hollywood, the iconography and stereotypes whereby it attempted to fix myths of women as natural and universal, a dislocation could be brought about between patriarchal ideology and the language used to perpetuate it that would provide the basis for strategies of subversion (see Feminist film theory, p. 492). At the same time, Johnston, like Wollen, believed that feminist oppositional film-making should not entirely sacrifice the pleasures of mainstream cinema. In this respect, she posed counter-cinema against the dominant mode of 1970s feminist cinema, documentary.

Johnston's argument drew on *Cahiers*' category 'e' (see p. 450) and on post-structuralist versions of auteur theory that challenged the idea of the director as intentional source of meaning, redefining it in terms of the unconscious preoccupations that could be decoded in the formal network of film texts and that were often outside the control of the director concerned. Johnston took issue with the idea that mainstream cinema was monolithically closed to intervention by women film-makers, arguing that the work of those few women directors who had managed to build up a body of work in the Hollywood system was of interest to feminists precisely because of the ways in which their unconscious preoccupations could be seen to turn sexist ideology on its head, manipulating the codes of mainstream cinema in order to criticise it, or to make it 'strange'.

Johnston used Dorothy Arzner and Ida Lupino as examples of women directors whose work manifested an internal criticism of mainstream ideology.

Johnston's ideas were challenged by later feminist theorists (for example, Bergstrom, 1979), but her counter-cinema argument was influential, both on feminist film-makers and on theory. One of the most significant aspects of the argument (that mainstream cinema was not ideologically closed) was more fully developed in her work with Pam Cook on Dorothy Arzner (1975; reprinted in Penley, 1988).

Women directors in Hollywood: Dorothy Arzner

One of the first tasks undertaken by 1970s feminist film criticism was that of rewriting the history of cinema to include the contribution of women film-makers, notably missing from traditional auteur pantheons. This new history quickly revealed the virtual absence of successful women directors within the Hollywood industry and, perhaps more surprisingly, the relatively small number of women who had worked independently in documentary and avant-garde cinema. Although the development of lightweight equipment and cheap film stock after World War II seemed to promise wider access to the means of production, the absence of women from the independent sector too seemed to suggest that ideological and economic factors played a greater part than technology in determining the place of women in cinema's history. In the case of Hollywood, feminist film criticism found that although women had worked as editors and scriptwriters, and of course as stars, very few ever made it to positions of power as directors or producers. One of the major contributions of feminist film history has been to draw attention to the hierarchical conditions of production and the ideological bias that have militated against the possibility of women having significant control over the kinds of films produced by the industry (see also Benton, 1975; Contemporary women directors, p. 68). Sometimes this discovery has led to an overvaluation of the work of those women directors who managed to survive and a tendency to construct their films as positive feminist statements, or as feminist 'art', as in the case of Dorothy Arzner (for example, Peary, 1974).

The counter-cinema position was different, in that it insisted that the writing of a history of the cinema to include the contribution of women directors should recognise that a simple chronology that 'redressed the balance' in favour of female auteurs would not be enough. Instead, what was required was a theoretical understanding of the complex relationship between ideological, technological and institutional factors that precisely made it impossible for positive feminist statements to emerge from the Hollywood system of production (see Johnston, 1975). A history of women's cinema did not simply already exist to be unearthed, it would have to be constructed, and the terms of that construction debated.

This feminist work on Dorothy Arzner proved controversial. It ruffled the feathers of male auteurist critics who could not accept that Arzner's films merited a place in their canons. Some feminist critics at the time objected to the ahistorical perception of women directors as 'unconscious discourse', and later, a challenge was mounted to the perceived 'heterosexist' bias of this account, which ignored the possibility that Arzner was a lesbian (Mayne, 1995). And Doty (1993) argued for a reappraisal of *Cahiers'* category 'e' with respect to queer readings of Arzner's work – the wheel appeared to have come full circle (see Auteurism and women directors, p. 468; Auteurs and alterity, p. 477). All this testifies to the continuing relevance of Dorothy Arzner in film studies. However, the response has tended to occlude the central question: how can the contribution of women directors to the history of cinema be recognised without simply replicating the existing tenets and canons of auteurism, in which they are inevitably marginalised?

Despite its theoretical underpinnings, the early feminst work on Arzner was really a reinterpretation of auteur theory's conception of the director in opposition to the industrial context of Hollywood cinema, nuanced by post-structuralist notions of the authorial discourse emerging from and constituted by the film text (see The author as 'discursive subject', p. 461). The problems with such 'radical readings' of Hollywood films have been pointed out elsewhere (see *Cahiers du cinéma*'s 'John Ford', p. 462). Clearly, an approach based on textual analysis does not tell us much about the actual conditions of production and reception of Arzner's films in the 1930s and 1940s: in that sense, it attempts to construct these films as contradictory texts without recourse to a traditional historiography. However, by focusing on the activity of 'rereading' and 'rewriting', it does raise important questions about the nature of ideology and the possibility of intervention within it. Dorothy Arzner disclaimed any feminist intention on her part: a rereading of her work can show that meaning is not necessarily fixed according to the author's intentions, and that a film text can accumulate meanings through different readings at different historical moments. Thus films with no immanent political content can be used to raise political questions in a different context.

Dorothy Arzner began her career typing scripts in Hollywood in the 1920s. After World War I, the film industry was fairly open and she soon became an editor and scriptwriter. She was given her first directorial assignment (*Fashions for Women*) by Paramount/Famous Players-Lasky in 1927 and went on to direct several comedies and dramas in the category of the women's picture. Although many women worked as editors and writers in Hollywood at this time, few became directors. To understand

Pioneer and survivor: Hollywood director Dorothy Arzner

DOROTHY ARZNER

Dance, Girl, Dance (USA 1940 *p.c* – RKO Radio Pictures; *d* – Dorothy Arzner)

Dance, Girl, Dance was the personal project of Erich Pommer, the former head of Germany's Ufa studio, then in exile in Hollywood: he had conceived, cast and started shooting the film and called in Dorothy Arzner to replace another RKO director. She reworked the script and sharply defined the central conflict as a clash between the artistic inspirations of Judy (Maureen O'Hara) and the commercial, gold-digging Bubbles (Lucille Ball). It is a mixed-genre film combining the conventions of the chorus/working-girl film (backstage musical) and the sophisticated romantic comedy. It is arguable that this combination produces a particularly acute contradiction in the film between, on one hand, an image of woman as spectacle and, on the other, as the subject of her own desires, both of which are seen to be ultimately controlled by men. The film has been seen as playing with the generic conventions to point up this contradiction, using irony and parody to bring ideology to the surface of the film in its mise en scène (see Johnston, 1988; Cook, 1988). For instance, it has been argued that genre conventions are reworked to displace the male discourse and focus on the woman's point of view; the scene in which Judy turns on and interrogates the burlesque audience is particularly striking in this context. The film uses class stereotypes to point up differences in Judy's and Bubbles's aspirations: however, these class differences seem to be transcended by the similarities between the two women's problems within male-dominated society.

The same argument sees the 'happy ending' of this film as ironic, pointing up the power structures within which male–female relationships exist under patriarchy. Rather than attribute this irony entirely to Arzner, the film might be discussed in the context of the ironic endings characteristic of the women's picture (see Melodrama, p. 316).

PAM COOK

the nature of Arzner's extraordinary achievement, it would be necessary to look at the structure of the industry at that time and the way it affected her work. She claims to have had considerable freedom on her projects (see Peary and Kay, 1975); at the same time, she was publicised as a woman director and was limited to the women's picture, a fact that raises questions about the status of women in the Hollywood industry during the 1920s and 1930s. There are significant differences between the films she directed before the arrival of synchronised sound and those she made afterwards, and again between the films she directed for different studios. The unevenness of her work, and the difficulty of assimilating it to a coherent oeuvre as auteur study prescribes, could be seen to confirm the proposition put forward by a theoretical analysis of her films: that any challenge to the prevailing ideology they may offer presents itself in the form of symptoms rather than as a direct statement (see Cook, 1988).

At the edges of Hollywood: Stephanie Rothman

The context for feminist discussion of Rothman's work is slightly different, though still emerging from the counter-cinema arguments. During the 1960s and 1970s, Rothman, a film school graduate and an avowed feminist, worked as producer and director for Roger Corman, first for AIP and then for Corman's independent production and distribution company, New World Pictures. A number of factors, including the reorganisation of the classical Hollywood studio system (within which Arzner had worked) following World War II, and the dissolution of the mass popular audience into niche markets, contributed to a growth in the independent sector. Through AIP and New World, which was initially geared to fast, low-budget production, Corman offered many young film-makers, including Rothman, the chance to direct (see Roger Corman, p. 416). New World Pictures developed

STEPHANIE ROTHMAN

The Student Nurses (USA 1970 *p.c* – New World Pictures; *d* – Stephanie Rothman)

This was the first of Rothman's major films for Corman's New World studio, made in the 'student nurse' genre that Corman is said to have invented. Working in the sexploitation, soft-porn genre produced mainly (but not exclusively) for male audiences, Rothman introduced several jarring notes that seem to be incompatible with the generic project. Her use of strategies such as parody and mixed styles could be seen to highlight the underlying preconceptions of sexploitation material, bringing them to the surface and exposing their sexism.

On another level, like many New World films, the film deals explicitly with social issues such as abortion, here presented from the perspective of the women characters and questioning masculine attitudes to female sexuality in a manner that would seem to be incompatible with the demands of sexploitation films. However, it might also be argued that abortion is just one more sensational element in a genre that depends for its existence on the exploitation of women's bodies as objects of erotic contemplation.

Despite owing something to exploitation aesthetics in its episodic narrative and formulaic acting styles, the film has comparatively high production values and clearly borrows from art cinema (especially in the fantasy sequence at the beach party) (see Cook, 2005).

PAM COOK

Terminal Island/Knuckle-men (USA 1973 *p.c* – Dimension Pictures; *d* – Stephanie Rothman)

This is an example of a film made by Rothman for her own production company, Dimension Pictures, continuing in the tradition of exploitation cinema. It can be argued that Rothman works on the action-sexploitation genre to challenge the pleasures it usually offers its audience, and so create new meanings out of basically uncongenial material. Comparison with other exploitation films could indicate how far the film's potential audiences might be expected to perceive the feminist criticism of exploitation genre conventions. During the 1970s, under the influence of feminism, there was a call for more positive representations of women in cinema, and an expanding audience of female viewers (see Cook, 2005).

The film is set in an island prison community in which there are opposing camps – one hierarchical and patriarchal, the other exploring the feasibility of a new social order in which notions of sharing and community, group discussion and responsibility are proposed. While relying on the conventions of the action-sexploitation genre, Rothman parodies them and uses role-reversal to subvert generic expectations.

The bee-stinging sequence in particular exemplifies a sadistic reversal of conventions that parodies male fantasies. Joy's (Phyllis Davis) exit from the pool, for example, is a parodic reversal of normal striptease procedure, as she emerges naked and then dresses herself, before the bees are let loose on her aroused, would-be mate. Another generic reversal can be seen in the fact that it is the women's knowledge and ingenuity in turning the island's resources to their own use that eventually brings about the takeover by the radical group of the enemy camp. Many exploitation films employ a form of 'positive heroine' stereotype that mirrors male aggression, and one would expect the action genre to validate this stereotype. In this film, by contrast, the new social order is based on a division of labour that gives men and women equal but different roles, arguably questioning the patriarchal system in which women are seen as mirror images of the male.

PAM COOK

Stephanie Rothman overturns exploitation expectations in *Terminal Island*

Freewheeling style: Sandrine Bonnaire as Mona in Agnès Varda's *Sans toit ni loi*

a reputation for dealing with serious political themes within the format of 'exploitation' film production (that is, cheap remakes of more upmarket productions in order to make a quick profit), acquiring a name as something of a feminist studio because of its promotion of 'positive female' stereotypes influenced by popular versions of 'Women's Lib' (see Hillier and Lipstadt, 1981).

However, in spite of the apparent potential of this situation for a declared feminist such as Rothman, it is arguable that exploitation films depend for their success on the image of woman as the object of male fantasy, just as much as, if not more than, classic Hollywood. Rothman often parodied the codes of exploitation genres to expose their roots in male fantasies and so undermine them, and it is this use of formal play to subvert male myths of women that has interested some feminists and that, it has been argued, places Rothman's work in the tradition of women's counter-cinema (see Cook, 2005). Rothman is also of interest to feminists because for a short period she owned her own company (with husband Charles Swarz), Dimension Films, thus achieving an unusual level of control within the industry. The company was dissolved in 1974 and Rothman has since gone back to writing scripts (see Fox, 1976).

Recent years have seen a revival of feminist interest in the potential of 'exploitation' film-making for offering women opportunities to enter the industry, and also to use the comic-book aesthetics of exploitation genres for subversive ends (see Despineux and Mund, 2000).

Outside Hollywood: Agnès Varda

Agnès Varda began her long directorial career in the context of the Nouvelle Vague (see p. 405), although she is rarely accorded the visibility of her male colleagues. Her husband, Jacques Demy, was a Nouvelle Vague director whose primary interest was in reworking the conventions of the Hollywood musical to point up its 'utopian' qualities (for example, *The Umbrellas of Cherbourg/Les Parapluies de Cherbourg*, 1964). It might be suggested that his interest in utopian fantasies informed Varda's *Happiness/Le Bonheur* (1965), where it was transformed into an ironic reflection on bourgeois marriage.

Varda's prolific body of work covers a wide range of forms, from documentary and short film essays to narrative features and art installations. She started out as a photographer, and her preoccupation with the relationship of film images to reality can be seen in films from *Cléo from 5 to 7/Cléo de 5 á 7* (1962), which appears to document in 'real' time a young woman's wait for news of her illness, to the freewheeling style of *Vagabond/Sans toit ni loi* (1985) and the 'poetic realism' of *The Gleaners and I/Les Glaneurs et la glaneuse* (2000). All her work is distinctly personal (see, for example, her touching tribute to her husband, *Jacquot de Nantes*, 1991), and she has kept her distance from feminism. This may be one of the reasons why feminist writing on her films has been sporadic, despite the major contribution she has made, and continues to make, to cinema history. As she approaches her eighties, it would seem to be a good time to reassess that contribution (see Flitterman-Lewis, 1996; Smith, 1998).

Varda's films seem to lean towards the art cinema strand of the Nouvelle Vague (cf. Marguerite Duras). However, they cannot be seen as lying unproblematically within the art cinema tradition. It could be argued that she is interested in investigating the basic processes by which cinematic images captivate the audience, which would place her in the avant-garde tradition within art cinema rather than in the counter-cinema tradition of Godard.

Selected Reading

Pam Cook, *Screening the Past: Memory and Nostalgia in Cinema*, New York and Oxford, Routledge, 2005.

Claire Johnston, 'Women's cinema as counter-cinema', in *Notes on Women's Cinema*, London, SEFT, 1974.

Judith Mayne, *Directed by Dorothy Arzner*, Bloomington, Indiana University Press, 1995.

Alison Smith, *Agnès Varda*, Manchester, Manchester University Press, 1998.

AGNÈS VARDA

Happiness/Le Bonheur (France 1965 *p.c* – Parc Film; *d* – Agnès Varda)

Varda was the only woman director associated with the Nouvelle Vague (Marguerite Duras belonged rather within the avant-garde); this film could be interestingly compared with early films of Godard and Truffaut for the way it questions the romantic point of view of its male protagonist, who conceives of 'freedom' in bourgeois terms. The theme of individual freedom and the impossibility of attaining it was central to many early Nouvelle Vague films (for example, *Breathless/A bout de souffle*, 1960; or *The 400 Blows/Les Quatre cents coups*, 1959) but the problem is usually presented entirely from the male protagonist's viewpoint, which is validated. It is arguable that Varda undermines that viewpoint by showing that it rests on an image, or myth, of woman that is oppressive.

Although the film presents a romantic fantasy of love and marriage, it places that fantasy as male and shows how it controls the production of images for women to identify with. This is illustrated by the treatment of the wedding preparations, the taking of photographs after the ceremony and the images of motherhood at the reception, all of which are seen to be caught up in a process of image-making at the same time as they present an ideal image of happiness. As François (Jean-Claude Druot), the husband, makes love to his mistress, shots of his wife (Claire Druot) shopping with the children provide an ironic commentary on his idea of happiness. It could be argued that Varda attempts to take a distance on the male point of view and open it up to criticism.

PAM COOK

An ironic portrayal of romantic love and marriage: François replaces his dead wife with his mistress (Marie-France Boyer, above)

AUTEURISM IN THE 1990s

NÖEL KING AND TOBY MILLER

In the Afterword to the 1998 edition of *Signs and Meaning in the Cinema*, Peter Wollen wrote: 'I am still an auteurist'. It is tempting to see the coincidence of auteurism and millennialism contained in the notion 'auteurism in the 1990s' as meaning 'the author is back'. Something of this attitude is suggested by Dudley Andrew's remark: 'After a dozen years of clandestine whispering we are permitted to mention, even to discuss, the auteur again' (Andrew, 1993), and by the fact that in 1995 both *Film Criticism* and *Film History* ran special issues on auteurism. The editorial of *Film Criticism* claimed its theme of 'The new auteurism' had emerged organically, by sifting through 'our favourites' among submitted manuscripts. This was heralded as a landmark moment, spontaneously offering a new wave of auteur criticism complete with the 'necessary corrective' of a more contextual and cautious perspective purged of the 'adulatory enthusiasms' of earlier versions. It was now possible to recognise the director as 'always a human function' in the collaborative process of film-making.

If these comments suggest that a long period of looking elsewhere in film theory has been rolled back to permit the re-emergence of auteurists, in practice, auteurism continued unabated after its initial adoption into Anglo-American film criticism in the 1960s. The different trajectories of structuralist auteurism, and thereafter the emergence of an increasingly pluralistic critical environment, certainly had an impact on what articles were carried in what journals. But rather than constituting a surpassing of auteurism, this was more a bypassing, and sometimes, in the case of queer theory (see p. 505), a refocusing.

A David Lynch film: *Eraserhead*

Auteur theory seemed to survive incognito for a while, waiting for the paradigms that had displaced it to grow tired or themselves seem old-fashioned. Yet perhaps it was more a matter of waiting for different domains of work to connect and reconnect. Although Roland Barthes and Michel Foucault routinely are cited as providing two death-knells to auteurism, in each case the alleged killing now appears to have constituted a much more modest project of redirecting forms of critical attention. Barthes's celebrated declaration of the 'death of the author' was a strategic way of permitting two births: that of textuality, conceived as 'a tissue of quotations drawn from the innumerable centres of culture' (Barthes, 1977, p. 146) and that of the reader/viewer, conceived as 'the space on which all the quotations that make up writing are inscribed' (Barthes, 1977, p. 148). Barthes's voice can be heard in Stephen Heath's conception of the author as part of a mutually constituting activity of writing–reading/viewing. In this understanding, the author is a rhetorical figure or trope, part of a 'fan of elements ... of a certain pleasure which begins to turn the film' and thereby ensnare the viewer. And the legacy of privileging reader power is apparent in David Thomson's 1997 reconsideration of *The Searchers* (1956) where he imagines a different conclusion, one that sees Ethan 'riding on with Debbie, being utterly with her, not uncle but lover'. This speculation is justified because, 'We are beyond auteurism now; the films that last endure because of things no maker owns' (Thomson, 1997, p. 31). Similarly, when Michel Chion describes the initial circulation of Lynch's *Eraserhead* (1976), he seems close to Barthes's perspective: 'In the beginning there was not an author, just a film ... the film was perfect; it still belonged completely to its public, and the shadow of the author had not yet fallen on the screen'. After saying 'The author always represents to some extent the work's downfall,' Chion provides suggestive reconfigurings of auteurism in such formulations as, 'There is nothing more common nowadays than an auteur. Auteur films (which create their auteur) are rarer stuff' (Chion, 1995, p. 3).

In this way, there are many things we can say about a text before we say 'who writes it', or, as Chion might argue, before we are conditioned to look for all the idiosyncratic moments that constitute, for some, what a David Lynch film is.

1970s to 1990s: the auteur in the industry

Michel Foucault's insistence that authors are constituted through discourses and institutions drew attention to the protocols of reading needing to be in place in order to 'find' an author. His suggestion that authorship 'names' a particular way of handling texts is confirmed in two 1990s descriptions of the way the cultural category of auteurism has entered film production and distribution practices. Timothy Corrigan's (1991) account of 'the commerce of auteurism' and Justin Wyatt's (1996)

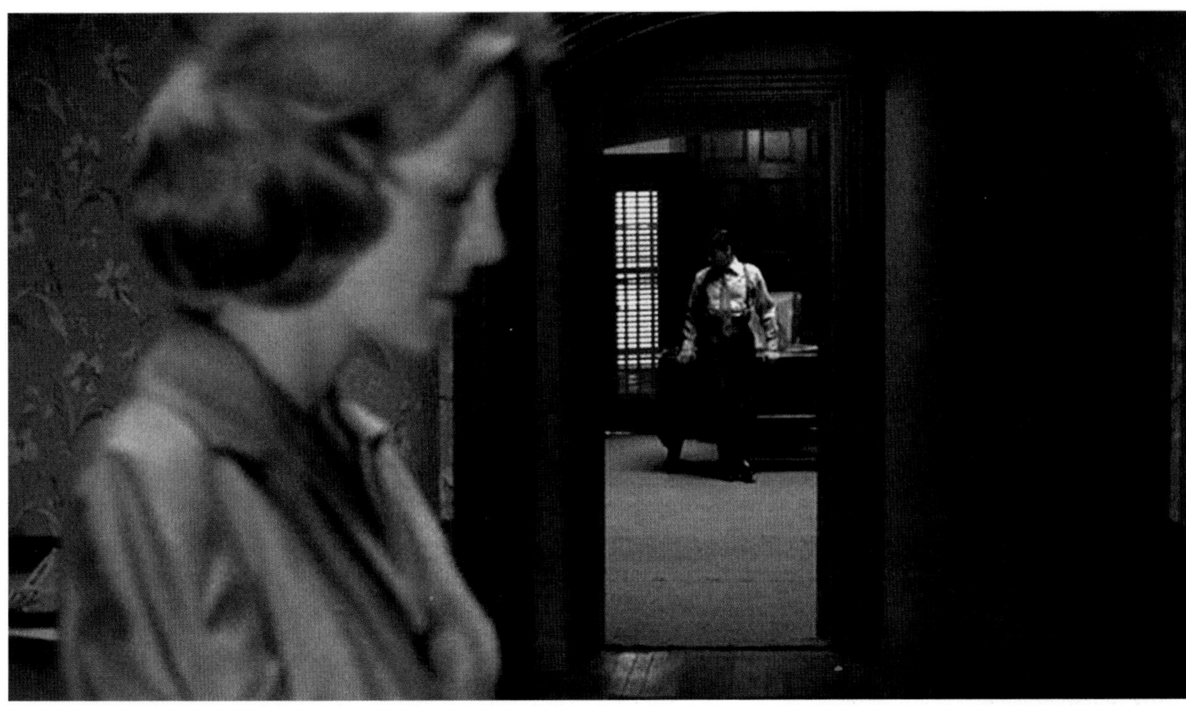

Auteurism redefined in the New Hollywood: Francis Ford Coppola's *The Godfather*

studies of Francis Coppola and the New Hollywood, and of Robert Altman, show how, since the mid-1970s, film-critical auteurism has become a crucial part of film publicity, marketing and film journalism.

Corrigan says the author 'has rematerialized in the eighties and nineties as a commercial performance of the business of being an auteur' (Corrigan, 1991, p. 104), and refers to 'the survival – and, in fact, increasing importance – of the auteur as a commercial strategy for organizing audience reception, as a critical concept bound to distribution and marketing aims that identify and address the potential cult status of an auteur' (Corrigan, 1991, p. 103). Since 'institutional and commercial agencies define auteurism almost exclusively as publicity and advertisement', it has become possible 'to already know ... the meaning of the film in a totalizing image that precedes the movie in the public images of its creator' (Corrigan, 1991, p. 106). Certain directors enjoy a celebrity that 'produces and promotes texts that invariably exceed the movie itself, both before and after its release' (Corrigan, 1991, p. 107). Corrigan's examples are Coppola, Kluge and Ruiz, but his point is also demonstrated by noting the difference between the lengthy 'crawl' of credits at the end of films – a carefully attained and finely monitored union achievement identifying personnel whose work appears on screen – and those occasions when films are presented to us as 'A Steven Spielberg Film' or 'Martin Scorsese Presents' even though these men are not directing. Their marquee value is a promotional device as well as the result of a whole package of 'deals' struck between personal and studio publicists (see also The function of authorship in cinema, p. 388).

Justin Wyatt's work on Coppola supports Corrigan's views by arguing that Hollywood studios, as economic-entrepreneurial entities, were happy to adopt auteurism, seeing it as simply the most recent (mid-1970s) description of established film-industry practices of contracting talent and marketing product (Wyatt, 1996, p. 19). So Paramount financed the short-lived Director's Company as a way of bringing together three hot directors of the moment – Coppola, Friedkin and Bogdanovich. Only three films were produced – Coppola's *The Conversation* (1974) and Bogdanovich's *Paper Moon* (1973) and *Daisy Miller* (1974). According to Wyatt, this initiative from Frank Yablans, Paramount's Chief Executive, only seems 'to accept the auteur theory when the real plan was for a "recontextualisation of auteurism within the studio structure"' (Wyatt, 1996, p. 16).

Thus the 1970s constitutes a historical moment of overlap between film-critical auteurism and an auteurism incorporated into studio film-making practice: the studios' 'ready acceptance of American auteur cinema in the 1970s was the result of characteristic industry-wide cautiousness' (Wyatt, 1996, p. 2) and if a film failed, studio executives could 'avoid culpability' by pointing to the auteur. The mid-1970s also saw a number of 'university-educated auteurs' and others working at the fringes or outside the formal education system, such as Spielberg, prepared to 'subtly update the safe studio genre package' (Wyatt, 1996, p. 45), resulting in 'big-budget auteur films' (Wyatt, 1996, p. 22) such as *The Godfather* (1972), *Jaws* (1975) and *Star Wars* (1977). This 'ongoing redefinition of auteurism in the new Hollywood' (Wyatt, 1996, p. 148) generated the paradoxical situation whereby 'the dazzling box-office success of expensive auteurist movies ... led to an industry-wide focus on blockbuster box-office revenues' (Wyatt, 1996, p. 22). The result: directors dependent on studios to finance and distribute 'big' personal films.

In a later piece, Wyatt sees 'the industrial and institutional factors impacting (Robert) Altman's career over the past twenty-five years' as revealing 'the complexity of the "author-name" as a means to account for the economic aspects of authorship' (Wyatt, 1998, p. 64). He traces the way 'economic constraints and opportunities in the film marketplace' used auteurism to promote Altman at various times across 30 years of film-making. Altman's 'third' career phase, aligned with the independents in the 1990s, shows how 'media constructions – around advertising, subject matter, and the auteur – are crucial to the major independents' careers as a form of marketing'.

Fine Line promoted *The Player* (1992) by stressing 'Altman's alienation from the studio system', repositioning him 'as a famous

Robert Altman's *The Player* denounced the lack of auteurs in contemporary Hollywood, but was marketed on its director's name

director returning to artistic form' (Wyatt, 1996, p. 62), a '"rejuvenated" auteur' (Wyatt, 1996, p. 64). The same auteurist plug was used with *Short Cuts* (1993), Altman's film derived from some Raymond Carver short stories: 'From two American masters comes a movie like no other'. No doubt, too, that some irony or cynical marketing is evident in the fact that Altman could make a film such as *The Player*, whose message contains a 'romantic auteurist' denunciation of the impossibility of an auteurist director's cinema in contemporary Hollywood, only to have that film marketed as an exemplary instance of a director's vision.

Auteur criticism in the 1990s

While auteurism as a critical description of distinctive thematic-stylistic cinematic achievements was being absorbed into the promotional and publicity domains of film-making, it was also continuing as an energetic film-critical paradigm. In 1984, *Wide Angle* had a special issue on film authorship and the 1990s produced some of the best discussions of this critical orientation: James Naremore (1990) on 'Authorship and the cultural politics of film criticism'; Dudley Andrew (1993) on a revitalised auteurism; Timothy Corrigan (1991) on 'The commerce of auteurism'; Alexander Doty's (1993) rethinking of auteurism by way of queer theory; and other new work on John Huston (Studlar and Desser, 1993) and Rainer Werner Fassbinder (Elsaesser, 1996; Kardish and Lorenz, 1997; *New German Critique*, 1994) are all products of this time. As was ever the case, auteurism continues to be practised in different ways with different consequences. James Naremore claimed that first-wave auteurism (if that is what we can call 1950s/1960s auteurism) 'took on different political meanings at different conjunctures'. While mounting 'an invigorating attack on convention', it also 'formed canons and fixed the names of people we should study' (Naremore, 1990, p. 21). That remains an accurate description of such 1990s auteur criticism as Bernard Eisenschitz's (1993) biography of Nicholas Ray – where an 'old-style' auteurism is supplemented by additional empirical information on the studio context – and Jay Boyer's (1996) study of Bob Rafelson. The title of Boyer's book, *Bob Rafelson: Hollywood Maverick*, announces its link to the 1950s/1960s France, UK and US mode of auteurism that required a few artist-mavericks to be destroyed or at least rejected/marginalised by 'the system' in order to be consecrated as auteurs. A revealing moment of heroic auteurism comes when Boyer is placing *Man Trouble* (1992) within Rafelson's oeuvre: 'Things that do not make much sense in the film often fall right into line when you consider the film is Rafelson's' (Boyer, 1996, p. 120).

On other occasions, critics tried to practise auteurism differently. So, in his reconsideration of Peckinpah's *Pat Garrett & Billy the Kid* (1973), Jim Kitses (whose 1969 *Horizons West* was a landmark Anglo-American rendering of first-wave author-genre criticism) distances himself from those perpectives that seek to lionise Peckinpah as an artistic victim of philistine studio front-office intervention (Kitses, 1998, p. 230). Auteurism was also practised differently in some mid-1990s studies of Rainer Werner Fassbinder that, in their care to distance themselves from earlier unhesitatingly auteurist studies of the director, encapsulate many of the various directions of auteur criticism as interpretative tool in the 1980s and 1990s. In 1992, on the tenth anniversary of his death, several reassessments of Fassbinder's 43 films, 14 plays, four radio plays and many essays came forward. A special issue of *New German Critique* (1994) placed Fassbinder's work in a changed German social-political climate; the Museum of Modern Art issued a publication (Kardish and Lorenz, 1997) to accompany the first complete retrospective of Fassbinder's work shown in the US (made possible by the Rainer Werner Fassbinder Foundation) and Thomas Elsaesser (1996) published his long-awaited book on Fassbinder. Elsaesser said Fassbinder was an 'undisputed auteur' whose films had been overwhelmed by the details of a pathological and sensational life, and admitted his project might seem an old-fashioned, 'not to say a "retrograde" one, seemingly wishing to reinstate the "author" as the locus (and the work as the material manifestation) of an intentional plenitude, whose stages and intricacies it is the task of the critic to reconstruct' (Elsaesser, 1996, p. 9). To forestall this possibility, Elsaesser's book uses Fassbinder's work as a prism permitting a scrutiny of a 'politics of "self" and "identity"' that works to 'define differently what it means to be representative' and that also helps redefine 'the cinema and its representations of history' (Elsaesser, 1996, p. 43).

Drawing on retrospectives and conferences held in Berlin, Munich and at Dartmouth College, *New German Critique* justified its re-examination of the 'controversial legacy and … relevance for the present' of Fassbinder's cultural work by saying they hoped to prevent the twin traps of oblivion or mummification within the film-cultural museum.

> Historicizing Fassbinder from today's standpoint means engaging his work in current debates about film-making, auteurism, and personal cinema; about the writing and rewriting of German film history; about questions of genre; about questions of gender and homosexuality; but it also means engaging his work with problems the current political situation is presenting. Here Fassbinder's films could be made to speak about questions of identity and nationality, marginality, foreigners, and representing a troubled past to an audience who knows these troubles only through other representations – all issues which are setting the political agenda of the 1990s for a unified Germany. (*New German Critique*, 1994)

Here the historicising distance means that current critical discussions of Fassbinder are far less likely to participate in gossipy biographical auteurism that raids both films and life to posit some explanatory revelation; and are also less likely to be overwhelmed by the aesthetic-charismatic notion of Fassbinder constituting a crossover emblematic figure for New German Cinema, carrying it single-handedly to an enthusiastic critical reception.

Gaylyn Studlar and David Desser's 1993 collection of articles on John Huston makes a move similar to the ones that justify the re-embrace of Fassbinder's work. When Studlar says the project is not driven by 'some nostalgic wish to elevate the director to a pantheon of directors from which he was formerly excluded' (p. 4), this refers to Andrew Sarris's (1968) book *The American Cinema*, where Huston provides the opening entry for a section ('Less than Meets the Eye') devoted to directors 'with reputations in excess of inspirations. In retrospect it always seems that the personal signatures were written in invisible ink' (Sarris, 1968, p. 155). Sarris's revised (1980) assessment of Huston is included in the collection, which claims as its principal aim the demonstration that 'a director-centered anthology, while "auteurist" in some sense of the word, need not perpetuate some idealistic notion of personalized cinematic authorship transcending the boundaries of either institutional or ideological constraints'. Instead the collection seeks to show how 'mutiple determinants' structure films directed by Huston, showing 'the ways in which Huston could be used to explore issues of authorship and sexual identity – and vice-versa'.

These different varieties of auteurism show that different modes of activating an auteurist critical gaze will achieve different results. For example, Paul Willemen (1994) adapts Yuri Lotman (author as structure to be constructed) and Stephen Heath (author as fan of elements) to generate his distinctive account of the author (Amos Gitai) as a crossroad where discursive chains meet and are held in a constellation by the text in context. This is quite different from the strand of relatively unproblematic 1990s auteurism that has repeated the 1950s version on such things as pop-music videos and the work of Quentin Tarantino. It is as if a romantic, literary notion of the author has been succeeded by a designer notion of the author: the author is now depicted as an irrepressible individuality appreciated and paid for by his or her ability to contribute to product differentiation, a process whose results are then redescribed by the film publicity-marketing system in terms of the conventional romantic notions of the author. This is convenient for business and promotional purposes, as the author shifts between two statuses: exemplary individual and brand name/corporate logo.

Since auteurism is not a unified critical practice, it is not surprising that the writing that seeks to establish the vision and sensibility of the author (equating film-makers with writers of world literature, a stockmarket version of the canon) is not the same discourse as Willemen's author-as-crossroads concept. Still, when Elsaesser says that any single-author study 'continues to have a powerful attraction for readers' (Elsaesser, 1996, p. 9), his point seems abundantly proved by such ventures as Faber's widely available 'Projections' and 'x on x' series (for example, *Malle on Malle*, 1992), which began in 1989 with *Scorsese on Scorsese*, and Twayne's 'Film-makers' series. Each testifies to a continuing public interest in what film-makers have to say about the films they make.

But even within an overarching auteurist publishing project, individual studies might treat auteurism differently. For example, Susan Hayward's (1998) study of Luc Besson appears in a series on French directors. Hayward claims Besson deliberately departs from the Nouvelle Vague generation of cinephilia and romantic auteurism. Although he writes, produces and directs his films, Besson describes himself as a metteur en scène, and is always keen to acknowledge the contribution of his crew, technicians and actors. According to Hayward, this is a calculated break with the narcissistic aesthetic of 1950s auteurism, which had 'glossed over the real complexities of the means of production (production practices)'.

Auteurs and alterity

Today, when some radical political writing seeks to promote the work of those marginalised from cinema by virtue of their sex or race (Dyer, 1997, pp. 14, 16), a form of authorship can emerge that denies individual vision and requires of directors that they be legitimate representatives of minorities or tangentially of entire national cinemas (for example, Tracey Moffatt or Isaac Julien). An example is the white media's obsession with Spike Lee, who is regularly regarded as a sage on the inner city – his films are not evidence, but 'he' is. (Discussion of the problem of Italian-American gangsterism does not see Martin Scorsese called upon to represent 'his' people.)

Another consideration of the issue of otherness and cinema comes in some writing from Judith Mayne and Alexander Doty, each concerned to theorise sexual preference and film authorship. At the outset of her piece on 'lesbian authorship', Mayne claims there is a potential contradiction in any critical enterprise that seeks to bring 'authorship into a discussion of lesbian representation' (Mayne, 1991, p. 177), arising from the (alleged) fact that 'within the context of cinema studies, the very notion of authorship is far more evocative of traditional, patriarchal film criticism than even is the case in literary studies' (Mayne, 1991, p. 177). Mayne explores this self-produced dilemma via a reading of Midi Onodera's short film *Ten Cents a Dance: Parallax* (1985), and its controversial reception, and eventually decides that 'the lesbian author is defined as both complicit in and resistant to the sexual fictions of patriarchal culture' (Mayne, 1991, p. 183).

In the course of the encounter between queer theory and auteurism conveyed in a discussion of George Cukor and Dorothy Arzner, Alexander Doty writes that queer auteurs can emerge by the practising in today's context of Andrew Sarris's late-1960s auteurism and/or could emerge if a critic adopted the category 'e' dimension of *Cahiers du cinéma*'s 1969 reworking of auteurism (see *Cahiers*' category 'e', p. 450; Auteurism and women directors, p. 468). In this case, the earlier auteurism attains a contemporary radicalism by being recruited to a 'hidden from film history' project. At the same time, Doty also argues for a notion of queer authorship as 'a use of auteurism which considers that meanings are constructed within and across film texts through the interplay of creators, cultures, and audiences. As a result, queer auteurs could either be "born" or "made"' (Doty, 1993, p. 46) by way of the interplay of 'queer people on all sides of the camera – before it, behind it, and in the audience' (Doty, 1993, p. 48). A case could be made for a director, star, writer 'as queer on the basis of their being queer ... or on the evidence that many of their films hold, or have held, a particularly meaningful place within queer cultural history, with or without knowledge of the director's sexuality' (Doty, 1993, p. 46). In addition, queer auteurs would be formed 'when the films of non-queer identified directors become interesting to queerly-positioned spectators for their (sub)texts'. By this stage, the auteurism on offer seems closer to the Roland Barthes and Michel Chion formulations cited earlier.

Auteurism now

Making films is such an obviously collective and artisanal (producers, stars, scriptwriters, cinematographers, editors, costume and set designers, music composers) activity in its 'division of labour, disparate skills and shared responsibilities' (Coward, 1987, p. 79) that speaking in terms of individual authorship becomes increasingly problematic the more film scholarship uncovers the detail of these other contributions. Is it feasible to consider popular film as great art expressive of an individual vision without accounting for Ken Adam's art direction in the James Bond cycle, Saul Bass's titles in Hitchcock's films or Edith Head's classical Hollywood costume design? Alternatively, the example of ethnographic cinema offers a complex amalgam of authorship. Anthropologist and film-maker frequently form a two-person crew, with the former recording sound and explaining language and other phenomena and the latter shooting (Asch, 1990). Who is the author here?

The identification of directors as auteurs is a move critics make based on a retrospective account of a body of work. And that is why we should position auteur criticism inside the wider sweep of film history and its conditions for authorial discourses, rather than subordinating social and industrial forces to an individual expressive totality. As Edward Buscombe (1981) wrote a quarter of a century ago, before we rank individuals as a priority for film theory, we should go looking for the social impact of and on the cinema and the intertextual and industrial interconnections of films upon one another. And Dudley Andrew reminds us that André Bazin wanted auteurism practised in tandem with discussions of 'a genre or a national trend or a social movement' (Andrew, 1993, p. 78), and that Wollen's desire in *Signs and Meaning in the Cinema* was to isolate 'the auteur's signal within the noise of the text' (Wollen, 1998, p. 79).

Sometimes that 'noise' will come from the recognition and description of those other artisanal contributions, as indicated above. At other times, the 'noise' will indicate the changed global circumstances of film production, circulation and exhibition. As more and more countries try to compete with Hollywood in a suddenly deregulated world TV market, one in which blockbusters and associated promotional costs wipe out other genres and nations, the issue of how to measure the creativity of a film arises in a new way – how many creative principals should come from a given country or region in order for the film to qualify for public support? This leads to a focus on producers, distributors, exhibitors, scriptwriters, actors and directors, which problematises existing notions of authorship across the cultural field.

There is now a certain tendency to examine how particular sites and practices produce the author, a concentration on how films circulate, the contexts in which they are apprehended and the rules that govern their interpretation. This approach contends that authorship is produced through such cultural apparatuses and technologies as: interview, criticism, publicity and curriculum, and also makes the important point that one should try to take account of the different conditions of possibility for creative claims. For example, the history of women scriptwriters in Hollywood is one of dominance prior to the advent of the mature studio system, with opportunities to move into directing and producing, then virtual exile throughout the studio system's heyday. Paradoxically, in contemporary Hollywood female studio heads and producers are in the situation of overseeing diminished earnings potential, while the capacity to become producers and directors and hence influence the conduct of production has not increased (Biebly and Biebly, 1996). Kathryn Bigelow (Cook, 2005) is an exception: a woman scriptwriter who has carved out some generic licence to write, produce and direct action-adventure. Large increases in the number of white women producers and studio executives have not seen salaries or power commensurate with those of men (Ryan, 1995; see also Contemporary women directors, p. 68).

It would be wrong to suggest that authorship as a category has ended or is irretrievably problematised. But whatever variety of it is practised in our contemporary context should attend to Jonathan Rosenbaum (2000) when he argues that, now more than ever, film criticism must detach itself from the seductions of film publicity. Rosenbaum claims that film critics do not raise sufficiently often 'the question of how often aesthetic agendas are determined by business agendas. When it comes to the role of business interests in shaping certain aspects of cinephilia, criticism is often simply in denial'. Rosenbaum is discussing the category of 'cult' films and the question of exactly how 'independent' independent cinema is in the late 1990s, in a context where the Sundance Festival (its premier showcase) is part sponsored by *Entertainment Weekly* and the *New York Times*. The 'independence' of the auteur and their 'vision' – as an element distinct from the rest of the cinema business – therefore remains a major issue for industry and criticism alike.

Selected Reading

Dudley Andrew, 'The unauthorised auteur today', in Collins *et al.* (eds), *Film Theory Goes to the Movies*, London and New York, Routledge, 1993.

Michel Chion, *David Lynch*, London, BFI Publishing, 1995; trans. Robert Julian.

Alexander Doty, 'Whose text is it anyway?: queer cultures, queer auteurs and queer authorship', *Quarterly Review of Film and Video* 15 (1): 41–54, 1993.

Peter Wollen, *Signs and Meaning in the Cinema*, London, BFI Publishing, 1998. Revised edition.

AUTHORSHIP REVISED AND REVIVED

PAM COOK

As the discussion in this section shows, authorship in cinema is alive and well, thriving in many different locations. While film theory and criticism continue to worry away at its cultural, institutional and ideological impact, they also endlessly find ways to reinvent it. Meanwhile, as has always been the case, the film industries and wider film cultures unashamedly use the notion of individual authorship and its associated pleasures to captivate readers and viewers. These promotional strategies have intensified in the context of global multimedia technologies and the expansion of tie-in possibilities through outlets such as TV, DVD, CD, print media and the Internet. As auteurism has been disseminated over multiple media sites, the distinction between commerce and art that was central to traditional auteur theory has dissolved. Many contemporary film-makers actively participate in and/or control the commercial spin-offs from their films. Auteur study today, then, needs to spread its net wider than film texts, and take into consideration surrounding discourses of production, promotion and various reception contexts.

A significant development in what might be called 'post-auteurism', referring to a period of transition between the apparent demolition of the author in post-structuralist discussion (see Auteur study after structuralism, p. 460) to its qualified return as an approach that can be used to pose methodological questions for film studies, has been the notion of contextualisation. We can take this to mean attention to the social and industrial contexts of particular film-makers, or to the cultural contexts in which scholars, critics and historians choose to employ one or more of many auteurist models to approach their subject. Thus auteur analysis today is required to justify itself, to set out the contexts that account for its persistence and value. In a sense, then, it has grown up. This is not to say, however, that unreconstructed auteurists no longer exist; indeed, they make up an important part of the market for film and related audiovisual media, and are recognised as such in promotional campaigns, film festival programmes and magazine articles.

At the same time, with the rise of globalised production, distribution and exhibition, attention has turned to the significance of auteurism for film-makers themselves, vying for attention and resources in volatile and highly competitive international markets. In such circumstances, auteur status can be seen as a strategic necessity, endowing film-makers with the 'creative capital' they need to negotiate the complexities of contemporary transnational audiovisual industries, and enabling them to establish themselves as a brand. This is one way in which independent film-makers can achieve serious bargaining power with major companies and funding agencies. Such negotiations are not always successful, however, and can result in the relegation of those whose interests may not coincide with those of the markets (see Contemporary women directors, p. 68).

Cinematic authorship hinges on notions of agency and control, traditionally vesting these in the figure of the director, whether this can be substantiated by historical research or not. With the 'historical turn' in film studies, scholars have returned to the archives to investigate evidence of the fine details of aesthetic and financial decision-making in order to uncover the significant contributions of others involved in the film-making process. Sometimes this may result simply in the displacement of authorial agency from the director to another member of the creative team; but this approach has the potential to highlight the difficulty of assigning authorship to one figure or another in a fluctuating situation where different creative functions achieve ascendancy at different times, and multiple signatures compete for visibility. Individual agency and control thus become less important than the social, industrial and personal factors that govern the collaborative business of film production at specific historical moments. Indeed, the motivating fantasy of auteurism, the attribution of agency and control to a single creative source, is revealed as myth – albeit a very powerful one that refuses to go away.

In this respect, it is significant that on the current scene there are successful directors who deny their auteur status, and assert their function as enabling others, such as actors, writers, editors, designers and producers, to fulfil their own creative ambitions (for example, Stephen Frears, p. 435). On the other hand, Danish auteur Lars von Trier has lent his name and international reputation to the Advance Party initiative, a collaborative transnational venture that aims to build an infrastructure for independent Scottish cinema. In the post-auteurist period, multiple and competing models of authorship in cinema continue to proliferate, and authorship's ever-mutating forms remain a central revitalising force in film studies. This situation nurtures a 'radical pluralism' in which no approach can be identified as 'correct' and different aspects of authorship conflict and collide in different contexts. Some of the multiple, conflicting dimensions of authorship can be traced through the branding strategies employed by four contemporary film-makers.

Four contemporary directors

Kathryn Bigelow

Kathryn Bigelow achieved the status of auteur as a result of a series of edgy, violent genre films made in the late 1980s and 1990s that appropriated the conventions of the horror film (*Near Dark*, 1987), the cop movie (*Blue Steel*, 1990), the buddy movie (*Point Break*, 1991) and the sci-fi action film (*Strange Days*, 1995). *Strange Days*, which confronted issues of 'extreme' sexuality, had a mixed critical reception, but it has achieved, along with Bigelow's earlier work, a cult reputation on fan websites. Like many of her female peers (see Contemporary women directors, p. 68), Bigelow worked in television, and directed three episodes of the melancholic police series *Homicide: Life on the Street* between 1998 and 1999. Her next film project, *The Weight of Water* (2000), was R-rated for its graphic depiction of violence and sex, and centred on a woman photographer (Catherine McCormack) who investigates a series of brutal murders of women that took place a 100 years earlier. This film had both detractors and supporters, which was also the case with *K-19: The Widowmaker* (2002) starring Harrison Ford and set on board a Russian nuclear submarine. In 2004, Bigelow directed an episode of the TV series

Invading male territory: Keanu Reeves and Patrick Swayze in Kathryn Bigelow's surfing action movie *Point Break*

Karen Sisco. She is rumoured to have a current project in pre-production with Voltage Pictures, *The Hurt Locker*, a war film set in Iraq that she co-scripted, due for release in 2008.

Despite the uneven response to her recent films, Bigelow has established a reputation as a stylish and innovative film-maker and, perhaps more unusually, as a superlative action-film director. Though not on the 'A' list, she has successfully negotiated the transition from low-budget to mainstream film-making by working with independent companies as well as major studios, and has co-written many of her projects. Her success can be put down to a number of strategic factors: her early films were deliberately controversial in their graphic portrayals of sex and violence, and in interviews Bigelow asserted her interest in controversy and in breaking the boundaries of what was considered suitable form and subject matter for women directors. She also developed a distinctive personal style that was cool and androgynous, deliberately crossing gender boundaries (Cook, 2005). Thus she built an identity as a maverick, at odds with the assumptions of the Hollywood industry – a version of the classic auteur – that attracted attention and support from major players such as James Cameron and Oliver Stone, with whom she collaborated. Indeed, she has consistently collaborated with male film-makers, and is an interesting example of a woman director at ease in what is conventionally considered masculine territory. Many of her films (*Near Dark*, *Blue Steel*, *Strange Days*, *The Weight of Water*) explore themes of transgression and the permeable boundaries of identity (see also Jermyn and Redmond, 2002). They often mimic the visceral style of male-centred action movies, highlighting the difficulties faced by women directors in maintaining a distinctive voice in mainstream cinema.

Sofia Coppola

Sofia Coppola was born into the film-making dynasty headed by her father, Francis Ford Coppola, one of the 'movie brat' generation that helped to change Hollywood in the 1960s and 1970s. This lineage has proved both help and hindrance: on one hand, it has provided her with artistic credentials, on the other, her father's monumental status in American cinema is frequently used as a measure of her own achievements. Moreover, the aura of privilege surrounding the Coppola name has sometimes aroused disproportionate envy and malice in critics. Nevertheless, Sofia Coppola has forged a distinct identity for herself and produced a body of work for which she has won international recognition.

Like Kathryn Bigelow, Coppola comes from an art-school background. Her interest in fashion design is well known, and she is associated with a new creative elite that crosses areas of popular culture such as music, fashion, art and film. With friend and colleague Wes Anderson, she has been branded one of contemporary American cinema's 'play group' (a term apparently coined by *Vanity Fair* that resonates ironically with the 'movie brat' tag). While Coppola maintains a distance from such labels, her association with this hip younger generation, which occupies a space somewhere between independent cinema and Hollywood (see *Lost in Translation* case study, p. 59), helped to consolidate her identity as cool style icon.

Coppola's debut feature, *The Virgin Suicides* (1999), a darkly ironic take on the teenpic that she also scripted, earned her a place as one of new American cinema's 'smart' directors, whose use of irony and focus on surface style masked a melancholy nihilism (Sconce, 2002). Her second film, *Lost in Translation* (2003), which she also produced and wrote, starred Bill Murray and

What lies beneath: small-town life devastated by teenage suicide in Sofia Coppola's *The Virgin Suicides*

Scarlett Johansson as Americans adrift in Tokyo and gained her an Academy Award for Best Original Screenplay as well as establishing her as one of the most powerful women in Hollywood. *Lost in Translation* was a personal film in the tradition of European art cinema, and Coppola, who is well aware of the importance of art cinema in contemporary American cinema, has compared her style to that of the Nouvelle Vague. Her third feature, *Marie Antoinette* (2006), an ambitious costume drama about the early life of the notorious queen, was an elegantly mounted, impressionistic piece that focused on the emotional journey of a young woman out of her depth in the hostile environment of the French court. Coppola used broad strokes to sketch in the historical background, and received a hostile response from some critics as a result. But *Marie Antoinette* was perfectly in tune with Coppola's persona as an artist/auteur unafraid to take risks with style and subject matter, and confirmed her status as an accomplished director with strong visual flair and an idiosyncratic voice.

In interviews, Coppola uses discourses of artistic production to describe her work and her approach, asserting that creative freedom is her priority. Her 'brand' as an artist/auteur has been established across a range of media, from glossy fashion magazines and teen publications, to television and tie-ins, such as spin-off albums of her movies' soundtracks. Her next film project has been mooted as a film version of Sarah Waters's lesbian novel *Tipping the Velvet*.

Baz Luhrmann

Baz Luhrmann's gestation as auteur has a complicated history. It was established retrospectively, on the basis of three films that make up the Red Curtain trilogy: *Strictly Ballroom* (1992), *William Shakespeare's Romeo + Juliet* (1996) and *Moulin Rouge!* (2001). There is a tension between Luhrmann's identity as author of those films and his collaborative working practices. A further tension is evident in the films' national identity: while *Strictly Ballroom* is perceived as Australian, *Romeo + Juliet* and *Moulin Rouge!* both have mixed origins characteristic of transnational global production patterns. Luhrmann himself has a mixed identity as an Australian and as an international figure.

Luhrmann's background is in theatre and opera: *Strictly Ballroom* was developed from his successful stage play, and before his feature-film debut, he had established a reputation as an innovative theatre director in Australia, and he continued to stage operas until 2002. Through the Sydney-based company Bazmark Inq, founded with Catherine Martin in 1997, Luhrmann was also involved in music production and organisation of live events, including fashion shows. *Strictly Ballroom* was a huge success at the 1992 Cannes Film Festival, generating immediate interest from Hollywood studios. In interviews, Luhrmann stressed the collaborative nature of his work, consistently acknowledging the contribution of his Australian creative team: designer Catherine Martin (who he married in 1997), scriptwriter Craig Pearce, cinematographer Don McAlpine and editor Jill Bilcock among them. *Strictly Ballroom* was credited with kick-starting the mid-1990s Australian cinema revival, and was linked with two other films: *Muriel's Wedding* and *The Adventures of Priscilla, Queen of the Desert* (both 1994). This trio was characterised by brash pop-culture aesthetics, which proved controversial with some critics. The association of *Strictly Ballroom* with the so-called 'glitter cycle' diminished once it was re-branded as the first of the Red Curtain trilogy following the theatrical release of *Moulin Rouge!* and the subsequent production of DVD editions of *Romeo + Juliet* and *Moulin Rouge!* with extra materials. In 2002, a Special Edition boxed set was issued, titled 'Baz Luhrmann's Red Curtain Trilogy' and including an additional disc, 'Behind the Red Curtain', that offered extensive coverage of Luhrmann's working methods and the genesis of the films. The boxed set established both the Red Curtain brand and Luhrmann's role as creative source, testified to in interviews with his main collaborators. Bazmark was responsible for the design of the DVDs and accompanying material, though copyright of the discs and the film versions of *Romeo + Juliet* and *Moulin Rouge!* remained with 20th Century Fox, with whom Bazmark had signed a 'first look' deal in 1998. This relationship with Fox has continued, with adjustments and renegotiations, to the present day. According to Luhrmann, it has enabled him to keep his creative independence.

While *Strictly Ballroom* can be seen as a prime example of medium-budget art cinema tailored to film festival and art-house circulation, both *Romeo + Juliet* and *Moulin Rouge!* are examples of the 'popular art movie' that has emerged over the last two decades with the rise of the major independents in the US (see The major independents, p. 54). They are design-led, high-concept event-movies featuring stars as well as lesser-known actors that cross over from art-house to mainstream audiences. They also consciously celebrate the cross-fertilisation of high and low, art and popular culture. This hybrid quality can be seen as Luhrmann's most distinctive trait: his identity and that of his work are characterised by oscillation between poles of national/transnational, local/global, art/popular culture and individual auteurism/collective artisanal activity. The Luhrmann brand holds all these contradictory elements together, epitomising in a way the shifting, unstable terrain of contemporary global film culture.

Luhrmann's current production, due for release in 2008, is a lavish historical epic, financed by Fox, titled *Australia* and dealing with little-known aspects of the country's history in the 1930s and 1940s. It is likely that this all-Australian venture, while moving away from the deliberately artificial 'studio' aesthetic of the Red Curtain trilogy, will nevertheless embody the hybrid production methods and postmodern style that constitute the Luhrmann trademark.

Wong Kar-wai

Like Baz Luhrmann, with whom he shares a number of traits, Wong Kar-wai's authorial identity is characterised by contradiction. His roots are firmly based in the cultures and film industry of Hong Kong – at the same time, he transcends those contexts, incorporating transnational influences. While his films draw on the popular genres of Hong Kong and American cinema, they are reinvented through art cinema aesthetics and his own distinctive style of storytelling, which is indebted to world literature and poetry (see Teo, 2005). Like Hong Kong itself, Wong's work reflects global traffic between east and west, and seems to celebrate and mourn a culture that is constantly in transition.

Wong Kar-wai has a reputation as a film-maker who will not compromise his vision and is constantly at odds with the market-led film industry. This, combined with his art cinema lineage and self-confessed cinephilia, qualifies him as an auteur in the most traditional sense. Indeed, despite his flamboyantly postmodern aesthetic, Wong's nostalgic relationship to his Hong Kong heritage has been viewed by some as conservative, as resisting change and progress. Moreover, his preoccupation with 'superficial' style and gesture has been perceived as an addiction to fashion, reflected in his self-presentation as style-

Baz Luhrmann reinvents the teenpic: Leonardo DiCaprio as Romeo in *William Shakespeare's Romeo+Juliet*

A bitter-sweet essay on love lost and found: Faye Wong in Wong Kar-wai's *2046*

obsessed celebrity. All this has only enhanced his cult persona among aficionados, who see him as an artist *maudit*, a wayward and misunderstood figure in a commerce-driven industry. In fact, as Teo (2005) points out, the Hong Kong film industry is well able to accommodate Wong's idiosyncratic working methods (see also Hong Kong cinema, p. 224).

Wong's oeuvre has gained greater prominence with the increasing interest in transnationalism in film studies (see p. 508). In a way, his films embody the very idea of transnationalism: the sense of enforced mobility, cultural flow, fragmentary experience and loss of stable identities are not there just as themes, but are embedded in their texture and structure, so that style and meaning are inextricable.

Wong studied graphic design before moving into a brief apprenticeship in television between 1980 and 1982, where he learned many of the working practices that he follows today. He started in the film industry as a scriptwriter, contributing ideas as part of a collective process rather than producing completed scripts. This toing and froing and exchange of ideas characterises the methods he employs on his own films, and contributes to their famously protracted production schedules (although he is surpassed in this respect by Baz Luhrmann, whose film *Australia* took more than six years to bring to fruition). His first feature film, *As Tears Go By/Wiangjiao Kamen* (1988), was an energetic reworking of the gangster movie indebted to popular Hing Kong cinema and the visceral style of early Scorsese. It was Wong's next production, *Days of Being Wild/A Fei Zhengzhuan* (1990), that began his long-standing collaboration with cinematographer Christopher Doyle, who contributes so much to the look of the films. Doyle is the most visible and widely acclaimed of Wong's many creative collaborators, who have been somewhat obscured by the director's reputation as auteur. Like other contemporary directors considered here, Wong tends to work with a repertory company of technical and creative personnel as well as actors.

It was *Chungking Express/Chongqing Senlin* (1994) that catapulted Wong onto the international stage. But it is characteristic of Wong's films that they refer back and forth to one another as well as to outside influences, and each appears to rework the others so that the entire oeuvre appears as an ever-evolving work in progress. The same characters reappear, adding to the sense of collapsed time/time passing, with *Days of Being Wild* intimately connected to the elegiac *In the Mood for Love/Huayang Nianhua* (2000) and the bittersweet essay on love lost and found, *2046* (2004). This creation of a group of films as part of a continuing project that has the quality of an obsession plays a vital role in perceptions of Wong's authorial identity. Wong has just completed his first English-language film, *My Blueberry Nights* (2007), starring singer Norah Jones as a young woman journeying across America in search of love.

Selected Reading

Pam Cook, 'Fictions of identity: style, mimicry and gender in the films of Kathryn Bigelow', in *Screening the Past: Memory and Nostalgia in Cinema*, Oxford and New York, Routledge, 2005.

David A. Gerstner and Janet Staiger (eds), *Authorship and Film: Trafficking with Hollywood*, London and New York, Routledge, 2003.

Jeffrey Sconce, 'Irony, nihilism and the new American "smart" film', *Screen* 43 (4): 349–69, winter 2002.

Stephen Teo, *Wong Kar-wai*, London, BFI Publishing, 2005.

PART 7

Developments in Theory

River Phoenix in *My Own Private Idaho*

FEMINISM AND FILM SINCE THE 1990s

BARBARA CREED

Feminist film theory will soon be entering its 40th year. While some post-feminists have declared that the feminist movement is over, others are more optimistic, preparing to celebrate the dictum that, on the contrary, 'life begins at 40'. A quick glance at the diverse range of new books and articles, not to mention films directed by women, that are produced each year confirms the view that not only is feminist theory alive and well but that it also now enjoys wide popular appeal. By the 1990s, it became clear that feminist theory had been instrumental in establishing gender theory in the academy, which may have fostered the erroneous view that the former had all but withered on the vine. However, some feminist critics, such as Ruby Rich (1998), remain convinced that feminist film culture atrophied in the 1990s, having been eclipsed by queer studies, multiculturalism and cultural studies. Others such as Patricia Mellencamp (1995) assert that despite the fact the 1990s has been referred to as the era of post-feminism, there is still much to be done and that women should enjoy the fact that feminist film theory now speaks from many diverse positions.

Inspired by second-wave feminism of the late 1960s, feminist film theory of the 1970s and 1980s was strongly influenced by Marxist, semiotic and psychoanalytic approaches – particularly the latter. It was primarily concerned with the gendered structure of representation, specifically the representation of women as an absence or lack in film. In the mid-1980s, growing uncertainty about the monolithic nature of patriarchal ideology and its influence on cinematic representation led some feminists to question aspects of feminist film theory such as the hegemony of the male gaze and the view that female characters were invariably represented as passive objects of male desire. Some, for instance, argued that contrary to the popular view, female characters in the rape-revenge and horror film genres were frequently represented as powerful and terrifying. These differences led to what Judith Mayne has described as the 'theory wars' (Mayne, 2000, p. xi). Critics of feminist theory argued that its reliance on psychoanalytic theory resulted in a binaristic view of female and male sexuality. Lesbians asked questions about the representation of lesbianism in film; black women raised the crucial question of race; and other groups drew attention to the absence of discussion about age and class.

By the 1990s, feminist film theory had settled into a new phase of its development. Influenced by a call for greater diver-

Resistance to the male order: Geena Davis and Susan Sarandon take over the road movie in Ridley Scott's *Thelma & Louise*

sity, as well as by postmodernism's attack on master discourses, feminist film theory began to move away from the psychoanalytic paradigm in order to explore a range of new areas that opened up the field of study (Pietropaolo and Testaferri, 1995). These included postmodernism and postcolonialism as well as debates around body theory and the emergence of two new images of women in film – the female action hero and the female avenger of *fin-de-siècle* culture. Another key influence on feminist theory has been the development and proliferation of new technologies. In addition, theorists and critics have continued to present new work in relation to ongoing areas of film study such as melodrama (White, 1994; Williams, 1998; Gledhill, 2000); the female friendship film (Hollinger, 1998); history and memory (Kuhn, 2004; Cook, 2005); the female spectator (Gordon, 2004; Klinger, 2006); and psychoanalytic theory (Walker, 2001; Neroni, 2004; Creed, 2005). Feminist theorists also began to address critically the growing number of films made by independent women directors who themselves had been influenced by feminism (Smelik, 1998).

Postmodernism

Postmodernism has proved particularly difficult to define, as the concept itself is critical of all attempts to establish definitive meanings. While some argue that the term simply sets out to undermine all meaning, others see it as offering a critique of key modernist values, particularly those associated with the grand narratives of the west such as 'Progress', 'Science', 'Democracy' and 'Religion'. The feminist view is that these narratives signify masculinist and phallocentric values and as such uphold the so-called superiority of men over women. In response, some feminists stated that 1970s and 1980s feminist film theory itself was in danger of becoming a master discourse.

In so far as postmodernism represents a critique of representation and delights in collapsing boundaries between classical dichotomies such as high art and popular culture, sacred and profane, male and female, feminist film theorists were quick to embrace postmodern theory. According to Alice Jardine, postmodernism signifies the 'delegitimation' of the 'paternal fiction' (Jardine, 1985, p. 67). Drawing on a postmodernist delight in parody, play and irony as a means of destabilising the paternal signifier, feminist theorists have interpreted various contemporary genres such as the horror film, science fiction and the road movie as undermining traditional boundaries between states of normality and abnormality, masculine and feminine, truth and fiction. *Thelma & Louise* (1991), for instance, playfully undermined the conventions of the road movie, in which the main protagonists are almost always male, by placing two women in the lead roles. This change of gender also meant that the film was able to explore women's issues such as rape as well as women's resistance to the male symbolic order. Other films presented a postmodern play with gender boundaries designed to undermine the paternal signifier; these include *The Last Seduction* (1993), *Basic Instinct* (1992) and *Bound* (1996). Postmodernism also emphasises the idea of gender as a performance in which so-called proper gender roles are enacted, thus emphasising the idea that gender is a construct (Butler, 1990). Yvonne Tasker argued that postmodernism's fragmentation of generic boundaries is related to the development of 'shifting "masculine" identities for women' that do not simply reduce women to pseudo men (Tasker, 1993, p. 132). In this context, feminist and postmodernist theory is related to queer theory (see also Postmodernism and film, p. 546; Queer theory and New Queer Cinema, p. 505).

Postcolonialism

By the late 1980s, feminists such as Jane Gaines, bell hooks and Lola Young were voicing strong criticism of feminist film theory's failure to discuss the representation of women in film in relation to racial difference. Their work pointed to the need to historicise studies of sexual difference in relation to colour. The failure to address race was particularly pronounced in relation to films, both documentary and fiction, dealing with the postcolonial world. There was a clear need to address issues such as colonised peoples and anti-colonial resistance, the Third World, diasporic cultures and feminine experience in a postcolonial world.

Anne McClintock argued that because the term 'postcolonialism' appears to herald the end of colonialism, its usage runs the risk of covering over those aspects of colonial power that continue into the present (McClintock, 1994, p. 294). Despite this difficulty, feminist film theory offered a number of concepts and strategies that could be readily adapted to an analysis of gender and race in postcolonial cinema. These strategies included: a critique of essentialism that questioned the presentation of unified categories of 'woman' and 'race'; a focus on representation and the construction of 'blackness' and 'whiteness' as signifying categories; a theory of the spectatorial gaze as an ideological construct leading to the notion of an 'imperial' or 'colonial' gaze; and an analysis of filmic narrative and discourse that demonstrated how these structures were readily sexualised and racialised. Theorists such as Homi K. Bhabha (1992) demonstrated how Freud's theories of castration and fetishism, which were central to feminist theory, were particularly relevant in an analysis of racial stereotyping. He argued that the fetishised stereotype in film is used to reactivate in the colonial subject the imaginary fantasy of an ideal unified white self.

Feminists wrote a number of key articles and books on the topic. Gina Marchetti (1993) focused on Hollywood films about Asians and interracial sexuality. Informed by feminist postcolonial theory, Marchetti drew on concepts of feminine masquerade and spectatorship, refiguring these notions in relation to race. Gaylyn Studlar and Matthew Bernstein (1997) adopted an interdisciplinary approach, with a strong emphasis on feminist film theory, to examine the way in which films are imbued with orientalism from the silent period to the present. Inspired by Gyatri Spivak (1988), E. Ann Kaplan (1997) explored the concept of the interracial look in her analysis of the 'imperial gaze'. Lalitha Gopalan (1997) and Jyotika Virdi (1999) wrote about the representation of violent women in Indian cinema.

This period also saw an increasing number of women making their own films around postcolonial issues. These included Moufida Tlatli's *Silences of the Palace/Les Silences du palais* (1994), Trinh T. Minh-ha's *Surname Viet, Given Name Nam* (1989), Tracey Moffatt's *Night Cries: A Rural Tragedy* (1990) and Deepa Mehta's *Earth* (1998). These films represent women's experience within a historical context and from a postcolonial perspective; they focus on the social and cultural specificities of the lived experience of their heroines. In discussing women's films in general, Alison Butler maintains it is possible that many represent a kind of feminism that is very different from that represented by feminism's film theory, which has focused more on 'the deconstruction of theoretical femininity' than on the lived experiences of actual women (Butler, 2000, p. 77).

Reflecting on women's lived experiences from a postcolonial perspective: Deepa Mehta's *Earth*

Body theory

The initial allegiance of feminist theory to psychoanalytic theory meant that there was greater focus on the unconscious workings of the text and the repressed psychic life of the heroine. In the 1990s, notions of embodiment replaced those associated with disembodiment and the unconscious. The turn to the body in feminist theory witnessed a concomitant focus in film on the new performative, physical heroine of popular cinema. Like the action hero of the new blockbuster, the action heroine was also a potent, visceral protagonist. Critical focus on the gender boundaries of such a heroine have led to a postmodern and queer questioning of any essentialist notion of sex or gender (Stacey, 2003). Emphasis on the fluid, dispersed nature of femininity seemed to call for an end to binary notions of gender – indeed of gender itself as a construct. Deleuze and Guattari's notion of a 'body without organs' also influenced film theorists working on gender (Hills, 1999; Pisters, 2001). Key studies in body and performance theory were produced by Judith Butler (1990), Yvonne Tasker (1993) and Chris Straayer (1996).

The new 1990s heroine takes at least two forms. The first is the tough action heroine of popular genres such as science fiction (*Alien*^{3}, 1992; *Alien Resurrection*, 1997; and *Terminator 2 Judgment Day*, 1991), the police film (*The Silence of the Lambs*, 1991; *Blue Steel*, 1990; *The Long Kiss Goodnight*, 1996) and the boxing film (*Girlfight*, 2000; *Million Dollar Baby*, 2004). The second is the deadly avenger who enacts revenge on a patriarchal world for its treatment of women (*Kill Bill Vol. 1*, 2003; *Monster*, 2003; *The Book of Revelation*, 2006). Two films directed by women about avenging heroines created a censorship controversy in France and elsewhere: *Romance* (1999) and *Baise-moi* (2000). This shift in the representation of the heroine has led to debates about the 'true' nature of sex and gender. Some argue that the action heroine is not a woman but a male substitute or pseudo male (Clover, 1992) and that the avenging heroine is a pornographic fantasy and as such supports phallocentrism. Others argue that sex and gender exist on a continuum and such images can only challenge patriarchal ideology, particularly its insistence on the binaristic division of sex and gender. The latter claim that the new action heroine offers a point of resistance that assists women in exploring the cultural and social changes promoted by feminism (Hills, 1999; Inness, 2004).

New technologies

New technologies such as the Internet, video games, digital film production, the camcorder and virtual technologies have also influenced production and theory. Because these technologies are less expensive and more accessible than the older analogue formats, women artists and film-makers now enjoy greater access to the means of production. Some feminists are optimistic about these developments. Alison Butler (2000) discusses the work of performance artist and film-maker Valie Export in relation to these developments. Export argues that because the body in cyberspace 'is a sign without a referent', it is potentially liberating.

Getting some action: Michelle Rodriguez in Karyn Kusama's *Girlfight*

Butler is more cautious. She suggests that cyberspace also signifies a loss of historical reality, which she argues has always functioned as an important factor in women's film-making.

New technologies have also influenced a shift away from the close textual analysis of the first decades of feminist film theory. Referring to the 1970s focus on the 'unattainable text', Judith Mayne argues that the emergence of new technologies has made 'the unattainable text attainable' (Mayne, 2000, p. xiv). The ability of DVD technology to exploit the freeze-frame and slow motion, for example, has made detailed and intricate textual analysis far more accurate and accessible. Ironically, this may have influenced theory's turn away from close textual analysis. Mayne sees this change as a key factor in theory's increasing focus on a new field of enquiry – the spectator. Laura Mulvey (2006) argues that the new digital media affect the way in which the spectator actually experiences film. The new media's capacity for close analysis enables the viewer to explore the very essence of film and its relationship to the viewer's sense of mortality. Mulvey offers new perspectives on a number of her own theories, such as visual pleasure, fetishism and gendered spectatorship, that have been central to feminist film theory over the past three decades.

The Internet has transformed the possibilities for critical discussion; for example, women now debate areas of feminist theory online. Global technologies have opened up the possibility of virtually instant global communication for a new generation of women interested in the transformative possibilities of feminist film theory in the future. After nearly four decades of feminist film theory, there is now a welcome plurality of voices, positions and passions.

Selected Reading

Alison Butler, 'Feminist theory and women's films at the turn of the century', *Screen* 41 (1): 73–8, 2000.

Judith Mayne, *Framed: Lesbians, Feminists and Media Culture*, Minneapolis and London, University of Minnesota Press, 2000.

Patricia Mellencamp, *A Fine Romance: Five Ages of Film Feminism*, Philadelphia, Temple University Press, 1995.

B. Ruby Rich, *Chick Flicks: Theories and Memories of the Feminist Film Movement*, Durham, NC, Duke University Press, 1998.

FEMINIST FILM THEORY

ANNEKE SMELIK

Feminism is a social movement that has had an enormous impact on film theory and criticism. Cinema is taken by feminists to be a cultural practice representing myths about women and femininity, as well as about men and masculinity. Issues of representation and spectatorship are central to feminist film theory and criticism. Early feminist criticism was directed at stereotypes of women, mostly in Hollywood films (Haskell, 1973; Rosen, 1973). Such fixed and endlessly repeated images of women were considered to be objectionable distortions that would have a negative impact on the female spectator. Hence, the call for positive images of women in cinema. Soon, however, the insight dawned that positive images were not enough to change underlying structures in film. Feminist critics tried to understand the all-pervasive power of patriarchal imagery with the help of structuralist theoretical frameworks such as semiotics and psychoanalysis. These theoretical discourses have proved very productive in analysing the ways in which sexual difference is encoded in classical narrative. For over a decade, psychoanalysis was to be the dominant paradigm in feminist film theory. More recently, there has been a move away from a binary understanding of sexual difference to multiple perspectives, identities and possible spectatorships. This opening up has resulted in an increasing concern with questions of ethnicity, masculinity and hybrid sexualities.

Classic film narrative

Claire Johnston was among the first feminist critics to offer a sustained critique of stereotypes from a semiotic point of view. She put forward a view of how classic cinema constructs the ideological image of woman. Drawing on Roland Barthes's notion of myth, Johnston investigated the myth of 'woman' in classic cinema. The sign 'woman' can be analysed as a structure, a code or convention. It represents the ideological meaning that 'woman' has for men. In relation to herself, she means no-thing (Johnston, 1991, p. 25): women are negatively represented as 'not-man'. The 'woman-as-woman' is absent from the text of the film (Johnston, 1991, p. 26).

The important theoretical shift here is from an understanding of cinema as reflecting reality, to a view of cinema as constructing a particular, ideological, view of reality. Classic cinema never shows its means of production and is hence characterised by veiling over its ideological construction. Thus, classic film narrative can present the constructed images of 'woman' as natural, realistic and attractive. This is the illusionism of classic cinema.

In her groundbreaking article 'Visual pleasure and narrative cinema' (see also Structuralism and its aftermaths, p. 524), Laura Mulvey used psychoanalysis to understand the fascination of Hollywood cinema. This fascination can be explained through the notion of scopophilia (the desire to see), which is a fundamental drive according to Freud. Sexual in origin, like all drives, *der Schautrieb* is what keeps the spectator glued to the silver screen. Classic cinema stimulates the desire to look by integrating structures of voyeurism and narcissism into the story and the image. Voyeuristic visual pleasure is produced by looking at another (character, figure, situation) as our object, whereas narcissistic visual pleasure can be derived from self-identification with the (figure in the) image.

Mulvey analysed scopophilia in classic cinema as a structure that functions on the axis of activity and passivity. This binary opposition is gendered. The narrative structure of traditional cinema establishes the male character as active and powerful: he is the agent around whom the dramatic action unfolds and the look gets organised. The female character is passive and powerless: she is the object of desire for the male character(s). In this respect, cinema has perfected a visual machinery suitable for male desire such as that already structured and canonised in the tradition of western art and aesthetics.

Mulvey disentangled the ways in which narrative and visual techniques in cinema make voyeurism into an exclusively male prerogative. Within the narrative of the film, male characters direct their gaze towards female characters. The spectator in the theatre is made to identify with the male look, because the camera films from the optical, as well as libidinal, point of view of the male character. There are thus three levels of the cinematic gaze (camera, character and spectator) that objectify the female character and make her into a spectacle. In classic cinema, voyeurism connotes women as 'to-be-looked-at-ness' (Mulvey, 1989, p. 19).

Mulvey tackles narcissistic visual pleasure with Lacan's concepts of ego formation and the mirror stage. The way in which the child derives pleasure from the identification with a perfect mirror image and forms its ego ideal on the basis of this idealised image is analogous to the way in which the film spectator derives narcissistic pleasure from identifying with the perfected image of a human figure on the screen. In both cases, however, during the mirror stage and in cinema, identifications are not a lucid form of self-knowledge or awareness. They are rather based on what Jacques Lacan calls '*méconnaissance*' ('misrecognition'), that is to say they are blinded by the very narcissistic forces that structure them in the first place. Ego formation is structurally characterised by imaginary functions. And so is cinema. At about the same time as Christian Metz worked on this analogy in his essays on psychoanalysis and cinema, Mulvey argued that cinematic identifications were structured along the lines of sexual difference. Representation of 'the more perfect, more complete, more powerful ideal ego' (Mulvey, 1989, p. 20) of the male hero stands in stark opposition to the distorted image of the passive and powerless female character. Hence the spectator is actively made to identify with the male rather than with the female character in film.

There are then two aspects to visual pleasure that are negotiated through sexual difference: the voyeuristic-scopophilic gaze and narcissistic identification. Both these formative structures depend for their meaning upon the controlling power of the male character as well as on the objectified representation of the female character. Moreover, according to Mulvey, in psychoanalytic terms, the image of 'woman' is fundamentally ambiguous in that it combines attraction and seduction with an evocation of castration anxiety. Because her appearance also reminds the male subject of the lack of a penis, the female character is a source of much deeper fears. Classic cinema solves the threat of castration in one of two ways: in the narrative structure or through fetishism. To allay the threat of castration on the level of narrative, the female character has to be found guilty. The films of Alfred Hitchcock are a good example of this kind of narrative plot (see Modleski, 1988). The woman's 'guilt' will be sealed by either punishment or salvation and the film story is then resolved through the two traditional endings made available to women: she must either die (as in *Psycho*, 1960) or marry (as in *Marnie*, 1964). In this respect, Mulvey provocatively says that a story demands sadism.

Tippi Hedren imprisoned by Sean Connery in Htchcock's *Marnie*

In the case of fetishism, classic cinema reinstates and displaces the lacking penis in the form of a fetish, that is, a hyper-polished object. Mulvey refers here to Josef von Sternberg's fetishisation of Marlene Dietrich. Marilyn Monroe is another example of a fetishised female star. Fetishising the woman deflects attention from female 'lack' and changes her from a dangerous figure into a reassuring object of flawless beauty. Fetishism in cinema confirms the reification of the female figure and thus fails to represent 'woman' outside the phallic norm.

The notion of 'the male gaze' has become a shorthand term for the analysis of complex mechanisms in cinema that involve structures such as voyeurism, narcissism and fetishism. These concepts help to illuminate how Hollywood cinema is tailor-made for male desire. Because the structures of Hollywood cinema are analysed as fundamentally patriarchal, early feminists declared that a woman's film should shun traditional narrative and cinematic techniques and engage in experimental practice: thus, women's cinema should be a counter-cinema.

A feminist counter-cinema

What should a feminist counter-cinema look like? For Mulvey, feminist cinema was to be an avant-garde film practice that would 'free the look of the camera into its materiality in time and space and the look of the audience into dialectics and passionate detachment' (Mulvey, 1989, p. 26). That such a counter-cinema would destroy the visual pleasure of the spectator was no problem for women; according to Mulvey, they would view the decline of classic film narrative with nothing more than 'sentimental regret' (Mulvey, 1989, p. 26).

Feminist counter-cinema took its inspiration from the avant-garde in cinema and theatre, such as the montage techniques of Sergei Eisenstein, the notion of *Verfremdung* (distanciation) of Bertolt Brecht and the modernist aesthetic of Jean-Luc Godard. As such, it was very much part of 1970s political film-making.

The privileged examples of feminist counter-cinema are Chantal Akerman's *Jeanne Dielman 23, Quai du Commerce, 1080 Bruxelles* (1975), Laura Mulvey and Peter Wollen's *Riddles of the Sphinx* (1977) and Sally Potter's *Thriller* (1979). It is interesting to note that the radical films of Marguerite Duras have drawn much less attention from anglophone feminist film critics. Important American experimental films are Yvonne Rainer's *Lives of Performers* (1972) and *Film about a Woman Who . . .* (1974), and *Sigmund Freud's Dora* (1979).

How does feminist counter-cinema avoid the conventions of classic cinema and how does it accommodate a female point of view? In the short experimental film *Thriller*, for example, this is achieved by deconstructing a classic melodrama, Puccini's opera *La Bohème* (1895). The film splits the female character into two: Mimi I, who is placed outside of the narrative in which she is the heroine, Mimi II. The first Mimi investigates how she is constructed as an object in the melodramatic narrative. According to Ann Kaplan (1983), the investigation is both psychoanalytic and Marxist–materialist. On the psychoanalytic level, Mimi I learns how the female subject is excluded from male language and classic narrative. The only position she can occupy is that of asking questions: 'Did I die? Was I murdered? What does it mean?'. On the Marxist–materialist level, Mimi I learns to investigate Mimi II's role as a seamstress and as a mother. As in Potter's second film, *The Gold Diggers* (1983), it is a woman of colour with a deep French-accented English voice (Colette Lafont) who does the critical questioning of the patriarchal image of white womanhood. Thus, in both films it is the 'foreign' female voice that speaks the discourse of theory and criticism.

Thriller communicates these theoretical discourses both visually and acoustically. The soundtrack includes the dominant female voice, as well as a repeated laugh, a repeated shriek and the sound of a heartbeat. These are typical components of the classical thriller and horror genres, while the film narrative does not give rise to any such suspense. Instead, it refocuses the attention of the spectator on the enigmas surrounding the female subject in classical discourse. *Thriller* deliberately violates conventional realist codes. The melodramatic story is partly told in shots that are pictures of photographs of a stage performance, and partly in reconstructed scenes in which the actors employ highly stylised movements. Another visual device is the use of mirrors. For Kaplan (1983), the play with repeated and jarring mirror shots illustrates the mental processes that Lacan's mirror phase involves psychoanalytically. For example, when Mimi I recognises herself as object, her shadow is thrown up on the screen. Mimi I is then shown with her back to the mirror, facing the camera. This image is repeated in a series of mirrors behind her (instead of 'correctly' reflecting the back of her head). This complex shot signals Mimi I's recognition of her split subjectivity. The investigation leads the women to understand they are not split in themselves, nor should they be split narratively. The film ends symbolically with both Mimis embracing.

Deconstructing patriarchal myths: Laura Mulvey and Peter Wollen's *Riddles of the Sphinx*

Feminist counter-cinema did not only pertain to fictional film, but also to documentary. The problems of finding an appropriate form and style were perhaps even more acute for documentary film, because traditional documentary uses illusionism and realism to capture 'truth' or 'reality'. For many feminist film-makers in the 1970s, this idealism was unacceptable. It could not include self-reflexivity, one of the starting points of feminist film practice. Feminist documentary should manufacture and construct the 'truth' of women's oppression, not merely reflect it (Johnston, 1991). However, other voices were also heard. Because many stylistically traditional documentaries have been important historical documents for the women's movement, this kind of feminist formalism was questioned. Alexandra Juhasz (1994) criticised this kind of orthodoxy, which proscribed anti-illusionist techniques undermining identification. She pointed to the paradox that the unified subject that was represented in early feminist documentaries presented the feminist viewer in fact with a 'radical, new and politicized reinterpretation of that female subjectivity, one which mobilized vast numbers of women into action for the first time' (Juhasz, 1994, p. 174).

We witness a theoretical contradiction of feminism here: while feminists need to deconstruct the patriarchal images and representations of 'woman', they historically need to establish their female subjectivity at the same time. That is to say, they have to find out and redefine what it means to be a woman. A relentless formalism may be too much of a one-sided approach to the complex enterprise of (re)constructing the female subject.

Counter-cinema represents only a small fraction of the many films produced by women since the mid-1970s. Yet, these experimental films have been overpraised for their subversive powers while realist women's films were overcriticised for their illusionism (see Kuhn, 1982; Kaplan, 1983). The suspicion of collusion cast on realist or narrative film has resulted in either a concentration of critical efforts on classic Hollywood cinema or in a largely unjustified acclaim of experimental women's cinema among the elected few who get to see it. This has resulted in a paradoxical neglect of contemporary popular films made by women for a wider audience; a lack of academic attention that continued long into the 1980s and even 1990s (see Humm, 1997; Smelik, 1998). Teresa de Lauretis (1984; 1987) was among the first to claim that feminist cinema should not destroy narrative and visual pleasure, but rather should be 'narrative and oedipal with a vengeance' (de Lauretis, 1987, p. 108). According to her, feminist cinema in the 1980s should define 'all points of identification (with character, image, camera) as female, feminine, or feminist' (de Lauretis, 1987, p. 133).

The female spectator

The account of 'the male gaze' as a structuring logic in western visual culture became controversial in the early 1980s, as it left no room for the female spectator nor for a female gaze. Yet, women did and do go to the movies. Mulvey was much criticised for omitting the question of female spectatorship. In a later essay, she addressed the vicissitudes of female spectatorship in her analysis of the western *Duel in the Sun* (King Vidor, 1946). Mulvey suggested that the female spectator may not only identify with the slot of passive femininity that has been programmed for her, but is also likely to enjoy adopting the masculine point of view. Mulvey elaborated on the notion of transsexual identification and spectatorship by pointing to the pre-oedipal and phallic fantasy of omnipotence that for girls is equally active as for boys, and hence, from a Freudian perspective, essentially 'masculine'. In order to acquire 'proper' femininity, women will have to shed that active aspect of their early sexuality. Mulvey speculates that female spectators may negotiate the masculinisation of the spectatorial position in Hollywood cinema, because it signifies for them a pleasurable rediscovery of a lost aspect of their sexual identity. Even so, the female spectator remains 'restless in [her] transvestite clothes' (Mulvey, 1989, p. 37).

Who owns the gaze? Gregory Peck and Jennifer Jones in *Duel in the Sun*

It was not until the end of the 1980s that female spectatorship was theorised outside the dichotomous categories of psychoanalytic theory. An account of female spectatorship in all its cultural contexts and multiple differences was then undertaken in a special issue of *Camera Obscura*, entitled 'The spectatrix' (1989). Editors Janet Bergstrom and Mary Ann Doane chose to give a comprehensive survey of international research on and theories of the female spectator in film and television studies.

The female masquerade

It has become a general assumption of feminist film theory that female spectators are more fluid in their capacity to identify with the other gender. For example, in her study of the fan phenomenon, Miriam Hansen (1991) used the idea of spectatorial flexibility to explain why women in the 1920s were drawn to the feminine positioning of Rudolph Valentino.

This spectatorial transvestism of the woman viewer points to a female masquerade. The concept of masquerade was first introduced into feminist film theory by Johnston (1975). The notion of masquerade was inspired by the role of the female character who cross-dressed as a male pirate. For Johnston, the female masquerade signified not only a masking but also an 'unmasking' in the deconstructionist sense of exposing and criticising.

Mary Ann Doane (1991) explored the notion of masquerade further to understand woman's relation to the image on the screen. Drawing on the psychoanalytic work of Joan Rivière, Doane understands the masquerade, not as cross-dressing, but on the contrary as a mask of femininity. Rivière had noticed in her clinical observations that women who find themselves in a male position of authority put on a mask of femininity that functions as compensation for their masculine position.

How does this concept of the masquerade relate to issues of identification and spectatorship? As we have seen, the male gaze involves voyeurism. Voyeurism presupposes distance. Doane argues that the female spectator lacks this necessary distance because she is the image. Femininity is constructed as closeness, as 'an overwhelming presence-to-itself of the female body' (Doane, 1991, p. 22). The female spectator can adopt 'the masochism of over-identification' or 'the narcissism entailed in becoming one's own object of desire' (Doane, 1991, pp. 31–2). Doane argues that the female spectator is consumed by the image rather than consuming it. This position can be avoided not only through a transsexual identification, but also through the masquerade. The masquerade is effective in that it manufactures a distance from the image. By wearing femininity as a mask, the female spectator can create the necessary difference between herself and the represented femininity on the screen.

In a study of the woman's film of the 1940s, Doane (1987) returned to the rather negative ways in which Hollywood constructs female identification and subjectivity. For Doane, the female spectator of those melodramas is involved in emotional processes like masochism, paranoia, narcissism and hysteria. The woman's film, in spite of its focus on a female main character, perpetuates these processes and thus confirms stereotypes about the female psyche. The emotional investments of the viewer lead to overidentification, destroying the distance to the object of desire and turning the active desire of both the female character and the female spectator into the passive desire to be the desired object. Mere 'desire to desire' seems to be, then, the only option for women.

The female look

Do these rather dire interpretations of female spectatorship imply that the female look is impossible and that the look or gaze is necessarily male? In the early 1980s, this seemed the case in feminist theory. In her analysis of Hollywood woman's films of the 1970s and 1980s, Ann Kaplan (1983) argued that female characters can possess the look and even make the male character the object of her gaze, but, being a woman, her desire has no power. The neo-feminist Hollywood movies involve a mere reversal of roles in which the underlying structures of dominance and submission are still intact. The gaze is not essentially male, 'but to own and activate the gaze, given our language and the structure of the unconscious, is to be in the "masculine" position' (Kaplan, 1983, p. 30).

The difficulties of theorising the female spectator made Jackie Stacey (1987) exclaim that feminist film critics have written the darkest scenario possible for the female look as being male, masochist or marginal. There have been some different voices, however. Gertrud Koch (1980) is one of the few feminists who early on recognised that women could also enjoy the image of female beauty on the screen. In particular, the vamp, an image exported from Europe and integrated into Hollywood cinema, provides the female spectator with a positive image of autonomous femininity. Koch argues that the image of the vamp revives for the female spectator the pleasurable experience of the mother as the love object in early childhood. Moreover, the sexual ambivalence of the vamp, for example Greta Garbo and Marlene Dietrich, allows for a female homoerotic pleasure that is not exclusively negotiated through the eyes of men. In Koch's view, the vamp is a phallic woman rather than a fetishised woman, as she offers contradictory images of femininity that go beyond the reifying gaze. The vamp's ambiguity can be a source of visual pleasure for the female spectator. The disappearance of the vamp in cinema, therefore, means a great loss of possible identifications and visual pleasure for the female audience.

A similar focus on the pre-oedipal phase and on the mother as love object and potential source of visual pleasure has been developed by Gaylyn Studlar (1988), though from a very different angle. Analysing films made by Josef von Sternberg starring Marlene Dietrich, she investigates the Deleuzian notion of masochism. Deleuze views masochism as the desire of the male to merge with the mother and subvert the father's phallic law. Its violence is contractual and consensual, in a way that sadism is not. Sadism negates the difference of the mother and exults in the power of the father. Studlar argues that visual pleasure in cinema resembles more the psychic processes of masochism than of sadism. Cinema evokes the desire of the spectator to return to the pre-oedipal phase of unity with the mother, and of bisexuality. The female spectator can thus identify with and draw pleasure from the powerful femme fatale in cinema. This is a sort of re-enactment of the symbiosis through which the spectator wishes to subject herself or himself to the powerful mother image. The condition of this active masochistic desire is that it be suspended, which is achieved by means of performance and masquerade on the part of the female character. These ritualisations of fantasy keep desire under control. For Studlar, the masquerade serves as a defensive strategy for women, by which they deflect and confuse the male gaze. She thus creates a place for the pleasure and desire of the female subject-spectator, albeit the pleasurable pain of desire.

Bisexual identification has also emerged in studies of very different film genres. In her study of the modern horror film, Carol Clover (1992) argues that both female and male spectators identify bisexually. She rests her case on the narrative role of the 'Final Girl': the one girl in the film who fights, resists and survives the killer-monster. The final girl acquires the gaze, and dominates the action, and is thus masculinised. Slasher films, such as *Halloween* (1978), *Friday the 13th* (1980) and *A Nightmare on Elm Street* (1984) (and their sequels), openly play on a difference between appearance (sex) and behaviour (gender). Clover argues that it is this 'theatricalization of gender' that feminises the audience. Whereas in classic horror (such as films by Hitchcock and Brian De Palma), the feminisation of the audience is intermittent and ceases when the final girl becomes the designated victim (as with Marion Crane in *Psycho*), in the modern horror film the final girl becomes her own saviour (see The horror film, p. 356). Her self-rescue turns her into the hero and it is at that moment that the male viewer 'gives up the last pretence of male identification'. For Clover, the willingness of the male spectator to throw in his emotional lot with a woman in fear and pain points to masochism. Although Clover is aware of the misogyny of the genre of the slasher film, she claims a subversive edge in that it adjusts gender representations and identifications.

Female subjectivity

The question of female spectatorship and the female look circle around the issue of subjectivity. Female subjectivity has been explored not only in relation to spectatorship, but also with respect to the narrative structure of film. One of the key figures in this field is Teresa de Lauretis, who examined the structural representations of 'woman' in cinema (1984; 1987).

De Lauretis (1984) emphasised that subjectivity is not a fixed entity but a constant process of self-production. Narration is one of the ways of reproducing subjectivity; each story derives its structure from the subject's desire and from its inscription in social and cultural codes. Narrative structures are defined by oedipal desire, which should be understood as both a socio-political economy dominated by men's control of women and as a way of emphasising the sexual origin of subjectivity. Sexual desire is bound up with the desire for knowledge, that is, the quest for truth. The desire to solve riddles is a male desire par excellence, because the female subject is herself the mystery. 'Woman' is the question and can hence not ask the question nor make her desire intelligible. In Hitchcock's *Vertigo* (1958), for example, Scottie's desire for the enigmatic Judy/Madeleine structures the narrative of the film.

Narrative is not oedipal in content but in structure, by distributing roles and differences, and thus power and positions. One of the functions of narrative, de Lauretis argues, is to 'seduce' women into femininity with or without their consent. The female subject is made to desire femininity. This is a cruel and often coercive form of seduction. Here de Lauretis turns Mulvey's famous phrase around: not only does a story demand sadism; sadism demands a story. She refers to the ways in which the female characters in *Vertigo*, but also in a 'woman's film' such as *Rebecca* (Hitchcock, 1940), are made to conform to the ideal image that the man has of them. The function of portraits of female ancestors in both films is highly significant in this respect: they represent the dead mother, the ideal that the male hero desires to have and forces upon the female heroine. For de Lauretis, the desire of the female character is impossible and the narrative tension is resolved by the destruction (Judy/Madeleine in *Vertigo*) or territorialisation of women (the new Mrs de Winter in *Rebecca*). Desire in narrative is intimately bound up with violence against women, and the techniques of cinematic narration both reflect and sustain social forms of oppression of women.

De Lauretis is hardly more optimistic than Mulvey about the female spectator. Not that she assumes identification to be single or simple; femininity and masculinity are identifications that the subject takes up in a changing relation to desire. De Lauretis distinguishes two different processes of identification in cinema. The first set is an oscillating either/or identification. In *Vertigo*, it consists of a masculine, active identification with the gaze (Scottie) and a passive, feminine identification with the image (Judy/Madeleine). The second set is a simultaneous both/and identification. It consists of the double identification with the figure of narrative movement (the protagonist, the new Mrs de Winter in *Rebecca*) and with the figure of narrative image (here the image of Rebecca). This set of figural identifications enables the female spectator to take up both the active and passive positions of desire: 'Desire for the other, and desire to be desired by the other' (de Lauretis, 1984, p. 143). This double identification may yield a surplus of pleasure, but it is also the very operation by which a narrative solicits the spectators' consent and seduces women into femininity.

The notion of the female subject, then, seems to be a contradiction in terms, so much so that de Lauretis sometimes refers to the female subject as a 'non-subject' (de Lauretis, 1987, p. 36). 'Woman' is fundamentally unrepresentable as subject of desire; she can only be represented as representation (de Lauretis, 1987, p. 20). Feminist theory is built on the very paradox of the unrepresentability of woman as subject of desire, and historical women who know themselves to be subjects. For de Lauretis, the self-conscious experience of being both 'woman' and 'women' is the productive contradiction of feminism. Women's films such as *Les Rendez-vous d'Anna* (1978), *Jeanne Dielman*, *Thriller* or *Sigmund Freud's Dora* are her privileged examples of films that explore and explode that very contradiction.

Female desire

A feminist critic who also approached the question of female desire within psychoanalytic discourse was Kaja Silverman (1988). Drawing on Lacanian psychoanalysis, Silverman argues that each subject is structured by lack or symbolic castration. In western culture it is, however, the female subject who is made to bear the burden of that lack in order to provide the male subject with the illusion of wholeness and unity. Silverman suggests that in cinema this displacement is enacted not only through the gaze and the image but also through the auditory register. Contrary to the more frequent disembodiment of the male voice in cinema, the female voice is restricted to the realm of the body. This amounts to keeping it outside discourse. The female voice can hardly reach a signifying position in language, meaning or power and is hence all too easily reduced to screams, babble or silence in dominant cinema.

Silverman discusses the cultural fantasy of the maternal voice that surrounds the infant like an acoustic blanket. This fantasy for the maternal enclosure negatively signifies the fear of being swallowed up by the mother, whereas it positively signifies a regression to the state of harmony and abundance when mother and child are still one. Silverman argues that both these fantasies equate the maternal voice to pure sound and deny the mother any cultural role as a discursive agent. In her rereading of psychoanalysis, Silverman attempts to make room for the mother and for female desire within discourse and the symbolic order.

Reinterpreting Freud's account of the psychological development of the little girl, Silverman puts great emphasis on the signifying role of the mother in early childhood. The entry into language means the end of the unity between mother and child as well as of an unmediated access to reality. The loss and separation entailed by the acquisition of language lead the child to desire the mother. The girl redirects her desire to the mother in what is called the negative Oedipus complex. This can only happen *after* the pre-oedipal stage, because distance from the mother is necessary for her to be constructed as an erotic object for the daughter. Silverman thus recuperates female desire for the mother as fully oedipal, that is, within the symbolic order, within language and signification.

It is after the event of the castration crisis, the dramatic onset of sexual difference, that the girl leaves the negative Oedipus complex and enters the positive oedipal phase, learning to redirect her desire to the father. For the rest of her life the female subject remains split between the desire for the mother and for the father. The two desires are the site of a constitutive contradiction and are consequently irreconcilable. For Silverman, the daughter's erotic investment in the mother can be a subversive force for a 'libidinal politics' because it is a form of desire that is opposed to the normative desire for the father. Silverman emphasises the negativity of the female negative Oedipus complex as a political potential. She argues that it is paramount for feminism to draw on the libidinal resources of the 'homosexual-maternal fantasmatic' (Silverman, 1988, p. 125).

Silverman also revises the traditional view on the divergence of identification and desire. In her view, these two psychic paradigms are not always mutually exclusive and can actually coalesce. In the negative Oedipus complex, the girl both identifies with and desires the mother, while the father figures neither as an object of desire nor of identification: for the girl, he is merely 'a troublesome rival' (Freud quoted in Silverman, 1988, p. 153). In this stage of development, the girl forms her identity through the incorporation of the mother's imago; she both wishes to possess and to be the mother. There is then a conjunction of identification and eroticism, which Silverman believes to have a vital relation to female narcissism. For her, feminism's libidinal struggle against the phallus lies in the intersection of desire for and identification with the mother.

In Silverman's reading, a fantasy of the maternal enclosure is the organising principle of *Riddles of the Sphinx*. In this experimental film, the figure of the Sphinx occupies the position of an 'imaginary narrator', a distinctly fictionalised voice-over. This disembodied voice speaks a wide variety of discourses about motherhood, from psychoanalysis to feminist politics, thus firmly establishing the maternal voice within the symbolic order. The film is centred upon the female desire to recover the oedipal or symbolic mother, represented by the Sphinx. *Riddles* springs off from the mother–daughter relationship, of Louise and her child Anna. The maternal fantasy can be found not only in the pre-oedipal dyad, but also in the homosexual-maternal ménage à trois of mother, grandmother and child. The film opens this maternal enclosure up to a feminist community of women, including Louise's friend Maxine, and the voice and work of artist Mary Kelly. This female collectivity, like female subjectivity, is based upon the passionate desire for the mother.

Sexual difference and its discontents

Although feminists have not always agreed about the usefulness of pyschoanalysis, there has been general agreement about the limitations of an exclusive focus on sexual difference. One such limitation is the reproduction of a dichotomy, male–female, that needs to be deconstructed. The fear was that this binary opposition would somehow tie questions of pleasure and identification to anatomical difference. Especially within American feminism, the term sexual difference was therefore replaced by a renewed interest in the sex–gender distinction that Gayle Rubin had introduced in 1975. The term gender generally seemed to indicate a clearer distinction between anatomy (sex) and social construction (gender), and equally between sexual practice and gender identity. Another limitation of the exclusive focus on sexual difference within psychoanalytic film theory is its failure to focus on other differences such as class, race, age and sexual preference.

Lesbian feminists were among the first to raise objections to the heterosexual bias of psychoanalytic feminist film theory. Indeed, feminist film theory – not unlike the Hollywood cinema it criticised so fiercely – seemed unable to conceive of representation outside heterosexuality. The journal *Jump Cut* wrote in its special issue on Lesbians and Film (1981): 'It sometimes seems to us that lesbianism is the hole in the heart of feminist film criticism' (p. 17). Apparently, almost ten years later matters had improved very little, as Judith Mayne (1990; 1994) complained that the denial of the lesbian identity of Hollywood director Dorothy Arzner pointed to a curious gap in feminist film theory, indeed, to the 'structuring absence' of lesbianism (Mayne, 1994, p. 107). As Patricia White (1991) observed, the 'ghostly presence of lesbianism' does not only haunt Hollywood Gothic but also feminist film theory.

In spite of the increasing focus on female spectatorship in feminist scholarship (see Spectatorship and audience research, p. 538), the homosexual pleasures of the female spectator were indeed largely ignored. Yet, it is interesting to know what happens for the female spectator when a classic narrative features two female characters. This question arose as early as Julia Lesage's (1980/81) pioneering analysis of the improvisational interplay of the two female characters in Jacques Rivette's *Céline and Julie Go Boating/Céline et Julie vont en bateau* (1974). She shows that the abandonment of the classic story based on male–female distinctions produces new and previously unimaginable narrative permutations.

Stacey (1987) argued that in Hollywood films with two female protagonists, such as *All about Eve* (1950) or *Desperately Seeking Susan* (1985), an active desire is produced by the difference between the two women. These stories are about women wanting to become the idealised other. An interplay of difference and otherness prevents the collapse of that desire into identification, prompting Stacey to argue that the rigid psychoanalytic distinction between desire and identification fails to address different constructions of desire. She suggests that a more flexible model of cinematic spectatorship is needed so as to avoid a facile binarism that maps homosexuality onto an opposition of masculinity and femininity.

De Lauretis (1988) has drawn attention to the difficulties of imagining lesbian desire within a psychoanalytic discourse that predicates sexual difference on sexual *in*difference. She here follows Luce Irigaray's notion of the symbolic law representing only one and not two sexes: patriarchy is deeply '*hommosexual*', as it erects the masculine as the one and only norm. Discussing the same problematic in a later essay, de Lauretis (1991) observed that the institution of heterosexuality defines all sexuality to such an extent that is difficult to represent homosexual-lesbian desire. She criticises both Stacey and Silverman for conceiving of desire between women as woman-identified female bonding and failing to see it as sexual. Here, and more extensively in her later book *The Practice of Love* (1994), de Lauretis returns to Freudian theory to account for the specificity of lesbian desire in terms of fetishism.

In answer to de Lauretis's criticism, Stacey (1994) argued in her study of female spectatorship that she is not concerned with a specifically lesbian audience but with a possible homoeroticism for all women in the audience. Her point is not to de-eroticise desire, but to look for ways in which a film may eroticise identification. The female spectator is quite likely to encompass erotic components in her desiring look, while at the same time identifying with the woman-as-spectacle. The homoerotic appeal of female Hollywood stars has indeed been widely recognised. Weiss (1992), for example, discusses the attraction of Hollywood stars for lesbian spectators in the 1930s. The androgynous appearances of Marlene Dietrich in *Morocco* (1930) (see case study), Greta Garbo in *Queen Christina* (1933) (see Spectatorship and audience research, p. 544) and Katharine Hepburn in *Sylvia Scarlett* (1936) were embraced as images of a gender-in-between and of sexual ambiguity. The star image of sexual androgyny served as point of identification outside conventional gender positions.

While these discussions of lesbian spectatorship are part of a wider movement in film studies to include the heterogeneity of the spectatorial situation, most discussions of spectatorship have been about white audiences. De Lauretis was criticised for not taking into account racial dynamics in the lesbian film *She Must Be Seeing Things* (1987). The issue of

Exploring sexual difference: Rosanna Arquette and Aidan Quinn in Susan Seidelman's *Desperately Seeking Susan*

black lesbian spectatorship has so far hardly been raised. The collection *Queer Looks* (Gever *et al.*, 1993) addressed the combination of racial difference and homosexuality, but it focused more on gay and lesbian film-making than on spectatorship as such.

Gay and lesbian criticism

The shift away from the restrictive dichotomies of psychoanalytic feminist film theory has resulted in a more historical and cultural criticism of cinema by gay and lesbian critics. This involved rereadings of Hollywood cinema, for example of the implicit lesbianism of the female buddy film. In order to avoid that 'danger', Hollywood films often include explicit scenes denying any lesbian intent. In *Julia* (1977), Jane Fonda slaps a man in the face when he suggests that her friendship with Julia (Vanessa Redgrave) was sexual. Other films put a 'real' lesbian in the story as a way of showing that the female friendship of the two heroines is not 'that way' (*Girl Friends*, 1978). In some films, the female buddies, however, become lovers, as in *Lianna* (1982) and *Personal Best* (1982). Several critics have pointed out that the lesbian subject matter of these films is acceptable to all kinds of audiences, because its eroticism feeds into traditional male voyeurism (Williams, 1986; Merck, 1993). Ellsworth (1990) investigated lesbian responses to *Personal Best* and found that many lesbian spectators actively rewrote the film by imagining a different ending. Her research shows that lesbian spectators use interpretative strategies to challenge the dominant reading of a film.

The theme of lesbianism still runs strong in more recent female buddy films. *Fried Green Tomatoes at the Whistle Stop Cafe* (1991) is one of those films about female friendship in which lesbianism remains unspoken, although it is a source of strength and inspiration. In *Thelma & Louise* (1991), the lesbian attraction between the women can only be expressed in a kiss on the mouth just before they leap to their death into the Grand Canyon. *Basic Instinct* (1992) features lesbian and bisexual characters as pathological killers, harking back to the time-old association in Hollywood films of lesbianism with death and pathology. What else is new? Angela Galvin (1994) suggested that the novelty may well lie in the heroine's absence of a moustache. The controversy over *Thelma & Louise* and *Basic Instinct* shows some of the various responses of feminist and lesbian criticism. While the films have been criticised for their reactionary representation of strong women and for their exploitation of voyeuristic themes, some spectators have appropriated them as 'lesbian films', enjoying images of empowered women who escape the Law (Tasker, 1993; Graham, 1995).

Alongside rereadings of Hollywood films, gay and lesbian criticism turned to films made by lesbians and gay men. Early films of European art cinema were rediscovered, such as *Girls in Uniform/Mädchen in Uniform* (1931). Rich (1984) argues that the anti-Fascist politics of *Mädchen in Uniform* is interconnected with its lesbian theme and its struggle against authoritarian structures and sexual repression. Rich places the film in the historical context of Weimar Germany with its vibrant lesbian subculture, especially in Berlin.

Mädchen in Uniform does not stand alone, but is part of a tradition of gay and lesbian film-making within early cinema (see Dyer, 1990; Weiss, 1992). Other films were made by gay or lesbian film-makers, such as the surrealist shorts of Germaine Dulac. Her films have been read as critiques of heterosexuality (Flitterman-Lewis, 1990). Fantasy plays an important role in these experimental films. In *The Smiling Madame Beudet/La Souriante Madame Beudet* (1922), a woman fantasises murdering her bully of a husband and escaping from her bourgeois marriage, and *The Seashell and the Clergyman/La Coquille et le clergyman* (1927) exposes oedipal male fantasies about the mystery of 'woman'.

Jean Genet's prison film *A Song of Love/Un chant d'amour* (1950) is a classic that has become enormously popular with gay audiences to the present day and that also has influenced gay film-makers. Dyer (1990) discussed the film's eroticism in terms of the tension between politics and pleasure. While some gay critics have reprimanded the film for its 'oppression' of gay men or were disturbed by its 'homophobic' representation of erotic pleasures, others took a more permissive or even celebratory attitude to the sado-masochism of the film. Dyer argues that the renewed political interest in perverse sexualities opened up a Foucauldian reading of the film's eroticism in terms of the social and historical relation between sexuality and power.

The play of power and desire has become the theme of some gay and lesbian films in the 1980s, which Dyer calls a 'Genetesque' tradition. A ritualisation of power and desire can, for example, be found in the Sadean theatre of *Seduction: The Cruel Woman/Verführung: die grausame Frau* (1985) by Elfi Mikesch and Monika Treut. This highly formalised and aestheticised exploration of sado-masochism was one of the first films to bring female desire and lesbian sexuality within the domain of power and violence. Another film-maker who must be mentioned in this context is Ulrike Ottinger, whose fantasmatic films from *Madame X/Madame X eine absolute Herrscherin* (1978) to *Johanna D'Arc of Mongolia* (1989) humorously deconstruct traditional femininity and perversely celebrate nomadic lesbian subjectivities (Longfellow, 1993).

These films are very different from the lesbian romance *Desert Hearts* (1985), a lesbian independent feature that made use of Hollywood conventions and was a box-office success. As Jackie Stacey (1995) points out, the film, quite surprisingly, was not followed by other successful lesbian romances nor did it receive much academic attention. She suggests that this may have to do with the popular lesbian romance film being 'a virtual contradiction in terms' (Stacey, 1995, p. 112). The film has, however, remained popular with lesbian audiences.

Feminist theory and race

Persistent critique of psychoanalytic film theory has also come from black feminists, who criticised its exclusive focus on sexual differences and its failure to deal with racial difference. Jane Gaines (1988) was one of the first feminist critics to point to the erasure of race in film theories that are based on the psychoanalytic concept of sexual differences. She pleaded for an inclusion of black feminist theory and of a historical approach into feminist film theory in order to understand how, in cinema, gender intersects with race and class.

White film critics have universalised their theories of representations of women, while black women have been excluded from those very forms of representation. The signification of the black female as non-human makes black female sexuality the great unknown in white patriarchy, that which is 'unfathomed and uncodified' and yet 'worked over again and again in mainstream culture because of its apparent elusiveness' (Gaines, 1988, p. 26). The eruptive point of resistance presents black women's sexuality as an even greater threat to the male unconscious than the fear of white female sexuality.

The category of race also problematises the paradigm of the male gaze possessing the female image. The male gaze is not a universal given but it is rather negotiated via whiteness: the black man's sexual gaze is socially prohibited. Racial hierarchies in ways of looking have created visual taboos, the neglect of which reflects back on film theory, which fails to account for the ways in which some social groups have the licence to look openly, while others can only 'look' illicitly. The racial structures of looking also have repercussions for structures of narrative. Gaines discusses the construction of the black man as rapist, while in times of slavery and long after, it was the white man who raped black women. The historical scenario of interracial rape explains much of the penalty of sexual looking by the black man, who was actually (rather than symbolically) castrated or lynched by white men. For Gaines, this scenario of sexual violence, repression and displacements rivals the oedipal myth.

Interventions such as Gaines's show that the category of race reveals the untenability of many one-sided beliefs within feminist film theory, and points to the necessity of contextualising and historicising sexual difference. Thus, Lola Young (1996) examines the representation of black female sexuality by situating British films in their historical and social context. Intersecting theories of sexual difference with those of differences of race and sexual preference, along with ethnicity and class, will eventually make other forms of representation thinkable, although Young argues convincingly that white and black film-makers find it hard to challenge stereotypical images of black women.

Almost simultaneously with Young's book a special issue of *Camera Obscura* (1995) was published, the focus of which was: 'Black women, spectatorship, and visual culture'. In her reading of Neil Jordan's films *Mona Lisa* (1986) and *The Crying Game* (1992), Joy James came to a similar conclusion as Young: these films fail to fulfil the promise of transgressive relationships and ultimately reproduce stereotypes of black female sexuality. Deborah Grayson examined the iconic representation of black women's hair in visual culture. Looking at diverse media and popular practices, she identified the racialised signification of hair within American health and beauty culture. In a similar vein, Marla Shelton analysed the crossover stardom of Whitney Houston. While Shelton celebrates Houston's successful construction of her own image and formation of different audiences, she points to the inherent conflicts that converge around this 'rainbow icon'. For example, Houston has found it hard to escape negative interpretations of her sexuality and of her role as a wife and mother. And while she has always had enormous crossover appeal, according to Shelton, in more recent years Houston had to embrace and express her blackness in order to maintain a large audience.

Generally, little research has been available about black audiences (see Spectatorship and audience research, p. 538). One of the exceptions is the work of Jacqueline Bobo (1995) on Steven Spielberg's *The Color Purple* (1985). The film was attacked in the black press for its racism. Yet, this critical view is mixed with reports of black spectators who found the film empowering. Bobo set out to research this apparent contradiction and interviewed a group of black women. The black female spectators were quite unanimously impressed by the film – 'Finally, somebody says something about us' – and felt strengthened by the triumph of the female protagonist Celie. They thought the criticism of the film (and also of Alice Walker's novel), particularly on the part of black men, quite unjustified. The women do recognise that the film continues the tradition of racist representations of blacks; Spielberg's interpretation of Sofia and Harpo is not considered to be successful. However, Bobo argues that, as black spectators, the women are by sheer necessity used to filtering out offensive racist images from what they see in cinema. The women negotiated their appreciation of the film through their personal history and past viewing experience. Moreover, Bobo found that certain technical aspects of the film contributed to spectatorial pleasure: *The Color Purple* introduced an innovative way of photographing black people so that they stood out against the background. This photographic technique made black people appear more distinctly on the screen than in the cinematic tradition of Hollywood.

The influential feminist critic bell hooks confirms that black viewers have always critically responded to Hollywood. Black female spectators do not necessarily identify with either the male gaze or with white womanhood as lack. Rather, they 'construct a theory of looking relations where cinematic visual delight is the pleasure of interrogation' (hooks, 1992, p. 126). For hooks, this is a radical departure from the 'totalizing agenda' of feminist film criticism, and the beginning of an oppositional spectatorship for black women.

A search for an oppositional subjectivity can also be found in the practice of film-making. Ngozi Onwurah's film *The Body Beautiful* (1990), for example, inscribes new subject positions for the diasporan daughter of a British mother and a Nigerian father. Combining documentary with fictional elements, this hybrid film centres on the relation between the body of the mother and that of her daughter by foregrounding questions of authenticity and authority. In a rewriting of the Freudian primal scene – the daughter watching the lovemaking of her mature white mother with a young black man – the film takes on the ethnographic gaze at the 'Other', radically subverting traditional psychoanalytic discourse.

Richard Dyer (1993) is one of the few film critics who has written about whiteness in cinema. He argues that it is difficult to think about whiteness, because it is often revealed as emptiness and absence. Because whiteness is constructed as the norm, it is unmarked. Yet, or rather, as such, it can represent everything. This eerie property of whiteness, to be nothing and everything at the same time, is the source of its representational power. In his reading of *Jezebel* (1938), Dyer points to the narrative technique of Hollywood colonial movies, where the white, sexually repressed heroine lives her emotions through the black servant. Such films conventionally oppose the chastity and virginity of white womanhood to the vitality and sexuality of the black woman, usually the white woman's servant. Its closure is the acquired ideal of white womanhood, although much of the pleasure of the film lies in the transgression of Jezebel (Bette Davis), exposing that ideal to be quite an ordeal.

On masculinity

While feminists have convincingly exposed western culture as male-dominated, this has not automatically produced a feminist theory of male subjectivity and sexuality. Pam Cook's essay 'Masculinity in crisis?' in a special issue of *Screen* (1982) opened up a new area of investigation: the riddled question of masculinity in the age of feminism. Much as the dominant paradigm of feminist film theory raised questions about the male look and the female spectacle, it also raised questions about the eroticisation of the male body as erotic object. What if the male body is the object of the female gaze or of another male gaze; and how exactly does the male body become the signifier of the phallus?

In the discussion of masculinity in cinema, the issue of homosexual desire was raised (Dyer, 1982; Neale, 1983). Most critics agree that the spectatorial look in mainstream cinema is implicitly male. While for Dyer this means that images of men do not automatically 'work' for women, according to Neale the erotic element in looking at the male body has to be repressed and disavowed so as to avoid any implications of male homosexuality. Yet, male homosexuality is always present as an undercurrent; it is Hollywood's symptom. The denial of the homoeroticism of looking at images of men constantly involves sado-masochistic themes, scenes and fantasies. Hence, the highly ritualised scenes of male struggle that deflect the look away from the male body to the scene of the spectacular fight.

The image of the male body as object of a look is fraught with ambivalences, repressions and denials. Like the masquerade, the notion of spectacle has such strong feminine connotations that for a male performer to be put on display or to don a mask threatens his very masculinity. Because the phallus is a symbol and a signifier, no man can fully symbolise it. Although the patriarchal male subject has a privileged relation to the phallus, he will always fall short of the phallic ideal. Lacan notices this effect in his essay on the meaning of the phallus, 'the curious consequence of making virile display in the human being itself seem feminine' (Lacan, 1977, p. 291). Male spectacle, then, entails being put in a feminine position. The immanent feminisation of male spectacle brings about two possible dangers for the posing or performing male: functioning as an object of desire, he can easily become the object of ridicule, and within a heterosexist culture, accusations of homosexuality can be launched against him (Neale, 1983; Tasker, 1993).

Masculinity studies became established in feminist film theory in the 1990s. In a special issue of *Camera Obscura* (1988) on 'male trouble', Constance Penley and Sharon Willis argued that the great variety of images of contemporary masculinity are organised around hysteria and masochism. As they point out, these two symptomatic formations are a telling displacement of voyeurism and fetishism, the terms that have so far been used in feminist film theory to describe male subjectivity and spectatorship. Lynne Kirby, for example, describes male hysteria in early cinema. She argues that the disturbing shock effects of early cinema (the rollercoaster ride, the speeding train shots) construct a hystericised spectator. Hysteria was seen as a quintessential female condition, but with modern technology men were equally subjected to shock and trauma and hence responded with hysteria. Male hysteria and masochism are further explored in books on male subjectivity by Tania Modleski (1991) and Kaja Silverman (1992).

Most studies of masculinity point to the crisis in which the white male heterosexual subject finds himself, a crisis in which his masculinity is fragmented and denaturalised (Easthope, 1986; Kirkham and Thumim, 1993; Tasker, 1993; Jeffords, 1994). The signifiers of 'man' and 'manly' seem to have lost all of their meaning, which makes Hollywood desperate to find a 'few good white men', in the words of Susan Jeffords. Yet, the crisis in masculinity is welcomed by gay critics as a liberatory moment. In his book on male impersonators, Mark Simpson (1994) takes great pleasure in celebrating the deconstruction of masculinity as authentic, natural, coherent and dominant.

Queer theory

Gay studies of masculinity often border on camp readings of the male spectacle (Medhurst, 1991b; Simpson, 1994). Camp can be seen as an oppositional reading of popular culture that offers identifications and pleasures that dominant culture denies to homosexuals. As an oppositional reading, camp can be subversive for bringing out the cultural ambiguities and contradictions that usually remain sealed over by dominant ideology.

This characteristic brings camp into the realm of postmodernism, which also celebrates ambivalence and heterogeneity. Subcultural camp and postmodern theory share a penchant for irony, play and parody, for artificiality and performance, as well as for transgressing conventional meanings of gender. This queer alliance between camp and postmodernism has often been noted. Medhurst provocatively states that 'postmodernism is only heterosexuals catching up with camp' (Medhurst, 1991a, p. 206). It is indeed an easy leap from Babuscio's understanding of camp as signifying performance rather than existence, to Judith Butler's notion of gender signifying performance rather than identity. Just as Babuscio claims that the emphasis on style, surface and the spectacle results in incongruities between 'what a thing or person *is* to what it *looks* like' (Babuscio, 1984, p. 44), Judith Butler (1990) asserts that the stress on performativity allows us to see gender as enacting a set of discontinuous if not parodic performances. Thus, it also became an available notion for lesbians (see Graham, 1995). Both camp and postmodernism denaturalise femininity and masculinity.

It is significant that, in the 1990s, the notion of 'camp' is often replaced by the term 'queer'. Camp is historically more associated with the closeted homosexuality of the 1950s and only came to the surface in the 1960s and 1970s. Postmodernism of the 1980s and 1990s brought campy strategies into the mainstream. Now, lesbians and gay men identify their oppositional-reading strategies as 'queer'. Away from the notions of oppression and liberation of earlier gay and lesbian criticism, queerness is associated with the playful self-definition of a homosexuality in non-essentialist terms. Not unlike camp, but more self-assertive, queer readings are fully inflected with irony, transgressive gender parody and deconstructed subjectivities.

Conclusion

The diversity of contemporary feminist film theory reflects the variegated production of women's cinema of the 1990s. Women film-makers have increasingly conquered Hollywood. Several of them have been able to maintain a consistent production in diverse genres: comedy (Penny Marshall), romantic drama (Nora Ephron) and action movies (Kathryn Bigelow), to name just a few. This has also been the case for several women film-makers in Europe, such as Margarethe von Trotta (Germany), Diane Kurys (France), Claire Denis (France) and Marion Hänsel (Belgium). In a more non-commercial pocket of the market, there has been a significant increase in films made by lesbian, black and postcolonial directors: film-makers as diverse as Monika Treut and Patricia Rozema, Julie Dash and Ngozi Onwurah, Ann Hui and Clara Law. This decade has witnessed the popular success of feminist art films, such as *Orlando* by Sally Potter (1992), and the Oscar-winning films *The Piano*, a costume drama by Jane Campion (1993), and *Antonia's Line*, a matriarchal epic by Marleen Gorris (1995) (see case study). Dropping a few names and titles in no way does justice to the scale of women's cinema of this decade. It merely indicates a prolific diversity that resonates with film audiences in this decade of hybridity. The polyphony of voices, multiple points of view, and cinematic styles and genres, signify women's successful struggle for self-representation on the silver screen.

Selected Reading

Jacqueline Bobo, *Black Women as Cultural Readers*, New York, Columbia University Press, 1995.

Annette Kuhn, *Women's Pictures: Feminism and Cinema*, London, Routledge and Kegan Paul, 1982. Revised edition 1994.

Teresa de Lauretis, *Alice Doesn't: Feminism, Semiotics, Cinema*, Bloomington, Indiana University Press, 1984.

Anneke Smelik, *And the Mirror Cracked: Feminist Cinema and Film Theory*, London, Macmillan, 1998.

Morocco (USA 1930 *p.c* – Paramount; *d* – Josef von Sternberg)

For many feminist film critics, Josef von Sternberg's star vehicle for Marlene Dietrich (see Stars after sound, p. 123) has been the privileged example of the fetish image of woman in classic cinema. *Morocco* features Dietrich as the cabaret singer Amy Jolly, stranded in Morocco. In her first American movie, and in the many that would follow, the plot illustrates a repeated pattern in which the Dietrich character is caught between the desires of two men. Here, she must choose between wealthy European aristocrat La Bessière (Adolphe Menjou) and foreign legionnaire Tom Brown (Gary Cooper). Dietrich is the image of glamorous eroticism and perfectly chiselled beauty. Claire Johnston reads the fetishised image of Amy Jolly as an illustration of the absence of woman as woman in classic cinema. Woman is a sign, a spectacle, a fetish. For Johnston, the image of woman as a semiotic sign denies the opposition man/woman; the real opposition is male/non-male. This is illustrated by Dietrich's famous cross-dressing at the beginning. The masquerade signals the absence of man; the fetishised image merely indicates the exclusion and repression of women (Johnston, 1991, p. 26).

For Laura Mulvey (1989), too, Dietrich is the ultimate (Freudian) fetish in the cycle of Sternberg's films. In order to disavow the castration anxiety that the female figure evokes, she is turned into a fetish; a perfected object of beauty that is satisfying rather than threatening. In this respect, it is significant that Sternberg produces the perfect fetish by playing down the illusion of screen depth; the image of the fetishised woman and the screen space coalesce. In this kind of 'fetishistic scopophilia', the flawless icon of female beauty stops the flow of action and breaks down the controlling look of the male protagonist. The fetish object is displayed for the immediate gaze and enjoyment of the male spectator without the mediation of the male screen character. For example, at the end of *Morocco*, Tom Brown has already disappeared into the desert when Amy Jolly kicks off her gold sandals and walks after him into the Sahara. The erotic image of the fetishised woman is established in direct rapport with the spectator. The male hero, says Mulvey, does not know or see (Mulvey, 1989, pp. 22–3).

It is in this possible subversion of the male gaze that the female star can manipulate her image. Kaplan (1983) argues that Dietrich deliberately uses her body as spectacle. Her awareness of Sternberg's fascination with her image accounts for a displayed self-consciousness in her performance before the camera. According to Kaplan, this creates a tension in the image that, together with Dietrich's slightly ironic stance, makes the (female) spectator aware of her construction as fetish (Kaplan, 1983, p. 51). For

Marlene Dietrich's excessive femininity in Sternberg's *Morocco*

Mary Ann Doane (1991, p. 26), this use of the woman's own body as a disguise points to the masquerade; the self-conscious hyperbolisation of femininity. This excess of femininity is typical of the femme fatale. For Doane, too, the masquerade subverts the masculine structure of the look, in defamiliarising female iconography.

For Gaylyn Studlar (1988), the film expresses a masochistic mode of desire. In Sternberg's films, the masochistic subject is represented by a male character. In *Morocco*, Amy Jolly's repeated rejection and public humiliation of La Bessière points to his masochistic self-abnegation. Masochistic desire thrives on pain and La Bessière is indeed shown to relish the public moments of humiliation. The pleasurable humiliation is increased by the entry of the rival and it is no surprise that he helps Amy to find the man she loves, legionnaire Brown. Studlar reads the exquisite torture of the older, richer and higher-class man by the femme fatale (either a prostitute or a promiscuous woman) as a sustained attack on the symbolic father and phallic sexuality. At the end of the film, La Bessière is reduced to the position of a helpless and abandoned child.

Studlar argues that in the masochistic scenarios of Sternberg's films, sex roles and gender identities are confused. In *Morocco*, La Bessière is the top-hatted, tuxedoed suitor to Amy. While Amy undermines his symbolic masculinity and social status, she in turn becomes the top-hatted, tuxedoed suitor to Brown. Dietrich's cross-dressing is counterpointed by the feminised masculine beauty of Tom Brown. The feminisation of the femme fatale's object of desire is further emphasised by the active female gaze. It is Dietrich who singles out Brown in the nightclub where she sings and who looks him over with an appraising gaze. She throws him a flower, which he wears behind his ear. Studlar argues that Dietrich's active look undermines the notion that the male gaze is always one of control.

Marlene Dietrich's tantalising masculinisation added to her androgynous appeal. Andrea Weiss (1992) argued that her sexual ambiguity was embraced as a liberating image by lesbian spectators. Rumour and gossip had already been shared in the gay subculture as early as in the 1930s. Dietrich's rumoured lesbianism has even been exploited by Paramount's publicity slogan for the release of *Morocco*: 'Dietrich – the woman all women want to see'. In the cross-dressing scene, Amy Jolly performs a French song in a nightclub. She walks down into the audience looking at a woman at a table. She looks over her entire body, turns away and hesitates before looking at the woman again. Then she kisses the woman on her lips, takes her flower and gives it to Tom Brown in the audience. Amy Jolly inverts the heterosexual order of seducer and seduced, while her lesbian flirtation and her butch image make the scene even more subversive. However fleeting and transitory such moments may be in classic cinema, Dietrich's star persona allows the lesbian spectator a glimpse of homoerotic enjoyment.

ANNEKE SMELIK

Reassemblage (USA 1982 *p* – Jean-Paul Bourdier; *d* – Trinh T. Minh-ha)

Reassemblage is the first film by Vietnamese-American film-maker Trinh Minh-ha. On the surface, it is a documentary about Senegalese women. However, it can also be seen as a poetic impression of the daily life of women living and working in a village in Senegal; or as a self-reflexive study of the position of the documentary film-maker. The film is definitely an exercise in finding a new language to film the 'other'.

Trinh Minh-ha's work challenges First World feminism. Her focal point is the postcolonial female subject. Both in her writing and films, she explores questions of identity, authenticity and difference.

The focus of feminist film theory on a psychoanalytic understanding of difference as sexual difference has produced a dichotomy that does not allow for any understanding of the complexities of the many differences in women's lives. Within a racialised context, difference means essentially division, dismissal or even worse, elimination. Trinh Minh-ha dedicates her words and images to understanding difference, so as to be able to 'live fearlessly with and within difference(s)' (Trinh, 1989, p. 84). She also relies on post-structuralist philosophies of difference, notably Deleuze's nomadology, in order to explore the possibility of positive representations of difference; as something else than merely 'different-from'. She thus combines creative experimentation with theoretical sophistication.

Reassemblage is fully aware of the anthropological tradition in filming difference and its appropriation of the gaze of the radical other. It is this kind of cinema that the film defies. It provides the spectator with images of village life, singling out the women for close-up attention and concentrating on the rhythms of their daily activities – shucking corn, grinding grain, washing babies. Repetition of certain shots adds to the rhythm of the montage: the albino child clinging to his black mother, the rotting carcasses of animals.

Trinh Minh-ha breaks with tradition by experimenting with sound. Originally an ethno-musicologist (and still a composer), she has used music to create a contest between the image and the sound. The sound is asynchronous with the images, abruptly shifting from music, to voice-over, to silence in the same scene. Moreover, the voice-over is not 'the voice of God' of traditional documentary. Trinh Minh-ha herself speaks the commentary and critically reflects on her position as film-maker and on the anthropological recording method. She challenges the objectivity of the camera ('The best way to be neutral and objective is to copy reality in detail, giving different views from different angles'), flatly contradicting her ironical commentary in the images that are shown on the screen. In *Reassemblage*, Trinh Minh-ha struggles to find a way of approaching the African other. She refuses to speak for the other women, rather, she wants to speak nearby the Senegalese. Her self-reflexively critical voice unsettles not only the subject filmed, but also the filming subject.

Reassemblage can be seen as an example of the counter-cinema that Claire Johnston and Laura Mulvey advocated (see p. 492). The film challenges the illusionism and the conventions that deliver the impression of reality. However, the film deconstructs mainstream documentary rather than classic Hollywood, and therefore it deals with issues of the gaze in an altogether different context. The gaze here is not the male gaze that objectifies the woman, but the western gaze that tries to objectify the racial other. This gaze bestows difference upon the other. The issues are thus not centred on visual pleasure and voyeurism, but on conventions of seeing the other. Trinh Minh-ha suggests that one can never really 'see' the other. There is no direct translation possible that makes the radical other accessible or available. The images, which are often strangely framed, or jarringly edited, also suggest that there is no unmediated gaze at the other. Difference is fundamentally incommensurable and that is the source of its strength and fascination.

ANNEKE SMELIK

Antonia's Line/Antonia (Netherlands/Belgium/UK 1995 *p.c* – Antonia's Line/Bergen/Prime Time/Bard Entertainment/NPS/Eurimages/European Co-production Fund (UK); *d* – Marleen Gorris)

Marleen Gorris was the first woman director to win an Oscar for a feature film: the Academy Award for the Best Foreign Film for *Antonia's Line* in 1996. This is all the more remarkable because she is known as an outspoken feminist film-maker. Her first film, *A Question of Silence/De stilte rond Christine M.* (1982), won many prizes at festivals and became a classic feminist hit. The reception was, however, mixed, and many male critics condemned it for its radical feminism, as was the case with her second film, *Broken Mirrors/Gebroken spiegels* (1984).

Antonia's Line breaks away from the focus on women's oppression and male violence of Gorris's earlier films. It features the almost utopian history of a matriarchal family within a European country village. Yet, Gorris's particular style can still be recognised in many of her 'authorial signatures'. Humm (1997) therefore argues that Gorris should be viewed as a feminist auteur. Her authorship can be situated, for example, in the genre subversion, the camera direction, the representation of silence as woman's voice, the importance of female friendships, subtle lesbian inflections in the story and biblical references.

Antonia's Line is a film that reflects de Lauretis's call for a feminist cinema that is 'narrative and oedipal with a vengeance'. It is narrative, but without a male hero, and hence without the voyeuristic pleasures of the male gaze. It is oedipal in the sense that it is about a family, but instead of featuring the triangle of father, mother and child, the film establishes a line of mothers and daughters. The film opens with the old Antonia telling her great-granddaughter Sarah that today she will die. In its exploration of the epic genre, the film tells the story of Antonia's line. Upon her mother's death after the war, Antonia returns with her daughter Danielle to the village where she was born to take over the family farm. When Danielle expresses her wish for a child without a husband, Antonia takes her to town and mother and daughter choose a good-looking stud for impregnation. Danielle gives birth to daughter Therèse, who turns out to be a prodigy and a genius. Therèse, in her turn, becomes mother of the red-haired Sarah.

The establishment of a female genealogy without fathers (or sons, for that matter) is remarkable enough. In that sense, Antonia's family is truly matriarchal. The film's politics lie, furthermore, in the representation of what Silverman would call the homosexual–maternal fantasmatic. It is within the embrace of mutual love between mothers and daughters that the women can ruthlessly pursue their own desires. As their desires are at odds with patriarchy, they have to fight the bigotry of the village people and especially of the church. It is Antonia's wilful strength that enables women's autonomy for generations to come.

Female desire is represented in all of its diverse manifestations: Antonia's wish for independence, Danielle's quest for artistic creativity, Therèse's pursuit of knowledge and Sarah's curiosity about life in general. The life of the mind – mathematics, music, philosophy – is eroticised in the film. This is matched by different kinds of female desires, such as their friend Letta who wishes to procreate and produces thirteen children. The most moving moments of the film are, however, the scenes in which the women explore sexual desire. When Danielle meets the love of her life, Therèse's female teacher Lara, she sees the object of her desire in her mind's eye as the Venus of Botticelli. When Antonia is already a respected grandmother, she tells the farmer Bas that she will not give him her hand, but that she is willing to give him her body – on her conditions. After their first sexual encounter, the film cuts to branches of cherry blossom blowing in the wind. The film thus creates an unexpected link between an older woman's sexuality and the fertility of spring.

History told through the maternal line of mothers and daughters in Marlene Gorris's *Antonia's Line*

Antonia's Line certainly idealises the productive and reproductive power of the homosexual maternal community. It is an inclusive community of family and friends that transcends class, age and religion, where the lesbian, the mentally handicapped, the unmarried mother, the lonely and the weak, and even men, can find refuge. However, this idealisation does not mean that the women are immune to the violence of the world outside. They are confronted with sadistic incest and brutal rape. But together they find the strength to survive and to punish the culpable men.

One of the distinctive features of the film is the use of a disembodied female voice, revealed in the last scene as Sarah's. It is a poetic voice that recounts the passing of time and the cycle of life and death. The voice-over brings once more the female fantasmatic firmly within language and history; that is, within the symbolic.

ANNEKE SMELIK

QUEER THEORY AND NEW QUEER CINEMA

JACKIE STACEY

In his discussion of queer film theory, Ellis Hanson suggests that rather than being limited to a particular sexual identity or practice, the term 'queer' might be most fruitfully understood as referring to perverse desires, in the psychoanalytic sense of 'the odd, the uncanny, the undecidable' (Hanson, 1993, p. 137). Queer sexuality, he suggests, is a term best deployed to gesture towards 'that no-man's land beyond the heterosexual norm' (p. 138). Following Hanson, we might introduce the notion of queer cinema as that which explores the perverse and the deviant within the sexual domain, rather than as one that produces a reassuring space of positivity or a potential route through which those outside the heterosexual norm seek to win the tolerance or acceptance of wider audiences.

Hanson's specification of queer as designating undecidability offers a way around the problem of supplying an introductory definition, while simultaneously acknowledging that the term queer defies a neat synthesis. Indeed, part of the discursive force of the term has involved undoing existing conceptual categories of sexuality and undermining traditional notions of sexual identity. Like postmodernism, queer has struggled to keep open its own signification against academic imperatives towards conclusive definition. Queer has successfully evaded such conceptual closure and maintained some of the slipperiness of its original impetus – perhaps because it has always also belonged as much to film- and video-makers, festival programmers, journalists and political activists as to academics.

B. Ruby Rich's announcement of 'the new queer cinema' in 1992 generated a debate within film studies that has continued ever since. Rich's pinpointing of the emergence of New Queer Cinema both offered an indicative reading of the cumulative impact of this highly diverse work and predicted its potential to reconfigure the field of lesbian and gay film studies: 'Definitively breaking with older humanist approaches and the films and tapes that accompanied identity politics, these works are irreverent, energetic, alternately minimalist and excessive. Above all, they're full of pleasure' (Rich, 2004, p. 54).

Coinciding with the emergence of queer theory in the academy (an interdisciplinary, theoretical dialogue between post-structuralism and political accounts of 'perverse' sexualities) and with a theatrical and experimental AIDS activism

The flowering of new queer cinema in the 1990s included Gregg Araki's *The Living End*

beyond it, New Queer Cinema promised a generative space in which to combine academic and political agendas concerned with representing non-normative sexualities through audiovisual media. Significantly, it was the screening of new independent, queer work at international film festivals (including New York, San Francisco, Utah, Toronto, Amsterdam, Berlin and London) in the early 1990s that precipitated Rich's intervention. Engaging with concepts in queer theory and issues in AIDS activism, New Queer Cinema included work such as *Poison* (Todd Haynes, 1991), *Swoon* (Tom Kalin, 1992), *Tongues Untied* (Marlon Riggs, 1989), *Paris Is Burning* (Jennie Livingston, 1990), *The Living End* (Gregg Araki, 1992), *Edward II* (Derek Jarman, 1991) and *My Own Private Idaho* (Gus Van Sant, 1991) (Benshoff and Griffin, 2004, p. 11). For Rich, the breadth of this international presence at film festivals and its historical reach in terms of its inclusion of work by film- and video-makers of different generations constituted a significant moment of consolidation and potentiality:

> For one magical Saturday afternoon in Park City, there was a panel that traced a history: Derek Jarman at one end on the eve of his 50th birthday; and Sadie Benning at the other, just joining the age of consent. The world had changed enough that both of them could be there, with a host of cohorts in between. (Rich, 2004, p. 59)

In film studies, queer thus entered the arena through discussions of specific films and videos and often through an identification of their directors as queer practitioners. The emergence of New Queer Cinema was constituted through the combination of this new work, which, for Rich, announced a break with the past, and the simultaneous reconfiguration of the significance of existing work, which was now given a new genealogical frame. The newness of this work lay in what she saw as the convergence of deconstructive cinematic style, irreverent celebration of sexual perversities, fierce and vocal political protest and compelling theoretical innovation within the academy; the reconfigured existing cohort began to include film-makers such as Ulrike Ottinger, Richard Fung, Monica Treut, Sheila McLaughlin, Su Friedrich and Pedro Almodóvar. In an uneven and fractured way, queer has continued to constitute its subjects, drawing on the political and visual practices of many generations of marginal activists and independent practitioners.

Queer may have been associated with so-called high theory (post-structuralism, postmodernism and psychoanalysis) but it has rarely shed its political allegiance to social and cultural transformation. The use of the term in the early 1990s was taken to be emblematic of a new mood, a new sense of entitlement and a new defiance (Jagose, 1996). To be queer was to be passionate about your sexuality and your politics and to adopt an 'in your face' strategy or lifestyle that made no concessions to mainstream tastes and sensibilities. Queer saw itself as embracing perversity and diversity by establishing alliances between gays, lesbians, bisexuals, transgender people and some 'like-minded' (oppositional, perverse, outrageous?) heterosexuals. Indeed, it sought to blur the boundaries around and between such classifications and categories. In this sense, queer was thought of not so much as an identity, but as a discursive position open to all those opposing 'heteronormative sexualities' (Berlant and Warner, 1998). In this context, queer cinema defined itself very firmly as daring to take risks, to explore deviance and to look at the 'underbelly' of sexual desire. Films such as *She Must Be Seeing Things* (Sheila McLaughlin, 1987) and *Swoon* examined questions of violence, jealousy, power imbalances, possessiveness and betrayal within gay and lesbian relationships. Coming from the independent sector, these films used techniques from art cinema to explore deviant sexualities, while also relying on familiar narrative and generic strategies, albeit somewhat self-reflexively (see case study).

For those who embraced both its politics and its filmic aesthetics, New Queer Cinema offered a much-needed response to the widely rehearsed problems of 'positive images' and to the limits of the political strategy of greater lesbian and gay visibility (Russo, 1981; Dyer, 1977). New Queer Cinema was hailed as offering a direct challenge to what was seen as the humanist trap of lesbian and gay cinema of the 1970s and 1980s that appealed for acceptance through bids for normality, naturalness and common humanity. In contrast, New Queer Cinema opened up a dynamic set of theoretical, aesthetic and political issues: perhaps cinematic representations of desire and sexuality should be disturbing and unsettling; perhaps greater visibility is not a political solution but is a central part of a broader representational problematic about the illusory union of image, knowledge and identity; and perhaps any assumed stability or continuity within individual or collective sexualities abnegated the fractures and fissures of both sexual and political subjectivities (Muñoz, 1999; Benshoff and Griffin, 2004; Aaron, 2004). But to typify all lesbian and gay cinema before the queer turn as concerned with positive images, humanism and identity politics would be as misleading as to characterise the shift from lesbian and gay to queer through a linear progress narrative. For such an account obscures the many tensions and differences within the longer history of so-called lesbian and gay cinemas and ignores the many continuing aesthetic and political concerns across the two periods (see Dyer, 1990; Stacey and Street, 2007). As some queer theorists have argued, these categories (of lesbian/gay and queer) are often mutually informing rather than mutually exclusive (see Warner, 2000).

For some, the idea of queer cinema is so firmly rooted in the independent audiovisual sector that using the category to discuss mainstream cinema and television is anathema. Since queer found its impetus in independent film and video, many would see the inclusion within its critical remit of more conventional narrative films as a distortion only permitted by the ill-advised diluting of the category over time. However, mainstream cinema (and later television) has had its place in the development of queer screen studies as a field. As Rich's original article made clear, even Hollywood had its role to play in the emergence of queer cinema, if initially by default. She highlights the coincidence of the opening of Paul Verhoeven's *Basic Instinct* and Derek Jarman's *Edward II* in 1992 in New York, followed only days later by the prestigious New Directors/New Films Festival premiering of four new 'queer' films. For Rich, the ultimate paradox was that: '*Basic Instinct* was picketed by the self-righteous wing of the queer community (until dykes began to discover how much fun it was) while mainstream critics were busily impressed by the "queer new wave"' (Rich, 2004, p. 54).

The problem of holding open a radical space that is not tainted by commercial control or popular forms continues to be a crucial aspect of the politics of queer audiovisual cultures for some critics, but for others, claiming a space within mainstream film has always been part of the project of 'queering culture'. Within this framework, films such as *Bagdad Café* (Percy Adlon, 1987); *Ballad of Little Jo* (Maggie Greenwald, 1993); *The Adventures of Priscilla, Queen of the Desert* (Stephan Elliott, 1994); *Bound* (Andy and Larry Wachowski, 1996); *Boys Don't Cry* (Kimberly Peirce, 1999); *Far from Heaven* (Todd Haynes, 2002) and *Brokeback Mountain* (Ang Lee, 2005) all belong to the now more generalised category of queer cinema. For scholars such as Richard Dyer (2002), Alexander Doty (1993) or Andy Medhurst (1993), popular culture has always been of interest as a queer space as much for reasons of class politics (the refusal to condemn popular pleasures as necessarily conservative, or to elevate bourgeois representational practices associated with experimental or independent traditions to the site of radical intervention) as for sexual politics (the practice of reading beyond the heteronormativity of popular culture to the camp, homoerotic or homosocial pleasures that have always been central to its appeal). As Medhurst points out, often this 'beyond' is a short journey. For example, it is easy to see why the British classic *Brief Encounter* (David Lean, 1945), a film about forbidden love scripted by Noël Coward, entered gay subculture as an iconic reference point. Medhurst's reading of it through questions of queer biography and subcultural knowledge (Medhurst, 1991), queer film-maker Richard Kwietniowski's reworking of it as a gay romance, *Flames of Passion* (1989), and Dyer's 1993 monograph on the film, which is written through a thoroughly queer sensibility, combine to enact a queering of popular cinema that demonstrates the full potential of what it means for queer film scholars and practitioners to 'read against the grain'.

Power imbalances in Sheila McLaughlin's *She Must Be Seeing Things*

Although Ruby Rich decried the co-opting of the New Queer Cinema movement into 'just another niche market' by dominant culture by 1995 (Rich, 2000, p. 22), its impact has continued to be remarkably successful in the current, rather conservative, academic climate (see Bronski *et al.*, 2006). Queer film studies now constitutes a considerable body of work around which courses, conferences and publications are organised.

Selected Reading

Michele Aaron (ed.), *New Queer Cinema: A Critical Reader*, Edinburgh, Edinburgh University Press, 2004.

Harry Benshoff and Sean Griffin (eds), *Queer Cinema: The Film Reader*, London and New York, Routledge, 2004.

Jackie Stacey and Sarah Street (eds), *Queer Screen: A Screen Reader*, Oxford and New York, Routledge, 2007.

NEW QUEER CINEMA

Tom Kalin's *Swoon* (1992), shot in black and white, used a stylish noir aesthetic to trace the intimacies of a homosexual couple engaged in child abduction and homicide; Sheila McLaughlin's *She Must Be Seeing Things* (1987) drew on queer performance work to explore cinematic pleasures beyond the heterosexual gaze and to play with the meanings of forbidden (or certainly at that time unpopular) issues, such as the fluid boundary between lesbian and heterosexual desire, the pleasures of voyeurism and 'stalking', and the tensions of interracial romance. Despite their obvious differences, both films were in critical dialogue with dominant modes of cinema, through their own versions of art-house style. *She Must Be Seeing Things*, for example, included obtrusive formal self-reflexivity by incorporating a film-within-a-film that commented on the main narrative but that was essentially an avant-garde film being made by the main protagonist, inserted into an otherwise more linear narrative (see de Lauretis, 1991). The narrative premise of *Swoon* was inspired by Hitchcock's *Rope* (1948), creating an intertextual link with the earlier film by exploiting, and making explicitly queer, its murderous, pathological, homosexual subtext (see Wallace, 2000). If the films were disturbing, even shocking, to many lesbian and gay audiences, as well as to straight ones, they were clearly intended to be. Debates raged about their form and their content: did *Swoon*'s stylish mise en scène somehow aestheticise homosexual violence, and did the narrative inextricability of their desire from their intention to kill pathologise homosexuality (yet again)? Did *She Must Be Seeing Things* offer an uncritical set of voyeuristic spectatorial pleasures that legitimised female psychopathology, denying the specificity of lesbian desire, or did it, as Teresa de Lauretis (1991) argued, do precisely the opposite through its formal innovations?

JACKIE STACEY

TRANSNATIONAL FILM STUDIES

DINA IORDANOVA

Transnational film studies approaches the cycle of film production, dissemination and reception as a dynamic process that transcends national borders and reflects the mobility of human existence in the global age; it explores the narrative and stylistic features of films that come about as a result of this supranational cycle of film-making and reception.

The growing impact of globalisation and new multicultural realities was first registered in other disciplines. Benedict Anderson's idea of the nation as an imagined community triggered observations on the 'limiting imagination of national cinema' (Higson, 2001). Influences came from fields encapsulating 'practices and processes of cultural translation, transfer and adaptation' (Bergfelder, 2005, p. 315), such as comparative literature and translation studies (Chow, 1993; Moretti, 1999); cultural studies (Ang, 2001; Chambers, 1993; Chen, 1998); studies of postcoloniality and postmodernism (Bhabha, 1990; Gilroy, 1993; Hall, 1991; Jameson, 1992; Said, 1993); and the sociological study of globalisation (King, 1991; Sassen, 1998; Urry, 2002). The work of influential anthropologists scrutinising the dynamics of migrancy and transnational systems (Appadurai, 1996; Clifford, 1997; Hannerz, 1996; Ong, 1999) was instrumental in mobilising film scholars' views on transnationalism, and so were writings on race, ethnicity and transnational feminism (Anzaldúa, 1987; Grewal and Kaplan, 1994; Shohat, 1999). Scholarship exploring identity-building mechanisms enhanced by the workings of global media was also influential (Featherstone, 1991; Morley and Robins, 1995; Sinclair, Jacka and Cunningham, 1996; Wilson and Dissanayake, 1996).

After the end of the Cold War in the late 1980s, global migration and diasporic cultural consumption intensified, imposing a new understanding of transnational human interactions. Countries that used to be traditional sources of emigration were transformed by immigration; worlds that were unlikely to touch or collide now intersected and overlapped. The expanding universe of multicultural conviviality transcended strictly defined and discrete national frameworks. World cinema could no longer be treated as a mosaic of discrete cultural phenomena (see also National cinemas in the global era, p. 168). It was increasingly recognised that the localities of production were spatially disjointed and that audiences were scattered around the globe.

While radically subverting Hollywood's hegemony, transnational cinema studies differed in impetus from that of Third Cinema, which polemically challenged Eurocentric dominance

Turkish-German identities explored in Fatih Akin's *Head-On*

through alternative narratives and iconographies (see Third World and postcolonial cinema, p. 97). Where Shohat and Stam (1994) exposed imperialist agendas inherent in entrenched cross-cultural representations, transnational cinema studies tackled such issues by investigating the growing body of films that displaced western-centrism emerging from peripheral locations.

Studies that recognised the increasing migrancy among film-makers broached concepts of interstitiality and accented mode of production (Naficy, 2001) and intercultural cinema (Marks, 2000). The 'floating lives' project (Cunningham and Sinclair, 2001) offered a new dialectical model by developing a framework of transnational flows that encompassed the interactions between cinematic output, the ever-changing diasporas and their dynamic consumption patterns. New dimensions of cinephilia were investigated (Rosenbaum and Martin, 2003). Scholarship tackled the dynamics of worldwide distribution of Indian films (Kaur and Sinha, 2005) directed at a global audience of diasporic, non-resident Indians but equally popular in countries without a significant Indian diaspora (Eleftheriotis and Iordanova, 2006; Larkin, 1997), and looked at films that reflected the narrative of diasporic existence (Desai, 2004). Pioneering work was done in the area of Chinese transnational cinemas, encompassing the cinematic cultures of Taiwan, Hong Kong, Singapore and the far-flung Chinese diaspora (Berry and Farquhar, 2006; Dissanayake *et al.*, 1999; Lu, 1997; Marchetti, 2006). Other transnational traditions explored included transatlantic Hispanic cinemas, the cinemas of the Francophone diaspora, Arab, pan-African and Balkan cinema.

Led by the realisation that cinema was transnational from the early days, a strand of scholarship focused on early manifestations of the phenomenon (Bergfelder, 2006; Maltby and Higson, 1999; Street, 2002). With the growing importance of Internet distribution and cyberspace word-of-mouth publicity among virtual communities (and Chris Anderson's influential theory of the 'long tail', 2006), these vernacular but vibrant channels of transnational dissemination are likely to proliferate. Examples of transnational film-making include the diaspora-reliant cinemas of Palestine or Kurdistan, Turkish German cinema, black British cinema (Malik, 1996), French beur cinema (Tarr, 2005) or selected indigenous media production practices (Ginsburg *et al.*, 2002). A transnational mode of work is evident in the careers of artists who work both at home and in the diaspora – actors such as Hong Kong's Chow Yun-fat or Mexico's Gael García Bernal, and directors such as New York/Uganda-based Indian Mira Nair.

In recent years, transnational cinema has yielded works that foreground questions of place and passage and explore diasporic life, as well as concepts such as cosmopolitan and insular, global and local. It features a variety of locations, traditionally interpreted as dependent and subaltern. Its key themes are defined by a growing awareness of instability and change brought about by incessant journeying and border-crossing. This is compounded by the foregrounding of locations that signify isolation and marginality, or presuppose a context that allows for reflection on fragile, mutating identities; where the meanings of 'belonging' and 'return' are questioned; where concepts of 'centre' and 'periphery' are challenged and gradually taken over by lively interactions between peripheries that put the centre in parentheses; and where diasporas-in-the-making, itinerants and travellers subtly problematise hierarchical notions of place. Previously entrenched divisions dissolve, enabling new genres and forms of representation. In some cases, the more ethnically defined concept of diaspora that implies ethnic unity and spatial dispersal (and is often associated with exile and traumatic rupture) is abandoned in favour of a more optimistic vision of the ethnically diverse but spatially convergent global city (Ang, 2001). A new, culturally significant space has come into being, one that allows the members of the growing community of global migrants to overcome the brand-mark ethos of lost homelands and experience a meaningful and coherent existence, one in which place is perpetually transformed by movement.

Selected Reading

Stuart Cunningham and John Sinclair (eds), *Floating Lives: The Media and Asian Diasporas*, New York, Rowman and Littlefield, 2001.

Laura U. Marks, *The Skin of the Film: Intercultural Cinema, Embodiment, and the Senses*, Durham, NC, Duke University Press, 2000.

Hamid Naficy, *An Accented Cinema: Exilic and Diasporic Filmmaking*, Princeton, NJ, Princeton University Press, 2001.

Ella Shohat and Robert Stam (eds), *Multiculturalism, Postcoloniality, and Transnational Media*, New Brunswick, NJ, Rutgers University Press, 2003.

Floating Life (Australia 1996 *p.c* – Hibiscus Films; *d* – Clara Law)

Clara Law, a Macau-born Hong Kong director whose entire work is preoccupied with the issues of migration and hybridity, made *Floating Life* (the first Australian non-English-language film) shortly after she migrated to Australia from Hong Kong in 1995. In *Floating Life*, the members of the Chan family are shown dispersing all over the world – to Australia, Canada and Germany – in anticipation of the 1997 takeover of Hong Kong by China. The film deals with their efforts to settle and keep close in their new, dispersed mode of existence. Moving around brings disquieting experiences, but staying in one place is no longer possible. The transient, diasporic nature of Hong Kong creates a sense of urgency that sends the protagonists on voyages they are not sure they want to undertake. They appear lonely and insecure, as they cling to a bag of fragrant tea or a photograph of a village house – yet they take on the challenges of adjusting to their new 'floating' identities and soon rejoin their extended families gathering in cyberspace.

DINA IORDANOVA

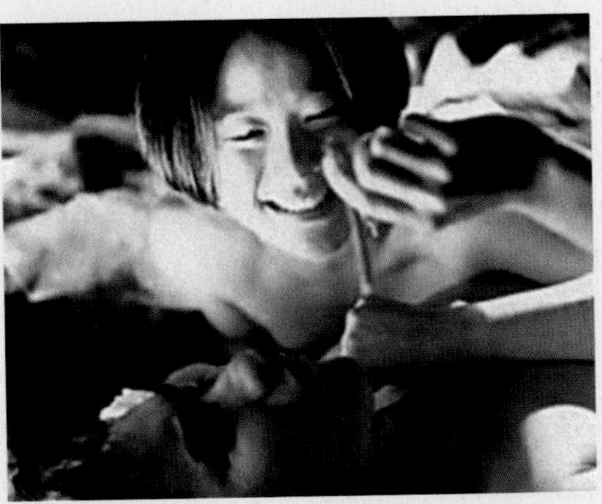

Lives disrupted by migration in Clara Law's *Floating Life*

STRUCTURALISM AND ITS AFTERMATHS

JOHN THOMPSON

An important strand of film theory could be said to have turned 'structuralist' in the 1970s. But what does 'structuralist' mean? The first thing to be clear about is that the structures involved are the structures of language. Structuralism derives from structural linguistics, which is first and foremost a method for dealing with phonemes (minimal sound units), morphemes (minimal meaning units) and sentences.

While obviously there is a 'lot of language around' in the cinema, even in the silent cinema, no one showed much interest in applying the insights of structural linguistics to the sentences on the soundtrack. Instead, the 'structuralist enterprise' is best thought of as the exploration, more or less systematic, of a series of analogies: what is *language like* about phenomenon x? For a period in the 1950s and 1960s in France, a number of leading intellectuals made brilliant use of that analogy to restructure their disciplines. In part, the influence of structuralism on anglophone film theory can be seen as fuelled by a kind of intellectual fandom: the French structuralist intellectuals were exciting writers, and it seemed natural to wish to bring that excitement across the Channel to reinvigorate writing on film.

However, the francophone thinkers who made a difference within film theory were not numerous. There was the grandfather of structuralism, Ferdinand de Saussure, whose posthumously published *Course in General Linguistics* (1916) initiated the structuralist 'mind-set'; then there were Roman Jakobson in linguistics; Claude Lévi-Strauss in anthropology; Jacques Lacan in psychoanalysis; Louis Althusser in Marxist philosophy; Roland Barthes in literary criticism; and Christian Metz in film studies proper. Someone frequently associated with structuralism, but who robustly repudiated the association, was historian Michel Foucault; and philosopher Jacques Derrida, in subjecting the thought of Saussure, Lévi-Strauss and Lacan to vigorous 'deconstruction', opened up a line of thought sometimes referred to as 'post-structuralist'.

But was 'structuralism' not always 'post-structuralism'? No doubt there was a certain 'scientistic' rhetoric about the structuralist enterprise at times. (Just as structural linguistics has allowed linguistics to turn itself into a science, so with structuralist anthropology, structuralist psychoanalysis, and so forth.) But in fact each of the major structuralist thinkers deployed the language analogy idiosyncratically, and each was perfectly willing to abandon the analogy whenever it began to get in the way of their work.

It should also be said that it was often not the most 'structuralist' side of these thinkers that attracted film theorists to them. A plausible way of characterising *Screen* theory of the 1970s is that it envisaged a four-way synthesis of linguistics, psychoanalysis, Marxism ('historical materialism') and a renewed literary criticism. (This once led David Bordwell, rather unflatteringly, to coin the phrase SLAB theory: Saussure, Lacan, Althusser, Barthes.) But it was not Lacan's formulation 'the unconscious is structured like a language' that was at the heart of his utilisation by film theory; and Althusser's intricate constructions around questions of ideology may in the end owe more to Nietzsche than to Saussure.

Structural linguistics: Ferdinand de Saussure

Saussure started his scholarly life as a brilliant student of historical linguistics, the study of language change. But, by the time he delivered the lecture course in Geneva that became his major work, he had formulated a very different picture of what was needed if theoretical linguistics were to move forward.

Four key oppositions structure Saussure's thought. (The preceding sentence, by the way, is a good example of 'structuralese': as we are about to see, the notion of opposition is central to the enterprise.) First, there is the opposition between the diachronic study of language and the synchronic study of language. At first, Saussure had specialised in the diachronic – in the study of how language changes across (dia) time (chronic). Subsequently, however, he was looking for a way of studying language as it existed at a particular point in time: how does one bit of the system 'go with' (syn) the other bits, at the present time or at a particular time in the past? A filmic example: the 'language' of current cinema is clearly different from the 'language' of early silent cinema – which is why the latter appears somehow foreign to us, until we watch enough silent films to 'learn the language'.

The notion of a 'system' of language relates to the second of Saussure's oppositions: that between *langue* and *parole*. In French, the former means roughly 'language', the latter 'speech', but Saussure bends ordinary usage a bit to make them fit his thought. *Parole* is an actual bit of utterance: the sound of conversation in a pub is the sound of *parole*, just as any particular bit of film would be, by analogy. But *langue* is a more abstract, more puzzling thing. It is the system, a synchronic totality, that is somehow shared by speakers of a language and that allows for comprehension. If I am sitting in a pub in Poland, I will hear as many *paroles* as if I am sitting in a pub in Paddington; but I will not be able to understand many of them, because I lack the *langue* that is Polish.

How is *langue* structured? According to Saussure, both at the level of the sounds of language (phonemes) and of the meanings of language (morphemes), the key idea is that structures are sets of oppositions. In English, it is just the difference between 'p' and 'b' that allows us to distinguish between 'pin', a sharp sewing tool, and 'bin', a receptacle for trash. And there is no possibility for grounding meaning, where language is concerned, in something else – in a 'natural' relationship between sound and meaning, for instance. The fact that other languages have completely different words for 'pin' and 'bin' shows this. Saussure expressed this fact by way of his third key opposition, that between signifier and signified. The signifier is, roughly, the sound-shape, while the signified is the meaning. Thus, a single signifier can, in the *langue* that is English, be brought into systematic relation with two signifieds (as 'bank' means both the boundary of a river and the place where one deposits money); or, in the case of nearly exact synonyms, a single meaning, or signified, can be expressed by two different signifiers. Saussure used the term 'sign' to express the unity of a signifier with a signified. Again, in the Polish pub, I come into contact

Dean Martin in Hawks's western *Rio Bravo*, which became a key text for structuralist critics

with a stream of signifiers, but, lacking the *langue*, I cannot process these as full signs, as signifier–signified units.

The fourth of Saussure's oppositions, syntagmatic versus paradigmatic (Saussure's own term for the latter was 'associative', but Jakobson's usage has prevailed), proposes a two-dimensional schema for locating the operations of difference within the stream of signs. The syntagmatic dimension of an utterance is the utterance itself, as made meaningful by 'one difference after another'. (In either Poland or Paddington, overindulgence in alcohol may lead to slurred speech, which is difficult to comprehend precisely because the normal differentials are lost.) More abstract is the paradigmatic dimension of an utterance. Here one must imagine, 'behind' each element of the utterance, the other possible elements that could fill that slot – or that could not. It is a fact about English that the substitution of 'p' for 't' in an 'in' context produces a viable English word, while the substitution of 'h' does not. A school of linguistics influential in the UK, Australia and Canada, systemic grammar, proposed a more direct terminology for this distinction: chain versus choice. Applied to film, 'chain' (the syntagmatic) would be the film itself as it unfolds, while 'choice' (the paradigmatic) would draw attention to what is 'there on screen' as meaningful through its contrast with what might have been there. (We see a close-up of a character, as part of the chain of the film; but part of the weight of the shot derives from our consciousness that other shot lengths would have been possible: how about a long shot? What difference would that difference make?)

Stepping back from the Saussurean oppositions in detail, we can see that they all bear on the reconstruction, in theory, of a shared 'something' that, at a given moment in time, allows there to be communication between a speaker and a hearer, or more generally an addresser and an addressee. Call that something '*langue*', or 'code', or (with linguist Noam Chomsky from the 1950s onwards) 'competence': the classic structuralist enterprise was to set out the rule system necessarily shared among members of the communicational community if its signs are to make interpersonal sense.

The early work of Christian Metz: applying Saussure

Christian Metz, whose academic formation was as a linguist, was in an excellent position to pioneer the exploration of the cinema-as-language analogy. He did so consciously as part of a reaction against the then dominant theoretical position of *Cahiers du cinéma*'s founder, André Bazin, to which we will return (see Bazin, p. 525).

Metz believed that the cinema should be regarded not as an automatic, 'objective' process of registration (the Bazinian position), but as a language: a means of communication that organises and encodes its raw material in accordance with a set of cultural conventions. He hoped to discover the rules that governed film language and to lay the groundwork for a semiotics of the cinema: a theory and taxonomy of film as a sign system. In doing so, he addressed two problems: that of determining where the artifice that renders cinema a language can be found; and that of isolating those features common to all films on which a systematic classification might be based.

The cinema: *langue* or *langage*?

This question, which forms the title of one of Metz's longest early essays (see Metz, 1974), distinguishes between two French words; although both can be translated into English as 'language', they designate slightly different concepts. *Langue* is spoken and written language in the restricted linguistic sense. *Langage* is a broader, generic term meaning any system of signs used for communication, including systems that may lack either the rigour (such as the Victorian 'language of flowers') or the subtlety (such as the language of computers, at least in the 1970s) of *langue* proper. To see cinema as *langage* is relatively uncontroversial and even commonplace: Bazin, for example, had no doubt that cinema was *langage*. To assimilate cinema to *langue* is more problematic – while being, of course, just what classic structuralism would be bound to attempt to do.

In addressing the question of whether cinema could be held to possess attributes analogous to verbal language, Metz applied criteria drawn from the work of the structural linguist André Martinet. According to Martinet, *langue* is distinguished from less systematic communicative modes by what he called its 'double articulation'. Any linguistic utterance can be analysed first into smaller individually meaningful components, known as *morphemes* or *monemes*, and second into the distinctive but not in themselves meaningful *phonemes* that each moneme or morpheme contains. Thus the utterance 'I like Ike' contains three monemes, and these monemes, as it happens, between them require the use of only three phonemes ('i', 'l', 'k'). The number of phonemes in a language is strictly limited (most natural languages have about 30 or 40), but because of the way language is articulated they can be used to generate an infinite number of possible utterances.

What makes the second articulation both possible and necessary is the arbitrary nature of the linguistic sign, the absence of a natural or analogical relationship between an object and the sign that stands for it. The cinema, however, is founded on the photographic resemblance between image and object. Whereas a new sentence in language is simply a new combination of a finite number of elements, each new film image is, strictly speaking, unique. It is also the case, Metz observed, that the cinema cannot be broken down into units smaller than the shot, and each shot is at least equivalent, in semantic content, to a whole sentence in language (not just a morpheme).

Metz concluded that there was no equivalent in the cinema of Martinet's second articulation (that between moneme and phoneme) and that even the first articulation (that between the sentence as a whole and its successive components) existed only at the level of the relations between large signifying units. Cinema therefore did not qualify as a *langue*, but it was a *langage*; more precisely it was a *langage d'art*, an expressive mode adapted to the communication of one-way messages. This did not mean that there was no scope for semiological analysis on the linguistic model, but it did imply that any such analysis could best be conducted not at the level of the shot but at the level of what he called the *grande syntagmatique*, the articulation of successions of shots into meaningful sequences.

The *grande syntagmatique*

It was in the elaboration of the notion of the *grande syntagmatique* that Metz found a reply to his first question about the artifice that qualifies the cinema as a language: the organisation of images into a narrative structure. Reality itself 'does not tell stories' – film can thus be considered as *langage* to the extent that it imposes a narrative logic upon the events it portrays.

The *grande syntagmatique* aimed to present a filmic syntax, to identify and classify the segments of narrative – the autonomous shot and seven kinds of longer sequences called 'syntagmas' – which, articulated together, produce the sequence of changing spaces over time that 'tells the story' of the film. Metz classified the segments according to a simple taxonomy of binary oppositions that, he hoped, would be exhaustive (see Metz, 1974, pp. 119–46). He believed that by charting the frequency of the various syntagmas in different films, it would be possible to describe their style with greater precision than before and to pinpoint changes in film language diachronically, over a historical period.

In spite of the many difficulties that Metz's proposed scheme quickly ran into, it remains an important landmark in the history of film theory. Devised (in 1966–7) at a moment when a need was felt for an alternative to auteurism, it initiated a series of attempts to find a rigorous methodology for dissecting films. Whatever its defects, it was the first and arguably to date the only major classification of narrative designed specifically for the cinema, whereas other structuralist and formalist analyses were conceived originally for other narrative media (myths, folk tales, novels). The general question it addresses – how is it possible that we so easily view as continuous, and continuously narrating, the succession of shots in classic narrative cinema – remains a valid one.

Metz himself moved on from the position taken up in his early essays. His desire to revise the *grande syntagmatique* was already evident in the copious errata and addenda sprinkled throughout the article when it was republished in *Essais sur la signification au cinéma* in 1968. Like many of his contemporaries, he regarded his research as work in progress rather than as a closed-off, definitive system. And his developing interest in psychoanalysis left him less interested in pursuing analogies between cinema and linguistic syntax than in exploring the cinema and dreamwork analogy – where, to be sure, still in a semi-structuralist idiom, 'dream syntax' and 'dream semantics', via the mechanisms of metaphor and metonymy, had their place (Metz, 1974). It may still be the case, however, that it was contingent rather than inevitable that neither Metz himself nor any other theorist at the time settled down to the task of 'debugging' the *grande syntagmatique*.

Criticisms of Metz

The *grande syntagmatique* was attacked from the start on a number of counts. Attacks took two forms: criticism of detail, and criticism of the project more generally.

Where detail was concerned, it turned out – and this was itself not an uninteresting finding – that applying Metz to the syntax of a particular film was harder and more problematic than should have been the case. Although the syntagmas appear to be clearly defined, in practice they are difficult to identify. The analyst is often confronted with a segment that either could fall into more than one of Metz's categories or does not seem to belong to any of them. Jack Daniel (1976) argues that a comparison of the successive versions of the system reveals it to be based on 'current observations' and that the impressive-looking diagram of 'successive dichotomies' is an unsuccessful attempt to impose a rigorous theoretical structure upon a random list of categories. The would-be analyst trying to apply Metz is also quickly confronted, as so often in cinema theory, by its visual bias: as suggested by the title '*grande syntagmatique* of the image track', the breakdown into syntagmas is dictated by the visual component of film. Difficulties arise where there is asynchronous or overlapping sound that does not match the division of images. The analysis of *Citizen Kane* (1941) in *Film Reader I* (1975) found this to be a major drawback.

These are the sorts of difficulties that the collaborative work of researchers in an area of study might well have been able to overcome. That no general will manifested itself along 'let's fix this!' lines is to be accounted for by the fact that a nervousness about the perceived reductive nature of the early Metzian project overall was rapidly felt. 'Do we want to be doing (only) this?' and 'Doesn't this restrict us to considering (only) a restricted group of films?' were questions quickly, perhaps too quickly, posed.

Metz had demarcated his study in a way that confined it to *denotative* rather than *connotative* meaning, as those terms were used by the linguist Louis Hjelmslev and in the semiotics of the early Roland Barthes (see Roland Barthes: the analysis of narrative, p. 517). Denotation, in the cinema, is the literal meaning of the spectacle; connotation encompasses all its allusive, symbolic meanings (Metz, 1974, p. 96). The artistic status of the cinema arguably resides in its connotative qualities, but it is, Metz argued, through the procedures of denotation that the cinema is *langage*. He hoped that eventually the semiotic model could be refined sufficiently to analyse both these strata and their interplay in producing meaning. (Indeed, the eventual Metzian 'psychoanalytic turn' could be seen as a move towards the analysis of connotation.) Meanwhile, however, it should confine itself in the first instance to the denotative level.

His critics found this proposal restrictive because of the way it confined narrative to what it is perceived to be by a rather literalist audience. His model deliberately remains on the overt level at which the film 'tells its story', excluding visual subtleties such as 'framing, camera movements and light "effects"', which he saw as belonging to the realm of connotation. The classical mise-en-scène analysis, which examines whether and how the story is underlined or (on occasions) undermined by connotative visual strategies, is absent from the Metzian system, banished by the decision to concentrate on relationships between shots rather than shot form. The system also excludes the possibility of multiple levels of narrative signification, where the deceptively calm surface of the film may conceal all kinds of undercurrents of repressed meanings. Finally, it excludes a theory of the interaction between film and viewer. It is the viewer, according to 'Notes towards a phenomenology of narrative' (1974), who perceives, recognises, defines narrative; on the contrary, argues more recent theory, it is the narrative that in part defines the viewer.

Another source of animus against Metz was his lack of interest in 'alternative cinemas'. The *grande syntagmatique* is designed for a specific type of film that could be broadly described as realist. Since each syntagma is defined by its logical, temporal and/or spatial relationship to the preceding and following ones, Metz's system presupposes that the film creates a consistent, self-enclosed fictional world. There is no provision for anti-realist juxtapositions of contradictory points of view (as in Godard's *Tout va bien*, 1972) or surrealist disruptions of traditional causality (as in Buñuel's *Un chien andalou*, 1928).

This bias was no accident. In Metz's view, the evolution of film language went hand in hand with the rise to ascendancy of the realist narrative film. 'It so happens that these (specifically cinematographic) procedures were perfected in the wake of the narrative endeavour . . . It was in a single movement that the cinema became narrative and took over some of the attributes of language' (Metz, 1974, pp. 95–6). Thus Metz found a solution for his second initial problem. The feature common to all films and on which an exhaustive classification of syntagmas could be based is, he posited, narrative – indeed, narrative and cinema are identified as one and the same. In his 1966 essay on 'The modern cinema and narrativity' (1974), he maintained that even the apparently anti-narrative films of the Nouvelle Vague could be assimilated into the narrative tradition. The 'other avant-garde', which, rather than experimenting with new modes of representation, works towards an abstract, non-representational aesthetic, was given short shrift by Metz, who deplored its 'gratuitous and anarchic images' and 'heterogeneous percussions' (Metz, 1974, p. 225).

A system that purports to be comprehensive but that can only account for a certain type of film is, on the face of it, in trouble. Moreover, later debates within British film criticism on the 'classic realist text' questioned the endorsement implicit in Metz's early work of the direction in which the cinema has developed (see The classic realist text, p. 519). How far, it has been asked, was the development of the narrative film as we now have it really inevitable? Should an analytic method that presents itself as neutral and descriptive, rather than prescriptive, support the domination of a single aesthetic? Especially one that has been claimed in the course of these debates to have a regressive, repressive ideological function?

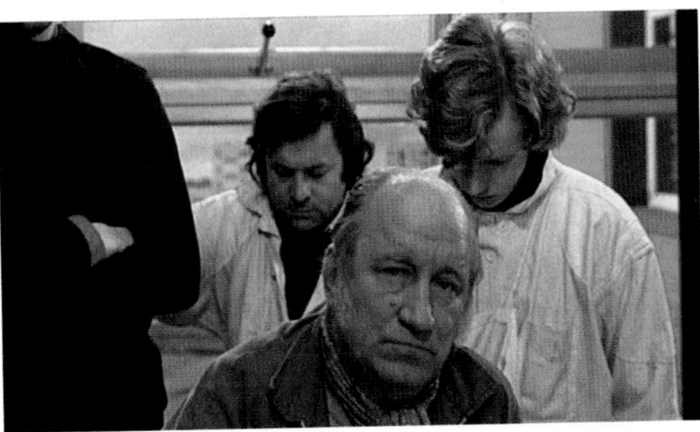

A challenge to structuralist analysis: Godard's *Tout va bien*

Still later, it is possible to feel that the 1970s reaction against the early, structuralist Metz involved accusing him of not doing everything, in a context in which the hope that everything could be done by a single (albeit complex) theory was still alive. Later, the move from structuralism to formalism was to involve a greater pluralism, a willingness to accept that one bit of the text, or one kind of text, may yield their secrets to an approach that other bits or genres resist. Questioning Metz's classic narrative bias was salutary, precisely because his analytical breakdown of classic narrative film syntax clarified what might be involved in the fight for other syntaxes. Equally, someone who wanted to pursue mise en scène analysis would hardly find the *grande syntagmatique* a barrier to doing so: different 'compartments of the text' are involved. And the same goes for someone who wanted to pursue ideological analysis.

Why read early Metz in the late 1990s? At the very least, it seems productive to approach the *Essais sur la signification au cinéma* as a heuristic device, an aid to learning. Applying the *grande syntagmatique* to individual films can both bring out how they work in mainstream cinema language terms and, on occasion, focus attention on their irregularities, ambiguities and unusual features. The possibility of a 'debugged' theory has since been raised in France and Germany. But the fate of Metz's initiative bears witness to how difficult, if not impossible, it is to carry a 'cinema as language' position through with rigour.

While the work of Metz was taken up as a demonstration of structuralism within an explicitly film studies context, even more intellectual exhilaration was felt by 1970s film scholars when they grappled with the powerful theoreticians whose own work made no reference to film at all (Lévi-Strauss) or only marginal reference to film (Barthes).

METZ

Adieu Philippine (France/Italy 1962 *p.c* – Unitec France/Alpha-Productions/Rome-Paris Films/Euro-International Films; *d* – Jacques Rozier)

The first attempts to develop a cinema semiotics operated at a general, theoretical level and seemed to exclude the detailed examination of individual texts. For this reason, the only example in Metz's first book of the structural analysis of a specific film occupies a unique place both within the evolution of his thought and within the history of cinema semiotics as a whole. Though aware that this work was then (1967) still very much in its infancy, Metz believed that the part of his programme concerned with narrative was 'sufficiently far advanced to be applied to the image track of an entire film' and that it was possible to make a '*complete* inventory' (Metz's emphasis) using the eight basic categories outlined in the *grande syntagmatique* (Metz, 1974, p. 177).

For the early Metz, narrative realism was the essence of the cinema, and even the apparent innovations of the Nouvelle Vague were for him no exception, despite some self-acknowledged difficulties with Godard's *Pierrot le fou* (1965) (Metz, 1974, pp. 217–19). *Adieu Philippine*, chosen, it seems, largely for reasons of personal taste and the availability of a shooting script and print, is described as a 'realist' film that presents few problems to a syntagmatic analysis. However, closer inspection reveals a number of points of resistance at which the film strains against the categories imposed on it by the *grande syntagmatique*. For example, the first syntagma is demarcated from the second by nothing more than Metz's imperial definition of the 'real action' of the film as 'individualised characters pursuing a definite goal' (Metz, 1974, p. 150) – a definition that is by no means self-evident. Similarly, the autonomous shot (syntagma 4) of Michel (Jean-Claude Aimini) sitting idle in the television studio is identified as a directorial comment on the action ('this interpolative status . . . is "real" and not subjective') and thus defined as a 'displaced diegetic insert' (Metz, 1974, p. 153). But the shot could be a subjective insert, representing the thoughts of either Michel (a three-quarter profile shot of him precedes it) or the two girls (a shot of them succeeds it).

Apparently a minor quibble, this illustrates a significant feature of Metz's analysis: the way in which he endows a sequence with a meaning that is deliberately held in abeyance by the film itself. The *grande syntagmatique* attempts to assimilate *Adieu Philippine* to the realist narrative tradition at the expense of contradictions that can be found in Rozier's film and also, perhaps, in even the most 'classic' conventional text.

Metz saw the film as primarily a documentary on modern youth. But Rozier's initial idea was to trace the history of a young man conscripted to fight in Algeria (1960–2 was the period of the Franco-Algerian war) and to show the 'disturbed side of his character'. Public pressures against such reference to the Algerian question (witness the banning of Godard's 1960 film *The Little Soldier/Le Petit soldat* by the French censor board and the minister of information) dictated that the serious theme be masked by employing the structure of a musical comedy romance (see Zand, 1963). A reading of *Adieu Philippine* that aims to pull out this political strand would need to point to the fact that Michel's departure for Algeria overarches the narrative (he discloses at the airfield that he is to be called up in a couple of months, and the film ends as he leaves for the army), as well as to the characters' growing malaise (is it only due to romantic rivalry?) and the eloquent silences: note (in the airfield sequence) Michel's poignantly unanswered questions to the girls reading his palm about where his imminent 'long journey' will take him ('où ça?', not translated in the subtitles) and what his life-line reveals. Metz's analysis, in contrast, collapses this scene together with the two preceding episodes, 'for alone they are treated too allusively for them to acquire any autonomy', under the general rubric of 'Sunday outing' (Metz, 1974, p. 153). The effect is to privilege an account of the film as a documentary about 'youth and its flirtations' at the expense of the other meanings (for instance, the shadow of Algeria) that are struggling to emerge and are as crucial as the things that are overtly said.

The point here is not to impose a 'more correct' reading, but to show that Metz's apparently objective, unimpeachable analysis and the conclusions he draws from it about the work's thematic concerns are the result of a series of choices that remain unacknowledged (probably even unconscious), laying early structural analyses such as this open to charges of presenting ideologically loaded readings in the guise of impartial science. Rather than passively discerning and describing the immanent and 'true' meaning, it is objected, critical enquiry actively produces a meaning in a process of interaction with the artistic text, and should therefore openly discuss, reflect upon and, if necessary, even call into question its own operations.

SHEILA JOHNSTON

All Is Well/Tout va bien (France/Italy 1972 *p.c* – Anouchka Films/Vicco Films (Paris)/Empire Films (Rome); *d* – Jean-Luc Godard/Jean-Pierre Gorin)

Tout va bien represents an attempt by Godard/Gorin to develop an alternative strategy of political film-making that would be more accessible than the resolutely anti-narrative Maoist 'Dziga-Vertov' films such as *Le Vent d'est* (1969). The decision to appropriate elements of 'mainstream' cinema such as international stars (Jane Fonda, Yves Montand) and a clearly defined story (preferably with love interest) was in some respects a major compromise dictated by the dissolution of a militant audience in the aftermath of May 1968 (see MacCabe, 1980, pp. 66–7). The film's ironic opening and closing sequences lay out the concessions enforced by the need to make the film commercially attractive, and the movie concludes with a caption 'a tale for the foolish one who still needs it', which seems to question the indispensability of narrative.

Tout va bien is on one level a film about the conditions of political film-making and aims to problematise the sections in which the narrative is centred on the intellectual, middle-class couple. But Andrew Britton (1976) succeeds, by downplaying the importance of the framing sequences, in producing a reading that runs directly counter to the director's intentions. Britton sees the main concerns of the film as played out in the confrontation between Susan/Fonda and Jacques/Montand, which focuses on the psychological development of 'two human individuals', the crisis in their personal relationship and their progress towards greater political consciousness (see also MacCabe, 1980, pp. 70–3).

This is where the value of a syntagmatic analysis comes in. The discipline of analysis foregrounds the fact that the central sections dealing with Susan, Jacques and the strike cannot be detached, as in Britton's account, from the overall structure of the film. Meanwhile, the difficulty of demarcating and defining syntagmas brings out the extent to which the film deviates from the conventions of classic narrative (see Thompson, 1976). More particularly, it demonstrates the way in which the film disrupts the traditional alignments of sound and image, appearance and reality – alignments that are assumed by Metz's *grande syntagmatique*. Note, for example, the indeterminate status of the 'radical song' sung by the workers, which could be classed as non-diegetic, but is allowed equal status with the framing interview sequences by Thompson, who sees the two stances taken up by the worker (submission and defiance) as two 'alternatives cut in together', neither of which is privileged as 'reality'.

Analysis of the film using Metz's categories can, therefore, be used to open up two sets of questions: first, to debate whether the use of narrative compromises the film or whether the text successfully resists being absorbed into the realist narrative tradition; and second, to reflect upon the usefulness of the *grande syntagmatique* itself.

SHEILA JOHNSTON

Claude Lévi-Strauss: the structural study of myth

Claude Lévi-Strauss writes as an anthropologist. The project of much of his work is to discover a hidden logic behind aspects of the life of traditional (so-called 'primitive' or 'savage') societies. His early work was devoted to demonstrating the elaborate logic of the rules governing marriage and kinship relationships; later he turned to the study of myth, using as his corpus the tales of the American Indian cultures of South America, and it is this work that proved influential within film theory, either directly or (because he 'aroused excitement among many different brands of intellectual'; Leach, 1974, pp. 8–9) indirectly through other disciplines (notably, the particular version of psychoanalysis that has become entrenched in film studies drawing on the work of Jacques Lacan that derives from Lévi-Strauss in certain key respects).

At first sight, the myths studied by Lévi-Strauss appear rambling and arbitrary, and their surface themes seem to have little in common with the subject matter of contemporary western narratives. Yet, he believed, they can be shown to be driven by an internal dynamic of formidable formal power, while, at this deeper level, their concerns are not dissimilar to those of our own culture.

Mythological systems, for Lévi-Strauss, have crucial similarities to language systems. They operate according to a set of codes and conventions: as in Saussure's model of language, each individual utterance (*parole*), in this case each single version of a myth, conforms to the overall symbolic system (*langue*), the language or group of myths and all the rules that govern its permutations. Just as the language of a community binds its members together, so does myth; just as learning the language of its community represents for the child, moving from infancy (from the Latin *infans*, speechless) into speech, a process of integration into the social group, so are 'the novices of the society who hear the myths for the first time . . . being indoctrinated by the bearers of tradition' (Leach, 1974, p. 59). In order to understand these myths, it is necessary to learn the grammar of their language. By comparing a number of different versions, the mythographer finds an underlying system governing the differences. This system can then be related to the society in which the myths are functional: the bizarre dramatis personae of myths, which may bring together plants, animals, gods and/or human figures, function as symbols of the tribal subgroups and the power relations between them; similarly, the narrative events illustrate tribal beliefs and taboos.

Lévi-Strauss took what was in the end, after the wonderful ingenuity of his formal analyses, a functionalist view of myth: myths 'express unconscious wishes which are somehow inconsistent with conscious experience . . . The hidden message is concerned with the resolution of unwelcome contradictions' (Leach, 1974, pp. 57–8). The embellishments, digressions and repetitions of the narrative all help to disguise these. This sense of a disguised logic of myth rendered Lévi-Strauss's approach appealing to intellectuals of the left interested in the analysis of contemporary ideology: the aim of a structural analysis, it might seem, would be a 'demythologising', stripping away the camouflage and laying the contradictions bare. There was also an appeal to those persuaded by the psychoanalytic account of symptomatic repetition-compulsion: if we assume that the purpose of a myth is to embody contradictions while repressing them from its surface, it is only by attending to their compulsive recurrence (via the juxtaposing of as many variants as possible) that we force it to yield up its meaning.

Lévi-Strauss and film culture

Lévi-Strauss's name was initially linked with the moment in British film theory known as auteur structuralism, a phrase first used by the late Charles Eckert (1973). The attempt to connect

Lévi-Strauss with an auteurist approach might seem curious given that a central premise of his work is that myths have no single creative source: this indeed is what allows him to consider myth as a collective cultural phenomenon. He claims, in a celebrated and much-quoted passage, to demonstrate

> not how men think in myths, but how myths operate [*se pensent* – literally, 'think themselves'] in men's minds without their being aware of the fact. And . . . it would perhaps be better to go further and, disregarding the thinking subject completely, proceed as if the thinking process were taking place in the myths, in their reflection upon themselves and their interrelation. (Lévi-Strauss, 1970, p. 12)

Here we see the usual strategic question that is always raised when a theory about x is applied to y: is it more productive to insist on the specificity of realm x, to see realm x and realm y as crucially similar, or to use the partial similarity of the realms as a tool with which to explore their differences? There are obvious differences between the orally transmitted narratives of primitive tribes and the cultural products of an advanced industrial society, and Lévi-Strauss's own project was precisely to illuminate those differences with an animus – some would say a nostalgia – in favour of the former. The myths he analyses are very much not products of a capitalist culture industry, and there is a poignancy about their only-too-likely vanishing once the television sets arrive. On the other hand, the formal tools used to treat one myth as a transformation of another might perfectly well lend themselves to the treatment of one film as a transformation of another, and thus feed either an auteurist focus on how a 'strong director' develops his own 'mythology' (clearly a tempting strategy when considering figures such as Ford, Hawks, Lang or Hitchcock) or a more institutional focus on the groupings of films that emerge when one takes the industrial and collective nature of their production fully seriously. Thus, an auteur structuralist in the early 1970s such as Peter Wollen could take from Lévi-Strauss the emphasis on recurrences within an oeuvre operating without the author's awareness of the fact (seeing the director as an 'unconscious catalyst', synthesising contradictory elements into an 'unintended meaning'; Wollen, 1972, pp. 167–8) while still differing from the anthropologist in identifying a kind of dominant voice, or 'voice beneath the voice', as that of an individual auteur. On the other hand, Charles Eckert, taking from Lévi-Strauss the emphasis on the collective, communal nature of myth, could propose as a suitable object of a structuralist analysis not a group of films sharing the same auteur signature, but 'communal blocks' selected on the basis of studio, production unit, movement or genre (Eckert, 1973, p. 49). And a sceptic such as Brian Henderson could retort that such a 'non-auteurist structuralism' (Henderson, 1973, p. 32) still blurred the question of whether films could properly be considered as myths, whatever their organising principle (see also Auteur structuralism under attack, p. 454).

Will Wright's book on the western, *Sixguns and Society* (1975), remains the one full-length study of the cinema to take Lévi-Strauss's work as its main 'idea and inspiration' (Wright, 1975, p. 16). For Wright, there is no doubt that 'the western, though located in a modern industrial society, is as much a myth as the tribal myths of the anthropologist' (Wright, 1975, p. 187). He sees it as performing a mythic function: disseminating 'simple and recognisable meanings which reinforce rather than challenge social understanding'. Wright claims that 'the structure of myth corresponds to the conceptual needs of social and self-understanding required by the dominant social institutions of that period', tracing a direct link between economic changes over some four decades of American history and transformations in the narrative structure of westerns (see The western, p. 378). Various criticisms of Wright's methodology have been offered, but at least for some readers the problem with his work is precisely the straightforwardness with which he proposes to match changes in myth structure with changes in social structure: in Lévi-Strauss, and in structuralism generally, the structures of language and of other language-like systems are granted considerably more autonomy than that. A general argument can be offered here: if changes in the western match changes in American history, and the latter is, after all, a single 'thing', then changes in all other Hollywood genres should equally be able to be shown to match the historical changes – a strong, and on the face of it an implausible, claim.

The continuing influence of Lévi-Strauss on film studies lies less in the possibility of making wholesale application of his mythographic method to a corpus of films (however that corpus is established) than in drawing some lessons from his structuralist habit of thought. Lévi-Strauss takes his myths apart, so to speak, by looking at their thematic material as involving sets of oppositions, just as the sound system of language does. A key opposition in the first volume of *Mythologiques* (1970), for instance, turns out to be that between raw food and cooked food. By the same token, a key opposition within the western genre has long been recognised to be that between 'the wilderness' (wild space) and 'the garden' (domestic space). The deployment of this opposition and a few more (masculine/feminine, illiterate/literate, lawlessness/legislation) can make the material of such a western as John Ford's *The Man Who Shot Liberty Valance* (1962) yield many unsuspected riches.

PROPP

To Have and Have Not (USA 1944 *p.c* – Warner Bros.; *d* – Howard Hawks)

Hawks's films, which in Robin Wood's view exhibit 'a continual tendency . . . to move towards myth' and whose figures are, he argues, elaborations on basic archetypes (Wood, 1968, pp. 26 ff.), could be used to illuminate Propp's approach to characterisation.

Frenchy (Marcel Dalio) is clearly a would-be dispatcher and 'approaches the hero with a request' three or four times. Harry Morgan (Humphrey Bogart) is, for Wood (1968, p. 27), the vessel of 'a certain heroic ideal'; here, however, his 'heroic attributes', in particular his extreme individualism, are posed as a problem. Acting purely for oneself, in the style of the fairytale prince, is no longer self-evidently heroic, and becomes redefined by the historical context (it is worth noting that some critics see Morgan's hesitation as a metaphor for America's isolationism in the first years of World War II).

The villains are soon unmasked: Johnson, the minor villain, 'causes harm or injury' (the attempt to cheat Morgan) on a purely private level, and his displacement early in the film by the main villain in the bulky personage of Captain Renard (Dan Seymour) signals the progressive compounding of personal conflicts by political ones.

The princess is harder to identify. Molly Haskell (1974) argues that Slim is not simply a 'sought-for' person but also a helper ('the peer comrade'), quoting Hawks's intention to make her 'a little more insolent' than Morgan/Bogart. Interestingly, her 'sought-for' status is shared, on another level, with the Free French. Hélène de Brusac's (Dolores Moran) resemblance to Slim (Lauren Bacall) in physique and dress is a kind of doubling. Robin Wood (1973, p. 34) suggests that the splitting of the female lead enables Hawks to hold apart the two narrative strands of love interest and the need for political commitment. In structural terms, it could be argued that it is only the presence of Hélène that releases Slim from a straightforward (and more passive) 'princess' role. This could perhaps be an opportunity to examine the 'spheres of action' open to women in the classical narrative cinema. How many of Propp's seven basic roles are gender specific?

Though Propp anticipated that a single figure could occupy several spheres of action, or conversely, that several figures might share the same one (Propp, 1968, pp. 80–1), Fell complains that the splintering of functions in Hawks's films resists Proppian analysis: 'When personae commit human mitosis and divide into separate personalities, they muddle the conventional formulae by developing relationships with each other' (Fell, 1977, p. 27). He also tends to focus on details such as spittoons or the location of hotel rooms, which seems to miss Propp's point that such features are surface variables peripheral to the basic narrative structure. This suggests that certain self-styled 'structuralist' criticism takes over only the superficial trappings (terminology; impressive-looking diagrams) of the methodology it claims to employ.

SHEILA JOHNSTON

Kiss Me Deadly (USA 1955 *p.c* – Parklane Pictures; *d* – Robert Aldrich)

In his Proppian analysis of this film, Fell (1977) claims that, like its source, a novel of the same name by Mickey Spillane, it is a crude, routinely conventional text. Other critics, however, have been struck by its formalistic visual style, and Claude Chabrol's review for *Cahiers du cinéma* (1956) puts forward an auteurist reading of the movie as a silk purse brilliantly created by the director out of 'the worst, most lamentable . . . the most nauseous product of the genre fallen into putrefaction'. Stylised film noir conventions are much in evidence (see Silver, 1975), as, for example, in the fragmented montage of the pre-credit sequence, extreme camera angles and the breaks of the 180° rule. Fell argues that the use of the devices remains strictly within the bounds of standardised formulae, while for other critics, it veers towards an excess that, in the view of one of them, turns *Kiss Me Deadly* into a 'purely formal film . . . (of) terrible beauty' (Durgnat, 1962).

Fell's moralistic condemnation of the hero (or anti-hero) as 'sadistic, manipulative, brutishly suspicious and loutishly vulgar' is also open to debate. In Proppian terms, Mike Hammer might more suitably be considered as a character-function in the 'hard-boiled' detective genre. Durgnat (1962) describes Aldrich's women as androgynous, forceful, threatening, and Hammer as 'passive, sardonic and frigidly resistant'. This sexual ambiguity is interesting in relation to Fell's suggestion that Propp's schema assumes stereotypical role-playing (sexual or otherwise) and breaks down where this is not present.

The first eight minutes of the film are useful in discussion of Propp's opening functions. The customary 'initial situation' of his tales, the state of equilibrium whose disruption and restoration propel the Proppian narrative, appears to be missing. How right is Fell in seeing the first function as 'the hero leaves home'? Is Propp's schema, centred as it is on the home and the family, inappropriate to deal with the 'absent family of film noir'? (see Harvey, 1978).

Fell argues that the thriller/detective genre, with its theme of the quest and 'energetic, visibly active plots' is particularly suitable for a morphological analysis. In the light of the above comments, it could be considered whether the noir thriller lacks the requisite stability and containment. More generally, how correct are 'Proppian' critics such as Fell (1977) and Erens (1977) in pointing to the potential of his method as a means of inter- and trans-generic comparisons? Are there certain genres that strain against his categories?

SHEILA JOHNSTON

Roland Barthes: the analysis of narrative

Roland Barthes's *S/Z*, first published in France in 1970 and translated into English in 1974, was to prove to be of the greatest importance not only in its home field of literary studies but as a model for film theory's engagement with textual analysis and with questions of the relationship between reader and text.

The narrative dissected by Barthes in *S/Z* – a novella, *Sarrasine*, written in 1830 by Honoré de Balzac – is proposed as an example of a realist text. Traditionally identified with the creation of a plausible and familiar world, realism is defined by Barthes in rather broader terms. Realist texts, in his view, make up the greater part of western literature, and *Sarrasine* is a realist text, even if its unholy cast of degenerate aristocrats and *demi-mondaines* and its improbably melodramatic narrative hardly seem straightforwardly the stuff of realism.

The common-sense equation of realism with plausibility is discounted in *S/Z*. Rather than assessing the credibility of Balzac's worldview, Barthes traces from a post-structuralist perspective a gradual and cumulative structuring process. The 'texture' of the realist text is, for him, created by the interweaving of different codes, each less important in itself than for the way in which they are combined. His 'slow-motion' reading of *Sarrasine* aims to show how the narrative is put together.

Clearly, this relationship between realism and narrative is quite different from that conceived by André Bazin, who saw film as a neutral medium for recording phenomena, and viewed with suspicion any attempt to organise and interpret what was for him a fundamentally ambiguous world. S/Z takes the opposite view: that highly organised narrative is an ingredient essential to the impression of realism. For Barthes, reality itself is not something passively revealed or reflected in art, but an impression constructed with care and artifice.

The point of reference of the realist text is not some independently existing 'real world'. Instead, the realist text is seen as involving the convergence of two sets of relations. On one hand, the work is subject to its own tight internal logic, its intra-textual economy. Characters act consistently; the narrative 'obeys a principle of non-contradiction' even if temporary snares may be set for the reader (S/Z, p. 156); actions follow predictable consequences so that, for instance, the disclosure that a character is asleep presupposes that at some future state she will wake up (see the code of actions, or proairetic code, S/Z, p. 18); and in general, 'everything holds together' (S/Z, pp. 181–2), that is, every detail, every action will play some – preferably more than one – functional role in the unfolding of the narrative, though ideally this functionality should not be too obvious (S/Z, pp. 22–3). Crucially, all the main enigmas posed in the course of the story must be resolved by the end.

On the other hand, the work depends on a set of external relationships, its position within a grid of other cultural texts: its intertextuality. Realism, Barthes argues, 'consists not in copying the real, but in copying a depicted copy of the real' (S/Z, pp. 54–6). In *Sarrasine*, for example, Marianina's marvellous beauty can only be defined in terms, not of some unmediated ultimate beauty, but of another cultural representation of it – 'the fabled imagination of the Eastern poets' (S/Z, pp. 32–4). The text convinces by being in harmony with, drawing on the credit of, other texts.

This definition of realism in terms of a work's formal operations rather than its subject matter leads Barthes into a distinction between the realist and the modernist text. The writerly (*scriptible*) text is modernist, non-representational, bereft of 'a narrative structure, a grammar or a logic', refusing definitive interpretation, opening up endless possibilities of meaning. The readerly (*lisible*) text is the other pole of the opposition: realist, representational, pre-eminently narrative, offering up only one, unequivocal meaning (S/Z, pp. 3–7). The 'writerly' and the 'readerly' should be seen as the notional extremes of a spectrum, with real texts somewhere between the extremes. *Sarrasine* would at first seem to fall near the readerly end of the spectrum, but, given the breakdown of meaning at important moments in the story, and Balzac's 'excessive' use of intertextuality, it does not succeed in suppressing the artifice deployed in its own production. It can be celebrated as an imperfectly realist text, writerly enough to make a lazy and passive reading of itself difficult.

Reader/viewer and text

Part of the project of S/Z was to argue for the emancipation of readers from the role of passive consumers currently assigned them by the 'culture industry'. This, Barthes believed, had not always been the reader's fate: it is the product of a division of labour and commodification of art peculiar to the development of capitalism. This division of labour is not thereby inevitable. Barthes recalled in retrospect that 'what I tried to begin in S/Z was a kind of identification of the notions of writing and reading: I wanted to squash the two together' (Heath, 1971, p. 47). Rather than humbly, scrupulously attending to the text in order to discern its 'singular, theological meaning' (theology being historically the field in which 'getting right' the one true meaning of the sacred text has been most assiduously, at times murderously, pursued), the reader/viewer should take up a less reverent attitude, seeking to change it by contributing to the process in which new meanings are generated: 'a form of work . . . a labour of language' (S/Z, pp. 10–11). Which is not to say that this active reader is 'free' to change the text at will: the relationship between reader and text is a dialectical one. Not only does the reader act upon, 'produce' the text, but equally it acts upon, 'produces' them. In the same way that the text is not a pregiven, self-sufficient entity but an unstable, multiply determined and ever-developing process, so too, the argument runs, is the person who reads or views it.

This is an attractive picture, since it affords the text an important but not oppressive role in the lives of its reader/viewer. One of the types of semiotic object that contributes to the formation of the human psyche is the artistic text. Each time we read a novel or view a film, we are perhaps, if only in a tiny way, reinforced (or, as the case may be, challenged) in our secure feeling of personal identity and all the preconceptions and prejudices that go with it. And each time we encounter the text, it cannot help but be ours.

Questions of method

S/Z is a work of system that at the same time is self-confidently and programmatically unsystematic. The minimal units into which it segments the text are determined as 'a matter of convenience' (S/Z, pp. 13–14: compare, for instance, the lengthy deliberations of Metz on precisely how to establish the minimal unit in a film). It claims to provide neither an exhaustive reading of *Sarrasine* nor a universal narrative structure. Its strategies are in sharp contrast to initial attempts by structuralist critics to anatomise the operations of narrative and other social sign systems. Their aim had been to develop exhaustive and immutable schemas. Such attempts to found a scientific poetics may have been necessary in order to break with traditional criticism; by 1970, however, the problems with this approach were becoming apparent. (Metz's *grande syntagmatique* and its difficulties provide an example of this; see p. 512.) The notion that culturally determined sign systems could be explained by an Olympian observer in a neutral metalanguage, supposedly immune from those very determinants, collapsed.

In his 1966 'Introduction to the structural analysis of narratives', Barthes had attempted to fashion 'a single descriptive tool', a hypothetical model that could be applied to 'different narrative species' in 'their historical, geographical and cultural diversity' (Barthes, 1966, pp. 80–1). Analysis should concentrate on the ways in which individual narratives conform to and depart from this universal model. In the opening pages of S/Z, however, he distances himself from such an attempt 'to see all the world's stories . . . within a single structure', now holding it to be 'a task as exhausting . . . as it is ultimately undesirable'. The reason given for this change of heart is that by forcing a text into 'a great narrative structure', it 'thereby loses its difference' (S/Z, p. 3).

Barthes was using the term 'difference' in a manner inflected by the influence of his younger contemporary, the philosopher Jacques Derrida. In a post-Saussurean sense, Derrida argued that signifying practices in general, on the model of language, depend on the network of differences among signs. Each work of literature differs, obviously, from other works; equally, however, it defers to them, that is, relies on them for its distinctive meaning (see Derrida, 1979). This formulation can still be seen as breaking with traditional notions of 'uniqueness' or 'individuality' as hermetic, essential qualities. Meaning cannot be established by considering a text in isolation, only by locating it within a network of differences and similarities. And because difference is determined within a cultural matrix that expands and changes shape through history, it is therefore itself also subject to historical change.

A work of art should not be seen as a closed system, a completed, inert object that will always remain the same, but dynamically, as an endless process of rereading and rewriting. The uncovering of fresh information, the advent of later works may place a text in a new light. This model of the text proposes that it acquires its meaning(s) not primarily at the moment of production but at the various moments of reception.

How far does this imply the demoting of the author as originating source of meaning? Barthes offers an epigram: 'the birth of the reader must be at the cost of the death of the Author' (1977, p. 148). But S/Z itself is a flamboyantly 'authorial' text. The prose style is dense, allusive and peppered with neologisms, colourful images and surprising comparisons. Barthes felt that 'the fact that S/Z may be subject to certain values of style in the traditional sense is important, for . . . to accept style is to refuse language as pure instrument' (Heath, 1971, p. 46). This is to refuse the scientism of early structuralism. At the same time, may not the reader wish at least sometimes to put into play, precisely, authorially based models of textual meaning?

S/Z and film theory

In assessing the influence of S/Z, it is necessary to recall that it too, like *Sarrasine*, is subject to the principle of intertextuality. It was only one product of the intense theoretical speculation being generated in France at that time. S/Z appeared in 1970, the same year as the equally influential *Cahiers*' collective text on Ford's *Young Mr Lincoln* (see *Cahiers du cinéma*'s 'John Ford', p. 462). As the ideas formulated in such analyses became assimilated by Anglo-American film culture, diffusion rather than 'application' in any strict sense turned out to be the order of the day. Less attention has been devoted to the specific features of S/Z's breakdown of narrative (for example, its proposed five codes) than to its more general propositions on the one hand and its exemplary status as a tour de force of attention to textual complexity on the other.

In fact, S/Z turned out to be a hard act to follow. Stephen Heath's 1975 analysis of *Touch of Evil* in *Screen* was probably the closest anyone came in English to providing an analysis with equal ambitions, with the work of Raymond Bellour and Marie-Claire Ropars in France needing acknowledgment too. But on the whole, the enterprise of 'ultra-close reading' of films has been marginalised, with the sceptical side of S/Z playing no small part in this process: in dramatising its own method as a kind of fiction, Barthes's text opened the way for less methodical, more modest and/or more focused 'probes' of film texts for particular purposes. It should also be said that the development of 'queer theory' for the cinema in the 1980s and 1990s, to which S/Z can be seen in content terms as making a strong, distinctive contribution, has tended to eschew the very pleasurable but undeniably rather elitist mandarin qualities of Barthes's critical procedures (see also Queer theory and new queer cinema, p. 505).

Narrative and audience

An important shift in emphasis occurred in the course of 'working through structuralism'. The first wave of structuralism analysed texts as autonomous, self-contained entities. But what if meaning is not immanent and pre-existing, but is created anew in every encounter between reader/viewer and text? Attention would have to be directed to what happens in the course of this encounter. The change of focus is described succinctly in the introduction to the 1976 *Edinburgh Film Festival Magazine*: 'The main problem of film criticism can no longer be restricted to the object cinema, as opposed to the operation cinema (a specific signifying practice which places the spectator)' (1976, p. 4).

Just as Barthes moved from structuralist scientism to a concern with the actual experience of reading and the pleasures (cerebral, visceral and sometimes even erotic) that it provides, Metz moved from a concentration on 'film language' to the essays collected in *Psychoanalysis and Cinema* (Metz, 1982) concerned with problems such as the effect produced upon us, the audience, by 'the operation cinema' and (a deceptively simple question) why we enjoy watching movies.

While an interest in developing a psychoanalytically informed account of the cinema was one impetus behind this move away from free-standing textual analysis, it was the political commitment of *Screen* in the 1970s that most influenced the way in which theory was developed and consolidated. Under the pressure of the political events of May 1968 and its aftermath and the international economic crisis of the 1970s (and, it must be remembered, well before 'Thatcherism' was even glimpsable as the political future for the UK), it was increasingly felt that the kind of theory that was needed was one that would provide some insight not just into the mechanical nuts-and-bolts structure of narrative, but also into its ideological effects. Political commitment very much informed the way in which approaches to narrative theory and analysis pioneered in France were mediated by British film culture. *Screen*, the main platform for these debates, had a consciously 'interventionalist' policy. Its aim was not only to describe but also to change its object of study (see, for instance, Stephen Heath's remarks on the desirable 'emphases and options' for *Screen*, 1974, p. 126). Primary concerns for theoretical writing became: first, to work towards a greater understanding of the relationship between viewer and film; second, to assess the ideological implications of this process; and third, to do so not so much in the interests of scientific accuracy or high scholarly endeavour but rather with the political aim to develop 'a new social practice of the cinema'.

The classic realist text

One of the most accessible routes into this terrain proved to be Colin MacCabe's (1974) influential concept of 'the classic realist text'. MacCabe summarised this concept in the form of two theses: (1) 'The classic realist text cannot deal with the real as contradictory'; (2) 'In a reciprocal movement the classic realist text ensures the position of the subject in a relation of dominant specularity' (1974, p. 12).

In the first of these theses, MacCabe addressed himself to the formal organisation of the text, its internal consistency and cohesion – characteristics that had been identified by Barthes as hallmarks of the 'readerly' work. The classic realist text might seem able to accommodate contradiction in the form of different discourses of viewpoints vying for supremacy, usually assigned to various characters in the narrative. But this apparent pluralism is actually, he argued, illusory: irreconcilable contradiction would threaten the inner stability of the text. This threat is neutralised by according the warring discourses unequal status, and arranging them in a hierarchy. The one at the top, the dominant discourse, acts as the voice of truth, overruling and interpreting all the others.

The second thesis, on specularity, was developed along the following lines. Whereas in the nineteenth-century novel, a form that has often been seen as the direct historical predecessor of mainstream cinema, MacCabe suggested that the voice of truth is the 'narrative prose', the impersonal 'metalanguage' that constantly comments on and subsumes the 'object languages' of individual figures within the world of the fiction, in film the position of knowledge is taken over by the narration of events through images. Thus 'the camera shows us what happens – it tells the truth against which we can measure the other discourses' (MacCabe, 1974, p. 10). In support of this view, he referred to scenes in *Klute* (Alan J. Pakula, 1971) and in *Days of Hope* (Ken Loach, 1975), where the 'erroneous' information purveyed on the soundtrack is played off against the 'truth' of what is seen (MacCabe, 1976b). The commonsense assumption that we can 'trust the evidence of our own eyes' indicates how potent our confidence in the visual can be.

This approach was at the time seen as constituting a break with the tradition within cinema aesthetics that conceives of the photographic image as an authentic record of the 'real world', a view found, for instance, in certain of Bazin's writings (see Bazin, p. 525). MacCabe was read as insisting that the realist narrative film bears no relation whatever to any 'essential reality', though it aims to give this impression. In fact, MacCabe's respect for Bazin was always considerable. It is precisely because of the strength of Bazinian intuitions about photography's relationship to the real that it becomes necessary to note how a voice-of-truth effect takes place. (The whole thrust of Bazin's interest in arguing for photographic techniques capable of sustaining ambiguity was, correspondingly, to work towards a cinema that would disperse or dialogise the singular voice of truth.) The problem is that the particular image comes to function as a guarantor of truth too simply and monolithically, that it is taken as truth as such by the viewer. Their position is one of overseer, of 'dominant specularity', which is however illusory: a 'pseudo-dominance'. The hierarchy of discourses within the film favours a singular meaning, and the viewer, offered apparently unimpeded access to knowledge, is discouraged from working to create their own reading. The viewer remains passive, placed 'outside the realm of contradiction and action – outside of production'. This 'petrification' of the viewer sustains the opposition between work production and leisure consumption that is an integral feature of capitalism.

The Althusserian background to MacCabe's position needs mentioning, though it is clearer looking back now than in the 1970s that what was being asserted hardly stands or falls with 'Althusserianism'. The tragic events of Louis Althusser's later life and the eclipse of the kind of possibility for the future felt to be represented in the 1970s (rather amazingly, it has to be said in retrospect) by the likes of the French Communist Party or forces to its left do not allow us to ignore the genuine interest and productivity of Althusserian thought. Althusser recast the classical Marxist model of economic base/ideological superstructure so as to propose for the latter a far more active role in society than had hitherto been allowed in the Marxist tradition. This gave the student of cultural forms a more important, even crucial, role in the political struggle than heretofore.

Ideology takes the form of systems of representation that can have a political effectivity of their own. The political order is secured, in most societies, not so much by coercion as by consent. The main agencies for organising and holding in place this consent are what Althusser calls the ideological state apparatuses. Of these, the most important are institutions such as the education system, church and family. Art, too, is seen as comprised within the apparatuses that contribute to the unconscious formation of individuals by 'interpellating' them in various ways, summoning them to take up their role in society (Althusser, 1971). It is not a question here of the indoctrination of one class/subclass by another (as some vulgar Marxist theories have it), since interpellation takes place at an unconscious level and in all men and women, but rather of a process of socialisation, an essential condition of communal existence within any economic order. In short, Althusser proposes that individuals are placed as social subjects in subtle and largely imperceptible ways – ways that simultaneously promote in them the impression of being consistent, rational and free human agents.

MacCabe's account of 'classic realism' sees the realist text as one more device for 'placing' or positioning individuals as social subjects, via the (interpellating) voice of truth and the authoritative 'speech' of the photographic image. The metaphor of the textually 'positioned subject' was indeed to become central to much 1970s theory: the effect of the operations of the realist text is to 'place' the subject in a fixed position of knowledge towards the text. At first sight, this seems a curious assertion. Surely sharp disagreement is perfectly possible between individuals even about what might seem the most unambiguously classic of realist texts; how then can one speak in such general terms of a single 'subject-position'? Naturally enough, the objection was raised that the 'viewing subject' is a meaningless abstraction, with little bearing on 'real' audiences in their social and historical diversity. Such criticism was in the first instance countered by introducing a conceptual distinction. On one hand, there is the empirical spectator whose interpretation of film will be determined by all manner of extraneous factors such as personal biography, class origins, previous viewing experience, the variables of conditions of reception and so forth. On the other hand, there is the abstract notion of a 'subject-position', which could be defined as the way in which a film solicits, demands even, a certain closely circumscribed reading from a viewer by means of its own formal operations (see Ellis, 1978). This distinction seemed fruitful to the degree that it allowed us to accept that different individuals can interpret a text in different ways, while insisting that the text itself imposes definite limits on their room to manoeuvre. In other words, it promised a method that would avoid the two extremes of an infinite pluralism that posits as many possible readings as there are readers, each equally legitimate, and an essentialism that asserts a single 'true' meaning (see Spectatorship and audience research, p. 538).

The 'positioning' model or picture was elaborated along other lines as well. A whole approach to space in the cinema was mobilised in this cause. The development of single perspective in painting, which took place at a particular historical moment (the early years of the 15th century in Italy, the period known as the Quattrocento) and which is absent from many non-western art traditions, seemed analogous to MacCabe's sense of a single voice of truth or position of truth; and it was noted that, despite the possibilities offered by distorting lenses, the cinema depicts space in a manner very similar to Renaissance art. In fact, the mechanical aid devised by Quattrocento painters to correct perspective errors, the camera obscura or darkened chamber, was the forerunner of the modern camera used for still and motion photography. This might seem to challenge the widespread notion that film technology has, thanks to scientific progress (the advent of sound, deep-focus cinematography and colour), moved steadily towards the ever more efficient and accurate reproduction of 'reality'; rather, the end in view is the embodiment of specifically humanist values and beliefs (see Ogle, 1977; Williams, 1977; see also Technologies, p. 139). Following this line of argument led some writers to argue that cinema is already suffused with ideological assumptions at the level of the individual shot, that is, before the construction of narrative, by the very nature of its own machinery (see Baudry, 1974/75; Bailblé, 1979/80). The organisation of components within the picture is not only informed by a particular worldview; it also demands of the spectator a certain complicity in these operations if they are to decipher its meaning.

More psychoanalytically orientated, but equally suitable for utilisation by the 'positioners' was the concept of 'suture'. Originally used by surgeons to denote the stitching that joins the edges of a wound, the term 'suture' was borrowed in the 1960s by Lacanian psychoanalysis as a means of understanding the relationship between the conscious and unconscious forces that produces the human subject. This relationship is seen in terms of an uneasy alliance between the two forms of psychic organisation called by Lacan the 'Imaginary' and the 'Symbolic'. The former, which is characterised by the unity it confers upon subject and object, bears a privileged relationship to vision: in early infancy, the child discovers its reflection in a mirror, its first apprehension of the body as unified. This moment (which Lacan calls the 'mirror stage') is central to the operation of the human psyche, providing the basis of our narcissistic relationship to the rest of the world, in which others are seen as versions of ourselves and we each experience ourselves as unified beings at the centre of the world (see MacCabe, 1976b, p. 13).

However, the fact that the mind does not develop and function in a vacuum casts doubt on our assumption of total individual autonomy. Just as Saussure insisted on the trans-individual, systemic nature of language, Lacanians argue that humanist accounts of the 'human individual' fail to recognise that from birth onwards this individual must define its identity (and be defined) within and against systems of pre-existing cultural relations. Successful social interaction requires individuals to engage in a complex network of rules and conventions (described by Lacanians as 'entry into the Symbolic'). This process begins from earliest childhood, decisive stages being the learning of language, and the acquisition of a fixed (hetero)sexual identity, preparing ('positioning') the child for cultural 'normality'.

This argument (which, it should be noted in passing, is rather more a construct of the first wave of anglophone importation of Lacan than a definitively Lacanian one, though not necessarily less interesting for that) suggests that the chief constraints at work in the evolution of the subject lie beyond our conscious control. Thus while manipulating the elementary codes essential to everyday activities like holding a conversation, or watching and understanding a film, we 'forget' the intricate symbolic structures that are necessary to any meaningful social activity. Our psychic life is a perpetual flux and reflux between the favoured realm of the imaginary, which functions not as a temporary phase on the road to maturity, but as a recurrent desire of the individual to seek and foster the wholeness of a unified ideal ego; and that, less congenial to us, of the symbolic, which forces our acknowledgment of the morass of determinations at work in the construction of the psyche. It is here that the concept of 'suture' comes into play, understood as the constant striving of the ego to fill in these gaps, and to impose unity on the conflicting forces of the unconscious. Within film theory, suture was used to name the imposition of unity across not only these general 'symbolic' codes but across disunifying formal features specific to film, notably the diversity of shots and of gazes. Bluntly, 'suture' is a psychoanalytically underpinned name for continuity editing. And continuity editing, once again, was seen as positioning the subject and imposing upon them a single voice of truth.

Criticism of classic realism

Once proposed, MacCabe's concept of the classic realist text, and the whole family of closely related theories that might be grouped together under the rubric of 'positioned subject theory', seemed both to advance and to constrict the field. Is it, or 'suture', or 'apparatus theory' (Baudry, 1974/75) not too ambitious in attempting to provide a prototype applicable to all realist narrative? Might not the model of classic realism become a grid within which each text is inserted a little too smoothly as yet another revamping of the same old pattern? To unmask a text as formally realist (whether it be classic or progressive in its content) is in a sense to denounce it as acting on the viewer in a repressive way. So some of this work on realism was seen as tending to dismiss the mainstream narrative film wholesale as an ideological monolith, a purely manipulative 'ideological state apparatus' for 'the reproduction of labour power'. What possible productive engagement with popular cinema could survive this line? MacCabe's category of classic realism avoids a charge of intellectual snobbery by spanning the high-art/mass-culture divide, 'lumping together *The Grapes of Wrath* and *The Sound of Music*' (MacCabe, 1974, p. 12) – a formulation that in turn just may have inspired Richard Dyer to mount an influential and spirited defence of *The Sound of Music* – but it can sound uncomfortably close to implying a blanket condemnation ('lumping together' indeed!).

Today, a rather different problem seems to be the key one. It is not so much 'unfairness to the text', more polysemous and dialogic than the voice-of-truth account proposes, of which the theory stands accused (indeed, the endless defence of individual films by showing them to be complex and ambiguous can itself become monotonous and politically rather naive, as Paul Willemen, 1994, has pointed out), but 'unfairness to the viewer'. The split between the empirical viewer and a sort of 'ideal viewer' is not the real issue: it is hard to imagine any theory of reception that does not make some such move. The trouble is that any sense of agency on the part of the theorised viewer is minimised. The positioned subject is thus a very subjected subject.

This arises in part from the structuralist roots of the account. Language really is a good example of a system to which we are subjected, in a strong sense, even though the creativity of the speaker/hearer, as Noam Chomsky would put it, is precisely made possible by this subjection. But as the 1980s unfolded, it became clear, if not always very palatable, that the privileged social science providing the model underpinning more local models had shifted from linguistics to (classic) economics; and, while the activities of rational economic people are no less abstract than those of Saussurean *langue*-speaking people, they do involve such elements as agency and choice. The notion that agency and choice are somehow humanist or bourgeois illusions seems itself a rather strange illusion, born perhaps out of the sense of blocked dreams of the left that characterised the Cold War era.

One is indeed 'constrained' to understand a text, but one chooses, both whether to consume the text in the first place and what judgment to make of it once consumed. (Or perhaps we should say that, empirically, people have more or less choice – there are always constraints and limitations, and there is such a thing as addiction – but that any account of the media audience has to build choice into the model: this then makes particular cases of absence of choice interesting, and perhaps addressable.)

This way forward from 'positioned spectator' theories was anticipated by two lines of investigation arising out of textual-analytic observation. The first of these was stimulated by the practice, in non-'classic' cinema, of the long take. If film is

Does the audience identify with Cary Grant's point of view in Hitchcock's *North by Northwest?*

unlike painting or still photography in one major respect, namely in providing not a single image but a series of images from ceaselessly shifting positions, so that the spectator is continually displaced within the fictional scene, this norm (no doubt 'domesticated' by continuity editing) is itself challengeable by the long, static take. These, as in, for instance, some of Chantal Akerman's films, far from providing a reassuringly secure viewing position, appear to disrupt the illusion of reality (see Heath, 1977/78). Certainly, there is an impatience/discomfort commonly felt by audiences when a shot is held a little 'too long'. But should the long take not be more positioning/reassuring for an audience rather than less? The key to this puzzle could be seen as lying in the peculiar nature of film as narrative, which, in contrast to the single image, depends heavily on duration and performance, the holding of the viewer over an extended period of time. This feat requires a delicate balancing act, the playing out of a tension between 'process (with its threat of incoherence or loss of mastery) and position (with its threat of stasis, fixity or of compulsive repetition, which is the same thing in another form)' (Neale, 1980, p. 26). Stability alone would soon lead to impatience and boredom, and what is needed is a perpetual oscillation between delicious instants of risk and repeated temporary returns to equilibrium. Some writers believe that the pleasurability of the cinema resides in precisely this process of limited risk (see Heath, 1977). Such a model of the spectator's response might seem to contrast sharply with MacCabe's more static formulation of 'dominant specularity'; but what is even more important is to note that the spectator can choose to explore the 'held image' productively rather than be repulsed by it. No doubt this 'choice' may require training, 'cultural capital' and so forth, but these too are 'choosable', developable. The implacable Bazinian practice of the film-makers Straub/Huillet is one that is unintelligible save in terms of an imagined viewer capable of exercising agency and cognitively exploring the image actively; and if such a viewer is imaginable for these texts, why not imagine him or her for the texts of the 'delicate balancing act' too?

The second line of investigation focused on point of view (pov), one of the medium's major rhetorical figures. In a pov shot, the camera assumes the spatial position of one of the characters within the narrative in order to show us what she or he sees (see Branigan, 1975). Most directors use this device to varying extents, one of its acknowledged masters being Hitchcock (see Bellour, 2001). The MacCabe framework allows some very interesting questions to be raised about pov. If the use of pov shots is linked to the discourses of different characters, are these subsumed, in the mainstream cinema, by an impersonal, dominant discourse comparable to the 'omniscient narrator' of realist prose (see Heath on *Touch of Evil*, 1975); and can it be argued that certain texts resist or undermine this voice of authority, the case sometimes made for the modernism of film-makers such as Dreyer or Bresson (see Nash, 1976)? But, in a classic and unusually definitive argument, Nick Browne (1975/76) demonstrated something very striking about pov through a close analysis of a sequence from *Stagecoach* (1939). This sequence is dominated by pov shots, but these are ascribed to a 'good woman' character whose prejudices vis-à-vis a prostitute character we are clearly not invited to share: indeed, the meaning of the passage, in a strong sense, is: 'these prejudices are cruel'. This is a striking case, because, on one hand, it is as good a demonstration as any of, precisely, a MacCabe-like voice-of-truth effect coming through the text as an overall dominant discourse. (It is interesting to speculate about what an empirical audience member who did feel that sitting down to eat at the same table as a prostitute was something to be avoided would make of the sequence: scriptwriter and director certainly go to some trouble to make such a viewer uncomfortable!) Yet, on the other hand, in so far as the MacCabe model might have predicted that the figure of pov would 'position' a viewer definitively ('I look through these eyes so I must take this position'), the sequence demonstrates how undetermining of judgment a particular bit of 'film form' is. And this opens up the 'likelihood', once again, that the viewer is a chooser of positions and an agent in terms of their uptake on what is there on the screen and on the soundtrack.

Psychoanalysis and film

However, another line of thought in the 1970s was to prove to be powerful, reinforcing the anti-agency bias of the theory of the time while opening up an exciting new range of phenomena to view. This was psychoanalysis, but especially psychoanalysis at the service (far from historically always the case!) of feminism (Feminist film theory, p. 491).

Psychoanalysis is by its very nature a scheme of concepts designed to deal with the layer of our experience where we find ourselves not very agent-like, or in the grip of some sort of 'agency' that is both ourself and foreign to our thought of ourself, an agency acting 'behind our backs'. In a clinical context, the patient seeks the psychoanalyst precisely because over a significant range of his or her life, he or she seems strangely incapable of acting rationally and economically. And even where what is at issue is not a matter of pathology, the layer of experience where we become aware of something 'below' or 'beyond' our agency in what we do and what we make has seemed suited to exploration using the psychoanalytic armory.

Film has from its outset felt 'uncanny' enough to trigger psychoanalytic approaches. One of the most enduring problems facing film theory and criticism is the elusive quality of their own object. Images have a tangible existence on celluloid, yet this materiality is constantly belied by the conditions under which we receive them. On one level, there are the practical difficulties of access to facilities for studying actual films – still with us in the video age, but significantly greater earlier. But also, more fundamentally, the very nature of film seems to reside in a relentless flow of images, the pleasures and fascinations it offers stemming from a fleeting ephemerality that defies attempts to arrest and contain it. Empirical audience research accordingly seems inadequate if what is envisaged is accounting fully for the viewing experience, and for the relation between film narrative and spectator. The more or less vague, but cohesive and reasoned memory we retain from a visit to the cinema has little in common with the complex and subtle, barely perceptible processes that move us while we are actually watching a film. The sociological approach therefore appeared to need, at the very least, complementing by work on an altogether different plane.

The tools and methods of psychoanalysis offered film theorists a means of understanding the operations at a micro-level of the 'mental machinery' activated by the passage of images on screen. The idea of suture, introduced above (see p. 521), seemed a useful way of defining the minute shifts and revisions that take place in our state of mind throughout the viewing of a film: a constant movement of the spectator between the dual domains of the imaginary and the symbolic, a movement that 'holds us in place' (positioning theory again!) as we watch and enjoy the film. To elaborate further this difficult concept (see Miller *et al.*, 1977/78), the process has been described as something like this. At the beginning of each shot, the spectator enjoys a secure imaginary relationship to the film, a feeling bound up with the illusion of privileged control over and unmediated access to its fictional world. A moment later, though, this illusion is dispelled as the spectator gradually becomes conscious of the image frame, and hence of the fact that the fictional space is after all narrowly circumscribed. This realisation stimulates the desire to see and find out more, and the former illusion of the image as offering a 'window on the world' yields to an unpleasant perception of the film as artefact, a system of signs and codes that lie outside the spectator's control. However, this recognition is soon overcome by the advent of the next shot, which apparently restores the previous condition of the spectator's imaginary unity with the images and starts the cycle off again (Miller *et al.*, 1977/78).

Such an account of the satisfaction afforded by 'invisible' continuity editing emphasises usefully the shot/reverse-shot pattern of narrative cinema and the involvement of the viewer in an intricate network of 'looks'. The pov shot unattached to a particular character draws the spectator into the text by positing him or her as the privileged observer of the image, in the place of an imagined character occupying the position of the camera (see Dayan, 1974). In the following reverse-angle shot, the point of origin of that look is assigned to a character within the fiction, thereby assuring that the viewer is not addressed directly by the film but remains safely outside it. In this way, the viewer is, in topographical terms, right inside the fictional space, yet never actually part of the action. No doubt the shot/reverse-shot figure is only one part of the total repertoire

Woman as object, man as 'bearer of the look' in *Under Capricorn*

of film language, but it does afford a particularly clear model of the more general relationship, dubbed by Heath (1974) 'separation in identification', of spectator to the events taking place on the screen.

The concept of 'separation in identification' was echoed in contemporaneous theories of 'the look' or 'the gaze'. These also saw film narrative as a process generated primarily out of an interplay of looks: not only those exchanged between the characters on screen, epitomised by the pov pattern, but also the look of the viewer, sitting in the cinema, at this fictional world, a look that the suturing process attempts to efface.

Metz was among those fascinated by the voyeuristic aspect of film viewing. In an essay first published in French in 1975 ('History/discourse', 1976), he argued through this idea by comparing a visit to the cinema with a visit to the theatre. The performance of a play deliberately sets out to be a collective experience, an event that acknowledges the gathered populace implicitly or indeed sometimes even explicitly, as in direct asides to the audience. Thus 'actor and spectator are present to each other . . . [in] a ceremony which has a certain civic quality, engaging more than the private man'. Film, by contrast, 'is exhibitionistic and it is not'; it 'knows that it is being looked at and does not know . . . All the viewer requires – but he requires it absolutely – is that the actor should behave as though he is not being seen, and so cannot see him, the voyeur'.

The peculiar nature of film as a not-quite performing art is reflected both in its conditions of production (the fact that, unlike the theatre, actors and audience are never physically present in the same place), and of its reception (the individual's immobility and sense of isolation from other spectators, the total darkness, the self-contained nature of the event, lack of interval to break up the narrative flow, and so forth). In a striking image, Metz compared the cinema audience to fish gathered round the side of an aquarium, 'looking out' onto the fictional world, 'absorbing everything through their eyes and nothing through their bodies'; the activity of looking becomes disproportionately important to the filmgoer compared to the more integrated physical experience of theatre-going. Suggestively, he linked this difference to the much later historical origins of the cinema, which 'was born at a period when social life was strongly marked by the concept of the individual' and which 'belongs to the private man' (Metz, 1976).

In retrospect, this is an interesting anticipation of the 'decline of the public sphere' argument associated with the name of Jürgen Habermas, destined to be so influential in the 1980s and 1990s; it also in some ways paints a curiously individualistic picture, since from other perspectives it is precisely the highly social nature of the mass cinema audience of the first half of the 20th century that gets eroded by the domestic practice of television viewing. However, the chief destiny of this emphasis on the voyeuristic nature of cinema was to feed into a full-bloodedly social account of gendered spectatorship.

Laura Mulvey on visual pleasure

If psychoanalysis is a conceptual system whose main purchase is on the layer of human experience where accounts stressing rationality, agency and autonomy are at their weakest, then the emergence of feminist theory in the 1970s and beyond, with its irresistible demonstration of the irrationality and at the same time the continuing grievousness of gender hierarchy, involved making good use of what psychoanalysis has to say about the origins and maintenance of gender distinction. It fell to Laura Mulvey in 1975 to propose, in one of the most influential contributions to 1970s theory (Mulvey, 1989), an account of how the voyeuristic aspect of cinema spectatorship both arises from and perpetuates patriarchy (see also Feminist film theory, p. 491).

Mulvey returns to the question of 'the look' from a feminist standpoint. She presents a picture of spectatorship familiar

Woman as problem for the macho male order in Nicholas Ray's *The Lusty Men*

from suture-based accounts, with an uneasy and labile relationship between the forward drive of narrative and the potential of the static image to resist it, but adds to this a key factor: in the classic Hollywood film, these two functions were almost always gender specific, reflecting and perpetuating the values of 'a world ordered by sexual imbalance'. In other words, the active, narrative role of making things happen and controlling events usually fell to a male character, while the female star, often virtually peripheral to functional events, remained more passively decorative. She functioned as the locus of masculine erotic desire, a spectacle to be looked at by both male characters and spectators, the latter, whatever their actual gender, being assumed to be and addressed as male by the operations of the film.

The Sternberg/Dietrich cycle has been seen as an extreme example of this tendency – Sternberg's celebrated remark that his films could well be projected upside down was cited by Mulvey as evidence that for him spectacle tends to take priority over narrative. Hitchcock was used as the contrasting example: here, the figure of the woman, representing a 'trouble' within the classic narrative, needs punishing by it to atone for the threat of narrative disruption, however voyeuristically pleasurable that spectacle has been. (The spectacle, threatening the stalling of the fictional flow, is treated as triggering the viewers' unpleasant awareness of themselves as looking that the mechanisms of cinema are usually concerned to repress.) Various compromises between spectacle and narrative are imaginable; a striking generic case is that of the backstage musical, which overtly employs the convention of the woman as showgirl, her spectacular performance of a song and/or dance anticipating this problem by 'matching' the look of the audience with that of male characters within the film, thus momentarily reconciling the tension between narrative and spectacle.

But why should the (sexually charged) image of the woman work so differently from that of the man? In 'demonstrating the way the unconscious of patriarchal society has structured film form', Mulvey drew on Freudo-Lacanian theories of child development. The key moments here are those involved with the discovery of sexual difference, notably the moment at which the male child sees (or realises, or . . .) that his mother lacks a phallus, that she is 'castrated', and fears for the first time that he might suffer such a dire fate. A conservative tendency within classic psychoanalysis saw this as a moment universally necessary as part of the entry of the growing child into the symbolic order (with the little girl's 'acceptance' of 'castration' equally necessary). Feminist theorists were concerned to call this inevitability into question, reformulating the process as a specific cultural phenomenon. Indeed, it is precisely the bizarreness, from any rational-agency perspective, of a gender-related ascription of more rationality and agency to the male than to the female that suggests that a psychoanalytic 'take' on the phenomenon might be appropriate. If the phallus becomes a privileged source of meaning, a 'positive term', despite its patent functioning only in terms of the diacritical functioning, à la Saussure, of gender difference, then this is a symptom of social pathology on a grand scale. The most miserable upshot of the weird overvaluation of the phallus is the devaluation it imposes on women. Instead of being defined by her own sexual attributes, her 'difference', 'woman' is perceived only negatively, as a lack: 'representation of the female form ... speaks castration and nothing else'.

Mulvey saw the main project of the classic Hollywood narrative cinema as the generation of pleasures for the male viewer that depended on deploying the body of the female star as a defence against the threat of castration she evokes. Her article drew attention to the ideological implications of the interdependence of deep-seated psychic processes and the operations of narrative cinema, each feeding on and reinforcing the other. The trenchancy of its writing is one of its most notable features:

> It is said that analysing pleasure, or beauty destroys it. That is the intention of this article . . . Not in favour . . . of intellectualised unpleasure, but to make way for a total negation of the ease and plenitude of the narrative fiction film . . . in order to conceive a new language of desire. (Mulvey, 1989)

Written 'compactly' to the point of presenting the reader with a real challenge, and refusing all the 'and yet . . .' clauses that would get one's favourite movies off the hook, the article made its impact because, of all the work considered so far, it most redescribes so as to make visible features of mainstream cinema that had not been visible before, and that patently deserved to be challenged. It generated a huge amount of debate, with much invested through the 1980s and 1990s in 'domesticating' it, so to speak, by advancing a fairer or more tolerant or more nuanced 'larger view'; but it is the clear and uncompromising nature of Mulvey's original formulations that has made the article such a classic (see also Feminist film theory, p. 491).

Aftermaths: the structuralist controversy fades

So much was acquired in the 1970s in film theory – and, necessarily, some acquisitions now look in better shape than others. This is not the place to attempt to cover everything that happened to film theory once the very specific 'conjuncture' that produced the theoretical writing discussed above had become 'deconjoined'. But three topics may give a flavour of the way discussion has moved on: the fate of a pre-structuralist thinker, André Bazin; the fate of a post-structuralist thinker, Gilles Deleuze; and the prospects for formalism now.

Bazin

Any theorist proposing some sort of 'naive realism', some sort of 'window on the world' theory of cinema would have been expected to draw heavy fire in the 1970s. André Bazin, however, was not just 'any theorist'. It was recognised at the time that his reputation rested upon an impressively substantial body of film theory and criticism, upon the editorial conducting of a journal, *Cahiers du cinéma*, which was a model of the 'magazine that matters', and upon his direct influence on the directors of the Nouvelle Vague. Still, his unabashed commitment to the importance of some kind of 'access to the real', available distinctively via photography, made his thought very hard to assimilate at a point where what seemed most important was to insist on cinema as language, language as arbitrary/diacritical, and ideology as omnipresent within cultural texts.

What was one to make of a crucial essay ('The evolution of the language of cinema') that both rehabilitated certain products of the American cinema (crucially for later authorship debates), moved discussion on from a simple 'talkies are reactionary' line that blocked critical appreciation of what was actually happening in the cinema post-sound, gently debunked the widespread critical tendency to fetishise the accomplishments of a certain moment of the Soviet cinema at the expense of other styles and practices – but also proposed a dichotomy between 'directors who believe in the image and directors who believe in reality'? Reality?

Directors with 'faith in the image' had historically tended to favour montage as a technique that allowed them to impose an interpretation on the events they portrayed. The effect, according to Bazin, was to create a 'meaning not objectively present in the images but derived purely from their juxtaposition'. This style was typified by the work of D. W. Griffith, Sergei Eisenstein and Alfred Hitchcock. The other kind of director, in contrast, would prefer long takes that preserved as far as possible the unity of time and space. Examples given by Bazin of practitioners of this approach included Erich von Stroheim, Jean Renoir and Orson Welles. Bazin made it clear that his sympathies lay with the latter method. The film image should, in his view, be evaluated 'according not to what it adds to reality but to what it reveals of it'.

These ideas followed on from those put forward in the 1945 essay 'The ontology of the photographic image', where Bazin propounded the scandalous thesis that there is a sense in which, looking at a photograph, we are looking directly at the object photographed, and where, correspondingly, photography is praised as a 'process of mechanical reproduction from which man is excluded . . . All the other arts are based on the presence of man; only in photography do we take pleasure in his absence' (Bazin, Vol. 1, 1958, p. 15).

It was inevitable that Bazin's belief that the film image should ideally be the transparent mediator of a putative 'reality' with minimal human intervention should have been attacked by structuralism-influenced critics. Bazin was held to have denied that film is a culturally determined language system. For him, the relationship between signifier and signified in cinema was not arbitrary but intimate and existential. This hypothesis is evidenced in Bazin's celebrated analogies between the photograph and the death mask or fingerprint; and indeed it would have been interesting to see what alternative theorisations of death-mask or fingerprint signs would have been offered by the anti-Bazinian camp, had they deigned to.

The richness of Bazin's legacy was never invisible in the 1970s, and indeed, in so far as the period was a time of 'importing from France', his unmistakable influence on such 'accepted' figures as Metz could hardly be denied. Careful readers of his work grasped how, as an exceptionally perceptive critic as well as a theorist and aesthetician, he constantly stressed the actuality rather than the ideal. Perfect transparency was, he realised, precluded by the current limitations of film technology and might indeed never be possible. Even the 'Ontology' essay, after developing the carefully elaborated argument that photography is an impartial, automatic process of registration, ends with the rider: 'On the other hand, of course, cinema is also a language'. This ambivalence is again found in one of Bazin's favourite images for the relation between film and reality: an asymptote, a curve that gradually approaches a straight line but that meets it only at infinity.

Indeed, in his essay on Italian Neo-realism, Bazin went so far as to claim that the need to enlist artifice to give the illusion of transparency generated a creative tension that was crucial to the work of art; true mimesis would result only in a flat and unheightened naturalism.

> We must beware of setting aesthetic refinement against a kind of crudeness, a kind of instant effectiveness of a realism satisfied just to show reality. Not the least of the merits of the Italian cinema will be, in my view, to have recalled once again that there is no 'realism' in art which is not first and foremost profoundly 'aesthetic'. . . Realism in art can only be achieved in one way – through artifice. (Bazin, Vol. 4, 1962, pp. 20–1)

Bazin's notion of realism was certainly rather more complex than is sometimes admitted. Ideally, he wanted the cinematographic image to have the status of an objective record; in actuality, though, he saw this as neither possible nor, in the last analysis, desirable. Positing that 'there is not one but several realisms' (Bazin, Vol. 1, 1958, p. 156), he set out to identify the very diverse methods by which these can be constructed. Most crucially, he always spoke for the creative energies of the historical moment in which he was writing: he was, instinctively and on principle, the least 'retro' or grumpy of theorists imaginable. Regrettably, the real accomplishment of the missed dialogue between Bazin and structuralism, now that both are in that past the redemption or preservation of which so preyed on Bazin's mind, still lies in the future.

BAZIN

Citizen Kane (USA 1941 *p.c* – Mercury Productions/RKO; *d* – Orson Welles)

In his book on Orson Welles and the essay on the evolution of the language of cinema, Bazin cites this film as exemplary of the tendency towards the long take and staging in depth, techniques that, he believed, allowed the viewer to perceive the inner unity of events.

However, *Citizen Kane* manifests an abundance of the trick effects that are roundly condemned by Bazin in his article 'The virtues and limitations of montage' (Gray, 2005). Bazin acknowledges the presence of these elements in the film, but accounts for them as a counterpointing device to set off the sequences that employ long takes and deep-focus. Equally, however, it could be objected that in view of the profusion of other modes of representation, the long take could not be accurately described as the dominant feature of Welles's style.

Second, Bazin's opposition of the long take versus montage accounts for only one aspect of the film, suppressing the myriad factors at work in producing meaning. For instance, although the scenes at the office of the *Inquirer* and in Xanadu are both in deep-focus, other elements such as, in the former case, specially constructed ceilings and low camera angles convey an impression of cramped and old-fashioned accommodation and, together with the characterisation of the staff, a blinkered and traditionalist editorial policy. In the latter case, vast rooms, high ceilings (often not visible), the towering statuary and mantelpiece that dwarf Kane (Orson Welles) and his wife Susan (Dorothy Comingore), combined with the use of lighting and sound, all build up an atmosphere of bleakness and

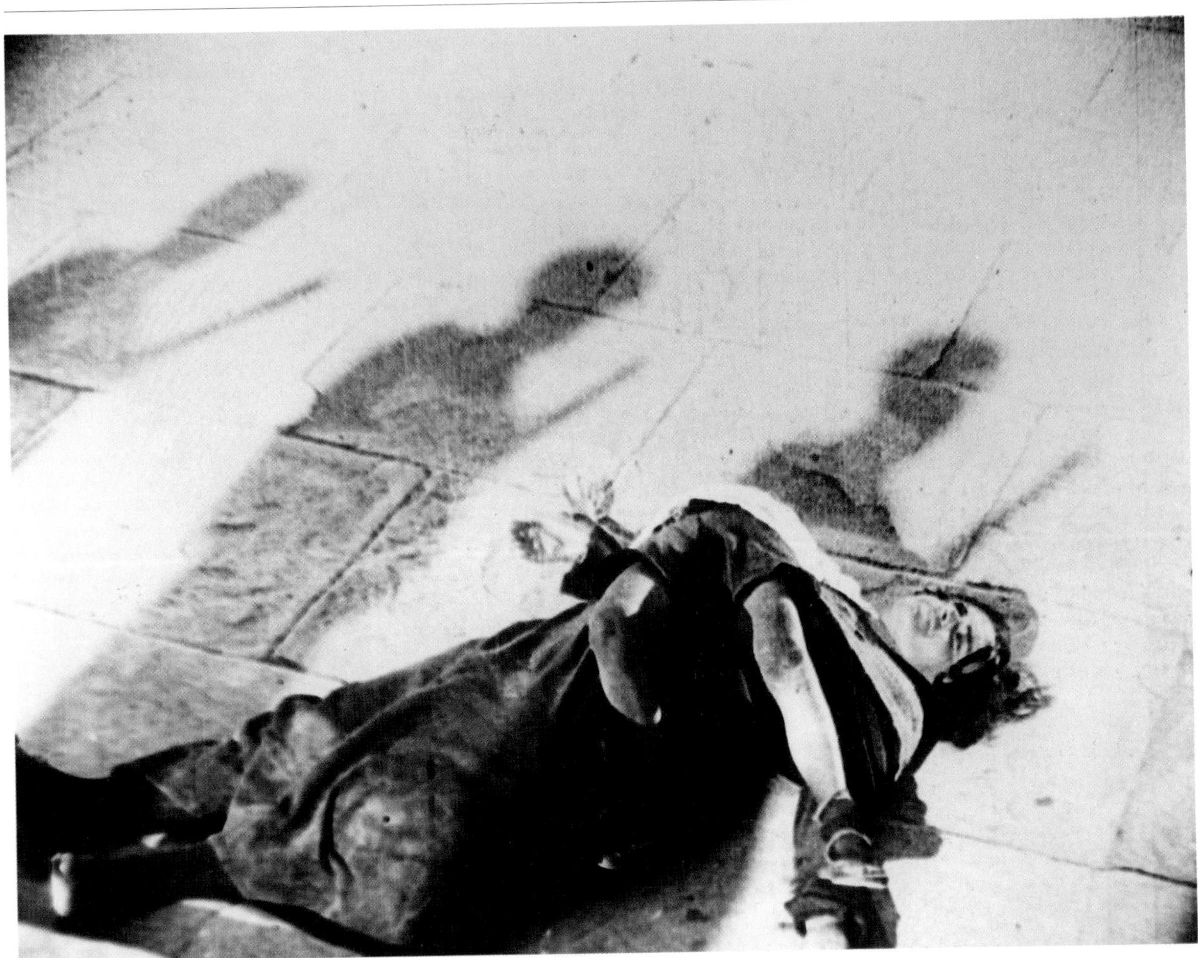

Eisenstein's revolutionary use of montage editing in *Battleship Potemkin*

those represented by Soviet director and theorist Sergei Eisenstein and those following French critic André Bazin.

Eisenstein is a representative of the most extreme faith in the ability of editing to produce aesthetic shocks and conflicts. Montage editing in its strictest definition is a reliance on the power of rapid cutting to create meaning. Rather than depending upon 'real' time and space to deliver information, Eisenstein privileged montage editing to create dialectical materialist works: thesis (shot no. 1) and antithesis (shot no. 2) create a synthesis (something greater than either shot independently). Such an approach revels in the discursive function of cinema and its potential to reorganise reality. For instance, during the famous 'Odessa steps' sequence in *Battleship Potemkin/Bronenosets Potemkin* (1925), the temporal and spatial relations are purely fictitious: at one moment it seems that a mother's child has fallen behind her, but a subsequent shot reveals he is now below her, and just when it seems that all the fleeing people have made it to the bottom of the steps, it seems to begin all over again. Real time and space cues are secondary to the manipulative functions of montage (see case study; and Soviet cinema, p. 244).

At the other end of the spectrum is André Bazin, for whom excessive dependence upon montage editing violates the essence of the cinema and its aesthetic development. Bazin encouraged film-makers to preserve the illusion of real time and space by relying less upon the 'trickery' of manipulative editing and more on staging in long takes, in deep space or planes of action. He favoured continuity devices (eyeline matches, the 180° rule) only when editing was necessary. For Bazin, unlike Eisenstein, cinema's 'evolution' is a continuous progression towards providing more convincing representations that mirror the complexity of our real experience of the world, which to him was complex, ambiguous and dense.

Most film-makers work in between these extreme positions, moving to one end of the spectrum or the other when there is a formal or narrative justification. Classic Hollywood cinema (see Classic Hollywood narrative, p. 45), for instance, stands as a compromise between these two ideologies of montage, following continuity editing regularly to make the editing unobtrusive when possible, but resorting to rapid montages for violent scenes (the shower scene in Hitchcock's *Psycho*, 1960) or the quick passing of time (the 'whirlwind romance' in *The Awful Truth*, Leo McCarey, 1937).

Film language

Critical consideration of 'film language' has matured during the 20th century, paralleling and absorbing developments in the arts and linguistics, structuralism and semiotics. For instance, early textbooks defined and discussed 'film grammar' (usually by listing various film devices), complete with 'good' and 'bad' examples. Raymond J. Spottiswoode (1951) set out to clarify 'the language and grammar which the film, as a prospective art form, has to acquire'. Many production manuals are underpinned by a similar approach as they recount, for instance, the best way to stage, shoot and edit someone falling down for comic or tragic effects. By the 1960s, however, stricter attempts to define where meaning is created in the cinema were tied closely and explicitly to theories of language, notably those of linguists Ferdinand de Saussure and Louis Hjelmslev. By adapting linguistic models of signification and carefully defining the specificity of film codes, theorists such as Christian Metz began to analyse rigorously film's marks of punctuation (for instance, fades on the one hand and wipes on the other) and various systems of signification (see The early work of Christian Metz, p. 511).

The result of such analysis is to understand the wide range of options or codes open to film-makers and to test the spectator's ability to decode, or 'read', various film techniques. In this analysis, film is conceived of as a 'text' of multiple signifying or discursive structures (editing codes, sound codes, narrative formulae and so on). 'Textual analysis' is really the activity of testing a film or group of films for specific, pertinent language-system codes, some of which, like the shot/reverse-shot, may be specific to the cinema, while others, like low-key lighting, are shared with other visual media (photography, painting, theatre). In the end, textual analysis is the cautious semiotic labour of explaining just how a film makes meaning and how its functional codes change from one era to another, one national cinema to another, and even one director to another.

Narration

While one can analyse the cinema from many perspectives, for most of us, movies are primarily interesting because they tell stories. Narrative in any medium is a double process of what is told, the represented story, and how it is told, or the narration. Narratology is the study of stories (involving characters, actions, dialogue) and, in the case of cinema, the filmic presentation and elaboration of stories. Most film criticism derives in part from narratological methods and adopts vocabulary from outside film studies proper – Russian formalism, semiotics, psychoanalysis, post-structuralism – which is modified in the light of the specificities of filmic experience and cinematic vocabulary.

Narrative study typically begins with defining a film's story structures and themes. Story is understood as a series of interrelated events, characters and actions out of which the audience creates a diegesis, or larger fictional world. Since most stories come to us with gaps and information narrated out of order, one of the spectator's primary tasks is to reconstruct the tale in terms of its fictional time and space, but also to clarify the cause–effect relations between elements. Film studies often speaks therefore of the story not as a passive object, but rather as a dynamic text, full of cues, repetitions, false paths, parallels and contrasts that are only available to the viewer in bits and pieces that must be sorted through, extrapolated and reorganised to be fully understood. For this reason, narrative study of the cinema usually draws up narrative categories by distinguishing group styles from individual styles, or classic Hollywood cinema, with its predictably generic stories, from the diversity of European art cinema (see Art cinema, p. 83).

The second aspect of fiction film analysis is the study of narration. A fiction film's narration involves the discursive process of telling the story via various narrating systems such as the selection and ordering of story elements, the narrative voice and pov, musical interventions, mise en scène, sound-to-image relations and editing strategies. The textual analysis of any individual film or group of stories involves precisely the investigation of which narration devices are at work for which effects. For instance, discussion of something as general as 'suspense' in an Alfred Hitchcock film depends as much on Hitchcock's narration (manipulative camera positions, melodramatic music, continuity editing patterns, low-key lighting) as on what the characters actually do or say. Such study tends then to create a critically constructed narrator or narrative voice behind any story. For some, this narrator is simply synonymous with the director or auteur, but much film criticism since the 1980s depends more on a narrator who is constructed from the textual cues and labelled a 'narrative instance' rather than a 'real' person, operating everything single-handedly behind the scenes. Thus, a narrator functions as an abstract force and is understood via the marks of narration within the fiction film text.

Film and the spectator

One of the liveliest areas of enquiry in cinema studies involves investigating and defining models of spectatorship. Even posing a simple question like: 'If films create meaning, what is the spectator's role in that process?' leads to surprisingly diverse approaches, since filmgoing is not a simple, singular 'process' at all. Researchers have considered the viewer from a wide variety of perspectives that relate to the social, economic, physical and psychological conditions of spectatorship (see Spectatorship and audience research, p. 538). The issue of spectatorship is particularly pertinent and problematic for discussions of the cinema and its apparatus, since motion pictures depend upon so many more technological, industrial and perceptual factors than does the novel. Reading a book depends upon very complex linguistic and psychological operations, but seeing and hearing a movie involves additional, specific operations. Consequently, most literary definitions of readers do not automatically fit the cinematic spectator and the processes of perception and meaning construction that constitute film spectatorship. The battle lines in film theory have long been drawn over which questions should even be asked concerning film viewing, much less which vocabulary should be employed, and while the debates parallel those in literary criticism, they are not identical.

The ultimate issue at stake in defining or explaining the film spectator concerns the problem of isolating how or where meaning is finally produced in the individual viewer (or in a group, society or mass audience for cultural critics). While competing models of spectatorship, like psychoanalytical and cognitive theories, may never agree on shared methodology or conclusions, the important thing for the film student is to acknowledge that a workable model for film viewing must incorporate a basic understanding of the series of operations that are continuously at work in our perception and comprehension of the sights and sounds we put together during the 'cinematic experience'. The most useful initial conception of a viewer therefore will be one that can account for how humans process the cinematic elements (shot/reverse-shots, dissolves, voice-over, three-point lighting and so on) into an understanding of a story, but then also how spectators relate those techniques to more general meaning construction.

The spectator must, therefore, be considered as actively perceiving images and sounds that can be related to each other within this specific film (as in the recognition of repeated low, canted camera angles on various characters in Spike Lee's *Do the Right Thing*, 1989) and from other textual or intertextual experiences (Expressionism has taught us to interpret tilted

A collision of classic Hollywood with European art cinema: Dustin Hoffman and Anne Bancroft in Mike Nichols's *The Graduate*

cameras as signifiers of psychological imbalance). Thus viewers perceive, identify, interpret, make hypotheses, sense emotions, fill in gaps and build fictional cause–effect relations as films unfold. Rather than becoming a static, ideologically determined subject, the spectator works actively on many levels simultaneously, consciously and unconsciously processing visual and audio cues. Various modes of production and competing filmic traditions will obviously expect and/or demand different sorts of specific variations on these operations from their spectators – the labour of sorting out story time in *Stagecoach* will be different than for Alain Resnais's *Hiroshima mon amour* (1959), for instance.

A spectating model based on the forward progression of hypothesis-making, memory and textual and intertextual comparisons is not unlike the semiotic model of diagramming syntagmatic and paradigmatic ordering. We look for scene-to-scene connections and consider options as we (and the text) advance. The viewing situation, with the continuing series of sounds and images, requires the audience to proceed via expectation ('The soldier mentioned in passing that Geronimo is on the warpath, therefore I wouldn't be surprised if there will be a fight later on') and retrospection ('I wondered why that banker seemed so nervous, now I realise the narrator was cueing me not to believe everything he said; he is in fact a thief'). The stronger the spectator's background in watching various modes of film-making (classic Hollywood films, art films, films by the same director, genre, film movement or national cinema), the easier it will be for the viewer to pick up on the codified cues. Purely ideological or psychoanalytic models of viewing too often sidestep the actual operations and procedures of the cinematic experience. Most narrative-theory models work more systematically to prove how processes of narration control the audience's perception and comprehension, and try to demonstrate how the viewer makes sense of and interprets film texts.

While there is no single theory of the cinema, nor any one critical approach, the study of film in its aesthetic or social dimensions must as systematically as possible confront the essence of film as an apparatus, a signifying practice and a narrative instance. The cinema's power, artistry and specific pleasure call for close analysis of all the traits it shares with other media but also of all that makes the cinema unique. Film analysis has a long and diverse history, but what unifies all important theories and critical approaches is their fascination with defining and assessing the relations between the very functioning of the cinematic illusion, the filmic options open to film-makers across time, and the narrative patterns and traditions that allow meaning to accrue to those two-dimensional images that keep flashing at a set rate upon a white rectangular screen.

Selected Reading

Richard Neupert, *The End: Narration and Closure in the Cinema*, Detroit, MI, Wayne State University Press, 1995.

Battleship Potemkin/Bronenosets Potemkin (USSR 1925 *p.c* – Goskino; *d* – Sergei Eisenstein)

One of the most famous scenes in *Battleship Potemkin*, the 'Odessa steps sequence', provides a striking example of Eisenstein's dialectical editing style in which montage functions to create conflict on many levels at once, motivating intricate and multiple reactions from the audience. The immediate function certainly is to prove the brutality of the Tsar's soldiers, who appear as an inhuman line of boots, rifles and shadows as they massacre hundreds of civilians. This theme is reinforced by tiny dramas (a war veteran with no legs hops acrobatically down the steps, a small group appeals for mercy and is gunned down, a doctor tries to help fallen victims amid the gunfire and chaos). But one of the larger responses engineered by Eisenstein is that the Tsar's soldiers win because they are more disciplined than the civilians, who outnumber the soldiers but have no unity or guns. The mutineers on the ship, by contrast, are unified and armed, thus allowing them to respond with their big guns at the end of this scene.

The sequence builds tension by the use of these visual elements, but even more so by its unconventional editing. The Odessa steps become an impossible narrative space, since establishing shots are not used consistently with the cut-ins, and time and space are distorted rather than clarified. For instance, the first half of the sequence includes montages of townspeople celebrating the triumph of the mutineers on the Potemkin in the harbour. But then, as David Bordwell writes, '"Suddenly": one of the most famous titles in world cinema introduces four percussive shots of a woman's body jerking spasmodically. Barely comprehensible in projection, the jump-cut series of shots functions, Eisenstein remarks, as the detonator in an explosion' (Bordwell and Thompson, 1993, p. 74). The actual frame lengths for these four disorienting shots are seven, five, eight and ten!

The entire sequence layers discontinuous shots onto one another according to precise rhythmic and graphic conflicts, until time and space become subjective and discursive rather than representational. By the middle of the massacre, when it seems everyone should be dead or have reached the bottom of the steps, the entire cycle of running and dying seems to begin anew. This is when the longest single action of the scene – a young mother is shot and her baby's carriage rolls down the steps – is fragmented into 35 shots, which are intercut with 25 further shots that do not include the mother or the carriage (such as the shot of the rifles, the older woman looking and people scurrying in different directions). Eisenstein's intricate dialectical approach to film form here constructs its most emotional and intellectual effects.

RICHARD NEUPERT

The Graduate (USA 1967 *p.c* – Embassy Pictures/ Lawrence Turman Inc; *d* – Mike Nichols)

The Graduate proves a particularly lively text, as it allows the analyst to test for and locate a wide variety of narrative strategies. There are radical examples of montage: for example, in one scene, a naked Mrs Robinson (Anne Bancroft) runs into a bedroom to startle the naive Ben (Dustin Hoffman) – he turns his head three times, as if on Eisenstein's Odessa steps, and his perception of her body is delivered via incredibly short takes (three to five frames). But there are also elegant long takes that allow the spectator to leisurely scan the widescreen image. The scene where Ben, who is now having an affair with Mrs Robinson, asks whether they cannot at least 'liven it up with a little conversation first this time', demonstrates both the value of long takes and the cleverness of creative widescreen framing.

This pivotal scene can be contrasted with the preceding scene in which Ben's mother tries in vain to get him to talk to her. The scene between Ben and his mother lasts only 73 seconds and is composed of eight shots (average shot length nine seconds). The scene between Ben and Mrs Robinson lasts nine minutes and 15 seconds, and it too is composed of eight shots (average shot length 70 seconds). Ben's attempt at conversation leads first comically then dramatically to information about the Robinson household, including the revelation that Mrs Robinson was pregnant with Elaine when the Robinsons married. The most jarring and shortest shots (5 and 6) happen at the point when Elaine becomes an issue.

During this scene, we see Ben rebel against Mrs Robinson's control, first by turning on the lights when she wants them off, but finally by crouching over her on the bed as she cowers in the corner of the frame in shadows. The moment when she stretches her leg across the screen as he tries to decide whether to leave clinches the argument, and Ben stays. This is not only exemplary scene construction but also a fascinating combination of story information and film style.

Nichols employs the widescreen framing and depth to isolate multiple zones of action for the characters to move into and to punctuate the dialogue during the unusually long takes. But he also manipulates the lighting and lack of colour (their flesh provides the only real colour in the scene), and shifts the camera level to reinforce the powerful performances and make the narration intricately cinematic. *The Graduate*, certainly a parody of conventional romantic comedies, collides classic Hollywood style with self-conscious devices of the modern European art cinema. André Bazin and Sergei Eisenstein would both be intrigued.

RICHARD NEUPERT

Three Colours White/Trois couleurs blanc (France/Switzerland/Poland 1994 *p.c* – MK2/CAB Productions/Zespol Filmowy Tor; *d* – Krzysztof Kieslowski)

Three Colours White, the second film in Kieslowski's trilogy (the others are *Three Colours Blue/Trois couleurs bleu*, 1993, and *Three Colours Red/Trois couleurs rouge*, 1994), employs many of the director's recurring narrative strategies, especially his cross-cutting of several actions to suggest connections between characters and places before those relations are clarified by the story's time and space. *White*, in particular, relies on a challenging plot structure and the use of techniques not normally found in classic texts, such as flash-forwards and subjective depth of information whose source cannot readily be assigned to a character.

White opens with a shot of a tattered suitcase on a conveyor belt. Next the narrator reveals a somewhat hesitant and uncomfortable young man outside the Palais de Justice in Paris. This sets up in the spectator's mind a connection between the suitcase and the young man. As the man enters the building, the film cuts several more times to the slowly moving suitcase to reinforce the abstract connection. Once inside, we learn that the man, Karol Karol (Zbigniew Zamachowski), is Polish and is being divorced by his French wife, Dominique (Julie Delpy). Viewers looking for immediate significance in the editing logic will perhaps make the connection that Karol, who speaks very little French, is being manhandled and discarded by the judicial system much like the suitcase. But the film's narrative strategy will soon reveal how the narrative is based partly on pieces of a puzzle that may not fit together until much later, if at all.

During the trial – a scene built mostly on straight alternating shots of Karol on one side, Dominique on the other – Karol protests that he wants time to prove their love is not yet dead. There is a cut from Karol's concerned face to a travelling shot following Dominique, in her wedding dress, down a church aisle and out into blinding white light. This shot, however, is not followed by one of Karol again (which would cue us in conventional fashion that he was thinking about their wedding day). Instead, Dominique sits up as if coming out of a daydream and asks 'I beg your pardon?' of the judge. During the 21-second shot in the church, the judge apparently has asked Dominique a question that she, and the audience, did not hear.

Thus Kieslowski embeds what may be a subjective memory or flashback in the middle of a scene but does not clarify whose vision it is. Such tactics, coupled with the suitcase inserts, establish a pattern of revelation from different temporal or spatial points in the diegetic world without firmly anchoring them. Finally, this opening scene ends without clarifying these shot relations, but rather complicates them further: the fleeing Dominique pulls Karol's suitcase – the same one from the earlier shots on the conveyor belt – out of her car in front of the Palais de Justice and drives away. The problem for the attentive audience member is that the suitcase is not as tattered here as in the earlier shots. Only later will the film reveal that the beginning shots of the suitcase were flash-forwards to a time when a desperate Karol will punch airholes in his suitcase and climb inside to be shipped home to Poland. Thus *White* provides an exemplary test case for analysing audience hypothesis-making (expectation and retrospection), editing that breaks unity of time and space and the creative use of specifically filmic narrative devices.

RICHARD NEUPERT

Putting together the pieces of the puzzle: Julie Delpy in *Trois couleurs blanc*

SPECTATORSHIP AND AUDIENCE RESEARCH

PAMELA ROBERTSON WOJCIK

The often fraught and contested concept of the film spectator has been central to film theory since the 1970s. Different notions of spectatorship are deployed to determine the ideological effects of the cinema, spectatorial pleasure in the cinema and how spectators can possibly resist the ideological positioning of the cinema. As Judith Mayne states:

> Spectatorship is not only the act of watching a film, but also the ways one takes pleasure in the experience, or not; the means by which watching movies becomes a passion, or a leisure-time activity like any other. Spectatorship refers to how film-going and the consumption of movies and their myths are symbolic activities, culturally significant events. (Mayne, 1993, p. 1)

Broadly, theorists distinguish between, on one hand, the concept of the film spectator as a correlate institution of the cinema and a hypothetical point of address by filmic discourse and, on the other hand, individual empirical viewers as members of plural, socio-historical audiences. Miriam Hansen identifies the two central questions facing film theorists in a consideration of these two different notions of spectatorship:

> When, how, and to what effect does the cinema conceive of the spectator as a textual term, as the hypothetical point of address of filmic discourse? And once such strategies have been codified, what happens to the viewer as a member of a plural, social audience? (Hansen, 1991, p. 2)

This section focuses primarily on the latter question, the ways in which researchers in film theory and history have attempted to define and analyse the viewer, through historiographic approaches, audience research, investigations of fans, and viewer ethnographies. But while the distinction between the hypothetical spectator and the viewer is important, much of the work on viewers, audiences and fans still overlaps with and responds to work on the film spectator. In order to comprehend the agenda and importance of viewer-based research, therefore, it is necessary to understand the concept of the spectator conceived as a hypothetical construct. (See also Structuralism and its aftermaths, p. 510; Feminist film theory, p. 491.)

The cinematic apparatus and textual systems

The concept of the film spectator can be traced back to 1970s semiotic and psychoanalytic theories of spectatorship. The spectator was conceptualised under the post-structuralist category of the subject, as understood through the writings of the psychoanalyst Jacques Lacan, and corresponding notions of ideology, especially as elaborated by the Marxist philosopher Louis Althusser.

Lacan appropriates the model of structural linguistics from Saussure and argues that our unconscious is a sign system that functions like a language. According to Lacan, the individual self is not a unified ego, but is consistently produced and transformed by the activity of the unconscious, which is itself produced through the language and perceptions of others. Althusser draws on Lacan's theories to reformulate Marx's concepts of alienation and identity into a theory of the subject. Althusser recasts the classic Marxist model of economic base/superstructure. He views ideology as 'relatively autonomous' of the economic base and determined by it only 'in the last instance'. Ideology takes the form of systems of representation that can have a political effectivity of their own. Althusser distinguishes between repressive state apparatuses (RSAs) (such as the police or army) that establish political order through force, and institutional state apparatuses (ISAs) (for example, the church, schools, the family, art) that establish order through consent. ISAs contribute to the unconscious formation of individuals by 'hailing' or 'interpellating' them as certain kinds of subjects, summoning them to take up their 'appropriate' role in society. In short, Althusser proposes that individuals are interpellated as social subjects in subtle and largely imperceptible ways – ways that promote in them the illusion that they are consistent, rational and free human agents.

Arguing from psychoanalytic and Marxist perspectives, film theorists have analysed how the cinema, and especially the classic Hollywood cinema, works to interpellate the film spectator, binding his or her desire with dominant ideological positions, and, above all, how it conceals this ideological process by providing the spectator with the comforting assurance that they are a unified, transcendent, meaning-making subject. Methodologically, the contributions of 1970s film theory to theories of spectatorship can be defined along two separate but related trajectories (for examples of both trajectories, see Rosen, 1986).

First, works influenced by and identified with Metz and Baudry centre on the concept of the cinematic apparatus, the cinema understood as an institutional and ideological machine. The apparatus refers to the general conditions and relations of cinematic spectatorship, and apparatus theory considers the subject effects specific to cinema, to the kind of machine it is, to the kind of viewing situation it generally involves. Due to the specific ways the cinema is arranged spatially, perceptually and socially (the darkness of the cinema, the spectator's seeming isolation, the placement of the projector behind the spectator's head, and the framing and structure of the film image), the cinematic apparatus is theorised in terms of Plato's prison cave, the mirror stage (as formulated by Lacan), principles of Renaissance perspective and idealist philosophy. Through these arrangements, as well as through the 'realist effect' of the cinema, the spectator, according to apparatus theory, is positioned as the transcendent vanishing point of filmic address. Returned to a regressive state of imaginary wholeness, the spectator imagines himself or herself as a transcendent meaning-making subject (mobile rather than immobile, active rather than passive, creating rather than absorbing meaning). The cinema, according to apparatus theory, works to acculturate and interpellate viewers to structures of fantasy, dream and pleasure that are aligned with dominant ideology.

The second axis of 1970s film theory, while overlapping with apparatus theory in many ways, emphasises the specifically textual operations of the cinematic institution. Rather than the spatial, perceptual and social arrangements of the apparatus, theorists such as Raymond Bellour, Thierry Kuntzel and Stephen Heath provided extremely detailed analyses of individual classic Hollywood films that were seen to represent the cinematic institution. Relying on the linguistic concept of enunciation (taken from Emile Benveniste) as well as psychoanalysis and semiotics, these text-based theories of spectatorship analyse how the textual system of particular films solicits and interpellates the spectator's understanding and subjectivity – organising knowledge, authority, pleasure and identification through systematic processes of vision and narration. The subject of textual analysis seems superficially to be more active than the subject of the cinematic apparatus, in so far as the subject of textual analysis is asked to take part in a hypothetical reading. Yet, both apparatus theory and analyses of textual systems imply that the spectator's imaginary participation in the filmic event depends upon the illusion that they are the enunciating author of filmic fiction.

In both apparatus theory and text-based systemic analyses, the spectator represents a term of discourse, an effect of signifying structures, and not an empirical moviegoer. The emphasis in these theories is on the way in which the cinematic institution inscribes certain viewing positions that the social viewer is asked to take up, a process of identification and desire that predetermines the viewer's subject position. Both apparatus theory and analyses of textual systems have been criticised for positing too monolithic and globalising a view of the film spectator. Critics have argued, first, that such abstract and generalisable conceptions of film spectatorship fail to account for how subjects are constituted differently by sexual, gendered and racial differences. And, second, critics claim that the attention to domination and control and the enforcement of assigned ideological positions seem to offer little room to imagine models of resistance to the dominant ideology and ways to change the signifying systems.

Feminist interventions

Feminist film theory offered the first important critique of these models. The earliest feminist psychoanalytic interventions into spectator theory were articulated by Stephen Heath and Julia Lesage, but crystallised in Laura Mulvey's 1975 'Visual pleasure' essay. Mulvey's essay critiques both the apparatus model and the text-based model of spectatorship theory for not taking into account the importance of the representation of the female form in the cinema's symbolic order and she points out that classic spectatorship is fundamentally gendered as masculine, which makes dominant routes of identification problematic for the female spectator (see Mulvey, 1989, p. 353).

Since the 1970s, feminist film theorists have grappled with Mulvey's provocative claims about the 'male gaze', often in contention with her bleak assessment of the female spectatorial position (see Bergstrom and Doane, 1989; Doane, 1991; Pribram, 1988; Gamman and Marshment, 1989; Hansen, 1986). Initially, feminist film theorists criticised Mulvey for duplicating the problem she identifies, because in 'Visual pleasure' she leaves the female spectator out of her analysis. Addressing this problem in 'Afterthoughts on "Visual pleasure and narrative cinema"' (1989), Mulvey envisions the female spectator's activity as an either/or hopscotch between positions of identification; she pictures the female spectator shifting unconsciously between an active masculine and a passive feminine identity.

Mary Ann Doane has argued that in opposition to transvestitism, the concept of female masquerade offers a more radical concept of spectatorship. Joan Rivière's 1929 essay (1986) has been taken up in feminist theory as a divining rod pointing to the 'performative status' and 'imitative structure' of the feminine. Doane suggests that 'a woman might flaunt her femininity, produce herself as an excess of femininity, in other words, foreground the masquerade' in order to 'manufacture a lack in the form of a certain distance between oneself and one's image' (Doane, 1991, pp. 25–6). Doane uses the example of *Stella Dallas*'s heroine's self-parody as an instance of 'double mimesis' or self-conscious masquerade. When Stella effectively parodies herself, pretending to be an even more exaggeratedly embarrassing mother than she is in the rest of the narrative, she demonstrates her recognition of herself as a stereotype (a pose, a trope) while making the excessiveness of her role visible and strange, depriving the initial mimesis of its currency. Although Doane locates distanciation primarily in the text, rather than reception, she underlines the masquerade's potential usefulness for understanding the spectator's activity as well as the performer's: 'What might it mean to masquerade as a spectator? To assume the mask in order to see in a different way?' (Doane, 1991, p. 26). The trope of the masquerade, then, helps to describe a process of negotiation between textual address and the viewer. The concept of negotiation implies a continuing process of give and take. It suggests that a range of positions of identification may exist within any text; and that, rather than having their response wholly determined by the text, audiences may shift subject positions as they interact with the text.

An interest in determining the specific mechanisms of female spectatorship has led many feminists to consider how specific genres and films address a female spectator. They have investigated certain films and genres that were specifically and historically aimed at a female audience, such as Rudolph Valentino films (Hansen, 1986) or the woman's film (Gledhill, 1987; Doane, 1987). These studies are interested in the ways that a specific address to woman complicates a Mulveyian model that assumes an address to the male spectator. They suggest that in these moments, the cinematic institution foregrounds its market orientation to a female consumer and thus opens up a potential gap or contradiction (albeit fleeting) between patriarchal ideology, on one side, and the recognition of female experience, desires and fantasies, on the other.

Theories of the gaze

Feminist film theory has provided a crucial forum for discussing, and models for understanding, modes of spectatorship for other empirical viewers who share the female spectator's alienation from the dominant – gays and lesbians, and racial or ethnic minorities. One avenue of research in feminist film theory and theories of spectatorship has been what, for purposes of abbreviation, can be called 'gaze theory'. Gaze theory tries to ascertain whether there are alternative gazes operating in the cinema, such as a 'female gaze' (Gamman and Marshment, 1989), a 'gay', 'lesbian' or 'queer gaze' (Doty, 1993; Evans and Gamman, 1995; Gever *et al.*, 1993; Hamer and Budge, 1994), or a 'black gaze' (Roach and Felix, 1989).

Conceptualising alternative gazes to Mulvey's 'male gaze' offers ways to reconsider the film text as less monolithic in its address and tends to focus on contradictions and gaps in the cinematic institution's dominant ideology and, therefore, on ways the cinema might be seen as less controlling and more flexible in its constitution of the subject (see Feminist film theory, p. 491). For instance, by considering a 'queer gaze', theorists have suggested ways we might reinterpret the fetishistic spectacle of masses of female bodies in Busby Berkeley musical numbers. Rather than predicate their assessment of Berkeley's sexual politics on the assumption that Berkeley's numbers are unequivocally addressed to a masculine spectator and that they wholeheartedly support the patriarchal ideology that they undoubtedly portray, queer theory focuses on how lesbian spectators might locate a lesbian eroticism in the numbers (Doty, 1993, pp. 13–14). A number like the title song of Ray Enright's 1934 *Dames* (which features images of women two by two in bed, exercising in sexy pyjamas and bathing together before turning into black-and-white abstractions) seems equally available to be read as lesbian imagery as well as in terms of the girl–girl eroticism favoured in straight male pornography. Even assuming a masculine address, then, different notions of the gaze help to understand these and other potentially oppositional ways in which viewers might be able to negotiate their experience of these texts.

The application of gaze theory to alternative models of spectatorship has been critiqued, however, for producing overly rigid models of social relationships and for sticking too closely to the terms of the monolithic apparatus and text-based models of spectatorship (Evans and Gamman, 1995; Williams, 1995). The single, unitary spectator of gaze theory has gradually been challenged by theories and histories of diverse viewing positions.

The questions feminist film theorists have raised about female spectatorship and the methods and models they offer have thus served as a springboard for a reconsideration of spectatorship models as determined by the semiotic-psychoanalytic framework. Theorists of female spectatorship and spectatorship among other minority groups have increasingly begun to analyse the social and historical factors that shape film spectatorship. Scholars influenced by the Frankfurt School and British cultural studies have attempted to give the concept of the spectator historical specificity and/or ethnographic precision to account for different kinds of readings and possible forms of subcultural resistance. Some of the most important areas for a reconsideration of spectatorship and empirical viewers have taken place through revisionist histories of the cinematic institution and its audience, reception, research on fans and ethnographic research.

Pre-classic spectatorship

In the 1970s, film theory and film history were largely separate areas of enquiry. In the 1980s, however, attention increasingly turned to 'the contradictions posed by film history' (Hansen, 1991, p. 5) to challenge the theoretical model of the spectator as passive subject, pure absorber of dominant ideology, as well as the model of a singular dominating male voyeur. Concentrating on pre-classic and post-classic moments in film history, film theorists and historians questioned

> the orthodoxies of a classical spectatorship without abandoning the fundamental insight that there is something to be learned from the moving picture and its apparatus about the spectators who gaze at it, look at it, glance at it, or avert their eyes from it. (Williams, 1995, p. 4)

Many of the most important challenges to the classic model of spectatorship have taken place in revisionist histories of early cinema practices. These histories oppose the technological determinism of apparatus theory, which suggests that once the technological apparatus was invented, classic cinema and its codes of realism followed. Revisionist histories and theories suggest, instead, that more than technology was involved in the invention of classic cinema and that early cinema offered alternative models of spectatorship (see Early and pre-sound cinema, p. 3).

Perhaps the most influential among theorists of early cinema practice is Tom Gunning, whose terms 'the cinema of attractions' and, to a lesser degree, 'aesthetics of astonishment' (Gunning, 1990; 1995) now vie with Mulvey's 'male gaze' as the most frequently cited formulations in the field. Gunning plays on Eisenstein's theory of attraction as well as the term's more colloquial use in the context of fairgrounds, amusements and other commercial entertainment venues. He discusses how early cinema adopted a display aesthetic similar to these commercial attractions, an aesthetic that was defined by the goal of astonishing viewers with sensational displays and direct address, as opposed to suturing them into a classic narrative. Gunning points out that: 'Early cinema was not dominated by the narrative impulse that later asserted its sway over the medium' but was instead an exhibitionist cinema, 'a cinema that displays its visibility, willing to rupture a self-enclosed fictional world for a chance to solicit the attention of the spectator' (Gunning, 1990, pp. 56–7). Gunning sees an affinity between early cinema and late avant-garde cinema, both of which can be described as cinemas of 'attractions'.

In addition to providing a better understanding of film spectatorship in early and avant-garde cinema, Gunning's theories of attractions and astonishment point to aspects of spectatorship that have been ignored and undervalued in apparatus theory and under gaze paradigms. Rather than see these spectatorial relations to cinema as exclusive to early cinema, theorists have adopted Gunning's terms to account for pleasures in all forms of cinema that are irreducible to more technologically determined modes of ideological absorption and the voyeuristic look. The notion of 'attractions', especially, has opened up theories of film spectatorship to consider the power of diverse spectacles in cinema to undermine and challenge narrative's realist grip.

Miriam Hansen has also re-evaluated early cinema practices and reception to challenge the seeming inevitability of classic spectatorship and to consider how the cinema provided the conditions for an alternative public sphere. She views the cinema itself as a public sphere 'defined by particular relations of representation and reception' and dependent upon 'processes specific to the institution of cinema, that is, the uneven development of modes of production, distribution, and exhibition' (Hansen, 1991, p. 7). Hansen considers the relationship between the cinema and other aspects of public life to determine 'how the public, as a collective and intersubjective horizon, is constituted and constitutes itself under particular conditions and circumstances' (Hansen, 1991, p. 8). During a crucial phase of the cinema's development, Hansen claims, it depended on peripheral social groups (immigrants, women, members of the newly urbanised working class) and thus necessarily catered to people with specific needs, anxieties and fantasies. She views the elaboration of classic modes of narration and spectator positioning as a response to the problem of making the cinema available to these diverse, unruly and sexually mixed audiences. Instead of a teleology of classic cinema, however, Hansen sees early cinema as a composite public sphere that allowed a margin of improvisation, interpretation and unpredictability that made cinema a public event open to reappropriation by film viewers of diverse backgrounds and interests.

Audience composition

Historians have also been interested in the social make-up of early cinema audiences and have addressed issues of ethnicity, class and urban geography to provide a crucial counter-argument to more monolithic notions of spectatorship (Allen, 1979; Gomery, 1982; Jowett, 1974; Merritt, 1985). These histories often focus on Manhattan's nickelodeon boom, which has functioned as a shorthand for the birth of the movies in general. Often historians concentrate on identifying changes in the class composition of nickelodeon and picture-palace audiences, frequently focusing on European immigrants as audiences or exhibition in ethnic white neighbourhoods. Counter to traditional histories of the cinema that framed early cinema as a lower-class amusement, revisionist historians starting in the 1970s emphasised the degree to which middle-class audiences altered the cinema, managing to appropriate and 'uplift' the cinema to suit their tastes and objectives (much as they had uplifted vaudeville). Robert C. Allen's (1979) text is key in this revisionist impulse. Allen examines the location of nickelodeons and claims that the majority of them were not in immigrant neighbourhoods but in putatatively middle-class neighbourhoods or traditional entertainment districts that served a variety of social types.

In her emphasis on how classic cinema responds to early immigrant and working-class audiences, and not exclusively to middle-class interests, Hansen's work can be seen as a crucial modification of this view. Ben Singer's work (1995) on nickelodeons also calls the revisionist argument into question. Supplementing Allen's data, remapping the nickelodeons' placement in the city and reviewing urban geography of the period, Singer finds that the immigrant and working-class foundations of cinema in traditional histories may not have been myth but a fairly accurate characterisation of early audiences.

Historical audience research has also focused on minority groups who, until recently, were marginalised by film theory and history. For instance, still working within American social history, Mary Carbine has examined African-American spectatorship in Chicago to challenge the emphasis on European immigration in histories of the nickelodeons. She notes that the nickelodeon boom also coincided with the 'Great Migration' of southern blacks to northern cities in America. Examining the 'culturally specific' ways black spectators used early cinema, Carbine claims that the 'dynamic of reception was inflected with the dynamic of black performance', and especially the live performance of African-American blues and jazz (Carbine, 1990, p. 23). Carbine thus challenges notions of the seemingly isolated and passive spectator and points to the ways in which different audiences can transform the cinematic institution according to their own cultural needs and fantasies.

In a different vein, Richard deCordova has analysed the children's audience and the rise of matinées. He analyses reformist audience studies of the 1920s and 1930s and suggests that 'an investigation of the practices through which researchers attempted to understand the child audience may tell us something about audience research today and the various power relations that subtend it' (deCordova, 1990, p. 92). He points out the oddity of the child's neglect in film history, since the image of the child has functioned as a precondition of audience research generally (in its paternalistic reformist mode – and, we might add, in psychoanalytic theory as well). Rather than simply fill a gap in audience research, deCordova's research, along with Carbine's, suggests the degree to which traditional concepts of spectatorship are constructed according to exclusionary and ahistorical models.

Reception theory

Overlapping with the new historiographic impulse in studies of spectatorship, but approaching the question from a somewhat different angle, is a burgeoning interest since the mid-1980s in reception. Rather than focusing on production or the cinematic text, reception studies take into account a broad range of extra-cinematic materials – including, as above, social history and audience composition, as well as reviews, commentary, fan discourse, star images or texts, commodity tie-ins, scandal, and other discourses and events that produce the conditions of reading and reception for the film text.

Janet Staiger, for instance, takes what she describes as a historical materialist approach to reception studies of individual films. She considers how films become encrusted with meaning over time and analyses how the discourses surrounding individual films become part of their meaning and help to determine their reception in different periods. Her analysis includes not only contemporary reviews and discourses around films, but also later transformations of a film's reception and various discourses surrounding films, including academic readings. In her analysis of Griffith's *The Birth of a Nation*, for example, Staiger considers the initial controversy surrounding the film's release in 1915, related to questions of racism, and how racist attitudes intersect with other tacit assumptions – about 'what constitutes acceptable historiography; whether a film should be judged on the content or effects of its subject matter, narrational procedures, or some combination of them; and whether censorship of certain representations is more important than free speech' (Staiger, 1992, p. 146). She then shows how debates in the 1930s transformed the reception of *The Birth of a Nation*, as the film was appropriated by progressive radicals as a symptom of Fascist and monopoly capitalist ideologies and to demonstrate the links between racism and class exploitation.

British cultural studies

In addition to a renewed interest in historiography, film studies and theories of spectatorship have been profoundly influenced by cultural studies. The Birmingham Centre for Contemporary Cultural Studies, especially under the leadership of Stuart Hall, can justifiably lay claim to being the key institution in the widely expanding field of cultural studies. The Centre's Marxism was aligned with the work of Antonio Gramsci, and especially his notion of hegemony. Gramsci's theory of hegemony holds that cultural domination, or, more precisely, cultural leadership, is not achieved through force or coercion, but secured through the consent of those it will ultimately subordinate. The subordinated groups consent to the dominant because they accept as 'common sense' the view of the world offered to them by the dominant group. The concept of hegemony differs from Althusser's ISAs (institutional state apparatuses) in viewing cultural domination as not inevitably produced through language or ISAs but as the product of complex negotiations and alignments of interest. The achievement of hegemony is sustained only through the continuing process of winning consent. In emphasising consent and 'common sense', Gramsci's concept of hegemony also provides a point of entry into imagining resistance. As opposed to 'top-down' theories of ideology, which reduce the subject to a passive dupe of the culture industry, Gramsci's concept of hegemony appealed to cultural studies because it offered a 'bottom-up' theory that attributes power to the subject and to subcultural groups to intervene in the signifying and political systems and to produce change. Gramsci envisions a class of organic intellectuals who can produce counter-hegemonic ideas, resistant worldviews that can alter dominant ideology and effect change.

Considering how viewers might be seen as resisting dominant ideology has led researchers influenced by cultural studies to consider the active role of the viewer in interpreting texts. Stuart Hall's 1980 essay 'Encoding/decoding' has been particularly influential for rethinking how viewers interpret texts. Hall argues against those who explain the processes of communication as a direct line from sender to receiver. As Graeme Turner explains, Hall points out that

> just because a message has been sent, this is no guarantee that it will arrive; every moment in the process of communication, from the original composition of the message (encoding) to the points at which it is read and understood (decoding) has its own determinants. (Turner, 1992, p. 89)

While some viewers accept the dominant as encoded, and others adopt an opposing position, most viewers engage in negotiated decoding practices that acknowledge the dominant definitions of the world but may still lay claim to exceptions in local or specific cases as determined by geography, ethnicity, class or gender, for example.

This attention to the positions viewers bring to texts can be seen in subcultural studies. Emphasising the minority, rather than the majority, the subordinate rather than the dominant, subcultural studies examined the strategies subcultures used to negotiate or oppose the dominant to make their own meanings by actively appropriating and transforming the dominant through manipulating its codes (Hebdige, 1979).

Influenced by cultural studies, later film theory has been marked by a developing interest in viewers, to see how they resist ideological positioning through decoding practices and 'fail' to take up dominant positions. This relates to many of the aforementioned challenges to the model of passive spectatorship, such as 'gaze theory', concepts of negotiated readings, and the interest in gaps and contradictions at the textual level – in fact, to any analysis of ideology that does not simply posit a theory of passively absorbent spectatorship. What distinguishes cultural studies research most clearly in its analysis of reception is the introduction of pleasure as a category separate from ideology. Within earlier formations, pleasure was seen as part of the deceptive apparatus and was interrogated for the politics it concealed. A competing perspective, however, has viewed pleasure as a dimension of cultural decoding that is in some way resistant to dominant ideologies.

Stars and fans

Star studies have proved an especially fruitful area of investigation for theorists interested in the joint process of encoding and decoding (see Gledhill, 1991; Dyer, 1979; 1986; also The star system, p. 110). The star text consists of cinematic and extra-cinematic elements (such as fan discourse, song sheets, publicity stills and interviews). From the perspective of ideological encoding, star studies emphasises the contradictions and gaps in star texts. Stars, as Richard Dyer argues, represent a 'structured polysemy, that is, the finite multiplicity of meanings and affects they embody and the attempt to structure them so that some meanings and affects are foregrounded and others are masked or displaced' (Dyer, 1979, p. 3). Rather than a simplistic relation between a given star text and a single ideology, Dyer claims that stars exist 'within and between ideologies' so that they may either manage and resolve contradictions, expose contradictions 'or embody an alternative or oppositional ideological position (itself usually contradictory) to dominant ideology' (Dyer, 1979, p. 38). From the perspective of decoding, star studies emphasises the ways in which members of different classes, genders, races, ethnicities and sexualities appropriate or read the star text and how their readings manage, expose or resolve those contradictions. Dyer's analysis of Paul Robeson's star text, for instance, investigates the contradiction between the emphasis on blackness in Robeson's image – 'musically, in his primary association with Negro folk music, especially spirituals; in the theatre and films, in the recurrence of Africa as a motif; and in general in the way his image is so bound up with notions of racial character, the nature of black folks, the Negro essence, and so on' (Dyer, 1986, p. 67) – and his status as a crossover star who appealed to white and black audiences alike. Dyer's analysis of the discourses surrounding Robeson in relation to his films shows that the discourse of blackness in Robeson's star image was managed differently by white and black audiences. Where Robeson represented a positive view of atavistic folk blackness as a radical alternative to white western culture, he could be seen simultaneously as fitting into white stereotypes of 'Sambo', Uncle Tom and the black brute.

Concomitant with an interest in stars, cultural studies has also opened the way for researchers to consider fans as active users of popular culture. Theorists have analysed fandom as an extreme case of viewer activity, a stigmatised activity marked by deviance and pathology; as a marker of cultural taste; and as a sensibility that helps construct coherent identities (see Lewis, 1992). Theorists have also analysed fans to determine the nature of spectatorial pleasure in texts and stars, and how fans read against the grain to construct oppositional meanings. Much of this research is still text-based and focuses on fan discourse in popular magazines, reviews, box-office sales, interviews, publicity materials and stars' performances in particular films to ascertain what elements of a star's persona fans respond to (Gaines, 1986; Roberts, 1993; Robertson, 1996). As with other areas of research, investigation of fans tends to focus on the way in which gender, race, ethnicity, class and sexuality shape fan responses. Shari Roberts, for instance, notes that while Carmen Miranda's star text 'offers various negative images of Latin Americans and of women, her persona also reveals these images as stereotypes, allowing for negotiated readings by fans' (Roberts, 1993, p. 4). Roberts notes that some fans were able to understand Miranda's stereotypical image as a kind of masquerade and 'were, thereby, through interpretation and fantasy, able to identify with her as one way to negotiate or cope with their own minority status in society' (Roberts, 1993, p. 18).

Ethnographic research

To determine how 'real' viewers and fans actually decode texts, many theorists since the mid-1980s have turned to ethnographic analysis of viewers. The ethnographic approach has been more visible in television studies than in cinema (see Ang, 1985; Brunsdon, 1981; Hobson, 1982; Jenkins, 1992; Morley, 1980; Penley, 1991; Seiter, 1991). This is partly because television watching is the most representative and common spectating activity in contemporary industrial societies, but it also relates to film studies' suspicion of sociological approaches in analysing media. In his article on ethnographic research into children's audiences, Richard deCordova (1990) reminds us that current interest in audience and ethnography represents a return to a set of interests and methods that characterised the earliest researches on film. But, as he suggests, this return to the repressed has arisen largely as a means of complicating psychoanalytic and semiotic models of spectatorship. Where early sociological studies viewed cinema as a threat to presumably vulnerable audiences such as women and children, more recent ethnographic research has arisen as a response to the passive model of spectatorship in 1970s film theory – it has as its avowed aim the empowerment of spectators and an interest in how viewers actively interpret texts and take pleasure in them.

Using the encoding/decoding model, Jacqueline Bobo interviewed African-American female viewers of Spielberg's *The Color Purple* (1985) to 'examine the way in which a specific audience creates meaning from a mainstream text and uses the reconstructed meaning to empower themselves and their social group' (Bobo, 1988, p. 93). Against the largely negative reception of the film among both black and white reviewers, Bobo finds that African-American female viewers discovered something progressive and useful in the film. As sophisticated oppositional viewers of black representation in Hollywood, the African-American women Bobo interviewed were able to filter out the negative stereotypes, and they engaged with the film as part of a broader movement among African-American women to construct and consume more works orientated to African-American women's experiences and their history.

Other analysts have tried to reconstruct viewers' responses historically by asking viewers to send letters and fill out questionnaires about their memories of certain films and stars. Using this approach, Richard Dyer has analysed gay men's subcultural camp response to Judy Garland; Helen Taylor has investigated the lasting appeal of *Gone With the Wind* (1939) among female fans; and Jackie Stacey has analysed the meanings and affects of 1940s female stars for British women. More than simply telling us about why certain people like certain film and stars, these ethnographic studies help us to understand the social dimensions of film viewing, and especially to consider the social and historical dimensions of identification. Dyer, for instance, notes the socio-historical dimension of gay men's attendance at Garland concerts that 'constituted a kind of going public or coming out before the emergence of gay liberationist politics' (Dyer, 1979, p. 145). Taylor counters the notion of singular spectator positioning by pointing to 'the varied and contradictory ways in which this one work has accumulated significance in their lives, making the notion of a single *Gone With the Wind* impossible' (Taylor, 1989, p. 232). And Stacey (1994) underlines the importance of extra-cinematic practices, such as copying stars' style and clothing, or imitating their mannerisms, as important dimensions of cinematic identification.

Ethnographic research revealed the complexity of viewers' responses to Vivien Leigh and Hattie McDaniel in *Gone With the Wind*

Ethnographic research has posed some methodological and ideological problems for film theorists. First, theorists have raised questions about the degree to which the subjects' statements can be taken at face value or need to be interpreted, an issue that raises the related problem of the researcher's position vis-à-vis their subjects, the degree to which they will read into their statements what they want to hear. A second problem is that since much interest in film spectatorship takes classic Hollywood films and stars as its subject, ethnographic research interested in viewers' initial responses to films must be reconstructed from viewers' memories and are thus potentially modified by nostalgia, changed perspectives or other shifts in their attitudes towards the films and stars they discuss. While these problems are still being debated, ethnographic research has, nonetheless, enriched spectator studies.

Conclusion

This overview of spectatorship and audience research has been necessarily schematic in tracing the trends in approaches to spectators and viewers. Trends can, however, be trendy. Since the late 1980s, there has been a tendency to categorise spectatorship too schematically as an either/or proposition, particularly in relation to pleasure, an impulse 'to categorise texts and readings/responses as either conservative or radical, as celebratory of the dominant order or critical of it' (Mayne, 1993, p. 93). The 'dominant' model, which focuses on the hypothetical spectator, argues that the cinematic apparatus and texts interpellate viewers into essentialist positions of subjecthood and so believes that the ties to those texts must be broken. These models tend to view pleasure as a form of cultural domination, passively imbibed, which renders us all cultural dupes. The 'dominant' model rightfully points out the problem with unexamined pleasure, its complicity with an oppressive sexual regime. Still, these models do not provide a means to name the pleasures viewers do take.

On the other side of the debate, however, the 'resistance' model's assumption that the activity of making meaning resides solely with viewers falls into a similar determinism. Cultural studies in particular has been identified with the resistance model, which valorises pleasure as redemptive. Meaghan Morris sums up the typical mode of argument in this 'banal', 'vox pop style': 'People in modern mediatised societies are complex and contradictory, mass cultural texts are complex and contradictory, therefore people using them produce complex and contradictory culture' (Morris, 1990, p. 30). In ascribing unqualified power to viewer response, this model suggests that, rather than interpellating viewers, the text produces a multiplicity of meanings from which the viewer can choose his or her point of identification. If the conservative model reifies pleasure in seeing texts as 'dominant' and audiences as dupes, the viewer-orientated model similarly reifies pleasure in ignoring the force of dominant ideology in favour of a free-for-all textual and cultural ambiguity. In ascribing an unqualified power to viewers' pleasure, this model often fails to account for the ways in which pleasure can merely affirm the dominant order.

Researchers have been trying increasingly to negotiate between these extremes. The historiographic models discussed above make a crucial intervention into the debate and help to mediate between positions. This process of negotiation between models must continue if we are to understand the genuinely contradictory mechanisms at play in film spectatorship, the ideological effects of the cinema and spectatorial pleasure.

Selected Reading

Robert C. Allen, 'From exhibition to reception: reflections on the audience in film history', *Screen* 31 (4): 79–91, winter 1990. Reprinted in Kuhn and Stacey (eds), *Screen Histories: A Screen Reader*, Oxford, Oxford University Press, 1998.

Judith Mayne, *Cinema and Spectatorship*, London and New York, Routledge, 1993.

Janet Staiger, *Interpreting Films: Studies in the Historical Reception of American Cinema*, Princeton, NJ, Princeton University Press, 1992.

Melvyn Stokes and Richard Maltby (eds), *American Movie Audiences: From the Turn of the Century to the Early Sound Era*, London, BFI Publishing, 1999.

Queen Christina (USA 1933 *p.c* – MGM; *d* – Rouben Mamoulian)

In her analysis of lesbian spectatorship, Andrea Weiss (1991) foregrounds the important role that rumour and gossip have played in gay subcultures and the ways in which gossip about stars affected viewers' responses to their films. Weiss claims that because dominant ideology seeks to make homosexuality invisible, gay history has been necessarily located in rumour, innuendo and coded language. She describes how Hollywood marketed the suggestion of lesbianism in such stars as Marlene Dietrich, Katharine Hepburn and Greta Garbo, to address straight male voyeuristic interest in lesbianism, but argues that this innuendo enabled female viewers to 'explore their own erotic gaze without giving it a name, and in the safety of their private fantasy in a darkened theatre' (Weiss, 1991, p. 286). These fantasies were supported by gossip about the presumed 'real life' lesbianism of the actresses, especially Dietrich and Garbo.

Weiss claims that in *Queen Christina*, Garbo gives her portrayal sufficient sexual ambiguity so that her actions and manner become coded for lesbian viewers. In addition to the scene where Garbo's Christina kisses Countess Ebba (Elizabeth Young) on the lips, Weiss identifies other coded lesbian elements. These include Garbo's androgyny, Christina's dressing in men's clothes, her choice of desire over duty, the interaction between women in the film, and the film's complicated attitude towards marriage. For instance, Christina, who opts to die a 'bachelor' and not an 'old maid', asserts that Molière said that marriage is shocking, contradicting the sentiment that the queen's refusal to marry is shocking. She relates his comment about enduring the idea of sleeping with a man in the room. For viewers privy to the gossip about Garbo's affair with scriptwriter Salka Viertel, this comment offers an inside lesbian joke.

In Weiss's reading, then, gossip and rumour serve as means for lesbian spectators to define and empower themselves against dominant heterosexual ideology. Spectatorship is thus seen as an oppositional act of appropriation. But, as Weiss suggests, Hollywood texts such as *Queen Christina* are already inflected with queer and camp codes, albeit intended to appeal to heterosexual men. Thus, queer readings redefine the dominant even as they appropriate it. In Alexander Doty's terms, they make the notion that mass culture is 'straight' a 'highly questionable given' (Doty, 1993, p. 104).

PAMELA ROBERTSON WOJCIK

Gone With the Wind (USA 1939 *p.c* – Selznick International/Loew's Inc; *d* – Victor Fleming)

Helen Taylor's ethnographic analysis of female viewers of *Gone With the Wind* takes a viewer-orientated approach to spectatorship that contradicts many of the assumptions of text-based analyses of the film. Taylor placed ads in a wide

Greta Garbo's androgyny encourages oppositional readings of *Queen Christina*

range of British publications asking readers who were fans of *Gone With the Wind* to write to her about their memories, experiences and views of both Margaret Mitchell's novel and the film. She received a total of 427 letters and amassed 355 questionnaires, mostly from women (25 men responded). The respondents represented a cross-section of women of all ages, from different backgrounds, including a handful of black women and a few dozen Americans.

Taylor's analysis points to the importance of the social situation of viewing, as many women recalled seeing the film with other women as part of a friendship ritual. It also underlines the importance of the book as a context for understanding the film. Text-based analyses of films rarely take into account the structure of expectations created by a novel when it is adapted. Taylor's respondents tended, on the whole, to have read the novel and seen the film several times; they viewed their experiences of these texts as separable but not isolated events. This tendency towards multiple, even obsessive, viewing and reading suggests that women's pleasure in the text exceeds plot and focuses instead on the affective dimension of the narrative and on an identification with and interest in Scarlett as a character.

Taylor also indicates how changes in the women's lives and consciousness affected their reading of the film. For many women, *Gone With the Wind* evoked a rich source of nostalgia, tied to the film's evocation of a past that is both real and mythic, and a treasured part of many women's personal histories. At the same time, viewers' attitudes towards the film, and especially its racism, have altered over time, so that many viewers reported their increasing embarrassment and horror at the film's support of the Ku Klux Klan and in its racial stereotyping. Also, young viewers more frequently criticised the book's racism than older viewers. Attitudes towards the film's racism were also affected by respondents' race. Many white women distinguished between Mammy and Prissy, viewing the former as a figure of nobility and dignity and the latter as a more irritating and offensive stereotype. Black viewers, by contrast, tended to see both characters as offensive stereotypes.

In addition to providing a larger social and historical context for understanding the film, Taylor's approach also challenges one of the most basic tenets of classic film theory. Text-based readings often emphasise the importance of closure and resolution in classic narrative. *Gone With the Wind*, however, has a famously unresolved ending, one that raises new enigmas rather than solving the old, and one that resists the clear happy ending of romance. Respondents seemed to prefer the unresolved ending to what they perceived as the unbelievable option of a 'Hollywood' one. This related both to their knowledge of the book and their desire to have the film be true to Margaret Mitchell's intentions, and to their pleasure in constructing their own fantasy endings. Unlike a definite ending, which could close off viewer participation, the ambiguous ending demanded a creative response from viewers, who were free to choose different versions of what would happen 'tomorrow'.

PAMELA ROBERTSON WOJCIK

POSTMODERNISM AND FILM

NÖEL KING

Postmodernism presents the paradox of a ubiquitous but elusive cultural presence. According to John Rajchman, it took ten years for postmodernism to grow from a disputed critical category 'in a few obscure journals of architecture and dance into a field of academic specialization' (Rajchman, 1991, p. 118). So wide-ranging is the cultural presence of postmodernism that it is used to describe anything from an inner-urban cityscape to restaurant interiors and gallery spaces. It denotes 'the decor of a room, the design of a building, the diegesis of a film, the construction of a record, or a "scratch" video, a TV commercial, or an arts documentary, or . . . the layout of a page in a fashion magazine' (Hebdige, 1986, p. 78). No wonder that Umberto Eco called postmodernism 'a term *bon à tout faire*' (Eco, 1985, p. 65) and suggests that it is best regarded as 'a *Kunstwollen*, a way of operating' (Eco, 1985, p. 66).

Controversies surround the use of postmodernism to demarcate a break with modernism, and there is much dispute over whether it should be thought of as a historical period, a 'cultural logic' or a set of representational practices. There is also the problem of grasping the specificity of postmodernism across different media forms. Definitions that work for architecture, dance, painting or literature might not hold for film, television or video.

Dana Polan describes postmodernism as a 'machine for generating discourse' (Polan, 1988, p. 49). The emergence of the concept obliged other critical orientations and paradigms, such as post-structuralism, modernism, Marxism, feminism and postcolonialism, to define their positions in relation to it (see also Feminism and film since the 1990s, p. 488). John Frow argues that the persistence of the term indicates that whatever is at stake cannot be shrugged off as 'theoretical fashion' (Frow, 1997, p. 23), while Hebdige adopts Raymond Williams's idea in *Keywords* that whenever substantial levels of nuance and complexity attach to a word, it can be seen to occupy 'a semantic ground in which something precious and important (is) felt to be embedded' (Hebdige, 1986, p. 79).

Although some of the dust surrounding debates about postmodernism has settled, Frow points out that even if we can assume that there is a consensus on how the term is used, the

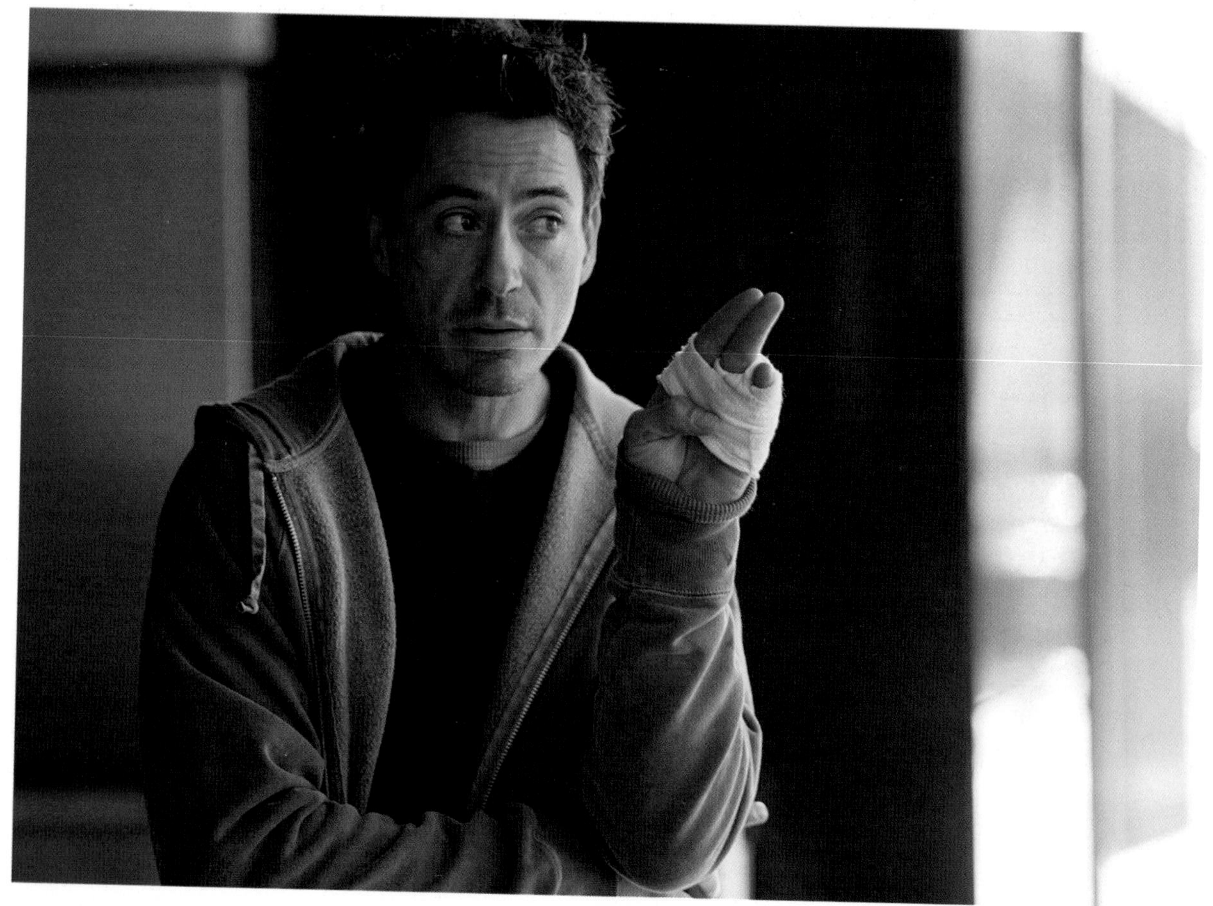

Postmodernism for a movie-aware audience: Robert Downey Jr in Shane Black's playful skit on crime thrillers *Kiss Kiss Bang Bang*

'definition of the concept shifts with the objects taken to exemplify it' (Frow, 1997, p. 27). Stuart Hall suggests that David Hare's film *Wetherby* (1985) contains 'emergent "postmodernist" elements' (Hall, 1986, p. 47) in so far as 'there is no story in the old sense' (Hall, 1986, p. 47). Hall then says that postmodernism is the current name given to the way old conceptual-explanatory certainties began to be doubted (Hall, 1986, p. 47), echoing Fredric Jameson's influential 1984 article in *New Left Review*. There, Jameson diagnosed a 'new depthlessness' (p. 58) as a distinguishing feature of the postmodern, and discerned a loss of faith in the traditional status of commentary and ideological critique devoted to the recovery of hidden meanings. The advent of postmodernism allegedly challenged the tenets of Marxism, psychoanalysis, existentialism and semiotics.

Many commentators seize on the notion of 'surface' as a definitive element of postmodernism. For Hall, postmodern society overwhelms us with a diverse plurality of surfaces just as modern cultural production enables us 'endlessly to simulate, reproduce, reiterate' (Hall, 1986, p. 49), something Peter Wollen (1986) identified when using video music clips as the centrepiece for his discussion of postmodernism to elaborate his idea of an updated 'imaginary museum' in which texts oscillate, combine and recombine. The technology of the video clip can enable a deceased Nat King Cole to sing in shared image-frame with his daughter Natalie, just as a car advertisement could have Dennis Hopper driving along in a new car only to find his earlier incarnation as 'Billy' from *Easy Rider* (1969) come alongside him on a motorbike, causing distinct cinematic-cultural histories of image-personae to conflate in a play of quotation and citation. Wyatt and Rutsky (1988) have linked postmodernism with the notion of 'high concept' to discuss 1980s US cinema, while Telotte suggests that the *Terminator* films 'play with appearances' (Telotte, 1992, p. 26) and are best approached by thinking in terms of surfaces. The postmodernist emphasis on pastiche, the play of simulacra and simulation, and intensified reflexivity implies new models for thinking about critical distance and commentary. In 1981, Rosalind Krauss identified a 'paraliterary space' defined by quotation and contestation rather than 'unity, coherence or resolution' (Krauss, 1985, p. 292). Documentary 'essay' films such as *Sunless/Sans soleil* (1983) and *The Gleaners & I/Les Glaneurs et la glaneuse* (2000) could be seen as cinematic manifestations of Krauss's notion of paraliterary texts.

If the initial impact of postmodernism was linked to its problematisation of other methods of organising knowledge and pedagogic strategies, postmodernism soon became an influential paradigm in its own right. Film studies created a canon of postmodernist works that included 1982's *Blade Runner* (see Bruno, 1987) and *Blue Velvet* (1986). Television programmes such as the self-reflexive *Moonlighting* (1985–9) and the work of the MTV network were also subsumed under postmodernism. More recently, Wes Anderson's *The Royal Tenenbaums* (2001), and Baz Luhrmann's *William Shakespeare's Romeo + Juliet* (1996) and *Moulin Rouge!* (2001) have been identified as postmodernist. These films deploy an eclectic mix of cinematic references to dissolve boundaries of time and place, celebrating the creative processes involved in historical reconstruction. Postmodernism's continuing impact on cinema is epitomised by films such as *Adaptation* (2002), which is used in university courses on screenwriting, so that students reading Robert McKee's screenwriting manual *Story* (1998) watch an actor playing McKee on screen. *Adaptation* and *Kiss Kiss Bang Bang* (2005) play with postmodernism as meta-narrative and/or meta-fiction (see case study). In the 21st century, texts work with postmodernism at the same time as working within it, and it has become 'a way of operating' (Eco, 1985) used by creative practitioners and cultural critics alike.

Selected Reading

Umberto Eco, *Reflections on The Name of the Rose*, London, Secker and Warburg, 1985; trans. William Weaver.

John Frow, 'What was postmodernism?', in *Time and Commodity Culture: Essays in Cultural Theory and Postmodernity*, Oxford, Clarendon Press, 1997.

Fredric Jameson, 'Postmodernism, or, the cultural logic of late capitalism', *New Left Review* 146: 58–92, July/August 1984.

Justin Wyatt and R. L. Rutsky, 'High concept: abstracting the postmodern', *Wide Angle* 10 (4), 1988.

Kiss Kiss Bang Bang (USA 2005 *p.c* – Warner Bros./Silver Pictures; *d* – Shane Black)

Kim Newman described the screenplays that brought Shane Black to fame – *Lethal Weapon* (1987), *Last Action Hero* (1993) and *The Long Kiss Goodnight* (1996) among them – as purveying 'broad-appeal postmodernism for a movie-aware audience' (Newman, 2005, p. 14). With *Kiss Kiss Bang Bang*, writer-director Black created a hybrid of witty, neo-screwball romantic comedy and literate action-thriller made up of playful allusions to older stories and modes of storytelling.

From the opening credits with their references to earlier credit sequences, to Robert Downey Jr's voice-over advising viewers that this is a retelling of past events as he introduces himself as the narrator, the film offers a commentary on its own mechanisms. Chapter headings ('How Harry Got to the Party', 'How Harmony Got to the Party', 'Lady in the Lake', 'Farewell My Lovely') simultaneously recall the literary conceits of eighteenth-century novels and specific Raymond Chandler thrillers. *Kiss Kiss Bang Bang* is an example of postmodernism's capacity for 'irony, metalinguistic play, enunciation squared' (Eco, 1985, p. 68), while it also retains traditional genre plotting in its investigative structure.

Along with its intertextual citational play, *Kiss Kiss Bang Bang* foregrounds the cinematic context itself. When Robert Downey Jr's voice-over interrupts the flow of sounds and images, viewers are confronted with a frozen, spliced image that could be film viewed on an editing machine. This reference to the passage of celluloid through the projector is 'rhymed' with the switching off of what appears to be a DVD or television image in the concluding 'Epilogue'. It is difficult not to see this as a knowing comment on the lucrative DVD and other ancillary markets that *Kiss Kiss Bang Bang* fed into after its theatrical release, and an acknowledgment of the importance of the home-entertainment environment to contemporary cinema.

NÖEL KING

BIBLIOGRAPHY

PART 1: Hollywood Cinema and Beyond

EARLY AND PRE-SOUND CINEMA

Richard Abel, *French Cinema: The First Wave, 1915–1929*, Princeton, NJ, Princeton University Press, 1984.

Richard Abel, *The Ciné Goes to Town: French Cinema, 1896–1914*, Berkeley, University of California Press, 1994.

Richard Abel (ed.), *Silent Film*, New Brunswick, NJ, Rutgers University Press, 1995.

Richard Abel, *The Red Rooster Scare: Making Cinema American, 1900–1910*, Berkeley, University of California Press, 1999.

Richard Abel (ed.), *Encyclopedia of Early Cinema*, London and New York, Routledge, 2005.

Richard Abel, *Americanizing the Movies and 'Movie-Mad' Audiences, 1910–1914*, Berkeley, University of California Press, 2006.

Richard Abel and Rick Altman (eds), *The Sounds of Early Cinema*, Bloomington, Indiana University Press, 2001.

Joanne Bernardi, *Writing in Light: The Silent Scenario and the Japanese Pure Film Movement*, Detroit, MI, Wayne State University Press, 2001.

Ivo Blom, *Jean Desmet and the Early Dutch Film Trade*, Amsterdam, Amsterdam University Press, 2003.

David Bordwell, Janet Staiger and Kristin Thompson, *The Classical Hollywood Cinema: Film Style and Mode of Production to 1960*, New York and London, Routledge & Kegan Paul, 1985. Revised edition 1987.

Eileen Bowser, *The Transformation of Cinema, 1907–1915*, New York, Scribner's, 1991.

Ben Brewster, 'Deep staging in French films 1900–1914', in Elsaesser and Barker (eds), *Early Cinema*, 1990a.

Ben Brewster, 'A scene at the movies', in Elsaesser and Barker (eds), *Early Cinema*, 1990b.

Ben Brewster and Lea Jacobs, *From Theatre to Cinema: Stage Pictorialism and the Early Feature Film*, Oxford, Oxford University Press, 1997.

Noël Burch, 'Primitivism and the avant-gardes: a dialectical approach', in Rosen (ed.), *Narrative, Apparatus, Ideology*, 1986.

Noël Burch, *Life to Those Shadows*, Berkeley, University of California Press, 1990.

Leo Charney and Vanessa Schwartz (eds), *Cinema and the Invention of Modern Life*, Berkeley, University of California Press, 1995.

Karl Dibbets and Bert Hogenkamp (eds), *Film and the First World War*, Amsterdam, Amsterdam University Press, 1995.

Thomas Elsaesser and Adam Barker (eds), *Early Cinema: Space, Frame, Narrative*, London, BFI Publishing, 1990.

Thomas Elsaesser, 'Comparative style analyses for European films, 1910–1918', Lecture at the *Deuxième colloque international de Domitor*, Lausanne, July 1992.

John Fell (ed.), *Film Before Griffith*, Berkeley, University of California Press, 1984.

John Fullerton, 'Contextualizing the innovation of deep staging in Swedish film', in Dibbets and Hogenkamp (eds), *Film and the First World War*, 1995.

André Gaudreault, 'Temporality and narrative in early cinema, 1895–1908', in Fell (ed.), *Film Before Griffith*, 1984.

Lee Grieveson and Peter Krämer (eds), *The Silent Cinema Reader*, London and New York, Routledge, 2004.

Tom Gunning, 'The "cinema of attractions": early cinema, its spectator and the avant-garde', *Wide Angle* 8 (3/4): 63–70, fall 1986. Reprinted in Elsaesser and Barker (eds), *Early Cinema*, 1990.

Tom Gunning, *D. W. Griffith and the Origins of American Narrative Film*, Urbana, University of Illinois Press, 1991.

Tom Gunning, 'Now you see it, now you don't: the temporality of the cinema of attractions', *The Velvet Light Trap* 32: 3–12, fall 1993.

Miriam Hansen, *Babel & Babylon: Spectatorship in American Silent Film*, Cambridge, MA, Harvard University Press, 1991.

Miriam Hansen, 'Early cinema, late cinema: transformations of the public sphere', *Screen* 34 (3): 197–210, autumn 1993. Reprinted in Williams (ed.), *Viewing Positions: Ways of Seeing Film*, New Brunswick, NJ, Rutgers University Press, 1995.

Miriam Hansen, 'Fallen women, rising stars, new horizons: Shanghai silent film as vernacular modernism', *Film Quarterly* 54 (1): 10–22, autumn 2000.

Lewis Jacobs, *The Rise of the American Film: A Critical History*, New York, Harcourt Brace, 1939.

Charlie Keil, *Early American Cinema in Transition: Story, Style, and Filmmaking, 1907–1913*, Madison, University of Wisconsin Press, 2001.

Charlie Keil and Shelley Stamp (eds), *American Cinema's Transitional Era: Audiences, Institutions, Practices*, Berkeley, University of California Press, 2004.

Jean Mitry, *Histoire du cinéma: art et industrie*, Vol. 1, Paris, Editions Universitaires, 1968.

Charles Musser, *The Emergence of Cinema: The American Screen to 1907*, New York, Scribner's, 1991a.

Charles Musser, *Before the Nickelodeon: Edwin S. Porter and the Edison Manufacturing Company*, Berkeley, University of California Press, 1991b.

Kathy Peiss, *Cheap Amusements: Working Women and Leisure in Turn-of-the-Century New York*, Philadelphia, PA, Temple University Press, 1986.

Lauren Rabinovitz, *For the Love of Pleasure: Women, Movies, and Culture in Turn-of-the-Century Chicago*, New Brunswick, NJ, Rutgers University Press, 1998.

Terry Ramsaye, *A Million and One Nights: A History of the Motion Picture through 1925*, New York, Simon and Schuster, 1926. Reprinted 1964.

Philip Rosen (ed.), *Narrative, Apparatus, Ideology: A Film Theory Reader*, New York, Columbia University Press, 1986.

Barry Salt, *Film Style and Technology: History and Analysis*, London, Starword, 1983; 1992. Revised edition 2003.

Shelley Stamp, *Movie-Struck Girls: Women and Motion Picture Culture after the Nickelodeon*, Princeton, NJ, Princeton University Press, 2000.

Kristin Thompson, *Exporting Entertainment: America in the World Film Market, 1907–1934*, London, BFI Publishing, 1985a.

Kristin Thompson, 'From primitive to classical', in Bordwell, Staiger and Thompson, *Classical Hollywood Cinema*, 1985b.

Kristin Thompson, 'The international exploration of cinematic expressivity', in Dibbets and Hogenkamp (eds), *Film and the First World War*, 1995.

Yuri Tsivian, 'Bauer and Hofer: on two conceptions of space in European film culture', *Celebrating 1895: An International Conference on Film before 1929*, Bradford, 19 June 1995.

William Uricchio and Roberta Pearson, *Reframing Culture: The Case of Vitagraph Quality Films*, Princeton, NJ, Princeton University Press, 1993.

Paolo Cherchi Usai, *Burning Passions: An Introduction to the Study of Silent Cinema*, London, BFI, 1994. Revised edition, *Silent Cinema: An Introduction*, 2000.

Ruth Vasey, *The World According to Hollywood, 1918–1939*, Madison, University of Wisconsin Press, 1997.

Zhang Zhen, *An Amorous History of the Silver Screen: Shanghai Cinema, 1896–1937*, Chicago, University of Chicago Press, 2005.

THE RISE OF THE AMERICAN FILM INDUSTRY

Richard Abel, *The Ciné Goes to Town: French Cinema, 1896–1914*, Berkeley, University of California Press, 1994.

Robert C. Allen, 'William Fox presents *Sunrise*', *Quarterly Review of Film Studies* 2 (3): 327–38, August 1977. Reprinted in Staiger (ed.), *The Studio System*, 1995.

Tino Balio (ed.), *The American Film Industry*, Madison, University of Wisconsin Press, 1976. Revised edition 1985.

John Belton, *American Cinema/American Culture*, New York, McGraw-Hill, 1994. Revised edition 2004.

Gregory Black, *Hollywood Censored: Morality Codes, Catholics and the Movies*, New York, Cambridge University Press, 1994.

Joel W. Finler, *The Hollywood Story*, London, Wallflower Press, 2003.

Douglas Gomery, *The Hollywood Studio System: A History*, London, BFI Publishing, 2005.

Ephraim Katz, *The International Film Encyclopedia*, London, Macmillan, 1980. Revised edition 1998.

Geoffrey Nowell-Smith, 'Silent cinema 1895–1930', in *The Oxford History of World Cinema*, Oxford, Oxford University Press, 1996.

Thomas Schatz, *The Genius of the System: Hollywood Filmmaking in the Studio Era*, London, Faber & Faber, 1998.

Anthony Slide, *The Big V: A History of the Vitagraph Company*, Metuchen, NJ, Scarecrow Press, 1976.

Janet Staiger (ed.), *The Studio System*, New Brunswick, NJ, Rutgers University Press, 1995.

Robert Stanley, *The Celluloid Empire: A History of the American Movie Industry*, New York, Hastings House, 1978.

THE CLASSIC STUDIO SYSTEM

Tino Balio (ed.), *The American Film Industry*, Madison, University of Wisconsin Press, 1976. Revised edition 1985.

Tino Balio (ed.), *Hollywood in the Age of Television*, London and Boston, Unwin Hyman, 1990.

David Bordwell, Janet Staiger and Kristin Thompson, *The Classical Hollywood Cinema: Film Style and Mode of Production to 1960*, New York and London, Routledge & Kegan Paul, 1985. Revised edition 1987.

Harry Braverman, *Labor and Monopoly Capital*, New York, Monthly Review Press, 1974.

Douglas Gomery, *The Hollywood Studio System*, New York, St Martin's Press, 1986.

Mae D. Huettig, 'The motion picture industry today', in Balio (ed.), *The American Film Industry*, 1985.

Paul Kerr (ed.), *The Hollywood Film Industry*, London, Routledge, 1986.

Gorham Kindem (ed.), *The American Movie Industry: The Business of Motion Pictures*, Carbondale, University of Illinois Press, 1982.

Thomas Schatz, *The Genius of the System: Hollywood Filmmaking in the Studio Era*, New York, Pantheon, 1988.

Robert Stanley, *The Celluloid Empire: A History of the American Movie Industry*, New York, Hastings House, 1978.

Janet Wasko, *Hollywood in the Information Age: Beyond the Silver Screen*, Oxford, Polity Press, 1994.

Paramount Pictures

Tino Balio (ed.), *The American Film Industry*, Madison, University of Wisconsin Press, 1976. Revised edition 1985.

Kevin Brownlow, *Hollywood: The Pioneers*, New York, Knopf, 1979.

I. G. Edmonds and Reiko Mimura, *Paramount Pictures and the People Who Made Them*, New York, A. S. Barnes, 1980.

Joel W. Finler, *The Hollywood Story*, New York, Crown Publishers, 1988. Reprinted by Wallflower Press, 2003.

Douglas Gomery, *The Hollywood Studio System*, New York, St Martin's Press, 1986.

Leslie Halliwell, *Mountain of Dreams: The Golden Years at Paramount*, New York, Farrar, Straus and Giroux, 1982.

Thomas Schatz, *The Genius of the System: Hollywood Filmmaking in the Studio Era*, New York, Pantheon, 1988.

Metro-Goldwyn-Mayer

Tina Balio (ed.), *The American Film Industry*, Madison, University of Wisconsin Press, 1985. 'Metro-Goldwyn-Mayer' (December 1932) and 'Loew's Inc' (August 1939).

Bosley Crowther, *The Lion's Share: The Story of an Entertainment Empire*, New York, E. P. Dutton, 1957.

John Douglas Eames, *The MGM Story*, New York, Crown Publishers, 1975.

Joel W. Finler, *The Hollywood Story*, New York, Crown Publishers, 1988.

Hugh Fordin, *The World of Entertainment*, Garden City, NY, Doubleday, 1975.

Douglas Gomery, *The Hollywood Studio System*, New York, St Martin's Press, 1986.

Thomas Schatz, *The Genius of the System: Hollywood Filmmaking in the Studio Era*, New York, Pantheon, 1988.

Warner Bros.

Edward Buscombe, 'Walsh and Warner Bros', in Hardy (ed.), *Raoul Walsh*, Edinburgh, Edinburgh Film Festival, 1974.

Russell Campbell, 'Warner Bros in the 30s: some tentative notes', *The Velvet Light Trap* 1, June 1971.

Russell Campbell, 'Warners, the depression and FDR', *The Velvet Light Trap* 4, spring 1972.

John Davis, 'Notes on Warner Bros' foreign policy 1918–1948', *The Velvet Light Trap* 4, spring 1972.

Douglas Gomery, 'Writing the history of the American film industry: Warner Bros and sound', *Screen* 17 (1): 40–53, spring 1976.

Daniel J. Leab, 'Viewing the war with the brothers Warner', in Dibbets and Hogenkamp (eds), *Film and the First World War*, Amsterdam, Amsterdam University Press, 1995.

Nick Roddick, *A New Deal in Entertainment: Warner Brothers in the 1930s*, London, BFI Publishing, 1983.

James R. Silke, *Here's Looking at You, Kid: 50 Years of Fighting, Working and Dreaming at Warner Bros*, Boston, Little, Brown and Co, 1976.

The Velvet Light Trap 15, 1975. Special issue on Warners Revisited.

Robin Wood, 'To have (written) and have not (directed)', *Film Comment* 9 (3): 30–5, May/June 1973.

Columbia Pictures

Tino Balio (ed.), *The American Film Industry*, Madison, University of Wisconsin Press, 1976. Revised edition 1985.

Edward Buscombe, 'Notes on Columbia Pictures Corporation, 1926–41', *Screen* 16 (3), autumn 1975.

John Cogley, 'The mass hearings', in Balio (ed.), *The American Film Industry*, 1985.

Michael Conant, 'The impact of the Paramount Decrees', in Balio (ed.), *The American Film Industry*, 1985.

Tom Flinn, 'Letter', *The Velvet Light Trap* 11: 62, winter 1974.

John Kobal, *Rita Hayworth: The Time, the Place and the Woman*, London, W. H. Allen, 1977.

Rochelle Larkin, *Hail Columbia*, New Rochelle, NY, Arlington House, 1975.

Robert H. Stanley, *The Celluloid Empire: A History of the American Movie Industry*, New York, Hastings House, 1978.

20th Century Fox

Robert C. Allen, 'William Fox presents *Sunrise*', *Quarterly Review of Film Studies* 2 (3): 327–38, August 1977.

Robert C. Allen, 'Case study: the background of *Sunrise*', in Allen and Gomery, *Film History: Theory and Practice*, New York, McGraw-Hill, 1985.

Charles Eckert, 'Shirley Temple and the house of Rockefeller', *Jump Cut* 2, July/August 1974. Reprinted in Gledhill (ed.), *Stardom: Industry of Desire*, London, Routledge, 1991.

Editors of *Cahiers du Cinéma*, 'Collective text on John Ford's *Young Mr Lincoln*', *Screen* 13 (3): 5–44, autumn 1972.

Steven N. Lipkin, '*Sunrise*: a film meets its public', *Quarterly Review of Film Studies* 2 (3), August 1977.

Roy Pickard, *The Hollywood Studios*, London, Frederick Muller, 1978.

Rebecca Pulliam, '*The Grapes of Wrath*', *The Velvet Light Trap* 2, August 1971.

John Howard Reid, 'The best second fiddle', *Films and Filming* 9 (2), November 1962.

Tony Thomas and Aubrey Solomon, *The Films of 20th Century-Fox: A Pictorial History*, Secaucus, NJ, Citadel Press, 1979.

RKO Radio Pictures

John Davis, 'RKO: a studio chronology', *The Velvet Light Trap* 10, autumn 1973.

Ron Haver, 'The mighty show machine', *American Film* 3 (2), November 1977.

Richard B. Jewell with Vernon Harbin, *RKO Story*, New York, Random House, 1985.

Pauline Kael, *The Citizen Kane Book*, London, Secker and Warburg, 1971.

Paul Kerr, 'Out of what past? Notes on the "B" film noir', *Screen Education* 32/33: 45–65, autumn/winter 1979/80.

Betty Lasky, *RKO: The Biggest Little Major of Them All*, New York, Roundtable Publishing, 1989.

Russell Merritt, 'RKO Radio: the little studio that couldn't', in *Marquee Theatre*, Madison, University of Wisconsin Extension Television Centre, 1973.

James L. Neibaur, *The RKO Features*, Jefferson, NC, McFarland, 2004

Tim Onosko, 'RKO Radio: an overview', *The Velvet Light Trap* 10, autumn 1973.

Gerald Peary, 'A speculation: the historicity of *King Kong*', *Jump Cut* 4: 11–12, November/December 1974.

Joel Siegel, *Val Lewton: The Reality of Terror*, London, Secker and Warburg/BFI, 1972.

Universal

Tino Balio, 'A mature oligopoly: 1930–1948', in *The American Film Industry*, Madison, University of Wisconsin Press, 1976. Revised edition 1985.

Connie Bruck, *When Hollywood Had a King*, New York, Random House, 2004.

Allen Eyles, 'Universal and International', *Focus on Film* 30, June 1978.

Michael G. Fitzgerald, *Universal Pictures: A Panoramic History in Words, Pictures and Filmographies*, New Rochelle, NY, Arlington House, 1977.

Charles Higham, *The Films of Orson Welles*, Berkeley, University of California Press, 1970.

Joseph McBride, *Orson Welles*, London, Secker and Warburg/BFI, 1972.

Dennis McDougal, *The Last Mogul: Lou Wasserman, MCA and the Hidden History of Hollywood*, New York, Da Capo Press, 2001.

James Naremore, *The Magic World of Orson Welles*, New York, Oxford University Press, 1978.

Stephen Pendo, 'Universal's golden age of horror', *Films in Review* 26 (3), March 1975.

Robert Sklar, *Movie-Made America: A Cultural History of American Movies*, New York, Vintage, 1994.

Robert Stanley, *The Celluloid Empire: A History of the American Movie Industry*, New York, Hastings House, 1978.

CLASSIC HOLLYWOOD NARRATIVE

Charles Barr, 'CinemaScope: before and after', *Film Quarterly* 16 (4): 4–24, summer 1963. Reprinted in Mast and Cohen (eds), *Film Theory and Criticism*, Oxford and New York, Oxford University Press, 1974.

Roland Barthes, *The Pleasures of the Text*, New York, Hill and Wang, 1975; trans. Richard Miller.

Roland Barthes, 'Introduction to the structural analysis of narratives', in *Image-Music-Text*, London, Fontana, 1993; trans. Stephen Heath.

David Bordwell and Kristin Thompson, *Film Art: An Introduction*, New York, McGraw-Hill, 2004. Revised edition.

Leo Braudy and Marshall Cohen (eds), *Film Theory and Criticism: Introductory Readings*, New York and Oxford, Oxford University Press, 2004.

Nick Browne, 'The spectator-in-the-text: the rhetoric of *Stagecoach*', *Film Quarterly* 29 (2): 26–38, winter 1975/76. Reprinted in Braudy and Cohen (eds), *Film Theory and Criticism*, 2004.

Noël Burch, *Theory of Film Practice*, Princeton, NJ, Princeton University Press, 1981.

Pam Cook, 'Duplicity in *Mildred Pierce*', in *Screening the Past: Memory and Nostalgia in Cinema*, Oxford and New York, Routledge, 2005.

Thomas Elsaesser and Adam Barker (eds), *Early Cinema: Space, Frame, Narrative*, London, BFI Publishing, 1990.

Tom Gunning, 'The "cinema of attractions"', *Wide Angle* 3 (4): 63–70, 1986. Reprinted in Elsaesser and Barker (eds), *Early Cinema*, 1990.

Alfred Guzzetti, 'Narrative and the film image', *New Literary History* 6 (2): 379–92, 1975.

Tania Modleski, 'The master's doll house: *Rear Window*', in *The Women Who Knew Too Much: Hitchcock and Feminist Theory*, London, Methuen, 1988.

Laura Mulvey, 'Visual pleasure and narrative cinema', *Screen* 16 (3), autumn 1975. Reprinted in *Visual and Other Pleasures*, London, Macmillan, 1989.

Steve Neale, 'New Hollywood cinema', *Screen* 17 (2): 117–22, summer 1976.

GLOBAL HOLLYWOOD

Post-war globalisation

Tino Balio, *United Artists: The Company That Changed the Film Industry*, Madison, University of Wisconsin Press, 1987.

Vincent Canby, 'Overseas films', *Variety* 2 May 1962, p. 18.

Thomas Guback, *The International Film Industry: Western Europe and America since 1945*, Bloomington, Indiana University Press, 1969.

Peter Lev, *The Euro-American Cinema*, Austin, University of Texas Press, 1993.

Toby Miller, Nitin Govil, John McMurria and Richard Maxwell, *Global Hollywood*, London, BFI Publishing, 2001.

Toby Miller, Nitin Govil, John McMurria, Richard Maxwell and Ting Wang, *Global Hollywood 2*, London, BFI Publishing, 2004.

Geoffrey Nowell-Smith and Steven Ricci (eds), *Hollywood and Europe: Economics, Culture, National Identity 1945–95*, London, BFI Publishing, 1998.

Kerry Segrave, *American Films Abroad: Hollywood's Domination of the World's Movie Screens*, Jefferson, NC, McFarland, 1997.

Variety, 'Stix Still Nix British Pix', 18 June 1947, pp. 1, 16.

Alexander Walker, *Hollywood UK: The British Film Industry in the Sixties*, New York, Stein & Day, 1974.

The major independents

Peter Biskind, *Down and Dirty Pictures: Miramax, Sundance, and the Rise of Independent Film*, New York, Simon and Schuster, 2004.

Geoff King, *American Independent Cinema*, London, I. B. Tauris, 2005.

Geoff King, *Indiewood, USA: Where Hollywood Meets Independent Cinema*, London, I. B. Tauris, 2008.

Steve Neale and Murray Smith (eds.), *Contemporary Hollywood Cinema*, London and New York, Routledge, 1998.

Yannis Tzioumakis, *American Independent Cinema: An Introduction*, Edinburgh, Edinburgh University Press, 2006.

Michael Wayne, 'Working Title Mark II: a critique of the atlanticist paradigm for British cinema', *International Journal of Media and Cultural Politics* 2 (1): 59, January 2006.

Justin Wyatt, 'The formation of the "major independent": Miramax, New Line and the New Hollywood', in Neale and Smith (eds), *Contemporary Hollywood Cinema*, 1998.

New Hollywood

Raymond Bellour, 'To analyse, to segment', *Quarterly Review of Film Studies* 1 (3): 331–43, 1976.

John Belton, *American Cinema/American Culture*, New York, McGraw-Hill, 1994.

James Bernardoni, *The New Hollywood: What the Movies Did with the New Freedom of the Seventies*, Jefferson, NC, McFarland, 1991.

David Bordwell, *Making Meaning: Inference and Rhetoric in the Interpretation of Cinema*, Cambridge, MA, Harvard University Press, 1989.

David Bordwell and Janet Staiger, 'Since 1960: the persistence of a mode of film practice', in Bordwell, Staiger and Thompson, *Classical Hollywood Cinema*, 1985.

David Bordwell, Janet Staiger and Kristin Thompson, *Classical Hollywood Cinema: Film Style and Mode of Production*, London and New York, Routledge & Kegan Paul, 1985.

Jacob Brackman, Harold Clurman and John Simon, 'Anti-heroes', a series of articles on *Five Easy Pieces*, in Denby (ed.), *Film 70/71: An Anthology by the National Society of Film Critics*, New York, Simon and Schuster, 1971.

Stuart Byron, '*The Searchers*: cult movie of the New Hollywood', *New Yorker Magazine* 5 March 1979, pp. 45–8.

Noël Carroll, 'The future of allusion: Hollywood in the seventies (and beyond)', *October* 20: 51–78, 1982.

David Colker and Jack Virrel, 'The new New Hollywood', *Take One* 6 (10): 19–23, September 1978.

Jim Collins, Hilary Radner and Ava Preacher Collins (eds), *Film Theory Goes to the Movies*, New York, Routledge, 1993.

Timothy Corrigan, *A Cinema without Walls: Movies and Culture After Vietnam*, London, Routledge, 1991.

David Denby, 'Can the movies be saved?', *New Yorker Magazine* 19 (28): 23–35, 1986.

Thomas Elsaesser, 'Why Hollywood?', *Monogram* 1: 4–10, 1971.

Thomas Elsaesser, 'The pathos of failure: the unmotivated hero in Hollywood of the 1970s', *Monogram* 6: 13–19, 1975.

Manny Farber and Patricia Patterson, 'The power and the gory', *Film Comment* 12 (3), 1976. Reprinted in *Negative Space: Manny Farber on the Movies*, New York, Da Capo Press, 1998.

Stephen Farber, 'Easy pieces', *Sight and Sound* 40 (3): 128–31, summer 1971.

Jean-Luc Godard and Pauline Kael, 'The economics of film criticism: a debate', *Camera Obscura* 8/9/10: 162–85, fall 1982.

Douglas Gomery, 'The American film industry in the seventies', *Wide Angle* 5 (4): 52–9, 1983.

Tom Gunning, 'The "cinema of attractions": early cinema, its spectator and the avant-garde', *Wide Angle* 8 (3/4): 63–70, fall 1986. Reprinted in Elsaesser and Barker (eds), *Early Cinema: Space, Frame, Narrative*, London, BFI Publishing, 1990.

Jim Hillier, *The New Hollywood*, London, Studio Vista, 1992.

J. Hoberman, 'Ten years that shook the world', *American Film* 10 (8): 38–9, 42–9, 52–9, 1985.

Kevin Jackson (ed.), *Schrader on Schrader and Other Writings*, London, Faber & Faber, 1990.

Diane Jacobs, *Hollywood Renaissance: The New Generation of Filmmakers and Their Works*, New York, Delacorte, 1980.

Pauline Kael, 'Why are the movies so bad?: or, the numbers', in *Taking It All In*, New York, Holt, Rinehart and Winston, 1984.

Lucy Kaylin, 'Independents' day', *GQ*, October 1995.

Jon Lewis, *Whom God Wishes to Destroy: Francis Coppola and the New Hollywood*, Durham and London, Duke University Press, 1995.

Kimball Lockhart, 'Blockage and passage in *The Passenger*', *Diacritics* 15 (1): 72–87, spring 1985.

Axel Madsen, *The New Hollywood: American Movies in the 70s*, New York, Thomas Y. Crowell Co, 1975.

Steven Marcus, 'Introduction', in Dashiell Hammett, *The Continental Op*, New York, Random House, 1974.

Eileen R. Meehan, 'Holy commodity fetish, Batman!': the political economy of a commercial intertext', in Pearson and Urrichio (eds), *The Many Lives of the Batman: Critical Approaches to a Superhero and His Media*, London, BFI Publishing, 1991.

James Monaco, *American Film Now: The People, The Power, The Money, The Movies*, New York and Oxford, Oxford University Press, 1979.

Steve Neale, 'Hollywood corner', *Framework* 19: 37–9, 1982.

Steve Neale and Murray Smith (eds), *Contemporary Hollywood Cinema*, London, Routledge, 1998.

William Paul, 'Hollywood Harakiri', *Film Comment* 13 (2): 40–3, 56–61, 1977.

William Paul, 'The K-mart audience at the mall movies', *Film History* 6 (4): 487–501, 1994.

Michael Pye and Lynda Myles, *The Movie Brats: How the Film Generation Took Over Hollywood*, New York, Holt, Rinehart and Winston, 1979.

Robert B. Ray, *A Certain Tendency of the Hollywood Cinema 1930–1980*, Princeton, NJ, Princeton University Press, 1985.

Brooks Riley, 'BBS Productions', in Roud (ed.), *Cinema: A Critical Dictionary* Vol. 1, London, Secker and Warburg, 1980.

Jonathan Rosenbaum, '*Rocky Horror* playtime vs shopping mall home', in *Moving Places: A Life at the Movies*, New York, Harper & Row, 1980.

Andrew Sarris, 'After *The Graduate*', *American Film* 3 (9): 32–7, July/August 1978.

Thomas Schatz, *Old Hollywood/New Hollywood*, Ann Arbor, UMI Research Press, 1983.

Thomas Schatz, *The Genius of the System: Hollywood Filmmaking in the Studio Era*, New York, Pantheon, 1988.

Thomas Schatz, 'The New Hollywood', in Collins *et al.* (eds), *Film Theory Goes to the Movies*, New York, Routledge, 1993.

Eben Shapiro and Thomas King, 'Production costs put a tarnish on tinseltown', *Wall Street Journal*, reprinted in the *Sydney Morning Herald*, January 1996.

Anne Thompson, 'Little giants', *Film Comment* 31 (2): 56, 58–60, 63, 1995.

David Thomson, *Overexposures: The Crisis in American Filmmaking*, New York, William Morrow, 1981.

David Thomson, 'The decade when movies mattered', *Movieline* August 1993, pp. 43–7, 90.

Mim Udovich, 'Tarantino and Juliette', *Details*, February 1996, pp. 112–17.

Maggie Valentine, *The Show Starts on the Sidewalk: An Architectural History of the Movie Theatre, Starring S. Charles Lee*, New Haven and London, Yale University Press, 1994.

Wide Angle 5 (4), 1983. Special issue on The New Hollywood.

Justin Wyatt, *High Concept: Movies and Marketing in Hollywood*, Austin, University of Texas Press, 1994.

Contemporary women directors

Ally Acker, *Reel Women: Pioneers of the Cinema 1896 to the Present*, New York, B. T. Batsford, 1991.

Janis Cole and Holly Dale, *Calling the Shots: Profiles of Women Filmmakers*, Kingston, Ontario, Quarry Press, 1994.

Pam Cook, 'No fixed address: the women's picture from *Outrage* to *Blue Steel*', and 'Fictions of identity: style, mimicry and gender in the films of Kathryn Bigelow', in *Screening the Past: Memory and Nostalgia in Cinema*, Oxford and New York, Routledge, 2005.

Pam Cook and Philip Dodd (eds), *Women and Film: A Sight and Sound Reader*, London/Philadelphia, PA, Scarlet Press/Temple University Press, 1993.

Michelle Goldberg, 'Where are the female directors?'. Available at: <www.salon.com/ent/movies/feature/2002/ 08/27/women_directors>. Accessed 6 February 2007.

Claire Johnston, 'Women's cinema as counter-cinema', in *Notes on Women's Cinema*, London, Society for Education in Film and Television, 1974. Reprinted in Thornham (ed.), *Feminist Film Theory: A Reader*, New York, New York University Press, 1999.

Claire Johnston (ed.), *Dorothy Arzner: Towards a Feminist Cinema*, London, BFI Publishing, 1975.

Kathleen Rowe Karlyn, 'Allison Anders's *Gas Food Lodging*: independent cinema and the new romance', in Evans and Deleyto (eds), *Terms of Endearment: Hollywood Romantic Comedy of the 1980s and 1990s*, Edinburgh, Edinburgh University Press, 1998.

Christina Lane, *Feminist Hollywood: From 'Born in Flames' to 'Point Break'*, Detroit, MI, Wayne State University Press, 2000.

Christina Lane, 'Just another girl outside the neo-indie', in Holmlund and Wyatt (eds), *Contemporary American Independent Film*, New York, Routledge, 2004.

Martha Lauzen, 'The celluloid ceiling: behind-the-scenes employment of women in the top 250 films of 2005'. Available at: http://moviesbywomen.com/marthalauzenphd/stats2005.html. Accessed 25 January 2007.

Judith Mayne, *The Woman at the Keyhole: Feminism and Women's Cinema*, Bloomington, Indiana University Press, 1990.

Judith Mayne, *Directed by Dorothy Arzner*, Bloomington, Indiana University Press, 1995.

Laurie Ouellette, 'Reel women: feminism and narrative pleasure in new women's cinema', *The Independent Film and Video Monthly*, April 1995, pp. 28–34.

Barbara Koenig Quart, *Women Directors: The Emergence of a New Cinema*, New York, Praeger, 1988.

Yvonne Tasker (ed.), *Fifty Contemporary Filmmakers*, London and New York, Routledge, 2002.

Rachel Williams, '"They call me 'Action Woman'": the marketing of Mimi Leder as a new concept in the high concept "action" film', in Tasker (ed.), *Action and Adventure Cinema*, London, Routledge, 2004.

AT THE EDGES OF HOLLYWOOD
New distribution, exhibition and reception contexts

Charles R. Acland, *Screen Traffic: Movies, Multiplexes, and Global Culture*, Durham, NC, Duke University Press, 2003.

Robert C. Allen, 'Home alone together: Hollywood and the "family film"', in Stokes and Maltby (eds), *Identifying Hollywood Audiences*, London, BFI Publishing, 1999.

Aaron Barlow, *The DVD Revolution: Movies, Culture, and Technology*, Westport, CT, Praeger, 2005.

Uma Dinsmore-Tuli, '"The pleasures of home cinema", or watching movies on telly: an audience study of cinephiliac VCR use', *Screen* 41 (3): 315–27, 2000.

John Geirland and Eva Sonesh-Kedar, *Digital Babylon: How the Geeks, the Suits, and the Ponytails Tried to Bring Hollywood to the Internet*, New York, Arcade Publishing, 1999.

Douglas Gomery, *Shared Pleasures: A History of Movie Presentation in the United States*, Madison, University of Wisconsin Press, 1992.

Ann Gray, *Video Playtime: The Gendering of a Leisure Technology*, London, Routledge, 1992.

Michele Hilmes, *Hollywood and Broadcasting: From Radio to Cable*, Champaign-Urbana, University of Illinois Press, 1990.

Barbara Klinger, *Beyond the Multiplex: Cinema, New Technologies, and the Home*, Berkeley, University of California Press, 2006.

Peter Krämer, 'The lure of the big picture: film, television, and Hollywood', in Hill and McLoone (eds), *Big Picture, Small Screen: Relations between Film and Television*, Luton, University of Luton Press, 1996.

Moya Luckett, '"Filming the family": home movie systems and the domestication of spectatorship', *The Velvet Light Trap* 36: 21–32, fall 1995.

Toby Miller, Nitin Govil, John McMurria and Richard Maxwell, *Global Hollywood*, London, BFI Publishing, 2001.

Tony Ming, 'China fights copying menace', 21stcentury.chinadaily.com.cn, 21 June 2001.

Eric Pfanner, 'Hollywood takes new tack against film piracy', *International Herald Times*, 24 March 2006, <www.iht.com/articles/2006/03/23/yourmoney/movies/php>.

David Pogue, 'Why the world doesn't need hi-def DVDs', *New York Times* 11 May 2006, sec. C, pp. 1, 10.

Kerry Segrave, *Movies at Home: How Hollywood Came to Television*, Jefferson, NC, McFarland, 1999.

Ben Singer, 'Early home cinema and the Edison Projecting Kinetoscope', *Film History* 2 (1): 37–70, winter 1988.

Brett Sporich, '2004 home video wrap', <www.hollywoodreporter.com>. Accessed 31 January 2005.

Janet Wasko, *Hollywood in the Information Age: Beyond the Silver Screen*, Austin, University of Texas Press, 1994.

Frederick Wasser, *Veni, Vidi, Video: The Hollywood Empire and the VCR*, Austin, University of Texas Press, 2001.

Haidee Wasson, 'The world on your doorstep: 16mm, film libraries, and the cosmopolitan home', in Maltby, Stokes and Allen (eds), *Going to the Movies: The Social Experience of Hollywood Cinema*, Exeter, University of Exeter Press, 2007.

African-American cinema: Oscar Micheaux

Donald Bogle, *Toms, Coons, Mulattoes, Mammies and Bucks: An Interpretive History of Blacks in American Films*, New York, Continuum, 1997. Revised edition 2003.

Pearl Bowser and Louise Spence, *Writing Himself into History: Oscar Micheaux, His Silent Films, and His Audience*, New Brunswick, NJ, Rutgers University Press, 2000.

Pearl Bowser and Louise Spence, 'Oscar Micheaux's *The Symbol of the Unconquered*: text and context', in Bowser, Gaines and Musser (eds), *Oscar Micheaux and His Circle*, 2001.

Pearl Bowser, Jane Gaines and Charles Musser (eds), *Oscar Micheaux and His Circle: African American Filmmaking and the Race Cinema of the Silent Era*, Bloomington, Indiana University Press, 2001.

Gerald R. Butters Jr, 'From homestead to lynch mob: portrayals of black masculinity in Oscar Micheaux's *Within Our Gates*', *Journal of Multimedia History* 5, 2000. Available at: <www.albany.edu/jmmh/vol3/micheaux/micheaux.html>.

Corey K. Creekmur, 'Telling white lies: Oscar Micheaux and Charles W. Chesnutt', in Bowser, Gaines and Musser (eds), *Oscar Micheaux and His Circle*, 2001.

Thomas Cripps, 'Movies in the ghetto B. P. (Before Poitier)', *Negro Digest* 18 (4): 21–7, 45–8, February 1969.

Thomas Cripps, *Slow Fade to Black: The Negro in American Film, 1900–1942*, New York and Oxford, Oxford University Press, 1977.

Thomas Cripps, 'The films of Spencer Williams', *Black American Literature Forum* 12 (4): 128–34, winter 1978.

Manthia Diawara (ed.), *Black American Cinema*, New York and London, Routledge, 1993.

Niamh Doheny, *No Longer 'On the Outside Looking In': Oscar Micheaux's Role in the Construction of a Black American Film Form*, PhD thesis, University of Southampton, 2004.

Jane Gaines, 'Fire and desire: race, melodrama and Oscar Micheaux', in Diawara (ed.), *Black American Cinema*, 1993.

Jane Gaines, *Fire and Desire: Mixed-Race Movies in the Silent Era*, Chicago and London, University of Chicago Press, 2001.

Susan Gillman, 'Micheaux's Chesnutt', *PMLA* 114: 1080–8, October 1999.

Ronald Green, *Straight Lick: The Cinema of Oscar Micheaux*, Bloomington, Indiana University Press, 2000.

Ronald Green and Horace Neal Jr, 'Oscar Micheaux and racial slur: a response to "The rediscovery of Oscar Micheaux"', *Journal of Film and Video* 40 (4): 66–71, fall 1988.

Arthur Jaffa, 'The notion of treatment: black aesthetics and film', in Bowser, Gaines and Musser (eds), *Oscar Micheaux and His Circle*, 2001.

Phyllis Klotman, 'The black writer in Hollywood, circa 1930: the case of Wallace Thurman', in Diawara (ed.), *Black American Cinema*, 1993.

Theophilus Lewis, 'Review of *Daughter of the Congo*', *New York Amsterdam News*, 16 April 1930.

Charles Musser, 'To redream the dreams of white playwrights: reappropriation and resistance in Oscar Micheaux's *Body and Soul*', in Bowser, Gaines and Musser (eds), *Oscar Micheaux and His Circle*, 2001.

Bernard L. Peterson, 'A filmography of Oscar Micheaux: America's legendary black filmmaker', in Platt (ed.), *Celluloid Power: Social Film Criticism from The Birth of a Nation to Judgment at Nuremberg*, Metuchen, NJ, Scarecrow Press, 1992.

Charlene Regester, 'The African-American press and race movies, 1909–1929', in Bowser, Gaines and Musser (eds), *Oscar Micheaux and His Circle*, 2001.

Henry Sampson, *Blacks in Black and White: A Sourcebook*, Metuchen, NJ, Scarecrow Press, 1995. Revised edition.

James Snead, *White Screens/Black Images: Hollywood from the Dark Side*, New York and London, Routledge, 1994.

D. Ireland Thomas, 'Review of *A Son of Satan*', *New York Amsterdam News*, 31 January 1925.

Gladstone L. Yearwood, '*Sweet Sweetback's Baaadasssss Song* and the development of the contemporary black film movement', in *Black Cinema Aesthetics*, Athens, Ohio University Press, 1982.

Joseph Young, *Black Novelist as White Racist: The Myth of Black Inferiority in the Novels of OM*, Westport, CT, Greenwood, 1989.

Documentary

Erik Barnouw, *Documentary: A History of the Non-Fiction Film*, Oxford, Oxford University Press, 1993.

Barry Keith Grant and Jeannette Sloniowski (eds), *Documenting the Documentary: Close Readings of Documentary Film and Video*, Detroit, MI, Wayne State University Press, 1998.

Kevin Macdonald and Mark Cousins (eds), *Imagining Reality: The Faber Book of Documentary*, London and Boston, Faber & Faber, 1998.
Bill Nichols, *Representing Reality*, Indianapolis, Indiana University Press, 1991.
Bill Nichols, *Blurred Boundaries: Questions of Meaning in Contemporary Culture*, Indianapolis, Indiana University Press, 1994.
Bill Nichols, *Introduction to Documentary*, Indianapolis, Indiana University Press, 2001.
Michael Renov (ed.), *Theorizing Documentary*, London and New York, Routledge, 1993.
Michael Renov, *The Subject in Documentary*, Minneapolis, University of Minnesota Press, 2004.
Alan Rosenthal (ed.), *New Challenges for Documentary*, Berkeley, University of California Press, 1988.

Art cinema

David Bordwell, 'Art-cinema narration', in *Narration in the Fiction Film*, Madison, University of Wisconsin Press, 1985.
David Bordwell, 'Visual style in Japanese cinema, 1925–1945', *Film History* 7 (1): 5–31, spring 1995.
Mike Budd, 'The National Board of Review and the early art cinema in New York: "The Cabinet of Dr Caligari" as affirmative culture', *Cinema Journal* 26 (1): 3–18, autumn 1986.
Tony Guzman, 'The Little Theatre Movement: the institutionalization of the European art film in America', *Film History* 17 (2/3): 261–84, 2005.
Peter Lev, *The Euro-American Cinema*, Austin, University of Texas Press, 1993.
Michel Marie, *The French New Wave: An Artistic School*, Oxford, Blackwell, 2003.
Steve Neale, 'Art cinema as institution', in Fowler (ed.), *The European Cinema Reader*, London and New York, Routledge, 2002.
Robert B. Ray, *A Certain Tendency of the Hollywood Cinema, 1930–1980*, Princeton, NJ, Princeton University Press, 1985.
Donald Richie, *A Hundred Years of Japanese Film*, Tokyo, New York and London, Kodansha International, 2001. Revised edition 2005.
Alain Robbe-Grillet, *Last Year at Marienbad*, London, John Calder, 1962.
Andrew Sarris, 'Notes on the auteur theory in 1962', *Film Culture* 27: 1–8, winter 1962/63. Reprinted in Sitney (ed.), *Film Culture Reader*, New York, Cooper Square Press, 2000.
Michael Temple and Michael Witt, 'Introduction 1960–2004: a new world', in Temple and Witt (eds), *The French Cinema Book*, London, BFI Publishing, 2004.
François Truffaut, 'A certain tendency of the French cinema' [1954], in Nichols (ed.), *Movies and Methods* Vol. I, Berkeley, University of California Press, 1976.
John E. Twomey, 'Some considerations on the rise of the art-film theater', *The Quarterly of Film Radio and Television* 10 (3): 239–47, spring 1956.
Ginette Vincendeau, 'The art of spectacle: the aesthetics of classic French cinema', in Temple and Witt (eds), *The French Cinema Book*, London, BFI Publishing, 2004.
Barbara Wilinsky, *Sure Seaters: The Emergence of Art House Cinema*, Minneapolis and London, University of Minnesota Press, 2001.
Yingjin Zhang, *Chinese National Cinema*, New York, Routledge, 2004.

Animation

Michael Barrier, *Hollywood Cartoons: American Animation in the Golden Age*, New York and Oxford, Oxford University Press, 1999.
Elizabeth Bell, Lynda Haas and Laura Sells (eds), *From Mouse to Mermaid: The Politics of Film, Gender and Culture*, Bloomington, Indiana University Press, 1995.
Philip Brophy and Julie Ewington (eds), *Kaboom!: Explosive Animation from Japan and America*, Sydney, Museum of Contemporary Art, 1994.
Alan Bryman, *Disney and His Worlds*, London and New York, Routledge, 1995.
Suzanne Buchan (ed.), *Animated Worlds*, London and Paris, John Libbey, 2006.
Eleanor Byrne and Martin McQuillan, *Deconstructing Disney*, London and Sterling, Pluto Press, 1999.
John Canemaker (ed.), *Storytelling in Animation: The Art of the Animated Image: 002*, Los Angeles, American Film Institute, 1988.
Alan Cholodenko (ed.), *The Illusion of Life: Essays on Animation*, Sydney, Power/Australian Film Commission, 1991.
Karl F. Cohen, *Forbidden Animation: Censored Cartoons and Blacklisted Animators in America*, Jefferson, NC, and London, McFarland, 1997.
Amy Davis, *Good Girls and Wicked Witches: Changing Representations of Women in Disney's Feature Animation, 1937–2001*, London and Paris, John Libbey, 2002.
Terence Dobson, *The Film Work of Norman McLaren*, London and Paris, John Libbey, 2006.
Maureen Furniss, *Art in Motion: Animation Aesthetics*, London and Montrouge, John Libbey, 1998.
Daniel Goldmark, *Tunes for 'Toons: Music and the Hollywood Cartoon*, Berkeley and London, University of California Press, 2005.
Daniel Goldmark and Yuval Taylor (eds), *The Cartoon Music Book*, Chicago, A Cappella Books, 2002.
Peter Hames (ed.), *Dark Alchemy: The Films of Jan Svankmajer*, Trowbridge, Wiltshire, Flicks Books, 1995.
Stefan Kanfer, *Serious Business: The Art and Commerce of Animation in America from Betty Boop to Toy Story*, New York, Scribner's, 1997.
Norman M. Klein, *Seven Minutes: The Life and Death of the American Cartoon*, New York and London, Verso, 1993.
John A. Lent (ed.), *Animation in Asia and the Pacific*, London and Paris, John Libbey, 2001.
Esther Leslie, *Hollywood Flatlands: Animation, Critical Theory and the Avant-Garde*, London and New York, Verso, 2002.
Antonia Levi, *Samurai from Outer Space: Understanding Japanese Animation*, Chicago and La Salle, IL, Open Court/Carus, 1996.
Jay Leyda (ed.), *Eisenstein on Disney*, London, Methuen, 1988.
Lev Manovich, *The Language of New Media*, Cambridge, MA, MIT Press, 2001.
Ajanovic Midhat, *Animation and Realism*, Zagreb, Croatian Film Club Association, 2004.
Susan Napier, *Anime: From Akira to Princess Mononoke*, New York, Palgrave, 2001.
Fred Patten, *Watching Anime, Reading Manga*, Berkeley, CA, Stone Bridge Press, 2004.
Gerald Peary and Danny Peary (eds), *The American Animated Cartoon*, New York, Dutton, 1980.
Michele Pierson, *Special Effects: Still in Search of Wonder*, New York, Columbia University Press, 2002.
Jayne Pilling (ed.), *That's Not All Folks: A Primer in Cartoonal Knowledge*, London, BFI Publishing, 1984.
Jayne Pilling (ed.), *Women and Animation: A Compendium*, London, BFI Publishing, 1992.
Jayne Pilling (ed.), *A Reader in Animation Studies*, London and Paris, John Libbey, 1997.
Floriane Place-Verghnes, *Tex Avery: A Unique Legacy 1942–1955*, London and Paris, John Libbey, 2006.
Chris Robinson, *Estonian Animation: Between Genius and Utter Illiteracy*, London and Paris, John Libbey, 2004.
Chris Robinson, *Unsung Heroes of Animation*, London and Paris, John Libbey, 2005.
Eric Smoodin, *Animating Culture: Hollywood Cartoons from the Sound Era*, Oxford, Roundhouse Publishing, 1993.
Eric Smoodin (ed.), *Disney Discourse: Producing the Magic Kingdom*, London and New York, Routledge/American Film Institute, 1994.
Carol A. Stabile and Mark Harrison (eds), *Prime Time Animation: Television Animation and American Culture*, London and New York, Routledge, 2003.
Janet Wasko, *Understanding Disney: The Manufacture of Fantasy*, Cambridge and Malden, Polity Press, 2001.
Steven Watts, *The Magic Kingdom: Walt Disney and the American Way of Life*, New York, Houghton Mifflin, 1997.
Paul Wells, *Around the World in Animation*, London, BFI/MOMI Education, 1996.
Paul Wells, *Understanding Animation*, London and New York, Routledge, 1998.
Paul Wells, 'Art of the impossible', in Andrew (ed.), *Film: The Critics' Choice*, Lewes, E. Sussex, Ivy Press, 2001.
Paul Wells, *Animation and America*, Edinburgh, Edinburgh University Press, 2002.
Paul Wells, *Animation: Genre and Authorship*, London, Wallflower Press, 2002.
Paul Wells, *The Fundamentals of Animation*, Lausanne, Ava Publishing, 2006.

Avant-garde and counter-cinema

Arts Council of Great Britain, *Film as Film*, London, Arts Council of Great Britain, 1979.

Janet Bergstrom, '*Jeanne Dielman, 23 Quai du commerce, 1080 Bruxelles* by Chantal Akerman', *Camera Obscura* 2, fall 1977.

Andrew Britton, 'Living historically: two films by Jean-Luc Godard', *Framework* 3, 1976.

Camera Obscura Collective, 'Yvonne Rainer: interview', *Camera Obscura* 1, fall 1976.

Ian Christie, 'French avant-garde film in the twenties: from "specificity" to surrealism', in Arts Council of Great Britain, *Film as Film*, 1979.

Pam Cook, '*The Gold Diggers*: interview with Sally Potter', *Framework* 24, 1984. Reprinted in *Screening the Past: Memory and Nostalgia in Cinema*, Oxford and New York, Routledge, 2005.

Pam Cook, 'The point of self-expression in avant-garde film', in Caughie (ed.), *Theories of Authorship*, London and New York, Routledge, 2001.

David Curtis, *Experimental Cinema*, London, Studio Vista, 1971.

Phillip Drummond, 'Textual space in *Un Chien Andalou*', *Screen* 18 (3), autumn 1977.

Phillip Drummond, 'Notions of avant-garde cinema', in Arts Council of Great Britain, *Film as Film*, 1979.

Deke Dusinberre, 'The ascetic task: Peter Gidal's *Room Film 1973*', in Gidal (ed.), *Structural Film Anthology*, 1978.

Peter Gidal (ed.), *Structural Film Anthology*, London, BFI Publishing, 1978.

Birgit Hein, 'The futurist film', in Arts Council of Great Britain, *Film as Film*, 1979.

David E. James, *Allegories of Cinema*, Princeton, NJ, Princeton University Press, 1989.

Claire Johnston, *Notes on Women's Cinema*, London, SEFT, 1974.

Claire Johnston, 'Women's cinema as counter-cinema', in *Notes on Women's Cinema*, 1974. Reprinted in Thornham (ed.), *Feminist Film Theory: A Reader*, New York, New York University Press, 1999.

E. Ann Kaplan, *Looking for the Other: Feminism, Film and the Imperial Gaze*, New York and London, Routledge, 1997.

Rudolf E. Kuenzli (ed.), *Dada and Surrealist Film*, New York, Willis Locker and Owen, 1987.

Teresa de Lauretis, *Technologies of Gender*, Bloomington, Indiana University Press, 1987.

Teresa de Lauretis, 'Guerrillas in the midst: women's cinema in the 80s', *Screen* 31 (1), spring 1990.

Standish D. Lawder, *The Cubist Cinema*, New York, New York University Press, 1975.

Scott MacDonald, *A Critical Cinema 2: Interviews with Independent Filmmakers*, Berkeley and Los Angeles, University of California Press, 1992.

Patricia Mellencamp, *A Fine Romance: Five Ages of Film Feminism*, Philadelphia, PA, Temple University Press, 1995.

Annette Michelson, 'Paul Sharits and the critique of illusionism: an introduction', in *Projected Images*, Minneapolis, Walker Art Centre, 1974.

Laura Mulvey, 'Visual pleasure and narrative cinema', *Screen* 16 (3), autumn 1975. Reprinted in *Visual and Other Pleasures*, London, Macmillan, 1989.

Laura Mulvey, 'Feminism, film and the avant-garde', *Framework* 19, 1979. Reprinted in *Visual and Other Pleasures*, 1989.

Constance Penley and Janet Bergstrom, 'The avant-garde – histories and theories', *Screen* 19 (3), autumn 1978.

Yvonne Rainer, 'More kicking and screaming from the narrative front/backwater', *Wide Angle* 7 (1/2), 1985.

A. L. Rees, *A History of Experimental Film and Video*, London, BFI Publishing, 1999.

Sheldon Renan, *The Underground Film*, London, Studio Vista, 1968.

Robert Russett and Cecile Starr, *Experimental Animation*, New York, Da Capo, 1988.

Paul Sandro, *Diversions of Pleasure: Luis Buñuel and the Crises of Desire*, Columbus, Ohio State University Press, 1987.

P. Adams Sitney, *Visionary Film*, Oxford, Oxford University Press, 1974. Second edition 1979.

Michelle Wallace, 'Multiculturalism and oppositionality', *Afterimage* (USA) 19 (3), October 1991.

Paul Willemen, *Looks and Frictions: Essays in Cultural Studies and Film Theory*, London, BFI Publishing, 1994.

Linda Williams, *Figures of Desire: A Theory and Analysis of Surrealist Film*, Urbana, University of Illinois Press, 1981.

Peter Wollen, 'The avant-gardes: Europe and America', *Framework* 14, 1981.

Peter Wollen, 'Godard and counter-cinema: *Vent d'est*'; 'The two avant-gardes'; '"Ontology" and "materialism" in film'; and 'Semiotic counter-strategies: retrospect 1982', in *Readings and Writings*, London, Verso, 1982.

Third World and postcolonial cinema

Barbara Abrash and Catherine Egan (eds), *Mediating History: The MAP Guide to Independent Video*, New York, New York University Press, 1992.

Aijaz Ahmad, 'Jameson's rhetoric of otherness and the "national allegory"', *Social Text* 15, autumn 1986.

Manuel Alvarado, John King and Ana Lopez (eds), *Mediating Two Worlds: Cinematic Encounters in the Americas*, London, BFI Publishing, 1993.

Benedict Anderson, *Imagined Communities: Reflections on the Origin and Spread of Nationalism*, London, Verso, 1983.

Roy Armes, *Third World Filmmaking and the West*, Berkeley, University of California Press, 1987.

Victor Bachy, *Tradition orale et nouveaux médias*, Brussels, OCIC, 1989.

Erik Barnouw and S. Krishnaswamy, *Indian Film*, New York, Columbia University Press, 1963. Revised edition, Oxford University Press, 1980.

Charles Ramirez Berg, *Cinema of Solitude: A Critical Study of Mexican Film, 1967–1983*, Austin, University of Texas Press, 1992.

Chris Berry (ed.), *Perspectives on Chinese Cinema*, London, BFI Publishing, 1991.

'Black British cinema', *ICA documents 7*, London, ICA, 1988.

Julianne Burton, 'Marginal cinemas and mainstream critical theory', *Screen* 26 (3/4): 3–21, May/August 1985.

Julianne Burton (ed.), *Cinema and Social Change*, Austin, University of Texas Press, 1986.

Julianne Burton (ed.), *The Social Documentary in Latin America*, Pittsburgh, PA, University of Pittsburgh Press, 1990.

Sumita Chakravarty, *National Identity in Indian Popular Cinema*, Austin, University of Texas Press, 1993.

Mbye B. Cham and Claire Andrade-Watkins (eds), *Blackframes: Critical Perspectives on Black Independent Cinema*, Cambridge, MA, MIT Press, 1988.

Mbye B. Cham, *Ex-Iles: Caribbean Cinema*, Trenton, NJ, Africa World Press, 1991.

Michael Chanan, *Chilean Cinema*, London, BFI Publishing, 1976.

Michael Chanan, *Santiago Alvarez*, London, BFI Publishing, 1980.

Michael Chanan (ed.), *Twenty-Five Years of the New Latin American Cinema*, London, BFI/Channel Four Television, 1983.

Michael Chanan, *The Cuban Image*, London, BFI Publishing, 1985.

Helen W. Cyr, *A Filmography of the Third World*, Metuchen, NJ, Scarecrow Press, 1986.

Manthia Diawara, 'Oral literature and African film: narratology in *Wend Kunni*', in Pines and Willemen (eds), *Questions of Third Cinema*, 1989.

Manthia Diawara, *African Cinema*, Bloomington, Indiana University Press, 1992.

Manthia Diawara, *Black American Cinema*, London, Routledge, 1993.

John D. H. Downing (ed.), *Film and Politics in the Third World*, New York, Autonomedia, 1987.

Frantz Fanon, *The Wretched of the Earth*, New York, Grove Press, 1964.

Rosa Linda Fregoso, *The Bronze Screen: Chicana and Chicano Film Culture*, Minneapolis, University of Minnesota Press, 1993.

Coco Fusco, *Reviewing Histories: Selections from New Latin American Cinema*, Buffalo, NY, Hallwalls, 1987.

Coco Fusco, *Young, British and Black*, Buffalo, NY, Hallwalls, 1988.

Teshome Gabriel, 'Towards a critical theory of third world films', in Pines and Willemen (eds), *Questions of Third Cinema*, 1989.

Behroze Ghandy and Rosie Thomas, 'Three Indian film stars', in Gledhill (ed.), *Stardom: Industry of Desire*, 1991.

Christine Gledhill (ed.), *Stardom: Industry of Desire*, London and New York, Routledge, 1991.
Beverly G. Hawk (ed.), *Africa's Media Image*, Westport, CT, Greenwood Publishing Group, 1993.
Paul Hockings (ed.), *Principles of Visual Anthropology*, The Hague, Mouton, 1995.
Fredric Jameson, 'Third World literature in the era of multinational capitalism', *Social Text* 15: 65–88, autumn 1986.
Fredric Jameson, *The Geopolitical Aesthetic: Cinema and Space in the World System*, London, BFI Publishing, 1992.
Randal Johnson, *Cinema Novo X 5: Masters of Contemporary Brazilian Film*, Austin, University of Texas Press, 1984.
Randal Johnson and Robert Stam (eds), *Brazilian Cinema*, Rutherford, NJ, Fairleigh Dickinson University Press, 1982.
'The last "special issue" on race?' *Screen* 29 (4): 2–11, autumn 1988.
'Latin American dossier', parts 1 and 2, *Framework* 10: 11–38, spring 1979; and 11: 18–27, autumn 1979.
John A. Lent, *The Asian Film Industry*, Austin, University of Texas Press, 1990.
Jay Leyda, *Dianying: Electric Shadows – An Account of Films and the Film Audience in China*, Cambridge, MA, MIT Press, 1972.
Lizbeth Malkmus and Roy Armes, *Arab and African Filmmaking*, London, Zed Press, 1991.
Angela Martin (ed.), *BFI Dossier 6: African Films: The Context of Production*, London, BFI, 1982.
Richard A. Maynard, *Africa on Film: Myth and Reality*, Rochelle Park, NJ, The Hayden Book Co, 1974.
David McDougall, 'Beyond observational cinema', in Hockings (ed.), *Principles of Visual Anthropology*, 1995.
Carl J. Mora, *Mexican Cinema: Reflections of a Society 1896–1988*, Berkeley, University of California Press, 1988.
Laura Mulvey, 'Ousmane Sembène 1976: the carapace that failed', *Third Text* 16/17: 19–37, autumn/winter 1991.
Hamid Naficy, *The Making of Exile Cultures: Iranian Television in Los Angeles*, Minneapolis, University of Minnesota Press, 1993.
Hamid Naficy and Teshome H. Gabriel (eds), *Otherness and the Media: The Ethnography of the Imagined and the Image*, Langhorne, PA, Harood, 1993.
Chon Noriega (ed.), *Chicanos and Film: Essays on Chicano Representation and Resistance*, New York, Garland Publishing, 1982. Reprinted by University of Minnesota Press, 1991.
Françoise Pfaff, 'Three faces of Africa: women in Xala', *Jump Cut* 27: 27–31, 1982.
Françoise Pfaff, *The Cinema of Ousmane Sembène*, Westport, CT, Greenwood, 1984.
Zuzana M. Pick (ed.), *Latin American Film-Makers and the Third Cinema*, Ottawa, Carleton University Press, 1978.
Zuzana M. Pick, *The New Latin American Cinema: A Continental Project*, Austin, University of Texas Press, 1993.
Jim Pines, *Blacks in Films: A Survey of Racial Themes and Images in the American Film*, London, Studio Vista, 1975.
Jim Pines and Paul Willemen (eds), *Questions of Third Cinema*, London, BFI Publishing, 1989.
Geoffrey Reeves, *Communications and the 'Third World'*, London, Routledge, 1993.
Mark A. Reid, *Redefining Black Film*, Berkeley, University of California Press, 1992.
Edward W. Said, *Orientalism*, London, Routledge & Kegan Paul, 1978. Reprinted by Penguin, 1991.
Edward W. Said, *Culture and Imperialism*, New York, Knopf, 1993.
Hala Salmane (ed.), *Algerian Cinema*, London, BFI Publishing, 1976.
Jorge A. Schnitman, *Film Industries in Latin America: Dependency and Development*, Norwood, NJ, Ablex, 1984.
Screen 24 (2), 1983. Special issue on Racism, Colonialism and Cinema.
Screen 26 (3/4), 1985. Special issue on Other Cinemas, Other Criticisms.
Ella Shohat, *Israeli Cinema: East/West and the Politics of Representation*, Austin, University of Texas Press, 1989.
Ella Shohat, 'Notes on the postcolonial', *Social Text* 31/2: 99–113, 1992.
Ella Shohat and Robert Stam, *Unthinking Eurocentrism: Multiculturalism and the Media*, London, Routledge, 1994.
Ella Shohat and Robert Stam (eds), *Multiculturalism, Postcoloniality and Transnational Media*, New Brunswick, NJ, Rutgers University Press, 2003.
Fernando Solanas and Octavio Getino, 'Towards a third cinema' (1969), in Chanan (ed.), *Twenty-Five Years of the New Latin American Cinema*, 1983.
Peter Stevens (ed.), *Jump Cut: Hollywood, Politics and Counter-Cinema*, Toronto, Between the Lines, 1986.
Clyde Taylor, 'Decolonizing the image', in Stevens (ed.), *Jump Cut: Hollywood, Politics and Counter-cinema*, 1986.
Rosie Thomas, 'Indian cinema: pleasures and popularity', *Screen* 26 (3/4): 116–32, May/August 1985.
Robert Farris Thompson, *African Art in Motion: Icon and Act*, Berkeley, University of California Press, 1973.
Trinh T. Minh-ha, *Woman, Native, Other*, Bloomington, Indiana University Press, 1989.
Trinh T. Minh-ha, *When the Moon Waxes Red*, New York, Routledge, 1991.
Trinh T. Minh-ha, *Framer Framed*, London, Routledge, 1992.
Gaizka S. de Usabel, *The High Noon of American Films in Latin America*, Ann Arbor, MI, UMI Research Press, 1982.
Allen L. Woll, *The Latin Image in American Film*, Los Angeles, UCLA Latin American Center Publications, 1980.
Allen L. Woll and Randall M. Miller, *Ethnic and Racial Images in American Film and Television*, New York, Taylor & Francis, 1987.
Ismail Xavier, *Allegories of Underdevelopment: Aesthetics and Politics in Modern Brazilian Cinema*, Minneapolis, University of Minnesota Press, 1997.

PART 2: The Star System

THE HOLLYWOOD STAR MACHINE

Tino Balio, *United Artists: The Company Built by the Stars*, Madison, University of Wisconsin Press, 1976.
Tino Balio (ed.), *The American Film Industry*, Madison, University of Wisconsin Press, 1976. Revised edition 1985.
Simone de Beauvoir, *Brigitte Bardot and the Lolita Syndrome*, London, André Deutsch/Weidenfeld & Nicolson, 1960.
Jane Clarke, Mandy Merck and Diana Simmonds, *BFI Dossier No. 4: Move over Misconceptions: Doris Day Reappraised*, London, BFI, 1981.
Jane Clarke, Mandy Merck and Diana Simmonds, 'Doris Day case study', in Gledhill (ed.), *Star Signs*, 1982.
Commission on Educational and Cultural Films, *The Film in National Life*, London, 1932.
Pam Cook, 'Star signs', *Screen* 20 (3/4), winter 1979/80.
Pam Cook, 'Stars and politics', in Gledhill (ed.), *Star Signs*, 1982. Reprinted in *Screening the Past: Memory and Nostalgia in Cinema*, New York and Oxford, Routledge, 2005.
Richard deCordova, *Picture Personalities: The Emergence of the Star System in America*, Urbana, University of Illinois Press, 2001.
Philip Davies and Brian Neve (eds), *Cinema, Politics and Society in America*, Manchester, Manchester University Press, 1982.
Richard Dyer, *Teachers' Study Guide I: The Stars*, London, BF1 Education, 1979.
Richard Dyer, '*A Star Is Born* and the construction of authenticity', in Gledhill (ed.), *Stardom*, 1991.
Richard Dyer with Paul McDonald, *Stars*, London, BFI Publishing, 1998. Revised edn.
John Ellis, 'Star/industry/image', in Gledhill (ed.), *Star Signs*, 1982.
John Ellis, 'Stars as cinematic phenomenon', in *Visible Fictions: Cinema, Television, Video*, London and New York, Routledge, 2000.
Anne Friedberg, 'Identification and the star: a refusal of difference', in Gledhill (ed.), *Star Signs*, 1982.
Christine Geraghty, 'Re-examining stardom: questions of texts, bodies, and performance', in Gledhill and Williams (eds), *Reinventing Film Studies*, London, Arnold, 2000.
Christine Gledhill (ed.), *Star Signs: Papers from a Weekend Workshop*, London, BFI Education, 1982.
Christine Gledhill (ed.), *Stardom: Industry of Desire*, London, Routledge, 1991.
Molly Haskell, *From Reverence to Rape*, New York, Holt, Rinehart and Winston, 1974.

Norman Mailer, *Marilyn*, London, Hodder & Stoughton, 1973.

Richard Maltby, 'The political economy of Hollywood: the studio system', in Davies and Neve (eds), *Cinema, Politics and Society in America*, 1982.

Robert Mazzocco, 'The supply-side star', *New York Review of Books* 1 April 1982.

Patrick McGilligan, *Cagney: the Actor as Auteur*, South Brunswick, NJ/London, A. S. Barnes/Tantivy, 1975.

Joan Mellen, *Big Bad Wolves: Masculinity in the American Film*, London, Elm Tree Books, 1978.

Edgar Morin, *The Stars*, New York, Grove Press, 1960.

Laura Mulvey, 'Visual pleasure and narrative cinema', *Screen* 16 (3), autumn 1975. Reprinted in *Visual and Other Pleasures*, London, Macmillan, 1989.

Geoffrey Nowell-Smith, 'On the writing of the history of cinema: some problems', *Edinburgh Magazine* 2, Edinburgh, Edinburgh Film Festival, 1977.

David Pirie, 'The deal', in Pirie (ed.), *Anatomy of the Movies*, London, Windward, 1981.

Murray Ross, *Stars and Strikes*, New York, Columbia University Press, 1941.

James F. Scott, *Film: The Medium and the Maker*, New York, Holt, Rinehart and Winston, 1975.

Jackie Stacey, *Star Gazing: Hollywood Cinema and Female Spectatorship*, London, Routledge, 1993.

Janet Staiger, 'Seeing stars', *The Velvet Light Trap* 20, summer 1983. Reprinted in Gledhill (ed.), *Stardom*, 1991.

Stuart, Halsey and Co, 'The motion picture industry as a basis for bond financing', in Balio (ed.), *The American Film Industry*, 1985.

John O. Thompson, 'Screen acting and the commutation test', *Screen* 19 (2): 55–69, summer 1978. Reprinted in Gledhill (ed.), *Stardom*, 1991.

ACTING IN CINEMA

Charles Affron, *Star Acting: Gish, Garbo, Davis*, New York, Dutton, 1977.

Cynthia Baron, Diane Carson and Frank P. Tomasulo (eds), *More Than a Method: Trends and Traditions in Contemporary Film Performance*, Detroit, MI, Wayne State University Press, 2004.

David Bordwell, *Figures Traced in Light: On Cinematic Staging*, Berkeley, University of California Press, 2005.

Ben Brewster and Lea Jacobs, *Theatre to Cinema: Stage Pictorialism and the Early Feature Film*, Oxford, Oxford University Press, 1997.

Cineaste (New York), 31 (4), 2006. Special supplement on Acting in the Cinema.

Richard Dyer, *Stars*, London, BFI Publishing, 1979. Revised edition 1998.

Alan Lovell and Peter Krämer (eds), *Screen Acting*, London and New York, Routledge, 1999.

James Naremore, *Acting in the Cinema*, Berkeley, University of California Press, 1988.

Roberta E. Pearson, *Eloquent Gestures: The Transformation of Performance Style in the Griffith Biograph Films*, Berkeley, University of California Press, 1992.

V. I. Pudovkin, *Film Technique and Film Acting*, New York, Bonanza Books, 1949; trans. Ivor Montague.

Lesley Stern and George Kouvaros (eds), *Falling for You: Essays on Cinema and Performance*, Sydney, Power Publications, 1999.

Virginia Wright Wexman, *Creating the Couple: Love, Marriage, and Hollywood Performance*, Princeton, NJ, Princeton University Press, 1993.

Pamela Robertson Wojcik (ed.), *Movie Acting: The Film Reader*, London and New York, Routledge, 2004.

Carole Zucker (ed.), *Making Visible the Invisible: An Anthology of Original Essays on Film Acting*, Metuchen, NJ, The Scarecrow Press, 1990.

STARS BEFORE SOUND

Katherine Albert, 'They said Joan was "high hat"', *Photoplay* 43: 65, 112–13, August 1931.

Ruth Biery, 'The story of a dancing girl as told by Joan Crawford', *Photoplay* 34 (4): 35, 122–3, September 1928.

Marquis Busby, 'Weddings that never happened', *Motion Picture Magazine* October 1931, pp. 28–30.

Gary Carey, *Doug & Mary: A Biography of Douglas Fairbanks and Mary Pickford*, New York, E. P. Dutton, 1977.

Alistair Cooke, *Douglas Fairbanks: The Making of a Screen Character*, New York, Museum of Modern Art, 1940. Reprinted 2002.

Richard deCordova, *Picture Personalities: The Emergence of the Star System in America*, Urbana and Chicago, University of Illinois Press, 1990.

Lori Landay, 'The flapper film: comedy, dance, and Jazz Age kinaesthetics', in Bean and Negra (eds), *A Feminist Reader in Early Cinema*, Durham, NC, Duke University Press, 2003.

Paul McDonald, *The Star System: Hollywood's Production of Popular Identities*, London, Wallflower Press, 2000.

Lawrence J. Quirk and William Schoell, *Joan Crawford: The Essential Biography*, Lexington, University of Kentucky Press, 2002.

Margaret Reid, 'Has the flapper changed? F. Scott Fitzgerald discusses the cinema descendants of the type he has made so well known', *Motion Picture Magazine* July 1927, pp. 28–9, 104.

Richard Schickel and Douglas Fairbanks Jr, *The Fairbanks Album*, Boston, MA, New York Graphic Society, 1975.

Ernest Thompson Seton, *How to Play Indian*, Philadelphia, PA, Curtis, 1903.

Gaylyn Studlar, 'The perils of pleasure? Fan magazine discourse as women's commodified culture in the 1920s', *Wide Angle* 13 (1): 6–33, 1991.

Gaylyn Studlar, *This Mad Masquerade: Stardom and Masculinity in the Jazz Age*, New York, Columbia University Press, 1996.

STARS AFTER SOUND

Béla Balázs, *Der sichtbare Mensch* [1924], Frankfurt am Main, Suhrkamp, 2001. In English: Erica Carter (ed.), *Visible Man*, Oxford, Berghahn, 2008; trans. Rodney Livingstone.

Cynthia Baron, 'Crafting film performances: acting in the Hollywood studio era', in Lovell and Krämer (eds), *Screen Acting*, 1999.

Donald Bogle, *Toms, Coons, Mulattoes, Mammies and Bucks: An Interpretive History of Blacks in American Films*, New York and London, Continuum, 2001. Revised edition.

David Bordwell, Janet Staiger and Kristin Thompson, *The Classical Hollywood Cinema: Film Style and Mode of Production to 1960*, London and New York, Routledge, 1985. Revised edition 1987.

Erica Carter, *Dietrich's Ghosts: The Sublime and the Beautiful in Third Reich Film*, London, BFI Publishing, 2004.

Danae Clark, 'The subject of acting', in Fischer and Landy (eds), *Stars: The Film Reader*, 2004.

Donald Crafton, *The Talkies: American Cinema's Transition to Sound, 1926–1931*, Berkeley, University of California Press, 1997.

Mary Ann Doane, *Femmes Fatales: Feminism, Film Theory, Psychoanalysis*, New York and London, Routledge, 1991.

Richard Dyer, 'Paul Robeson: crossing over', in Fischer and Landy (eds), *Stars: The Film Reader*, 2004.

Charles Eckert, 'Shirley Temple and the house of Rockefeller', in Gledhill (ed.), *Stardom*, 1991.

Lucy Fischer, 'Rene Clair, *Le Million*, and the coming of sound', *Cinema Journal* 16 (2): 34–50, spring 1977.

Lucy Fischer and Marcia Landy (eds), *Stars: The Film Reader*, London and New York, Routledge, 2004.

Jane Gaines (ed.), *Classical Hollywood Narrative: The Paradigm Wars*, Durham and London, Duke University Press, 1992.

Gerd Gemünden and Mary J. Desjardins (eds), *Dietrich Icon*, Durham and London, Duke University Press, 2007.

Christine Gledhill (ed.), *Stardom: Industry of Desire*, London and New York, Routledge, 1991.

Lea Jacobs, *The Wages of Sin: Censorship and the Fallen Woman Film, 1928–1942*, Madison, University of Wisconsin Press, 1991.

Gertrud Koch, 'Exorcised: Marlene Dietrich and German nationalism', in Cook and Dodd (eds), *Women and Film: A Sight and Sound Reader*, London/Philadelphia, PA, Scarlet Press/Temple University Press, 1993.

Siegfried Kracauer, *The Mass Ornament: Weimar Essays*, Cambridge, MA, Harvard University Press, 1995; ed. and trans. Thomas Levin.

Alan Lovell and Peter Krämer (eds), *Screen Acting*, London and New York, Routledge, 1999.

Richard Maltby and Ian Craven, *Hollywood Cinema: An Introduction*, Oxford, Blackwell, 1995.

Paul McDonald, *The Star System: Hollywood's Production of Popular Identities*, London, Wallflower Press, 2000.

Laura Mulvey, 'Visual pleasure and narrative cinema', in *Visual and Other Pleasures*, London, Macmillan, 1989.

James Naremore, *Acting in the Cinema*, Berkeley, University of California Press, 1988.

New York Times 6 December 1930.

Charles O'Brien, *Cinema's Conversion to Sound: Technology and Film Style in France and the US*, Bloomington, Indiana University Press, 2005.

Alastair Phillips and Ginette Vincendeau (eds), *Journeys of Desire: European Actors in Hollywood*, London, BFI Publishing, 2006.

Johannes Riis, 'Naturalist and classical styles in early sound film acting', *Cinema Journal* 43 (3): 3–17, spring 2004.

Gianluca Sergi, 'Actors and the sound gang', in Lovell and Krämer (eds), *Screen Acting*, 1999.

Martin Shingler, 'Bette Davis: malevolence in motion', in Lovell and Krämer (eds), *Screen Acting*, 1999.

Janet Staiger, 'The Hollywood mode of production, 1930–60', in Bordwell, Staiger and Thompson, *The Classical Hollywood Cinema*, 1985; 1987.

Gaylyn Studlar, *In the Realm of Pleasure: Von Sternberg, Dietrich, and the Masochistic Aesthetic*, Urbana and Chicago, University of Illinois Press, 1988.

Variety 18 September 1934.

Christian Viviani, 'The "foreign woman" in classical Hollywood cinema', in Phillips and Vincendeau (eds), *Journeys of Desire*, 2006.

Andrea Weiss, *Vampires and Violets: Lesbians in Film*, Harmondsworth, Penguin, 1993.

STARS IN POSTWAR CINEMA

Dennis Bingham, '"Before she was a virgin ...": Doris Day and the decline of female film comedy in the 1950s and 1960s', *Cinema Journal* 45 (3): 3–31, spring 2006.

Steven Cohan, *Masked Men: Masculinity and the Movies in the Fifties*, Bloomington, Indiana University Press, 1997.

Richard Dyer with Paul McDonald, *Stars*, London, BFI Publishing, 1998. Revised edition.

Joshua Gamson, *Claims to Fame: Celebrity in Contemporary America*, Berkeley, University of California Press, 1994.

Christine Gledhill (ed.), *Stardom: Industry of Desire*, London and New York, Routledge, 1991.

Stephen Gundle, 'Sophia Loren: Italian icon', in Fischer and Landy (eds), *Stars: The Film Reader*, London and New York, Routledge, 2004.

Barbara Klinger, *Melodrama and Meaning: History, Culture, and the Films of Douglas Sirk*, Bloomington, Indiana University Press, 1994.

Rachel Moseley, *Growing up with Audrey Hepburn: Text, Audience, Resonance*, Manchester, Manchester University Press, 2002.

Tessa Perkins, 'The politics of "Jane Fonda"', in Gledhill (ed.), *Stardom*, 1991.

Hilary Radner and Moya Luckett (eds), *Swinging Single: Representing Sexuality in the 1960s*, Minneapolis, University of Minnesota Press, 1999.

Jackie Stacey, *Star Gazing: Hollywood Cinema and Female Spectatorship*, London and New York, Routledge, 1993.

Virginia Wright Wexman, *Creating the Couple: Love, Marriage, and Hollywood Performance*, Princeton, NJ, Princeton University Press, 1993.

CONTEMPORARY STARDOM

'ABC7 – Gov. Schwarzenegger's tax returns released'. Cited at: <en.wikipedia.org/wiki/Arnold_Schwarzenegger>. Accessed 29 December 2006.

Nigel Andrews, *True Myths: The Life and Times of Arnold Schwarzenegger: From Pumping Iron to Governor of California*, New York, Bloomsbury, 2003.

Michael De Angelis, *Gay Fandom and Crossover Stardom*, Durham, NC, Duke University Press, 2001.

Thomas Austin and Martin Barker (eds), *Contemporary Hollywood Stardom*, London, Arnold, 2003.

Daniel Bial, *Arnold Schwarzenegger: Man of Action*, New York, Franklin Watts, 1998.

Andrew Britton, 'Stars and genre', in Gledhill (ed.), *Stardom*, 1991.

Rich Cohen, 'Already a classic', *Vanity Fair* November 2006, pp. 340–50.

John Connolly, 'Arnold the barbarian', *Premiere*, March 2001, pp. 89–92, 119.

David A. Cook, *Lost Illusions: American Cinema in the Shadow of Watergate and Vietnam 1970–1979*, Berkeley, University of California Press, 2000.

Richard Dyer, *Stars*, London, BFI Publishing, 1979. Revised edition 1998.

Lucy Fischer and Marcia Landy (eds), *Stars: The Film Reader*, New York and London, Routledge, 2004.

'George Clooney biography: personal quotes'. Available at: <www.imdb.com/name/nm0000123/bio>. Accessed 29 December 2006.

Christine Geraghty, 'Re-examining stardom: questions of texts, bodies and performance', in Gledhill and Williams (eds), *Reinventing Film Studies*, 2000.

Christine Gledhill (ed.), *Stardom: Industry of Desire*, London and New York, Routledge, 1991.

Christine Gledhill and Linda Williams (eds), *Reinventing Film Studies*, London, Arnold, 2000.

Whoopi Goldberg, *Book*, New York, Avon Books, 1997.

Chris Holmlund, *Impossible Bodies: Femininity and Masculinity at the Movies*, London and New York, Routledge, 2002.

Chris Holmlund, 'Wham! Bam! Pam!: Pam Grier as hot action babe and cool action mama', *Quarterly Review of Film and Video* 22 (2): 97–112, April/June 2005.

Jeff Hudson, *George Clooney: A Biography*, London, Virgin Books, 2003.

Gary Indiana, *Schwarzenegger Syndrome: Politics and Celebrity in the Age of Contempt*, New York and London, New Press, 2005.

Barry King, 'Articulating stardom', in Gledhill (ed.), *Stardom*, 1991.

Barry King, 'Embodying an elastic self: the parametrics of contemporary stardom', in Austin and Barker (eds), *Contemporary Hollywood Stardom*, 2003.

Lea DeLaria, 'Lesbian at work', *The Advocate* 7 February 1995, pp. 46, 48–52.

Laurence Leamer, *Fantastic: The Life of Arnold Schwarzenegger*, New York, St. Martin's Press, 2005.

David Martindale, 'Whoopi Goldberg', *Biography Magazine*, April 2000, n.p.

Paul McDonald, 'Supplementary chapter: reconceptualising stardom', in Dyer, *Stars*, 1998.

Paul McDonald, *The Star System: Hollywood's Production of Popular Identities*, London, Wallflower Press, 2000.

Angela Ndalianis and Charlotte Henry (eds), *Stars in Our Eyes: The Star Phenomenon in the Contemporary Era*, Westport, CT, and London, Praeger, 2002.

Diane Negra, '"Queen of the indies": Parker Posey's niche stardom and the taste cultures of independent film', in Holmlund and Wyatt (eds), *Contemporary American Independent Film*, London and New York, Routledge, 2005.

Pamela Noel, 'Who is Whoopi Goldberg and what is she doing on Broadway?', *Ebony* 40: 27–8, 30, 34, March 1985.

Stephen Prince, *A New Pot of Gold: Hollywood under the Electronic Rainbow, 1980–1989*, Berkeley, University of California Press, 2002.

Andrea Stuart, '*The Color Purple*: in defense of happy endings', in Gamman and Marshment (eds), *The Female Gaze*, Seattle, Real Comet Press, 1989.

Arthur De Vany, *Hollywood Economics: How Extreme Uncertainty Shapes the Film Industry*, London and New York, Routledge, 2004.

Andy Willis (ed.), *Film Stars: Hollywood and Beyond*, Manchester and New York, Manchester University Press, 2004.

Justin Wyatt, *High Concept: Movies and Marketing in Hollywood*, Austin, University of Texas Press, 1994.

PART 3: Technologies

INTRODUCTION

Rick Altman, 'The evolution of sound technology', in Belton and Weis (eds), *Film Sound*, 1985.

Rick Altman, *Sound Theory, Sound Practice*, New York and London, Routledge, 1992.

Tino Balio (ed.), *The American Film Industry*, Madison, University of Wisconsin Press, 1985.

Charles Barr, 'CinemaScope: before and after', in Mast and Cohen (eds), *Film Theory and Criticism*, 1974.

John Belton, *Widescreen Cinema*, Cambridge, MA, Harvard University Press, 1992.

John Belton and Elisabeth Weis (eds), *Film Sound: Theory and Practice*, New York, Columbia University Press, 1985.

Edward Buscombe, 'Sound and color', *Jump Cut* 17, April 1978. Reprinted in Turner (ed.), *The Film Cultures Reader*, London and New York, Routledge, 2002.

James Cameron, 'Technology and magic', *CineFex* 51, August 1992.

Charles Eidsvik, 'Machines of the invisible: changes in film technology in the age of video', *Film Quarterly* 42 (2), winter 1988/89.

A. R. Fulton, in Balio (ed.), *The American Film Industry*, 1985.

Philip Hayward and Tana Wollen (eds), *Future Visions: New Technologies of the Screen*, London, BFI Publishing, 1993.

Stephen Heath and Teresa de Lauretis (eds), *The Cinematic Apparatus*, London, Macmillan, 1980.

Gerald Mast and Marshall Cohen (eds), *Film Theory and Criticism*, New York, Oxford University Press, 1974.

Stephen Neale, *Cinema and Technology: Image, Sound, Colour*, London, BFI Publishing/Macmillan, 1985.

Frank Rickett, 'Multimedia', in Hayward and Wollen (eds), *Future Visions*, 1993.

Paul Virilio, *Guerre et cinéma 1: logistique de la perception*, Paris, Cahiers du Cinéma, 1984. In English: *War and Cinema*, London, Verso, 1989.

Brian Winston, *Technologies of Seeing*, London, BFI Publishing, 1996.

Peter Wollen, 'Cinema and technology: an historical overview', in Heath and de Lauretis (eds), *The Cinematic Apparatus*, 1980.

SOUND

Rick Altman, *Sound Theory, Sound Practice*, New York, Routledge, 1992.

Tim Amyes, *Technique of Audio Post-Production in Video and Film*, Oxford, Focal Press, 1990. Revised edition 1998.

Tino Balio (ed.), *The American Film Industry*, Madison, University of Wisconsin Press, 1976. Revised edition 1985.

Evan William Cameron (ed.), *Sound and the Cinema*, New York, Redgrave Publishing Co, 1980.

Michel Chion, *L'Audio-vision*, Paris, Editions Nathan, 1990. In English: *Audio-vision: Sound on Screen*, New York, Columbia University Press, 1994; trans. Claudia Gorbman.

Douglas Gomery, 'The coming of the talkies: invention, innovation and diffusion', in Balio (ed.), *The American Film Industry*, 1985.

Stephen Jones, 'A sense of space: virtual reality, authenticity and the aural', *Critical Studies in Mass Communication* 10 (3), 1993.

Patrick L. Ogle, 'Development of sound systems: the commercial era', *Film Reader* 2: 198–211, January 1977.

COLOUR

Tom Gunning, 'Colorful metaphors: the attraction of colour in early silent cinema', *Fotogenia* 1, 1995. Available at: <www.muspe.unibo.it/period/fotogen/num01/eng01.htm>.

Gorham Kindem, 'Hollywood's conversion to color: the technological, economic and aesthetic factors', *Journal of the University Film Association* 31 (2): 29–36, spring 1979.

Vincente Minnelli, *I Remember It Well*, London, Angus & Robertson, 1975.

Stephen Neale, *Cinema and Technology: Image, Sound, Colour*, London, BFI Publishing/Macmillan, 1985.

Angela Dalle Vacche, *Cinema and Painting: How Art Is Used in Film*, Austin, University of Texas Press, 1996.

Angela Dalle Vacche and Brian Price (eds), *Color: The Film Reader*, New York and Oxford, Routledge, 2006.

Brian Winston, *Technologies of Seeing*, London, BFI Publishing, 1996.

DEEP-FOCUS

Charles Barr, 'CinemaScope: before and after', in Mast and Cohen (eds), *Film Theory and Criticism*, New York, Oxford University Press, 1974.

Charles H. Harpole, 'Ideological and technological determinism in deep-space cinema images', *Film Quarterly* 33 (3): 11–22, spring 1980.

Patrick L. Ogle, 'Technological and aesthetic influences upon the development of deep-focus cinematography in the United States', *Screen* 13 (1): 45–72, spring 1972. Reprinted in Ellis (ed.), *Screen Reader* 1, London, SEFT, 1977.

Gavin Smith, 'A man of excess: Paul Schrader on Jean Renoir', *Sight and Sound* 5 (1), January 1995.

George E. Turner, 'Gregg Toland, ASC', *American Cinematographer* 63 (11), November 1982.

Christopher Williams, 'The deep-focus question: some comments on Patrick Ogle's article', *Screen* 13 (1): 73–6, spring 1972. Reprinted in Ellis (ed.), *Screen Reader* 1, London, SEFT, 1977.

LIGHTING

Peter Baxter, 'On the history and ideology of film lighting', *Screen* 16 (3), autumn 1975.

Richard Dyer, *White: Essays on Race and Culture*, London and New York, Routledge, 2002.

T. Earle-Knight, 'Studio lighting 1930–1980', *The BKSTS Journal*, January 1981.

Charles W. Handley, 'History of motion picture studio lighting', *Journal of the SMPTE* 63: 129–33, October 1954.

WIDESCREEN

Charles Barr, 'CinemaScope: before and after', in Mast and Cohen (eds), *Film Theory and Criticism*, 1974.

John Belton, *Widescreen Cinema*, Cambridge, MA, Harvard University Press, 1992.

David Bordwell, 'Widescreen aesthetics and mise-en-scène criticism', *The Velvet Light Trap* 21: 18–25, summer 1985.

David Bordwell, Janet Staiger and Kristin Thompson, *The Classical Hollywood Cinema*, New York, Columbia University Press, 1985. Revised edition 1987.

Philip Hayward and Tana Wollen (eds), *Future Visions: New Technologies of the Screen*, London, BFI Publishing, 1993.

Stephen Huntley, 'Sponable's CinemaScope: an intimate chronology of the invention of the CinemaScope optical system', *Film History* 5 (3): 298–320, September 1993.

Gerald Mast and Marshall Cohen (eds), *Film Theory and Criticism*, New York, Oxford University Press, 1974.

Victor Perkins, '*River of No Return*', *Movie* 2, September 1962.

The Velvet Light Trap 21, summer 1985. Special issue on Widescreen, with articles by André Bazin and David Bordwell.

Fred Waller, 'The archaeology of Cinerama', *Film History* 5 (3), September 1993.

Tana Wollen, 'The bigger the better: from CinemaScope to Imax', in Hayward and Wollen (eds), *Future Visions*, 1993.

CAMERAS

Stephen Neale, *Cinema and Technology: Image, Sound, Colour*, London, BFI Publishing/Macmillan, 1985.

David Samuelson, 'Cine equipment over fifty years', *The BKSTS Journal* 63 (1), January 1981.

Brian Winston, *Technologies of Seeing*, London, BFI Publishing, 1996.

ALTERNATIVE PRODUCTION FORMATS

Hugh Baddeley, '"Sub-standard": the development of 16mm', *The BKSTS Journal* 63 (1), January 1981.

Lili Berko, 'Surveying the surveilled: video, space and subjectivity', *Quarterly Review of Film and Video* 14 (1/2), 1992.

Laura Hudson, 'Promiscuous 8', *Coil* 2, November 1995.

Stuart Marshall, 'Video: from art to independence: a short history of a new technology', *Screen* 26 (2), March/April 1985.

Rodger J. Ross, 'The development of professional Super 8', *American Cinematographer* 56 (11), November 1975.

Patricia R. Zimmerman, 'Trading down: amateur film technology in fifties America', *Screen* 29 (2), spring 1988.

DIGITAL VIDEO

Mike Figgis, *Digital Filmmaking*, London, Faber & Faber, 2007.

James Knight and Katrina Manson, 'Interview with Idrissa Ouédraogo', BBC World Service website, 2005. Available at: <www.bbc.co.uk/worldservice/specials/1458_latestnews/page7.shtml>. Accessed 26 October 2006.

Martin Lister, Jon Dovey, Seth Giddings, Iain Grant and Kieran Kelly, *New Media: A Critical Introduction*, London and New York, Routledge, 2003.

Ron Magid, 'Exploring a new universe: George Lucas discusses his ongoing effort to shape the future of digital cinema', *American Cinematographer* 83 (9), September 2002.

EDITING

Les Paul Robley, 'Digital offline video editing: expanding creative horizons', *American Cinematographer* 74 (4/7), April/July 1993.

Barry Salt, *Film Style and Technology: History and Analysis*, London, Starword, 1983; 1992. Revised edition 2003.

Janet Wasko, *Hollywood in the Information Age*, Cambridge, Polity Press, 1994.

MULTIMEDIA TECHNOLOGIES

Robin Baker, 'Computer-technology and special effects in contemporary cinema', in Hayward and Wollen (eds), *Future Visions*, 1993.

Frank Beacham, 'Movies for the future: storytelling with computers', *American Cinematographer* 76 (4), April 1995.

Frank Biocca and Mark R. Levy, *Communication in the Age of Virtual Reality*, Hove and New Jersey, Lawrence Erlbaum Associates, 1995.

Andrew Cameron, 'Dissimulations: the illusion of interactivity', *Millennium Film Journal* 28, spring 1995.

Bob Cotton and Richard Oliver, *Understanding Hypermedia: From Multimedia to Virtual Reality*, London, Phaidon, 1993.

Charles Eidsvik, 'Machines of the invisible: changes in film technology in the age of video', *Film Quarterly* 42 (2), winter 1988/9.

Bob Fisher, 'Dawning of the digital age', *American Cinematographer* 73 (4), April 1992.

Philip Hayward and Tana Wollen (eds), *Future Visions: New Technologies of the Screen*, London, BFI Publishing, 1993.

Malcolm Le Grice, 'Kismet, protagony and the zap splat factor: some theoretical concepts for an interactive avant-garde cinema', *Millennium Film Journal* 28, spring 1995.

Nicholas Negroponte, *Being Digital*, London, Hodder & Stoughton, 1995.

Joan Pennefather, 'From cinema to virtual reality', *Intermedia* 22 (5), October/November 1994.

Michele Pierson, *Special Effects: Still in Search of Wonder*, New York, Columbia University Press, 2002.

Jannine Pourroy, 'Through the proscenium arch', *Cinefex* 46, May 1991.

Gregory Solman, 'The illusion of a future', *Film Comment* 28 (2), March/April 1992.

David Tafler, 'Beyond narrative: notes towards a theory of interactive cinema', *Millennium Film Journal* 20/1: 116–31, autumn/winter 1988/89.

John Watkinson, *An Introduction to Digital Video*, Oxford, Focal Press, 1994.

Grahame Weinbren, 'In the ocean of streams of story', *Millennium Film Journal* 28, spring 1995.

Virtual Reality

Frank Biocca and Mark R. Levy, *Communication in the Age of Virtual Reality*, Hove and New Jersey, Lawrence Erlbaum Associates, 1995.

Karen Carr and Rupert England (eds), *Simulated and Virtual Realities: Elements of Perception*, London, Taylor & Francis, 1995.

Ron Magid, 'ILM magic is organised mayhem', *American Cinematographer* 75 (12), December 1994.

Nicholas Negroponte, *Being Digital*, London, Hodder & Stoughton, 1995.

Howard Rheingold, *Virtual Reality*, London, Secker and Warburg, 1991.

Barrie Sherman and Phil Judkins, *Glimpses of Heaven, Visions of Hell*, London, Hodder & Stoughton, 1992.

PART 4: World Cinemas

NATIONAL CINEMAS IN THE GLOBAL ERA

Richard Abel, *The Red Rooster Scare: Making Cinema American, 1900–1910*, Berkeley, University of California Press, 1999.

Benedict Anderson, *Imagined Communities: Reflections on the Origin and Spread of Nationalism*, London, Verso, 1983.

Roger Clarke, 'The life and Seoul of the party', *Independent* 27 April 2001.

Natasa Durovicovà and Kathleen E. Newman (eds), *World Cinemas, Transnational Perspectives*, New York and London, Routledge, 2007.

Elizabeth Ezra and Terry Rowden (eds), *Transnational Cinema: The Film Reader*, London and New York, Routledge, 2006.

Mette Hjort and Scott Mackenzie (eds), *Cinema and Nation*, London and New York, Routledge, 2000.

Valentina Vitali and Paul Willemen (eds), *Theorising National Cinema*, London, BFI Publishing, 2006.

Alan Williams (ed.), *Film and Nationalism*, New Brunswick, NJ, Rutgers University Press, 2002.

AUSTRALIAN CINEMA

John Baxter, *The Australian Cinema*, Sydney, Angus & Robertson, 1970.

Ina Bertrand (ed.), *Cinema in Australia: A Documentary History*, Kensington, New South Wales University Press, 1989.

Annette Blonski, Barbara Creed and Freda Freiberg (eds), *Don't Shoot Darling!: Women's Independent Film-Making in Australia*, Melbourne, Greenhouse Publications, 1987.

Diane Collins, *Hollywood Down Under: Australians at the Movies, 1896 to the Present*, Sydney, Angus & Robertson, 1987.

Felicity Collins and Therese Davis, *Australian Cinema after Mabo*, Cambridge, Cambridge University Press, 2004.

Susan Dermody and Elizabeth Jacka, *The Screening of Australia: Anatomy of a National Cinema*, 2 vols., Sydney, Currency Press, 1987 and 1988.

Scott Hocking (ed.), *100 Greatest Films of Australian Cinema*, Melbourne, Scribal Publishing, 2006.

Chris Long, 'Silent film until 1914', in McFarlane, Mayer and Bertrand (eds), *Oxford Companion to Australian Film*, 1999.

Peter Malone (ed.), *Myth & Meaning: Australian Film Directors in Their Own Words*, Sydney, Currency Press, 2001.

Brian McFarlane, *Words and Images: Australian Novels into Film*, Melbourne, Heinemann, 1983.

Brian McFarlane, 'Six degrees of aspiration', *The Australian Book Review*, November 2006.

Brian McFarlane and Geoff Mayer, *New Australian Cinema: Sources and Parallels in American and British Film*, Melbourne, Cambridge University Press, 1992.

Brian McFarlane, Geoff Mayer and Ina Bertrand (eds), *The Oxford Companion to Australian Film*, Melbourne, Oxford University Press, 1999.

Bruce Molloy, *Before the Interval: Australian Mythology and Feature Films, 1930–1960*, St Lucia, University of Queensland Press, 1990.

Albert Moran and Tom O'Regan (eds), *An Australian Film Reader*, Sydney, Currency Press, 1985.

Albert Moran and Tom O'Regan (eds.), *The Australian Screen*, Ringwood, Victoria, Penguin, 1989.

Scott Murray (ed.), *The New Australian Cinema*, Melbourne, Thomas Nelson/Cinema Papers, 1980.

Scott Murray (ed.), *Back of Beyond: Discovering Australian Film and Television*, Sydney, Australian Film Commission, 1988.

Scott Murray (ed.), *Australian Film 1978–1994*, Melbourne, Oxford University Press/Cinema Papers/Australian Film Commission, 1995.

David Myers, *Bleeding Battlers from Ironbark: Australian Myths in Fiction and Film: 1890s–1980s*, Rockhampton, Qld, Capricornia Institute Publications, 1987.

Tom O'Regan, *Australian National Cinema*, London and New York, Routledge, 1996.
Andrew Pike and Ross Cooper, *Australian Film 1900–1977*, Melbourne, Oxford University Press, 1980. Revised edition 1998.
Neil Rattigan, *Images of Australia: 100 Films of the New Australian Cinema*, Dallas, TX, Southern Methodist University, 1991.
Jonathan Rayner, *Contemporary Australian Cinema*, Manchester, Manchester University Press, 2000.
Eric Reade, *History and Heartburn: The Saga of Australian Films, 1896–1978*, Sydney, Harper & Row, 1979.
James Sabine (ed.), *A Century of Australian Cinema*, Melbourne, Heinemann, 1995.
Graham Shirley and Brian Adams, *Australian Cinema: The First Eighty Years*, Sydney, Angus & Robertson/Currency Press, 1983.
David Stratton, *The Last New Wave: The Australian Film Revival*, London and Sydney, Angus & Robertson, 1980.
David Stratton, *The Avocado Plantation*, Sydney, Macmillan, 1990.
John Tulloch, *Legends on the Screen: The Australian Narrative Cinema 1919–1929*, Sydney, Currency Press and the Australian Film Institute, 1981.
John Tulloch, *Australian Cinema: Industry, Narrative and Meaning*, Sydney, Allen & Unwin, 1982.
Graeme Turner, *National Fictions: Literature, Film and the Construction of Australian Narrative*, Sydney, Allen & Unwin, 1993.

BRITISH CINEMA

Introduction

Justine Ashby and Andrew Higson (eds), *British Cinema, Past and Present*, London and New York, Routledge, 2000.
Bruce Babington (ed.), *British Stars and Stardom: From Alma Taylor to Sean Connery*, Manchester, Manchester University Press, 2001.
Charles Barr (ed.), *All Our Yesterdays: 90 Years of British Cinema*, London, BFI Publishing, 1986.
Charles Barr, *Ealing Studios*, Moffat, Cameron and Hollis, 1998. Revised edition.
Raymond Durgnat, *A Mirror for England: British Movies from Austerity to Affluence*, London, Faber & Faber, 1971.
Sue Harper, *Women in British Cinema: Mad, Bad and Dangerous to Know*, New York, Continuum, 2000.
Andrew Higson (ed.), *Dissolving Views: Key Writings on British Cinema*, London, Cassell, 1996.
Andrew Higson, *Waving the Flag: Constructing a National Cinema in Britain*, Oxford, Clarendon Press, 1997.
Andrew Higson, *English Cinema, English Heritage: Costume Drama Since 1980*, Oxford, Oxford University Press, 2003.
Geoffrey Macnab, *J. Arthur Rank and the British Film Industry*, London and New York, Routledge, 1993.
Geoffrey Macnab, *Searching for Stars: Stardom and Screen Acting in British Cinema*, New York, Continuum, 2000.
Robert Murphy, *The British Cinema Book*, London, BFI Publishing, 1997. Revised edition 2002.
Duncan Petrie, *The British Cinematographer*, London, BFI Publishing, 1996.
Amy Sargeant, *British Cinema: A Critical and Interpretive History*, London, BFI Publishing, 2005.
Andrew Spicer, *Typical Men: The Representation of Masculinity in Popular British Cinema*, London, I. B. Tauris, 2003.
Sarah Street, *British National Cinema*, London, Routledge, 1997.
Sarah Street, *Transatlantic Crossings: British Feature Films in the USA*, New York, Continuum, 2002.
Michael Williams, *Ivor Novello: Screen Idol*, London, BFI Publishing, 2003.

The British film industry

Ealing Studios

Charles Barr, *Ealing Studios*, London, Cameron & Tayleur/Newton Abbot, David & Charles, 1977. Revised edition 1998.
John Ellis, 'Made in Ealing', *Screen* 16 (1): 78–127, spring 1975.
Christine Geraghty, *British Cinema in the Fifties: Gender, Genre and the New Look*, London and New York, Routledge, 2000.
Sue Harper and Vincent Porter, *British Cinema of the 1950s: The Decline of Deference*, Oxford, Oxford University Press, 2003.
'Interview with Alexander Mackendrick', *Positif* 92, 1968.
Geoffrey Macnab, *J. Arthur Rank and the British Film Industry*, London and New York, Routledge, 1993.
Robert Murphy (ed.), *The British Cinema Book*, London, BFI Publishing, 1997. Rev. edn 2002.
Tim Pulleine, 'A song and dance at the local: thoughts on Ealing', in Murphy (ed.), *The British Cinema Book*, 1997.

Gainsborough Pictures

Sue Aspinall and Robert Murphy (eds), *BFI Dossier 18: Gainsborough Melodrama*, London, BFI, 1983.
Charles Barr, *English Hitchcock*, Moffat, Cameron & Hollis, 1999.
Pam Cook, *Fashioning the Nation: Costume and Identity in British Cinema*, London, BFI Publishing, 1996.
Pam Cook (ed.), *Gainsborough Pictures*, London and Washington, Cassell, 1997.
Sue Harper, *Picturing the Past: The Rise and Fall of the British Costume Film*, London, BFI Publishing, 1994.
Geoffrey Macnab, *J. Arthur Rank and the British Film Industry*, London and New York, Routledge, 1993.
Tom Ryall, *Alfred Hitchcock and the English Cinema*, London, Croom Helm, 1986. Revised edition, Athlone, 1996.
Sarah Street, '*The Lodger*', in Forbes and Street (eds), *European Cinema: An Introduction*, Basingstoke, Palgrave Macmillan, 2000.
Michael Williams, *Ivor Novello: Screen Idol*, London, BFI Publishing, 2003.

Hammer Productions

Allen Eyles, Robert Adkinson and Nicholas Fry (eds), *The House of Horror: The Complete Story of Hammer Films*, London, Lorrimer, 1973.
Peter Hutchings, *Hammer and Beyond: British Horror Film*, Manchester, Manchester University Press, 1993.
James L. Limbacher, *The Influence of J. Arthur Rank on the History of the British Film*, Dearborn, MI, Henry Ford Centennial Library, n. d.
Little Shoppe of Horrors 4, April 1978.
Robert Murphy, *Sixties British Cinema*, London, BFI Publishing, 1992.
Kim Newman (ed.), *The BFI Companion to Horror*, London, Cassell/BFI Publishing, 1996.
George Perry, *The Great British Picture Show*, London, Hart-Davis MacGibbon, 1974.
David Pirie, *A Heritage of Horror: the English Gothic Cinema 1946–1972*, London, Gordon Fraser, 1973.
David Pirie, *Hammer: A Cinema Case Study*, London, BFI Education, 1980.

British social realism 1959–63

Sue Aspinall and Robert Murphy (eds), *BFI Dossier 18: Gainsborough Melodrama*, London, BFI, 1983.
Michael Balcon, 'Interview in "In the picture"', *Sight and Sound* 28 (3/4): 133, summer/autumn 1959.
Geoff Brown, 'Paradise found and lost: the course of British realism', in Murphy (ed.), *The British Cinema Book*, 1997.
Raymond Durgnat, *A Mirror for England: British Movies from Austerity to Affluence*, London, Faber & Faber, 1971.
Andrew Higson, 'Space, place, spectacle: landscape and townscape in the "kitchen sink" film', in *Dissolving Views*, London and New York, Cassell, 1996.
John Hill, 'Ideology, economy and the British cinema', in Barrett, Corrigan, Kuhn and Wolff (eds), *Ideology and Cultural Production*, London, Croom Helm, 1979.
John Hill, *Sex, Class and Realism: British Cinema 1956–1963*, London, BFI Publishing, 1986.
Alan Lovell, 'The British cinema: the unknown cinema', London, BFI Education Dept Seminar Paper, 1969.
Robert Murphy, *Sixties British Cinema*, London, BFI Publishing, 1992.
Robert Murphy, *The British Cinema Book*, London, BFI, 1997. Revised edition 2002.
George Perry, *The Great British Picture Show*, London, Hart-Davis MacGibbon, 1974.
Alexander Walker, *Hollywood, England: The British Film Industry in the 60s*, London, Michael Joseph, 1974.

Peter Wollen, *Signs and Meaning in the Cinema*, London, Secker and Warburg/BFI, 1969. Revised edition 1972; expanded edition, BFI Publishing, 1998.

Contemporary British cinema

Paul Dave, *Visions of England: Class and Culture in Contemporary Cinema*, Oxford, Berg, 2006.

Lester Friedman (ed.), *Fires Were Started: British Cinema and Thatcherism*, London, Wallflower Press, 2006.

John Hill, *British Cinema in the 1980s*, Oxford, Clarendon Press, 1998.

Nigel Mather, *Tears of Laughter: Comedy-drama in 1990s British Cinema*, Manchester, Manchester University Press, 2006.

Robert Murphy (ed.), *The British Cinema Book*, London, BFI Publishing, 1997. Revised edition 2002.

Robert Murphy (ed.), *British Cinema of the 1990s*, London, BFI Publishing, 1999.

Julian Petley and Duncan Petrie (eds), 'New British cinema', *Journal of Popular British Cinema* 5, 2002.

Scottish cinema

David Bruce, *Scotland the Movie*, Edinburgh, Polygon/Scottish Film Council, 1996.

John Caughie, 'Representing Scotland: new questions for Scottish cinema', in Dick (ed.), *From Limelight to Satellite*, 1990.

Pam Cook, *I Know Where I'm Going!*, London, BFI Publishing, 2002.

Cairns Craig, *Out of History: Narrative Paradigms in Scottish and British Culture*, Edinburgh, Polygon, 1996.

Eddie Dick (ed.), *From Limelight to Satellite: A Scottish Film Book*, London, British Film Institute/Scottish Film Council, 1990.

Eddie Dick, Andrew Noble and Duncan Petrie (eds), *Bill Douglas: A Lanternist's Account*, London, British Film Institute/Scottish Film Council, 1993.

Forsyth Hardy, *Scotland in Film*, Edinburgh, Edinburgh University Press, 1990.

David Martin-Jones, '*Orphans*, a work of minor cinema from post-devolutionary Scotland', *Journal of British Cinema and Television* 1 (2): 226–41, 2005.

Colin McArthur (ed.), *Scotch Reels: Scotland in Cinema and Television*, London, BFI Publishing, 1982.

Colin McArthur, *Braveheart, Brigadoon and the Scots: Distortions of Scotland in Hollywood Cinema*, London, I. B. Tauris, 2003a.

Colin McArthur, *Whisky Galore! and The Maggie*, London, I. B. Tauris, 2003b.

Jonathan Murray, 'Contemporary Scottish film', *The Irish Review* 28: 75–88, 2001.

Jonathan Murray, 'Convents or cowboys?', in Hill and Rockett (eds), *Studies in Irish Film I: National Cinemas and Beyond*, Dublin, Four Courts, 2004.

Jonathan Murray, 'Kids in America?: narratives of transatlantic influence in 1990s Scottish cinema', *Screen* 46 (2): 217–25, summer 2005.

Duncan Petrie, *Screening Scotland*, London, BFI Publishing, 2000.

Duncan Petrie, *Contemporary Scottish Fictions*, Edinburgh, Edinburgh University Press, 2004.

Welsh cinema

David Berry, *Wales and Cinema: The First 100 Years*, Cardiff, University of Wales Press, 1996.

Steve Blandford (ed.), *Wales on Screen*, Bridgend, Seren/Poetry of Wales Press, 2000.

Peter Stead, *Acting Wales: Stars of Stage and Screen*, Cardiff, University of Wales Press, 2002.

CHINESE CINEMA

Chris Berry (ed.), *Perspectives on Chinese Cinema*, London, BFI Publishing, 1991.

Chris Berry and Mary Farquhar, *China on Screen: Cinema and Nation*, New York, Columbia University Press, 2005.

David Bordwell, *Planet Hong Kong: Popular Cinema and the Art of Entertainment*, Cambridge, MA, Harvard University Press, 2000.

Jubin Hu, *Projecting a Nation: Chinese National Cinema before 1949*, Hong Kong, Hong Kong University Press, 2002.

Leo Ou-fan Lee, 'The tradition of modern Chinese cinema: some preliminary explorations and hypotheses', in Berry (ed.), *Perspectives on Chinese Cinema*, 1991.

Feii Lü, *Taiwan Dianying 1994–1999: Zhengzhi, Meixue, Jingji* [*Taiwan Cinema 1994–1999: Politics, Aesthetics, Economics*], Taipei, Yuanliu, 1998.

Sheldon H. Lu and Emilie Yueh-yu Yeh (eds), *Chinese-Language Film: Historiography, Poetics, Politics*, Honolulu, University of Hawaii Press, 2004.

Ni Zhen, *Memoirs from the Beijing Film Academy: The Genesis of China's Fifth Generation*, Durham, NC, Duke University Press, 2003; trans. Chris Berry.

Stephen Teo, *Hong Kong Cinema: The Extra Dimensions*, London, BFI Publishing, 1997.

Yingjin Zhang, *Chinese National Cinema*, New York, Routledge, 2004.

Zhang Zhen, *An Amorous History of the Silver Screen: Shanghai Cinema, 1896–1937*, Chicago, University of Chicago Press, 2006.

DANISH CINEMA

Dogme 95

Stig Björkman (ed.), *Trier on von Trier*, London and New York, Faber & Faber, 2004.

Robert Bresson, *Notes on the Cinematographer*, London, Quartet, 1986.

Mike Figgis, *Digital Filmmaking*, London and New York, Faber & Faber, 2007.

Tag Gallagher, *The Adventures of Roberto Rossellini: His Life and Films*, New York, Da Capo Press, 1998.

Mette Hjort and Scott Mackenzie (eds), *Purity and Provocation: Dogma 95*, London, BFI Publishing, 2003.

Richard Kelly, *The Name of This Book Is Dogme 95*, London and New York, Faber & Faber, 2000.

Richard Raskin (ed.), 'Aspects of Dogma 95', *P.O.V. A Danish Journal of Film Studies* 10, December 2000. Special issue.

Peter Schepelern, 'Filmen ifolge Dogme. Spilleregler, forhindringer og befrielser', *Dansk Film* 10 (1), spring 1999.

Patricia Thomson, '*The Idiots* plays by von Trier's rules', *American Cinematographer* 81 (1), January 2000.

Lars von Trier, *Idioterne. Manuskript og dagbog*, Copenhagen, Gyldendal, 1998.

Thomas Vinterberg, *Festen*, Copenhagen, Per Kofod, 1998.

FRENCH CINEMA

Introduction

Richard Abel, *French Cinema: The First Wave, 1915–1929*, Princeton, NJ, Princeton University Press, 1984.

Richard Abel, *The Ciné Goes to Town, French Cinema 1896–1914*, Berkeley, University of California Press, 1994.

Roy Armes, *French Cinema*, London, Secker and Warburg, 1985.

Guy Austin, *Stars in Modern French Film*, London, Arnold, 2003.

Antoine de Baecque, *Nouvelle vague*, Paris, Cinémathèque Française/Hazan, 1998.

Antoine de Baecque, *La cinéphilie: invention d'un regard, histoire d'une culture 1944–1968*, Paris, Fayard, 2003.

Jean-Pierre Bertin-Maghit, *Le cinéma sous l'occupation: le monde du cinéma français de 1940 à 1946*, Paris, Perrin, 2002.

Noël Burch and Geneviève Sellier, *La drôle de guerre des sexes du cinéma français, 1930–1956*, Paris, Editions Nathan, 1996.

Colin Crisp, *The Classic French Cinema, 1930–1960*, Bloomington, Indiana University Press, 1993.

Carolyn A. Durham, *Double Takes: Culture and Gender in French Films and Their American Remakes*, Hanover, NH, University Press of New England, 1998.

Evelyn Ehrlich, *Cinema of Paradox: French Filmmaking under the German Occupation*, New York, Columbia University Press, 1985.

Jean-Pierre Esquenazi, *Godard et la société française des années 1960*, Paris, Armand Colin, 2004.

Sandy Flitterman-Lewis, *To Desire Differently: Feminism and the French Cinema*, New York, Columbia University Press, 1996.

Jill Forbes, *The Cinema in France after the New Wave*, London, Macmillan/BFI Publishing, 1992.

Naomi Greene, *Landscapes of Loss: The National Past in Postwar French Cinema*, Princeton, NJ, Princeton University Press, 1998.

Susan Hayward, *French National Cinema*, London and New York, Routledge, 1993.

Susan Hayward and Ginette Vincendeau, *French Film: Texts and Contexts*, London and New York, Routledge, 2000.

Diana Holmes and Robert Ingram, *François Truffaut*, Manchester, Manchester University Press, 1997.

Alex Hughes and James S. Williams (eds), *Gender and French Cinema*, Oxford and New York, Berg, 2001.

Sylvie Lindeperg, *Les ecrans de l'ombre: la seconde guerre mondiale dans le cinéma français, 1944–1969*, Paris, CNRS Editions, 1997.

Laurent Marie, *Le cinéma est à nous: le PCF et le cinéma français de la libération à nos jours*, Paris, L'Harmattan, 2005.

Michel Marie, *La nouvelle vague: une école artistique*, Paris, Editions Nathan, 1997. In English: *The French New Wave: An Artistic School*, Oxford, Blackwell, 2003; trans. Richard Neupert.

Judith Mayne, *Le Corbeau*, London, I. B. Tauris, 2006.

Lucy Mazdon, *Encore Hollywood: Remaking French Cinema*, London, BFI Publishing, 2000.

Alison McMahan, *Alice Guy-Blaché: Lost Visionary of the Cinema*, New York, Continuum, 2002.

Raphaëlle Moine, *Les genres du cinéma*, Paris, Editions Nathan, 2002.

Fabrice Montebello, *Le cinéma en France*, Paris, Armand Colin, 2005.

Richard Neupert, *A History of the French New Wave Cinema*, Madison, University of Wisconsin Press, 2002.

Martin O'Shaughnessy, *Jean Renoir*, Manchester, Manchester University Press, 2000.

Phil Powrie (ed.), *The Cinema of France*, London, Wallflower Press, 2005.

Henry Rousso, *The Vichy Syndrome: History and Memory in France since 1944*, Cambridge, MA, Harvard University Press, 1991; trans. Arthur Goldhammer.

Georges Sadoul, *French Film*, London, Falcon Press, 1953.

Geneviève Sellier, *La nouvelle vague: un cinéma au masculin singulier*, Paris, CNRS Editions, 2005.

Carrie Tarr with Brigitte Rollet, *Cinema and the Second Sex: Women's Filmmaking in France in the 1980s and 1990s*, London and New York, Continuum, 2001.

Michael Temple and Michael Witt (eds), *The French Cinema Book*, London, BFI Publishing, 2004.

Michael Temple, James S. Williams and Michael Witt (eds), *For Ever Godard*, London, Black Dog Publishing, 2004.

François Truffaut, 'Une certaine tendance du cinéma français', *Cahiers du cinéma* 31, January 1954. In English: 'A certain tendency of French cinema', in Nichols (ed.), *Movies and Methods Vol. I*, Berkeley, University of Calfornia Press, 1976.

Ginette Vincendeau, *The Companion to French Cinema*, London, BFI Publishing, 1996.

Ginette Vincendeau, *Stars and Stardom in French Cinema*, London and New York, Continuum, 2000.

Ginette Vincendeau, *Jean-Pierre Melville: An American in Paris*, London, BFI Publishing, 2003.

Alan Williams, *Republic of Images: A History of French Filmmaking*, London and Cambridge, MA, Harvard University Press, 1992.

French cinema in the 1930s

Richard Abel, *French Film Theory and Criticism: A History/Anthology 1907–1939, Vol. 2: 1929–1939*, Princeton, NJ, Princeton University Press, 1988. Revised edition 1993.

Dudley Andrew, *Mists of Regret: Culture and Sensibility in Classic French Film*, Princeton, NJ, Princeton University Press, 1995.

Pierre Billard, *L'âge classique du cinéma français*, Paris, Flammarion, 1995.

Jonathan Buchsbaum, *Cinema Engagé: Film in the Popular Front*, Urbana, University of Illinois Press, 1988.

Colin Crisp, *The Classic French Cinema, 1930–1960*, Bloomington, Indiana University Press, 1993.

Colin Crisp, *Genre, Myth, and Convention in the French Cinema, 1929–1939*, Bloomington, Indiana University Press, 2002.

Jean-Pierre Jeancolas, *Quinze ans d'années trente: le cinéma des français 1929–1944*, Paris, Stock, 1983.

Michèle Lagny, Marie-Claire Ropars and Pierre Sorlin, *Générique des années trente*, Paris, Presses Universitaires de Vincennes, 1986.

Martin O'Shaughnessy, *Jean Renoir*, Manchester, Manchester University Press, 2000.

Alexander Sesonske, *Jean Renoir: The French Films, 1924–1939*, Cambridge, MA, Harvard University Press, 1980.

Edward Baron Turk, *Child of Paradise: Marcel Carné and the Golden Age of French Cinema*, Cambridge, MA, Harvard University Press, 1989.

Ginette Vincendeau, *French Cinema in the 1930s: Social Text and Context of a Popular Entertainment Medium*, PhD thesis, University of East Anglia, 1985.

Ginette Vincendeau, 'Anatomy of a myth: Jean Gabin', *Nottingham French Studies* 32 (1): 19–31, 1993.

Ginette Vincendeau, *Pépé le Moko*, London, BFI Publishing, 1998.

The Nouvelle Vague

Roy Armes, *French Cinema since 1946: Vol. 2 The Personal Style*, London, Zwemmer, 1970.

Raymond Durgnat, *Nouvelle Vague: The First Decade*, Loughton, Essex, Motion Publications, 1963.

Peter Graham (ed.), *The New Wave: Critical Landmarks*, London, Secker and Warburg/BFI, 1968.

Susan Hayward, *French National Cinema*, London, Routledge, 1993.

Terry Lovell, 'Sociology of aesthetic structures and contextualism', in McQuail (ed.), *Sociology of Mass Communication*, 1972.

Denis McQuail (ed.), *Sociology of Mass Communication*, Harmondsworth, Middlesex, Penguin, 1972.

James Monaco, *The New Wave: Truffaut, Godard, Chabrol, Rohmer, Rivette*, New York and Oxford, Oxford University Press, 1976. Reprinted by Harbor Electronic Publishing, 2004.

Jacques Siclier, 'New wave and French cinema', *Sight and Sound* 30 (3), summer 1961.

Ginette Vincendeau (ed.), *The Companion to French Cinema*, London, Cassell/BFI, 1996.

French cinema since the 1980s

Guy Austin, *Contemporary French Cinema: An Introduction*, Manchester, Manchester University Press, 1996.

Martine Beugnet, *Marginalité, sexualité, contrôle dans le cinéma français contemporain*, Paris, L'Harmattan, 2000.

Christian Bosséno, 'Immigrant cinema: national cinema – the case of *beur* film', in Dyer and Vincendeau (eds), *Popular European Cinema*, London and New York, Routledge, 1992.

Serge Daney, 'Falling out of love', in Vincendeau (ed.), *Film/Literature/Heritage: A Sight and Sound Reader*, London, BFI Publishing, 2001.

Elizabeth Ezra and Sue Harris (eds), *France in Focus: Film and National Identity*, Oxford, Berg, 2000.

Susan Hayward, *Luc Besson*, Manchester, Manchester University Press, 1998.

Lucy Mazdon (ed.), *France on Film: Reflections on Popular French Cinema*, London, Wallflower Press, 2001.

Phil Powrie, *French Cinema in the 1980s: Nostalgia and the Crisis of Masculinity*, Oxford, Clarendon Press, 1997.

Phil Powrie (ed.), *French Cinema in the 1990s: Continuity and Difference*, Oxford, Oxford University Press, 1999.

René Prédal, *Le jeune cinéma français*, Paris, Editions Nathan, 2002.

James Quandt, 'Flesh & blood: sex and violence in recent French cinema', *Artforum International* 42 (6), February 2004.

Carrie Tarr, *Reframing Difference: Beur and Banlieue Filmmaking in France*, Manchester, Manchester University Press, 2005.

Carrie Tarr with Brigitte Rollet, *Cinema and the Second Sex: Women's Filmmaking in France in the 1980s and 1990s*, London and New York, Continuum, 2001.

GERMAN CINEMA

Introduction

Sean Allan and John Sandford (eds), *DEFA: East German Cinema, 1946–1992*, Oxford and New York, Berghahn, 1999.

Tim Bergfelder, Erica Carter and Deniz Göktürk (eds), *The German Cinema Book*, London, BFI Publishing, 2002.

Tim Bergfelder, *International Adventures: German Popular Cinema and European Co-productions in the 1960s*, Oxford and New York, Berghahn, 2005.

Barton Byg and Betheny Moore (eds), *Moving Images of East Germany: Past and Future of DEFA Film*, Washington, DC, Johns Hopkins Press, 2002.

Erica Carter, *How German Is She? Postwar West German Reconstruction and the Consuming Woman*, Ann Arbor, University of Michigan Press, 1997.

Erica Carter, *Dietrich's Ghosts: The Sublime and the Beautiful in Third Reich Film*, London, BFI Publishing, 2004.

Lotte H. Eisner, *The Haunted Screen: Expressionism in the German Cinema and the Influence of Max Reinhardt*, Berkeley, University of California Press, 1969.

Thomas Elsaesser, *Weimar Cinema and After: Germany's Historical Imaginary*, London and New York, Routledge, 2000.

Thomas Elsaesser and Michael Wedel (eds), *A Second Life: German Cinema's First Decades*, Amsterdam, Amsterdam University Press, 1996.

Thomas Elsaesser and Michael Wedel (eds), *The BFI Companion to German Cinema*, London, BFI Publishing, 1999.

Heide Fehrenbach, *Cinema in Democratizing Germany: Reconstructing National Identity after Hitler*, Chapel Hill, University of North Carolina Press, 1995.

Sabine Hake, *Passions and Deceptions: The Early Films of Ernst Lubitsch*, Princeton, NJ, Princeton University Press, 1992.

Sabine Hake, *Popular Cinema of the Third Reich*, Austin, University of Texas Press, 2002a.

Ursula Hardt, *From Caligari to California: Erich Pommer's Life in the International Film Wars*, Oxford and New York, Berghahn, 1996.

Siegfried Kracauer, *From Caligari to Hitler: A Psychological History of the German Film*, Princeton, NJ, Princeton University Press, 1947. Revised edition 2004.

Klaus Kreimeier, *The Ufa Story: A History of Germany's Greatest Film Company*, New York, Hill and Wang, 1996.

Alice A. Kuzniar, *The Queer German Cinema*, Stanford, Stanford University Press, 2000.

Johannes von Moltke, *No Place Like Home: Locations of Heimat in German Cinema*, Berkeley, University of California Press, 2005.

Eric Rentschler, *The Ministry of Illusion: Nazi Cinema and Its Afterlife*, Cambridge, MA, Harvard University Press, 1996.

Heide Schlüpmann, 'Melodrama and social drama in the early German cinema', *Camera Obscura* 22: 73–85, 1990.

Heide Schlüpmann, 'Cinema as anti-theatre: actresses and female audiences in Wilhelmine Germany', in Abel (ed.), *Silent Film*, London, Athlone, 1996.

Linda Schulte-Sasse, *Entertaining the Third Reich: Illusions of Wholeness in Nazi Cinema*, Durham, NC, Duke University Press, 1996.

Paolo Cherchi Usai and Lorenzo Codelli (eds), *Before Caligari: German Cinema, 1895–1920/Prima di Caligari: Cinema Tedesco, 1895–1920*, Pordenone, Biblioteca dell'Imagine, 1990.

Weimar cinema

Lotte H. Eisner, *The Haunted Screen: Expressionism in the German Cinema and the Influence of Max Reinhardt*, Berkeley, University of California Press, 1969.

Thomas Elsaesser, *Weimar Cinema and After: Germany's Historical Imaginary*, London and New York, Routledge, 2000.

Sabine Hake, *Passions and Deceptions: The Early Films of Ernst Lubitsch*, Princeton, NJ, Princeton University Press, 1992.

Ursula Hardt, *From Caligari to California: Erich Pommer's Life in the International Film Wars*, Oxford and New York, Berghahn, 1996.

Uli Jung and Walter Schatzberg, *Beyond Caligari: The Films of Robert Wiene*, Oxford and New York, Berghahn, 1999.

Anton Kaes, *From Hitler to Heimat: The Return of History as Film*, Cambridge, MA, Harvard University Press, 1989.

Siegfried Kracauer, *From Caligari to Hitler: A Psychological History of the German Film*, Princeton, NJ, Princeton University Press, 1947. Revised edition 2004.

Klaus Kreimeier, *The Ufa Story: A History of Germany's Greatest Film Company*, New York, Hill and Wang, 1996.

Johannes von Moltke, *No Place Like Home: Locations of Heimat in German Cinema*, Berkeley, University of California Press, 2005.

Bruce Murray, *Film and the German Left in the Weimar Republic*, Austin, University of Texas Press, 1990.

Frederick Ott, *The Films of Fritz Lang*, Secaucus, NJ, Citadel Press, 1979.

Julian Petley, *Capital and Culture: German Cinema 1933–45*, London, BFI Publishing, 1979.

Patrice Petro, *Joyless Streets: Women and Melodramatic Representation in Weimar Germany*, Princeton, NJ, Princeton University Press, 1989.

Hans Günther Pflaum and Hans Helmut Prinzler, *Cinema in the Federal Republic of Germany*, Bonn, Inter Nationes, 1993.

Eric Rentschler, *West German Film in the Course of Time*, Bedford Hills, NY, Redgrave, 1984.

David Robinson, *Das Cabinet des Dr Caligari*, London, BFI Publishing, 1997.

New German Cinema

Timothy Corrigan, *New German Film: The Displaced Image*, Bloomington, Indiana University Press, 1994.

Thomas Elsaesser, *New German Cinema: A History*, London, Macmillan/BFI, 1989.

James Franklin, *New German Cinema: From Oberhausen to Hamburg*, Boston, MA, Twayne, 1983.

Sandra Frieden, Richard W. McCormick, Vibeke R. Petersen and Laurie Melissa Vogelsang (eds), *Gender and German Cinema: Feminist Interventions*, Vols. 1 and 2, Providence, RI, and Oxford, Berg, 1993.

Anton Kaes, *From Hitler to Heimat: The Return of History as Film*, Cambridge, MA, Harvard University Press, 1989.

Julia Knight, *Women and the New German Cinema*, London and New York, Verso, 1992.

Richard W. McCormick, *Politics of the Self: Feminism and the Postmodern in West German Literature and Film*, Princeton, NJ, Princeton University Press, 1991.

October 46, autumn 1988. Special issue on Alexander Kluge.

Klaus Phillips (ed.), *New German Filmmakers*, New York, Frederick Ungar, 1984.

Eric Rentschler, *West German Film in the Course of Time*, Bedford Hills, Redgrave, NY, 1984.

John Sandford, *The New German Cinema*, London, Eyre Methuen, 1980.

Contemporary German cinema

Sean Allan and John Sandford (eds), *DEFA: East German Cinema, 1946–1992*, Oxford and New York, Berghahn, 1999.

Barton Byg and Betheny Moore (eds), *Moving Images of East Germany: Past and Future of DEFA Film*, Washington, DC, Johns Hopkins Press, 2002.

Thomas Elsaesser, 'German cinema in the 1990s', in Elsaesser and Wedel (eds), *The BFI Companion to German Cinema*, London, BFI Publishing, 1999.

Sabine Hake, *German National Cinema*, London and New York, Routledge, 2002b.

Johannes von Moltke, *No Place Like Home: Locations of Heimat in German Cinema*, Berkeley, University of California Press, 2005.

Eric Rentschler, 'From new German cinema to the post-wall cinema of consensus', in Hjort and Mackenzie (eds), *Cinema and Nation*, London and New York, Routledge, 2000.

HINDI CINEMA

Erik Barnouw and S. Krishnaswamy, *Indian Film*, New York, Columbia University Press, 1963. Revised edition, Oxford University Press, 1980.

Veena Das, 'The mythological film and its framework of meaning: an analysis of *Jai Santoshi Maa*', *India International Centre Quarterly* 8 (1), March 1980.

Chidananda Das Gupta, *The Cinema of Satyajit Ray*, New Delhi, Vikas, 1980.

Chidananda Das Gupta, 'The cultural basis of Indian cinema', in *Talking about Films*, New Delhi, Orient Longman, 1981.

Bagishwar Jha (ed.), *B. N. Sircar*, Calcutta, NFAI/Seagull Books, 1990.

Geeta Kapur, 'Revelation and doubt: *Sant Tukaram* and *Devi*', in Niranjana *et al.* (eds), *Interrogating Modernity*, 1993.

Ashis Nandy, 'An intelligent critic's guide to the Indian cinema', in *The Savage Freud and Other Essays on Possible and Retrievable Selves*, Princeton, NJ, Princeton University Press, 1995.

Tejaswini Niranjana, P. Sudhir and Vivek Dhareshwar (eds), *Interrogating Modernity: Culture and Colonialism in India*, Calcutta, Seagull Books, 1993.

Ashish Rajadhyaksha, 'The Phalke era: conflict of traditional form and modern technology', in Niranjana *et al.* (eds), *Interrogating Modernity*, 1993.

Ashish Rajadhyaksha and Paul Willemen (eds), *Encyclopaedia of Indian Cinema*, London, BFI Publishing, 1999. Revised edition.

Report of the Film Enquiry Committee (S. K. Patil, Chairman), New Delhi, Government of India Press, 1951.

Report of the Indian Cinematograph Committee 1927–28 (T. Rangachariar, Chairman), Calcutta, Government of India Central Publications Branch, 1928.

Andrew Robinson, *Satyajit Ray: The Inner Eye*, London, André Deutsch, 1989.

Kobita Sarkar, 'Influences on the Indian film', *Indian Film Quarterly*, January/March 1957.

Kobita Sarkar, 'Black and white', *Indian Film Review*, December 1958.

Kobita Sarkar, *Indian Cinema Today*, New Delhi, Sterling, 1975.

Kumar Shahani, 'The saint poets of Prabhat', *Filmworld Annual*, January 1980.

Kumar Shahani, 'Notes towards an aesthetic of cinema sound', *Journal of Arts & Ideas* 5, 1985.

Kumar Shahani, 'Film as a contemporary art', *Social Scientist* 18 (3), March 1990.

Kumar Shahani, 'Violence and responsibility', in 'Kumar Shahani Dossier', *Framework* 30/31, 1986.

Madan Gopal Singh, 'The space of encounter: a re-reading of *Sant Tukaram*', in Vasudev (ed.), *Frames of Mind*, 1995.

Aruna Vasudev (ed.), *Frames of Mind: Reflections on Indian Cinema*, New Delhi, UBS Publishers' Distributors, 1995.

Ravi Vasudevan, 'The melodramatic mode and the commercial Hindi cinema: notes on film history, narrative and performance in the 1950s', *Screen* 30 (3): 29–50, summer 1989.

Ravi Vasudevan, 'Shifting codes, dissolving identities: the Hindi social film of the 1950s as popular culture', *Journal of Arts & Ideas* 23/24, 1993.

Bollywood

Erik Barnouw and S. Krishnaswamy, *Indian Film*, New York and Oxford, Oxford University Press, 1980.

Anupama Chopra, *Dilwale Dulhaniya Le Jayenge*, London, BFI Publishing, 2003.

Rachel Dwyer, *Yash Chopra*, London, BFI Publishing, 2002.

Rachel Dwyer, *100 Bollywood Films*, London, BFI Publishing, 2005.

Rachel Dwyer and Divia Patel, *Cinema India: The Visual Culture of the Hindi Film*, London, Reaktion Books, 2002.

Tejaswini Ganti, *Bollywood: A Guidebook to Popular Hindi Cinema*, London, Routledge, 2004.

Ashis Nandy, 'An intelligent critic's guide to the Indian cinema', in *The Savage Freud and Other Essays on Possible and Retrievable Selves*, Princeton, NJ, Princeton University Press, 1995.

M. Madhava Prasad, *Ideology of the Hindi Film: A Historical Construction*, Delhi, Oxford University Press, 2000.

Ashish Rajadhyaksha and Paul Willemen, *Encyclopaedia of Indian Cinema*, London, BFI Publishing, 1999. Second edition.

Ravi Vasudevan (ed.), *Making Meaning in Indian Cinema*, Delhi, Oxford University Press, 2001.

HONG KONG CINEMA

David Bordwell, *Planet Hong Kong: Popular Cinema and the Art of Entertainment*, Cambridge, MA, Harvard University Press, 2000.

Frank Bren and Law Kar, *Hong Kong Cinema: A Cross-Cultural View*, Lanham, MD, The Scarecrow Press, 2004.

Yingchi Chu, *Hong Kong Cinema: Coloniser, Motherland and Self*, London, RoutledgeCurzon, 2002.

Fredric Dannen and Barry Long, *Hong Kong Babylon: An Insider's Guide to the Hollywood of the East*, London, Faber & Faber, 1997.

Poshek Fu and David Desser (eds.), *The Cinema of Hong Kong: History, Arts, Identity*, Cambridge and New York, Cambridge University Press, 2000.

Stefan Hammond and Mike Wilkins, *Sex and Zen & a Bullet in the Head: The Essential Guide to Hong Kong's Mind-Bending Movies*, London, Titan, 1997.

Leon Hunt, *Kung Fu Cult Masters: From Bruce Lee to Crouching Tiger*, London and New York, Wallflower Press, 2003.

Bey Logan, *Hong Kong Action Cinema*, London, Titan, 1995.

Sheldon Hsiao-peng Lu (ed.), *Transnational Chinese Cinemas: Identity, Nationhood, Gender*, Honolulu, University of Hawaii Press, 1997.

Sheldon H. Lu and Emilie Yueh-yu Yeh (eds), *Chinese-Language Film: Historiography, Poetics, Politics*, Honolulu, University of Hawaii Press, 2005.

Meaghan Morris, Siu Leung Li and Stephen Chan Ching-kiu (eds), *Hong Kong Connections: Transnational Imagination in Action Cinema*, Durham, NC, Duke University Press, 2006.

Laikwan Pang and Day Wong (eds), *Masculinities and Hong Kong Cinema*, Hong Kong, Hong Kong University Press, 2005.

Stephen Teo, *Hong Kong Cinema: The Extra Dimensions*, London, BFI Publishing, 1997.

Esther C. M. Yau (ed.), *At Full Speed: Hong Kong Cinema in a Borderless World*, Minneapolis, University of Minnesota Press, 2001.

IRISH CINEMA

Ruth Barton, *Jim Sheridan: Framing the Nation*, Dublin, The Liffey Press, 2002.

Ruth Barton, *Irish National Cinema*, New York and London, Routledge, 2004.

Luke Gibbons, *Transformations in Irish Culture*, Cork, Cork University Press, 1996.

John Hill, *Cinema and Northern Ireland: Film, Culture and Politics*, London, BFI Publishing, 2006.

John Hill, Martin McLoone and Paul Hainsworth (eds), *Border Crossing: Film in Ireland, Britain and Europe*, Belfast/London, Institute of Irish Studies/BFI Publishing, 1994.

Martin McLoone, *Irish Film: The Emergence of a Contemporary Cinema*, London, BFI Publishing, 2000.

Harvey O'Brien, *The Real Ireland: The Evolution of Ireland in Documentary Film*, Manchester, Manchester University Press, 2004.

Lance Pettitt, *Screening Ireland: Film and Television Representation*, Manchester, Manchester University Press, 2000.

Emer Rockett and Kevin Rockett, *Neil Jordan: Exploring Boundaries*, Dublin, The Liffey Press, 2003.

Kevin Rockett, *Irish Film Censorship: A Cultural Journey from Silent Cinema to Internet Pornography*, Dublin, Four Courts Press, 2004.

Kevin Rockett and John Hill (eds), *National Cinema and Beyond: Studies in Irish Film 1*, Dublin, Four Courts Press, 2004.

Kevin Rockett, Luke Gibbons and John Hill, *Cinema and Ireland*, New York and London, Routledge, 1988.

ITALIAN CINEMA

Zygmunt Baranski and Robert Lumley (eds), *Culture and Conflict in Postwar Italy*, Basingstoke, Palgrave Macmillan, 1990.

Giorgio Bertellini, *The Cinema of Italy*, London, Wallflower Press, 2004.

David Forgacs and Robert Lumley (eds), *Italian Cultural Studies: An Introduction*, Oxford, Oxford University Press, 1996.

Stephen Gundle, 'From neo-realism to *Luci Rosse*: cinema, politics, society, 1945–85', in Baranski and Lumley (eds), *Culture and Conflict in Postwar Italy*, 1990.

Stephen Gundle, 'Fame, fashion and style: the Italian star system', in Forgacs and Lumley (eds), *Italian Cultural Studies*, 1996.

Maggie Günsberg, *Italian Cinema*, Basingstoke, Palgrave Macmillan, 2005.

Marcia Landy, 'The family melodrama in the Italian cinema, 1929–1943', in Landy (ed.), *Imitations of Life: A Reader on Film and Television Melodrama*, Detroit, MI, Wayne State University Press, 1991.

Millicent Marcus, *Italian Film in the Light of Neo-realism*, Princeton, NJ, Princeton University Press, 1987.

Geoffrey Nowell-Smith with James Hay and Gianni Volpe, *The BFI Companion to Italian Cinema*, London, BFI Publishing/Cassell, 1996.

Pierre Sorlin, *Italian National Cinema 1896–1996*, London, Routledge, 1996.

Christopher Wagstaff, 'Cinema', in Forgacs and Lumley (eds), *Italian Cultural Studies*, 1996.

Mary P. Wood, *Italian Cinema*, Oxford, Berg, 2005.

Italian Neo-realism

André Bazin, *Qu'est-ce que le cinéma?* Vol. IV, Paris, Editions du Cerf, 1962. In English: Hugh Gray (ed.), *What Is Cinema?* Vol. 2, Berkeley, University of California Press, 1971. Revised edition 2005.

Peter Brunette, *Roberto Rossellini*, New York and Oxford, Oxford University Press, 1987.

Morando Morandini, 'Italy from fascism to neo-realism', in Nowell-Smith (ed.), *Oxford History of World Cinema*, 1996.

Geoffrey Nowell-Smith, *Visconti*, London, Secker and Warburg/BFI Publishing, 1967. Revised edition 1973.

Geoffrey Nowell-Smith (ed.), *The Oxford History of World Cinema*, Oxford, Oxford University Press, 1996.

Geoffrey Nowell-Smith with James Hay and Gianni Volpi, *The BFI Companion to Italian Cinema*, London, BFI Publishing/Cassell, 1996.

David Overbey (ed.), *Springtime in Italy*, London, Talisman Books, 1978.

Sam Rohdie, 'A note on Italian cinema during Fascism', *Screen* 22 (4): 87–90, 1981.

Christopher Wagstaff and Christopher Duggan, *Italy and the Cold War: Politics, Culture and Society*, Oxford, Berg, 1995.

JAPANESE CINEMA

Introduction

Joseph L. Anderson and Loren Hoekzema, 'The spaces between: American criticism of Japanese film', *Wide Angle* 1 (4): 2–6, 1977.

Joseph L. Anderson and Donald Richie, *The Japanese Film: Art and Industry*, Tokyo, Tuttle Company, 1959. Revised edition, Princeton University Press, 1982.

David Bordwell, *Ozu and the Poetics of Cinema*, Princeton, NJ, Princeton University Press, 1988.

David Bordwell, 'Visual style in Japanese cinema, 1925–1945', *Film History* 7 (1): 5–31, spring 1995.

Noël Burch, *To the Distant Observer: Form and Meaning in the Japanese Cinema*, Berkeley, University of California Press, 1979.

Carol Cavanaugh and Dennis Washburn (eds), *Word and Image in Japanese Cinema*, Cambridge, Cambridge University Press, 2001.

David Desser, *Eros Plus Massacre: An Introduction to the Japanese New Wave Cinema*, Bloomington, Indiana University Press, 1988.

Linda Ehrlich and David Desser (eds), *Cinematic Landscapes: Observations on the Visual Arts and Cinema of China and Japan*, Austin, University of Texas Press, 1994.

Kathe Geist, 'Playing with space: Ozu and two-dimensional design in Japan', in Ehrlich and Desser (eds), *Cinematic Landscapes*, 1994.

Kyoko Hirano, *Mr Smith Goes to Tokyo: Japanese Cinema under the Occupation, 1945–1952*, Washington, DC, Smithsonian Institution Press, 1992.

Hiroshi Komatsu, 'Some characteristics of Japanese cinema before World War I', in Nolletti and Desser (eds), *Reframing Japanese Cinema*, 1992.

John Lent, *The Asian Film Industry*, Austin, University of Texas Press, 1990.

Keiko McDonald, *Mizoguchi*, Boston, MA, Twayne Publishing, 1984.

Keiko McDonald, *Japanese Classical Theater in Films*, Rutherford, NJ, Fairleigh Dickinson University Press, 1994.

Arthur Nolletti and David Desser (eds), *Reframing Japanese Cinema: Authorship, Genre, History*, Bloomington, Indiana University Press, 1992.

James Quandt (ed.), *Kon Ichikawa*, Toronto, Toronto International Film Festival Group, 2001.

Donald Richie, *Ozu: His Life and Films*, Berkeley, University of California Press, 1974.

Donald Richie, *The Films of Akira Kurosawa*, Berkeley, University of California Press, 1984.

Stephen Teo, *Hong Kong Cinema: The Extra Dimensions*, London, BFI Publishing, 1997.

Kristin Thompson, 'Notes on the spatial system of Ozu's early films', *Wide Angle* 1 (4): 8–17, 1977.

Contemporary Japanese cinema

Joseph L. Anderson and Donald Richie, *The Japanese Film: Art and Industry*, Princeton, NJ, Princeton University Press, 1982.

Philip Brophy, *100 Anime*, London, BFI Publishing, 2005.

Steven T. Brown (ed.), *Cinema Anime*, Basingstoke, Palgrave Macmillan, 2006.

Noël Burch, *To the Distant Observer: Form and Meaning in Japanese Cinema*, London, Scolar Press, 1979.

Eric Cazdyn, *The Flash of Capital: Film and Geopolitics in Japan*, Durham, NC, Duke University Press, 2002.

Jonathan Clements and Helen McCarthy, *The Anime Encyclopedia: A Guide to Japanese Animation since 1917*, Berkeley, CA, Stone Bridge Press, 2001. Revised edition 2006.

Chris Desjardins, *Outlaw Masters of Japanese Film*, London, I. B. Tauris, 2005.

Keiko I. McDonald, *Reading a Japanese Film: Cinema in Context*, Honolulu, University of Hawaii Press, 2006.

Jay McRoy (ed.), *Japanese Horror Cinema*, Edinburgh, Edinburgh University Press, 2005.

Thomas Mes, *Agitator: The Cinema of Takashi Miike*, London, FAB Press, 2003.

Tom Mes and Jasper Sharp, *The Midnight Eye Guide to New Japanese Film*, Berkeley, CA, Stone Bridge Press, 2004.

Susan Napier, *Anime from Akira to Howl's Moving Castle: Experiencing Contemporary Japanese Animation*, Basingstoke, Palgrave Macmillan, 2001. Revised edition 2006.

Alastair Phillips and Julian Stringer (eds), *Japanese Cinema: Texts and Contexts*, Oxford and New York, Routledge, 2007.

Donald Richie, *A Hundred Years of Japanese Film*, Tokyo, Kodansha, 2001. Revised edition 2005.

Mark Schilling, *Contemporary Japanese Film*, New York and Tokyo, Weatherhill, 1999.

Isolde Standish, *A New History of Japanese Cinema: A Century of Narrative Film*, London and New York, Continuum, 2005.

Thomas Weisser and Yuko Mihara Weisser, *Japanese Cinema Encyclopedia: Horror, Fantasy, Science Fiction*, Miami, Vital Books, 1998.

SOVIET CINEMA

David Bordwell, *The Cinema of Eisenstein*, Cambridge, MA, Harvard University Press, 1993.

Ephraim Katz, *The Macmillan International Film Encyclopedia*, Basingstoke, Macmillan, 1980. Revised edition 2001.

Peter Kenez, *Cinema and Soviet Society 1917–1953*, Cambridge, MA, Cambridge University Press, 1992.

Jay Leyda, *Kino: A History of the Russian and Soviet Film*, London, George Allen and Unwin, 1973. Revised edition 1983.

Richard Taylor (ed.), *The Eisenstein Reader*, London, BFI Publishing, 1998.

Richard Taylor, *October*, London, BFI Publishing, 2002.

Richard Taylor and Ian Christie (eds), *The Film Factory: Russian and Soviet Cinema in Documents, 1896–1939*, New York and London, Routledge, 1988. Revised edition 1994.

Richard Taylor and Ian Christie (eds), *Inside the Film Factory: New Approaches to Russian and Soviet Cinema*, New York and London, Routledge, 1994.

Denise Youngblood, *Soviet Cinema in the Silent Era, 1918–1935*, Ann Arbor, MI, UMI Research Press, 1985. Revised edition, University of Texas Press, 1991.

SPANISH CINEMA

M. Esquirol and J. Ll. Fecé, 'Un freak en el parque de atracciones: *Torrente, el brazo tonto de la ley*', *Archivos de la Filmoteca* 39: 27–39, 2001.

European Audiovisual Observatory, *FOCUS 2006: World Film Market Trends/Tendances du marché mondial du film*, 2006.

Peter W. Evans (ed.), *Spanish Cinema: The Auteurist Tradition*, Oxford, Oxford University Press, 1999.

Barry Jordan and Rikki Morgan-Tamosunas, *Contemporary Spanish Cinema*, Manchester, Manchester University Press, 1998.

Alberto Mira, *The Cinema of Spain and Portugal*, London, Wallflower Press, 2005.

Antonio Lázaro Reboll and Andrew Willis (eds), *Spanish Popular Cinema*, Manchester, Manchester University Press, 2004.

Paul Julian Smith, *Desire Unlimited: The Cinema of Pedro Almodóvar*, London and New York, Verso, 1994. Revised edition 2000.

Paul Julian Smith, *Spanish Visual Culture: Cinema, Television, Internet*, Manchester, Manchester University Press, 2006.

Núria Triana-Toribio, *Spanish National Cinema*, London and New York, Routledge, 2003.

PART 5: Genre

HISTORY OF GENRE CRITICISM

Lawrence Alloway, *Violent America: The Movies 1946–64*, New York, Museum of Modern Art, 1971.

Rick Altman, *The American Film Musical*, Bloomington, Indiana University Press, 1987.

Rick Altman, *Film/Genre*, London, BFI Publishing, 1999.

André Bazin, 'The western, or the American film par excellence', and 'The evolution of the western', in Gray (ed. and trans.), *What Is Cinema?* Vol. 2, Berkeley, University of California Press, 1971. Revised edition 2005.

Gillian Beer, *The Romance*, London, Methuen, 1970.

Biograph Bulletins, 1896–1908, compiled by Kemp R. Niver, Los Angeles, Locaire Research Group, 1971.

Diane Blakemore, *Understanding Utterances: An Introduction to Pragmatics*, Oxford, Blackwell, 1992.

Jean-Loup Bourget, 'Social implications in Hollywood genres', in Grant (ed.), *Film Genre*, 1977. Reprinted in Grant (ed.), *Film Genre Reader III*, 2003.

Leo Braudy, *The World in a Frame*, Garden City, NY, Anchor Doubleday, 1976.

Edward Buscombe, 'The idea of genre in the American cinema', *Screen* 11 (2): 33–45, March/April 1970. Reprinted in Grant (ed.), *Film Genre Reader III*, 2003.

Edward Buscombe, 'Walsh and Warner Bros', in Hardy (ed.), *Raoul Walsh*, 1974.

John G. Cawelti, *The Six-Gun Mystique*, Bowling Green, OH, Bowling Green University Popular Press, 1971.

John G. Cawelti, *Adventure, Mystery and Romance: Formula Stories as Art and Popular Culture*, Chicago, University of Chicago Press, 1976.

Richard Collins, 'Genre: a reply to Ed Buscombe', *Screen* 11 (4/5): 66–75, July/October 1970. Reprinted in Nichols (ed.), *Movies and Methods Vol. 1*, Berkeley, University of California Press, 1976.

Steven Davis (ed.), *Pragmatics: A Reader*, Oxford, Oxford University Press, 1991.

Jacques Derrida, *Acts of Literature*, New York and London, Routledge, 1992.

Antony Easthope, 'Notes on genre', *Screen Education* 32/33, winter/spring 1979/80.

Nils Erik Enkvist, 'On the interpretability of texts in general and of literary texts in particular', in Sell (ed.), *Literary Pragmatics*, 1991.

Barry Keith Grant (ed.), *Film Genre: Theory and Criticism*, Metuchen, NJ, The Scarecrow Press, 1977.

Barry Keith Grant (ed.), *Film Genre Reader III*, Austin, University of Texas Press, 2003.

Barry Keith Grant, *Film Genre: From Iconography to Ideology*, London, Wallflower Press, 2007.

Phil Hardy (ed.), *Raoul Walsh*, Edinburgh, Edinburgh Film Festival, 1974.

Judith Hess, 'Genre film and the status quo', in Grant (ed.), *Film Genre*, 1977. Reprinted in Grant (ed.), *Film Reader III*, 2003.

Fredric Jameson, 'Magical narratives: romance as genre', *New Literary History* 7: 135–63, 1975.

E. Ann Kaplan (ed.), *Women in Film Noir*, London, BFI Publishing, 1978. Revised edition 1998.

Jim Kitses, *Horizons West*, London, Secker and Warburg/BFI, 1969. Revised edition, *Horizons West: The Western from John Ford to Clint Eastwood*, London, BFI Publishing, 2004.

Kleine Optical Company, *Complete Illustrated Catalog of Moving Picture Machines, Stereoptikons, Slides, Films*, Chicago, Kleine Optical Company, 1905.

Clayton Koelb, 'The problem of tragedy as a genre', *Genre* 8 (3): 248–66, September 1975.

Gunther Kress and Terry Threadgold, 'Towards a social theory of genre', *Southern Review* 21 (3): 215–43, 1988.

Geoffrey Leech, *The Principles of Pragmatics*, London, Longman, 1983.

Stephen C. Levinson, *Pragmatics*, Cambridge, Cambridge University Press, 1983.

Gregory Lukow and Steve Ricci, 'The "audience" goes "public": inter-textuality, genre, and the responsibilities of film literacy', *On Film* 12: 29–36, spring 1984.

John Lyons, *Language, Meaning and Context*, London, Longman, 1981.

Colin McArthur, *Underworld USA*, London, Secker and Warburg/BFI, 1972.

Colin McArthur, 'Iconography and iconology', London, unpublished BFI Education seminar paper, 1973.

Frank McConnell, *The Spoken Seen: Films and the Romantic Imagination*, Baltimore, MD, Johns Hopkins University Press, 1975.

Christian Metz, *Language and Cinema*, The Hague, Mouton, 1974.

Jacob L. Mey, *Pragmatics: An Introduction*, Oxford, Blackwell, 1993.

Charles Musser, 'The travel genre in 1903–04: moving toward fictional narratives', *Iris* 2 (1): 47–59, 1984. Reprinted in Elsaesser and Barker (eds), *Early Cinema: Space, Frame, Narrative*, London, BFI Publishing, 1990.

Stephen Neale, *Genre*, London, BFI Publishing, 1980.

Steve Neale, 'Questions of genre', *Screen* 31 (1): 45–66, spring 1990. Reprinted in Grant (ed.), *Film Genre Reader III*, 2003.

Steve Neale, 'Melo talk: on the meaning and use of the term "melodrama" in the American trade press', *The Velvet Light Trap* 32: 66–89, fall 1993.

Steve Neale, *Genre and Hollywood*, London, Routledge, 1999.

Steve Neale (ed.), *Genre and Contemporary Hollywood*, London, BFI Publishing, 2002.

Mary Louise Pratt, 'The short story: the long and the short of it', *Poetics* 10: 175–94, 1981.

Douglas Pye, 'Genre and movies', *Movie* 20, 1975. Reprinted in Grant (ed.), *Film Genre Reader III*, 2003.

Tom Ryall, *Teachers' Study Guide No. 2: The Gangster Film*, London, BFI Education, 1978.

Thomas Schatz, *Hollywood Genres: Formulas, Filmmaking, and the Studio System*, New York, Random House, 1981. Reprinted by McGraw-Hill, 1988.

Thomas Schatz, *Old Hollywood/New Hollywood: Ritual, Art, and Industry*, Ann Arbor, MI, UMI Research Press, 1983.

Roger D. Sell (ed.), *Literary Pragmatics*, London, Routledge, 1991.

Henry Nash Smith, *The Virgin Land*, Cambridge, MA, Harvard University Press, 1950.

Terry Threadgold, 'Talking about genre: ideologies and incompatible discourses', *Cultural Studies* 3 (1): 101–27, January 1989.

Tzvetan Todorov, 'The origin of genres', *New Literary History* 8 (1): 159–70, autumn 1976. Reprinted in Duff (ed.), *Modern Genre Theory*, London, Longman, 2000.

Andrew Tudor, *Theories of Film*, London, Secker and Warburg/BFI, 1974.

Marc Vernet, 'Genre', *Film Reader* 3, February 1978.

Robert Warshow, 'The gangster as tragic hero', and 'Movie chronicle: the westerner', in *The Immediate Experience*, New York, Atheneum Books, 1970.

Alan Williams, 'Is a radical genre criticism possible?', *Quarterly Review of Film Studies* 9 (2): 121–5, spring 1984.

Michael Wood, *America in the Movies, or Santa Maria, It Had Slipped My Mind*, New York, Delta, 1975.

Will Wright, *Sixguns & Society: A Structural Study of the Western*, Berkeley, University of California Press, 1975.

ACTION-ADVENTURE

Jose Arroyo, *Action/Spectacle Cinema: A Sight and Sound Reader*, London, BFI Publishing, 1999.

Joseph A. Boone and Michael Cadden (eds), *Engendering Men: The Question of Male Feminist Criticism*, New York, Routledge, 1990.

Andrew Britton, 'Blissing out: the politics of Reaganite entertainment', *Movie* 31 (2): 1–42, winter 1986.

J. A. Brown, 'Gender and the action heroine: hardbodies and the *Point of No Return*', *Cinema Journal* 35 (3): 52–71, spring 1996.

John G. Cawelti, *Adventure, Mystery and Romance: Formula Stories as Art and Popular Culture*, Chicago, University of Chicago Press, 1976.

Steven Cohan and Ina Rae Hark (eds), *Screening the Male: Exploring Masculinity in Hollywood Cinema*, London, Routledge, 1993.

Chris Holmlund, 'Masculinity as multiple masquerade: the "mature" Stallone and the Stallone clone', in Cohan and Hark (eds), *Screening the Male*, 1993.

Susan Jeffords, *The Remasculinization of America: Gender and the Vietnam War*, Bloomington, Indiana University Press, 1989.

Susan Jeffords, *Hard Bodies: Hollywood Masculinity in the Reagan Era*, New Brunswick, NJ, Rutgers University Press, 1994.

Douglas Kellner and Michael Ryan, *Camera Politica: The Politics and Ideology of Contemporary Hollywood Film*, Bloomington and Indianapolis, Indiana University Press, 1988.

Richard Koszarski, *An Evening's Entertainment: The Age of the Silent Feature Picture, 1915–1928*, New York, Scribner's, 1990.

Gina Marchetti, 'Action-adventure as ideology', in Angus and Thally (eds), *Cultural Politics in Contemporary America*, New York, Routledge, 1989.

Fred Pfeil, *White Guys: Studies in Postmodern Domination and Difference*, London, Verso, 1995.

Jeffrey Richards, *Swordsmen of the Screen: From Douglas Fairbanks to Michael York*, London, Routledge & Kegan Paul, 1977.

Joseph Sartelle, 'Dreams and nightmares in the Hollywood blockbuster', in Nowell-Smith (ed.), *The Oxford History of World Cinema*, Oxford, Oxford University Press, 1996.

Thomas Sobchack, 'The adventure film', in Gehring (ed.), *Handbook of American Film Genres*, Westport, CT, Greenwood Press, 1988.

Yvonne Tasker, *Spectacular Bodies: Gender, Genre and the Action Cinema*, London and New York, Routledge, 1993.

Brian Taves, *The Romance of Adventure: The Genre of Historical Adventure Movies*, Jackson, University of Mississippi Press, 1993.

Elizabeth G. Traube, *Dreaming Identities: Class, Gender and Generation in 1980s Hollywood Movies*, Boulder, CO, Westview Press, 1992.

Sharon Willis, *High Contrast: Race and Gender in Contemporary Hollywood Films*, Durham, NC, Duke University Press, 1998.

Robin Wood, *Hollywood from Vietnam to Reagan*, New York, Columbia University Press, 1986.

COMEDY

Joe Adamson, *Groucho, Harpo, Chico and Sometimes Zeppo: A History of the Marx Brothers and a Satire on the Rest of the World*, New York, Simon and Schuster, 1973. Reprinted 1983.

James Agee, *Agee on Film*, New York, McDowell, Obolensky Inc, 1958. Reprinted by Random House, 2000.

James Agee, 'Comedy's greatest era (1949)', in *Agee on Film*, 1958. Reprinted in *Agee on Film*, New York, Random House, 2000.

Robert C. Allen, *Vaudeville and Film, 1895–1915: A Study in Media Interaction*, New York, Arno Press, 1980.

Bruce Babington and Peter William Evans, *Affairs to Remember: The Hollywood Comedy of the Sexes*, Manchester, Manchester University Press, 1989.

Mikhail Bakhtin, *Rabelais and His World*, Cambridge, MA, MIT Press, 1968.

Tino Balio, *Grand Design: Hollywood as a Modern Business Enterprise, 1930–1939*, New York, Scribner's, 1993.

Charles Barr, *Laurel and Hardy*, London, Studio Vista, 1967.

John Belton, *American Cinema/American Culture*, New York, McGraw-Hill, 1994.

Henri Bergson, 'Laughter' [1900], in Sypher (ed.), *Comedy*, 1956.

Eileen Bowser, *The Transformation of Cinema, 1907–1915*, New York, Scribner's, 1990.

Andrew Britton, *Cary Grant: Comedy and Male Desire*, Newcastle-upon-Tyne, Tyneside Cinema, 1983.

Andrew Britton, *Katharine Hepburn: The Thirties and After*, Newcastle-upon-Tyne, Tyneside Cinema, 1984.

Scott Bukatman, 'Paralysis in motion: Jerry Lewis's life as a man', in Horton (ed.), *Comedy/Cinema/Theory*, 1991.

Duane Paul Byrge, 'Screwball comedy', *East–West Film Journal* 2 (1): 17–25, December 1987.

Noël Carroll, *An In-Depth Analysis of Buster Keaton's The General*, New York University PhD thesis, 1976, Ann Arbor, MI, UMI Dissertation Information Service, 1988.

Noël Carroll, 'Notes on the sight gag', in Horton (ed.), *Comedy/Cinema/Theory*, 1991.

Stanley Cavell, *Pursuits of Happiness: The Hollywood Comedy of Remarriage*, Cambridge, MA, Harvard University Press, 1981.

Jane Clarke, Mandy Merck and Diane Simmonds (eds), *BFI Dossier 4: Move over Misconceptions: Doris Day Reappraised*, London, BFI, 1981.

Jean-Pierre Coursodon, *Keaton et cie*, Paris, Seghers, 1964.

Jean-Pierre Coursodon, 'Jerry Lewis', in Coursodon and Sauvage, *American Directors*, 1983.

Jean-Pierre Coursodon, *Buster Keaton*, Paris, Atlas L'Hermier, 1986.

Jean-Pierre Coursodon and Pierre Sauvage, *American Directors*, New York, McGraw-Hill, 1983.

Donald Crafton, 'Pie and chase: gags, spectacle and narrative in slapstick comedy', in Karnick and Jenkins (eds), *Classical Hollywood Comedy*, 1995.

Ramona Curry, 'Goin' to town and beyond: Mae West, film censorship and the comedy of unmarriage', in Karnick and Jenkins (eds), *Classical Hollywood Comedy*, 1995.

Tom Dardis, *Keaton: The Man Who Wouldn't Lie Down*, London, André Deutsch, 1979.

Tom Dardis, *Harold Lloyd: The Man on the Clock*, New York, Viking Press, 1983.

Mary Ann Doane, 'The economy of desire: the commodity form in/of cinema', *Quarterly Review of Film and Video* 11 (1): 23–33, May 1989.

William Donnelly, 'A theory of the comedy of the Marx Brothers', *The Velvet Light Trap* 3, winter 1971/72.

Mary Douglas, 'The social control of cognition: some factors in joke reception', *Man* (new series) 3 (3): 361–76, September 1968.

Richard Dyer, 'Rock – the last guy you'd have figured', in Kirkham and Thumim (eds), *You Tarzan*, 1993.

Richard Dyer, *Pastiche*, Oxford and New York, Routledge, 2006.

Mick Eaton, 'Laughter in the dark', *Screen* 22 (2): 21–5, 1981.

Andy Edmonds, *Fatty: The Untold Story of Roscoe Fatty Arbuckle*, London, McDonald, 1991.

Barbara Ehrenreich, *The Hearts of Men: American Dreams and the Flight from Commitment*, London, Pluto Press, 1983.

Peter William Evans and Celestino Deleyto (eds), *Terms of Endearment: Hollywood Romantic Comedy of the 1980s and 1990s*, Edinburgh, Edinburgh University Press, 1998.

Film Comment 11 (1), 1975. Special issue on Animation.

Lucy Fischer, 'Sometimes I feel like a motherless child: comedy and matricide', in Horton (ed.), *Comedy/Cinema/Theory*, 1991.

Elizabeth A. Ford and Deborah C. Mitchell, 'Pygmalion problems', in *The Makeover in Movies: Before and After in Hollywood Films, 1941–2002*, London, McFarland, 2002.

Sigmund Freud, *Jokes and Their Relation to the Unconscious*, Harmondsworth, Penguin, 1976.

Sigmund Freud, 'Humour' [1927], in *Art and Literature*, Harmondsworth, Penguin, 1985.

Northrop Frye, *Anatomy of Criticism: Four Essays*, Princeton, NJ, Princeton University Press, 1957.

Roger Garcia and Bernard Eisenschitz (eds), *Frank Tashlin*, Locarno, Editions du Festival, 1994.

Jon Gartenberg, 'Vitagraph comedy production', in Bowser (ed.), *The Slapstick Symposium*, Brussels, Fédération Internationale des Archives du Film, 1988.

Wes D. Gehring, *Charlie Chaplin: A Bio-bibliography*, Westport, CT, Greenwood Press, 1983.

Wes D. Gehring, *W. C. Fields: A Bio-bibliography*, Westport, CT, Greenwood Press, 1984.

Wes D. Gehring, *Screwball Comedy: A Genre of Madcap Romance*, Westport, CT, Greenwood Press, 1986.

Wes D. Gehring, *The Marx Brothers: A Bio-bibliography*, Westport, CT, Greenwood Press, 1987.

Wes D. Gehring, *Laurel and Hardy: A Bio-bibliography*, Westport, CT, Greenwood Press, 1990.

Wes D. Gehring, *Groucho and W. C. Fields: Huckster Comedians*, Jackson, University of Mississippi Press, 1994.

Tom Gunning, 'Crazy machines in the garden of forking paths: mischief gags and the origins of film comedy', in Karnick and Jenkins (eds), *Classical Hollywood Comedy*, 1995.

Marybeth Hamilton, *The Queen of Camp: Mae West, Sex and Popular Culture*, London, Pandora, 1996.

Brian Henderson, 'Romantic comedy today: semi-tough or impossible?', *Film Quarterly* 31 (4): 11–23, summer 1978.

Sumiko Higashi, *Cecil B. DeMille and American Culture: The Silent Era*, Berkeley, University of California Press, 1994.

Claire Hines, 'Armed and fabulous: *Miss Congeniality*'s queer rom-com', in Abbott and Jermyn (eds), *Falling in Love Again: Romantic Comedy in Contemporary Cinema*, London, I. B. Tauris, 2008.

Andrew S. Horton (ed.), *Comedy/Cinema/Theory*, Berkeley, University of California Press, 1991.

Linda Hutcheon, *A Theory of Parody: The Teachings of Twentieth-Century Art Forms*, London, Methuen, 1985.

Henry Jenkins III, 'The amazing push-me/pull-you text: cognitive processing, narrational play, and the comic film', *Wide Angle* 8 (3/4): 35–44, fall 1986.

Henry Jenkins III, *What Made Pistachio Nuts? Early Sound Comedy and the Vaudeville Aesthetic*, New York, Columbia University Press, 1993.

Catherine Irene Johnson, *Contradiction in 1950s Comedy and Ideology*, Ann Arbor, MI, UMI Research Press, 1981.

Claire Johnston and Paul Willemen (eds), *Frank Tashlin*, Edinburgh, Edinburgh Film Festival, 1973.

Dan Kamin, *Charlie Chaplin's One-Man Show*, Metuchen, NJ, The Scarecrow Press, 1984.

Kristina Brunovska Karnick, 'Commitment and reaffirmation in Hollywood romantic comedy', in Karnick and Jenkins (eds), *Classical Hollywood Comedy*, 1995.

Kristina Brunovska Karnick and Henry Jenkins III (eds), *Classical Hollywood Comedy*, London, Routledge, 1995.

Karyn Kay, '"Part-time work of a domestic slave", or putting the screws to screwball comedy', in Kay and Peary (eds), *Women and the Cinema: A Critical Anthology*, New York, Dutton, 1977.

Pat Kirkham and Janet Thumim (eds), *You Tarzan: Masculinity, Movies and Men*, London, Lawrence & Wishart, 1993.

Norman M. Klein, *Seven Minutes: The Life and Death of the American Animated Cartoon*, London, Verso, 1993.

Susanne Kord and Elisabeth Krimmer, 'Running woman: Sandra Bullock', in *Hollywood Divas, Indie Queens and TV Heroines: Contemporary Screen Images of Women*, Oxford, Rowman and Littlefield, 2005.

Richard Koszarski, *An Evening's Entertainment: The Age of the Silent Feature Picture, 1915–1928*, New York, Scribner's, 1990.

Peter Krämer, 'Vitagraph, slapstick and early cinema', *Screen* 29 (2): 98–104, spring 1988.

Peter Krämer, 'Derailing the honeymoon express: comicality and narrative closure in Buster Keaton's *The Blacksmith*', *The Velvet Light Trap* 23, spring 1989.

Peter Krämer, 'The making of a comic star: Buster Keaton and *The Saphead*', in Karnick and Jenkins (eds), *Classical Hollywood Comedy*, 1995.

Frank Krutnik, 'The clown-prints of comedy', *Screen* 25 (4/5): 50–9, July/October 1984.

Frank Krutnik, 'The faint aroma of performing seals: the "nervous" romance and the comedy of the sexes', *The Velvet Light Trap* 26: 57–72, fall 1990.

Frank Krutnik, 'Jerry Lewis and the deformation of the comic', *Film Quarterly* 48 (4): 12–26, fall 1994.

Frank Krutnik, 'A spanner in the works? Genre narrative and the Hollywood comedian', in Karnick and Jenkins (eds), *Classical Hollywood Comedy*, 1995.

Frank Krutnik, *Inventing Jerry Lewis*, Washington, DC, Smithsonian Institution Press, 2000.

Frank Krutnik, 'Conforming passions?: Contemporary romantic comedy', in Neale (ed.), *Genre and Contemporary Hollywood*, London, BFI Publishing, 2002.

Frank Krutnik (ed.), *Hollywood Comedians: The Film Reader*, London and New York, Routledge, 2003.

Jean-Pierre Lebel, *Buster Keaton*, London, Zwemmer, 1967.

Tina Olsin Lent, 'Romance, love and friendship: the redefinition of gender relations in screwball comedy', in Karnick and Jenkins (eds), *Classical Hollywood Comedy*, 1995.

Leonard Maltin, *The Great Movie Comedians*, New York, Crown, 1982.

Leonard Maltin, *Of Mice and Magic: A History of American Animated Cartoons*, New York, Plume, 1987.

François Mars, *Le Gag*, Paris, Editions du Cerf, 1964.

Gerald Mast, *The Comic Mind: Comedy and the Movies*, New York, Random House, 1976.

Donald McCaffrey, *Four Great Comedians*, New York, Barnes, 1968.

Donald McCaffrey, *Three Classic Silent Screen Comedies Starring Harold Lloyd*, London, Associated University Presses, 1976.

Albert F. McClean, *American Vaudeville as Ritual*, Lexington, University of Kentucky Press, 1965.

Charles Musser, *The Emergence of Cinema: The American Screen to 1907*, New York, Scribner's, 1990a.

Charles Musser, 'Work, ideology and Chaplin's tramp', in Sklar and Musser (eds), *Resisting Images*, 1990b.

Charles Musser, 'Ethnicity, role-playing and American film comedy: from *Chinese Laundry* to *Whoopee* (1894–1930)', in Friedman (ed.), *Unspeakable Images: Ethnicity and the American Cinema*, Urbana, University of Illinois Press, 1991.

Charles Musser, 'Divorce, DeMille and the comedy of remarriage', in Karnick and Jenkins (eds), *Classical Hollywood Comedy*, 1995.

Steve Neale, 'Psychoanalysis and comedy', *Screen* 22 (2): 29–43, 1981.

Steve Neale, 'The *Big* romance or *Something Wild?*: romantic comedy today', *Screen* 33 (3): 284–99, 1992.

Steve Neale and Frank Krutnik, *Popular Film and Television Comedy*, London, Routledge, 1990.

Elder Olson, *The Theory of Comedy*, Bloomington, Indiana University Press, 1968.

Jerry Palmer, *The Logic of the Absurd*, London, BFI Publishing, 1987.

Jerry Palmer, *Taking Humour Seriously*, London and New York, Routledge, 1995.

Sylvain du Pasquier, 'Buster Keaton's gags', *Journal of Modern Literature* 13 (2): 269–91, April 1973.

William Paul, *Ernst Lubitsch's American Comedy*, New York, Columbia University Press, 1983.

William Paul, 'Charles Chaplin and the annals of anality', in Horton (ed.), *Comedy/Cinema/Theory*, 1991.

William Paul, *Laughing Screaming: Modern Hollywood Horror and Comedy*, New York, Columbia University Press, 1994.

Gerald Peary and Danny Peary (eds), *The American Animated Cartoon: A Critical Anthology*, New York, Dutton, 1980.

Susan Purdie, *Comedy: The Mastery of Discourse*, London, Harvester Wheatsheaf, 1993.

Joyce Rheuban, *Harry Langdon: The Comedian as Metteur-en-scène*, Rutherford, Fairleigh Dickson University Press, 1983.

Doug Riblet, 'The Keystone Film Company and the historiography of early slapstick', in Karnick and Jenkins (eds), *Classical Hollywood Comedy*, 1995.

David Robinson, *The Great Funnies*, London, Studio Vista, 1969.

David Robinson, *Chaplin: His Life and Art*, London, Paladin, 1986.

Margaret A. Rose, *Parody: Ancient, Modern, and Postmodern*, Cambridge, Cambridge University Press, 1993.

Kathleen Rowe, *The Unruly Woman: Gender and the Genres of Laughter*, Austin, University of Texas Press, 1995a.

Kathleen Rowe, 'Comedy, melodrama and gender: theorizing the genres of laughter', in Karnick and Jenkins (eds), *Classical Hollywood Comedy*, 1995b.

Jonathan Sanders, *Another Fine Dress: Role-play in the Films of Laurel and Hardy*, London, Cassell, 1995.

Thomas Schatz, *Hollywood Genres: Formulas, Filmmaking, and the Studio System*, New York, Random House, 1981.

Steve Seidman, *Comedian Comedy: A Tradition in the Hollywood Film*, Ann Arbor, MI, UMI Research Press, 1981.

David R. Shumway, 'Screwball comedies: constructing romance, mystifying marriage', *Cinema Journal* 30 (4): 7–23, summer 1991.

Ed Sikov, *Screwball: Hollywood's Madcap Comedies*, New York, Crown, 1989.

Ed Sikov, *Laughing Hysterically: American Screen Comedy of the 1950s*, New York, Columbia University Press, 1995.

Jean-Paul Simon and Daniel Percheron, 'Le gag', in Collet, Marie, Percheron, Simon and Vernet, *Lectures du film*, Paris, Albatross, 1976.

Robert Sklar and Charles Musser (eds), *Resisting Images: Essays on Cinema and History*, Philadelphia, PA, Temple University Press, 1990.

Raoul Sobel and David Francis, *Chaplin: Genesis of a Clown*, London, Quartet, 1977.

Michael Stern, 'Jerry Lewis b. Joseph Levita, Newark, New Jersey, 1926 res. Hollywood', *Bright Lights* 1 (3), 1975.

Kevin W. Sweeney, 'The dream of disruption: melodrama and gag structure in Keaton's *Sherlock Junior*', *Wide Angle* 13 (1): 101–20, January 1991.

Wylie Sypher (ed.), *Comedy*, New York, Doubleday, 1956.

Robert C. Toll, *On With the Show: The First Century of Show Business in America*, New York, Oxford University Press, 1976.

Robert C. Toll, *The Entertainment Machine: American Show Business in the Twentieth Century*, New York, Oxford University Press, 1982.

Alexander Walker, *Sex in the Movies: The Celluloid Sacrifice*, Harmondsworth, Penguin, 1968.

Gerald Weales, *Canned Goods as Caviar: American Film Comedy of the 1930s*, Chicago, Chicago University Press, 1985.

Arthur Wertheim, *Radio Comedy*, New York, Oxford University Press, 1979.

Mark Winokur, *American Laughter, Immigrants, Ethnicity and 1930s American Film Comedy*, London, Macmillan, 1996.

Katherine Solomon Woodward, *The Comedy of Equality: Romantic Film Comedy in America, 1930–1950*, University of Maryland PhD thesis, Ann Arbor, MI, UMI Dissertation Information Service, 1991.

CONTEMPORARY CRIME

The detective film

Richard Alewyn, 'The origin of the detective novel', in Most and Stowe (eds), *Poetics of Murder*, 1983.

Tino Balio, *Grand Design: Hollywood as a Modern Business Enterprise, 1930–1939*, New York, Scribner's, 1993.

David Bordwell, *Narration in the Fiction Film*, London, Methuen, 1985.

Eileen Bowser, *The Transformation of Cinema, 1907–1915*, New York, Scribner's, 1993.

Roger Caillois, 'The detective novel as game', in Most and Stowe (eds), *The Poetics of Murder*, 1983.

Ian Cameron (ed.), *The Movie Book of Film Noir*, London, Studio Vista, 1992.

John G. Cawelti, *Adventure, Mystery, and Romance: Formula Stories as Art and Popular Culture*, Chicago, Chicago University Press, 1976.

John Cawelti, '*Chinatown* and generic transformation in recent Hollywood films', in Grant (ed.), *Film Genre Reader II*, 1995.

Charles Derry, *The Suspense Thriller: Films in the Shadow of Alfred Hitchcock*, Jefferson, NC, McFarland, 1988.

Thomas Elsaesser, 'The pathos of failure: American film in the 1970s – notes on the unmotivated hero', *Monogram* 6: 13–19, 1975.

Michel Foucault, *Discipline and Punish*, New York, Vintage Books, 1979.

Edward Gallafent, '*Echo Park*: film noir in the seventies', in Cameron (ed.), *Movie Book of Film Noir*, 1992.

Daniel J. Gerould (ed.), *Five Filmmakers: Tarkovsky, Forman, Polanski, Szabo, Makavejev*, Bloomington, Indiana University Press, 1994.

Mick Gidley (ed.), *Modern American Culture: An Introduction*, London, Longman, 1993.

Barry Keith Grant (ed.), *Film Genre Reader II*, Austin, University of Texas Press, 1995.

Leighton Grist, 'Moving targets and black widows: film noir in modern Hollywood', in Cameron (ed.), *Movie Book of Film Noir*, 1992.

Cynthia Hamilton, 'American genre fiction', in Gidley (ed.), *Modern American Culture*, 1993.

Mary Beth Haralovich, 'Sherlock Holmes: genre and industrial practice', *Journal of the University Film Association* 31 (2): 33–57, spring 1979.

Gary Hoppenstand (ed.), *The Dime Novel Detective*, Bowling Green, OH, Bowling Green University Press, 1982.

Albert D. Hutter, 'Dreams, transformations, and literature: the implications of detective fiction', in Most and Stowe (eds), *Poetics of Murder*, 1983.

Ernst Kaemmel, 'Literature under the table: the detective novel and its social mission', in Most and Stowe (eds), *Poetics of Murder*, 1983.

Stephen Knight, *Form and Ideology in Crime Fiction*, Bloomington, Indiana University Press, 1980.

Richard Koszarski, *An Evening's Entertainment: The Age of the Silent Feature Picture, 1915–1928*, New York, Scribner's, 1990.

Larry Langman and Daniel Finn, *A Guide to American Silent Crime Films*, Westport, CT, Greenwood Press, 1994.

Ernest Mandel, *Delightful Murder: A Social History of the Crime Story*, London, Pluto Press, 1984.

Glenn W. Most and William W. Stowe (eds), *The Poetics of Murder: Detective Fiction and Literary Theory*, San Diego, CA, Harcourt Brace Janovich, 1983.

Stephen Neale, *Genre*, London, BFI Publishing, 1980.

Ian Ousby, *Bloodhounds of Heaven: The Detective in English Fiction from Godwin to Doyle*, Cambridge, MA, Harvard University Press, 1976.

Jerry Palmer, *Thrillers: Genesis and Structure of a Popular Genre*, London, Edward Arnold, 1978.

Leroy Lad Panek, *An Introduction to the Detective Story*, Bowling Green, OH, Bowling Green State University Press, 1987.

Leroy Lad Panek, *Probable Cause: Crime Fiction in America*, Bowling Green, OH, Bowling Green State University Press, 1990.

Geraldine Pederson-Krag, 'Detective stories and the primal scene', in Most and Stowe (eds), *Poetics of Murder*, 1983.

Dennis Porter, *The Pursuit of Crime: Art and Ideology in Detective Fiction*, New Haven, CT, Yale University Press, 1981.

Thomas Schatz, *Hollywood Genres: Formulas, Filmmaking and the Studio System*, New York, Random House, 1981.

Murray Smith, *Engaging Characters: Fiction, Emotion and the Cinema*, Oxford, Clarendon Press, 1995.

Matthew Solomon, 'Dime novels and early cinema as the nickelodeon period begins: outlaw and detective stories', Unpublished conference paper, 1995.

Richard F. Stewart, *... And Always a Detective: Chapters on the History of Detective Fiction*, Newton Abbot, David & Charles, 1980.

Julian Symons, *Bloody Murder: From the Detective Story to the Crime Novel*, London, Pan Books, 1992.

Kristin Thompson, *Breaking the Glass Armor: Neoformalist Film Analysis*, Princeton, NJ, Princeton University Press, 1988.

Tzvetan Todorov, *The Poetics of Prose*, Ithaca, NY, Cornell University Press, 1977.

The gangster film

Lawrence Alloway, *Violent America: the Movies 1946–64*, New York, Museum of Modern Art, 1971.

Peter Brooks, *The Melodramatic Imagination*, New Haven, CT, and London, Yale University Press, 1976.

Charles Eckert, 'The anatomy of a proletarian film: Warners' *Marked Woman*', *Film Quarterly* 27 (2): 10–24, winter 1973/74. Reprinted in Nichols (ed.), *Movies and Methods Vol. II*, Berkeley, University of California Press, 1985.

Philip French, 'Incitement against violence', *Sight and Sound* 37 (1), winter 1967/68.

Gangsters: 16+ Guide, London, BFI National Library, n. d.

Barry Keith Grant (ed.), *Film Genre Reader II*, Austin, University of Texas Press, 1995.

Robert B. Heilman, *Tragedy and Melodrama*, Seattle, University of Washington Press, 1968.

Nick James, *Heat*, London, BFI Publishing, 2002.

Steve Jenkins, *The Death of a Gangster*, London, BFI Education, 1982.

Thomas Leitch, *Crime Films*, Cambridge, Cambridge University Press, 2002.

Alan Lovell, *Don Siegel: American Cinema*, London, BFI Publishing, 1975.

Colin McArthur, *Underworld USA*, London, Secker and Warburg/BFI, 1972.

William Park, 'The police state', *Journal of Popular Film* 6 (3), 1978.

Nick Roddick, *A New Deal in Entertainment: Warner Bros in the 1930s*, London, BFI Publishing, 1983.

Tom Ryall, *Teachers' Study Guide 2: The Gangster Film*, London, BFI Education, 1978.

Thomas Schatz, *Hollywood Genres: Formulas, Filmmaking and the Studio System*, New York, Random House, 1981.

Jack Shadoian, *Dreams and Dead Ends: The American Gangster/Crime Film*, Cambridge, MA, MIT Press, 1977.

Andrew Tudor, *Image and Influence*, London, Allen and Unwin, 1974.

Robert Warshow, 'The gangster as tragic hero', in *The Immediate Experience*, New York, Atheneum Books, 1970.

Richard Whitehall, 'Crime Inc', *Films and Filming* 10 (4/6), January/February/March 1964.

Robin Wood, *Howard Hawks*, London, Secker and Warburg/BFI, 1968. Revised edition, BFI Publishing, 1981. New edition by Wayne State University Press, 2006.

The suspense thriller

Michael Balint, *Thrills and Regressions*, London, Hogarth Press, 1959.

Brian Davis, *The Thriller: The Suspense Film from 1946*, London, Studio Vista, 1973.

Charles Derry, *The Suspense Thriller: Films in the Shadow of Alfred Hitchcock*, Jefferson, NC, McFarland Press, 1988.

George N. Dove, *Suspense in the Formula Story*, Bowling Green, OH, Bowling Green State University Popular Press, 1989.

Gordon Gow, *Suspense in the Cinema*, New York, Castle, 1968.

Lawrence Hammond, *Thriller Movies: Classic Films of Suspense and Mystery*, London, Octopus, 1974.

Larry Langman and Daniel Finn, *A Guide to American Crime Films of the Thirties*, Westport, Greenwood Press, 1995a.

Larry Langman and Daniel Finn, *A Guide to American Crime Films of the Forties and Fifties*, Westport, CT, Greenwood Press, 1995b.

François Truffaut (with Helen G. Scott), *Hitchcock*, New York, Simon and Schuster, 1967. Revised edition 1985.

COSTUME DRAMA

Stella Bruzzi, *Undressing Cinema: Clothing and Identity in the Movies*, London and New York, Routledge, 1997.

Judith Butler, *Gender Trouble*, Oxford and New York, Routledge, 2006.

Pam Cook, *Fashioning the Nation: Costume and Identity in British Cinema*, London, BFI Publishing, 1996.

Pam Cook, *Screening the Past: Memory and Nostalgia in Cinema*, Oxford and New York, Routledge, 2005.

Pam Cook, 'Portrait of a lady: Sofia Coppola', *Sight and Sound* 16 (11): 36–40, November 2006.

Jennifer Craik, *The Face of Fashion: Cultural Studies in Fashion*, London and New York, Routledge, 1994.

Sybil DelGaudio, *Dressing the Part: Sternberg, Dietrich and Costume*, Madison, NJ, Fairleigh Dickinson University Press, 1993.

Richard Dyer, *Stars*, London, BFI Publishing, 1979. Revised edition 1998.

Jane Gaines and Charlotte Herzog (eds), *Fabrications: Costume and the Female Body*, New York, Routledge, 1991.

Marjorie Garber, *Vested Interests: Cross-Dressing and Cultural Anxiety*, London, Routledge, 1992.

Christine Gledhill, *Home Is Where the Heart Is: Studies in Melodrama and the Woman's Film*, London, BFI Publishing, 1987.

John Harvey, *Men in Black*, London, Reaktion Books, 1997.

Dick Hebdige, *Subculture: The Meaning of Style*, London, Routledge, 1995.

Andrew Higson, *English Heritage, English Cinema: Costume Drama since 1980*, Oxford, Oxford University Press, 2003.

Andrew Higson, 'Re-presenting the national past: nostalgia and pastiche in the heritage film', in Friedman (ed.), *Fires Were Started: British Cinema and Thatcherism*, London, UCL Press, 1993.

Anne Hollander, *Seeing Through Clothes*, Berkeley, University of California Press, 1993.

Barbara Klinger, *Melodrama and Meaning: History, Culture and the Films of Douglas Sirk*, Bloomington, Indiana University Press, 1994.

Annette Kuhn, *The Power of the Image: Essays on Representation and Sexuality*, London, Routledge, 1985.

Elizabeth Leese, *Costume Design in the Movies*, London, Dover Press, 1991.

Edward Maeder, *Hollywood and History: Costume Design and Film*, London, Thames and Hudson, 1987.

Claire Monk and Amy Sargeant (eds), *British Historical Cinema*, London and New York, Routledge, 2002.

Rachel Moseley, *Fashioning Film Stars: Dress, Culture, Identity*, London, BFI Publishing, 2005.

Julianne Pidduck, *Contemporary Costume Film: Space, Place and the Past*, London, BFI Publishing, 2004.

Pierre Sorlin, *Film in History: Restaging the Past*, Oxford, Blackwell, 1983.

Sarah Street, *Costume and Cinema: Dress Codes in Popular Film*, London, Wallflower Press, 2002.

Gainsborough costume melodrama

Sue Aspinall and Robert Murphy (eds), *BFI Dossier 18: Gainsborough Melodrama*, London, BFI, 1983.

Pam Cook, *Fashioning the Nation: Costume and Identity in British Cinema*, London, BFI Publishing, 1996.

Sue Harper, *Picturing the Past: The Rise and Fall of the British Costume Film*, London, BFI Publishing, 1994.

J. P. Mayer, *British Cinemas and Their Audiences*, London, Dennis Dobson, 1948.

Heritage cinema

Cairns Craig, 'Rooms without a view', in Vincendeau (ed.), *Film/Literature/Heritage*, 2001.

Richard Dyer, 'Nice young men who sell antiques: gay men in heritage cinema', in Vincendeau (ed.), *Film/Literature/Heritage*, 2001.

Andrew Higson, 'Re-presenting the national past: nostalgia and pastiche in the heritage film', in Friedman (ed.), *Fires Were Started: British Cinema and Thatcherism*, London, UCL Press, 1993.

Andrew Higson, 'The heritage film and British cinema', in Higson (ed.), *Dissolving Views: Key Writings on British Cinema*, London, Cassell, 1996.

Andrew Higson, *English Heritage, English Cinema: Costume Drama since 1980*, Oxford and New York, Oxford University Press, 2003.

John Hill, *British Cinema in the 1980s*, Oxford, Clarendon Press, 1999.

Fredric Jameson, *Postmodernism or, The Logic of Late Capitalism*, London, Verso, 1991.

Alison Light, 'Englishness', *Sight and Sound* 1 (3): 63, July 1991.

Claire Monk, 'Sexuality and heritage', in Vincendeau (ed.), *Film/Literature/Heritage*, 2001.

Claire Monk, 'The British heritage-film debate revisited', in Monk and Sargeant (eds), *British Historical Cinema*, London and New York, Routledge, 2002.

Julianne Pidduck, '*Elizabeth* and *Shakespeare in Love*: screening the Elizabethans', in Vincendeau (ed.), *Film/Literature/Heritage*, 2001.

Julianne Pidduck, *Contemporary Costume Film: Space, Place and the Past*, London, BFI Publishing, 2004.

Phil Powrie, *French Cinema in the 1980s: Nostalgia and the Crisis of Masculinity*, Oxford, Clarendon Press, 1997.

Raphael Samuel, *Theatres of Memory Vol I: Past and Present in Contemporary Culture*, London, Verso, 1994.

John Urry, *The Tourist Gaze*, London, Sage, 2002. Revised edition.

Ginette Vincendeau, 'Unsettling memories', in *Film/Literature/Heritage*, 2001a.

Ginette Vincendeau (ed.), *Film/Literature/Heritage: A Sight and Sound Reader*, London, BFI Publishing, 2001b.

Tana Wollen, 'Nostalgic screen fictions', in Corner and Harvey (eds), *Enterprise and Heritage: Crosscurrents of National Culture*, London and New York, Routledge, 1991.

EXPLOITATION CINEMA

David Andrews, *Soft in the Middle: The Contemporary Softcore Feature in Its Contexts*, Columbus, Ohio State University Press, 2006.

Mark Betz, 'Art, exploitation, underground', in Jancovich *et al.* (eds), *Defining Cult Movies*, 2003.

Michael J. Bowen, 'Embodiment and realization: the many film-bodies of Doris Wishman', *Wide Angle* 19 (3): 64–90, July 1997.

Carol J. Clover, *Men, Women and Chain Saws*, Princeton, NJ, Princeton University Press, 1992a.

Carol J. Clover, 'Getting even', *Sight and Sound* 2 (1): 16–18, May 1992b.

David A. Cook, *Lost Illusions: American Cinema in the Shadow of Watergate and Vietnam 1970–1979*, Berkeley, University of California Press, 2002.

Pam Cook, 'Exploitation films and feminism', *Screen* 17 (2): 122–7, summer 1976.

Pam Cook, 'The pleasures and perils of exploitation films', in *Screening the Past: Memory and Nostalgia in Cinema*, Oxford and New York, Routledge, 2005.

Jonathan L. Crane, 'A lust for life: the cult films of Russ Meyer', in Mendik and Harper (eds), *Unruly Pleasures*, 2000.

Pamela Church Gibson (ed.), *More Dirty Looks: Gender, Pornography and Power*, London, BFI Publishing, 2003.

Elena Gorfinkel, 'The body as apparatus: Chesty Morgan takes on the academy', in Mendik and Harper (eds), *Unruly Pleasures*, 2000.

Matt Hills, *The Pleasures of Horror*, New York, Continuum, 2005.

Mark Jancovich, Antonio Lázaro Reboll, Julian Stringer and Andy Willis (eds), *Defining Cult Movies: The Cultural Politics of Oppositional Taste*, Manchester, Manchester University Press, 2003.

Peter Lehman (ed.), *Pornography: Film and Culture*, New Brunswick, NJ, Rutgers University Press, 2006.

Moya Luckett, 'Sexploitation as feminine territory: the films of Doris Wishman', in Jancovich *et al.* (eds), *Defining Cult Movies*, 2003.

Maitland McDonagh, *Filmmaking on the Fringe: The Good, the Bad, and the Deviant Directors*, New York, Citadel Press, 1996.

Xavier Mendik and Graeme Harper (eds), *Unruly Pleasures: The Cult Film and Its Critics*, Guildford, Surrey, FAB Press, 2000.

Xavier Mendik and Steven Jay Schneider, *Underground USA: Filmmaking Beyond the Hollywood Canon*, London, Wallflower Press, 2002.

Kim Newman, 'Exploitation and the mainstream', in Nowell-Smith (ed.), *The Oxford History of World Cinema*, Oxford, Oxford University Press, 1996.

Mike Quarles, *Down and Dirty: Hollywood's Exploitation Filmmakers and Their Movies*, Jefferson, NC, and London, McFarland, 1993. Revised edition 2001.

Jacinda Read, *The New Avengers: Feminism, Femininity and the Rape-Revenge Cycle*, Manchester, Manchester University Press, 2000.

Frank Rich, 'Naked capitalists', *New York Times Magazine* 20 May 2001, pp. 51–92. Cited in Williams, *Porn Studies*, 2004, p. 21.

Eric Schaefer, *'Bold! Daring! Shocking! True!' A History of Exploitation Films, 1919–1959*, Durham, NC, and London, Duke University Press, 1999.

Eric Schaefer, *Massacre of Pleasure: A History of the Sexploitation Film, 1960–1979*, Durham, NC, Duke University Press, 2008.

Jeffrey Sconce, '"Trashing" the academy: taste, excess, and an emerging politics of cinematic style', *Screen* 36 (4): 371–93, winter 1995.

Jeffrey Sconce (ed.), *Sleaze Artists: Cinema at the Margins of Taste, Style and Financing*, Durham, NC, Duke University Press, 2007.

Linda Williams, *Hardcore: Power, Pleasure, and the 'Frenzy of the Visible'*, London, Pandora Press, 1991.

Linda Williams (ed.), *Porn Studies*, Durham, NC, and London, Duke University Press, 2004.

Linda Ruth Williams, *The Erotic Thriller in Contemporary Cinema*, Edinburgh, Edinburgh University Press, 2005.

Linda Ruth Williams, 'Women in recent US cinema', in Williams and Hammond (eds), *Contemporary American Cinema*, Maidenhead, Berkshire, Open University Press/McGraw-Hill, 2006.

Blaxploitation

Donald Bogle, *Toms, Coons, Mulattoes, Mammies, and Bucks: An Interpretive History of Blacks in American Films*, New York, Continuum, 2003. Revised edition.

Thomas Cripps, *Black Film as Genre*, Bloomington, Indiana University Press, 1978.

Manthia Diawara, *Black American Cinema*, New York and London, Routledge, 1993.

Nelson George, *Blackface: Reflections on African-Americans and the Movies*, New York, HarperCollins, 1994.

Ed Guerrero, *Framing Blackness: The African American Image in Film*, Philadelphia, PA, Temple University Press, 1993.

Amanda Howell, 'Spectacle, masculinity, and music in blaxploitation cinema', *Screening the Past* 18, 29 July 2005. Available at: <www.latrobe.edu.au/screeningthepast/firstrelease/fr_18/AHfr18a.html>.

Daniel J. Leab, *From Sambo to Superspade: The Black Experience in Motion Pictures*, New York, Houghton Mifflin, 1975.

Tommy Lee Lott, 'Documenting social issues: *Black Journal*, 1968–70', in Klotman and Cutler (eds), *Struggles for Representation: African American Documentary Film and Video*, Bloomington, Indiana University Press, 1999a.

Tommy Lee Lott, *The Invention of Race: Black Culture and the Politics of Representation*, New York and Oxford, Blackwell, 1999b.

Paula J. Massood, *Black City Cinema: African American Urban Experiences in Film*, Philadelphia, PA, Temple University Press, 2003.

James P. Murray, *To Find an Image: Black Films from Uncle Tom to Super Fly*, New York, Bobbs-Merrill, 1973.

Huey P. Newton, '"He won't bleed me": a revolutionary analysis of *Sweet Sweetback's Baadasssss Song*', *The Black Panther Intercommunal News Service* 6, 19 June 1971. Extract reprinted in Van Peebles, *Sweet Sweetback's Baadasssss Song*, 2004.

Mark A. Reid, *Redefining Black Film*, Berkeley, University of California Press, 1993.

Jesse Algernon Rhines, *Black Film/White Money*, New Brunswick, NJ, Rutgers University Press, 1996.

Clyde Taylor, 'The LA rebellion: new spirit in American film', *Black Film Review* 2: 2, 1986.

Clyde Taylor, 'We don't need another hero: anti-theses on aesthetics', in Cham and Andrade-Watkins (eds), *Blackframes: Critical Perspectives on Black Independent Cinema*, Cambridge, MA, MIT Press, 1988.

Melvin Van Peebles, *Sweet Sweetback's Baadasssss Song: A Guerrilla Filmmaking Manifesto*, New York, Lancer Books, 1971. Reprinted by Avalon, 2004.

Renee Ward, 'Black films, white profits', *Black Scholar* 7 (8): 13–24, 1976.

S. Craig Watkins, *Representing: Hip Hop Culture and the Production of Black Cinema*, Chicago, University of Chicago Press, 1998.

Gladstone Yearwood, 'The hero in black film: an analysis of the film industry and problems in black cinema', *Wide Angle* 5 (2): 42–50, 1982.

FILM NOIR

Raymond Borde and Etienne Chaumeton, *Panorame du film noir americain*, Paris, Editions de Minuit, 1955. Reprinted in part as 'Sources of film noir', *Film Reader* 3, 1978.

Ian Cameron (ed.), *The Movie Book of Film Noir*, London, Studio Vista, 1992.

John Cawelti, '*Chinatown* and generic transformation in recent Hollywood films', in Grant (ed.), *Film Genre Reader II*, Austin, University of Texas Press, 1995.

Pam Cook, 'Duplicity in *Mildred Pierce*', in Kaplan (ed.), *Women in Film Noir*, 1978; 1998. Reprinted in *Screening the Past: Memory and Nostalgia in Cinema*, Oxford and New York, Routledge, 2005.

Joan Copjec (ed.), *Shades of Noir*, London, Verso, 1993.

Elizabeth Cowie, 'Film noir and women', in Copjec (ed.), *Shades of Noir*, 1993.

Bruce Crowther, *Film Noir, Reflections in a Dark Mirror*, London, Virgin Books, 1988.

James Damico, 'Film noir: a modest proposal', *Film Reader* 3, February 1978. Reprinted in Silver and Ursini (eds), *Film Noir Reader*, 1996.

Mary Ann Doane, *The Desire to Desire: The Woman's Film of the 1940s*, Bloomington, Indiana University Press, 1987.

Raymond Durgnat, 'The family tree of film noir', *Cinema* (UK) 6/7: 48–56, August 1970. Reprinted in *Film Comment* 10 (6), November/December 1974; and in Silver and Ursini (eds), *Film Noir Reader*, 1996.

Richard Dyer, 'Resistance through charisma: Rita Hayworth and *Gilda*', in Kaplan (ed.), *Women in Film Noir*, 1978; 1998.

Herbert Eagle, 'Polanski', in Gerould (ed.), *Five Filmmakers: Tarkovsky, Forman, Polanski, Szabo, Makavejev*, Bloomington, Indiana University Press, 1994.

Tom Flinn, 'Three faces of film noir', *The Velvet Light Trap* 5, summer 1972. Reprinted in McCarthy and Flynn (eds), *Kings of the 'B's: Working within the Hollywood System*, New York, Dutton, 1975.

Edward Gallafent, '*Echo Park*: film noir in the seventies', in Cameron (ed.), *Movie Book of Film Noir*, 1992.

Christine Gledhill, '*Klute* 1: a contemporary film noir and feminist criticism', and '*Klute* 2: feminism and *Klute*', in Kaplan (ed.), *Women in Film Noir*, 1978; 1998.

Leighton Grist, 'Moving targets and black widows: film noir in modern Hollywood', in Cameron (ed.), *Movie Book of Film Noir*, 1992.

Larry Gross, 'Film après noir', *Film Comment* 12 (4): 44–9, July/August 1976.

Tom Gunning, *Fritz Lang: Allegories of Vision and Modernity*, London, BFI Publishing, 2000.

Sylvia Harvey, 'Woman's place: the absent family of film noir', in Kaplan (ed.), *Women in Film Noir*, 1978; 1998.

Reynold Humphries, *Fritz Lang: Genre and Representation in His American Films*, Baltimore, MD, Johns Hopkins Press, 1988.

Florence Jacobowitz, 'The man's melodrama: *The Woman in the Window* and *Scarlet Street*', in Cameron (ed.), *Movie Book of Film Noir*, 1992.

Stephen Jenkins, *Fritz Lang: The Image and the Look*, London, BFI Publishing, 1981.

Stephen Jenkins, 'Dashiell Hammett and film noir', *Monthly Film Bulletin* 49 (586), November 1982.

Paul M. Jensen, *The Cinema of Fritz Lang*, London, Zwemmer, 1969.

Claire Johnston, '*Double Indemnity*', in Kaplan (ed.), *Women in Film Noir*, 1978; 1998.

E. Ann Kaplan (ed.), *Women in Film Noir*, London, BFI Publishing, 1978. Revised edition 1998.

E. Ann Kaplan, 'Introduction', in *Women in Film Noir*, 1978; 1998.

Paul Kerr, 'Out of what past? Notes on the B-film noir', *Screen Education* 32/33: 45–65, autumn/winter 1979/80. Reprinted in Silver and Ursini (eds), *The Film Noir Reader*, 1996.

Frank Krutnik, *In a Lonely Street: Film Noir, Genre, Masculinity*, London and New York, Routledge, 1991.

Richard Maltby, 'Film noir: the politics of the maladjusted text', in Cameron (ed.), *Movie Book of Film Noir*, 1992.

Colin McArthur, *Underworld USA*, London, BFI/Secker and Warburg, 1972.

Steve Neale, *Genre and Hollywood*, London, Routledge, 1999.

Brian Neve, *Film and Politics in America: A Social Tradition*, London, Routledge, 1992.

R. Barton Palmer, *Hollywood's Dark Cinema: The American Film Noir*, New York, Twayne, 1994.

J. A. Place, 'Women in film noir', in Kaplan (ed.), *Women in Film Noir*, 1978; 1998.

J. A. Place and L. S. Peterson, 'Some visual motifs of film noir', *Film Comment* 10 (1), January/February 1974. Reprinted in Silver and Ursini (eds), *Film Noir Reader*, 1996.

Dana Polan, *Power and Paranoia: History, Narrative, and the American Cinema, 1940–1950*, New York, Columbia University Press, 1986.

Robert Porfirio, 'No way out', *Sight and Sound* 45 (4), autumn 1976.

Pulp Fictions: The Film Noir Story (NYCVH/BBC, tx. BBC2, 4 August 1995).

Thomas Schatz, *Hollywood Genres: Formulas, Filmmaking and the Studio System*, New York, Random House, 1981.

Paul Schrader, 'Notes on film noir', *Film Comment* 8 (1), spring 1972. Reprinted in Silver and Ursini (eds), *The Film Noir Reader*, 1996.

Alain Silver and James Ursini (eds), *The Film Noir Reader*, New York, Limelight Editions, 1996.

Alain Silver and Elizabeth Ward (eds), *Film Noir*, London, Secker and Warburg, 1981. Reprinted as *Film Noir: An Encyclopedic Reference to the American Style*, Woodstock, NY, The Overlook Press, 1992. Revised edition 1996.

J. P. Telotte, *Voices in the Dark: The Narrative Patterns of Film Noir*, Urbana, Illinois University Press, 1989.

Deborah Thomas, 'Hollywood deals with the deviant male', in Cameron (ed.), *Movie Book of Film Noir*, 1992.

Marc Vernet, 'Film noir on the edge of doom', in Copjec (ed.), *Shades of Noir*, 1993.

Diane Waldman, '"At last I can tell it to someone!": feminine point of view and subjectivity in the Gothic romance film of the 1940s', *Cinema Journal* 23 (2): 29–40, winter 1983.

Michael Walker, 'Film noir: introduction', in Cameron (ed.), *Movie Book of Film Noir*, 1992.

MELODRAMA

Guy Barefoot, 'Hollywood, melodrama and twentieth-century notions of the Victorian', in Bratton *et al.* (eds), *Melodrama: Stage, Picture, Screen*, 1994.

Guy Barefoot, *Gaslight Melodrama: From Victorian London to 1940s Hollywood*, New York, Continuum, 2001.

Jeanine Basinger, *A Woman's View: How Hollywood Spoke to Women, 1930–1960*, London, Chatto & Windus, 1993.

Jean-Loup Bourget, 'Faces of the American melodrama: Joan Crawford', *Film Reader* 3: 24–34, 1978.

Jacky Bratton, Jim Cook and Christine Gledhill (eds), *Melodrama: Stage, Picture, Screen*, London, BFI Publishing, 1994.

Peter Brooks, *The Melodramatic Imagination*, New Haven, CT, Yale University Press, 1976.

Charlotte Brunsdon, '*Crossroads*: notes on soap opera', *Screen* 22 (4), 1981. Reprinted in *Screen Tastes: From Soap Opera to Satellite Dishes*, London and New York, Routledge, 1997.

Jackie Byars, *All That Hollywood Allows: Re-reading Gender in 1950s Melodrama*, London, Routledge, 1991.

Camera Obscura 19 (3), September 2004. Special issue on Todd Haynes.

Bert Cardullo, '*Way Down East*: play and film', in *Indelible Image*, Lanham, MD, University Press of America, 1987.

Pam Cook, 'Duplicity in *Mildred Pierce*', in Kaplan (ed.), *Women in Film Noir*, 1978; 1998. Reprinted in *Screening the Past: Memory and Nostalgia in Cinema*, Oxford and New York, Routledge, 2005.

Pam Cook, 'Rethinking nostalgia: *In the Mood for Love* and *Far from Heaven*', in *Screening the Past: Memory and Nostalgia in Cinema*, Oxford and New York, Routledge, 2005.

Barbara Creed, 'The position of women in Hollywood melodramas', *Australian Journal of Screen Theory* 4: 27–31, 1977.

Wimal Dissanayake (ed.), 'Special issue on melodrama and cinema', *East–West Film Journal* 5 (1), January 1991.

Wimal Dissanayake (ed.), *Melodrama and Asian Cinema*, Cambridge, Cambridge University Press, 1993.

Mary Ann Doane, 'The "woman's film": possession and address', in Doane, Mellencamp and Williams (eds), *Re-Vision: Essays in Feminist Film Criticism*, Frederick, MD, University Publications of America/AFI, 1983.

Mary Ann Doane, *The Desire to Desire: The Woman's Film of the 1940s*, Bloomington, Indiana University Press, 1987.

Richard Dyer, *Pastiche*, Oxford and New York, Routledge, 2006.

Barbara Ehrenreich, *The Hearts of Men*, London, Pluto Press, 1983.

Lotte Eisner, *Murnau*, London, Secker and Warburg, 1973.

Thomas Elsaesser, 'Tales of sound and fury: observations on the family melodrama', *Monogram* 4, 1972. Reprinted in Grant (ed.), *Film Genre Reader II*, Austin, University of Texas Press, 1995.

John Fell, *Film and the Narrative Tradition*, Norman, University of Oklahoma Press, 1974.

Lizzie Francke, *Script Girls: Women Screenwriters in Hollywood*, London, BFI Publishing, 1994.

Brandon French, *On the Verge of Revolt*, New York, Ungar, 1978.

Christine Gledhill (ed.), *Home Is Where the Heart Is: Studies in Melodrama and the Woman's Film*, London, BFI Publishing, 1987.

Jon Halliday, *Sirk on Sirk*, London, Secker and Warburg/BFI, 1971.

Molly Haskell, *From Reverence to Rape*, Harmondsworth, Penguin, 1979.

Marina Heung, '"What's the matter with Sara Jane?": daughters and mothers in Douglas Sirk's *Imitation of Life*', *Cinema Journal* 26 (3): 21–43, spring 1987.

Lea Jacobs, 'Censorship and the fallen woman cycle', in Gledhill (ed.), *Home Is Where the Heart Is*, 1987.

Lea Jacobs, *The Wages of Sin, Censorship and the Fallen Woman Film, 1928–1942*, Madison, University of Wisconsin Press, 1991.

E. Ann Kaplan (ed.), *Women in Film Noir*, London, BFI Publishing, 1978. Revised edition 1998.

E. Ann Kaplan, 'Mothering, feminism and representation: the maternal in melodrama and the woman's film from 1910 to 1940', in Gledhill (ed.), *Home Is Where the Heart Is*, 1987.

E. Ann Kaplan, *Motherhood and Representation: The Mother in Popular Culture and Melodrama*, London, Routledge, 1992.

Stanley Kauffmann, 'D. W. Griffith's *Way Down East*', *Horizon* 14 (2): 50, spring 1972.

Vance Kepley, '*Broken Blossoms* and the problem of historical specificity', *Quarterly Review of Film Studies* 3 (1): 37–47, winter 1978.

Chuck Kleinhans, 'Notes on melodrama and the family under capitalism', *Film Reader* 3: 40–7, 1978. Reprinted in Landy (ed.), *Imitations of Life: A Reader on Film and Television Melodrama*, 1991.

Barbara Klinger, *Melodrama and Meaning: History, Culture, and the Films of Douglas Sirk*, Bloomington and Indianapolis, University of Indiana Press, 1994.

Sarah R. Kozloff, 'Where Wessex meets New England: Griffith's *Way Down East* and Hardy's *Tess of the d'Urbervilles*', *Literature/Film Quarterly* 13 (1): 35–41, 1985.

Marcia Landy (ed.), *Imitations of Life: A Reader on Film and Television Melodrama*, Detroit, MI, Wayne State University Press, 1991.

Robert Lang, *American Film Melodrama: Griffith, Vidor, Minnelli*, Princeton, NJ, Princeton University Press, 1989.

Arthur Lennig, 'The birth of *Way Down East*', *Quarterly Review of Film Studies* 6 (1): 105, winter 1981.

Burns Mantle, 'Review of *Way Down East*', *Photoplay* 19 (1), December 1920.

Judith Mayne, *Directed by Dorothy Arzner*, Bloomington, University of Indiana Press, 1994.

Tania Modleski, 'The search for tomorrow in today's soap operas: notes on a feminine narrative form', *Film Quarterly* 33 (1): 12–21, autumn 1979.

Laura Mulvey, '*Fear Eats the Soul*', *Spare Rib* 30, 1974.

Laura Mulvey, 'Notes on Sirk and melodrama', *Movie* 25, 1977/78. Reprinted in Gledhill (ed.), *Home Is Where the Heart Is*, 1987.

Laura Mulvey, 'Afterthoughts on "Visual pleasure and narrative cinema" inspired by King Vidor's *Duel in the Sun* (1946)', *Framework* 15/16/17, summer 1981. Reprinted in *Visual and Other Pleasures*, Bloomington, Indiana University Press, 1989.

Stephen Neale, *Genre*, London, BFI Publishing, 1980.

Steve Neale, 'Melodrama and tears', *Screen* 27 (6): 6–22, 1986.

Steve Neale, 'Melo talk: on the meaning and use of the term "melodrama" in the American trade press', *The Velvet Light Trap* 32 (3): 66–89, fall 1993.

Geoffrey Nowell-Smith, 'Minnelli and melodrama', *Screen* 18 (2): 113–18, summer 1977. Reprinted in Gledhill (ed.), *Home Is Where the Heart Is*, 1987.

Michael Paris, *From the Wright Brothers to Top Gun: Aviation, Nationalism and Popular Cinema*, Manchester University Press, 1995.

Griselda Pollock, 'Report on the weekend school', *Screen* 18 (2): 105–13, summer 1977.

Frank Rahill, *The World of Melodrama*, Philadelphia, Pennsylvania State University Press, 1967.

D. N. Rodowick, 'Madness, authority and ideology in the domestic melodrama of the 1950s', *The Velvet Light Trap* 19: 40–5, 1982. Reprinted in Gledhill (ed.), *Home Is Where the Heart Is*, 1987.

Thomas Schatz, *Hollywood Genres: Formulas, Filmmaking and the Studio System*, New York, Random House, 1981.

Richard Schickel, *D. W. Griffith*, New York, Limelight Editions, 1996.

Ben Singer, 'Female power in the serial-queen melodrama: the etiology of an anomaly', *Camera Obscura* 22: 90–129, January 1990.

Stephen Teo, *Wong Kar-wai*, London, BFI Publishing, 2005.

Nicholas Vardac, *From Stage to Screen: Theatrical Method from Garrick to Griffith*, Boston, MA, Harvard University Press, 1949.

Christian Viviani, 'Who is without sin?: The maternal melodrama in American film 1930–39', *Wide Angle* 4 (2), 1980.

Diane Waldman, '"At last I can tell it to someone!": feminine point of view and subjectivity in the Gothic romance film of the 1940s', *Cinema Journal* 23 (2): 29–40, winter 1983.

Michael Walker, 'Melodrama and the American cinema', *Movie* 29/30: 2–38, summer 1982.

Andrea S. Walsh, *Women's Film and Female Experience, 1940–1950*, New York, Praeger, 1984.

Paul Willemen, 'Distanciation and Douglas Sirk', *Screen* 12 (2): 63–7, summer 1971.

Linda Williams, '"Something else besides a mother": *Stella Dallas* and the maternal melodrama', *Cinema Journal* 24 (1): 2–27, fall 1984. Reprinted in Gledhill (ed.), *Home Is Where the Heart Is*, 1987.

Linda Williams, 'Melodrama revised', in Browne (ed.), *Refiguring American Film Genres: Theory and History*, Berkeley, University of California Press, 1998.

THE MUSICAL

Rick Altman (ed.), *Genre: The Musical*, London, Routledge, 1981.

Rick Altman, *The American Film Musical*, Bloomington, Indiana University Press, 1987.

Rick Altman, 'The musical', in Nowell-Smith (ed.), *The Oxford History of World Cinema*, Oxford, Oxford University Press, 1996.

Bruce Babington and Peter William Evans, *Blue Skies and Silver Linings: Aspects of the Hollywood Musical*, Manchester, Manchester University Press, 1985.

Tino Balio, *Grand Design: Hollywood as a Modern Business Enterprise, 1930–1939*, New York, Scribner's, 1993.

Richard Barrios, *A Song in the Dark: The Birth of the Musical Film*, New York, Oxford University Press, 1995.

Gerald Bordman, *American Operetta: From HMS Pinafore to Sweeney Todd*, Oxford, Oxford University Press, 1981.

Gerald Bordman, *American Musical Comedy: From Adonis to Dreamgirls*, Oxford, Oxford University Press, 1982.

Gerald Bordman, *American Musical Revue: From the Passing Show to Sugar Babies*, Oxford, Oxford University Press, 1985.

Leo Braudy, *The World in a Frame: What We See in Films*, New York, Anchor, 1976.
Steven Cohan, 'Feminizing the song-and-dance man: Fred Astaire and the spectacle of masculinity in the Hollywood musical', in Cohan and Hark (eds), *Screening the Male*, 1993.
Steven Cohan (ed.), *Hollywood Musicals: The Film Reader*, New York and London, Routledge, 2002.
Steven Cohan and Ina Rae Hark (eds), *Screening the Male: Exploring Masculinities in Hollywood Cinema*, London and New York, Routledge, 1993.
Jim Collins, 'The musical', in Gehring (ed.), *Handbook of American Film Genres*, New York, Greenwood Press, 1988.
Jerome Delameter, 'Performing arts: the musical', in Kaminsky (ed.), *American Film Genres*, 1974.
Jerome Delameter, *Dance in the Hollywood Musical*, Ann Arbor, MI, UMI Research Press, 1981.
Richard Dyer, '*The Sound of Music*', *Movie* 23, 1976/77.
Richard Dyer, 'Entertainment and utopia', *Movie* 24, 1977. Reprinted in Cohan (ed.), *Hollywood Musicals*, 2002.
Richard Dyer, '*A Star Is Born* and the construction of authenticity', in Gledhill (ed.), *Stardom: Industry of Desire*, London and New York, Routledge, 1991.
Thomas Elsaesser, 'Vincente Minnelli', in Altman (ed.), *Genre: The Musical*, 1981.
Greg S. Faller, *The Function of Star-Image and Performance in the Hollywood Musical: Sonja Henie, Esther Williams, and Eleanor Powell*, PhD thesis, Northwestern University, 1987, Ann Arbor, MI, UMI Dissertation Information Service, 1992.
Jane Feuer, *The Hollywood Musical*, London, Macmillan, 1982. Reprinted by Indiana University Press, 1993.
Jane Feuer, 'The self-reflexive musical and the myth of entertainment', in Grant (ed.), *Film Genre Reader III*, Austin, University of Texas Press, 2003.
Lucy Fischer, 'The image of woman as image: the optical politics of *Dames*', in Altman (ed.), *Genre: The Musical*, 1981.
Hugh Fordin, *The Movies' Greatest Musicals: Produced in Hollywood USA by the Freed Unit*, New York, Ungar, 1975.
Beth Eliot Genne, *The Film Musicals of Vincente Minnelli and the Team of Gene Kelly and Stanley Donen, 1944–1958*, PhD thesis, University of Michigan, 1984, Ann Arbor, UMI Dissertation Information Service, 1992.
Barry K. Grant, 'The classic Hollywood musical and the "problem" of rock 'n' roll', *Journal of Popular Film and Television* 13 (4), winter 1986.
Stuart Kaminsky, *American Film Genres*, Dayton, OH, Pflaum, 1974.
Richard Kislan, *The Musical: A Look at the American Musical Theater*, Englewood Cliffs, NJ, Prentice-Hall, 1980.
Arthur Knight, 'The movies learn to talk: Ernst Lubitsch, René Clair, and Rouben Mamoulian', in Weis and Belton (eds), *Film Sound: Theory and Practice*, 1985.
John Kobal, *Gotta Sing, Gotta Dance: A Pictorial History of Film Musicals*, London, Hamlyn, 1971.
Bill Marshall and Robynn Stilwell (eds), *The Musical: Hollywood and Beyond*, London, Intellect Books, 2000.
Alain Masson, 'George Sidney: artificial brilliance/the brilliance of artifice', in Altman (ed.), *Genre: The Musical*, 1981.
Gerald Mast, *Can't Help Singin': The American Musical on Stage and Screen*, Woodstock, NY, Overlook Press, 1987.
Vincente Minnelli with Hector Arce, *I Remember It Well*, Garden City, NY, Doubleday, 1974.
Ethan Mordden, *The Hollywood Musical*, New York, St Martin's Press, 1982.
Ethan Mordden, *The Hollywood Studios: House Style in the Golden Age of the Movies*, New York, Knopf, 1988.
John Mueller, 'Fred Astaire and the integrated musical', *Cinema Journal* 24 (1): 28–40, autumn 1984.
John Mueller, *Astaire Dancing: The Musical Films*, New York, Wings Books, 1985.
James Naremore, *The Films of Vincente Minnelli*, Cambridge, Cambridge University Press, 1993.
Stephen Neale, *Genre*, London, BFI Publishing, 1980.
Sue Rickard, 'Movies in disguise: negotiating censorship and patriarchy through the dances of Fred Astaire and Ginger Rogers', in Lawson-Peebles (ed.), *Approaches to the American Film Musical*, Exeter, Exeter University Press, 1996.
Nick Roddick, *A New Deal in Entertainment: Warner Bros in the 1930s*, London, BFI Publishing, 1983.
Mark Roth, 'Some Warners musicals and the spirit of the New Deal', in Altman (ed.), *Genre: The Musical*, 1981.
Martin Rubin, *Showstoppers: Busby Berkeley and the Tradition of Spectacle*, New York, Columbia University Press, 1993.
Thomas Schatz, *The Genius of the System: Hollywood Filmmaking in the Studio Era*, New York, Pantheon Books, 1988.
Cecil Smith and Glenn Litton, *Musical Comedy in America*, New York, Theatre Arts Books, 1981.
Aubrey Solomon, *Twentieth Century-Fox: A Corporate and Financial History*, Metuchen, NJ, Scarecrow Press, 1988.
Joseph P. Swain, *The Broadway Musical: A Critical and Musical Survey*, Oxford, Oxford University Press, 1990.
J. P. Telotte, 'A sober celebration: song and dance in the "new" musical', *Journal of Popular Film and Television* 8 (1): 2–14, spring 1980.
Richard Traubner, *Operetta: A Theatrical History*, Oxford, Oxford University Press, 1983.
Variety, 'This is operetta', 20 February 1946, p. 49.
Alexander Walker, *The Shattered Silents: How the Talkies Came to Stay*, New York, William Murrow, 1979.
Elisabeth Weis and John Belton (eds), *Film Sound: Theory and Practice*, New York, Columbia University Press, 1985.
Alec Wilder, *American Popular Song: The Great Innovators, 1900–1950*, Oxford, Oxford University Press, 1972.
Charles Wolfe, 'Vitaphone shorts and *The Jazz Singer*', *Wide Angle* 12 (3): 58–78, July 1990.
Peter Wollen, *Singin' in the Rain*, London, BFI Publishing, 1992.
Michael Wood, *America in the Movies*, London, Secker and Warburg, 1975.
Robin Wood, 'Art and ideology: notes on *Silk Stockings*', in Altman (ed.), *Genre: The Musical*, 1981.
Robin Wood, *Howard Hawks*, London, BFI Publishing, 1981. New edition by Wayne State University Press, 2006.

SCIENCE FICTION AND HORROR

Science fiction

Erik Barnouw, *The Magician and Cinema*, New York, Oxford University Press, 1981.
John Baxter, *Science Fiction in the Cinema*, London, Zwemmer, 1970.
John Brosnan, *Movie Magic: The Story of Special Effects in the Cinema*, London, MacDonald Press, 1974.
John Brosnan, *Future Tense: The Cinema of Science Fiction*, New York, St Martin's Press, 1978.
Giuliana Bruno, 'Ramble city: postmodernism and *Blade Runner*', in Kuhn (ed.), *Alien Zone*, 1990.
Noël Carroll, 'The future of allusion: Hollywood in the seventies (and beyond)', *October* 20: 51–81, spring 1982.
James Donald (ed.), *Fantasy and Cinema*, London, BFI Publishing, 1989.
Victor Erlich, *Russian Formalism: History, Doctrine*, New Haven, CT, Yale University Press, 1981.
John Frazer, *Artificially Arranged Scenes: Th Films of Georges Méliès*, Boston, G. K. Hall, 1979.
Paul Hammond, *Marvellous Méliès*, New York, St Martin's Press, 1974.
Donna Haraway, 'A manifesto for cyborgs: science, technology and socialist feminism in the 1980s', *Socialist Review* 80: 65–108, 1985. Reprinted in *Simians, Cyborgs and Women: The Reinvention of Nature*, New York and London, Routledge, 1991.
Phil Hardy, *The Encyclopedia of Science Fiction Movies*, London, Octopus Books, 1986.
Richard Hodgens, 'A brief, tragical history of the science fiction film', *Film Quarterly* 13 (2): 30–9, winter 1959.
David Hutchison, *Film Magic: The Art and Science of Special Effects*, New York, Prentice-Hall, 1987.

Edward James, *Science Fiction in the Twentieth Century*, Oxford, Oxford University Press, 1994.

Judith B. Kerman (ed.), *Retrofitting Blade Runner: Issues in Ridley Scott's Blade Runner and Philip K. Dick's Do Androids Dream of Electric Sheep?*, Bowling Green, OH, Bowling Green State University Popular Press, 1991.

Annette Kuhn (ed.), *Alien Zone: Cultural Theory and Contemporary Science Fiction Cinema*, London, Verso, 1990.

Annette Kuhn (ed.), *Alien Zone II: The Spaces of Science Fiction Cinema*, London, Verso, 1999.

Steve Neale, 'Hollywood strikes back: special effects in recent Hollywood movies', *Screen* 21 (3): 101–5, 1980.

Steve Neale, 'Issues of difference: *Alien* and *Blade Runner*', in Donald (ed.), *Fantasy and Cinema*, 1989.

Constance Penley, Elisabeth Lyon, Lynn Spigel and Janet Bergstrom (eds), *Close Encounters: Film, Feminism and Science Fiction*, Minneapolis, University of Minnesota Press, 1991.

Michele Pierson, *Special Effects: Still in Search of Wonder*, New York, Columbia University Press, 2002.

David Pringle (ed.), *The Ultimate Encyclopedia of Science Fiction*, London, Carlton, 1997.

Michael Pye and Lynda Myles, *The Movie Brats: How the Film Generation Took Over Hollywood*, New York, Holt, Rinehart and Winston, 1979.

Robert B. Ray, *A Certain Tendency of the Hollywood Cinema, 1930–1980*, Princeton, NJ, Princeton University Press, 1985.

Thomas Schatz, *Old Hollywood/New Hollywood: Ritual, Art, and Industry*, Ann Arbor, MI, UMI Research Press, 1983.

Vivian Sobchack, *The Limits of Infinity: The American Science Fiction Film 1950–1975*, New York, Ungar, 1980.

Vivian Sobchack, *Screening Space: The American Science Fiction Film*, New York, Ungar, 1988.

Jean-François Tarnowski, 'Approche et définition(s) du fantastique et de la science-fiction cinématographique (1)', *Positif* 195/6: 57–65, July/August 1977.

J. P. Telotte, *Replications: A Robotic History of the Science Fiction Film*, Urbana, University of Illinois Press, 1995.

Justin Wyatt, *High Concept: Movies and Marketing in Hollywood*, Austin, University of Texas Press, 1994.

The horror film

Rhona J. Behrenstein, *Attack of the Leading Ladies: Gender, Sexuality and Spectatorship in Classic Horror Cinema*, New York, Columbia University Press, 1996.

Andrew Britton, Richard Lippe, Tony Williams and Robin Wood (eds), *American Nightmare: Essays on the Horror Film*, Toronto, Festival of Festivals, 1979.

Philip Brophy, 'Horrality: the textuality of contemporary horror films', *Screen* 27 (1): 2–13, January/February 1986. Reprinted in Gelder (ed.), *The Horror Reader*, London and New York, Routledge, 2000.

Ivan Butler, *Horror in the Cinema*, London, Zwemmer, 1970.

Noël Carroll, 'Nightmare and the horror film: the symbolic biology of fantastic beings', *Film Quarterly* 34 (3): 16–25, spring 1981.

Noël Carroll, *The Philosophy of Horror*, New York and London, Routledge, 1990.

Carlos Clarens, *Horror Movies: An Illustrated Survey*, London, Secker and Warburg, 1968.

Carol J. Clover, *Men, Women and Chain Saws*, Princeton, NJ, Princeton University Press, 1992.

Pam Cook, 'Review of *Dead Ringers*', *Monthly Film Bulletin* 56 (660): 3–4, January 1989.

Jonathan Lake Crane, *Terror and Everyday Life*, London, Sage, 1994.

Barbara Creed, 'Horror and the monstrous-feminine: an imaginary abjection', *Screen* 27 (1): 44–70, January/February 1986. Reprinted in *The Monstrous-Feminine*, 1993.

Barbara Creed, 'Phallic panic: male hysteria and *Dead Ringers*', *Screen* 31 (2): 125–46, summer 1990.

Barbara Creed, *The Monstrous-Feminine: Film, Feminism, Psychoanalysis*, London and New York, Routledge, 1993.

Barbara Creed, *Phallic Panic: Film, Horror and the Primal Uncanny*, Melbourne, Melbourne University Press, 2005.

Charles Derry, *Dark Dreams: A Psychological History of the Modern Horror Film*, London, Thomas Yoseloff, 1977.

Mary Ann Doane, Patricia Mellencamp and Linda Williams (eds), *Revision: Essays in Feminist Film Criticism*, Frederick, MD, University Publications of America/AFI, 1983.

Lotte Eisner, *The Haunted Screen: Expressionism in the German Cinema and the Influence of Max Reinhardt*, London, Thames and Hudson, 1969.

T. R. Ellis, *A Journey into Darkness: The Art of James Whale's Horror Films*, Ann Arbor, MI, University Microfilms, 1985.

Walter Evans, 'Monster movies: a sexual theory', *Journal of Popular Film* 2 (4): 353–65, autumn 1973.

Walter Evans, 'Monster movies and rites of initiation', *Journal of Popular Film* 4 (2): 124–42, autumn 1975.

Roy Huss and T. J. Ross (eds), *Focus on the Horror Film*, Englewood Cliffs, NJ, Prentice-Hall, 1972.

Steve Jenkins, 'Review of *The Thing*', *Monthly Film Bulletin* 49 (583): 158–60, August 1982.

Robert E. Kapsis, '*Dressed to Kill*', *American Film* 7: 52–6, March 1982.

Harlan Kennedy, 'Things that go howl in the id', *Film Comment* 18 (2), March/April 1982.

Julia Kristeva, *The Powers of Horror: An Essay on Abjection*, New York, Columbia University Press, 1982.

Annette Kuhn, 'Border crossing', *Sight and Sound* 2 (3): 13, July 1992.

Ernest Larsen, 'Hi-tech horror', *Jump Cut* 22, November 1977.

Laura Lederer (ed.), *Take Back the Night*, New York, William Morrow and Co, 1980.

Susan Lurie, 'Pornography and the dread of woman', in Lederer (ed.), *Take Back the Night*, 1980.

Brian Murphy, 'Monster movies: they came from beneath the 50s', *Journal of Popular Film and Television* 1 (1): 31–44, winter 1972.

Stephen Neale, *Genre*, London, BFI, 1980a.

Steve Neale, 'Hollywood strikes back: special effects in recent American cinema', *Screen* 21 (3): 101–5, 1980b.

David Pirie, *A Heritage of Horror: The English Gothic Cinema 1946–72*, London, Gordon Fraser, 1973.

Michael Pye and Lynda Myles, *The Movie Brats: How the Film Generation Took Over Hollywood*, New York, Holt, Rinehart and Winston, 1979.

Otto Rank, *The Double*, New York, Signet, 1979; trans. Harry Tucker Jr.

W. H. Rockett, 'Perspectives', *Journal of Popular Film and Television* 10 (3), autumn 1982.

Chris Rodley (ed.), *Cronenberg on Cronenberg*, London, Faber & Faber, 1992.

T. J. Ross, 'Introduction', in Huss and Ross (eds), *Focus on the Horror Film*, 1972.

Gianluca Sergi, 'A cry in the dark: the role of post-classical film sound', in Neale and Smith (eds), *Contemporary Hollywood Cinema*, London, Routledge, 1998.

Stephen Snyder, 'Family life and leisure culture in *The Shining*', *Film Criticism* 7 (1): 4–13, fall 1982.

Andrew Tudor, *Image and Influence: Studies in the Sociology of Film*, London, Allen and Unwin, 1974.

Andrew Tudor, *Monsters and Mad Scientists*, Oxford, Blackwell, 1989.

Linda Williams, 'When the woman looks', in Doane *et al.* (eds), *Revision: Essays in Feminist Film Criticism*, 1983.

Linda Williams, 'Discipline and fun: *Psycho* and postmodern cinema', in Gledhill and Williams (eds), *Reinventing Film Studies*, London, Arnold, 2000.

Tony Williams, 'American cinema in the 70s: family horror', *Movie* 27/28, winter/spring 1980/81.

Robin Wood, *Hitchcock's Films*, New York, A. S. Barnes, 1965.

Robin Wood, 'Introduction', in Britton *et al.* (eds), *American Nightmare*, 1979.

Slavoj Zizek, *For They Know What They Do*, Verso, London, 1991.

TEENPICS

Theodor W. Adorno, *Prisms*, London, Neville Spearman, 1967.

Theodor W. Adorno, 'Culture industry reconsidered', *New German Critique* 6: 12–19, fall 1975. Reprinted in *The Culture Industry*, New York and London, Routledge, 2002.

Theodor W. Adorno, 'On popular music', in Frith and Goodwin (eds), *On Record*, 1990.

Bruce A. Austin (ed.), *Current Research in Film: Audiences, Economics and Law*, Vol. 2, Norwood, NJ, Ablex, 1986.

Richard Benjamin, 'The sense of an ending: youth apocalypse films', *Journal of Film and Video* 56 (4): 24–49, December 2004.

Jonathan Bernstein, *Pretty in Pink: The Golden Age of Teenage Movies*, New York, St Martin's Press, 1997.

Alan Betrock, *The I Was a Teenage Juvenile Delinquent Rock 'N' Roll Horror Beach Party Book: A Complete Guide to the Teen Exploitation Film, 1954–1969*, London, Plexus, 1986.

David Considine, 'The cinema of adolescence', *Journal of Popular Film and Television* 9 (3), 1981.

David Considine, *The Cinema of Adolescence*, Jefferson, NC, McFarland, 1985.

Thomas Doherty, 'Teenagers and teenpics, 1955–1957: a study of exploitation filmmaking', in Austin (ed.), *Current Research in Film*, 1986.

Thomas Doherty, *Teenagers and Teenpics: The Juvenalization of American Movies in the 1950s*, Boston, MA, Unwin Hyman, 1988.

Simon Frith and Andrew Goodwin (eds), *On Record: Rock, Pop and the Written Word*, New York, Pantheon, 1990.

James Gilbert, *A Cycle of Outrage: America's Reaction to the Juvenile Delinquent in the 1950s*, New York and Oxford, Oxford University Press, 1986.

Harvey J. Graff, *Conflicting Paths: Growing up in America*, Cambridge, MA, Harvard University Press, 1995.

James Hay, '"You're tearing me apart!": the primal scene of teen films', *Cultural Studies* 4 (3): 331–8, October 1990.

Dick Hebdige, *Subculture: The Meaning of Style*, London, Methuen, 1979.

bell hooks, '*Kids*: transgressive subjects – reactionary film', in *Reel to Real: Race, Sex and Class at the Movies*, New York and London, Routledge, 1996.

Brigine E. Humbert, '*Cruel Intentions*: adaptations, teenage movie or remake?', *Literature/Film Quarterly* 30 (4): 270–86, December 2002.

Fredric Jameson, *Postmodernism or, The Cultural Logic of Late Capitalism*, London, Verso, 1992.

Roz Kaveney, *Teen Dreams: Reading Teen Film and Television from 'Heathers' to 'Veronica Mars'*, London, I. B. Tauris, 2006.

Joseph F. Kett, *Rites of Passage: Adolescence in America, 1790 to the Present*, New York, Basic Books, 1977.

Peter Krämer, 'Bad boy: notes on a popular figure in American cinema, culture and society, 1895–1905', in Fullerton (ed.), *Celebrating 1895: The Centenary of Cinema*, London, John Libbey, 1998.

Paul Lazarus, 'Audience research in the movie field', *Annals of the American Academy of Political and Social Science* 254, 1947.

Jon Lewis, *The Road to Romance and Ruin: Teen Films and Youth Culture*, New York and London, Routledge, 1992.

Richard Maltby (ed.), *Dreams for Sale: Popular Culture in the 20th Century*, London, Harrap, 1989.

Linda Martin and Kerry Segrave, *Anti-Rock: The Opposition to Rock 'n' Roll*, New York, Da Capo Press, 1993.

Jay McRoy, 'Italian neo-realist influences', in Rombes (ed.), *New Punk Cinema*, Edinburgh, Edinburgh University Press, 2005.

Gary Morris, 'Beyond the beach: social and formal aspects of AIP's beach party movies', *Journal of Popular Film and Television* 21 (1): 2–11, spring 1993. Also in *Bright Lights Film Journal* 21, May 1998; available online.

E. Muller and D. Farris, *That's Sexploitation: The Forbidden World of 'Adults Only' Cinema*, London, Titan Books, 1997.

Martin Quigley, 'Who goes to the movies and who doesn't', *Motion Picture Herald* 10 August 1957.

Eric Schaefer, *"Bold! Daring! Shocking! True!": A History of Exploitation Films, 1919–1959*, Durham and London, Duke University Press, 1999.

Paul Schrader, 'Babes in the hood', *Artforum International* 23 (9): 74–9, May 1995.

Timothy Shary, *Generation Multiplex: The Image of Youth in Contemporary American Cinema*, Austin, University of Texas Press, 2002.

Timothy Shary, *Teen Movies: American Youth on Screen*, London, Wallflower Press, 2005.

Gavin Smith, '*Gummo*', *Sight and Sound* 8 (4): 24, April 1998.

Amy Taubin, 'Chilling and very hot', *Sight and Sound* 5 (11): 16–19, November 1995.

Sarah Thornton, *Club Cultures: Music, Media and Subcultural Capital*, London, Polity Press, 1995.

Robin Wood, 'Part time or can't hardly wait for that *American Pie*: Hollywood high school movies of the 90s', *CineAction!* 58: 2–10, June 2002.

THE WESTERN

André Bazin, 'The western, or the American film par excellence', and 'The evolution of the western', in Gray (ed. and trans.), *What Is Cinema?* Vol. 2, Berkeley, University of California Press, 1971. Revised edition 2005.

Raymond Bellour, 'Alternation, segmentation, hypnosis: interview with Raymond Bellour', *Camera Obscura* 3/4, 1979.

Edward Buscombe, 'The idea of genre in the American cinema', *Screen* 11 (2): 33–45, March/April 1970. Reprinted in Grant (ed.), *Film Genre Reader III*, Austin, University of Texas Press, 2003.

Edward Buscombe (ed.), *The BFI Companion to the Western*, London, BFI/André Deutsch, 1988.

Edward Buscombe and Roberta Pearson (eds), *Back in the Saddle Again: New Essays on the Western*, London, BFI Publishing, 1998.

Ian Cameron and Douglas Pye (eds), *The Movie Book of the Western*, London, Cassell/Studio Vista, 1996.

John Cawelti, *The Six-Gun Mystique*, Bowling Green, OH, Bowling Green University Popular Press, 1971.

John Cawelti, *The Six-Gun Mystique Sequel*, Bowling Green, OH, Bowling Green University Popular Press, 1999.

Richard Collins, 'Genre: a reply to Ed Buscombe', *Screen* 11 (4/5): 66–75, July/October 1970. Reprinted in Nichols (ed.), *Movies and Methods Vol. 1*, Berkeley, University of California Press, 1976.

Pam Cook, 'Women and the western', in *Screening the Past: Memory and Nostalgia in Cinema*, Oxford and New York, Routledge, 2005.

William Cronon, George Miles and Jay Gitlin (eds), *Under an Open Sky: Rethinking America's Western Past*, New York, W. W. Norton, 1992.

Christopher Frayling, 'The American western and American society', in Davies and Neve (eds), *Cinema, Politics and Society in America*, Manchester, Manchester University Press, 1981a.

Christopher Frayling, *Spaghetti Westerns: Cowboys and Europeans from Karl May to Sergio Leone*, London, Routledge & Kegan Paul, 1981b.

Philip French, *Westerns*, London, Secker and Warburg/BFI, 1973.

Stuart Hall and Paddy Whannel, *The Popular Arts*, London, Hutchinson Educational, 1964.

Jim Kitses, *Horizons West*, London, Secker and Warburg/BFI, 1969. Revised edition, *Horizons West: The Western from John Ford to Clint Eastwood*, London, BFI Publishing, 2004.

Jim Kitses, 'An exemplary postmodern western: *The Ballad of Little Jo*', in Kitses and Rickman (eds), *The Western Reader*, New York, Limelight Editions, 1998.

Jacqueline Levitin, 'The western: any good roles for feminists?', *Film Reader* 5: 95–108, 1982.

Patricia Nelson Limerick, *The Legacy of Conquest: The Unbroken Past of the American West*, New York, W. W. Norton, 1987.

Patricia Nelson Limerick, Clyde A. Milner II and Charles E. Rankin (eds), *Trails: Towards a New Western History*, Lawrence, University Press of Kansas, 1991.

Alan Lovell, 'The western', *Screen Education* 41, September/October 1967. Reprinted in Nichols (ed.), *Movies and Methods Vol. 1*, Berkeley, University of California Press, 1976.

Colin McArthur, 'The roots of the western', *Cinema* (UK) 4, October 1969.

Tania Modleski, 'A woman's gotta do ... what a man's gotta do? Cross-dressing in the western', in *Old Wives' Tales: Feminist Re-visions of Film and Other Fictions*, London, I. B. Tauris, 1999.

Laura Mulvey, 'Afterthoughts on "Visual pleasure and narrative cinema" inspired by King Vidor's *Duel in the Sun* (1946)', *Framework* 15/16/17: 12–15, summer 1981. Reprinted in *Visual and Other Pleasures*, Bloomington, Indiana University Press, 1989.

Stephen Neale, *Genre*, London, BFI Publishing, 1980.

Douglas Pye, 'Genre and history: *Fort Apache* and *Liberty Valance*', *Movie* 25: 1–11, winter 1977/78. Reprinted in Cameron and Pye (eds), *The Movie Book of the Western*, London, Studio Vista/Cassell, 1996.

Jean-Louis Rieupeyrout, 'The western: a historical genre', *Quarterly of Film/Radio/Television* 3, winter 1952.

Tom Ryall, 'The notion of genre', *Screen* 11 (2): 22–32, March/April 1970.

Richard Slotkin, *Gunfighter Nation: the Myth of the Frontier in Twentieth-Century America*, New York, Atheneum, 1992.

Jane Tompkins, *West of Everything: The Inner Life of Westerns*, New York, Oxford University Press, 1992.

Jean Wagner, 'The western: history and actuality', in Agel (ed.), *Le western*, Paris, Lettres Modernes, 1961.

Robert Warshow, 'Movie chronicle: the westerner', in *The Immediate Experience*, New York, Atheneum Books, 1970.

The Western, London, BFI National Library Selected Bibliography, n. d.

Paul Willemen, 'Voyeurism, the look and Dwoskin', *Afterimage* (UK) 6: 40–50, 1976.

Will Wright, *Sixguns & Society: A Structural Study of the Western*, Berkeley, University of California Press, 1975.

PART 6: Authorship and Cinema

INTRODUCTION

David Bordwell, 'The art cinema as a mode of film practice', *Film Criticism* 4 (1): 56–64, 1979. Reprinted in Fowler (ed.), *The European Cinema Reader*, London and New York, Routledge, 2002.

Michel Foucault, 'What is an author?', *Screen* 20 (1): 13–33, spring 1979. Reprinted in Rabinow (ed.), *The Foucault Reader*, New York, Pantheon Press, 1984.

Graham Murdock, 'Authorship and organisation', *Screen Education* 35: 19–34, summer 1980. Reprinted in Alvarado, Buscombe and Collins (eds), *The Screen Education Reader*, New York, Columbia University Press, 1997.

Mark Nash, *Dreyer*, London, BFI Publishing, 1977.

Stephen Neale, 'New Hollywood cinema', *Screen* 17 (2): 117–22, summer 1976.

FOR A NEW FRENCH CINEMA: THE *POLITIQUE DES AUTEURS*

Alexandre Astruc, 'The birth of a new avant-garde: la caméra-stylo', *Ecran Français* 144, 1948. In English: Peter Graham (ed. and trans.), *The New Wave*, London, Secker and Warburg/BFI, 1968.

André Bazin, 'La politique des auteurs', *Cahiers du Cinéma* 70, April 1957. In English: Peter Graham (ed. and trans.), *The New Wave*, London, Secker and Warburg/ BFI, 1968.

André Bazin, *Jean Renoir*, Paris, Editions Champ Libre, 1971. In English: Da Capo Press, 1992; 2001; trans. W. W. Halsey and William H. Simon.

Robert Benayoun, 'Le roi est nu', *Positif* 46, June 1962.

Peter Bogdanovich, *Fritz Lang in America*, London, Studio Vista, 1968.

Edward Buscombe, 'Ideas of authorship', *Screen* 14 (3): 75–85, autumn 1973. Reprinted in Caughie (ed.), *Theories of Authorship*, 1981; 2001.

Cahiers du Cinéma 99, September 1959. Special issue on Fritz Lang.

John Caughie (ed.), *Theories of Authorship*, London, Routledge & Kegan Paul/BFI, 1981. Reprinted 2001.

Goffredo Fofi, 'The cinema of the Popular Front in France, 1934–38', *Screen* 13 (4): 5–57, winter 1972/3.

Tom Gunning, *The Films of Fritz Lang*, London, BFI Publishing, 2000.

John Hess, '*La politique des auteurs*: Part one: world view as aesthetics', and 'Part two: Truffaut's manifesto', *Jump Cut* 1: 19–22, May/June 1974, and *Jump Cut* 2: 20–2, July/August 1974. Available online.

Steve Jenkins (ed.), *Fritz Lang: The Image and the Look*, London, BFI Publishing, 1981.

Claire Johnston, *Study Unit 10: Fritz Lang*, London, BFI Education Dept, January 1969. Revised edition 1977.

Anton Kaes, *M*, London, BFI Publishing, 2000.

Siegfried Kracauer, *From Caligari to Hitler: A Psychological History of the German Film*, Princeton, NJ, Princeton University Press, 1947.

David Lusted, *Study Notes for the Slide Set from 'The Big Heat'*, London, BFI Education Dept, June 1979.

Colin McArthur, *The Big Heat*, London, BFI Publishing, 1992.

Martin O'Shaugnessy, *Jean Renoir*, Manchester, Manchester University Press, 2000.

V. F. Perkins, *La Règle du jeu (The Rules of the Game)*, London, BFI Publishing, 2003.

Julian Petley, *BFI Distribution Library Catalogue 1978*, London, BFI, 1978.

Jean Renoir, *My Life and My Films*, London, Collins, 1974; trans. Norman Denny.

Jacques Rivette and François Truffaut, 'Renoir in America', *Sight and Sound* 24 (1), July/September 1954.

François Truffaut, 'A certain tendency of the French cinema', *Cahiers du Cinéma* 31, January 1954. In English: Bill Nichols (ed.), *Movies and Methods Vol. 1*, Berkeley, University of California Press, 1976.

Peter Wollen, '"Ontology" and "materialism" in film', *Screen* 17 (1): 7–23, spring 1976. Reprinted in *Readings and Writings*, London, Verso, 1982.

Auteurs and metteurs en scène

Charles Barr, *English Hitchcock*, Moffat, Cameron & Hollis, 1999.

André Bazin, 'Hitchcock versus Hitchcock', in LaValley (ed.), *Focus on Hitchcock*, Englewood Cliffs, NJ, Prentice-Hall, 1972.

Raymond Bellour, 'Hitchcock the enunciator', *Camera Obscura* 2: 66–91, fall 1977.

Robert E. Kapsis, *Hitchcock: The Making of a Reputation*, Chicago, University of Chicago Press, 1992.

Tania Modleski, *The Women Who Knew Too Much: Hitchcock and Feminist Theory*, New York, Routledge, 1988.

Laura Mulvey, 'Visual pleasure and narrative cinema', *Screen* 16 (3), autumn 1975. Reprinted in *Visual and Other Pleasures*, London and New York, Macmillan, 1989.

V. F. Perkins, *Film as Film: Understanding and Judging Movies*, London, Penguin, 1972.

Tom Ryall, *Blackmail*, London, BFI Publishing, 1993.

Tom Ryall, *Alfred Hitchcock and the British Cinema*, New York, Continuum, 1996.

John Smith, 'Conservative individualism: a selection of English Hitchcock', *Screen* 13 (3): 51–70, autumn 1972.

François Truffaut, *Hitchcock*, London, Secker and Warburg, 1968. Revised edition, Simon and Schuster, 1985.

Elisabeth Weis, *The Silent Scream: Hitchcock's Sound Track*, Madison, NJ, Fairleigh Dickinson University Press, 1982.

Linda Williams, 'Learning to scream', *Sight and Sound* 4 (12): 14–17, December 1994.

Linda Williams, 'Discipline and fun: *Psycho* and postmodern cinema', in Gledhill and Williams (eds), *Reinventing Film Studies*, London, Hodder Arnold, 2000.

Peter Wollen, 'Hitchcock's vision', *Cinema* (UK), June 1969, pp. 2–4.

Robin Wood, *Hitchcock's Films*, New York, Yoseloff, 1978.

Robin Wood, *Hitchcock's Films Revisited*, New York, Columbia University Press, 1989.

Auteur and studio

André Bazin, *Orson Welles: A Critical View*, London, Elm Tree Books, 1978; trans. Jonathan Rosenbaum.

André Bazin, 'William Wyler or the Jansenist of mise-en-scène', in Williams (ed.), *Realism and the Cinema*, London, Routledge & Kegan Paul/BFI Publishing, 1980.

Robert L. Carringer, *The Making of 'Citizen Kane'*, Berkeley, University of California Press, 1992.

Stephen Heath, 'Film and system: terms of analysis Part I', *Screen* 16 (1): 7–77, spring 1975; 'Part II', *Screen* 16 (2): 91–113, summer 1975.

Clinton Heylin, *Despite the System: Orson Welles vs the Hollywood Studios*, Edinburgh, Canongate Books, 2006.

Pauline Kael, *The Citizen Kane Book*, London, Secker and Warburg, 1971.

Laura Mulvey, *Citizen Kane*, London, BFI Publishing, 1992.

V. F. Perkins, *The Magnificent Ambersons*, London, BFI Publishing, 1999.

Peter Wollen, *Study Unit No. 9: Orson Welles*, London, BFI Education, 1969. Reprinted 1977.

The Nouvelle Vague

Don Allen, *François Truffaut*, London, Secker and Warburg/BFI, 1974.

David Bordwell and Kristin Thompson, *Film Art: An Introduction*, Reading, Berkshire, Addison-Wesley, 1979. Fourth edition, 1993; revised edition, New York, McGraw-Hill, 2004.

Wheeler Winston Dixon, *The Films of Jean-Luc Godard*, New York, State University of New York Press, 1997.

Susan Hayward, *French National Cinema*, London, Routledge, 1993.

Marsha Kinder and Beverle Houston, *Close-Up: A Critical Perspective on Film*, New York, Harcourt Brace, 1972.

Colin MacCabe, *Godard: A Portrait of the Artist at Seventy*, London, Bloomsbury, 2003.

Robert Stam, *François Truffaut and Friends: Modernism, Sexuality and Film Adaptation*, New Brunswick, NJ, Rutgers University Press, 2006.

François Truffaut, 'A certain tendency of the French cinema', *Cahiers du Cinéma* 31, January 1954. In English: Bill Nichols (ed.), *Movies and Methods Vol. I*, Berkeley, University of California Press, 1976.

Christopher Williams, 'Politics and production: some pointers through the work of Jean-Luc Godard', *Screen* 12 (4): 6–24, winter 1971/72.

THE AUTEUR THEORY

James Agee, *Agee on Film: Reviews and Comments by James Agee*, London, Peter Owen, 1963.

Geoff Andrew, *The Films of Nicholas Ray: The Poet of Nightfall*, London, BFI Publishing, 2004.

David Bordwell and Kristin Thompson, *Film Art: An Introduction*, Reading, Berkshire, Addison-Wesley, 1979. Fourth edition, 1993; revised edition, New York, McGraw-Hill, 2004.

Pam Cook, 'The art of exploitation: or how to get into the movies', *Monthly Film Bulletin* 52 (623): 367–9, December 1985.

Pam Cook, 'Women and the western', in *Screening the Past: Memory and Nostalgia in Cinema*, Oxford and New York, Routledge, 2005.

Roger Corman and Jim Jerome, *How I Made a Hundred Movies in Hollywood and Never Lost a Dime*, New York, Da Capo Press, 1998.

Wheeler W. Dixon, 'In defense of Roger Corman', *The Velvet Light Trap* 16: 11–15, fall 1976.

Bernard Eisenschitz, *Nicholas Ray: An American Journey*, London, Faber & Faber, 1993.

Tom Gunning, *D. W. Griffith and the Origins of American Narrative Film: The Early Years*, Champaign, University of Illinois Press, 1993.

Molly Haskell, *From Reverence to Rape*, New York, Holt, Rinehart and Winston, 1974.

Jim Hillier, 'The economics of independence: Roger Corman and New World Pictures', *Movie* 31/32: 43–53, winter 1986.

Pauline Kael, *The Citizen Kane Book*, London, Secker and Warburg, 1971.

J. F. Kreidl, *Nicholas Ray*, Boston, MA, Twayne Publishers, 1977.

Alison McMahan, *Alice Guy Blaché: The Lost Visionary of the Cinema*, New York, Continuum, 2002.

Gary Morris, 'Introduction to New World Pictures', *Bright Lights* 1 (1), autumn 1974.

Gary Morris, 'Interview with Roger Corman', *Bright Lights* 1 (2), spring 1975. Available online.

Edward Murray, *Nine American Film Critics*, New York, Frederick Ungar, 1975.

The New American Cinema Group, 'The first statement of the group', *Film Culture* 22/23, summer 1961.

Geoffrey Nowell-Smith, 'Six authors in pursuit of *The Searchers*', *Screen* 17 (1), spring 1976. Reprinted in Caughie (ed.), *Theories of Authorship*, London and New York, Routledge & Kegan Paul/BFI, 1981; 2001.

V. F. Perkins, 'The cinema of Nicholas Ray', in Cameron (ed.), *Movie Reader*, London, November Books, 1972.

Andrew Sarris, 'Notes on the auteur theory in 1962', *Film Culture* 27, winter 1962/63.

Andrew Sarris, *The American Cinema: Directors and Directions 1929–1968*, New York, Dutton, 1968.

Andrew Sarris, *'You Ain't Heard Nothing Yet': The American Talking Film, History and Memory, 1927–1949*, New York, Oxford University Press, 1998.

Yannis Tzioumakis, *American Independent Cinema: An Introduction*, Edinburgh, Edinburgh University Press, 2006.

David Will and Paul Willemen (eds), *Roger Corman: The Millennic Vision*, Edinburgh, Edinburgh Film Festival, 1970.

Mike Wilmington, 'Nicholas Ray: the years at RKO: Parts I and II', *The Velvet Light Trap* 10, autumn 1973; and 11, winter 1973/74.

AUTEUR THEORY IN BRITAIN

Lindsay Anderson, '*Paisà*', *Sequence* 2, winter 1947.

Lindsay Anderson, 'The last sequence of *On the Waterfront*', *Sight and Sound* 24 (3): 127–30, January/March 1955.

Ian Cameron (ed.), *Movie Reader*, London, November Books, 1972.

Raymond Durgnat, *A Mirror for England: British Movies from Austerity to Affluence*, London, Faber & Faber, 1971.

Colin Gardner, *Karel Reisz*, Manchester, Manchester University Press, 2006.

Kevin Gough-Yates (ed.), *Michael Powell in Collaboration with Emeric Pressburger*, London, BFI, 1971.

O. O. Green [Raymond Durgnat], 'Michael Powell', *Movie* 14, October 1965.

Erik Hedling, *Lindsay Anderson: Maverick Filmmaker*, London, Cassell, 1998.

John Hill, 'Ideology, economy and the British cinema', in Barrett, Corrigan, Kuhn and Wolff (eds), *Ideology and Cultural Production*, London, Croom Helm, 1979.

John Hill, *Sex, Class and Realism: British Cinema 1956–1963*, London, BFI Publishing, 1986.

Raymond Lefèvre and Roland Lacourbe, *Trente ans de cinéma britannique*, Paris, Editions Cinéma 76, 1976.

Alan Lovell, *The British Cinema: The Unknown Cinema*, London, BFI Education Dept Seminar Paper, 1969.

Alan Lovell, 'Free cinema', in Lovell and Hillier, *Studies in Documentary*, London, Secker and Warburg/BFI, 1972.

Alan Lovell, *Don Siegel: American Cinema*, London, BFI, 1975.

Alan Lovell, 'Brecht in Britain: Lindsay Anderson', *Screen* 16 (4): 62–72, winter 1975/76.

Alan Lovell, 'The unknown cinema of Britain', *Cinema Journal* 11 (2): 1–8, spring 1972.

Robert Murphy (ed.), *The British Cinema Book*, London, BFI Publishing, 1997.

Victor Perkins, 'The British cinema', in Cameron (ed.), *Movie Reader*, 1972.

Karel Reisz, 'Interview', *Cinéma International* 16, 1967.

Sam Rohdie, 'Review: *Movie Reader*, *Film as Film*', *Screen* 13 (4): 135–45, winter 1972/73.

Paul Ryan (ed.), *Never Apologise: The Collected Writings of Lindsay Anderson*, Medford, NJ, Plexus, 2004.

Movie and mise en scène analysis

Charles Barr, '*King and Country*', in Cameron (ed.), *Movie Reader*, 1972.

Charles Barr, 'CinemaScope: before and after', in Mast and Cohen (eds), *Film Theory and Criticism*, New York, Oxford University Press, 1974.

David Bordwell and Kristin Thompson, *Film Art: An Introduction*, Reading, Berkshire, Addison-Wesley, 1979. Fourth edition, 1993; revised edition, New York, McGraw-Hill, 2004.

Ian Cameron (ed.), *Movie Reader*, London, November Books, 1972.

Michel Ciment, *Kazan on Kazan*, London, Secker and Warburg/BFI, 1974.

Michel Ciment, *Conversations with Losey*, London, Methuen, 1985.

Richard Collins, 'Media/film studies', in Gledhill (ed.), *Film and Media Studies in Higher Education*, 1981.

Paul Filmer, 'Literary criticism and the mass media, with special reference to the cinema', in Wollen (ed.), *Working Papers on the Cinema*, 1969.

Colin Gardner, *Joseph Losey*, Manchester, Manchester University Press, 2004.

Christine Gledhill (ed.), *Film and Media Studies in Higher Education*, London, BFI Education, 1981.

Brian Henderson, 'The long take', in Nichols (ed.), *Movies and Methods Vol. I*, 1976.

Jim Hillier, '*East of Eden*', *Movie* 19: 22–3, winter 1971/72.

Raymond Lefèvre, 'Interview with Joseph Losey', *Image et son* 202, February 1967.

Paul Mayersberg, 'Contamination', in Cameron (ed.), *Movie Reader*, 1972.

Bill Nichols (ed.), *Movies and Methods Vol. I*, Berkeley, University of California Press, 1976.

V. F. Perkins, '*America, America*', *Movie* 19: 35–8, winter 1971/72.

V. F. Perkins, *Film as Film: Understanding and Judging Movies*, London, Penguin Books, 1972.

V. F. Perkins, 'A reply to Sam Rohdie', *Screen* 13 (4): 146–51, winter 1972/73.

Pierre Rissient, *Losey*, Paris, Editions du Cinéma, 1966.

Richard Roud, 'The reluctant exile', *Sight and Sound* 48 (3): 145–7, summer 1979.

Richard Schickel, *Elia Kazan: A Biography*, London, HarperCollins, 2005.

Roger Tailleur, *Elia Kazan*, Paris, Editions Seghers, 1971.

Michael Walker '*Splendor in the Grass*', *Movie* 19: 32–4, winter 1971/72.

Peter Wollen (ed.), *Working Papers on the Cinema: Sociology and Semiology*, London, BFI Education Dept, 1969.

Robin Wood, 'The Kazan problem', *Movie* 19: 29–31, winter 1971/72.

British auteurs

Ian Christie, 'The scandal of *Peeping Tom*', in *Powell, Pressburger and Others*, 1978.

Ian Christie (ed.), *Powell, Pressburger and Others*, London, BFI Publishing, 1978.

Ian Christie, *Arrows of Desire*, London and Boston, MA, Faber & Faber, 1994. Rev. edn.

Mark Connolly, *The Red Shoes*, London, I. B. Tauris, 2005.

Pam Cook, *I Know Where I'm Going!*, London, BFI Publishing, 2002.

Raymond Durgnat, *A Mirror for England: British Movies from Austerity to Affluence*, London, Faber & Faber, 1971.

Richard Dyer, *Brief Encounter*, London, BFI Publishing, 1993.

John Ellis, 'Art, culture and quality: terms for a cinema in the forties and seventies', *Screen* 19 (3): 9–49, autumn 1978. Revised in Higson (ed.), *Dissolving Views: Key Writings on British Cinema*, London, Cassell, 1996.

Kevin Gough-Yates (ed.), *Michael Powell in Collaboration With Emeric Pressburger*, London, British Film Institute, 1971.

O. O. Green [Raymond Durgnat], 'Michael Powell', *Movie* 14, October 1965.

Raymond Lefèvre and Roland Lacourbe, *Trente ans de cinéma britannique*, Paris, Editions Cinema 76, 1976.

Kevin Macdonald, *Emeric Pressburger: The Life and Death of a Screenwriter*, London, Faber & Faber, 1996.

Geoffrey Macnab, *J. Arthur Rank and the British Film Industry*, London and New York, Routledge, 1993.

Andrew Moor, *Powell and Pressburger: A Cinema of Magic Spaces*, London, I. B. Tauris, 2005.

Duncan Petrie, *The British Cinematographer*, London, BFI Publishing, 1996.

Screen 46 (1), spring 2005. Special issue on Michael Powell.

Sarah Street, *Transatlantic Crossings: British Feature Films in the USA*, New York, Continuum, 2002.

Contemporary British directors

Lester Friedman (ed.), *Fires Were Started: British Cinema and Thatcherism*, London, Wallflower Press, 2006.

Christine Geraghty, *My Beautiful Laundrette*, London, I. B. Tauris, 2004.

Andrew Higson (ed.), *Dissolving Views: Key Writings on British Cinema*, London and New York, Cassell, 1996.

Sarita Malik, 'Beyond "the cinema of duty"? The pleasures of hybridity: black British film of the 1980s and 1990s', in Higson (ed.), *Dissolving Views*, 1996.

Sarita Malik, *Representing Black Britain: Black and Asian Images on Television*, London, Sage Publishing, 2001.

Murray Smith, *Trainspotting*, London, BFI Publishing, 2002.

British cinema: auteur and studio

Charles Barr, *Ealing Studios*, London/Newton Abbot, Cameron & Tayleur/David & Charles, 1977. Revised edition, Moffat, Cameron & Hollis, 1999.

Ian Christie, 'Introduction', in Christie (ed.), *Powell, Pressburger and Others*, London, BFI Publishing, 1978.

Bernard Cohn, 'Interview with Mackendrick', *Positif* 92, February 1968.

Ian Conrich, 'Traditions of the British horror film', in Murphy (ed.), *The British Cinema Book*, London, BFI Publishing, 1997.

Pam Cook, 'Mandy: daughter of transition', in *Screening the Past: Memory and Nostalgia in Cinema*, Oxford and New York, Routledge, 2005.

John Ellis, 'Made in Ealing', *Screen* 16 (1): 78–127, spring 1975.

John Ellis, 'Art, culture and quality: terms for a cinema in the forties and seventies', *Screen* 19 (3): 9–49, autumn 1978. Revised in Higson (ed.), *Dissolving Views*, London and New York, Cassell, 1996.

Christine Geraghty, *British Cinema in the Fifties: Gender, Genre and the New Look*, London and New York, Routledge, 2000.

Peter Hutchings, *Hammer and Beyond: British Horror Film*, Manchester, Manchester University Press, 1993.

Peter Hutchings, *Terence Fisher*, Manchester, Manchester University Press, 2001.

Philip Kemp, *Lethal Innocence: The Cinema of Alexander Mackendrick*, London, Croom Helm, 1991.

Philip Kemp, 'The long shadow: Robert Hamer after Ealing', *Film Comment* May/June 1995, pp. 71–8. Revised in MacKillop and Sinyard (eds), *British Cinema of the 1950s: A Celebration*, Manchester, Manchester University Press, 2003.

Little Shoppe of Horrors 4, April 1978. Special issue on Hammer.

Colin McArthur, *Scotch Reels*, London, BFI, 1982.

Colin McArthur, *Whisky Galore! and The Maggie*, London, I. B. Tauris, 2002.

David Pirie, *A Heritage of Horror: The English Gothic Cinema 1946–1972*, London, Gordon Fraser, 1973.

Tim Pulleine, 'A song and dance at the local: thoughts on Ealing', in Murphy (ed.), *The British Cinema Book*, London, BFI Publishing, 1997.

Philip Simpson, 'Directions to Ealing', *Screen Education* 24: 5–16, autumn 1977.

AUTEUR THEORY AND STRUCTURALISM

Louis Althusser, *For Marx*, Harmondsworth, Penguin, 1969; trans. Ben Brewster.

Louis Althusser, *Lenin and Philosophy and Other Essays*, London, New Left Books, 1971; trans. Ben Brewster.

Catherine Belsey, *Critical Practice*, London, Methuen, 1980.

Jonathan Culler, *Structuralist Poetics*, London, Routledge & Kegan Paul, 1975.

Sylvia Harvey, *May '68 and Film Culture*, London, BFI Publishing, 1978.

Stephen Heath, *The Nouveau Roman: A Study in the Practice of Writing*, London, Elek Books, 1972.

Edmund Leach, *Lévi-Strauss*, London, Fontana, 1970.

Geoffrey Nowell-Smith, *Visconti*, London, Secker and Warburg/BFI, 1967. Revised edition 1973.

Lee Russell [Peter Wollen], 'Jean-Luc Godard', *New Left Review* 38, September/October 1966.

Peter Wollen, *Signs and Meaning in the Cinema*, London, Secker and Warburg/BFI, 1969. Revised edition 1972; expanded edition, London, BFI, 1998.

Robin Wood, 'Jean-Luc Godard', *New Left Review* 38, September/October 1966.

Structuralism, individualism and auteur theory

Louis Althusser, *Lenin and Philosophy and Other Essays*, London, New Left Books, 1971; trans Ben Brewster.

Alexander Astruc, 'The birth of a new avant-garde: la caméra-stylo' [1948], in Graham (ed.), *The New Wave: Critical Landmarks*, New York, Doubleday, 1968.

Jean-Marie Benoist, 'The end of structuralism', *20th Century Studies* 3, May 1970.

Jacques Lacan, 'The mirror stage as formative of the function of the I', in *Ecrits: A Selection*, London, Tavistock Publications, 1977; trans. Alan Sheridan.

Edmund Leach, *Lévi-Strauss*, London, Fontana, 1970.

Geoffrey Nowell-Smith, 'Cinema and structuralism', *20th Century Studies* 3, May 1970.

Cultural politics and auteur theory

Jean-Louis Comolli and Jean Narboni, 'Cinema/ideology/criticism', *Cahiers du Cinéma*, October 1969. In English: Nick Browne (ed.), *Cahiers du Cinéma 1969–1972: The Politics of Representation*, Cambridge, MA, Harvard University Press, 1989.

Thomas Elsaesser, 'Tales of sound and fury', *Monogram* 4: 2–15, 1972. Reprinted in Gledhill (ed.), *Home Is Where the Heart Is: Studies in Melodrama and the Woman's Film*, London, BFI Publishing, 1987.

Jon Halliday, *Sirk on Sirk*, London, Secker and Warburg/BFI, 1971a.

Jon Halliday, 'Notes on Sirk's German films', *Screen* 12 (2): 8–13, summer 1971b.

Jon Halliday, '*All That Heaven Allows*', in Mulvey and Halliday (eds), *Douglas Sirk*, 1972.

Sylvia Harvey, *May '68 and Film Culture*, London, BFI Publishing, 1978.

Barbara Klinger, *Melodrama and Meaning: History, Culture, and the Films of Douglas Sirk*, Bloomington, Indiana University Press, 1994.

Laura Mulvey, 'Notes on Sirk and melodrama', *Movie* 25, winter 1977/78. Reprinted in Gledhill (ed.), *Home Is Where the Heart Is: Studies in Melodrama and the Woman's Film*, BFI Publishing, 1987.

Laura Mulvey and Jon Halliday (eds), *Douglas Sirk*, Edinburgh, Edinburgh Film Festival, 1972.

Screen 12 (2), summer 1971. Special issue on Douglas Sirk.

Paul Willemen, 'Distanciation and Douglas Sirk', *Screen* 12 (2): 63–7, summer 1971.

Auteur structuralism under attack

Richard Dyer, *Stars*, London, BFI Publishing, 1979. Revised edition 1998.

Charles Eckert, 'The English cine-structuralists', *Film Comment* 9 (3): 46–51, May/June 1973. Reprinted in Caughie (ed.), *Theories of Authorship*, London and New York, Routledge & Kegan Paul/BFI, 1981. Reprinted 2001.

Molly Haskell, *From Reverence to Rape: The Treatment of Women in the Movies*, Chicago, University of Chicago Press, 1987.

Brian Henderson, 'Critique of cine-structuralism, Part I', *Film Quarterly* 27 (1): 25–34, autumn 1973; 'Part II', *Film Quarterly* 27 (2): 37–46, winter 1973/74.

Jim Hillier and Peter Wollen (eds), *Howard Hawks: American Artist*, London, BFI Publishing, 1996.

Peter Wollen, *Signs and Meaning in the Cinema*, London, Secker and Warburg/BFI, 1969. Revised edition 1972; expanded edition, London, BFI, 1998.

Robin Wood, *Howard Hawks*, London, Secker and Warburg/BFI, 1968. Revised edition, BFI Publishing, 1981; new edition by Wayne State University Press, 2006.

Robin Wood, 'To have (written) and have not (directed)', in Nichols (ed.), *Movies and Methods Vol. I*, Berkeley, University of California Press, 1976.

AUTEUR STUDY AFTER STRUCTURALISM

Lindsay Anderson, '*The Searchers*', *Sight and Sound* 26 (2), autumn 1956. Reprinted in Caughie (ed.), *Theories of Authorship*, 1981; 2001.

Lindsay Anderson, *About John Ford*, London, Plexus, 1981.

André Bazin, 'The evolution of the language of cinema', in Gray (ed. and trans.), *What Is Cinema?* Vol. I, Berkeley, University of California Press, 1971. Revised edition 2005.

Ben Brewster, 'Notes on the text "Young Mr Lincoln" by the editors of *Cahiers du Cinéma*', *Screen* 14 (3): 29–43, autumn 1973.

Edward Buscombe, 'Ideas of authorship', *Screen* 14 (3): 75–85, autumn 1973. Reprinted in Caughie (ed.), *Theories of Authorship*, 1981; 2001.

Edward Buscombe, *Stagecoach*, London, BFI Publishing, 1992.

John Caughie, 'Teaching through authorship', *Screen Education* 17, winter 1975/76.

John Caughie (ed.), *Theories of Authorship*, London and New York, Routledge & Kegan Paul/BFI, 1981. Reprinted 2001.

Editors of *Cahiers du Cinéma*, 'John Ford's *Young Mr Lincoln*', *Cahiers du Cinéma* 223, 1970. In English: *Screen* 13 (3): 5–44, autumn 1972.

John Ellis, 'Teaching authorship: Ford or fraud?', in Gledhill (ed.), *Film and Media Studies in Higher Education*, London, BFI Education, 1981.

Tag Gallagher, *John Ford: The Man and His Films*, Berkeley, University of California Press, 1988.

Stephen Heath, 'Comment on "The idea of authorship"', *Screen* 14 (3): 86–91, autumn 1973. Reprinted in Caughie (ed.), *Theories of Authorship*, 1981; 2001.

Charles Higham and Joel Greenberg, *Hollywood in the 40s*, London, Tantivy Press, 1968.

Jim Kitses, *Horizons West: The Western from John Ford to Clint Eastwood*, London, BFI Publishing, 2004. Revised edition.

Alan Lovell, *Don Siegel: American Cinema*, London, BFI, 1975.

Geoffrey Nowell-Smith, 'Six authors in pursuit of *The Searchers*', *Screen* 17 (1): 26–33, spring 1976. Reprinted in Caughie (ed.), *Theories of Authorship*, 1981; 2001.

Andrew Sarris, *The John Ford Movie Mystery*, London, Secker and Warburg/BFI, 1976.

Screen Education 17, winter 1975/76. Special issue on *The Searchers*.

Gaylyn Studlar and Matthew Bernstein (eds), *John Ford Made Westerns: Filming the Legend in the Sound Era*, Bloomington, Indiana University Press, 2001.

Peter Wollen, *Signs and Meaning in the Cinema*, London, Secker and Warburg/BFI, 1969. Revised edition 1972; expanded edition, London, BFI, 1998.

Robin Wood, *Howard Hawks*, London, Secker and Warburg/BFI, 1968. Revised edition, BFI Publishing, 1981; new edition by Wayne State University Press, 2006.

THE AUTHOR NEVER DIES

Raymond Bellour and Mary Lea Bandy (eds), *Jean-Luc Godard: Sound + Image*, New York, Museum of Modern Art, 1992.

'The Estates General of the French cinema, May 1968', *Screen* 13 (4): 58–88, winter 1972/73.

Peter Harcourt, *Six European Directors*, Harmondsworth, Penguin, 1974.

Colin MacCabe, *Godard: Images, Sound, Politics*, London, Macmillan/BFI, 1980.

Colin MacCabe, *Godard: A Portrait of the Artist at Seventy*, London, Bloomsbury, 2004.

V. F. Perkins, *Film as Film: Understanding and Judging Movies*, Harmondsworth, Penguin, 1972.

Michael Temple, James S. Williams and Michael Witt (eds), *For Ever Godard: The Work of Jean-Luc Godard, 1950 to the Present*, London, Black Dog Publishing, 2003.

Peter Wollen, *Signs and Meaning in the Cinema*, London, Secker and Warburg/BFI, 1969. Revised edition 1972; expanded edition, London, BFI, 1998.

Peter Wollen, 'Counter-cinema: *Vent d'est*', *Afterimage* (UK) 4, autumn 1972, and 'The two avant-gardes', in Hardy, Johnston and Willemen (eds), *Edinburgh '76 Magazine*, Edinburgh, Edinburgh Film Festival, 1976. Reprinted in *Readings and Writings*, London, Verso, 1982.

Auteurism and women directors

Sarah Benton, *Patterns of Discrimination Against Women in the Film and Television Industries*, London, Association of Cinematograph Television and Allied Technicians, 1975.

Janet Bergstrom, 'Re-reading the work of Claire Johnston', *Camera Obscura* 3/4: 21–31, summer 1979.

Pam Cook, 'Approaching the work of Dorothy Arzner', in Johnston (ed.), *Dorothy Arzner: Towards a Feminist Cinema*, London, BFI Publishing, 1975. Reprinted in Penley (ed.), *Feminism and Film Theory*, 1988.

Pam Cook, '"Exploitation films" and feminism', *Screen* 17 (2): 122–7, summer 1976.

Pam Cook, 'The pleasures and perils of exploitation films', in *Screening the Past: Memory and Nostalgia in Cinema*, New York and Oxford, Routledge, 2005.

Anne Cottringer, 'Representation and feminist film practice', in Cowie (ed.), *Catalogue of British Film Institute Productions 1977–1978*, London, BFI, 1978.

Carla Despineux and Verena Mund (eds), *Girls Gangs Guns*, Marburg, Schüren, 2000.

Alexander Doty, 'Whose text is it anyway?: queer cultures, queer auteurs and queer authorship', *Quarterly Review of Film and Video* 15 (1): 41-54, 1993.

Sandy Flitterman-Lewis, *To Desire Differently: Feminism and the French Cinema*, New York, Columbia University Press, 1996. Revised edition.

Terry Curtis Fox, 'Fully female', *Film Comment* 12 (6): 46–52, November/December 1976.

Sylvia Harvey, *May '68 and Film Culture*, London, BFI Publishing, 1978.

Jim Hillier and Aaron Lipstadt, *BFI Dossier 7: Roger Corman's New World*, London, BFI, 1981.

Claire Johnston, 'Women's cinema as counter-cinema', in *Notes on Women's Cinema*, London, SEFT, 1974. Reprinted in Thornham (ed.), *Feminist Film Theory: A Reader*, New York, New York University Press, 1999.

Claire Johnston, 'Dorothy Arzner: critical strategies', in *Dorothy Arzner: Towards a Feminist Cinema*, London, BFI, 1975. Reprinted in Penley (ed.), *Feminism and Film Theory*, 1988.

Terry Lovell, *Pictures of Reality*, London, BFI, 1980.

Barbara Martineau, 'Subjecting her ob-jectification', in Johnston (ed.), *Notes on Women's Cinema*, London, SEFT, 1974.

Judith Mayne, *Directed by Dorothy Arzner*, Bloomington, Indiana University Press, 1995.

Laura Mulvey, 'Feminism, film and the avant-garde', *Framework* 10, spring 1979. Reprinted in *Visual and Other Pleasures*, Bloomington, Indiana University Press, 1989.

Steve Neale, 'Art cinema as institution', Screen 22 (1), 1981. Reprinted in Fowler (ed.), *The European Cinema Reader*, London and New York, Routledge, 2002.

Gerald Peary, 'Dorothy Arzner', *Cinema* (USA) 34, autumn 1974.

Gerald Peary and Karyn Kay, 'Interview with Dorothy Arzner', in Johnston (ed.), *Dorothy Arzner: Towards a Feminist Cinema*, London, BFI Publishing, 1975.

Constance Penley (ed.), *Feminism and Film Theory*, New York and London, Routledge, 1988.

Alison Smith, *Agnès Varda*, Manchester, Manchester University Press, 1998.

Peter Wollen, 'The two avant-gardes', in Hardy, Johnston and Willemen (eds), *Edinburgh '76 Magazine: Psychoanalysis/Cinema/Avante-Garde*, Edinburgh, Edinburgh Film Festival, 1976. Reprinted in *Readings and Writings*, London, Verso, 1982.

AUTEURISM IN THE 1990s

Dudley Andrew, 'The unauthorised auteur today', in Collins, Radner and Collins (eds), *Film Theory Goes to the Movies*, 1993.

Timothy Asch, 'Collaboration in ethnographic filmmaking: a personal view', in Rollwagen (ed.), *Anthropological Filmmaking*, Amsterdam, Harwood Academic, 1990.

Roland Barthes, 'The death of the author', in *Image-Music-Text*, New York, Hill and Wang, 1977; trans. Stephen Heath. Reprinted in Caughie (ed.), *Theories of Authrorship*, 1981; 2001.

André Bazin, 'La politique des auteurs', in Hillier (ed.), *Cahiers du Cinéma: The 1950s: Neo-Realism, Hollywood, The New Wave*, Cambridge, MA, Harvard University Press, 1985.

Denise D. Bielby and William T. Bielby, 'Women and men in film: gender inequality among writers in a culture industry', *Gender & Society* 10 (3): 248–70, June 1996.

Geraldine Bloustein, 'Jane Campion: memory, motif and music', *Continuum* 5 (2): 29–39, 1992.

Jay Boyer, *Bob Rafelson: Hollywood Maverick*, New York, Twayne, 1996.

Edward Buscombe, 'Ideas of authorship', in Caughie (ed.), *Theories of Authorship*, 1981; 2001.

John Caughie (ed.), *Theories of Authorship*, London and New York, Routledge & Kegan Paul/BFI, 1981. Reprinted 2001.

Michael Chion, *David Lynch*, London, BFI Publishing, 1995; trans. Robert Julian.

Jim Collins, Hilary Radner and Ava Preacher Collins (eds), *Film Theory Goes to the Movies*, New York, Routledge, 1993.

Timothy Corrigan, *A Cinema without Walls: Movies and Culture after Vietnam*, New York, Routledge, 1991.

Rosalind Coward, 'Dennis Potter and the question of the television author', *Critical Quarterly* 29 (4): 79–87, 1987.

Stuart Cunningham, *Featuring Australia: The Cinema of Charles Chauvel*, Sydney, Allen & Unwin, 1991.

Gilles Deleuze, *Negotiations 1972–1990*, New York, Columbia University Press, 1995; trans. Martin Joughin.

Alexander Doty, 'Whose text is it anyway?: queer cultures, queer auteurs and queer authorship', *Quarterly Review of Film and Video* 15 (1): 41–54, 1993.

Richard Dyer, *White*, London and New York, Routledge, 1997.

Bernard Eisenschitz, *Nicholas Ray: An American Journey*, London, Faber & Faber, 1993; trans. Tom Milne.

Thomas Elsaesser, *Fassbinder's Germany: History, Identity, Subject*, Amsterdam, Amsterdam University Press, 1996.

Film Criticism 19 (3), 1995. Special issue on The New Auteurism.

Film History 7 (4), 1995. Special issue on Auteurism Revisited.

Elliot Forbes and David Pierce, 'Who owns the movies?', *Film Comment* 30 (6): 43–50, 1994.

Michel Foucault, 'What is an author?', in Lodge (ed.), *Modern Criticism and Theory: A Reader*, London, Longman, 1988. Also in Rabinow (ed.), *The Foucault Reader*, New York, Pantheon Press, 1984.

Philip French, *Malle on Malle*, London, Faber & Faber, 1992.

Diana Fuss (ed.), *Inside/Out: Lesbian Theories, Gay Theories*, New York, Routledge, 1991.

Susan Hayward, *Luc Besson*, Manchester, Manchester University Press, 1998.

Laurence Kardish with Juliane Lorenz, *Rainer Werner Fassbinder*, New York, Museum of Modern Art, 1997.

Jim Kitses, '*Pat Garrett and Billy the Kid*', in Kitses and Rickman (eds), *The Western Reader*, New York, Limelight Editions, 1998.

Annette Kuhn, *Queen of the 'B's: Ida Lupino behind the Camera*, Westport, CT, Praeger, 1995.

Janet Maslin, 'So, what's wrong with this picture?', *New York Times* 5 June 1998, pp. E1, E18.

Judith Mayne, 'A parallax view of lesbian authorship', in Fuss (ed.), *Inside/Out*, 1991.

L[loyd] M[ichaels], 'Editor's note', *Film Criticism* 19 (3): 1, 1995.

Anthony Mosawi, 'The control by novelists of film versions of their work', *European Law Review* 6 (3): 83–7, 1995.

James Naremore, 'Authorship and the cultural politics of film criticism', *Film Quarterly* 44 (1): 14–22, 1990.

New German Critique 63, autumn 1994. Special issue on Fassbinder.

Jessie Algeron Rhines, *Black Film/White Money*, New Brunswick, NJ, Rutgers University Press, 1996.

Jonathan Rosenbaum, *Movie Wars: How Hollywood and the Media Limit What We Can See*, New York, A Cappella, 2000.

James Ryan, 'And the producer of the movie is . . .', *New York Times* 24 September 1995.

Andrew Sarris, *The American Cinema: Directors and Directions 1929–1968*, New York, E. P. Dutton, 1968.

Jane Shattuc, *Television, Tabloids, and Tears: Fassbinder and Popular Culture*, Minneapolis, University of Minnesota Press, 1993.

Gaylyn Studlar and David Desser (eds), *Reflections in a Male Eye: John Huston and the American Experience*, Washington, DC, Smithsonian Institution Press, 1993.

David Thomson, *A Biographical Dictionary of Film*, London and New York, André Deutsch, 1997.

Wide Angle 6 (1), 1984. Special issue on Authorship in Cinema.

Paul Willemen (ed.), *Amos Gitai: A Montage*, London, BFI Publishing, 1994.

Peter Wollen, *Signs and Meaning in the Cinema*, London, BFI Publishing, 1998. Expanded edition.

Justin Wyatt, 'Economic constraints/economic opportunities: Robert Altman as auteur', *The Velvet Light Trap* 38: 51–67, autumn 1996.

Justin Wyatt, 'The formation of the "major independent": Miramax, New Line and the New Hollywood', in Neale and Smith (eds), *Contemporary Hollywood Cinema*, London and New York, Routledge, 1998.

AUTHORSHIP REVISED AND REVIVED

Jose Arroyo, 'Kiss kiss bang bang', *Sight and Sound* 7 (3): 6–9, March 1997. Reprinted in Vincendeau (ed.), *Film/Literature/Heritage: A Sight and Sound Reader*, London, BFI Publishing, 2002.

Pam Cook, 'Fictions of identity: style, mimicry and gender in the films of Kathryn Bigelow', in *Screening the Past: Memory and Nostalgia in Cinema*, Oxford and New York, Routledge, 2005.

Pam Cook, 'Portrait of a lady: Sofia Coppola', *Sight and Sound* 16 (11): 36–40, November 2006.

Pam Cook, *Baz Luhrmann*, London, BFI Publishing, 2008.

David A. Gerstner and Janet Staiger (eds), *Authorship and Film: Trafficking with Hollywood*, London and New York, Routledge, 2003.

Deborah Jermyn and Sean Redmond (eds), *The Cinema of Kathryn Bigelow: Hollywood Transgressor*, London, Wallflower Press, 2002.

Jeffrey Sconce, 'Irony, nihilism and the new American "smart" film', *Screen* 43 (4): 349–69, winter 2002.

Stephen Teo, *Wong Kar-wai*, London, BFI Publishing, 2005.

PART 7: Developments in Theory

FEMINISM AND FILM SINCE THE 1990s

Homi K. Bhabha, 'The Other question: the stereotype and colonial discourse', in Merck (ed.), *The Sexual Subject: A Screen Reader in Sexuality*, London and New York, Routledge, 1992.

Alison Butler, 'Feminist theory and women's films at the turn of the century', *Screen* 41 (1): 73–8, 2000.

Judith Butler, *Gender Trouble: Feminism and the Subversion of Identity*, New York and London, Routledge, 1990. Second edition 1999.

Carol J. Clover, *Men, Women and Chain Saws: Gender in the Modern Horror Film*, Princeton, NJ, Princeton University Press, 1992.

Pam Cook, *Screening the Past: Memory and Nostalgia in Cinema*, Oxford and New York, Routledge, 2005.

Barbara Creed, *Media Matrix: Sexing the New Reality*, Sydney, Allen & Unwin, 2003.

Barbara Creed, *Phallic Panic: Film, Horror and the Primal Uncanny*, Melbourne, Melbourne University Press, 2005.

Christine Gledhill, 'Rethinking genre', in Gledhill and Williams (eds), *Reinventing Film Studies*, London, Arnold, 2000.

Lalitha Gopalan, 'Avenging women in Indian cinema', *Screen* 38 (1): 42–59, spring 1997.

Suzy Gordon, '*Breaking the Waves* and the negativity of Melanie Klein: rethinking "the female spectator"', *Screen* 45 (3): 206–25, autumn 2004.

Elizabeth Hills, 'From "figurative males" to action heroines: further thoughts on active women in the cinema', *Screen*, 40 (1): 38–50, spring 1999.

Karen Hollinger, *In the Company of Women: Contemporary Female Friendship Films*, Minneapolis and London, University of Minnesota Press, 1998.

Sherrie A. Inness, *Action Chicks: New Images of Tough Women in Popular Culture*, Basingstoke, Palgrave Macmillan, 2004.

Alice Jardine, *Gynesis: Configurations of Woman and Modernity*, Ithaca, NY, and London, Cornell University Press, 1985.

E. Ann Kaplan, *Looking for the Other: Feminism, Film and the Imperial Gaze*, New York and London, Routledge, 1997.

Barbara Klinger, 'The art film, affect and the female viewer: *The Piano* revisited', *Screen* 47 (1): 19–42, spring 2006.

Annette Kuhn, 'Heterotopia, heterochronia: place and time in cinema memory', *Screen* 45 (2): 106–14, summer 2004.

Gina Marchetti, *Romance and the 'Yellow Peril': Race, Sex and Discursive Strategies in Hollywood Fiction*, Berkeley, University of California Press, 1993.

Judith Mayne, *Framed: Lesbians, Feminists and Media Culture*, Minneapolis and London, University of Minnesota Press, 2000.

Ann McClintock, 'The angel of progress: pitfalls of the term "post-colonialism"', in Williams and Chrisman (eds), *Colonial Discourse and Post-Colonial Theory: A Reader*, New York, Columbia University Press, 1994.

Patricia Mellencamp, *A Fine Romance: Five Ages of Film Feminism*, Philadelphia, PA, Temple University Press, 1995.

Laura Mulvey, *Death 24x a Second: Stillness and the Moving Image*, London, Reaktion Books, 2006.

Hilary Neroni, 'Jane Campion's jouissance: *Holy Smoke* and feminist film theory', in McGowan and Kunkle (eds), *Lacan and Contemporary Film*, New York, Other Press, 2004.

Laura Pietropaolo and Ada Testaferri (eds), *Feminisms in the Cinema*, Bloomington and Indianapolis, Indiana University Press, 1995.

Patricia Pisters (ed.), *Micropolitics of Media Culture: Reading the Rhizomes of Deleuze and Guattari*, Amsterdam, Amsterdam University Press, 2001.

B. Ruby Rich, *Chick Flicks: Theories and Memories of the Feminist Film Movement*, Durham, NC, Duke University Press, 1998.

Anneke Smelik, *And the Mirror Cracked: Feminist Cinema and Film Theory*, Basingstoke, Macmillan, 1998.

Gayatri Chakravorty Spivak, 'Can the subaltern speak?', in Nelson and Grossberg (eds), *Marxism and the Interpretation of Culture*, Urbana and Chicago, University of Illinois Press, 1988.

Jackie Stacey, 'She is not herself: the deviant relations of *Alien Resurrection*', *Screen* 44 (3): 251–76, autumn 2003.

Chris Straayer, *Deviant Eyes, Deviant Bodies*, New York, Columbia University Press, 1996.

Gaylyn Studlar and Matthew Bernstein (eds), *Visions of the East: Orientalism in Film*, New Brunswick, NJ, Rutgers University Press, 1997.

Yvonne Tasker, *Spectacular Bodies: Gender, Genre and the Action Cinema*, London and New York, Routledge, 1993.

Jyotika Virdi, 'Reverence, rape – and then revenge: popular Hindi cinema's "woman's film"', *Screen* 40 (1): 17–37, 1999.

Janet Walker, 'Trauma cinema: false memories and true experience', *Screen* 42 (2): 211–16, 2001.

Mimi White, 'Women, memory and serial melodrama', *Screen* 35 (4): 336–54, 1994.

Linda Williams, 'Melodrama revised', in Browne (ed.), *Refiguring American Film Genres: Theory and History*, Berkeley, University of California Press, 1998.

FEMINIST FILM THEORY

Jack Babuscio, 'Camp and the gay sensibility', in Dyer (ed.), *Gays and Film*, New York, Zoetrope, 1984. Revised edition.

Janet Bergstrom and Mary Ann Doane (eds), *Camera Obscura: A Journal of Feminism and Film Theory* 20/21, May/September 1989. Special issue on The Spectatrix.

Jacqueline Bobo, *Black Women as Cultural Readers*, New York, Columbia University Press, 1995.

Judith Butler, *Gender Trouble: Feminism and the Subversion of Identity*, New York and London, Routledge, 1990.

Diane Carson, Linda Dittmar and Janice R. Welsch (eds), *Multiple Voices in Feminist Film Criticism*, London and Minneapolis, University of Minnesota Press, 1994.

Rowena Chapman and Jonathan Rutherford (eds), *Male Order: Unwrapping Masculinity*, London, Lawrence & Wishart, 1988.

Carol J. Clover, *Men, Women and Chain Saws: Gender in the Modern Horror Film*, Princeton, NJ, Princeton University Press, 1992.

Pam Cook, 'Masculinity in crisis? Tragedy and identification in *Raging Bull*', *Screen* 23 (3/4): 39–46, Sept/October 1982. Reprinted in *Screening the Past: Memory and Nostalgia in Cinema*, Oxford and New York, Routledge, 2005.

Pam Cook and Philip Dodd (eds), *Women and Film: A Sight and Sound Reader*, London, Scarlet Press, 1993.

Mary Ann Doane, 'Film and the masquerade: theorising the female spectator', *Screen* 23 (3/4): 74–87, September/October 1982. Reprinted in *Femmes Fatales: Feminism, Film Theory, Psychoanalysis*, New York and London, Routledge, 1991.

Mary Ann Doane, *The Desire to Desire: The Woman's Film of the 1940s*, Bloomington, Indiana University Press, 1987.

Richard Dyer, 'Don't look now: the male pin-up', *Screen* 23 (3/4): 61–73, September/October 1982.

Richard Dyer, *Now You See It: Studies on Lesbian and Gay Film*, London, Routledge, 1990.

Richard Dyer, 'White', in *The Matter of Images: Essays on Representations*, London and New York, Routledge, 1993.

Antony Easthope, *What a Man's Gotta Do: The Masculine Myth in Popular Culture*, London, Paladin, 1986.

Elizabeth Ellsworth, 'Feminist spectators and *Personal Best*', in Erens (ed.), *Issues in Feminist Film Criticism*, 1990.

Patricia Erens (ed.), *Issues in Feminist Film Criticism*, Bloomington, Indiana University Press, 1990.

Sandy Flitterman-Lewis, *To Desire Differently: Feminism and the French Cinema*, Urbana and Chicago, University of Illinois Press, 1990. Revised edition, New York, Columbia University Press, 1996.

Jane Gaines, 'White privilege and looking relations: race and gender in feminist film theory', *Screen* 29 (4): 12–27, autumn 1988.

Angela Galvin, '*Basic Instinct*: damning dykes', in Hamer and Budge (eds), *The Good, the Bad and the Gorgeous: Popular Culture's Romance with Lesbianism*, London, Pandora, 1994.

Martha Gever, John Greyson and Pratibha Parmar (eds), *Queer Looks: Perspectives on Lesbian and Gay Film and Video*, New York and London, Routledge, 1993.

Christine Gledhill and Linda Williams (eds), *Reinventing Film Studies*, London, Arnold, 2000.

Paula Graham, 'Girl's camp? The politics of parody', in Wilton (ed.), *Immortal, Invisible: Lesbians and the Moving Image*, London and New York, Routledge, 1995.

Deborah Grayson (ed.), *Camera Obscura* 36, 1995. Special issue on Black Women, Spectatorship and Visual Culture.

Deborah Grayson, 'Is it fake? Black women's hair as spectacle and spec(tac)ular', *Camera Obscura* 36: 13–30, 1995.

Miriam Hansen, *Babel and Babylon: Spectatorship in American Silent Film*, Cambridge, MA, Harvard University Press, 1991.

Molly Haskell, *From Reverence to Rape: The Treatment of Women in the Movies*, Chicago and London, University of Chicago Press, 1973. Revised edition 1987.

bell hooks, *Black Looks: Race and Representation*, Boston, MA, South End Press, 1992.

Maggie Humm, *Feminism and Film*, Edinburgh, Edinburgh University Press, 1997.

Joy James, 'Black femmes fatales and sexual abuse in progressive white cinema', *Camera Obscura* 36: 33–47, 1995.

Susan Jeffords, *Hard Bodies: Hollywood Masculinity in the Reagan Era*, New Brunswick, NJ, Rutgers University Press, 1994.

Claire Johnston, 'Women's cinema as counter-cinema', in *Notes on Women's Cinema*, London, SEFT, 1974. *Screen* reprint 1991. Reprinted in Thornham (ed.), *Feminist Film Theory: A Reader*, New York, New York University Press, 1999.

Claire Johnston, 'Femininity and the masquerade: *Anne of the Indies*', in Johnston and Willemen (eds), *Jacques Tourneur*, Edinburgh, Edinburgh Film Festival, 1975.

Alexandra Juhasz, 'They said we wanted to show reality – all I want to show is my video: the politics of feminist, realist, documentaries', *Screen* 35 (2): 171–90, summer 1994.

Jump Cut 24/25, March 1981. Special issue on Lesbians and Film.

E. Ann Kaplan, *Women and Film: Both Sides of the Camera*, New York and London, Methuen, 1983.

Lynne Kirby, 'Male hysteria and early cinema', *Camera Obscura* 17: 113–31, May 1988.

Pat Kirkham and Janet Thumim (eds), *You Tarzan: Masculinity, Movies and Men*, London, Lawrence & Wishart, 1993.

Gertrude Koch, 'Warum Frauen ins Männer kino gehen', in Nabakowski, Sander and Gorsen (eds), *Frauen in der Kunst, Band I*, Frankfurt am Main, Suhrkamp, 1980.

Annette Kuhn, *Women's Pictures: Feminism and Cinema*, London, Routledge & Kegan Paul, 1982. Revised edition, London, Verso, 1994.

Jacques Lacan, 'The signification of the phallus', in *Ecrits: A Selection*, London, Tavistock, 1977; trans. Alan Sheridan.

Teresa de Lauretis, *Alice Doesn't: Feminism, Semiotics, Cinema*, Bloomington, Indiana University Press, 1984.

Teresa de Lauretis, *Technologies of Gender: Essays on Theory, Film and Fiction*, Bloomington, Indiana University Press, 1987.

Teresa de Lauretis, 'Sexual indifference and lesbian representation', *Theatre Journal* 40 (2): 155–77, May 1988. Reprinted in *Figures of Resistance: Essays in Feminist Theory*, Champaign, University of Illinois Press, 2007.

Teresa de Lauretis, 'Film and the visible', in Bad Object-Choices (eds), *How Do I Look? Queer Film and Video*, Seattle, WA, Bay Press, 1991.

Teresa de Lauretis, *The Practice of Love: Lesbian Sexuality and Perverse Desire*, Bloomington, Indiana University Press, 1994.

Julia Lesage, 'Subversive fantasy in *Celine and Julie Go Boating*', *Jump Cut* 24/25, winter 1980/81.

Brenda Longfellow, 'Lesbian phantasy and the other women in Ottinger's *Johanna d'Arc of Mongolia*', *Screen* 34 (2): 124–36, summer 1993.

Judith Mayne, *The Woman at the Keyhole: Feminism and Women's Cinema*, Bloomington, Indiana University Press, 1990.

Judith Mayne, *Directed by Dorothy Arzner*, Bloomington, Indiana University Press, 1994.

Andy Medhurst, 'That special thrill: *Brief Encounter*, homosexuality and authorship', *Screen* 32 (2): 197–208, summer 1991a. Reprinted in Stacey and Street (eds), *Queer Screen: A Screen Reader*, Oxford and New York, Routledge, 2007.

Andy Medhurst, '*Batman*, deviance and camp', in Pearson and Uricchio (eds), *The Many Lives of the Batman: Critical Approaches to a Superhero and His Media*, London, BFI Publishing, 1991b.

Mandy Merck, *Perversions: Deviant Readings*, London, Virago, 1993.

Tania Modleski, *The Women Who Knew Too Much: Hitchcock and Feminist Theory*, New York and London, Methuen, 1988.

Tania Modleski, *Feminism without Women: Culture and Criticism in a 'Postfeminist' Age*, New York and London, Routledge, 1991.

Laura Mulvey, 'Visual pleasure and narrative cinema', and 'Afterthoughts on "Visual pleasure and narrative cinema" inspired by King Vidor's *Duel in the Sun* (1946)', in *Visual and Other Pleasures*, London, Macmillan, 1989.

Constance Penley (ed.), *Feminism and Film Theory*, New York and London, Routledge/BFI Publishing, 1988.

Constance Penley and Sharon Willis (eds), *Camera Obscura* 17, fall 1988. Special issue on Male Trouble.

Steve Neale, 'Masculinity as spectacle', *Screen* 24 (6): 2–16, 1983. Reprinted in Cohan (ed.), *Screening the Male: Exploring Masculinities in Hollywood Cinema*, London and New York, Routledge, 1993.

B. Ruby Rich, 'From repressive tolerance to erotic liberation: *Maedchen in Uniform*', in Doane, Mellencamp and Williams (eds), *Revision: Essays in Feminist Film Criticism*, Los Angeles, University Publications of America/AFI, 1984.

Marjorie Rosen, *Popcorn Venus: Women, Movies and the American Dream*, New York, Avon, 1973.

Gayle Rubin, 'The traffic in women: notes on the "political economy" of sex', in Reiter (ed.), *Toward an Anthropology of Women*, New York, Monthly Review Press, 1975.

Maria Shelton, 'Whitney is every woman?: cultural politics and the pop star', *Camera Obscura* 36: 135–53, 1995.

Kaja Silverman, *The Acoustic Mirror: The Female Voice in Psychoanalysis and Cinema*, Bloomington, Indiana University Press, 1988.

Kaja Silverman, *Male Subjectivity at the Margins*, New York and London, Routledge, 1992.

Mark Simpson, *Male Impersonators: Men Performing Masculinity*, London, Cassell, 1994.

Anneke Smelik, *And the Mirror Cracked: Feminist Cinema and Film Theory*, London, Macmillan, 1998.

Jackie Stacey, 'Desperately seeking difference', *Screen* 28 (1): 48–61, winter 1987. Reprinted in Evans and Hall (eds), *Visual Culture: The Reader*, London, Sage Publications/The Open University, 1999.

Jackie Stacey, *Star Gazing: Hollywood Cinema and Female Spectatorship*, London and New York, Routledge, 1994.

Jackie Stacey, '"If you don't play you can't win"': *Desert Hearts* and the lesbian romance film', in Wilton (ed.), *Immortal, Invisible: Lesbians and the Moving Image*, London and New York, Routledge, 1995.

Gaylyn Studlar, *In the Realm of Pleasure: Von Sternberg, Dietrich and the Masochistic Aesthetic*, New York, Columbia University Press, 1988.

Yvonne Tasker, *Spectacular Bodies: Gender, Genre and the Action Cinema*, London, Routledge, 1993.

Trinh T. Min-ha, *Woman, Native, Other: Writing, Postcoloniality and Feminism*, Bloomington, Indiana University Press, 1989.

Andrea Weiss, *Vampires and Violets: Lesbians in the Cinema*, London, Jonathan Cape, 1992.

Patricia White, 'Female spectator, lesbian specter: *The Haunting*', in Fuss (ed.), *Inside/Out: Lesbian Theories, Gay Theories*, New York and London, Routledge, 1991.

Linda Williams, '*Personal Best*: women in love', in Brunsdon (ed.), *Films for Women*, London, BFI Publishing, 1986.

Lola Young, *Fear of the Dark: 'Race', Gender and Sexuality in the Cinema*, London and New York, Routledge, 1996.

QUEER THEORY AND NEW QUEER CINEMA

Michele Aaron (ed.), *New Queer Cinema: A Critical Reader*, Edinburgh, Edinburgh University Press, 2004.

Harry M. Benshoff and Sean Griffin (eds), *Queer Cinema: The Film Reader*, London and New York, Routledge, 2004.

Lauren Berlant and Michael Warner, 'Sex in public', *Critical Inquiry* 24 (2): 547–66, winter 1998. Special issue on Intimacy.

Michael Bronski, Terri Ginsberg, Roy Grundman, Kara Keeling, Liora Moriel, Yasmin Nair and Kirsten Moana Thompson, 'Queer film and pedagogy', *GLQ* 12 (1): 117–34, 2006.

Alexander Doty, *Making Things Perfectly Queer: Interpreting Mass Culture*, Minneapolis, University of Minnesota Press, 1993.

Richard Dyer (ed.), *Gays and Film*, London, BFI Publishing, 1977.

Richard Dyer, *Now You See It: Studies in Lesbian and Gay Film*, London, Routledge, 1990.

Richard Dyer, *Brief Encounter*, London, BFI Publishing, 1993.

Richard Dyer, *The Culture of Queers*, London, Routledge, 2002.

Ellis Hanson, 'Technology, paranoia and the queer voice', *Screen* 34 (2): 137–61, summer 1993.

Annamarie Jagose, *Queer Theory: An Introduction*, New York, New York University Press, 1996.

Teresa de Lauretis, 'Film and the visible', in Bad Object-Choices (eds), *How Do I Look? Queer Film and Video*, Seattle, Bay Press, 1991.

Andy Medhurst, 'That special thrill: *Brief Encounter*, homosexuality and authorship', *Screen* 32 (2): 197–208, summer 1991. Reprinted in Stacey and Street (eds), *Queer Screen*, 2007.

Andy Medhurst, 'It's as a man that you've failed: masculinity and forbidden desire in *The Spanish Gardener*', in Kirkham and Thumim (eds), *You Tarzan: Masculinity, Movies and Men*, London, Lawrence & Wishart, 1993.

José E. Muñoz, *Disidentifications: Queers of Colour and the Performance of Politics*, Minneapolis, University of Minnesota Press, 1999.

B. Ruby Rich, 'New queer cinema', *Sight and Sound* 2 (5): 30–5, September 1992.

B. Ruby Rich, 'Queer and present danger', *Sight and Sound* 10 (3): 22–4, March 2000.

B. Ruby Rich, 'A queer sensation: new gay film', in Benshoff and Griffin (eds), *Queer Cinema*, 2004.

Vito Russo, *The Celluloid Closet: Homosexuality in the Movies*, New York, Harper & Row, 1981.

Jackie Stacey and Sarah Street (eds), *Queer Screen: A Screen Reader*, Oxford and New York, Routledge, 2007.

Lee Wallace, 'Continuous sex: the editing of homosexuality in *Bound* and *Rope*', *Screen* 41 (4): 369–87, 2000. Reprinted in Stacey and Street (eds), *Queer Screen*, 2007.

Michael Warner, *The Trouble with Normal: Sex, Politics, and the Ethics of Queer Life*, Cambridge, MA, Harvard University Press, 2000.

TRANSNATIONAL FILM STUDIES

Benedict Anderson, *Imagined Communities*, London, Verso, 1986.

Chris Anderson, *The Long Tail: Why the Future of Business Is Selling Less of More*, New York, Hyperion, 2006.

Ien Ang, *On Not Speaking Chinese: Living Between Asia and the West*, London and New York, Routledge, 2001.

Gloria E. Anzaldúa, *Borderlands/La Frontera: The New Mestiza*, San Francisco, Aunt Lute Books, 1987.

Arjun Appadurai, *Modernity at Large: Cultural Dimensions of Globalization*, Minneapolis, University of Minnesota Press, 1996.

Tim Bergfelder, 'National, transnational or supranational cinema', *Media, Culture and Society* 27 (3): 315–31, 2005.

Tim Bergfelder, *International Adventures: German Popular Cinema and European Co-Productions in the 1960s*, Oxford, Berghahn Books, 2006.

Chris Berry and Mary Ann Farquhar, *China on Screen: Cinema and Nation*, New York, Columbia University Press, 2006.

Homi K. Bhabha (ed.), *Nation and Narration*, London, Routledge, 1990.

Iain Chambers, *Migrancy, Culture, Identity*, London and New York, Routledge, 1993.

Kuan-Hsing Chen (ed.), *Trajectories: Inter-Asia Cultural Studies*, New York and London, Routledge, 1998.

Rey Chow, *Writing Diaspora: Tactics of Intervention in Contemporary Cultural Studies*, Bloomington, Indiana University Press, 1993.

James Clifford, *Routes: Travel and Translation in the Late Twentieth Century*, Cambridge, MA, Harvard University Press, 1997.

Stuart Cunningham and John Sinclair (eds), *Floating Lives: The Media and Asian Diasporas*, New York, Rowman and Littlefield, 2001.

Jigna Desai, *Beyond Bollywood: The Cultural Politics of South Asian Diasporic Film*, London and New York, Routledge, 2004.

Wimal Dissanayake, Shirley Geok-lin Lim and Larry E. Smith (eds), *Transnational Asia Pacific: Gender, Culture and the Public Sphere*, Chicago, University of Illinois Press, 1999.

Dimitris Eleftheriotis and Dina Iordanova (eds), 'Indian cinema abroad: historiography of transnational cinematic exchanges', *South Asian Popular Culture* 4 (2), October 2006. Special issue.

Elizabeth Ezra and Terry Rowden (eds), *Transnational Cinema: The Film Reader*, London and New York, Routledge, 2006.

Mike Featherstone (ed.), *Global Culture: Nationalism, Globalisation and Modernity*, London, Sage, 1991.

Paul Gilroy, *The Black Atlantic: Modernity and Double Consciousness*, London, Verso, 1993.

Faye Ginsburg, Lila Abu-Lughod and Brian Larkin (eds.), *Media Worlds: Anthropology on New Terrain*, Berkeley, University of California Press, 2002.

Inderpal Grewal and Caren Kaplan (eds), *Scattered Hegemonies: Transnational Feminist Practices and Questions of Postmodernity*, Minneapolis, University of Minnesota Press, 1994.

Stuart Hall, 'The local and the global: globalisation and ethnicity', and 'Old and new identities', in King (ed.), *Culture, Globalisation and the World System*, 1991.

Ulf Hannerz, *Transnational Connections: Culture, People, Places*, London, Routledge, 1996.

Andrew Higson, 'The limiting imagination of national cinema', in Hjort and Mackenzie (eds), *Cinema and Nation*, London and New York, Routledge, 2001.

Dina Iordanova, 'Expanding universe: from the ethnic foodstore to blockbuster', *Framework: The Journal of Cinema and Media* 41: 54–70, autumn 1999.

Dina Iordanova, 'Displaced? Shifting politics of place and itinerary in international cinema', *Senses of Cinema* 14, 2001. Available at: <www.sensesofcinema.com/contents/01/14/displaced.html>.

Fredric Jameson, *The Geopolitical Aesthetic: Cinema and Space in the World System*, Bloomington, Indiana University Press, 1992.

Raminder Kaur and Ajay J. Sinha (eds), *Bollyworld: Popular Indian Cinema through a Transactional Lens*, London, Sage, 2005.

Anthony King (ed.), *Culture, Globalisation and the World System*, London, Macmillan, 1991.

Brian Larkin, 'Indian films and Nigerian lovers: media and the creation of parallel modernities', *Africa: Journal of the International African Institute* 67 (3): 406–40, 1997.

Sheldon H. Lu (ed.), *Transnational Chinese Cinemas: Identity, Nationhood, Gender*, Honolulu, University of Hawaii Press, 1997.

Sarita Malik, 'Beyond the "cinema of duty"? The pleasures of hybridity in black British film of the 1980s and 1990s', in Higson (ed.) *Dissolving Views: Key Writings on British Cinema*, London, Cassell, 1996.

Richard Maltby and Andrew Higson (eds), *Film Europe and Film America: Cinema, Commerce, and Cultural Exchange, 1920–1939*, Exeter, University of Exeter Press, 1999.

Gina Marchetti, *From Tian'anmen to Times Square: Transnational China and the Chinese Diaspora on Global Screens, 1989–1997*, Philadelphia, Temple University Press, 2006.

Laura U. Marks, *The Skin of the Film: Intercultural Cinema, Embodiment, and the Senses*, Durham, NC, Duke University Press, 2000.

Franco Moretti, *Atlas of the European Novel, 1800–1900*, London, Verso, 1999.

David Morley and Kevin Robins, *Spaces of Identity: Global Media, Electronic Landscapes and Cultural Boundaries*, London and New York, Routledge, 1995.

Hamid Naficy (ed.), *Home, Exile, Homeland*, New York and London, Routledge, 1999.

Hamid Naficy, *An Accented Cinema: Exilic and Diasporic Filmmaking*, Princeton, NJ, Princeton University Press, 2001.

Aihwa Ong, *Flexible Citizenship: The Cultural Logic of Transnationality*, Durham, NC, Duke University Press, 1999.

Jonathan Rosenbaum and Adrian Martin (eds), *Movie Mutations: The Changing Face of World Cinephilia*, London, BFI Publishing, 2003.

Edward Said, *Culture and Imperialism*, London, Chatto & Windus, 1993.

Saskia Sassen, *The Global City: New York, London, Tokyo*, Princeton, NJ, Princeton University Press, 1991.

Saskia Sassen, *Globalization and its Discontents: Essays on the New Mobility of People and Money*, New York, New Press, 1998.

Viola Shafik, *Arab Cinema: History and Cultural Identity*, Cairo, The American University of Cairo Press, 1998.

Dina Sherzer (ed.), *Cinema, Colonialism, Postcolonialism: Perspectives from the French and Francophone World*, Austin, University of Texas Press, 1996.

Ella Shohat (ed.), *Talking Visions: Multicultural Feminism in a Transnational Age*, Cambridge, MA, The MIT Press, 1999.

Ella Shohat and Robert Stam, *Unthinking Eurocentrism: Multiculturalism and the Media*, London and New York, Routledge, 1994.

Ella Shohat and Robert Stam (eds), *Multiculturalism, Postcoloniality, and Transnational Media*, New Brunswick, NJ, Rutgers University Press, 2003.

John Sinclair, Elizabeth Jacka and Stuart Cunningham (eds), *New Patterns in Global Television: Peripheral Vision*, London, Oxford University Press, 1996.

Sarah Street, *Transatlantic Crossings: British Feature Films in the USA*, London and New York, Continuum, 2002.

Carrie Tarr, *Reframing Difference: Beur and Banlieue Filmmaking in France*, Manchester, Manchester University Press, 2005.

John Urry, *The Tourist Gaze: Leisure and Travel in Contemporary Societies*, London, Sage, 2002. Revised edition.

Rob Wilson and Wimal Dissanayake (eds), *Global/Local: Cultural Production and the Transnational Imaginary*, Durham, NC, Duke University Press, 1996.

STRUCTURALISM AND ITS AFTERMATHS

Andrew Britton, 'Living historically: two films by Jean-Luc Godard', *Framework* 3, spring 1976.

'*Citizen Kane*' (collective text), *Film Reader* 1, 1975.

Jack Daniel, 'Metz's grande syntagmatique: summary and critique', *Film Form* 1 (1), spring 1976.

Colin MacCabe, *Godard: Images, Sounds, Politics*, London, Macmillan/BFI, 1980.

Christian Metz, *Essais sur la signification au cinéma*, Vols. I and II, Paris, Editions Klincksieck, 1968–72.

Christian Metz, *Film Language: A Semiotics of the Cinema*, New York and Oxford, Oxford University Press, 1974; trans. Michael Taylor.

Christian Metz, 'The modern cinema and narrativity' [1966], in *Film Language*, 1974.

Kristin Thompson, 'Sawing through the bough: *Tout va bien* as a Brechtian film', *Wide Angle* 1 (3): 38–47, 1976. Reprinted in *Breaking the Glass Armor: Neoformalist Film Analysis*, Princeton, NJ, Princeton University Press, 1988.

Nicole Zand, 'Le dossier Philippine', *Cahiers du Cinéma* 148, October 1963.

Claude Lévi-Strauss: the structural study of myth

Claude Chabrol, 'Review of *Kiss Me Deadly*', *Cahiers du Cinéma* 54, 1956.

Raymond Durgnat, 'The apotheosis of va-va-voom', *Motion* 3, spring 1962.

Charles Eckert, 'The English cine-structuralists', *Film Comment* 9 (3): 46–51, May/June 1973. Reprinted in Caughie (ed.), *Theories of Authorship*, London and New York, Routledge & Kegan Paul/BFI, 1981. Reprinted 2001.

Patricia Erens, '*Sunset Boulevard*: a morphological analysis', *Film Reader* 2: 92–4, 1977.

John L. Fell, 'Vladimir Propp in Hollywood', *Film Quarterly* 30 (3): 19–28, spring 1977.

Sylvia Harvey, 'The absent family of film noir', in Kaplan (ed.), *Women in Film Noir*, BFI Publishing, 1978. Revised edition 1998.

Molly Haskell, 'Howard Hawks – masculine feminine', *Film Comment* 10 (2): 34–9, March/April 1974.

Brian Henderson, 'Critique of cine-structuralism, Part I', *Film Quarterly* 27 (1): 25–34, autumn 1973; 'Part II', *Film Quarterly* 27 (2): 37–46, winter 1973/74.

Edmund Leach, *Lévi-Strauss*, London, Fontana, 1974.

Claude Lévi-Strauss, 'Overture', in *The Raw and the Cooked: Mythologiques Volume One*, London, Jonathan Cape, 1970; trans. John and Doreen Weightman. Reprinted by University of Chicago Press, 1983.

Christian Metz, 'Notes towards a phenomenology of narrative' [1966], in *Film Language: A Semiotics of the Cinema*, 1974.

Christian Metz, *Film Language: A Semiotics of the Cinema*, New York and Oxford, Oxford University Press, 1974; trans. Michael Taylor.

Vladimir Propp, *Morphology of the Folktale*, Austin, University of Texas Press, 1968; trans. Laurence Scott.

Alain Silver, '*Kiss Me Deadly* – evidence of a film style', *Film Comment* 11 (2): 24–30, March/April 1975.

Peter Wollen, *Signs and Meaning in the Cinema*, London, Secker and Warburg/BFI, 1969; 1972. Expanded edition, London, BFI Publishing, 1998.

Robin Wood, *Howard Hawks*, London, Secker and Warburg/BFI, 1968. Revised edition, BFI Publishing, 1981. New edition by Wayne State University Press, 2006.

Robin Wood, 'To have (written) and have not (directed)', *Film Comment* 9 (3), May/June 1973. Reprinted in Nichols (ed.), *Movies and Methods Vol. I*, Berkeley, University of California Press, 1976.

Robin Wood, 'Hawks de-Wollenised', in *Personal Views: Explorations in Film*, London, Gordon Fraser, 1976. Revised edition, Wayne State University Press, 2006.

Will Wright, *Sixguns & Society: A Structural Study of the Western*, Berkeley, University of California Press, 1975.

Roland Barthes: the analysis of narrative

Roland Barthes, 'Introduction to the structural analysis of narratives', *Communications* 8, 1966. Reprinted in *Image-Music-Text*, 1993.

Roland Barthes, *S/Z*, Paris, Editions du Seuil, 1970. In English: New York, Hill and Wang, 1974; trans. Richard Miller.

Roland Barthes, *Image-Music-Text*, London, Fontana, 1977; trans. Stephen Heath. Reprinted 1993.

Rosalind Coward and John Ellis, *Language and Materialism*, London and New York, Routledge & Kegan Paul, 1977. Reprinted 1994.

Jacques Derrida, *L'écriture et la différance*, Paris, Editions du Seuil, 1967. In English: *Writing and Difference*, London, Routledge & Kegan Paul, 1979; trans. A. Bass.

Stephen Heath, 'A conversation with Roland Barthes', in Heath, MacCabe and Prendergast (eds), *Signs of the Times: Introductory Readings in Textual Semiotics*, Cambridge, Granta, 1971.

Stephen Heath, 'Film and system: terms of analysis, Part I and Part II', *Screen* 16 (1): 7-77, spring 1975; and 16 (2): 91-113, summer 1975. Reprinted in *Questions of Cinema*, Bloomington, Indiana University Press, 2004.

Narrative and audience

Louis Althusser, 'Ideology and ideological state apparatuses', in *Lenin and Philosophy and Other Essays*, London, New Left Books, 1971; trans. Ben Brewster.

Claude Bailblé, 'Programming the look: a new approach to teaching film technique', *Screen Education* 32/33: 99–131, autumn/winter 1979/80.

Jean-Louis Baudry, 'Ideological effects of the basic cinematographic apparatus' [1970], *Film Quarterly* 28 (2): 39–47, winter 1974/75; trans. Alan Williams. Reprinted in Braudy and Cohen (eds), *Film Theory and Criticism: Introductory Readings*, Oxford, Oxford University Press, 2004.

André Bazin, *Orson Welles: A Critical View*, London, Elm Tree Books, 1978; trans. Jonathan Rosenbaum.

André Bazin, 'William Wyler or the Jansenist of mise-en-scène', in Williams (ed.), *Realism in the Cinema*, London, Routledge & Kegan Paul/BFI, 1980.

Raymond Bellour, 'System of a fragment (on *The Birds*)', in Penley (ed.), *The Analysis of Film*, Bloomington, Indiana University Press, 2001.

Edward Branigan, 'Formal permutations of the point-of-view shot', *Screen* 16 (3): 54–64, autumn 1975.

Nick Browne, 'The spectator-in-the-text: the rhetoric of *Stagecoach*', *Film Quarterly* 29 (2): 26–38, winter 1975/76. Reprinted in Braudy and Cohen (eds), *Film Theory and Criticism: Introductory Readings*, Oxford, Oxford University Press, 2004.

Daniel Dayan, 'The tutor-code of classical cinema', *Film Quarterly* 28 (1): 22–31, autumn 1974.

John Ellis, 'Watching death at work: an analysis of *A Matter of Life and Death*', in Christie (ed.), *Powell, Pressburger and Others*, London, BFI Publishing, 1978.

Stephen Heath, 'Lessons from Brecht', *Screen* 15 (2): 103-28, summer 1974.

Stephen Heath, 'Film and system: terms of analysis Part I and II', *Screen* 16 (1): 7–77, spring 1975; and 16 (2): 91–113, summer 1975.

Stephen Heath, 'Film performance', *Cinetracts* 1 (2), 1977. Reprinted in *Questions of Cinema*, Bloomington, Indiana University Press, 2004.

Stephen Heath, 'Notes on suture', *Screen* 18 (4), winter 1977/78. Reprinted as 'On suture', in *Questions of Cinema*, Bloomington, Indiana University Press, 2004.

Brian Henderson, 'The long take', *Film Comment* 7 (2), summer 1971. Reprinted in Nichols (ed.), *Movies and Methods Vol. I*, Berkeley, University of California Press, 1976.

Colin MacCabe, 'Realism and the cinema: notes on some Brechtian theses', *Screen* 15 (2): 7–27, summer 1974.

Colin MacCabe, '*Days of Hope* – a response to Colin McArthur', *Screen* 17 (1): 98–101, spring 1976a.

Colin MacCabe, 'Theory and film: principles of realism and pleasure', *Screen* 17 (3): 7–27, autumn 1976b.

Christian Metz, *Psychoanalysis and Cinema: The Imaginary Signifier*, London, Macmillan, 1982.

Mark Nash, '*Vampyr* and the fantastic', *Screen* 17 (3): 29–67, autumn 1976.

Stephen Neale, *Genre*, London, BFI Publishing, 1980.

Screen 14 (1/2), spring/summer 1973. Special issue on Cinema Semiotics and the Work of Christian Metz.

Paul Willemen, *Looks and Frictions: Essays in Cultural Studies and Film Theory*, London, BFI Publishing, 1994.

Psychoanalysis and film

Elizabeth Cowie, *Representing the Woman: Cinema and Psychoanalysis*, London, Macmillan, 1997.

Daniel Dayan, 'The tutor-code of classical cinema', *Film Quarterly* 28 (1): 22–31, autumn 1974.

Stephen Heath, 'Lessons from Brecht', *Screen* 15 (2): 103–28, summer 1974.

Christian Metz, 'History/discourse – a note on two voyeurisms', in Hardy, Johnston and Willemen (eds), *Edinburgh '76 Magazine* 1: 21–5, 1976.

Christian Metz, *Psychoanalysis and Cinema: The Imaginary Signifier*, London, Macmillan, 1982.

Jacques-Alain Miller, Jean-Pierre Oudart and Stephen Heath, 'Dossier on suture', *Screen* 18 (4): 23–96, winter 1977/78.

Laura Mulvey, 'Visual pleasure and narrative cinema', *Screen* 16 (3), autumn 1975. Reprinted in *Visual and Other Pleasures*, London, Macmillan, 1989.

Laura Mulvey, *Fetishism and Curiosity*, London, BFI Publishing, 1996.

Slavoj Zizek, *Looking Awry: An Introduction to Jacques Lacan through Popular Culture*, Cambridge, MA, MIT Press, 1991.

Aftermaths: the structuralist controversy fades

Note: Quotations from Bazin in the text have been translated directly from:

André Bazin, *Qu'est-ce que le cinéma?*, Vols. 1 and 4, Paris, Editions du Cerf, 1958; 1962. Some of these articles have been translated in Gray (ed.), *What Is Cinema?*, Vols 1 and 2, 2005; 'William Wyler or the Jansenist of mise-en-scène', in Williams (ed.), *Realism and the Cinema*, London, Routledge & Kegan Paul/BFI, 1980.

Dudley Andrew, *André Bazin*, New York, Oxford University Press, 1990.

David Bordwell, *Making Meaning: Inference and Rhetoric in the Interpretation of Cinema*, Cambridge, MA, Harvard University Press, 1989.

Gilles Deleuze, *Cinéma 1: L'image-mouvement*, Paris, Editions de Minuit, 1983. In English: *Cinema 1: The Movement-Image*, London, Athlone Press, 1986; trans. Hugh Tomlinson and Barbara Habberjam.

Gilles Deleuze, *Cinéma 2: L'image-temps*, Paris, Editions de Minuit, 1985. In English: *Cinema 2: The Time-Image*, London, Athlone Press, 1989; trans. Hugh Tomlinson and Robert Galeta.

Gilles Deleuze and Felix Guattari, *Anti-Oedipus: Capitalism and Schizophrenia*, Minneapolis, University of Minnesota Press, 1983.

Paul Patton, 'Review of Gilles Deleuze, *Cinema 1: The Movement-Image* and *Cinema 2: The Time-Image*', *Screen* 32 (2): 238–43, 1991.

David N. Rodowick, *Gilles Deleuze's Time Machine*, Durham, NC, Duke University Press, 1997.

Marie-Claire Ropars-Wuilleumier, 'The cinema, reader of Gilles Deleuze', *Camera Obscura* 18: 120–6, September 1988. Reprinted in Boundas and Olkowski (eds), *Gilles Deleuze and the Theatre of Philosophy*, London and New York, Routledge, 1994.

Kristin Thompson, *Breaking the Glass Armor: Neoformalist Film Analysis*, Princeton, NJ, Princeton University Press, 1988.

POST-THEORY, NEO-FORMALISM AND COGNITIVISM

Joseph D. Anderson, *The Reality of Illusion: An Ecological Approach to Cognitive Film Theory*, Carbondale, Southern Illinois University Press, 1996.

Daniel Barratt and Jonathan Frome (eds), *Film Studies: An International Review* 8, 2006. Special issue on Film, Cognition and Emotion.

David Bordwell, *Narration in the Fiction Film*, Madison, University of Wisconsin Press, 1985.

David Bordwell, 'A case for cognitivism', *Iris* 9: 11–40, 1989.

David Bordwell and Noël Carroll (eds), *Post-Theory: Reconstructing Film Studies*, Madison, University of Wisconsin Press, 1996.

David Bordwell, Janet Staiger and Kristin Thompson, *The Classical Hollywood Cinema: Film Style and Mode of Production to 1960*, New York, Columbia University Press, 1985. Revised edition 1987.

Edward Branigan, *Narrative Comprehension and Film*, London and New York, Routledge, 1992.

Noël Carroll, *Mystifying Movies: Fads and Fallacies in Contemporary Film Theory*, New York, Columbia University Press, 1988.

Noël Carroll, *The Philosophy of Horror, or Paradoxes of the Heart*, New York, Routledge, 1990.

Torben Grodal, *Moving Pictures: A New Theory of Film Genres, Feelings, and Cognition*, Oxford, Clarendon Press, 1997.

Hugo Münsterberg, *The Photoplay: A Psychological Study*, New York, D. Appleton, 1916. Reprinted in Langdale (ed.), *Hugo Münsterberg on Film: The Photoplay: A Psychological Study and Other Writings*, London and New York, Routledge, 2002.

Carl Plantinga and Greg M. Smith (eds), *Passionate Views: Film, Cognition, and Emotion*, Baltimore, MD, Johns Hopkins University Press, 1999.

Murray Smith, *Engaging Characters: Fiction, Emotion, and the Cinema*, Oxford, Clarendon Press, 1995.

Ed S. H. Tan, *Emotion and the Structure of Narrative Film: Film as an Emotion Machine*, Mahwah, NJ, Lawrence Erlbaum, 1996; trans. Barbara Fasting.

Kristin Thompson, *Breaking the Glass Armor: Neoformalist Film Analysis*, Princeton, NJ, Princeton University Press, 1988.

LOOKING AT FILM

Jacques Aumont, Alain Bergala, Michel Marie and Marc Vernet, *Aesthetics of Film*, Austin, University of Texas Press, 1992; trans. Richard Neupert.

David Bordwell and Kristin Thompson, *Film Art: An Introduction*, New York, McGraw-Hill, 1993. Revised edition 2004.

Christian Metz, *Film Language: A Semiotics of the Cinema*, Oxford and New York, Oxford University Press, 1978; trans. Michael Taylor.

Richard Neupert, *The End: Narration and Closure in the Cinema*, Detroit, MI, Wayne State University Press, 1995.

Karel Reisz and Gavin Millar, *The Techniques of Film Editing*, New York, Hastings House, 1953.

Raymond Spottiswoode, *A Grammar of the Film*, Berkeley, University of California Press, 1951.

SPECTATORSHIP AND AUDIENCE RESEARCH

Robert C. Allen, 'Motion picture exhibition in Manhattan, 1906–1912: beyond the nickelodeon', *Cinema Journal* 18 (2): 2–15, spring 1979.

Robert C. Allen, 'From exhibition to reception: reflections on the audience in film history', *Screen* 31 (4): 79–91, winter 1990. Reprinted in Kuhn and Stacey (eds), *Screen Histories: A Screen Reader*, Oxford, Oxford University Press, 1998.

Louis Althusser, 'Ideology and ideological state apparatuses', in *Lenin and Philosophy and Other Essays*, London, New Left Books, 1971; trans. Ben Brewster.

Ien Ang, *Watching 'Dallas': Soap Opera and the Melodramatic Imagination*, London, Methuen, 1985.

Ien Ang, *Desperately Seeking the Audience*, London, Routledge, 1991.

Bruce A. Austin, *The Film Audience: An International Bibliography of Research*, Lanham, MD, Scarecrow Press, 1983.

Bruce A. Austin, *Immediate Seating: A Look at Movie Audiences*, Belmont, CA, Wadsworth, 1989.

Janet Bergstrom and Mary Ann Doane (eds), *Camera Obscura* 20/21, May/September 1989. Special issue on The Spectatrix.

Jacqueline Bobo, '*The Color Purple*: black women as cultural readers', in Pribram (ed.), *Female Spectators: Looking at Film and Television*, 1988.

Charlotte Brunsdon, '*Crossroads*: notes on soap opera', *Screen* 22 (4): 32–8, 1981. Reprinted in *Screen Tastes: From Soap Opera to Satellite Dishes*, London and New York, Routledge, 1997.

Mary Carbine, '"The finest outside the loop": motion picture exhibition in Chicago's black metropolis', *Camera Obscura* 23: 8–41, May 1990.

Richard deCordova, 'Ethnography and exhibition: the child audience, the Hays Office and Saturday matinées', *Camera Obscura* 23: 90–107, May 1990.

Philip Corrigan, 'Film entertainment as ideology and pleasure: a preliminary approach to a history of audiences,' in Curran and Porter (eds), *British Cinema History*, London, Weidenfeld & Nicolson, 1983.

Mary Ann Doane, *The Desire to Desire: The Woman's Film of the 1940s*, Bloomington, Indiana University Press, 1987.

Mary Anne Doane, 'Film and the masquerade: theorizing the female spectator', and 'Masquerade reconsidered: further thoughts on the female spectator', in *Femmes Fatales: Feminism, Film Theory, Psychoanalysis*, New York, Routledge, 1991.

Alexander Doty, *Making Things Perfectly Queer: Interpreting Mass Culture*, Minneapolis, University of Minnesota Press, 1993.

Richard Dyer, *Stars*, London, BFI Publishing, 1979. Revised edition 1998.

Richard Dyer, *Heavenly Bodies: Film Stars and Society*, New York, St Martin's Press, 1986.

Caroline Evans and Lorraine Gamman, 'The gaze revisited, or reviewing queer viewing', in Burston and Richardson (eds), *A Queer Romance: Lesbians, Gay Men and Popular Culture*, London, Routledge, 1995.

Anne Friedberg, *Window Shopping: Cinema and the Postmodern*, Berkeley, University of California Press, 1993.

Jane Gaines, 'War, women, and lipstick: fan mags in the forties', *Heresies* 19, January 1986.

Lorraine Gamman and Margaret Marshment (eds), *The Female Gaze: Women as Viewers of Popular Culture*, Seattle, WA, The Real Comet Press, 1989.

Martha Gever, John Greyson and Pratibha Parmar (eds), *Queer Looks: Perspectives on Lesbian and Gay Film and Video*, London, Routledge, 1993.

Christine Gledhill (ed.), *Home Is Where the Heart Is: Studies in Melodrama and the Woman's Film*, London, BFI Publishing, 1987.

Christine Gledhill (ed.), *Stardom: Industry of Desire*, London, Routledge, 1991.

Douglas Gomery, 'The growth of movie monopolies: the case of Balaban and Katz', *Wide Angle* 3 (1): 54–63, 1979.

Douglas Gomery, 'Movie audiences, urban geography, and the history of the American film', *The Velvet Light Trap* 19: 23–9, spring 1982.

Antonio Gramsci, *Selections from the Prison Notebooks*, London, Lawrence & Wishart, 1971; trans. Quentin Hoare and Geoffrey Nowell-Smith.

Tom Gunning, 'The "cinema of attractions": early film, its spectator and the avant-garde', in Elsaesser and Barker (eds), *Early Cinema: Space, Frame, Narrative*, London, BFI Publishing, 1990.

Tom Gunning, 'An aesthetic of astonishment: early film and the (in)credulous spectator', in Williams (ed.), *Viewing Positions*, 1995.

Stuart Hall, 'Encoding/decoding', in *Culture, Media, Language*, Birmingham, Centre for Contemporary Cultural Studies, 1980.

Diane Hamer and Belinda Budge (eds), *The Good, the Bad, and the Gorgeous: Popular Culture's Romance with Lesbianism*, London, Pandora, 1994.

Miriam Hansen, 'Pleasure, ambivalence, identification: Valentino and female spectatorship', *Cinema Journal* 25 (4): 6–32, summer 1986.

Miriam Hansen, *Babel and Babylon: Spectatorship in American Silent Film*, Cambridge, MA, Harvard University Press, 1991.

Dick Hebdige, *Subculture: The Meaning of Style*, London, Methuen, 1979.

Dorothy Hobson, *'Crossroads': The Drama of a Soap Opera*, London, Methuen, 1982.

Henry Jenkins, *Textual Poachers: Television Fans and Participatory Culture*, London, Routledge, 1992.

Garth Jowett, 'The first motion picture audiences', *Journal of Popular Film* 3 (1): 39–54, winter 1974.

E. Ann Kaplan (ed.), *Women in Film Noir*, London, BFI Publishing, 1978. Revised edition 1998.

Lisa Lewis (ed.), *The Adoring Audience: Fan Culture and Popular Media*, London, Routledge, 1992.

Judith Mayne, 'Immigrants and spectators', *Wide Angle* 5 (2): 32–41, 1982.

Judith Mayne, *Cinema and Spectatorship*, London and New York, Routledge, 1993.

Russell Merritt, 'Nickelodeon theaters, 1905–1914: building an audience for the movies', in Balio (ed.), *The American Film Industry*, Madison, University of Wisconsin Press, 1985.

David Morley, *The 'Nationwide' Audience: Structure and Decoding*, London, BFI Publishing, 1980.

David Morley, *Family Television: Cultural Power and Domestic Leisure*, London, Routledge, 1986.

Meaghan Morris, 'Banality in cultural studies', in Mellencamp (ed.), *Logics of Television: Essays in Cultural Criticism*, Bloomington, Indiana University Press, 1990.

Laura Mulvey, 'Visual pleasure and narrative cinema', and 'Afterthoughts on "Visual pleasure and narrative cinema" inspired by King Vidor's *Duel in the Sun* (1946)', in *Visual and Other Pleasures*, Bloomington, Indiana University Press, 1989.

Constance Penley, 'Brownian motion: women, tactics, and technology', in Penley and Ross (eds), *Technoculture*, Minneapolis, University of Minnesota Press, 1991.

Deirdre Pribram (ed.), *Female Spectators: Looking at Film and Television*, London, Verso, 1988.

Janice A. Radway, *Reading the Romance: Women, Patriarchy, and Popular Literature*, Chapel Hill, University of North Carolina Press, 1984. Reprinted 1991.

Joan Rivière, 'Womanliness as masquerade', in Burgin, Donald and Kaplan (eds), *Formations of Fantasy*, London, Methuen, 1986.

Jacqui Roach and Petal Felix, 'Black looks', in Gamman and Marshment (eds), *The Female Gaze*, 1989.

Shari Roberts, '"The lady in the tutti frutti hat": Carmen Miranda, a spectacle of ethnicity', *Cinema Journal* 32 (3): 3–23, spring 1993.

Pamela Robertson, *Guilty Pleasures: Feminist Camp From Mae West to Madonna*, Durham, NC, Duke University Press, 1996.

Philip Rosen (ed.), *Narrative/Apparatus/Ideology: A Film Theory Reader*, New York, Columbia University Press, 1986.

Ellen Seiter, Hans Borchers, Gabriele Kreutzner and Eva-Marie Warth (eds), *Remote Control: Television, Audiences, and Cultural Power*, London and New York, Routledge, 1991.

Ben Singer, 'Manhattan nickelodeons: new data on audiences and exhibitors', *Cinema Journal* 34 (3): 5–35, spring 1995.

Jackie Stacey, *Star Gazing: Hollywood Cinema and Female Spectatorship*, London, Routledge, 1994.

Janet Staiger, *Interpreting Films: Studies in the Historical Reception of American Cinema*, Princeton, NJ, Princeton University Press, 1992.

Melvyn Stokes and Richard Maltby (eds), *American Movie Audiences: From the Turn of the Century to the Early Sound Era*, London, BFI Publishing, 1999.

Helen Taylor, *Scarlett's Women: 'Gone with the Wind' and Its Female Fans*, London, Virago, 1989.

Graeme Turner, *Introduction to British Cultural Studies*, London and New York, Routledge, 1992.

Andrea Weiss, '"A queer feeling when I look at you": Hollywood stars and lesbian spectatorship in the 1930s', in Gledhill (ed.), *Stardom: Industry of Desire*, 1991.

Linda Williams (ed.), *Viewing Positions: Ways of Seeing Film*, New Brunswick, NJ, Rutgers University Press, 1995.

POSTMODERNISM AND FILM

Giuliana Bruno, 'Ramble city: postmodernism and *Blade Runner*', *October* 41: 61–74, summer 1987. Reprinted in Kuhn (ed.), *Alien Zone: Cultural Theory and Contemporary Science Fiction Cinema*, London, Verso, 1990.

Umberto Eco, *Reflections on the Name of the Rose*, London, Secker and Warburg, 1985; trans. William Weaver.

John Frow, 'What was postmodernism?', in *Time and Commodity Culture: Essays in Cultural Theory and Postmodernity*, Oxford, Clarendon Press, 1997.

Stuart Hall, 'On postmodernism and articulation: an interview with Stuart Hall', *Journal of Communication Inquiry* 10 (2): 45–60, 1986.

Dick Hebdige, 'Postmodernism and the "other side"', *Journal of Communication Inquiry* 10 (2): 78–98, 1986.

Fredric Jameson, 'Postmodernism, or, the cultural logic of late capitalism', *New Left Review* 146: 59–92, July/August 1984.

Rosalind Krauss, 'Poststructuralism and the paraliterary', in *The Originality of the Avant-Garde and other Modernist Myths*, Cambridge, MA, MIT Press, 1985.

Kim Newman, 'Screwball thrills', *Sight and Sound* 15 (12): 14, 16, December 2005.

Dana Polan, 'Postmodernism and cultural analysis today', in Kaplan (ed.), *Postmodernism and Its Discontents: Theories and Practices*, London, Verso, 1988.

John Rajchman, 'Postmodernism in a nominalist frame', in *Philosophical Events: Essays of the 80s*, New York, Columbia University Press, 1991.

'Shane Black talks to Stephen Dalton', *Sight and Sound* 15 (12): 16–17, December 2005.

J. P. Telotte, '*The Terminator*, *Terminator 2* and the exposed body', *Journal of Popular Film and Television* 20 (2): 26–34, 1992.

Peter Wollen, 'Ways of thinking about music videos (and postmodernism)', *Critical Quarterly* 28 (1/2): 167–70, 1986.

Justin Wyatt and R. L. Rutsky, 'High concept: abstracting the postmodern', *Wide Angle* 10 (4), 1988.

INDEX

Page references in **bold** refer to featured subjects of Case Studies; those in *italic* denote illustrations.

M

S